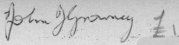

THE CLASSICAL GAZETTEER

WILLIAM HAZLITT

The Classical Gazetteer

First published in 1851 by Whittaker & Co., London

This edition published in 1995 by Senate, an imprint of
Studio Editions Ltd, Princess House, 50 Eastcastle Street,
London W1N 7AP, England

ISBN 1 85958 046 7

Printed and bound in Guernsey by
The Guernsey Press Co. Ltd

(BY PERMISSION.)

THIS VOLUME,

INTENDED AS AN AID TO INSTRUCTION,

IS RESPECTFULLY DEDICATED

TO THE MOST HON.

THE MARQUESS OF LANSDOWNE, K.G.

LORD PRESIDENT OF THE COUNCIL,

IN GRATITUDE FOR THE MUCH WHICH,

AMID EXTREME DIFFICULTIES,

HE HAS ALREADY DONE TO PROMOTE EDUCATION

IN THIS COUNTRY,

AND FOR THE MUCH MORE WHICH HE IS KNOWN

TO DESIRE AND TO DESIGN.

PREFACE.

THE compiler, under the most advantageous circumstances, of a work of reference must be prepared, upon a review of its first edition, to find more or less of commission and of omission, alike to be regretted. There is especial apprehension of this where, as in the present instance, the materials were not ready at hand, subsisting in some similar form of combination, but had to be collected, by laborious researches extending over several years, from works as various in period and language as they are different in their plan, and, to a very large extent, contradictory in their general theories, and in their particular definitions, allocations, and identifications. I have no doubt that in revising these pages I shall meet in them with much to correct; but I can conscientiously say, that in their preparation I have used my best endeavours to render them as free from error as was practicable in a work of such complicated, and, to me, novel labour, prosecuted concurrently with much, and much wearing, work, and amid circumstances not the most favourable for that tranquil application of the mind and judgment which is essential to the effectual development of such a production.

I have neither space nor inclination to set forth the long list of authorities that have been consulted in the preparation of this volume. I will simply state, that I have made it my business to have constantly before me (aided herein by the extensive resources, most liberally administered, of the London Library) all the old and new works that I had ascertained to be the best on the subject, general and particular. My own strong feeling of interest in the matter has led me to bestow especial, and, I hope, productive pains upon the identification of modern localities with ancient sites. The general plan of the work speaks for itself. I could more easily have made individual details fuller, but this would have been incompatible with the contemplated use of the work in Schools. Had the work been extended in size, its price also must, of necessity, have been enlarged, and this would at once have most materially impaired that usefulness which I earnestly desire may be found a prominent attribute of the work.

5, South Square, Gray's Inn.
　　Feb., 1851.

NOTE.—The chief abbreviations used in this work are the following:—
　　bet. *between.*
　　fl. *flumen.*
　　ins. *insulæ.*　　isl. *island.*
　　m. mons, *mountain;* after a numeral, *miles.*
　　pal. *palus.*
　　prom. *promontorium, promontory.*
　　sin. *sinus.*
The figures in brackets indicate the distance of the place described from the locality immediately preceding the bracket.
A capital placed after the name of a river indicates the bank of the river, Left or Right, on which the place described stood.

THE

CLASSICAL GAZETTEER.

A.

AAD, a district of Arabia Felix, on the s. coast; afterwards occupied by the Chatramotitæ.

ABA, a town of Arabia Felix.

ABACÆNA (Abacænum), I. a town of Caria; II. of Media; III. of Sicily, near the source of Helicon fl. s.w. of Messana. *Near Tripi.*

ABÆ, I. a town of Phocis, s.e. of Hyampolis, built by Abas of Argos; noted for an oracle of Apollo, older than that at Delphi. *Near Exarcho.* II. of Lycia.

ABÆRA, a town of Arabia Deserta, towards Petra.

ABALA (Avalites Emporium), capital of the Abali, Æthiopia, at the head of Abalites sinus. *Zeyla.*

ABALITÆ (Abali, Avalitæ), a tribe of Troglodytæ, Æthiopia, on Erythræum mare, s. of the Adulitæ.

ABALITES sinus, a bay of Erythræum mare, s. w. of Dire prom. *Gulf of Zeyla.*

ABALLABA, a town of the Otadeni, Britannia, at Hadriani murus, N. bet. Congovata and Amboglanna. *Watchcross.*

ABALLO, a town of the Mandubii, Lugdunensis I., bet. Sidelocum (24) and Autesiodorum (33). *Avalon.*

ABALUS (Basilia, Baltia), a district of Scandinavia, deemed by the ancients an island, and noted for its amber. *Northern Sweden.*

ABANA fl., Amana, a stream of Syria, rising in Anti-Libanus, 16 m. N. w. from Damascus, and, after a short course, falling into the Chrysorrhoas. *Fidji.*

ABANTES, a people who from Thrace settled at various periods in Phocis, Ionia, Chios, Thesprotia, and Eubœa.

ABANTIA, *postea* Amantia, a town of the Atintanes, Illyria, on Polyanthes fl. 30 m. s.e. from Apollonia; built by the Eubœan Abantes, on their way home from Troy. *Near Nivitza.*

ABANTIS ins., i. q. Eubœa.

ABAORTÆ, a people of India, on the Indus.

ABARA, a town of Babylonia, bet. Dorista and Curraphus.

ABARBINA, a town of Hyrcania, w. of Maxera fl. *Astrabad.*

ABARI, i. q. Sabiri.

ABARIM m., m. of Palestine, e. of the Dead Sea, separating Moabitis from Arabia Deserta. *Ije-Abarim.*

ABARIMON, a district of Scythia Asiatica, the people of which, from wearing a particular kind of sandal, were fabled to have their feet turned backwards.

ABARIS, a maritime town of Egypt, e. of Pelusium.

ABARNE, a town of Gumathene, Armenia, w. n. w. of Amida.

ABARNIS, I. a town of Byzacene, noted for its fishing-rods. II. of Mysia, at Abarnis prom. III. a pr. of Mysia, on the Hellespont, N. of Lampsacus, noted for its truffles.

ABARRAZA, a town of Syria, bet. Cyrrhus and Edessa.

ABAS fl., Albania, i. q. Alazon.

ABĂSES, a name given by Strabo to the African Oases.

ABASGI (Abaschi), a people of Sarmatia Asiatica, N. of the Apsili, extending along the Euxine, and inland towards Caucasus.

ABASGUS fl., a r. of the Abasgi, rising in Corax mons, and falling into the Euxine between Nitice and Nesis.

ABASITES, i. q. Abbaites.

ABASSUS (Ambassus, Alarnassus, Amadasse), a town of Phrygia Magna, on Alandrus fl. towards Tyscon.

ABASTANI, a people on the Indus. .

ABATHUBA, a town of Marmarica.

ABĂTOS ins., an isl. in the Nile, near Philæ, abounding in flax and papyrus. Priests only were permitted to enter it. *Biggeh.* .

ABBA, a town of Africa, near Carthage.

ABBAITES, a people of Phrygia Epictetus, extending into Mysia, at its S. E. angle.

ABDADA, a town of Galatia.

ABDEA, a town of Mesopotamia, bet. Ad Pontem and Atra.

ABDĒRA, I. a town of the Bastuli, Bætica, bet. Sexitanum W. and Murgis E. A Phœnician settlement. A Roman Colonia. *Adra.* II. *postea* Polystylus, cap. of the Bistones, Thrace, on the Ægean, E. of Nestus fl., S.W. of Pistyrus; founded by Timesius of Clazomenæ; recolonized by Teian fugitives from Ionia; the birthplace of Democritus and Protagoras. Noted for its mullets, and its people for fits of a peculiar phrenzy. *Asprorosa.*

ABDIABDA, a town of Albania Asiat., on the Caspian.

ABDON, a Levitical city of Asher.

ABDUA fl., i. q. Addua.

ABEL-BETH-MAACHA (Abel Maim), a town of Napthali, S. E. of Cæsarea Philippi. The death-place of Sheba.

ABEL CHARMAIM, a town of Reuben, 7 m. from Rabbath Ammon.

ABEL MAIM, i. q. Abel-beth-Maacha.

ABEL MEHOLA (Abel Mèa), a town of Manasseh, bet. Bethsan (10) and Shechem, where the Midianites took refuge from Gideon. The birth-place of Elisha.

ABEL MIZRAIM, a place in Ephraim, bet. Jericho and the Jordan, where the Israelites, whom the Canaanites mistook for Egyptians, mourned for Jacob. Bethagla afterwards rose on the site.

ABEL SITTIM, a town of Moabitis, near the Jordan, and over against Jericho, where the Israelites sinned with the Moabitish women.

ABELLA, a town of Campania, on Clanius fl. towards its source; N. E. of Nola. A Chalcidian settlement, noted for its filberts and apples. *Avella Vecchia.*

ABELLĪNUM (Avellana), I. cap. of the Marsi, Lucania, on Aciris fl. towards its source; N. E. of Casilinum. *Marsico Vetere.* II. Surnamed Protropum, a town of the Hirpini, Samnium, bet. Beneventum (16) and Picentia (12). *Avellino.*

ABELTERIUM, a town of the Celtici, Lusitania, bet. Scalabis W. N. W. and Septem Aræ S. E.

ABENS fl., a r. of Vindelicia, falling into the Danube below Abusina. *Abens.*

ABĒSAMIS, a town of Syria, built by Semiramis.

ABĒSTE, a town of Drangiana, N. of Elymandrus fl. *Bost.*

ABHORRAS fl. (Aburas), i. q. Chaborras.

ABIÆ, a town of Messenia, on Messeniacus sin., 9 m. s. from Pheræ. The Ira of Homer.

ABIETA, i. q. Abinta.

ABII, a people of Scythia extra Imaum, of uncertain position, noted for their peaceful integrity of life.

ABĬLA, I. a town of Ammonitis, 7 m. from Philadelphia; the residence of Jephtha; II. a town of Cœle-Syria, cap. of Abilene, on Abana fl., bet. Heliopolis (32) and Damascus (15), the burial-place of Abel. *Nebi-Abel.* III. a town of Decapolis, near Hieromax fl., bet. Gadara (12) and Capitolias. IV. a town of Spain.

ABILENE, a district of Cœle-Syria, about Abila.

ABILONCÆ, the people of Abila, Syria.

ABILUNUM, a town of the Juthungi, Germania Magna, on Campus fl. towards its source; N. E. of Usbium.

ABIMAEL, a district of Arabia Felix, s. of Themud.

ABINA, a town of Susiana.

ABINTA (Abieta), a town of the Jazyges Metanastæ, on Bollia fl., above Anabum.

ABISAMA (Abisa), Gosa, a port of the Adramytæ, Arabia, bet. Arabiæ Felicis Emporium and Cane. *Abin.*

ABISARIS (Ambisaris), a district of India, E. of the Hydaspes.

ABISSA, a port of the Omanitæ, Arabia, bet. Corodamum prom. and Cosara. *Abisagi.*

ABLĂTA, a town of Pontus, near Polemonium.

ABLIANA, a town of Albania, on the Caspian, bet. Albianus fl. and Cyrus fl.

ABLĬTI, a people of Mysia, near Pergamus.

ABNICII, a maritime people of Syrtica Regio, w. of Sabrata.

ABNICUM, a town of Armenia. *Ani. Anisi.*

ABNŎBA (Arnoba, Arnova), m. of Germania Mag., running N.W.—S.E. bet. the Rhine, about Aliso, and the Danube, towards its source. *Black Forest; Baar, Abenow, &c.*

ABOBRICA, a marit. town of the Grovii, Tarraconensis, bet. Spacorum vicus and Minius. *Betanzos.*

ABOCCIS (Abuncis), a town of the Nubæ, on the Nile, bet. Premuthis and Cambysis Ærarium. Here was a celebrated temple of Athor (Venus). *Aboo-Simbel.*

ABODIACUM (Abuzacum), a town of the Licates, Vindelicia, on Licus fl., bet. Augusta Vindelicorum (31) and Parthanum (30). *Peisenberg.*

ABOLANI, a people of Latium, towards Alba.

ABOLLA, a town of Sicily, at the mouth of Erineus fl.

ABŎNA æstuar., an æstuary of the Cornavii, Britannia, E. of Vervedrum prom. *Dornoch Frith.*

ABŎNE, a town of the Belgæ, 9 m. N.W. of Aquæ Solis. *Compton Greenfield.*

ABŎNOTEICHOS (Aboni-Mœnia), *prius* Colussa, *postea* Iŏnopolis, a port of the Heneti, Paphlagonia, 20 m. s.w. from Æginetes. The birth-place of Alexander, the pseudo-Æsculapius. *Ineboli.*

ABORACA, a town of Sarmatia Europæa, towards Mæotis palus.

ABORIENSE, a town of Africa Propria.

ABORĬGĬNES, "from the beginning;" generally nations whose origin cannot be traced; specially the primitive population of Italy, the Umbri, Opici, and Ænotri; and, more peculiarly, the people about Reate, called also Casci, Prisci, Sacrani.

ABORON, a town of Ancobaritis, Mesopotamia, on the Euphrates, bet. Thilutha and Olabus.

ABOTIS, a town of Thebais, on the Nile L., bet. Hypsele and Aphroditopolis, opposite Antæopolis.

ABRAGANA, a town of Serica, on Bautisus fl.

ABRAVANNUS æstuarium, a bay of the Novantæ, Britannia, E. of Novantorum prom. *Glenluce Bay.*

ABRETA, an early name of Mysia, from the nymph Brettia.

ABRETTENE, a district of Mysia, bet. Macistus fl., towards its source and Rhyndacus fl.

ABRINATÆ, a people of Pontus.

ABRINCA, i. q. Obringa.

ABRINCATUI, I. a maritime people of Lugdunensis II., bounded N. by the Bajocasses and Unelli, s. by the Redones and Aulerci-Diablintes, E. by the Viducasses. *Diocese of Avranches.* II. *prius* Ingena, their cap., E. of Aletum. *Avranches.*

ABROSTOLA, a town of the Tolistoboii, Galatia, bet. Pessinus (24) and Amorium.

ABROTŎNUM, a town of Syrtica Regio, of uncertain position. Identified by Mannert with Sabrata.

ABSIDRI, a tribe of Carduchi, Assyria, N. of Calachene.

ABUCÆI, a people of Arabia Felix, on Persicus sinus, about Coromanus.

ABUCINI portus, a town of the Sequani, Maxima Sequanorum, on the Arar, s.w. of Luxovium. *Port sur Saone.*

ABUNIS, a town of the Agoritæ, Sarmatia, s.E. of Suruba.

ABUR, a town of the Saringæ, India, N.W. of Orthura.

ABURATHA, a port of Taprobane, N. bet. Mordula and Bocana.

ABUS æstuarium, an æstuary of Britain, E. at Ocellum prom. *Humber.*

ABUS fl., a r. of the Coritani, Brit., falling into Abus æstuar. *Ouse.*

ABUS m. (Aba), a ridge of Anti-Taurus, in Armenia Maj., bet. Arsissa palus and Lychnitis palus. *Agri-dagh, Koh-i-nuh* ("mountain of Noah").

ABUSINA, a town of the Runicates, Vindelicia, on Abens fl. near its confluence with the Danube, 12 m. s.w. of Regina. *Abensberg.*

ABUZACUM, i. q. Abodiacum.

ABUZATHA, a town of Adiabene, on the Tigris, N. of Ctesiphon.

ABỸDOS, I. a town of Byzacene, bet. Mazara and Byzacium; II. a town of Mysia, on the Hellespont, 3¾ m. s.w. from Sestos; a Thracian settlement, enlarged by Milesians. Noted for its horses, for Xerxes' bridge, for the loves of Hero and Leander, and for its resistance to Philip. On *Cape Nagara.* III. a town of Pæonia, on the Axius; IV. a town of Thebais, on the Nile, bet. This and Diospolis Parva. A Milesian settlement. The burial-place of Osiris. *El Matfoon* ("the buried").

ABỸLA m., a pr. of Mauritania Tingitana, at the inner entrance, s. of the Mediterranean. One of the Pillars of Hercules, the other being the opposite pr. of Calpe. *Cabo Ximiera; Apes' Hill.*

ABYSTRUM. *Vide* Aprustum.

ABZIRITANUM, a town of Africa Propria.

ABZOÆ, a town of Scythia, on Borealis oceanus.

ACABE m., a pr. of Thebais, on the Red Sea, above Nichesia.

ACABENE, a district of Mygdonia, Mesopotamia, on the Tigris, N. of Cæne.

ACABIS, baths of Cyrenaica.

ACABICONTEICHOS, a town of Mauritania, under Atlas m.

ACACESIUM, a town of Arcadia, on Acacesius m., founded by Acacus, S. of Lycaon.

ACACESIUS m., a m. of Arcadia; 1 m. from Praseæ, whence Mercury derived the appellation Acacesius.

ACADAMA, a town of Syria, on the Euphrates.

ACADARA, I. a town of India e. Gangem, N.E. of Agimothra. II. of Arabia Felix.

ACADINUS fons, a fountain of Sicily, near Palica, endued with the quality of testing oaths, those written falsely sinking at once to the bottom.

ACALANDRA, a town of Lucania, on the Acalandrus. Salandra.

ACALANDRUS fl., a r. of Lucania, falling into Tarentinus sinus, E. of Thurii. Salandrella.

ACALE, a town of Arabia Felix.

ACALISSUS (Acalia, Ascandalis), a town of Lycia.

ACAMANTIS, a name, I. of Cyprus, from Acamas prom. ; II. of Teos.

ACAMANTIS m., a m. of Cyprus w.

ACAMANTIUM, a town of Phrygia Magna, built by Acamas, son of Theseus.

ACAMAS, I. the N.W. extremity of Cyprus, rising in two semi-globular summits. Cape Amant : Salizano. II. a town of Cyprus, at Acamas prom. Grusocco.

ACAMPSIS fl., i. q. Apsarus.

ACANNÆ (Psygmi portus), a port of Æthiopia, at Elephas prom.

ACANTHONITIS, a district of Carmania, on the confines of Gedrosia.

ACANTHUS, I. an isl. of Mysia, in the Propontis, near Ophiusa ; II. m. of Athamania, bet. the Arachthus and the Inachus. Tzumerka. III. a town (Doulonpolis) of Cnidus penins., Caria, near Bubassus; IV. of Acte penins., Macedonia, on Strymonicus sinus, at the E. extremity of Xerxes' ditch—an Andrian settlement, noted for its wines. V. of Ægypt, on the Nile R., bet. Aphroditopolis and Scenæ-Mandræ. Dashur. VI. of Athamania, under Acanthus m., s.w. of Tetraphylia.

ACAPEATÆ, a people of Sarmatia Europ., on Mæotis palus.

ACĂRA, I. a town of Pannonia. II. of Gallia Cispadana, near Rhegium Lepidum.

ACAREA fons, a fountain of Corinth, where Iolas cut off the head of Eurystheus.

ACARMAN, a town of Arabia Felix.

ACARNANES, "unshorn," a tribe of Leleges, Acarnania ; so named to distinguish them from the Curetes, or traditionally, from Acarnan, s. of Alcmæon.

ACARNANIA, a division of Epirus, bounded w. and s. by Ionium mare, E. by Achelous fl., N. by Ambracius sin. Noted for its horses. Carnia, Carlelia.

ACARNE. Vide Acharræ.

ACATHARTUS sinus, a bay of Arabicus sinus, s.

ACATHRA ins., I. an isl. of the Sinæ. II. of Arabia Felix.

ACAVATHA, a town of Palmyrene, bet. Matthana and Cholle, S.S.E. of Thapsacus.

ACCAD, a town of Sittacene, 9 m. s.w. from Ctesiphon. Built by Nimrod. Akker-koof.

ACCARŎN, prius Ekron, a city of Judæa, bet. Jamnia and Azotus. The metropolis of the Philistæi. Aker.

ACCHITÆ, a people of Arabia Felix, on the Red Sea.

ACCI, a town of the Bastitani, Bætica, on the Bætis, E.N.E. of Illiberis. A colonia (Julia Gemella Accitana) ; the station of the 3rd and 6th legions. Guadix el Viejo.

ACCION lacus, i. q. Lemanus lacus.

ACCIPITRUM ins. (Hieracum), an isl., I. of Arabia Felix, in the Red Sea, N.W. of Mamala ; II. of Sardinia, w. above Plumbia ins. San Pietro.

ACCISI, a people of Sarmatia As., on Mæotis palus.

ACCO (Akē), a city of Asher, on the Mediterranean, at the mouth of Belus fl., 30 m. s. from Tyrus. A colonia (C. Claudii Cæsaris) ; called also, circa 100 B.C., Ptolemais, in honour of Ptolemy. Acca; Acre.

ACCUSIORUM colonia, i. q. Gratianopolis.

ACDEI, a people of Sarmatia Asiatica, on Mæotis palus.

ACEDĬCI, a people of Latium, subject to the Æqui.

ACĒLA, I. a town of Lycia, named from Acelus, s. of Hercules. II. of the Regni, Brit., bet. Vindomis and Vagniaca.

ACĒLUM, a town of the Veneti, Venetia, N.W. of Tarvisium. Asolo.

ACĒMA m., i. q. Cema.

ACER fl., a river of Lucania, falling into the Sora at Grumentum.

ACERNUM, a town of Picenum, 15 m. E. from Salernum. Acerno.

ACERONIA, a town of Lucania, bet. Forum Popilii (9) and Marcelliana (9). Brienza.

ACERRÆ, a town, I. of the Insubres, Gallia

Transpadana, on the Addua, bet. Cremona (13) and Laus Pompeia (22) on Via Posthumia. *Gherra.* II. of Campania, on Clanius fl., near its source, N.W. of Nola, dest. by Hannibal, col. by Augustus. *Acerra.*

ACERVETIS, i. q. Calatis, Thraciæ.

ACERVO, a town of the Latovici, Pannonia Sup., 18 m. from Æmona. *Seussenburg.*

ACĒS fl. Ind. i. q. Acesines.

ACESIA, a village of Lemnos, so named from Philoctetes having been cured there.

ACESĪNES fl. (Aces), I. a r. of India e. Gangem, rising in Imaus m. and falling into the Indus. *Chunab, Jenaub.* II. i. q. Tanais. III. of Sicily, falling into Siculum mare under Ætna m. N. of Acis fl. *Cantaro.*

ACESTA, i. q. Ægesta.

ACHABYTUS m., a m. of Rhodes, on which stood a temple of Jupiter.

ACHÆI, I. a name generally of the Greeks; II. a tribe of Pelasgi, originally from Achaia, Thessaly, who, driven from their settlements in Laconia by the Heraclidæ, seized upon Ionia in Peloponnesus, and gave it their name. III. Orchomenian settlers in Sarmatia Asiat., on the Euxine, S.E. of the Toreatæ, afterwards named Zichi, Ziketi. IV. -scopuli, rocks of Triphylia, near Samos.

ACHÆIUM, a town of Troas, on the coast, opposite Tenedos ins.

ACHÆMÆNIA, a name of Persia, from the Achæmænidæ.

ACHÆUS fl. (Burcas), a r. of the Achæi Sarmat., falling into the Euxine 15 m. s. from Hercules prom.

ACHAĪA, I. a district of Phthiotis, Thessaly N.W., the early seat of the Achæi. II. a country of Peloponnesus, bounded, including Sicyonia, N. by Corinthiacus sinus, s. by Arcadia and Elis, E. by Corinthia, w. by Ionium mare. First named Ægialus, "shore," and peopled by Pelasgi; then Ionia, when the population was enlarged by an immigration of Ionians; and next Achaia, when occupied by Achæi from Laconia. *Livadia.* III. a Roman province, comprehending Peloponnesus and Græcia extra Peloponnesum, s. of Thessaly. IV. a town of Crete. V. capital of the Achæi, Sarmat., on Cerceticus sinus. VI. surnamed Vetus, the earlier settlement of the same people, 15 m. N.W. from the preceding; VII. the early name of Jalysus, in Rhodes.

ACHAIACALA, a town of Auranitis, Babylonia, on an isl. of the Euphrates, s. of Olabus.

ACHAIORUM littus, I. the coast of Cyprus N., bet. Aphrodisia and Carpasia. Named from the Greeks, who landed here under Teucer. *Near Jalousa.* II. portus, a port of the Callipedæ, Sarmatia, w. of Olbia. *Porto Buono.* III. of Troas, 2½ m. s. from the mouth of the Scamander, the assembling-place of the Greek fleet. IV. statio, the tomb of Hecuba, in Thracius Chersonesus, over against Sigæum.

ACHAIS, I. a town of Aria. II. of Hyrcania, built by Antiochus in honour of his brother.

ACHANA fl., a r. of Arabia, towards the Euphrates.

ACHANI (Acharni), a p. of Scythia.

ACHAR, i. q. Nizibis.

ACHARACA, I. a town of Lydia, bet. Tralles and Nysa, where was the cave Charonium, in which sick persons were directed to their cure in a dream. II. of Lycaonia, w. of Iconium.

ACHARDEUS fl., a r. of Sarmatia Asiat., rising in Caucasus m., and falling into the Tanais towards its mouth. *Manitsch, Egorlik.*

ACHARITANUM, a town of Africa, towards Cyrenaica.

ACHARNÆ, a demus of Attica, s.w. of Hymettus, the population of which, chiefly charcoal-burners, were proverbial for their uncouth manners. *Near Menidi.*

ACHARRÆ (Acharne), a town of Dolopia, Thessaly, on Vanusus fl., below Theuma. *Achari.*

ACHASA, a district of Scythia extra Imaum, bet. the Chattiæ and the Chamanæi.

ACHĀTES fl., a r. of Sicily, falling into the Mediterranean s.E. of Gela. In it agates, thence named, were first found. *Drillo.*

ACHĒLŌUS fl., I. a r. (*prius* Thoas, "swift," Thestius, *postea* Pachilola) of Græcia extra Peloponnesum, rising in Pindus m. N. of Dolopia, and, after separating Acarnania from Aperantia and Ætolia, falling into Ionium mare by two mouths at Œniadæ and Nasus. *Aspro-potamo.* II. of the Malienses, Thessaly, falling into Maliacus sinus at Phalara. III. of Thesoa, Arcadia, falling into Alpheus fl.

ACHERDUS, a demus of Attica, of the tribe Hippothoontis.

ACHĒRON fl., "joyless," I. a r. 1. *postea* Zoonautes, of Bithynia, falling into the Euxine near Heraclea. II. of Bruttium, falling into Crathis fl., near Consentia, the death-place of Alexander, king of the Molossi. *Maresanto.* III. of Epirus, rising N.w. of Passaron, and, after running for some distance under ground, falling into the Adriatic at Glykys portus. There was an oracle on its banks, where the dead were evoked. The extreme gloom of its scenery suggested it to Homer as one of the rivers of Erebus. *Souli.* IV. of Triphylia, falling into Alpheus fl. near Typana; Pluto, Proserpine, and Ceres were peculiarly venerated on its banks. V. lacus (Acheruns), a sulphureous lake of Baiæ, Campania, so hemmed in by hills that only the sun at noonday penetrated thither. Reputed a resort of witches.

ACHERONTIA (Acherontum), a town of the Peuceti, Lucania, "nestling" on a hill s.e. of Ferentum. *Acerenza.*

ACHERUSIA palus, I. a lake of Campania, bet. Misenum and Cumæ. *Lago di Fusaro.* II. of Thesprotia, Epirus, formed by Acheron fl. towards its source.

ACHERUSIA specus, a cavern on the coast of Bithynia, e. of Heraclea; reputed the entrance to Orcus, by which Hercules descended in search of Cerberus.

ACHIBI, a people of Sarmatia, contiguous to the Savari.

ACHILLEA ins., i. q. Achillis.

ACHILLEI cursus, penins. (Achilleos Dromos), a long narrow peninsula of Sarmatia E., bet. Sagaricus sin. and Carcinites sin. Named from the races and other games established there by Achilles.

ACHILLEIUM, I. a town of Dandarica, Sarmat. As., on Mæotis palus, at the entrance of Cimmerius Bosporus. *Near Buschuk.* II. of Lydia, near Ænea. III. on Sigæum prom., built around the tomb of Achilles.

ACHILLEIUS portus, a port of Laconia, on Laconicus sin., w.n. of Psamothus. *Porto-Kallio.*

ACHILLIS ins., I. Leuce, an isl. of Dacia, off Pselon Ost. II. i. q. Achillei cursus. III. of Samos, towards Ampelus prom.

ACHINDANA fl., a r. of Carmania, falling into Persicus sinus e. of Corius fl.

ACHISARMI, a people of Africa.

ACHMETHA, Heb. " treasure-fortress," i. q. Ecbatana.

ACHNÆ, the early name of Casus ins.

ACHOLAI, a town of Arabia Felix.

ACHOLLA (Acolitanum oppidum, Acilla), a maritime town of Byzacena, bet. Sullectis and Brachodes prom. A Mitylenean settlement. *Near Elalia.*

ACHOR, "distress," a valley of Benjamin, along the Jordan, near Jericho; the scene of Achan's punishment.

ACHRADUS, a demus of Attica.

ACHRIANE, a town on the Caspian.

ACHRUA, a town of Arabia Felix.

ACHZIB (Achsaph, Ecdippa), I. a town of Asher, on the Mediterranean, 10 m. n. of Acco. *Zib.* II. a town of Judah.

ACIACUM, a town of the Morini, in Tervanensis pagus. *Auchy.*

ACĬBI, a town of Sarmatia Europ., n.e. of Riphæi m.

ACĬDALUS fons, I. a fountain of Campania, the water of which was good for sore eyes; II. of Bœotia, near Orchomenus, sacred to the Graces.

ACIDAS (Acidon, Jardanus) fl., a r. of Tryphylia, Elis, falling into Anigrus fl. towards the sea. Near it was the tomb of Jardanus.

ACIDAVA, I. a town of the Burideenses, Dac., bet. Cedonia (24) and Apulum (14); II. of the Potulatenses, Dac., on Aluta fl., L. bet. Romula (13) and Rusidava (24). *Lucavez.*

ACIDII, a village of Lucania, n. of Grumentum.

ACIENSES, a people of Latium, above Albanus m.

ACĬLA, Arabia, i. q. Ocelis.

ACILISĒNE, a district of Sophene, Arm., e. of Chorzene. *Ekelis.*

ACILLA. *Vide* Acholla.

ACIMBRO, i. q. Acinippo.

ACIMINCUM, a town of Pannonia, on the Danube, above its confluence with the Tibiscus, bet. Bononia and Cusum. *Alt-Salankemen.*

ACĬNA, a town of Arabia.

ACINAI, a people of Bactriana, bet. the Chomi and the Tambyzi.

ACINXCIS fl., a r. of Colchis, falling into the Euxine, bet. Phasis fl. and Acampsis fl.

ACINCUM (Aquincum), a town of Valeria, Pannon., on the Danube, bet. Crumerum and Campona. The station of the Legio II. adjutrix. *Alt Buda,* near *Buda.*

ACINIPPO (Acimbro), a town of the Turdetani, in Bætica, w. of Arunda.

ACINTANI, a people of Spain, worshippers of Neco, a form of Mars.

ACĬRIS fl., a r. of Lucania, rising n.w. of Abellinum Marsicum, and falling into Tarentinus sin. at Heraclea. *Agri.*

ACIS fl., I. a r. of Sicily, *quasi* "swift as an arrow (Acinius)," rising in Ætna m., and, after a course of about a mile, falling into Siculum mare at Acis, bet. Acesines fl. and Adrix, n. of Catana. Named from the loves of Galatea. *Iaci.* II. a town of Sicily, e. at the mouth of Acis fl. *Castel d' Iaci.* III. ins., one of the Cyclades ins., towards Crete.

ACITAVONES, a people of the Alpes Cottiæ, contiguous to the Salassi. *Val de la Vanoise.*

ACITHIS fl. (Acithius, Atys), a r. of Sicily, falling into Africum pelagus, N. of Lily-bæum prom. *Carabi.*

ACITIA, a name of Melos.

ACITODUNUM, a town of the Lemovices, Aquitania, S.E. of Prætorium. *Ahun.*

ACITORIZIACUM GALATIÆ, i. q. Androsia.

ACIUS fl., Thestius, a river of Ætolia.

ACMŌDA (Æmōdæ), seven islands in Deucalidonus oceanus. *Shetland.*

ACMŌNIA (Acmōna), a town, I. of the Potulatenses, Dacia, s. of Tiriscus. II. of Phrygia Epictetus, bet. Cotyæum (35) and Alydda (25), near the source of Thymbres fl. ; built by Acmon, s. of Manes.

ACOLA, a town of Media.

ACŎNE, "whetstones," the port of Heraclea, in Bithynia. Besides whetstones, its district was very productive of the plant hence called ' aconite.'

ACONITES, a people of Italy, over against Sardinia.

ACONTIA, a town of the Vaccæi, Tarraconensis, on the Durius.

ACONTISMA (Saltus Sapæorum, Symbolum), a defile between the mountains of the Sapæi in Thrace and the coast; S.E. of Philippi.

ACONTIUM, a town of Arcadia, named from Acontius, s. of Lycaon.

ACONTIUS fl., I. a r. of Bœotia, rising in Acontius m., and falling into Copais lac. ; II. mons, a m. of Bœotia, on the confines of Phocis, s. of Abæ.

ACORABA, Syria, i. q. Androna.

ACORIS, I. a town of Heptanomis, on the Nile, R. bet. Cynopolis and Speos Artemidos. *Tehené.* II. of the Jazyges, Sarmat., on Palus Mæotis, E. of Byce lac.

ACRA, I. a town of Bruttium. II. (Acracomion), a town of Taurica Chersonnesus, s., at the w. entrance of Cimmerius Bosporus. III. Mœsiæ, i. q. Tetrisia. IV. ins., an isl. of Mauritania Cæsar., opposite the mouth of Siga fl. IV. i. q. Japygium prom. V. LEUCE (Castrum Album), " white castle," a town of the Contestani, Tarraconensis, on Illicitanus sin., s. of Alebus. Built by Hamilcar. *Denia.* VIII. MELÆNA, a town of the Thyni, in Bithynia, at Melæna prom. *Calin Acra.*

ACRABA, a town of Osrhoene, s.w. of Carrhæ.

ACRABATENE, a toparchy of Samaria, s. about Acrabbim.

ACRABATĒNE, a toparchy of Judæa, on the borders of Idumæa.

ACRABBIM, capital of the toparchy of Acrabatene, Samaria, 9 m. E. from Sichem. *Akrabah.*

ACRACANUS, Babylonia, i. q. Maarsares.

ACRÆ, I. a town of Ætolia, N.W. of Trichonius lac., near Thestia. II. of Sicily, near the source of Helorus fl., 24 m. s.w. of Syracuse. Built by the Syracusans 665 B.C. *Arcia.*

ACRÆPHIA (Acræphium, Acræphinon), a town of Bœotia, on the w. slope of Ptous m., near Copais lacus. Considered by some the Arne of Homer. *Near Karditza.*

ACRAGAS, I. a town of Eubœa. II. (Agragas), the Greek name of Agrigentum.

ACRĂGAS fl., a r. of Sicily, falling into Africum pelagus, below Agrigentum. *Girgenti.*

ACRASUS, a town of Lydia.

ACRAVISCI, a people of Mœsia Superior, N.W.

ACRE, a town of Cyprus, where was a temple of Venus, to which women were not admitted.

ACRIA, I. a town of Laconia, on Laconicus sinus, 4 m. s. from Helos, with a temple of Cybele. *San Giorgio.* II. of the Turdetani, Bætica, near Hispalis.

ACRIDOPHAGI, I. a people of Ethiopia, living upon salted locusts, and dying at an early age of *morbus pediculosus.* There was another nation of locust-eaters in Parthia.

ACRILLÆ (Acilla), a town of Sicily, on Anapus fl., R. bet. Acræ and Syracusæ.

ACRIOTERI palus (Pisidicus lacus), a lake of Pisidia, bet. Termessus and Sagalassus. *Igridi.*

ACRISIONE, a town of Argolis, N.E. of Argos.

ACRĪTAS prom., I. Leucatas, a pr. of Bithynia, at the E. entrance of Astacenus sin., 37 m. from Nicomedia. II. the s. headland of Messenia, opposite Theganassa ins. *Cape Gallo.*

ACROATHON. *Vide* Acrothoon.

ACROCORINTHUS m., *prius* Epope, a hill of Corinth, s.w. of the city ; on it stood the citadel of Corinth, and a temple of Venus, attended by 1000 slave-priestesses.

ACROCERAUNII (Ceraunii), m. of Epirus, extending along the coast nearly to Buthrotum, and inland to Tomarus m. ; in part dividing Illyria from Epirus. Terrible for their lightning-storms, whence the name. *Kimara.*

ACROCERAUNIUM prom., the N.W. extremity

of Acroceraunii, on the Adriatic, opposite Sasonius. *C. Linguetta.*

ACROCOMÆ, a people of Thrace, so named from their wearing the hair long in front.

ACROCON saltus. *Vide* Oca.

ACROLISSUS, the citadel of Lissus, in Illyria, E. of the town. *Alessio.*

ACROLOCHIAS prom., a pr. of Egypt at Alexandria, on which the Pharos stood.

ACRŌNIUS lacus, a lake formed by the Rhine, after passing through Venetus lacus.

ACROPŎLIS, I. the citadel of Athens, built by Cecrops. II. Iberia, i. q. Harmoziaca.

ACROREA regio, a mountainous district of Elis, on the borders of Arcadia.

ACROTADUS ins., an isl. in Persicus sinus.

ACROTERIUM prom., a pr. of Lycia, 6¼ m. E. of Antiphellas.

ACROTHON prom. (Acroathon), the S.E. extremity of Acte, in Macedonia. *C. Monte Santo.*

ACRŎTHOOS (Acrŏthon), a town on the upper region of Athos m., overwhelmed by an earthquake, as a punishment for the impiety of its inhabitants, and succeeded by Apollonia.

ACRUNUM, a fortress of Bithynia, at one of the passes of Olympus m.

ACRURIUM m., *postea* Galate, a m. of Phocis, near Pharygæ.

ACTANIA ins., one of the Electrides ins., Germ., off the mouth of Flevus fl., N.E. *Heligoland.*

ACTE, "sea-shore," I. the early name of Attica. Traditionally named from Actæus, a king of the country. II. MITYLENARUM, a portion of the coast of Mysia, s. of Cisthene, the seat of several Mitylenean colonies. III. penins., the E. penins. of Chalcidice, Maced., bet. Singiticus sin. and Strymonicus sin.

ACTIUM prom., I. a pr. of Corsica, w. *Cape d'Acciajuola.* II. a city of the Agræi, in Acarnania, at the inner entrance, s. to Ambracius sinus, 5 m. E. from Anactorium. Off this point, in the Anactorius sinus, was fought the battle in which Augustus defeated Antony. *La Punta.*

ACTRIDA, a town of Arabia Felix.

ACULIA, Hispan., i. q. Acontia.

ACUNUM, a town, I. of the Tricastini, in Gallia Narbonensis, bet. Senomagus (18) and Batiana (12). *Ancone.* II. of Pannonia, i. q. Acimincum.

ACUR, a town of Pandionis regnum, Ind., near Agaricus sin.

ACUSIO, Galliæ, i. q. Acunum.

ACUTÆ ins., isl. near the Echinades.

ACYPHAS, I. a town of the Malienses, on Sperchius fl., above Anticyra. II. (Doridis), i. q. Pindus opp.

ACYTUS ins., i. q. Melos.

AD ABUM, a town of the Coritani, Brit., on Abus fl., R. bet. Petuaria and Prætorium.

AD ÆNUM, i. q. Pons Æni.

AD AMBRUM, a town of the Consuanetæ, Vindel, on Ambra fl., bet. Isunisca (32) and Augusta Vindelicorum (27). *Furstenfeld.*

AD AMMONEM, a small village of Syrtica, around a temple of Ammon, bet. Sabrata and Casæ.

AD AMMONTEM, a town of Ituræa, bet. Cæsarea Paneas s.w. and Damascus N.E.

AD ANAM, a town of the Celtici, Lusitania, on the Anas, below Pax Augusta.

AD ANGITULAM, a town of Bruttium, at the mouth of Angitula fl., bet. Ad Turres (13) and Nicotera (25), on Via Aquilia.

AD ANSAM, I. a town of the Trinobantes, Brit., bet. Colonia and Canonium. II. Othona, a town of the Trinobantes, on Idumania fl., 15 m. from Combretonium. *Near Dedham.*

AD AQUAS, baths, I. 1. of the Potulatenses, Dac., on Sergetiafl., 14 m. E. of Zarmizegethusa, bet. *Hatzeg* and *Vaj da Hunyad* N. II. *postea* Belga Uvella, Theorodunum. of the Belgæ, Britannia. *Wells.* III. of the Lusitani, bet. Lama, N.W., and Lancia Transcudana, S.E. IV. of the Mœsi, Mœsia Sup., on the Danube, bet. Pons Trajani and Dorticum. V. of Picenum, on Truentus fl., bet. Ad Centesimum (4) and Asculum (10). *Aqua Santa.* VI. of Pæonia, on the borders of Mœsia, bet. Amavasarium (12) and Scopi (21). *Banja.* VII. -ALBULAS, a town of the Latini, Latium, on Anio fl., bet. Rome (14) and Tibur (6), on Via Tiburtina. *Solfatara.*

AD ARAS, a town of the Turduli, Bætica, bet. Astigi, s.w., and Corduba, N.E.

AD ARNUM, a town of Etruria, on Arnus fl., L. bet. Florentia (18) and In Portu (4).

AD ARVALLA, a town of Numidia, bet. Sibus and Vicus Valeriani.

AD AUREOS, a town of the Veneti, Venetia, bet. Vicetia (11) and Cadianum (10). *Montebello.*

AD BIVIUM, a station on Via Lavicana, at its junction with Via Latina, N.W. of Anagnia. *Sant' Ilario.*

AD CABALLOS, a town of Gallia Transpadana. *Bagnocavallo.*

AD CAHALIS, a town of Numidia, bet. Zyrna Maseli and Ad Germani.

AD CALEM, a town of Umbria, bet. Ad Ensem (14) and Ad Intercisa (9), on Via Flaminia. *Cagli.*

AD CALOREM, a town of Lucania, on Calor fl., R. bet. Ad Silarum and Marcelliana.

AD CANALES, a town, I. of Messapia, under Aulon m., w.n.w. of Tarentum. *Canile.* II. of the Pentri, Samnium, on Via Trentana, bet. Ad Pirum (10) and Bovianum (11).

AD CAPSUM ULTIMUM, a town of the Psylli, Africa, on Syrtes Maj., at Hippi prom.

AD CASAS CÆSARIANAS (Ad Fines), a town of Etruria, on the Via Cassia, bet. Arretium (25) and Florentia (25). *S. Giovanni.*

AD CASTORIS, a town of the Cenomanni, Gallia Transpad., bet. Cremona and Bedriacum.

AD CASTRA, I. a town of the Carni, Venetia, on Frigidus fl., bet. Ad Fornulos (12) and Ad Pirum. II. (Legio XXX. Ulpia Trajana), of the Gugerni, Germania, on the Rhine, bet. Vetera Castra (1½) and Colonia Trajana. *In der Poll Alpen.*

AD CEDROS, a town of the Tectosages, Narbonensis I., bet. Ebromagus and Carcaso.

AD CENTENARIAS, a town of Numidia, bet. Tenebreste and Ad Rubras.

AD CENTESIMUM, a town of Picenum, on Via Salaria, bet. Badies (10) and Asculum Picenum (12). *Quintodecimo.*

AD CENTURIONES (Ad Centenarium), a town of the Sardones, Narbonensis I., n.w. of Juncaria. *Cervera.*

AD CEPASIAS, a town of Venetia, on Via Æmilia, bet. Feltria (28) and Opitergium (28). *Abbazia.*

AD CONFLUENTES, a marit. town of Gallia Cispadana, N. of Rubico fl.

AD DECIMUM, I. a town of Calabria, on Via Egnatina, bet. Egnatia (10) and Speluncæ (11). II. of the Insubres, Gallia Transpadana, bet. Ticinum (10) and Mediolanum (10). *Casa Dico.* III. of the Latini, Latium, on Via Latina, bet. Rome (10) and Roboraria (6). IV. of the Taurini, Gall. Transpadana, on Aurelia Via, bet. Augusta Taurinorum (10) and Quadrata (12). V. of the Treveri, Belgica I., on Mosella fl., below Augusta Treverorum.

AD DIANAM, I. a town of Cestrine, in Epirus, bet. Buthrotum (8) and Glykis portus (13). II. of the Eordeti, Illyria, on Genusus fl., bet. Trajectum Genusi (7) and Candavia (2). III. of Numidia, on the coast, bet. Tuniza (15) and Hippo Regius.

AD DRACONES, I. a town of Armenia Minor, bet. Olotœdariza (26) and Aza (24)—probably the Charax of Ptolemy. II. of Mauritania Cæsar., bet. Regiæ and Albula.

AD DRINUM, a town of the Triballi, Mœs., on Drinus fl., R. above Gensis.

AD DUODECIM, I. a town of the Ædui, Lugdunensis I., bet. Cabillonum (18) and Augustodunum (16½). *Conches.* II. of the Batavi, Germania II., bet. Noviomagus (18), and Grinnes (9), near *Yssendorn.* III. of Calabria, 12 m. N.W. from Hydruntum. *Borgogne.* IV. of the Mediomatrici, Belgica I., bet. Decem Pagi (18) and Divodurum (18). V. of the Sapæi, Thrace, on Egnatia Via, bet. Drapescas and Philippi. VI. of the Segusini, Gallia Transpadana, on Duria min. fl., R. bet. Segusio (12) and Ad Fines (12), on Via Aurelia. *Giaconera* or *Burgone.* VII. of the Veneti, Venetia, bet. Patavium (12) and Ad Nonum (11), on the Via Æmilia. *Near Miraus.*

AD DUOS PONTES, a town of the Lucenses, in Gallæcia, at the mouth of Læron fl.

AD DURIUM, a town of the Durotriges, Britannia, on Durius fl., s.w. of Moridunum. *Totness.*

AD ENSEM, a town of Umbria, bet. Helvillum (10) and Ad Calem (14), on Via Flaminia. *La Scheggia.*

AD FICUM, a town of the Psylli, Africa prop., on Syrtis Maj., bet. Auzui and Prætorium.

AD FIGLINAS, a town of the Euburiates, Liguria, on Via Aurelia, bet. Hasta (3) and Genua (7). *Finale.*

AD FINEM, a town of the Veneti, Venetia, on Meduacus min. fl., bet. Vicetia (11) and Patavium (10). *Arlesega.*

AD FINES, I. a town of the Agesinates, Aquitania II., bet. Limonum (30) and Argantomagus (31½). *Haintz.* II. of the Arverni, Aquitania I., bet. Ubinum and Acitodunum. *Croisseacoigne.* III. of the Atrebates, in Belgica II., bet. Castellum (21½) and Nemetacum (21½). *Bethune* or *Annezin.* IV. of the Caturiges, Narbonensis II., bet. Davianum (12) and Vapincum (11). *Blaynie Sept Fons.* V. of the Cenomanni, in Lugdunensis III., bet. Suindinum (24) and Cæsarodunum (30). *Trois Bornes,* near *Château du Loir.* VI. of the Colapini, Pannon., on Colapis fl., bet. Quadrata (14 E.) and Siscia. *Glina.* VII. of the Curiosolites, in Lugdunensis III., bet. Fanum Martis (10½) and Condate. *Autrain.* VIII. of Dacia Medit., in Mœsia Sup., bet. Hammenum and Vendenæ. IX. of Illyria, on the confines of Pannonia, bet. Servitium and Ad

Ladios. X. of the Læetani, Tarraconensis, on Rubricatus fl., R. towards its mouth. XI. of the Levici, in Belgica II., bet. Nasia (21) and Tullum (6). *Foug.* XII. of the Mandubii, Lugdunensis I., near Alesia. *Fins.* XIII. of the Nitrobriges, Aquitania II., bet. Vesubium (30) and Aginnum (22½). *La Marque.* XIV. of the Pelagones, Macedonia, bet. Ad Herculem (8) and Anavasarum (35). XV. of the Petrocorii, Aquitania II., bet. Vesunna (31½) and Augustoritum (31¼). *La Tour Blanche,* bet. Vaux and Chante. XVI. of the Senones, Lugdunensis IV., bet. Aquæ Segestæ (22) and Genabum (15); bet. *Cour-Dieu* and *Philissanet.* XVII. of the Suessiones, Belgica II., bet. Durocortorum (18) and August. Suessionum (18). *Fismes.* XVIII. of the Tasconi, Aquitania I., on Tarnis fl., bet. Tolosa and Cosa. XIX. of the Taurini, Gallia Transpad., on the Aurelia Via, bet. Ad Duodecim (12) and Ad Octavum (8); bet. *Camarelleto* and *Castelleto.* XX. of the Tectosages, Narbonensis I., bet. Elusio and Sestomagus. XXI. of the Tugeni, Rhætia, bet. Vitodurum (30) and Arbor Felix (30). *Pfyn.* XXII. of the Verodunenses, in Belgica II., bet. Verodunum (15) and Ibliodurum (9). *Marcheville.*

AD FLEXUM, I. a town of the Boii, Pannon., bet. Gerulata (16) and Quadratum. *Ovar, Altenburg?* II. of the Cenomanni, Gallia Transp., on Clusius fl., bet. Brixia (11) and Beneventum (10), on Via Æmilia. *Bettola.* III. of the Volsci, Latium, on Via Latina, bet. Casinum (8) and Venafrum (8). *S. Pietro in fine.*

AD FONTICULOS, a town of the Anamares, Gallia Transpad., bet. Florentia (5) and Fidentia (5), on the Via Æmilia. *Fontana.*

AD FORNULOS, a town of the Carni, Venetia, on Frigidus fl., bet. Ad Undecim (12) and Ad Castra (12). *Verloza.*

AD FRATRES, a marit. village of Mauritania Cæsar., bet. Artisiga and Lemnis.

AD GALLINAS, a village round a villa of Livia, on the Tiber, near Rubras. *Civitella d' Arno.*

AD GALLUM (Gallinacium), a town of Zeugitana, on Bagradas fl., R. near its mouth, bet. Utica (12) and Carthage (15). *Gella.*

AD GEMELLAS, a town of the Balari, Sardinia, s.w. of Olbia.

AD GERMANI, a town of Numidia, bet. Ad Cahalis and Buglata.

AD GRADUS, the name given by the Romans to the E. mouth of the Rhone. *Gras.*

AD GRÆCAS, a town of Etruria, on Palus Clusina, bet. Ad Novas (9) and Ad Joglandem (12), on Via Cassia. *Fojano.*

AD HARNABAM, *apud* Livium, i. q. Arna Umbriæ.

AD HERCULEM, I. a town of the Balari, Sardinia, bet. Turris Libyssonis and Erucium. II. of Etruria, 12 m. S.S.E. from Pisæ. *Violino.* III. of Mesopotamia, bet. Dicate and Atra. IV. of Pannonia Inf., on the Danube, bet. Salva and Cirpis (10). V. of the Pelagones, Macedonia, bet. Præsidium (9) and Ad Fines (8). VI. of the Triballi, Mœsia, on Margus fl., bet. Naissus and Hammenum.

AD HONORATIANUM, a town of the Hirpini, Samnium, on Via Numicia, bet. Ad Matrem Magnam (15) and Venusia (28).

AD HORREA, a marit. town of the Digauni, Narbonensis II., bet. Antipolis (12) and Forum Voconii (24). *Horibel.*

AD INTERCISA (Petra Pertusa), a town of Umbria, bet. Ad Calem (4) and Forum Sempronii (9) on Via Æmilia. *Furlo.*

AD JOGLANDEM, a town of Etruria, on Via Cassia, bet. Ad Græcas (12) and Biturgia (10), E. of Arretium. *Coggiano.*

AD JOVEM, a town of the Tectosages, Narbonensis I., bet. Bucco (10½) and Tholosa (10½). *Teula* or *Chaubet.*

AD LABORES, a town of the Hercuniatæ, Pannonia, on the Danube, bet. Donatiana and Teutoburgium. Named from the arduous battle here bet. Constantine and Licinius. *Near Vucovar.*

AD LACUM FELICIS, a town of Valeria, Pannonia, on the Danube, 18 m. E. from Azaum. *Neudorf?*

AD LANARIUM, a town of Sicily, s.w. near Mazara. *Campo Bello.*

AD LAPIDEM, I. a town of Britain. *Stoneham.* II. a village of Numidia, bet. Tibilis and Gasaupala.

AD LECTOCE, a town of the Cavares, in Gallia Viennensis, on the Rhone, above Arausio (13). *Passe du Lez.*

AD LIBRAS, a town of the Sardiæi, Illyria, N.E. of Tilurium.

AD LIPPOS, a town of the Vettones, Lusitania, N. of Capara.

AD LULLIA, a town of the Morini, Belgica II., bet. Durocoregum (16½) and Lintomagus. *St. Pol.*

AD LUNAM, a town of the Chætuari, Germania, at Hadriani Vallum, N.E. of Clarenna.

AD MAJORES, a town of Numidia, bet. Audus m. and Palladis lac., w. of Ad Medias.

AD MALAS, a town of Numidia, on fl. bet. Vasidica and Tipasa.

AD MALUM, I. a town of Histria, bet. Anesica (18) and Ad Titulos (17). *Jablonovitz.* II. of the Mœsi, Mœs. Sup., on the Danube, bet. Bononia and Ratiaria.

AD MARTIS, I. a town of Etruria, on Via Claudia, bet. Pistoria (8) and Luca (12); II. of Picenum, on Truentus fl., L. 16 m. N.E. from Falacrinum. *Arquata.* III. of the Segovii, Gallia Transpadana, bet. Gesdao (9) and Segusio (16) on the Via Aurelia. *Oulx.* IV. of Umbria, on Via Flaminia, bet. Narnia (17) and Mevania. *Massa.*

AD MATREM, a town of the Hirpini, Samnium, near the source of Cerbalus fl., on Via Numicia, bet. Equus Tuticus (10) and Ad Honoratianum (15). *Villanova.*

AD MATRICES, a town of the Plærœi, Illyria, on Naro fl., bet. Bistue Vetus and Bistue Nova.

AD MAUROS, a town of Noricum. *Maurkirch.*

AD MEDERA, I. a town of Cœle-Syria, bet. Damascus S.W. and Thelsia N.E. II. of Numidia, on Ardali fl., bet. Ad Mercurium and Mutia. A colonia.

AD MEDIAS, I. a town of the Æchilenenses, Sardinia, bet. Forum Trajani and Macopsista. II. of the Albocenses, Dacia, bet. Trans-Tierna and Fontes Herculis. III. of the Lingones, Gallia Cispadana, bet. Forum Gallorum (12) and Bononia (13). *Samoggia.* IV. of Numidia, above Palladis lac., w. of Cerva. V. of the Taurini, Liguria, on Padus fl., R. bet. Rigomagus (10) and Ad Cottias (13) on the Via Aurelia. *Castagna,* near *Casale.* VI. of the Volsci, Latium, bet. Forum Appii s. (9) and Tarracina (10). *Mesa.*

AD MENSULA, a town of Etruria, on Umbro fl., bet. Mantiana (18) and Sena Julia, on Via Cassia. *Montalcino.*

AD MERCURIAS, a town, I. of Mauritania Tingit., on the coast, bet. Zilia and Tingis. II. of Mauritania Ting., on the coast, bet. Dyas fl. and Sala.

AD MERCURIUM, I. a town of Numidia, bet. Buglata and Aquæ Cæsaris. II. of Numidia, on Ardali fl., near its source, bet. Thebeste and Ad Medera. III. of Zeugitana, on Bagradas fl., bet. Ad Pertusa and Unuca. IV. of Zeugitana, bet. Aves and Vina.

AD METIUM, *apud* Livium, i. q. Martius Collis.

AD MONILIA, a maritime town of Liguria, bet. Ad Solaria (6) and Bodetia. *Moneglia.*

AD MORUM, a town of the Bastitani, Tarraconens., on Osca fl., above Ilorcum.

AD MUROS, a town of the Boii, Noricum, E. of Quadrata.

AD NAVALIA, a town of the Ingauni, Liguria, bet. Alba Docilia (13) and Hasta (7), on Via Aurelia, at the mouth of Labona fl. *Noli?*

AD NONAS, I. a town of Etruria, bet. Armenta (9) and Cosa (22). II. of Etruria, on Via Claudia, bet. Ad Sextum (9) and Sabate (4). III. of the Tectosages, in Narbonensis I., bet. Tholosa (9) and Ad Vicesimum (11). *Pont Pertusat.* IV. of the Triballi, Mœsia, bet. Viminacium and Municipium.

AD NONUM, I. a town of the Insubres, Gallia Transpadana, bet. Mediolanum (7) and Laus Pompeia (9), on Via Æmilia. *Marignano.* II. of the Latini, Latium, bet. Rome (9) and Aricia (7), on the Via Appia. *Frattochie.* III. of the Latovici, Pannonia Sup., bet. Longaticum and Æmona. IV. of the Sidicini, Campania, bet. Pons Campanus (9) and Casilinum (6), on Via Appia. V. of the Veneti, Venetia, bet. Ad Duodecim (11) and Altinum (9). *Mestre.*

AD NOVAS, I. a town of Campania, on the Via Appia, bet. Calatia (6) and Caudium (9). *Nova.* II. of the Consuanetæ, Vindelicia, on Licus fl., bet. Augusta Vindelicorum and Abodiacum. *Epfach.* III. of the Delmates, Illyria, bet. Bitubium and Aufustianæ. IV. of Etruria, on the Via Cassia, bet. Clusium (9) and Ad Græcos (9). *Montepulciano.* V. of Gallia Cispadana, on the coast, N.E. of Cesena. *Cesenatico.* VI. of Mauritania Ting., bet. Ad Mercuri and Babba Julia. VII. of the Mœsi, Mœsia Inf., on the Danube, bet. Danum and Jatrum. VIII. of Valeria, Pannonia, on the Danube, bet. Antiana and Donatiana. IX. Phœniciæ, i. q. Ornithonpolis. X. of the Taulantii, in Illyria, bet. Apollonia (24) and Clodiana (25). XI. of the Triballi, Mœsia, on the Danube, bet. Cuppa and Ad Scrofulas.

AD OCTAVUM, I. a town of the Sidicini, in Campania, on Via Appia, bet. Capua (8) and Pons Campanus (9). II. of the Taurini, in Gallia Transpadana, bet. Ad Fines (8) and Augusta Taurinorum (8), on the Via Aurelia. III. of the Triballi, Mœsia Sup., on Margus fl., bet. Idomus and Horreum. IV. of Umbria, on the Metaurus fl., bet. Forum Sempronii (9) and Fanum Fortunæ (8).

AD PADUM, a town of the Ananes, Liguria, on Padus fl., bet. Placentia (20) and Quadrata (7). *Citta Padulina.*

AD PALATIUM, a town of the Cenomanni,

Venetia, on Athesis fl., bet. Sarnis and Vennum. *Pozzoalta.*

AD PALMAM, I. a town of Byzacene, on Syrtis Min., bet. Lacene and Tacape. II. of Byzacene, bet. Ad Medias and Thala. III. of Numidia, bet. Villa Sele and Cirta. IV. of the Psylli, in Africa Proper, on Syrtis Maj., bet. Iscina and Transmariciolum. V. of Tripolis Afric., bet. Leptis Maj. and Quintiliana.

AD PALUDES, a town of Chaldæa, s.w. of Vologesia.

AD PANNONIAS, a town of the Potulatenses, Dacia, 9 m. N. from Prætorium.

AD PERTUSA, a town of Zeugitana, bet. Tunis and Ad Mercurium.

AD PICTAS TABERNAS, a town of the Hernici, Latium, on Via Latina, bet. Roboraria (7) and Anagnia (15). *Macere.*

AD PINUM, a town of Lucania, bet. Venusia (12) and Opinum (12). *Spinazzola.*

AD PIRUM, I. a town of Apulia, on the Via Frentana, bet. Geronium (9) and Ad Canales (10). *Campolieto.* II. of the Carni, Venetia, bet. Ad Castra and Longaticum (12), under Pirum m. III. of Umbria, at the mouth of Sena fl., bet. Fanum Fortunæ and Senogallia, on Via Flaminia. *Cesano.*

AD PISINAS, a town of Numidia, bet. Rustici and Velefis.

AD PONTEM, I. a town of the Coritani Brit., bet. Crocolana and Margidunum (7). *Near Southwell* (9). II. of Etruria, on Tiberis fl., bet. Rome (3) and Ad Rubras (6), on Via Flaminia. *Ponte Molle.* III. of Mesopotamia, bet. Zagura and Abdia. IV. of the Turdetani, Bætica, at the bridge which formerly connected Cotinussa ins. with the mainland.

AD PONTEM ISIS, a town of the Boii, Noricum, on the Danube, at the confluence of Isis fl. *Ips?*

AD PONTES, I. a town of the Albocenses, Dacia, on the Danube, 12 m. s. from Arcidava. II. of the Atrebatii Brit., on Tamesis fl., bet. Calleva fl. and Londinium.

AD PONTES TESSENII, a town of the Licates, Rhætia, bet. Ad Ambram (40) and Parthanum (20).

AD PORTUM VENETUM, *postea* Brintesia, a port of the Veneti, Venetia, at the mouth of Meduacus Maj., bet. Meduacus Maj. (3) and Altinum (16). *Fusina? Portesine.*

AD PRÆTORIUM, I. a town of Armenia Minor, bet. Arane (28) and Pisonus (32). II. of Byzacene, bet. Diolele Præsidium and Capsa.

AD PUBLICANOS, I. a town of the Centrones,

Alpes Penninæ, bet. Casuaria and Mantala (16), N.W. of Darantasia. *Conflans.* II. of Pannonia Sup., bet. Adrans (6) and Ad Quatuordecim (11).

AD PUTEA, I. a town of the Characitani, Tarraconens., N.E. of Alternia. II. of the Mœsi, Mœsia, bet. Castra Nova and Œscus.

AD PUTEUM, a town of Cyrenaica, on Syrtis Maj., bet. Cocynthon and Mendrion.

AD PYRENÆUM, a town of the Sardones, Narbonensis I., bet. Ad Stabulum (16) and Summus Pyrenæus (5). *Château du Reart.*

AD QUATUORDECIM, a town of Pannonia Sup., bet. Ad Publicanos and Ad Savum.

AD QUINDECIM PEUCETIÆ, i. q. Rudiæ.

AD QUINTANAS, a town of the Hernici, Latium, on Via Lavicana, bet. Rome (15) and Ad Bivium (15). *Quadri.*

AD QUINTUM, a town of the Eordeti, Illyria, on Genusus fl., bet. Clodiana (15) and Scampis (5), on the Egnatia Via.

AD RADICES, a town of the Tilatæi, Mœsia Inf., near the source of Jaterus fl., bet. Sostra and Monte Imo.

AD RHENUM, a town of the Tugeni, Rhætia, on the Rhine, at its issue from Venetus lacus, bet. Arbor Felix (9) and Brigantia (10). *Rheinek.*

AD ROTAM, I. a town of Lydia, towards the sea. II. of Numidia, on Ampsagas fl., bet. Lacus Regius and Thamugadis.

AD ROTAS, a town of the Insubres, Gallia Transpad., bet. Tres Tabernæ (5) and Placentia (11), on the Via Æmilia. *Orio.*

AD RUBRAS, I. a town of the Celtici, Bætica, N.E. of Præsidium. II. of Etruria, on Tiberis fl., bet. Ad Pontem (6) and Ad Vicesimum (11), on Via Flaminia. *Prima Porta.* III. of Mauritania Cæsar., on Siga fl., R. bet. Calama and Albula. IV. of Mauritania Cæsar., bet. Ad Fratres and Albula, s.w. of Siga. V. of Numidia, bet. Ad Centenarias and Gasaupala.

AD SABBATUM, a town of Bruttium, on Sabbatus fl., bet. Consentia (12) and Ad Turres (18), on Via Aquilia.

AD SABRINAM, a town of the Belgæ, Britannia, on Sabrina fl., near its mouth. *Portishead, or Portbury.*

AD SALICES, a town of the Peucini, Mœsia Inf., at the s.w. extremity of Halmyris lac., N.W. of Istros.

AD SALSUM, a maritime village of Mauritania Cæsar., bet. Siga and Gilva.

AD SAMARUM, a town of the Pentri, Samnium, on Tamarus fl., near its source, bet. Bovianum and Equus Tuticus.

AD SANOS, a town of the Veneti, Venetia, on

Plavis fl., L. bet. Altinum (12) and Concordia (11), on Via Æmilia.

AD SAVA (Assafensis), a town of Mauritania Cæsar., on Sava (Audus) fl., 25 m. w.s.w. from Sitifis.

AD SAVUM, a town of Pannonia, on Savus fl., near Emona.

AD SCROFULAS, a town of the Triballi, Mœsia, on the Danube, bet. Ad Novas and Tallata.

AD SEPTEM ARAS, a town of Lusitania.

AD SEX INSULAS, a town of Mauritania Ting., towards Rusadir.

AD SEXTUM, I. a town of Etruria, bet. Massa Veternensis and Sena Julia. *Filotta.* II. of Etruria, on Via Claudia, bet. Rome (6) and Cære (9). III. of the Tectosages, Narbonensis I., bet. Augusta Ausciorum (9) and Hungunuera (10½). *Ollet* or *La Lique.*

AD SILANOS, a town of the Carni, Venetia, on Sontius fl., bet. Aquileia (35) and Tarvisetum. *Sella.*

AD SILANUM, a town of the Gabali, Aquitania I., on Divona fl., s. of Anderitum.

AD SILARUM, a village of Lucania, on Silarus fl., bet. Ad Tanarum and Ad Calorem.

AD SILMA, a town of Numidia, on the frontiers of Zeugitana, bet. Armosela and Bulla Regia.

AD SOLARIA, I. a town of Etruria, bet. Florentia (9) and Hellana (9). *Near Poggio.* II. of the Ilercales, Liguria, bet. Ricina (15) and Monilia (7), on the Via Aurelia. *Zara.*

AD SPELUNCAS, a town of the Psylli, Africa P., on Syrtis Maj., bet. Charax and Œsporis.

AD STABULUM, a town of the Sardones, Narbonensis I., s.w. of Illiberis. *St. Martin.*

AD STATUAS, I. a town of the Amantini, Pannon., on the Danube, bet. Chertobalus and Bregetio. II. of the Contestani, Tarracenensis, N.E. of Sætabis. III. of the Latini, Latium, on Via Latina, bet. Quintana (3) and Ad Pictas (7). *Osteria San Cesario.*

AD STOMA, a town of the Peucini, Mœsia, at the mouth of Pulchrum Ostium.

AD SUMMUM PYRENÆUM, I. a town of the Indigetes, Tarraconensis, in the Pyrenees, E., bet. Illiberis N. and Juncaria S.S.E. II. of the Jaccetani, Tarraconensis, in the Pyrenees w., bet. Forum Ligneum N. and Jacca SS.E.

AD TANARUM, a maritime town of the Picentini, on Tanarus fl., near its mouth, bet. Picentia and Pæstum.

AD TARUM, a town of the Anamares, Gall. Cispad., on Tarus fl., bet. Fidentia (8) and Parma (7). *Castel Guelfo.*

AD TAUM, a town of the Iceni, Brit., on Taus fl., s. of Venta Icenorum. *Tasborough.*

AD TEMPLUM, a town of Gætulia, bet. Putea and Laminie.

AD TINE RICINA, a town of Sabinium, bet. Fanum Fugitivi and Tres Tabernæ, s. of Spoletium.

AD TITULOS, a town of Histria, bet. Ad Malum (17) and Tarsaticum (17). *Starada.*

AD TRICESIMUM, a town of the Carni, Venetia, on Turrus fl., R. bet. Julium Carnicum (30) and Aquileia (30). *Trigesimo.*

AD TROPÆA, a town of Bruttium, on Tyrrhenum mare, near Portus Herculis, named from the victory of Sextus Pompeius.

AD TURREM, I. a town of the Salyes, Narbonensis II., bet. Matavonium (14) and Tegulata (16). *Tourves.* II. Sardiniæ, i. q. Turris Libyssonis.

AD TURRES, I. a town of Bruttium, on Via Aquilia, bet. Ad Sabbatum (18) and Angitula (13). *Maida.* II. of Byzacene, bet. Speculum and Capsa. III. of Liburnia, bet. Tarsatica and Senia. IV. of Etruria, on Via Aurelia, bet. Lorium (10) and Pyrgi (12). V. of the Manii, Illyria, bet. Narona and Diluntum. VI. of the Oretani, Tarraconensis, on the Anas, above Ilucia. VII. of the Volsci, Latium, on Via Severiana, bet. Circeii (4) and Tarracina (9). *Torre Olevola.* VIII. Albas, a port of the Volsci, Latium, bet. Astura, (9) and Circeii (9), on the Via Severiana. *Mura di San Donato.*

AD UNDECIMUM, I. a town of the Carni, Venetia, on Turrus fl., bet. Aquileia (11) and Ad Fornulos (12). *Zillina.* II. *postea* Furfane, of Apulia, on Via Egnatia, bet. Herdonia (15) and Canusium (11).

AD (Templum) VENERIS, a town of Calabria, on Via Egnatia, bet. Norva (8) and Egnatia (8). *Monte San Pietro.*

AD VICESIMUM, I. a town of Armenia Minor, bet. Trapezuntium (20) and Zigana (32). II. of Pannonia, i. q. Alicanum. III. of the Demetæ, Britannia, w. of Maridunum. *Castle Flemish.* IV. of Etruria, bet. Ad Rubras (11) and Aqua Viva (7), on Via Flaminia, N.E. of Veii. *Castel Novo.* V. of Lucania, bet. Cylistarnus and Thurii (20). VI. of the Tectosages, Narbonensis I., bet. Salsulæ and Narbo. VII. of the Tectosages, Narbonensis I., bet. Ad Nonum (11) and Elusio (9). *Visconti.*

Ad Victoriolas, a town of Gallia Cispadana, on Via Æmilia, bet. Mutina (3) and Forum Gallorum.

Adaca, a town of Palmyrene.

Adăda (Adadata, Odada), a town of Pisidia, E. of Prostama.

Adæ, a town of Æolis Asiat., on Elæatrius sin., bet. Cyme and Hydra prom. (5).

Adam, a town of Reuben, on the Jordan, in Amoritis, Peræa, over against Jericho, where the Jordan stayed its course for the passage of the Israelites.

Adamas fl., a r. of India i. Gangem, falling into Gangeticus sin. N.E. of Mana fl. Its banks produced diamonds, whence its name. *Bramni,* or *Soank.*

Adăna, a city of Cilicia Campestris, on Sarus fl., 30 m. above its mouth, founded by Adanus the Phœnician, son of Uranus and Terra. *Adana.*

Adana (Athane), i. q. Arabiæ Felicis Emporium.

Adanates, a people of the Alpes Cottiæ, E. of the Medulli. Part of the *Val de la Maurienne.*

Adani ins., two islets of Arabia Felix, in the Red Sea, N.W. of Muza.

Adapera, a town of the Trocmi, Galatia, bet. Eccobriga (24) and Tavium (24).

Adari, a port of the Leanitæ, Arabia, on Persicus sin., s. of Cheldone prom.

Adarima, a town of Limyrica, India, E. of Melinda.

Adarin, a town of Cœle-Syria, 10 m. N.E. from Ad Medera.

Adaristus, a town of Macedonia.

Adasa, a town of Ephraim, 4 m. from Bethhoron.

Adata, I. Commagene, the local name of Germanicia. II. of Cappadocia, in Saravene præfectura. III. of Palmyrene, bet. Tyba and Evaria.

Adaugmadum, a town of the Bagigætuli, Libya, bet. Tillabari and Thabunagdi.

Addaa, Babylonia, i. q. Is.

Addŭa fl. (Abdua, Adouas), a r. of Gallia, Transpad., rising in the Alpes Rhætiæ, and running through Larius lac., into the Padus, 6 m. w. of Cremona. *Adda.*

Addyma, a town of Mauritania Cæsariensis.

Adëba, a town of the Ilercaones, Tarraconensis, on the Iberus, R. towards its mouth. *Amposta.*

Adeda, a town of the Cassanitæ, in Arabia Felix, on the Red Sea, s. of Mamala. *Attuie.*

Adellum, a town of the Contestani, Tarraconensis, W.N.W. of Centum.

Ades, I. a town of Cilicia Trachea, near Laertes. II. of Zeugitana, at the s.w. head of Carthaginens. sin. A colonia, Maxula. The locality of the first defeat of the Carthaginians by Regulus. *Rhades.*

Adesa fl. (Ædesa), a r. of Lycia, running by Choma.

Adiabas fl., i. q. Kaprus.

Adiabaræ, a people of Meroe, on the right bank of the Nile, next to Dodecaschœnai.

Adiabene, I. a name of Assyria. II. the chief of the six provinces of Assyria, on Lycus (Caprus) fl.

Adiabla, a town of Albania Asiatica.

Adida, a town of Judæa, towards Jerusalem.

Adiënus (Odintus), I. a r. of Pontus, falling into the Euxine 7½ m. N. from Ascuris fl. *Mapourah.* II. a town of Pontus, at the mouth of Adienus fl.

Adisamum, a town of Taprobane, on the Ganges.

Adisathri, a people of India, on Adisathrus m.

Adisathrus m., m. of India i. Gangem, extending s.w.—N.E. from above Carura to about Nagaruris.

Admah (Adama), I. the easternmost of the four cities in the valley of Siddim that shared the fate of Sodom. II. a town of Peræa, on the shore of the Dead Sea, near the site of the earlier cognominal city.

Adōnis fl., a r. of Phœnicia, rising in Libanus, and falling into the Mediterranean s. of Byblus. The red colour of its waters, caused by the nature of the soil, connected it with the fable of Adonis (Thammuz). *Nahr Ibrahim.*

Adopissus, a town of Lycaonia.

Adoraim (Dora), a town of Juda, s. of Thappuah.

Adoreus m., a ridge of Didymus m. in Phrygia Magna, towards the s. border of Galatia.

Adorsi, i. q. Aorsi.

Adrabæcampi, a people of Germ. Mag., bet. the Marus and the Danube, contiguous to the Sudini and the Quadi.

Adraha (Edrei), I. a town of Auranitis, Syria, 24 m. N.W. from Bostra. *Draa.* II. of Arabia Petræa. III. of Liburnia.

Adraistæ, a people of India i. Gangem, about Pimprama.

Adramitæ, a maritime people of Arabia Felix, s. of the Chatramotitæ. *Hadramaut.*

Adramyttēnus sin., a gulf of the Ægean,

E. of Lectum prom., bet. Gargara prom. and Pyrrha prom. *Gulf of Edremit.*

ADRAMYTHIS ins., an isl. of Lycia.

ADRAMYTTĪUM, *prius* Pedasus, a town of Æolis Asiatica, near the head of Adramyttenus sin., 16 m. E. from Antandrus. Named after Adramys, brother of Crœsus, by whom it was greatly enlarged. It also received a colony of Athenians. The seat of a conventus juridicus. The birth-place of the orator Xenocles. Adramyn (Mercury) was peculiarly venerated here. *Edremit.*

ADRANA fl., a r. of the Chatti, rising in Bacenis Silva, and falling into the Visurgis, N. of Nuæsium. *Eder.*

ADRANS m., I. a ridge of Cetius m. in Noricum, w. of Celeia. *Trajaner Berg;* II. a town of Pannonia Sup., on the confines of Noricum, bet. Celeja and Ad Publicanos (6). *Dragemel?*

ADRANUM, a town of Sicily, on Adranus fl., near its junction with Cyamosurus fl., N.W. of Ætna. Founded by Dionysius the Elder, and named after the god Hadranus. *Aderno.*

ADRANUS fl., a r. of Sicily, rising in Nebrodes m., and by its junction with Cyamosurus fl. at Adranum forming Symæthus fl.

ADRAPSA, I. a town of Bactria, E. of Bactra. II. of Hyrcania, s. of Socana fl.

ADRASTĪA, I. a fountain of Sicyonia. II. a district of Mysia, on Granicus fl., towards its mouth. III. (Adrastus), a town of Mysia, bet. Parium and Priapus. Built by Adrastus.

ADRIA Elid., i. q. Andria.

ADRIA, &c. *Vide* Hadria, &c.

ADRIUS. *Vide* Ardius.

ADRUS ins., I. an isl. Clota, of Valentia, in Clota æstuar. II. Edrus, of Hibernia E. III. a r. of Lusitania, falling into the Anas, near Pax Augusta.

ADRYX, a maritime town of Sicily, E. bet. Acis and Catana.

ADUATICI. *Vide* Atuatici.

ADULA m., I. a generic name of Alpes Rhæticæ. II. a ridge of the Alpes Rhæticæ, whence the Rhine flows. *Mt. St. Gothard.*

ADŬLIS (Aduli portus), capital of the Adulitæ, Æthiopia, at the head of Adulitanus sin. The port of Axume. *Zulla.*

ADULITÆ, a tribe of Troglodytæ, on the Red Sea, w. bet. the Colobi and the Abaliæ.

ADULITANUS sin., a gulf of the Red Sea, w. of Adulis, bet. Orine Chersonesus and Colobanorum prom.

ADULLAM, I. a town of Judæa, 10 m. E. from Eleutheropolis. A royal city of the Canaanites. II. a cavern on the borders of the Dead Sea, 6 m. s.w. of Bethlehem, in the side of a ravine, now called Wady Khureitum. David's place of refuge.

ADUMMIM, a pass on the borders of Judah and Benjamin, bet. Jerusalem and Jericho. Infamous from the many murders committed there by robbers. The scene of the parable of the good Samaritan.

ADUNAS fl., a r. of Susiana, falling into the Eulæus.

ADUNICATES, I. a people of Gallia Narbonensis, contiguous to the Nemanturi. II. their city. *Aiglun.*

ADURNI portus, a port of the Regni, Brittania, bet. Anderida and Trisanton fl.

ADYLISUS m., m. of Bœotia, towards Thebæ.

ADYRMACHIDÆ, a people of Libya, extending from the Nile to Catabathmus, or, according to Herodotus, to Pleunos.

ÆA, I. a town of Colchis, on Phasis fl., above Phasis (15). The reputed birth-place of Medea. Probably identical with Male. II. fons, a fountain of Amydon, in Amphaxitis Macedoniæ.

ÆEÆ ins., probably one of the Ægates ins., Sicily.

ÆANE, a town of Elymea, Macedon, on Haliacmon fl., N.E. of Phylace. Founded by Æanus, s. of Elymas the Tyrrhenian. *Vanitches.*

ÆANTEUM, the tomb of Ajax, on the coast of Mysia, near Rhœteum. *Intepe.*

ÆANT prom., the headland N.W. at the entrance of Heroopolitanus sin.

ÆANTIS, a tribe or ward of Attica, named after Ajax, son of Telamon.

ÆANTIUM prom., a headland of Magnesia, Thessaly, at the E. entrance of Pagasæus sin., over against Pteleum. *C. Trikeri; C. Volo.*

ÆAS fl. (Aous), a r. of Illyria, rising in Lacmon m., and falling into the Adriatic at Apollonia. *Voioussa.*

ÆBALIA, a name of Tarentum.

ÆBŪDÆ (Hebrides), islands of Caledonia, N.W. *Hebrides.*

ÆBŪRA (Libōra, Æpora, Apora), a town of the Carpetani, s.w. of Toletum. *Cuerva.*

ÆCÆ, a town of Apulia, on Via Egnatia, bet. Equus Tuticus and Ad Pirum. *Troia.*

ÆCHILENSES, a maritime people of Sardinia, N. of Tyrsus fl., towards its mouth.

ÆCULANUM (Æclanum), a town of the Hirpini, on Via Appia, 13 m. s.E. from Beneventum. *Le Grotte,* near Mirabella.

ÆDEPSUS, a town of Eubœa, on Opuntius sinus, over against Halæ in Locris (15), with warm springs, sacred to Hercules. *Dipso.*

ÆDIMUS sin., a bay of the Mediterranean at Loryma, Caria.

ÆDONIUS m., a m. of Thrace, whence the term Ædonius for Thracian.

ÆDONIS ins. (Ædonia, Sidonia), an island of Marmarica, off Batrachos.

ÆDUI (Hedui, Ædussi), an Insubrian people of Lugdunensis I., on the confines of Aquitania I., bet. the Liger and the Arar fl., N. of the Sequani ; the earliest allies of Rome in Gaul. *Departments of Saone et Loire, Nièvre, and a portion of Côte d'Or.*

ÆGÆ (Agæa), I. a town of Achaia Propria, on Crathis fl. near its source ; extinct in Strabo's time. II. of Ætolia, i. q. Ægitium. III. of Æolis Asiat., or, according to Ptolemy, of Lydia, E.N.E. of Temnus. *Cassaba.* IV. of Cilicia Campestris, where Apollonius Tyanæus studied under Euxenes. *Ajas-cala (Castle of Ajax).* V. Edessa, *postea* Bodina, capital of Emathia and metropolis of Macedonia, until the seat of royalty was transferred to Pella ; then the place of sepulture for the Macedonian princes ; on Astræus fl., bet. Cellæ (28) and Pella (28) on the Egnatia Via ; called Ægæ, because a flock of goats indicated the site to its founder Caranus. *Vodina.* VI. of Eubœa, on Opuntius sin., s. of Ædepsus. According to Strabo, this town gave name to the Ægean. *Akio.* VII. of the Locri Opuntii. VIII. of Mauritania. IX. (Meloboteria), of Pallene in Macedonia, on Toronaicus sin., s.w. of Mecyberna. X. of Syria, under Amanus m. XI. Augeæ, of Laconia, 3½ m. N. from Gythium.

ÆGÆA, PIERIÆ, i. q. Agassæ.

ÆGEÆ ins., is. of Ionia.

ÆGÆUM mare, the portion of the Mediterranean bounded N. by Macedonia and Thrace, w. by Greece, and E. by Asia Minor. Named from Ægæ, Eubœa ; or from Æx ins. ; or from the resemblance of its islands to a herd of goats ; or from its sudden squalls (aigis) ; or from Ægia, queen of the Amazons, drowned in it ; or from Ægæus, father of Theseus, also drowned in it. *Archipelago* (Aigaion-Pelagos), *Ægean.*

ÆGÆUS m., a summit of Dicte m., E. of Lyctus, where was the cave in which Jupiter was fed by the bees.

ÆGALEUS m., I. a hill of Attica, N.w. of Athens, whence Xerxes viewed the battle of Salamis. *Skaramanga.* II. of Messenia, overlooking Pylos. *Agio Elio.*

ÆGARA, Lydia (Æolis), i. q. Ægæ.

ÆGATES ins., Æguades, Ægusæ, three isl. (Hiera, Bucina, and Ægusa) on the w. coast of Sicily, N.w. of Lilybæum prom., the locality of the termination of the first Punic war ; and, in Virgil, of the loss of Anchises.

ÆGEIS, a ward of Attica, named after Ægeus, father of Theseus.

ÆGELEON, a town of the Malienses Paralii, Thessaly, near Larissa Cremaste.

ÆGESTA (Acesta, Segeste), a town of Sicily, S.E. of Eryx, named after its founder Ægestus, of Troy ; called Segeste by the Romans, to avoid the indelicacy in their language of the term Ægesta (excrements). The locality, under Æmilius Censorinus, of the story of a brazen horse, similar to that of the brazen bull of Perillus. *Near Barbara.*

ÆGESTANUM emporium, the port of Ægesta, at the mouth of the Simois. *Castel a mare.*

ÆGETINI, the people of Azetium or Netium, Peucetia.

ÆGIALE, a town of Amorgos ins., on the w. coast. *Porto Sant' Anna.*

ÆGIALEES, a Pelasgic tribe, the first settlers of Achaia, in Peloponnesus, who, with their Ionian fellow-colonists, were expelled by Achæans from Laconia, under Tisamenius, son of Orestes, circa 1104 B.C.

ÆGIALUS, I. capital of Ægialus. Paphlagonia, 7½ m. E. from Cytorus. II. the coast of Paphlagonia, extending 12 m. w. from Carambis prom.

ÆGYDA, *postea* Justinopolis, a town of Histria, on Tergestinus sin., E. of Caprea, at the mouth of Formio fl., on an island connected with the continent by a bridge. *Capo d'Istria.*

ÆGIDIORUM ins., an island of India i. Gangem, w. of Taprobane.

ÆGIDIS ins., the isl. of Histria, on which Ægida stood.

ÆGILA, a town of Laconia.

ÆGILIA, a demus of Attica, of the tribe Antiochis, on Saronicus sin., s. of Lampra ; famous for its figs. Named after the hero Ægilus. *Elimbos.*

ÆGILIA ins. (Ægile), I. an isl. of Eubœa, opposite Cynosura prom., in Attica. *Stouri.* II. of Laconia, 15 m. s.E. from Cythera. *Cerigotto.*

ÆGILIPS Ithacæ, i. q. Ægireus.

ÆGILIUM ins., Etruriæ, i. q. Igilium.

ÆGILODES sinus, a bay of the Ægean, in Laconia, at Ægila.

ÆGILON, the Greek name of Capraria ins.

ÆGIMURUS ins. (Ægimorus), an isl. of Zeugitana, at the s. entrance of Carthaginensis sin., 30 m. from Carthage. It gradually sank, all but two peaks, called Aræ, which were adopted by the Romans and Carthaginians as the boundary of their respective empire. *Galetta.*

ÆGINA, I. *prius* Ænoa, Ænone, Ænopia, an isl. of Argolis, in Saronicus sin., 20 m. s.w. from Athens; re-named after Ægina, mother of Æacus. Its inhabitants were called Myrmidones, "ants," from their extreme application to agriculture and their thrift. They were the first people who coined silver money, hence called Æginæum. *Enghia.* II. its capital, on the N.W. coast. Built by Æacus.

ÆGINETES fl., I. a r. of Paphlagonia, falling into the Euxine at Æginetes. II. a port of the Heneti, Paphlagonia, 20 m. E. from Aboniteichos. *Ginuc.*

ÆGINIUM, a town of Estiæotis, Thessaly, on Peneus fl., N.W. of Phaloria. *Stagous; Kalabachi.*

ÆGIPLANCTUS m., a hill of Megaris, one of Æneus' range.

ÆGIRA, *prius* Hyperesia, one of the Twelve Cities of Achaia, on Corinthiacus sin., 1½ m. from the sea, N.W. of Pellene. With an oracle, whose priests derived their inspirations from bulls' blood. Named Ægira after a flock of goats, the ingenious use of which saved the town from an assault of the Ionians. *Bloubouki.*

ÆGIRÆ portus, the harbour of Ægira, Achaia, 1½ m. from the city. *Mauro Lethari.*

ÆGIREUS, a district of Ithaca ins.

ÆGIROESSA, one of the Twelve Cities of Æolis Asiat., on the Ægean, over against Mitylene, N.E. Renovated by Attalus Philadelphus, and named Attalia Agroira. *Ajasmikevi.*

ÆGIRUS, a town of Lesbos ins., E. near Methymna.

ÆGIRUSA, a town of Megaris, near Tripodiscus.

ÆGISSUS (Ægypsus), a town of the Peucini, Mœsia, on the Danube, bet. Noviodunum and Ad Stoma.

ÆGISTHENÆ, *vide* Ægosthenæ.

ÆGITA, a town of Mœsia Superior.

ÆGITHALLUS prom., *postea* Acellus, I. a pr. of Sicily, w. above Lilybæum prom. *Capo di San Teodoro.* II. a fortress of Sicily, at Ægithallus prom.

ÆGITHARSUS prom. Sic., i. q. Ægithallus.

ÆGITIS, a fortress of Arcadia.

ÆGITIUM (Ægæ), a town of the Apodoti, Ætolia, under Corax m., E. 10 m. from the sea, N. of Tichium.

ÆGIUM, one of the Twelve Cities of Achaia, near Corinthiacus sin., bet. Rhypæ and Helice. The early seat of the Achæan Council, and the place where Jupiter was suckled by a goat (whence the name). *Vostizza.*

ÆGLE, an early name of Syme ins.

ÆGONEA (Ægone, Econia), a town of the Malienses, Thessaly, near Phalara.

ÆGONIA, i. q. Itonia, in Pontus.

ÆGOS POTĂMOS, I. a stream of Chersonnesus Thracius, falling into the Hellespont over against Lampsacus. II. a town of Chersonesus Thracius, at the mouth of Ægos Potamos fl. The locality of the decisive defeat of the Athenians by the Lacedæmonians. *Galata.*

ÆGOSTHÊNÆ, I. a town of Megaris, on Alcyonium mare, under Onæus m. E. of Pagæ. *Porto Germano.* II. of Phocis.

ÆGOSTIS, a town of the Locri Opuntii.

ÆGUSA ins., an isl. of Sicily, one of the Ægates ins., s. of Bucina. Perhaps the Æeæ of Homer. *Favignana.*

ÆGUSÆ ins., Sicil., i. q. Ægates.

ÆGYLLUS, a village of Bithynia, near Nicomedia.

ÆGYPTUS ("land of the Copts"), *heb.* Mitsraim, *cophtice,* Chami, "dark-loam land," a country of Africa (by Herodotus considered a country of itself, and by other writers assigned to Asia), bounded N. by the Mediterranean, s. by Ethiopia, w. by Libya, E. by Palestine, Arabia Petræa, and the Red Sea. It was divided into Inferior, extending from the sea to Memphis; Middle, or Heptanomis, extending thence to s. of Hermopolis; and Superior, or Thebais, extending thence to Ethiopia at Hiera-Sycaminos. The original population appears to have been a Caucasian immigration from the N.E. *Egypt. Misr.*

ÆGYS, a town of Laconia, on the borders of Messenia, N.W. of Belemina. *Ægia Eirene.*

ÆLĂNA (Ailah, *hebraicè* Eloth, Ailoth, Ailath, Elath), a town of the Nabathæi in Arabia, at the head (E.) of Ælaniticus sin., one of the two ports by which Solomon traded with the East. *Akaba.*

ÆLANITICUS sin., the E. termination of the Red Sea, extending from Phocarum ins. to Ælana. *Bahr el Akaba.*

ÆLIA, I. a town of Byzacene, bet. Terentum and Tysdrus, a colony from Zama. II. of Dacia Medit., in Mœsia Sup., bet. Pantalia and Sardica. III. Capitolina, a name given to Jerusalem by Adrian, after his own name, Ælius, and a temple of Jupiter Capitolinus erected by him there.

IV. Castra, a town of the Ilergetes, Tarraconensis, on the Iberus, above Allobon.

ÆLII pons, a town of Maxima Cæsariensis, Britannia, at Hadriani murus.

AELU, a town of the Sabæi, Arabia Felix, on the Red Sea, 16 m. s. from Pudnu. *Loheia.*

AELVIONES, Germaniæ, i. q. Helvicones.

ÆMATÆ, a town of Illyricum, s. of the Savus, below Ad Fines. *Smiania.*

ÆMATHIAS, i. q. Macedonia Prop.

ÆMILIANA, a town of Tarraconensis, towards the sources of the Anas.

ÆMINES portus, a port of the Salyes, in Narbonensis II., bet. Massilia and Telo Martius. Near *Cassis.*

ÆMINIUM, a town of the Lusitani, on Munda fl., R., above Conimbrica (10).

ÆMINIUS fl., Lusitania, i. q. Munda.

ÆMÖDÆ. *Vide* Acmodæ.

ÆMÖNA (Emona), capital of the Latovici, Pannonia, bet. Nauportus and Adrans (25). *Laybach.*

ÆMÖNIA I. an early name of Macedonia. II. a town of the Potulatenses, Dacia, s.e. of Zarmizegethusa.

ÆNARE, an isl. of Asia Minor, towards Samos.

ÆNÄRIA (Inarĭme, Pithecŭsa), an isl. of Campania, at the n.w. end of Cumanus sin., s.w. of Prochyta. Colonised by Eretrians and Chalcidians, but deserted on account of its volcanic eruptions, whence the identification of the island with Homer's Land of the Arimi, the locality of Typhœus' torments. The island abounded with copper, whence its Latin name ; and with apes, whence its Tuscan and Greek names. *Ischia.*

ÆNEA, I. a town *surn.* Nova, of Acarnania, on the Achelous r., near Ænea Vetus. *Trigardon.* II. *surn.* Vetus, of Acarnania, on the Achelous r., 8½ m. from its mouth. *Palæo Catouna.* III. of Chalcidice, Macedonia, on Thermaicus sinus, at Æneium prom., 15 m. s.w. from Thessalonica. Built by Æneas, in whose honour games and sacrifices were annually celebrated here. *Panomi.* IV. (Nea-come) of Mysia, on Æsepus fl., bet. Polichna and Palæscepsis (6¼). Noted for its silver mines, and for a temple of Minerva, around which the rain never fell. *Eskupi.* V. an early name of Rome.

ÆNEIS, a ward or tribe of Athens, named after Æneus, grandson of Cadmus.

ÆNEIUM prom. (Ænelon), a pr. of Chalcidice, in Macedonia, on Thermaicus sinus, 15 m. s.w. from Thessalonica. *C. Panomi.*

ÆNESIPPAS ins. (Ænesipasa), an isl. of Marmarica, off Apis.

ÆNESISPHY (Ennesyphöra), a port of the Zygritæ, Marmarica, bet. Geræ and Syce.

ÆNIANES (Enienes), a tribe of Pelasgi, who, from Dotius Campus in Magnesia, Thessaly, settled for a time in Epirus, and then established themselves in Æniania.

ÆNIANIA, the country of the Ænianes, Thessaly, bounded s. by Phocis, Doris, and Ætolia, n. by Dolopia, w. by Aperantia, e. by Maliensis.

ÆNIANUM sinus, Thessaliæ, i. q. Maliacus sinus.

ÆNNUM (Ægypti), i. q. Philotera.

ÆNON, a town, I. of Samaria, on the Jordan, 8 m. s.e. from Bethsan. Here John baptized. II. of Trachonitis, Syria, 37 m. n. of Canatha.

ÆNONA (Civitas Prasini), a town of Liburnia, on the Adriatic, n. of Jadera, opposite Cissa ins. *Nona.*

ÆNUS fl., I. a r. of Thessaly, running by Ænus. II. a town of Caria, e. of Rhodes. III. of the Locri Ozolæ. IV. of Pelasgiotis, Thessaly, under Ossa m.

ÆNOS (Absynthus, *prius* Poltyobria), I. cap. of the Apsynthii, in Thrace, at the issue e. of Stentoris palus. A Mitylenean colony anterior to the siege of Troy, enlarged by Æneas in honour of Polydorus, whose tomb stood here. Remarkable for its extreme cold. *Enos.* II. m., a m. of Cephallenia. *Monte Leone.*

ÆNŸRA, a town of Thasos ins., on the e. coast, bet. Thasos and Cænyra.

ÆOLI, a tribe of Thessalians who invaded Ætolia, and, for a time, communicated their name to it.

ÆOLIA, i. q. Strongyle.

ÆOLLÆ ins. (Vulcăniæ, Hephæstïades, Lipărĕæ, Planctai ?), seven isl. of Sicily N., Lipari, Hiera, Strongyle, Didyme, Ericusa, Phœnicusa, Euonymus, q. v. The kingdom of Æolus.

ÆOLIS, I. *prius* Curetis, *postea* Ætolia. II. a country of Asia Minor, extending along the Ægean, bet. Caïcus fl. and Hermus fl. Settled *circa* 1124 b.c., by Æolians from Thessaly. III. the early name of Thessaly. IV. a town of Phocis, towards Panopea.

ÆOLIUM mare (Mysium), the Ægean, on the coast of Æolis Asiat.

ÆPASIUM (Elid), i. q. Hypæsia.

ÆPĒA, I. a town of Crete. II. of Cyprus, on Clarius fl., near Soli. III. of Messenia, the early name of Corone. IV. i. q. Thuria.

ÆPIATICUS portus, a maritime town of the Menapii, in the Nervicanus pagus. *Oudenborg.*

ÆPOLIUM, a maritime town of Dacia, bet. Tremniscus and Neoptolemi turris.

ÆPY, a town of Messenia.

ÆQUA, a village of Campania, on Cumanus sinus, E. of Surrentum. *Equa.*

ÆQUANUS VICUS, a town of Campania, near Surrentum. *Vico.*

ÆQUESILIA, in Ptolemy, i. q. Aquæ Celenæ.

ÆQUI (Æquïcŏli), a tribe of Sabines in Latium, bet. the Latini w., the Volsci and Hernici s., the Marsi E., and the Sabini N. Noted for their incessant guerilla warfare against Rome.

ÆQUINOCTIUM, a town of the Boii, Pannonia, on the Danube, bet. Vindobona (14) and Carnuntum (14). *Fischament.*

ÆQUUM COLONIA, a town of the Dalmates, Illyria, on Tilurus fl., above Tilurium, E.N.E. of Salona.

ÆQUUM FALSICUM, a town of Sabinium, on Tiberis fl., near Aqua Viva.

ÆERE, a town of Trachonitis, N.W. of Zara.

ÆRENOSII, a tribe of Celtiberi, contiguous to the Bargusii.

ÆRETICE, a district of Armenia Min.

ÆRIA, a city of the Vocontii, Viennensis, N. of Massilia. *Auriac, near the Château de Lers.*

ÆROPUS m., m. of Illyria, on the Æas fl., opposite Asnaus m. *Monte Trebeeshna.*

ÆROSA, a name of Cyprus, from the brass produced there.

ÆSACUS fl., a r. of Troas, rising in Ida m.

ÆSARIS fl., i. q. Auser.

ÆSARONENSES, a maritime port of Sardinia, bet. the Carenses N. and the Barbaricini s.

ÆSARUS fl., a r. of Bruttium, falling into Ionium mare at Crotona. *Esaro.*

ÆSCULAPII ins. (Tiberina), I. an isl. in the Tiber, at Rome, formed of the corn thrown by the people into the river from the Campus Martius, as having been sown by Tarquin. II. nemus, a town of Phœnicia, bet. Berytus and Sidon.

ÆSEPUS fl., a r. of Mysia, rising in Colytus m., near the Scamander, and falling into Propontis E. of Granicus fl. *Boklu.*

ÆSERNIA, a town of the Caraceni, Samnium, on Via Numicia, bet. Aufidena (18) and Bovianum (12). *Isernia.*

ÆSICA, I. fl., a r. of Britain. II. a town of the Otadeni, Brit., on Hadrianus murus, N. bet. Amboglanna and Procolitia. The station of the Cohors Prima Asturum. *Greatchester.*

ÆSICI, a people of Arabia Petræa, towards Chaldæa, s. of the Caucabeni.

ÆSIS, I. a r. of Italy, rising in the Apennines, near Malitica, and, after dividing Umbria from Picenum, falling into the Adriatic near Ancona. The ancient boundary, in this direction, of Gallia Cisalpina. *Fiumesino.* II. (Æsium), a town of the Senones, on Æsis fl., near its mouth, founded by Aisis, a Pelasgian hero, *circa* 1300 B.C. A colonia. *Iesi.*

ÆSON, I. a r. of Pieria, Macedonia, falling into the Leucus fl. at Pydna. II. (Æsonia), a town of Magnesia, Thessaly.

ÆSONA, a town of the Lacetani, Tarraconensis, w. of Setelsis. *Isona.*

ÆSTRÆI, a people of Macedonia, N.E. of Pelagonia.

ÆSTRÆUM (Astræa, Asterion), capital of the Æstræi, Macedonia, on Pontus fl., above Bylazora. *Vistrizza.*

ÆSTRÆUS fl., a r. of Bottiæa, falling into Axius fl.

ÆSTRIA ins., an isl. of Dalmatia, s. of Corcyra Nigra.

ÆSTUARIUM, the w. mouth of the Bætis.

ÆSTYÆI (Hæsti, Æstri), a people of Sarmatia Europ., on Codanus sinus, N. of the Venedi.

ÆSULA (Æsulum, *rectius* Æsculum), a town of the Latini, Latium, bet. Tibur and Præneste. Extinct in Pliny's time.

ÆSYME (Œsyme, *postea* Emathia), a town of the Pieres, Thrace, on Strymonicus sinus, opposite Thasos ins. *Eski Kavala.*

ÆSYROS fl., a r. of Bithynia, falling into Propontis towards Astacenus sinus.

ÆTHALIA, the Tyrrhenian name of Lemnos ins. and Ilva ins.

ÆTHALIDÆ, a demus of Attica, of the tribe Leontis.

ÆTHALŒIS fl. (Etheleus), a stream of Troas, falling into Æsepus fl. below Scepsis.

ÆTHEA, a town of Messenia, on the borders of Laconia.

ÆTHERIA (Æthria, Æria), the ancient name of Ethiopia, of Thasus, of Rhodes, of Cyprus, of Crete, and of Thessaly.

ÆTHICES, a people of Thessaly, in the N.W. angle of Estiæotis, among whom the centaurs sought refuge. Extinct in the time of Strabo.

ÆTHIOPE, the ancient name of Lesbos.

ÆTHIŌPES HESPERII, a tribe of Æthiopes, on the Atlantic, and extending inland, s. of the Daradæ. *Sierra Leone, Gold Coast, Ivory Coast, Ashantee, &c.*

ÆTHIOPIA, I. a country of Africa, bounded N. by Egypt, s. by Terra Incognita, w. by Libya Int., E. by Erythræum mare. The term, indicating "land of dark faces," was applied by several of the ancient geographers to all the more s. and E. countries of the world. *Nubia, Sennaar, and part of Abyssinia.* II. Egypti, i. q. Dodeca-schœnus. III. a district of Lydia, on the Hyllus, whence Diana was entitled Æthiopica.

ÆTHIOPICI m., a range of hills w. of the Nile.

ÆTHIOPICUS sinus, the Erythræum mare, on the coast of Æthiopia.

ÆTNA, I. a volcanic m. of Sicily, on the E. coast, bet. Tauromenium and Catana. *Mongibello, Etna.* II. *prius* Inessa, a town of Sicily, towards the base of Ætna m., s. bet. Centuripæ and Catana. *Castro.*

ÆTOLI, a people of Elis, who, under Ætolus, son of Endymion, invaded Curetis and gave their name to it.

ÆTŌLIA, I. *prius* Curetis, a country of Græcia E., Peloponnesum, bounded N. by Epirus, s. by Corinthiacus sinus, w. by Epirus and Acarnania, E. by Doris and Locris. It was divided into Ætolia Antiqua, extending along the coast from Achelous fl. to Calydon, and inland up to Stratus; and Ætolia Epictētus ("acquired"), the inland portion from about Stratos, N., to the Locri Ozolæ, E. Made a province of Rome 146 B.C. *Vlakia.* II. a town of Laconia.

ÆTORYNCHUS prom., a pr. of Bithynia, on Bosporus Thracius. Named from its resemblance to an eagle's beak.

ÆTUATII (Ætuates), a people of Maxima Sequanorum, on the Rhine.

ÆTULANA, a district of Armenia Minor N.

ÆTUS, I. an early name of the Nile. II. a r. of Scythia, which by its overflow destroyed the gardens of one Prometheus, whence the fable of his liver being consumed by an eagle.

ÆX (Ægos) prom., a pr. of Æolis Asiat., on the Ægean, bet. Chios and Tenedos. Named, from its supposed resemblance to a goat.

ÆXŌNE, a demus of Attica, of the tribe Cecropis, on Saronicus sinus, opposite Hydrusa ins. Noted for mullets. The people were proverbial as slanderers. *Axaona.*

ÆZANI (Azani), a city of Phrygia Epictetus, on Rhyndacus fl., near its source. Founded by Æzen, son of Tantalus. *Tjaudere Hissar.*

AFFLIANUS m., a hill E. of the Tiber, whence the Aqua Claudia flowed.

AFRICA, I. *Græce* Libya, one of the three great ancient *partes* of the world; bounded N. by the Mediterranean, w. and s. by the Atlantic, E. by Indicus oceanus and Erythræum mare. Named either from the Greek term indicating "without cold," or from a Phœnician word implying fertility. II. PROPRIA (Vetus Carthaginiensis), a maritime region of Africa, bet. Tusca fl. and Syrtis Minor; afterwards a Roman province, bet. Ampsagus fl. and Aræ Philænorum. It comprised Byzacena, Tingitana, and Tripolitana. *Tunis and parts of Tripoli.*

AGALASSA, a town of the Caspiræ Ind., on Acesines fl., L., above its junction with Hydaspes fl.

AGALINGUS fl., a r. of Sarmatia Europæa, falling into Sagaris fl. above Istrianorum portus.

AGAMANANA, a town of Mesopotamia, on the Euphrates, s. of Haditha. *Kahem.*

AGAMATHÆ, a people of Sarmatia Asiat., on Mæotis palus.

AGAME, a district of Tenesis, Æthiopia, s.w. of Adulis.

AGAMEDE, a town of Lesbos, near Pyrrha. Extinct in Pliny's time.

AGAMIA, a town of Troas, on a headland s. of Sigæum. The scene of the rescue of Hesione by Hercules.

AGAMZAGA (Agamzua), a town of Media.

AGANAGARA, I. a town of the Marundæ, Ind., on the Ganges, bet. Orcophanta and Talarga. II. of the Sindi, Ind., on Magnus sinus N.W.

AGANIPPE fons, a fountain of Bœotia, on Helicon m. Sacred to the Muses.

AGANTEI, a people of Sarmatia Asiat., on the Tanais.

AGARA, I. a town of India i. Gangem, on Agaricus sinus. II. of the Philitæ, in India i. Gangem, on Jomanes fl. *Agra.* III. of Susiana Cissia, on the Choaspes, s.w. of Susa. IV. of Susiana Melitene, on the Tigris, above Araca.

AGARI, a town of Byzacene, 16 m. from Thapsus.

AGARIABÆ, a town of Syrtica regio, bet. Augarmi and Tamalleni turris, w. of Zuchis.

AGARICUS sinus, a bay of Ind. oceanus, bet. India i. Gangem s.E., and Taprobane N.W.

AGARUM prom., a pr. of Sarmatia E., on Palus Mæotis, near the mouth of Agarus fl., opposite Heraclea Taurica. *Fetodowa.*

AGARUS fl., a r. of Sarmatia E., falling into Palus Mæotis near Agarum prom. *Berda.*

AGASSÆ (Ægæa, Agessus), a town of Pieria, Macedonia, bet. Beræa and Bala. *Near Cojani.*

AGĀSUS portus, a port of Daunia, Apulia, under Garganus m., N.E. of Sipontum. Perhaps the Apenestæ of Ptolemy. *Porto Greco.*

AGATHA, I. a town of the Volcæ Arecomicæ, in Narbonensis I., at the mouth of the Arauris fl. Founded by the Phocæans *circa* 630 B.C. *Agde.* II. ins., an isl. of Narbonensis I., off Agatha. III. of Lycia.

AGATHARTUS prom., the N.W. prom. of Sicily, at Cetaria.

AGATHOCLIS I. ins., two isl. in Indicus oceanus, s. of the Red Sea. II. turris, a fortress of Zeugitana, 30 m. s.w. of Utica.

AGATHOPOLIS, i. q. Araura.

AGATHONIS ins., an isl. of Dodecaschœnus, in the Red Sea, S.E. of Berenice.

AGATHOS DÆMON, I. the w. branch of the Nile, from above Letopolis, to the point where it divides into the Canopic and Bolbitic branches, below Naucratis. II. an isl. of India e. Gangem, N.W. of Sindæ ins. *Nicobar?*

AGATHYRNA (Agathyrsa, Agathyrsum), a maritime town of Sicily, N. bet. Tyndaris and Aluntium. Built *circa* 1100 B.C. by Agathyrnus, son of Æolus. *Near Sant' Agata.*

AGATHYRSI, a people from Sarmatia Europæa, N.W. of the Neuri, who migrated to Central Dacia, in Carpathus m., towards the source of Mariscus fl.

AGAU (Agava), a town of Æthiopia, towards the source of Astaboras fl. Noted for its great fairs.

AGAVI, a people of Scythia, of simple life, subsisting chiefly on mares' milk.

AGAZACA, a town under Parapomisus m.

AGAZZARI, a tribe of Venedi, Germania. The same with the Chazarii.

AGBATANA, the more correct form of Ecbatana.

AGBIA, a town of Zeugitana, bet. Musti and Tionica.

AGDANITIS, a maritime district of Carmania, bet. Rudiane w., and Corius fl. E.

AGDISTIS m. Galatiæ, i. q. Dindymus.

AGEDI, a people of Sarmatia Asiatica, on Mæotis palus.

AGELOCUM (Segelocum, Adelocum), a town of the Coritani, Brit., bet. Danum and Lindum (14). *Near Littleborough.*

AGENDICUM (Agedincum, Agedīcum), *postea* Senones, capital of the Senones, Lugd. IV., on Icauna fl., bet. Condate (21) and Clanum (25). *Sens.*

AGER CAMERE, a district of Bruttium, on Crathis fl., towards its mouth.

AGESINATES, I. a tribe of Pictones, in Aquitania II. *Archdeaconry of Aisenai.* II. their capital. *Lusignan.*

AGDAN, a town of Cyrenaica, bet. Maranthis and Echinos.

AGGAR (Aggersel), I. a town of Byzacene, bet. Manange and Aquæ Regiæ. II. of Gætulia, on Tritonis pal., w. of Puteus. III. Nepte, of Libya Int., w. of Thusari. IV. of Zeugitana, bet. Mediocera and Ulesippira.

AGIDANA ins. (Oaracta), an isl. of Carmania, in Persicus sinus, bet. Tarsias prom. and Organa ins., opposite the mouth of Corius fl.

AGIMOTHRA, a town of the Bari, Ind., on Serus fl., above Tomara.

AGINA, a town of Iberia, on Araxes fl., above Vasanda.

AGINIS, a town of Susiana Cissia, on Eulæus fl. The Beth Zaper of Scripture. *Ahwaz.*

AGINNUM, capital of the Nitiobriges, Aquitania II., on Garumna fl., R., bet. Excisum (20) and Lactora. *Agen.*

AGIRIA, a town of the Edetani, Tarraconensis, S.S.E. of Bilbilis.

AGISYMBA, the name given by Ptolemy to the Terra Incognita of Africa, under the Equator.

AGMA, a town of the Bagi-Gætuli, Libya, bet. Augemmi and Ausilindum.

AGMANISPHE, a port of the Homeritæ, Arabia Felix, E. of Arabiæ Fel. Emporium.

AGNA fl., a r. of Mauritania Tingit., falling into the Atlantic s. of Ussadium prom.

AGNAVIS, a town of the Potulatenses, 14 m. s.e. from Tibiscus. *Kertschina.*

AGNI CORNU prom., a pr. of Egypt, near Bolbiticum Ostium.

AGNION, a port of Crete, bet. Tretus prom. (6½) and Cisamus (11).

AGNOTES, I. a maritime people of Aquitania II., bet. the Pictones and the Santones. *District of Ack.* II. their capital. *Aber-Ack.*

AGNUS, a demus of Attica, of the tribe Acamantis, near Pallene.

AGOCE, a town of Æthiopia.

AGŌNES, I. *ap.* Ptolem., i. q. Euganes. II. a town of Gallia Transpadana, towards Novaria. *Agonale.*

AGONIDA ins., an isl. of Bætica w., one day's sail S.E. from the mouth of the Anas.

AGŌRA, a town of Thracius Chersonesus, bet. Aphrodisias and Callipolis, on the Egnatia Via. *Malagra.*

AGORANIS fl., a r. of India i. Gang. rising near the Ganges, and joining that river 7 m. w. from Patna. *Sagra;* or, according to Mannert, *Gowrah.*

AGORESUS, a town of Caria; an Argive settlement.

AGORETÆ, a port of Sarmatia As., on Vardanes fl.

AGORRA, Susiana, i. q. Aginis.

AGRADATAS fl., Persia, i. q. Cyrus.

AGRÆ, a village of Attica, on the Ilissus fl., near Athens.

AGRÆI (Agrinæ), I. a people of Acarnania, an Ætolian tribe, originally independent, occupying both sides of Achelous fl., s. of Amphilochia. II. of Arabia Deserta, i. q. Hagareni.

AGRAIS, capital of the Agræi, Acarnania, E. of Argos Amphilochus. *Agriada.*

AGRANUM, a town of Babylonia, on one of the canals of the Euphrates; it was destroyed by the Persians or Parthians.

AGRAULE (Agrule), I. Inferior, a demus of Attica, of the tribe Erectheis, near Athens, s.E., where the court called Ardettus was held. II. Superior, a demus of Attica, of the tribe Erectheis, s.E. of Agraule Inferior, under Hymettus m.

AGRAVONITÆ, a people of Illyria.

AGREDICUM, a town of the Senones, Lugdunensis IV., s.E. of Melodunum.

AGREMONES, a town of Ætolia.

AGRI, a people of Sarmatia As., E. of the Zichi. DECUMATES, a district of Germania Magna, the original seat of the Marcomanni, extending into Vindelicia, granted on the tenure of paying a tithe of the produce to the Gauls who attended in the Roman train after the expulsion of the Marcomanni.

AGRIANE, a town of Pontus, bet. Simos and Ibora.

AGRIANES, I. fl., *postea* Ergina, a r. of Thrace, rising in Hæmus m. and falling into Hebrus fl., below the mouth of Artiscus fl. *Ergene.* II. a people of Pæonia, Macedonia, under Scordus m.

AGRIASPÆ, *vide* Ariaspæ.

AGRIGENTUM (Acrăgas), a city of Sicily, on Acragas fl., near its confluence with Hypsa fl., 3 m. from the sea. Built by the Gelenses, B.C. 581. The capital of Phalaris. The birth-place of Empedocles. *Girgenti.*

AGRILIUM, a town of Bithynia, on Sangarius fl., bet. Nicæa (24) and Dorilæum (35). *Vizirkhan.*

AGRINIUM, a town of the Agræi, Ætolia Epictetus, N.W. of Thermon. *Vrachori.*

AGRIOMĒLUS fl., i. q. Sperchius.

AGRIOPHAGI, I. a people of Ethiopia. II. of India e. Gangem.

AGRIOPIUM, a place on Moloeis fl., in Bœotia, towards Platææ.

AGRIPPENSIS, a town of Bithynia.

AGRIPPINENSIS COLONIA (Civitas Agrippinensium), a city of the Ubii, in Germania II., on the Rhine, L., bet. Novesium (24) and Bonna (16). *Cologne.*

AGRIPPENSIS (Agrippias), the name given to Anthedon, Jud., when rebuilt by Herod.

AGRITIUM, a town of Bithynia, s.w. of Tottaium. *Belidjek.*

AGRIUM, a town on the N. coast of Crete, 4 m. E. of Rithymna. *Ario.*

AGRIZALA, a town of the Tectosages, in Galatia.

AGROSPI, a town of Ethiopia, on the Nile.

AGROIRA (Alloira), a name of Attalia, in Lydia.

AGSTANITIS, a district of Sophene, Armen., on Nymphius fl., bet. Tigranocerta and Amida. *Aghdsunikh.*

AGUBENI, a people of Arabia Deserta, w. of the Roabeni.

AGUNTUM (Aguntus), a town of the Ambidravi, in Rhætia, near the source of Dravus fl., bet. Littanum (23) and Loncium (18). *Innichen.*

AGYLLÆ, Etruria, the ancient name of Cœre.

AGȲRIUM, a town of Sicily, bet. Centuripæ and Assorus; the birth-place of Diodorus Siculus. *Near San Filippo d'Agiro.*

AHAVA fl., a r. of Assyria, of uncertain position, on which Ezra assembled the returning Jews.

AI (Aiath, Aija), a town of Ephraim, 5 m. E. of Bethel, the scene of Joshua's defeat and subsequent victory. *Deir Diwan.*

AIAS m. (Æas), a prom. of Thebais, on the Red Sea, s. of Philotera.

AII, a maritime port of India i. Gangem, about Coltiara.

AILA (Ailath), Arabia, i. q. Ælana.

AIN, a town of Judæa, and afterwards of Simeon, N.N.w. of Arad.

AIOPOLIS, Babylon, i. q. Is.

AISACUS fl. (Atagis), a r. of Rhætia, which, after its junction with the Byrrhus, falls into the Athesis.

AISUMAI m., m. of Asia, a ridge of Masius m., w. of Izala m.

AJALON, I. a valley of Dan, bet. Jerusalem and Ekron, the scene of Joshua's miracle. *Merj ibn Omeir.* II. a town in the cognominal valley, 2 m. N.E. from Nicopolis. *Yalo.* III. a town of Zebulun, the burial-place of Elon. IV. a town of Juda.

AKRABBI, a town of Samaria, s.E. of Sichem.

AKRABBIM (Maaleh Akrabbim), a pass in the mountains of Akrabattene, Judæa.

ALA I. (Halah), Mesopotamia, i. q. Aluana. II. FLAVIANA, i. q. Vindobona. III. NOVA, a town of the Boii, Pannon., bet. Æquinoctium and Carnuntum.

ALABANDA, a city of Caria, N. of Stratonicea, bet. two hills, "like an ass with a packsaddle :" traditionally founded by the hero Alabandus; noted for its dark marble, and named, as the term imports, from some great "horse-victory." The seat of a Conventus Jurid. *Arabi-hissar.*

ALABASTRON (Alabastropolis), a town of Heptanomis, N.E. of Cynopolis. Noted for its alabaster works.

ALABASTRUS fl., a r. of Æolis Asiat., rising in Ida m. and falling into Adramyttenus sin.

ALABASTRĪTES m. (Alabastrinus), a ridge of Arabici m., S.E. of Alabastropolis, named from its alabaster quarries. *Gebil el Kalil.*

ALĀBUS fl. (Alābon), a r. of Sicily, falling into Siculum mare at Megara, bet. Xyphonia and Thapsus. *Cantaro.*

ALÆ, a town of Cilicia Campestris, w. of Pyramus fl.

ALÆNUS fl., i. q. Alaunus.

ALÆSA (Halesa), a maritime town of Sicily, N. bet. Calacta and Cephalœdium. Built by Arconides, of Herbita, 403 B.C. Near it was a fountain that seemed to dance at the sound of a flute.

ALÆSUS fl. (Halesus), a r. of Sicily, falling into Tyrrhenum mare at Alæsa. *Pitineo.*

ALAGMA, a town of Osrhoene, on Belias fl., bet. Comisimbela and Ichnæ.

ALAGONIA, a town of Messenia, 4 m. N.E. from Gerenia.

ALALÆU ins. (Aliæu), islands of the Adulitæ, in the Red Sea, off Adulis. (Panis, Macaria.)

ALALCOMĒNÆ (Alcomenæ), I. a town of Asteris ins., or, according to Plutarch, of Ithaca ins. Named after Alalcomenes, foster-father of Minerva. II. of Bœotia, on the s.w. bank of Copais lac., w. of Haliartus, 4 m. from Ocalea. Sacred to Minerva, hence surnamed Alalcomeneis. *Near Sulinari.*

ALALCOMENIA fons, a fountain of Arcadia, N. of Mantina.

ALĀLIA, i. q. Corsica, the Phœnician name of Aleria.

ALALIS, a town of Palmyrene, on the Euphrates, s.w. of Sura. *Elamora.*

ALAMATA, a town of Palmyrene, on the Euphrates, bet. Zenobia and Thapsacus.

ALAMBATERON (Alambatis) prom., a pr. of Gedrosia, bet. Casia pr. and Daranabilla, at the E. extremity of Paragon sin.

ALAMONS (Alabon, Alapuntis), a town of the Caturiges, Narbonensis II., on Druentia fl., R., between Vapincum (17) and Segustero (16). *Monestier d'Allamont.*

ALAMUS, I. a town of Albania As., N.W. of Albana. II. Babylonia, i. q. Olabus.

ALANDER fl., a r. of Phrygia Magna, rising near Bendos, and falling into Sangarius fl. N.E. of Dorylæum. *Al Haur.*

ALANI (Alauni), I. a people of Albania As., S.E. of Legæ. II. mons, a m. of Scythia extra Imaum, N.

ALANORSI, a people of Scythia i. Imaum, towards the Alani.

ALANTON, a town of the Varduli, Tarraconensis, 9 m. s.w. of Pompelo.

ALAPTA, a town of Chalcidice, Macedonia, near Stagira.

ALAPUNTIS. *Vide* Alamons.

ALARA fl., a r. of Germania Mag., rising in Melibocus m., and falling into Visurgis fl. below Tuliphurdum.

ALARNASSUS. *Vide* Abassus.

ALASI, a town of the Garamantes, Africa.

ALATA, I. a town of the Labeatæ, Illyria, on Barbana fl., N. of Birziminum. II. of the Læceni, Arabia, w. of Itamus port.

[ALATA castra (Castrum Puellarum) a fortress of the Damnii, 2 m. from Lindum. *Edinburgh.*]

ALATERVA, a town of the Damnii, on Bodotria æstuar., 5 m. w. of Lindum. *Cramond.*

ALATIS, a town of Palmyrene, on the Euphrates, bet. Sura and Attis.

ALATRIUM, a town of the Hernici, Latium, E. of Ferentinum, on the borders of Sabinium. A municip. and colonia. *Alatri.*

ALAUNA, I. a town of the Damnii, Brit., at Severi murus, bet. Coria and Lindum. II. of the Osismii, Lugdunensis II., N.E. of Coriallum (14). *Alleaume,* near *Valogne.* III. of the Unelli, Lugdunensis III., N.E. of Crociaconum.

ALAUNI, a tribe of Boii, Noricum, bet. Stiria fl. and Œnus fl., s. of the Levaces.

ALAUNIUM, a town of the Salyes, Narbonensis II., bet. Segustero (24) and Apta Julia. *Passage of the Lauzon at Mont Laurs.*

ALAUNUS fl. I. a r. of Britain, falling into the German Ocean N. of Vedra fl., the N. limit of Valentia and Maxima Cæsariensis. *Aln.* II. of the Regni, falling into the sea w. of Vectis ins. III. of the Durotriges, Britannia, falling into the sea w. of the preceding. *Brit.* IV. m., m. of Sarmatia, E., towards Tanais fl., N.N.W. of Mæotis palus.

ALAZIA, capital of the Alazones, Bithynia, near the junction of the Macestus and Rhyndacus.

ALAZONES, I. a town of Sarmatia Europæa, on both sides of Hypanis fl., towards its mouth. II. of Bithynia, on Rhyndacus fl.

ALAZONIUS fl., I. a r. of Tarraconensis, i. q. Clodianus. II. of Albania, falling into Cyrus fl. above Osica. *Aloson; Alacks.*

ALBA, I. a town of the Oretani, Tarraconensis, N.N.E. of Laccuris. II. AUGUSTA, i. q. Alba Helviorum. III. DOCILIA, of the Ingauni, Liguria, bet. Vicus Virginis (13) and Ad Navalia (13), on the Via Aurelia. *Albizzola.* IV. FUCENTIA, of the Marsi, Sabinium, near the N.W. extremity of Fucensis lac., bet. Carseoli (24) and Marrubium (13), on Via Valeria. A colonia 304 B.C. Its citadel was used by the Roman senate as a state prison. 1 *m. from Alba.* V. HELVIORUM (Alba Augusta), capital of the Helvii, in Narbonensis, near the Rhone, N. of Senomagus. *Aps; Apt.* VI. JULIA, a later name of Apulum, Dacia, from the Gyula family. VII. LONGA, of the Latini, Latium, 20 m. S.E. from Rome, on Albanus m., overlooking the E. shore of Albanus lac. A Siculian town, successively occupied by Aborigines and Pelasgi. Destroyed by Tullus Hostilius. Traditionally founded by Ascanius, and named from the white sow of Æneas. *Palazzolo.* VIII. POMPEIA, of the Statielli, Liguria, on Tanarus fl., bet. Pollentia (35) and Hasta (16). A municip., named after Sextus Pompeius. The birth-place of Pertinax. *Alba.*

ALBACUS m., a m. of Caria.

ALBANA, capital of Albania Asiat., on the Caspian, N. of Albanus fl. *Darubandi.*

ALBANI, I. a people of Illyria, bet. the Partheni and the Penestæ, N.W. of Lychnitis palus. II. a tribe of Massagetæ, occupying Albania Asiatica.

ALBANIA, I. a country of Asia, bounded N. by Sarmatia Asiatica, at Cæsius fl., s. by Armenia Major, at Cyrus fl., w. by Iberia and Armenia Maj., E. by the Caspian. *Daghistan* and *Lazestan.* II. a town of Adiabene, Assyria, E. of Hatra. *Halvan.*

ALBANIÆ portæ (pylæ), defiles in Caucasus m., leading from Iberia into the maritime portion of Albania, s.w. of Albana. *Pass of Derbend.*

ALBANOPOLIS, capital of the Albani, in Illyria. *Croia.*

ALBANUM, a town of Latium, on the w. shore of Albanus lacus, N. of Aricia. *Albano.*

ALBANUS, I. a r. of Albania, falling into the Caspian N. of Cyrus fl. *Bilbana.* II. a lake of Latium, at Alba Longa, occupying the crater of an extinct volcano. Its waters, which threatened to submerge the adjacent country, were partially carried off by an artificial canal, a mile and a half long,

cut through the solid rock, still extant at Castel Gandolfi. *L. d'Albano.* III. (Albius), a ridge of m. intersecting Illyria, from Alpes Carnicæ to Scordus m. IV. a m. of Latium, overlooking Alba Longa. Sacred to Jupiter Latialis. Here were celebrated the Feriæ Latinæ, and the triumphs of many of the Roman generals. *Monte Cavo.*

ALBIANA, a town at the s. extremity of Corsica, below Palla.

ALBIANUM, a town of the Genauni, Rhætia, near Œnus fl., 38 m. E. from Veldidena. *Seebauen.*

ALBIGA (Albix), a town of the Ruteni, Aquitania I., on Tarnis fl., w.s.w. of Condatomagus. *Alby.*

ALBIN, "high land," a name of Caledonia.

ALBINGAUNIUM (Albium Ingaunum), capital of the Ingauni, in Liguria, on the Via Aurelia, bet. Lollupice (8) and Lucus Bormanni (15), on the Ligusticus sin. *Albenga.*

ALBINIA (Almina) fl., a r. of Etruria, rising N. of Saturnia, and falling into Inferum mare s. of Telamon (4). *Albegna.*

ALBINIANA, a town of the Frisii, Germ., on the Rhine, bet. Lugdunum (10 E.) and Trajectum. *Alphen.*

ALBINTEMELIUM (Albium Intemelium), capital of the Intemeli, in Liguria, near the mouth of Rutuba fl., on the Via Aurelia, bet. Costa Balenæ (16) and Lumo (6). *Vintimille.*

ALBIŒCI (Albici), *postea* Reii, I. a people of Narbonensis II., contiguous to the Memini, in the mountains N.E. of Massilia. II. their earlier capital. *Albiosc.*

ALBION ins., Britannia, I. an isl. of the Atlantic, bet. Gallia and Hibernia. Peopled by various immigrations from the continent. *Great Britain.* II. Inferior, a division of Albion, comprehending Maxima Cæsariensis and Valentia. III. Superior, a division of Albion, comprehending Britannia I., Flavia Cæsariensis, and Britannia II. IV. Ulterior (Albion Borealis, Albion Barbara), a division of Albion, comprehending the countries of the Pictones, or Vecturiones, Caledonii, Attacottæ, and Horestæ.

ALBIS fl. (Elfa), a r. of Germania Magna, rising in Asciburgius m., near Strevinta, and falling into Germanicus oc. N. of Visurgis fl. *Elbe.*

ALBOCENSES, a people of Dacia, on the Danube, bet. Tibiscus fl. and the Saldenses.

ALBONA, a town of Liburnia, on Flanaticus sin., N.W. bet. Flanona and Nesactium.

ALBONICA, a town of the Edetani, Tarraconens., E. of Lutia.

ALBUCELLA (Arbucala), a town of the Vaccæi, Tarracon., bet. Pontia and Amallobriga. *Villa Fasila.*

ALBŪLA, I. the old Latin name of the Tiber. II. a town of Mauritania Cæsar., bet. Ad Rubras and Ad Dracones, S.E. of Siga.

ALBULATES fl., a r. of Picenum, falling into the Adriatic N. of Cupra. *Vibrata.*

ALBUM prom., I. a pr. of Palestine, marking the S. termination of Phœnicia, above Alexandroscenæ. II. littus of Marmarica.

ALBŪNĒA nemus et fons, a grove and fountain of Latium, near Tibur.

ALBURNUS m., a ridge of m. in Lucania, bet. Tanager fl. and Calor fl. *Alburno; Monte di Postiglione.*

ALBUS portus, I. a port of Arabia, i. q. Jamnia. II. of Bætica, w. of Calpe. *Algesiras.*

ALCATHOE, an appellation of Megara Nisæa, from Alcathous, s. of Pelops.

ALCE, a town of the Carpetani, Tarraconens., near the Anas, w.s.w. of Munda.

ALCES, a r. of Bithynia.

ALCIMEDON campus, a plain of Arcadia, 4 m. w. from Mantinea.

ALCIMUNNIS (Alcimœnis), a town of Germania Magna, on Alcis fl., at its junction with the Danube.

ALCIMUS prom., the w. extremity of Munychium prom. at Athens. The burial-place of Themistocles.

ALCIS fl., a r. of Germania Magna, falling into the Danube at Alcimunnis.

ALCOMENÆ, a town of Pelagonia Deuriopis, in Macedonia, on Erigonus fl., below Bryanium.

ALCONIS opp. et ins. *Vide* Alonis.

ALCYONIA palus, a pool of Argolis, near Lerna, of depth reputed unfathomable, through which Bacchus descended in search of Semele.

ALCYONIUM mare, the Corinthiacus sin., bet. Bœotia, Megaris, and Corinthia.

ALĒA, I. a town of Arcadia, 2¼ m. w. from Tegea. II. of Thessaly. III. of the Vettones, Lusitania, s. of Lacipea.

ALEBUS fl., a r. of Tarraconensis, falling into Illicitanus sin. bet. Acra Leuce s. and Artemisium prom. N.

ALEISIUM (Alesiæum), a town of Pisatis, Elis, bet. Olympia and Elis, on Aleisius fl., near Amphidoli. Noted for a great monthly fair.

ALEISIUS fl., a r. of Pisatis, falling into Alpheus fl. s.s.E. of Salmone.

ALEIUS campus, the district of Cilicia Cam-

pestris, bet. Sarus and Pyramus fl. The death-place of Bellerophon.

ALELE, a city of Libya, on Ger fl. *Helel.*

ALEOS fl., a r. of Ionia, falling into Erythræus sin. at Erythræ. Its water promoted the growth of hair.

ALEMANNI, a people of Germania Magna, at first bet. the Rhine, the Danube, and the Mænus ; afterwards extending to the Alps. The descendants of a tribe of them, settled by Theodoric in Venetia, N. of Verona, still retain almost entirely the language and manners of their ancestors.

ALĒRIA, I. a town of the Biturges Cubi, Aquitania II., on Audria fl., bet. Argantomagus (21) and Avaricum (40). *St. Vincent d'Ardentes.* II. *prius* Alalia, of Corsica, at the mouth of Rhotanus fl. A Phocæan settlement. A colonia. *Aleria.*

ALESIA (Alexia), capital of the Mandubii, Lugdunensis I., N.E. of Aballo, traditionally built by Hercules. Memorable for its siege by Cæsar. *Alise ; Sainte Reine, on Mt. Auxois.*

ALESIÆ, a town of Laconia, on Eurotas fl., above Amyclæ.

ALESIUM m., a m. of Arcadia, at Mantinea.

ALETIUM, a town of the Salentini, in Japygia, bet. Uxentum (12) and Neretum (10), N.W. of Japygium prom. A municipium. *Santa Maria della Lizza.*

ALETUM, a maritime town of the Curiosolites, Lugdunensis III., w. of Ingena. *On Cape Guich Alet. near St. Malo.*

ALEUS, a village of Cos ins.

ALEX fl., a r. of Bruttium, separating the Regini from the Locrenses, and falling into the sea at Peripolium.

ALEXANDRA m., a summit of Ida m., overlooking Antandros. The immediate scene of the Judgment of Paris (Alexandros).

ALEXANDRI, I. ARÆ, altars placed by Ptolemy in Sarmatia, under Riphæi m., and fabulously attributed by him to Alexander the Great. II. COLUMNÆ, columns erected in honour of Alexander, in Sarmatia A., under Hippici m., E. III. DIVERSARIUM, a caravanserai near Leontecephale, in Phrygia. IV. ins., Persia, i. q. Aracia.

ALEXANDRIA, I. (Alexandriopolis), the later capital of Arachosia, on Arachotus fl., near Gundava. II. ARIANA, of Aria, on Arius fl., N. of Artasana. *Pulki.* III. *prius* Racotis (the No of Scripture), a town of Egypt, on the coast, s.w. of Canopus (12). Rebuilt by Dinocrates, at the command of Alexander, 332 B.C. *Skanderik, Alexandria.* IV. of Drangiana, on Etymandrus fl., above its mouth. V. of Gedrosia, i. q. Ora. VI. of India i. Gangem, at the junction of the Indus and Hyphasis. VII. *surnamed* Sogdiana, of India, on the Indus, below Alexandria ad Hyphasin. VIII. *postea* Antiochia, of Margiana, on Margus fl., E. of Apavartice. Destroyed by the barbarians and rebuilt by Antiochus, son of Seleucus, and named by him Antiochia. *Mawri; Schah Djehan.* IX. of the Orsipi, Bactria, under Parapomisus m., bet. Saragana and Ortospana, on Dargomanes fl. X. of Mysia, i. q. Antandrus. XI. of Oxiana, S. of Maracanda, on Oxus fl., S.W. of Alexandria Ultima. XII. *surnamed* ad Issum, of Cilicia, on Issicus sin., 16 m. s. from Baiæ. Built by Alexander in memory of the battle of Issus. *Scanderoon; Alessandretta.* XIII. *surnamed* ad Latmum, of Caria, towards Latmos m. XIV. *surnamed* Ultima (Alexandroschata), of Sogdiana, on Jaxartes fl., towards its source. Built by Alexander. *Near Khodjend.* XV. SUSIANÆ, *vide* Charax. XVI. *surnamed* Troas, *prius* Antigonia, a maritime city of Troas, s. of Sigæum. Built by Antigonus, enlarged by Lysimachus. Under Rome a colonia. It was hence St. Paul and St. Luke sailed for Macedonia; and it was here that St. Paul restored Eutychus to life. The birth-place of Hegesianax, of Histiæa, and of Hegemon. *Eski Stamboul.*

ALEXANDRÏOPOLIS (Sauloe), a town of Parthia-Siracene, N.E. of Hecatompylos.

ALEXANDRIUM, a town of Acrabbatene, Samaria, E.N.E. of Silo. Built by Alexander Jannæus. *Kuryzeb.*

ALEXANDROSCENÆ, a maritime town of Galilæa Superior, bet. Album prom. and Achzib.

ALEXIA, i. q. Alesia.

ALGÆ, a maritime town of Etruria, on Via Aurelia, bet. Centumcellæ (3) and Rapio (3). *Torre Nuovo.*

ALGÏDUM, a town of the Æqui, Latium, 16 m. S.E. of Rome, on the Via Latina. *Rocca del Papa.*

ALGIDUS m., a range of hills in Latium, E. of Albanus m.

ALIASSUS, a town of the Trocmi, Galatia, on the Halys, L., N. of Aspona (18).

ALIBACA, a town of the Pentapolis, Cyrenaica, S.E. of Berenice.

ALICANUM (Heclitanum, *rectius* Raclinatum), a town of Pannonia Superior, on Murus fl., 40 m. S.W. from Sabaria. *Szerdahely.*

ALICODRA, a town of Bactriana, w. of Oxus fl.

ALIGOMARI fons, a sacred stream and fountain of Lydia, running near Mossine.

ALII, a town of Phrygia.

ALILÆI (Hevila), a people of Arabia Felix, on the Red Sea, bet. the Cinædocolpitæ and the Cassanitæ. Named from the goddess Alilat (Urania). *Halil.*

ALIMALA, Lyciæ, i. q. Amelas.

ALIMNE, Lyciæ, i. q. Amelas.

ALIMUS, a demus of Attica, of the tribe Leontis, near Colias prom., 4½ m. S.E. from Athens. The birthplace of Thucydides. *Mysta.*

ALINA ins., an isl. of Caria, off Crya.

ALINDA, a town of Caria, bet. Stratonicea and Cosimia. *Aleina.*

ALINDÆA (Calindæa), a town of Mygdonia, in Macedonia, on Axius fl., S.E. of Idomene.

ALINZA (Orosa), a town of Media, E. of Nazada. *Near Talvar.*

ALIPHERA, a town of Arcadia, on the confines of Triphylia, s.w. of Melænæ. *Nerovitza.*

ALISARNA (Elisarne, Haliserne), a town of Mysia, near Pergamum.

ALISCA, a town of Valeria, Pannonia, 7 m. S.E. from Ala Nova. *Szexard.*

ALITROPE, i. q. Alope, Thessal.

ALISINCUM, a town of the Ædui, Lugdunensis I., w. of Augustodunum. *Anizy le Grand.*

ALISO, I. a r. of the Bructeri Majores, Germania, falling into Lupia fl., R., at Aliso. II. (Tropæa Drusi), a town of the Bructeri Majores, Germania, on Aliso fl., at its junction with Lupia fl. Built by Drusus. *Lisborn.*

ALISTA, a maritime village of Corsica, 5 m. w. from Graniacum prom. *Torre Salenzara.*

ALISTUS, a town of the Viruni, Germania, s. of Laciburgium. *Near Schwerin.*

ALISUM, a town of the Usipetes, Germania, on the Rhine, below Asciburgium. *Wesel.*

ALITROPHAGI, a people of Serica.

ALIUM, a town of Acroria, Elis, N.W. of Thraustus.

ALLAN, a town of Mesopotamia, on the Euphrates, bet. Basilia and Contra Birtha.

ALLAREA, a town of Crete.

ALLARODII, Pontus, i. q. Chalybes.

ALLAVA fl. I. (Alba, Allaba), a r. of Sicily, rising in Cratas m. and falling into Africum pelagus E. of Thermæ Selinuntiæ. *Callata Bellota.* II. a town of Sicily, on Allava fl., L., towards its mouth, 12 m. from Cena. *Ribera.*

ALLAVONA (Allabone), a town of the Ilergetes, Tarraconensis, 16 m. N.W. from Cæsarea Augusta. *Alagon.*

ALLIA fl., a r. of Sabinium, rising near Nomentum and falling into the Tiber about 11 m. above Rome. The locality of the defeat of the Romans by Brennus, B.C. 390. *Aia.*

ALLIANA, I. REGIO, a district of Gallia Cisalpina, bet. the Padus and Ticinus fl. Noted for a wool called Retovina. *About Rebbio.* II. a town of the Lævi, Gallia Transpadana, N. of Laumellum.

ALLIËNI FORUM, *postea* Forum Arrii, a town of the Lingones, Gallia Cisalpina, on Voluta fl., N.w. of Spina. *Ferrara.*

ALLĪFÆ, a town of the Pentri, Samnium, on Via Numicia, bet. Ebritiana (9) and Sepinum (16). Here was a manufactory of large drinking-cups. A col. of the triumvirs. *Allife.*

ALLINGOS, a town of Crete.

ALLOBRŎGES, a people of Narbonensis, bet. the Rhodanus and the Isura fl. *Departments of Drome, Isère et Mt. Blanc, and Leman, W.*

ALLOBROGIA, *postea* Sabaudia, the country of the Allobroges.

ALLOSYNGA, a maritime town of the Calingæ Ind., at the E. mouth of Tyndis fl.

ALLOTRIGES, a town of Tarraconensis, N.

ALMA fl., a rivulet of Etruria, falling into Inferum m., bet. Prile fl. (19) and Scabris portus (6).

ALMĀNA, a town of Pelagonia, in Macedonia, on Axius fl., above Europus. *Gradiska.*

ALMATH, Almon, i. q. Bahurim.

ALMIA, a town of the Siracæ, Sarmatia As., under Corax m., s. of Euriapa.

ALMINA fl., Etruria, i. q. Albinia.

ALMO fl., a stream rising near Bovillæ, and falling into the Tiber near Rome. *Almone, Aquatacio.*

ALMODATH, a district of Arabia Felix, partially in the Desert, subsequently occupied by the Alumeotæ.

ALMON (Almonia), the early name of Minya, in Thessaly.

ALMON DIBLATHAIM, one of the stations of the Israelites on their way from Mount Hor.

ALMOPEIA, I. Macedonia, generally. II. the country of the Almopes.

ALMOPES, a tribe of Pæonians, on Erigonus fl., towards its source. Anterior of date to the conquests of the Temenidæ; named after the giant Almops.

ALMUS fl., I. a r. of Mœsia Superior, falling into the Danube at Almus. II. a m. of Pannonia, on the Danube, towards Sirmium, on which Probus planted the first vine in Germany. III. a town of the Mœsi, Mœsia Superior, on the Danube,

bet. Remetodia and Pomodiana, at the mouth, R., of Almus fl.

ALOCIÆ ins., three isl. of Germania Magna, off Cimbrica Chersonesus.

ALOIUM, a town of Thessaly, near Tempe.

ALONE, I. a town of the Brigantes, Brit., s.E. of Glanaventa. The station of the Cohors Tertia Nerviorum. *Ambleside.* II. the Contestani, Tarraconensis, w. of Lucentum, near the mouth of Tader fl. A Massilian settlement. *Torre di Salinas.*

ALONI, a people of Adiabene, Assyria, on Caprus fl.

ALONIANUM, a town of Byzacene, bet. Cerva and Thala.

ALONIS, I. (Alconis) an isl. on the coast of Narbonensis II., over against Alconis. *Ile de la Fournigue.* II. a maritime town of the Verucini, Narbonensis II., bet. Heraclea Caccabaria and Olbia. *At Pointe des Gourdons.*

ALONTA fl. (Alonda), a r. of the Alontæ, Sarmatia, falling into the Caspian, N. of Telaeba. *Terek.*

ALONTÆ (Olondæ), a people of Sarmatia As., on the Caspian, about Alonta fl.

ALONTIGECELI, a town of the Turtetani, Bætica, bet. Iluro s.w. and Aratispi N.

ALŎPE, I. a town of the Locri Opuntii, on Opuntius sin., bet. Daphnus and Cynus; II. of Pontus, the birth-place of the Amazon Penthesilea.

ALOPĔCE, I. (Alŏpecia, Atech) an isl. of Sarmatia Asiat., 12 m. w. from the E. mouth of the Tanais. II. a demus of Attica, of the tribe Antiochis, N. of Hymettus m., 1½ m. from Athens, the birth-place of Socrates and Aristides.

ALOPECONNĒSUS, an Æolian town of Chersonnesus Thracius, on Melas sin., opposite Imbros ins. Famous for its truffles. *Alexi.*

ALOPES, the early name of Ephesus.

ALŌRUS, a town of Bottiæa, Macedonia, on Thermaicus sin., at the mouth of Haliacmon fl. *Near Kapsochori.*

ALOS (Halos), *surnamed* Phthioticum or Achaicum, a town of Phthiotis, in Thessaly, bet. Phylace and Demetrium, on Amphrysus fl., near its mouth. Founded by Athamas.

ALOSTIGI, a town of the Turtetani, Bætica, bet. Silia N.w. and Carruca E.

ALOSTU, a maritime town of Taurica Chersonesus, s.E. bet. Lampas and Lagyra.

ALPĒNI (Alpēnas, Alponus), a town of the Locri Epicnemidii, on Maliacus sin., s. of Thermopylæ.

ALPES m., I. a chain of m. separating Italy

from Gaul and Germany, extending in a semicircle of 600 m. from above Vada Sabbatia to Flanaticus sin. The various ridges, in total extent about 1000 m., were distributed by Augustus into Alpes Carnicæ, A. Cottiæ, A. Graiæ, A. Maritimæ, A. Noricæ, A. Penninæ, A. Rhætiæ. The word *Pen* is Celtic for "high." II. BASTARNICÆ, i. q. Alpes Carpatæ. III. CARNICÆ, i. q. Juliæ. IV. CARPATÆ, the N.E. range, in the country of the Carpi. *Krapak. Carpathian m.* V. COTTIÆ, the range above Alpes Maritimæ, separating the Garoceli and Vagienni of Gallia Cisalpina from Gallia Narbonensis. Named after Cottius, the client of Augustus. *Cottian Alps, Mt. Genèvre.* VI. GRAIÆ, the range above Alpes Cottiæ, separating Gallia Cisalpina from Narbonensis. It was by one of its defiles that Hannibal passed into Italy. *Graian Alps. Little St. Bernard.* VII. *idem*, a province of Narbonensis, extending above Alpes Graiæ m. *Valais and Savoy.* VIII. JULIÆ (Carnicæ), the range of Alps on the N. confine of Histria, terminating in Albius m. *Carnischen Alpen.* IX. LEPONTIÆ (Summæ), the range separating the Lepontii of Rhætia from Helvetia. *Mt. St. Gothard.* X. MARITIMÆ, the range bet. Nicæa and Vesulus m. *M. di Tenda. Maritime A.* XI. *idem*, a province of Narbonensis II., extending above Alpes Maritimæ m. *Nice and Dauphiny E.* XII. NORICÆ, the range in Noricum separating the Ambisontii from the Alauni, extending to the head of Plavis fl. *Norischen Alpen. Noric Alps.* XIII. PENNINÆ (Pænæ), the range separating the Veragri of Gallia Narbonensis from the Salassi of Gallia Cisalpina; extending from Summus Penninus to the sources of Rhodanus and Rhenus fl. *Great St. Bernard.* XIV. RHÆTĬCÆ (Tridentinæ), the range separating the Cotuantii of Rhætia from the Brixentii. *Mt. Brenner.* XV. SUMMÆ, i. q. Alpes Lepontiæ. XVI. TRIDENTINÆ, i. q. Alpes Rhætiæ.

ALPESA, a town of the Celtici, Lusitania, N.W. of Pax Augusta.

ALPHĒUS fl., a r. of Elis, rising 1½ m. from Asea. Near its source it is joined by Eurotas fl., with which it runs for above three miles; they then enter a subterraneous channel, and emerge, the Eurotas near Bilmina in Laconia, the Alpheus near Megalopolis. The Alpheus falls into the Cyparissius sin. at Litrine; but the poets feign that, from love for the nymph Arethusa, it passes under the sea and rises in

Sicily at Arethusa fons. Its waters were considered good for leprosy. Towards its source, *Karilena;* after its reappearance, *Rofea.*

ALPIS MARITIMA, capital of Alpes Maritimæ, bet. Albintemelium (9) and Cemenelium (9). *Nôtre Dame de Bon Voyage.*

ALPŌNIS, a m. and town of Macedonia or Thessaly.

ALSA, I. a r. of the Carni, Venetia, falling into the Adriatic bet. Varanus fl. and Aquileia. The death-place of Constantine. *Ausa.* II. a port of the Carni, at the mouth of Alsa fl. *Ausa.*

ALSADAMUS m., m. of Decapolis, S.E., separating it from Arabia Deserta.

ALSIETINUS lacus, a lake of Etruria, formed by Alsium fl. *Lago di Martignano.*

ALSIUM, a maritime town of Etruria, on Via Aurelia, bet. Bibiana (6) and Pyrgi (10). *Statua.*

ALSUGA, Venetiæ, i. q. Ausugum.

ALTA ripa, I. a pr. of the Meretæ, Britt., N. of Vara æstuar. II. a town of Valeria, Pannon., on the Danube, 18 m. from Lussonium. *Tolna.* III. of the Vangiones, Germania I., on the Rhine, bet. Barbetomagus and Noviomagus. *Altrip.*

ALTABA, a town of Numidia, bet. Justis and Thebeste.

ALTANUM, a town of Bruttium, on Locrensis sin., bet. Locri and Scylla, on Via Trajana.

ALTERNIA, a town of the Celtiberi, Tarraconensis, bet. Characa N.W., and Valentia S.E.

ALTHA, a town of Messene Inferior, Babyl., W.S.W. of Charax.

ALTHÆA (Carteia), *postea* Urcesa, capital of the Olcades, Tarraconensis, N.W. of Consabrum. The population was removed by Hannibal to Africa. *Orgaz.*

ALTIAIA, *postea* Alteium, a town of the Treveri, near the Rhine, N.W. of Barbetomagus. *Altzheim; Eltz.*

ALTIBURUS (Altuburus), a town of Byzacene, bet. Mutia and Atteserra.

ALTINA, a town of Pannonia I., on Savus fl., bet. Bassiana (12) and Singidunum (8).

ALTINUM, I. a town of Valeria, Pannonia, 22 m. S.W. from Ad Statuas. *Czektso.* II. of the Veneti, Venetia, on Silis fl., R., near its mouth, bet. Ad Nonum (9) and Sanos (12), on Via Æmilia. Noted for its wool. The death-place of L. Antonius Verus. *Altino.*

ALTIS, the sacred grove of Olympia, in Elis; the burial-place of Pelops.

ALTUS, a fortress of Amphaxitis, in Macedonia, near Thessalonica.

ALUACA, a town of Assyria, on Lycus fl., towards its source.

ALUANA (Ala), a town of Gauzonitis, Mesopotamia, on Chaborrus fl., w. of Singara.

ALUIA, a town of Corsica, on Circidius fl., R., above Tarabenorum Vicus.

ALUMEOTÆ, a people of Arabia Felix, N. of the Sophanitæ, in the district previously called Almodath.

ALUNTIUM (Haluntium), a maritime town of Sicily N., at the mouth of the Chydas fl. Built *circa* 1100 B.C. *San Filadelfo*.

ALUTA fl., *postea* Tausis, a r. of Dacia, rising in Carpathus m. N. of Prætoria Augusta, and falling into the Danube over against Anasamus. *Alt, Olt*.

ALUTRA, a town of the Euganei, in Gallia Transpadana, N.E. of Brixia.

ALVEA, I. a town of Corsica, N.E. from the mouth of Liamon fl. *Vico*. II. of the Vaccæi, Taraconensis, E.S.E. of Sentica.

ALVUM (Histria), i. q. Albona.

ALYATTA, I. a town of Bithynia, towards Pessinus. II. of Phrygia, towards Caballus.

ALYBES, i. q. Chalybes.

ALYBE, Mysiæ, probably Ænea.

ALYCHME (Lyciæ), i. q. Amilas.

ALYCUS fl., a r. of Sicily, falling into the sea bet. Gela and Camarina. *Vrillo*.

ALYDDA (Attalyda), a town of Phrygia Epictetus, bet. Acmonia (25) and Philadelphia.

ALYI, a town of Lower Egypt, on the Nile, R., bet. Thimonepsus and Hipponon.

ALYSIS m., a m. of Crete, whence Jupiter was named Alysius.

ALYSSUS fons, a fountain of Arcadia, near Cynætha. Reputed, as the name imports, to cure hydrophobia.

ALYZIA (Leuxia), a town of Acarnania, on the w. coast, 2 m. from the sea, 15 m. N.E. from Leucas. *Ælias*.

AMADOCA, capital of the Amadoci, Sarmatia, on the Borysthenes, above Sarum.

AMADOCI, a people of Sarmatia Europæa, about Amadoca.

AMADOCUS lac., I. a lake of the Amadoci, Sarmatia Europæa, N. of Niossum, whence issued the N.E. source of the Borysthenes. II. m., m. of Sarmatia Europæa, separating the Amadoci from the Navari.

AMÆA, a town of the Vettones, Lusitania, on Arda fl., above Interamnesia.

AMAGETOBRIGA (Magetobria), a town of the Sequani, in Maxima Sequanorum, N.W. of Visontio. The locality of the defeat of Ariovistus. *Amage*.

AMALCHIUM mare, "frozen sea;" the Greek name of Borealis oceanus.

AMALEKITÆ, a nomadic people, bet. Palestine and Egypt. Of date long anterior to the Amalek from whom some authors describe them to be descendants; they were finally exterminated by David.

AMALLOBRIGA, a town of the Vaccæi, Tarraconensis, E.N.E. of Nardinium. *Medina*.

AMAMASSUS, a maritime town of Cyprus.

AMANA, I. a peak of Hermon m., whence issues Amana (Abana) fl. II. a r., i. q. Abana.

AMANDRA, a district of India, on the Indus.

AMANICÆ portæ (Amanides pylæ), a defile of Cilicia Campestris, in Amanus m., N. of Ciliciæ pylæ, by which Darius passed from Syria into Cilicia, prior to the battle of Issus, on the same night that Alexander passed from Cilicia into Syria by the Ciliciæ pylæ. *Demir-capi*.

AMANIENSES Cilic., i. q. Eleutherocilices.

AMANTIA, Illyria, i. q. Abantia.

AMANTINI (Amantes), a people of Pannonia Inferior, E. of the Boii, N. of the Aravisci.

AMANUS I. m., a ridge of Taurus, extending S.E. from about Melitene, bet. Cilicia and Syria, to the Mediterranean at Rhossicus scopulus. *Monte Negro. Al Lucan*. II. portus, the early name of Flaviobriga.

AMARA, a maritime town of Arabia Felix, N. of Didymi prom.

AMARDI (Mardi, "plunderers"), I. a people of Media, bet. Amardus fl. s., and Jasomus m. w. of the Cadusii. II. on the Caspian, bet. the Anariacæ and Hyrcania.

AMARDUS fl., a r. of Media, rising in Nisæi Campi, and falling into the Caspian s. of Cyropolis; it separates Media Atrobatene from Media Magna. *Sefid Rud*.

AMARES, a people of Bactriana, s. of the Scordi.

AMARI lac., several lakes or ponds of peculiarly bitter water, near Arsinoe (*Suez*).

AMARISPI, a people of Bactria, under Parapomisus m., s.w. of the Drepsiani.

AMARUSA (Marusia), a town of Hyrcania. *Bistam*.

AMARYNTHUS, a town of Eubœa, 1 m. from Eretria. Noted for its annual festivals in honour of Diana.

AMASENUS fl., a r. of Latium, one of the streams which formed the Pomptinæ Paludes.

AMASIA, I. a city of Pontus, on Iris fl., below Sebastopolis; under Rome, the metropolis of Pontus. The birth-place of Strabo. *Amasieh*. II. Germania. *Vide* Amisia.

AMASSI, a people of Sarmatia, on the Tanais.

AMASTOROS, a town of Cyrenaica, at Drepanum prom.

AMASTRIS (Mastrum), *prius* Sesamus, capital of Paphlagonia, on a peninsula, 11¼ m. E. from Parthenius fl. A Milesian settlement, enlarged and renamed by Amastris, queen of Heraclea. *Amasera.*

AMATHŬS, I. capital of Cyprus, on the S. coast, E. of Curium. Sacred to Adonis and the bearded Venus. A colony from Hamath, Syria. The people were said to grow horned. *Near Limasol.* II. *Hebraicè* Betharamathon, a town of Gad, Galeaditis, 22 m. S. from Pella. *Amatah.* III. (Psamathus), of Laconia, at Tænarum prom. *Porto Quaglio.* IV. (Pamisus), *postea* Mamaus, a r. of Triphylia, Elis, near Pylus.

AMATHUSIA, an early name of Cyprus.

AMAXA, a town of Bithynia.

AMAXIA, a port of Cilicia Trachea, E. of Syedra. Its district, noted for its cedar timber, was given by Mark Antony to Cleopatra.

AMAZONES, a fabulous confederation of women, variously placed in Scythia, Asia Minor, &c.

AMAZONIUS, I. a surname of Thermodon fl., Pontus. II. of Paryadres m., Pontus.

AMBACIA, a town of the Turones, Lugdunensis III., near Cæsarodunum. *Amboise.*

AMBARRI (Ambiari), a people of Lugdunensis I., on the Arar, S. of the Sequani, supposed by some antiquaries to be cognate with the Umbri of Italy, and with the Ambrones. *About Amberrieux.*

AMBASTÆ, a people of India e. Gangem, about the mouth of Ambastus (Lanos) fl.

AMBASTUS fl. Indiæ, i. q. Lanos.

AMBE, a port of the Alilæi, Arabia Felix, on the Red Sea, bet. Badea and Mamala.

AMBIANI, I. a maritime people of Belgica II., bounded N. by the Morini, S. by the Calleti and Bellovaces, E. by the Veromandui. *Dept. of Somme.* II. *prius* Samarobriva, their capital, on Samara fl., R., N.W. of Augusta Veromanduorum. *Amiens.*

AMBITARINUS vicus (Ambiatinus vicus), a town of the Treveri, in Germania II., on the Rhine, bet. Confluentes and Bontobrica. *Near Reuse.*

AMBIDRAVI, a people of Noricum, on Dravus fl., towards its source.

AMBILIATES, a people of Armorica, contiguous to the Biducesii. *About Lamballe.*

AMBILIATI, a tribe of Ambiani, Gallia. *About Abbeville.*

AMBILATRI, a tribe of Pictones, Aquitania, N.E. of Limonum. *About Chatellerault.*

AMBILICI, a people of Noricum, bet. the Dravus and the Savus fl.

AMBISUNTES (Ambisontii), a people of Noricum, towards Alpes Noricæ. *Valley of the Boita.*

AMBITUI, a people of Galatia, of uncertain position, said to have been a colony of Ambiani from Gaul.

AMBIVARETES, I. a people of Germania, between the Scaldis and the Mosa, on Amblava fl.

AMBLADA, a town of Pisidia, towards Antiochia. Noted for a peculiar medicinal wine.

AMBLAVA, I. a r. of the Ambivaretes, Gallia, falling into one of the tributaries of the Mosa. *Ambleve.* II. their capital, on Amblava fl. *Amblet.*

AMBOGLANNA, a town of the Otadeni, Britannia, on Hadriani murus, N. bet. Aballaba and Æsica. The station of the Cohors Prima Ælia Dacorum. *Burdswald.*

AMBRA fl., I. a r. of Etruria, falling into Arnus fl. N. of Ad Joglandem. *Ambra.* II. of Vindelicia, rising in Alpes Rhæt., above Coveliace, and falling into Isara fl. above Jovisara. *Amber.*

AMBRĂCIA, *prius* Paralia, a city of Epirus, on Arachthus fl., 11 m. from Ambracius sin. Built by Ambrax, enlarged by Corinthians 650 B.C. The royal city of Pyrrhus, and afterwards the seat of a republic. *Near Arta.*

AMBRACĬUS sinus, a gulf of the Adriatic, bet. Epirus and Acarnania. *Golfo de l'Arta.*

AMBRACUS, a fortress of Ambracia, S.W. of the city. *Fidio Castro.*

AMBRONES, a people of Maxima Sequanorum, N.E. of Lemanus lacus. *In Berne, Southern, Unterwald, &c.*

AMBRUSSUM, a town of the Volcæ Arecomicæ, Narbonensis I., bet. Nemausum (15) and Sextatio (15). *Pont Emberieu.*

AMBRŸSAS, a town of Phocis, N.E. of Anticyra. Noted for its cochineal and its vines. *Near Dystomo.*

AMELAS (Alimala, Alychme), a town of Lycia, near Myra. *Almali.*

AMELETUM, a town of Pontus, on the Euxine, 19 m. w. from Phauda.

AMENANUS (Ammanus) fl., a r. of Sicily, falling into Siculum mare s. of Catana.

AMENIA, a town of Pontus, near Genesintis prom.

AMĔRIA, a town of Umbria, bet. Castellum Amerinum (9) and Tuda (16), N.W. of Narnia. Founded 1045 B.C. A colonia. The birth-place of Roscius. *Amelia.*

AMERIA, the early name of Neocæsarea, in Pontus. Famous for the great temple of Men Pharnaces.

AMERIOLA, a town of Sabinium, N.W. of Tibur.

AMERUS m., a ridge of Acroceraunii m. in Epirus, towards Illyria.

AMÉSELUM, a town of Sicily, on Cyamosurus fl., R. near Argyrium. *Ragalbuto.*

AMESTRATUS, a town of Sicily, towards the N. coast, bet. Nomæ and Apollonia.

AMÏDA (*prius* AMMÆA), a city of Sophene, Armen., on the Tigris, R., s.w. of Tigranocerta. Restored by Constantine, and named by him Constantia. The locality of a defeat of the Romans by Sapor. Noted for its gold and silver mines. *Kara Amid; Diarbekir.*

AMILUS, I. a village of Arcadia, bet. Orchomenus and Stymphalus. II. (Anulus), a r. of Mauritania.

AMÏNA ins., an isl. of India i. Gangem, s. of Monacha.

AMINACHÆ, a people of India i. Gangem, under Bepurrus m. E., on Œdanes fl. L.

AMÏNEA, a village of Campania, s. of Sinuessa. Noted for its vineyards.

AMINIUS fl., a r. of Arcadia, falling into Helisson fl., R. below Megalopolis.

AMISIA, I. (Amasia, Amisius), a r. of Germania Magna, rising s. of Teutoburgium and falling into Germanicus oc., w. of the Visurgis. *Ems.* II. a fortress erected by Drusus, near the mouth of the preceding. *Delf-Zyl.* III. a town of the Istævones, Germania, on Amisia fl., near Stereontium. *Near Soest.*

AMISUS (Piræus), capital of Pontus, on Amisenus sin., 112¼ m. S.E. from Sinope. A Milesian settlement, enlarged by Athenians. *Samsun.*

AMÏTERNUM, a town of Sabinium, on Aternus fl. R., towards its source, N.W. of Prifernum. The birth-place of Sallust. *Near San Vittorino.*

AMMÆA, *vide* Amida.

AMMAUS, *vide* Hamath.

AMMITES fl., a r. of Chalcidice, Macedonia, falling into Bolbe palus, E. of Olynthias fl.

AMMOCHOSTOS prom., a "sandy" prom. of Cyprus, N.E. of Pedalium prom. *C. Grego.*

AMMODES prom., a pr. of Cilicia Campestris, bet. Cydnus fl. and Sarus fl.

AMMON BALITHONOS prom., Byzacene, i. q. Brachodes.

AMMONII prom. (Cabubathra), a pr. of Arabia Felix, 25 m. w. from Arabiæ Felicis Emp. *C. Hargiah.*

AMMONIS ins., an isl. of Marmarica, w. of Antipyrgos.

AMMONÏTIS, the country of the Ammonites, descendants of Ammon or Benimmi, the younger son of Lot, in Peræa, bounded N. and N.E. by Jabbok fl., s. by Moabitis, w. by Gilead m. (but earlier by the Dead Sea and Jordan), S.E. by Arabia.

AMMONUM, an oasis of Marmarica, on the confines of Libya, s. of Parætonium, 160 m. from the Mediterranean. Here was the great temple of Jupiter Ammon, and a fountain (Fons solis), the water of which, in the morning and evening, was warm, at noon cold, and at midnight boiling hot. *Oasis of Siwah.*

AMNIAS fl., a r. of Paphlagonia, falling into Halys fl., 30 m. s. from Sinope. *Kara Su.*

AMNICIA, a town of Bruttium, bet. Ad Angitulam (4) and Vibo Valentia (10), on Via Aquilia.

AMNISUS, I. a river of Crete, falling into the Ægean at Amnisus. *Apostolemi.* II. (Monesus), a town on the N. coast of Crete, E. of Heracleum. The E. port of Gnossus.

AMORDOCIA, a marshy district of Babylonia, s. of the Euphrates, towards its confluence with the Tigris.

AMORGOS, one of the Sporades, bet. Naxos and Astypalæa. Noted for its fine flax. Under the Romans a place of banishment. The birth-place of Simonides. *Amorgo.*

AMORITIS, the country of the Amoritæ (descendants of Canaan), in Peræa, bounded E. by Ammonitis, N. by Jabboc fl., s. by Moabitis, and w. by the Dead Sea and Jordan fl. The district was conquered by Moses, and divided between Reuben and Gad.

AMORIUM, a town of the Tolistoboii, Galatia, on Sangarius fl., bet. Abrosta (23) and Laodicea Catacecaumene (20). *Amoria.*

AMOS, a town of Caria.

AMPALOONTIS, a maritime town of Cyrenaica, w. bet. Boreum prom. and Berenice.

AMPE, I. Chaldæa, i. q. Charax. II. a r. of Crete, falling into the sea at Ampelus. *Sacro.* III. a town of Crete, at Ampelus prom. *Sacro.* IV. hills intersecting Samos ins. *Ambelona.* V. a headland of Crete, s. of Sammonium prom. *C. Sacro.* VI. the N. extremity of Ampelus m., Samos, opposite Icarus ins. *C. San Domenico.* VII. its s. extremity. *C. Colonni.* VIII. (Toronæum), the s. extremity of Sithonia penins., Macedonia. Famous for its wine. *C. Falso.*

AMPELÜSIA (Cotes), the N.W. extremity of Africa, at the s. entrance of Herculis Fretum. *Cape Spartel.*

AMPHÆA, a town of Messenia, on the frontiers of Laconia, near the source of Amphitus fl. *Cochla.*

AMPHANÆ, I. a town, of Doris. II. (Amphanæum), of Magnesia, Thessaly, near Pagasæ.

AMPHAXITIDIS ABYDON, i. q. Amydon.

AMPHAXITIS, a district of Mygdonia, Macedonia, on Axius fl. L., towards its mouth.

AMPHIALE prom., a pr. of Attica, on Saronicus sin., over against Salamis, the w. extremity of Corydallus m. *C. Daphne.*

AMPHIARAI fons, I. a fountain of Argolis, falling into Lerna palus. II. of Bœotia, near the temple of Amphiaraus at Oropus.

AMPHICÆA (Amphiclæa, Ophitea), a town of Phocis, at the N. foot of Parnassus m., 8 m. N.E. from Lilæa. *Dadi.*

AMPHIDOLI, a town of Pisatis, Elis, on Alpheus fl. R., N.W. of Olympia.

AMPHIGENIA, a town of Messenia, on the borders of Triphylia.

AMPHILOCHIA, the country of the Amphilochi, the N.E. portion of Acarnania, on the borders of Epirus, Athamania, and Aperantia. Afterwards annexed to Ætolia.

AMPHILYSSUS fl., a r. of Samos ins., rising in Assarus m.

AMPHIMALLA (Amphipalia, Pantomatrium), a town on the N. coast of Crete, at the head of Amphimallius sin. *Near Armiro.*

AMPHIMALLE fl., a r. of Crete, falling into Amphimallius sin., E. of Amphimalla.

AMPHIMALLIUS sin., a bay of the Ægean, in Crete, bet. Rithymna and Drepanum prom. *G. d'Armiro.*

AMPHIMATRIUM, Pantomatrium, i. q. Amphimalle.

AMPHIPAGUS prom., a headland of Corcyra ins., on the W. coast, below Phalacrum prom. *C. Sant' Angelo.*

AMPHIPOLIS ("river-surrounded"), *postea* Chrysopolis, I. capital of the Edones, Thrace, and subsequently of Macedonia I., on an island of Strymon fl., near its egress from Cercinatis palus, 3 m. from Strymonicus sin., bet. Argilus (10) and Domerus (13). Founded by Agnon, son of Nicias, the Athenian. *Emboli ; Jeni-keui.* II. THAPSACUS, so named by Seleucus Nicator. III. Messenia, i. q. Amphidoli.

AMPHISSA ("among the mountains"), capital of the Locri Ozol., at the head of Crissæus sin., 7½ m. N.W. of Delphi. *Salona.*

AMPHISSIUM prom., a pr. of Bruttium, towards Scylletium.

AMPHITROPE, a demus of Attica, of the tribe Antiochis, N.E. of Thricus. *Metropisi.*

AMPHITUS fl., a r. of Messenia, rising near Amphæa and falling into Pamisus fl. N.E. of Ithome m. *Zeza.*

AMPHRYSUS fl., a r. of Phthiotis, Thessaly, rising in Othrys m., and falling into Pagasæus sin. N. of Alos. On its banks Apollo fed the flocks of Admetus. *Armiro.*

AMPSAGA fl., a r. of Africa, rising N. of Thamugadis, and, after separating Numidia from Mauritania, falling into the Mediterranean at Pacciana. *Wad el Kebir.*

AMPSALIS, a port of the Zichi, Sarmatia, bet. Herculis prom. and Achæus fl.

AMPSIVARII, Germania, i. q. Ansibarii.

AMSANCTI lacus, a sulphureous lake of the Hirpini, Campania, s.w. of Trivicum. On its banks was a temple of Mephitis. *Lago di Mefiti.*

AMUDIS, a town of Mygdonia, Mœsia, w. of Nisibis.

AMUTRIUM, *postea* Altinum, a town of the Saldenses, Dacia, s. of Drubetis. *Near Brancowar.*

AMYCI PORTUS, a port of Bithynia, on Thracius Bosporus, N. of Nicopolis. The burial-place of king Amycus. *Lamia.*

AMYCLÆ, I. a city of the Ausones, Latium, on Amyclanus sin., s.w. of Fundi. A colony from Amyclæ, Laconia. The population was said to have been destroyed by serpents. II. of Laconia, 5 m. s. of Sparta, on Eurotas fl. The birth-place of Castor and Pollux, and the burial-place of Hyacinthus. *Aia Kyriaèi or Sclavo-Chorio.*

AMYCLÆUM, a maritime town of Crete.

AMYCLANUS, I. lacus, i. q. Fundanus. II. sin. (Fundanus), a bay of Tyrrhenum mare at Amyclæ.

AMYDON (Abydon), a town of Amphaxitis, in Macedonia, on Axius fl.

AMYMONE fons, one of the streams contributing to Lerna palus in Argolis. Named after one of the daughters of Danaus.

AMYRUS, I. a r. of Magnesia, Thessaly, rising in Ossa m., near Lacerea, and falling into the Ægean below Amyrus. II. a town of Magnesia, Thessaly, on Amyrus fl., s.w. of Melibœa.

AMYSTIS fl., a r. of India, falling into the Ganges towards its source. *Patterea.*

AMYZON, a fown of Caria, bet. Heraclea and Alabanda. *Baffi.*

ANAB, a town of Judæa, s.E. of Hebron, Judæa. *Anab.*

ANABIS, a town of the Surdaones, Tarraconensis, bet. Ilerda and Jespus.

ANABON, a district of Drangiana, N. of Aria lacus. *E. Sedjestan.*

ANABUCIS, Cyrenaica, i. q. Aulomalax.

ANABUM, a town of the Carpi, Sarmatia, on the Danube, near the mouth of Granua fl.

ANABŪRA, a town of Phrygia Magna, bet. Beudos and Abassus.

ANACÆA, a demus of Attica, of the tribe Hippothoontis.

ANACTORIA, I. a district of Asia Minor, on both sides the Mæander fl. Named from Anax, prince of Caria. II. the early name of Miletus.

ANACTŌRIUM, a city of the Agræi, Acarnania, on Ambracius sin., at its s. entrance, bet. Nicopolis, of which it was the port, and Thyreum, s.e. of Actium. Its people, a colony of Corcyreans and Corinthians; were transferred by Augustus to Nicopolis. *Aghios Petros.*

ANACTORIUS sin., the entrance to the Ambracius sin., in which was fought the battle of Actium. *G. di Trevesa.*

ANADYNATA, a town of Paphlagonia, bet. Antoninopolis (28) and Gangra (36).

ANÆA, a town of Lydia, on the coast, bet. Ephesus and Panionium. The burial-place of the Amazon Anæa. The birth-place of Menelaus the Peripatetic.

ANAGNIA, capital of the Hernici, Latium, on Via Latina, bet. Ad Bivium and Ferentinum. A Colonia of Drusus. *Anagni.*

ANAGNUTES, a people of Novem Populana. *About Agnos, Basses Pyrénées.*

ANAGOMBRI m., a m. of Marmarica, w. of Ammonium.

ANAGOME, a town of Lysia, near Caystrus fl., under Tmolus m., bet. Hypæpa (9) and Ephesus (34). *Bainder.*

ANAGURDES, a fortress of Bithynia.

ANAGYRUS, a demus of Attica, of the tribe Erectheis, on Saronicus sin., s. of Æxone. Named from a fetid plant that grew here, which, the more you rubbed it, the more fetid it grew; whence the proverb.

ANAIZETES, a people of Pannonia Inferior, bet. Dravus fl. and Savus fl., e. of the Jassi.

ANAKIM, a gigantic race, occupying the country between Jerusalem and Hebron, divided into three tribes, descended from and named after the three sons of Anak, Ahiman, Sesai, and Talmai. They were exterminated by Joshua and Caleb.

ANALIBA, a town of Armenia Minor, on Euphrates fl. R., bet. Caltiorissa (24) and Zimara (15). *Derindeh.*

ANAMĀNI (Anamares, Ananes), a people of Gallia Cispadana, extending into Liguria, along the s. bank of the Padus.

ANAMARORI, a tribe of Anamani, Gallia, on the Trebia, s. of the Marici. *About Marsaglia.*

ANANUS fl. (Andanis, Azarius?), a r. of Carmania, falling into Persicus sin. 25 m. w. from Sabis fl.

ANANA, a town of Phrygia Magna, on Ascania pal. n., bet. Apamea Cibotus and Ceretape.

ANANES, a people of Liguria, n.e. along the Padus, w. of the Anamares.

ANAO PORTUS, a harbour of the Vediantii, Liguria, e. of Olivula (12).

ANAPHE ins., one of the Sporades, e. of Thera, named from Apollo's "suddenly appearing" there to the Argonauts. *Anphio.*

ANAPHLYSTUS, a demus of Attica, of the tribe Antiochis, on Saronicus sin., at Astypalæa prom. *Anaphiso.*

ANĀPUS fl., I. a r. of Acarnania, falling into Achelous fl. R., s. of Stratus. *Aetos.* II. of Sicily, falling into Siculum mare, at Syracusæ, s. *Alfeo.*

ANAR, a town of Chaldæa, on the Euphrates, L., bet. Aserga and Ampe.

ANAREI m., a ridge of Imaus, in Scythia i. Imaum. *Altai m.*

ANARIACÆ, a people of Media Magna, on the Caspian, bet. the Drybices and the Amardi.

ANARISMUNDI prom., a pr. of Taprobane, w. bet. Soanus fl. and Margana.

ANARITÆ, a tribe of Ichthyophagi, Arabia, on Persicus sin., e. of Atta.

ARARTOPHRACTI, a people of Sarmatia Europ., contiguous to the Burgundiones.

ANARTI (Anartes), a tribe of Agathyrsi, Dacia, on Tibiscus fl., towards its source.

ANAS fl., a river of Hispania, rising near Laminium, and, after separating Bætica from Lusitania, falling by two mouths into the Atlantic, e. of Balsa. Its name arose from its characteristic, towards its source, of diving like a duck below the surface, from time to time. *Guadiana (Wadi-Ana).*

ANASAMUS, a town of the Mœsi, Mœsia Inferior, on the Danube, bet. Utus and Nicopolis, at the mouth R. of Noes fl.

ANASSUS, I. fl., a r. of the Carni, Venetia, falling into the Adriatic at Anassus. *Revonchi.* II. a port of the Carni, in Venetia, s.e. of Apicilia. *Porto di Lignano.*

ANASTASII MŒNIA, Thraciæ, i. q. Macrontichos.

ANASTASIOPOLIS, Mesopotamia, *vide* Dara.

ANATHA (Phathusis, Bethauna), a town of Auranitis, Babylonia, on an isl. of the Euphrates, below Corsote. *Anah.*

ANATHOTH, a Levitical city of Benjamin, 3½ m. n. from Jerusalem. The birth-place of Jeremiah. *Anata.*

ANATILI, a people of Narbonensis I., occupying the Delta of the Rhone.

ANATIS fl., Mauritania, i. q. Asama.

ANAUNES, *vide* Genaunes.

ANAUNIUM, *postea* Naunium, Anagnis, capital of the Genaunes, Rhætia, N.W. of Tridentum. *Castel Nano.*

ANAURUS, I. a name of the Nile. II. a r. of Magnesia, Thessaly, rising in Pelion m. and falling into the Pagasæus sin. below Tolcos. It was in this stream that Jason lost his sandal.

ANAVA (Anaus, Sanaus, Sanis, Sanaos), a town of Phrygia Magna, on the N. shore of Anavus lacus. *Alan-Kevi.*

ANAVASARIUM, a town of Almopæia, Macedonia, bet. Ad Fines (35) and Ad Aquas (12).

ANAVUS lacus, a salt lake of Phrygia Magna, E. of Colossæ, near the source of Mæander fl. *Hajee Ghieul.*

ANAXIA (Hamaxia), a maritime town of Pamphylia, 9 m. N.E. from Ptolemais.

ANAZARBA (Cesarea ad Anazarbum), *postea* Ainzarjat, a town of Cilicia Campestris, on Pyramus fl., bet. Mopsuestia (11) and Flavias (18). Under Theodosius, cap. of Cilicia. The birth-place of Dioscorides and of Appian. *Anzarba.*

ANAZARBUS m., a summit of Taurus m., Cilicia, overlooking Anazarba.

ANBUREUM, *vide* Œsporis.

ANCALITES, a people of Britain, W. of the Trinobantes. *In Berkshire.*

ANCHIÄLE, a city of Cilicia Campestris, E. of Zephyrium prom., "on the sea shore," at the mouth of Anchiales fl. Founded by Sardanapalus "in one day with Tarsus." Traditionally named from Anchiale, daughter of Japetus.

ANCHIALES fl., a r. of Cilicia Campestris, rising in Taurus m., and falling into the Mediterranean at Anchiale. *Mersyn.*

ANCHIALUS, a town of the Crobyzi, in Thrace, on a gulf of the Euxine, s. of Mesembria. *Akkali.*

ANCHISMUS m., a summit of Pentelicus m., N.E. of Athenæ. *Mt. San Giorgio.*

ANCHISIA m., a m. of Arcadia, N.W. of Mantinea. The burial-place of Anchises.

ANCHITÆ, a people of Arabia Felix, on the edge of the Desert, s. of the Catanitæ.

ANCHOE, a place in Bœotia, N. of Larymna Inferior, at which Copais lacus discharged itself by several channels into the Euripus. *Potzumadi.*

ANCLACÆ, a people of Sarmatia Asiat., in Caucasus m.

ANCOBARITIS, a district of Mesopotamia, occupying its s. extremity.

ANCÖN, I. a port of Pontus, 20 m. E. from Amisus, at Ancon prom., at the mouth of Isis fl. *Tscherschembi*. II. a prom. of Caria, at the E. "elbow" of Glaucius sin.

ANCÖNA, a maritime city of Picenum, above Cumerium prom., S.E. of Senogallia. A Dorian city, enlarged by Syracusans, fugitives from Dionysius; enlarged and its port constructed by Trajan. Noted for its purple dye. *Ancona.*

ANCORARIUS m., a m. of Mauritania Cæsar., below Cartenna.

ANCÖRE, Bithynia, i. q. Nicæa.

ANCUS, a town of the Jabades, Illyria, under Albanus m., E. bet. Epidotium and Ausancalis.

ANCŸRA, I. capital of the Abbaites Mysi, in Phrygia Epictetus, near the source of Macestus fl., towards Sinnaus. II. a town of Sicily, on Halycus fl., above Legum. III. capital of the Tectosages, Galatia, bet. Gordium and Halys fl. Built by Midas. Named from an anchor found on its site, and long preserved in the temple of Jupiter here. In its neighbourhood was the fountain where Midas caught Silenus. Here was discovered the famous Marmor Ancyritanum. *Angouri. Angora.*

ANCYRIUM prom., a pr. of Bithynia, marking the Asiatic entrance of Bosporus Thracius. Named from a rock taken hence as an anchor by the Argonauts.

ANCYRONPOLIS, a town of Heptanomis, on the Nile, R., bet. Thimonepsus and Aphroditopolis. Named from the stone anchors made there. *Eggeron.*

ANDABILIS (Andavilis), a town of Cappadocia, bet. Sasima (16) and Tyana (16).

ANDACA (Andraca), a town of Arachosia, towards the junction of Cophes fl. with Choaspes fl.

ANDAGA, a town of Siracene, Armenia, on Harpasus fl. R., below Chorsa. *Ani.*

ANDANIA (Æchalia), the early capital of Messenia, on the confines of Arcadia, bet. Messene and Megalopolis, near Carnucium nem.

ANDANIS fl., Carmania, i. q. Anamis.

ANDARÆ, a people of India.

ANDATIS, a town of Ethiopia, on the Nile.

ANDECAMULUM, a town of the Lemovices, N.W. of Augustoritum. *Rançon.*

ANDECAVI, *vide* Andes.

ANDEIRA, a town of Æolis Asiat., N.E. of Gargara. Noted for its orichalcum, and for a remarkable cavern. Cybele was peculiarly worshipped here.

ANDEMADUNUM, *postea* Lingones, capital of the Lingones, Lugdunensis I., near the source of Matrona fl., N.E. of Alesia. *Langres.*

ANDERICA, a town of Cissia, Susiana, on Coprates fl., 25 m. N.W. from Susia. Here Darius settled a colony of Eretrians.

ANDERŸCA, a port of the Regni, Brit. I., bet. Othona portus and Adurni portus. *Seaford.*

ANDERIS, a town of the Cantii, Brit. *Rye.*

ANDERITUM, I. the early capital of the Gabali, Aquitania I., S.E. of Aquæ Calidæ. *Anterrieux.* II. a town of the Parisii, Lugdunensis IV., on Sequana fl., R., at the junction of Isara fl.

ANDES, I. (Andecavi, Ondicavai), a people of Lugdunensis III., on Liger fl., having the Turones E., Namnetes w., Pictones s., and Aulerci N. *Department of Mayenne.* II. their capital, near Liger fl., w.N.w. of Cæsarodunum, *postea* Juliomagus, in honour of Julius Cæsar. *Angers.* III. a village near Mantua, s.E. The birth-place of Virgil. *Pietola.*

ANDESINA, a town of the Leuci, Belgica I., N.E. of Tullum (16). *Nancy or d'Essay.*

ANDETHANNA, a town of the Treveri, in Belgica I., bet. Orolaunum (22½) and Augusta Treverorum (20½). *Nieder Anwen.*

ANDETRIUM, a fortress of the Dalmatæ, in Illyria, 3 m. N.w. from Salon. *Clissa.*

ANDIUM, an isl. of Britain.

ANDŌMATIS fl., i. q. Sonus.

ANDOSII, a people of Celtiberia, N. of the Ærenosii. *About Altousane, near Pons.*

ANDRACA, a town of Cappadocia, towards Zama.

ANDRAPA, *postea* Neoclaudiopolis, a town of Paphlagonia, S.E. of Olgasys m. s., 9 m. N.w. from Galea.

ANDRIA, I. a town of Phrygia. II. of Triphylia, Elis, on the coast, near Pyrgos.

ANDRIACA, I. a town of Lycia, at the mouth of Andriacus fl., ½ m. E. from Simena. The port of Myra. *Andraki.* II. of Media Magna, bet. Ecbatana and Parachoana.

ANDRIACUS fl., a r. of Lycia, falling into the Mediterranean at Andriaca. *Andraki.*

ANDRICUS, I. a r. of Cilicia Campestris. II. a summit of Taurus, in Cilicia Trachea, overlooking Charadrus.

ANDRIUS fl., a r. of Troas, falling into the Scamander below Cebrene fl. *Lidjick Deressetchai.*

ANDRONA (Acoraba), baths of Chalybonitis, N.w. of Salaminias. *Haman.*

ANDROPOLIS, a town of Egypt, on Agathos Dæmon fl., N. of Cynecopolis. *Chabur.*

ANDROPOPHAGI, cannibals, variously placed in N.E. Africa and elsewhere.

ANDRORI (Andres), a tribe of Ananianes, Liguria. *About Casteggio.*

ANDROS, I. (Lasia, Cauros, Nonagria, Hydrussa, Epagris) one of the Cyclades ins., bet. Geræstus prom. (10) and Ceos (39).

Andro. II. its capital, on the w. coast. *Andro.*

ANDROSIA (Acitoriziacum), a town of Galatia, on Halys fl., 33 m. from Eccobriga.

ANDUETIUM, a town of Rhætia, near the Danube, bet. Carnuntum and Gerulatis.

ANDUSIA, a town of the Volcæ Arecomici, Narbonensis, on Vardo fl., N.w. of Ambrussum. *Anduze.*

ANĒMO fl., a r. of Gallia Cispadana, rising s. of Mutila, and falling into the Adriatic s. of Spineticum Ostium. *Amone.*

ANEMOESSA, a place in Arcadia, on Helisson fl., N.w. of Bucolion.

ANĒMORIA, "blown by the mountain wind," a town of Phocis, near Hyampolis, under Calopterius m.

ANEMURIUM, I. a town of Cilicia Trachea, at Anemurium prom. *Anamour.* II. a pr. of Cilicia, the s. extremity of Asia Minor, over against Crommyon prom. in Cyprus (23½). *C. Anamour.*

ANESICA, a town of Histria, bet. Fons Timavi and Ad Malum (18), N.E. of Tergeste, *Senasetsch.*

ANEU ins., an isl. of Arabia Felix, in the Red Sea, over against Hippus m. *Maaman.*

ANGARII, the early name of the Angrivarii.

ANGARIS, a m. of Judæa, on the coast N. of Gaza.

ANGELE, a demus of Attica, of the tribe Pandionis, N.w. of Brauron. *Apangellaki.*

ANGELOCOME, a fortress of Bithynia, towards Nicæa.

ANGITES fl., a r. of Thrace, rising in Cercius m. E., and separating the Odomanti from the Edones. *Anghista.*

ANGILLÆ, a town of the Turduli, Bætica, on Singilis fl. above Singilis.

ANGITIA, a town of the Marsi, Sabinium, N. of Lucus Angitiæ.

ANGITULA fl., a r. of Bruttium, falling into Hipponiates sin. at Ad Angitulam. *Angitola.*

ANGLI, a tribe of Suevi, who, from the E. side of the Albis, migrated to the w. side, and settled about Lagnus sin., N. of the Saxones. *Schleswig and part of Holstein.*

ANGRĪVĀRII, a tribe of Ingævones, on the Visurgis, N. of the Cherusci. *About Angern.*

ANGUILLARIS, a town of Etruria, on the Sabatinus lac., 25 m. N.w. of Rome.

ANGŬLUS, a town of the Vestini, Picenum, on Salina fl. L., bet. Hadria and Salinæ. *Citta Sant' Angelo.*

ANGUSTIA, a town of the Cotenses, Dacia, on Ararus fl. R.

ANI, I. a town of Chorzene, Arm., on Pyxirates fl., below Aziris. II. of the Taurisci, Noricum, on Anisus fl., 17 m. E. from Vocarium. *Radstadt.*

ANIAS fl., Arcadia, i. q. Aroanius.

ANIDUS fl., Africa, i. q. Asama.

ANIESES, a people of Sogdiana, about the sources of the Jaxartes.

ANIGRÆA, a district of Argolis, on Argolicus sin., N. of Thyrea. Noted for its olives.

ANIGRIADUM fons, a fountain of Triphylia, Elis, falling into Anigrus fl. near its source. Reputed good for cutaneous disorders.

ANῙGRUS fl. (Minyeus), a r. of Triphylia, Elis, rising in Lapitha m., and losing itself in a marsh on the sea-coast, near Samia. Remarkable in connexion with the story of the Centaurs and of Hercules. *Mavropotamo, Sidero.*

ANINETUM (Aninesum), a town of Lydia.

ANIO, I. *prius* Anienus, a r. of Italy, rising near Trebia, and falling into the Tiber at Antemnæ. Named from Anius, king of the Etruscans. Noted for its cataract ; whence its title, Præceps. *Teverone.* II. Novus, Aqua Claudia, an aqueduct from Anio fl. to Rome, constructed under Claudian.

ANISTORGIS, Hispania, i. q. Conistorgis.

ANISUS fl. (Anasus), a r. of Noricum, rising E. of Vacorium, and falling into the Danube at Lauriacum. *Ens.*

ANITHA, a town of Moabitis, s. of Mephaat.

ANNAMATIA, a town of Valeria, Pannonia, bet. Salinum (22) and Intercisa, N.E. of Volcea lac. *Duna Pentele.*

ANNEIANUM, I. a town of the Magelli, Etruria, bet. Florentia (20) and Castellum (25). II. of the Veneti, Venetia, bet. Vicus Varianus (18) and Ateste (20). *Legnano.*

ANNIBI m., m. of Serica. *Altai Alin.*

ANNINA, a district of Tenesis, Æthiopia, N.W. of Abala.

ANNUM, a town of the Frentani, Samnium, on Sagrus fl., bet. Anxanum (4) and Pallanum (12).

ANONUM fons, a fountain of Laconia, at Derrhium.

ANOPÆA, a defile of the Malienses, bet. Asopus and Alpenus, by which the Persian army turned the position of the Greeks at the battle of Thermopylæ.

ANSIBARII (Ansivarii), a tribe of the Chauci, on the w. bank of the Visurgis. *About Minden in Westphalia.*

ANT.ÆÖPÖLIS, a town of Thebais, on the Nile, R., bet. Muthis and Passalon. Named from Antæus. *Quaou.*

ANTANDRUS, a town of Æolis Asiat., on Adramyttenus sin., at the foot of Alexandria m., opposite Coryphas, 16 m. w.

from Adramyttium. An Æolian colony, Settled also by Cimmerii and Edones from Thrace. *Antandro.*

ANTARĂDUS, a town of Phœnicia, on the coast, over against Aradus. Named Constantia after Constantius. *Tortosa.*

ANTEIS (Antiæ), a town of the Salyes, Narbonensis II., bet. Forum Julii and Matavonium. *Draguignan.*

ANTELIA, a town of Cappadocia, in Saravene præfectura.

ANTEMNÆ, a Sicilian town of Sabinium, locally in Latium, on Anio fl.

ANTEUS fl., a r. of Pisidia, at Antiochia. *Cazma.*

ANTHEA, I. a town of Achaia, the inhabitants of which were removed to Patræ. II. Euanthea, a name of Tralles. III. a name of Messenia.

ANTHEDON (Anthedonius portus, Atheniensis portus), I. a town of Argolis, on Saronicus sin., N.W. of Spiræum prom. *Francolimni.* II. of Bœotia, on Euripus, bet. Anchoe (7) and Salganeus (9). The birth-place of the sea-god Glaucus. III. of Simeon, Judæa, on Besor fl., near its mouth, 5 m. N.W. from Gaza. Rebuilt by Herod, and named Agrippias.

ANTHELE, a town of Malienses, Thessaly, near Asopus fl., w. of Thermopylæ.

ANTHĒMUS, I. a r. of the Apsilæ, Sarmatia, falling into the Euxine at Dioscurias. II. a district of Mygdonia, Macedonia, N.E. of Thessalonica. III. a lake of Mygdonia, at Anthemus. IV. capital of Anthemus regio, on Anthemus lac., N.E. of Thessalonica. *Near Langaza.* V. i. q. Samos.

ANTHEMUSIA, I. a district of Osrhoene, Mesopotamia, N.W. on Euphrates fl., w. of Gauzonitis. II. its capital, bet. Dacara and Coræa, w. of Edessa.

ANTHENE, I. a town of Argolis, on the confines of Laconia, S.E. of Tegea. Named after Anthe, daughter of Neptune. II. of the Damasæ, Ind., on Doanas fl. III. one of the Pisistratidæ ins., Ionia.

ANTHYLLA, a town of Lower Egypt, on the Canopic branch of the Nile, S.E. of Alexandria; the revenues of which were assigned by the Persian conquerors to the queens of Persia for shoe money.

ANTIANA, a town of Valeria, Pannonia, on the Danube, 24 m. N. from Mursa. *Batina.*

ANTIBOLE ostium, the E. and principal mouth of the Ganges.

ANTICASIUS m., m. of Cassiotis, Syria, s. of Casius m.

ANTICINOLIS, a port of Paphlagonia, 7½ m. E. from Cinolis.

ANTĬCYRA (Anticirrha), I. a town of Phocis, on a bay of the Corinthiacus sinus, bet. Cirrha and Medeon. Noted for its helle-bore. *Aspro Spiti.* II. of Æniania, Thes-saly, on Maliacus sin., at the mouth of Sperchius fl. Also noted for its helle-bore.

ANTICRAGUS m., lofty cliffs of Lycia, on Glaucius sin., N.W. of Telmessus, in some sort the back of Cragus m. *Soum-bourlou.*

ANTIGONĔÆ fauces, a defile of the Acro-cerauni m., bet. Illyria and Chaonia.

ANTIGONIA, I. *prius* Sigia, an earlier name of Alexandria Troas, from Antigonus. II. a town of Chaonia, Epirus, w. of Omphalium. *Argyro Castro.* III. of Crucis, Chalcidice, Maced., N.E. of Com-brea. IV. the early name of Nicæa, Bithynia. V. surnamed Psaphara, a town of Pelagonia, on Thermaicus sin., near Æneum prom. VI. of Seleucis, Syria, near Antiochia, whither its inhabitants were removed by Seleucus Nicator.

ANTIGONIS, a tribe or ward of Attica, named after Antigonus, father of Demetrius Poli-orcetes. Afterwards named Attalis, in honour of king Attalus.

ANTILIBANUS m., m. of Cœle-Syria, parallel E. with Libanus m., and blending with the m. of Trachonitis. *Jebel el Gharbi.*

ANTINOË (Antinŏŏpolis, *prius* Besa), a town of Heptanomis, on the Nile, bet. Speos-Artemidos and Pesla, nearly oppo-site Hermopolis. Enlarged by Hadrian, and re-named by him after his favourite Antinous, drowned here. *Sheikh Abadeh.*

ANTINUM (Atina), a town of the Marsi, Sa-binium, on Liris fl., 5 miles s.w. from Angitiæ. A municip. *Citta d'Antina.*

ANTIOCHI SŌLEN, a port of the Adulitæ, on the Red Sea, 60 geog. m. s.e. from Adulis.

ANTIOCHIA, I. *prius* Reblata, a city of Apamene, Syr., cap. of Syria, on both sides of the Orontes, 30 m. from the sea. Founded by Seleucus Nicator, and named after his father; surnamed Epidaphnes, from the neighbouring Daphne; Tetra-polis, from its four quarters; and, later, Theopolis, from its earnest reception of Christianity. By Strabo it is ranked the third city of the world. *Antakia; An-tioch.* II. ad Cragum, a town of Cilicia Trachea, on Cragus m. *Antiochetta.* III. Lamotis, capital of Lamotis Regio, Cilicia, at the mouth of Lamus fl. IV. ad Mæ-andrum, *prius* Pythopolis, a city of Caria, bet. Mæander fl. and Orsinus fl., near their junction. Enlarged and re-named by

Antiochus, son of Seleucus. Noted for the fig Triphylla. The birth-place of Dio-trephis the sophist. *Jeni-Sher.* V. of Pisidia, bet. Apamea Cibotus (69) and Iconium (65). Founded by Antiochus Soter, 250 B.C. A colonia (Colonia Cæ-sarea) of Tiberius. Prominent in the his-tory of St. Paul. *Yalobatch.* VI. ad Py-ramum, ad Sarum, a town of Cilicia Cam-pestris, bet. Pyramus and Sarus fl., 19 m. E. from Mallus. VII. ad Taurum, a town of Commagene, Syr., under Amanus m., N.W. *Bahasna.* VIII. of Margiana, i. q. Alexandria. IX. ad Callirrhoen, Mesopo-tamia, i. q. Edessa. X. of Mesopotamia, i. q. Nisibis. XI. of Susiana, i. q. Charax.

ANTIOCHIANA, the s. division of Lycaonia.

ANTIOCHIS, I. a tribe or ward of Attica, named after Antiochus, son of Hercules; II. a district of Syria, about Antioch; III. of Cilicia, i. q. Lamotis.

ANTIPATRIA, a town of Phœbatis, Illyria, s.e. of Chrysondio.

ANTIPATRIS, *prius* Kapharsaba, a t. of Sa-maria, towards the sea, 12 m. N.E. from Joppa. Enlarged by Herod, and named by him Antipatris, in honour of his father. *Kaffr Suba.*

ANTIPHELLUS, a port of Lycia, over against Megiste ins. (6¼), s.e. of Phellus. *Vathry; Antifilo.*

ANTIPHILÆ, a maritime town of Dacia, bet. Arpis and Cremniscus.

ANTIPHRA, I. an isl. of Marmarica, over against Antiphra. II. a maritime town of Marmarica, e. of Catabathmus Major.

ANTĬPŎLIS, capital of the Deciates, Narbo-nensis II., on the coast bet. Var fl. (10) and Ad Horrea (12). Founded by the Phocæans circa 500 B.C. *Antibes.*

ANTIPYRGOS, a port of Marmarica, bet. Scythranius portus and Petræ parvæ portus.

ANTIQUARIA, a town of the Turtetani, Bætica, bet. Astapa N.W. and Ilipula Magna N.E. *Antiquera.*

ANTIRRHIUM prom. (Rhium Molycricum, Rhium Ætolicum), a headland of Ætolia, at the inner entrance to the Corinthiacus sin., over against Rhium in Arcadia, from which it is distant 5 stadia, according to Strabo, 7 according to Thucydides, 10 ac-cording to Scylax.

ANTISSA, a town of Lesbos ins., N. of Sigrium prom. The birth-place of Ter-pander. *Calas Limneonas.*

ANTISTIANA, a town of the Læetani, Tarra-conensis, N.W. of Carthago vetus.

ANTITAURUS, a ridge of Taurus m., running

through Cappadocia to the Euphrates. *Alidagh.*

ANTIUM, I. the early name of Genua. II. capital of the Volsci, Latium, on Mare Inferum, bet. Lavinium (17) and Astura (7), on the Via Severiana. Founded by Anthias, son of Circe, or by Ascanius. A colonia. 468 B.C. The birth-place of Nero, and of the historian Valerius ; the death-place of Coriolanus. Here were found the Apollo Belvedere, the Fighting Gladiator, &c. ; and hence were taken the beaks of the ships, which were formed into the chief Rostrum of the Forum at Rome. *Porto d'Anzo and Nettuno.*

ANTIVESTÆUM prom., i. q. Bolerium.

ANTOBROGES, a people of Aquitania, N. of the Tasconi. *About Antouin, in the diocese of Cohors, and in the diocese of Montauban.*

ANTONA fl., i. q. Avona.

ANTONACUM, a town of the Treveri, Germania II., on the Rhine, bet. Bonna (16½) and Confluentes (13½). *Andernach.*

ANTONINI vallum, Britannia, a renovation by Lollius Urbicus, under Antoninus Pius (A.D. 140), of the second wall of Agricola, bet. Glota æstuarium and Bodotria æstuarium. *Græme's Dyke.*

ANTONINOPOLIS, I. a town of Bithynia, 28 m. from Anadynata. Founded by Antoninus. *Tscherkiesch.* II. Tela, of Mesopotamia, E. of Edessa and Dara. Named by Constantius Constantia, and by Maximian Maximianopolis. *Tel Kiuran.*

ANTRON (Antronæ), a town of Phthiotis, Thessaly, S.E. of Pteleum, at the entrance of Pagasæus sin. Noted for its millstones. *Agios Teodoros.*

ANTROS ins., an isl. of Aquitania II., at the mouth of Garumna fl. It was reputed to rise and fall with the tide. *Corduan.*

ANUATH, a town of Samaria, bet. Silo N.E. and Geba s.

ANUBINGARA, a port of Taprobane, N. bet. Phasis and Nagadiba.

ANUROGRAMMUM, a city of Taprobane, under Galibi m. W., 8 m. E. from Jogana. *Anarodgurro.*

ANXA, Japygiæ, i. q. Callipolis.

ANXANTIA, *postea* Anxino, Ansuino, a town of the Marsi, Sabinium, on Fucinus lac., N.W. above Lucus Angitiæ. *Poggio Filippo.*

ANXĂNUM, I. a town of Daunia, Apulia, at the mouth of Cerbalus fl., bet. Sipontum and Salinæ. *Rivoli.* II. (Anxia, Anxa), of the Frentani, Samnium, bet. Ortona (10) and Annum (4), on Via Flaminia. A colonia. *Lanciano Vecchio.*

ANXIA, a town of Lucania, on Casuentus fl. L., bet. Potentia (15) and Grumentum (18). *Anzi.*

ANXUR, the Volscian name of Tarracina, Latium.

ANYDRUS, I. an isl. of Ionia, in Hermius sin., over against Clazomenæ. II. one of the summits of Hymettus m. *Lampro Vouni.*

ANYGATH, *postea* Angadrat, a town of Æthiopia, w. towards the Niger. *Aghade.*

ANZITENE (Azetene), a district of Sophene, Arm., on the Euphrates, L., above Amida. *Hanozith.*

AOI stena, a defile of Æropus m., on the confines of Illyria and Epirus, through which Aous fl. runs. *Near Clissura.*

AONES, a tribe of Leleges, occupying Aonius Campus in Bœotia, prior to the invasion of Cadmus. Named after Aon, son of Neptune.

AONIA, the primitive name of Bœotia.

AONIUS campus, Bœotia, the plain in which Thebes stood.

AORATA saltus, a defile in Lentiani colles, bet. Cyzicus and Lopadium.

AORNOS, I. a fortress of the Assacani, India, on a rock at the junction of the Cophes with the Indus. Deemed impregnable until taken by Alexander. II. of Bactriana, situate on a high rock near Bactra.

AORSI (Adorsi), a people of Sarmatia Asiat., who from the N.W. shore of the Caspian removed to the Tanais.

AORUS fl., Arcadia, i. q. Arsanius.

AÖÜS fl. (Alorus), Illyr., i. q. Æas.

APÆSUS, I. a r. of Mysia, falling into Propontis, w. of Priapus. *Beiram-dere.* II. Pæsus, a town of Mysia, bet. Parium and Lampsacus, on Apæsus fl. A Milesian settlement.

APAITÆ, a later name of the Cercetæ, in Pontus.

APAMARIS (Arimara), a town of Cyrrhestica, Syr., on the Euphrates, bet. Eragiza and Serrhæ (8).

APAMEA, *prius* Pella, I. a city of Apamene, near the Orontes, N. of Larissa. Built by Antigonus ; re-named by Seleucus Nicator after his queen. *Kalaat el Medyk ; Phamiat.* II. of Bithynia, 24 m. N. of Prusa, built on the site of Myrtea, by Prusias, and named after his queen. A colonia of Julius Cæsar (Julia Concordia). *Modania.* III. (Arsace), surnamed Ragiana, Raphiana, of Medea-Choarene, 10 geog. m. s. of Caspiæ portæ, S.E. of Ragæ. IV. (Seleucia), of Osrhoene, on the Euphrates, and opposite Zeugma, with which it was connected by a bridge. Built by Seleucus. *Roum-Kala*, 2 m. N. from El Bir. V. *prius* Cibotus, a city of Phrygia Magna, on Mæander fl., above its junction with Glaucus fl., E.N.E. of Chonæ. Built by Antiochus Soter, and named after his mother Apama. The second commercial city of Asia Minor. *Deenare.* VI. of Babyl., on the Tigris, at the confluence of the Euphrates. *Korna.*

APAMENE, a district of Syria, E. of Cassiotis.

APANÆSTE, a town of Peucetia, on Via Frentana, bet. Barium (22) and Egnatia (15). *S. Vito.*

APARNI (Parnæ), a people of Sogdiana.

APARTHENI, a people of Sarmatia Asiat., about the sources of Imites fl.

APASIDA, a town of Colchis, at the mouth of Acinasis fl.

APATURUS (Apaturum), a town of Chersonesus Taurica, near Cimmerium prom. Named from a temple of Venus Apatura.

APAVARTICE (Abarbina), capital of Apavarcticene, Margianæ.

APAVARCTICENE (Arcticene), a district of Parthia, S.E. The seat of the Abii.

APERLÆ (Aperræ), a town of Lycia, at Acroterium prom., 7½ m. w. from Simena.

APELAURUS m., a m. of Arcadia, 1¼ m. from Stymphalus.

APENNINUS m., m. running through Italy from Alpes Maritimæ, about Genua, to the coast of the Adriatic, near Ancona, Garganus prom., then inclining to Inferum mare, and terminating, after a course of 700 m., at Leucopetra prom. *Apennines.*

APERANTIA, I. a district of Ætolia, bounded N. by Athamania, w. by Amphilochia, E. by Æniania and Dolopia. *Carpenitze.* II. its capital, on Campylus fl. *Carpenitze.*

APERŎPIA ins., an isl. of Argolis, in Hermionus sin. *Dhoko.*

APESAS m. (Apesus, Apæsantus), a m. of Argolis, E. of Nemea, whence Theseus took his flight.

APHARSITES, a colony from Chaldæa settled in Samaria.

APHAS, a r. of the Molossi, Epirus.

APHEK (Aphaka), I. a city of Asher, bet. Heliopolis and Byblus, on Adonis fl. Noted for a temple of Astarte (Venus), and for a lake, the water of which bore any weight, however ponderous. *Afka.* II. of Gaulonitis, bet. Gaulon and Hippus. III. of Judæa, on the borders of Judah and Benjamin, E. of Jerusalem, where the Philistines took the Ark from the He-

brews. *Feik.* IV. of Issachar, a royal city of the Canaanites, N. of Jezreel. In its neighbourhood occurred the battle fatal to Saul and Jonathan.

APHEREMA, i. q. Ephraim.

APHĒTÆ, a port at the w. entrance of the Pagasæus sin., below Larissa, deriving its name from the *departure* hence of the Argonauts. *Fetio.*

APHIDANTES, a tribe of Molossi, Epirus.

APHIDNA, I. a demus of Attica, of the tribe Leontis, near Deceleia, 15 m. N.W. from Athens, where Theseus concealed Helena. II. a town of Laconia.

APHLE, a town of Chaldæa, on the Euphrates, below its confluence with the Tigris.

APHNITIS palus, a lake of Mysia, E. of Zelea.

APHORA (Gephora), a maritime town of Tripolis, Africa, bet. Getullum and Megerthis.

APHRODISIAS, I. an isl. of Bætica, i. q. Junonis ins. II. Læa, an isl. of Cyrenaica, N.W. of Darnis. III. a maritime district of Æolis Asiat., opposite Lesbos. IV. a prom. of Caria, in Doridis sin., bet. Schœnus sin. and Thymnias sin. V. a town of Aphrodisias ins., Cyrenaicæ. VI. *prius* Leleges, Megalopolis, Ninoe, a town of Caria, on Orsinus fl., 8 m. above Antiochia ad Mæandrum, on the borders of Phrygia. *Gheira.* VII. of Cilicia Trachea, at Zephyrium prom. (w.). VIII. of Laconia, on the E. shore of Bæaticus sin., s. of Cotyrta. Founded by Æneas. IX. of Thrace, at the entrance of Chersonnesus Thracius, bet. Apri (34) and Callipolis (35), on Egnatia Via.

APHRODISUM (Pyrenæum, Veneris), I. a prom. of Tarraconensis, the termination of the Pyrenees, on the Mediterranean, N. of Rhodes. *C. Creux.* II. a town of Arcadia. III. of Cyprus, on the N. coast, 8¾ m. N. from Salamis. IV. of Zeugitana, on Neapolitanus sin., N. of Hadrumetum. V. a haven of Numidia, s. of Hippo Regius. *El Berber.* VI. the middle basin of Piræus, Athen.

APHRODITE. *Vide* Myos Hormus.

APHRODITIS, a town of Thebais, bet. Didymis and Compasis.

APHRODITOPOLIS, I. a town of Heptanomis, on the Nile, R., bet. Ancyronpolis and Acanthus. *Atfyh.* II. of Lower Egypt, on the Bubastic branch of the Nile, above Bubastus. III. of Thebais, on the Nile, L., bet. Abotis and Crocodilopolis. *Tachta.*

APHÝTIS, a town of Pallene, Macedonia, on Thermaicus sin., s. of Potidæa.

APIA, the early name of Peloponnesus; from Apis, son of Apollo, or from Apis, son of Telchin.

APIÆ campus, a plain of Mysia, above Thebe and Adramyttium, N. of Temnus m.

APIARIUM, a town of the Contestani, Tarraconens., bet. Salaria w. and Ibis E.

APIATES, a people of Novem Populana, w. of the Bigerrones. *About Accous.*

APICILIA, a town of the Carni, Venetia, on Tilavemptus Major fl., L., bet. Concordia (9) and Ad Undecim (10), on Via Æmilia. *Latisana.*

APIDĂNUS fl., a river of Achaia, in Phthiotis, Thessal., rising near Xynias lac., and falling into Peneus fl. at Phacium. *Vlacho Ioni.*

APILAS fl., a r. of Pieria, Macedonia, falling into Thermaicus sin. at Heracleium.

APINA, a town of the Monades, Apulia, towards Arpi.

APIRA (Aparisdocome), a town of Phrygia Pacatiana.

APIS, I. a town of Cyrenaica, on the coast bet. Euschœnus and Diarrhoæ. II. of Lower Egypt, on Mareotis palus, s. III. of Libya Ægypti, 5 m. w. from Parætonium. According to Scylax, the w. boundary of Egypt.

APO, a town of the Albocenses, Dacia, on Apus fl.

APOBATANA, i. q. Ecbatana Mediæ.

APOBATHMI, a place of Argolis, on Argolicus sin., near Anigræa, where Danaus first landed.

APOBATHRA, a point on the coast, near Sestos, where Xerxes' ship struck against the ice.

APOCOPA m. (Poinætheŏn), I. a m. of India i. Gangem, N.E. of Canthy sin. II. the coast of Azania, Æthiopia.

APOCREMNUS prom. (Hypocremnus), a prom. of Ionia, at Chytrium, opposite Drymusa ins. *Esomeno.*

APODOTI, a people of Ætolia, occupying the country s. of Evenus fl.

APOLLINARIUM, a town of the Helvii, Narbonensis. *Aubenas.*

APOLLINIS prom., a pr. of Mauritania Cæsar., E. of Chinalaph fl. *C. Mostagan.* II. MINOR CIVITAS, a town of Thebais, on the Nile, L., bet. Lycopolis and Hypsele.

APOLLINOPOLIS MAGNA (Apollinos Superior), I. a town of Thebais, on the Nile, L., bet. Hieracanpolis and Contra-Toum. The inhabitants were great enemies to crocodiles. *Edfu.* II. PARVA, *postea* Maximianopolis? a town of Thebais, on the Nile, R., bet. Coptos and Thebæ.

APOLLONIA, I. a town of the Apodoti, Æto-

lia, N.W. of Potidania. II. capital of Apolloniatis Assyr., on Physcus fl., S.E. of Dara. III. Albanum, i. q. Heraclea-Albaca. IV. of Chalcidice, in Macedonia, on the Egnatia Via, bet. Heraclea (11) and Bromiscus (11). *Pollina.* V. of Crete, on the N. coast, bet. Cytæum and Gnossus. *Near Candia.* VI. *postea* Sozusa, of Cyrenaica, 10 m. N.E. from Cyrene. *Marza Susa.* VII. a town on one of Echinades ins. VIII. of Judæa, bet. Assur N. and Joppa s. *Orsuf.* IX. AD RHYNDACUM, of Mysia, on a peninsula at the N.W. extremity of Apolloniates lac. *Abulliona.* X. of Mysia, near Assus. XI. *prius* Margium, of Phrygia Magna, bet. Apamea Cibotus (24) and Antiochia ad Pisidiam. *Ketsi Bourlu.* XII. of Pisidia, 24 m. E. from Apamea. *Sandakleh.* XIII. of Sicily, bet. Calacta and Aluntium. XIV. of Siphnos ins., on the E. coast. *Castro.* XV. of the Taulantii, Illyria, on Æas fl., R., about 7 m. from its mouth. A Corcyrian colony, celebrated for its laws and its cultivation of literature, especially the Greek, which Augustus studied here. *Polina.* XVI. *postea* Sozopolis, of the Odrysæ, Thrace, on the Euxine, s. of Anchialus. A Milesian settlement. *Siseboli.* XVII. of the Sapæi, Thrace, on the Strymonicus sin., bet. Acontisma and the mouth of Nestus fl. XVIII. *surnamed* Macrobia, on the site of Acrothoos. The inhabitants were said to live longer than other men.

APOLLONIAS, I. *prius* Thynias, an isl. of Bithynia, in the Euxine, 3 m. E. from Rhoe. II. an isl. of Lycia. III. a town of Apollonias ins., Bithynia.

APOLLONIS (Apollonoshieron), I. a town of Lydia, s. of Hiera Cæsarea, 37½ m. from Pergamum. *Bullene.* II. a town of Crete.

APOLLŌNIĀTIS, I. a district of Assyria, bet. Chalonitis and Sittacene. *Arioch.* II. a lake of Mysia, on the borders of Bithynia, principally formed by Rhyndacus fl. *Lake Abulliona.*

APOLLONIEIS, a demus of Attica, of the tribe Acamantis.

APOLLONIUM prom. (Pulchrum), a pr. of Zeugitana, at the N. entrance of Carthaginensis sin.

APOLLONOSHIERON, Lydiæ, i. q. Apollonis.

APOLOGUS, a town of Characene, Babylonia, on one of the artificial issues of the Euphrates, w. of Charax.

APONI fons (Aquæ Patavinæ), baths of Venetia, 6 m. s.w. from Patavium, whose waters, besides being considered to cure "without pain," were reputed prophetic. The birth-place of Livy. *Bagni d'Abano.*

APORISDOCOME, i. q. Apira, in Phrygia.

APOSTANA, a maritime town of Persis, bet. Areon fl. and Bagrada fl.

APPHA, a town of Parthia, s.w. of Tabas.

APPHADANA, *apud* Ptolemæum, i. q. Dara, Mesopotamia.

APPHANA ins., an isl. of Susiana, in Persicus sin., off Sacer sin.

APPIA, a town of Phrygia, near Synnada.

APPIANUM, a town of the Tridentini, Rhætia, N.E. of Ennemasæ.

APPIARIA, a town of the Getæ, Mœsia, on the Danube, bet. Transmarisca and Tegræ.

APPIOLÆ, a town of the Volsci, Latium, bet. Setia and Privernum. Dest. by Tarquinius Priscus.

APROSITOS ins., i. q. Pluvialia.

APRUS, a town of the Apsynthii, Thrace, on Melas fl., bet. Zesutera (12) and Bedizus (12). A colonia of Claudius.

APRŪSA fl., a r. of Umbria, falling into the Adriatic s. of Ariminum. *Ausa.*

APRUSTUM (Abystrum), a town of the Bruttii, Lucania, N.W. of Thurii. *Argusto.*

APSALUS, a town of Almopœia, Macedonia, on Trigonus fl., w. of Anavasarium.

APSĂRUS, I. (Apsarrus, Acampsis), a r. of Pontus, forming the junction of Glaucus and Lycus fl., and falling into the Euxine, 2 m. N. from Apsarum. *Tchoroksou.* II. (Apsyrtus), a port of Pontus, bet. Achabis fl. (7½) and Apsarus fl. (2). Named Apsyrtus from Medea, whose tomb was shown in the vicinity. *Gonieh.*

APSILÆ (Apsilii), a town of Colchis, on the Phasis, bet. the Abasgi and the Lazi.

APSŎRUS, I. chief of the Apsyrtides ins., Liburniæ, s. of Apsyrtium. *Osero.* II. its capital, at the N. extremity.

APSUS fl. (Thapsus), a r. of Illyria, rising in Bercetesius m., s.e. of Codrion, and falling into the Adriatic below Asparagium, 15 m. s. from Genusus fl. *Ergent; Beratino.*

APSINTHII, a people of Thrace, on the Melas sinus, N.W. of Chersonnesus Thracius. Their district was noted for the plant called after them.

APSINTHUS, Thraciæ, i. q. Ænos.

APSYRTIDES ins., *prius* Brigeides, four isl. of Liburnia, in the Adriatic, off Polaticum prom. Named from Apsyrtus, brother of Medea.

APSYRTIS ins., an isl. of Liburnia, s. of Crepsa ins. *Ferosina.*

APSYRTIUM ins., one of Apsyrtides ins., Liburniæ, s. of Apsarus. *Cherso.*

APTA JULIA (Civitas Aptensium), a town of the Vulgientes, Narbonensis II., bet. Cabellio (12) and Alaunium. A colonia. *Apt.*

APTERA, a town of Crete, in the s.e. angle of Martilus sin., 10 m. w. from Cydonia. The locality of the defeat of the Syrens by the Muses, whence the name "wingless." *Palæo-castro.*

APTUCHI FANUM, *postea* Aptungis, Balacra, a maritime town of Pentapolis, Cyrenaicæ, 15 m. s.w. from Physcus.

APUA, capital of the Apuani, in Liguria, N. of Luna.

APUĀNI, a people of Liguria, contiguous to the Briniates, afterwards removed to Samnium.

APULI, descendants of the Osci, settled with the Dauni, in Apulia.

APULIA, originally the district of Italy, along the E. coast, s.e. of the Frentani, occupied by the Apuli. Later the entire s.e. of the peninsula E. of Lucania and Samnium, s. of the Frentani.

APULIA DAUNIA, Plana, *vide* Daunia.

APULUM (Apula, Augustum), *postea* Alba Julia, a town of the Burideenses, Dacia, on Marisus fl., 8 m. N. from Blandiana. A colonia. *Weissenburg.*

APUS fl., a r. of Dacia, falling into the Danube below the junction of Margus fl. *Nera.*

AQUA FERENTINA, the source of Ferentina fl., near Apiolæ, Latium. The council place of the confederate Latin cities.

AQUA MARTIA, a canal from Facinus lac. to Rome, through Tibur.

AQUA TEPULA, a watercourse from Tusculum to Rome, constructed by the censors Cæpio and Longinus, and M. Agrippa. *Tepiduccia.*

AQUA VIRGO, a watercourse from Tusculum to Rome. *Aqua Vergine.*

AQUA VIVA, I. a town of Etruria, on Tiberis fl., R., bet. Ad Centesimum (7) and Ocriculum, on Via Flaminia, s.e. of Falerii. *Aqua Viva.* II. of the Jassii, Pannonia, on Dravus fl., R., bet. Ramista (10) and Populi.

AQUÆ, I. baths of Germania Magna, N.E. of Cambete. (Civitas Aurelia Aquensis). *Baden.* II. baths of Mauritania Cæsar., bet. Suffasar (26) and Tanaramusa. A colonia. *Hamam Meriga.* III. of the Tigurini, Maxima Sequanorum, s.w. of Augusta Rauracorum. IV. of Zeugitana, 19 m. s.e. from Musti. V. of Zeugitana, near Aves. VI. ALBULEÆ, a sulphureous lake, with floating islands, at Tibur, emptying itself into the Tiber. It gave name to the Tiburtine Sibyl. VII. ANGÆ, baths of Bruttium, N.W. of Lametus. VIII. APOLLINARES, of Etruria, on Minio fl., bet. Sabate (10) and Tarquinii (12), on Via

Claudia. *Bagni di Stigliano.* IX. ARA-VENÆ, of Cappadocia, s. of Zama. X. ARDEATÆ, of Latium, near Ardea. *Solforata.* XI. AUGUSTÆ, Gallia, i. q. Tarbellicæ. XII. BALISSÆ, of the Oseriatæ, Pannonia, bet. Varianæ and Inicerum (25). *Near Daruvar.* XIII. BILBILITANÆ, of the Celtiberi, Tarraconensis, on Salo fl., L., 16 m. w. from Bilbilis. *Alhama.* XIV. BORBONIÆ (Bormonis), of the Bituriges Cubi, Aquitania I., bet. Sitilia (24) and Tinconium. *Bourbon l'Archambault.* XV. CÆRETANÆ, of Etruria, near Cære. *Bagni di Sasso.* XVI. CÆSARIS, of Numidia, bet. Ad Mercurium and Theveste (7). XVII. CELINÆ, of the Celinæ, Tarraconensis, s. of Iria Flavia. *Caldas del Rey.* XVIII. CALIDÆ, baths of the Arverni, Aquitania I., N. of Augustonemetum. *Vichy.* XIX. of Astica, Thrace, bet. Anchialus and Calybe. XX. of the Gabali, Aquitania I., N.W. of Anderitum (27). *Aigues Chaudes.* XXI. CALDENSES, of the Læetani, Tarraconensis, bet. Subis and Iluro. XXII. CONVENARUM, bet. Oppidum Novum and Lugdunum (26). *Bagnères en Bigorre.* XXIII. CUMANÆ, of Cumæ, Campania. XXIV. CUTILIÆ, of Cutiliæ, Sabinium. The death-place of Vespasian. XXV. DACICÆ, of Mauritania Ting., bet. Gilda and Volubilis. XXVI. ELLOPIÆ, of Ellopia, Eubœa, towards Histiæa. XXVII. FLAVIÆ, of the Bracari, Tarraconensis, E.N.E. of Bracara August. *Chaves.* XXVIII. HELVETIÆ (Castellum Aquarum), of Tugēnus pagus, S.E. of Vindonessa. XXIX. HERCULIS, of Numidia, s.w. of Calceus Herculis, under Audus m., N. XXX. HYPSITANÆ, of Sardinia, at Forum Trajani. XXXI. JASSIÆ, of the Jassii, Pannonia, N.E. of Pœtovium. XXXII. LABANÆ, of Sabinium, near Nomentum. *Bagni di Grotta Marozza.* XXXIII. LABODES, Sicily, i. q. Thermæ Selenuritiæ. XXXIV. LESITANÆ, of Sardinia, near Lesa. XXXV. MATTIACÆ, of the Mattiaci, Germania, N.W. of Moguntiacum. *Wisbaden.* XXXVI. NEAPOLITANÆ, of Sardinia, S.E. of Neapolis. *Acqua di Corsari.* XXXVII. NERÆ, of the Bituriges Cubi, Aquitania I., bet. Mediolanum (18) and Cantilia (22). *Neris.* XXXVIII. NISENII, of the Ædui, Gallia, on Niveris fl., R., below Pocrinium. *Bourbon Lancy.* XXXIX. ONESIORUM, of the Onesii, Novem Populana, near Aquæ Convenarum. *Bagnères-Ozon, near Bagnères en Bigorre.* XL. ORIGENIS, of the Lucenses, Tarraconensis, on Minius fl., L., above the junction of Bilbilis fl. *Orense.*

XLI. PANNONIÆ, of the Boii, Pannonia, s. bet. Vindobona and Scarabantia (31). *Baden.* XLII. PASSERIS, of Etruria, near Fanum Voltumnæ, s. of Volsinius lac., bet. Forum Cassii and Vulsinii, on Via Cassia. *Bagni di Serpa.* XLIII. PISANÆ, of Etruria, 3 m. N.E. from Pisæ. *Bagni di Pisa.* XLIV. POPULONIÆ, of Etruria, s. of the mouth of Lynceus fl., on Falesia portus, bet. Manilia and Populonium, on Via Aurelia. *Caldane.* XLV. QUERQUENNÆ, of the Bracari, Tarraconensis, on Limia fl., L., above Limia. *Banos de Molgas.* XLVI. QUINTIANÆ, of the Lucenses, Tarraconensis, on Navius fl., L., near its source. XLVII. REGIÆ, of Epirus, near Chimera. *Argyro-Castro.* XLVIII. of Byzacene, bet. Aggarsel (14) and Terentum. XLIX. SEGETÆ, of the Segusiani, Lugdunensis I., near the sources of Liger fl., bet. Forum Segusianorum (13½) and Icidmagus (25½). L. SEGESTÆ, of the Senones, Lugdunensis IV., bet. Agenticum (33) and Ad Fines (22). *Near Sceaux.* LI. SEXTIÆ, of the Salyes or Salluvii, Narbonensis II., bet. Tegulata (15) and Massilia (15). The first Roman settlement in Gaul. A colonia of the Consul Sextus Calvinus, 123 B.C. Enl. by Augustus. The locality of a great defeat of the Cimbri by Marius. *Aix.* LII. SICCÆ, baths of the Consorani, Novem Populana, bet. Calagorris (16) and Vernosola (15). *Aigues Sèches.* LIII. SINUESSANÆ, of Latium, near Sinuessa. Deemed beneficial for barrenness in women and insanity in men. *Bagni.* LIV. SOLIS, *rectius* Sulis, *postea* Balnia, Badiza, Bathonia, of the Belgæ, Brit., on Aufona fl., R., bet. Abone and Verlucio. A colonia. Its baths were noted 800 B.C. Sacred to the goddess Sulis. *Bath.* LV. STATIELLÆ (Ad Aquas), of the Statielli, Liguria, bet. Crixia (20) and Dertona, on Bormias fl. Memorable for the defeat of the Carthaginian Mago. *Acqui.* LVI. TACAPITANÆ, of Africa, 16 m. w. from Tacape. LVII. TARBELLICÆ, (Augustæ), *postea* Aquensis Urbs, of the Tarbelli, Novem Populana, on Aturus fl., S.E. of Mosconnum (24). *D'Aqs.* LVIII. TAURI, of Etruria, 3 m. E. from Centumcellæ. Said to have been discovered by a bull, whence the name. *Bagni di Ferrata.* LIX. TEANÆ, of the Sidicini, near Teanum. *Acqua delle Caldarelle.* LX. TIBILITANÆ, of Numidia, N.W. of Tibilis, bet. Cirta and Hippo Regius. *Anuouna.* LXI. VETULONIÆ (Velinæ), of Etruria, on the coast, w. of Velutonium, bet. Populonium (16) and Vada Volaterrana (23). *Vetuli.* LXII.

Voconis, of the Ausetani, Tarraconensis, s.e. of Gerunda. *Caldas de Malavella.* LXIII. Volaterranæ, of Etruria, n.w. of Volaterræ. *Monte Cerberi.*

Aquartille, a town of Numidia, bet. Cirta and Numiturianum.

Aquila, I. Major (Jagath), a town of Mauritania Ting., at the mouth of Tamuda fl., bet. Phœbi prom. and Tænia longa. II. Minor, a town of Mauritania Ting., on the Mediterranean, bet. Abyla and Phœbi prom.

Aquilaria, a town of Zeugitana, on Carthaginensis sin., s.w. of Mercurii prom., 22 m. from Clupea.

Aquĭlēia, I. a city of the Carni, Venetia, on Natisus fl., 8 m. above its mouth, bet. Timavus and Ad Undecimum, on the Via Æmilia. Founded by the Argonauts, 1350 b.c. The ninth city of the empire, and the entrepôt of the commerce between Rome and Illyria. The name was given from the augury of an eagle. *Aquila.* II. a town of Rhætia, bet. Ad Luna (20) and Opie (18). *Gunzburg.* III. of Etruria, on Arnus fl. L., bet. Biturgia (14) and Florentia (15), on Via Cassia. *Incisa.*

Aquilianis Nova, a town of Zeugitana, bet. Armoscla and Picus.

Aquilo, a town of Daunia-Apulia, on Via Egnatina, bet. Equus Tuticus and Æcæ. *Buccola di Troja.*

Aquĭlonia, I. a town of the Hirpini, Samnium, on Via Appia, bet. Sub Romula (11) and Pons Aufidi (6). *Lacedogna.* II. of the Pentri, Samnium, towards the confines of Latium, 20 m. n.w. from Bovianum. *Agnone.*

Aquinates, a people of Gallia Cispadana, towards Forum Livii.

Aquinum, I. a town of the Boii, Gallia Cispadana, s. of Mutina. *Acquario.* II. of the Volsci, in Latium, on Via Latina, bet. Fabratera (8) and Casinum (9). A colonia. The birth-place of Juvenal. *Aquino.*

Aquis Granum (*prius* Vegerra), baths of the Eburones, Germania II., s.w. of Marcodurum. Founded by Granus, brother of Nero. *Aach; Aix-la-Chapelle.*

Aquitani, Gallia, i. q. Tarbellici.

Aquitania, a province of Gaul, under Augustus. Bounded n. and e. by the Liger, s. by the Pyrenees, w. by the sea. It comprised the subdivisions of Novem Populana, Aquitania I. and Aquitania II.

Aquitania I., the e. subdivision of Aquitania, bounded (generally), n. and e. by the Liger, s. by the Garumna, w. by a line bet. Tasciaca, n. and e. of Agen-

num, s. *Departments of Cher, Indre, Allier, Cantal, Puy de Dôme, Tarn et Garonne, Corrèze, Haute Vienne.*

Aquitania II., the w. subdivision of Aquitania. Bounded n. by the Liger, s. by the Garumna, w. by the sea, e. by Aquitania I. *Departments of Vendée, Deux Sèvres, Vienne, Charente Inférieure, and portions of Lot et Garonne and Gironde.*

Ar (Rabbah-Moab, Rabmathon, Rabbath Moma, Areopolis), the metropolis of Moab, n.w. of Zoar, 25 m. s. of Arnon fl. *El Rabbi.*

Araducta, a town of the Bracari, Tarraconensis, s.e. of Catraleucum.

Ara Minervæ ins. (Ara Palladis), an islet of the Troglodytæ, in the Red Sea, off Mnemium prom. *Magarzawe.*

Ara Tutelæ, a maritime village of Corsica, e. bet. Mariana and Alista.

Ara Ubiorum, the early name of Agrippina Colonia.

Arabia, the country of the Arabes, descendants of Joktan. Bounded n. by Palestine and the Syrian Desert, n.e. by Persicus sin., e. and s.e. by Erythræum mare, s.w. by Arabicus sinus, w. by Egypt. It comprised Arabia Deserta, Arabia Felix, and Arabia Petræa.

Arabia Deserta (Erēmos), the inland portion of Arabia n. towards the Desert of Syria.

Arabia Felix (Eudaimōn), the maritime portions of Arabia. *Yemen and Hejoz.*

Arabia Petræa, the n.w. portion of Arabia, bet. Palestine and Arabicus sin.

Arabiæ Felicis Emporium, Arabia Felix (Eden, Ophir? *postea* Adane), a port of the Homeritæ, Arabia, bet. Ammonii prom. and Abisama. *Aden.*

Arabici montes, m. of Egypt, e. of the Nile. *Djebel Mokkatam.*

Ababĭcus sin., i. q. Rubrum mare.

Arabingara, a maritime town of Taprobane, on the s.w. coast. *Colombo.*

Arabis fl. (Arbis, Arabius), I. a r. of Gedrosia, falling into Terabdon sin. e. of Pagala. It separates the Oritæ from the Arabitæ. *Purally.* II. capital of the Arabitæ, Gedrosia, on Arabis fl. *Pura.* III. a town of Meroe, on the Nile, R., bet. Primis parva and Napata.

Arabisci, a tribe of Scordisci in Pannonia, bet. the Danube and the Savus.

Arabissus, a town of Cappadocia, on Pyramus fl., bet. Plandari (22) and Osdara (28).

Arabitæ (Arabies), a people of Gedrosia, extending 25 geog. m. along the coast bet. the Indus and the Arabis. *Luz.*

ARABITEUS m., m. of the Arabitæ, in Gedrosia, parallel with the Indus, and terminating over against Bibacte ins.

ARABRACÆ, a town of Cappadocia.

ARACA, a town of Susiana-Cissia, on the Tigris, below Agra.

ARACELI, a town of the Varduli, Tarraconensis, bet. Tritium N.W. and Alanton S.E.

ARACHNÆUS m. (Hysselinus, *prius* Sapyselaton), a m. of Argolis, on the confines of Corinthia, N. of Lessa. *Monte Sophico.*

ARACHOSIA, a division of Aria, bounded N. by Bactria, S. by Gedrosia, W. by Drangiana, at Etymandrus fl., E. by India, at the Indus. *Harauwatish; Kutch-Gundava.*

ARACHOTÆ (Arachoti, Arachotri), the people of Arachosia.

ARACHOTUS (Cophen, Culis), I. capital of Arachosia, N.E. of Arachotus fl., bet. Ortospana (50 geog. m.) and Prophthasia (100 geog. m.). Built by Semiramis. II. a river of Arachosia, rising in Parapomisus m. and falling into Etymandrus fl. at Bestia. *Urghundab? Harauwoti?* III. a lake of Arachosia, formed by Arachotus fl.

ARACHTHUS fl. (Arĕthon, Aræthus), a r. of Epirus, rising in Tymphe m., separating Epirus from Athamania, and falling into the Ambracius sin. below Ambracia. *Arta.*

ARACIA ins. (Alexandri ins.), an isl. of Persis, in Persicus sin., bet. Chersonnesus prom. and Hyperis fl.

ARACILLUM, a town of the Autrigones, Tarraconensis, on Saunium fl., N. of Juliobriga.

ARACYNTHUS m., I. a m. of Ætolia, towards the w. coast, bet. the Achelous and the Evenus fl. *Zigos.* II. a m. of Bœotia.

ARAD, a city of Judæa, bet. Malatha (4) and Hebron (20).

ARADEN (Anopolis), a town of Crete.

ARADRISPE (*postea* Aspadana, Aspacana), a town of Media, on the borders of Persis. *Ispahan.*

ARADUS, I. an isl. of Arabia, in Persicus sin., s. of Pylora ins. II. Phœnicia, i. q. Arvad.

ARÆ, I. a people of Carmania, on the confines of Gedrosia. II. a town of Mauritania Cæsar., bet. Tatitti and Zabi. III. ALEXANDRI, of Cilicia Campestris, under Amanus m., near Issus. IV. FLAVIÆ, of Vindelicia, E. of Tarodurum. *Rothweil.* V. MUTIÆ, of the Capenates, Etruria, near

Artena. VI. PHILÆNORUM, of Africa Propria, on Syrtis Major, bet. Benidedari and Automalax, around two altars raised by the Carthaginians to the brothers Philæni, whose self-devotion extended the limits of Carthage hither, much further into the territory of Cyrene than previously obtained. The altars were extinct in Strabo's time. VII. SESTIANÆ (Tres Aræ), three altars raised to Augustus, on Nerium prom., Tarraconensis.

ARÆÆ ins., three islets of Caria, about Syme ins.

ARÆGENUÆ, capital of the Saii or Sesuvii, Lugdunensis II., bet. Viducasses (36) and Nudionum (60). *Argentan.*

ARÆTHUS (Arethas fl.), i. q. Arachthus.

ARÆTHYREA, the early name of Phlius, in Argolis, from Aræthyria, daughter of Arus.

ARAGUS fl. (Arrabo), a r. of Iberia, rising towards Caucasiæ pylæ, and falling into the Cyrus near Harmozia. *Aragvi.*

ARAINUS, a town of Laconia, on Laconicus sin., w. bet. Teuthrome and Las, where was the monument of Las.

ARAM, the Scripture name of Syria, Mesopotamia, Chaldæa, and Assyria, from Aram, fifth son of Shem.

ARAMÆI, the Persian appellation of the Sacæ.

ARAMAGARA, a maritime town of Limyrica, Ind., bet. Tyndis (5) and Callicarias prom. *Carwar.*

ARANDIS, a town of the Lusitani, on the Tagus, R., above Tubucci.

ARANE (Aranis), a town of Armenia Minor, 24 m. s.w. from Euspœna.

ARANGÆ, a town of Cappadocia, bet. Hispa (18) and Ciaca (9).

ARANNI, a town of the Cynetes, Lusitania, s.w. of Myrtilis. *Ourique.*

ARANTIA, the earlier name of Phliasia.

ARANTINUS m., a hill of Argolis, on Asopus fl., overlooking Phlius. *Agros-basili.*

ARAPACHITIS, a district of Assyria, N.E. on the confines of Armenia Major. Named from Arphaxad, s. of Shem. *Arphachsad; Aghbak.*

ARAPHÆA, an isl. of Caria.

ARAPHEN, a demus of Attica, of the tribe Ægeis, near Myrrhenus. *Raphena.*

ARAPLUS, a town of Thracius Chersonnesus, on the coast s.E. of Alopeconnesus.

ARAR fl. (Arăris), *postea* Saucona, Sangona, a r. of Lugdunensis I., rising in Vogesus m., and falling into the Rhone at Lugdunum. *Sâone.*

ARARAT, I. a Scriptural name of Armenia Major. II. a district of central Armenia

Major. III. a ridge of Gordyæi m., in Ararat regio, bet. Artaxata and Arsissa-Thospitis lacus. On one of its peaks the ark rested.

ARARUS fl., Dacia, i. q. Aluta.

ARAS, the first name of Phliasia, Pelop.

ARASAXA, a town of Morimene, Cappadocia, bet. Coduzabala (24) and Comana.

ARASSUS (Ariassus, Aarassus), a town of Pisidia, according to Artemidorus, of Pamphylia, according to Hierocles, s.w. of Atalia, on Atalicus sin.

ARATHA, a town of Margiana, E. of Sina.

ARATISPI, a town of the Turtetani, Bætica, N. of Alontigeceli.

ARATU, a town of the Zygritæ, Marmarica, on the coast bet. Zygræ and Geræ.

ARAURA, I. i. q. Cessero. II. a town of the Volcæ Arecomici, on Arauris fl., R., above Agathe.

ARAURACA, a town of Armenia Minor, on Euphrates fl., bet. Suissa (18) and Carsagis (24).

ARAURIS fl. (Rauraris), a r. of Narbonensis I., rising in Cebenna m., N.E. of Condatomagus, and falling into Gallicus sin. at Agatha. Towards its mouth it was called Petrosus, from its rocky bed. *L'Erault.*

ARAUSA, a town of the Dalmates, Illyria, on Titius fl. L., N.E. of Scardona.

ARAUSIO (Civitas Arausiensis, Civitas Arausicorum, Colonia Secundanorum), capital of the Cavares, Gallia Viennensis, on the Rhone, above Avenio. A colonia. *Orange.*

ARAVENE, a western portion of Cataonia, Cappadocia.

ARAVISCI, a people of Pannonia Inf., s. of the Amantini.

ARAXA, a town of Lycia, near Carmylessus.

ARAXENE (Araxenus Campus), a district of Armenia Major, on the Araxis, below Artaxata. *Erasskhadsor.*

ARAXES, I. generally an appellation of great rivers. II. (Arosis), a river of Persis Prop., rising on the confines of Susiana Cabandene s., and falling into a lake s.E. of Persepolis. *Bend-emir.* III. a r. of Armenia Major, rising in Abus m., and, after separating Armenia from Media, falling into the Cyrus above Taga, or, according to Strabo, into the Caspian, s. of the Cyrus. *Arras; Eräschk.*

ARAXUS prom., a pr. of Achaia, s.w. of Rhium. *C. Papas.*

ARBA (Kirgath-Arba), the early name of Hebron.

ARBALO, a town of the Bructeri Minores, Germ., s.E. of Aliso.

ARBE, the capital of Scardona ins., Liburnia.

The name was sometimes applied to the island itself. *Arbe.*

ARBEJA, a town of the Brigantes Brit., E. of Virosidum.

ARBELA, I. a town of Galilæa, bet. Dio Cæsarea w. and Tiberias E. II. capital of Arbelitis Assyr., E.S.E. of Nineveh. Near it, at Gaugamela, was gained the victory of Alexander over Darius. *Arbil.*

ARBELITIS, a district of Adiabene, Assyr., about Arbela. *Arbah.*

ARBIS fl., I. Gedrosia, i. q. Cophen. II. a town of Egypt, on the Nile, R., above Moru.

ARBIUS m., a m. of Crete, where Jupiter was nurtured.

ARBOR FELIX (*postea* Arbonense Castrum), I. a town, of the Tugeni, Rhætia, on Venetus lac. w., bet. Ad Fines (30) and Brigantia (20). *Arbon.* II. of the Lingones, Gallia. *Arbot-sur-Aube.*

ARBUCALA, a town of the Vettones, Lusitan., near Salmantica.

ARCA, I. a r. of Phœnicia, falling into the sea 1 m. N. from Eleutherus fl. II. a town of Chaldæa, N.E. of Gera. *Erech ?* III. a town of Asher, Phœnicia, at the mouth of Arca fl. Afterwards named Cæsarea, as the birth-place of Alexander Severus.

ARCADES, the people of Arcadia, in Peloponnesus, of such antiquity that they boasted to be older than the moon.

ARCADIA, I. (Arcades), a town of Crete, bet. Gortys and Lyctus (16), the streams around which sympathetically ceased to flow when the town was taken by the Gnossians, and only resumed their course upon their expulsion six years afterwards. *Arcadioti.* II. Ægypti, i. q. Heptanomis. III. (Pelasgia, Lycaonia, Parrhasia), a country of Peloponnesus, bounded N. by Achaia, s. by Messenia and Laconia, w. by Elis, E. by Argolis. Settled by Pelasgi from Thessaly 1521 B.C. Named from Arcas, son of Jupiter and Callisto. IV. a fortress of Zacynthus ins., s.w. of Zacynthus.

ARCAIARIS (Carcha), a town of Agstanitis Armen., bet. Sardeva and Samachis.

ARCAS, Cappadocia, i. q. Carmala.

ARCESINE, a town of Amorgos ins., on its N. coast. *Arkesini.*

ARCEUTHUS fl., a river of Apamene, Syria, falling into the Orontes towards Antiochia. *Jaghra ?*

ARCHALLA, a town of Cappadocia, s. of Cadyna. *Erklé.*

ARCHANDROPOLIS, a town of Lower Egypt, on the Canopic branch of the Nile, bet.

Chereu and Hermopolis parva. Built by Archandrus, son-in-law of Danaus.

ARCHABIS fl., Arabis, a r. of Colchis, 8 m. w. from Apsarus fl.

ARCHELAÏS, I. a town of Cappadocia, in Præfectura Garsauritis, on Halys fl., R., bet. Argustana (16) and Mocissus (12). Built by Archelaus, last king of Cappadocia. A colonia of Claudius. *Akserai.* II. of Judæa, N. of Jericho. Built by Archelaus, son of Herod. Noted for its palm-trees.

ARCHELAIUM (Auraclea demus), a town of Galatia, on the confines of Phrygia, bet. Dorylæum (30) and Germa (20).

ARCHI, a town of Ephraim, bet. Bethel and Bethoron. The birth-place of Hushai.

ARCHILACHITÆ, a people of Taurica Chersonesus.

ARCHILE, a town of Pentapolis Cyrenaicæ, N.E. from Cyrene.

ARCHIPPE, a town of the Marsi, Sabinium, at the s. extremity of Fucinus lacus, by which it was almost entirely swallowed up. *Arciprete.*

ARCHYRES, a people of Sarmatia Asiat., towards Sintica.

ARCI, I. a people of Germania Magna, on the Vistula, bet. the Burii s. and the Naharvali N. II. of Canaan, about Arca. III. a town of the Turtetani, Bætica, bet. Lastigi E.N.E. and Xera W.S.W.

ARCIACA, a town of the Tricasses, Lugdunensis IV., bet. Augustobona (18) and Durocatalaunus (33). *Arcis sur Aube.*

ARCIAS, a village of Bruttium, near Metaurus.

ARCIDAVA, a town of the Albocenses, Dacia, 12 m. N. from Ad Pontes. *Slatina.*

ARCILACIS, a town of the Oretani, Tarraconensis, S.E. of Laminium.

ARCINNA, a town of the Ciagisi, Dacia, bet. Arcidava and Phrateria.

ARCIOTA, a town of Carmania Deserta, bet. Pantyene and Caumata.

ARCOBADARA, a town of the Cistoboci, Dacia, on Parata fl., L., towards its source.

ARCOBRIGA, a town of the Celtiberi, Tarraconensis, on Salo fl., R., near its source, 91 m. w. from Cæsar Augusta. *Arcos.*

ARCONNESUS, I. i. q. Aspis ins., Ioniæ. II. an isl. of Caria, in Ceramicus sin., over against Halicarnassus. *Orakadasi.*

ARCTAUNUM (Taunus), a town of the Mattiaci, Germ., under Taunus m., at Drusi Vallum, N.E. of Aquæ Mattiacæ.

ARCTONNESUS, a name of the isl. on which Cyzicus stood.

ARCTOUS OCEANUS, i. q. Borealis.

ARCTU prom. (Ursa), a pr. of Sardinia, N.E.

above Columbarium prom. *Capo dell' Orso.*

ARDA fl., a r. of Thrace, rising S.E. of Nicopolis, and falling into Hebrus fl. above Ascadama.

ARDALI fl., a r. of Numidia, rising N. of Thebeste, and falling into Bagradas fl., R., above Mutia.

ARDANIS prom. (Ardania, Ardanaxes, Cardame), a pr. of Marmarica, bet. Petræ Magnæ portus and Catæonium prom.

ARDAUDA, Taurica Chersonesus, i. q. Theodosia.

ARDAXANUS fl. (Artatus), a r. of the Cavii, Illyria, a branch of the Mathis, falling into the Adriatic below Lissus. *Orocha.*

ARDĔA I. a town, of Persis Prop., on the border of Susiana Cabandene S. II. capital of the Rutuli, Latium, about 20 m. S.E. from Rome and 3 from the sea. A Greek city, traditionally founded by Danæ, mother of Perseus. The city of Turnus. A colonia. The retreat of Camillus. *Ardea.*

ARDELICA, a town of the Cenomanni, Gallia Transpadana, at the s. extremity of Benacus lac., at the issue of Mincius fl., bet. Brixia (32) and Verona (13). *Peschiera.*

ARDIÆI, a people of Dalmatia, about Ardion m.; removed hither from the coast by Augustus, on account of their piracies.

ARDION m. (Ardius), a ridge of the Alpes Juliæ, intersecting Dalmatia lengthwise. *Tartari.*

ARDOBRICA, a town of the Lucenses, Tarraconensis, at the mouth of Juvia fl., R., bet. Artabrum prom. N. and Caranicum s. *Ferrol.*

ARDUENNA SILVA, a chain of woody hills, in Belgica II., extending from the Treveri to the Nervii; in length 250 m., in breadth 100. *Ardennes.*

ARDULA, a fortress of Cappadocia, bet. Mazaca and Eremosgræa.

ARDYES, a people of Maxima Sequanorum, on the Rhone, R., w. of Octodunum.

AREBRIGIUM, I. a town of the Salassi, Gallia Transpadana, on Duria Maj. fl., L., bet. Artolica (6) and Augusta Prætoria (25). *Pré St. Didier.* II. of the Centrones, Alpes Penninæ, bet. Augusta Prætoria (25) and Bergintrum (18). *Giorgen, Pont de Seran.*

ARECOMÏCI, a portion of the Volcæ, Gallia, about Nemausus.

AREDATE, Noricum, i. q. Arelate.

AREGEVIA, a town of the Teuriochæmæ, Germania, w. of Calægia. *Near Halberstadt.*

ARELATE (Arlape), I. a r. of Noricum, falling into the Danube at Arelate. *Erlaf.*

II. (Arlape), a town of the Boii, Noricum, on the Danube, bet. Ad Pontem Isis (8) and Namare. *Pohlarn.* III. (Arelas, Arelatum) capital of the Salyes, Gallia Narbonensis, on the Rhone, bet. Ernaginum and Fossa Mariana. The city lay on both sides the river, and that on the L. bank was called Constantia, in honour of Constantine. A colonia of the 6th legion. Surnamed Julia Paterna, in honour of the father of Tiberius; Gallula Roma, as a favourite retreat of the Romans; and Mamillaris (*Græcè* Thelene), from its fancied shape, or from the fertility of the district. *Arles.*

ARENÆ m., sand hills on the w. coast of Bætica, about Olontigi. *Arenas Gordas.*

ARENATIUM, a town of the Bructeri, Germania, N.E. of Noviomagus (10). *Arth, near Herwen.*

ARENE, a village of Triphylia, Elis, near Lepræum. *Sarene.*

ARENIUM, Frentanorum, i. q. Larinium.

ARENOSUM littus, the coast of Corsica w., above Rhium prom.

AREON, I. a r. of Persis, falling into Persicus sin. bet. Gogana and Apostana. II. a town of Cappadocia.

AREOS ins., Pontus, i. q. Aretias.

ARES fl., a r. of Bruttium, falling into Hipponiates sin. over against Ligia ins. *Rivale.*

ARETHUSA fons, I. a fountain or lake, of Eubœa, at Chalcis. II. of Ithaca, on the s. coast. *Near Koraka.* III. of Armenia, i. q. Arsissa. IV. of Sicily, near Syracuse, fabled to have a connexion with Alpheus fl. V. a town of Chalcidice, Macedonia, on Bolbe fl., w. of Stagira, near Bromiscus. The burial-place of Euripides. VI. of Apamene, Syria, on the Orontes, 16 m. N. from Emesa. *Restan.*

ARETIAS (Areios, Area), an isl. of Pontus, in the Euxine, over against Pharnacia (3¾). In it was a temple of Mars, erected by the Amazons Otrere and Antiope.

AREUS fl., a r. of Bithynia, falling into Propontis towards Astacenus sin.

AREVA fl. (Areba), a r. of Tarraconensis, falling into the Durius. The E. boundary of the Arevacæ. *Urcero.*

AREVACÆ, a people of Tarraconensis, on the Durius and Areva, bet. the Pelendones E. and the Vaccæi N.

AREVACE (Arebace), a town of the Arevacæ, Tarraconensis, s.w. of Segontia.

ARGA, I. a town of the Arsæ, Arabia, on the coast, w. of Jatrippa. II. of Gileaditis, s.E. of Pella. III. of the Nabathæi, on Ælaniticus sin.

ARGADINA, a town of Margiana w. *Near Meshed.*

ARGÆUS m., m. of Cappadocia, extending 80 m. bet. Cæsarea E. and Galatia w. *Argisch.*

ARGANTHONIUS (Arganthus) m., a m. of Bithynia, above Prusias. Named from Arganthone, wife of Rhesus. The scene of the story of Hylas.

ARGANTOMAGUS, a town of the Bituriges Cubi, Aquitania I., bet. Augustoritum (31½) and Alerta. *Argenton.*

ARGARA, a town of India i. Gangem, on Argaricus sin. s. *Arlingurry.*

ARGARICUS sin., a bay of Indicus Ocean., at Argara, over against the N.W. extremity of Taprobane. *Palk B.*

ARGEADES fl. (Arciades), a sacred stream of Bruttium, falling into Metaurus fl. E. of Portus Orestis.

ARGELIA, a town of Germania Magna, on the Albis. *Torgau.*

ARGENIS fl., a r. of Lugdunensis III., running into the sea N.W. of Curiosolites.

ARGENNUM, I. an isl. of Ionia, over against Trogilium prom. II. a pr. of Ionia, s.w. of Erythræ, looking towards Posidium prom. *C. Bianco.* III. a pr. of Sicily, E. above Tauromenium. *C. Sant' Alessio.*

ARGENOMESCUM, a town of the Autrigones, Tarraconensis, s.E. of Vereasueca.

ARGENTA, I. a town of Estiæotis, Thessaly, on the borders of Athamania, s.w. of Gomphi. II. of Gallia Cispadana, on Padus fl., near Spina.

ARGENTANUM, a town of Bruttium, N. of Hetriculum. *Argentina.*

ARGENTARIA, a town of the Breuci, in Illyria, bet. Ad Drinum and Staneclum.

ARGENTARIUS, I. a pr. of Etruria, terminating the peninsula on which Cosa stands, over against Igilium ins. *M. Argentaro.* II. m. of Tarraconensis, about the sources of the Bætis.

ARGENTEUM ostium, a name of Spineticum Ostium, Gall. Cisalp.

ARGENTEUS, I. a r. of Gallia Narbonensis, rising near Ad Turrim, and falling into the Ligusticus sin. at Forum Julii. *Argens.* II. a town of the Salyes, Narbonensis II., bet. Reii Apollinares and Forum Julii.

ARGENTIA I. regio (Ophir), a district of India e. Gangem, on the R. bank of Dorius fl. *Aracan.* II. a town of the Cenomanni, in Gallia Transpadana, bet. Mediolanum (12) and Pons Aureoli (10). *Gorgonzuola.*

ARGENTIOLUM, a town of the Astures, Tarraconensis, s.s.w. of Asturica Augusta.

ARGENTORATUM (Argentina, *postea* Stratæburgus, Strateburgum), capital of the Ribocci, Germania I., on the Rhine, above Saletia. One of the 50 forts built by Drusus. The seat of a prefecture. *Strasburg.*

ARGENTUARIA, a town of the Rauraci, Maxima Sequanorum, on the Rhine, L., bet. Cambe (33) and Helellum (18). *Artzenheim.*

ARGENUS fl., a r. of Lugdunensis II., separating the Boiocasses from the Viducasses, and falling into the sea E. of Grannonum, over against Carocotinum. *Arguenon.*

ARGENUS, a town of the Viducasses, on Argenus fl., towards its mouth.

ARGESIS, *postea* Ergasteria, a town of Mysia, 30 m. S. from Phemenium.

ARGESTÆUS campus, the district of Argos Oresticum.

ARGEUS sinus. *Vide* Argolicus.

ARGIBÆUM, a name of Eubœa, from the white colour of its oxen.

ARGIDAVA, a town of the Potulatenses, Dacia, under the mountains, E. bet. Aluta and (Syl.) fl. *Argisch?*

ARGIÆ, I. a town of Dolopia, Thessaly, N. of Othrys m., S.E. of Sosthenis. *Argaie.* II. ins., 20 islets bet. Rhodes and Caria.

ARGĪLUS, a town of Bisaltia, Macedonia, on Strymonicus sin., bet. Bromiscus (10) and Amphipolis (10), on Egnatia Via. An Andrian settlement.

ARGINUSA, a town of Æolis Asiat., opposite Arginusæ ins.

ARGINŪSÆ ins., 3 isl. of Æolis Asiat., 15 m. S.E. from Mitylene. Remarkable for the defeat of the Spartan fleet by the ten Athenian commanders. *Ianot.*

AGRIPPÆI (Phalacri, "*bald* heads"), a caste of priests in Scythia, of uncertain position, living upon vegetables, and deemed sacred by their neighbours. Possibly the ancestors of the Brahmins of India.

ARGISSA (Argusa), a town of Perrhœbia, Thessaly, N.W. of Larissa. *Argissa.*

ARGITHEA, a town of Athamania, on the borders of Epirus, S.W. of Ethiopia. *Gardikaki.*

ARGITA fl., a r. of the Robogdii, Hibernia, 7 m. E. from Vidua fl. *Bann.*

ARGIVI, a general name of the Greeks.

ARGIZA (Argesis, Erezii), a town of Mysia, bet. Pæmanenus (30) and Pergamus (35).

ARGOB I. a district of Bashan, assigned to the half-tribe of Manasseh; lying along Jordan fl. E. towards the Sea of Galilee. *Ergab.* II. (Raguba), its capital, N.E. of Gerasa.

ARGOLĬCUS sin., a gulf of the Ægean, bet.

Argolis and Laconia. *Golfo di Napoli* or *Nauplia.*

ARGŎLIS (Argeia), a country of Peloponnesus, bounded N. by Corinthia and Achaia, S. by Laconia and Argolicus sin., E. by Saronicus sin., W. by Arcadia. First occupied by Pelasgi from Epirus; and established as a state by Inachus, 1856 B.C.

ARGOS (Argi), I. capital of Argolis, at the junction of Inachus and Charadrus ff., 5 m. S.W. from Mycenæ; sacred to Juno. Variously surnamed Achaicum, Hippium, Pelasgicum, Poludipsion, Polupothelon, and Inachium. Founded by Argus, son of Niobe, 1711 B.C. The birth-place of Ageladas and Polycletus, the sculptors. It was here Pyrrhus was killed. *Argo.* II. a town of Nisyrus ins., on the E. coast. III. surnamed Amphilŏchicum, capital of Amphilochia, Acarnania, on Inachus fl., at the S.E. extremity of the Ambracius sin., bet. Olpæ and Crenæ, 22 m. S.E. of Ambracia. Founded by the Argive Amphilochus, son of Amphiaraus, on his return from Troy; or, according to Ephorus, by Alcmæon, brother of Amphilochus. Its inhabitants were transferred by Augustus to Nicopolis. *Neokhori, near Vlikha.* IV. Oresticum, i. q. Orestia. V. Pelasgicum, Thessaliæ, i. q. Larissa.

ARGOŬS portus, a port of Ilva ins. Named from the expedition of the Argonauts. *Porto Ferrajo.*

ARGUS I. campus, a sort of common, at Mantinea, E. of the city. II. castellum, a fortress of Cappadocia, under Taurus m., near Nora. III. fl., Salassororum, i. q. Orgus.

ARGUSTANA, a town of Cappadocia, bet. Nitazus (13) and Archelais (16). *Artan.*

ARGYNA, a town of Locris Ozol.

ARGYPHIA, a maritime town of Messenia.

ARGYRA, I. a town of Achaia, on a cognominal stream, near Boline. In ruins in the time of Pausanias. II. of Eubœa, bet. Eretria and Tamynæ. III. of Jubadii ins., at its N. extremity. IV. of Pontus, on the Euxine, 2½ m. E. from Tripolis.

ARGYRIPA (Argos-hippium), the early name of Arpi in Apulia.

ARGYRONIUM prom., a headland in Bithynia, on Bosporus Thracius, near which was the hill called the Bed of Hercules.

ARGYRUNTUM, a town of Liburnia, at the mouth of Tedanius fl., N.E. of Corinium.

ARIA, I. a region of Asia, bounded N. by Margiana and Bactriana, at Sariphi m., S. by Gedrosia, W. by Parthia, E. by India. It comprehends the Parapomisadæ and Arachosia. *Hareia; part of Chorasan*

Sedgestan, and Afghanistan. II. lacus, a lake of Drangiana, towards Carmania, formed by Etymandrus, Ophradus, and Pharnacotus fll.

ARIACA, a central district of India i. Gangem, bet. Limyrica and Mæsolia.

ARIACÆ, a people of Scythia i. Imaum, bet. the Oxus and the Jaxartes.

ARIALBINUM, a town of the Rauraci, Maxima Sequanorum, bet. Augusta Raurac. (9) and Cambe (10½). *Binningen.*

ARIANA, a region of Asia, comprehending Susiana, Parthia, Persis, Drangiana, Gedrosia, Carmania Drangiana. *Eeriene.*

ARIANI m., Hispan., i. q. Marianus m.

ARIANZUS, a village near Nazianzus, in Cappadocia.

ARIARATHIA, a town of Cappadocia, in Chammanene præfectura, bet. In Medio (25) and Coduzabala (20).

ARIASPÆ (Agriaspæ), a people of Arachosia Drangiana, on Etymandrus fl. Named Euergitæ by Cyrus, from the prompt aid they gave him in his Scythian expedition.

ARIASPE, capital of the Ariaspæ, Drangiana, on Etymandrus fl., R. *Near Pulki.*

ARICA ins., an isl. of Britain. *Sark.*

ARICHI (Arrechi), a town of Sarmatia Asiat., on Vardanes fl., R., towards its source.

ARICĬA, a town of the Latini, Latium, on Via Appia, bet. Ad Nonum (6) and Tres Tabernæ (7). A Siculian city, traditionally founded by Hippolitus Virbius, who was worshipped here. A colonia of Sylla. Noted for its leeks. Here was a temple of Diana, whose priest held his office by the tenure of superior force. *La Riccia.*

ARICONIUM, a town of the Silures, Brit., 11 m. N. of Blestium. *Weston?*

ARĬETIS FRONS prom., i. q. Cruimetopon.

ARIGÆUM, a town of India, towards Euaspla fl.

ARII, I. the people of Aria, on Arius fl. II. a tribe of Lygii, Germania.

ARIMA m., a volcanic m. of Cilicia Trachea, above Corycus. According to Strabo, the locality of Typhœus' torments.

ARIMANTHOS, a town of Cyrenaica, bet. Echinos and Philonos.

ARIMARA, Syriæ, i. q. Apammaris.

ARIMASPI, a people assigned to Scythia Asiatica, but probably fabulous; said to have had but one eye, and to have been always at war with the Gryphons.

ARIMATHEA, a town of Judæa, s.w. of Lydda. The birth-place of Joseph. *Ramleh.*

ARIMI, a people in Homer, of uncertain position; variously placed in Asia Minor, in Ænaria ins., &c.

ARĬMINUM, a city of Umbria, at the mouth of Ariminus fl., N.W. of Pisaurum. A colonia 230 B.C. It was considered the key of the E. coast of Italy. Its seizure by Julius Cæsar confirmed the civil war. *Rimini.*

ARIMĬNŬS fl., a r. of Umbria, falling into the Adriatic at Ariminum. *Marecchia.*

ARIMPHÆI, a people assigned to Scythia, towards Riphæi m. From the description, probably the same with the Argippæi.

ARINDELA, a town of Idumæa, s.s.E. of Bazrah.

ARINTHA, a town of Bruttium, near Consentia. *Rende.*

ARIOLA, a town of the Remi, Belgica II., bet. Fanum Minervæ (24) and Caturigæ. *Montgarni.*

ARIOLICA, a town of the Brannovices, Lugdunensis I., on Niveris fl., above Pocrinium. *Roure; Cartelas.*

ARIOMACIS arx, a fortress of Oxiana, Sogd., near Alexandria.

ARION m., Apul., i. q. Garganus.

ARIORICA, a town of the Sequani, in Maxima' Sequanorum, bet. Urba and Filomusiacum. *Arc sous Cicon? Pontarlier?*

ARIORUM m., i. q. Mariani m.

ARIS, I. fl., a r. of Messenia, falling into Pamisus fl., N.W. of Thuria. II. a town of Megaris, towards the coast.

ARISABIUM, a town of the Nangalogæ, India, near the source of Dorius fl., E. of Tugma.

ARISBA, I. a town of Lesbos ins., N.W. of Pyrrha. Destroyed by an earthquake. *Sumakia.* II. (Barispe) of Mysia, on Hellespont, at the mouth of Selleis fl., s.w. of Percote. A Milesian colony. Named after Arisba, daughter of Teucer. The abode of the hospitable Axylus. The scene of the great defeat of the Greeks by Prusias. *Gangerlee.*

ARISERRIA, a town of Cyrrhestica, Syria, N.W. of Zeugma.

ARISTERA ins., an isl. of Argolis, in Argolicus sin., near Pityusa.

ARISTIUM, a town of Phrygia Pacatiana.

ARISTON, Thebais, i. q. Hydreuma.

ARISTONAUTÆ, the port of Pellene, in Achaia, 8 m. from the city. Named after the Argonauts, who touched here.

ARITIUM PRÆTORIUM, a town of the Celtici, Lusitania, on the Tagus, L., towards its mouth.

ARIUS fl., a r. of Aria, rising by two sources in Parapomisus and in Sariphi m., losing itself in a lake towards Margiana. *HeriRud.*

ARIUSIA regio, the N. portion of Chios ins., especially famous for its wines. *Arvisia.*

ARIVATES, a people of Pannonia Sup., contiguous to the Azali.

ARKA, the capital of the Arkitæ, a tribe of Canaanites in Syria, 25 m. N. of Tripolis. *Arka.*

ARMA (Horma), a town of Simeon, s. of Hazezon Thamar.

ARMACTICA, i. q. Harmosia.

ARMADILLUS AGER, the district of Sarmadillum in Japygia.

ARMAGEDDON m., a name of Carmel m., or of a peak of that m. overlooking Megeddon.

ARMALAUSI, a tribe of Hermunduri, on the Danube, w. of the Narisci. *About Oberpfalz.*

ARMALIBA fl. *Vide* Naarmaliba.

ARMANNI, a people of Scythia i. Imaum, on the E. Rha.

ARMAURIA, a town of Colacene, Armen. *Anigara, Armavir.*

ARMAXA, a town of Cilicia in Cappadocia, bet. Eulepa (24) and Marandara (28).

ARMENDON ins., an isl. of Crete, N. of Sammonium prom.

ARMĒNE (Harmene), I. a port of Paphlagonia, w. of Sinope. Noted for the stupidity of its inhabitants, who walled it round to keep out the cold. II. of Pontus, bet. Prytanis fl. (3) and Pyxites fl. (8¼).

ARMĒNIA (Harim), a country of Asia, divided by the Euphrates into Armenia Major and Armenia Minor.

ARMENIA MAJOR, the E. division of Armenia, bounded N. by Iberia and Albania, s. by Mesopotamia, Assyria, and Media, w. by Armenia Minor and Pontus, E. by Albania and the Caspian. Named, according to some, from Aram, son of Shem; according to Strabo, from Armenius, a companion of Jason.

ARMĒNIA INTERIOR, a district of Armenia Major, on the borders of Armenia Minor and Pontus, N. of Sephene. *Bartshaikh.*

ARMĒNIA MINOR, the w. division of Armenia, bounded N. by Pontus, s. by Cappadocia, at Melas fl., w. by Cappadocia, E. by Armenia Major, at the Euphrates. At one period it extended N. to the Euxine; and, in the time of Ptolemy it comprised Melitene, Lavianense, and Aravene of Cappadocia. Its districts were Orbalisene and Ætulana (N.), Æretice, Orsena (Central), and Orbesine (s.) *Arabkir, Devriki, Erzinghan, and Turuberan.*

ARMENIUM, a town of Pelasgiotis, Thessaly, w. of Bæbe lac. The birth-place of Armenus, colonizer of Armenia Asiat.

ARMENOCHALYBES, a people of Cappadocia, towards Armenia Major.

ARMENTA (Armina), I. a r. of Etruria, rising in Tuniata m., and falling into Inferum Mare below Armenta. *Fiore.* II. a town of Etruria, on Armenta fl., towards its mouth, bet. Forum Aurelii and Ad Novas (7), on Via Aurelia.

ARMIANA, a town of Aria, w. of Chaurina, towards the border of Parthia.

ARMISSA, a town of Germania Magna, bet. Samulocenna and Grinario.

ARMONIACUS fl. (Armua), a r. of Africa, falling into the Mediterranean, bet. Hippo Regius and Tabraca. *Mafragg.*

ARMORICA, generally the w. coast of Gaul: specially, in the time of Pliny, Aquitania; later, the coast bet. the Sequana and the Liger, or the modern *Bretagne* and *Normandie.*

ARMORIUM, a town of the Tolistoboii, Galatia, E. of Germa. *Amoria.*

ARMOSATA. *Vide* Arsamosata.

ARMOSCLA I. a r. of Zeugitana, falling into Bagradas fl., L., above Thacia. II. a town of Zeugitana, on Armoscla fl.

ARNA, I. a town of Chalcidice, Macedonia, s.E. of Apollonia. II. of Lyciæ, i. q. Xanthus. III. of Umbria, near Tiber fl., R., 1 geog. m. E. of Perusia. *Civitella d' Arno.*

ARNE, I. a city of Phthiotis, Thessaly, near Demetrias. Founded, according to Strabo, by a colony of Bœotians, driven from their homes by the Pelasgi; or, according to Thucydides, itself the original seat of the Bœotians, who, expelled hence by the Thessalians, settled in Bœotia, B.C. 1124. II. of Bœotia, the early name of Chæronea or of Acræphia, and of Bœotia itself. III. fons, a fountain of Arcadia, ¼ m. E. from Mantinea.

ARNISSA, I. a town of Eordæa, Macedonia, E. of Cellæ. II. of the Taulantii, Illyria, on Genusus fl., L., towards its mouth.

ARNON fl., a r. of Peræa, rising on the confines of Arabia, and falling into the Dead Sea, N.w. of Rabbath Moab. The boundary—first, bet. Moabitis and Ammonitis, then bet. Moabitis and Amoritis, and, lastly, bet. Moabitis and Reuben. *Wady Mudschab.*

ARNUS, a r. of Etruria, rising in the Apennines, near Anneianum, 15 m. w. of the sources of the Tiber, and, after running by Florentia and Pisæ, falling into the Tyrrhenum mare at Portus Pisanus. *Arno.*

ARO fl., a rivulet of Etruria, falling into the sea at Fregenæ. *Aroue.*

AROANIUS (Anius, Aorus) fl., a r. of Arcadia,

rising in the m. N. of Pheneus, and falling into Ladon fl. near its source. Its fish were reputed musical.

AROCHA fl., a r. of Bruttium, falling into Scylleticus sin., N.E. of Scylacium. *Crocha* or *Crocchio.*

AROE, an ancient town of Achaia, occupying part of the site of Patræ; built by Triptolemus, and identified with his agriculture.

AROER, I. a town of Gad, in Gileaditis, on Jabbok fl., w. of Rabbath Ammon. II. of Reuben, Ammonitis, on Arnon fl., N.E. of Rabbath Moab; standing partly on an isl. of the river and partly on its bank. *Araayr.* III. of Simeon, Judæa, E.S.E. of Beerseba.

AROGARASSA, a fortress of Armenia, towards Elegia.

AROLUS, a town of Bisaltia, Macedonia, N. of Callithera. *Lakaneh.*

ARŌMATA, I. a town of Æthiopia, at Aromatum prom. II. (Arōma) of Lydia, under Messogis m., near Acharaca. Noted for its fragrant wine. III. *prius* Noticornu, a pr., the N.E. extremity of Africa, on Erythræum m., over against Dioscoridis ins. *C. Guardafui.*

AROSIS fl., I. a r. of Asia, rising in the m. of the Uxii, and, after separating Susiana from Persis, falling into Persicus sin. below Oroatis. Towards its mouth it was called Oroatis. *Tab; Rasain.* II. i. q. Araxes.

AROTHRIA, the early name of Eretria, Eubœa.

ARPAD (Arphad), a city of Syria, near Damascus.

ARPI, *prius* Argyrippa, a town of Daunia, Apulia, bet. Sipontum (21) and Prætorium Laverianum (9). Founded by Daunus, father of Diomedes, a Pelasgic chief, poetically identified with the Diomed of Homer. *Arpi.*

ARPĪNUM, a town of the Volsci, Latium, on Fibrenus fl., s.w. of Sora. The birthplace of Cicero and Marius. *Arpino.*

ARPIS, a maritime town of Dacia, above Psilon Ost.

ARRA, a town of Chalcidice, Syria, bet. Cappareas (23) and Chalcis (20). *Maarraab.*

ARRĀBO, I. (Narrabo), a r. of Pánnonia S., falling into the Danube near Arrabo. *Raab.* II. *vide* Aragus. III. a town of the Boii, Pannonia, on Arrabo fl., L., bet. Sabaria (20) and Alicanum. *Tsakany.*

ARRABŌNA, a town of Pannonia Inf., on Arrabo fl., R., near its mouth, 27 m. S.E. from Ad Flexum. *Raab.*

ARRAPACHITIS, a district of Aturia, Mesopotamia.

ARRĒTIUM (Arretium Vetus), one of the twelve cities of Etruria, near the N.E. extremity of Clusina palus, N.W. of Cortona. A colonia and municipium. Noted for its terra cotta. *Arezzo.*

ARRĒTIUM FIDENS, a town of Etruria, near Arretium. *Castiglione.*

ARRETIUM JULIUM, a town of Etruria, near Arretium. *Subliano.*

ARRHENE, a district of Armenia Major, w. of Arsissa. *Harkh.*

ARRHIANA, a town of Chersonesus Thracius, on the Hellespont, bet. Cynossema and Idacus.

ARRIACA, a town of the Arevacæ, Tarraconensis, N.E. of Complutum.

ARRIANA castra, a town of the Boii, Noric., on the Danube, bet. Canabiaca and Trigisamo.

ARRIANUS fl., i. q. Arius.

ARROSIUS fl., a r. of Lugdunensis, falling into the Liger below Bibracte. *Arrou.*

ARRUBIUM, a town of the Mœsi, on the Danube, bet. Dinogitia and Troesmis.

ARSA, a town of the Turtetani, Bætica, on Singulis fl., near its mouth.

ARSACE, Mediæ-Choarene, i. q. Apamea.

ARSACIA, Parthia, i. q. Nisæa.

ARSÆ, a people of Arabia Felix, on the Red Sea, bet. the Banizomenes and the Cinædocolpitæ.

ARSAMOSATĂ (Armosata), a town of Anzitene, Armenia, on Arzanias fl., 7 geog. m. from its junction with the Euphrates. *Randia.*

ARSANIUS fl. (Arsanias, Arsametus, Teleboas), a r. of Armenia Major, rising in Abus m., and falling into the Euphrates, L., below Arsamosata. *Ardjis, Arsen.*

ARSEN fl., a r. of Arcadia, falling into Ladon fl.

ARSENARIA (Arsinna), a town of Mauritania Cæsar., w. of Cartenna, 3 m. from the sea. A colonia. *Arzen.*

ARSĒNIUM, a town of the Arii, Germ., N.W. of Carrhodunum. *Radom.*

ARSĒSA, Arm., i. q. Arsanene.

ARSIA fl., a r. of Histria, falling into the Adriatic at Nesactum. The boundary of Italy in that direction, as fixed by Augustus. *Arsa.*

ARSICUA, a town of the Quadi, Germ., N. of Singone. *Kremnitz.*

ARSIĒTÆ, a people of Sarmatia Europ., towards the Burgundiones.

ARSINARIUM prom., a pr. of Libya, on the Atlantic, N. of Rissadium prom. *C. Corveiro, C. Bianco, C. Las Barbas.*

ARSINAS fl., i. q. Erasinus.

ARSINOË, I. a pr. of Cyprus, S.E. of Zephyrium prom. II. a city of Ætolia, on or near Cyathus fl., E. of Conope. Built by and named after Arsinoë, wife of Ptolemy Philadelphus. *Angelo Castron.* III. surnamed Epidires (Berenice, Isidisportus, Dire), a town of the Avalitæ, at Dire prom. *Assab.* IV. of Cilicia Trachea, E. of Posidium prom. V. of Cilicia Trachea, in Selinitis regio, near Jotape. VI. of Cyprus, near Ammochostos prom. VII. of Cyprus, on the S. coast, bet. Ammochostos prom. and Salamis. *Poli.* VIII. *prius* Marium, of Cyprus, on the N.W. coast, 4 geog. m. from Acamas prom. Extinct in Pliny's time. IX. of Egypt, at the mouth of Heroopolites sin. X. (Baal Zephon), *postea* Cleopatris, of Lower Egypt, at the head of the Red Sea. *Suez.* XI. *prius* Crocodilopolis, of Heptanomis, bet. the Nile and Mœris lac., S.S.W. of Memphis. Here crocodiles were worshipped. *Near Medinet el Faioum.* XII. *prius* Tauchira, of Pentapolis Cyrenaicæ, bet. Berenice and Ptolemais. *Teukira.*

ARSISSA, I. a district of Armenia Major, on Arsissa pal. N. *Turuberan.* II. pal. (Mantiana, Thospitis), a lake of Armenia Major, bet. Abus m. and Niphates m., S.W. of Artaxata, in circuit 240 m. It produced natron, and one kind of fish only. Upon its surface the heaviest substances were said to float. *Lake of Van* or *Ard-isch.*

ARSITIS, a district of Hyrcania, in Laputa m., W. of Astabene.

ARSŌPÆ, a people of Sarmatia Europæa.

ARSULÆ, a town of Umbria, near Carseoli. *Arsoli.*

ARTABRI (*Græc.* Artotrebæ), a tribe of Callæci, Tarraconensis, on the N.W. coast.

ARTABRORUM PORTUS, a bay of the Atlantic, on the coast of the Artabri, Tarraconensis, s. of Artabrum prom.

ARTĂBRUM prom. (Celticum, Nerium), a pr. of Tarraconensis, on the Atlantic, s.w. of Trileucum prom. *Cabo di Finisterra.*

ARTACANA, a town of Parthia, w. of Appha.

ARTACÆON ins., an isl. immediately contiguous to Cyzicus, in Mysia.

ARTACE, I. a m. of Mysia, over against Cyzicus. II. a fountain of Cyzicus. III. a town on Artacæon ins.

ARTACENE, *vide* Arāctene.

ARTACINA, a town of Crete. *Near Aptera.*

ARTACOANA (Astacana, Artokakna, Artalavan, Artacabane, Articaudna), capital of Aria, on Arius fl., s. of Alexandria Arion. *Dushak, near Hindmend? Nubendan?*

ARTÆI (Arteatæ), a people of Parthia S., the progenitors of the Persæ.

ARTAGĪRA, I. a town of Bagravandene, Armenia, W.N.W. of Artaxata. The deathplace of Caius Cæsar. *Artagers?* II. a town of Æthiopia, on Gir fl., S.E. of Thumelitha. *Bornu.*

ARTALBINUM, Maxima Sequanorum, i. q. Arialbinum.

ARTALESON, a town of Chorzene ; of uncertain position.

ARTAMIS, I. a town of Pentapolis Cyrenaicæ, bet. Cœnopolis and Balacræ. *Dakash.* II. a r. of Bactria, rising in Paropamisus and falling into Oxus fl.

ARTANE, a port of the Thyni, Bithynia, at the mouth of Artanes fl., 19 m. E. from Melæna prom.

ARTANES fl., a r. of the Thyni, Bithynia, falling into the Euxine at Artane.

ARTANISSA, a town of Iberia, N.E. of Surra. *Telawe.*

ARTASIGIRTA (Arsinia?), a town of Gumathene, Armenia, bet. Thospitis lac. and Amida.

ARTATUS fl., i. q. Ardaxanus.

ARTAXĂTA (Artaxiasata), *postea* Neronea, capital of Armenia Major, on the Araxes, L., bet. the s.w. extremity of Lychnitis lac. and Ararat. Built for king Artaxas, under the direction of Hannibal. Destroyed by Carbulo ; restored by Tiridates. *Tactterdat* ("throne of Tiridates") *at Artaschat.*

ARTEMIA ins., one of the Echinades ins.

ARTEMISIA ins., an isl. of Etruria, s. E. of Igilium. *Gianuti.*

ARTEMISIUM (Dianium), I. a hill of Peloponnesus, w. of Œnoe, separating in that direction Argolis from Arcadia. *Monte Mallevo.* II. of Caria, the w. extremity of Glaucius sin., 7½ m. N. from Pedalium prom. *C. Bokomadhi.* III. of Eubœa, w. of Histiæa, over against Proanna in Thessaly. Off this headland was fought one of the great battles between the Greeks and Persians. *C. Syrochori.* IV. (Ferrarium), of Tarraconensis, at the N. extremity of Illicitanus sin., over against Etusus ins. *C. Artemus. C. San Martino.* V. a Greek town of Bruttium, near Balbra. *Sant' Agata.* VI. a fortress of Chalcidice, Macedonia, at the mouth of Chabrias fl. VII. (Hemeroscopium), of the Contestani, Tarraconensis, at Artemisium prom. *Denia.* VIII. of Sicily N., at the mouth of Melas fl. Off it occurred the defeat of Sextus Pompeius by Augustus, B.C. 36.

ARTEMITA, I. one of the Oxeæ ins. *Oxia.*

II. (Chalusar, Halusar), a city of Apollo-niatis, Assyria, on Silla fl., 62 m. N.N.E. from Ctesiphon. *Shereban.* III. a town of Thospitis, Armenia, on Arsissa lac. s., above As'acana. *Van.*

ARTENA, l. a town of the Volsci, Latium, s.E. of Asculum. II. of the Veientes, Etruria, on Larus fl., L., near Sabatinus lac.

ARTENES fl., Mœsia, i. q. Utus.

ARTENIA, a town of the Carni, Venetia. *Artegna.*

ARTHEDON ins., an islet on the coast of Troas.

ARTIGI, a town of the Turtuli, Bæturia, bet. Percejana s.w. and Contosolia N.E.

ARTISCUS fl., a r. of Thrace, rising in Hæmus m., falling into Hebrus fl. below Hadrian-opolis. *Bujuk-dere.*

ARTISIGA, a maritime town of Mauritania Cæsar., near Gypsara.

ARTOBRIGA, a town of the Consuanetæ, Rhætia, bet. Bedacum (16) and Juvavia (17). *Teisendorf.*

ARTOLICA, a town of the Salassi, Gallia Transpadana, bet. Arebrigium (6) and Alpes Graia (6), on Via Aurelia. *La Tuile.*

ARTONA, Latii, i. q. Hortona.

ARTYNIA lacus, Mysiæ, i. q. Miletopolis.

ARTZES (Arzes), a town of Arsissa, Armenia, towards the E. extremity, N. of Arsissa lac. *Ardschisch.*

ARULA fl., a r. of Maxima Sequanorum, ris. towards Lacus Lausannus, and falling into the Rhine at Confluentes.

ARULIS (Arudis), a town of Cyrrhestica, on the Euphrates, N. of Zeugma. Perhaps the same with Capersana. *Bir ? Roum-kala ?*

ARULOS fl., i. q. Ascordus.

ARUMAH (Rumah), a village near Shechem. The abode of Abimelech.

ARUNCI, a town of the Celtici, Bætica, s.w. of Nertobriga.

ARUNDA, a town of the Turtetani, Bætica, on Barbesula fl., above Sæpona. *Ronda.*

ARUPENUM, a town of the Japodes, in Illyria, bet. Bilbilis and Avendum. *Near Mod-rush.*

ARUSNATI, a tribe of Euganei, in the m. N. of Verona. *In the Val Pullicella.*

ARUTELA, a town of the Burideenses, Dacia, on Aluta fl., bet. Prætorium and Castra Trajana (9).

ARVA, a town of the Turtuli, Bætica, on the Bætis, above Canama.

ARVAD (Arpad, Arphad, Aradus), capital of the Arvaditæ, on a cognominal island in the Mediterranean, 25 m. N. of Tri-

polis in Syria, over against Antaradus. *Ruad.*

ARVARNI, a maritime people of India i. Gangem, E. bet. the Sorineæ and Mæso-lius fl.

ARVERNI, a people of Aquitania, s.E. of the Lemovices. *Department of Corrèze, Haute Vienne, Creuze, Puy de Dôme.*

ARVERNUM, i. q. Augustonemetum.

ARVII, a tribe of Cenomanni, Lugdunensis III., bet. the Aulerci Diablintes and the Andes.

ARX, I. a town of the Volsci, Latium, on Melpis fl., bet. Arpinum and Aquinum. Near it was Arcanum, the villa of Quintus Cicero. *Arce.* II. BRITANNICA, a fort-ress of the Frisii, at one of the N. mouths of the Rhine, s.w. of Flevus lac. Accord-ing to some, the Pharos, built by Caligula in commemoration of his sham conquest of Britain, stood here. *T'huis Britten ?* III. CALELA, a fortress of Apulia, on the borders of the Frentani, 6 m. s.E. of Larinum. *Casa Calenda.* IV. CARVENTANA, a fortress of the Latini, on Algidus m., towards Corbio. V. TAOCHORUM, capital of the Taochi, Armenia Inferior, near Boas fl., N.W. of Andaga.

ARXAMA, Mesopotamia, i. q. Arzamo.

ARYCANDA, a town of Lycia, at the junction of Arycandus fl. with Limyrus fl.

ARYCANDUS fl., a r. of Lycia fl., falling into Limyrus fl.

ARYMAGDUS fl., a r. of Cilicia, rising in Taurus m. and falling into Aulon Cilicius E. of Anemurium. *Direk Ondessy.*

ARZAMO, I. a r. of Mesopotamia, rising in Masius m., at Mejacarire, and falling into Mygdonius fl. above its junction with Cha-boras fl. II. a town of Mygdonia, Meso-potamia, on Arzamo fl., R., bet. Horre and Macharta.

ARZENENE (Arxane, Arsane), a district of Armenia Major, N. of Arsissa Thospitis lac. *Arzen.*

ARZES (Atranutzium), a town of Armenia, towards the source of the Euphrates. *Ar-zenrum* (" Arzen of the Romans "), *Erze-roum.*

ARZUS fl. (Assus), a r. of the Odrysæ, in Thrace, falling into Hebrus fl., E. of Sub-supara. *Tchorlu.*

ASAAC (Arsaac), the local name of Nisæa, Parthia. The capital of Arsaces. (See Nisæa.)

ASABO m., a m. of Arabia Felix, on the N.E. coast, terminating in Asabon prom.

ASÆI (Asæ), Sarmatia Asiatica, i. q. Aspur-gitani.

ASAMA (Anatis, Adanis) fl., a r. of Mauritania Tingitana, falling into the Atlantic 25 geog. m. s.w. from Sala fl. *Ommirabih; Morbeya,*

ASAMON m., m. of Galilæa, near Dio Cæsarea.

ASAMUM, a port of the Encheleæ, Illyria, bet. Zizium and Epidaurus.

ASANAMARÆ, a town of India e. Gangem, near the source of Œdanes fl.

ASANCA, a town of the Sidones, Sarmatia, s.e. of Carrhodunum.

ASAS LUPERCI, a town of Syrtica Regio, bet. Martæ and Augarmi, w. of Zuchis.

ASCA, Arabia Felix, i. q. Nesca.

ASCACANCI m., m. of the Sacæ.

ASCALINGIUM, a town of the Cherusci, Germania, on Visurgis fl., L., n.e. of Teutoburgium. *Near Minden.*

ASCĀLON, a city of Judæa, one of the five capitals of the Philistines, on the Mediterranean, 12 m. s. of Gaza. Under the Romans a free city, with a magnificent temple of Venus Urania. The birth-place of Herod the Great, hence surnamed Ascalonites. Noted for its scallions (eschalots). *Asklan; Scalona.*

ASCANDALIS, Lyciæ, i. q. Acalissus.

ASCANIA, I. the country about Ascanius lac., Bithynia. II. one of the Sporades, s.w. of Thera. *Christiana.* III. a lake of Phrygia Magna, on the borders of Pisidia, n.e. of Sagalassus. Remarkable for crystallizing salt naturally. *L. Bourdour.* IV. a town of Bithynia, on Ascanius lacus.

ASCANIUS (Cius), I. a r. of Bithynia, discharging the waters of Ascanius lacus into Cianus sin. at Cius. II. a lake of Bithynia, at Cius, under Olympus m., 10 m. long by 4 wide. Its water was strongly nitreous. III. a port of Æolis Asiatica, bet. Phocæa and Cyme.

ASCAUCALIS, a town of the Burgundiones, Germania, n. of Setidava.

ASCERRIS, a town of the Lacetani, Tarraconensis, n.w. of Orgia.

ASCETÆ, a people of Arabia Felix, in Asichon Regio.

ASCIBURGIUM, I. a town of the Gugerni, Germania II., on the Rhenus, L., bet. Vetera Castra (13) and Novesium (21). Fabled to have been built by Ulysses. One of the fifty citadels constructed by Drusus on the Rhine. *Aesberg.* II. a town of the Chamavi, Germania, on Sala fl. *S. of Xanten.*

ASCIBURGIUS m., a m. of Germania, bet. the Albis and Viadrus. *Riesengebirge.*

ASCITÆ, a maritime people of Arabia Felix, s. bet. Syagrus prom. and Didymi prom.

ASCOMARCI, a people of Sarmatia Asiatica, on Mæotis pal.

ASCORDUS fl., a r. of Pieria, Macedonia, rising in Bermius m., and falling into the Haliacmon, s.e. of Beræa. *Vendjia.*

ASCRA, a town of Bœotia, on a summit of Helicon, 5 m. w. from Thespiæ. The birth-place of Hesiod. Almost extinct in Pausanias' time. *Pyrjaki.*

ASCRIVIUM, a town of the Siculotæ, Illyria, on Rhizonicus sin., w. of Vicinium. *Cattaro.*

ASCŬLUM, I. a town of Daunia, Apulia, 6 m. s.w. from Herdonia. The locality of the battle of Pyrrhus with Dentatus. *Ascoli.* II. capital of Picenum, on Truentus fl., R., bet. Ad Centesimum (12) and Ad Aquas, on Via Flaminia. A colonia and municipium. Memorable for its siege by Pompey. The birth-place of the orator Barrus. *Ascoli.*

ASCURIS, I. a r. of Pontus, falling into the Euxine, 3¾ m. n. from Rhizius portus. II. a lake of Perrhæbia, in Thessaly, n.w. of Gonnus. *Mauro Limni.*

ASDOD (Aschdod, Azotus-Paralias), I. a city of Judah, near the Mediterranean, bet. Joppa and Askelon, 16 m. n.e. of Gaza. One of the five chief cities of the Philistines, and noted for the great temple of Dagon, destroyed by Jonathan Asmonæus. *Esdud.* II. PISGAH, a city of Reuben.

ASEDO, i. q. Asindum.

ASEA, a town of Arcadia, e. of Megalopolis, 2¼ m. from Athenæum, 5 furlongs from the source of Alpheus fl. *Francobrissi.*

ASEKA, a town of Judah, Judæa, bet. Jerusalem n.e. and Eleutheropolis s.s.w.

ASERGA, a town of Chaldæa, on the Euphrates, L., bet. Dablan and Anar.

ASERIA, a town of the Hylli, Liburnia, bet. Barnum and Blandona, n.w. of Scardona.

ASFINIS, a town of Thebais, on the Nile, L., bet. Latopolis and Hermonthis. *Asfun.*

ASGILIA ins. (Tharo), an isl. of the Anaritæ, Arabia, in Persicus sin. *Scharedsje.*

ASHAN (Chorashan), a town of Judah, 25 m. s.w. of Jerusalem. Afterwards assigned to Simeon.

ASHER, I. a tribe of Israel (descended from Asher, son of Jacob by Zilpah), bounded n. by Lebanon, s. by Issachar, w. by the coast of Phœnicia, e. by Zebulun and Napthali. II. a town of Samaria, bet. Sichem and Bethsan. III. of Judæa, bet. Cæsarea and Apollonia.

ASHTAROTH (Ashteroth-Karnaim), a town of Auranitis, n.e. of Jabesh-Gilead; the capital of Bashan, with a great temple of Asta-roth (Astarte). *Mezaraib.*

ASIA, I. one of the three divisions of the world known to the ancients. Bounded N. by Tanais (or, according to Herodotus and Plato, the Phasis), the Euxine, the Bos-phorus, and the Hellespont; S. by the Oceanus Indicus; W. by the Red Sea and the Isthmus Ægypti (or, according to He-rodotus, Mela, and others, the Nile); E. by the unascertained limits of Scythia and Serica. It was divided into Asia Citerior, or Minor, and Asia Ulterior, or Magna. The name is variously derived from Asia, wife of Prometheus; from Asius, grand-son of Manes; from Asi, *Phœnicè* "inter-mediate;" from Asis, *Grœcè* "mud," in relation to Asia palus; and from the Asæ (Aspurgitani), the subjects of Wodin. II. MAGNA, Asia, E. of the Euphrates. III. MINOR, vel Citerior, the division of Asia W. of the Euphrates. Bounded N. by the Euxine, the Propontis, and the Hellespont; S. by the Mediterranean; W. by the Ægean; E. by Apsarus fl., Scydiscus m., Euphrates fl., Taurus m., and Amanus m. It comprised Æolis, Armenia Minor, Bi-thynia, Cappadocia, Caria, Cilicia, Galatia, Ionia, Lycia, Lycaonia, Lydia, Mysia, Pamphylia, Paphlagonia, Pisidia, Pontus, and Troas. Under the Romans it was divided into two provinces, Asiana and Pontica. Its population was originally derived from Asia Magna, and augmented from time to time by Iones, Pelasgi, and other tribes from Europe. *Anadoli.* IV. PALUS, marshes on Caystrus fl., in Asia Regio. Frequented by water-fowl, the property of the priests of Ephesus. V. PROPRIA (Consularis), a Roman division of Asia Minor, comprising Ephesus, Smyrna, Pergamus, and Sardes. VI. REGIO, a district of Lydia, on Caystrus fl., from its mouth towards Tmolus m. and Sardis. The Asia of Homer, which, before the time of Herodotus, had communicated its name to the entire Asiatic continent. VII. its capital, of uncertain position. Here the three-stringed harp was invented. VIII. (Isia), Bruttii, i. q. Tisia.

ASIBA, a town of Pontus, on the confines of Cappadocia.

ASICHON regio, a maritime district of Arabia Felix, w. of Syagrus prom.

ASINÆUS sinus, a name of Messeniacus sin., from Asine.

ASINĀRUS fl., a r. of Sicily, falling into Si-culum mare, bet. Abolla and Helorum. *Falconara; Fiume di Noto.*

ASINDUM, I. a town of Bætica, 5 m. s.w.

from Hispalis. A colonia (Cæsariana). II. of Argolis, on Argolicus sin., bet. Philano-rum and Phlius. Founded by Dryopes from Parnassus. *Vivares.* III. of Laco-nia, the early name of Hypsus. IV. of Messenia, *prius* Hyamia, at the E. ex-tremity of Asinæus sin., 5 m. E. from Acritas prom. A colony from Asine, Ar-golis.

ASIONGABER (Esiongeber), i. q. Berenice.

ASIONES, a people of Asia Minor, about Asium pratum.

ASIOTÆ (Jotæ), a people of Scythia e. Imaum, contiguous to the Aorsi.

ASIUS m., a hill of Laconia, on Laconicus sin. w., overlooking Las.

ASMIRÆA, a town of Serica, on Asmiræi sin.

ASMIRÆI m., a m. of Central Serica. *West Da-Uri.*

ASMURA, a town of Arsitis, Hyrcania, near Maxera fl. *S. of Bistam.*

ASNAUS m., a m. of Epirus, on Æas fl., op-posite Æropus m. *Monte Melchiovo.*

ASOCHIS, a town of Galilæa, towards Sa-maria.

ASOPIA, a district of Sicyonia, on Asopus fl.

ASŌPUS fl., I. a r. of Achaia, rising in Cæ-lossa m., N.w. of Lyrcea, and falling into Corinthiacus sin. below Sicyon. *Basilico.* II. of Bœotia, rising in Cithæron m., near Platæa, and, after separating the territories of Platæa and Thebes, falling into Euripus, near Oropus. *Asopo.* III. of Mali-ensis, Thessaly, rising in Œta m., and falling into Maliacus sin., near Thermo-pylæ. IV. of Phrygia Magna, falling into Lycus fl. near Laodicea. V. a town of Laconia, on Laconicus sin., close to Cypa-rissa, 8 m. s. from Acriæ. *Esapo.*

ASOS, an inland town of Crete.

ASPABŌTA, a town of Scythia i. Imaum, on the Caspian, N.E. of the mouth of the Oxus.

ASPACARA, a town of Serica, near Bautisus fl., towards its source.

ASPALATHIA, capital of Carnus ins., Acar-nania.

ASPALUCA, cap. of the Aspiates or Apiates, Novem Populana, bet. Forum Ligneum and Iluro (18). *Aspe, at Accous, near Pont Lesquit.*

ASPALATHOS, a town of the Dalmatæ, 3 m. from Salon. The birth-place of Diocle-tian, and the locality of his palace. *Spa-latro.*

ASPARAGIUM, a town of the Taulantii, Illy-ria, above the mouth of Apsus fl.

ASPAVIA, a town of Bætica, N. of the Bæ-tis, near Corduba.

ASPENDI portus, the port of Aspendus, in

Pamphylia, at the mouth of Eurymedon fl. Memorable for the double defeat in one day of the Persian fleet and army by Cimon. The death-place of Thrasybulus.

ASPENDUS, *postea* Trimupolis, a town of Pamphylia, on Eurymedon fl., 7½ m. from its mouth. An Argive colony.

ASPHALTITES lac. (Mare Salsum, Mare Mortuum), a lake of Palestine, formed by the Jordan, below Tiberias lac., in length 40 m., in breadth 8 m. At one time the vale of Siddim, the locality of Sodom and Gomorrah, and the three other cities destroyed with them. *Bahr-Lut*, " *sea of Lot.*" *Dead Sea.*

ASPIA fl., a r. of Picenum, falling into Miseus fl. near its mouth. *Aspido.*

ASPII, a people of India, E. of Cophes fl.

ASPIS ins., an isl. of Argolis, in Saronicus sin., over against Spiræum prom. II. (Arconnesus), of Ionia, over against Lebedus. *Carabash.* III. of Lycia, over against Cragus m. IV. a prom. of the Troglodytæ, on the Red Sea, above Diogenis prom. V. of Zeugitana, i. q. Taphnitis. VI. (Iaspis), a town of the Contestani, Tarraconensis, N.W. of Ilicis. *Aspe.* VII. of the Macæ, Zeugitana, N. of Euphranta. *Isa.*

ASPISI, I. a people of Scythia i. Imaum, inhabiting Aspisii m. II. m. of Scythia, E. of Norossus m.

ASPITHRA, I. a r. of India e. Gangem, falling into Magnus sin. N.E. II. capital of the Aspithræ, Ind., at the mouth of Aspithra fl.

ASPITHRÆ, a people of India e. Gangem, on Aspithra fl.

ASPLEDON, *postea* Eudielos, a town of Bœotia, near the N.W. bank of Copais lac., on Melas fl., 2½ m. N.E. of Orchomenus. Named after Aspledon, son of Neptune. Deserted for want of water, the Melas suddenly disappearing.

ASPONA, a town of the Tectosages, Galatia.

ASPARENUS, a m. of Mysia, near Pergamus, sacred to Cybele.

ASPRON, a later name of Ophiusa, Dacia.

ASPURGITANI (Asæ, Asturicani), a people of Sarmatia Asiatica, bet. Lycus fl. and Vardanes fl.

ASPURGIUM, capital of the Aspurgitani, Sarmatia. The Asgard of the Goths, and by them deemed the original seat of Wodin.

ASSA, a town of Sithonia, Macedonia, at the N.W. extremity of the Singiticus sinus. *San Niccolo.*

ASSA PAULINI, a town of the Brannovices, Lugdunensis I., on Arar fl., bet. Lugdunum (15) and Luna (15). *Anse.*

ASSACENI (Astaceni), a people of India i. Gangem, N.E. of Cophes fl.

ASSARIA, a port of Tripolis Afric., bet. Pisindon and Pontes.

ASSERIATES, a people of Histria, on Arsia fl.

ASSESSUS, a town of Ionia, near Miletus.

ASSHUR, the Scriptural name of Assyria.

ASSISIUM, a town of Umbria, S.E. of Arna. *Assisi.*

ASSORUS, I. a summit of Ampelus m., in Samos ins. II. a town of Anthemus, Macedonia, on Echedorus fl., below Grestone. III. of Sicily, on Chrysas fl., L., bet. Enna and Agyrium.

ASSURÆ (Oppidum Azuritanum), a town of Zeugitana, S.E. of Sicca Venerea. *Reff.*

ASSUS, I. a r. of Phocis, rising in Œta m., and falling into Cephissus fl. near Parapotamii. II. of Thrace, i. q. Arzus. III. *prius* Apollonia, a town of Æolis Asiat., above Adramyttenus sin., E. of Lectum prom. A colony from Lesbos. The birth-place of Cleanthes the stoic. A residence of Aristotle. Noted for its fine wheat, reserved for the tables of the Persian kings. Here St. Luke rejoined St. Paul after his journey from Alexandria Troas. The vicinity produced a sort of quick-lime stone, called sarcophagus, used for coffins. *Beriam Kalesi.*

ASSYRIA (Asshur, Aturia), a country of Asia, bounded N. by Armenia Maj., at Udacespes m., S. by Babylonia, at the Tigris, W. by Mesopotamia and part of Babylonia, at the Tigris, and by Armenia Maj., at Gordyæi m., E. by Media, at Choatrus m. and Zagrus m., and by Susiana at Zagrus m. Named from Asshur, grandson of Noah. *Part of Kurdistan.*

ASTA, I. a town of the Taurini, Liguria, on Tanarus fl., L., below Alba Pompeia. *Asti.* II. surnamed REGIA, of the Turtetani, Bætica, near Xera, N.W., 3 geog. m. from the sea. A colonia. *Mese de Asta.*

ASTABENI, a maritime people of Hyrcania, w. of Maxera fl.

ASTABORAS fl., the E. branch of the Nile, above Meroe, flowing from Pseboa (Coloe) lac. *Tacazze; Atbarra.*

ASTACAMPRA (Astacapra), a maritime town of Larica, Ind., S. of Papica prom.

ASTACANA (Vastauna), a town of Thospitis, Armen., at the S.E. extremity of Arsissa lac. *Ostan.*

ASTACENUS sin. (Albianus), a bay of Propontis, at Astacus, E. of Cianus sin. *Golfo d'Isnid.*

ASTACURES (Aristuriani), a people of Libya, W.N.W. of the Garamantes.

ASTĂCUS, I. a town of Acarnania, on Ionium mare, opposite Ithaca ins. *Tragameste.* II. a r. of Bithynia, falling into Astacenus sin. III. (OLBIA), a city of Bithynia, on Astacenus sin., E. above Nicomedia. Settled by colonists from Megara Nisæa 711 B.C. Extended by an Athenian colony. Nearly destroyed by Lysimachus, and its inhabitants transferred to Nicomedia.

ASTÆ, the people of Astica, in Thrace.

ASTAPA, a town of the Turtetani, Bætica, on the Bætis, R., N. of Astigi.

ASTĂPUS fl. (Abahius), the w. branch of the Nile, above Meroe. *Abawi; Bahr el Azergue.*

ASTELEPHUS fl., a r. of the Apsilæ, Sarmat., falling into the Euxine 12½ m. s. of Dioscurias. *Aksu; Mokoi.*

ASTERIA, a name of Rhodes, Delos, &c.

ASTERIS ins., an island of the Ionium mare, bet. the N.E. extremity of Cephallenia ins. and Ithaca ins., where the suitors lay in wait for Telemachus. *Didaskalio.*

ASTERIUM fl., a stream of Argolis, rising in Eubœa m.

ASTERIUM, i. q. Piresiæ.

ASTERUSIA m., a m. of Crete, near Lebena. *Astrizzi.*

ASTRAGI, a town of the Psylli, Africa Prop., on Syrtis Maj., bet. Prætorium and Putea nigra.

ASTIANENE, a district of Armenia Maj., bet. Aziris and the Euphrates. *Haschteank.*

ASTIBUS, a town of Pæonia, Macedonia, on Axius fl., bet. Tranupara (20) and Pantalia (50). *Istib.*

ASTĬCA, a country of Thrace, lying along the Euxine, N.W. of Byzantium.

ASTĬGI, I. capital of the Turtetani, Bætica, on Singilis fl. towards its junction with the Bætis. A colonia (Augusta firma). *Ecija.* II. VETUS, surnamed Juliensis, the early capital of the Turtetani, Bætica, N.W. of Antiquaria.

ASTRÆUS fl., a r. of Bottiæa, Macedonia, rising in Bermius m. w. of Berœa, and falling into the Pellæus lac. at its N.W. extremity. *Vistritza.*

ASTRAGON, a fortress of Caria, near Stratonicea.

ASTROGONDA, a maritime town of Cyrenaica, w. above Crocodilum prom.

ASTROMELA, I. a town of the Avantici, Alpes Marit., at the issue of the cognom. lake. *At Cap d'Œil.* II. a salt lake of the Avantici, in Alpes Maritimæ. *Estouma.*

ASTRON fl., a r. of Æolis Asiat., rising in Ida m., and falling into Adramyttenus sin.

ASTUIA, a town of the Viruni, Germania, s. of Alistus.

ASTURA, I. a r. of Latium, falling into the sea at Astura. Memorable for the decisive defeat of the Asturiates and other Latin tribes by the Romans. *Stura.* II. (Asturica), a r. of Tarraconensis, falling into the Durius above Ocelum. *Tuerto.* III. a town of Mysia, bet. Adramyttium and Antandros. IV. a town of Mysia, s. of Abydus; noted for its gold mines. Extinct in Strabo's time. V. of the Boii, Noricum, i. q. Cetium. VI. (Stura), of the Volsci, Latium, at the mouth of Astura fl., bet. Antium S.E. (7) and Ad Turres Albas (9). *Astura.*

ASTŬRES, a people of Tarraconensis, N.W. bet. the Cantabri N., the Vaccæi s., the Callæci w., and the Celtiberi E. Noted for their valour, and for a breed of ambling horses called Asturcones. *Part of Asturia, of Leon, and about Valladolid.*

ASTURICA fl., i. q. Astura.

ASTURĬCA AUGUSTA, capital of the Astures, Tarraconensis, on Urbius fl., L., bet. Vallata N.E. and Valobria s.w. A colonia. *Astorga.*

ASTYPALÆA, I. an isl. of the Ægean, bet. Amorgos and Cos; one of the Sporades, 88 m. in circuit. So infested at one time with hares, that the interposition of the gods was solicited to extirpate them. *Stanpalia.* II. a pr. of Attica, on Saronicus sin. S.E. of Zoster prom. *C. Anaphiso.* III. a pr. of Caria, N. of Zephyrium prom. *C. Pasha Limen.* IV. the capital of Astypalæa ins., on the N. coast. V. a fortress of Samos ins., opposite Panionium. Built by Polycrates.

ASYPHUS m., m. of Marmarica.

ATABYRIS m., a m. of Rhodes s.w. Sacred to Jupiter.

ATABYRIUM (Itabyrion). *Vide* Thabor.

ATACINI, a tribe of Tectosages in Narbonensis I., on Atax fl.

ATACINUS vicus, capital of the Atacini, Narbonensis, about 10 m. s.s.w. of Narbo. The birth-place of Varro. *Aussiere.*

ATAGIS, the local name of Athesis fl.

ATALANTA, I. an isl. of Attica, near Psyllalea ins., off Athens. *Talantous.* II. an isl. of the Locri Opuntii, in Opuntius sin., opposite Opus; severed from the continent by an earthquake. *Talanta.* III. (Allante, Allantium), a town of Emathia, Macedonia, on the confines of Pelagonia, bet. Gortynia and Europus.

ATALMO, a district of Tenesis in Æthiopia, w. of Axome.

ATARNEI, a people of Sarmatia Asiaticæ, contiguous to the Auchetæ.

ATARNEUS, a town of Æolis Asiatica, over against Mitylene. A residence of Hermias of Assus. *Near Dikheli.*

ATARBECHIS, a town of the Delta, Egypt.

ATAX (Attagus), a r. of Gallia Narbonensis, rising in the Pyrenees near the source of the Ruscino fl., and falling into the Gallicus sin. below Narbo. *Aude.*

ATELLA, an Oscan town of the Sidicini in Campania, bet. Capua (9) and Neapolis (9), on the Via Domitiana. Here the farces called Fabulæ Atellanæ were first performed. A colonia of Augustus. *Sant' Elpidio.*

ATENE, a demus of Attica, of the tribe Antiochis.

ATER m., m. of Cyrenaica.

ATERNUM, a port of the Vestini, Marrucini and Peligni, on the Adriatic, at the mouth of Aternus fl., S.E. of Hadria. *Pescara.*

ATERNUS, a r. of Italy, rising near Amiternum, and, after separating the Piceni from the Vestini and Marrucini, falling into the Adriatic at Aternum. *Pescara.*

ATESTE, a town of Venetia, on Eretenus fl. *Este.*

ATESUI (Ætusiates), a people of Lugdunensis IV., contiguous to the Segusiani. *About Atteux,* or *St. Etienne en Forêt.*

ATHACUS, a town of Lyncus, Macedonia, on the Erigonus fl., above its junction with Bevus fl.

ATHAGAI, a town of Tenesis, Æthiopia, s.w. of Pseboa lac.

ATHAMANES, an Epiriot people of Athamania. Extinct as a nation in Strabo's time.

ATHAMANIA, a district of Ætolia, N. of Aperantia, bounded w. and N. by Epirus, to which it originally belonged, and E. by Thessaly.

ATHAMANTIUM, a name of Teos in Ionia, from Athamas, the leader of the Minyæ, who colonized it.

ATHAMANTIUS campus, I. a plain of Bœotia, on the S.E. bank of Copais lac., below Acræphium. Named after Athamas. II. of Thessaly, i. q. Crocius campus.

ATHAMANTIS, the early name of Teos in Ionia, from Athamas.

ATHANA, Arabiæ, i. q. Adana.

ATHANAGRA, capital of the Ilergetes, Tarraconensis, on Cinga fl., N.E. of Osca. *Agramant.*

ATHAR m., a m. of Cappadocia, overlooking Nazianzus.

ATHAROTH, I. a town of Ammonitis, above Machærus. II. of Judæa, N.W. of Gophna.

ATHENAGURA, a town of the Pasalæ, Ind., N.E. of Talarga.

ATHENÆ, I. a town of Acarnania, founded by Athenians. II. capital of Attica, 5 m. from Saronicus sin., over against Salamis. Built by Theseus, 1234 B.C. *Athens, Setines (Es tan, Athenas).* III. of Bœotia, on Copais lac. IV. of Pontus, 10 m. N. from Condyle. V. surnamed Diades, a town of Eubœa, on Opuntius sin., over against Cynus, in Locris Op. Founded by Dias, son of Abas. *Calos.*

ATHENÆUM, a portion of Athamania in Ætolia, on the confines of Thessaly, s. of Potnæum. II. portus (Scythotauricus portus), a port of Taurica Chersonesus, 5 geog. m. w. from Theodosia.

ATHENOPOLIS, a marit. town of the Salyes, in Narbonensis II., near Antipolis. A Massilian settlement. *St. Tropez.*

ATHER prom., a headland of Cephallenia ins., on its N.W. coast, over against Leucate prom. *C. Athera.*

ATHESINUS, a r. rising in the Alpes Carnicæ and falling into Ænus fl. *Sill.*

ATHESIS (Atesia, Atagis) fl., a r. of Venetia, rising in Alpes Rhæticæ, and falling into the Adriatic below Fossis, after a course of 190 m. *Etsch; Adige.*

ATHMONIA (Athmonum), a demus of Attica, of the tribe Cecropis, S.E. of Hephæstiadæ, where Diana Amarusia was worshipped. *Marousi.*

ATHOS m., a m. of Acte, Macedonia, at the S. extremity of the peninsula; reputed of enormous altitude; 3353 feet in actual height. Traditionally named from the giant Athos. *Agion Oros; Monte Santo.*

ATHRIBIS, a town of the Delta, Egypt, on the Bubastic branch of the Nile, above Aphroditopolis, N.W. of Patumos. *Athryb; Trieb.*

ATHRIBITICUM Ostium Nili, the name of the Sebennytic branch of the Nile, towards Athribis.

ATHRITÆ, a people of Arabia Felix, bet. the Magitæ and the Thameditæ.

ATHRULLA, a town of Arabia Felix, towards Asca.

ATHRYS fl., Mœsia, i. q. Jatrus.

ATINA, I. a town of Lucania, near Tanager fl., R., S.E. of Forum Popilii. *Diano.* II. of the Marsi, i. q. Antinum. III. of the Volsci, Latium, on Melas fl., near its source, S.E. of Arpinum, under Nivosus collis. A colonia of Nero. Of date as early as the Trojan war. *Atino.*

ATINTANIA, the country of the Atintanes in Illyria, bounded N. by Apsus fl., s. by

Epirus, w. by the Adriatic, E. by Macedonia.

ATLANTICUM mare (Magnum, Occiduum, Hesperium, Exterum), the ocean washing the w. coasts of Europe and Africa. *Atlantic.*

ATLANTIS ins., according to Plato, an isl. in the Atlantic, over against Gaditanum Fretum, larger than Asia and Africa together, with smaller isl. around it. Its people held sway over Western Africa and Spain, their further conquests in Europe having been prevented by the Athenians. The isl. was submerged by an earthquake.

ATLAS, a r. of Mœsia Inferior, falling into the Danube at Sagadava.

ATLAS MAJOR m., *loc.* Dyrin, m. of Africa, intersecting Mauritania Tingitana s.w.— N.E. from about the mouth of Sala fl. to Numidia. Named by the Greeks from the Titan Atlas, and said, indeed, to be the giant himself transformed. *Atlas; Daran, Darah.*

ATLAS MINOR m., a chain of m. in Mauritania Tingit., extending parallel with its N. coast, from about Tingis.

ATMONI, a tribe of Carpi, Sarmatia.

ATRÆ, a maritime town of Daunia, Apulia, bet. Matinum and Sipontum.

ATRAX, a town of Pelasgiotis, Thessaly, on Peneus fl., 10 m. w. from Larissa. Noted for the green marble found in its vicinity, and for the magic cultivated by its inhabitants.

ATRIA, ADRIA, ADRIATICUM, &c. *Vide sub* H.

ATREBĀTES, I. (Atrebatæ, Atrebatii), a people of Gallia Belgica, s.E. of the Morini. *Pas de Calais.* II. a people of Britannia I., on the Thames s., bet. the Belgæ w. and the Regni E. *In Berkshire.*

ATROPATĒNE, the N.W. division of Media, above Amardus fl. Named from the prefect Atropates, the successful opponent of Alexander. The country of Zerdushit (Zoroaster). *Aderbeitzein.*

ATTA, a town of Arabia Felix, on Persicus sin., s. of Gerrha. *Adsjar.*

ATTABUS fl., a r. of Aurea Chersonesus, falling into Perimulicus sin., N. of Coli.

ATTACORI, a people of Serica, contiguous to the Tochari.

ATTACUM, a town of the Celtiberi, Tarraconensis, on Salo fl., L., above Bilbilis. *Atteca?*

ATTÆA, Mysiæ, i. q. Attalia.

ATTALIA, I. a city of Pamphylia, at the head of Attalicus sin., at the mouth of Catarrhactes fl., E., immediately opposite Olbia, with which, in process of time, it became

joined. Founded by Attalus Philadelphus. Hence Paul and Barnabas sailed for Antioch. *Palaia Attalia; Sattalia.* II. AGROIRA, the name given to Ægiroessa, of Æolis Asiatica, when renovated by Attalus Philadelphus.

ATTASII (Attasini), a people of Sogdiana, towards the Chorasmii.

ATTEGUA, a town of the Turtetani, Bætica, near Salsus fl., towards its source, s.E. of Astapa.

ATTELEBUSA ins., an isl. of Lycia, over against Cyprus. *Rashat.*

ATTESERRA, a town of Zeugitana, bet. Aliburus and Assuræ.

ATTICA (Atthis), *prius* Acte and Mopsopia, a country of Græcia e. Pelop., bounded N. by Bœotia, s. and E. by the Ægean, w. by Megaris and Saronicus sin. Settled by Cranai, a Pelasgic tribe under Cranaus; organized as a kingdom by Cecrops, B.C. 1556.

ATTICELLÆ, a town of Zeugitana, on Bagradas fl., R., bet. Valli and Chidibbela.

ATTICI, a town of Cyrenaica, w. bet. Tinci and Noetu.

ATTĬCITUS fl. (Anticites), a N. branch of Vardanus fl., Sarmatia Asiatica, falling into the Palus Mæotis. Noted for a fine pickle-fish (sturgeon ?).

ATTIDIUM, a town of Umbria, on Æsis fl., L., towards its source. *Attigio.*

ATTIS, a town of Palmyrene, on the Euphrates, bet. Alatis and Barbalissus.

ATTIUM prom., a pr. of Corsica, N. below Tilox prom. *Punta di Acciuolo.*

ATTUARII, i. q. Chasuarii.

ATUATUCI, a tribe of Tungri, in Germania II., bet. the Nervii and Mosa fl. *In Luttich and Namur.*

ATUATICA (Aduatica, Atuacua, Atuacutum, Tungri), capital of the Aduatuci, in Germania II., near Mosa fl., L., w.N.w. of Aquis Granum. *Tongres.*

ATUBI, a town of the Turtuli, Bætica, bet. Corduba N.N.w. and Ulia s.s.w. A colonia (Claritas Julia).

ATYRA, *prius* Poros, a town of Thrace, on Propontis, bet. Rhegia and Selymbria.

ATURES, I. a people of Novem Populana, on Aturis fl., towards its source. II. *postea* Vicus Julii, their capital, on Aturis fl., s.w. of Elusa. *Aire.*

ATURIA, I. a r. of Tarraconensis, falling into Cantabricum mare, w. of Magrada fl. ? II. a district of Adiabene, Assyria, about Nineveh. The name was sometimes applied to Assyria generally.

ATURIS fl. (Aturus), a r. of Novem Populana, rising towards Aquæ Convenarum, and falling into the sea at Lapurdum. *Adour.*

ATURNUS fl., a rivulet of the Pentri, Samnium, rising in Eribanus m. and falling into Vulturnus fl. below Falsulæ.

ATUSIA, a town of Phrygia, on Caprus fl.

ATYS fl., Siciliæ, i. q. Acithis.

AUCHA fl., a r. of the Quadi, Germania, falling into the Danube w. of Celmantia.

AUCHETÆ, a people of Sarmatia Asiatica, to vards the Asampetæ.

AUCHISÆ (Ausariani), a people of Cyrenaica, s. of the Cabali.

AUCIS (Ausciates, Ulces), in Gallia Cisalpina, i. q. Ad Martis.

AUCULA, a town of Etruria, on Pallia fl., N.E. of Saturnia.

AUDARISTUS, a town of Pelagonia, Macedonia, on Erigonus fl., bet. Stobi (12) and Alcomenæ.

AUDENA fl., a r. of Liguria, falling into the Magra. *Aulla.*

AUDIZETES, a people of Pannonia Inferior, on Dravus fl., R.

AUDUM prom., a pr. of Mauritania Cæsar., at the w. entrance of Numidicus sin. *C. Carbon.*

AUDUS, I. a r. of Mauritania Cæsar., falling into the Mediterranean at Audum prom. *Adous or Zowah.* II. (Aurasius), a ridge of m. in S. Numidia, their sides rugged, but their summits level, fertile plains.

AUFIDĒNA (Aufidenum, Aufina), I. capital of the Caraceni, Samnium, on Via Valeria, bet. Sulmo (15) and Æsernia (18). *Alfidena.* II. a town of Daunia, Apulia, at the mouth of Aufidus fl., bet. Salinæ (40) and Barduli (6). *Torre del Ofanto.*

AUFĪDUS fl., a r. of Apulia, rising in Balade m., s. of Sub Romula, and falling into the Adriatic at Aufidenum. *Ofanto.* II. of Latium, i. q. Ufens.

AUFONA (Avona, Antona) fl., I. a r. of the Cornavii, Brit. Rom., falling into Sabrina fl. above Glevum. *Avon.* II. of the Iceni, Britan., falling into Germanicus Oceanus, s.w. of Brannodunum. *Ouse.* III. of the Iceni, Britan., falling into the Germanicus Oceanus below Burgiodunum. *Waveney.* IV. of the Regni, Britan., falling into the sea towards Magnus Portus. *Wiltshire Avon.* V. a town of the Belgæ, *vide* Abone. VI. of the Iceni, on Aufona fl. *Bungay.* VII. of the Vestini, Picenum, s.e. of Prifernum. *Ofena.*

AUFUSTIANÆ, a town of the Naresii, Illyria, N.N.W. of Narona.

AUGÆ, Pamphylia. i. q. Ptolemais.

AUGALI, a people of Sogdiana, s. of the Tachori.

AUGARMI, a town of Syrtica Regio, bet. Asao Luperci and Agariabæ, w. of Zuchis.

AUGASII, a tribe of the Massagitæ.

AUGEÆ, an inland town of the Locri Epicnemedii ; extinct in Strabo's time.

AUGEMMI, a town of the Bagi Gætuli, in Libya, bet. Thabalati and Agma.

AUGILA, a city of Cyrenaica, s. of Philonos, s.e. of Aræ Philænorum. It gave the name of Augilæ to the Nasamones.

AUGINUS m., a ridge of the Apennines, N. of the Apuani.

AUGUSTA, I. a town of Cilicia Campestris, in Bryelice Regio. II. a town of the Hernici, Latium, on Anio fl., below Sublaqueum. III. of Gallia Cispadana, bet. Butrium (11) and Sagis ad Padum (12). *Salle di Agosta.* IV. AUSCIORUM, *prius* Elimberris, *postea* Ausci, capital of the Ausci, Novem Populana, s. of Lactora. *Auch.* V. CÆSAREA, Tarraconensis, *vide* Cæsar Augusta. VI. EMERITA, a town of the Vettones, Lusitania, on the Anas, below Metellinum. Appointed a colony of military pensioners (Emeriti) by Augustus. A colonia and proprætorial seat. *Merida.* VII. GEMELLA, Bætica, *vide* Tucci. VIII. NEMETUM, *vide* Noviomagus. IX. NOVA, a town of Tarraconensis, *vide* Augustobriga. X. of the Vangiones, Germania, on Hadriani Vallum, e.n.e. of Noviomagus. XI. PRÆTORIA, a town of the Burideenses, Dacia, s.w. of Pirum. A prætorian colony of Augustus. *Cronstadt; Brasson.* XII. capital of the Salassi, Gallia Cisalpina, on Duria Major fl., L., bet. Arebrigium (25) and Vitricium (25), on Via Aurelia. Founded by Augustus, on the site of the camp of Terentius Varro. *Aosta.* XIII. RAURACORUM, *postea* Rauraci, capital of the Rauraci, Maxima Sequanorum, on the Rhine, bet. Basilea (6) and Sanctio. A colonia of Augustus. *Augst; Kayser.* XIV. SUESSIONUM (Noviodunum?), *postea* Suessiones, capital of the Suessiones, Belgica II., on Axona fl., bet. Bibe and Noviomagus, N.w. of Durocortonum. *Soissons.* XV. TAURINORUM, *prius* Taurasia, capital of the Taurini, Liguria, on Padus fl., bet. Ad Octavum (8) and Ad Decimum (10), on Via Aurelia. A colonia. *Torino; Turin.* XVI. TIBERII, Vindelicia, i. q. Reginum. XVII. TREVERORUM, *postea* Treveri, capital of the Treveri, Belgica I., on Mosella fl., N.E. of Andethanna. A colonia of Augustus. The residence of several of the Roman emperors, and denominated by Ausonius the second metropolis of the empire. *Trier; Trèves.* XVIII. TRICASTINORUM, capital

of the Tricastini, Gallia Viennensis, on
Druna fl., R., bet. Dea Vocontiorum (23)
and Valentia (22). *Aoust en Diois.* XIX.
TRINOBANTUM, i. q. Londinium. XX.
ULPIA TRAJANA, i. q. Sarmizegethus.
XXI. VAGIENNORUM, *postea* Bagienna,
Baienna, capital of the Vagienni, Liguria,
s. of Pollentia. *Bene.* XXII. VEROMAN-
DUORUM, capital of the Veromandui, Bel-
gica II., on Samara fl., near its source,
bet. Camaracum (27) and Contra-Aginnum
(19½). *St. Quentin.* XXIII. VINDELI-
CORUM, capital of the Licates, Vindelicia,
on Licus fl., near its junction with Vindo fl.
A colonia of Augustus, B.C. 12. *Augsburg.*

AUGUSTAMNICA, a later name of the Egyptian Delta s.

AUGUSTANA CASTRA, a town of the Runicates, Vindelicia, on the Danube, bet. Regina
and Serviodurum (29). *Azelburg.*

AUGUSTI FOSSA, a canal in Latium, cut
from Feroniæ to Ufens fl., s.e. of Cora.

AUGUSTI TROPHÆA, an arch erected by Augustus on Alpis Maritima, above Portus
Herculis Monaci, to mark the limits of
Italy in that direction. On it were en-
graved the names of the Alpine tribes he
had subdued. *La Turbia.*

AUGUSTOBONA (Augustomana), *postea* Tri-
casses, Trecæ, capital of the Tricasses,
Lugdunensis IV., on Sequana fl., n.e. of
Agedincum. *Troyes.*

AUGUSTOBRIGA, I. a town of the Vettones,
Lusitania, s.w. of Libora. *Puente de Ar-
zobispo.* II. (Nova Augusta, Nudaugusta),
a town of the Pellendones, Tarraconensis,
bet. Numantia w.s.w. and Cæsar Augusta
s.e. *Alvea el Muro.*

AUGUSTODUNUM, *prius* Bibracte, capital of
the Ædui, Lugdunensis I., e. of Alisincum.
Famous as a resort of learning. A colonia
(Flavia). *Autun.*

AUGUSTODURUS, a town of the Lexovii,
Lugdunensis II., bet. Croneiaconnus (31½)
and Viducasses (19). *Bayeux.*

AUGUSTOMĂGUS, *postea* Silvanectes, capital
of the Silvanectes, Belgica II., on Isara fl.,
s.w. of Augusta Suessionum. *Senlis.*

AUGUSTOMANA, i. q. Augustobona.

AUGUSTŎNEMETUM (Nemossus), *prius* Ar-
verna, *postea* Clarus mons, the later
capital of the Arvérni, Aquitania I., on
Elaver fl., n. of Gergovia. *Clermont.*

AUGUSTOPOLIS, I. a town of Arabia Petræa.
II. of Phrygia Salutaris.

AUGUSTŎRITUM, cap. of the Lemovices,
Aquitania I., bet. Ad Fines (31½) and
Argantomagus (31½) w. of Augustoneme-
tum. *Limoges.*

AUGUSTUM, a town of the Allobroges, Gallia

Viennensis, on Rhodanus fl., bet. Etanna
and Vienna.

AULÆ, a port of Cilicia Campestris, bet.
Tarsus and Anchiale.

AULAHON, a town of the Psylli, Africa Prop.,
on Syrtis Major, bet. Oesporis and
Iscina.

AULÆI-TĪCHOS (Aulæi-Mœnia, Thera), a
town of Astica in Thrace, on the Euxine,
s. of Apollonia. *Rouzeh.*

AULERCI, a people of Lugdunensis III.,
comprising the A. Cenomanni, N. of the
Turones; the A. Diablintes, contiguous to
the Sesuvii; and the A. Eburovices, e. of
the Lexovii. *Dioceses of Mans and Eu-
reux.*

AULIS, a town of Bœotia, on Euripus, over
against Chalcis (3 m.), the rendezvous,
with Bathys portus, of the Grecian fleet
destined against Troy.

AULOCRENE lac., a lake of Phrygia Magna,
e. of Celænæ. Noted for its fine reeds.
The scene of the punishment of Marsyas.

AULON, I. a district of Apulia, on Galæsus
fl., L., n.e. of Tarentum. Celebrated for
its fertility. *Terra di Melone.* II. the
valley of Arethusa, in Chalcidice. III.
(Campus Magnus), the valley bet. Asphal-
tifes lac. and Tiberias lac., on the Jordan.
El Gour. IV. CILICIUS, the strait separating Cyprus from Cilicia. V. a district
of Messenia, on Neda fl., on the borders
of Triphylia and Arcadia. VI. a town of
Aulon reg., Messenia, on Neda fl., towards
its mouth. VII. a mining village of Attica, on Laurium m. VIII. a town of the
Taulantii, Illyria, at the n.e. extremity of
Aulonicus sin. *Valona.*

AULONICUS sin., a gulf of the Adriatic, s. of
Apollonia.

AUNEDONACUM, a town of the Santones,
Aquitania II., bet. Mediolanum (24½) and
Rauranum (30) w.n.w. of Sermanicoma-
gus. *Aunay.*

AUNIOS ins., an isl. of Tarraconensis, in the
Atlantic, s. of Corticata ins. *Ons.*

AURÆI, a town of Venetia, bet. Vicetia
(11) and Cadiana. *Montebello.*

AURANITIS (Hauran), a district of Peræa,
bet. Trachonitis and Gaulonitis. *Hauran.*

AURASIUS m., Numidiæ, i. q. Audus.

AUREA CHERSONESUS, I. a peninsula of
India e. Gangem, bet. Indicum mare and
Eous oceanus. *Malacca.* II. a prom. of
Aurea Chersonesus, at its w. commence-
ment, opposite Bazacata ins.

AUREA regio, a district of India e. Gangem,
on the L. bank of Darius fl. *Pegu.*

AURELIANI, I. a tribe of Carnutes, Lugdunensis IV., n.e. of the Turones. *Depart-*

ment of Loiret, and part of Cher. II. their capital, i. q. Genabum.

AUREUS m., I. m. of central Corsica, about Mora. In direction N.E. and S.E., forming an elbow. *Monte d'Oro.* II. of Mœsia Sup., overlooking Aureus m. It was planted with vines by Probus. III. a town of the Triballi, Mœsia, on the Danube, bet. Tricornium and Margus, at the foot of Aureus m. *Crozca.*

AURICORNU prom., a pr. of the Bosporus Thracius, over against Calchedon.

AURICULA, a town of the Æqui, N.E. of Tibur.

AURIGANI, Tarraconens., i. q. Autrigones.

AURINIA, the early name of Saturnia, Etruria.

AURITINA, a town of Cyrenaica, s. of Cyrene.

AURONUS fl., a r. of Dacia, falling into Parata fl.

AURU, a town of the Garamantes, Libya, bet. Vinaza and Thentei.

AURUNCA, the early capital of the Aurunci, in Latium, near Suessa Auruncorum. *Church of Santa Croce.*

AURUNCI, an Iberian or Sicanian people, settled at first in S.E. Latium, above the Ausones, and driven thence into N.W. Campania.

AUSA, capital of the Ausetani, Tarraconens., bet. Cortona w. and Secerræ E. *Vique d'Ossona.*

AUSANCALIO, a town of Liburnia, bet. Ancus and Clambete.

AUSAR (Æsar, Ausa) fl., a r. of the Apuani, in Etruria, rising in Balista m., and falling formerly into Arnus fl. at Pisæ, but now into the sea by a distinct channel. *Serchio.*

AUSARA, capital of the Ausaritæ, Arab., on the coast, N. of Syagrus prom.

AUSAVA, a town of the Treveri, Belgica I., bet. Beda (18) and Icorigium (12). *Oos.*

AUSCII, a people of Aquitania, bet. the Aturis and the Garumna. *Hautes Pyrénées.*

AUSER fl., a r. of Syrtica reg., falling into the Mediterranean E. of Zuchis.

AUSES (Ausenses), a people of Libya, towards Triton fl., who celebrated peculiar games in honour of Minerva.

AUSETANI, a people of Tarraconensis, on the Mediterranean, s., bet. the Indigetes N. and the Læetani s.

AUSIGDA (Nausida), a maritime town of Pentapolis Cyrenaicæ, bet. Ptolemais and Aptuchi fanum. *Zadra.*

AUSILINDUM, a town of the Bagi Gætuli,

Libya, bet. Berezei and Agma, under Girgiris m.

AUSIRA (Lysira), i. q. Lystra.

AUSOBA æstuar., an æstuary of the Magnatæ, Hibernia, on the Atlantic, at Magnata. *Galway Bay.*

AUSŎNA, capital of the Ausones, Latium, N. of Minturnæ. *Sonnino.*

AUSŌNES, a Sicanian people, settled on the coast of Latium, bet. the Volsci and Aurunci, long prior to the siege of Troy. Subjugated by Rome 335 B.C. Their name was poetically applied to the whole peninsula.

AUSŎNIA, a poetical designation of Italy, from the Ausones ; specially, the district about Ausona.

AUSONIUM mare, that portion of the Mare Ionium which washes the shores of Sicily E., Bruttium, and Magna Græcia.

AUSTRAGENA, a district of Parthia, noted for its naphtha.

AUSTRALIS oc., i. q. Indicus.

AUSTRAVIA, i. q. Glessaria ins., Germ.

AUSUGUM, *postea* Alsuga, a town of the Tridentini, Venetia, on Meduacus Mag. fl., bet. Tridentum (24) and Feltria (30). *Valsugana.*

AUSURIANI, a people of Africa Propria, towards Cyrenaica.

AUTACÆ, a people of Sarmatia As., towards Mæotis palus.

AUTARIĀTÆ, a people of Illyria, contiguous to the Triballi.

AUTHETANI, the Greek form of Ausetani.

AUTHIANDÆ, a people of Sarmatia Asiat., towards Mæotis palus.

AUTIPSIDA, a town of Byzacene, bet. Avula and Uzappa.

AUTISSIODORI, a people of Aquitania I., N.W. of the Ædui, about Autissiodorum.

AUTISSIODORUM, a town of the Autissiodori, and afterwards of the Senones, Lugdunensis IV., bet. Aballo (33) and Eburobrica (18). *Auxerre.*

AUTORI, a people of Hibernia, N. of the Gangani. *Galway.*

AUTOBA (Atteva), a town of the Evonymitæ, on the Nile, bet. Tasitia and Phturis. *Soleb.*

AUTOLŎLA ins., Africa, i. q. Junonis ins.

AUTŎLŎLES, a tribe of Gætuli, Libya, on Asama fl., towards its mouth. *Morocco.*

AUTOMALAX (Automala, Automalaca, Anabucis), a fortress of Cyrenaica, on Syrtis Maj., E. of Philænorum.

AUTOMATE ins. (Hiera), one of the Sporades ins., bet. Thera and Therasia.

AUTOMELA, capital of the Horatæ, Ind.. on an island. *Cochin.*

AUTRI, a people of Arabia Petræa, N. of Arsinoe.

AUTRĬCUM, *postea* Carnutes, capital of the Carnutes, Lugdunensis IV., bet. Durocasses and Suindinum. The locality of the judicial sittings of the Gaulish Druids to decide disputes among the nobles. *Chartres.*

AUTRIGONES, a tribe of Cantabri, bet. the Caristi E. and the Turmodigi W.

AUTURA fl., a r. of Lugdunensis II., falling into the Sequana at Uggadis. *Eure.*

AUZARA, a town of Arabia, on the Euphrates, bet. Rahaba and Dura.

AUZIA (Auza), a fortress of Mauritania Cæsariensis, bet. Cæsarea and Sitifis. A colonia. *Hamza.*

AUZUI, a town of the Macæ, Africa Propria, on Syrtis Mag., S. bet. Chosol and Ad Ficum.

AUGIA m., m. of Syrica. *Atai, N.*

AUXENNA, a town of the Remi, Belgica II., on Axona fl., bet. Ninittacum (13½) and Durocortorum (15). *Menneville.*

AUXIMA, ap. Florum, i. q. Uxama, Tarraconens.

AUXĬMUM (Auxŭmum), a town of Picenum, on Miseus fl., bet. Ancona and Ricina, on Via Flaminia. *Osimo.*

AUXIQUA, a town of Tripolitana, near the Cinyps, S.W. of Leptis Major.

AUZACI m., m. of Scythia e. Imaum and Serica.

AUZACIA, a town of Scythia e. Imaum, on Œchardus fl., towards its source.

AUZACĬTÆ, a people of Scythia e. Imaum, on Auzaci m.

AVALĬTÆ. *Vide* Abalitæ.

AVANTICI, a people of Alpes Maritimæ, N. of the Bodiontici.

AVARA, I. a r. of Lugdunensis II., falling into the Autura fl. below Mediolanum. II. Havarra, a town of Arabia Petræa, N.E. from Ælana.

AVARENI, a people of Sarmatia E., on Vistula fl. *About Cracow.*

AVARES, a tribe of Sarmatians settled in Germania Magna, under Carpathus m.

AVARĬCUM, *postea* Bituriges, cap. of the Bituriges Cubi, Aquitania I., bet. Condate and Alerta, on Autura fl., L., near its source. *Bourges.*

AVARPI, a tribe of Vindili, Germ., bet. the Viruni W. and the Rheudigni E.

AVARUM prom., a pr. of Gallæcia, w. of Bracara. *Cabo di Viana.*

AVATICORUM STAGNUM, i. q. Astromela.

AVEIA, a town of the Vestini, Picenum, on Aternis fl., R., bet. Prifernum (7) and Frustemæ (2). *Fossa.*

AVELDIUS fl., a r. of Apulia, falling into the sea bet. Barduli and Turenum.

AVEN, a valley of Syria, in Lebanon, 30 m. N. of Damascus. *About Baalbek.*

AVĒNIO, a city of the Cavares, Gallia Viennensis, on the Rhine, L., near its junction with Druentia fl. A Massilian settlement. *Avignon.*

AVENDUM, a town of Liburnia, bet. Arupenum and Senia.

AVENS, a r. of the Sabines, whence the name Aventinus was given to Mt. Aventine.

AVENTIA, a rivulet of Etruria, falling into Tyrrhenum mare S. of Luna. *Lavenza.*

AVENTICUM, cap. of the Ambrones, Maxima Sequanorum, bet. Minodunum (19½) and Petinesca (21). A colonia of Vespasian. (Colonia Flavia; Via Flavia.) *Avenches.*

AVERNUS lac. (Aornos, "without birds"), a salt lake of Campania, at Cumæ, communicating with Lucrinus lac. by a narrow channel; formed into a harbour called Portus Julius by M. Agrippa. It was surrounded on all sides, except at the outlet, by dark wooded cliffs, sacred to Hecate, and its depth was reputed unfathomable. Its sulphureous exhalations, fatal to birds (whence the name), occasioned it to be identified as the locality of Ulysses' descent into hell. *Lago d'Averno.*

AVERNUS specus, a cavern near Avernus lac., the cave of the Cumæan sibyl. One of the fabled entrances to hell. *Averno?*

AVES, a town of Byzacene, s. of Silesua.

AVIA fl., a r. of Arcadia, in Pheneus campus.

AVIMI (Avites, Hivites), an early people of Canaan, on the coast about Ascalon, expelled or destroyed by the Philistines.

AVIONES, a tribe of Vindili, Germ., on Albus fl.

AVIRETH, a town of Osrhoene, bet. Batnæ and Comisimbela.

AVITTA, a town of Zeugitana, bet. Bisica and Thubarbis Maj.

AVIUM, I. ins., an isl. of Arabia Felix, on Erythræum m., S.E. of Abisama. II. oppidum, Phœniciæ, i. q. Ornithonpolis. III. prom., Taprobane, i. q. Orneum.

AVULA, a town of Byzacene, bet. Leggo and Antipsida.

AVUS fl., a r. of Tarraconensis, falling into the Atlantic bet. Celadus fl. N. and Durius fl. S. *Ave.*

AXANTIS ins., an isl. of Lugdunensis III., N.W. of Gobæum prom.

AXATI (Olaura), a town of the Turtuli, Bætica, on the Bætis, above Arva. A municipium. *Lora.*

AXEIUM, a town of the Sagii, in Lugdunensis II., s. of Sagium.

AXELLODUNUM, a town of the Brigantes, Brit.,
at Hadriani murus. The station of the
Cohors I. Hispanorum. *Burgh on the
Sands.*

AXENUS, the earlier name of the Euxine,
from the " inhospitality" of its people.

AXIA, a fortress of Etruria, near Tarquinii.

AXIACÆ, I. a people of Sarmatia Europæa,
bet. Axiaces fl. and the Hypanis. Noted
for their honest simplicity of life. II.
Their capital, on the Hypanis, i. q. Olbia.

AXIACES fl., a r. of Sarmatia Europæa,
falling into Sagaricus sin., w. of the
Hypanis.

AXILIS, Marmarica, *vide* Azilis.

AXIMA, I. a town of the Centrones, Alpes
Penninæ, bet. Bergintrum (9) and Daran-
tasia (10). *Aisme.* II. of Persia, on
Oroatis fl.

AXINUM, a town of the Celtiberi, Tarraconensis.

AXIOPŎLIS, a town of Mœsia Inferior, on the
Danube, bet. Capidava and Succidava. It
was from this point, according to Ptolemy,
that the Danube was called Ister. *Ras-
sova.*

AXIUM, a town of Amphaxitis, Macedonia,
on Axius fl., 7 m. N.W. of Thessalonica.
Vardari.

AXIUM fl., I. a r. of the Damnonii, falling
into the sea below Axela. *Axe.* II. *postea*
Bardarus, of Macedonia, separating Bottiæa from Mygdonia, rising in Scardus m.,
near Scopia, and falling into the Thermaicus sin. at Chalastra. *Vardari.*

AXON fl., a r. of Caria, falling into Indus fl.,
near Calynda.

AXŎNA fl., a r. of Belgica II., falling
into Isara fl. below Augusta Suessionum.
Aisne.

AXUENNA, a town of the Remi, Belgica II.,
bet. Basilia (18) and Verodunum (25½).
Vienne la Ville.

AXŪME (Aixūme), I. a country of Africa,
s.e. of Meroe. *Tigré and part of Abyssinia.* II. its capital, s.w. of Adule, near
the source of Astaboras fl. Thence came
the celebrated obelisk, one of forty-five
originally standing there. *Axum.*

AXYLOS REGIO, "without wood," a district
of Phrygia, on the s.w. confines of Galatia.

AZA, I. a town of Armenia Minor, bet. Dra-
contes (24) and Satala (24). II. i. q.
Gaza.

AZABITIS, a district of Sarmatia Asiatica, bet.
Rhombites Major fl. and Theophamus fl.
Baschcrosch.

AZAGARIUM, a town of the Amadoci, Sarmatia, on the Borysthenes, L., above Amadoca. *Czernobol ?*

AZALA, a village of Bithynia, near Heracleum.

AZALI, a people of Pannonia Superior, under
Cetius m., s. of Vindobona.

AZAMORA, a fortress of Cappadocia, in
Cataonia Præfectura.

AZANI, capital of Azanitis, Phrygia, on Rhyndacus fl., L., towards its source, N. of
Cadi.

AZANIA, I. one of the three districts into
which Arcas divided Arcadia, extending
from Orchomenus to Alpheus fl., and
named after his son Azan. II. a maritime
country of Ethiopia, s. of Egypt. *Zanguebar; Ajan.*

AZANITIS, a district of Phrygia Epictetus,
N.W.

AZANIUM mare, that portion of the Oceanus
Indicus which borders Azania.

AZANIUS fons (Clitorius), a fountain at Clitor
m., Arcadia, sacred to Cybele, the waters
of which created a distaste for wine.

AZANUS fl., a r. of Taprobane, falling into
the sea bet. Odoca and Nabarta.

AZARA, I. a town of Armenia Major, on the
Araxes. II. *potius* Zara (Urzan, Ram Or-
muz), of the Elymæi, Susiana, on Hedyphon
fl., with a temple of Zara (Diana). III. of
the Themeotæ, Sarmatia Asiatica, on
Mæotis pal., at the mouth of Theophanius fl.

AZARABA, a town of the Tyrambæ, Sarmatia
Asiatica, on Rhombites fl., L., towards
its mouth.

AZARI portus, a port of Bithynia, on Bosporus Thracius, at the N. mouth of Azaritia
fons.

AZARITIA fons, a stream of Bithynia, falling
into Bosporus Thracius at Nicopolis. It
was said to contain crocodiles.

AZAUM, a town of Valeria, Pannonia, on the
Danube, above Acincum.

AZEKAH, a town of Judah, 12 m. E. of Bethlehem, where the Amorites were destroyed
by hailstones.

AZEM, a town of Simeon.

AZENIA, a demus of Attica, of the tribe
Hippothoontis, on Saronicus sin., w. of
Sunium prom. *Alegrana.*

AZĒTIUM, a town of Peucetia, N.E. of Grumum.

AZIBINTHA ins., one of the Sporades ins.

AZILIS (Naxilis, Naziris, Axilis), a port of
Pentapolis Cyrenaicæ, bet. Chersonesus
Magna and Darnis.

AZIRIS, I. a district of Armenia Inferior, on
Pyxirates fl., L. *Arhind.* II. (Ereza),

its capital, on Pyxirates fl., towards its junction with Lycus fl. III. *vide* Basgædariza.

AZIZIS (Ahihis, Aixi), a town of the Potulatenses, Dacia, 12 m. N. from Bersovia.

AZOCHIS, a town of the Absidri, Assyria, N.W. of Ecbatana.

AZONES, a people of Central Assyria, E. under Choatrus m.

AZŌRUS, a town of Pelagonia Tripolis, Thessaly, bet. Doliche and Oxynia (15). *Vuvula.*

AZOTA, a town of Colchis, S.E. of Apasida.

AZŌTUS, Syriæ, i. q. Asdod.

AZURITANUM OPPIDUM, Byzacene, i. q. Assura.

B.

BAAL-BEK, the local name, "City of the Sun," of Heliopolis, Phœnicia.

BAAL-GAD, i. q. Baal-Hermon.

BAAL-HERMON (Baal-Gad), a town of Galilæa, under Hermon m., E. of Sarepta.

BAAL-MEON (Beth-Meon, Beth-Baal-Meon), baths of Reuben, 9 m. s.w. from Heshbon.

BAAL-PERAZIM, a village of Rephaim Vallis, s.w. of Jerusalem.

BAAL-ZEPHON, "northern light-house," the scriptural name of Arsinoe-Cleopatris, Egypt.

BABA (Hileja, Eleju), a town of Mygdonia, Mesopotamia, bet. Thebeta and Singara.

BABANOMUS (Bamonitis), a district of Galatia, on Halys fl., R.

BABBA, a town of Mauritania Ting., 40 m. s.E. from Lixus, under Atlas Minor. A colonia of Augustus (Julia Campestris). *Bani Teude.*

BABỸLON (Babel, Sheshach), I. capital of Babylonia, on both sides of the Euphrates, s.w. of Seleucia. Founded by Belus, 247 B.C.; enlarged by Semiramis. Here was the tower of Babel, a temple of Belus (*Birs Nemrood*). II. *postea* Fostat, a town of Lower Egypt, on the Nile, R., s.E. of Cercasorum. *Old Cairo; Musr el Ateekeh.*

BABYLONIA, a country of Asia, bounded N. by Mesopotamia, at Medius murus, and by Assyria at the Tigris; s. by Persicus sin. and Arabia; w. by Arabia Deserta; and E. by the Tigris. *Irak Arabi.*

BABYRSA, a fortress of Armenia, near Artaxata.

BABYTACA, Susiana, i. q. Badaca.

BACA, I. a fortress of Cilicia. II. a town of the Jazyges Metanastæ, N.W. of Acimincum. III. of Mauritania, i. q. Vaccæ.

BACARI, a town of India i. Gangem, w. at the mouth of Barius fl., bet. Podoperura and Melinda. *Calicut.*

BACAS-CHAMIRI, a town of the Zamareni, Arabia, N.E. of Aramana. *Svica-Shamary.*

BACASIS, a town of the Ausetani, Tarraconensis, on Rubricatus fl., L., N.E. of Selensis. *Baga.*

BACATAILLI, a town of Cassiotis, Syria, E. of Laodicea. *Bellulca; Bahhlulie.*

BACCANÆ, a town of Etruria, on Via Cassia, bet. Veii (9) and Sutrium (12). *Baccano.*

BACCHI urbs, a town of Taprobane, N.E., at the mouth of Baracus fl., bet. Bocana and Cytæum prom.

BACCHIA, a town of Albania, w. of Sanua.

BACĒNIS silva, the portion of Hercynia silva bet. the Cherusci and the Catti.

BACHETIUM (Bucenta), a fortress of Cassopæia, at the E. extremity of Acherusia palus. *Castri.*

BACHILITÆ (Anchitæ), a people of Arabia, towards the s.E. coast, E. of the Kithebanitæ. *Tribe of Beni Kahtany.*

BACHIS, a town of Heptanomis, on Mœris lac. E.

BACTRA, capital of Bactria, on Bactrus fl., N.W. of Aornos. *Balkh.*

BACTRIA (Bactriana), a country of Asia, bounded N. by Sogdiana, at Oxus fl.; s. and E. by Aria, at Parapomisus m.; and w. by Margiana. *Balkh.*

BACTRUS fl., I. Armeniæ, i. q. Araxes. II. (Dargidus), a r. of Bactria, falling into Oxus fl. below Bactra. *Balkh; Dehasch.*

BACUATES, a people of Mauritania Tingit., s. of Atlas Min., w. of the Macanitæ.

BACUNTIUS fl., a r. of Pannonia Inferior, falling into Savus fl. at Sirmium. *Bossut.*

BADACA (Babytacæ), a town of the Cossæi, Susiana, on the Eulæus, under Cossæi m.

BADACUM, i. q. Bedajum.

BADARA, a town of Gedrosia Pardene, s.w. of Cottobara.

BADATIUM, a town of Taurica Chersonesus, N.E. of Satarche.

BADEA REGIA (Vadea), a town of the Cinædocolpitæ, Arabia, on the Red Sea, s.w. of Macolaba, of which it was the port. *Ras Bad.*

BADERA, a town of the Volcæ Tectosages, Narbonensis I., s.E. of Tolosa, bet. Ad Novum and Ad Vigesimum. *Basiege.*

BADIA, a later name of Pax Augusta.

BADIAMÆI, a people of India i. Gangem, on Tyndis fl., R., towards its mouth.

BADIAS, a town of Numidia, bet. Audus m. and Palladis lac., w. of Ad Majores.

BADIS, I. a town of Carmania, at Carpella

prom. II. of Etruria, i. q. Vicus Badies.

BADIZA, Bruttii, i. q. Besidiæ.

BADUHENNA lucus, a sacred grove of the Frisii, Germania, bet. Flevus lac. and the sea.

BÆA m., a m. on the w. coast of Cephallenia, bet. Pale and Taphos. Named after Bæus, the steersman of Ulysses.

BÆBE, I. a town of Caria. II. of Crete, near Gortys.

BÆBERDON, a town of Cappadocia.

BÆCOR, a town of Spain.

BÆCULA, I. a town of the Ausetani, Tarraconensis, on Alba fl., L., above Gerunda. II. of Bætica, N. of Baniana.

BÆLO, I. a r. of Bætica, falling into the Atlantic near Bæsippo. *Barbate.* II. a port of Bætica, E. of Bælo fl. A colonia. *Balonia.*

BÆNUM, Arabia, i. q. Catabanum.

BÆONES ins. (Barace), an isl. of Larica, India, S. of Barygazenus sin. *Peram.*

BÆSIPPO, a port of the Turtetani, Bætica, bet. Junonis prom. w. and Bælo E. *Vejer.*

BÆTANA, a city of Ariaca, India, 50 m. S.E. from Omenogara. *Beder.*

BÆTERRÆ (Beterræ, Blitarra), *surnamed* Septimanorum, a town of the Tectosages, Narbonensis, bet. Cessero and Narbo, on Orbris fl., L. A colony of the 7th legion. *Bezières.*

BÆTICA (Turtitania), a division, by Augustus, of Hispania Ulterior, separated from Lusitania by Anas fl., and from Tarraconensis by a line from Portus Magnus, at Murgis s. to Ilucia N. Named from the Bætis. *Andalusia, and parts of Alemtejo, Estremadura, and La Mancha.*

BÆTIS (Perkis) fl., *prius* Tartessus, a r. of Hispania, Bætica, rising in Tugiensis saltus, near Tugia, and falling into the Atlantic by two mouths, the N.W. at Tartessus, the S.E. above Gades. *Guadalquivir (Arabicè, Wad el Kebir, " great river ").*

BÆTIUS, I. a r. of Arabia Felix, falling into the Red Sea, 1 m. N. from Badei. *Bardili.* II. a m. of Asia, dividing Gedrosia from Arachosia.

BÆTULO fl., a r. of Tarraconensis, falling into the Mediterranean w. of Bætulo. *Besos.* II. a town of the Læetani, Tarraconensis, on Bætulo fl., N.E. of Barcino. *Badalona.*

BÆTURIA, the N.W. district of Bætica, bet. the Anas and Marianus m.

BAGA, i. q. Vaga.

BAGĀCUM (Baganum, Basiacum, Bavacum), the early capital of the Nervii, Belgica II., bet. Camaracum (27) and Vodgoriacum (18). *Bavay.*

BAGADAONIA, a district of s. Cappadocia, under Taurus m.

BAGÆ, a town of the Massagetæ, Sogdiana, N. of Tribactra.

BAGAZE, a port of Libya Int., N. of Soloentium prom.

BAGE, a town of Lydia, on Hermus fl., R., above Attalia.

BAGISARA, a port of the Ichthyophagi, Gedrosia, bet. Calyba and Malana.

BAGISTĀNA, a town of Media, S.E. of Ecbatana. Upon a rock here are figures and cuneiform inscriptions, illustrative of the victories of Darius Hystaspes. *Behistun.*

BAGISTANUS m., a m. of Media, at Bagistana, sacred to the Bagas (gods of Media).

BAGOUS m., m. intersecting Aria N.W. and extending into Arachosia S.E. *Gaur.*

BAGRADAS fl. (Bagadras, Braca), I. a r. of Africa, rising in Numidia, E. of Justis, and falling into the Mediterranean at Utica. On its banks occurred the adventure of the army of Regulus with the serpent. *Medscherda; Brada.* II. of Agizymba, Africa, losing itself in the sands. *Wad el Mezzeran.* III. of Asia, falling into Persicus sin., E. of Apostana. The boundary of Persis Prop. and Carmania. *Divrud.*

BAGRAVANDENE, a district of Armenia Major, bet. the Araxes and the Euphrates, w. of Ararat. *Bagrevend.*

BAGRUM, a town of Lycaonia, bet. Tolistochorium and Vetestum.

BAHAREIN ins., an isl. of Arabia Felix, S.E. of Gherra.

BAHURIM, a city of Benjamin, E. of Jerusalem.

BAIÆ, I. a town of Cilicia Campestris, on Issicus sin., s. of Issus, 16 m. from Castabolum. *Bayas.* II. baths of Campania, on Puteolinus sin., N. of Misenum. Named from Baius, a companion of Ulysses. Sacred to Venus. *Baia.*

BAINIS fl., Callæcia, i. q. Minius.

BAIOCASSES, I. (Badiocasses), a tribe of Lexovii, Lugdunensis II., E. of the Unelli. *In Le Bessin.* II. *prius* Augustodurus, their capital, i. q. Augustodurum.

BAJOBARI, i. q. Bojoarii.

BALA (Bada, Valla), a town of Pieria, Macedonia, 7 m. w. from Olympus. *Servitza.*

BALACRÆ, a town of Pentapolis Cyrenaicæ, bet. Cyrene and Artamis.

BALAGAIA, a town of Arabia, on the Euphrates, above Belesi.

BALANÆA, a town of Cassiotis, Syria, on the Mediterranean, bet. Paltus (8) and Carnus, 74 m. N. from Tripolis.

BALANSTRA, a town of the Triballi, Mœsia, bet. Translitæ and Meldia.

BALARI, a people of Sardinia, bet. the Corsii and the Cunustani.

BALARUM, a haven of Bruttium, towards Scylla.

BALBIA, a town of Bruttium. *Altomonte.*

BALBURA, a town of Lycia, near Cibyra.

BALCEA, a town of Mysia. *Bali-Kesri.*

BALEĀRES ins. (Balearides, Gymnasiæ, Chæ-arades, Chærades), two isl. of Tarraconensis, N.E. of Pityusæ ins. Named from the skill of the inhabitants with the sling. *Majorca and Minorca.*

BALEPATNA, a port of Ariaca, India, s. of Simylla prom. *Terrapur.*

BALETIUM (Valetium), a maritime town of Calabria, bet. Pactius fl. (10) and Lupia (15). *San Pietro Vernotico.*

BALISTA m., a summit of the Apennines, in Liguria, N.W. of Letus m. *Mt. Balistra.*

BALLATHA, Mesopotamia, i. q. Balnæ.

BALNEUM REGIS, baths of Etruria, S.E. of Vulsinii. *Bagnara.*

BALOMUM, a port of Gedrosia, 50 m. from Barna.

BALONGA, a port of Aurea Chersonesus, near Thagora.

BALSA, a town of the Cuneus, Lusitania, bet. Cuneum prom. and Esuris (24). A municipium. *Tavira.*

BALTIA ins., i. q. Abalus.

BALYRA fl., a r. of Messenia, falling into the Pamisus. Named from the lyre of Thamyris. *Mauro-Zoumena.*

BALZANUM, a town of the Tridentini, Rhætia, on Athesis fl., below its confluence with the Atagis. *Bolsano; Botzen.*

BAMBALA, a port of India i. Gangem, w. bet. Cottiara and Comaria prom. (10.) *Manpoly.*

BAMBOTUS fl., of Libya, i. q. Nia.

BAMBYCE, Syria, a second Greek name of Hierapolis.

BANA, Arabia, i. q. Catabana.

BANACHATH, a town of Arabia Deserta, towards Persicus sin. The seat of the children of Nahath.

BANASA, a town of Mauritania Tingitana, on Sudus fl., L., 50 m. s. of Lixus. A colonia of Augustus (Valentia). *Mahmora.*

BANATIA, a town of the Caledonii, Brit., w. of Victoria.

BANAVASI, a town of Ariaca, Ind., s.w. of Omenogara. *Puna.*

BANDOTIĒNE, a district of India i. Gangem, on Choaspes fl.

BANDRITUM, a town of the Senones, Lugdunensis IV., bet. Autissiodorum s.w. and Eburobrica N.W.

BANIANA, a town of the Turtuli, Bætica, N.E. of Illiturgis.

BANIURÆ, a tribe of Gætuli, in Mauritania Cæsariensis, on Siga fl., towards its source.

BANIZŎMĔNES (*i. e.* Beni Zomran), a people of Arabia Felix, on the Red Sea, N. of the Arsæ. The descendants of Zimran, son of Keturah. *Tribe of Beni Omran.*

BANNAVANTA (Bennavenna), a town of the Catavellauni, Maxima Cæsariensis, 17 m. s.E. from Venonæ. *Daventry.*

BANNOMANNA ins. (Bantomanna), i. q. Rauronia.

BANTIA, I. capital of the Callicæni, Illyria, on Genusus fl., bet. Cerax and Deboma. II. a town of Lucania, 6 m. w.n.w. from Silvium. The death-place of Marcellus. *Vanza.*

BANUBARI, a people of Arabia Felix, on the Red Sea, about Charmothus, N.W. of the Arsæ.

BAPHYRUS fl., Maced., i. q. Helicon.

BAPTANA, capital of Cambadene, Media, s.w. of Ecbatana. *Near Kirmanschah.*

BARA, I. an æstuary of Britain. *Murray Frith.* II. (Pharos), an isl. of Calabria, over against Brundusium.

BARABA. *Vide* Taraba.

BARACA, a maritime town of Albania, N. of Cyrus fl. *Pakovan.*

BARACE, I. an isl. of India, i. q. Bæones. II. a bay of Indicus Oceanus, at Barace ins. *Gulf of Cambay W.*

BARACUM, a town of Phazania, N.W. of Saba.

BARACURRA, a port of Cirrhadia, India, s. of Catabeda fl.

BARACUS fl., a r. of Taprobane, falling into Indicus Oceanus at Bacchi urbs.

BARAMALCUM, Arab., i. q. Mariaba.

BARANGE, a town of Hyrcania, N.E.

BARAXMALCHA, a town of Mesopotamia, on the Euphrates, s. of Olabus.

BARATHA (Barate), a town of Lycaonia, bet. Iconium (50) and Tyana (39). *Bore?*

BARATHRA, i. q. Sirbonis palus.

BARBA, a town of the Turtetani, Bætica, N.E. of Teba.

BARBALISSUS, a town of Chalybonitis, on the Euphrates, bet. Attis and Eragiza. The residence of the satrap Baleses. *Balés.*

BARBANA fl., a r. of the Labeates, Illyria, rising in Scordus m., and, after passing through Labeatis palus, forming below Scodra, with Clausula fl., the r. Oriuns. *Moracca.*

BARBARIA, i. q. Azania.

BARBARIANA, I. a town of the Turtetani. Bætica, on the Mediterranean, N. of Calpe (10). II. of the Berones, Tarraconensis, near Lumberita.

BARBARICINI, a maritime people of Sardinia, bet. the Æsaronenses N. and the Salsitani s.

BARBARICUM EMPORIUM, a town of India i. Gangem, at the mouth of the Nile. *Debil, Divl-Sind.*

BARBARIUM, I. prom., a pr. of Lusitania, s. of Magnum prom. *Cabo de Espichel.* II. sin., the portion of Indicus Oceanus on the coast of Barbaria (Azania). *Gulf of Zanguebar.*

BARBESULA, I. (Chrysus), a r. of Bætica, falling into the Mediterranean at Barbesula. *Guadiaro.* II. a port of Bætica, E. above Barbariana. *Torre Guadiaro.*

BARBOSTHENES m., a summit of Menelaium m., Laconia, at Xarax.

BARCÆI (Barchitæ), a people of Cyrenaica, about Barce.

BARCANI, a people of Parthia, on the borders of Hyrcania.

BARCE, I. capital of the Barcæi, Cyrenaica, s.w. of Cyrene. Enlarged B.C. 560, by Greeks from Cyrene. *Merdsjeh.* II. prom. a pr. of Cyrenaica, at Ptolemais.

BARCĬNO (Barchino), capital of the Laletani, Tarraconensis, on the sea, s. of Prætorium. Founded by Hamilcar Barcas, 235 B.C. A colonia (Faventia). *Barcelona.*

BARDA? a town of Drangiana, on Etymandrus fl., R., above Palacenti.

BARDERATE, a town of Liguria, on the Padus, at the confluence of Duria fl. *Verrua.*

BARDINES, Phœnicia, the local name of the Chrysorrhoas.

BARDOARA, a town of the Doani, Ind., on Doanas fl., above Berabe.

BARDULUM, a maritime town of Apulia, on Via Frentana, bet Aufidus fl. (6) and Aveldius fl. (9). *Barletta.*

BAREA, a town of the Bastitani, Tarraconensis, N.E. of Urci.

BARENE, a town of Media Magna, bet. Phraasa and Ecbatana.

BARGĂSA, a town of Caria, on Ceramicus sin., E. of Ceramus. Founded by Bargasus, s. of Hercules and Barge.

BARGULUM, a fortress of the Parthini, Illyria.

BARGUS (Birgus) fl., I. a r. of Hibernia s., falling into the Atlantic N. of Dabrona fl. *Barrow.* II. of Thrace, falling into the Hebrus.

BARGUSI, i. q. Bergusii.

BARGYLIA (Andanus), a town of Caria, on Jassicus sin., N.E. of Caryanda. Built by Bellerophon. The birth-place of Protarchus the Epicurean. Noted for a statue of Diana, exempt from moisture.

BARGYLIACUS sin., Cariæ, i. q. Jassicus.

BARGYLUS m., a m. of Phœnicia, towards Arca fl.

BARIANA, a town of Mesopotamia, bet. the Tigris and the Saocoras.

BARIS, I. a town of Calabria, i. q. Veretum. II. of India, N. of Sagalassus. *Isbarteh.* III. a ridge of Taurus, in Armen. Major, E. of Abus m. *Varaz.*

BARISBE (Bares), Mysiæ, i. q. Arisbe.

BARIUM, a maritime town of Peucetia, on Via Egnatia, bet. Butuntum (11) and Turris Julianæ (11). A colony from Bæra ins. A municipium. *Bari.*

BARIUS fl., a r. of India i. Gangem, the s. limit of Limyrica. *Peraru.*

BARNA, a port of Gedrosia, 70 m. E. of Cophas.

BARNACIS, a town of the Celtiberi, Tarraconensis, bet. Parietinum s.w. and Salticum N.

BARNICHIUS fl., i. q. Enipeus, Thessal.

BAROMACUS, Britannia, i. q. Cæsaromagus.

BARNUS, Macedonia, i. q. Arnissa.

BARRA, the early capital of the Orobii, Gallia Cisalp., bet. Comum and Bergomum. Extinct in Pliny's time. *Barra Vico.*

BARRUS m., a m. of the Orobii, at Barra. *Monte di Barra.*

BARSA ins., an isl. of the Cangi, Britannia II., s. of Canganorum prom. *Bardsey.*

BARSACUM, Sarmatia, i. q. Sarbacum.

BARSITA, i. q. Barsippa.

BARUSSÆ ins., isl. of India e. Gangem, parallel w. with Bonæ Fortunæ ins. Inhabited by Anthropophagi.

BARYGAZA, a port of India e. Gangem, on Barygazenus sin., 7 m. from the mouth of Namadus fl. *Baroatsch.*

BARYGAZENUS sin., a bay of Indicus Oceanus, at Barygaza. *Gulf of Cambay E.*

BARZALA (Barsalium), a town of Commagene, on the Euphrates, 8 geog. m. s.e. from Claudias. *Bersel.*

BASACOTES, i. q. Vasates.

BASAGI (Abissagi), a port of the Omanitæ, Arabia, s.w. of Corodamum prom. *Bassœs.*

BASANARÆ, a people of India e. Gangem, on Doanas and Lanos fl., N. of Chalcitis regio.

BASANITES m., a m. of Egypt, bet. Syene and Berenice. Named from its quarries of touch-stone (basanite). *Om Kerrebeh.*

BASANTE (Basiana), a town of Pannonia Inferior, on Savus fl., R., bet. Mursonia and Saldis.

BASAROPEDA, a district of Armenia Interior, N., above Theodosiopolis.

BASCATIS fl., a r. of Sogdiana, falling into the Jaxartes. *Fersan.*

BASCISI m., m. of Africa, separating Cyrenaica and Marmarica from Libya Int.

BASGÆDARIZA (Agiris, Eriza), a fortress of Armenia Minor, s.e. of Satala. Built by Mithridates. *Bakorey.*

BASHAN, *postea* Batanea, a country E. of Jordan, extending from Hermon m. to the m. of Gilead, S. On the defeat of its king, Og, it was assigned to the half tribe of Manasseh.

BASI, a town of the Bogistani, Tarraconensis, N. of Bergidum.

BASILIA, I. a town of the Rauraci, Germania I., on the Rhine, above Cambete. Built by Valentinian I. *Basle.* II. of Mesopotamia, on the Euphrates, bet. Maguda and Allan. III. of the Remi, Belgica II., bet. Durocortorum N.W. and Fanum Minervæ.

BASILICA, I. a town of Mauritania Cæsar., bet. Choba and Sitifis. II. surnamed Diadumene, of Numidia, bet. Lambæsa and Symmachi.

BASILICÆ (Basilidæ), Sarmatia, i. q. Scythæ Regii.

BASILINOPOLIS, Bithynia, i. q. Mytheopolis.

BASILIPOTAMUS fl., i. q. Eurotas.

BASILIPPUM, a town of the Turtetani, Bætica, on the Anas, bet. Carmara N.N.E. and Hispalis S.W. *El Biso.*

BASILIS, a town of Arcadia, on the Alpheus. Founded by Cypselus. *Kuparissia.*

BASILISENE, a district of Armenia Major, towards the source of the Araxes. *Vagharschavan.*

BASSÆ, a town of Arcadia, at the foot of Cotylius m. From the Temple of Apollo Epicurius here, came the friezes in the British Museum of the battle with the Amazons and the battle of the Centaurs and Lapithæ. *Le Colonne.*

BASSANIA, a town of the Taulantii, Illyria, on Mathis fl., S.E. of Acrolissus.

BASSI, Galliæ, i. q. Hassi.

BASSIANA, I. a town of the Boii, Pannonia, on Arrabo fl., L., bet. Mursella and Sabaria (18). *Sarvar.* II. of Pannonia Inferior, on Savus fl., 12 m. from Novicianum. *Near Dobrinu.*

BASTA, a town of the Sallentini, Japygia, S. of Sallentia. *Vaste.*

BASTARNÆ, a people of Sarmatia Europ., on Hypanis fl., bet. Tyra fl. and Tanais fl.

BASTIA (Mentesa Bastia), capital of the Bastitani, Tarraconensis, N.E. of Acci. *La Guardia? Baza.*

BASTITANI, a people of Bætica and Tarraconensis, N.E. of the Bastuli.

BASTERBINI, the people of Basta in Japygia.

BASTULI (Bætuli), a mixed population of Spaniards and Phœnicians, occupying the coast of Bætica, bet. Junonis prom. and Magnus portus.

BATÆ, a people of Serica, S. of the Aspacaræ.

BATANA, a district of Osrhoene, Mesopot., S. of Anthemusia.

BATANÆA, generally Bashan; specially, a district of Decapolis, S. of Trachonitis.

BATAVA CASTRA, a town of the Runicates, Vindelicia, on the Danube, at the mouth L. of Œnus fl. Named from the Cohors Batava. *Passau.*

BATAVI, a people of Germania II., on both banks of the Rhine, towards its mouth.

BATAVORUM ins., I. the insulated country at the mouths of the Rhine and Vahalis, occupied by the Batavi. II. oppidum, a town of the Batavi, Germania II. *Batenberg.*

BATAVODURUM, a town of the Batavi, on Mosa fl., 21 m. w. from Arenatium. *Wykby-Duurstede.*

BATE, I. a demus of Attica, of the tribe Ægeis. II. (Pagra), a port of the Toreatæ, Sarmat., on the Euxine, 50 m. S.E. from Sindicus portus. *Zudzuk Kale.*

BATHIA, i. q. Pax Augusta.

BATHINUS fl., a r. of Pannonia.

BATHOS, a place in Arcadia, near Alpheus fl., 1½ m. from Basilis. The locality of the mysteries of the Great Goddesses.

BATHNÆ (Batnæ), I. (Bithias, Corea Bathæ, locally Zarug), capital of Batana, Osrhoene, bet. Edessa and Hierapolis S.W. Here a great fair for Indian and Chinese goods was held in September. *Serondjse.* II. (Baina), a town of Cyrrhestica, bet. Hierapolis N.E. (18) and Beræa W.S.W. (54). *Basbe.*

BATHURA, Phœnicia, i. q. Ecbatana.

BATHYLLUS fons, a fountain of Megalopolis, Arcadia, falling into the Helisson.

BATHYS fl., I. of Phrygia, i. q. Tymbris. II. of Pontus, i. q. Acampsis. III. of Sicily, falling into Segestanus sin., bet. Parthenicum and Segestanum Emporium. *Jati.* IV. portus, the S. port of Aulis, in Bœotia. *Vathi.* V. a port of the Troglodytæ, on the Red Sea, N. of Dioscoron portus. *Arecca.*

BATI, a maritime people of India i. Gangem, E., on the S. bank of Chaberis fl.

BATINA, a town of Atropatene, Media, S.E. of Sincar. *Sulthanie.*

BATIANA, a town of the Segetani, Viennensis, on the Rhone, at the confluence of the Druna, bet. Acunum and Umbennum. *Bancs, opposite Baix.*

BATINI (Butones), a tribe of Marcomanni, Germ., on Albis fl., towards its source.

BATINUS fl., a r. of Picenum, falling into the sea N. of Castrum Novum. *Tordino.*

BATNÆ. *Vide Bathnæ.*

BATOGABRA, a town of Judæa, 16 m. N.E. from Ascalon.

BATRACHOS, a port of Marmarica, bet. Petræ parvæ portus and Paliurus. *Batraka, Patriarka.*

BATRII, a people of Arachosia, on Arachotus fl., towards its junction with Etymandrus fl.

BATRASABBA, a town of the Omanitæ, Arabia, s. of Asaborum prom. *Sabee.*

BATTI, a tribe of Chatti, Germ., on Adrana fl., R., towards its source.

BATULUM, a town of the Pentri, Samnium, E. of Beneventum. *Paduli.*

BATUS fl., a r. of Bruttium, falling into Siculum m. w. of Halex fl. *Bato.*

BAUCIDIAS ins., one of Pelopidis ins., Argolis.

BAUDOBRICA, a town of the Treveri, Germania I., bet. Belginum E. and Ad Decimum w.

BAULI, *prius* Boaulia, a town of Campania, above Misenum, on Puteolinus sin., where Hercules landed with the oxen of Geryon. Here were the famous fish-ponds of Hortensius. The death-place of Agrippina.

BAUMÆ, a town of Osrhoene, on the Euphrates, above Nicephorium.

BAUOTA, i. q. Basta, in Japygia.

BAUTÆ, a town of the Allobroges, Viennensis, bet. Geneva and Ad Casuaria. *Vieux Anneci.*

BAUTISUS fl., a r. of Serica, rising in Casii m., and falling into Œchardes fl. *Hoang-Ho.*

BAVO ins. *Vide* Boas.

BAXALA, a town of Mesopotamia, on Saocorus fl., s. of Nisibis.

BAZACATA ins., one of the Salinæ ins., Indiæ, opposite Tacola. *Chedube.*

BAZIRA, a town of India i. Gangem, towards Aornos.

BAZIS, a town of Tyanitis, Cappadocia.

BAZIUM prom., a pr. of Dodecaschœnus, on the Red Sea, s. of Berenice. *Ras el Naschef.*

BEACÆ, a town of Chaonia, on the confines of Illyria.

BEBASE, Mesopot. *Vide* Bezabde.

BEBERACUS lacus, a lake of Mygdonia, Mesopot., S.E. of the source of Chaborras fl. *Chatonie.*

BEBIANA, a village of Etruria, bet. Lorium (5) and Alsium (6), on Via Aurelia.

BEBII m., a s.E. continuation of Albanus m., separating Liburnia and Dalmatia from Pannonia.

BEBRIACUM, a more correct reading of Bedriacum, q. v.

BEBRŸCES, I. a tribe of Bryges, the early possessors of the coast of Bithynia. II. a colony from Bithynia, settled in Gaul, about Narbo. *Departments of Pyrénées Orientales and Aude S.*

BEBRYCIA, the early name of Maritime Bithynia.

BECHIRES, a people of Pontus, on the coast, bet. the Macrones and the Byzeres.

BECIUS m., m. of Drangiana, s.

BECHUNI, Rhætia, i. q. Euganei.

BEDA, a town of the Treveri, Belgica I., bet. Ausava N. and Augusta Treverorum s.

BEDAJUM (Badacum), a town of the Alauni, Noricum, bet. Pons Æni (18) and Artobriga. *Seebruck.*

BEDESA (Badesa), a town of the Castellani, Tarraconensis, on Alba fl., L., below Egosà.

BEDĒSIS fl., a r. of Gallia Cispadana, flowing by Ravenna into the sea. *Ronco.*

BEDIRUM, a town of the Garamantes, Libya, near the source of Cinyps fl.

BEDIZUS, a town of the Odrysæ, Thrace, on the Egnatia Via, bet. Apri and Bisanthe.

BEDRIĀCUM (Bebriacum), a village of the Cenomanni, Gallia Transp., on Ollius fl., R., bet. Cremona (15) and Mantua, on Via Posthumia. Memorable for the defeat of Galba by Otho, and of Otho by Vitellius. *Cividale.*

BEDUNIA, a town of the Astures, Tarraconensis, on Urbius fl., below Asturica Augusta.

BEER, "well," a place bet. Jerusalem and Shechem.

BEER-ELIM, a place in Moabitis.

BEER-LAHAI-ROI, a spring of Canaan, bet. Kadesh and the Desert of Shur, on the borders of Edom, where Hagar was visited by the angel.

BEEROTH, a town of Benjamin, at the foot of Gibeon m., 7 m. N.E. from Jerusalem. *Bir.*

BEERSEBA (Berosabe, Bersaba, Barsubæ), a town of Judah, and afterwards of Simeon, 20 m. s. from Hebron. Named from Abraham's oath at the well.

BEGA, a district of Æthiopia, s. of the Memnones.

BEGORRITES lac., a lake of Eordæa, Macedonia, S.E. of Cellæ. *Kitrini.*

BELA, the early name of Zoar.

BELACI, I. a people of Alpes Maritimæ, w. of the Segusini. *Valle de Bardonache.* II. *postea* Belac, Beulas, Bedularium, Beolarium, their capital. *Beaulard.*

BELBINA ins., an isl. of Attica, s.w. of Sunium prom. *San Giorgio d'Arbora.*

BELCA, a town of the Carnutes, Lugdunensis IV., on the Liger, R., bet. Gergovia and Brivodurum.

BELCIANAS, a town of Elegosine, Armen. s.w. of Arsamosata.

BELDEAS, a town of Mesopotamia, on the Tigris, above Labbana.

BELEMINA (Bellina, Blemmina), a town of Laconia, in its N.W. angle, 12½ m. from Pellane. *Bourainos.*

BELENDI, I. a people of Novem Populana, on the coast, w. of the Vasates. II. their capital. *Belin.*

BELERIDÆ ins. (Balarides), three islets of Sardinia, E. above Ficariæ ins. *Sanguinarie.*

BELERIUM prom., Antivestæum (Belir, *Celticè*, "western rock"), Bolerium, the w. extremity of Britannia I., opposite Cassiterides ins. *Cape Cornwall.*

BELESI (Biblada), a town of Tingene, Mesop., on the Euphrates, bet. Giddara and Euphrates ins.

BELGA UVELLA (Theodorodurum), *vide* Ad Aquas.

BELGÆ, I. a mixed population of Celts and Germans settled in Belgica I. and II. II. Colonists from Gaul settled in Britannia I., bet. the Damnonii w., the Regni E., the Dobuni and Atrebatii N., and the Durotriges and Regni s. *Somerset N. and part of Wilts and Hants.*

BELGICA I., a division of Gaul, N.E., comprehending the Treveri, the Mediomatrici, and the Leuci. *Duchy of Trèves, part of Luxembourg. Departments of the Meuse, Moselle, Meurthe, and Vosges.*

BELGICA II., a division of Gaul, N.W., comprehending the Morini, Nervii Bellovaci, &c. *Departments of Ardennes, Seine et Oise, Pas de Calais, &c.*

BELGICA, a town of the Ubii, Germania II., N.E. of Marcomagus.

BELGINUM, a town of the Treveri, Germania I., bet. Baudobrica w. and Dumnissus E.

BELIJA, a town of the Caristii, Tarraconens., s. of Flaviobriga. A colonia. *Belchite.*

BELGITÆ, a people of Pannonia, on the Savus.

BELIAS fl. (Belicha, Balissus), a r. of Mesopotamia, rising in Masius m., near Dabana, and falling into the Euphrates towards Callinicum.

BELGORITIA, a town of the Brigantes, Brit., S.E. of Derventio. *Near Millington.*

BELISAMA æstuar., an æstuary of Britain, bet. Seteja æstuary and Setantiorum portus. *Mouth of the Ribble.*

BELION fl., Gallæc., i. q. Limia.

BELLENE, a village of Mauritania Cæsar., bet. Castra Nova and Mina, under Ancorarius m. s.

BELLI, an early people of Tarraconensis, about Segobriga.

BELLINTUM, a town of the Desuviates, Vien-

nensis, on the Rhone, above Tarasco. *Barbentane.*

BELLOCASSES, Gallia, i. q. Vellocasses.

BELMINATIS, i. q. Belemina.

BELLŎVĂCI, a people of Belgica II., bet. the Ambracii, Veromandui, and Suessiones N., the Veliocasses, Parisii, and Melli s., the Caleti and Veliocasses w., and the Suessiones E. *Departments of Oise et Somme.*

BELOCOME, a fortress of Bithynia, bet. Nicæa and Cius.

BELOIUM, a town of the Carni, Venetia, N. of Aquileia (30).

BELUNUM (Berunum), a town of Rhætia, on Plavis fl., above Quercus, N.E. of Feltria. *Belluno.*

BELSINUM, a town of the Tornates, Novem Populana, bet. Augusta Ausciorum N. and Lugdunum s.

BELUS fl. (Beleus), a r. of Judæa, rising from Cendevia lac., and falling into the Mediterranean at Acco. Its sand was of a peculiar fine quality. *Nahr Halou.*

BEMBINA, a town of Argolis, on Nemea fl., N.W. of Nemea. *Agios Giorgios.*

BEMMARA, a town of Mesopotamia, bet. Zeugma (20) and Edessa (25).

BENĀCUS lac., a lake of Gall. Transpad., bet. Sebinus lac. and Atagis fl. Catullus calls it Lydiæ undæ lac., in reference probably to the contiguous (Lydian) Veneti. *Lago di Garda.*

BENADEDARI, a town of the Psylli, Africa Prop., on Syrtis Maj., bet. Tagulis and Aræ Philænorum.

BENAVASA, a town of Ariaca, India, N. of Murzupale.

BENE, a town of Crete, near Gortys. The birth-place of the poet Rhianus.

BENEHARNI, a tribe of Osquidates, Novem Populana. *In Bearn.*

BENEHARNUM, capital of the Beneharni, Novem Populana, bet. Aquæ Tarbellicæ N.W., and Iluro s.s.E. *Castelnon, bet. Maslacq and Lagor.*

BENEMARIUM (Nemrim), a village of Moabitis, N. of Zoar.

BĔNĔVENTUM, I. a town of the Catavellauni, Brit., bet. Tripontum and Lactodurum. II. of the Cenomanni, Gall. Transp., at the s.w. extrem. of Benacus lac., bet. Ad Flexum (10) and Ardelica. III. *prius* Maleventum, a town of the Hirpini, in Samnium, on Via Appia, bet. Caudium (11) and Eclanum (15). Traditionally built by Diomed. The change of name, as of better augury, took place when the town became a colonia, 271 B.C. Here Pyrrhus was defeated by Curius, B.C. 274, and in the vicinity was the triumphal arch of Trajan, erected 114. The birthplace of the grammarian Arbelius. *Benevento.*

BENDA fl. *Vide* Renda.

BEN HINNOM (Gehinnon), a valley of Judæa, E. of Jerusalem. The locality of Tophet.

BENJAMIN, a tribe of Juda, bounded by Ephraim at Hazor, and Lus, S. by Juda at Ephrata, W. by Dan, near Bethhoron, E. by the Jordan.

BENLAUNI, a people of Rhætia, on Ænus fl., L., below Veldidena.

BENNAVENNA. *Vide* Bannavanta.

BENNI, a tribe of Odrysæ, on Hebrus fl.

BEPYRUS m., m. of India e. Gangem, towards the sources of the Ganges.

BER (Bera), a town of Juda, 8 m. N. from Bethogabris.

BERABONNA, a port of Argentea regio, Indiæ, on Gangeticus sin., S. of Sada. *Barabon.*

BERANDA, a town of Amordocia, Babylonia, s. of Orrhoe.

BERCORATES, I. a tribe of Boates, Novem Populana, about Losa. II. their capital, *postea* Barcou. *Jouanon.*

BERCETESIUS m., m. of Macedonia, at the N.W. extremity of Canalovii m.

BERDERIS, a town of the Ambastæ, Ind., E. of Bacari.

BERDRIGEI, a people of Bactria, towards the Oxus.

BERE, a town of the Soræ, Ind., E. of Sora.

BEREBIS, a town of the Hercuniatæ, Pannon., on Dravus fl., R., bet. Jovallium and Seronis.

BERECYNTHUS m., I. Dictynnæus, the w. continuation of Ida m. in Crete, in whose recesses the Idæi Dactyli first applied fire in the preparation of metals. II. a m. of Phrygia Magna, on Mæander fl., s.w. of Apamea Cibotus. Sacred to Cybele, hence called Berecynthia. Named from the Berecynthii, a tribe of Bryges settled here prior to the Trojan war.

BEREGRA, a town of Prætutia, Picenum, s. of Interamna. A colonia.

BERENĬCE, I. (Dire, Epidiris, Isidis portus), Æthiopiæ, i. q. Arsinoe. II. of Cilicia Trachea, E. of Celenderis. III. (Esiongebar), of the Nabathæi, Arabia Petræa, at the head of Ælanites sin. IV. (Hesperis), a city of Pentapolis, Cyrenaica, on Pseudopenias prom., near the mouth of Lathon, or Eccius fl. Here were the "gardens of the Hesperides," of which vestiges still remain. *Bernie; Benegaye.* V. (Panchrysos), of

Thebais, on the Red Sea, N.E. of Coptos, over against Leuce Come, s.w. *Sakayt el Kublee.*

BERENICIDÆ, a tribe of Attica, of the tribe Ptolemais.

BERETHIS, a town of Meroe, on the Nile, R., bet. Boon and Gerbo.

BERETIS, Pannonia, i. q. Verea.

BEREUM, a town of Mœsia, on the Danube, bet. Troesmis and Cium.

BEREZII, a village of Gætulia, bet. Veri and Ausilindum.

BERGA, a town of the Siropæones, Thrace, on Strymon fl., below Euporia. The birthplace of Antiphanes, the comic writer. *Begkevi.*

BERGIA, a port of Syrtica, E. of Leptis Magna.

BERGIDIUM (surnamed Flavium), a town of the Astures, Tarraconensis, E.S.E. of Lucus Augusti. A colonia. *La Vega.*

BERGIDUM (Vergium), capital of the Bergistani, Tarraconensis, S.E. of Bergusia. *Vierzo.*

BERGINE, capital of the Nearchi, Gallia, at the mouth of the Rhone.

BERGINTRUM, a town of the Centrones, Alpes Penninæ, on Isara fl., R., above Axima. *Belantre.*

BERGISTANI (Vergistani), a people of Tarraconensis, in the Pyrenees, N.W. of the Ausetani.

BERGIUM, a town of the Hermanduri, Germania, on Mœnus fl., above Divona. *Bamberg.*

BERGŎMUM ("mountain home"), capital of the Orobii, Gallia Transpad., bet. Pons Aureoli (13) and Tollegata (12), on Via Æmilia. A municipium. *Bergamo.*

BERGUSIA, I. capital of the Bergusii, Tarraconensis, in the Pyrenees, on Sicoris fl., above Ilerda. *Barège.* II. a town of the Allobroges, Viennensis, bet. Augustum E. and Ad Decem w. *Balaguer.*

BERGUSII (Bargusii), a tribe of Ilergetes, Tarraconensis, on Sicoris fl.

BERIBRACES, a people of Tarraconensis, on the coast, N. of Caprasia prom.

BERIS fl., a r. of Pontus, falling into the Euxine 11 m. s.E. from Themiscyra.

BERISSA, a town of Pontus, bet. Phiara (12) and Gaziura.

BERITINI, a tribe of Salyes, Narbonensis, on Varus fl., towards its source. *Vallées de St. Pierre and de Pene.*

BERMIUS m., m. of Emathia, Macedonia, a N.W. continuation beyond the Haliacmon of Olympus. Within its valleys were the celebrated rose-gardens of Minos. *Zero Livado.*

BERNUS (Barnus), a town of the Penestæ, Illyria, under Bernus m., on Via Egnatia, near Lychnidus.

BERNUS m. (Bora), the s. continuation of Scardus m., separating s.e. Illyria from Almopeia, Pelagonia, and Lyncus.

BEROBE, a town of the Doani, India e. Gangem, near the mouth, R., of Doanus fl. *Syriam.*

BERŒA (Berrhæa), I. *prius* Chalybon, a town of Chalybonitis, Syria, on Chalus fl., s.w. of Alexandria (90). Named Berhæa by the Macedonians. *Aleppo; Chaleb; Haleb.* II. a town of the Bessi, Thrace, on Harpessus fl., s.w. of Carasura. Named Irenopolis in honour of Irene. *Eski-Zadra.* III. a town at the foot of Bermius m., 30 m. s.w. from Pella. *Kara Veria.*

BERONES, a tribe of Celtiberi in Tarraconensis, bet. the Iberus n., Idubeda m. s., the Autrigones w., and the Edetani e.

BEROTHA, a town of Napthali, Galilee Sup., near Kedesa.

BERRALIS, a town of Gauzonitis, Mesopot., w. of Thallaba.

BERSABE. *Vide* Beerseba.

BERSIMA, a town of Osrhoene, on the Euphrates, below Barbalissus.

BERSOVIA, I. a r. of Dacia, below Bersovia. *Karassa.* II. (Berzobis), a town of the Biephi, Dac., on Bersovia fl., 12 m. n.n.w. from Centum Putea. *Near Karaschowa.*

BERSULA fl., a r. of the Ananes, Liguria, falling into Padus fl., e. of Ad Padum.

BERTA, a town of Bisaltia, Macedonia, on the Bisaltes fl., below Ossa.

BERTISCHUS m., a n.w. continuation of Scardus m., separating Illyria from w. Mœsia. *Djamous Dagh.*

BERTULA ins., an isl. of Sardinia, n.w. of Tharros. *Coscia di Donna; Malventre.*

BERŸTUS (Berothai), a maritime city of Phœnicia, 42 m. s.w. from Tripolis. Built by Saturn. A colonia (Felix Julia). *Beirut.*

BERZEO, a town of Mauritania Cæsar., bet. Modolana and Fons Camerata.

BERZIMINUM, a town of the Labeates, Illyria, on Barbana fl., bet. Alata and Cinna. *Podgoritza.*

BESA, I. a demus of Attica, of the tribe Antiochis. *Near Sunium.* II. the early name of Antinoe in Heptanomis, from an Egyptian god.

BESBICUS ins., an isl. of Mysia, in Propontis, over against the mouth of Rhyndacus fl., n. Severed from the continent by an earthquake. *Kalolimni.*

BESIDIÆ, a town of Bruttium, on Crathis fl., R. *Bisignano.*

BESOR fl., a r. of Judæa, falling into the Mediterranean 5 m. below Gaza.

BESSA, a town of Locri Epicnemidii, extinct in Strabo's time.

BESSAPARA, a town of the Odrysæ, Thrace, on Hebrus fl., above Philippopolis. *Bazardjick.*

BESSECHANA, a town of Aniobaritis, Mes., on the Euphrates, bet. Ozogarda and Naharra.

BESSI, a tribe of Satræ, Thrace, bet. Rhodope and Hæmus m., extending to Nestus fl.

BESTIA DESOLUTA (Parabeste, Abeste), a town of Arachosia, at the junction of Arachotus fl. with Etymandrus fl.

BESYNGA (Babysenga), I. a r. of India e. Gangem, falling into Gangeticus sin. below Bessynga. *Setang.* II. a town of Argentea regio, India i. Gangem, on Besynga fl., towards its mouth. *Pegu.*

BESUCHIS, a fortress of Babylonia, bet. Ctesiphon and Maogamalcha.

BETASII, I. a people of Germania II., contiguous to the Sunici. II. their capital. *Beetz or Biez, near Brussels.*

BETHABARA, a village of Benjamin, Judæa, at a ford of the Jordan, 30 m. n.e. of Jerusalem, where the Israelites passed dry-shod. Here John baptized.

BETHAGLA, a town of Benjamin, Judæa, on the Jordan, bet. Jericho, n.w., and Beth-Jesimoth.

BETHAMMARIA (Bethammali, Barsampse), a town of Syria, on the Euphrates, below Cæciliana (14).

BETHANY, a town of Judæa, under the Mount of Olives, 2 m. e. from Jerusalem. The locality of the miracle of Lazarus, and of the Ascension.

BETHAR (Betari, Bither), a village of Ephraim, Judæa, 18 m. s. from Cæsarea.

BETHARAMATHON, i. q. Amatha, Peræa.

BETHARANPHTHA (Bethharan), a town of Peræa, on the Jordan, 12 m. s.e. from Jericho, and re-named Livias in honour of Julia Livia.

BETHAVEN, a town of Benjamin, in Judæa, e. of Bethel.

BETHAUNA, Mesopotamia, i. q. Anatho.

BETH CHERIM, Indæa, i. q. Herodium.

BETH DAGON, a town of Judæa, s.e. of Joppa.

BETH DIBLATHAIM, a town of Moabitis.

BETHEDEN Vallis, i. q. Bikah.

BETHEL, *prius* Luz, a town of Judæa, 12 m. n. from Jerusalem. Named Bethel by Jacob, in relation to his vision. *Beitsin.*

BETH GAMUL, a town of Batanæa, bet. Boztra N.E. and Thantia S.W.

BETHHACCEREM m., a hill near Bethlehem, S.E. *Jebel el Fareidis.*

BETHHARAN. *Vide* Betharanphtha.

BETHIA (Bycta), a town of Media-Sigrianes, bet. Seva and Ragæ.

BETH-JESIMOTH, i. q. Bethsimoth.

BETHLEHEM (Bethlemoon, Ephratah), a village of Judah, 6 m. s. from Jerusalem. The birth-place of our Saviour, and of David; the burial-place of Jesse. *Beitlahm.*

BETHLEPHTHENE, a toparchy of Judæa, s. of Emaus.

BETHMARCABATH, a town of Simeon.

BETHOGABRIS, Judæa, i. q. Eleutheropolis.

BETH-SITTA, a town of Galilee, on the confines of Samaria, E.N.E. of Jezreel.

BETHURAI, a suburb of Tiberias, Galilee.

BETH-ZACHARIAS, a town of Juda, S.W. of Thekoa.

BETHORON Inf., a village of Judæa, E. of Bethoron Sup.

BETHORON (Betaron Sup.), a village of Judæa, 12 m. N.W. of Jerusalem. Rebuilt by Solomon. *Beitur el Foka.*

BETHPHAGE, a village near Bethany, under the Mount of Olives. *Abu Dis.*

BETHSAIDA, I. a town of Galilee, on the Jordan, above Bethsaida-Julias. The birth-place of Andrew, Peter, and Philip. II. of Gaulonitis, on the Jordan, near its influx into Tiberias lac. Afterwards named Julias by Herod.

BETHSAN, a city of Decapolis, on the Jordan, 15 m. s. from Tiberias. Named Scythopolis, from some Scythian emigrants, who settled here B.C. 631. *Beisan.*

BETHSHEMES, I. the Scriptural name of Heliopolis, Egypt. II. (Irshemesh), a Levitical town of Judah, bet. Methogabris (10) and Emmaus, 30 m. S.W. from Jerusalem. III. a town of Naphthali.

BETHSIMOTH (Bethgeshimoth, Bethsi nuth), a town of Moabitis, near the Dead Sea, 10 m. E. from Jericho.

BETHSOLOCE. *Vide* Carcha.

BETHZAR (Bethsura, Bethsoron), a town of Judah, Judæa, 20 m. s. from Jerusalem. *Bethsar.*

BETHULIA, a town of Galilæa, near Dothaim.

BETONIM (Bothnim), a town of Gad, in Gileaditis, bet. Abel Sittim S.W., and Ramoth Gilead N.E.

BETTIGI, a people of India i. Gangem, under Bettigus m., s.

BETTIGUS m., m. of India i. Gangem, on

the w. coast, terminating in Comaria prom.

BETULLO fl., a river of Tarraconensis, falling into the Mediterranean, s. of Jovis prom. *Ter.*

BETUMA (Betousa), a town of Acabene, Mesopot. on the Tigris, above Libana.

BEUDOS (Budea), a town of Phrygia Magna, N.E. of Synnada (5). *Beiad.*

BEVA, a town of Lyncus, Macedonia, on Bevus fl., opposite Nicia. *Filorino.*

BEVUS fl., a r. of Lyncus, Macedonia, rising in Bernus m., and falling into Erigonus fl. below Heraclea.

BEZEK, a town of Judah, bet. Sichem (17) and Bethshan.

BEZETHA, a suburb of Jerusalem, s.

BEZOBDE (Beth-Zabda, Zabda, Gosarta, Zebedara, Sappha), a town of Gordyene, Armen., on the Tigris, N.E. of Nizibis. *Djesirat ibn omar; Gozart.*

BEZOR (Bosor, Boso̅ra), a city of Reuben, in Ammonitis, E. of Kirjathaim.

BIABANNA, a town of Gorda, Arabia, w. of Mariaba. *Bubban.*

BIAS fl., a r. of Messenia, falling into Messeniacus sin., N. of Corone.

BIASARI, i. q. Abisare.

BIBACLA ins. (Bibaga), an isl. of Gedrosia, bet. Portus Mulierum and Crocela ins.

BIBACUM, a town of the Narisci, Germania, N. of Reginum.

BIBÆ, a town of Zeugitana, bet. Onellana and Mediocera, N.W. of Hadrumetum.

BIBALÆ, a tribe of Bracaræ, Tarraconensis.

BIBASIS fl., i. q. Hypasis, India.

BIBE, a town of the Suessiones, Belgica II., bet. Augusta Suessionum w. and Ad Fines E.

BIBIANA, a town of Etruria, 6 m. N. from Alsium.

BIBIUM, a town of the Caritni, Germania, on the Rhine, bet. Saletio and Argentoratum.

BIBLIS fons, a sacred fountain of Caria, near Miletus.

BIBRACTE, I. the early name of Augustodunum. So called from the goddess Bibracte. II. capital of the Bibroci, Britannia. *Bray.*

BIBRAX, a town of the Remi, Belgica II., bet. Augusta Suessionum w. and Axuenna E. *Bièvre.*

BIBROCI, a tribe of the Atrebatii, Britan.

BICARDIUM, a town of the Teuriochæmæ, Germ., s. of Argeira. *Erfurt.*

BIDA (Bidil), a town of Mauritania Cæsar., bet. Tigisis and Tubusuptus (40). *Blida.*

BIDACUM (Bidarum), i. q. Badacum.

BIDIS (Beidis, Beido.), a town of Sicily,

near the source of Anapus fl., 15 m. s.w. from Syracuse. *Ch. of San Giovanni di Bidini.*

BIDUCESII, I. a maritime people of Lugdunensis III., bet. Tetus fl. and the Curiosolites. II. their capital, *postea* Bidué. *St. Brieux.*

BIECRUM Ost., the issue of Halmyris lac. into the Euxine, N. of Istros.

BIENNA (Biennos), a town on the s.e. coast of Crete, e. of Erythræum prom. Named after the hero Biennos. *Agioi Saranta.*

BIENON, a town on the w. coast of Crete, bet. Inachorium and Lissus.

BIEPHI, a people of Dacia, on the Tibiscus, N. of the Albocenses.

BIESSI, a people of Sarmatia, in Carpathus m.

BIFRACTUS m., a m. of the Ædui, w. of Augustodunum, and by some geographers considered the early site of Bibracte. *Mt. Beuvrai.*

BIGERRI, cap. of the Bigerrones, Novem Populana, N.E. of Iluro.

BIGERRA, a town of the Bastitani, Tarraconens., E. of Laminium. *Bogarra.*

BIGERRONES, a people of Novem Populana, bet. the Tarbelli and the Convenæ. *Bigorre.*

BIGIS (Bis), a town of Drangiana-Anabon, s.e. of Pharazana.

BIKAH vallis (Bucca, Beth-eden), a valley of Cœle-Syria, bet. Libanus and Anti-Libanus. *Bokah.*

BILBANA (Bilana, Bilæna), Arabiæ, i. q. Pallon.

BILBILIS, I. a r. of Tarraconensis, falling into Salo fl. below Forum Cigurrorum. *Bibey.* II. a town of the Celtiberi, Tarraconensis, on Bilbilis fl., at its junction with the Salo, 81 m. w. from Cæsar Augusta. A colonia (Augusta). The birthplace of Martial. *Baubola.*

BILIANDRUM, a town of the Taurisci, Noricum, 14 m. s.e. from Tarnasix. *Grades.*

BILITIO, a town of the Mesiates, Gallia Transpadana, on Ticinus fl. *Bellinzona.*

BILUIÆ, Arabiæ, i. q. Bliulæi.

BILLÆUS fl., a r. of Asia Minor, rising in Olympus m., near Cratia, Paphlagonia, and falling into the Euxine at Tium. The early limit of Bithynia and Paphlagonia.

BINAGARA, a town of Pulinda, India, N.W. of Barygaza, *Beckur.*

BINDA, I. one of the three mouths of Nanaguna fl., Ind. II. a town of Æthiopia.

BINGIUM, a town of the Vangiones, Germania I., at the confluence of the Rhine and Nava fl., bet. Vosalia and Moguntiacum (18). Built by Drusus. *Bingen.*

BIORA (Biotha), Sardinia, i. q. Bitia.

BIRGUS fl., i. q. Bargus.

BIRICIANA, a town of Rhætia, 7 m. s.w. from Leiniacum.

BIRTHA (Byrthum), I. a town of Acabene, Mesopotamia, on the Tigris, s. of Bithiga. II. of Palmyrene, on the Euphrates, bet. Circesium and Zenobia. III. i. q. Seleucia (Apamea) Mesopotamiæ.

BIS, a town of Parapomisus, on Etymandrus fl. *Bost.*

BISA fl., a stream of Pisatis (Bisatis), Elis, falling into the Alpheus, R., near Cycesium. It probably gave name to the district.

BISALTÆ, a people of Macedonia, bet. Bolbe lac. and the Strymon. The hares of their country were fabled to have two livers.

BISALTES fl., a r. of Bisaltia, Macedonia, falling into Cercinitis palus.

BISANTHE (*postea* Rhædestus), a town of the Odrysæ, Thrace, on the Propontis, bet. Bedizus and Heræum. A Samian colony. *Rodosti.*

BISCARGIS, a town of the Ilercaones, Tarraconensis, on the Iberus, below Octogesa. A colonia. *Berrus.*

BISICA-LUCANA, a town of Zeugitana, bet. Choreva and Avitta.

BISTŎNES, a maritime people of Thrace, bet. the Sapæi and the Cicones. The name is sometimes applied to the whole of Thrace.

BISTŎNIS lac., a salt lake of the Bistones, at the mouths of Compsatus and Travus fl., N.E. of Abdera. *Bourikhane.*

BITAXA, a town of Aria, on the border of Margiana, N. of Alexandria Arion. *Badkis.*

BITHIAS, Mesop., i. q. Batnæ.

BITHIGA (Virta), a town of Mygdonia, Mes., 3 geog. m. N. from Nisibis.

BITHRA, a town of Babylonia, on the Euphrates, L., s. of Neapolis.

BITHYNIA, a country of Asia Minor, bounded N. by the Euxine, s. and s.e. by Phrygia, w. by Thracius Bosporus, Propontis, and Mysia, e. by Paphlagonia, at Parthenius fl., and, according to some geographers, at Sangarius fl. Peopled from Thrace. *Kodavendkhiar and Kodjaili.*

BITHYNIUM (*postea* Claudiopolis), the early capital of Bithynia under Lyperus m., s. of Tium. Built by king Zipoetes. Named Claudiopolis under Tiberius. The birthplace of Antinous, the favourite of Hadrian. Under Theodosius, the metropolis of the province Honorias. Destroyed by an earthquake. *Boli (i. e. Polis).*

BITIA, I. (Batia), a town of Cassopeia, in Epirus, N.E. of Elatia. *Castri.* II. (Biora,

Biotha), a maritime town of Sardinia, s., bet. Herculis portus and Tegula. *Sant' Isidoro di Teulada.*

BITURGIA (Bituriza), a town of Etruria, on Arnus fl., bet. Ad Joglandem and Ad Fines Cæsarianas. *Monte Vachi.*

BITURIGES CUBI, I. a people of Aquitania I., bet. the Carnutes N., the Lemovices and Arverni s., the Turones and Agesinates w., and the Ædui E. *Departments of Vienne, Indre, and Cher.* II. their capital, i. q. Avaricum.

BITURIGES VIVISCI (Josci, Ubisci), a Celtic people of Aquitania II., on the Garumna, about Burdigala. *Department of Gironde.*

BITYLA, Laconiæ, i. q. Œtylus.

BIUM, a town of Taurica Chersonesus, N. of Portacra.

BIZONE, a town of the Crobyzi, Mœsia, on the Euxine, bet. Cruni (10) and Tetrisia. Destroyed by an earthquake.

BIZYA, a town of Astica, Thrace, N.w. of Salmydessus. The citadel of king Tereus. *Bizya.*

BLAENE, a district of Central Paphlagonia.

BLANDA, I. a town of Lucania, on Via Aquilia, s. of Scidrus. *Maratea.* II. of the Læetani, Tarraconensis, at the mouth of Larnum fl. *Blanes.*

BLANDENONA, a town of Liguria, 10 m. s. from Ticinum. *Broni.*

BLANDIANA, a town of the Burideenses, Dac., bet. Gernichera (9) and Apulum, on Marisus fl., L. *East of Muhlenbach.*

BLANDUSIÆ fons., a fountain of Sabinium, near Mandela.

BLANNOVICES (Blannovii, Brannovices), a people of Lugdunensis I., on the s. confines of the Ædui. *Brionnais.*

BLANONA, a town of Illyria, on the borders of Dalmatia. *Zara.*

BLARIACUM, a town of the Taxandri, Germania II., on the Mosa, L., bet. Cevelum and Menapiorum castrum.

BLASCON ins., an isl. of the Volcæ Arecomici, Narbonensis, off Agatha, now joined to the mainland by a mole. *Brescon.*

BLASTOPHŒNICES, a tribe of Phœnicians or Arabs, settled on the s.w. coast of Bætica.

BLATUM-BULGIUM, a town of the Selgovæ, Britan., E. of Carbantorigum. *Middleby.*

BLAUDON, Phrygiæ, i. q. Blaundus.

BLAUNDUS, I. a town of Lydia, on Hippurius fl., near Ancyra. A Macedonian settlement. II. of Pontus, bet. Sebastia (24) and Euspæna (28).

BLAVIA, a port of the Veneti, Lugdunensis III., N.w. of Dortoritum. *Port Louis.*

BLAVIUM, a town of the Santones, Aqui-

tania II., on the Garumna, R., at the confluence of the Duronius. *Blaye.*

BLEMMYÆ, a people of Æthiopia, s. of the Adiabaræ, bet. the Troglodytæ and the Nile. They were reputed to be destitute of heads, and to have their faces in their breasts.

BLENDIUM, a port of the Caristi, Tarraconensis, E. of Vereasueca. *Santander.*

BLERA, I. a town of Etruria, on Via Claudia, bet. Forum Claudii (16) and Tuscana (9). *Bieda.* II. of Messapia, on Via Appia, bet. Silvium (16) and Sub Lupatia (14). *Gravina.*

BLESTIUM, a town of the Silures, Brit. II., N.E. from Burrium. *Monmouth.*

BLETISA, a town of the Vettones, Lusitania, bet. Ocelum N.w., and Salmantica s.E.

BLIULÆI (Biluiæ), a people of Arabia Felix, in the mountains N.w. of Basag. The descendants of Adbeel. *Tribe of Beni Boo-Allee.*

BLOUCIUM (Castellum Luceium), a town of the Tolistoboii, Galatia, near Pessinus. The residence of king Deiotarus.

BLUBION, a town of the Tectosages, Galatia.

BOACTEA (Boaclea), a town of the Apuani, Liguria, at the junction of Boactes fl. with Macra fl., above Luna. *Vezzano.*

BOACTES fl. (Boacea), a r. of Liguria, falling into Macra fl. at Boactea. *Vara.*

BOAGRIUS fl. (Manes), a r. of the Locri Epicnemedii, falling into Maliacus sin. at Scarphe.

BOARIA ins. (Boaris), an isl. of Sardinia, s. *Toro.*

BOAS, I. the name of Apsarus fl., in Pontus, towards the upper portion of its course. II. ins. (Bavo), one of the Liburnides ins., off Tragurium. A place of banishment for Roman criminals. *Bua.*

BOCANUM HEMERUM, a town of Mauritania Tingit., towards the Mediterranean. *Morocco.*

BOCARUS fl., I. a r. of Cyprus, rising in Acamas m., and falling into the sea below Palæ Paphos. II. of Salamis, falling into the sea opposite Ægina.

BOCCHŌRUM, a town of Balearis Mag. In ruins in Pliny's time.

BOCCHYRIS, a town of Marmarica, near Paliurus fl., E., towards its mouth.

BODENCOMAGUS (" on Bodencus"), the Ligurian name of Industria, Liguria.

BODENCUS (*Celticè*, "deep"), the Ligurian name of Padus fl.

BODENI, i. q. Budini.

BODERIA æstuar., i. q. Bodotria.

BODETIA, a maritime town of the Apuani,

Liguria, bet. Ad Monilia and Portus Veneris.

BODIONTICI, a tribe of Albioeci, Alpes Maritimæ, s. of the Avantici. *Diocèse de Digne.*

BODOTRIA æstuar. (Boderia), an æstuary of Britain, bet. Tina fl. and Alaunus fl. *Frith of Forth.*

BODUNI, Britannia, i. q. Dobuni.

BŒÆ, a town of Laconia, on Bœaticus sin. N. of Malea prom. *Vathiki.*

BŒATICUS sin., a gulf of the Ægean, in Laconia, bet. Onugnathus penins. and Malea prom. *G. di Vathiki.*

BŒBE, a town of Pelasgiotis, Thessaly, on the S.W. shore of Bœbeis lac., N.W. of Pheræ. *Hadgine.*

BŒBEIS lac. (Bœbias), a lake of Pelasgiotis, Thessaly, on the confines of Magnesia, S.E. of Larissa. *L. Carlas.*

BOE COLEN m., m. of Cyrenaica, a w. cont. of Bascisi m.

BŒONOA, Elid, i. q. Ephyre.

BŒOTI ("husbandmen"), a tribe of Pelasgi, who from Thessaly superseded the Leleges in Bœotia.

BŒOTIA ("land of husbandmen"), a country of Græcia e. Peloponnesum, bounded N. by Maliacus sin., S. by Corinthiacus sin., Megaris, and Attica, w. by Phocis, E. by Euripus. Settled by Aones, and other Lelegian tribes; then (1493 B.C.) by Phœnicians, under Cadmus, from Eubœa, and finally (1124 B.C.) by Bœotians from Thessaly. *Part of Livadia.*

BŒRUS, a town of Paraxia, Macedonia, on the Axius fl., N.W. of Carabia.

BOEUM, a town of Taurica Chersonesus, bet. Theodosia and Parosta.

BOGADIUM, a town of the Bructeri Mag., N.E. of Asciburgium, 6 m. w. from Amisus fl. *Munster.*

BOGARDI, a tribe of Agræi, Arab., on Persicus sin., about Cadara.

BOII, I. a people of Lugdunensis IV., s. of the Senones, on the Liger, a migration of whom settled in Gallia Cispadana s., about Bononia, to which they gave name; whence they were removed by the senate to Germania Magna, bet. Vindilici m. and the Danube (called after them Boiohemum, "home of the Boii," *Bohemia*). The Marcomanni drove them from these settlements into Noricum and Pannonia, bet. Isara fl. and Arrabo fl. There was a tribe of them, called also Boates, on the coast of Novem Populana, s.w. of Burdigala. II. capital of the Boii, Lugdunensis. *Boui, near Entrain.* III. Boates, capital of the Boii, Novem Populana. *Tête de Buch.*

BOIODŪNUM (Boiodurum), cap. of the Boii, Noricum, on the Danube, at the confluence of Ænus fl. *Innstadt.*

BOIUM, I. a town of the Dassaretæ, Illyria, on the w. shore of the Lychnitis palus, s. of Sation. II. of Doris, S.E. of Erineus. *Mariolates.*

BOLA (Volæ), a town of the Latini, or, according to Livy, of the Æqui, Latium, bet. Præneste and Tolerium. An Alban settlement. *Poli.*

BOLBÆ, Caria, i. q. Heraclea.

BOLBE, I. a lake of Anthemus, Mygdonia, E. of Anthemus lacus. *Betchik.* II. a town on the N. shore of the lake. *Betchik.*

BOLBENE (Balabilene), a district of Armenia Minor, on the borders of Sophene, N. of Anzitene. *Balahovidh.*

BOLBITENE, a town of Lower Egypt, at the mouth of Bolbiticum Ostium Nili, L.

BOLBITICUM OSTIUM (Bolbitinum), a mouth of the Nile, E. of Canopicum Ostium.

BOLBULA ins., an isl. of Ionia, towards the mouth of Caystrus fl.

BOLEI, a town of Argolis, on Argolicus sin., bet. Didymus and Philanorium.

BOLELASGUS, a town of the Trocmi, Galatia, bet. Ancyra (24) and Sarmalia (24).

BOLENTIUM, a town of Pannonia Inferior, on Dravus fl., R., bet. Mariniana and Sirota.

BOLINÆUS fl., a r. of Achaia, falling into Corinthiacus sin. below Boline.

BOLINE, a town of Achaia, bet. Argyra and Erineus portus, on Bolinæus fl. Extinct in the time of Pausanias.

BOLISSUS, a town of Chios ins., at its N.W. extremity. *Volisso.*

BOLLIA fl., a r. of Germania Magna, of uncertain position. Represented by some geographers as falling into the Danube E. of Anabum.

BOMAREI, a people of Bactria, near the Oxus.

BOMBUS fl., a r. of Cilicia Campestris.

BOMIUM, I. a town of Ætolia, N. of Ægitium, near the source of Evenus fl. II. of the Belgæ, Britannia, 15 m. N. from Leucarum. *Near Bridgewater, at the confluence of the Tone and Parret.* III. (Bovium), of the Silures, bet. Isca Silurum and Nidus. *Boverton; Ervenny.*

BOMO, "cattle," the name given to Eubœa by its Arabic colonists under Cadmus (Kademah).

BONÆ FORTUNÆ ins., an isl. of India e. Gangem, parallel w. with Aurea Chersonnesus, and extending S.E. to Jabadii ins. Inhabited by Anthropophagi. *Great Andaman isl.*

BONCHÆ, Mesopotamia, i. q. Batani.

BONCONICA (Bauconica), a town of the Vangiones, Germania I., on the Rhine, bet. Moguntiacum (11) and Borbetomagus (19½). *Oppenheim.*

BONDELIA, a town of Etruria, N. of Luca. *Pedona.*

BONIS, a town of India-Gedrosia, s.w. of Alexandria Sogdiorum.

BONNA, *Celticè* Buhn, *postea* Verona, a town of the Ubii, Germania I., on the Rhine, above Colonia Agrippina. The quarters of the Sixth Legion. *Bonn.*

BONOCHÆMÆ, a tribe of Hermunduri, Germania, on Albis fl., L.

BŎNŌNIA, *prius* Felsina, I. an Etruscan city of Gallia Cispadana, bet. Ad Medias (7) and Claterna (15), on Via Æmilia Lepida. Taken by the Gauls 194 B.C. A colonia 1101 B.C. *Bologna.* II. a town of the Mœsi, Mœsia Superior, on the Danube, bet. Dorticum and Ad Malum. *Bodon?* III. of Pannonia Inferior, on the Danube, bet. Milata (16) and Sirmium (19). *Illock?* IV. A later name of Gessoriacum.

BONTOBRICA, a town of the Treveri, Germania I., on the Rhine, bet. Bingium and Confluentes. *Boppart.*

BOON, a town of Meroe, on the Nile, R., bet. Pnups and Berethis.

BOONA, Pontus, *vide* Genetes.

BOOSCÆTE, Bithyniæ, i. q. Helgas.

BOOSURA prom., Cyprus, i. q. Dinaretum.

BOPOS, a town of Thebais, on the Nile, R., bet. Chenoboscia and Cœnopolis.

BORACTA, a town of India e. Gangem, on the Ganges, at its junction with Sarabus fl.

BORANI, a tribe of Bastarnæ, Sarmatia.

BORBETOMĂGUS (Augusta Vangionum), *postea* Warmatia, a town of the Vangiones, Germania I., on the Rhine, above Bonconica. *Worms.*

BORBORUS fl., a stream of Bottiæa, falling into Pellæus lac.

BORCANII, Parthia, i. q. Barcani.

BORCOVICUS, a town of the Brigantes, Britan., at Hadriani mur, s. bet. Æsica and Citurnum. The station of the Cohors Prima Tungrorum. *Housesteads.*

BOREALIS OCEANUS, a name of the Arctic Ocean.

BOREUM, I. a m. of Arcadia, bet. Megalopolis and Tegea. II. OSTIUM, a mouth of the Danube, bet. Pseudo Ostium and Psilo Ostium. III. a pr. of Cyrenaica, w. marking the termination of the *northern* horn of Syrtis Major. IV. of Cyrenaica, w. bet. Caminus and Ampalaontes, s. of Berenice. *Cape Tejuni.* V. the N.W. extremity

of Hibernia, below Venicnium prom. *Malin Head.* VI. the N. extremity of Taprobane.

BORGYS, I. a r. of the Heniochi, Sarmatia, falling into the Euxine above Abasgus fl. II. a port of the Heniochi, at the mouth of Borgys fl. *Ketchili.*

BORMANNI, a town of the Camatullicini, Narbonensis, N.E. of Olbia. *Bormes.*

BORMANUM, a town of the Jazyges Metanastæ, E. of Uskenum.

BORON, a town of the Apuani, Liguria, on Boactes fl., bet. In Apennino (2) and Luna.

BORRAMA, a fortress of Phœnicia, on the coast, bet. Tripolis and Aradus.

BORSIPPA (Borsippon, Barsita), a town of Babylonia, on Naarsares fl., near Babylon. The seat of a college of Chaldæan astronomers. Noted for its flax manufactures. *Semaue; Cufa.*

BORTINÆ, a town of the Vescitani, Tarraconensis, w.N.w. of Osca. *Almuderar.*

BORUSCI, a people of Sarmatia, towards Riphæi m. The probable progenitors of the Prussians.

BORYSTHENES, I. an isl. of Sarmatia, E. at the outer mouth of the Borysthenes. II. fl., *postea* Danapris, a r. of Sarmatia E. rising in Budinus m. and falling into the Euxine E. of the mouth of Hypanis fl. *Dnieper.* III. a name of Olbia, Sarmatia.

Bos prom., a pr. of Bithynia, on Bosporus Thracius, bet. Calchedon and Chrysopolis. Named from the landing here of Io.

BOSA, a maritime town of the Coracenses, Sardinia, w. bet. Cornus and Carbia, at or near the mouth of Temus fl. *Buosa.*

BOSARA, a port of Arabia Felix, N.E. of Basag. *Masora; Mizi.*

BOSPORUS, *quasi* "fordable by a bullock," I. CIMMERIUS, the strait communicating bet. the Euxine and Palus Mæotis, and separating, at that point, Europe from Asia. *Bosporus; Stretto di Zabache; S. di Cafa; S. di Feodosia.* II. (THRACIUS, MYSIUS, CALCHEDONIÆ), the strait bet. Thrace and Mysia, connecting the Euxine with the Propontis. Traditionally named from the passage of Io. *Bosporus.* III. i. q. Panticapæum.

BOSTRA, *vide* Bozra.

BOSTRENUS fl., a r. of Phœnicia, falling into the sea at Sidon.

BOTRYS (Teros), a town of Phœnicia, on the coast, 12 m. N. from Byblus.

BOTTÆUM, a town of Lycaonia, on Tattæa pal.

BOTTIÆA (Bottiæis), a district of Macedonia, bet. the Haliacmon and the Axius, s. of Emathia.

BOTTIÆI, a people of Cretan origin, settled first in Bottiæa, and then in Chalcidice about Therme and Olynthus.

BOTRODUS, a town of the Celtiberi, Tarraconensis, near Segobriga.

BOUM, a town of Æthiopia, on the Nile, L.

BOUTA, a town of the Bagi-Gætuli, Africa.

BŎVIĀNUM, capital of the Pentri, Samnium, on Via Numicia, bet. Æsernia (18) and Ad Tamarum (16). A colonia of Julius Cæsar. The parent city, of the same name, stood about 12 miles N.E. *Boiano.*

BŎVILLÆ, I. a town of the Hernici, or rather of the Volsci, Latium, towards Arpinum. *Banco.* II. surnamed Suburbanæ, of the Latini, Latium, 9½ m. S.E. from Rome, on Appia Via. A municipium and colonia. The death-place of P. Clodius. *Osteria delle Frattochie.*

BOVIUM, a town of the Ordovices, Brit., bet. Deva (10) and Mediolanum (20). *Harthill.*

BOXUM, a town of the Ædui, Lugdunensis I., bet. Augustodunum N.E. and Aquæ Nisenæ S.W.

BOZIATA, a town of Albania Asiatica.

BOZRAH (Bostra), I. capital of Auranitis, 24 m. S.E. from Adraa. A colonia of Trajan. *Ma Sherik Hauran.* II. of Edom, S.E. of the s. extremity of the Dead Sea, N. of Petra. *El Busaireh.*

BRACA, "standing pools," the local name of Bagradas fl., Africæ, from its slow course and its tendency, more especially towards its mouth, to form pools and lakes.

BRACĂRA AUGUSTA, capital of the Bracari, Tarraconensis, on Celadus fl., L., above Celiobriga. A colonia. *Braga.*

BRACARI, a tribe of Callæci, bet. Minius fl. N.W. and Durius fl. S.

BRACCHIUM, a town of the Brigantes, Britan., on Urus fl., R., towards its source.

BRACHEA, a name of the Red Sea, from its numerous shoals.

BRACHMANES, a people or, more probably, a caste of Indians, settled in Æmodi m. and elsewhere.

BRACHME, a town of India i. Gangem, in Æmodi m. A seat of the Brachmins.

BRACHŌDES prom. (Ammon Balithonos), a pr. of Byzacene, bet. Acholla and Ruspæ. *C. Capoudiah.*

BRADANUS fl., a r. of Italy, rising in the Apennines bet. Venusia and Potentia, and, after separating Lucania from Apulia, falling into Tarentinus sin. N.E. of Metapontum. *Bradano.*

BRAGODURUM, a town of the Leutrenses, Vindelicia, on the Danube, below Brigobanna.

BRAMMA, a port of the Aspithræ, on Magnus sin., s. of Aspithra.

BRANCHIDÆ, a people of Sogdiana, towards Nautaca.

BRANODUNUM, a town of the Iceni, Britan., at the s. entrance of Metaris Æstuar., N.W. of Venta Icenorum. A station of the Equites Dalmatæ. *Brancaster.*

BRANOGENIUM (Branovium), *locally* Wyreceaster, a town of the Dobuni, Britannia, on Sabrina fl., N. of Glevum. *Worcester.*

BRATANANIUM, a town of the Consuanetæ, Rhætia, on Isara fl., 12 m. N.E. from Urusa. *East of Gerezried.*

BRATTIA ins., an isl. of the Adriatic, one of the Liburnides ins., opposite Salona. Noted for its goats' cheese and its wine. *Brazzo.*

BRATUSPANTIUM, Belgica, i. q. Cæsaromagus.

BRAURON, a demus of Attica, of the tribe Æneis, near the mouth of Eresinus fl., bet. Pallene and Prusiæ. Here Iphigenia landed with the statue of Diana. *Palaio-Vronna.*

BRAVINIUM, a town of the Ordovices, Britannia II., S.E. of Mediolanum. *Ludlow.*

BREGÆTIUM (Brigantium), a town of the Amantini, Pannonia, on the Danube, below Carnuntum. A station of the Legio Prima Adjutrix. The death-place of Valentinian. *Szony.*

BREGMENTINI, a people of Æolis Asiatica, towards Pergamum.

BREMENIUM, a town of the Otadeni, Valentia, S.E. of Coria Gadenorum. *Richester.*

BREMENTONACUM (Bremeterracum), a town of the Brigantes, Britan., N. of Coccium (22). *Lancaster.*

BREMETERRACUM, Britannia, i. q. Brementonacum.

BRENDICE, a town of the Cicones, Thrace, on Egnatia Via, bet. Maximianopolis (20) and Trajanopolis (37).

BRETTIOI, the Greek name of the Bruttii of Italy.

BRENTÉSION, "stag's head," the Messapian name of Brundusium.

BRENTHE, a town of Arcadia, on Brentheates fl., half a mile from its junction with Alpheus. *Koritena.*

BRENTONICUM (Bretina), a fortress of the Euganei, Gallia Transpadana, bet. Benacus lacus N.E. and the Athesis. *Brentonico.*

BRETINA, Gallia, i. q. Brentonicum.

BREUCI, a people of Pannonia, on the Savus.

BREUNI (Breones), a people of Rhætia, bet. Ænus fl. and Alpes Venetæ. *About the Grand Brenner, &c.*

BREVIODURUM, a town of the Lexovii, Lugdunensis II., N.E. of Noviomagus. *Pont Autou.*

BRICINNIÆ, a town of Sicily, s. of Leontini, near the source of Pantagias fl.

BRIGACINI (Trigacini), a tribe of Astures, Tarraconensis, about Brigæcium.

BRIGÆ, a town of the Belgæ, Britannia I., 11 m. w. from Venta Belgarum. *Broughton Farm.*

BRIGÆCIUM, capital of the Brigacini, on Asturica fl., 40 m. s.e. from Aug. Asturica. *Near Benevente.*

BRIGANTES (*Celticè* "plunderers"), I. a people of Britain, occupying the whole of Maxima Cæsariensis, with the exception of the portion occupied s. of Alaunus fl. by the Otadeni. *Durham, Cumberland, Westmoreland, Lancashire, and Yorkshire.* II. of Hibernia, s. *Waterford and part of Tipperary.*

BRIGANTII, I. a people of Alpes Maritimæ. *Vallée de Brianconnet.* II. of Rhætia, on Brigantinus lacus, s.

BRIGANTINUS portus, a bay of the Atlantic, at Flavium. *Puerto de la Coruna; The Groyne.*

BRIGANTINUS lacus (Acronius), a lake of Rhætia and Vindelicia, bet. Brigantium E. and Constantia w., formed by the Rhine. *Lake of Constance; Bodensee.*

BRIGANTIUM (Brigomagensium Civitas), capital of the Brigiani, Alpes Maritimæ, bet. In Alpe N.E. and Rama s. *Briançon.* II. (Bregantio), capital of the Brigantii, Rhætia, s.w. of Campodunum, at the E. extremity of Brigantinus lacus. *Bregentz.* III. Pannonia, i. q. Bregætium.

BRIGIANI, a tribe of Salyes, Narbonensis, N.W. of the Nerusci. *Vallée de Briançon.*

BRIGINNUM, *postea* Brinnonus, a town of the Volcæ Arecomici, Narbonensis I., bet. Vatrus and Sextatio. *Brignon, W. of Uzez.*

BRIGOBANNA, a town of the Latobrigi, Vindelicia, towards the source of the Rhine. *Breunlingen.*

BRIGULUS fl., an early name of the Arar.

BRILESSUS m., a N. ridge of Pentelici m., Attica, on Charadrus fl. *Turko-Vouni.*

BRINIATES, a tribe of Liguria, above Tigulia. *About Brugnetto.*

BRISA prom., a pr. of Lesbos ins., on the s.w. coast, E. of Eressus.

BRIOVEVA (Briodurum), a town of the Unelli, Lugdunensis II. *St. Lo.*

BRISOANA fl. (Brizana), a r. of Persis Proper, falling into Persicus sin., 50 m. N.W. from Rhogonis fl.

BRITABLUM (Brutobria), a town of the Vaccæi, Tarraconensis, N.E. of Segobia.

BRITANNIA, *Celticè* "land of painted men," *vide* Albion.

BRITANNICUS OCEANUS, the sea on the s. coast of Britain. *British Channel.*

BRITOLAGI, a tribe of Getæ, Dacia, bet. the Tyras fl. and Parata fl.

BRIULA (Biula, Priula), a town of Lydia, near Nysa.

BRIVA ISARA, a town of the Veliocasses, Lugdunensis II., on the Isara, bet. Petromantalum w.N.W. and Lutetia s.E.

BRIVAS, a town of the Arverni, Aquitania I., on the Elava, s.E. of Augustonemetum. *Brioude.*

BRIVATES portus, a port of the Namnetes, Lugdunensis III., bet. the mouth of the Liger and the Herius. *Brivain, near Croisic.*

BRIVODURUM, a town of the Senones, Lugdunensis IV., on the Liger, bet. Belca and Condate.

BRIXANTÆ, i. q. Brigantii.

BRIXELLUM, a town of Gallia Cispadana, on Padus fl., 20 m. N.W. from Regium Lepidum. A colonia. The death-place of Otho. *Bresello.*

BRIXIA fl., a r. of Susiana, falling into Persicus sin. Noted for the quantities of mud it deposited.

BRIXIA, capital of the Cenomanni, Gallia Transpadana, on Gortia fl., L., bet. Tetellus (10) and Ad Flexum (11), on Via Æmilia. An Etruscan city. A colonia and municipium. *Brescia.*

BRIZACA, a town of Armenia Major.

BRIZANA fl., Persis, i. q. Brisoana.

BROCOMAGUS, a town of the Tribocci, Germania I., N.E. of Tres Tabernæ. *Brumat.*

BRODENTIA, a town of the Marcomanni, Germania, E. of Reginum.

BRODONTII, a people of Viennensis, N. of the Uceni. *About Mt. Brodon.*

BROCĂVUM, a town of the Brigantes, Brit., s.E. of Voreda. *Brougham.*

BROMAGUS, a town of the Ambrones, Maxima Sequanorum, bet. Minodunum N. and Viviscus s.

BROMISCUS, a town of Chalcidice, Macedonia, on Strymonicus sin., at the mouth of Bolbe fl., bet. Apollonia (11) and Argilus (10).

BROVONACÆ, a town of the Brigantes, Brit., on Ituna fl., 13 m. s.E. from Voreda. *Kirby Thore.*

BROXÆ, a town of Venetia, near Forum Julii. *Brischis.*

BRUCHI, a people of Colchis, in Caucasus, N. of the Abasgi.

BRUCIDA, *vide* Brygias.

BRUCLA, a town of the Burideenses, Dacia, 12 m. N. from Apulum, on Mariscus fl.

BRUCTĔRI, a people of Germania, s. of the

Frisii and Chauci, N. of the Luppia, and w. of the Visurgis. They were divided by Amisia fl. into Bructeri Majores and Bructeri Minores.

BRUCHI, a people of Iberia, on the confines of Sarmatia.

BRUGETIA, *postea* Brugeria, a town of the Volcæ Arecomici, Narbonensis I., bet. Andusia and Tedusia. *Brugnière.*

BRUNDISII prom., a headland at the entrance of the harbour of Brundusium. *Capo Cavallo.*

BRUNDUSIUM (Brindisium), a port of Calabria, on the Adriatic, bet. Speluncæ and Baletium. Of date prior to 700 B.C. A colonia 246 B.C. *Brindisi.*

BRUSILIANA, a town of Numidia, bet. Siguss (7) and Thacia (7).

BRUTIDÆ, a phratria of Attica.

BRUTTIUM, a region of Italy, occupying the "toe of the boot," bounded N. by Lucania, at Laus fl., and Crathis fl., and elsewhere by the sea. Settled by a body of slaves, fugitives, as the name imported, from Lucania. *Calabria Ultra.*

BRUTTIUS sinus, a bay of the Tyrrhenian sea, at Metaurum. *Golfo di Gioja.*

BRUXOS, Phrygia, i. q. Druzon.

BRYANIUM, a town of Pelagonia, Pæonia, on Erigonus fl., above Alcomenæ.

BRYAZON (Olachas), I. a r. of Bithynia, falling into Astacenus sin. Its water was reputed to choke perjurers. II. a town of Bithynia, on Bryazon fl., bet. Calchedon and Nicomedia.

BRYCHON fl., I. a stream of Magnesia, Thessaly, rising in Pelion m. and falling into Pagasæus sin. II. a r. of Pallene, Macedonia.

BRYCLICE, an inland district of Cilicia Campestris.

BRYGI (Brygii, Phrygi), a tribe of Dassaretæ, Illyria, on the confines of Macedonia.

BRYGIAS (Brygium, Brucida), capital of the Brygi, Illyria, E. of Lychnitis palus, on the Via Egnatia, bet. Lychnidus (13) and Scirtiana (4). *Presba.*

BRYLLIUM, a town of Bithynia, near Cius.

BRYSEÆ, a town of Laconia, under Taygetus M., s.w. of Amyclæ.

BRYSTACIA, a town of the Œnotri, Bruttium, 6 m. w. from Crimisa. *Umbriatico.*

BRYZON (Bruzus, Dryzon), a town of Phrygia M., bet. Ipsus and Sozopolis.

BUANA (Semiramoceria), a town of Thospitis, Armenia, on Arsissa lac., s. above Artemita.

BUBACENE, a district of Bactria, on Oxus fl.

BUBALIA (Budalia), a town of Pannonia

Inferior, near Sirmium. The birth-place of the emperor Decius.

BUBASTICUS fl., a cut from the Tanitic branch of the Nile at Phacusa, to Pelusium, terminating in Pelusiacum Ostium. Constructed by Pharaoh Neco.

BUBASTUS (Bubastis, Pe-biseth), a city of Lower Egypt, on the Bubastic branch of the Nile, s.w. of Tanis. Named from the worship of Bubasht (Diana). The burial-place of the Sacred Cats. *Tel-Basta.*

BUBINDA fl., a r. of Hibernia, E. separating the Usluntii from the Eblani. *Boyne.*

BUBŌN, *postea* Sophianopolis, a town of Lycia, near Cibyra.

BUBULCORUM OPPIDUM, a maritime town of Galilea Inferior, bet. Ptolemais and Cæsarea.

BUBULUS fl., a r. of Dacia, rising w. of Zarmizegethusa and falling into Tibiscus fl. towards the junction of Savus fl.

BUCA, a port of the Frentani, s.E. of Sagrus fl. *Penna.*

BUCCIANA ins. (Bucinna), an isl. of Sardinia, E. below Hermæa ins. *La Vacca.*

BUCCO, a town of the Volcæ Tectosages, Narbonensis I., bet. Hunganverro w. and Tolosa E.

BUCĔPHĂLA, a town of India i. Gangem, on the Hydaspes, below the junction of the Acesines and Hydraotes. Founded by Alexander, in memory of his horse. *Moultan; Mung?*

BUCEPHALUS, I. a pr. of Argolis, near Haliusa. *Machorma.* II. a harbour of Corinthia, on Saronicus sin., N. of Piræus portus.

BUCHÆTIUM (Buchĕta, Bucenta), a town of Molossis, Epirus, on Acherusia palus. *San Giovanni.*

BUCI LAPIS, a town of Cilicia Prefectura, in Cappadocia.

BUCINA ins., an isl. of Sicily, one of the Ægates ins., N. of Ægusa, E. of Hiera.

BUCINOBANTES, a tribe of Chatti, Germania, under Taunus m. N.

BUCOLICUM OSTIUM, one of the artificial mouths of the Nile.

BUCOLION, a town of Arcadia, near Orestheium. Built by Bucolion.

BUCRA prom., a pr. of Sicily, s. below Camerina. *C. di Scalami.*

BUDEA (Budeum), a town of Magnesia, Thessaly.

BUDINI (Bodeni), a people of Sarmatia, about Budinus m. *Podolia?*

BUDINUM m., a m. of Sarmatia, E. towards the N. source of the Borysthenes?

BUDORGIS, i. q. Budorigum.

BUDORIGUM (Budorgis), a town of the

Diduni, Germania, E. of the source of the Albis. *Ratibor ?*

BUDORIS, a town of the Teucteri, Germania, on the Rhine, bet. Colonia Agrippina and Bonna. *Dusseldorf.*

BUDORUS, I. a r. of Ellopia, Euboea, running into the Ægean, E. of Artemisium prom., near Cerinthus. II. a fortress of Salamis, nearly opposite Megara. *Monastery of the Phaneromeni.*

BUDROA ins., an isl. on the N. coast of Crete, towards Drepanum prom.

BUDUA, a town of the Vettones, Lusitania, w.N.W. of Augusta Emerita.

BUDUXI, a town of Numidia, bet. Sigus and Visalta.

BUGLATA, a town of Numidia, bet. Ad Germani and Ad Mercurium.

BULICAS, Arabia, i. q. Ocelis.

BULIS, a town of Phocis, 1 m. N. from Mychos portus.

BULLA, I. surnamed Minsa, i. q. Carthago. II. surnamed Regia, a royal city of Numidia, s. of Tabraca. *Badscha.*

BULLEUM, i. q. Burrium.

BUMADUS (Bumellus) fl., a r. of Adiabene, Assyria, falling into the Lycus below Gaugamela. *Chazir-Zou; Bohrus.*

BUMASINI, a people of Taprobane, on the w. coast, about Prasodes sin.

BUNIMA, a town of the Tymphæi, Epirus, bet. Trampya and Dodona. Founded by Ulysses.

BUNITIUM, a town of the Viruni, Germania, on Suevus fl., s.E. of Laciburgium. *Rostock.*

BUNOMUS, the early name of Pella, Macedonia.

BUPHAGIUM, a town of Arcadia, near the source of Buphagus fl., 5 m. s.E. from Melæneæ.

BUPHÀGUS fl., a r. of Arcadia, falling into Alpheus fl. near Buphagium.

BUPHIA, a town of Achaia, towards Sicyon.

BUPHRUS fl., a r. of Messenia, rising in Ægialeus m., and falling into the sea N. of Coryphasium prom. *Brisomeri.*

BUPORTHMUS prom., a pr. of Argolis, over against Aperopia ins.

BUPRÀSIUM, a town of Epea, Elis, s. of Larissa. Extinct in Strabo's time.

BURA, one of the twelve cities of Achaia, on Buraicus fl., s.E. of Cerynia; near the site of an earlier cognominal city, destroyed by an earthquake.

BURAICUS fl., a r. of Achaia, rising in Lampe m., and falling into Corinthiacus sin. below Bura. On its banks was an oracle of Hercules, consulted by dice-throwing. *Calavrita.*

BURCA fl., Sarmat., i. q. Achæus.

BURCHANA ins., one of the Electrides ins., off the mouth of Amisia fl. *Borcum.*

BURDIGÀLA, capital of the Bituriges Vivisci, Aquitania II., on the Garumna, L., towards its mouth. The birth-place of Ausonius. *Bordeaux.*

BURDIPTA, a town of the Odrysæ, Thrace, on Hebrus fl., bet. Subzupara and Hadrianopolis.

BURDEXTIUM, a town of the Cælatæ, Thrace, on Harpessus fl., bet. Rhamæ and Daphaba.

BURGENA, a town of Pannonia Inf., on the Danube, bet. Rittium (15) and Taurunum (10). *Near Tassa S.*

BURGINATIUM, a town of the Quaderni, Germania II., on the Rhine, at the confluence of the Vahalis. *Schankenschantz.*

BURGUNDIONES, a tribe of Vindili, German., bet. Viadrus fl. and Vistula fl., N. of the Omani. The progenitors of the Gaulish Burgundians.

BURÌDAVA, *postea* Taba, capital of the Buridenses, Dac., on Aluta fl., R., bet. Castra Trajani and Pons Aluti (13).

BURIDEENSES, a tribe of Agathyrsi, Dacia, about the sources of Marissus fl.

BURII, a tribe of Lygii, Germania, about Asciburgius m.

BURNUM (Burnium), a town of Illyria.

BURRIUM (Bulleum), a town of the Silures, Brit., on Isca fl., N. of Isca Silurum (9). *Usk.*

BURSAO (Bursada), a town of the Pelendones, Tarraconensis, towards Deobriga. *Borja.*

BURTUDIZUS, a town of the Odrysæ, Thrace, on Tearus fl., bet. Ostudizum and Bergula.

BURUNCA, a town of the Ubii, Germania I., on the Rhine, above Durnomagus.

BUSENTUS (Barentinus) fl., a r. of Bruttium, falling into the Crathis at Consentia. *Busiento.*

BUSITIS (Buzites), a district of Arabia Des. Named from Buz, second son of Nahor.

BUSIRIS, a city of Lower Egypt, on the Busiritic branch of the Nile, below Leontopolis. Built by Busiris. Sacred to Isis. *Aboussir.*

BUSIRITICUM OSTIUM NILI, the name of Phatmeticum Ostium, towards Busiris.

BUTEIA (Butadæ), a demus of Attica, of the tribe Æneis. Named after Butæus.

BUTHEMANEI, Arabia, i. q. Themanei.

BUTHROTUM, a town of Thesprotia, Epirus, at Posidium prom., 26 m. from Phœnice. Founded by Helenus, son of Priam. A colonia. *Butrinto.*

BUTHROTUS fl., a r. of Bruttium, falling into Locrensis sinus, 2 m. N. from Locri. *Novito.*

BUTHURUS, a town of Numidia, near the source of Bagradas fl.

BUTICUS lacus, a lake of Lower Egypt, at Butus, formed by the Saitic and Sebennytic branches of the Nile.

BUTRIUM, an Umbrian town of Gallia Cispad., bet. Ravenna (11) and Augusta (11). *Butrio ? Sant' Alberto ?*

BUTUA (Buthoe), a town of the Enchelees, on the Adriatic, bet. Rhizon (15) and Olcinium (90). Founded by Cadmus. *Boudoua.*

BUTUNTUM, a town of Peucetia, on Via Egnatia, bet. Rubi (11) and Barium (11). *Bitonto.*

BUTUS, a town of Lower Egypt, on Buticus lac., bet. Sais and Sebennyticum Ost. Noted for an oracle of Latona. *Kom-Kasir.*

BUXENTUM (Pyxus, "full of box-trees"), I. a r. of Lucania, falling into the sea N.W. of Blanda. *Busento.* II. a pr. of Lucania, at Buxentum. *Capo degli Infreschi.* III. a town of Lucania, at the mouth of Buxentum fl. Founded by Micythus, king of Rhegium, *circa* 471 B.C. A colonia 196 B.C. *Near Policastro.*

BUZARA m., m. of Mauritania Cæsariensis, a w. continuation of Audus m. *Tittery.*

BYBASSIA CHERSONESUS, the termination of Doris Chersonesus, Caria, above Cnidus.

BYBASSIUS sin., a bay of Schœnus sin. s., at the commencement of Bybassia Chersonesus. *G. Lithotronda.*

BYBLOS, I. Egypt, i. q. Aphroditopolis. II. *postea* Zebelet, a town of Phœnicia, towards the coast, bet. Berytus and Tripolis. Sacred to Thammuz (Adonis). *Dsjebal, Esbile.*

BYCE lac. (Buges, Sapra), a morass of Sarmatia E., formed by Palus Mæotis, at the entrance of Coretus sin. *Guiloé Moré.*

BYCES fl., a r. of Sarmatia Europ., falling into Byce lac.

BYLÆ, a town of Pontus, s. of Trapezus. Noted for its silver mines, whence the modern name. *Gumish-Nameh.*

BYLAZŌRA, a town of the Agrianes, Pæonia, on Pontus fl., below Æstræum. *Velesa.*

BYLLINI, a people of Illyria N.

BYLLIS, a town of the Taulantii in Illyria, on Æas fl., R., above Nymphæum, S.E. of Apollonia. A colonia (col. Byllidensis). *Gradista.*

BYLTÆ, a people of Scythia i. Imaum, on Indus fl., R., towards its source.

BYRIN m., m. of Africa, on both sides of Ampsaga fl.

BYRSI (Brysi, Bræsi), a tribe of Æmathi, Macedonia, about Scydra.

BYSNÆI, a tribe of Bebryces, in Bithynia.

BYZACENA (Byzacium), the s. division of Africa Propria, extending along the coast from Horrea to Meninx ins.

BYZACIA (Mamma), capital of Byzacene, on Syrtis Minor, N.E. of Tritonis pal. *Beghui.*

BYZANTES, the people of Byzacena, Africa.

BYZANTIUM, I. *prius* Lygos, a city of the Odrysæ, Thrace, on Thracius Bosporus, at the entrance of the Propontis. Founded by a colony from Megara-Nisæa, under Byzas, 715 B.C.; enlarged by immigrants from Lacedæmon, Miletus, and Athens; and made by Constantine the capital of the Eastern Empire, and named first Nea Roma, and then Constantinopolis. *Stamboul ("the city"), Constantinople.* II. surnamed Toparon, a port of Ariaca, India, on Barygazenus sinus.

BYZĒRES, a people of Pontus, on the coast, bet. Achabis fl. and Acampsis fl.

C.

CABADENE, a district of Carmania Deserta, on the confines of Drangiana.

CABALACA, Alban, i. q. Chabala.

CABALEA, a later name of Milyas, Lycia.

CABALEI (Lasonii), a Mæonian tribe, who settled in Milyas, Lycia.

CABALLICOME, a town of Lycaonia, 23 m. S.E. from Laodicea.

CABALSUS, a town of Thebais, bet. Hydræum Apollinis and Hydræum Cænon.

CABANA, I. a port of Arabia Felix, on Persicus sin., E. of Cadara. *Calba.* II. of the Oritæ, Gedros., bet. Cocala and Pagala.

CABANDENE, the E. portion of Susiana s.

CABALI, a people of Cyrenaica, s. of Cyrene.

CABAR SASIA, a town of Byzacene, near Hadrumetum. *Susa.*

CABARNIS ins., an early name of Paros ins.

CABASA, a town of Lower Egypt, on the Saitic branch of the Nile, L., below Sais. *Cabas el Melek.*

CABASSUS, a town of Cataonia.

CABELEES (Solymi), i. q. Cabalei.

CABELLIO, capital of the Cavares, Viennensis, on Druentia fl., S.E. of Avenio. *Cavaillon.*

CABERASA, a town of Media.

CABILLŌNUM (Caballinum, Cabillōnes), a town of the Ædui, Lugdunensis I., on the Arar, R., above Tinurtio. *Chalons sur Saone.*

CABIRA (Diopolis, Sebastopolis, Sebaste), a city of Pontus, on Lycus fl., R., 15 m. above Eupatoria, under Paryadres m. The favourite abode of Mithridates Eupator. Enlarged by Pompey and by Pythodoris.

CABUBATHRA m., the southernmost headland of Arabia Felix, E. of Catabania. *Capo St. Antonio.*

CABURA, Arachos, i. q. Ortospana.

CABURRO, a town of the Vagienni, Liguria. *Cavor, near Bagnolo.*

CABUSIACUM, a town of the Remi, Belgica II., bet. Verbinum N. and Ninitacum s.

CABYLE, a town of the Crobyzi, Thrace, w. of Anchialus.

CACHĂLES fl., a r. of Phocis, running by Tithorea into the Cephisus. *Kako-Rheuma.*

CACIDARI, the early name of the Arimaspi.

CACOBÆ, a people of India i. Gangem, under Emodi m., E. of the Aminachæ.

CACUTHIS fl., a r. of India e. Gangem, falling into the Ganges. *Gumty.*

CACYPĂRIS fl., a r. of Sicily, falling into the sea, s. of Longum prom. *Cassibile.*

CACYRUM, a town of Sicily, N. of Gela. *Cassaro.*

CADARA, a town of the Borgodi, Arabia, on Persicus sin., s.E. of Catara. *Godo.*

CADARÆ, *rectius* Cataræ, a tribe of Agræi, Arabia, on Persicus sin., N. of the Rhadamæi.

CADI, a town of the Abbaites, Phrygia Epictetus, on Peucella fl., s.w. from Synnaus. Noted for its scammony. *Kedous.*

CADIANUM, a town of the Cenomanni, Venetia, bet. Verona (10) and Ad Aureos (10), on Via Æmilia. *Caldiero.*

CADISTUS m., a w. summit of Berecynthus m., above Polyrrhenia. *M. Grabusa.*

CADMEIA, the early name of Thebes in Bœotia, after Cadmus.

CADMEIS, a name of Bœotia, from Cadmus.

CADMUS, I. a r. of Phrygia M., falling into Lycus fl. near Laodicea. II. a ridge of Taurus, in Lycia, extending to Laodicea. *Baba Dagh.*

CADRAITÆ, Arabia, i. q. Cedrei.

CADRUSI (Cetrosa), a town of the Gandarii, Arachosia, N.W. of Tazora. Built by Alexander.

CADUPI, a people of Ethiopia, on the Nile, R., near the great cataract.

CADURCI, I. a people of Aquitania I., bet. the Petrocorii and Nitiobriges w. and the Ruteni E. *Department of Lot.* II. their cap., i. q. Divona.

CADUSII (Gelæ), a people of Med. Atropatene, on the Caspian, s. of Caspiane. Memorable for their long warfare with the Medes. *Guilan?*

CADYNA, a town of Tyanitis, Cappadocia, s.w. of Castabala. *Nigdé.*

CADYTA (Cadytis), i. q. Jerusalem? Gath?

CÆCIÆ ins., two islets of Argolis, off Spiræum prom.

CÆCINUM, a town of Bruttium, on Cæcinus fl., R., near its mouth. *Satriano.*

CÆCINUS fl., a r. of Bruttium, falling into Scylleticus sin. s. of Scylletium. *Ancinale.*

CÆCŬBUS ager, the country about Amyclæ, Latium, celebrated for its wine.

CÆDESSA (Kedes), a city of refuge of Naphthali, Galilee Sup., towards Tyre.

CÆDIA, a town of the Sidicini, Campania, near Sinuessa.

CÆDITIÆ TABERNÆ, a post-house on Via Appia, in Campania, near Cædia.

CÆDITIUS CAMPUS, the district around Cædia, Campania.

CÆDIUM, a town of the Nertereani, Germ., s. of Pheugarum.

CÆDRUS fl., a r. of Sardinia, falling into the sea at Fanum Carisii.

CÆLA, the coast of Eubœa, bet. Geræstus prom. and Chalcis.

CÆLÆA ins., an isl. of the Omanitæ, Arabia.

CÆLADUS fl., a r. of Tarraconensis, falling into the Atlantic below Bracara Augusta.

CÆLE, the funeral suburb of Athens. The birth-place of Cymon and Thucydides.

CÆLATÆ, I. Majores, a tribe of Odrysæ, Thrace, under Hæmus m. II. Minores, a tribe of Odrysæ, under Rhodope m.

CÆLIANUM, a town of Lucania, on Bradanus fl., bet. Opinum (32) and Heraclea (25). *Cirigliano.*

CÆNA, I. a town of Acabene, Mesopotamia, on the Tigris, at the confluence of the Caprus. *Senn.* II. of Pontus, i. q. Ænus. III. of Tyanitis, Cappadocia, bet. Tyana (13) and Podandus (12).

CÆNE, a town of Lower Egypt, on the Nile, L., bet. Iseum and Tacona.

CÆNINA, a town of Sabinium, on the Anio, near Antemnæ. Colonized by Romulus. *Monticelli.*

CÆNON, a port of Cyrenaica, bet. Euschænus and Apis.

CÆNONCHORION, a fortress of Pontus, on Lycus fl., 5 geog. m. from Cabira. The treasure-fortress of Mithridates.

CÆNOPOLIS, I. a town (Vagharschapat) of Cotacene Armen., N.E. of Armauria. *Ardimed Khagbag.* II. of Laconia, i. q. Tænarum. III. of Cyrenaica, bet. Ptolemais (32) and Cyrene (33). IV. of Thebais, on the Nile, R., bet. Bopos and Coptos.

CÆNUS fl., a r. of Narbonensis, falling into the sea E. of Maritima Avaticorum. *Arc.*

CÆNỸRA, a town of Thasos ins. E., over against Samothrace.

CÆNYS prom., a pr. of Bruttium, over against Pelorus prom. *Punta del Pezzo; Coda del Volpe.*

CÆPIANA, a maritime town of the Celtici, Lusitan. w. of Cætobrix.

CÆPIONIS turris, a lighthouse at the N.W. extremity of Tartessus ins.

CÆRATUS, I. the early name of Gnossus. II. a r. of Crete, running by Gnossus into the sea at Heracleium. *Cartero.*

CÆRE, I. a Siculian city of Etruria, on Cæretanus fl., 4 m. from the sea, w.n.w. of Rome. It was taken by the Tyrrheni (who named it Agylla) and became one of their twelve Etrurian cities. The capital of Mezentius. A colonia and municipium. Extinct in Strabo's time. *Cer Vetere.* II. a town of the Vettones, Lusitania, on Cuda fl., near its source.

CÆRESII, a tribe of Tungri, Germania II., on Sura fl.

CÆRETANUS fl., a r. of Etruria, falling into the sea below Cære. *Vaccina.*

CÆSADA, a town of Tarraconensis, bet. Complutum and Bilbilis.

CÆSAR AUGUSTA, *prius* Salduba, a city of the Edetani, Tarraconensis, on the Iberus, at the confluence of the Gallicus, below Allobon. Colonized with the Emeriti of the 4th, 6th, and 10th Legions. *Saragossa, Zaragosa.*

CÆSARĒA, I. ins., *prius* Angia, an isl. of Lugdunensis II., s.e. of Sarnia ins. *Jersey.* II. *prius* Paneas (Banias), a city of Galilæa Superior, n.e. of Dan. Surnamed Philippi by Philip, son of Herod. III. *prius* Jol, capital of Mauritania Cæsar., on the coast, bet. Tipasa and Gunugio (12). Renamed by Juba. A colonia of Claudius. *Vacur.* IV. *prius* Turris Stratonis, a city of Samaria, on the coast, s.w. of Megiddo. Renovated and renamed by Herod. The birth-place of Eusebius. A colonia (Prima Flavia). *Kaisarieh.* V. Bithyniæ, i. q. Helgas. VI. Cappadociæ, i. q. Mazaca. VII. Ciliciæ, i. q. Anazarba. VIII. Lydiæ, i. q. Hiero Cæsarea.

CÆSARIANA (Cæsarina), I. a town of Lucania, on Tanager fl., towards its source, bet. Marcelliana (14) and Nerulum (28), on Via Aquilia. *Casal Nuovo.* II. of the Amantini, Pannonia, bet. Osones and Mogetiana.

CÆSAROBRIGA, a town of the Vettones, Lusitan., on the Tagus.

CÆSARODUNUM, *postea* Turones, capital of the Turones, Lugdunensis III., on the Rhone, L., bet. Robrica and Tasciaca. *Tours.*

CÆSARŎMĂGUS, I. *postea* Bellovaci, capital of the Bellovaci, Belgica II., bet. Curmiliaca n.w. and Litanobriga s.e. *Beauvais.* II. a town of the Trinobantes, Brit., bet. Canonium and Durolitum. *Widford, near Colchester.*

CÆSENA, surnamed Curva, a town of Gallia Cispadana, on Sapis fl., R., bet. Forum Popilii (6) and Compitum (6). *Cesena.*

CÆSIA silva, a forest of Germania Magna, on the Luppia. *Häserwald.*

CÆSIÆ littus, the coast of Corsica n., bet. Attium prom. and Tilox prom.

CÆSIUS fl., a r. of Asia, separating Albania from Sarmatia Asiatica, and falling into the Caspian.

CÆTE ins., an isl. on the n. coast of Crete, over against Cydonia. *San Teodoro.*

CÆTOBRIX, a town of Lusitania, 3 m. w. from Salacia.

CAGULATÆ, a people of Arabia, under Climax m., contiguous to the Elamitæ. *Tribe of Beni Kholan.*

CAHALETUS, a town of the Sellitæ, Thrace, on Hæmus m., bet. Soatræ and Anchialus.

CAICANDRUS ins., an isl. of Persia, off Ila.

CAICINUS fl., a r. of Bruttium, falling into Siculum mare, 10 m. w. from Herculeum prom. The boundary of the territories of Locria and Rhegium. On its Locrian side the Cicadæ were always chirping; on the other bank always mute. The death-place of Euthymus. *Amendolea.*

CAICUS fl., a r. of Mysia, rising in Temnus m. and falling into Elæaticus sin., 3 m. s. of Elæa. *Aksou* or *Bakirchay.*

CAIETA, a town of the Ausones, Latium, at Caietanum prom., s. of Formiæ. A Lacedæmonian settlement. Named from the nurse of Æneas buried there, or rather from the Spartan word *kaiata* " *cavern.*" *Gaeta.*

CAIETANUM prom., a pr. of Latium, at the n. entrance of Formianus sin. The burialplace of Æneas' nurse.

CAIETANUS sinus, i. q. Formianus.

CAINAS fl., a r. of India i. Gangem, rising in Vindius m. and (formerly) falling into the Ganges below its junction with Sittocacis fl. *Kan.*

CAISA, a town of Amordocia, Babylonia, s.w. of Orrhoe.

CALABANTIA, a maritime village of Lycia, 6 m. from Perdiciæ.

CALABRIA, the country of the Calabri, a tribe of Japyges, settled in the e. of Japygia, extending along the Adriatic from Turris Aureliana to Portus Tarentinus. *Terra di Lecce.*

CALACHENE (Calacina), a district of Adiabene, Assyria, on the Tigris, n. of Aturia.

CALACTA, a maritime town of Sicily, n. bet. Chydas fl. and Alæsa. Named from its beautiful coast scenery. *Near Caronia.*

CALADA fl., a r. of Zeugitana, falling into the Mediterranean at Tunis.

CALÆGIA, a town of the Calucones, Germania, s.e. of Melibocum. *Wittemberg ?*

CALĂGUM, a town of the Meldi, Lugdunensis

IV., bet. Jatinum N.W. and Riobe s.w. *Chailly.*

CALAGURRIS (Calagorina), *surnamed* Nasica, I. capital of the Vascones, Tarraconensis, on the Iberus, R., above Græcurris. A colonia (Julia). Memorable for the famine it underwent in the Sertorian war. The birth-place of Quintilian. *Calahorra.* II. of the Vescitani, Tarraconensis, bet. Jacca N. and Osca s. *Surnamed* Fibularensis from the Fibulæ manufactured there. *Loarra.* III. a town of the Volcæ Tectosages, Narbonensis, on the Garumna, bet. Vernasole and Lugdunum.

CALAMA, I. a town of the Ichthyophagi, Gedros., bet. Cissa and Bagisara. *Calamat.* II. of Mauritania Cæsariensis, on Mulucha fl., towards its mouth. *Calaat el Wad?* III. of Numidia, on Rubricatus fl., R., above Tagaste. *Gelma.*

CALAMÆ, a village of Messenia, w. of Lymnæ. *Calamata.*

CALAMATIUS m., a m. of Lucania, near Pæstum. *Monte Capaccio.*

CALAMI, a port of Samos, over against Panionium.

CALAMISSUS, a town of the Locri Ozolæ, near Olpæ. *Calamitir.*

CALAMUS, a port of Phœnicia, on Rison fl., 3 m. s. from Sicaminos.

CALAMYDES, a town on the s. coast of Crete, bet. Lissus and Tarrha. *Colami.*

CALANTHIA, a village of Cilicia Trachea, 12 m. N.E. from Sebaste.

CALARNA (Turris Calarnea), a fortress of Chalcidice, Macedonia, on Strymon fl., N.W. of Acanthus.

CALASARNA, a town of Bruttium, near the source of Crimisa fl. *Campana.*

CALATHAI (Khaulothæi), a people of Arabia, s.w. of the mouth of the Euphrates. *Tribe of Beni Khaled.*

CALATHANA, a town of Dolopia, Thessaly, s.E. of Theuma.

CALATHE ins. (Galata), an isl. of Africa, off Tabraca. *Galita.*

CALATHIOS m., a m. of Messenia, near Gerenia, in which was a remarkable cavern. *Kalathi.*

CALATHUA, capital of the Calathæi, Arabia, w. of Jucara.

CALATIA (Galatia), I. a town of Campania, on Via Appia, bet. Capua (6) and Ad Novas (3), w.N.W. of Caudium. A colonia of Sylla and again of Julius Cæsar. *Galazze.* II. *potius* Caiatia, of the Pentri, Samnium, s. of Compulteria. *Cajazzo.*

CALAURIA ins., an isl. of Argolis, in Saronicus sin., over against Pogon portus. Exchanged by Latona with Neptune for Delos. The death-place of Demosthenes. *Isle des Corsaires.*

CALBIS fl., i. q. Chaus.

CALBIUM prom., a pr. of the Unelli, Lugdunensis, over against Sena ins. *Cape Raz.*

CALCARIA, I. a town of the Brigantes, s. of Eboracum (9). *Tadcaster.* II. of the Anatili, Narbonensis, on Astromela stagnum, N.W. of Solarium. *Calissane.*

CALCEUS HERCULIS, a town of Numidia, bet. Ad Duo Flumina and Aquæ Herculis.

CALCHEDON (Procerastes, Colpusa), a city of Bithynia, at the s. extremity of Bosporus Thracius. Enlarged by a colony from Megara Nisæa 732 B.C. Noted for its brass manufactures, whence the name. *Kadikeui.*

CALE, a demus of Attica. II. (Portus Cale, Portus Portus), a port of the Bracari, Tarraconensis, at the mouth, R., of Durius fl., 35 m. s.w. from Bracara Augusta. It gave name to Portugal. *Oporto (The Port).* III. of Mysia, towards Pergamum. IV. of the Parisii, Lugdunensis IV., on Matrona fl., bet. Jatinum and Lutetia. V. *surnamed* Parembole, of the Byzeres, Pontus, at the mouth of Calos fl.

CALECOME, a town of Chalybonitis, Syria, bet. Bathnæ and Chalcis.

CALEDONIA, the Latin form of *Caël-doch,* " land of the Gael."

CALEDONII, a people of Britannia Barbara, extending across the island s.w. to N.E., from Lelannonius sin. to Vara Æstuar.

CĂLĒLA, a town of Apulia, s.w. of Larinum. *Casa Calenda.*

CALENDA, a town of the Vaccæi, Tarraconensis, N.E. of Siptemanca.

CALENDERIS, a town of Argolis, on Pagon portus.

CALENTUM, a town of the Turtuli, Bætica, N.W. of Lacomurgi.

CĂLES (Calex), I. a r. of Bithynia, rising in Hypius m. and falling into the Euxine at Cales. II. a town of the Ausones, and afterwards of the Sidicini, Campania, on Via Latina, bet. Teanum (4) and Casilinum (7). A colonia, 333 B.C., and municipium. The emporium of the Falernian wine. *Calvi.* III. an emporium of Bithynia, on the Euxine, at the mouth of Cales fl., 15 m. from Elæa.

CALESIA, a town of the Diduni, Germania, bet. Setidava and Leucaristus. *Kalisch.*

CALETHE, a town of the Turtetani, Bætica, bet. Asindum and Carteia.

CALĒTI, a people of Lugdunensis II., on the coast, bet. the Sequana and the Phrudis ffl. *Pays de Caux.*

CALIGARA, a port of the Sinæ.

CALINAPAXA, a town of India i. Gangem, 2 m. from the Ganges, 167 m. below Rhodopha. *Canouge.*

CALINDA, Cariæ, i. q. Calymna.

CALINGÆ, a maritime people of India i. Gangem, bet. Tyndis fl. and Ganges fl.

CALINGII, a people of Arabia Felix, S.E. of Zames m. *Tribe of Beni Kaled.*

CALINGUM, capital of the Calingæ, India, on Tyndis fl. *Cullo.* II. prom., a pr. of the Calingæ, India. *Gordewar.*

CALIORDI, a people of Taurica Chersonesus.

CALITI, a people of Africa, towards the Nubæ.

CALLÆCI (Calläici, Gallæci), a people of Tarraconensis, bet. Cantabricum mare N., Durius fl. s., the Atlantic w., and the Astures E. *Entre Minho e Minho, Tras os Montes, Gallicia, and portions of Asturia and Leon.*

CALLAMÆON prom. (Calliuacron), a pr. of Marmarica, 5 m. w. of Laodamantius portus.

CALLAS fl., a r. of Eubœa, falling into the Ægean at Histiæa.

CALLATIS (Callatia, Cerastia), a town of the Crobyzi, Mœsia, on the Euxine, bet. Tomi (30) and Tetrisia. A mixed Milesian and Megarensian people.

CALLEVA (Calcua), capital of the Atrebatii, Britan., bet. Venta Belgarum and Ad Pontes. *Silchester.*

CALLIÆ, a people of Arcadia, towards Methydrium.

CALLIANE (Calliena), a port of India i. Gangem, bet. Simylla and Harmagara. *Surat.*

CALLIARUS, an inland town of the Locri Epicnemedii, extinct in Strabo's time.

CALLIBETUS, a town of Lydia, near Mæander fl., N. of Tripolis. Noted for its confectionary. *Eski Kaleh.*

CALLICA, a town of Bithynia, near Nicomedia.

CALLICÆNI, a tribe of Dassaretæ, Illyria, on the S.W. shore of Lychnitis palus.

CALLICHORUS fl., I. a stream of Eleusis, Attica, at which the female votaries assembled. II. of Bithynia, falling into the Euxine, E. of Sandaraca.

CALLICONE collis, a hill of Troas, near Troja Vetus, on Simois fl., whence Mars animated the Trojans.

CALLICULA m. (Eribanus), a ridge of m. in Italy, separating Campania from Samnium.

CALLIDRŎMUS m., the highest summit of Æta m., near Thermopylæ.

CALLIFÆ, a town of the Pentri, Samnium, 5 m. S.E. of Allifæ. *Calvisi.*

CALLIGERIS, a town of Ariaca, India, bet. Bætana and Hippocura. *Calliani.*

CALLIGICUM prom., Indiæ, i. q. Cory.

CALLIMACHE, a port of Caria, 7 m. from Dædala.

CALLINICUM, Mesopotamia, i. q. Nicephorium.

CALLIPEUCE SALTUS, a pass of Olympus m., towards Libethra. *Pieria.*

CALLIPIDÆ, a people of Sarmatia, E. on both sides the Borysthenes, towards its mouth.

CALLIPOLIS, "beautiful city," I. Ætoliæ, i. q. Callium. II. of Bithynia, on Craspedites sin. A colony from Mægara-Nisea, circa 700 B.C. III. of Caria, on Ceramicus sin. *Gallipoli.* IV. of Cilicia Campestris, s.w. of Cucusus. V. of the Sallentini, Japygia, on Tarentinus sin., N.W. of Leuca. Founded by a Lacedæmonian colonia under Leucippus. *Gallipoli.* VI. of Sicily, above Argenum prom. VII. of Thracia Chersonesus, 5 m. N.E. from Ægos Potamos. Traditionally founded by Callias, the Athenian. *Gallipoli.*

CALLIPOS fl., a r. of Lusitania, falling into the Mediterranean s. of Cetobriga. *Caldao ; Sadao.*

CALLIPO, a town of the Lusitani, on Callipo fl., N.E. of Ebura.

CALLIRRHŎE, "fine fountain," a town of Mesopotamia, i. q. Edessa. II. (Lasa), of Peræa, near the Dead Sea, s.w. of Heshbon.

CALLIS, a town of Pentapolis Cyrenaicæ, bet. Barca and Cænopolis.

CALLISTE, an early name of Thera ins.

CALLISTRATIA (Marsilla), a port of Paphlagonia, 3 m. E. from Carambis.

CALLITHERA, a town of Bisaltia, Macedonia, N.W. of Ossa. *Likovan.*

CALLIUM (Calliæ, Callipolis), a town of Ætolia, towards Heraclea Trachynia.

CALLONIANA (Caulonia), a town of Sicily, on Himera Magna fl., L., bet. Corconiana (12) and Enna.

CALLMUSA prom., a pr. of Cyprus, w. of Soloe.

CALLYDIUM (Clanudda), a fortress of Lydia, 35 m. from Philadelphia.

CALNE, Calno, Canneh, i. q. Ctesiphon, Babyloniæ.

CALOE, a village of Lydia, near Hypæpa. *Caliveh Khan.*

CALOGRÆA, a fortress of Bithynia, at one of the passes of Olympus m.

CALOLIMEN, "fair haven," a port on the s. coast of Crete, w. of Leon prom. *Calolimonia.*

CALON-STOMA. Danubii, i. q. Pulchrum Ostium.

CALOR, I. a r. of Lucania, rising s. of Marcelliana and falling into Silarus fl. below Ad Silarum. *Calore.* II. of Samnium, rising in Balade m. N.E. of Aceronia Lucaniæ and falling into Vulturnus fl. above Syllæ. *Calore.* III. a town of the Hirpini, Samnium, on Calor fl., L., bet. Nuceriola (6) and Eclanum (5), on Via Appia. *Calore.*

CALOS fl., I. a r. of Pontus, falling into the Euxine 3 m. E. from Psychrus fl.

CALOS PORTUS, a town of the Hylæ, Sarmatia, at the mouth of Carcinis fl., R.

CALPE, I. a pr. of Bætica, on Herculeum Fretum, E. The European pillar of Hercules. *Cape Gibraltar.* II. a town of Bætica, at Calpe prom. A colonia (Julia). *Gibraltar.* III. a pr. of Bithynia, w. of Prusa ins. *Kirpeh.* IV. of Bithynia, at Calpe prom. *Busadche.*

CALPITUS fl., a r. of Phrygia, towards Parnassus.

CALPURNIANA, a town of the Turtuli, Bætica, bet. Corduba (25) and Obulco.

CALTIORISSA (Callorissa), a town of Armenia Minor, bet. Seleoboria (15) and Analiba (24).

CALUCONES, I. a tribe of Hermunduri, Germania, on Albis fl., below the Bonochæmæ. II. of Rhætia, bet. the Rugusci and the Brixantes. *Val Calenca.*

CALUS, a town of Arcadia, bet. Arsen fl., L., (3) and Thelpusa (5).

CALVISIANA, a town of Sicily, bet. Hybla (24) and Agrigentum (44). *Butera.*

CALYCADNUS fl., a r. of Cilicia Trachea, falling into the sea below Seleucia. *Giuksou,* or *Kaly Kad.*

CALYCADNUS prom., Cilicia, i. q. Sarpedon.

CALYDNA ins., i. q. Calymna.

CALYDNÆ ins., islets of Troas, bet. Tenedos and Sigæum. *Kapperi.*

CALYDNUS, the early name of Thebes, in Bœotia, after king Calydnus.

CALYDON, a city of Ætolia, near Evenus fl., 7½ m. from the sea, 9 m. w. from Naupactus. The locality of the story of the Calydonian boar.

CALYDONA, a town of the Ubii, Germania II., towards Agrippina colonia. *In the Forêt de Caldnoven.*

CALYMNA ins., an isl. in the Icarium mare, chief of the Calydnæ ins., bet. Leros ins. and Cos ins. Noted for its honey. *Calimno.* II. capital of the cognominal isl. on the s. coast, E. of Notium.

CALYNDA, a town of Caria, near the junction of Indus fl. with Axon fl., N.W. of Dædala.

CALYNDICI m., m. of Caria, at Calynda, on Indus fl., R.

CALYPSO ins., a fabulous isl. placed by Scylax off Lacinium prom., Italia.

CAMALA, a town of the Astures, Tarraconensis, N.E. of Pallantia.

CAMARA, a town of Crete, on Didymi sin. w., 2 m. s. from Olus.

CAMARĀCUM, a town of the Nervii, Belgica II., on the Scaldis, bet. Nemetacum w.N.w. and Hermomacum E.N.E. *Cambray.*

CAMARIA ins., an isl. formed by Ostium Hispanicum and Ostium Metapinum Rhodani.

CAMATULLICINI, a maritime tribe of Salyes, Narbonensis, s. of the Verrucini. *About Ramatuelle.*

CAMBADENE (Kapada), a district of Media Magna, occupying its s.w. angle.

CAMBALA, a town of Armenia Int., N. of Theodosopolis.

CAMBALIDUS m., m. of Susiana, N.E.

CAMBERICHUM ostium, a mouth of the Ganges, bet. Magnum ost. and Pseudostomuin ost.

CAMBETE, a town of the Rauraci, Germania I., on the Rhine, above Stabula. *Kembs.*

CAMBETUM, a town of the Lucenses, Tarraconensis, at the mouth L. of Ulla fl., bet. Orium prom. N. and Nolla s.

CAMBIOVENCES, a people of Gaul, of uncertain position. Placed by Valois about Combrailles, in the Diocese of Limoges.

CAMBODUNUM, I. (Camulodunum), a town of the Brigantes, Brit., bet. Eboracum and Mancunium. II. capital of the Estiones, Vindel., on Ilargus fl., s.w. of Augusta Vindelicorum. *Kempten.*

CAMBOLECTRI, a people of Viennensis, bet. the Vocontii and the Tricorii.

CAMBONUM, capital of the Cambolectri, Viennensis, bet. Dea Vocontiorum and Vapincum. *Lacombe?*

CAMBORICUM, a town of the Iceni, Brit., on Devana Via, N.w. of Camulodunum. *Cambridge.*

CAMBREA, a town of Chalcidice, Macedonia, on Thermaicus sin., bet. Lisæ and Lipaxus.

CAMBRETONIUM, a town of the Iceni, s.w. of Sitomagus. *Grundesburgh.*

CAMBUNII m., m. separating Macedonia from Thessaly, and extending from Pindus m. to Olympus m.

CAMBUNIUS saltus (Volustana), a defile in Cambunii m., bet. Pelagonia and Macedonia *Volutza.*

CAMBYS ostium (Cambusum), the w. mouth of the Ganges.

CAMBYSENE, a district of Albania, on the confines of Armenia Maj., bet. Cyrus fl. and Alazonius fl. *Kakethi.*

CAMBYSES fl., I. a r. of Cambysene, Albania,

rising in Caucasus m., and falling into Alazonius fl. near its junction with Cyrus fl. *Jori.* II. of Media, falling into the Caspian s. of Cyrus fl. *Astara.*

CAMBYSIS ÆRARIUM, a fortress of the Nubæ, on the Nile, bet. Aboccis and Erchoas (6 geog. m.), where Cambyses deposited his military chest, on his expedition into Nubia. *Dubdi.*

CAMBYSU, a town of Egypt, on Ptolemæus fl., towards Heroopolis. Founded by Cambyses.

CAMECHIA, a town of Albania Asiat., bet. Albanus fl. and Cyrus fl.

CAMELIDÆ ins., two islets of Ionia, off the mouth of Mæander fl.

CAMELIOMAGUS, a town of the Ananes, Liguria, on Via Posthumia, bet. Iria (16) and Placentia (25). *Cigomol.*

CAMELOBOSCI, a people of Carmania, on the borders of Persis, extending to Persicus sin.

CAMERINA, *prius* Hyparia, a maritime town of Sicily, s. bet. Mesopotamium and Cimba. A Syracusan settlement. Near it was a cognominal marsh, the fatal consequences of draining which, against the advice of the oracle, gave rise to the proverb: *Ne moveas Camerinam. Torre di Camarina.*

CAMERINUM (Cameria), a town of Umbria, on the borders of Picenum, S.E. of Matilica. A colonia. *Camarana.*

CAMERS, the Umbrian name of Clusium, Etruria.

CAMERTE, a city of Umbria, midway bet. Tudes and Ameria. *Camero.*

CAMESENE, an early name of Latium, from Camese, sister and wife of Janus, or from the Eastern word *camas,* to lie hid.

CAMETAS, a town of the Triballi, Mœsia, on Margus fl., R., bet. Præsidium Dasmum and Præsidium Pompeii.

CAMINA ins., one of the Sporades.

CAMYCUS, I. fl., a r. of Sicily, falling into the sea w. of Agrigentum. *Naro.* II. a Sicanian town of Sicily, at the mouth of Camicus fl. The residence of Cocalus, the murderer of Minos. Its citadel was built by Dædalus.

CAMINUS, a maritime town of Cyrenaica, N. bet. Diachersis and Boreum.

CAMYRUS, I. an early name of Hierapytna, Crete. II. a town of Rhodes, on the N.W. coast. Founded by Camirus, son of Cercaphus. The birth-place of the poet Pisander. *Camiro.*

CAMYSA (Comassa), capital of Camisene, Pontus, on Halys fl., bet. Sebastia (24) and Zara.

CAMISENE regio, a district of Pontus, on

Halys fl., at its source, N.E. of Colopene regio.

CAMISTRUM, a town of the Mœsi, Mœsia Inferior, on the Danube, bet. Ciabrus and Regianum.

CAMPÆ (Cambe), a town of Cilicia prefect., Cappadocia, bet. Mazaea (16) and Siva (22).

CAMPÆ, Germanicæ, i. q. Adrabæcampi.

CAMPANIA, "open country," a region of Italy, bounded N. by Latium, s. by Lucania, at Silarus fl., w. by Tyrrhen. mare, E. by Samnium, at Tifata m. Occupied first by the Osci; next by the Tyrrheni, who founded here, also, twelve chief cities; and, lastly, by a mixed population of Osci, Tyrrheni, Samnites, and Greeks. *Terra di Lavoro.*

CAMPANUS sin., Campaniæ, i. q. Cumanus.

CAMPI CANINI, a valley of the Mesiates, in Rhætia Transpadana, on the Rhine, towards Verbanus lacus. *Graubundten.*

CAMPI LAPIDEI, *vel* Lapidarii, a plain of shingle in Viennensis, bet. Astromela Stagnum and the Rhone. The scene of the fight bet. Hercules and Albion and Bergion. *La Crau.*

CAMPI VETERES, a place in Lucania, near Potentia. The death-place of Tib. Gracchus. *Vietri.*

CAMPONA, a town of Valeria, Pannonia, on the Danube, bet. Acincum and Salinum. *Saint Endré.*

CAMPONI, a tribe of Bigerrones, Novem Populana, bet. the Convenæ E., and the Osquidates. *Vallée de Campan.*

CAMPSA (Capsa), a town of Chalcidice, Macedonia, on Thermaicus sin., near Combrea.

CAMPUS MAGNUS (Esdrelon Vallis), a district of Galilæa, on the confines of Samaria, bet. Mount Carmel w. and the Jordan E.

CAMPUS SERENUS, a district of Thrace, on the left bank of Agrianes fl., towards its source.

CAMPYLUS fl., a r. of Aperantia, Ætolia, falling into Achelous fl. *Carpenitze.*

CAMULODÜNUM (Camaldonum), capital of the Trinobantes, N.W. of Cæsaromagus. *Colchester.*

CAMUNI, a tribe of Euganei, in Gall. Cispad., about the source of Ollius fl., N. of Sebinus lac. *Val Camonica.*

CANA, I. a r. of Palestine, falling into the Mediterranean s. of Cæsarea. The boundary bet. Ephraim and Manasseh. *Nahr el Kasab.* II. a town of Palestine, near Dio Cæsarea. The locality of the miracle of water turned into wine. The birth-place of Simeon Canaanites and of Nathaniel. *Kanael Jelil.* III. a town of Asher, Phœnicia, near Sidon.

CANAAN, "lowlands," generally Palestine; specially, the coast of Phœnicia. Named from Canaan, son of Ham.

CANABIACA, a town of the Boii, Noricum, on the Danube, bet. Namare and Arriana Castra.

CANACA, a town of Bæturia, Hispania, on the Anas. *San Lucar.*

CANÆ, I. a pr. of Æolis Asiatica, at the entrance of Eleaticus sinus. *C. Colonni.* II. a town of Æolis Asiatica, at Canæ prom. A Locrian settlement.

CANAGARA, a maritime town of the Calingæ, India, 6 geog. m. s. from Manada fl. *Canara.*

CANALICUM, a town of the Epanterii, Liguria, on Via Æmilia Scaura, bet. Vada Sabata (12) and Crixia (10). *Carcaro.*

CANALIS REGIUS, a canal of Lower Egypt, leading from Bubasticus fl. above Patumos, by Heroopolis to Thaubastum.

CANALOVII m., a n. continuation of Pindus, bounding Elymæa w., terminating in Berecetius m.

CANAMA, a town of the Turtuli, Bætica, on the Bætis, above Italica.

CANARIA ins., one of the Fortunæ ins., Africæ.

CANASIS (Canthadis, Canate), a port of Gedrosia, on Paragon sin., bet. Samydace and Troca.

CANASTRÆUM prom., the s.e. extremity of Pallene, Macedonia, over against Derrhis prom. *C. Palliouri.*

CANATHA, I. (Kenath), a town of Manasseh, in Trachonitis, n.n.e. of Bostra. *Coneith.* II. ins., an isl. of India i. Gangem, s. of Vangania ins.

CANDACE, Ariæ, i. q. Cotace.

CANDALICÆ, a town of the Taurisci, in Noricum, 20 m. n.e. from Virunum. *Friesach.*

CANDAVA VIA, the Egnatia Via, on its passage over Candavii m.

CANDAVIA, a town of the Eordeti, Illyria, near Genusus fl., bet. Ad Dianam (2) and Tres Tabernæ (9).

CANDAVII m., a ridge of Canalovii m., Illyria, encircling Lychnitis pal., and separating Dassaretia from Lyncus. *Crasta.*

CANDIDIANA, a town of the Getæ, Mœsia, on the Danube, bet. Nigriniana and Transmarisca.

CANDIANUS fl., a r. of Gallia Cispadana, falling into the Adriatic at Portus Classis.

CANDIDUM prom., the s. extremity of Africa Prop., n.w. of Hippo Dyarrhitis. *Ras el Abiad.*

CANDIPATNA, a town of the Arvarni, India, on Tynna fl., R., n. of Poleur.

CANELATA, a town of Sicily, near Centurinum oppidum. *Torre di Farinole.*

CANDYBA, a town of Lycia, s.e. of Choma.

CANE, I. a port of the Adramitæ, w. of Prionotus sin., over against Aromata prom. Africæ n.w. *Hussan Ghorab, Cana-Canim.* II. a town of Phrygia, near Pessinus. *Kahé.* III. a village of the Tectosages, Galatia, s. of Cratia.

CANENTELUS fl., a r. of Aquitania II., falling into the sea n. of Carantonus fl. *Sèvre.*

CANETHUS m., a hill of Eubœa, at Chalcis.

CANGANORUM prom., a pr. of the Cangi, Brit., s.w. of Mona ins. *Cape Braich y Pwll.*

CANGI, a tribe of Ordovices, in the n.w. angle of Britannia II.

CANICULARIÆ ins., islets of Sardinia, in Fretum Gallicum.

CANINA ins., an isl. of Gedrosia, off Bagisara.

CANINEFATES (Cannanefates), a tribe of Batavi, bet. Helium ostium and Flevum ostium.

CANIS fl., a r. of Arabia Felix, falling into Persicus sin. e. of Cabana. *Zar or Lar* ("dog").

CANNA (Carna), a town of Lycaonia, n.w. of Iconium.

CANNABA, a town of Osrhoene, Mesopot., bet. Apamea and Bethmari.

CANNÆ, a village of Daunia, Apul., near Aufidus fl., L., bet. Canusium (5) and the sea. Destroyed, all but its citadel, 215 B.C., the year before the great battle which celebrates its name. *Canne.*

CANNARUM prom., a pr. of Mauritania Ting., on the Mediterranean, bet. Parietina and Russadir.

CANOGIZA, a town of the Tacoræi, India, on Œdanes fl., R.

CANONIUM, a town of the Trinobantes, Brit., n.e. of Cæsaromagus. *Near Kelvedon.*

CANOPICUM OSTIUM NILI (Heraclioticum), the w. mouth of the Nile, bet. Canopus and Alexandria. *Maadié.*

CANOPISSÆ, a maritime town of Zeugitana, above Tabraca.

CANOPUS (Canobus), a maritime city of Lower Egypt, bet. Alexandria (12) and Canopicum ostium. Built *circa* 1100 B.C., and named from Canopus, the steersman of Menelaus, buried there. Noted for its Temple of Serapis. *Near Aboukir.*

CANTABRAS fl., Indiæ, i. q. Hydraotes.

CANRAITÆ, Arabiæ, i. q. Cedrei.

CANTABRI, a maritime people of Tarraconensis, on the Iberus, towards its mouth. *Biscay and part of Asturia.*

CANTABRICUM mare, the sea washing the n. coast of Spain. *Bay of Biscay.*

CANTÆ, a people of Britannia Barbara, N. of the Caledonii. *Bet. Murray Frith and Dornoch Frith.*

CANTANUS, a town of Crete, on Leuci m., bet. Calamydes and Cydonia. *Candano.*

CANTECI, a people of Sarmatia Asiatica, on Ocharius fl.

CANTERIUS mons, a m. of Sabinium, near Reate. *Monte San Giovanni.*

CANTHARIUM prom., the w. extremity of Samos, over against Icarus ins. *C. Dominico.*

CANTHAROLETHRON, a place near Olynthus, Macedonia. Reputed fatal to black beetles.

CANTHI sin., a bay of Indicus Oceanus, E. of the mouth of the Indus. *Gulf of Cutch.*

CANTII (*Celticè* Canti, "end"), a people occupying the E. portion of Britannia I., E. of the Regni. *Kent and E. Surrey.*

CANTILIA, a town of the Arverni, Aquitania I., N. of Augustonemetum.

CANTIOBIS, a town of the Cenni, Germania, S.E. of Bergium. *Near Windsheim.*

CANTIUM (Acantium) prom., the N.E. extremity of Britannia. *N. Foreland.*

CANTOCAPTÆ, a people of Sarmatia Asiatica, towards Mæotis palus.

CANUSIUM, a Greek city of Daunia, Apulia, on Aufidus fl., R., 12 m. from its mouth, bet. Ad Undecim (11) and Rudiæ. A colonia of Hadrian. Noted for its red shining wool.

CAPARA, a town of the Vettones, Lusitania, N. of Rusticiana. *Venta de Caparra.*

CAPENA, a city of Etruria, 5 m. S.E. of Soracte m. A Veian settlement. *Civitucula.*

CAPERCOLIA, a town of Samaria, bet. Cæsarea and Ginea E.

CAPEDUNUM, a town of the Scordisci, Pannonia.

CAPELLANUM, Germaniæ, i. q. Palas.

CAPERNAUM, a town of Galilæa, on Tiberias lac., N.W. above Tiberias. Named from an adjacent spring of very pure water, deemed by Josephus a vein of the Nile. *Khan Minyeh.*

CAPERSANA, Mesopotamia, i. q. Porsica.

CAPEUS sin., a bay of Persicus sin., in Arabia, s. of Magorum sin. *Bahr Katiff.*

CAPHĂREUS prom., the S.E. headland of Eubœa, N.W. of Andros ins. Noted for the destruction of the Greek fleet on its return from Troy. *C. d'Oro.*

CAPHAS m., m. of Libya Inf., s. of Mandron m.

CAPHTORIM (Cophtoim, Caphtoræ), Egyptians, from Coptos, who, with the Philistine, occupied the coast of Palestine bet. Joppa and Egypt.

CAPHYÆ, a town of Arcadia, w. of Orcho-menus. Built by Capys, father of Anchises.

CAPIDAVA, a town of Mœsia Inf., on the Danube, bet. Carsum and Axiopolis.

CAPISSA, capital of Capissene, Arachosia. Destroyed by Cyrus. *Peshawur.*

CAPISSENE, a district of Arachosia, towards Paropamisus m., on the Indus. *Pishiauwada, Peshawur.*

CAPITIUM, a town of Sicily, N.N.W. of Galarina. *Capizzi.*

CAPITOLIAS, a town of Gaulonitis Sup., 16 m. N. of Adraha. *Mezareit.*

CAPITONIANA, a town of Sicily, on Eryx fl., bet. Gelasium Philosophiana and Catana (24). *Near Ramaceo.*

CAPITULUM, a town of the Hernici, Latium, bet. Præneste and Anagnia. A colonia of Sylla. *Paliano.*

CAPOTES m., a ridge of Antitaurus m., Armenia Maj. *Kapoit.*

CAPPADŎCIA (Magna Cappadocia), a country of Asia Minor, bounded N. by Galatia and Pontus, s. by Pamphylia and Cilicia, w. by Pisidia and Phrygia, E. by Armenia Minor. It, at one time, comprised Pontus, Armenia Minor, and a portion of Cilicia. Named from Cappadox fl.

CAPPADOX fl., a r. of Cappadocia, falling into Halys fl., R., above Siva, partially separating Galatia from Cappadocia. *Erkurous.*

CAPRĀRIA ins. (Ægilon, "goat island"), I. an isl. of Africa, s. of Junonis ins. *Gomera.* II. one of the Baleares ins., 12 m. s. from Major ins. *Cabrera.* III. an isl. of Etruria, N.W. of Ilva. *Capraia.* IV. a town of Numidia, bet. Tipasa and Tibilis.

CAPRASIÆ, a town of Lucania, on Via Aquilia, bet. Muranum (16) and Consentia (28). *Tarsia.*

CAPRASIÆ ostium, a mouth of Padus fl., bet. Spineticum ostium and Sagis ostium. *Bocca di bel Occhio.*

CAPREÆ ins., an isl. of Campania, w. of Surrentinum prom. *Capri.*

CAFRIA lac., a salt lake of Pamphylia, at the mouth of Cestrus fl. *Capri.*

CAPRIANUS m., m. of Sicily, s.w. above Thermæ Selinuntiæ.

CAPRUS fl. (Zerbis, Adiaba), I. a r. of Assyria, falling into the Tigris at Cœnæ. *Zab Asfal, Lesser Zab.* II. of Phrygia Magna, falling into Lycus fl. below Laodicea. *Giumiskoi.* III. an isl. of Chalcidice, Macedonia, off Stagira. IV. portus, the harbour of Stagira, Macedonia.

CAPSA, I. a town of Byzacene, bet. Veresvi and Gemellæ. A treasure fortress of Jugurtha, taken by Marius. A colonia. *Cafsa.* II. a town of Lybia Inf., near the source of the southern Bagradas.

CĂPŬA (Campua, "camp"), *prius* Vulturnum, a city of Campania, on Via Appia, bet. Casilinum (3 s.e.) and Calatia (6). Taken by Etruscans under Capys 800 B.C. A colonia. Infamous for its debauchery. *Church of Santa Maria di Capoa, near Capua* (2 m. s.e.).

CAPUT BOVIS, I. a town of Dacia, w. of Caput Bubali. II. BUBALI, a town of the Potulatenses, Dacia, near the source of Bugonis fl., 3 m. from Azizis. *Brebul.* III. BUDELLI, a town of Mauritania Cæsar., bet. Modolana and Culcul. IV. CILLANI, a town of Mauritania Cæsar., bet. Suffisar and Trinadi. V. TYRSI, a village of the Carenses, in Sardinia, at the source of Tyrsus fl. VI. VADA, a maritime town of Byzacene, s. of Brachodes prom. *Capoudia.*

CARABIA, a town of Paraxia, Macedonia, on the Axius fl., N.W. of Lete. *Arabli.*

CARABIS, a town of the Celtiberi, Tarraconensis.

CARACATES, a tribe of Vangiones, Germania I., on the Rhine, s. of the Treveri.

CARACENI (Carentini), a tribe of Samnites, occupying the s. portion of Samnium, on Sagrus fl. (whence it has been contended that their real name was Sarracini).

CARADA, Arabia, i. q. Cadara.

CARADOCHI castrum, a town of the Ordovices, Brit., on Sabrina fl., on the site of an encampment of Caradoc.

CARÆ, a town of Tarraconensis, 12 m. s. from Pompelo. *Puente de la Reyna.*

CARALÆ, a tribe of Sacæ, Sogdiana, on the Jaxartes.

CARĂLIS, capital of Sardinia, s., at the inner entrance E. of Caralitanum prom. Founded by an Æolian colony under Tolaus; enlarged by a Carthaginian colony 494 B.C. A municipium. *Cagliari.*

CARALITĀNUM prom., a pr. of Sardinia, s., at the E. entrance of Caralitanus sin. *Capo Sant' Elia.*

CARALITĀNUS sin., a bay of Tyrrhenium mare, at Caralis. *Golfo di Cagliari.*

CARALĪTIS palus, I. a lake of Isauria, w. of Iconium (14). *Pusgusa; Kereli.* II. of Pisidia, on the borders of Lycia, N.W. of Isionda.

CARALĬA, a town of Isauria, at the N. extremity of Caralitis lac. *Kereli.*

CARAMBIS prom., a pr. of Paphlagonia, w. of Lepte prom. *C. Kerempi.*

CARAMBIS, I. a town of Paphlagonia, at Carambis prom. II. fl., a r. of Sarmatia

Europæa, falling into Septentrionalis Oceanus. *Dwina.*

CARANA, Arabiæ. *Vide* Carman.

CARANICUM, a town of the Artabri, Tarraconensis, on Magnus portus, s., bet. Mearus fl. and Vir fl.

CARANITIS (Carenitis), a district of Armenia, s.w. of Chorzene. *Karin.*

CARANTANIA (Carastasei), a people of Sarmatia Asiatica, towards Mæotis palus.

CARANTANUM, the early name of Noricum, as the abode of the Carantani, a Latin form of the Sclavonian designation of its population. Hence the modern Carinthia.

CARANTOMAGUS, a town of the Ruteni, Aquitania I., bet. Varadetum w. and Segodunum E.

CARANTONUS fl., a r. of the Santones, Aquitania II., falling into the Atlantic at Uliarus ins. *Charente.*

CARASÆ (Garites), a town of the Tarbelli, Novem Populana, bet. Aquæ Tarbellicæ N. and Ad Summum Pyrenæum s.s.w. *Garis.*

CARASURA, a town of the Odrysæ, Thrace, bet. Cillium and Pala.

CARAVANTIS, a town of the Cavii, Illyria, on Mathis fl., bet. Æneum and Durnium.

CARAVI, a town of the Celtiberi, Tarraconensis, on the Iberus, R., above Malia.

CARBA, a fortress of Cappadocia, bet. Casaman and Ardula.

CARBÆ, Arabiæ, i. q. Cerbani.

CARBANTIA, a town of the Segusini, Gallia Cisalpina, 12 m. from Cottia.

CARBANTŎRĬGUM, a town of the Selgovæ, Brit., towards the mouth of Novius fl., R. *Kircudbright.*

CARBIA, a maritime town of the Coracenses, Sardinia, bet. Bosa and Nymphæus portus. *Algher.*

CARBINA, a town of Calabria, near Cœlium. *Carovigno.*

CARBIS fl. (Cambil), a r. of Gedrosia, falling into the sea at Cissa.

CARBONARIA ostium, a mouth of Padus fl., bet. Olane ost. and Fossa Philistina. *Po d' Ariono.*

CARBONARIUS m., a mountain of the Marsi, Italy, bet. Gravis m. (10) and Marrubium (8). *M. Carbonaro.*

CARBŬLA, a town of the Turtuli, Bætica, on the Bætis, L., at the confluence of Singulis fl. *Near Guadalcazar.*

CARCA, a town of the Bastitani, Tarraconensis, s.s.w. of Ilunum.

CARCĂSSO (Carcăsum), a town of the Volcæ Tectosages, Narbonensis I., on the Atax, L., bet. Ad Cedros and Tricesimum. *Carcassone.*

CARCICI, a town of the Commoni, Narbonensis, on the coast, bet. Portus Zao w. and Citharista E.

CARCATHIOCERTA, the early capital of Sophene, Armenia, near the source of the Tigris. Extinct in Ptolemy's time.

CARCHA, capital of the Garamæi, Assyria, on the Tigris, N. of Antiochia.

CARCHĒDO, the Greek form of the Phœnician Karth-hadtha, "new town," *Carthage.*

CARCHEMISH, the Scriptural name of Circesium, Mesopotamia.

CARCĬNE (Carcinitis), a town of the Hylæ, Sarmat., at the mouth of Carcines fl.

CARCINES fl. (Hypacaris), I. a r. of Bruttium, N. of Scylacæum prom. *Corace.* II. a town on Carcines fl., near its mouth.

CARCINITES sin., a bay of the Euxine, at the mouth of Carcines fl. *G. of Perekop.*

CARCOME, a maritime town of Mauritania Cæsar., bet. Chinalaph fl. and Carepula.

CARCORUM regio, a district of India i. Gangem, on Colchicus sin.

CARCURIUM, a town of the Turtuli, Bæturia, N.E. of Cotinæ.

CARDALENA, the coast of Arabia Felix, on Duatus sin. *Nahel.*

CARDAMENE ins., an isl. of Arabia Felix, on the Red Sea, s.w. of Pudnu. *Habur.*

CARDAMYLE, I. a port of Chios ins., N.E. of Pelinæus m. *Kardamili.* II. of Messenia, on Messeniacus sin., E. below Abia. *Scardamoula.*

CARDIA, "heart-shape" (*postea* Hexamilion), a port of Thracia Cherson., near Lysimachia. A mixed colony of Clazomenians and Milesians. The birth-place of Hieronymus the historian. The majority of its population were transferred to Lysimachia.

CARDU, a town of Marmarica, bet. Gounia and Jucundiæ.

CARDUCHI, i. q. Gordyæi.

CAREI, a people of India i. Gangem, s., about Colchicus sin.

CAREIA, a town of Etruria, on Larus fl., bet. Ad VI. (9) and Ad IX. (9), on Via Claudia. *Golera.*

CARĒNE, a town of Æolis Asiatica, w. of Peparene. *Chirin-Keui.*

CARĒNI, a maritime people of Britannia Barbara, in its extreme N.E. angle, w. of the Cornavi. *Sutherlandshire, N.*

CARENSES, a maritime people of Sardinia, E. of the Balari.

CARENTINI, *apud* Plin., i. q. Caraceni.

CARENTINUM, a town of the Caraceni, on Sagrus fl., R. *Citta di Sangro.*

CARENUSCA, a town of the Mediomatrices,

Belgica I., on the Mosella, bet. Ricciacum N.N.E., and Divodurum s.

CAREPULA, a maritime town of Mauritania Cæsar., bet. Carcome and Cartenna.

CARESA ins., one of the Lichades ins., Locris.

CARESENE reg., the district about Caresus in Troas.

CARESUS (Carseæ), a town of Troas, on Caresus fl.

CARESUS fl., a r. of Troas, rising near Mallus, and falling into Æsepus fl. at Caresus.

CARGIANA, a town of Dacia, 15 m. N.W. from Optatiana. *North of Czasz Regen.*

CARIA, a country of Asia Minor, bounded N. by Lydia and Ionia, at Mæander fl., s. by the Mediterranean, w. by Ionium mare, E. by Phrygia and Lycia. The people, a mixed Phœnician, Lelegian, and Ionian race (traditionally named from Car, brother of Lydus), were noted for their skill in war and navigation. *Muntesha.*

CARIATA, a town of Bactriana. The residence of Callisthenes.

CARIATHA, Arabiæ. *Vide* Carriata.

CARICON, a town of Africa, towards Lixus fl.

CARIMA, a town of the Tectosages, in Galatia.

CARINE, a town of Media Cambadene, bet. Corma and Zagri portæ.

CARINI, Germaniæ, i. q. Varini.

CARIONES, a people of Sarmatia E., on the Danube, L.

CARIPETA, Arabiæ, i. q. Carriata.

CARIPRÆA, a town of Parthia, near the source of Socanaa fl.

CARĬRIN ("shelter"), the Phœnician name of Caralis, in Sardinia.

CARIS fl., a r. of Gaul, rising among the Bituriges Cubi, and falling into the Liger w. of Cæsarodunum. *Cher.*

CARISSA, I. a town of the Trocmi, Galatia, bet. Etonea and Amasia. II. of the Turtetani, Bætica, bet. Nebrissa N.E. and Colobona s.s.w.

CARISTI (Carieti), a tribe of Cantabri, Tarraconensis, bet. the Iberus s., the sea N., the Autrigones w., and the Varduli E. *Part of Biscay.*

CARISTUM, the early capital of the Statielli, Liguria, s. of Aquæ Statiellæ. *Cartoso.*

CARITNI, a tribe of Alemanni, Germ., bet. the Rhine and Niter fl., s. of Intuergi.

CARIUS m., a m. of Lydia, overlooking Torrhebus.

CARLINA, an inland town of Venetia.

CARMACÆ, a people of Sarmatia Asiatica, towards Mæotis palus.

CARMALAS fl., a r. of Cataonia, rising in Antitaurus, and falling into Pyramus fl. above Arabissus. *Kermel-Sou.*

CARMAN regia, capital of the Minæi, Arabia, E.S.E. of Macoraba. *Karn-al-Manzil.*

CARMANA, capital of Carmania, N.W. of Apamea Raphane. *Kherman.*

CARMANIA, a country of Asia, bounded N. by Parthia, s. by Persicus sin. and Paragon sin., w. by Persis, E. by Drangiana and Gedrosia. Noted for its large grapes. *Kerman, Laristan E., and Moghistan.*

CARMANIA DESERTA, the N. portion of Carmania.

CARMANORIUS m., the early name of Tmolus m.

CARMARA, a town of the Arvarni, India, s.w. of Malanga.

CARMEL, a town of Judah, 10 m. s. from Hebron. The abode of Nabal. *El Carmel.*

CARMELUM prom., the termination of Carmelus m., in the Mediterranean, 15 m. s.w. of Acco. *Cape Carmel.*

CARMELUS m., m. of Galilæa Sup., parallel s. with Kison fl., terminating in Carmel prom. *Carmel.*

CARMELYSSUS, a fortress of Lycia, on the coast, near Telmissus.

CARMINIANUM, a town of Messapia, s.w. of Lupia. It became, together with its forest and territory, annexed to the privy purse of the Emperors. *Carmignano.*

CARMINNA ins. (Carmana), an isl. of India.

CARMONA, a town of the Turtetani, Bætica, bet. Ilipula Minor N.E., and Basilippo s.w. *Carmona.*

CARNÆ, a people of Sarmatia Asiat., towards Cissii m.

CARNA (Carnon) fl., a r. of Arabia Felix, falling into the Red Sea bet. Zuarain and Badei.

CARNALIS, I. a town of Morimene, Cappadocia. II. *apud* Pausan., i. q. Caralis Sardinæ.

CARNASIUM, a village, 1 m. from Andania, Messenia, with a sacred grove, in which were celebrated the rites of the great goddesses. *Krano.*

CARNI, a tribe of Taurisci, who from the Alpes Noricæ formed settlements in Venetia, N. of the Veneti, from whom they were separated by Tilavemptus fl. *Carniola.*

CARNION fl., a r. of Arcadia, rising near Ægys in Laconia, and falling into Alpheus fl.

CARNON, a town of the Minæi, Arabia. *Karn-al-Magsal.*

CARNONACÆ (Carnones), a people of Britannia Barbara, on its w. coast. bet. the Careni and the Vacomagi. *Sutherland W. and part of Ross.*

CARNŪTES (Carnutæ), a people of Lugdunensis IV., on the Liger, N. of the Bituriges Cubi, E. of the Aulerci Eburovices and Cenomanni. *Departments of Loire N., Loiret w., Eure et Loire, et Seine et Oise N.W.*

CARNUNTUM (Carnus), a town of the Boii, Pannonia, on the Danube, bet. Ala Nova and Anduætium. *Between Petronel and Altenburg.*

CARNUS, I. one of the Teleboiæ ins., Acarnania, E. of Taphus ins. Especially noted for its fine flour. *Calamo.* II. a town of Phœnicia, i. q. Antaradus.

CAROCA, a town of the Roxolani, on Mæotis palus, bet. Poritas fl. and Tanais.

CAROCOTINUM, a port of the Caleti, Gaul, 3 m. w. from Juliobona. *Harfleur.*

CARPACELIS, a town of Laviniasene, Cappadocia.

CARPASIA, a port of Cyprus, N.E., near Sarpedon prom. Built by Pygmalion. *Carpass.*

CARPASIÆ ins., islets of Cyprus, N. coast, w. of Carpasia. *Chiro.*

CARPĀTES m. (Carpatici, Alpes Bastarnicæ), an E. and s.E. continuation of the Alps, separating Sarmatia from Dacia, and intersecting the latter country in various ridges. *Krapak.*

CARPATHIUM mare, the portion of the Mediterranean, bet. Crete and Carpathus ins.

CARPATHUS ins., one of the Sporades, bet. Rhodes (15) and Crete. *Scarpanto.*

CARPELLA prom., the termination of Persici m., on Paragon sin., bet. Badis and Salarus fl., marking the boundary of Carmania and Gedrosia. *C. Jask.*

CARPENTORACTE, a town of the Vocontii, Viennensis, N.E. of Avenio. *Carpentras.*

CARPESSUS, a name of Carteia, Bætica, from the large shells found on its beach.

CARPETANI, a people of Tarraconensis, bet. Tagus fl. N., Anas fl. s., the Vettones w., and the Celtiberi E. *Provinces of Valladolid, Avila and Segovia, and parts of Guadalaxara and Toledo.*

CARPI (Carpiani), a tribe of Bastarnæ, Sarmat., about Alpes Carpatæ, N. of the Jazyges Metanastæ.

CARPIS, I. fl., i. q. Dravus. II. a town of Zeugitana, bet. Carthago (20) and Misua (40). *Gurbos.* III. (Cirpis, Ad Herculem), of Valeria, Pannon., on the Danube, bet. Salva (21) and Crumerum. *Visregrad.*

CARPRASIA prom., a pr. of Tarraconensis, E., at the s. extremity of Sucronensis sin., s.w. of the Iberus. *C. Penniscola.*

CARREA POTENTIA, a town of the Taurini, on Padus fl., R., 6 m. from Augusta Taurinorum. *Chieri.*

CARREI, a people of Arabia, E. of the Minæi, about Carriata.

CARRHA fl., a r. of Osrhoene, Mesop., falling into Belias fl. above Comisimbela.

CARRHÆ (Tharrana, Haran), I. a town of Osrhoene, on Carrha fl., bet. Batnæ and Sahal, 95¼ geog. m. w. from Nisibis. A colonia. The locality of the defeat of Crassus, and of the death of Caracalla. Hence Abraham departed for the land of Canaan. *Haran.* II. of Susiana-Cissia, on the Choaspes, bet. Badaca and Susa.

CARRHODUNUM, a town of the Consuanetæ, Vindel., on Ænus fl., above Turum. II. of the Jassii, Pannon., on Dravus fl., R., at its confluence with Murus fl. III. of Germania, on the Vistula, towards its source. *Cracow.*

CARRIATA (Giratha, Cariatha, Caripeta), capital of the Carrei, Arabia, E.N.E. of Thaumata. *Kariatain.*

CARRIENSIS AGER, the coast of Lusitania, N. of Munda fl.

CARRUCA, a town of the Turtetani, Bætica, bet. Sabora N.W. and Munda S.E.

CARSAGIS (Carsat), a town of Cappadocia, 28 m. w. from Sinera.

CARSËOLI, a town of the Æqui, Latium, on Via Valeria, bet. Lamnæ (10) and Alba Fucentia (24). A colonia 303 B.C. It was used by the Senate as a state prison. A law prevailed here against keeping foxes. *Celle di Carsoli.*

CARSIDAVA, a town of the Cistoboci, Dac., on the Parata fl., N.W. of Petrodava. *Near Choczim,* s.

CARSÜLÆ, a town of Umbria, s.w. of Spoletium, on Via Flaminia. *Carsoli.*

CARSUM, a town of Moesia Inf., on the Danube, bet. Cius and Capidava.

CARSUS fl., a torrent at Syriæ Pylæ, forming the boundary of Cilicia Campestris.

CARTA, Hyrcan., i. q. Zadracarta.

CARTASYNA, a town of the Gangaridæ, Ind., on Cambys ostium, at its mouth.

CARTEIA (Melcartheia, Heraclea, Carpessus), a port of Bætica, on Portus Albus, N.W. of Calpe. Founded by the Phœnician Hercules (Melcarthus). *Rocadillo.*

CARTENNA, a port of Mauritania Cæsar., bet. Carepula and Arsenaria. A colonia of Augustus. *Tennez.*

CARTENNUS fl., a r. of Mauritania Cæsar.,

falling into the Mediterranean at Cartenna.

CARTERONTYCHUS prom., a pr. of Sarmatia Asiat., on the Euxine, N. of Dioscurias.

CARTHAGO (Karth-hadtha, Carchĕdo, Betsura, Bosra, Byrsa), a city of Zeugitana, on a peninsula of Carthaginensis sin. Founded before 1180 B.C.; enlarged by the Tyrians under Elissa (Dido) 869 B.C. Destroyed by the younger Scipio 146 B.C. Restored nearly on the same site by Augustus, who nominated it a colony. The peninsula on which it stood has, by the withdrawal of the sea, become main land. *Carthage; Satcor.*

CARTHAGO NOVA (Massiena), capital of the Contestani, Tarraconensis, on Massienus sin., N.E., bet. Urci s.w. and Saturni prom. E. Built by Asdrubal Barcas 227 B.C. A colonia (Victrix Julia Nova). *Cartagena.*

CARTHAGE VETUS, a maritime town of the Læetani, Tarraconensis, near Ilerda. *Cartavieja.*

CARTHEA, a town of Ceos ins., on the s.E. coast. *Poles.*

CARTILIS, a maritime town of Mauritania Cæsar., bet. Gunugis and Lar.

CARTINAGA, a town of the Gangaridæ, Ind., on Cambys ostium, Ganget., above Cartasyna.

CARTRIS penins., i. q. Cimbrica Chersonesus.

CARUCA (Carula), a town of the Turtetani, Bætica, bet. Hispalis and Astigi.

CARURA, I. an isl. of Zeugitana, off Apollonium prom. II. baths of Caria, on the Mæander, bet. Laodicea (20) and Ephesus. III. capital of the Cerebothræ, India, on Chaberis fl., 30 m. from the sea. *Carur.*

CARUSA (Cressa), a Greek port of Paphlagonia, s. from Cyptasia 9 m. Founded *circa* 1180 B.C. *Kerzé.*

CARVO, a town of the Batavi, near the Rhine, w. of Arenatium. *Rheenen.*

CARUSADIUS m. (Carvancas), m. of Noricum, a s.w. continuation of Cetius m.

CARYÆ, I. a town of Arcadia, N. of Pheneus. II. of Laconia, under Parnon m., N.W. of Sellasia, with a temple of Diana Caryatis, in which the architectural form, hence called, Caryatides was first employed.

CARYANDA ins., I. an isl. of Caria, in Bargyliacus sin., over against Caryanda. The birth-place of Scylax the geographer. II. a town of Caria, on Bargyliacus sin., opposite the cognom. isl.

CARYDIUS saltus, a defile in Amanus m., bet. Podandus and Adana.

CARYSIS ins., an isl. of Caria, off Crya.

CARYSTUS, I. a town of Euboea, s., bet. Petalia prom. and Geraestus prom., at the foot of Oche m. A colony of Dryopes. Celebrated for its green marbles, and for its asbestos. *Castel Rosso.* II. of Laconia, near Ægys. Noted for its wine.

CASA, a town of Pamphylia, near Colobrassus.

CASA RUNONIANA, a town of the Macae, Africa Prop., on Syrtis Maj., w., bet. Macomades and Cisternae.

CASÆ ANICIORUM, I. a maritime town of Syrtica regio, bet. Ad Ammonem and Cypsaria. II. a town of Thebais, on the Nile, L., bet. Phylace and Lycopolis. III. CALVENTI, a maritime town of Mauritania Caesar., bet. Icosium (32) and Tipasa. *Bresch.*

CASALA, a town of Zeugitana, bet. Nephiris and Cucubis.

CASALINUS sin., a bay of Corsica, N.W., towards Attium prom. *G. di Calvi.*

CASAMA, a town of Syria, bet. Sattatha and Palmyra.

CASAMAN, a fortress of Cappadocia, bet. Mazaca and Carba.

CASANDRA ins., Persiae, i. q. Aracia.

CASCANTUM, a town of the Celtiberi, Tarraconensis, 1 geog. m. from the Iberus, R., above Carabis. A municipium. *Cascante.*

CASIA prom., a pr. of Gedrosia, on Paragon sin., bet. Talmena and Alambatis prom.

CASII m., m. of Serica, s. *Khara.*

CASILINUM, a town of the Sidicini, Campania, on both sides of Vulturnus fl., bet. Ad Nonum (6) and Capua (3), on Via Appia. A colonia of Julius Caesar. Memorable for its resistance to Hannibal. *Capua.*

CASINOMAGUS, a town of the Volcae Tectosages, Narbonensis I., bet. Ad Sextum w. and Hungunverro E. *Chabannes.*

CASINUM, *prius* Cascum (*Oscicè*, "old"), a town of the Volsci, Latium, on Via Latina, bet. Aquinum (9) and Ad Flexum. A colonia 314 B.C. *S. Germano.*

CASIOTIS (Casuch), I. a district of Lower Egypt, bet. Gerra and Ostracene. II. of Syria, S. of the Orontes, towards its mouth.

CASIUM prom., the termination of Casius m., Egypt, on Ecregma palus w. *C. del Kas,* " chisel."

CASIUM, the chief town of Casiotis, Egypt, bet. Pentaschoenon and Ostracene. The burial-place of Pompey. *Katieh.*

CASIUS m., I. a m. of Casiotis, Syria. Noted for its alleged immense altitude, and for

a temple of Jupiter Casius. *Jebel Okrab.* II. of Egypt, in Casiotis regio.

CASMENÆ, a town of Sicily, near the springs of Hippuris fl. Built by the Syracusans 645 B.C. *Comisi.*

CASMONATES, I. a tribe of Statielli, Liguria, s.w. of Aquae Statiellae. II. *postea* Casmonium (Gasmonium, Gasmundium), their capital. *Castelazzo.*

CASAS ins. (*prius* Astrabe), one of the Sporades, bet. Carpathus (9) and Crete (31). *Caso.*

CASPATYRUS, the early name of Peucela.

CASPEA, a town of Lycaonia, bet. Iconium and Isaura.

CASPERIA (Casperula), a town of Sabinium, near the source of Himella fl., s.w. of Reate. *Aspra.*

CASPIA, a town of Iberia, on the Cyrus, L., bet. Sura and Mestleta.

CASPIÆ portae, pylae, I. a defile in Caspius m., bet. Media and Parthia, 6 m. S.E. from Ragae. II. *apud* Tacitum, i. q. Caucasiae.

CASPII, I. m. of Media, bet. Cambyses fl. and Cyrus fl. II. a people of Media, in Caspii m.

CASPIANE, the country of the Caspii, Media. Ptolemy assigns it to Armenia, and Strabo to Albania.

CASPINGIUM, a town of the Batavi, on the Rhine, R., bet. Tablae and Grinnes.

CASPIRA, capital of the Caspiraei, Ind., N.E. of Taxila.

CASPIRÆI, a people of India e. Gangem, bet. the Hyphasis and the Ganges fl. *Part of Cashmir.*

CASPIRIA ins., Africae, i. q. Convallis.

CASPIUM mare, Hyrcanium, an inland sea of Asia, bet. Media and Armenia w., and Chorasmia E. Most of the ancients conceived it to be a bay of the northern sea, communicating with it by a narrow strait. Some geographers discriminate between Caspian mare and Hyrcanium, making the former the w., the latter the E. portion of the sea. *Caspian; Kaspüskoie Moré; Al Dhengiz.*

CASSÆ, a town of Cilicia.

CASSÆI, a people of Susiana-Corbiene, on Choaspes fl.

CASPIUS m., a ridge of Taurus, E. of Niphates, separating Armenia Magna from Media.

CASSANDRIA, a city of Chalcidice, on the isthmus connecting Pallene with the mainland. Built by Cassander close to Potidaea, and partly peopled by the inhabitants of that city. A colonia. *Kassandhra.*

CASSANDREI, Arabiae, i. q. Cassani.

CASSANITÆ (Gasandi, Cassandrei), a people of Arabia Felix, s. and E. of Macaraba, N. of the Elisari, with a few towns on the coast s.w.

CASSANITES m., m. of the Cassanitæ, Arabia. *Gazuan.*

CASSERA, Chalcid. Maced., i. q. Assera.

CASSI, a tribe of Trinobantes, Brit. *About Cassiobury, &c., Hertfordshire.*

CASSIDA, I. a people of Indiæ e. Gangem, on the Ganges, at its junction with Comenases fl. II. of the Pasalæ, Ind., near Œdanes fl., L., above Athenagura.

CASSILIACUM, a town of the Estiones, Vindelicia, w. N. w. of Cambodunum. *Isny.*

CASSINOMAGUS, a town of the Lemovices, Aquitania I., bet. Sermanicomagus w. and Augustoritum E.

CASSIOFE, I. a prom. of Corcyra ins., at its N.E. extremity, over against Onchesmus. *C. di Santa Caterina.* II. a port of Chaonia, over against Cassiope, Corcyra. III. of Corcyra ins., at Cassiope prom., 15 m. from Corcyra. Deriving its name from a noted temple of Jupiter Casius.

CASSIPOLIS, a town of Cilicia Campestris, w. of Aleius campus.

CASSITERĬDES ins. (Silurum, Sylinæ, Æstrymnides, Hesperides) isl. of the Damnonii, Britannia I., off Antivestæum prom. Hence the Phœnicians procured their tin, the Sanscrit name of which is *Kastira,* "shining." The name probably extended to Cornwall itself. *Scilly Isl. and W. Cornwall.*

CASSOPE, a town of Epirus, towards Pambotis lac.

CASSOTIS fons, a stream of Parnassus, flowing by Delphi into Pleistus fl.

CASTABALA, I. a town of Tyanitis, Cappadocia, N.E. of Calydna. Here was the statue of Diana Perasia, "brought from beyond sea," i. e. from Tauris, by Orestes. Her priestesses walked on burning cinders uninjured. *Kalat Masman.* II. of Cilicia, E. of Anazarbus. *Chamdun.*

CASTALIA fons, a stream of Parnassus, running from Phædriades m., by Delphi, into Pleistus fl. Sacred to the Muses. Its murmurs were reputed prophetic.

CASTAMON, a town of Paphlagonia, under Olgasys m., s.w. of Pompeiopolis. *Castamouni.*

CASTELLANI, a tribe of Ausetani, Tarraconensis, under the Pyrenees, bet. the Ceretani w., the Indigetes E., and the Ausetani s.

CASTANIA, a town of Messapia, near Tarentum.

CASTELLA DARII, fortresses erected by Darius in Sarmatia N., on the Tanais, E. of Alaunus m.

CASTELLUM, I. *postea* Chassalaba, Castella, a town of Germania, 84 m. N.N.E. from Moguntiacum. *Cassel.* II. AMERINUM, a fortress of Etruria, on Amerina Via, bet. Falerii (12) and Ameria (9). *Bassano.* III. CARACENORUM, of the Caraceni, Samnium, on Sagrus fl. *Castello di Sangro.* IV. FIRMANORUM, the port of Firmum in Picenum, bet. Potentia (12) and Truentium (24), on Via Flaminia. *Porto di Fermo.* V. MENAPIORUM, a fortress of the Menapii, on Mosa fl. *Kessel.* VI. MARINORUM, of the Morini, E. of Gessoriacum. *Montcassel.*

CASTHANÆA, a town of Magnesia, Thessaly, on the Ægean, bet. Melibœa and Sepias prom. Named from its fine chesnuts. *Tamukhari.*

CASTNIUS m., a m. of Pamphylia, overlooking Aspendus.

CASTOBOCI, a people of Sarmatia Europæa, towards the Carni.

CASTOLI campus, a plain of Lydia, on Castolus fl.

CASTRA, I. CÆCILIA (Celicis, Cæcilia Gemellina, Ad Sorores), a fortress of the Vettones, Lusitania, N. of Emerita. *Caceres.* II. CORNELIA, a town of Zeugitana, E. of Utica. Originally a camp of the Elder Scipio, whence the name. *Porto Farina.* III. EXPLORATORUM, of the Brigantes, Brit., towards the w. termination of Hadriani murus N. IV. GERMANORUM, a fortress of Mauritania Cæsar., near Cartilis. V. HANNIBALIS, a town of Bruttium, on Scylacius sin., bet. Scylacium (5) and Crotona. *Roccella?* VI. HERCULIS, of the Batavi, N.w. of Noviomagus. *Hervelt.* VII. JULIA (Trogilium), of the Vettones, Hispania, s.E. of Castra Cæcilia. *Truxillo.* VIII. NOVA, of the Mœsi, Mœsia Inf., on the Danube, bet. Variana and Utus, at the mouth, R., of Œscus fl. IX. NOVA, of Mauritania Cæsar., under Ancorarius m.. s., bet. Bellene and Tassacora. X. NOVA, of the Saldenses, Dac., 20 m. s.E. of Pelendova. Built by Constantine. *Forcas?* XI. PAREMBOLE, of the Dassaretæ, Illyria, on the confines of Macedonia, bet. Pylon (11) and Heraclea (12). XII. PYRRHI, of Orestis, Macedonia, on Æas fl., w. of Gyrtona. XIII. TRAJANA, of the Burideenses, Dac., on Aluta fl., R., bet. Arutela and Buridava (12). XIV. ULCISIA, of Valeria, Pannonia, N.w. of Acincum. XV. ZARBA, of the Odrysæ,

Thrace, on Harpessus fl., bet. Pala and Rhamæ.

CASTRI LUCUS, a town of Germania I., s. of Tablæ. *Mons.*

CASTRUM, I. EIRCTA, a fortress of Sicily, on the N. coast. II. FABATIANUM, a town of Numidia, near Cirta. III. GADAUM, of Mauritania Cæsar., under Ancorarius m., S.S.E. of Cartenna. IV. INNI, *vide* Castrum Novum, Etruriæ. V. MAURO-RUM, a fortress of Zabdicene, Armen., bet. Dara and Meride. *Catar-Tutha.* VI. MENAS, a town of Venetia, near Forum Julii. VII. MINERVÆ, of Japygia, bet. Hydruntum (8) and Veretum (15). *Castro.* VIII. of Bruttium, on Locanus fl., near its source. Built by Idomeneus, circa 1100 B.C. *Grotteria.* IX. MUTILUM, of Etru-ria, bet. Sarsina and Arretium. *Meldola.* X. NOVUM, of the Prætutii, Picenum, bet. Truentum (12) and Hadria (15), on Via Flaminia. *Giulia Nova.* XI. NOVUM (Castrum Inui), of Etruria, on Via Aurelia, bet. Pyrgi (8) and Centumcellæ (5). An Etruscan settlement. A colonia. Sacred to Inuus (Pan). *Torre Chiaraccia.* XII. PUERORUM, of Mauritania Cæsar., bet. Portus Deorum and Gilva. XIII. THEO-DORA, of Dacia, on the Danube, over against Pons Trajani. XIV. TINGITII, of Mauritania, on Chinalath fl., L., below Tiganda. XV. TRUENTUM (Truentinum), of Prætutii, Picenum, at Truentus fl., L., near its mouth, bet. Castellum Firmano-rum (24) and Castrum Novum (12), on Via Flaminia. A Liburnian settlement. *Monte Brandone.* XVI. VULTURNI, of Campania, at the mouth of Vulturnus fl., on Via Domitiana, bet. Sinuessa and Li-ternum (7). A colonia 196 B.C. *Vol-turno.*

CASTŬLO, a town of the Oretani, Tarraco-nensis, on Bætis, R., near its source, bet. Mentesa-Bastia N. and Tugia s. A Pho-cæan settlement. The birth-place of Imilce, Hannibal's wife. The hill on which it stood was bivertical, and hence the town was surnamed Parnassia. A co-lonia (Cæsari Venales). *Caslona; Ca-zorla.*

CASTULONENSIS saltus, a ridge of Mari-anus m., Tarraconensis, about Castulo. Noted for its silver mines. *Sierra di Cazorle.*

CASUARIA, a town of the Centrones, Alpes Penninæ, bet. Bautæ N.W. and Ad Pub-licanos S.E.

CASUENTUS fl., a r. of Lucania falling into Tarraconensis sin., s. of Metapontum. *Ba-sienti.*

CASULA, a town of Zeugitana, bet. Maxula (20) and Curubis (25). *Soleiman.*

CASURGIS, a town of the Burii, Germ., s.w. of Budorgis. *Near Troppau.*

CASUS (Achne), I. an isl. of the Carpathian sea, 7 m. s.w. from Carpathus. *Kahso.* II. its capital, on the s. coast. *Khaso.*

CATABANA (Cataba, Bana), capital of the Catabani, Arabiæ, 3 geog. m. N. from Arabiæ Emporium. *Kataba.*

CATABANI, a people of Arabia Felix, occu-pying its w. angle, w. of the Homeritæ. *Beni Kahtan.*

CATABATHMUS MAJOR ("descent"), a valley of Marmarica, running inland bet. Panor-mus and Syce, at one time the E. boundary of Marmarica, and by some geographers considered the E. boundary also of Africa, Egypt being assigned to Asia. *Akabah el Soloum.*

CATABATHMUS MINOR, a valley of Libya Ægypti, on the coast, E. of Phœnicus portus.

CATABATHRA, the tunnels, some natural, others artificial, by which the redundant waters of Copais lacus passed into the sea.

CATABEDA fl., a r. of India e. Gangem, fall-ing into Gangeticus sin., E. of Ganges fl. *Shatigan.*

CATABOLON, a port of Cilicia, 2 geog. m. N.E. from Issus. *Karabolat.*

CATACECAUMENE regio ("burnt up"), a volcanic district of Lydia, on Hermus fl., L., towards its source. According to some writers, the seat of the Arimi of Homer, and the scene of Typhœus' punishment. Noted for its wine.

CATADERBIS fl., a r. or inlet of Susiana, on Persicus sin., opposite Margastana ins.

CATADUBA, a town of the Gangani, Ind., on the Ganges, R., near its source.

CATADUPA, two cataracts on the Nile; the greater above Premis, the less above Ele-phantis ins. The contiguous people, called Catadubi, were said to lose their hearing from the roar of the water.

CATÆA ins., an isl. of Carmania, on Persicus sin., bet. Cecadrus ins. and Tarsias prom. It marked, according to Næarchus, the limit of Carmania and Persis Propr., and before the rise of Ormus was a great em-porium. *Keish, or Cais.*

CATÆONIUM prom., a pr. of Marmarica, bet. Menelai portus (9) and Scythranius portus.

CATALAUNI, a people of Belgica II., in the s. territory of the Remi. *Departments of Marne s. and Meuse w.*

CATALAUNUM, their capital, i. e. Durocatalauni.

CATALI, a people of Histria, s. of the Subocrini.

CĂTĂNA (Catina), a maritime city of Sicily, E. Built by a Chalcidian colony 753 B.C. A colonia. The birth-place of Charondas. Here was a temple of Ceres which only women were permitted to enter. *Catania.*

CATANGION sin., a bay of Bithynia, on Bosporus Thracius, N. of Oxyrrhoum prom.

CATANITÆ (Catanii), a people of Arabia Felix, under Zames m., s. *Tribe of Beni Kahtan.*

CATAONIA, a prefecture of Cappadocia, bet. Amanus m. and Anti-taurus. *Aladeuli.*

CATARA, capital of the Cataræi, Arabia, E.N.E. of Gerra. *Katura.*

CATARACTORIUM, a town of the Brigantes, Brit., s.w. of Vinovia. *Catterick.*

CATARÆI, a people of Arabia Felix, on Persicus sin., about Catara.

CATARI, a people of Pannonia.

CATARRHACTES fl., I. a r. of Crete, rising in Inatus m., and falling into Libycum m., 20 m. w. from Hierapytna. *Sudsuro.* II. of Pamphylia, running from Pisidicus lacus into the sea at Attalia. *Duden.* III. (Marsyas), of Phrygia M., running from Aulocrene lac. into Mæander fl., near Celænæ. IV. MAJOR, the great cataract of the Nile, N.W. of Tasitia. V. MINOR, the lesser cataract, N. of Philæ.

CATARZENE, a district of Armenia, towards Moschici m.

CATAVELLAUNI, a people of Flavia Cæsariensis, bet. the Iceni and Trinobantes, E., the Dobuni and Cornavii w., the Trinobantes and Dobuni s., and the Coritani N.

CATAZETI, a people of Sarmatia Asiatica, on the Tanais.

CATENATES (Clautinatii), a people of Vindelicia, on Licus fl., bet. the Danube and Ambra fl.

CATENNENSES, Pisidia, i. q. Etennenses.

CATHÆI, a town of India, on Hydraotes fl., N.W. of the Malli.

CATHENA m., a m. of Lucania, near Pæstum. *Monte Capaccio.*

CATHRAMOTITÆ, Arabiæ. *Vide Chathramotitæ.*

CATHRAPS fl., Carmania, i. q. Salsus.

CATONI, a people of Sarmatia Asiatica, on the Tanais.

CATOPTERIUS ("looking downwards") m., a summit of Parnassus, near Anemorium.

CATORISSIUM, a town of the Uceni, Viennensis, bet. Cularo N. and Melosecium E. *Petit-Chat.*

CATRALEUCUM, a town of the Bracari, Tarraconensis, on Avus fl., L., towards its source.

CATREA, a town of Crete, founded by Catreus the Arcadian.

CATTI (Chatti), a people of Germania Magna, s. of the Cherusci. *Hesse; Fulda; Franconia N., &c.*

CATTIGARA, a port of an isl. (Borneo) of India e. Gangem, s. of Cocoranagora. *Succadang.*

CATUALIUM, a town of the Taxandri, Germania II., N.W. of Teudurum.

CATUIACA, a town of the Memini, Narbonensis, E. of Apta Julia.

CATURÏGES, I. a people of Alpes Maritimæ, at first on Druentia fl., towards its source, w. of Vapincum, but afterwards largely extending themselves into Viennensis and Narbonensis. II. (Catorimagus), their capital, bet. Dea Vocontiorum and Ebrodunum. *Chorges.* III. a town of the Remi, Belgica II., bet. Ariola N.W. and Nasium. *Bar le Duc.*

CATVIACA, Vocontiorum, i. q. Ad Fines. (*Oppedete.*)

CATYEUCHLANI, Brit., i. q. Catavellauni.

CAUCA, a town of the Vaccæi, Tarraconensis, s. of Pallantia. *Coca.*

CAUCHABENI ("sons of the stars"), a tribe of Chaldæans in Arabia, N.E., on the Euphrates. *Tribe of Beni Cauchab.*

CAUCADÆ, a people of Sarmatia Asiatica, on Lagus fl.

CAUCANA portus, a port of Sicily, s., bet. Hermynius fl. and Bucra prom.

CAUCASIÆ portæ (Caspiæ, Sarmatæ), defiles of Caucasus, the chief pass from Sarmatia Asiat. into Iberia, N. of Harmozia. *Tatar-Topa.*

CAUCASIUM mare, i. q. Euxinus.

CAUCĂSUS m., m. of Asia, bet. the Euxine and the Caspian.

CAUCASUS INDICUS, a name given to the N.E. extension of Parapomisus m. by the soldiers of Alexander.

CAUCI campi, the plain bet. Pasitigris fl., towards its mouth and the Tigris.

CAUCOENSES, a tribe of Agathyrsi, Dacia, on Parata fl., N. of the Jassii.

CAUCON fl., a r. of Achaia, rising in Scollis m., and falling into the Teutheas fl. near Teuthea.

CAUCONES, a tribe of Pelasgi, the early occupants of Elis, and the portion of Achaia about Caucon fl., a colony of whom migrated to Asia Minor, about Parthenius fl. Extinct in Strabo's time.

CAUCONIA, the early name of Elis.

CAUCONII, a people of Caria, about Caunus.

CAUCUNA portus, a haven of Sicily, w. of Motychanus fl.

CAUDELLUM, a town of the Vulgientes, Narbonensis, on Druentia fl., s. of Apta Julia.

CAUDĪNÆ FURCÆ vel FURCULÆ, a defile of Samnium, near Caudium. The locality of the disgrace of the Roman army. *Val d'Arpaia.*

CAUDINI, a tribe of the Pentri, Samnium, on the borders of Campania, s. of Vulturnus fl.

CAUDIUM, capital of the Caudini, Samnium, bet. Ad Novas (9) and Beneventum (11). *Paolisi, or Cervinara.*

CAULARES fl., a r. of Phrygia M., falling into the Mæander fl. N. of Cibyra. *Zu.*

CAULONIA (Aulon), a city of Bruttium, on Locrensis sin., at the mouth of Sagrus fl., L., bet. Cocynthum prom. and Subsicivum. An Achæan settlement. Destroyed by Dionysius. *Castro Vetere.*

CAULUM, a village of Campania, near Capua. Noted for its wine. *Caulo.*

CAUMATA, a town of Carmania Deserta, bet. Arcioba and Aridarum.

CAUNUS, a maritime city of Caria, 4 m. s. from Pisilis, the people of which were reputed autochthonous. *Kaiguez.*

CAUPHIACA, a town of Persis Prop., w. of Pasargada.

CAURA, a town of the Turtetani, Bætica, on the Bætis, at the separation of its mouths.

CAURIUM, a town of the Vettones, Lusitania, w. of Rusticana. *Coria.*

CAUSENNÆ, a town of the Coritani, Brit., bet. Lindum (26) and Durobrivæ.

CAVĂRES (Cavări), a people of Viennensis, bet. the Rhodanus, the Druentia, and the Isara. *Departments of Vaucluse and Drome, w.*

CAVATURINES, a people of Liguria, towards Genua. *About Creverina.*

CAVICLUM, a maritime town of the Bastuli, Bætica, bet. Mænoba w. and Salambina E.

CAVII, a people of Illyria, bet. the Labeates and the Parthini.

CAVIONES, Germania, i. q. Chaibones.

CAYSTRA PEDION, a village of Phrygia Mag., bet. Ipsus and Julia.

CAYSTRUS, I. a r. of Ionia, rising in Tmolus m., towards Sardes, and falling into Ionium mare below Ephesus. *Kutchuk Mendere.* II. (Clistrus, Cestrus), a town of Cilicia

Trachea, on Calycadmus·fl., towards its w. source.

CAZECA, a port of Taurica Chersonesus s.

CEBA, a town of the Vagienni, Liguria, on Tanarus fl., R., E. of Augusta Vagiennorum. Noted for its cheese. *Ceva.*

CEBRENE, I. a r. of Troas, falling into Simois fl., near Cebrene. *Kazdagh-tchai.* II. a town of Troas, on the Simois, near its source. Named from the charioteer of Hector. Its inhabitants were transferred to Alexandria. *Kutchulan-Tepe.*

CECADRUS ins., an isl. of Carmania, in Persicus sin., bet. Sagdiana ins. and Catæa ins.

CECILIA, a town of Cyrrhestica, Syria, on the Euphrates, bet. Manurrhoa and Europus, 4 m. s.E. from Zeugma.

CECILIONICUM, a town of the Vettones, Lusitania, bet. Ad Lippos N.N.w. and Libora s.E.

CECROPIA (Cropia), I. a demus of Attica, of the tribe Leontis, N. of Phlya. Named after Cecrops. II. a name of Athens.

CECROPIDÆ, the name of the Athenians under Cecrops, and until the time of Erectheus.

CECROPIS, a tribe or ward of Attica.

CECRYPHALÆA ins. (Cecryphalos), an isl. of Argolis, in Saronicus sin., over against Epidaurus.

CEDARENI, Arabiæ, i. q. Cedrei.

CEDI or Cedæ, a demus of Attica, of the tribe Erectheis.

CEDONIÆ, a town of the Burideenses, Dacia, bet. Acidava and Stenarum (12).

CEDREI (Cedareni, Gedranitæ, Darræ), a people of Arabia Felix, s. of Arabia Petræa, bet. the Nabathæi and the sea. The descendants of Kedar. *In the Hedjaz.*

CEDREUS fl., a r. of Sardinia, falling into the sea N. of Saprus fl. *Galtelli.*

CEDRIUS m., a summit of Ida in Crete. *Mt. Psiloritz.*

CEIRIADÆ, a demus of Attica, of the tribe Hippothoontis, N. of Amphitrope. *Keratia.*

CELĂDUS fl., I. a r. of Arcadia, rising in Thesoa Regio and falling into the Alpheus. II. of Tarraconensis, bet. the Durius and Minius. *Celado.*

CELÆNÆ, I. a Phœnician town of Æolis Asiatica, on Heptaporus fl., N.E. of Adramyttium. II. capital of Phrygia Magna, at the source of Marsyas fl., s.E. of Apamea Cibotus, whither its inhabitants were transferred by Antiochus Soter. The locality of the legend of Midas.

CELEÆ, a town of Phlius, Argolis, ½ m. N.w. from its capital, where a festival in honour of Ceres was celebrated every fourth year.

CELEJA, a town of Pannonia, on Sana fl., 24 m. N.E. from Adrans. *Cilley.*

CELELATES, a people of Liguria, near the Ilvates. *About Celetta.*

CELENDERIS, a maritime city of Cilicia Trachea, 12½ m. N.E. from Meganda, on Is fl. A Phœnician settlement enlarged by Samians. *Kelindreh.*

CELENNA, a fortress of Samnium, near Batulum.

CELETRIUS lacus, a lake of Orestis, Macedonia, N.E. of Orestia. *Lago di Castoria.*

CELĒTRUM, a town of Orestis, Macedonia, on a peninsula at the N.W. extremity of Celetrius lacus. *Castoria.*

CELEUSUM, a town of Rhætia, on the Danube, 14 m. N.E. from Germiniacum. *Pföring.*

CELIA, a town of Peucetia, on Via Egnatia, bet. Butuntum (12) and Netium (9). *Ceglie.*

CELIDA, a town of Cyrenaica, near Cænopolis.

CELINA, I. a r. of Venetia, falling into Liquentia fl. *Cilina.* II. a town on the cognominal river. Extinct in Pliny's time.

CELLÆ (Cellæ Picentinæ, Cellæ Vicus), I. a town of Byzacene, on Syrtis Minor, 30 m. s. from Tasbalta. II. of Eordæa, Macedonia Consularis, on the Astræus fl., bet. Heraclea (34) and Ægæ (28), on Egnatia Via. *Kirl Derpend.* III. of Mauritania Cæsariensis, bet. Perdices (18) and Macri (25). *Mojanah.* IV. of the Odrysæ, Thrace, s. of Hebrus fl., bet. Opizus and Philippopolis.

CELMANTIA, a town of Germania Magna, on the Danube, at the confluence of Vagus fl. *Komorn.*

CELNIUS fl., a r. of the Caledonii, E. falling into the sea, w. of Tæzalum prom. *Doveran.*

CELONÆ, I. a town of Susiana Messabatice, bet. Racha and Corma. II. Assyriæ, i. q. Chala.

CELOSSA (Ceglossa), I. m. of Argolis, a N.W. continuation of Arachnæus m., towards Achaia. Named after Ceglusa, mother of Asopus. II. a fortress of Argolis, on Celossa m.

CELSA, a town of the Ilergites, Tarraconensis, on the Iberus, 6 m. S.E. of Cæsar Augusta. A colonia (Victrix Julia). *Xelsa.*

CELSITANI, a people of Sardinia, about Usellis.

CELTÆ, the early population of Gaul, migrations of whom peopled portions of Spain (on the Anas, in Gallæcia, &c.), Britain, &c.

CELTI, a town of the Turtuli, Bætica, N. of Ilipa.

CELTIBERI, a people of central Tarraconensis, bet. Iberus fl. N., Sucro fl. s., the Carpetani N. and Arevacæ s.w., and the Hercaones E. A tribe of Celtic immigrants mingled with the Iberi.

CELTICA, generally the Greek name of Gaul and Germania; specially, Gaul; with Cæsar, that portion of Gaul between the Garumna, the Sequana, the sea, and Cebenna m. Named from a giant called Celtus, or from Celtus, the old name of the Garumna, or from the idea the Greeks formed of the comparative civilization of its inhabitants.

CELTICO-FLAVIA, a town of the Vettones, Lusitania, near Salmantica, S.S.E.

CELTICUM prom., Hispaniæ, i. q. Artabrum.

CELTO-GALATIA, the name given by Ptolemy to Gaul.

CELTORII, Galliæ, i. q. Suelteri.

CELTZENE, a district of Armenia Interior, on Lycus fl., N.E. of Chorzene.

CELYDNA, a town of the Marundæ, India, on the Ganges, at its junction with Cossoanes fl.

CELYDNUS fl., a r. of Illyria, falling into the Adriatic at Oricum. In the time of Ptolemy the s. boundary of Macedonia.

CEMA m., a ridge of Alps, in Alpes Maritimæ. *Mont Lerres.*

CEMBIS portus, a haven of the Cempsi, Lusitania, N. of Gades.

CEMENELUM, a town of the Vediantii, Alpes Maritimæ, on Varus fl., L., bet. Vintium w. and Albintemelium. *Cimiers.*

CEMPSI, a people of Lusitania, occupying a portion of the Cuneus.

CENA, a town of Sicily, on the s.w. coast, bet. Allava and Agrigentum (18). *Mont' Allegro.*

CENÆUM prom., the N.W. headland of Eubœa ins., on Maliacus sin., over against Cnemis. *Lithada.*

CENAXE palus, a lake of the Tectosages, Galatia, near Ancyra.

CENCHREÆ, I. a town of Argolis, under Chaon m., s., bet. Trochos and Hysiæ. II. the E. port of Corinth, on Saronicus sin., 8½ m. S.E. from the city. *Kenchres.* III. a town of Troas, on Simois fl., s. of Næandria. The residence for a time of Homer. *Tchigri.*

CENCHREIS ins., an isl. of Argolis, in Saronicus sin., over against Spiræum prom.

CENCHRIUS fl., a r. of Ionia, rising in Solmissus m. and falling into Ionium mare at Ortygia.

CENDEVIA palus, a marsh formed by Belus fl., Phœniciæ, towards its mouth.

CENERIUM, a town of Messenia, on the coast, near Platamodes prom.

CENESTUM, a town of Corsica, on Sacer fl., L., towards its mouth. *Corte.*

CENETA (Cenitense Castrum), a town of the Veneti, Venetia, N. of Opitergium. *Ceneda.*

CENIMAGNI, a tribe of Iceni, Britan., N. of the Trinobantes. *Suffolk, Norfolk, and Cambridgeshire.*

CENION OSTIUM, an estuary of the Damnonii, Brit., at Voliba. *Falmouth Harbour.*

CENNI, a tribe of Curiones, Germania, on Mœnus fl.

CENO PORTUS, the port of Antium, Latium. *Porto d'Anzo.*

CENOMĀNNI, I. *vide* Aulerci Cenomanni. II. a colony of Gaulish Cenomanni, in Gallia Transpadana, on Padus fl., bet. Addua fl. w. and Athesis fl. E.

CENTAURI, a tribe of Pelasgi-Eordi, settled in and under Ossa m. Such skilled horse-tamers that they were poetically said to be half man and half horse.

CENTOBRIGA, i. q. Nertobriga.

CENTRITES fl., i. q. Nicephorius.

CENTRONES, a people of Alpes Graiæ, N. of the Segusini. *Tarentaise.*

CENTRONUM CIVITAS, Galliæ, i. q. Darantasia.

CENTUMCELLÆ (Trajani portus), a maritime town of Etruria, on Via Aurelia, bet. Castrum Novum (5) and Algæ. Noted for its fine harbour, constructed by Trajan. *Civita Vecchia.*

CENTUM PUTEA, a town of the Albocenses, Dacia, bet. Bersovia and Acidava, N.W. of Pons Trajani. *Near Oraviza.* II. wells of Palmyrene Syr., N.W. of Palmyra.

CENTURIA ins., one of the Fortunatæ ins., Africa, N.E. of Canaria. *Fuerteventura.*

CENTURINUM, a maritime town of Corsica, below Sacrum prom. *Centuri.*

CENTURIPÆ, a town of Sicily, on Cyamosurus fl., bet. Argyrium and Ætna. *Centorlu.*

CEOS ins. (Cea, Cos, Hydrussa), an isl. of the Ægean, 5 m. S.E. of Macris. Once a part of Eubœa. Noted for the elegant attire of its women. *Zea.*

CEPHA, a fortress of Gordyene, Armenia, on the Tigris, below its junction with Nymphæus fl. *Hesn-Keif.*

CEPHALÆ prom., a pr. of Africa, on Syrtis Major, w. above Macomades. *C. Canan or Mesra.*

CEPHALE, a demus of Attica, of the tribe Acamantis.

CEPHALLENIA ins., *prius* Samos, an isl. of Acarnania, s. of Leucate prom., 6 m. s.w. of Ithaca ins, 120 m. in circuit and 60 m. long. Named after Cephalus, the friend of Amphytrion. *Cephalonia.*

CEPHALLONESUS ins., an isl. of Sarmatia E., in Carcinites sin.

CEPHALŒDIUM (Cephalædium), a maritime town of Sicily, N. bet. Alæsa and Himera. *Cefalu.*

CEPHISSA, a demus of Attica, of the tribe Erectheis, on Cephissus fl., at the s. foot of Brilessus m., 6 m. from Athens. The favourite retreat of Herodes Atticus. *Kephisia.*

CEPHĪSUS fl., "roaring," *surnamed* Atticus, I. a r. of Attica, rising at Trinemei and falling into Saronicus sin. at Phalerum portus. *Podhonista.* II. *surnamed* Eleusinius, of Attica, rising in Cithæron m. and falling into Saronicus sin. below Eleusis. III. of Phocis, rising in Parnassus, near Lilæa, from a spring said to roar, at midday, like a bull, and falling into Copais lacus at Orchomenus. *Mauro Nero.*

CEPHISSUS palus, i. q. Copais.

CEPI, a town of Sarmatia Asiatica, near Cimmerius Bosporus. A Milesian settlement.

CEPRESICUM prom., Lusitaniæ, the early name of Sacrum prom.

CERAITÆ, a town of Crete, N.W. of Hierapytna.

CERAMICUS sinus, a bay of Carium mare, E. bet. Termerium prom. and Triopium prom. *L. Stanco or Boudroun.*

CERAMUS, a fortress of Caria, on Ceramicus sin. N. *Keramo.*

CERANÆ (Ceranorum forum), a town of Catacecaumene, Lydia, on the borders of Phrygia, w. of Blaundus.

CERASÆ, a town of Lydia, on Hermus fl., opposite Bagæ. *Sirghie.*

CERĀSUS, a town of the Mosynœci, Pontus, 9 m. from Coralla prom. A colony from Sinope. Here the 10,000 were encamped for ten days, and hence the cherry-tree was imported into Italy by Lucullus. *Skefie.*

CERATÆ, a hill of Attica, w. of Eleusis. The boundary between Attica and Megaris.

CERAUNII m., the S.E. termination of Caucasus m., on the Caspian, bet. Sarmatia Asiatica and Albania.

CERAUSIUS m., a w. summit of Lycæus m., in Arcadia, on the confines of Messenia.

CERAX, a town of Phœbatis, Illyria, on Genusus fl., bet. Gerunium and Bantia. *Koridje.*

CERBALUS fl., a r. of Apulia, falling into the Adriatic at or near Sipontum. Above its mouth it formed a lake. It was the boundary of Daunia Proper and Diomedis Campi. *Cervaro.*

CERBANI (Carbæ), a people of Arabia Felix, occupying the coast of the Red Sea N. of the Elamitæ, and extending inland N.E. to the Manitæ and the Uadeni. Descendants of Kedar. *Tribe of Beni Harb.*

CERBERIUM, the earlier name of Cimmerium.

CERBESII, a tribe of Bryges or Phryges, settled in Phrygia Magna prior to the Trojan war. Extinct in Strabo's time.

CERCAPHUS m., a m. of Ionia, near Colophon.

CERCAS, a town of Argolis, near Nauplia. The birth-place of the historian Acusilaus.

CERCASŌRA, a town of Lower Egypt, on the Nile, L., bet. Letopolis and Memphis. *El Arkas.*

CERCETÆ (Cæti, Apaitæ), a people of Sarmatia Asiatica, in Corax m., N.W. of the Zichi.

CERCETICUS sinus, a bay of the Euxine, N. of Toreticum prom.

CERCETIUS m. (Citius), I. the N. extremity of Pindus m., on the borders of Thessaly, Epirus, and Macedonia, extending E. to Cambunii m. *Zygos or Ian Cantara.* II. prom., the N.W. extremity of Samos, N. of Cantharium prom. *C. Kerki.*

CERCIDIATES, I. a people of Liguria, N. of the Ilvates. II. their capital. *Ceretto, towards Tortona.*

CERCIDIUS fl., a r. of Corsica, falling into the sea N. of Urcinium. *Liamone.*

CERCINA, I. an isl. of Byzacene, N. of Syrtis Minor, over against Thenæ, 25 m. long by 12½ m. broad. *Chercara.* II. its town.

CERCINE m., a m. of the Sinti, Pæonia, parallel with Pontus fl. Impassable on account of the thick forests which covered them. They form the boundary between Pæonia and Thrace. *Tchengel Dagh.*

CERCINETIS, a maritime town of Taurica Chersonesus, w. above Daudace.

CERCINITIS ins., I. an isl. of Byzacene, contiguous to Cercina ins. N.E., and joined to it by a bridge. II. palus, a lake of Thrace, formed by Strymon fl., a few miles above its mouth, 18 m. long by 6 broad. *L. Takinos.*

CERCINIUM, a town of Pelasgiotis, Thessaly, w. of Bæbe lacus.

CERCOPIA, a town of Phrygia Magna, near Synnada.

CERCUSIUM, Mesopotamiæ, i. q. Circesium.

CERDILIUM m., a hill of Bisaltia, Macedonia, near the mouth of Strymon fl.

CERDONIA, Dauniæ, i. q. Herdonia.

CEREATE (Cirrhæate), a village of the Volsci, Latium, bet. Anagnia and Sora. The residence, in his youth, of Marius.

CEREÆ, a town of Paphlagonia, 20 m. from Tycæ.

CEREBELLIACA, a town of the Segelauni, Viennensis, bet. Valentia N.W. and Augusta Tricastinorum s.E.

CERERIS SPECULA (Demetros scopias) prom., a pr. of Africa, on Arabicus sin., 9 geog. m. s. from Dioscoron portus.

CERESIUS lacus, a lake of the Orobii, Gallia Transpadana, bet. Verbanus lacus and Larius lacus. *Lago di Lugano.*

CERESSUS, I. a fortress of Bœotia, on Helicon m., N.E. of Ascra. II. of the Lacetani, Tarraconensis, N.E. of Telobis. *Cervera?*

CERETAPA, a town of Phrygia Magna, on Aulindenus fl., bet. Ascania lacus and Colossæ.

CEREURA, a port of Limyrica, Indiæ, s.E. of Bacari. *Cananor.*

CERFENNA, a town of the Marsi, near the N.E. extremity of Fucinus lacus, bet. Marrubium (7) and Alba Fucentia. *Sant' Felicita or Colli.*

CERILLÆ (Carillæ), a maritime town of Bruttium, bet. Laus and Clampetia (40), on Via Aquilia. *Cirella Vecchia.*

CERINTHUS, a town of Ellopia, Eubœa, near Budorus fl., E. of Artemisium prom. Founded by Cothon. *Geronda.*

CERMORUS sinus, i. q. Strymonicus sin.

CERNE ins., an isl. of Ethiopia, in the Atlantic, s.w. of Atlas Major, according to Hanno, two days' sail s. and one E. from Herculeum Fretum. From its agreeable climate it is called by Dionysius Periegetes, Tempe. It was colonized by Hanno. *Arguin.*

CERNEATIS ins., a name in Lycophron of Corsica.

CERONES (Creones), a maritime tribe of Caledonii, w. below the Vacomagi. *Parts of Argyleshire and Inverness.*

CERRETANI (Cerretani Juliani, Cerretani Augustani), an Iberian people of Tarraconensis, N. and N.E. of the Ilergetes. *N. Catalonia.*

CERSIE, a town of the Ratacenses, Dacia, bet. Parolissum and Cargiana (17). *Near Kemetzel.*

CERSUNUM, a town of Corsica, on Tavola fl., L., above Talcinum.

CERTIMÆ (Alce), a town of the Turtetani, Bætica, N.E. of Munda.

CERVÆ, a town of Byzacene, bet. Ad Turres and Alonianum (20).

CERVÆRIÆ, I. a pr. of Narbonensis, s.E. of Cervaria, the s. boundary at that point of

Gaul. II. a fort of the Sardones, Narbonensis, under the Pyrenees, s.e. of Illiberis. *Cervera.*

CERYCIUS m., a m. of Bœotia, towards Oropus. The birth-place of Mercury.

CERYNEA, *rectius* Ceraunia, one of the twelve cities of Achaia, on Cerynites fl., s.e. of Helice.

CERYNIA m., a m. of Achaia, on the borders of Arcadia.

CERYNITES fl., a r. of Achaia, rising in Cerynia m., and falling into Corinthiacus sin. near Cerynia. *Bokhusia.*

CESPEDIUM, a citadel of Pisidia, near Selge.

CESSERO, a town of the Volcæ Tectosages, Narbonensis, near Agatha. *St. Thyberi.*

CESTIÆ, a town of the Taurini, Liguria, on Padus fl., R., bet. Quadrata (11) and Rigomagus, on Via Aurelia. *Cizzengo.*

CESTRINE, I. (Cestria), a district of Epirus, on the coast bet. Chaonia and Thesprotia, and extending inland to Tomarus m. Noted for its oxen. II. *prius* Cammania, its capital, on Cestrines fl., under Tomarus m. s.w. Named from Cestrinus, son of Helenus. *Philates.*

CESTRINUS fl., a r. of Cestrine, rising in Tomarus m., and falling into the Thyamis at Gitanæ. *Ceramitza.*

CESTRUS fl., a r. of Pamphylia, rising n.e. of Sagalassus, and falling into the sea 8 m. e. of Attalia. *Ak Sou.*

CETARIA, I. a maritime town of Etruria, under Argentarius m. n., opposite Cetaria Domitiana (3). II. surnamed Domitiana, of Etruria, on Via Aurelia, bet. Cosa and Telamon. *Calla della Scuarciatore?* III. of Sicily, n. bet. Bathys fl. and Panormus.

CETEII, a name, with Homer, of the Mysian subjects of Eurypylus.

CETEIUS fl., a r. of Mysia, rising in Pindasus m., and falling into Caicus fl. below Teuthrania. *Barmakpatras-tchay.*

CETIA prom., a pr. of Crete, dividing Didymi sin. into two portions. *C. Sitia.*

CETIS (Cinnatis), a district of Cilicia Trachea, on Calycadnus fl., towards its e. source.

CETIUM (Citium), a town of the Boii, Noricum, under Cetius m., n. of Comageni. A colonia (Ælia Cetiensis).

CĒTIUS m., a ridge of Alps, the n.w. boundary of Pannonia and Noricum. *Kahlenberg.*

CETOBRIGA (Cætobrix), a maritime town of the Celtici, Lusitania, bet. Cepiana w. and Malceca e. Named from its fishery. *Setuval.*

CETTI, a demus of Attica, of the tribe Leon-

tis. The birth-place of Eubulus, the comic writer.

CEVELUM, a town of the Taxaudri, Germania II., on the Mosa, L., bet. Grinnes and Blariacum.

CEVENNA m., m. of Aquitania I. and Narbonensis, running s.w.—n.e. bet. Carcasso and Vienna-Allobrogum. *Cevennes.*

CHAA, a town of Triphylia, Elis, bet. Lepræum and Samos. Extinct in Strabo's time.

CHAALA, a district of Arabia Felix, in the m. bet. Tabala and Nagara. *Chaulan.*

CHABALA (Cabalaca), a city of Albania, s.w. of Albania. *Khablas Var.*

CHABARZUBA, the early name of Antipatris, Samariæ.

CHABĒRIS, I. a r. of India i. Gangem, rising in Bettigus m., and falling into Indicum mare by several mouths, n. of Taprobane ins. *Cavery.* II. a town of India i. Gangem, 4 m. n. from the mouth of Chaberis fl., bet. Carura portus and Podoca. *Caverypatam.*

CHABINUS m., Arabiæ, *vide* Lœmus.

CHABLASII (Chablatæi), a people of Arabia Felix, n.e. on Achana fl.

CHABORA (Nabagath), a town of Tingene, Mesopot., on the Euphrates, at its junction with the Chaboras, opposite Circesium.

CHABORAS (Aborras, Chabur) fl., a r. of Mesopotamia, rising in Masius m. at Ressaina, and falling into the Euphrates over against Circesium. *Al Khabur.*

CHABRIAS fl., a r. of Chalcidice, Macedonia, rising near Heraclea, and falling into the Thermaicus sin. below Cissus.

CHABUATA, a town of the Cottabani, Arabiæ, s.e. of Rhabana Regia. *Gabbi.*

CHABUL, a district of Galilee Sup., given by Solomon to Hiram.

CHABUR? fl., a r. of Gordyene, Arm., falling into the Tigris, L., below Bezabde.

CHADABA, a town of Albania Asiat.

CHADISIUS, I. a r. of Pontus, falling into the Euxine 12½ m. w. from Ancon. II. a town at its mouth.

CHÆANOTÆ, a people of Sarmatia, on the Euxine n.e.

CHÆDINI, a people of Scandia ins. w.

CHÆMÆ, a tribe of the Longobardi, Germania.

CHÆNIDES, a people of Sarmatia Asiat., near the Rha, s. of the Suardeni.

CHÆRIPHI ost., the fourth mouth of the Indus from the w.

CHÆRU saltus, a forest of Messenia, on the confines of Laconia, 2½ m. e. from Abia.

CHÆRONEA, a town of Bœotia, on Cephissus

fl., R., bet. Orchomenus and Daulis. Named from Chæron, son of Apollo, and by some considered the Arne of Homer. The birth-place of Plutarch. Memorable for the defeat of the Athenians by the Bœotians, 447 B.C.; for the defeat of the Athenians and Bœotians by Philip, B.C. 338 ; for the defeat of Archelaus by Sylla, 86 B.C. *Kaprena.*

CHÆTUORI (Armalausi), a tribe of Alemanni, Germ., on the confines of Vindelicia.

CHALA (Chelonæ), capital of Chalonitis, Assyr., under Zagrus m., N. of Zagri portæ, E.N.E. of Artemita. *Adsjem Kanikin.*

CHALADRA (Ghaladræ), a town of Eordæa, under Chaladrus m., N.W. of Agassa. *Cogliana.*

CHALADRUS m., a m. of Eordæa, Macedonia, separating that district from Orestis and Elymæa.

CHALÆON, a town of Locris, on Crissæus sin., N.W. of Cirrha. *Larnaki.*

CHALASTRA, a town of Amphaxitis, Macedonia, at the mouth of Axius fl. The inhabitants were removed to Thessalonica by Cassander.

CHALBICI, a people of Narbonensis, on the Rhodanus. *About Chablais.*

CHALCA (Talca, Talge) ins., an isl. in the Euxine, near the mouth of Maxera fl. Said to abound in spontaneous corn and fruits, sacred to the gods.

CHALCERITIS ins., i. q. Aretias.

CHALCĒTORES (Chalcetorium), a town of Caria, s. of Miletus.

CHALCIA ins., one of the Sporades, S.E. of Telos, with a cognominal town.

CHALCĬDĬCE, I. a peninsula of Macedonia, bounded N. by Mygdonia, s. and w. by Thermaicus sin., E. by Strymonicus sin. Colonized and named by Chalcidians of Eubœa. II. a district of Syria, about Chalcis.

CHALCIS, I. a maritime district of Ionia, bet. Corycum prom. and Teos. II. one of the Echinades ins. III. (Chalcia), a m. of Ætolia, overlooking Chalcis. *Varasova.* IV. a pr. of Ionia, E. of Corycum prom., with a grove of Alexander the Great, where games in his honour were celebrated by the Ionian states. *Vromo.* V. a r. of Triphylia, Elis, falling into the sea s.w. of Scillus. *Mundritza.* VI. (Chalcia, Hypochalcis), a town of Ætolia, at the mouth of Evenus fl., under Chalcis m. *Galata.* VII. capital of Chalcidice, Syr., s.w. of Beræa, on Chalus fl. *Near Kinnasrin.* VIII. a town of Corinthia, on Corinthiacus sin., bet. Lechæum and Coronea. IX. *postea* Euripos, capital of Eubœa, on the Euripus, over against (N.E.) Aulis. A city anterior to the siege of Troy; enlarged by an Ionian colony from Athens, under Cottius. It was connected with the continent by a wooden bridge, constructed B.C. 410. The birth-place of Lycophron. *Egripo, Negropont.* X. a town of Triphylia, Elis, on Chalcis fl.

CHALCITIS, I. regio, a district of India, on Lanos fl., N. of the Acadræ. II. ins., one of the Demonesi ins., Bithynia, s. of Calchedon. *Karkia.*

CHALDÆA, generally, Babylonia; specially, a district of Babylonia, on the Euphrates, R., towards its junction with the Tigris.

CHALDÆI, I. a people of Arabia, bet. the Euphrates and the N.W. coast of Persicus sin. *Tribe of Beni Khaled.* II. of Armenia, i. q. Chalybes.

CHALDAICI lac., several lakes of Babylonia, formed by the Euphrates towards its confluence with the Tigris.

CHALDONE prom., a pr. of Arabia Felix, on Persicus sin., over against Salsum fl.

CHALI, a people of Cimbrica Chersonesus, N. of the Cobandi. *N. Schleswig and S. Jutland.*

CHALIA, a town of Bœotia, on the Euripus, N. of Oropus.

CHALION, I. a town of the Locri Ozolæ, at the N.W. extremity of Crissæus sin. *Agia Eufemia.* II. its port. *Monastir Contziro.*

CHALIS, a maritime town of Sicily s., bet. Phalarium and Calvisiana.

CHALONITIS, a district of Assyria, bet. Apolloniatis and Zagrus m., in length 15. geog. m. *Kizil-Kubat.*

CHALTAPETIS, the N. portion of Susiana.

CHALUS fl., a r. of Syria, falling into a lake, s. of Chalcis. *Koeik.*

CHALUSUS fl., a r. of Germania Mag., falling into Lagnus sin., after separating the Saxones from the Teutones. *Trave.*

CHALYBES (Chaldæi, Chaldi), a people, or perhaps rather a caste, scattered about the coast of Pontus and Paphlagonia, bet. Armenia and Halys fl. Noted as workers in iron.

CHALYBONITIS, a district of Syria, on Chalus fl.

CHALYBS fl., Tarraconensis, i. q. Callipos.

CHAMĀVI (Franci), a tribe of Istævones, Germ., bet. the Rhine, the Amisus, and the Luppia.

CHAMMANENE, a prefecture of Cappadocia, towards Pontus, N. of Cilicia prefectura.

CHANES fl., a r. of Albania, falling into the Cyrus.

CHANUNIA (Chaonia), a town of Cyrrhestica, bet. Doliche and Cyrrhus.

CHAON m., a m. of Argolis, overlooking Trochos.

CHAONIA, a district of Epirus (at one time an independent state), on the confines of Illyria, extending along the coast to Cestrine, and inland to a considerable but uncertain distance. Named after Chaonus, who married Andromache after the death of Pyrrhus I. Settled by Pelasgi.

CHARACA, capital of the Characitani, Tarraconensis, s.s.w. of Segobriga.

CHARACARBA, a town of Bactriana, on the Oxus, near the confluence of the Ochus. *Maru Amu.*

CHARACENE, I. a district of Cilicia, N. of Seleucia. II. of Susiana Elymais, on Persicus sin. *Kars.*

CHARACITANI, a tribe of Celtiberi, Tarraconensis, on Sucro fl., towards its source.

CHARACOMA, a town of Laconia, on Eurotas fl., bet. Sparta and Pellane. *Peribolia.*

CHARACOMETES fons, hot springs at Charax, Lydia.

CHARADEÆ, a people of Gedrosia, on the borders of Carmania.

CHARADRA, a town of Phocis, on Charadrus fl., 2½ m. N.w. from Lilæa. Destroyed by Xerxes. *Mariolates.*

CHARADRUS fl., I. a r. of Achaia, falling into Corinthiacus sin. s.w. of Rhium. II. of Argolis, falling into Argolicus sin. near Temenium. *Planitza.* III. of Attica, rising in Lycabellus m., and falling into the Ægean below Phegus. *Kenusio.* IV. of Messenia, running into Leucas fl. s.w. of Andania. V. of Molossis, Epirus, rising towards Passaro, and falling into Ambracius sin. N.E. of Nicopolis. *Lourtcha.* VI. of Phocis, falling into Cephisius fl. near Charadra. VII. a fortress of Cilicia Trachea, under Andriclus m., 12½ m. s.E. from Aragus prom. *Karadran.* VIII. a town of Molossis, Epirus, on Charadrus fl., N.w. of Ambracus. *Rogous.*

CHARAX, I. a fortress of Ætulane, Armenia Minor. II. of Bithynia, on Astacenus sin., near Nicomedia. III. of the Cadusii, Med., on the Caspian, N. of Cyropolis. IV. of Corsica, w. above Circidius fl. V. of Egypt, on Barathra palus. Built by Chabrias. VI. of Lydia, in the immediate vicinity of Tralles. VII. of Media Ragiana, w. of Caspiæ Portæ. *Kesker.* VIII. of Perrhæbia, Thessaly, on Peneus fl., L., at the entrance of Tempe. IX. (Alexandri), of Phrygia, near Celænæ, on the site of an encampment of Alexander. X. a town of the Psylli, Africa P., on Syrtis Maj., bet. Zur and Ad Speluncas. A mercantile

establishment of the Carthaginians. Misnamed by Ptolemy Pharax. *Eneura.* XI. capital of Susiana, Characene, on the Tigris, towards its mouth. Built by Alexander, and named Alexandria; restored by Antiochus, and called Antiochia and Charax, from its strong position; and afterwards enlarged by Spasines, an Arabian chief and called Spasines. *Jali Agasp.* XII. (Castrum Gurzubitense), a maritime fortress of Taurica Chersonesus, N.E. of Criumetopon prom. *Alupka.*

CHARBANUS m., m. of Asia, separating Media from Susiana.

CHARCHA, a town of Mesopotamia, towards Besabde.

CHARECLA, a town of Pentapolis Cyrenaicæ, E. of Berenice.

CHARGATA, I. a district of Arabia, N. of the Catanitæ. *Kardje.* II. a town on the Red Sea, opposite Jerachæorum ins. *Kardje.*

CHARIDEMUM prom., a pr. of Bætica, bet. Magnus Portus N. and Massienus sin. N.E. *Cabo de Gata.*

CHARIEIS fl., *vide* Charisius.

CHARIMALÆ, a people of Pontus, under Moschici m.

CHARMÆI, Arabiæ, i. q. Carman regia.

CHARMOTHUS portus, a port of the Thamydeni, on the Red Sea, s. of Chersonesus Acra. *Sharmo.*

CHARINDA fl., a r. of Media Magna, falling into the Caspian on the borders of Hyrcania.

CHARISIA, a village of Arcadia, 1¼ m. N. from Scias. Built by Charisius, son of Lycaon.

CHARISIUS (Charieis, Charistus, Charus) fl., a r. of Colchis, falling into the Euxine, N. of Phasis fl.

CHARRACARTA, a town of Sogdiana, on Polytimetus fl., below Bactra.

CHARUDES, a people of Cimbrica Chersonesus, N.E. of the Chali.

CHARYBDIS, a whirlpool in Siculum Fretum, N. over against Scylla, having strong tidal currents.

CHASTIA, a demus of Attica, of the tribe Æneis, N.w. of Acharnæ. *Kastia.*

CHASUARII (Chattuarii, Attuarii), a tribe of Ingævones, on the confines of the Istævones, bet. the Ansibarii N. and the Angrivarii s.

CHATENI, a people of Arabia Felix, on Capeus sin. about Istriana.

CHATRAMIS, a district of Arabia Felix, bet. Persicus sin. and the Blieulei.

CHATRAMOTITÆ, a people of Arabia Felix, N. of the Adramitæ. *Hadramaut.*

CHATRIÆI, a people of India i. Gangem, about Apocopa m., s. and w. of the Caspiræi.

CHATTUARII, i. q. Chasuarii.

CHAUCI (Cauchi), a tribe of Germania, bet. Amisus fl. and Albis fl. There was a colony of them on Flevus lac., N.W. another colony in Hibernia E., bet. the Eblani N. and the Menapii s.

CHAUCLEI, Arabiæ, i. q. Chaldæi.

CHAULOTHÆI, Arabiæ, i. q. Chaldæi.

CHAUNARIUM (Cannarium) prom. a pr. of Libya, s. of Cosenus fl. *Cap de Non.*

CHAURANA, a town of Scythia e. Imaum, under Emodi m.

CHAUS (Calbis) fl., a r. of Phrygia, falling into Indus fl., L.

CHAVELÆI, Arabia, i. q. Chaldæi.

CHAVON (Chaon), Media, i. q. Choana.

CHAVUM, a town of Taurica Chersonesus, E. of Palacium.

CHAZA, a town of the Syrbotæ, Africæ, on Astapus fl., w. of Sirbitium.

CHEBAR fl., *apud* Ezekiel., i. q. Chaborras.

CHEIMO (Chi), a port of Marmarica, 1 m. w. from Posirion.

CHELÆ, a village of Bithynia, on Thracius Bosporus, near Pantichium.

CHELÆ, a town of Bithynia, on the Euxine, 3 m. E. from Apollonia ins.

CHELIDONIA, Phrygiæ, i. q. Diniæ.

CHELIDONIÆ ins., islets of Lycia, over against Sacrum prom. In Strabo's time three, at present five.

CHELIDONIUM prom., Lyciæ, i. q. Sacrum.

CHELONIDES lac., I. a lake of Libya, formed by Gir fl. II. ins., an isl. of the Trogloditæ, in the Red Sea, off Satyrorum prom.

CHELONITES, I. prom., a pr. of Epia in Elis, s.w. of Hyrmine prom. *C. Tornese.* II. sin., a bay of the Ionian Sea in Elis, at Chelonites pr.

CHELONOPHAGI, a people on the coast of Gedrosia and Carmania, who lived on the flesh of turtles, and roofed their huts with the shells.

CHELYDOREA m., a m. of Arcadia, contiguous to Cyllene m., where Mercury found the shell which he formed into a lyre.

CHEMMIS (Chennis), the local name of Panopolis in Thebais.

CHEMMITES NOMOS, Egypti, i. q. Phthenotes.

CHEN (Chenæ), a town of Laconia, near Malea prom. The birth-place of Miso.

CHENOBOSCIA, a town of Thebais, on the Nile, over against Diospolis Parva.

CHEPHIRAH, a town of Benjamin.

CHEREÆ ins., islets of Euboea, near Ægilia ins. *Kavalleri.*

CHEREU, a town of Lower Egypt, bet. Hermupolis (24) and Alexandria (20). *Keriun.*

CHERITH fl., a stream of Palestine, falling into the Jordan. The locality of Elijah's concealment. *Wady-Kelt.*

CHERSIS, a maritime town of Cyrenaica, bet. Zephyrium prom. (9) and Erythron.

CHERSONESUS, I. a pr. of Ætolia, w. of Chalcis. *Missolonghi.* II. surnamed Magna, of Africa, bet. Paliurus and Azilis, marking the limits of Marmarica and Cyrenaica. III. a port of Marmarica, at Chersonesus prom. *Rasalin.* IV. a pr. of Corinthia, on Saronicus sin., w. of Rheitum prom. V. of Crete, at Chersonesus. *Capo di Corbo.* VI. of Egypt, near Alexandria, N. VII. of Euboea, on the E. coast, N. of Zarax prom. *C. Cherronesi.* VIII. of India i. Gangem, w. below Byzantium. IX. surnamed Acra, of the Leanitæ, Arabiæ, on Persicus sin., N. of Icara ins. *Ras el Char.* X. of Persis, bet. Sitiogagus fl. and Aracia ins. XI. the s. extremity of Sardinia. *C. di Teulada.* XII. THRACIA, a peninsula of Thrace, extending along Melas sin. s., and the Hellespont N. XIII. TAURICA, a peninsula of Sarmatia Europæa, bet. the Euxine and Mæotis palus. *Crimea.* XIV. a town of Astrea, Thrace, E. of Sizeboli. XV. a town of Crete, on the w. shore of Didymi sin., s. of Zephyrium prom. The port of Lyctus. *Spina Longa.* XVI. a town on the w. coast of Crete, bet. Phalasarna and Rhamnus. *San Marco.* XVII. surnamed Heracleotica (Cherrone). XVIII. a maritime town of Taurica Chersonesus, w. above Palacium, at the entrance s. of Ctenus portus. *Near Gurtschi.* XIX. surnamed Vetus, a maritime town of Taurica Chersonesus, w. below Chersonesus. The earlier settlement of the Megarenses. XX. a port of the Troglodytæ, on the Red Sea, N. of Mnemion Acron. *Komol.*

CHERSUS fl., Ciliciæ, i. q. Lycus.

CHERTOBALUS, a town of the Amantini, Pannonia, on the Danube, E. of the confluence of the Arrabo.

CHERUSCI, a tribe of Hermiones, Germ., bet. the Angrivarii and Longobardi N., the Chatti s., the Bructeri w., and the Semnones and Calucones E.

CHESINUS fl., a r. of Sarmatia Europ., falling into Codanus sin. N. of Turuntes fl. *Dwina.*

CHESIUM prom., a pr. of Samos, near Samos opp.

CHESIUS fl., a r. of Samos, falling into the sea at Chesium prom.

CHESULOTH, a town of Galilæa, bet. Nazareth N.w. and Thabor m.

CHETÆA, a maritime village of Marmarica, bet. Zygræ and Zagylis.

CHIDIBBELA, a town of Zeugitana, on Bagradas fl., R., bet. Atticellæ and Choreva.

CHILIOCOMON, I. a district of Assyria, N.E. of Arapachitis. *Arphad.* II. of Pontus, on Iris fl., L., bet. Amasia and Phazemon. III. of Phrygia Epict., near Dorylæum.

CHIMÆRA, I. a summit of Olympus in Lycia, near Phaselis, which, emitting a constant flame without smoke or stone, gave rise to the fable of Chimæra. II. a maritime town of Chaonia, under Acrocerannii m., bet. Palæste and Panormus. *Kimaro.*

CHIMARRUS fl., a r. of Argolis, running bet. Lerna and Argos into Argolicus sinus.

CHIMERIUM prom., a pr. of Thesprotia, bet. Sybola portus and Toryne, opposite Paxos ins. *C. Saracinico.*

CHINALAPH fl., a r. of Mauritania Cæsar., rising in Cinnaba m., and falling into the Mediterranean s. of Apollinis prom. *Shellib.*

CHINNEROTH (Chinnereth, Cinneroth), i. q. Tiberias.

CHIOS, I. ins. (Æthalia, Macris, Pityusa), an isl. of Ionia, bet. Erythræ and Psyra ins. Successively occupied by Leleges and Carians, Pelasgi from Thessaly, and Abantes (or Ionians) from Eubœa. In circuit 125 m. The birth-place of Ion, Theopompus, Theocritus, Metrodorus, and Scymnus. Noted for the beauty of its women, and for its wine, the finest in all Greece. *Scio, Chio.* II. its capital, on the E. coast, opposite Erythræ. *Chio.*

CHITABANITÆ, a people of Arabia Felix, contiguous to the Anchitæ. *Beni Salem.*

CHIRIPPE, a town of Amordocia, Babyl., on Pallacopas canalis, w. of Altha.

CHISIDUS, a town of Zeugitana, on Bagradas fl., L., bet. Turris and Membrissa.

CHITONE, a demus of Attica.

CHIZARUS, a town of Pontus, at the s. extremity of Stephane lac.

CHLIARA, warm-baths of Lydia, w. of Sipylus m.

CHLIAT, a town of Armenia, near Arzes.

CNUMIS (Chnubis), the local name of Contra-Latopolis, Egypti.

CHOANA, I. a town of Bactriana, on Oxus fl. II. (Chavon), of the Sidices, Media, near Bagistana. Here were gardens planted by Semiramis.

CHOARENE, I. a district of Arachosia, under Bœtius m. II. of Media Magna, on the borders of Parthia, bet. Jasonius m. and Caspius m.

CHOAS fl., the early name of Achelous fl., Ætoliæ.

CHOASPES fl., I. (Zuastus, Guræus) a r. of Paropamisus, India, falling into the Indus s. of Cophes fl. *Attok.* II. (Eulæus, the Ulai of Scripture) of Susiana, rising in Zagrus m. N. of Zagri portæ. For some distance its course is subterranean; then, rising N. of Susa, it falls into the Tigris by a cut called Pasitigris, below its junction with the Euphrates. Its water, peculiarly sweet, was sacred to the use of the Persian kings. *Kerrah.*

CHOATHRAS m., i. q. Zagrus.

CHOATRÆ, a people of Sarmatia Asiatica.

CHOATRES fl., Parthiæ, i. q. Zioberis.

CHOBA (Chobat), a maritime town of Mauritania Cæsariensis, 38 m. w. from Igilgilis. *Budscha; Boudgié.*

CHOBAR (Chebar), one of the canals between the Euphrates and the Tigris, w. of the Maarsares. Named from its constructor, Gobares.

CHOBOTA, a town of Albania, S.E. of Albaniæ pylæ. *Kuba.*

CHOBUS fl., I. a r. of Ecretice, Colch., falling into the Euxine 27 m. s. from Singames fl. *Schijani; Kelenhel.* II. a town of Colchis, on Chobus fl., at its junction with Charisius fl.

CHODDA, a town of Gedrosia, on Pomanus fl.

CHŒNIDES, a tribe of Perierbidi, Sarmatia, on the Tanais.

CHŒRADES ins., "rocky," i. q. Baleares. II. two islets in the Tarentinus sin., over against Tarentum. *San Pietro e San Paolo.*

CHOES fl. (Coas, Euaspla), a r. of Parapomisus, falling into the Cophen, L. *Semil.*

CHŒTÆ, a town of Anthemusia, Macedonia.

CHOLARGUS (Cholargeis), a tribe of Atticæ, of the tribe Acamantis.

CHOLBESINA, a town of Sogdiana, s. of Maruca.

CHOLLE, a town of Palmyrene, bet. Palmyra N.E. and Thapsacus.

CHOLLIDÆ, a demus of Attica, of the tribe Ægeis or Leontis.

CHOLMADARA, a town of Commagene, on the Euphrates, bet. Heba and Samosata.

CHOLUA (Coloris), a town of Colchis, on the confines of Armenia, s.E. of Azota.

CHOMA, I. a place of Arcadia, under Boreum m. The boundary between Tegea and Megalopolis. II. a defile in the N.E. m. of Phrygia, towards Lycaonia. III. a town of Lycia, on Adesa fl.

CHOMARA, capital of the Chomari, Margiana, on Ochus fl., s. of Alicodra.

CHOMARI (Chomi), a people of Margiana, s.w. of the Salateræ.

CHONE, capital of the Chones, Bruttium, N.

of Crimisa. A settlement of Philoctetes. *Ciro; Casabuona?*

CHONES, a mixed tribe of Japyges and Ænotri, contiguous to the Leutarni.

CHORÆNIS arx, a fortress of Sogdiana, S.E. of Alexandria Oxiana.

CHORASMII, a people of Sogdiana, on both sides the Oxus, towards its mouth. *Uvarazm-iya.*

CHORAZAN, a town of Galilee, 2 m. N.W. from Capernaum.

CHORDYLE, a port of Colchis, bet. Athenæ and Arcadis fl.

CHOREVA, a town of Zeugitana, on Bagradas fl., R., S.E. of Musti. *Gloukieh.*

CHOROANA, a district of Parthia, occupying its S.W. angle.

CHORODNA (Corea), a town of Persis Proper, S.W. of Persepolis.

CHOROMITRENE, a district of Media Magna, bet. Amardus fl. and Parthia, E. of Jasonius m.

CHORSA (Chadus), a town of Siracene, on Harpasus fl., R., towards its source. *Karut.*

CHORSABIA, a town of Ætulana, Armenia Minor.

CHORZENE (Chorzanene), a district of Armenia Interior, on the borders of Armenia Minor, w. of Astianene. *Khosan; Khordsen.*

CHOSOL, a town of the Macæ, Africa Proper, on Syrtis Major, s. bet. Dissio and Auzui.

CHREMETES fl., Libyæ, i. q. Nia.

CHRENDI, a people of Hyrcania, s.

CHRETES fl., Libyæ, i. q. Subur.

CHRETINA, a maritime town of the Lusitani, W.N.W. of Olisipo. *Cintra.*

CHRONUS fl., a r. of Sarmatia E., falling into Codanus sin. E. of the Vistula. *Pregel.*

CHRYSA, I. an isl. on the s. coast of Crete, over against Hierapytna. *Gaidronisi.* II. a Syro-Phœnician town of Æolis Asiatica, bet. Astyra (2½) and Thebe (6¼). The town of Chryseis. III. *surnamed* Dia, of Troas, on the coast, s. of Alexandria.

CHRYSAORIUM, a village of Caria, bet. Eunomus and Stratonicea. With a temple of Jupiter Chrysaorius, in which were held the assemblies of the Carian states.

CHRYSAS fl., a r. of Sicily, rising N. of Assorus and falling into Symæthus fl. above Murgantia. *Dittaino.*

CHRYSE, "golden," I. a district of India e. Gangem E. Deemed an island. *Ava.* II. a name of Thasos ins. III. an isl. of Lemnos ins., which, according to Pausanias, was submerged by an earthquake,

another island, called Hiera, rising in its place. The retreat of Philoctetes, who was here bitten by the serpent.

CHRYSOANA fl., a r. of Aurea Chersonesus, falling into Indicus Oc. opposite Salinæ ins. *Tanasserim.*

CHRYSOBALLUM, a village of Tyanitis, Cappadocia, near Podandus.

CHRYSOCĒRAS, I. the harbour of Byzantium. Named from its rich draughts of fish. *The Golden Horn.* II. a pr. of Thrace, near Byzantium.

CHRYSONDIO, a town of Phœbatis, Illyria, w. of Gerunium.

CHRYSOPOLIS, I. a later name of Amphipolis, Thrace. II. the E. port of Calchedon, Bithynia, opposite Byzantium. *Scutari.* III. of Gallia Cisalpina, a designation of Parma.

CHRYSORRHOAS fl., "golden," I. a r. of Argolis, running into Saronicus sin. below Trœzene. II. of Phrygia Magna, falling into Mæander fl. below Hierapolis. Its water was of a strongly petrifying quality. III. of Syria, composed of Abana, Pharphar, and numerous other streams, which, after watering Damascus, loses itself in a morass about 15 m. from the city. *Barradi.*

CHRYSUS OSTIUM, the third mouth from the w. of the Indus.

CHTHONIA, an early name of Crete.

CHULLU, Africæ, *vide* Cullu.

CHULOBETENE, a district of Armenia Major. Named from Chul, s. of Aram.

CHUNI, a people of Sarmatia E., bet. the Rheucanali and the Amadoci, E. of the Borysthenes.

CHUS, the Scriptural name, according to some writers, of Ethiopia; according to others, of Arabia.

CHYDAS fl., a r. of Sicily, falling into the Tyrrhenian sea at Aluntium.

CHYTONA (Ghytana), a town of Cestrine, at the junction of Cestrinus and Thyanus fll. A colony from Clazomene. *Palæo Venetio.*

CHYTRIUM (Chytrus), I. a town of Cyprus, bet. Cerynia and Salamis. Noted for its honey. *Chytri.* II. a town of Ionia, on Hermius sin. s.w., above Clazomenæ. *Tcharpau.*

CIABRUS (Cebrus, Ciambrus), I. a r. of Mœsia, rising in Scomius m. and falling into the Danube at Ciabrus. *Zebris.* II. a town of the Mœsi, Mœsia Inferior, on the Danube, bet. Modiana and Camistrum, at the mouth, R., of Ciabrus. *Zebris.*

CIACA, a town of Melitene, Cappadocia, bet. Arangæ (9) and Melitene (18). A colonia (Ala Prima Augusta).

CIAGISI, a people of Dacia, on the Danube, bet. the Saldenses and the Piephigi.

CIANUS sinus, a bay of Propontis, Bithynia, at Cius. *Gulf of Mondanich.*

CIBALÆ, a city of Pannonia Inferior, on Bacuntius fl., bet. Ulpianum and Mursa. The birth-place of Gratian. The locality of the defeat of Licinius by Constantine. *Vinkouckze.*

CIBOTUS, a maritime village of Bithynia, towards Astacenus sin.

CIBYRA, I. a town of Milyas, Lycia, near Laodicea. Restored by Tiberius and assigned to Phrygia; still later to Caria. Noted for its excellent laws. II. *surnamed Parva* (Cyberna), of Pamphylia, on the coast, 7½ m. s.e. from Melas fl.

CICÆ ins., isl. of Tarraconensis, in the Atlantic, over against the mouth of the Minius. *Cies.*

CICHỸRUS, a later name of Ephyre, Thesprotia.

CICIMENI, a people of Sarmatia Asiatica.

CICISA, a town of Zeugitana, on Bagradas fl., R., near Carthage.

CICŎNES, a maritime people of Thrace, bet. the Bistones and Hebrus fl. It was on their coast that Ulysses was first shipwrecked.

CICONIA (Gallaicus, Brianticus, Priaticus Campus), the country of the Cicones, in Thrace.

CICONIUM, a town of Bithynia, on Thracius Bosporus, N. of Discus prom. A colony of Cicones from Thrace.

CICYNETHUS ins., an isl. of Magnesia, Thessaly, in Pagasæus sin., off Zelasium prom., with a cognominal town. *Trikeri.*

CICYNNA, a demus of Attica, of the tribe Acamantis.

CIDÆNIS, the early name of Elæa, in Æolis Asiatica.

CIDYSSUS, a town of Phrygia Epictetus, on the confines of Bithynia, N. of Dioclea.

CIGURRI, a town of the Autrigones, Tarraconensis, on the Iberus, R., above Velia.

CILBIANUS campus, a plain of Lydia, on Caystrus fl., extending from Imolus m. to Ephesus.

CILIANA, a town of the Celtici, Lusitania, on Calippus fl., near its mouth.

CILICIA, a country of Asia Minor, bounded N. by Pisidia, Lycaonia, and Cappadocia; s. by the Mediterranean; w. by Pisidia and Pamphylia; e. by Syria. Its e. portion was called, from the peculiar "rugged" character communicated to it by Taurus m., Cilicia Trachea; its e. portion, from its more open character, Campestris. Settled by the Hypachæi, a colony of Phœnicians, so called by the Greeks, and renamed after Cilix, son of Agenor. There were Cilices also in Troas, Cappadocia, and Mysia. *Itshil.*

CILICIÆ pylæ, a defile of Cilicia Campestris, bet. Amanus m. and the sea, extending from Ægæ to Baiæ. The pass by which Alexander entered Syria, on the same night, previous to the battle of Issus, that Darius entered Cilicia by the Amanicæ pylæ. *Strette di Scanderoon.*

CILICUM ins., an islet of Pontus, 2 m. e. from Jasonium prom.

CILINI, a tribe of Bracari, Tarraconensis.

CILIO, a town of Byzacene, 25 m. w. from Sufetula. *Casarin.*

CILIZA, a town of Cyrrhestica, bet. Zeugma and Onchæ.

CILLA, I. a Syro-Phœnician town of Æolis Asiatica, w. of Adramyttium. Extinct in Pliny's time. II. of Numidia, s. of Sicca Venerea.

CILLABA, a town of Phazania, e. of Hammamum. *Zuila.*

CILLÆUS fl., a r. of Æolis Asiatica, rising in Ida m. and falling into Adramyttenus sin. below Cilla. *Zikeli.*

CILLIUM, a town of the Odrysæ, Thrace, bet. Parembole and Carasura.

CILLUTA ins. (Cilloustin, Psillouskin), an isl. at the mouth of the Indus.

CILMA, a town of Zeugitana, s. of Maxula.

CILURNUM, a town of the Brigantes, Brit., on Hadriani murus, s. bet. Hunum and Procolitia. *Walwick-Chesters.*

CIMARA, a town of Chalcitis Regio, India, N.E. of Doana.

CIMARUS prom., Cretæ, i. q. Corycum.

CIMBA, a town of Sicily, on Hyrminius fl., R., bet. Camerina and Helorum.

CIMBIS portus, a haven of the Cempsi, Bætica.

CIMBRA, a town of Rhætia, 2 m. N.E. of Tesana. *Cimbra.*

CIMBRICA Chersonesus, a peninsula of Scandinavia. Named from the Cimbri, who, however, never dwelt there. *Denmark and Jutland.*

CIMBRIANA, a town of Pannonia, 25 m. N.W. from Tricciana. *Stuhl-Weissenburg.*

CIMBRORUM prom., the N. extremity of Cimbrica Chersonesus.

CIMETRA, a town of the Caudini, Samnium.

CIMIATA, *postea* Docea, a town of Paphlagonia, under Olgasys m., N.W. of Andrapa. *Tosia.*

CIMIATENE, a district of Paphlagonia, in its S.E. angle.

CIMINIA silva, *vide* Ciminus m.

CIMINUS lacus, a lake of Etruria, S.E. of Tarquinii. *L. di Vico; Ronciglione.*

CIMINUS m., a range of hills in Etruria, S. and E. of Tarquinii, under which, towards Rome, lay Ciminia silva.

CIMMERII, I. a people of Sarmatia Asiatica, on Mæotis palus, descendants of Gomer. Their name gradually assuming the form of Cimbri, they emigrated to the N.E. parts of Germany, it is uncertain to what particular locality, whence they invaded various portions of Europe. A body of them settled, circa 90 B.C. in Helvetia, and their name, at least, remains in the Welsh Cymry. II. CAMPANIÆ, the people of Cumæ.

CIMMERIS, an earlier name of Antandrus, Æolis.

CIMMERIUM, a town of Sarmatia Asiatica, on Palus Mæotis S., on Cimmerium prom., at the E. entrance of Bosporus Cimmerius, hence named. *Eski Krim.* II. mare, i. q. Euxinus.

CIMMERIUS m., a m. of Taurica Chersonesus, w. of Theodosia.

CIMOLIS (Cinolis), a port of Paphlagonia, 8 m. E. from Æginetes. *Kinla.*

CIMOLOS ins. (Echinusa), one of the Sporades, bet. Siphnos and Melos. Noted for its figs and for its excellent fuller's earth. *Argentiera; Cimoli.* II. Its capital, on the s.w. coast.

CINÆDOCOLPITÆ, a nickname of the Debæ, Arabiæ, stigmatizing their effeminacy.

CINÆDOPOLIS ins., an isl. of Caria, in Ceramicus sin.

CINÆI, Canaan, i. q. Kenites.

CINARUS ins. (Cines), one of the Sporades, N.E. of Amorgus. *Kinara.*

CINGA fl., a r. of Tarraconensis, rising in Edulius m. and falling into Sicoris fl. at Octogesa. *Cinca.*

CINGILIA, a fortress of the Vestini, Picenum, towards Cutina. *Citta Aretenga.*

CINGULARIUM (Zyganium), a town of Phrygia Paroria, near Mesonacte.

CINGULUM, a fortress of Picenum, on Miseus fl., s. of Cupra Montana. Built by Labienus. *Cingolo.*

CINIANA, a town of the Bracari, Tarraconensis, N.E. of Bracara Augusta.

CINIATA, a town of Paphlagonia, near Dadybra.

CINITHII, a people of Libya, on both sides of Triton fl.

CINIUM (Sineu), a town of Balearis Major, E. of Palma.

CINNA (Sinna), a town of the Labeates, Illyria, at the N.E. extremity of Labeatis palus, bet. Scodra (12) and Birziminum.

CINNABA m., m. of Mauritania Cæsar., a N.E. continuation of Madelhubadus m.

CINNAMOMŌFERA REGIO, "cinnamon-producing" (Aromatophoros), a region of Æthiopia, on the s.E. coast of Erythræum mare.

CINYPS fl. (Cinyphus), a r. of Syrtica Regio, falling into the sea, after a course of about 25 m., E. of Leptis Magna. *Wady Quahan.*

CIPHISUS, a maritime village of Cilicia Trachea, near Aphrodisias.

CIRCEII, a town of the Volsci, Latium, within Circeium prom., bet. Ad Turres Albas (9) and Tarracina (13), on Via Severiana. Founded by Tarquin. The fabled abode of Circe. Noted for its oysters and for its wild boars. The retreat of Lepidus. *San Felice.*

CIRCEUM prom., a pr. of Latium, at Circeii. The fabled abode of Circe. Here was the tomb of Elpenor. It was noted for a variety of poisonous herbs. *Monte Circello.*

CIRCĒSIUM (Carchemish, Carcusium, Phalegia), a city of Mesopotamia, on the Euphrates, at its junction with the Chaboras. *Kirkessieh.*

CIRCUS fl., a r. of Eubœa, which rendered the fleece of sheep white.

CIRNA m., m. of Zeugitana, N. of Bagradas fl. *Iskell.*

CIRPIS, Pannoniæ, i. q. Carpis.

CIRRHA, a town of Phocis, the port of Delphi, at the mouth of Pleistus fl., on Crissæus sin. Demolished for sacrilege, but restored by the Amphissians. *Xeno Peqadia.*

CIRRHADI, a people of India e. Gangem, on Gangeticus sin., s. of the mouth of Œdanes fl.

CIRTA, *postea* Constantina, capital of Numidia, on Ampsagas fl., L., bet. Ad Palmam and Sigus. A colonia of Cæsar, named from the leader of the colony, P. Sittius (Colonia Julia Sittianorum). *Constantina.*

CIRTISA (Certis), a town of Pannonia Inferior, bet. Cibalis and Leuconum. *Diakovar.*

CISAMUS, a port of Crete, at the head of Martilus sin. *Kisamo.*

CISIMBRUM, a town of the Turtuli, Bætica, bet. Ægabrum N.W. and Hippo Nova S.E.

CISSA, I. a r. of Colchis, falling into the Euxine, 16 m. s. from Apsarus fl. II. a fountain of Arcadia, under Ostracina m. III. (Zygopolis,) capital of the Cissii, at the mouth of Cissa fl. IV. (Lissa) a town of the Lacetani, Tarraconensis, on Ibcrus fl. *Guissona.*

CISSERUSSA ins., an isl. of Rhodes, towards Cnidus.

CISSI, a maritime village of Mauritania Cæsar., w. of Rusucurrum.

CISSIA, the central district of Susiana Elymais, about Seleucia. With Herodotus and Ptolemy an appellation of Susiana itself.

CISSIDES prom., a pr. of Lycia, 10 m. from Lagusa.

CISSII m., m. of Sarmatia Asiatica.

CISSUS, a town of Amphaxitis, Macedonia, near Thessalonica. The birth-place of Cisseus. *Cismé.* II. the port of Erythræ, Ionia.

CISTERNÆ, a town of the Macæ, Africa Proper, on Syrtis Major, w. of Trieron prom.

CISTHĒNE, a port of Æolis Asiatica, w. of Pyrrha prom. Near it were copper mines. Deserted in Strabo's time.

CISTOBOCI, a people of Dacia, bet. the Tyras and the Parata ffl., N. of the Harpii.

CISTOVIA, a town of Germania Magna, near Albis fl., E. of Cænocnum.

CISTRAMUM, a fortress of Cilicia Campestris, near Anazarba.

CITHÆRON m., a chain of m. separating Bœotia from Megaris and Attica, a w. continuation of Parnes m. Sacred to Jupiter Cithæronius and to Bacchus. The scene of the death of Actæon and of Pentheus, and of the exposure of Œdipus. *Elatea.*

CITHARASTA, I. a pr. of the Commoni, Narbonensis, bet. Taurentum and Olbia. *Cap Cepet.* II. a town on the cognominal prom. *Ciotat, near Ceireste.*

CITHARIZUM, a town of Sophene, Armenia, on the s. arm of the Euphrates.

CITIUM, I. a city of Cyprus s., at a cognominal prom. Founded by Belus. From its name the Scriptural designation of the Gentiles, *Chittim,* is supposed to have been derived. The death-place of Cimon the Athenian. The birth-place of Zeno and of Apollonias. *Chiti.*

CIUM, a town of Mœsia Inferior, on the Danube, bet. Bereum and Carsum.

CIUS fl., I. i. q. Ascanius Bithyniæ. II. i. q. Oescus. III. a city of Bithynia, on Cianus sin., at the mouth of Ascanius fl., R. The port of Nicæa. A Milesian colony. Destroyed by Philip, son of Demetrius; rebuilt by Prusias, and called for a time Prusias ad Mare. *Kio.*

CLADEUS fl., a r. of Elis, rising near Thraustus and falling into Alpheus fl., E. of Olympia. *Stauro-Kephali.*

CLAMPETIA, a maritime town of Bruttium,

bet. Cerillæ (40) and Tempsa (10), on Via Aquilia. *Amantia.*

CLANIS fl. (Glanis), an early name of the Liris. II. a r. of Etruria, rising near Arretium and falling into the Tiber N.E. of Vulsinii. *Chiana.*

CLANIUS fl., Campaniæ, i. q. Liternus.

CLANUM, a town of the Senones, Lugdunensis IV., bet. Agenticum w. and Augustobonâ E.N.E.

CLARENNA, a town of Germania Magna, on Niter fl., R., below Grinario.

CLARIUS fl., a r. of Cyprus.

CLAROS, a village of Ionia, on the coast, bet. Colophon and Ephesus. The seat of the oracle of Apollo Clarius, where Mopsus defeated Calchas. *Zille.*

CLASTIDIUM, a town of the Ananes, Liguria, E. of Iria. The locality of the defeat of Viridomarus by Claudius Marcellus. The principal dépôt of Hannibal's army while encamped on Trebia fl. *Casteggio.*

CLATERNA, a town of Gallia Cispadana, bet. Bononia (15) and Forum Cornelii (13), on Via Æmilia Lepida. *Quaderna.*

CLAUDA ins. (Claudus), I. an isl. on the s. coast of Crete, 25 m. s. from Phœnix portus. *Gafdanisi.* II. its town. *Gafda.*

CLAUDANUM, *vide* Pons Servilii.

CLAUDIAS (Claudiopolis, Arclaudia), a town of Laviniasene, Cappadocia, on Euphrates fl., below Melita.

CLAUDIOMERIUM, a town of the Artabri, Tarraconensis, E. of Artabrum prom.

CLAUDIOPOLIS, I. a later name of Bithynium, Bithynia. II. Cappadocia, i. q. Heraclea. III. a town of Cilicia Trachea, on Calycadnus fl., above Philadelphia. Founded by Claudius. *Mout.* IV. a town of the Trocmi, Galatia, on Halys fl., N.W. of Carissa.

CLAUDIS, a town of Numidia, s.s.E. of Cirta.

CLAUDIUS m., m. of Pannonia, towards Mœsia. *Bacherberg.*

CLAUDONIUM, a town of Noricum, near Tregisamum.

CLAUSENTUM, a town of the Regni, Brit., s.w. of Venta Belgarum. *Bittern Farm,* 1 *m.* N.E. *from Southampton.*

CLAUSULA fl., a r. of the Labeates, Illyria, falling into Barbanà fl. below Scodra, and forming with it Oriuns fl. *Drivasti.*

CLAUTINATII, Vindeliciæ, i. q. Catenates.

CLAVENNA, a town of the Orobii, Gallia Transpadana, bet. Tarvesedum (15) and Summus lacus (10). *Chiavenna.*

CLAZOMENÆ, one of the twelve cities of Ionia, at the s.w. extremity of Hermius sin., below Chytrium. Built by a colony of Cleonæans and Phliasians on a peninsula, afterwards connected with the main-land by Alexander the Great. The birth-place of Anaxagoras. *Vourla.*

CLEANDRIA, a town of Æolis Asiatica, 7½ m. N. from Celænæ, on Rhodius fl.

CLELA, a town of Bruttium, on Sabbatus fl., R., above Clampetia. *Pietramala.*

CLEONÆ, I. a town of Acte, Macedonia, on Singiticus sin., N.W. of Thyssus. A colony from Chalcis, Eubœa. II. of Argolis, bet. Corinth (10) and Nemea. Near it Hercules slew the Moliones. *Cortese.*

CLEOPATRIS, Egypti, i. q. Arsinoe Heroopolitana.

CLEPIDAVA, a town of Sarmatia E., on or near Tyras fl., above Patridava.

CLEPSYDRA fl., a stream near Messene.

CLEUSIS fl., i. q. Clusius.

CLIBANUS, a town of Isauria.

CLIBANUS m., a ridge of the Apennines, in Bruttium, parallel with Neæthus fl., R. *Monte Visardo.*

CLIDES prom., Cypri, i. q. Dinaretum.

CLIMAX, " ladder," I. a defile in Artemisium m., bet. Mantinea and Argos, s. of Prinus. A part of the ascent was cut in steps, whence the name. *Scalatou Bey.* II. of Solymei m., Lycia, on the sea-shore, E. of Phaselis. III. Pisidiæ, i. q. Termessus. IV. *surnamed* Magnus, bet. Susiana-Challapetis and Persis, s.w. of Aspadana. V. m. of Arabia Felix, the w. boundary of the Chatramotitæ. *Djebil Nakhil.* VI. a port of Paphlagonia, 6 m. E. from Crobiolus.

CLIMBERRIS, i. q. Augusta Ausciorum.

CLISOBRA (Surapuru), a town of the Suraseni, India, on Diamana fl., near its junction with Sambus fl.

CLISURA, a defile of Taurus, in Armenia, 8 m. from Phison.

CLITÆ, I. a tribe of mountaineers in Cilicia Trachea. II. a town of Bithynia, on Billæus fl., E. of Hadrianopolis. III. a town of Pallene, Macedonia, near Cassandræa.

CLITERNIA, a maritime town of Daunia, Apulia, s.E. of Tifernus fl. *Sacchione.*

CLITERNUM, capital of the Æqui, Latium.

CLITOR, a town of Arcadia, under Aroanius m., w. of Pheneus. Founded by Clitor, son of Azan. *Katzanes.*

CLITORIUS fl., I. a r. of Arcadia, falling into Aroanius fl. at Clitor. Its fish were said to sing. II. fons, i. q. Azanius.

CLITUMNUS fl., a sacred r. of Umbria, rising near Ad Montes and falling into the Tiber above Vettuna. *Clitunno.*

CLODIANA (Castra Claudiana), a town of the

Eordeti, Illyria, on the site of an encampment of Appius Claudius, on the Egnatia Via, bet. Epidamnus (43) and Scampis (20).

CLODIANUS fl. (Fluvia Alba), a r. of Tarraconensis, falling into the Mediterranean at Emporiæ. *Muga; Lobregat Menor.*

CLUACARIA, a town of Zeugitana, bet. Elephantaria and Tuburbis Minor.

CLUANA, a town of Picenum, on Tinna fl., 3 m. from its mouth. *Sant' Elpidio.*

CLUDRUS fl., Phrygia, i. q. Glaucus.

CLUNIA, I. capital of the Arevacæ, Tarraconensis, N.W. of Uxama. A colonia. *Corunna del Conde.* II. a town of the Rugusci, Rhætia, on the Rhine, 16 m. N. from Magia.

CLUNIUM, a maritime town of Corsica, E. above Mantinorum opp. *San Catarina.*

CLUPEA, *vide* Clypea.

CLUSINA palus, a marsh of Etruria, w. of Trasimenus lacus. *Val di Chiana.*

CLUSIUM, *prius* Camers, one of the Twelve Cities of Etruria, bet. Volsinii (30) and Ad Novas Statuas (12), on Via Cassia. The capital of Porsenna.

CLUSIUS fl. (Cleusis), a r. of Gallia Cisalpina, falling into the Ollius at Bedriacum. The E. boundary of the Insubres. *Chiese.*

CLUSO fl., a r. of Gallia Transpadana, rising in Alpes Cottiæ, near Scincomagus, and falling into Padus fl. below Forum Vibii. *Chissone.*

CLUSORA (Clausa), a town of the Centrones, Galliæ. *Cluse.*

CLUTERNUM, a town of Samnium, 9 m. s.w. from Æsernia. *Capriati.*

CLUVIA, a town of the Hirpini, Samnium, 10 m. N.E. from Beneventum. *Montechiodi.*

CLYDÆ (Chydæ, Lydæ), a port of Caria, w. of Crya.

CLYLIPENUS sinus, a gulf of Sarmaticus Oceanus. *Gulf of Finland.*

CLYPEA (Taphitis, Aspis), I. a pr. of Zeugitana, s. of Mercurii prom. Named from its resemblance to a shield. II. a maritime town of Zeugitana, bet. Mercurii prom. and Curubis (30), on the cognominal prom. Built by the Sicilians under Agathocles.

CLYSMA, a town of Arabia, on the Red Sea, below Arsinoe. *Kolzum.*

CLYSTRUS, Ciliciæ, *vide* Caystrus.

CNACADIUS m., a m. of Laconia, near Las.

CNACION fl., a r. of Laconia, falling into the Eurotas, near Lacedæmon. *Pantalimona; Trypiotiko.*

CNEMIDES, a fortress of the Locri Epicnemidii, N.E. of Thronium, over against Cenæum prom.

CNEMIS m., m. of Locris, towards Bœotia, which gave name to the Locri Epicnemidii.

CNIDUS, a city of Caria, at Triopium prom. The metropolis of Doris Asiatica. Founded by a Lacedæmonian colony. Here was the statue of the Cnidian Venus by Praxiteles. The birth-place of Eudoxus, Agatharchides, &c.

Co, a town of Heptanomis, on the Nile, L., bet. Tamontum and Ibium. *Samallut.*

COA, Chaldeæ, i. q. Ur-choa, i. e. Ur.

COAS fl., i. q. Choes.

COBANDI, a tribe of Saxones, Germania, on Chalusus fl.

COBE, a port of Æthiopia, on Erythræum mare, opposite Cane, in Arabia, bet. Mosyticum prom. and Niloptolomæum. *Chaji.*

COBIALUS (Crobialus), i. q. Ægialus, Paphlagonia.

COBIOMACUM, a town of Volcæ Tectosages, Narbonensis I., bet. Tolosa and Narbo. *Cambiac.*

COBOLITÆ (Bolitæ), a tribe of Paropamisadæ, Arachosia, E. of the Sallagydæ. *Cabool.*

COBORIS ins., an isl. of Arabia Felix, s. of Asaborum prom., bet. Labatanis ins. and Sambracate.

COBRYS portus, the harbour of Cardia, Chersonesus Thracia.

COBUCTA, a maritime town of Mauritania Ting., N. bet. Tœnia Longa and Parietina.

COBULATUS fl., a r. of Pisidia, falling into Caralitis palus.

COCALA, a maritime town of the Oritæ, Gedrosia, bet. Ora and Cabana.

COCCIUM, Brit., i. q. Rigodunum.

COCCYGIUS m., *prius* Thornax, a m. of Argolis, bet. Halice and Hermione. Named from the metamorphosis of Jupiter into a coccyx.

COCHE (Choche), a town of Saccea, Arabia, near Sabe.

COCHLEARIA, a port of Sardinia, s. of Olbia. *Porto Pedrami.*

COCHLIA, a port of Caria, 6 m. from Orya.

COCINTHION, a town of Cyrenaica, on Syrtis Major, bet. Tiniodirum and Ad Puteum.

COCINTHUM (Stilida), I. a pr. of Bruttium, at the s. entrance of Scylleticus sin., the separation of Ionium mare from Siculum mare. It is the longest prom. in Italy. *Capo di Stilo.* II. a town at the prom., bet. Scylacium (22) and Succeianum (20). *Stilo.*

COCLEARIA, a maritime town of the Carenses, Sardinia E., bet. Olbia and Feronia.

COCOSA (Coequosa), capital of the Cocosates, Novem Populana, on the Aturis, L., bet. Tellonum and Aquæ Tarbellicæ. *Causseque.*

COCOSATES, *surnamed* Sexsignani, a people of Novem Populana, on Aturis fl., w. of the Tarusates. *About Chalosse.*

COCYLIUM, a town of Troas, bet. Næandria and Alexandria. Extinct in Pliny's time. *Kutchulan.*

COCYLUS fl., a r. of Thesprotia, Epirus, falling into Acheron fl. Its waters were extremely nauseous.

CODANI, a maritime people of Arabia Felix, on Betius fl., L.

CODANONIA ins. (Candanovia), a supposed isl. in Codanus sin.

CODANUS sinus, the s.w. portion of Suevicum mare. *Baltic.*

CODRION, a fortress of Phœbatis, Illyria, near the source of Apsus fl. *Codras.*

CODRONA, a town of Gedrosia, Pardene, N.W. of Alexandria Sogdiorum.

CODRYLA (Cordylus, Cordyla), a town of Pamphylia.

CODUZABALA, a town of Cappadocia, bet. Ariarathia (20) and Comana (24).

CŒLÆ ins., two islets on the coast of Troas.

CŒLE-SYRIA, "hollow Syria," the district of Syria, bet. Libanus and Anti-Libanus. *El Bakaah.*

CŒLIOBRIGA, a town of the Bracari, Tarraconensis, near Bracara Augusta ?

CŒLIUM, a town of Messapia, N. 8 m. from the sea. *Ceglie.*

CŒLIUS mons, a town of the Estiones, Vindelicia, on Ilargus fl., bet. Cambodunum and Viana.

CŒLUS, a town of Chersonesus Thracia, on the Hellespont, N. of Madytus. *Boix.*

CŒNON GALLICANON, a town of Bithynia, bet. Dablæ (24) and Dadastana.

CŒNUS fl., one of the mouths of the Rhodanus. *Gras de Foz.*

CŒRESI, a people of Germania II., bet. the Condrusi and the Eburones. *About Carolgau.*

COEUS fl., a r. of Messenia, falling into Electra fl., at Electra.

COGAMUS fl., a r. of Lydia, falling into Hermus fl. below Philadelphia.

COGNI, a people of Germania Magna, on the Danube, S.E. of the Lygii.

COHIBUS fl., i. q. Chobus.

COISSA, a town of Gumathene, Armenia, bet. Corra and Amida.

COLACCA, a town of Maliensis, Thessaly, destroyed by the Thessalians.

COLANCORUM, a town of the Silingi, Germania, N. of Susudata.

COLANICA, a town of the Damnii, Britannia Barbara, s.w. of Lindum. *Lanark.*

COLAPINI, a people of Pannonia s., bet. Colapis fl. and Savus fl., E. of the Latovici.

COLAPIS fl., a r. of Pannonia, rising in Liburnia and falling into the Savus at Siscia. *Kulpe.*

COLARNI, a town of the Lusitani, E.N.E. of Conimbrica.

COLATIO, a town of Noricum, 22 m. s.E. from Virunum.

COLBUSA, a name of Calchedon.

COLCHI, I. a town of India i. Gangem, s.E. on Colchicus sin. *Collatoor.* II. i. q. Macrones, Pontus.

COLCHICUM mare, i. q. Euxinus.

COLCHICUS sinus, a bay of Indicum mare, at Colchi, India, bet. Comaria prom. and Cory ins.

COLCHIS, I. a country of Asia, bounded N. by Sarmatia Asiatica, at Corax fl., s. by Armenia, according to Strabo, at Trapezus; according to Ptolemy, at Phasis; according to others, at Acampsis, w. by the Euxine, E. by Iberia. Peopled by Egyptians. II. a town of Elegosine, Armenia, N. of Thospitis lac.

COLENTUM ins., an isl. of Liburnia, s. of Cratcæ ins. *Mortero.*

COLETIANI, a people of Pannonia s., bet. Arrabo fl. and Murus, s. of the Boii.

COLI, a port of Aurea Chersonesus, w. bet. Attabus fl. and Perincula. *Peira.*

COLIACUM prom., *vide* Cory.

COLLÆUM, a town of Phrygia Epictetus, bet. Dioclea and Conni. The birth-place of Æsop, and of Alexander the Grammarian. *Kutaya.*

COLIAS prom., I. a headland of Attica, 2⅓ m. from Phalerum prom. *Colias or Tryspyrgoi.* II. *vide* Cory.

COLICARIA, a town of Gallia Cispadana, on Padus fl., R., bet. Hostilia (25) and Mutina (25). *Mirandola.*

COLLA, a town of the Apsynthii, Thrace, bet. Ænos and Zollana.

COLLATIA, a town of the Ambilici, Noricum, bet. Juenna and Upellæ. II. of Daunia, Apulia, s. of Pantanus lac., under Garganus m. *Collatina.* III. of the Latini, Latium, N. of Gabii, 4 m. E. of Rome. A colony from Alba. Memorable from the story of Lucretia. *On Monte Castellaccio.*

COLLENTUM, a town of Scardona ins.

COLLODE ins., an isl. of Sardinia, N.E. of Sarabus.

COLLOPS MAGNUS, I. Numidiæ, i. q. Cullu. II. PARVA, i. q. Cullucitanæ.

COLOBANORUM prom., a pr. of Æthiopia, on the Red Sea, at the N. entrance of Adulitanus sin. The boundary of the Colobi and Adulitæ.

COLOBATUS fl., a r. of Pisidia, falling into Catarrhactes fl. towards Isionda. *Estenaz.*

COLOBI, a tribe of Troglodytæ, on the Red Sea, w. above the Adulitæ.

COLOBONA, a town of the Turtetani, Bætica, bet. Carissa, N.N.E. and Asta Regia s.s.w.

COLOBRASSUS, a town of Pamphylia, on the borders of Cilicia, s.E. of Etenna.

COLOE (Pseboa), I. a lake of Tenesis, Æthiopia, s.w. of Axume. II. a town of Pontus, bet. Piala (12) and Pida (10). III. of Tenesis, Æthiopia, bet. Axume and Adulis.

COLONÆ, I. a town of Mysia, near Lampsacus. A Milesian colony. II. of Troas, on the coast below Alexandria, 15 m. s.w. from Troja. The city of Cycnus, father of Tennes. Its inhabitants were removed to Alexandria Troas.

COLONIA, I. a town of the Damnii, Brit., on Glota fl., R., above Vanduaria. *Carstairs?* II. of Cappadocia, on Lycus fl., R., s.E. of Cabira. *Koulei-hissar.* III. of the Trinobantes, Brit., bet. Combretonium and Ad Ansam. IV. AGRIPPINA (Oppidum Ubiorum), capital of the Ubii, Germania I., on the Rhine, above Burunca. A colonia of Agrippa, enlarged by Agrippina. *Cologne; Koln.* V. EQUESTRIS, Maxima Sequanorum, i. q. Noviodunum. VI. MARITIMA, of the Avatici, Narbonensis, on Astromela Stagnum, w. above Fossæ Marianæ. VII. TRAJANA (Castra Ulpia), of the Gugerni, Germania II., on the Rhine, bet. Burginatium and Vetera Castra. The station for the 30th legion, and hence surnamed Tricesima. *Kellen.*

COLONIDES (Colone), a town of Messenia, on Messeniacus sin., 5 m. s. of Corone. A colony from Attica. *Saratcha.*

COLONIS ins., an isl. of Argolis, in Argolicus sin. *Spezia-Pulo.*

COLONUS, *surnamed* Hippios, a demus of Attica, of the tribe Ægeis, bet. Athens and Cropia, with a cognominal hill, whither Œdipus retired on his banishment.

COLÖPHON, one of the twelve cities of Ionia, on the coast, bet. Lebedos and Ephesus. Founded by Andræmon, son of Codrus. The birth-place of the poets Mimnermus, Phœnix, Antimachus, Hermesianax, and Nicander; of Polymnestus, the musician, and Xenophanis; it also laid claim to

Homer. Noted for its fine cavalry, and for the *resina Colophoniana*.

COLOPHONIORUM portus, the N. harbour of Torone in Sithonia, Macedonia.

COLORINA, a town of Auranitis, Babyl., on the Euphrates, bet. Achajacala and Olabus.

COLOSSÆ, *postea* Chonæ, a city of Phrygia Mag., N.E. of Laodicea, bet. Mæander fl. and Lycus fl. Noted for its wool trade. Destroyed by an earthquake in the time of Nero; restored, somewhat more w., under the name of Chonæ, by one of the Byzantine emperors. The birth-place of Nicetas, the historian, of Epaphras, the disciple of St. Paul, and the bearer hither of his Epistle to the Colossians, and of Onesimus. *Konas.*

COLPUSA, the early name of Calchedon in Bithynia.

COLSA, a town of the Mardi, Armen., N.W. of Moranda. *Kors.*

COLTHENE, a district of Armenia, on Lychnitis lac.

COLUBRARIA ins. (Ophiusæ), islets of Tarraconensis, N.W. of Ebusus ins. *Columbretes.*

COLUMBARIA ins., an isl. of Etruria, near Ilva ins. *Palmarola.*

COLUMBARIUM prom., a pr. of Sardinia, N.E. below Arcti prom. *C. di Sarda.*

COLUMEN, a town of the Latini, Latium, near Labicum.

COLUMNA, I. (Statua Regina), a pillar (around which grew a town), set up S. of Scylla prom. in Bruttium, to mark the narrowest point of Fretum Siculum. *La Catona.* II. a place in Etruria, bet. Telamon port. and Ambro fl., where a body of Gauls, retreating from the battle of Telamo, were destroyed by Paulus Æmilius. *Colonna.*

COLUMNARUM FRETUM, i. q. Herculis Fretum; so named from the Columns of Hercules.

COLUSSA, Paphlagonia, the early name of Aboniteichos.

COLYERGIA prom., a pr. of Argolis, on Hermionicus sin., at Hermione.

COLYPES, a demus of Attica, of the tribe Ægeis.

COLYTHUS, a suburban demus of Athens. The birth-place of Plato; the abode of Æschines and of Timon the misanthrope. The children here were noted for a peculiarly precocious speech.

COMAGENE, a town of the Boii, Noricum, bet. Piratortum (8) and Asturis.

COMĀNA, I. (Cruse), a city, first of Cataonia, Cappadocia, and afterwards of Armenia, on Sarus fl., towards its source, bet. Mazaca (64) and Circusus (62). Named from the hair of Orestes, deposited here by him in the temple of Ma (Bellona). A colonia. *Al Bostan.* II. surnamed Pontica, a town of Pontus, on Iris fl., towards its source, 30 m. w. of Zela. *Komanak.*

COMARI, a port of India i. Gangem, E. *Conniacombri.*

COMARIA (Comar) prom., the S. extremity of India i. Gangem, over against Taprobane ins. *C. Comorin.*

COMARUS portus, a haven of Molossis, Epirus, bet. Glykis portus and Nicopolis. *Near Canali.*

COMBA, a town of Lycia, towards Araxa.

COMBARISTUM, a town of the Andecavi, Lugdunensis III., bet. Sipia N.W. and Juliomagus S.E.

COMBREA, a town of Chalcidice, Macedonia.

COMBRETONIUM, a town of the Cenimagni, Brit., on Sturius fl., R., bet. Sitomagus (22) and Colonia. *Woodbridge.*

COMBUSTA ins., I. an isl. of Arabia Felix, on the Red Sea, S.W. of Cardamene ins. II. a town of the Volcæ Tectosages, Narbonensis I., bet. Sulsulæ N. and Ruscino.

COMBUSTICA, a town of the Mœsi, Mœs. Sup., bet. Ratiaria and Timacus Min.

COMEDARUM m., m. of Asia, separating Bactria and Sogdiana.

COMEDAVA, a town of the Ratacenses, Dac., N.W. of Ramidava.

COMENASIS fl., a r. of India i. Gangem, falling into the Ganges N. of Agoranes fl. *Caramnassa;* or (Mannert) *Sagra.*

COMICIANA, a town of Sicily, under Maro m., S. bet. Agrigentum and Ancyra.

COMINIUM, a town of the Volsci, N.E. of Atina, near the source of Fibrenus fl. *S. Maria del Campo.*

COMINIUM (Ceritum), a town of the Pentri, Samnium, N.W. of Telesia. *Cereto.*

COMISENE, the N.E. district of Parthia.

COMISIMBELA, a town of Osrhoene, on Belias fl., bet. Avireth and Alagma.

COMMAGENE, a district of Syria, bounded N. by Cappadocia at Taurus m., S. by Cyrrhistica, E. by the Euphrates, w. by Syria Prop.

COMMANIA, the early name of Cestrine in Epirus.

COMMINICA (Commica), i. q. Lugdunum Convenarum.

COMMORIS, a fortress of the Eleutherocilices, Cilicia Trachea, in Amanus m.

COMMONI, a maritime tribe of Salyes, Narbonensis, s. of the Sueltri, E. of Massilia.

COMO, a town of Pentapolis, Cyrenaicæ, bet. Hadrianopolis and Arsinoe.

COMPASIS, a town of Thebais, bet. Aphroditis and Diospolis, E. of Apollinopolis Magna.

COMPITUM ANAGNINUM, a station on the Via Latina, near Anagnia, named from the junction here of the Via Latina and the Via Prænestina. *Villamagna.*

COMPITUM, a town of Gallia Cispad., bet. Cæsena (6) and Ariminum (12), on Via Æmilia Lepida.

COMPLUTICUM, a town of the Bracari, Tarraconensis, E. of Bracara Augusta.

COMPLUTUM, a town of the Vaccæi, Tarraconensis, N.N.E. of Titulcia. *Alcala de Henarez.*

COMPSA, a town of the Hirpini, Samnium, on the confines of Lucania, S.E. of Aletrum. *Conza.*

COMPSATUS (Cossinates, Consintus) fl., a r. of the Bistones, Thrace, rising in Rhodope m., and falling into the Ægean at Bistonis lacus, w. of Dicæa.

COMPULTERIA (Cupulteria), a town of the Pentri, Samnium, N. of Calatia, under Callicula m. *Cuttere.*

COMUM, a town of the Orobii, Gall. Transpadana, at the s.w. extremity of Larius lac., bet. Summus lac. (60) and Mediolanum (18). A colonia of Julius Cæsar, and municipium. The birth-place of Pliny Secundus. *Como.*

CONADIPSAS, a district of Scythia i. Imaum, E. of the Materi.

CONAPSENI, a maritime people of Sarmatia Asiat., on the Palus Mæotis, about the N. mouth of the Vardanes.

CONCABAR (Chaone), a town of Media Magna, bet. Ecbatana and Baptana. *Kenkobar.*

CONCANA, a town of Tarraconensis, N.E. of Juliobriga. *Santillana.*

CONCANGIUM, a town of the Brigantes, Brit., S.E. of Diolum.

CONCORDIA, I. a town of the Carni, Venetia, on Romatinus fl., R., towards its mouth, bet. Ad Sanos (11) and Apulia (9) on Via Æmilia. A colonia of Julius Cæsar. *Concordia.* II. of the Lusitani, bet. Tubucci S.E. and Sellium N.W. III. of the Tribocci, Germania I., w.N.w. of Tabernæ. *Weissenburg.*

CONDATE, "at the bend of the river," I. a town of the Allobroges, Viennensis, on the Rhodanus, bet. Geneva and Etanna. II. of the Arverni, Aquitania I., on the Liger, R., bet. Revessio E. and Aquæ Calidæ s.w. III. of the Aulerci Eburovices, Lugdunensis II., bet. Noviomagus N.W. and Durocasses. IV. of the Cornavii, Brit. Romana, bet. Mancunium (18) and Deva. *Northwich.* V. of the Petrocorii, Aquitania II., on Duronius fl., opposite Vatedo. VI. *postea* Redonum, capital of the Re-

dones, Lugdunensis III., bet. Legedia w.N.w. and Sepia. *Rennes.* VII. of the Santones, Aquitania II., on Carantonus fl., L., bet. Mediolanum and Sarrum. VIII. of the Senones, Lugdunensis IV., N.W. of Agenticum. IX. of the Senones, Lugdunensis IV., on the Liger, bet. Brivodurum and Massava.

CONDATOMAGUS, a town of the Ruteni, on Tarnis fl., L., bet. Carantomagus and Forum Neronis.

CONDERATES, a people of Vienniensis, bet. the Segusiani and the Rhodanus. *About Condrieux.*

CONDERCUM, a town of the Otadeni, Brit., on Hadriani murus, N. bet. Hunum and Segedunum. *Benwell.*

CONDIVICNUM, *postea* Namnetes, capital of the Namnetes, Lugdunensis III., on the Liger, bet. Corbilo and Juliomagus. *Nantes.*

CONDOCHATES fl., a r. of India i. Gangem, falling into the Ganges towards Corygaza. *Gunduk.*

CONDRUSII, a tribe of Tungri, Germania II., on the Mosa, above the Eburones. *About Condroz.*

CONDYLEA, a village of Arcadia, adjoining Caphyæ.

CONFLUENTES, I. a town of Pannonia Inf. on the Danube, bet. Taurunum and Singidunum. II. of the Tigurini, Germania I., on the Rhine, at the confluence of the Arula. III. of the Treveri, Germania I., on the Rhine, at the confluence, R., of the Mosella. *Coblentz.*

CONGAVALA, a town of the Otadeni, Brit., on Hadriani murus N., opposite Luguvallum. *Stanwicks.*

CONGUSTUS, a r. of Lycaonia, bet. Pegella (20) and Perla (15).

CONII, Lusitania, i. q. Cunetes.

CONIMBRIGA, a town of the Lusitani, near Munda fl., s. of Talabriga. *Two m. S. of Coimbra.*

CONISTURGIS (Anistorgis), capital of the Cynetes, Lusitania, on the Anas, towards its mouth, opposite Præsidium.

CONNI (Cona, Cone, Conipolis), a town of Phrygia Magna, 32 m. from Nacolea, near the source of Thymbres fl.

CONÖPE, I. a lake of Ætolia, near Conope, the scene of the metamorphosis of Cycnus. *L. Angelo-Castron.* II. a town of Ætolia, on Achelous fl., L., bet. Phanæ and Metropolis, immediately contiguous to Arsinoë. *Angelo-Castron.*

CONOPEIUM, a maritime town of Pontus, on the border of a cognominal marsh or lake, 5 m. s. from Naustathmus. *Coumjougaz.*

Conovium, a town of the Ordovices, Brit., on Toesobis fl., at its mouth, L., near Segontium. *Caer-rhyn.*

Conozus fl., according to Plutarch, the early name of Strymon fl.

Consabrum, a town of the Carpetani, Tarraconensis, 28 m. N.W. from Murum. *Consuera.*

Consentia, capital of Bruttium, on Crathis fl., near its source, bet. Caprasiæ (28) and Sabbatus fl. (12). *Cosenza.*

Consilinum, a fortress of Lucania, of uncertain position.

Consorani, I. a people of Novem Populana, extending into Narbonensis I., under the Pyrenees, bet. the Convenæ w. and the Sardones E. *In Le Couserans.* II. their capital. *Lizier.*

Constantia, I. a town of the Unelli, Lugdunensis II., bet. Crociaconum N. and Abrincatui s. *Constance.* II. Mesopotamiæ, *vide* Antoninopolis. III. Africæ, i. q. Cirta.

Constantiana, a town of Mœsia Inf., bet. Tomi and Pteron prom.

Consuanetes (Consuantoi, Contuantii), a town of Vindelicia, N. of Brigantinus lacus. *About Kœnigseck.*

Contadesdus fl., a r. of Thrace, rising in Hæmus m., and falling into Agrianes fl. s.E. of Ostudizum. *Saradjala.*

Contenebra, a town of Etruria, near Tarquinii.

Contestani, a maritime people of Tarraconensis s.E., bet. Sucronensis sin. N.E. and Massienus sin. s.w. *S. Valencia and Murcia.*

Conthyle, a demus of Attica, of the tribe Pandionis.

Contoparia Via, the road bet. Corinth and Mycenæ.

Contosolia, a town of the Turtuli, bet. Metellinum N.W. and Mirobriga s.E.

Contra Acincum, *postea* Pessium, a town of the Jazyges Metanastæ, on the Danube, over against Acincum. *Pesth.*

Contra-Apollinopolis, a town of Thebais, on the Nile, nearly opposite Apollinopolis Magna.

Contra-Birtha, a town of Mesopotamia, on the Euphrates, opposite Birtha, bet. Allan and Circesium.

Contra-Coptos, a town of Thebais, on the Nile, L., opposite Coptos.

Contra-Latopolis (Chnubis), a town of Thebais, on the Nile, R., opposite Latopolis.

Contra-Margum, a town of the Albocenses, Dacia, on the Danube, opposite Margus.

Contra-Ombos, a town of Thebais, on the Nile, L., above Ombi s., 24 m. from Contra-Syene.

Contra-Pselcis, i. q. Metacompso.

Contra-Syene, a town of Thebais, on the Nile, L., below Syene. *Gharly-Assuan.*

Contra-Talmis, a town of Dodecaschœnus, on the Nile, R., opposite Talmis.

Contra-Taphis, a town of Dodecaschœnus, on the Nile, R., opposite Taphis.

Contra-Toum, a town of Thebais, on the Nile, L., below Toum.

Contrebia (Leucas), I. *postea* Cantabria, a town of the Berones, Tarraconensis, on the Iberus, opposite Varia. II. of the Carpetani, Tarraconensis, N.E. of Toletum. *Santaver?*

Contributa, a town of the Celtici, Bæturia, bet. Nertobriga s.w. and Julipa N.E. A colonia (Julia). *San Bartholome del Villar.*

Coos fl., a r. of Messenia, towards Cyparissia.

Convallis (Nivaria, Caspiria) ins., one of the Fortunatæ ins., Africæ. *Teneriffe.*

Convenæ, a people on the Garumna, towards its source. *Diocese of St. Bernard de Comminge.*

Copæ, a town of Bœotia, on Copais lac., N.E. bet. Acræphia and Holmones. *Topolias.*

Copais (Haliartius, Orchomenius, Cephissius, Leuconis) palus, a lake of Bœotia, formed by Cephissius, Termesius, and other streams, and discharging itself by numerous subterraneous channels into Hytice palus and the sea. Noted for its eels. *L. Topolias.*

Copar, a town of the Debæ, Arab., on the Red Sea, bet. Betius fl. and Jambia. *Rabegh, Arbric.*

Cophanta, a port of Gedrosia, bet. Barna (75) and Assa, at the mouth of Arbis (Cophen) fl.

Cophen (Arbis), I. a r. of Gedrosia, falling into Indicus Oc. at Cophanta. *Mend.* II. Arachosiæ, i. q. Arachotus.

Cophes (Cophen) fl., a r. of Paropamisus, falling into the Indus at Spatura? *Cow.*

Cophos, "soundless," the s. harbour of Torone in Sithonia, Macedonia.

Copiæ, i. q. Sybaris.

Coprates fl., a r. of Susiana, rising in Media, and falling into the Pasitigris near Susa.

Copria (Sterquilinium) littus, the coast of Sicily N.E., bet. Tauromenium and Charybdis. Named from the wrecks of ships, thrown there from Charybdis.

Coptos, "privation" (Chemmis), a town of Thebais, near the Nile, R., bet. Cænopolis and Apollinopolis parva. The seat of great trade, carried on by a mixed population of Egyptians and Arabs. Named from the tradition that Isis here *deprived* herself of her hair in token of mourning for Osiris ; and hence, also, the priests of Isis always kept their heads shaved. *Keft.*

CORA, I. a town of the Volsci, s.w. of Signia, near Ulubræ. An Alban colony. A municipium and colonia. According to Pliny, founded by Dardanius. *Cora.* II. a town of the Mandubii, Lugdunensis I., bet. Autissiodorum N.W. and Aballo S.E. *Ville-Auxerre.*

CORACÆ, a town of Magnesia in Thessaly, near Methone.

CORACESIUM, a maritime town of Cilicia Trachea, on the borders of Pamphylia, w. of Syedra. The stronghold of the pirate Diodotus Tryphon. *Alaza.*

CORACENSES, a people of Sardinia, occupying its N.W. angle.

CORACIUM (Corycium) prom., a headland of Bithynia, near the N. mouth of Thracius Bosporus.

CORACODES portus (Corax), a port of the Æchilenenses in Sardinia w., s.w. of Cornus. *Algeri.*

CORALIUS (Cuarius) fl., Bœotia, i. q. Phalarus.

CORALLA, a port of Pontus, 15 m. s.w. from Hieronoros. *Kourelih.*

CORANCALI, a people of India e. Gangem.

CORANITÆ, a people of Arabia Felix, w. of the Leanitæ. Descendants of Korah, son of Esau.

CORASSIÆ (Corsiæ) ins., islets of Samos, bet. Cantharium prom. and Melantii Scopuli. *Formiche.*

CORAX, I. a r. of the Apsilæ, Sarmat., falling into the Euxine N. of Dioscurias. The N. boundary of Colchis. II. a ridge of Œta m., Ætolia, on the coast ; a continuation of Taphiassus m. *Koraka.* III. (Coracium), an E. continuation of Corycus m., s. of Smyrna. IV. a ridge of Caucasus, along the N.E. shore of the Caspian. V. a prom. of Taurica Chersonesus, s., below Athenæum portus. *Kirkinos-Burnu.*

CORAXI, I. a people of Sarmatia As., on the Euxine, under Corax m., above the Apsilæ. Noted for the fine wool of their sheep. II. of Scythia, N. of the Orgasi.

CORBASA (Colbasa), a town of Philyas, Pisidia, bet. Attalia and Termessus.

CORBEUS (Gorbeus), a town of the Tectosages, Galatia, bet. Ancyra (21) and Rosologia (12). The residence of Saveondarius, the son-in-law of Deiotarus. *Corbega.*

CORBIENE, capital of Susiana-Corbiene, bet. Ecbatana and Arderica. *Khourimabad.*

CORBILO, a town of the Namnetes, Lugdunensis III., at the mouth of the Liger. *Corsep.*

CORBIO, I. a town of the Latini, Latium, s.E. of Tusculum. *Rocca Priora.* II. capital of the Suessetani, Tarraconens., on Pallantias fl., R., below Belsinum. *Solsana ?*

CORBULONIS MONUMENTUM, a fortress erected by Corbulo, on the sea-coast of the Frisii. *Groningen.*

CORCARA, a town of Adiabene, Assyr., N. of Ecbatana.

CORCONAGÆ, a people of India i. Gangem, on Cambys ost., Ganget., R.

CORCONIANA, a town of Sicily, bet. Agrigentum (13) and Calloniana (12). *Naro.*

CORCONTII, a tribe of Marcomanni, German., under Asciburgius m., s.w.

CORCURA, a maritime town of India i. Gangem, w., bet. Melinda and Elancum.

CORCYRA (Drepane, Scheria, Phæacia) ins., I. an isl. of Epirus, bet. Osichesmus and Sybota. Colonized by Phæacians from Liburnia ; settled by Corinthians under Chersicrates, 758 B.C. *Corfu.* II. its capital, on the E. coast, s.w. of Buthrotum. *Corfu.* III. surnamed Nigra (Melæna), from its dark woods, an isl. of the Adriatic, one of the Liburnides ins., near Pharos. Colonized by Cnidians. *Curzola.*

CORDA, a town of the Selgovæ, Brit., on Vidogara fl., s.w. of Colania. *Old Cumnock.*

CORDES fl., a r. of Mesopotamia, running by Dara into the Chaborras.

CORDUBA, a city of Bætica, on the Bætis, above Decuma, N.E. of Astigi. Built by the first Marcellus. The first Roman colony in Spain, and surnamed Patricia from the high rank of its leading inhabitants. The birth-place of the two Senecas, and of Lucan. *Cordova.*

CORDUENI (Carduchi, Cordiæi), a people of Armenia, s.E., on the borders of Assyria. *Kordhaikh.*

CORDYLE, I. a town of the Bechires, Pontus, 12½ m. E. from Odienus. II. a port of the Macrones, Pontus, 5 m. s.E. from Hieronoros.

CORDYLUSA ins., an isl. of Rhodes.

COREA, a town of Samaria, N.E. of Silo.

COREATIS, a town of India, on the Indus, 3 m. below Caumana.

CORENSE littus, the coast of Bætica, w., about Gades.

CORESSUS (Corissia), a town of Ceos ins., on the N.W. coast. The port of Julis. Deserted in Strabo's time.

CORĒTUS sin., a bay of Palus Mæotis, on the E. side of the isthmus of Taurica Chersonesus.

CORFINIUM, capital of the Peligni, Italy, on ViaValeria, bet. Stabulæ (7) and Interpromium (12), for a short time the metropolis of the Marsic confederacy, and then called Italicum. *Church of San Pelino and Pentima.*

CORGATHA, a port of Aurea Chersonesus, E., above Throana.

CORIA, I. a town of the Damnii, Brit., bet. Vanduaria and Alauna. *Castle Cary.* II. *surnamed* Gadenorum, of the Otadeni, Britannia Barbara, S.E. of Alaterva. *Jedburgh.*

CORIALLUM (Cortallum), a port of the Osismii, Lugdunensis III., w.N.w. of Cosidia. *Cherbourg.*

CORIANDI, a people of Hibernia, w. of the Brigantes.

CORIDORGIS, a town of the Batini, Germ., N.E. of Reginum.

CORINEA, a district of Osrhoene, Mesop., on the frontier of Armenia Maj.

CORINIUM, Brit., i. q. Durocornovium.

CORINTHIA, a country of Peloponnesus, bounded N. by Corinthiacus sin., s. by Argolis, w. by Achaia, E. by Saronicus sin. Established as a kingdom by Sisyphus, B.C. 1376.

CORINTHIACUS isthmus, the isthmus connecting Peloponnesus with Græcia extra Peloponnesum, in breadth, at the narrowest part, six miles. The seat of the Isthmian games. Attempts to cut through the isthmus were made, but wholly in vain, by Demetrius Poliorcetes, by Julius Cæsar, Caligula, Nero, and Herodes Atticus.

CORINTHIACUS sin., a gulf of Ionium mare, washing the coasts of Achaia N., Corinthia N., Megaris N., Bœotia s., Phocis s., Locris Ozol., and Ætolia. *G. di Lepanto.*

CORINTHUS, *prius* Ephyre, *surnamed* Bimaris, from its position, capital of Corinthia, Peloponnesus. Built by Corinthus, son of Marathon, B.C. 1520; rebuilt B.C. 1410; destroyed by Lucius Mummius B.C. 146; restored by Julius Cæsar, who erected it into a colonia, under the name of Laus Julia. *Corinth.*

CORINUS fl., a r. of the Dobuni, Brit., falling into the Isis below Durocornovium. *Churn.*

CŎRIŎLI, a city of the Volsci, Latium, bet. Velitræ and Lanuvium. Its capture con-

ferred the surname of Coriolanus upon C. Marcius. *On Monte Giove.*

CORIONDI, a people of Hibernia, s. and s.w. of the Menapii. *S. Wexford and Kilkenny.*

CORIOVALLUM, a town of the Eburones, Germania II., bet. Juliacum and Pons Mosæ. *S. Finisterre.*

CORISOPITI, I. a people of Armorica, on the s. coast of the Osismii. II. their capital. *Quimper-Corentin.*

CORISSIA. *Vide* Coressus.

CORITANI, a people of Britain, occupying the N.E. angle of Flavia Cæsariensis, bet. Abus fl. and Metaris æst., E. of the Cornavii. *Counties of Derby, Notts, Lincoln, Leicester, Rutland, and part of Northampton.*

CORIUS (Coros) fl., a r. of Carmania, falling into Persicus sin. opposite Oaracta ins.

CORMA fl., I. a r. of Media Cambadene, falling into Choaspes fl. at Ruttarata. II. (Carmsin), a town of Media Cambadene, on Corma fl., s.w. of Ecbatana.

CORMALUS fl., a r. of Æolis Asiat., rising in Ida m., and falling into Adramyttenus sin.

CORMASA, a town of Pisidia, 40 m. N.W. of Perga.

CORMONES, a town of the Carni, Venetia, s. of Forum Julii. *Cormons.*

CORNA, a people of Lycaonia, bet. Iconium and Barate.

CORNACUM, a town of Pannonia, on the Danube, bet. Teutoburgium (16) and Cuccis. *Illok.*

CORNAVII, I. a people of Britannia Barbara, on its extreme N. coast. II. of Flavia Cæsariensis, bet. the Coritani E., the Ordovices w., Belisama fl. N., and Avona fl. s. *Cheshire, Shropshire, Staffordshire, Worcestershire, Warwickshire.*

CORNE, a town of Laviniasene, Cappadocia, on Euphrates fl.

CORNELII (Cornelia, Corneliana, Scipionis Vallum) castra, a town built on the encampment of Cornelius Scipio, in the Second Punic war, at Pulchrum prom., 1½ m. from Utica.

CORNIASPA, a town of the Trocmi, Galatia, bet. Tavia and Pardosena.

CORNICLANUM, Cyren., i. q. Tinci.

CORNICULANA, a town of Gallia Cispad., bet. Neronia (6) and Hadria (6). *Mezzogaro.*

CORNICULANI colles, hills of Sabinium, about Corniculum and Cænina. *Monti Monticelli and Sant' Angelo.*

CORNICULUM, a town of Sabinium, N.E. of

Cænina. The birth-place of Servius Tullius. *Sant' Angelo.*

CORNUS, a town of Sardinia, under Insani m., N. of Thyrsus fl., 18 m. s. from Bosa. *On Monte Santo.*

COROBILIUM, a town of the Catalauni, Belgica II., bet. Durocatalauni N. and Segessera.

COROC, a town of Drangiana, s.w. of Prophtasia.

CORODAMUM prom., a pr. on the E. extremity of Arabia Felix, at the entrance of Omanus sin. *Ras al Hhad.*

COROMANUS, capital of the Abucæi, Arabia, bet. Teredon and 'Adari. *Grane.*

CORODUNUM, a town of the Convenæ, Novem Populana, on the Garumna. *Gourdan.*

CORŌNE, *prius* Æpia, a town of Messenia, on Messeniacus sin., 5 m. N. from Colonides. *Coron.*

CORONEA, I. a peninsula of Attica, on the Ægean, N. of Potamos. *Corugni.* II. a city of Bœotia, under Laphystius m., w. of Alalcomenæ, 27 m. N.W. from Platæa. Noted for the victory of Agesilaus over the Thebans, 394 B.C. Near it was a temple of Minerva Itonis, in which the Bœotian states assembled. *Korunies.* III. a town of Corinthia, on Corinthiacus sin., bet. Corinth and Sicyon, at the mouth of Nemea fl. IV. a town of Phthiotis, in Thessaly, towards Thaumaci.

CORONTA, a town of Acarnania, s.w. of Stratus, near Medeon.

CORONUS m., a ridge of Caspius m., on the borders of Hyrcania.

CAROPESTUS, a town of Lycaonia, on the borders of Cappadocia, bet. Sabatra and Archelais.

COROS fl., Carmania, i. q. Corius.

COROTHOS, a town of Cyrenaica, E. of Drepanum prom.

CORPICENSES, a people of Sardinia, on Tyrsus fl., s., bet. the Æchilenses w. and the Barbaricini E.

CORPILLI, a people of Thrace, on Hebrus fl.

CORRA, a town of Gumathene, Arm., bet. Arsinia and Amida.

CORRAGUM. *Vide* Corax.

CORSEA (Corseæ), a town of Bœotia, under Cyrtonius m. N.W., w. of Larymna.

CORSEÆ ins., an isl. in Icarium mare, bet. Samos and Patmos. *Furnis.*

CORSEÆ PERRHÆBIÆ, i. q. Orthe.

CORSĬCA (*prius* Cyrnus) ins., an isl. of Italy, N. of Sardinia. Its original population was augmented, at intervals, by Phocæans from Asia Minor, Carthaginians, and Romans. It was noted for its wax. *Corsica.*

CORSII, Corsican settlers in Sardinia, over against Corsica.

CORSIO (Herculea), a town of the Amantini, Pannonia, bet. Osones and Gurtiana.

CORSŌTE, a town of Mesopotamia, on the Euphrates, below Zaitha.

CORSTOPĪTUM, a town of the Brigantes, Brit., on Vedra fl., L., bet. Epiacum and Pons Ælii. *Near Corbridge.*

CORSULA, a Pelasgic town of Sabinium, 8 m. s.E. of Reate. *Contigliano.*

CORSURA ins., Zeugitana, i. q. Ægimurus.

CORTALLIA, capital of the Daoni, Ind.

CORTE (Cortia Prima), a town of Dodecaschœnus, on the Nile, bet. Metacampsi and Hiera Sycaminos (4). The first town, as its affix indicates, from the Æthiopian border, N. *Korty.*

CORTICATA, I. an isl. of Tarraconensis, on the Atlantic, off the mouth of Olla fl., s. of Orium prom. II. a town of the Turtuli, Bæturia, bet. Mirobriga N.N.E. and Mellarea s.s.w. *Cortegana.*

CORTONA, I. one of the twelve Tyrrhenian cities of Etruria, bet. Trasimenus lac. and Arretium (14). A colonia of Sylla. *Cortona.* II. a town of the Lacetani, on Rubricatus fl., R., above Bacasis.

CORTORATE, a town of the Petrocorii, Aquitania II., bet. Condate s.w. and Crinaccum E.

CORUSIA, a town of the Melibi, Sarmat., on Vardanes fl., towards its source.

CORVORUM ins. (" crow's nests"), three small islands in Ladon fl., Arcadia, at its junction with Alpheus fl.

CORVORUM nidus, a biforked mount of Cilicia.

CORY, I. an isl. of India i. Gangem, off Cory prom. *Ramanan Coil.* II. (Colias, Coliacum), a prom. of India i. Gangem, E., separating Colchicus sin. from Agaricus sin. *Ramanan Coil.*

CORYBANTIUM, a town of Troas, on the coast, s. of Hamaxitus.

CORYBISSA, a district of Troas, towards Scepsis.

CORYCA ins., an isl. of Crete, over against Corycum prom. *Carabusa.*

CORYCIUM antrum, I. a large stalactite cavern, on the s. slope of Parnassus, above Delphi, 330 feet long by 200 wide. Sacred to the Corycian nymphs, and to Pan. II. the crater of an extinct volcano in Arima m., 2 m. inland from Corycium prom., Cilicia. According to Strabo, and others, the locality of Typhœus' torments.

CORYCIUM prom., I. a pr. of Cilicia Trachea, at Corycus. II. of Crete, N.W., the termination of Corycus m. *C. Carabusa.* III. of Ionia, over against Cercetius m., the s. termination of Corycus m. *C. Kourko.*

CORYCUS, I. the coast of Lycia, E. of Olympus. II. the coast of Pamphylia, about Corycus. III. m., on the N.W. coast of Crete, terminating in Tretum prom. IV. a ridge of Mimas m., extending from behind Erythræ, Ionia, to Corycum prom. V. a maritime town of Pamphylia, near Phaselis, s.w. VI. a port of Cilicia Trachea, at Corycium prom., E. of Pulchrium Coracesium portus. *Korghoz.* VII. a port of Ionia, w. of Corycum prom. *Sikya.*

CORYDALLA (Coridillus), a town of Lycia, 29 m. w. from Phaselis.

CORYDALLUS, I. a tribe of Attica, N.W. of Athens. The haunt of the robber Procrustes. *Daphni Bouni.* II. a demus of Attica, of the tribe Hippothoontis, under Corydallus m.

CORYGAZA, a town of the Marundæ, Ind., on the Ganges, bet. Salimbothra and Celydna.

CORYLEUM, a town of Paphlagonia, near Gangra.

CORYNÆUM prom., a pr. of Ionia, at the N. entrance of Erythræus sin.

CORYNE, I. a town of Epea, Elis, on Peneus fl., near its mouth. *Gastonni.* II. of Ionia, at Corynæum prom.

CORYPHANTIS, I. a town of Æolis, Asiat., on Adramyttenus sin. A Mitylenæan settlement. II. of Bithynia. Extinct in Pliny's time.

CORYPHASIUM prom., a pr. of Messenia, on the approach to which the later portion of Pylos stood. *Monte San Niccolo.*

CORYTHEIS, a village of Arcadia, s. of Tegea.

COS, I. (Merope, Cea, Nymphæa), an isl. of Caria, off Halicarnassus (15). In circuit 65 m. Colonized by Thessalians, and then by Dorians from Megara. Noted for its fine silk manufactures. *Stanco.* II. *prius* Astypalæa, its capital, within Scondarium prom., with a temple of Æsculapius, in which were the Antigonus and the Venus Anadyomene of Apelles. The birth-place of Apelles, Philetas, Hippocrates, &c. *Stanco.*

COSA, I. a r. of Latium, falling into Liris fl. below Frusino. II. (Cossa), a maritime city of Etruria, on Via Aurelia, bet. Ad Novum (9) and Telamon. A colony from Volsinii. A colonia 274 B.C., and again of Augustus (col. Julia). The locality of the defeat of M. Æmilius Lepidus by Lutatius Catulus. *Ansedonia.* III. a town of Lucania, near the source of Cylistarnus fl., N.W. of Sybaris. The death-place of T. Annius Milo. *Civita, near Cossano.* IV. of the Parapiotæ, Ind., on Sambris fl., R., towards its source. Noted for its diamonds. *Cotta.* V. of the Cadurci, Aquitania I., s. of Divona.

COSAMBA, a port of India, near the w. mouth of the Ganges. *Balasor.*

COSĀNUM prom., a pr. of Etruria, at Cosa.

COSARA, a maritime town of Arabia Felix, opposite Serapidis ins.

COSCINIA (Coscinus), a town of Caria. *China.*

COSEDIA, a town of the Osismii, Lugdunensis III., bet. Reginea w.s.w. and Legedia E.N.E. *La Cousiniere.*

COSEGANES fl., a r. of India e. Gangem, falling into the Ganges above Celydna.

COSETANI, a people of Tarraconensis, on Rubricatus fl., R., towards its mouth.

COSSÆI, a people of Susiana, N.W. of the Uxii.

COSSINI, a tribe of Veneti, Lugdunensis, on the coast. *About Coueznou.*

COSSIUM (*postea* Vasatæ), capital of the Vasates, Novem Populana, bet. Alingo and Tres Arbores. *Bazas.*

COSSURA ins., an isl. of the Mediterranean, midway bet. Sicily and Africa. Abounding in olives and pasture. *Pantalaria.*

COSSOANUS (Cosoagus) fl., a r. of India i. Gangem, falling into the Ganges. *Cosa.*

COSSUS m., a summit of Olympus, Bithynia.

COSTA BALÆNA, a maritime town of the Intemelii, Liguria, bet. Albintemelium (16) and Lucus Bormanni (16). *Costa Rainera.*

COSTOBOCI, i. q. Cistoboci.

COSYLINUM, a town of Lucania, near Tanager fl., R. *Near Padula.*

COTACE, Ariæ, i. q. Candace.

COTACENE, a district of Armenia Maj., w. of Lychnitis lac. *Cotaikh.*

COTÆNA, a town of Morimene, Cappadocia.

COTARZENE (Chorzene), a district of Armenia Maj., s. of Sacasene. *Vanand.*

COTE ins., an isl. of Crete, 20 m. s.E. from Dictynium. *San Teodoro.*

COTENSES, a tribe of Agathyrsi, Dac., on Ararus fl.

COTES prom. ("vine-producing"), the local name of Ampelusia prom., Maurit.

COTHOCIDÆ, a demus of Attica. The birth-place of Æschines.

COTHON ("cup"), the inner harbour of Carthage. An artificial structure.

COTINÆ, a town of the Turtuli, Bæturia, bet. Sisapo s.w. and Carcurium N.E.

COTINUSA ins., Bætica, the isl. on which Gades stood.

COTOMBA, a town of the Sabæi, Persia, on Cyrus fl., s. of Pasargada.

COTONIS ins., one of the Echinades ins.

COTTABANI (Catabeni), a people of Arabia Felix, in the mountains, N. of the Omanitæ. *Tribe of Beni Kahtan.*

COTTÆ, a people of Sarmatia Asiatica.

COTTÆOBRIGA, a town of the Vettones, Lusitania, s.w. of Salmantica.

COTTIA, a town of Gallia Transpadana, on the Via Posthumia, bet. Ad Medias (13) and Laumellum (12). *Cozzo.*

COTTIARA (Cottona, Cottonara), capital of Limyrica, India, on the coast, bet. Elancum and Bambala. *Cotschin?*

COTTIARIUS fl., a r. of the Sinæ, falling into Eous Oceanus at Cattigara. *Cambodia.*

COTTOBARA, a town of Gedrosia-Pardene, bet. Codrona and Musarna.

COTTONA, Indiæ, i. q. Cottiara.

COTYÆUM, a town of Phrygia Epictetus, N.E. of Azeni. The birth-place, according to some authorities, of Æsop. *Kutaya.*

COTYLÆUM m., a m. of Eubœa, near Tamynæ.

COTYLE, the early name of Aquæ Cutiliæ.

COTYLIUS m., a w. summit of Lycæus m., in Arcadia, 5 m. s. of Phigalea.

COTYORA, a port of the Tibareni, Pontus, 10 m. s.E. from Genetæum prom., where the 10,000 encamped during forty-eight days previous to their embarkation for Heraclea. The people were afterwards transported to Pharnacia. *Ordou.*

COTYRGA, a town of Sicily, N.W. of Ancyra.

COTYRTA, a fortress of Laconia, near Boeæ.

COVELIACE, a town of the Focunates, Vindel., bet. Esco Nova and Parthanum (20).

COVENNUS ins. (Counos), an isl. of Cantium, N. *Canvey.*

CRAGUS, I. a chain of m. in Lycia, with seven, or according to Strabo eight, summits. Scylax describes it as the boundary of Caria and Lycia. Named from Cragus, s. of Tremilus. *Yedi Bouroun.* II. a prom. of Cilicia Trachea, s.E. of Nephilis prom. III. a town of Lycia, under the cognom. m.

CRAMBUSA ins., I. an isl. of Cilicia Trachea, off Cruni prom. *Papadoula.* II. (Dionysia) of Lycia, E. of Sacrum prom. According to Strabo, a town on the opposite mainland. *Grambousa.*

CRANÆ ins., an isl. of Laconia, on Laco-

nicus sin., over against Gythium, whither Paris first carried Helena. *Marathonisi.*

CRANAUS, a town of Caria, near Antiochia, whither its inhabitants were transferred by Antiochus.

CRANIA, a village of Epirus, near Ambracia.

CRANII, a town of Cephallenia ins., over against Palle, partly settled by Messenians from Pylos. *San Giovanni.*

CRANON, I. a m. of Epirus, on the Arachthus fl., overlooking Crania. II. a town of Athamania, in Ætolia, on Achelous fl., below Theium. Named after Cranon, son of Pelasgus. *Crania.* III. of Pelasgiotis, Thessaly, bet. Larissa and Pharsalus. The city of the Scopadæ of Herodotus. Memorable for the defeat of the Greeks by the Macedonians, under Antipater, 322 B.C. In its vicinity was a warm spring, which, mixed with wine, retained its heat for several days. *Near Hadjilar.*

CRASPEDITES sin., "edge," a bay of Astacenus sin., at its w. entrance, over against Acrita prom.

CRASSUM prom., Sardiniæ, i. q. Pachia.

CRATAIS fl., a r. of Bruttium, N. of Scylla, and named from the mother of Scylla. *Solano,* or *Fiume dei Pesci.*

CRATAS m., m. of Sicily, running s.E. from below Panormus.

CRATEÆ ins., isl. in the Adriatic; two of the Liburnides.

CRATER sin., Camp., i. q. Cumanus.

CRATHIS, I. a r. of Achaia, rising in Crathis m., and falling into Corinthiacus sin., N.W. of Ægira. *Acratha.* II. of Bruttium, rising s. of Consentia, and falling into Tarentinus sin. below Sybaris. Named from the Achaian Crathis. Its water turned the hair grey. *Crati.* III. a m. of Arcadia, on the border of Achaia, N.W. of Pheneus.

CRATIA (Flavíopolis), a town of Bithynia, on Billæus fl., near its source, bet. Claudiopolis and Ancyra (24). *Near Tereboli.*

CRAUGIÆ ins., two isl. of Argolis, in Saronicus sin., over against Spiræum prom.

CRAUSINDON fl., a stream of Magnesia, Thessaly, rising in Pelion m., and falling into Pagasæus sin.

CREMASTI, a mining village of Mysia, behind Abydos.

CREMERA fl., a r. of Etruria, rising near Baccanæ, and falling into the Tiber at Ad Rubras. Memorable for the fate of the 300 Fabii. *Valca.*

CREMNA, I. a fortress of Pisidia, 4. m. N. from Sagalassus, near Baris. *Kebrinaz.* II. a town of the Jazyges, Sarmat., on Palus Mæotis, at Agarum prom.

CREMNISCUS, a maritime town of Dacia, bet. Antiphilæ and Œpolium. A Milesian colony.

CREMONA, a city of the Cenomanni, in Gallia Transpadana, on Padus fl., bet. Acerræ (13) and Bedriacum (15), on Via Posthumia. A colonia (219 B.C.). Destroyed by the army of Vespasian, and restored by that emperor. Its territory was distributed by Augustus among his veterans. *Cremona.*

CREMONIS JUGUM, an early name of Alpes Graiæ.

CRENÆ, "fountains," a place in Amphilochia, Acarnania, s. of Argos Amphilochus. *Kouphara.*

CRENIDES, "fountains," I. the early name of Philippi, Thrace. II. a town of Bithynia, on the Euxine, 8 m. from Sandaraca.

CREON m., a summit of Lepitymnus m. in Lesbos.

CREONIUM, a town of the Callicæni, Illyria, E. of Bantia.

CRESIUS collis, a hill of Arcadia, near Tegea.

CRESSA I. (Critea), a town of Chersonesus Thracia, near Crithote. Founded by Miltiades. II. of Peræa, Caria, on the coast. *Karagash.*

CRESSÆUS sin., a bay of the Mediterranean, in Caria, at Cressa. *G. Karagash.*

CRESTONE (Grestone), I. capital of Crestonia, on Echedorus fl., below Terpillus. II. *apud* Herod, i. q. Crotona, Italiæ.

CRESTONIA (Grestonia), a district of Mygdonia, Macedonia, N. of Anthemus. Long occupied by a tribe of Pelasgi, who retained their primitive language and manners. Suttee was practised by them. Infested by lions. *Caradagh.*

CRETA (Æria, Doliche, Idæa, Telchinia) ins., an isl. of the Ægean, bet. the Cyclades ins. and Africa. Settled by Minæi from Arabia, by Curetes (Cretes), Pelasgi, Dores, Dactyli, &c. Named after Cres, son of Jupiter and Idæa. Organized as a state by Minos, son of Jupiter and Europa, *circa* 1015 B.C. Celebrated for its hundred cities, for its labyrinth, for the laws of Minos, and for the skill of its people as bowmen, whence, in Phœnician, its name. In length 270 m., in extreme breadth 50, in circuit 539. *Candia, Kirid, Creti.*

CRETHI, i. q. Philistæi.

CRETICUM mare, the portion of the Mediterranean bet. Peloponnesus and Crete.

CRETŎPŎLIS, a town of Pisidia, N. of Termessus. *Buttakli.*

CREUSIS (Creusa), the port of Thespiæ in Bœotia, on Alcyonium mare, N.W. of Pagæ. *Livadostro.*

CREVENIA, a town of the Cavii, Illyria, bet. Epicaria and Gabuleus.

CRIMISA, I. a r. of Bruttium, falling into the sea at Crimisa. *Fiumenica.* II. a pr. of Bruttium, at Crimisa. *Capo d'Alice.* III. *postea* Paternum, a town of Bruttium, at the mouth of Crimisa fl., bet. Roscianum (27) and Neæthus fl. (12), on Via Trajana. Built by Philoctetes, whose tomb was shown there. *Ciro.*

CRIMISUS (Crinisus, Crimesus) fl., a r. of Sicily, falling into Hypsa fl., s. of Entella. The locality of the decisive defeat of the Carthaginians by Timoleon. *San Bartolomeo.*

CRINACCUM, a town of the Petrocorii, Aquitania II., bet. Vesunna N.E. and Cortorate W.

CRISPIANA, a town of Pannonia, bet. Cimbriana (25) and Arrabo (25). *Sarkany.*

CRISSA, a town of Phocis, towards the N.E. extremity of Crissæus sin., bet. Cirrha and Delphi. Destroyed by order of the Amphictyonic council. *Crisso.*

CRISSÆUS campus, a plain in Phocis, bet. Cirrha and Crissa, where the Pythian games were celebrated.

CRISSÆUS sin., a bay of Corinthicus sin., bet. Phocis and Locris, extending to Cirrha. *G. di Salona.*

CRITALLA (Tiralli), a town of Cataonia, Cappadocia, where Xerxes assembled his land army.

CRITE, a town of the Crobyzi, Mœs., on the Euxine, bet. Odessus and Naulochus.

CRITHOTE, I. a pr. of Acarnania, over against Phorcys portus in Ithaca ins., N.W. of Astacus. *C. Candilla.* II. a town of Chersonesus Thracia, on the Hellespont, N. of Gallipolis. Founded by Miltiades.

CRIUMETŎPON pr., I. a pr. of the Damnonii, Brit. *Ram Head.* II. the s.w. extremity of Creta ins., over against Phycus prom. in Africa (125). *C. Crio.* III. the s. extremity of Taurica Chersonesus., s.e. of Palacium. *Ajadagh, Kandjes Borun.*

CRIUS fl., a r. of Achaia, falling into Corinthiacus sin., N.W. of Aristonautæ.

CRIVA, a demus of Attica, of the tribe Antiochis.

CRIXIA, a town of the Ilvates, in Liguria, on Via Æm. Scaura, bet. Canalicum (10) and Aquæ Statiellæ (22). *Near Cairo N.*

CROBYZI, a maritime people of Mœsia Inf., on the confines of Thrace.

CROCALA ins., an isl. of Gedrosia, off the w. mouth of the Indus (15).

CROCEÆ, a town of Laconia, bet. Harplea and Gythium. Noted for a fine hard stone.

CROCIACONUM (Crociatonum, Cronciaconnum, Croneiaconnum), a town of the Unelli, Lugdunensis II., bet. Alauna N.W. and Augustodurum S.E. *Turqueville, near Andouville.*

CROCIUS campus (Athamantius campus), a plain of Phthiotis, Thessaly, on both sides of Amphrysus fl., towards its source. *Krokos.*

CROCOCALANA, a town of the Coritani, Brit., bet. Lindum and Ad Pontem (7). *Near Warren House.*

CROCODILONPOLIS, I. a town of Thebais, on the Nile, L., bet. Aphroditopolis and Ptolemais Hermii (2 geog. m.). Here crocodiles were worshipped. *Embeshunda.* II. Ad Mœrin, i. q. Arsinoë.

CROCODILUM prom., a pr. of Cyrenaica, w. above Boreum prom.

CROCODILUS m., a summit of Amanus m., Ciliciæ, towards Issus.

CROCYLIUM, I. a town of the Apodoti, in Ætolia, s.w. of Tichium. II. a fortress of Ithaca.

CRODUNUM, a town of the Volcæ Tectosages, Narbonensis, bet. Tolosa and Narbo.

CROMI (Cromni), a town of Arcadia, 10 m. s.w. from Megalopolis. *Crano.*

CROMMYON, I. the extremity of Cyprus, w. of Lapethus, over against Anemurium prom., Cilicia. *C. Cormakiti.* II. a town of Corinthia, on Saronicus sin., bet. Sidus and Megara. Named after Crommus, son of Neptune. The haunt of the robber Sinis, slain by Theseus. *Kinetta.*

CROMNA, a Greek town of Paphlagonia, on the coast, 15 m. E. from Amestris, whither its inhabitants were transferred by Amestris. *Cromena.*

CROMON, a town of Arcadia.

CRONIUM mare, i. q. Pigrum.

CROTALLA, a town of Bruttium, on Crotalus fl. *Roccella.*

CROTALUS fl., a r. of Bruttium, falling into Scylleticus sin. N.E. of Scylletium. *Corace.*

CROTŌNA, a city of Bruttium, on Tarentinus sin., at the mouth of Æsarus fl., bet. Petelia (13) and Lacinium prom. (6). Founded by Myscellus of Achaia, *circa* 715 B.C.; named from the hero Croton. Memorable as the residence of Pythagoras. The birthplace of Milo, and of the physician Democedes. *Cotrone.*

CRUMERUM (Curta), a town of Valeria, Pannonia, on the Danube above Acincum. *Gran.*

CRUNI, I. a stream of Triphylia, Elis, near Chalcis. II. a pr. of Cilicia Trachea, 5½ m. N.E. from Pisurgia. *C. Crauni.* III. *postea* Dionysiopolis, a port of the Cro-

byzi, Mœs., on the Euxine, bet. Tetrisia and Odessus.

CRUPTORICIS VILLA, a town of the Frisii, where 400 Romans killed themselves to avoid falling into the hands of the barbarians. *Hem Ryk.*

CRUSINIA, a town of the Sequani, Maxima Sequanorum, on Dubis fl., L., bet. Visontio and Pons Dubis.

CRUSIS (Crossæa), a maritime district of Chalcidice, Macedonia, on Thermaicus sin., bet. Gigonium prom. and Olynthus.

CRUSTUMERIUM (Crustumium), a town of Sabinium, on the Tiber, 2 m. above Fidenæ. A colony from Alba. Subjugated by the elder Tarquin. Noted for its wine and its pears. *Marcigliano Vecchio.*

CRUSTUMIUS fl., a r. of Umbria, falling into the sea N.W. of Pisaurum. *Conca.*

CRYA (Criassus, Carya; *surnamed* Fugitivorum), a maritime town of Caria, E. of Caunus. *Cari.*

CRYON fl., a r. of Lydia, falling into Hermus fl. w. of Magnesia Ad Sipylum.

CRYPTA NEAPOLITANA, *vide* Pausilypus m.

CRYPTUS (Amithoscuta) portus, a port of the Omanitæ, Arabiæ, E. of Mysecros fl. *Muscat.*

CTENUS portus, a bay of Taurica Chersonesus, at Eupatoria.

CTESĪPHON, a city of Assyria, on the Tigris, opposite Seleucia. The later capital of the Parthian empire. *Al Modain.*

CTIMENE, a city of Dolopia, in Thessaly, towards the N.W. shore of Xynias lac. *Ctemeno.*

CUARIUS (Curalius) fl., a r. of Estiæotis, Thessaly, falling into Peneus fl. at Pharycadon.

CUBALLUS, a fortress of Galatia, on the borders of Phrygia Epict., N.E. of Plitendus.

CUBENA, a town of Armenia, s.E. of Artaxata. *Djulfa.*

CUCCIS, a town of Pannonia, on the Danube, bet. Cornacum (13) and Milata. *Near Suszey.*

CUCULLÆ (Castellum Cucullus), a town of the Alauni, Noricum, on Jovanus fl. above Juvavia (14). *Kuchl.*

CUCULUM, a mountain fortress of the Peligni, on the confines of the Marsi. *Cucullo.*

CUCUNDA, a town of the Zichi, Sarmat., E. of Masatica.

CUCUSUS, a town of Cataonia, Cappadocia, and subsequently of Armenia, near the source of Pyramus fl., s.E. of Comana, bet. Ariarathia (62) and Laranda. *Cocsou.*

CUDA fl., a r. of Lusitania, falling into the Durius near Roboretum. It separated the Lusitani from the Vettones. *Coa.*

CUDETUS fl., a r. of the Bistones, Thrace, falling into the Ægean below Pistyrus.

CUDUPÆ, a people of India e. Gangem, on Serus fl., N. of the Bari.

CULARO, *postea* Gratianopolis, a town of the Uceni, Viennensis, on the Rhone, L., N. of Catorissium. *Grenoble.*

CULCUA, Brit., i. q. Calleva.

CULCUL (Culcua), a town of Mauritania Cæsar., bet. Berzeo (25) and Igilgilis, w. of Cirta. A colonia.

CULICI, a general name with Pliny, of the Alutrenses, Asseriates, and several other small Alpine tribes.

CULICONES, a tribe of Rhæti, on the N.E. shore of Larius lac. *Val di Colico.*

CULLUCITANA (Collops Parvus), a port of Mauritania, 7 m. w, from Zaca. *At Ras Hadid.*

CULLU (Chulli, Collops Magnus), a town of Numidia, on Olcachites sin., w. bet. Rusicada (6 geog. m.) and Pacciana. Noted for its purple dye. *Collo.*

CUMANA, a fortress of Iberia, near Caspiæ Portæ.

CUMANUS (Crater, Campanus) sin., a bay of Tyrrhenium mare, at Neapolis, bet. Misenum prom. and Surrentinum prom. *G. di Napoli; Bay of Naples.*

CUMÆ, a maritime city of Campania, on Via Domitiana, bet. Liternum (6) and Puteoli (3). Founded by a colony from Eubœa, under Hippocles of Cyme and Megasthenes of Chalcis 1050 B.C. Taken by the Samnites 418 B.C. A colonia of Augustus and municipium. The oracle of the Cumæan Sibyl was in a chamber hewn out of the solid rock here. *Cuma.*

CUMÆUS sin., i. q. Elæaticus.

CUMERIUM prom., a pr. of Picenum, at Ancona. *Monte Comero, Monte Gnasco.*

CUMINARIUS vicus, a town of the Carpetani, Tarraconensis, near the Tagus, N.E. of Toletum. Named from its cumin. *San Cruz de la Zarza.*

CUNARUS m., a summit (considered the highest) of the Apennines, in the country of the Vestini, on the borders of Picenum, N. of Cutina. *Monte Corno, Il Gran Sasso.*

CUNAXA, a village of Babylonia, bet. the Euphrates and the Tigris, N.W. of Seleucia. The death-place of Cyrus.

CUNETIO, a town of the Atrebates, Brit., w. of Spinæ. *Marlborough.*

CUNEUM (Patanion) prom., a pr. of the Cuneus, Lusitan., bet. Ossonoba w. and Balsa E. *Cabo de Santa Maria.*

CUNEUS, the coast of Lusitania, bet. the Anas and the sea. Named from its supposed wedge-like form. *Algarve* (Arabic, "the west").

CUNEUS AUREUS, a town of the Venonetes, Rhætia, bet. Lapidaria (17) and Tarvesedum (10). *Splugen.*

CUNI, a town of India, bet. Alexandria Sogdiorum and Codrona.

CUNICI, a town of Balearis Maj., on the N.E. coast.

CUNICULARIÆ ins., islets of Sardinia, off Cunicularum prom. s.

CUNICULARUM prom., a pr. of Sardinia, at the w. entrance of Caralitanus sin. *Capo di Pula.*

CUNUSITANI, a people of Sardinia, on Tyrsus fl., towards its source, bet. the Balari N. and the Ruacenses s.

CUPPÆ, a town of the Triballi, Mœs., on the Danube, bet. Punicum and Ad Novas.

CUPRA MARITIMA, a Tyrrhenian town of Picenum, on the coast, s. of Castrum Firmanum. Named from a temple of Cupra, the Tyrrhenian Juno, restored by Hadrian. *Grotte a Mare,* or *Marano.*

CUPRA MONTANA, a Tyrrhenian town of Picenum, in the mountains, on the L. bank of Æsis fl. *Near Masaccio d' Iesi.*

CURENSIS fl., a r. of Sabinium, running by Cures into the Tiber, below Capena.

CURES, a Tyrrhenian city of Sabinium, N. of Eretum, on Curensis fl. The birth-place of Numa Pompilius, and further notable as the place whence the Romans derived the name of Quirites. S.E., at Mandela, stood the "Sabine farm" of Horace. *Correse.*

CURETES, "shorn," a tribe of Leleges, the original settlers of Ætolia, deriving their name from their custom of shaving off the frontal hair.

CURETIS, the early name of Ætolia.

CURGONII, Hispaniæ, i. q. Murbogii.

CURIA, I. a town of the Otadeni, Brit., 4 geog. m. from Colanica. *Borthwick Castle.* II. of the Suanitæ, Rhæt., bet. Lapidaria and Magia. *Coire.*

CURIANUM prom., a pr. of the Medulli, Aquitania II., at the s. entrance of the Garumna. *Pointe d'Arcachon.*

CURIAS prom., a peninsula of Cyprus, E. of Curium. *C. Gatto.*

CURICA (Curgia), a town of the Celtici, Bætica, N.W. of Ilipa.

CURICTA (Curiacte), an isl. of the Adriatic, one of the Liburnides ins., s. of Absyrtides ins. *Veglia.*

CURICTUM, a town of Curicta ins.

CURIONES, a tribe of Hermunduri, on Mœnus fl., towards its source.

CURIOSOLITES, I. a people of Lugdunensis IV., N.E. of the Osismii. *Diocèse de St. Malo.* II. their capital, N.W. of Condate. *Corseult*, 5 m. w. from *Dinan.*

CURIUS m., a m. of Ætolia, N. of Chalcis, overlooking Pleuron ; whence, according to some writers, the Curites of Ætolia derived their name.

CURIUM, an Argive city of Cyprus, s. within Treton prom., E. at the mouth of Lycus fl. Noted for its copper ore. *Episkopia.*

CURMILIACA, a town of the Bellovaci, Belgica II., bet. Samarobriva N. and Cæsaromagus.

CURRAPHUS, a town of the Strophi, Babyl., bet. Abara and Thamara.

CURTA, Pannoniæ, i. q. Crumerum.

CURTAIA, a port of the Omanitæ, Arabiæ, s.w. of Cryptus portus. *Kuriat.*

CURUBIS, a maritime town of Zeugitana, bet. Clypea and Neapolis (16). A colonia (Col. Fulvia). *Gurba.*

CURVANCAS m., a summit of the Alpes Carnicæ, N. of Tasinemetum.

CUSA fl., a r. of Mauritania Ting., falling into the Atlantic bet. Rusibis and Dyas fl.

CUSÆ, a town of Thebais, on the Nile, bet. Lycopolis (35) and Hermupolis (24). *Kusieh.*

CUSIBIS, a town of the Oretani, Tarraconensis, S.S.E. of Oretum.

CUSUM, a town of Pannonia Inf., on the Danube, bet. Acimincum and Milata (16).

CUSUS fl., *postea* Granua, a r. of the Quadi, Germania Magna, falling into the Danube at Acincum. *Gran.*

CUTATISION, Colch., i. q. Cytæa.

CUTILIÆ, I. a town of Sabinium, on Cutiliensis lac., R., bet. Reate (8) and Interocrea (6), on Via Salaria. An Umbrian settlement. *Paterno.* II. lacus, a lake of Sabinium, at Cutiliæ; called the umbilicus, or navel, of Italy, being equidistant (76 m.) from the two seas. *Pozzo Ratignano, Lago di Contigliano.*

CUTINA, a fortress of the Piceni, near Cunarus m. *Citta Aquana.*

CYAMON prom., a pr. on the N. coast of Crete, E. of Psacum prom. *C. Maleca.*

CYAMOSURUS fl., a r. of Sicily, rising in Nebrodes m. w. of Adrianus fl., and, by its junction with that stream at Adranum, forming Symæthus fl. *Trachino.*

CYANE fl., a stream of Sicily, springing from the opening in the earth made by Pluto when carrying off Proserpine, and falling into the Anapus. According to Ovid, a transformation of the nymph Cyane. II. a town of Lycia, near Aperiæ. *Tristomo.*

CYANEA ins., an isl. of Bithynia, S.E. of Coracium prom.

CYANEÆ (Symplegades, "dashers ;" Syndromades, Planctai, "wanderers") ins., two rocks within the entrance to the Bosporus Thracius. Fabled to be floating rocks, ever and anon dashing against each other. *Pavonare.*

CYANES (Gyenus), a town of Ecretice, Colch., at the mouth of Cyaneus fl.

CYANEUS fl., a r. of Colchis, falling into the Euxine, bet. Tarsuras fl. and Sicanabis, at Cyanes.

CYANUM prom., a pr. of Crete, s. of Dictamnium. *Cheronisi.*

CYATHUS fl., a r. of Ætolia, which, after running through lakes Trichonius and Conope, falls into Achelous fl. N. of Conope. *Neschio.*

CYBALE, a town of Chaldæa, bet. Thamara and Donantilia.

CYBELIA, a maritime town of Ionia, s. of Erythræ.

CYBISTRA, a town of Tyanitis, Cappadocia, N.E. of Tyana. *Kara-hissar.*

CYCALA, a demus of Attica, of the tribe Æantis.

CYCESIUM, a town of Pisatis, Elis, on Alpheus fl., w. of Olympia.

CYCHREA, the early name of Salamis, after the hero Cychreus.

CYCLADES ins., islands in the Ægean, around Delos. The islands comprehended within this designation were : Andros, Ceos, Cimolus, Cythnus, Delos, Gyarus, Melos, Myconus, Naxos, Olearus, Paros, Prepesinthus, Rhenea, Seriphus, Siphnus, Syros, and Tenos. Settled, 1. by Phœnicians, Carians, and Leleges ; 2. by Persians ; and 3. by Athenians.

CYCLADIUM, Bithyniæ, i. q. Lycadium.

CYCLOPES (Chirogasteres), a caste of Phœnicians, devoted to architecture. The authors of the Cyclopean edifices, still extant at Mycenæ, Argos, &c.

CYCLOPIS ins., an isl. of Rhodes, towards Syme ins.

CYCLOPUM SCOPULI, three Needle-islets of Sicily, E. bet. Acis and Adrix. *Fariglioni.*

CYDAMUS, a town of Libya Interior, w. of Thillabari.

CYDANTIDÆ, a demus of Attica, of the tribe Ægeis.

CYDATHENÆUM, a demus of Attica, of the tribe Pandionis. The birth-place of Nicochares, the comedian, and Andocydes, the orator.

CYDNA, a port of Lycia, 8 m. from Hiera prom.

CYDNI, a people of Pannonia, on Arrabo fl.

CYDNUS fl., a r. of Cilicia Campestris, rising in Taurus m. above Tarsus, and falling into the sea at Rhegma lacus. Noted for its excessive coldness, which nearly killed Alexander, and for the pageant of Cleopatra. *Tersoos.*

CYDONEA ins., one of Leucæ ins., Æolis, with warm springs.

CYDONIA, a town of Crete, on the N. coast, bet. Minoum and Aptera. *Jerami.*

CYDRARA, Phrygiæ, i. q. Laodicea.

CYDRIÆ, a town of the Brygi, Illyria, E. of Lychnitis palus, near Brygias.

CYINDA, a fortress of Cilicia Campestris, above Anchiale.

CYIZA, a maritime town of Gedrosia, bet. Alambatis prom. and Daranabilla.

CYLICRANES, a tribe of Malienses, Thessaly, towards Trachis.

CYLINDRINE, a district of India, about the source of the Ganges.

CYLISTARNUS fl., a r. of Lucania, falling into Tarentinus sin., s. of Siris fl. *Racanello.*

CYLLA (Chelidonia), a town of Phrygia Parorea, bet. Synnada and Antiochia Pisidia, E. of Metropolis.

CYLLANUS CAMPUS, the plain of Phrygia Parorea, about Cylla. *Sitshanli.*

CYLLENE, I. a m., the highest of the range which, extending E. from Erymanthus m., separates Arcadia from Achaia, situate bet. Stymphalus and Pheneus. Sacred to Mercury. *Zyria.* II. the harbour of Elis, on the N. coast, E. of Chelonatus prom., 15 m. from its capital. Named after Cyllenius, the Arcadian. The Pelasgic port of embarkation for Italy. *Lechena.*

CYLLENICUS sinus, a gulf of the Ionian s. at Cyllene, Elis.

CYMARIA, a port of Caria, 8 m. from Pasada.

CYME, chief of the twelve cities of Æolis Asiatica, on Cumæus (Eleaticus) sin., w. from Myrina, *surnamed* Phriconis from Phricium m., in Locris, the previous seat of its Æolian colonizers. Originally a Pelasgic city, and named from the amazon Cume. The residence of Homer's ancestors, and of the father of Hesiod. The birth-place of Ephorus, the Nestorian. *Sanderly.* II. a town of Euboea, near Chalcis, the seat of the colonizers of the Italian Cumæ.

CYMINE, Dolopiæ, i. q. Ctimene.

CYNÆTHA, a town of Arcadia, under Aroanius m., N.W. of Clitor. Its inhabitants were noted for their profligacy and barbarism. *Calavrita.*

CYNETES (Cynesii, Cunæi), the people of the Cuneus, Lusitania.

CYNETICUM LITTUS, the coast of Narbonensis, towards the Pyrenees.

CYNIA PALUS, a salt lake of Acarnania, on the s. coast, bet. Melite pal. and Uria pal., 7½ m. long by 2 broad. Probably an early mouth of Achelous fl. *Lago d'Antolico.*

CYNŎPŎLIS, I. a town of Heptanomis, on an island in the Nile, opposite Co. II. of Lower Egypt, on the Sebennytic branch of the Nile, 5 geog. m. w. from Thmuis. Named from the circumstance that dogs were worshipped there. *Busir?*

CYNORTIUM m., a m. of Argolis, near Epidaurus.

CYNOSCEPHÄLÆ, "dog's head," I. a place in Boeotia, bet. Leuctra and Thebes. II. a hill of Pelasgiotis, Thessaly, near Scotussa. The scene of the defeat of Philip of Macedon by Flaminius, 197 B.C.

CYNOSSĒMA, I. "dog's tomb," a place near Calydon, Ætolia, where Atalanta's dog, killed by the boar, was buried. II. a pr. of Attica, the E. termination of Pentelicus m. towards Marathon. III. (Onagnathos), a pr. of Caria, at the s. entrance of Doridis sin. *C. Aloupo,* or *Volpe.* IV. a town of Chersonesus Thracia, on the Hellespont. Named from the metamorphosis and death here of Hecuba. Noted for the victory of the Athenian fleet under Thrasybulus and Thrasyllus over the Peloponnesian allies. *Kelidil-bahar.*

CYNOSTHRIUM prom., a pr. of Pamphylia, bet. Cestrus fl. and Eurymedon fl.

CYNOSURA, "dog's tail," prom., a headland of Attica, in Saronicus sin., the w. extremity of Pentelicus m. *Cape Cavala.*

CYNTHUS m., a m. of Delos, giving their surname to Apollo and Diana.

CYNURIA, a district of Arcadia, on the confines of Argolis.

CYNOSURIA, an ancient district of Megaris.

CYNUS, the port of Opus Locrid., 7½ m. N.W. from the capital. The burial-place of Pyrrha. *Lebanitis.*

CYPARISSEIS fl., a r. of Messenia, rising in Ægaleus m., L., falling into Cyparissus sin. near Cyparissia. *Arcadhia.*

CYPARISSIA, I. a town of Laconia, on Laconicus sin., s. of Acriæ, close to Asopus. *Rupino; Rampino; Castel Kyparissi.* II. of Messenia, on Cyparissius sin., w. of Messine. *Arcadhia.* III. a name of Samos.

CYPARISSIUM prom., a headland of Messenia, the s. extremity of Cyparissius sin. *C. Konello,* or *C. Apidaglia.*

CYPARISSIUS sinus, a gulf of Ionium mare, extending 36 m. on either side from Cyparissia. *G. d'Arcadhia.*

CYPARISSUS, "full of cypresses," a town of Phocis, on Parnassus m., bet. Delphi and Lebadia. *Panies.*

CYPASIS, a town of Chersonesus Thracia, on Melas sin., s. of Cardia.

CYPHANTA, a town of Laconia, N.W. of Zarax, 1½ m. from the sea. In ruins in Pausanias' time. *Kyphanto.*

CYPHARA (Cypæra), a fortress of Dolopia, Thessaly, on the frontier of Phthiotis, on Phœnix fl., below Phalacthia. *Kyphara.*

CYPHUS, I. a m. of Perrhæbia, Thessaly, one of the Olympus range, overlooking the cognominal town. II. a town of Perrhæbia, Thessaly, towards Ascuris palus.

CYPRIÆ ins., three islets of Lycia, in the Lycium mare, towards Phaselis. *Trinesia.*

CYPRII, a demus of Attica.

CYPRUS ins., "cypress-growing" (Sphecia, Cerastis, Cryptus), an isl. of the Mediterranean, equidistant bet. Phœnicia and Cilicia. The third in extent of the seven great islands of the Mediterranean. In length 140 m., in greatest breadth 50. Colonized from Phœnicia, Greece, Crete, and Egypt. *Cyprus: Kibris.*

CYPSARIA, a maritime town of Syrtica Regio, bet. Casæ and Præsidium.

CYPSILA, I. a town of Arcadia, N.W. of Megalopolis. Founded by Cypsilus. II. of the Apsynthii, Thrace, on Egnatia Via, bet. Trajanopolis (29) and Siracella (30). *Ipsala.*

CYPTASIA (Cloptasa), Paphlagonia, i. q. Gurzubanthon.

CYRBA, an early name of Hierapytna, in Crete.

CYRE fl., a stream of Cyrenaica, near Cyrene, probably giving name to the district.

CYRENAICA, a district of Africa, bounded N. by the Mediterranean, s. by Libya, E. by Marmarica, at Chersonesus Magna, and w. by Africa Propria, at Philænorum Aræ. Made a Roman province circa 90 B.C., in conjunction with Crete. *Barca.*

CYRENE, capital of Cyrenaica, 10 m. inland, s.w. from its port, Apollonia. Built 630 B.C. by a Lacedæmonian colony from Thera ins., under Battus, from whom the Cyrenians were also called Battiadæ. The seat of the Aristippian or Cyrenaic sect. The district was noted for its fine horses. *Kayran; Kyreune; Kurin.*

CYRESCHATA (Cyropolis), a town of Sogdiana, N.E. of Maracanda. Built by Cyrus; destroyed by Alexander, but restored.

CYRETIÆ, a town of Perrhæbia, Thessaly, on Titaresius fl., below Oloossoon. *Tcheritchani.*

CYRHADÆ, a demus of Attica, of the tribe Acamantis.

CYRNUS, a town of Eubœa, near Carystus.

CYROPOLIS, I. a port of the Cadusii, Media, on the Caspian, N. of Amardus fl. *Reschd.* II. a town of Persis Proper, w. of Pasargada. III. of Sogdiana, i. q. Cyreschata.

CYRRHESTĬCA, I. a district of Emathia, Macedonia, about Cyrrhus. II. of Syria, bet. the plain of Antioch w., the Euphrates E., Commagene N., and Chalybonitis s.

CYRRHUS, I. capital of Cyrrhestica, Macedonia, 16 m. N.W. from Pella. *Palæo-Castro.* II. of Cyrrhestica, Syriæ, bet. Chanunia and Gindarus, N.E. of Antiochia. The birth-place of Avidius Cassius.

CYRTHANEUS portus, *vide* Scythranius.

CYRTII, a people of Persia, towards the Mardi.

CYRTONE, a town of Bœotia, 2½ m. N.W. from Holmones, on Ptoon m.

CYRUS fl. I. (Agradatas), a r. of Asia, rising N. of Pasargada and falling into Bagradas fl. E. of Apostana. II. (Corus, Cyrnus), of Asia, rising in Paryadrus m. below Artanissa, and, after separating Iberia and Albania from Armenia Major, falling into the Caspian by twelve mouths below Sanina. *Kur.* III. of Media, falling into the Caspian at Charax.

CYSSUS (Casystes), the s. port of Erythræ, Ionia. *Tchesmeh.*

CYTÆA (Cuta), I. capital of Colchis, near Phasis fl., R., below Surapona. The city of Medea. II. a maritime town of Taurica Chersonesus, s. bet. Cimmerium and Acra.

CYTÆUM, I. the N.E. extremity of Taprobane. II. a town on the N. coast of Crete, s.w. of Dium prom. *Near Policastro.*

CYTERIUM, a town of Bruttium, near Consentia. *Cerisano.*

CYTHERA, I. *prius* Porphyris, an isl. of Laconia, in the Ægean, 5 m. s.w. from Malea prom. Here Venus rose from the sea. *Cerigo.* II. its capital, on the s.E. coast, 1¼ m. from the sea.

CYTHERON (Cytherus), a demus of Attica, of the tribe Pandionis. One of the twelve divisions of Cecrops.

CYTHERUS fl., a r. of Elis, falling into Alpheus fl., E. near Heraclea. *Lintza.*

CYTHNUS, I. one of the Cyclades, bet. Ceos and Seriphus. Noted for its cheese. The scene of the Pseudo-Nero's adventures. Devastated by Amphytrion. *Thermia.* II. a m. of Delos. *Monte Cintio.* III.

capital of the cognominal island, on the w. coast. *Hevræo-Castro.*

CYTINIUM, a town of Doris, the chief of the Dorica Tetrapolis, w. of Parnassus, on the confines of Locri Ozolæ.

CYTONIUM (Certonium), a maritime town of Æolis Asiatica, s. of Carine. *Kidonia.*

CYTORUM, a Greek town of Paphlagonia, on the coast, 26 m. E. from Amastris, whither its inhabitants were removed by Queen Amastris. *Kidros.*

CYTŌRUS m., a m. of Paphlagonia, overlooking Cytorum. It was noted for its fine boxwood.

CYZICUS, a city of Mysia, on an island in Propontis, E. of Æsepus fl. Built by Cyzicus, son of Apollo, the chief of a Pelasgic colony from Thessaly. Permanently settled by Milesians; connected by a bridge with the continent by Alexander. Under Rome, a free city. Memorable for its siege by Mithridates. The birth-place of Agathocles, Neanthes, &c. *Atraki.*

CYZISTRA (Cosistra), a town of Cilicia Pref., Cappadocia.

D.

DABANA, a town of Mesopotamia, bet. Carræ and Calinicum, near the source of Belias fl.

DABENEGORA, a port of the Caludæi, Arabia Felix, s. of Asaborum prom. *Daba ; Dobba.*

DABERATH, a town of Zebulun, under Tabor m. *Dabira.*

DABLÆ, a town of Bithynia, bet. Tottæum (28) and Dadaslana (40).

DABLAN, a town of Chaldæa, on the Euphrates, L., bet. Donantilia and Aserga.

DABRŌNA fl., a r. of Hibernia s., 10 m. from Bargus fl. *Lee.*

DACHAREMOIZÆ, a people of Arabia Felix, N. of Marithæ montes. *Dar-al-Kharamatah.*

DACHARENI, a people of Arabia Felix, N. of Macoraba. *Tribe of Dwy Daher.*

DACHINABADES, "south land," the coast of India i. Gangem, s. of Larice pens. *Deccan.*

DACIA, a country of Europe, bounded N. by Sarmatia Europæa, at Tyras fl., s. by Mœsia, at the Danube, w. by Pannonia, at the Tibiscus, E. by the Euxine. The country of the Daci, *prius* Daoi. It was distributed into Alpensis under Carpatus m., Mediterranea (central Dacia), and Ripensis, the N. portion. *Transylvania, Wallachia, Moldavia (Bessarabia).*

DACIBYZA, a town of Bithynia, on Astace-nus sin., N. bet. Nicomedia and Lybissa. *Ghebze.*

DACOCA, a town of the Garamæi, Assyria, S.S.E. of Arbela.

DACORA (Daora), I. a town of Cilicene, Cappadocia, near Cæsarea-Mazaca. II. (Thiar), of Osrhoene, Mesopotamia, bet. Apamea and Anthemusias.

DACTONIUM, a town of the Lucenses, Tarraconensis, on Silis fl., R., below Forum Cigurrorum.

DACTYLESMA, a village of Arcadia, s. of Maniæ. The scene of one of Orestes' phrensies.

DADANCANA, a village of Bithynia, bet. Prusias ad Hypium and Bithynium.

DADARA, a town of Arabia, on the Euphrates, bet. Dura and Merrhan.

DADASTANA, a town of Bithynia, bet. Dablæ (40) and Juliopolis (26). The death-place of Jovian.

DADENA, a port of the Caludæi, Arabia, N. of Dabanegora. The abode of Dedan, grandson of Cush. *Daden.*

DADES prom., a pr. of Cyprus, E. of Citium. *C. Chiti.*

DADYBRA, a town of Paphlagonia, near the source of Amnias fl.

DÆANTIUS CAMPUS, the district about Dæas, in Phrygia.

DÆDĂLA, a town of Caria, on Glaucius sin., at the mouth of Ninus fl., 6¼ m. from Callimache. Named from Dædalus, who was bitten to death here by a serpent.

DÆDALIDÆ, a demus of Attica, of the tribe Cecropis.

DÆDALIUM, *prius* Omphale, a fortress of Sicily, s. bet. Agrigentum (18) and Phintæ. The citadel of Phalaris.

DÆMONUM ins., an isl. of Arabia Felix, in the Red Sea, S.E. of Berenice.

DÆTICHÆ, a people of India e. Gangem, bet. Hyphasis and Hesudrus ffl.

DAGDUANA, a town of Arsissa, Mesopotamia, on Arsissa pal. w. *Dedvan.*

DAGOLASSUS (Megalassus), a town of Cappadocia, bet. Zara (20) and Nicopolis (24).

DAGONA (Dogana), a town of Armenia Minor, bet. Sebastia Comassa (15) and Dagolassus (25).

DAGOSIRA, a port of Gedrosia, on Paragon sin., bet. Pasida and Samydace.

DAHÆ, I. a people of Hyrcania, about Hyrcania. II. (Dii, Machærophori), of Thrace, about Rhodope m.

DAIX fl., a r. of Scythia i. Imaum, falling into the Caspian E. of Rymmus fl. *Daik: Ural.*

DALA fl., a r. of Gaul, falling into the Rhodanus, E. of Lemanus lac. *Dala.*

DALANDA (Ladana), a town of Armenia Minor, on the Euphrates.

DALASIS, a maritime district of Cilicia, towards Charanice.

DALDES (Daldia), a town of Lydia, near Mæonia. The birth-place of Artemidorus. *Ghiuldiz.*

DALION fl., a r. of Triphylia, Elis, falling into Alpheus fl. N. of Typana.

DALISANDUS, a town of Cappadocia, near Cydnus fl.

DALITERNI, the early name of the Veragri, from Dala fl.

DALMANUTHA, a town of Galilee, on Gennesareth lacus.

DALMÄTÆ, a people of Illyria, extending along the coast of the Adriatic from Titius fl. to Barbana fl., and to a considerable distance inland.

DALMINIUM (Delmium), capital of the Dalmatæ, Illyria, towards Andetrium.

DAMANIA, a town of Tarraconensis, on Turia fl., L., below Lobetum.

DAMASCUS (Damasek, Darmasek), a city of Syria, and at one time its capital, 176 m. s.w. from Palmyra. Contemporary with Abraham. The scene of St. Paul's first preaching the Gospel. *Damascus; Demeshk; Es Sham.*

DAMASI m., m. of India e. Gangem, bet. Darius fl. and Doanas fl.

DAMASIA, a town of the Vindelici, Rhætia, on Licus fl.

DAMASTIUM, a town of the Perisadii, Illyria. Noted for its silver mines.

DAMNA, I. the largest of Orcades ins., N.E. of Ocetis.   II. a town of Serica, on Œchardes fl.

DAMNIA, a port of the Omanitæ, Arabiæ, s. of Acilla. *Dagma.*

DAMNII, a people of Valentia, Britan., extending across the island s.w. to N.E. from s. of Vidogara sin. to N. of Bodotria Æstuar.

DAMNONII (Dumnonii), a people occupying the w. portion of Britannia I., from w. of Vexalla Æstuar. N. and from E. of Isaca fl. s.   *Devonshire and Cornwall.*

DAMNONIUM prom.. i. q. Ocrinum.

DAN, I. a tribe of Israel, bounded N. by Ephraim at Geser, s. by Juda at Bethsemes, w. by the Mediterranean, and E. by Benjamin, w. of Bethhoron.   II. *prius* Laish, capital of Dan, bet. Cæsarea Panias E. and Rehob. The chief locality of Jeroboam's idolatry. The N. boundary of the Israelites. *Tel el Kady.*

DANA, I. Cappadocia, i. q. Tyana.   II. a port of Taprobane, s. bet. Cytæum prom. and Ornæum prom.   *Tanoal.*

DANAI, the Pelasgi of Argos, so naming themselves from Danaus.

DANALA, a village of Galatia, where the conference bet. Lucullus and Pompey was held.

DANAPRIS fl., i. q. Borysthenes.

DANASTER fl., i. q. Tyras.

DANDACE, a port of Taurica Chersonesus, w. above Eupatoria.

DANDAGULA, capital of the Calingæ, Indiæ, on Manada fl. *Calingaputam.*

DANDARI (Dandaridæ), a people of Sarmatia Asiatica, contiguous to the Sindi.

DANDARICA, a district of Sarmatia Asiatica, on Vardanes fl., R., towards its mouth.

DANDUTI, a tribe of Chatti, Germania, on Adrana fl., R., below the Batti.

DANEUM PORTUS, Ægypti, i. q. Arsinoe-Cleopatris.

DANTHALETÆ (Denseletæ), a tribe of Dardani, Thrace, N. of the Medi, bet. Strymon fl. and the Bessi, under Hæmus m., and in Mœsia, under Scomius m.

DANUBIUS fl., a r. of Europe, rising in Abnoba m. and falling, after a course of 1770 m., into the Euxine by several mouths (6 according to Pliny, 7 according to Strabo). From its mouth to its junction with Savus fl., its early name was Ister.   *Danube; Donau.*

DANUM, a town of the Brigantes, Britan., bet. Legeolium and Agelocum. *Doncaster.*

DAORSI, a tribe of Dalmatæ, Illyria, contiguous to the Ardiæi.

DAPHABA, a town of the Cælatæ, Thrace, on Harpessus fl., bet. Burdextium and Nice.

DAPHNE, I. a town of Lower Egypt, on Bubasticus fl., 16 m. s.w. from Pelusium. II. a fortress of Lycia.   III. a village of Syria, 5 m. s. from Antioch. Noted for its royal pleasure-gardens. It communicated the surname Epidaphne to Antioch. IV. the port of Trapezus.

DAPHNITIS ins., an isl. of the Colobi, in the Red Sea, opposite Sabæ. *Dollaca.*

DAPHNUS, I. a port of Æthiopia, on Erythræum mare, w. of Elephas fl.   II. warm baths of Ionia, in the territory of Clazomenæ.   III. a town of the Locri Opuntii, on Opuntius sin., 2½ m. E. from Cnemis. Extinct in Strabo's time.

DAPHNUSIS palus, a lake of Bithynia, formed by Hypius fl. below Prusias. *L. Effnanly.*

DARA, I. a r. of Carmania, falling into Persicus sin. bet. Bagrada fl. and Ila, opposite Sogdiana ins. It separates the Camelobosci from Rudiane. *Darabin.*   II. a town of Mygdonia, Mesopotamia, N. of

Nisibis. Named by Anastasius, Anasta-siopolis. *Dara-Kardin?*

DARADÆ, a people of Libya Interior, about the mouth of Daradus fl. *The Foulahs.*

DARADAX fl. (Dardes), a r. of Syria, falling into the Euphrates bet. Barbalissus and Eragiza. It separates Cyrrhestica from Syria Proper.

DARADRÆ, a people of Scythia e. Imaum, S.E. of the Byltæ.

DARADUS fl. (Dara), a r. of Libya Interior, falling into the Atlantic. *Senegal.*

DARÆ, a people of Libya Interior. *Darah.*

DARAGAMONIS fl., a r. of Bactria, falling into Oxus fl. E. of Bactrus fl.

DARANABILLA, a port of Gedrosia, bet. Alambatis prom. and Dendrobosa.

DARANDÆ, a people of Drangiana, on the borders of Aria.

DARANISSA, a district of Armenia Interior, N. of Chorzene. *Daranaghi.*

DARANON, a town of the Trocmi, Galatia, bet. Mogaron and Zela.

DARANTASIA (Forum Claudii), capital of the Medulli, Alpes Penninæ, on Isara fl., R., bet. Oblimum and Axima. *Moutiers en Tarentaise.*

DARAPSA, i. q. Drapsaca.

DARDĂNI, a tribe of Pelasgi, from Mœsia or Pæonia, who, under Dardanus their chief, son of Jupiter and Electra, colonized first Samothrace and then Dardania, in Asia Minor, circa 1506 B.C., allying themselves with their brethren the Teucri. Remark-able, amid great barbarism in other respects, for their delight in music.

DARDANIA, I. the portion of Mœsia Superior on the confines of Macedonia, settled by the Dardani. II. the district of Troas, in Asia Minor, colonized by the Dardani, ex-tending along the coast from Rhodius fl. to Rhœteum prom., and inland to the territo-ries of Zeleia, Assus, and Antandros.

DARDANIUM (Dardanis) prom., a pr. of Dar-dania Asiatica, s. of Abydus. *Kepoburun-Puntadei; Barbari.*

DARDĂNUS, I. the capital of Dardania Asiatica, at the foot of Ida m. II. a town of Dardania Asiatica, at Dardanium prom., 7½ m. s. from Abydus.

DARDI, an Illyrian tribe, whom, with the Monades, Diomed found in occupation of a portion of Daunia Apulia, about Trica, and whom he destroyed.

DAREIUM, a town of Parthia-Arpavarcticene, N. of Tabas. *Dehi-Muhammed.*

DARENTIACA, a town of the Tricastini, Vien-nensis, on Druna fl., R., above Augusta Tricastinorum.

DARGIDUS fl., Bactriæ, i. q. Bactrus.

DARGOMANES fl., a r. of Bactriana, rising in Parapomisus m. and falling into the Ochus.

DARINI, a people of Hibernia, E. bet. the Robogdii N. and the Usluntii s. *Down, Armagh, and Antrim.*

DARIORIGUM (Darioritum), capital of the Veneti, Lugdunensis, 14 geog. m. from Portus Namnetum. *Venne; Vannes;* locally, *Wenet.*

DARITIS, a district of Media Magna, w. of the Vadasi.

DARNIS (Zarine), one of the five chief towns of Pentapolis, Cyrenaicæ, bet. Azilis and Aphrodisias. *Derne.*

DAROMA, a toparchy of Judæa, N. of Ge-raritica.

DARON, a town of the Memnones, Meroe, E. of Meroe.

DARRÆ (Kedarræ), a people of Arabia Felix, on the Red Sea, bet. the Sideni and the Banubari. *About El Khedheyre.* There was a tribe of the same name on the S.E. coast, among the Omanitæ.

DARSA (Dyrzila, Zorzila), a town of Pisidia, bet. Cormasa and Lysinoe.

DARTORITUM, capital of the Veneti, Lugdu-nensis III., w.n.w. of Duretia.

DASCŎN, a fortress of Sicily, on the coast, N.E. of Plemmyrium prom.

DASCUSA, a town of Melitene Prefectura, Cappadocia.

DASCYLITIS (Dascylos) palus, a lake of Bithynia, on Rhyndacus fl., R., towards Dascylium, formed by Odrysses fl. *L. Diaskilo.*

DASCYLIUM, I. a name of Bithynia and Mysia, as a Persian Satrapy. II. a city of Bithynia, on Propontis, bet. Rhyndacus fl. and Gebes fl. *Diaskilo.*

DASEÆ, a town of Arcadia, 1 m. s. from Macareæ.

DASENA, a town of Arbelitis, Assyria, bet. Arbela and Gaugamela.

DASMENDA (Dasmena), *postea* Tzamandus, a fortress of Cappadocia, on the confines of Commagene.

DASSARETIA, the country of the Dassaretæ, Illyria, round Lychnitis palus. *Daulas.*

DASTARCUM, a fortress of Cataonia.

DATII, a tribe of Ruteni, Aquitania, on the Garumna, L., bet. Aginnum and Lactora. *About Testet.*

DATOS, a maritime town of the Edones, Thrace, close to Neapolis, and by Leake identified with it. Noted for its gold mines and its fertility. Founded by Calis-tratus the Athenian.

DAUCONES, a people of Scandia ins. s.

DAULIA, a town of the Eordeti, Illyria, N.E. of Asparagium.

DAULIS (Daulia, Daulium), a town of Phocis, 3½ m. w. from Panopeus. The scene of the story of Philomele and Procne. *Daulia.*

DAUNI, a people of Apulia, a mixed race of Illyrian Japyges and Osci, occupying the upper portion of the region above the Peuceti, from whom they were separated by a line drawn from Aufidus fl. to Silvium. Named from their king, Daunus, identified by tradition as the father-in-law of Diomed.

DAUTONIA, a town of the Oseriatæ, Pannonia, bet. Piretæ and Siscia.

DAVABA (Davada), a town of Scythia i. Imaum, E. of Asbabota.

DAVARA, a town of Cappadocia, in Taurus m., 6 geog. m. from Irenopolis. *Dalak.*

DAVIANUM, a town of the Vocontii, Viennensis, E.S.E. of Cambonum.

DAXATA, a town of Serica.

DAXIMONITIS, a district of Pontus, on Iris fl., below Comana.

DEA VOCONTIORUM, capital of the Vocontii, Gallia Viennensis, on Druna fl., R., bet. Lucus Augusti (12) and Augusta Tricastinorum (23). *Luc, near Vaugelas.*

DEBA, a town of Mesopotamia, on the Tigris, R., S.E. of Nisibis. *Eski-Mosul.*

DEBÆ (Dedebæ, nicknamed by the Greeks Cinædocolpitæ), a people of Arabia Felix, on Bætius fl. *Tribe of Zebeyde.*

DEBELTUS, a town of the Selletæ, Thrace, on the Euxine, bet. Anchialus and Apollonia.

DEBIR, *prius* Kirjath-Sepher, Kiriath-Sannai, I. a sacerdotal city of Juda, bet. Duma N.E. and Beerseba S.W. II. a town of Gad, E. of the Jordan. III. of Benjamin.

DEBOMA, a town of the Eordeti, Illyria, on Apsus fl., N.W. of Ilion. *Dobrin.*

DEBORAS, *surnamed* Inferior, a town of the Penestæ, on Drilo fl., below Deborus Superior. *Dibre.* II. Superior, of the Penestæ, on Drilo Niger fl., below Uscana. *Dibre.*

DEBOTES fl., a r. of Sardinia, falling into the sea towards Bitia. *Iscagessa.*

DEBRIS, a town of the Garamantes, Africæ.

DECANTÆ (Cantæi), a maritime tribe of Caledonii, E., about Vara Æst. and Tuæsis Æst. *On Cromarty Frith.*

DECAPOLIS, Bethsan, a district of Judea, principally E. of the Jordan, N. of Ammonitis. Named from its ten confederate cities.

DECASTADIUM, a town of Bruttium, bet. Peripolium and Leucopetra prom., on Via Trajana. *Castitio.*

DECELEIA, a demus of Attica, of the tribe Hippothoontis, bet. Cephissia and Oropus, (15). It was the Deceleians who indicated Helena's hiding-place to the Tyndaridæ. *Varibobi.*

DECEM PAGI, a town of the Mediomatrices, Belgica I., on Saravus fl., bet. Ad Duodecim and Pons Saravi. *Dieuze.*

DECETIA (Degena), a town of the Ædui, Lugdunensis I., on an island of the Liger, bet. Nivernum, N.W., and Aquæ Nisenæ, S.E. *Decise.*

DECIANA, a town of the Indigetes, Tarraconensis, N.E. of Juncaria.

DECIATES (Liguri Transalpini), I. a maritime tribe of Salyes, Narbonensis, about Antipolis, E. of the Oxybii. II. their capital, i. q. Antipolis.

DECIUM, a town of the Varduli, Tarraconensis, S.E. of Deva.

DECENNOVIUM, a canal of Latium, running from Forum Appii southwards, parallel with Via Appia.

DECTUNINES, a people of Alpes Maritimæ.

DECUMA, a town of the Turtuli, Bætica, on the Bætis, L., above Corbula.

DEDAN, a district of Arabia Petræa, S.E. of Idumæa. The seat of the children of Dedan, son of Jokshan. *Vide Daden.*

DEGLANE, a town of Albania, on Alazonius fl., 6 geog. m. N. from Nega.

DEHAVITES, a people of Persia.

DEIBICCÆ, a port of Margiana, on the confines of Parthia, E. of Apabarcticene.

DEIPNAS, a town of Thessaly, near Larissa, where Apollo was entertained on his return from Tempe.

DEIRADES, a demus of Attica, of the tribe Leontis.

DELAS fl., Assyriæ, i. q. Gorgus.

DELBIA, a name of Derbe, Lycaonia, from the juniper it produced.

DELGOVITIA, a town of the Brigantes, Brit., bet. Derventio (13) and Prætorium (25). *Near Skipton, N.*

DELIUM, I. a port of Bœotia, 5 m. N.E. from Tanagra, on the Euripus. Noted for the battle between the Athenians and Bœotians, in which Alcibiades saved the life of Socrates. *Dramisi.* II. (Edelium), a town of Laconia, on Argolicus sin., with an oracle of Apollo.

DELOS (Asteria, Ortygia, Cynthia), an isl. of the Ægean, the centre of the Cyclades, bet. Rhenea and Myconus. It arose from the sea, as a resting-place for Latona. Here was celebrated the quinquennial festival of the Greeks, called Delia. The birthplace of Apollo and Diana, whence the island was deemed so sacred that no burials were permitted in it. *Sdille* or

Delos. II. a m. of Bœotia, at Tegyra, sacred to Apollo.

DELPHI, *prius* Pytho, a city of Phocis, under Parnassus, N.E. of Crissa. The seat of the famous oracle. The original temple, built 1263 B.C. was of brass; the second, of stone, erected by Trophonius and Agamedes, was destroyed by fire 548 B.C.; the third, erected by the Alcmæonidæ, was commenced shortly afterwards. The fane of the temple was said to be on the exact centre of the earth. *Castri.*

DELPHINIUM, I. the port of Oropus, Attica, at the mouth of Oropus fl. II. of Chios ins., on the E. coast, opposite Œnussæ ins. *Porto Delfino.*

DELTA (Rahab, Rib), the portion of Lower Egypt, comprising the various mouths of the Nile. Named from its form, which, with Cercasura as the apex, and Canopus w. and Pelusium E. as the base, represents the Greek Δ. Some geographers describe two lesser deltas, within the greater.

DEMETÆ (*Celticè*, Di-moi-atta, "people of the southern plain"), a port of Britannia II., occupying the coast w. of the Silures, and s. of Stucia fl.

DEMETRIAS, I. a prom. of Assyria, near Arbela. *Kerkuk.* II. a ward or tribe of Athens. Named after Demetrius Poliorcetes; afterwards re-named Ptolemais, in honour of Ptolemy Lagus. III. capital of Magnesia, Thessaly, at the N. extremity of Pagasæus sin., to which it also gave name, 12 m. S.E. of Phenæ. Built by Demetrius Poliorcetes, B.C. 290. and peopled with the inhabitants of Pagasæ, Olizon, Nelia, Iolcos, Ormenium, Rhizus, Sepias, and Bæbe. *On Monte Goritza.* IV. the name given for a time to Sicyon, as rebuilt by Demetrius Poliorcetes.

DEMETRIUM, I. a port of Bithynia, bet. Lateæ (13) and Dusæ. II. of Phthiotis, Thessaly, on Pagasæus sin., w. of Pyrasus. Sacred to Demeter (Ceres). III. a town of Samothrace, on the s. coast, opposite Imbros ins., where Perseus was seized by the Romans, after the battle of Pydna.

DEMONISI ins., the islands Chalcitis and Pityodes, &c. of Bithynia. Noted for their brass.

DEMUS fl., a r. of Sogdiana, falling into the Jaxartes. *Marghinan.*

DENDROBASA, a port of Gedrosia, bet. Daranabilla and Cophas.

DENDROS ins., an isl. of Argolis, in Saronicus sin., over against Spiræum prom.

DENSILETÆ, Thraciæ, i. q. Danthaletæ.

DENTHELIA, a village of Messenia, near Limnæ.

DENTHIADÆ, a village of Laconia, near Pitane.

DEOBRIGA (Doubriga), a town of the Autrigones, Tarraconensis, on the Iberus, N.E. of Virovesca. *Brinnos.*

DEOBRIGULA, a town of the Murbogii, Tarraconensis, near Stantiyanes, w., near its parent-city, Deobriga.

DERÆI (Dersæi), a people of Thrace, on Strymon fl.

DERBÆ (Dardæ), a people in the N.E. mountains of India; famed for their gold mines.

DERBE (Delbia), a port of Lycaonia, at the w. extremity of a lake (not named) on the borders of Cappadocia, S.E. of Iconium. Noted in the history of St. Paul. *Benbir-Klissa.*

DERCON, a town of Astica, Thrace, on the Euxine, S.E. of Philea prom. *Dercono.*

DERRHIS (Deris), I. the S.E. extremity of Sithonia, Macedonia. *C. Drepano.* II. a prom. of Mauritania, 2 geog. m. N.W. from Leucaspis. *Cape Deras.* III. a town on the isthmus of Chersonesus Thracia, at the S.E. extremity of Melas sin., above Lysimachia.

DERRHIUM (Derrha), a town of Laconia, under Taygetus m., s.w. of Amyclæ.

DERTONA, a town of the Ananes, Liguria, bet. Aquæ Statiellæ (28) and Iria. A colonia. *Tortona.*

DERTOSA, capital of the Ilercaones, Tarraconensis, on the Iberus, L., above Adeba. A municipium and colonia (Julia Ilergavonia). *Tortosa.*

DERTUM, a maritime town of Apulia, on Via Frentana, bet. Turris Cæsaris (9) and Egnatia (9). *Torre del Orto.*

DERVENTIO, I. a r. of the Brigantes, Brit., falling into Urus fl. *Derwent.* II. a town of the Brigantes, Brit., bet. Eboracum and Delgovitia, on Derventio fl. *Little Chester.*

DERXENE, Armeniæ, i. q. Xerxene.

DESERTA BOIORUM, a district of Pannonia Sup., s. of Vienna, under Cetius m. E. *Wiener-wald.*

DESSOBRIGA, a town of the Turmodigi, Tarraconensis, bet. Laccobriga, w. and Segisamo, e.

DESUDABA, a town of the Mædi, Thrace, on Strymon fl., nearly opposite the mouth of Pontus fl.

DESUVIATES, a tribe of Salyes, Narbonensis, on the Rhone and Druentia ffl.

DEUCALION ins., a rock of Phthiotis, Thessaly, in Pagasæus sin., near Pyrrha prom.

DEULTUS, a town of the Odrysæ, Thrace, on the Euxine, s.w. of Anchialus.

DEURIOPIS, a district of Pelagonia, Pæonia, on Erigonus fl.

DEUSONA, a town of the Chattuarii, Germ., on the Rhine, opposite Asciburgium.

DEVA fl., a r. I. of Britannia Barbara, falling into the German ocean at Devana, s. of Tæzalum prom. *Dee.* II. of the Cornavii, Brit., falling into the Atlantic below Deva. *Dee.* III. of Tarraconensis, falling into Cantabricum mare bet. Nanasca fl. and Salis fl. *Deba.* IV. a r. of Tarraconensis, falling into Cantabricum mare bet. Aturia fl. and Vesperies. *Navion; Ybarychalval.* V. (Devana), a town of the Cornavii, Brit. Rom., on Deva fl., towards its mouth, bet. Condate (20) and Varæ. *Chester.* VI. (*Grævcè* Dèona), a town of the Varduli, Tarraconensis, at the mouth, R., of Deva fl. VII. a town of the Tæzali, Brit., 7 m. from the mouth of Deva fl.

DEVONA, a town of the Tursones, Germ., on Mænus fl., R., above Segodunum. *Schweinfurt.*

DEXARI, a people of Chaonia, about Amerus m.

DIA, I. an isl. on the N. coast of Crete, off Matium. *Standia.* II. (Diospolis), a town of Bithypia, on the Euxine, 8 m. E. from Hypius fl. III. a town of Caria, near Miletus. IV. of Taurica Chersonesus, bet. Nymphæum and Panticapæum.

DIABETÆ ins., islets of Caria, about Syme ins. *Kiskilles.*

DIABAS fl., Assyriæ, i. q. Gorgus.

DIABATE ins., an isl. of Sardinia, N.E. of Gordilanum prom. *Faluga.*

DIACHERSIA, a maritime town of Cyrenaica, bet. Zau Taberna and Caminos.

DIACHIRA, Mesopotamiæ, i. q. Idacara.

DIACOFENE a district of Galatia, S.E. of Ximane.

DIACRIA, a district of Attica, bet. Parnus m. and Braupn.

DIACRII SCOPULI, two rocks on the E. coast of Eubœa, N.E. of Nedon.

DIAGON fl., a r. of Elis, falling into the Alpheus.

DIALOGE (Thiagole), one of the mouths of the Danube.

DIAIUNA fl. (Jomanes), a r. of India e. Gangem, rising in Imaus m., and falling into the Ganges above Cassida. *Dschumna; Zmna.*

DIANA VETERANORUM, a town of Numidia, o the confines of Mauritania Cæsariens., bet. Lamasbua and Thabutis. *Tagou Aïnah.*

DIANÆ-DICTYNNÆ PROM., a pr. of Laconia, ot Laconicus sin., N. of Las.

DIANÆ-PORTUS, a port of Corsica, N. of Rhotanus fl. *Cervione.*

DIANIUM (Artemisium) ins., I. an isl. of Etruria, s.E. of Igilium ins. *Gianuti.* II. prom. and town. *Vide* Artemisium.

DIAPHANES (Thapsacus) fl., a r. of Cilicia Campestris, falling into Issicus sin., s. of Issus.

DIARRHEUSA ins., one of the Pisistratidæ ins. of Ionia.

DIARRHOÆ, a maritime town of Cyrenaica, s. of Serapium.

DIATONIUM, a town of Crete, towards Gortys, a colony from Lyctus.

DIAUNA, a town of Albania, N. of Casius fl. *Derbend.*

DIBIO, a town of the Lingones, Lugdunensis I., bet. Tilena N.E., and Vidubia s.w. *Dijon.*

DIBON (Dimon), a town of Gad, in Moabitis, 3 m. N. of the Arnon. *Diban.*

DICÆA (Stabulum Diomedis), a Greek city of the Bistones, Thrace, on the w. shore of Bistonis lacus. *Boâr Kalis.*

DICÆARCHIA, the Greek name of Puteoli.

DICATE, a town of Gauzonitis, Mesopotamia, bet. Zogorra and Ad Herculem.

DICTE, I. an E. continuation of Ida m., in Crete, terminating in Ampelus prom. *Sitia.* II. a summit of Ida, Asiat., towards Scepsis. III. a town of Crete, under Dicte m. Built by Jupiter.

DICTYNNÆUM (Dictamnum), a town of Crete, on Psacum prom. *Magny.*

DICTYNNÆUS m., Cretæ, i. q. Berecynthus.

DICTYS, a town of the Tectosages, Galatia.

DICUNTIA fl., a r. of Noricum, i. q. Arelate.

DIDATTIA, a town of the Sequani, Maxima Sequanorum, N.E. of Velatodurum. *La Cité.*

DIDMASA, i. q. Midmasa.

DIDUGUA (Digba), a town of the Strophi, Babyl., on the Tigris.

DIDUNI, a tribe of Lygii, Germ., on Viadrus fl., towards its source.

DIDURI, a people of Sarmatia Asiat., E. of the Sanari.

DIDYMA ins., I. (Euonymus) an isl. of Sicily, N. of Lipari. *Panaria.*

DIDYMI, I. islets of Cilicia Campestris, on Issicus sin., E. of Pyramus fl. II. m. of Arabia Felix, N. of Abissa. *Palheiros.* III. prom. (Gemelli), a pr. of Arabia Felix, N. of Syagrus prom. IV. sin., a bay of the Ægean, on the N. coast of Crete, E. of Zephyrium prom. *G. di Mirabel* w., *and G. di Setia* E. V. (Branchidæ, *postea* Melanudium), a village on the coast of Ionia, s.w. of Miletus, 2½ m. from the sea, bet. two hills.

DIDYMIS, a town of Thebais, bet. Phœnicon and Aphroditis, S.E. of Thebæ.

DIDYMOTEICHOS, a town of Mysia, on Granicus fl., s.w. of Priapus. *Dimotiko.* II. of the Odrysæ, Thraciæ, on Hebrus fl., above Zorinia. *Dimotiko.*

DIDYMUS, a town of Argolis, bet. Mazes and Boli (2¼). *Didymo.*

DIGBA, Babylon, i. q. Didigua.

DIGDIDA, a town of the Psylli, Africa Prop., w. of Aræ Philænorum.

DIGENTIA fl., a r. of Sabinium, falling into Curensis fl. *Licenza.*

DII, Thraciæ, i. q. Dahæ.

DIGLITO fl., a name of the Tigris, towards its junction with Nymphæus fl.

DIKELA, a district of Arabia Petræa, on the Red Sea, bet. the Sideni and the Darræ.

DILIS, a town of the Segoregii, Narbonensis, on the coast, w. of Incaro.

DIMALLUM (Dimalle), a fortress of the Parthini, Illyria, on Mathis fl., bet. Lissus and Epidamnus. *Malosse.*

DIMASTUS, I. a m. of Myconus ins. II. an isl. of Rhodes.

DINARETUM (Clides, Boosura, Olympus) prom., the N.E. extremity of Cyprus. With a temple of Venus Urania or Acræa, from which women were excluded. *C. Sant' Andria.*

DINDYMENE (Dindymus) m., m. of Phrygia Epictetus, running from about the source of Hermus fl., towards Mysia and Bithynia. Sacred to Rhea or Cybele. *Morad Dagh.*

DINDYMUS m., i. q. Dindymene.

DINIA, town of the Bodiontici, Alpes Maritimæ, N.w. of Sanitium. *Digne.*

DINIÆ, Phryg., i. q. Cylla.

DINOGITIA, a town of Mœsia, on the Danube, bet. Noviodunum and Arrubium.

DIOCÆSAREA, I. a town of Cilicia-Trachea, on Calycadnus fl., about Hyria. II. (Sephoris, Zippori), of Galilæa, 18 m. w.s.w. from Tiberias. Destroyed by Varus; restored by Herod Antipas. *Sefurieh.* III. of Garsauritis, Cappadocia, near Nazianzus.

DIOCLEA (Docela), a town of Phrygia Epict., bet. Cydissus and Cotyeum.

DIOCLETIANOPOLIS, a later name of Pella, Macedoniæ.

DIODŌRI ins., a commercial isl. at the entrance of the Red Sea, s.w. of Ocelis. *Parim.*

DIODURUM, a town of the Carnutes, Lugdunensis IV., s.w. of Lutetia.

DIOGENIS prom., a pr. of the Troglodytæ, on the Red Sea, above Satyrorum prom.

DIOLCOS OSTIUM NILI, one of the two lesser mouths of the Nile, E. of Sebennyticum ost.

DIOLELE præsidium, a fortress of Byzacene, s.w. of Capsa.

DIOLINDUM, a town of the Petrocorii, Aquitania II., on Duronius fl., bet. Vesunna N. and Divona s.E.

DIOLUM, a town of the Brigantes, Brit., s.E. of Morbium.

DIOMEDEA (Tremitus) ins., chief of the Diomedeæ ins., Apuliæ. The death-place of Augustus' grand-daughter Julia. *Isola San Domenico.*

DIOMEDEÆ ins., three islets of Apulia, off Uria. Named from the metamorphosis there of the companions of Diomed. *San Domenico ; San Nicola ; Caprara.*

DIOMEDIS campi, the district of Apulia, bet. Cerbalus fl. and Aufidus fl. Apportioned by Daunus to Diomed.

DIOMEDIS STABULUM, i. q. Dicæa.

DION, a town of Palestine, 2 m. N. from Pella. Noted for its water, sweet but very unwholesome.

DIONYS PORTUS, a port of Marmarica, near Chersonesus Magna.

DIONYSIA ins., a name of Naxos, from its fine wines.

DIONYSIADES ins., two isl. of Crete, in Didymus sin., over against Cætia prom. *Yanidzares.*

DIONYSIAS, I. a town of Heptanomis, near Arsinoe Crocodilopolis, s.w. II. Trachonitis, N.E. of Cranatha.

DIONYSII prom., a pr. of Byzacene at Hadrumetum s.

DIONYSIOPHANI, the port of Arsinoë II., Indiæ, i. q. Nagara.

DIONYSOPOLIS, a town of Phrygia Mag., N.E. of Hierapolis.

DIOPOLIS, I. a town of the Odrysæ, Thrace, s.w. of Bessapara. II. i. q. Cabira.

DIOSCORIDIS ins., an isl. of Æthiopia, on Erythræum mare, N.E. of Aromatum prom. Noted for its aloes. *Socotra.*

DIOSCŌRON PORTUS, a port of the Troglodytæ, on the Red Sea, E. of Napata. *Baahr al Fushaa.*

DIOSCŌRUM ins., an islet of Bruttium, s.E. of Ogygia ins. Now submerged.

DIOSCURIAS (*postea* Sebastopolis), a town of Ecretice, Colchis, on the Euxine, 4 m. s.E. from Pityus, at the mouth of Arthemus fl. Built by Castor and Pollux or, according to others, by their charioteers, the Heniochi.

DIOSHIERON, I. a town of Ionia, bet. Lebedos and Colophon. II. *postea* Christopolis, of Lydia, on Caystrus fl., in Cilianus campus.

DIOSPŎLIS, I. Bithyniæ, i. q. Dia. II. Judeæ, i. q. Lydda. III. Lydiæ, i. q. Dioshieron. IV. *surnamed* Magna, Egypti, i. q. Thebæ. V. Parva, a town of Thebais, on the Nile. *Hou.*

DIPÆA, a town of Arcadia, on Helisson fl., above Lycæa.

DIPÆNA, a town of Arcadia, towards Methydrium.

DIPO, a town of the Turtuli, Bæturia, bet. Augusta Emerita N.W. and Corduba S.E.

DIPOLIS, a surname of Lemnos ins., in reference to its two towns.

DIRCE fons, I. a stream of Achaia, near Pharæ. II. of Bœotia, at Thebes.

DIRE ("neck"), I. sin., the strait bet. Arabicus sin. and Erythræum mare. *Bab el Mandeb.* II. prom., a pr. of Æthiopia, at the w. entrance of the Red Sea, opposite Palindromus prom., in Arabia. *Ras Bel.*

DIRIDOTIS. *Vide* Teredon.

DIRPHOSSUS (Dirphys, Dirphe), a hill of Eubœa, N.E. of Chalcis. *Delphi.*

DISCUS, two shoals of Bithynia, on Bosporus Thracius, N. of Chrysopolis.

DISSIO (Aqua Amara), baths of Africa Prop., on Syrtis Maj., s., bet. Aspis and Chosol.

DITTHI (Dittani), an early people of Tarraconensis, bet. Sucro fl. and Turia fl.

DIUM, I. a prom. on the N. coast of Crete, N.E. of Cytæum. *C. Sassoso.* II. a town of Acte Macedoniæ, on Strymonicus sin., N.W. of Olophyxus. III. a town of Crete, at the cognominal prom. IV. (Diospolis), a city of Decapolis. V. of Ellopia, Eubœæ, E. of Histiæa. VI. of Magnesia, Thessaly, near Ormenium. VII. of Pieria, Macedonia, at the mouth of Baphyrus fl., on Thermaicus sin., at the foot of Olympus m., bet. Heraclea (12) and Pydna (20). A colonia. Here were the brass statues of Lysippus. *Standia.*

DIUR fl., a r. of Mauritania Ting., falling into Phthuth fl., R., near its mouth.

DIVODURUM (*postea* Mediomatrices, Mettis), capital of the Mediomatrices, Belgica I., on the Mosella, L., above Carenusca. *Metz.*

DIVONA (*postea* Cadurci), capital of the Cadurci, Aquitania I., on Œtis fl., bet. Diolindum N.W. and Varadetum E. *Cahors.*

DIZOATRA (Zizoatra), a town of Laviniasene, Cappadocia.

DOANA, capital of the Doani, Ind., on Doanas fl.

DOANAS fl., a r. of India e. Gangem, rising in Emodi m., and falling into Sarabicus sin. at Berobe. *Dongon.*

DOANI, a people of India e. Gangem, on Doanus fl., about its mouth.

DOBERUS, a town of Pæonia, on the w. shore of Prasias palus, under Dysorus m. *Doiran.*

DOBRATH (Itabyrium), a town of Galilæa, under Thabor m. N.W.

DOBUNI, (*Celticè*, Doff-uni, "on the bank of the river"), a people of Flavia Cæsariensis, bet. the Silures w., the Catavellauni and Trinobantes e., Avona fl. N., and the Belgæ s. *Gloucestershire, and parts of Warwickshire and Oxfordshire.*

DOCAS, Phrygia, i. q. Diniæ.

DOCEA, i. q. Cimiata.

DOCELA. *Vide* Dioclia.

DOCIDAVA, a town of the Anarti, Dac., w. of Parolissum.

DOCIMIA, a town of Phrygia M., N.E. of Synnada, where were the quarries which produced the fine Synnadic or Docimitic marble. *Doghanla.*

DODECASCHŒNUS (Æthiopia Ægypti), a district of Africa, on the Nile, bet. Thebais at Syene and Hiera-Sycaminos. Here, according to Herodotus, the course of the Nile was tortuous as that of the Mæander.

DODON fl., a r. of Epirus, rising near Dodona, and falling into Œas fl. below Fauces Aoi. *Vistrizza.*

DODONA (Bodona), I. a port of Perrhæbia, Thessaly, on Titaresius fl., L. Supposed by some writers to have been the original seat of the celebrated oracle. II. of Thesprotia, and afterwards of Molossis, Epirus, at the source of Thyamis fl., under Tomarus m., N. The seat of the famous oracle, the most ancient in Greece. Founded by the Pelasgi. *Mokari, near Delvinaki.*

DOEANTIUS campus, a district of Pontus, i. q. Themiscyra. Named from the chief Docas.

DOK, a town of Ephraim, Samaria, N.W. of Jericho.

DOLA, a maritime town of the Cantii, Brit., bet. Rutupæ and Dubræ.

DOLĬCHE ins., I. Arabiæ, i. q. Zenobii ins. II. one of the Echinades, i. q. Dulichium. III. a name of Creta ins. IV. a town of Pelasgiotis-Tripolītis, s.w. of Pythium. *Duklista.*

DOLICHISTE ins., an isl. of Lycia, off Aperlæ. *Kakava.*

DOLIONES, a primitive people of Mysia, bet. Æsepus fl. and Dascylitis.

DOLOMENE, a district of Aturia, Assyriæ.

DOLONCÏ, a people of Thrace, occupying the Chersonesus. Named after Doloncus, brother of Bithynus.

DOLOPIA, a district of Thessaly, bounded N.

by Estiæotis and Phthiotis, s. by Æniania and Maliensis, w. by Aperantia (into which at one time it extended), E. by Phthiotis. *Thamako ; Grituiano ; Agrapha.*

DOLUCA (Doliche), a town of Cyrrhestica, w. of Zeugma.

DOLUCENS, a town of the Morini, Belgica II., bet. Gessoriacum and Pontes.

DOMÆ ins., an isl. of Gedrosia, towards Saranga. *Tschilnay.*

DOMANA, a town of Armenia Minor, bet. Solonenica (18) and Satala (18). The station of the Equites Sagittarii Domanæ.

DOMANITIS, a district of Paphlagonia, N.E. of Blaene reg.

DOMITIOPOLIS, a town of Cilicia Trachea, on Arymagdus fl.

DONATIANA, a town of the Hercuniatæ, Pannonia, near the Danube, bet. Ad Novas and Ad Labores.

DONANTILIA, a town of Chaldæa, bet. Cybate and Dablan.

DONUSA. *Vide* Gonusa.

DONYSA ins., an isl. of the Ægean, one of the Sporades, bet. Naxos and Ios. Under the Romans a place of banishment. Famous for its green marble. *Raclia.*

DŌRA (Dorus, Dor), a maritime town of Phœnicia, bet. Calama N. and Cæsarea Palestina s. (9). *Tortura.*

DORA FONS, a town of the Darræ, Arabia Felix, N.W. of Abissa. *Dahra.*

DORAS, a town of Sicyonia.

DORBETA, a town of Sophene, Armeniæ, N. of Amida.

DORENI, Arabiæ, i. q. Zoreni.

DORES, a tribe of Pelasgi, who, driven from Estiæotis, Thessaly, by the Macedni, emigrated under Dorus, son of Hellen, to the country called after them Doris, expelling thence or subjugating the Dryopes, its original population. Circa 1104 B.C., in league with their guests the Heraclidæ, they invaded Peloponnesus, where they established Lacedæmon and other states.

DORICA TETRAPOLIS, i. q. Doris Asiat.

DORICANA, a town of Dacia, near Ulpianum.

DORIDIS sin., a bay of Carium mare, bet. Triopium prom. and Cynossema prom. *G. di Syme.*

DORIONES, a town of the Mœsi, Mœs. Inf., on Utus fl., R., bet. Storgosia and Melta.

DORIS (*prius* Dryopis, Æpalius), I. a country of Græcia e. Peloponnesum, bounded N. by Thessaly, s. by Locri Ozolæ, w. by Ætolia, E. by Phocis. *Lidoriki.* II. (Carius, Triopium) a peninsula of Caria, bet. Ceramicus sin., and Doridis sin.

DORISCUS, I. a plain of the Cicones in Thrace, along Hebrus fl., where Xerxes reviewed his army. II. a fortress of Thrace, on Hebrus fl., below Dyme, overlooking the cognominal plain. Built by Darius.

DORISTA, a town of Babylonia, bet. Seleucia and Abara.

DORIUM, *postea* Oluris, a town of Messenia, bet. Electra and the sea. The place where the Muses deprived Thamyris of his sight.

DORIUS fl., a r. of India e. Gangem, rising in Damasi m., and falling into Indicum mare, by several mouths, at the w. entrance of Sarabicus sin. *Pegu.*

DOROSTŌRUM, a town of the Getæ, Mœsia, on the Danube, bet. Sagadava and Tegulicium. The station of the Eleventh Legion. *Silistria ; Sistria.*

DORTICUM, a town of the Mœsi, Mœsia Sup., on Timacus fl., bet. Ad Aquas and Bononia.

DORUM URBS, a town of the Ordovices, Brit., towards the source of Sabrina fl., E. of Maglona.

DORVATIUS fl., Brit., i. q. Durius.

DORYLEUM, a town of Phrygia Epict., on Thymbris fl., R., towards its junction with Sangarius fl., S.E. of Cydissus. It had warm baths. *Eski Sher.*

DOSARENI, i. q. Zoreni.

DOSARON fl., a r. of the Callingæ, India, falling into the sea w. of Callinga.

DOSCI, Sarmatiæ Asiat., i. q. Psessii.

DOTHAM, a town of Samaria, 12 m. N. from Samaria. The place where Joseph was sold by his brethren.

DOTIUM, a town of Pelasgiotis, Thessaly, in Dotius campus, at the N.E. extremity of Bæbeis palus. *Djechani.*

DOTIUS campus, a district of Pelasgiotis, Thessaly, bet. Ossa m. and the N.E. shore of Bæbeis palus. The primitive seat of the Ænianes.

DOULONPOLIS, a name of Acanthus, in Cnidus.

DRABESCUS, a town of the Edones, Thrace, 12 m. N.W. of Philippi. *Drama.*

DRACO, I. a r. of Bithynia, falling into Propontis w. of Astacenus sin., after a peculiarly meandering course. *Dil.* II. of Campaniæ, i. q. Sarnus. III. a m. of Lydia, bet. Temnus m. and Tmolus m. *Kizzel-djeh ; Mousseh Dagh.*

DRACONTIS ins., an isl. of Africa, off Hippo, N.W.

DRACONUM, I. a m. of Icarus ins., where, according to the local tradition, Bacchus was born. II. prom., the E. extremity of

Icarus ins., over against Cantharium prom. (10). *C. Phanari.* III. a town of Icarus ins., near the cognom. prom. The residence, for a time, of Euripides.

DRACUINA, a town of Germania Mag., on the Danube, above the junction of Ilargus fl.

DRANCÆ, Oxydrancæ, a people of Sogdiana, contiguous to the Drybattæ.

DRANGÆ, the principal port of Drangiana, w. of Aria lacus.

DRANGIĀNA (Zarangia), a country of Asia, bounded N. by Aria, s. by Gedrosia, at Etymandrus fl., w. by Parthia and Carmania, E. by Arachosia, at Etymandrus fl. *Zaraka.*

DRAPSACA (Darapsa), a town of Bactriana, towards Maracodra. Built by Alexander.

DRATÆ (Dagræ), a town of Tyanitis, Cappadocia.

DRAUDACUM, a fortress of the Penestæ, Illyriæ, bet. Uscana and Æneum.

DRAVUS fl. (Drabus, Draus), a r. of Pannonia, rising E. of Vipitenum, and falling into the Danube at Teutoburgium. *Draave.*

DRECANUM prom., a pr. of Cos, on the N. coast, 22½ m. w. from Cos oppid.

DREPANE (*postea* Helenopolis, a town of Bithynia, on Propontis, E. of Prœnetus. Renamed by Constantine, in honour of his mother Helena. *Ersek.*

DREPANUM ("scythe-like"), I. the early name of Corcyra ins. II. prom., a pr. of Achaia, over against Rhium prom., deriving its name from the fable of Saturn's scythe. *Drepano.* III. of Crete, N., at the w. extremity of Amphimallius sin. *Drepano.* IV. of Cyrenaica, w., below Berenice. V. of Thebais, on the Red Sea, at the entrance to Heroopolites sin. VI. of Cyprus, on the w. coast, beyond Paphos. *C. Trapano.* VII. a maritime town of Sicily, w., bet. Eryx and Ægithallus. *Trapani.*

DREPSA, capital of the Drepsiani Bactrianæ, bet. the Oxus and the Jaxartes. *Waschgerd.*

DREPSIANI, a people of Bactria, s.w. of Vandabanda.

DRESIA, a town of Phrygia Magna, on Obrimus fl., towards Peltæ.

DRILÆ, a people of Pontus, in the m. above Trapezus, who ultimately became fused with the Sanni and adopted their name.

DRILLOPHILLITÆ, a people of India i. Gangem, under Uxentus m. s., on the right bank of Mana fl.

DRILON fl., a r. of Illyria, formed by the junction of two rivers, the Drilon Albus, rising in Bertischus m., and the Drilon

Niger, rising in Callicæni m., near Bantia; these, meeting at Gabuleus, fall together into the Adriatic below Lissus. *Drino.*

DRIMATI, a people of Arabia Felix, about Corodamum prom. *About Bunder Djuraim.*

DRINUS fl., a r. of Europe, rising in Bebii m. s.E. of Bersumnum, and, after separating Illyria from Mœsia, falling into Savus fl. *Drina.*

DRIOS m., a m. of Naxos ins. The birthplace of Bacchus.

DRIPPA, a town of the Apsynthii, Thrace, on the Egnatia Via, bet. Cypsela (12) and Siracella (14).

DRIPSINUM, a town of the Euganei, in the hills above Vicetia. *Tressino.*

DRIUM m., a summit of Garganus m., 12 m. N. of Matinum, on which were chapels of Calchas and Podalirius.

DRIZIUM, a fortress of Cappadocia, towards Commagene.

DROI, a people of Thrace, on Strymon fl.

DROSACA (Rosacha), a town of Serica.

DRUBETIS (Druphegis), a town of the Saldenses, Dacia, N.E. of Pons Trajani. *Crajova.*

DRUENTIA fl., a r. of Gaul, rising in Vesalus m. and falling into the Rhone at Avenio. *Durance.*

DRUNA fl., a r. of Gaul, falling into the Rhone, L., at Batiana. *Drome.*

DRUSI TROPÆA, a town of Germania, on Visurgis fl., E. of Pheugarum. The deathplace of Drusus.

DRUSILLANA, a town of Zeugitana, bet. Signese and Thacia.

DRUSOMAGUS, a town of the Catenates, Vindelicia, on Licus fl., near its confluence with the Danube. *Memmingen.*

DRUZIPARA, a town of the Odrysæ, Thrace, bet. Bergula and Turullus. *Karishtan.*

DRYBACTÆ, a people of Sogdiana, contiguous to the Candari.

DRYBICES, a people of Media Choromitrene, on the Caspian, bet. Amardus fl. and the Anariacæ.

DRYMÆA, *prius* Naubolus, a town of Phocis, 2½ m. from Tithronium. Destroyed by Xerxes. *Ogulnitza.*

DRYMUS, I. a village of Attica, near Panactum. II. a place in Ellopia, Eubœa, on Callas fl., near Histiæa.

DRYMUSA ins., an isl. of Ionia, in Hermius sin., over against Chytrium. *Isola Inglese.*

DRYOPES, a tribe of Thracians, the early settlers of the N. portion of Phocis, under Œta m., colonies of whom migrated to Epirus, about Ambracia, to Eubœa, Asia Minor, and to Peloponnesus. There were

Dryopes also on the s. shores of the Euxine.

DRYOPIS REGIO, the district around Ambracia, settled by Dryopes from Œta m.

DRYOSCEPHALÆ (Triscephalæ), a defile of Bœotia, in Cithæron m., on the confines of Attica, S.E. of Platæa.

DRYS, a maritime town of the Cicones, Thrace, E. of Serrhium prom. Built by Iphicrates the Athenian.

DRYUSA, a name of Samos.

DUATUS sinus, a gulf of the Red Sea, in Arabia Felix, s. of Orsa m. *Bahr al Madeha.*

DUBII, a town of Umbria, bet. Nuceria (8) and Prolaqueum (8), on Via Flaminia.

DUBIOS, a district of Otene, Armenia, E. of Artaxata. *Tuin.*

DUBIS fl., a r. of Maxima Sequanorum, falling into the Arar above Cabillonum. *Dour.*

DUBRÆ (Dubris), *postea* Derfrio, Doris, Dovoria, a maritime town of the Cantii E., bet. Dola and Lemanus portus. *Dover.*

DUDUM, Ganara, a town of Libya.

DUELTUS lacus, a lake of the Odrysæ, Thrace.

DULGIBINI (Dulgumnii), a tribe of Cherusci, Germania, on the confines of the Angrivarii, E. of Visurgis fl.

DULICHIUM (Doliche) ins., chief of the Echinades ins., about 2 m. from Cephallenia, submerged by an earthquake.

DUMA (Dumætha, Dumath), I. a town of Juda, Judæa, bet. Hebron N.E. and Debir, S.W. II. of the Saraceni, Arabia Petræa, N.E. of Bacas Chamiri. The abode of Dumah, sixth son of Ishmael. *Daumat al Ghendal.*

DUMNA ins., one of the Orcades ins., Brit. *Hay.*

DUMNISSUS, a town of the Treveri, Germania I., bet. Belginum w. and Bingium S.E.

DUMNONII, Brit., i. q. Damnonii.

DUMNUM, a town of the Vangiones, Germania I., s. of Bingium. *Near Stromberg.*

DUNGA, a town of Ariaca, Indiæ, bet. Goaris fl. (7) and Benda fl. *Pernalla.*

DUNIUM, Brit., i. q. Maridunium.

DUNUM, *Celticè,* high, I. a town of the Mœsi, Mœsia Inferior, on the Danube, bet. Securisca and Ad Novas. II. of the Usdiæ, Hibernia, 8 m. w. from Eblana. III. sinus, an estuary of Britain E., bet. Vedra fl. and Gabrantvicorum portus. *Robin Hood's Bay.*

DUODEA, a town of Chalcidice, Macedonia, bet. Thessalonica (13) and Heraclea (14), on the Egnatia Via.

DUR, an æstuary of Hibernia w. *Galway Bay.*

DURA, a plain of Babylonia, the locality of the idolatry of the golden image of Nabuchodonasar. II. (Durma), a town of Apolloniatis, Assyria, on the Tigris, bet. Peloriarca and Carcha. *Dor.* III. (Europus, Thelda), of Tingene, Mesopotamia, on the Euphrates, bet. Asicha and Merrhan. Built by the Macedonians.

DURANIUS fl., I. a r. of Aquitania, falling into the Garumna, R., near its mouth. *Dordogne.* II. a r. of the Jazyges Metanastæ, falling into the Danube. *Tyrna.*

DURETIA, a town of the Veneti, Lugdunensis III., N.W. of Condivicnum.

DURIA MAJOR fl., I. a r. of the Salassi, Gallia Transpadana, rising in Alpes Graiæ, w. of Arebrigium, and falling into Padus fl. at or near Industria. *Doria Baltia.* II. MINOR, of Gallia Transpadana, rising in Matrona m. and falling into Padus fl. below Augusta Taurinorum. *Doria Riparia.*

DURIUS (Dorvatius), I. a r. of Britain, falling into the Atlantic below Ad Durium. *Dart.* II. of Spain, rising in Caunus m. S.E. of Numantia, and, after separating Tarraconensis from Lusitania, falling into the Atlantic at Cale, bet. Avus fl. N. and Langobriga s. Its sands were reputed to contain gold. *Duero* (Sp.); *Douro* (Portug.).

DURNACUS, i. q. Turnacum.

DURNIUM, a town of the Cavii, Illyria, E. of Lissus.

DURNOMAGUS, I. a town of the Coritani, Brit., N.E. of Lindum. II. of the Ubii, Germania I., on the Rhine, above Novesium.

DURNOVARIA, a town of the Durotriges, Brit., E. of Maridunium. *Dorchester.*

DUROBRIVÆ (Durobrabis, Durobrisin, Rofusceaster), I. a town of the Cantii, Brit., bet. Vagniacæ (9) and Durovernum (25). *Rochester.* II. of the Catavellauni, Brit., bet. Causenna (30) and Durolipons (35).

DUROCASSES, a town of the Carnutes, Lugdunensis IV., bet. Condate Eburovic. and Diodurum. *Dreux.*

DUROCATALAUNI, capital of the Catalauni, Belgica II., on the Matrona, R., bet. Basilia N. and Arciaca s.

DUROCOBRIVÆ, a town of the Catavellauni, Brit., bet. Magiovintum (17) and Verolarnium (12). *Near Dunstable* s.

DUROCORNOVIUM (Corinium Dobunorum, Corin Ceaster), a town of the Dobuni, Brit., on Corinus fl., towards its source. *Cirencester.*

DUROCORTORUM, *postea* Remi, capital of the

Remi, bet. Ad Fines w. and Noviomagus E. *Reims.*

DUROLEVUM, a town of the Cantii, Brit., bet. Durobrivæ and Durovernum (19). *Faversham.*

DUROLIPONS, a town of the Iceni, N.W. of Camboricum. *Godmanchester.*

DUROLĪTUM, a town of the Trinobantes, Brit., bet. Cæsaromagus (16) and Londinium (15). *Romford.*

DURONIA, I. a r. of Samnium, falling into Trinius fl. below Duronia. *Durone.* II. a town of the Pentri, Samnium, on Duronia fl., N.E. of Æsernia. *Civita Vecchia.*

DURONIUS fl., a r. of Aquitania II., falling into the Garumna, R., towards its mouth.

DURONUM, a town of the Nervii, Belgica II., bet. Quarteus lacus N. and Verbinum S.

DUROTINCUM, a town of the Medulli, Viennensis, bet. Mellosecium w. and Stabatio S.E.

DUROTRIGES (*Celticè*, Dur-treig, "sea-tribe"), a people occupying the S. coast of Britannia I., bet. the Damnonii w., the Regni E., and the Belgæ N. *Dorsetshire.*

DUROVERNUM (Durobernia, Duroaverus, Darvernum), a town of the Cantii, Brit., bet. Durobrivæ (25) and Durolevum. *Canterbury.*

DURTIA, a town of the Tencteri, Germania, on the Rhine, over against Agrippina Colonia.

DURUS fl., I. Assyriæ, i. q. Gordus. II. a r. of Hibernia w., separating the Gangani from the Velibori.

DUSÆ AD OLYMPUM, a town of Bithynia, under Olympus m., bet. Demetrium and Bithynium (30).

DUSARE m., m. of Arabia Felix. Sacred to Dusares (Dionysius).

DYARDANES fl., Indiæ, i. q. Œdanes.

DYAS fl., a r. of Mauritania Tingit., falling into the Atlantic bet. Casa fl. and Ad Mercurias.

DŸME, *prius* Palla and Stratos, I. one of the twelve cities of Achaia, on Corinthiacus sin., 45 m. N.W. of Olenus. Settled by Caucones. A colonia. The burial-place of Sostratos, the friend of Hercules. II. a town of Thrace, on Hebrus fl., bet. Trajanopolis (13) and Cypsela (12), on the Egnatia Via.

DYPÆA, a town of Arcadia, on Helisson fl.

DYRAS fl., a stream of Maliensis, Thessaly, falling into Maliacus sin. 2⅜ m. S. of Sperchius fl. Feigned to have first sprung from the ground to save Hercules from the burning pyre.

DYRIN m., i. q. Atlas Major.

DYRRHACHIUM, the peninsula on which Epidamnus Illyr. was built, and which gave its later name to that city.

DYRZILA, Pisidia, i. q. Darsa.

DYSORUS (Hypsizorus) m., m. of Pæonia, N. of Prasias palus.

DYSPONTIUM, a town of Pisatis, Elis, N.W. of Olympia. The inhabitants were transferred to Epidamnus and Apollonia.

DYSTUS, a town of Eubœa, on the w. coast, S. of Eretria. *Disto.*

E.

EASIS, a town of Gedrosia, N.E. of Ora.

EBA, a town of Etruria, N. of Albinia fl. *Monte Po.*

EBAL m., a m. of Ephraim, N. of Sichem, over against Gerizim m. Famous for the Ratification of the Covenant.

EBELLINUM, a town of the Vascones, Tarraconensis, bet. Calagurris Nasica S.W. and Calagurris Fibularensis E.S.E.

EBLAIA, a town of Albania Asiatica.

EBLĀNA (Bal-a-cleigh, "town built on hurdles," Ashcled, Deblana, Dub-linn, "Black Pool"), capital of the Eblani, Hibernia, at the mouth of Libanius fl. *Dublin.*

EBLANI (Blanii), a people of Hibernia E., bet. the Usluntii N. and the Chauci S. *Meath and Dublin.*

EBLILÆI m., m. of Arabia Felix, terminating in Asaborum prom. *Aval.*

EBODE, a town of Arabia Petræa, S.E. of Fons Emischabales.

EBODURUM, a town of Vindelicia.

EBORA, I. a port of the Artabri, Callæcia, in the Atlantic, s. of Novium. A municipium. *Evora.* II. a town of the Celtici, Lusitania, bet. Olisipo w.N.W. and Augusta Emerita E.N.E. A colonia (Liberalitas Julia). *Evora.* III. of the Edetani, Tarraconensis, w.s.w. of Biscargis. IV. *surnamed* Cerealis, of the Turtuli, Bætica, bet. Mentesa N.E. and Ægabrum S.W.

EBORACUM, capital of the Brigantes, Brit., on Abus fl., I., bet. Isurnum and Derventio. A municipium and colonia. The death-place of Septimius Severus and Constantius Chlorus. The station of the Legio Sexta Victrix. *York.*

EBRIAPA, a town of Sarmatia Asiatica, on Gerrus fl., towards its source.

EBRO PORTUS, a port of Venetia, bet. Fossa Claudia (18) and Meduacus Minor (6). *Chiozza.*

EBROMAGUS, a town of the Volcæ Tectosages,

Narbonensis I., bet. Sestomagus w. and Ad Cedros E.

EBUDÆ (Hebrides, Mevaniæ) ins., isl. of Britannia Barbara, N.W. *Hebrides.*

EBUDUM prom., a pr. of Britannia Barbara, N.W. *Cape Wrath.*

EBURI, a town of the Picentini, Campania, above Picentia. *Eboli.*

EBURIATES, I. a people of Liguria, contiguous to the Statielli. II. their capital. *Burio*, 6 geog. m. s. *from Asti.*

EBUROBRICA, a town of the Senones, Lugdunensis IV., bet. Agenticum N.W. and Bandritum S.E.

EBUROBRITIUM, a maritime town of the Lusitani, s. of Collippo fl.

EBURODUNUM (Epeprodunum), I. a town of the Caturiges, Alpes Maritimæ, on Druentia fl., N.E. of Caturigæ. *Embrun.* II. of Maxima Sequanorum. *Yverdun.* III. of the Quadi, Germania, N. of Medoslanium. *Near Drosing.*

EBUROVICES, *vide* Aulerci.

EBURŌNES, a people of Germania II., on both banks of the Mosa, s. of the Toxiaudri. *About Hasselt.*

EBURUM, a town of the Gothini, Germania, on Viadrus fl., L., above Budorgis. *Olmutz ?*

EBUSMI REGINA, a town of Bactriana, N. of the junction of the Ochus with the Dargomanes.

EBŪSUS (Ebyssos), I. the larger of the Pityusæ ins., Tarraconensis, N. of Ophiusa. Noted for its pastures, its figs, and its exemption from all vermin except rabbits. *Ibiza; Yvica.* II. (Ebusa), its capital, S.E. A Carthaginian settlement. *Ibiza.*

EBUTIANA, a town of the Pentri, Samnium, on Via Numicia, bet. Cluturnum and Allifæ (9). *Ailano.*

ECBATĂNA, I. a city of Adiabene, Assyria, N. of Nineveh. The summer residence of the kings of Parthia. II. (Apobatana, Achmetha, Haghamata), capital of Media, under Orontes m. N., bet. Concabar and Maziniaman, S.E. of Arbela. The summer residence of the kings of Persia. Built by king Arphaxad. *Hamadan.* III. (Bathura), of Phœnicia, under Carmel m. N.E. The death-place of Cambyses. *Caiffa.*

ECCIUS fl., a r. of Cyrenaica, falling into the Mediterranean at Berenice.

ECCOBRIGA, a town of the Trocmi, Galatia, bet. Sarmatia (20) and Adapera (24).

ECDIPPA, Palestine, i. q. Achzib.

ECECHIRES, a tribe of Bechires, Pontus, towards Achabis fl.

ECETRA (Echetra), a town of the Volsci, near Velitræ.

ECHEDAMIA, a town of Phocis. Destroyed in the Sacred War.

ECHEDORUS (Chidorus) fl., a r. of Mygdonia, Macedonia, rising in the mountains of Grestonia and falling into Thermaicus sin. at Sindus. *Gallico.*

ECHEIA-NAUSICLEIA prom., a headland of Bithynia, on Bosporus Thracius.

ECHELIDÆ, a demus of Attica, of the tribe Erectheis, on Saronicus sin.

ECHETLA, a town of Sicily, midway bet. Leontini and Camarina. *Vizini.*

ECHEUTHEIS, a village of Arcadia, near Segea.

ECHINĂDES ins., formerly islands or rocks of various extent, on the s.w. coast of Acarnania, at the mouth of Achelous fl., subsequently annexed to the continent by the alluvial deposits of that river.

ECHĪNUS, I. a town of Acarnania, bet. Myrtuntium and Thyreum. *Agios Petros.* II. of Cyrenaica, bet. Agdan and Arimanthos. III. of the Malienses Paralii, Thessaly, 2½ m. from Larissa Cremaste. Founded by Echion, one of the progeny of the dragon's teeth. *Echinou.*

ECHYMNIA, a town of Acme, Macedonia, near Acanthus.

ECLANUM (Æculanum), a town of the Hirpini, Samnium, near Calor fl., R., on Via Appia, bet. Beneventum (15) and Sub Romula (21). *Grotte di Mirabella.*

ECNOMOS m., a m. of Sicily, on the s. coast, near the mouth of Himera Maj. fl. *M. di Licata.*

ECONIA, Thessaly, i. q. Ægonia.

ECREGMA palus, the mouth of Sirbonis palus, midway bet. Girrha and Ostracine.

ECRETICE, a district of Colchis, on the confines of Sarmatia Asiatica. *Egrissi.*

ECTENES, a tribe of Leleges, Bœotia, prior to the invasion of Cadmus.

EDAPTEIS, a demus of Attica.

EDENATES, a tribe of Avantici, Alpes Maritimæ, s. of the Tebavii. *Val d'Eynau.*

EDER (Adar), a village of Judæa, 1 m. from Bethlehem.

EDESSA (Callirrhoe), *prius* Ur, *postea* Orrhoa, capital of Osrhoene, Mesopotamia, on Scirtus fl., near its source, N.W. of Carrhæ. *Orfa.*

EDESSA, Emathiæ, i. q. Ægæ.

EDETA (Liria), capital of the Edetani, Tarraconensis, w. of Saguntum. *Lyria.*

EDETANI (Sedetani), a tribe of Celtiberi, Tarraconensis, bet. the Iberus, about Cæsar Augusta, and the Sucro, towards its mouth. *Valencia* E. *and* N., *and Arragon* s.

EDISSA, Siciliæ, i. q. Odyssea.

EDLANDUNIUM, a town of the Belgæ, w. of Sorbiodunum. *Wilton.*

EDOM (Idumæa, Idume), a region extending from the s. extremity of the Dead Sea, L., to Ælanites sin. Named from Edom (Esau). *Sherath.*

EDON m., a m. of Thrace, Bessica, with a temple of Bacchus, whence the priestesses of that god were named Edonidæ.

EDŌNES, a people of Thrace, in its s.w. angle. Bounded N. by the Odomanti, s. by the Pieres, w. by Strymon fl., and E. by the Sapæi. At one period extending beyond the Strymon into Macedonia. The name is sometimes poetically applied to the whole Thracian people.

EDONIS, "pleasant," a name of Thasos ins.

EDRINUS lacus, a lake of Gallia Transpadana, bet. Larius lac. and Benacus lac. *Lago d'Idro.*

EDRUM, a town of the Triumpilini, Gallia Transpadana, at the s. extremity of Edrinus lac. A municipium. *Idro.*

EDRUS ins., an isl. of the Eblani, Hibernia, N. of Eblana.

EDULIUS m., I. a summit of Parnassus. II. a ridge of the Pyrenees, about Jacca s.

EDYLIUM m., a m. of Bœotia.

EETIONEIA, a fort commanding, with Alcimus prom., the entrance to the Piræus at Athens. Named after Eetion. *Trapezona.*

EGARA, a town of the Læetani, Tarraconensis, near Rubricatus fl., L., above Rubricata.

EGDEVAMA, a town of Lycaonia, bet. Velestum (20) and Pegella (20).

EGDINI, a tribe of Albiœci, Alpes Maritimæ, under the Alpes, N.W. of the Vesubiani. *Val St. Etienne.*

EGELESTA, a town of the Celtiberi, near Sucro fl., L., N.E. of Libisosa. Noted for its mineral salts. *Yniesta.*

EGERIA fons, a r. of Latium, falling into Nemorensis lac.

EGERIÆ VALLIS, a valley of Latium, Rome, near the source of Almo fl., in which was Fons Egeriæ. Both sacred to the nymph Egeria. The retreat of Numa. *Caffarilla?*

EGITA, a town of the Mœsi, Mœsia Superior, near Pons Trajani.

EGITANIA (Igedita), a town of the Lusitani, bet. Lancia Oppidana N.N.W. and Norba Cæsarea. *Idalha Vieja?*

EGITNAPOLIS (Oxybiorum portus), a port of the Oxybii, near Agatha. *Napoule.*

EGLON, a town of Judah, on Eskol fl., R., 10 m. s.w. from Eleutheropolis.

EGNATIA, a port of Calabria, on Via Egnatia, bet. Dertum and Ad Decem (10). Here was found a peculiar sort of fire-stone. *Torre d'Agnazzo.*

EGOSA, a town of the Castellani, Tarraconensis, in the Pyrenees, on Alba fl., near its source.

EIONÆ, I. the port of Amphipolis, Thrace, at the mouth of Strymon fl. A colony ot Mende. Notable for the gallant defence and heroic death of Boges, Xerxes' general. *Contessa.* II. a town of Argolis, on Saronicus sin., N.w. of Scyllæum prom. Extinct in Strabo's time. *Paleochorio.*

EIRESIDÆ, a demus of Attica, of the tribe Acamantis.

EKRON, *vide* Accaron.

ELÆA, I. a stream of Bœotia, rising in Delos m. II. an islet of Bithynia, one of the Demonisi group. III. prom., a pr. of Cyprus, s. of Carpasiæ ins. *Chalebernau.* IV. a port of Pergaminus, 1½ m. s. from Caicus fl. Founded circa 1160 B.C., by Athenians. *Clisiakevi.* V. a town of Cassiopeia, Epirus, at the mouth of Acheron fl. VI. the N. port of the Sabæ, Æthiopia.

ELÆATICUS (Cumæus) sinus, a bay of the Ægean, at Elæa, Æolis, bet. Harmatus prom. and Hydra prom. *G. di Tchandeli.*

ELÆUM, a port of Bithynia, on the Euxine, at the mouth of Elæus fl., 8 m. E. from Lilæum.

ELÆUS (Elatas), I. a r. of Bithynia, rising in Hypius m., and falling into the Euxine at Elæus. II. an islet of Caria, off Loryma. *Barbanicolo.* III. a demus of Attica, of the tribe Hippothoontis. IV. a fortress of Ætolia, near Calydon. V. a town of Chaonia, under Tomarus m., N., bet. Hadrianopolis (24) and Pandosia. *Selio.* VI. a town of Chersonesus Thracia, on the Hellespont, N. of Mastusium prom. A Tean col. With a temple and shrine of Protesilaus, for defiling which the satrap Artayctes was put to death.

ELÆUSSA ins., I. an isl. of Æolis Asiat., opposite Cane prom. II. of Cilicia Trachea, off Sebaste. Now a peninsula. The favourite residence of Archelaus of Cappadocia.

ELAH vallis, a valley of Judah, 11 m. s.w. from Jerusalem. Named from its Terebinth trees, and noted as the place of encampment of the Israelites when David slew Goliath.

ELAIUS (Elæus) m., a N.W. summit of Lycæus m., in Arcadia, on the borders of Triphylia.

ELAM, the Scriptural designation of Susiana.

ELAMITÆ, a people of Arabia Felix, on the Red Sea, bet. the Alilæi and the Tomabei. *Beni el Yam.*

ELANCUM, a maritime town of India e. Gangem, w., bet. Corcura and Cottiara.

ELAPHITIS (Elaphusa) ins., I. an islet in the Adriatic, 12 m. from Melite. II. of Chios.

ELAPHONNESUS ("stag island"), an isl. of Mysia, contiguous to Proconnesus ins.

ELAPHUS torrens, a stream of Arcadia, falling into Helisson fl. e. of Megalopolis.

ELASORA, capital of the Elasori, Arabia Felix, s.e. of Thabba. *Elaser.*

ELASORI (Elesori, Asshurim), a people of Arabia, in the mountains, N.E. of Sisippi portus. The descendants of Asshur, son of Dedan. *Tribe of El Asyr.*

ELATÆA, a city of Phocis, on the e. bank of Cephissus fl., 22 m. e. from Amphicæa. Destroyed by Xerxes, but restored. *Elephta.*

ELATAS fl., Bithyniæ, i. q. Elæus.

ELATH, the Scriptural name of Ælana, in Arabia.

ELATIA (Iletia, Iletium), a town of Perrhæbia, Thessaly, on Peneus fl., s.w. of Gonnus.

ELATOS m., a m. of Zacynthus, at its s.e. extremity, opposite Ichthys prom., in Elis. *Monte Scopo.*

ELATRIA (Elatia), a town of Cassopeia, in Epirus, near the Charadrus fl., s.w. of Batia. *Ruins near Luro.*

ELAVER (Elaris, Elauris) fl., a r. of Gaul, rising in Cevenna m., and falling into the Liger, near Noviodunum. *Allier.*

ELBO ins., an isl. of Ægypt, in the Nile.

ELCEBUS, a town of the Tribocci, Germania I., bet. Argentoratum N.E. and Argentoravia s.w.

ELCETHIUM, a town of Sicily, towards the source of Selinus fl.

ELCOBARIS, a town of the Turtetani, on Vacca fl., R., near its source.

ELDAAH, Arabiæ, i. q Ludia.

ELDANA, I. a town of the Indapratæ, Ind., N.E. of Selampura. II. of the Vettones, Lusitania, bet. Acontia w. and Salmantica e.

ELEA prom., a pr. of Cyprus, N.E. of Salamis. *C. Elea.*

ELEALEH, a town of Reuben, in Amoritis, 2 m. N.E. from Heshbon. *El-aal.*

ELEATES (Veleates) sin., a bay of Inferum m. at Velia.

ELECTRA, I. a r. of Crete, i. q. Lethæus. II. of Messenia, falling into Balyra fl. III. a town of Messenia, on Electra fl., at its junction with Coeus fl., w. of Andania. *Alitouri.*

ELECTRIDES ins. ("amber-producing"), I. the Greek name of the Glessariæ ins., several isl. of the Frisii, German., bet. the mouths of Visurgis fl. and Flevus fl. II. islets at the mouth of the Padus, which by the deposits of soil have become lagunes.

ELECTRIS ins., chief of the Electrides ins.

ELEGIA, a town of Gumathene, Armen., on the Euphrates, bet. Claudias and Juliopolis. *Elija.*

ELEGIUM, a town of the Boii, in Noricum, 13 m. e. from Lauriacum. *Near Strengberg.*

ELEGOSENE, a district of Sophene, Armen., about Mazaca. The Tigris rises in it.

ELEIA (Hileja), a town of Mesopotamia, w. of Singara.

ELEON ("marshy"), a town of Bœotia, on Asopus fl., near Tanagra.

ELEPHANTARIA, I. a town of the Corsii, Sardinia, bet. Turobolis Minor and Tibula. II. of Zeugitana, under Cirna m., s., bet. Vaga and Cluacaria.

ELEPHANTINE (Elephantis) ins., an isl. in the Nile, s. of Syene, and within it a cognominal town. Here the navigation of the Nile formerly terminated, on account of the lesser cataract a short distance above. *Djesirat Assouan.*

ELEPHAS, I. a r. of Æthiopia, falling into Erythræum m. e. of Elephas prom. II. m. of Æthiopia, terminating in Aromatum prom. *Baba Felek.* III. a prom. of Æthiopia, on Erythræum mare, e. of Aromatum prom.

ELETHYA, Ægypti, i. q. Lucina.

ELEUSA, Cilicia, i. q. Sebaste.

ELEUSA ins., I. an isl. of Attica, in Saronicus sin., opposite Astypalæa prom. *Elissa.* II. Cariæ, i. q. Hyetusa.

ELEUSIS, I. a demus of Attica, of the tribe Hippothoontis, on Saronicus sin., bet. Athens (13) and Megara (13). Named after Eleusis, son of Mercury. The seat of the Eleusinian mysteries. *Lesina.* II. a town of Bœotia, near Copæ. III. of Thera ins.

ELEUTHERÆ, I. a town of Attica, bet. Œnoe and Dryoscephalæ. In ruins in the time of Pausanias. *Gypto-castro.* II. of Bœotia, near Oropus. Founded by Cothus and Æclus. III. of Crete, near Oaxus.

ELEUTHERNA, a town of Crete, 6 m. s. from Rithymna. Here amatory songs were first composed by Amitou. *Elefterna.*

ELEUTHERO CILICES, various tribes of marauding Cilicians occupying Amanus m. The object of Cicero's Cilician campaign.

ELEUTHEROPOLIS (Bethogabris), a town of

Judah, in Judæa, bet. Jerusalem N.E. and Libna S.W. *Beit-jibrin.*

ELEUTHĒRUS fl., I. a r. of Phœnicia, falling into the sea 3 m. N. from Tripolis. *Nahr el Kibir.* II. of Sicily, falling into the Tyrrhenian sea, bet. Soluntum and Panormus. *Bajaria.*

ELGOVÆ, i. q. Selgovæ.

ELIBERRI, i. q. Illiberis.

ELICA, Tarraconensis, i. q. Illici.

ELICOCI, Narbonensis, i. q. Helvii.

ELIMBERRIS ("new town"), i. q. Augusta Ausciorum.

ELINGUS (Silpia), a town of the Oretani, Tarraconensis, N. of Castulo.

ELIS, I. a country of Peloponnesus, bounded N. by Achaia, s. by Messenia, w. by the Ionium mare, E. by Arcadia. Settled by the Caucones. Named from Eleus, a descendant of Endymion. II. its capital, on Peneus fl., bet. Cyllene (15) and Thalamæ. It was long without walls, as being sacred to Jupiter Olympius. Here were the Venus Urania, in ivory and gold, and the Minerva, of Phidias. The birth-place of Phædo, and of Pyrrho. *Palæopoli.*

ELISSON fl., a r. of Achaia, falling into Corinthiacus sin. S.E. of Aristonautæ. *Melisso.*

ELIXUS fl., a r. of Ceos ins., falling into the sea at Coressia.

ELLANDUNUM, a town of the Belgæ, Brit., w. of Sorbiodunum.

ELLĒPŌRUS fl., a r. of Bruttium, falling into the sea s. of Scyllacium. Noted for the victory of Dionysius over the allied Magna-Grecians. *Callipari.*

ELLOMENUS, a port of Leucas ins., on its E. coast, s. of Leucas opp. *Porto Vlico.*

ELLOPIA, I. a name of Eubœa ins. II. a N.E. district of Eubœa, on Callas fl.

ELMANTICA, *apud* Polyb., i. q. Salmantica.

ELORUS fl., I. Bruttii, i. q. Elleporus. II. Sicily, i. q. Helorus.

ELUI, Galliæ, i. q. Helvii.

ELUSA, I. a city of Idumæa, s. of Beerseba. *El Khulasa.* II. (Elusaberris), capital of the Elusates, Novem Populana, bet. Scittium and Vanesia. *Eauze.*

ELUSĀTES, a people of Novem Populana.

ELUSIO, a town of the Volcæ Tectosages, Narbonensis I., between Ad Vicesimum w. and Ad Fines E.

ELVIA, a town of central Paphlagonia.

ELYMA, capital of the Elymi, in Sicily, near the mouth of Simois fl.

ELYMÆA (Elymæum), I. the country of the Elymiotæ, in Macedonia, bounded N. by Eordæa, s. by Thessaly, w. by Stymphalia, E. by Pieria. II. its capital, on Haliacmon

fl., N.W. of Phylace. Founded by Elymas, the Tyrrhenian. *Near Greuno.*

ELYMÆI, the principal port of Susiana, on Persicus sin.

ELYMAIS, I. a district of Media, bet. Choromitrene and Atropatene. II. the w. portion of Susiana.

ELYMI, a tribe of Sicani in Sicily, about Elyma, Entella, Sejesta, and Eryx m. According to some historians they were a Trojan colony.

ELYMIA, a town of Arcadia, bet. Mantinea and Orchomenus.

ELYRUS, a town of Crete, N.W. of its port Suia.

ELYSII, I. a tribe of Diduni, Germ., about Hegitmatia. II. i. q. Helysices, Narbonensis.

ELYSII CAMPI, plains of Bœotia, the beauty of which suggested the name to the poets as that of the abode of the blessed after death.

EMATHIA, a district of Macedonia, bounded N. by Pelagonia, s. by Bottiæa, w. by Deuriopæa, E. by Grestonia. The district first settled by the Temenidæ of Argos.

EMATHIA, Thraciæ, i. q. Æsyme.

EMBOLIMA, a town of India, at the confluence, w., of Coas fl., with the Indus.

EMBOLUS prom., a pr. of Lycia, near the mouth of Limyrus fl. *C. Finika.*

EMĒSA, a town of Apamēne, Syriæ, S.E. of Epiphania. Noted for its Temple of Elagābalus, one of whose priests became the Heliogabalus of Imperial Rome. The locality of the great battle between Aurelian and Zenobia. *Hems.*

EMIM, a race of giants in the country afterwards called Ammonitis and Moabitis.

EMISCHABALES FONS, a town and water station of Arabia Petræa, S.E. of Gaza. *Om-el-Yemal.*

EMMAUS (Hamath), I. baths of Galilæa, on Tiberias lac., near Tiberias. II. *postea* Nicopolis, of Judæa, S.E. of Arimathea. *Amvas.* III. a village near Jerusalem, the locality of the interview with the two disciples.

EMŌDI m., a N.E. extension of Parapomisus m., m. separating India e. Gangem from Scythia. *Part of Himalaya.*

EMONA, a town of the Latovici, Pannonia, on Savus fl., L., bet. Ad Savum and Nauportus, S.W. of Celeia. *Laybach.*

EMPORIÆ, a maritime district of Byzacene, on Tritonis palus and the coast of Syrtis Minor. The name was also applied generally to Byzacene, on account of its great productiveness.

EMPORIÆ (Emporium), a city of the Indigetes, Tarraconensis, at the mouth of Clodianus fl. A Massilian settlement. A colonia of Julius Cæsar. *Ampurias.*

EMPORICUS sin., a bay of the Atlantic, at Thymiaterium.

EMPORIUM PLACENTIÆ, the port of Placentia, in Gallia Cispadana, on Padus fl., at or near Placentia. *Ponte Nura?*

EMPULUM, a fortress of the Latini, Latium, 3 m. E. from Tibur. *Ampiglione.*

ENCHELANÆ, a town of the Pissantini, Illyria, at the s. extremity of Lychnitis palus.

ENCHELEI (Enchelees), a tribe of Dalmatæ, Illyria, towards Buthua, among whom Cadmus and his wife Hermonia ended their days.

ENDIDÆ, a town of the Nauni, Rhætia, on Atagis fl., L., bet. Pons Drusi (11) and Tridentum (16). *Eyna.*

ENDOR ("fountain of the house"), a town of Manasseh, in Galilæa, s. of Nazareth; the abode of the witch consulted by Saul.

ENGANNIM ("fountain of the garden"), I. a town of Issachar. *Vide* Ginea. II. a town of Judah.

ENGEDDI ("fountain of the kid", Hazezon-Thamar), a town of Judæa, on the Dead Sea, E.S.E. of Hebron, 30 m. S.E. from Jerusalem. *Ain-jiddy.*

ENGYUM, a town of Sicily, bet. Petra and Enna. A Cretan settlement. *Gangi.*

ENHYDRIUM, a town of Pelasgiotis, Thessaly.

ENINGIACUS, a district of Scandinavia, supposed by the ancients an island. *Finland.*

ENIPEUM prom., Lucaniæ, i. q. Posidium.

ENIPĒUS (Barnichius) fl., I. a r. of Elis, falling into Alpheus fl., towards Salmone. II. of Phthiotis, in Thessaly, rising in Othrys m. S.E. of Melitæa, and falling into Apidanus fl., near Pharsalus. *Goura.* III. of Pieria, Macedoniæ, rising in Olympus, and falling into the Thermaicus sin., N. of Heracleum. *Malathria.* IV. a town of Phthiotis, in Thessaly, on the cognominal river, towards Pharsalus.

ENNA, a town of Sicily, near the source of Himera Maj. fl., bet. Calloniana and Assorus; occupying the centre of Sicily. The locality of the rape of Proserpine. *Castro San Giovanni.*

ENNEACRONNOS fl., Athenar, i. q. Callirrhoe.

ENNEA ODOI, Thraciæ, the Greek form of Novem Viæ.

ENNEMASE, a town of Rhætia, 1 m. N. from Tridentum. *Meano.*

ENIRA, a demus of Attica.

ENOPE, Messen., i. q. Gerenea.

ENROGEL ("fountain of the foot"), a pool

of Benjamin, near the pool of Siloam. Memorable as the depository of the holy fire during the Babylonish captivity.

ENTELLA, I. a r. of Liguria, falling into Ligusticus sin. *Lavagna.* II. a town of Sicily, on Hypsa Major fl., R., s. of Macella. A Carthaginian settlement. *Entella.*

ENYDRA, a town of Phœnicia, near Marathos.

EODANDA DESERTA, the country N. of Abissa, Arabiæ.

EORDÆA, the country of the Eordi, Macedoniæ, bounded N.W. by Lyncus, N.E. by Bottiæa, s. by Elymæa, w. by Orestis, E. by Pieria.

EORDAICUS fl., a r. of Macedonia, rising in Candavii m., and, after traversing Orestis and Elymæa, falling into the Haliacmon below Phylace. *Bichlistas.*

EORDETI, a people of Illyria, bounded N. by the Albani and Parthini, s. by the Atintanes, w. by the Taulantii, E. by the Dassaretæ.

EORDI, the original appellation of the Leleges in Macedonia. They were also called Centauri.

EOUS OCEANUS, the ocean washing the E. shores of India e. Gangem and of Serica.

EPACRIA (Diacria), a district of Attica, on Pentelicus m.

EPAGERITÆ, a people of Sarmatia, in Caucasus m.

EPAGRIS, a name of Andros ins.

EPAMANDUODURUM, a town of the Sequani, Maxima Sequanorum, on Dubis fl., R., bet. Larga and Velatodurum. *Mandeure.*

EPANTERII, "dwellers on the heights," a people of Liguria, in the Alpes Maritimæ, above the Ingauni. *About Monte-Acuto.*

EPARA, a town of Characene, Babylonia, on the Euphrates, bet. Aphle and Charax.

EPEA (Elis Propria), the country of the Epei, in Elis, N. of Peneus fl., named from Epeus, son of Endymion.

EPETIUM, a town of the Dalmatæ, Illyria, s. of Naro fl. *Stobræa.*

EPHAH, a district of Arabia, on the Red Sea, N. of Charmothus Portus. The seat of the children of Ephah, eldest son of Midian. *About Makar Efa.*

EPHERA, a district of Arabia, on Ælaniticus sin., bet. Ælana and Modiana. The seat of the descendants of Epher, second son of Midian. *About Shor Afar.*

EPHESUS (Smyrna, Samorna, Trachea, Ortygia, Ptelea), the metropolis of Ionia, under Prion m., on Caystrus fl., L., just above its mouth, bet. Colophon and Magnesia, founded by the Amazons. A Lelegian town, settled by Attic Ionians, under Androclus, s. of Codrus. Celebrated for the temple of Diana, built by Chersiphron; burned by Herostratus 356 B.C.; rebuilt by Dinocrates; destroyed 260 A.D. Ephesus was the great commercial emporium of Asia, and, by the agency of St. Paul, became its Christian metropolis. It was the birthplace of Heraclitus the Obscure, Hermodorus, Hipponax, Artemidorus, Alexander Lychnus, Apelles, and Parrhasius. The people were said to be magicians. *Ayasluck.*

EPHIALTIUM prom., the N. prom. of Carpathus ins.

EPHRAIM, I. a tribe of Israel, bounded N. by Issachar, at Ebal m., and the half tribe of Manasseh at Kana fl., s. by Dan, (w. at Geser) and Benjamin, at Haza, w. by the Mediterranean, E. by the Jordan. II. m., m. of Judæa and Samaria, bet. Sechem N. and Jerusalem s. III. a town of Benjamin, 8 m. N. from Jerusalem.

EPHRATA, the ancient name of Bethlehem, and of the surrounding district.

EPHŸRE, I. an island of Argolis, in the Argolicus sin., over against Boli. *Hypsili.* II. the early name of Corinth. III. a town of Achaia, towards Corinthia. IV. of the Agræi, Acarnania. V. a town of Arcadia. VI. (Ænoe, Bæonoa), a town of Ephea, Elis, on Selleis fl., near its mouth, 15 m. s.w. from Elis. VII. *postea* Cichyrus, capital of Thesprotia, in Epirus, near the w. extremity of Acherusia palus, where Theseus and Pirithous were imprisoned for their attempt to carry off Proserpina. Built by Phidippus, grand-son of Hercules. The district was noted for the growth of poisonous drugs. *Near Castrizza.*

EPIACUM, a town of the Brigantes, Brit., on Vedra fl., R., bet. Vindolana and Corstopitum. *Lanchester.*

EPICARIA, a town of the Cavii, in Illyria, bet. Lissus and Crevenia.

EPICAROS, a town of Palestine, on the Dead Sea, s. of Callirrhoe.

EPICEPHISIA, a demus of Attica, of the tribe Æneis.

EPICHUS, a town of Syrtis Regio, Africæ, 25 m. from Meninx ins.

EPICRANE fons (Epicrene), a fountain of Bœotia.

EPIDAURUS, I. *prius* Epicarus, a city of Argolis, on Saronicus sin., opposite Pityonnesus ins. A Carian colony, enlarged by settlers from Epidaurus, Illyriæ. The birth-place of Æsculapius. *Epidaurs.* II. a town of the Dalmatæ, Illyria, on the Adriatic, s. of Naro fl. A colonia. *Ragusa Vecchia.* III. *surnamed* Limera or

Limenera, a town of Laconia, on the Ægean, 25 m. N. of Epidelium. Founded by the Argives. *Palæo Emvasia.*

EPIDAMNUS, *postea* Dyrrachium, capital of the Taulantii, in Illyria, N. of Petra prom. Founded by Corcyreans 625 B.C. A colonia. The name is by some authors said to have been changed from Epidamnus to Dyrrhachium, on account of the sinister meaning applicable to the former designation. Venus was especially worshipped here. *Durazzo.*

EPIDELIUM, a town of Laconia, on the Ægean, near Malea prom. *Sant' Angelo.*

EPIDERPON, Venetiæ, i. q. Opitergium.

EPIDIA ins., Inf. et Sup., two of the Ebudæ ins., Brit.

EPIDIUM prom., a pr. of the Epidii, Brit., opposite Robugdium prom. *Mull of Cantyre.*

EPIECIA, a town of Corinthia, on the confines of Argolis, N.E. of Bembina.

EPIEICĪDÆ, a demus of Attica, of the tribe Cecropis.

EPINA (Elidis), i. q. Harpenna.

EPIMARANITÆ, Arabiæ, i. q. Maranitæ.

EPIOROS ins. (Nanigeris), an isl. of Taprobane, over against Cory ins.

EPIPHANIA, I. a city of Apamene, Syria, on the Orontes, 23 geog. m. N.W. of Emèsa. *Hamah.* II. (*prius* Æniandus), of Cilicia Campestris, bet. Anazarba (30) and Antiochia (30). Built by Antiochus Epiphanes.

EPIRUS ("mainland"), a country of Europe, bounded N. by Illyria, s. by Acarnania, w. by the Ionium mare, E. by Athamania, or, earlier, by Achelous fl. Established as a kingdom by Pyrrhus, son of Neoptolemus and grandson of Neptune, B.C. 1170.

EPITALIUM, a town of Triphylia, Elis, s. of Phrixa. The Homeric Thryon or Thryoessa of Nestor.

EPIUM, a town of Triphylia, in Elis, N.E. of Macistus, on Alpheus fl., L.

EPOPEUS m., a volcanic m. of Ænaria ins., whose eruptions gave rise to the fables respecting the giant Typhœus in connexion with this island. *M. Epomeo; Monte San Niccolo.*

EPARA, a town of the Turtuli, Bætica, on the Bætis, L., above Corduba (28).

EPAREDIA ("horse-tamer"), a city of the Salassi, in Gallia Transp., on Duria Maj. fl., L., bet. Vitricium (21) and Vercellæ (33). A colonia and municipium. *Ivrea.*

EPOISSUM, a town of the Treveri, Belgica I., bet. Meduantum N.E. and Mosa s.w.

EPOTIUM, a town of the Vulgientes, Narbonensis, on Druentia fl., bet. Alabon and Segustero.

EPYRUS, a town of the Bistones, Thrace, on Egnatia Via, bet. Pistyrus (8) and Bistonia (20).

EQUABONA, a town of the Celtici, Lusitania, at the mouth, L., of the Tagus, opposite Olisipo. *Coyna.*

EQUITURRI, a tribe of Salyes, Narbonensis, on Varus fl., R., above the Nerusci. *In Entre-Deux.*

EQUUS TUTICUS ("great horse"), an Oscan town of the Hirpini, in Samnium, on Via Egnatia, bet. Forum Novum (12) and Æcæ (8). The place whose name Horace found impracticable. *Church of San' Eleuterio.*

ERACTUM, a town of Dacia, towards Clepidava.

ERÆ, Ioniæ, i. q. Geræ.

ERAGISA, a town of Cyrrhestica, Syr., on the Euphrates, bet. Barbalissus and Apammaris (16). *Rasek.*

ERANA, I. a fortress of the Eleutherocilices, in Amanus m. II. a town of Messenia, s. of Cyparissium prom. The Arene of Homer. *Ordina.*

ERANNOBOAS fl., a r. of India, falling into the Ganges, E. of Palimbothra.

ERASINUS fl., I. a r. of Argolis, falling into Argolicus sin., below Lerna. *Kefalari.* II. of Attica, rising near Pentele, and falling into the Ægean, below Brauron.

ERATYRA, a district of Elamea, in Macedonia.

ERAVISCI, a people of Pannonia.

ERBESSUS (Herbessa), a town of Sicily, N.E. of Agrigentum.

ERCALUM, a town of the Hylæ, Sarmat., on Carcines fl., towards its source.

ERCHEIA, a demus of Attica, of the tribe Ægeis. The birth-place of Xenophon and of Isocrates.

ERCHOAS, a town of the Nubæ, on the Nile, bet. Cambysis Ærarium and Satachta.

ERCOBRIGA, Hispaniæ, i. q. Talabriga.

ERCTA prom., a pr. of Sicily, N., above Panormus, or, according to some geographers, N. of Eryx.

ERDINI, a people of Hibernia, W., bet. the Venicnii, N., and the Magnatæ, s. *Sligo and Antrim.*

EREBANTIUM prom., the N. extremity of Sardinia. *Longo Sardo ; Cabo della Testa.*

EREBINTHODIS ins., an isl. of Bithynia, one of the Demonisi group.

ERECH, i. q. I. Araca. II. Edessa, Mesop.

ERECTHEIA, a demus of Attica, of the tribe Ægeis.

EREMOSGRÆA, a fortress of Cappadocia, bet. Ardula and Cucusus.

ERENEA, a village of Megaris, near Megara.

ERESII, Mysiæ, i. q. Argiza.

ERESSUS, a town of Lesbos ins., on the s.w. coast, 3½ m. S.E. from Sigrium prom. The birth-place of Theophrastus and Phanias. Noted for its fine flour. *Eresso.*

ERETĒNUS. *Vide* Eridanus.

ERETRIA (Arotria, Melaneis), I. a town of Eubœa, on the w. coast, opposite Delphinium, the largest in the island next to Chalcis. A colony from Eretria in Attica. Here was a famous school of philosophy and dialectics. *Castri.* II. of Phthiotis, Thessaly, bet. Pharsalus and Pheræ. *Near Tzangli.*

ERETUM, a town of Sabinium, on Tiberis fl., L., bet. Rome (18) and Vicus Novus (14), on Via Salaria. Sacred to Here (Juno). *Rimane.*

ERGASTERION, a mining town of Mysia, bet. Argesæ (15) and Cyzicus.

ERGAVĬCA (Ergavia), a town of the Vaccæi, Tarraconensis, E. of the source of the Tagus. A colonia and municipium.

ERGETIUM (Sergentum), a town of Sicily, S.E. of Enna, on Chrysas fl., R.

ERGINA fl., Thraciæ, i. q. Agrianes.

ERGISCE, a town of the Cicones, Thrace.

ERIBÆA, a town of the Paravæi, on the N. bank of Aous fl. *Eriboe.*

ERIBIANUS m., *apud* Ptol., i.q. Callicula m.

ERIBOLUM (Hyribolum, Eribæa), a village of Bithynia, on Astacenus sin., s., opposite Nicomedia. *Karamusal.*

ERICEIA, a demus of Attica, of the tribe Ægeis.

ERICINUM, a town of Perrhæbia, Thessaly, on the confines of Estiæotis. II. Sardiniæ, i. q. Erucium.

ERICUSA ins., an isl. of Sardinia, N. of Didyme ins. *Dattolo.*

ERIDANUS fl., I. a r. of Athens, running into the Ilissus, near the Lyceum. II. (Eretenos, Rhodanus, *postea* Reteno), a r. of Venetia, rising N.w. of Vicetia, and passing by Aponifontes, falling into the Adriatic, N. of Padus fl. Noted for its eels. *Bachiglione.* III. (Spineticum Ostium), the branch of Padus fl., falling into the Adriatic at Spineticum. *Po di Primaro.* IV. the Greek name of Padus fl. Associated poetically, with the fall of Phaeton, and the amber tears of his weeping sisters, from the circumstance that, of old, the Po produced amber.

ERINÆI, a people of Scythia, N. of the Serbi.

ERIMON, an inland town of the Ænotri, Bruttium.

ERINEUS, I. a r. of Siciiy, falling into Siculum mare, bet. Neustathmus portus and Asinarus fl. *Miranda.* II. a town of Attica, on Cephissus Eleusinius fl., near Eleusis. Here Pluto descended into the earth with Proserpine. III. of Doris, on Pindus fl. *Artotina.* IV. the harbour of Rhypæ, in Achaia, at the mouth of Phœnix fl., 1 m. from Ægium.

ERISANE, a town of Bætica.

ERISTHE, a port of Arabia Felix, s., towards Abisama. *Resem; Reschin.*

ERIX, a maritime town of the Apuani, in Liguria, the port of Luna, on Portus Lunæ. *Spezzia?*

ERIZA (Erezus), a town of Phrygia Mag., on the borders of Caria, on Caus fl., bet. Laodicea ad Lycum and Themisonium. *Bazarkhan.*

ERLAPI fl. *Vide* Arelate.

ERMIN STREET (Hermann Street), a Roman road in Britain, extending from Holborn, London, to St. David's, in Wales, with a branch to Southampton.

ERNODURUM, a town of the Bituriges Cubi, Aquitania I., bet. Avaricum, N.E. and Alerta, S.W.

ERNOLATIUM, a town of Noricum, on Amisus fl., L., bet. Tutatio (12) and Gabromagus (8). *Near Bongras,* N.

ERNAGO, a town of the Desuviates, Gallia Viennensis, N. of Arelate (7½). *St. Gabriel.*

EROCHUS, a town of Phocis, towards Panopeus.

ERŒADÆ, a demus of Attica, of the tribe Hippothoontis.

ERONOBOOS fl., Ind. i. q. Sonus.

ERUCIUM (Ericinum), a town of the Balari, in Sardinia, on Coquinas fl., S.E. of Tibula.

ERYANNUS fl., a r. of Æolis Asiat., rising in Ida m., and falling into Adramyttenus sin.

ERYCE (Eruca), a town of Sicily, near the source of Eryces fl., N.W. of Hybla Heræa.

ERŸCES fl., a r. of Sicily, rising near Eryce. *Palagonia.*

ERYMANTHUS, I. an early name of Psophis, Arcadia. II. a r. of Arcadia, rising in Lampe m., and falling into Alpheus fl. above Phrixus. *Dogana.* III. a range of m., on the N. frontier of Arcadia, bet. Scollis m. and Crathis m., where Hercules destroyed the boar. *Olonos.*

ERYMMI, a maritime town of Scythia, on the Rha.

ERYMNA, an early name of Tralles, in Lydia.

ERYMNÆ, Magnesia, i. q. Eurymenæ.

ERYTHIA ins., the isl. next to that on which Gades formerly stood. It is associated by the poets with the story of Geryon.

ERYTHINI, "red heaps," a maritime town of Paphlagonia, on the rocks, 8 m. E. from Amastris.

ERYTHRÆ, I. a town of Bœotia, s. of Platæa, on Asopus fl. Famous for its bread. In ruins in the time of Pausanias. II. a town of Crete, at Erythræum prom. III. of Dardania, near Gergitha. The birthplace of the Erythræan sibyl. IV. the port of Eupalium, in Locris, on Corinthiacus sin. *Kokino.* V. (Cnopupolis), one of the twelve cities of Ionia, on Erythræus sin., at the mouth of Aleos fl., opposite Chios opp. A Cretan and Lycian colony, under Erythrus; augmented subsequently by settlers from Attica, under Cnopus, son of Codrus. The seat of the elder Erythræan sibyl. Noted for its wine and fine flour. *Ritre.*

ERYTHRÆUM mare, the portion of the Indicus Oceanus; s. as Erythræum mare, specially; w. as Rubrum mare or Arabian sin., E. as Persicus sin., which washes the coasts of Arabia. Named from king Erythras, son of Perseus and Andromeda; or, according to Forster and others, from Edom (Esau)? II. prom. a pr. of Crete, on the S.E. coast, w. of Ampelus prom. *C. Langada.*

ERYTHRÆUS sin., a bay of Ionium mare, at Erythræ.

ERYTHRON, a maritime town of Pentapolis, Cyrenaicæ, bet. Chersis and Naustathmos.

ERYX, a city of Sicily, on the s. slope of Eryx m. *San Giuliano.*

ERYX m., a m. occupying the N.W. angle of Sicily; the highest in the island after Etna. On its summit was a temple of Venus Erycina. *Monte San Giuliano.*

ESAR, Meroe, i. q. Axume.

ESBUTA (Sebounta), a town of Idumæa, 10 m. N.N.E. from Ludia. The seat of the descendants of Ishbak. *Shobak.*

ESCĀMUS fl., a r. of Mœsia, falling into the Danube.

ESCADIA, Escua, a town of Bætica, N. of Obucula.

ESCIUS fl., Mæs. i. q. Œseus.

ESCO, a town of the Estiones, Vindelicia, on Vinda fl., towards its source, bet. Cambodunum (20) and Abodiacum (18).

ESCO NOVA, a town of the Licates, Vindelicia, on Licus fl., E. of Esco.

ESDRAELON VALLIS, Galileæ. *Vide* Campus Magnus.

ESHTAOL, a town of Judah, s.e. of Ascalon.

ESHTEMOA (Ashtemoh), a town of Judah, s. *Sema.*

ESIONGEBER (Asiongeber), the Scriptural name of Berenice Ælanitica.

ESKOL fl., a r. of Judæa, falling into the Mediterranean near Ascalon, s. In the cognominal valley through which it ran, the large bunch of grapes was cut by the scouts of Moses.

ESOPIS, I. a r. of Bruttium, falling into Locrensis sin., near Locri. II. a summit of the Apennines, at Locri, on which stood the citadel of that city.

ESROM, i. q. Hezron.

ESSEDONES, a people of Sarmatia Asiat., N. of the Napitæ.

ESSUI (Sagii, Saii), a people of Lugdunensis II., bet. the Aulerci Cenomanni s. and the Aulerci Eburovices N. *About Seez.*

ESTHEMOA, a sacerdotal city of Juda, s.e. of Lachis.

ESTIA lacus, a lake of Germania Magna. *Dammersee.*

ESTIA prom., a pr. of Bithynia, on Bosporus Thracius, e. of Argyronium prom. Here was the Hieron, a temple of Jupiter Urius, and an Altar of the Twelve Gods, consecrated by Jason.

ESTIÆOTIS, a district of Thessaly, on the confines of Athamania, N. of Dolopia; the territory principally of Medon. Originally the country of the Dorians.

ESTIONES, a tribe of Vindelici, Rhæt., bet. the Danube, N., the Focunates, s., the Licates, e., and the Lentienses, w.

ESTOBARA, a town of Bactriana, near the source of Ochus fl.

ESUBIANI, a people of the Alps, contiguous to the Edenates. *On the Vesubia.*

ESURIS, a maritime town of the Turtetani, Bætica, at the mouth of the Anas. *Castromaria.*

ETANNA, I. a town of the Allobroges, Viennensis, on Rhodanus fl., bet. Condate and Augusta. II. (Catenna, Atmenia), of Pisidia, e. of Selge.

ETAXALOS ins., an isl. of the Omanitæ, Arabiæ.

ETEOCRETES, "true Cretans," the primitive occupants of the s. coast of Crete.

ETEONUS, *postea* Scarphe, a town of Bœotia, on Asopus fl., R., bet. Siolus and Erythræ.

ETERA, a town of Crete, in Didymi sinus, bet. Camara (3) and Cetia prom. *Leopetro.*

ETHAM, I. a desert of Egypt and Arabia, at the head of the Red Sea. II. a town of Lower Egypt, near the w. branch of Amarus lacus, N.W. of Arsinoe, bet. Suchoth and Hiroth. The second stage of the Israelites after their departure from Raemsis (Heroopolis). III. a town of Judah, 1½ m. s. from Bethlehem. Built by Rehoboam. *Elitash.*

ETHOPA, a hill fortress of Athamania, in Ætolia, near Argithea, towards the confines of Thessaly.

ETIA, a town of Crete, w. of Itanus. The birth-place of the sage Miso.

ETIS, Etia, a town of Laconia, near Aphrodisias. Founded by Æneas.

ETOBĒMA (Etobesa, Honosca), a town of the Edetani, Tarraconensis, N.W. of Segobriga. *Oropesa.*

ETOCETUM, a town of the Cornavii, Brit. Rom., s.e. of Penocrucium. *Wall, near Lichfield.*

ETŌNE, *postea* Lemone, a town of Perrhæbia, N. of Elatia.

ETONEA, Tonia, a town of the Trocmi, Galatia, bet. Tavium (13) and Carissa.

ETONISSA (Etobema, Etovesa), a maritime town of the Ilercaones, Tarraconensis, bet. Caprasia prom. N.E. and Sepelaci s.w. *Segorbe.*

ETOSCA, Tarracon. *apud* Vell. Paterc., i. q. Osca.

ETRURIA, a region of Italy, bounded N.W. by Liguria, at Macra fl., N.E. by Gallia Cispadana, at the Apennines, w. by Tyrrhenum mare, e. by Umbria, at the Apennines and Tiberis fl., s. by Latium and Sabinium at Tiberis fl. For Etruria, in its larger signification, see Tyrrheni.

ETRUSCI, Tusci, i. q. Tyrrheni.

ETYMANDRUS fl., a r. of Aria, rising in Parapomisus m., and falling into Aria Palus. *Hilmend.*

EUASPLA fl., Indiæ, i. q. Cophen.

EUBŒA, I. " fine oxen " (Ellopia, Asopis, Abantia, *prius* Macris), an isl. of the Ægean, extending along the coasts of Phocis, Bœotia, and Attica. In breadth from 2 to 17 m., in length 150, in circuit 365. It was supposed to have been torn from the continent by an earthquake. Settled originally by Phœnicians, under Cadmus, and afterwards by Dryopes, and by Abantes from Abæ, in Phocis. The name is fabulously derived from the visit here of Io in her metamorphosis. *Egripo; Negropont.* II. m., a m. of Argolis, 2 m. from Mycenæ. III. a town of Sicily, on Simæthus fl., towards Mylæ.

EUBOIS, a town of Eubœa, swallowed up by an earthquake.

EUBULUM portus, Taurica Chersonesus, i. q. Symboli prom.

EUBURIATES, a mountain tribe of Liguria, above Genua.

EUCARPIA, a town of Phrygia Magna, w. of Synnada, N.E. of Eumenia (30). Noted for its fine grapes.

EUCRATIDIA, a town of Bactria, N.W. of Bactra. Built by king Eucratides.

EUDIELOS, Bœotia, i. q. Aspledon.

EUDIÊRUM, a fortress of Perrhæbia, Thessaly, N.E. of Ascuris palus. *Konospoli.*

EUDIPHUS, i. q. Eulepa.

EUDIXATA, a town of Armenia Minor.

EUDOCIA, a town of Pamphylia, near Termessus.

EUDON fl., a r. of Lydia, flowing by Tralles into Mæandrus fl.

EUDOSII, a tribe of Vindili, Germania, N. of the Semnones.

EUDOXIA, I. a town of Pontus, s.w. of Comana. II. of the Tolistoboii, Galatia, near Germa.

EUDRACINUM, a town of the Salassi, Gallia Transpadana, bet. Summus Penninus (10) and Augusta Prætoria (15).

EUERCES, *vide* Isaura.

EUGANEI, a primitive race of N.E. Italy, who, driven from their possessions in Venetia by the Etruscans, settled w. of Athesis fl., about the lakes Sebinus, Edrus, and Benacus, where they occupied 34 towns, which were admitted by Augustus to the rights of Latin cities.

EUGENIUM, a fortress of the Parthini, Illyria, s.w. of Dimallum. *Ichin.*

EUGION fl., a sacred stream of Bruttium, falling into Metaurus fl. E. of Portus Orestis.

EUGONE, i. q. Itonia in Pontus.

EUHIPPA, an early name of Thyatira, Lydia.

EULÆUS (Ulai), fl., Susianæ, i. q. Choaspis, or, according to some geographers, a r. of Susiana, falling into Cophrates fl. *Kuran.*

EULEPA, a town of Cappadocia, bet. Cæsarea (16) and Armaxata (24).

EUMÆA, a town of Pontus, on Halys fl., L., near Camisa.

EUMENES portus, Arabiæ, i. q. Orine.

EUMENIA, a town of Phrygia Magna, on Glaucus fl., N. of Peltæ. Founded by Eumenes. *Ishekle.*

EUMOLFIAS, the early name of Philippopolis, Thraciæ.

EUNÆ, a town of Caria.

EUNÆA, a town of Cynuria, Argolis.

EUONYMIA, a demus of Attica, of the tribe Erectheis.

EUONYMUS ins., Sicily, i. q. Didyme.

EUPAGIUM, a town of Acrorea, Elis, N. of Alium.

EUPALIUM (Eupolium), a town of the Locri Ozolæ, on the confines of Ætolia, N.E. of Naupactus.

EUPATÔRIA, *postea* Magnopolis, I. a town of Pontus, at the junction of Lycus fl. with Iris fl., N.W. of Cabira. Founded by Mithridates Eupator, completed by Pompey the Great. *Tchenikeh.* II. of Taurica Chersonesus, w. above Chersonesus. Built by Mithridates Eupator. *Eupatoria; Kaslov.*

EUPHORBIUM, a town of Phrygia Magna, bet. Synnada (37) and Apamea Cibotus (36), on Orgas fl. *Sandakli.*

EUPHRANTA, a fortress of the Psylli, Africæ, on Syrtis Major, bet. Putea Nigra and Macomades Psyllorum. In the time of Ptolemy, this was the boundary w. of Cyrenaica.

EUPHRÂTES (*biblicè* Pherath), fl., a r. of Asia, rising in Abus m., Armenia, and, after separating Asia Minor from Armenia Major, and Syria from Mesopotamia, falling, combined with the Tigris, after a course of 1147 m., into Persicus sin. There were various artificial canals connecting it with the Tigris about Seleucia and Babylon, " the rivers of Babylon " of the Psalmist. According to Pliny the Euphrates originally fell into Persicus sin. by a natural channel of its own, 7 m., or, according to some writers, 25 m. w. of the Tigris.- *Euphrates; Phrat.*

EUPHRATIS ins., islets in the Euphrates, above Phatusa.

EUPILIS lacus, a lake of the Orobii, Gallia Transpadana, s. of Larius lacus. *Pieve d'Incino.*

EUPLÆA ins., an islet of Campania, in Cumanus sin., under Pausilypus m. *La Gaiola.*

EUPOLIUM, a town of the Locri Ozolæ, inland from Erythræ, its port.

EUPOREA, a town of Bisaltia, Macedonia, on Strymon fl., bet. Gazorus (8) and Heraclea Sintica (17).

EURÆA, a town of Molossis, on the w. bank of Pambotis lacus, s.E. of Horreum. *Jannina.*

EURANIUM, a town of Caria.

EUREIS, I. a r. of Troas. II. a village of Troas, on Eureis fl., near Scepsis.

EURIA, a maritime town of Marmarica, bet. Plynos and Petræ Magnæ portus.

EURIAPA, a town of Sarmatia, E. of Corusia. *Rawkagskaia.*

EURÎPUS, I. the strait dividing Eubœa from

Bœotia. It was subject to extraordinary tides and currents. II. a bay of the Ægean, in Lesbos s.w. III. i. q. Chalcis, Eubœa.

EURIPYDÆ, a demus of Attica, of the tribe Leontis, near Cropia.

EURŎMUS (Eurŏpus), *prius* Idria and Chrysaoris, a town of Caria, towards the head of Issicus sin. Founded by Idreus, son of Car. *Mendelet.*

EURŎPA, "land of the evening, the West," one of the three divisions of the world known to the ancients. Bounded N. by Oceanus Borealis, s. by the Mediterranean, w. by the Atlantic, E. by the Tanais (or, according to Herodotus, &c., the Phasis), the Mæotis palus, the Euxine, the Propontis, the Hellespont, and the Ægean. The name is traditionally derived from Europa, daughter of Agenor. Its original population, scattered savages, was augmented at various periods from the E. (the expedition of the Argonauts up the Danube was in 1350 B.C.) and N.E.

EUROPUS, I. a town of Almopœia, Pæonia, w. of Apsalus. II. of Bottiæa, on the Ludias fl., above Ichnæ. III. of Cyrrhestica, on the Euphrates, bet. Ceciliana and Zeugma (14). Built by the Macedonians. *Jerabis.* IV. of Emathia, Macedonia, on the Axius fl. below Almana. V. Mediæ, i. q. Rhagæ.

EUROTAS fl., I. Japygiæ, i. q. Galæsus. II. a r. of Laconia, rising near Belemina and falling into Laconicus sin. w. of Helos. In its course it disappears for a time under ground, reappearing near Belmina. *Vide* Alpheus fl. *Ere ; Vasilico - Potamo,* "*royal river.*" III. Thessaliæ, i. q. Titaresius.

EURYAMPUS, a town of Magnesia, Thessaly.

EURYDICEA, a town of Pallene, Macedonia.

EURYELOS prom., a pr. of Sicily, near Syracuse.

EURYLEÆ, a village of Achaia, near Olenus.

EURYMEDON fl., a r. of Pamphylia, rising on the confines of Phrygia, E. of Sidera, and falling into the sea below Aspendus, w. of Side. Memorable for the double defeat, on sea and land, of the Persians by Cimon. *Caprisou.*

EURYMĒNÆ (Erymnæ), I. a town of Magnesia, Thessaly, on the coast, bet. Myræ and Rhizus. II. of Molossis, Epirus, towards Euræa. Destroyed by Cassander.

EURYNASSA ins., an isl. of Chios.

EURYTANES, a people of Ætolia, occupying the country from about Thermus N. to the borders of Thessaly. A very savage people, reputed to live on raw flesh.

EUSCHŒNUS, a maritime town of Cyrenaica w., bet. Hyphali and Cænon.

EUSEBIA AD ARGÆUM, the name given to Mazaca, Cappadocia, by Ariobarzanes Eusebes.

EUSEBIA AD TAURUM, a later name of Izana. Cappadocia.

EUSENE, a maritime town of Pontus, bet. Naustathmus (20) and Amisus (8).

EUSPÆNA, i. q. Phuphuena.

EUTHENE (Eutane), a town of Caria, on Doridis sin.

EUTHYMEDIA, Indiæ, i. q. Sagala.

EUTRESIS, a town of Bœotia, bet. Thespiæ and Platæa, N.E. of Leuctra, where Amphion and Zethus dwelt before they reigned in Thebes. Extinct in the time of Pausanias. *Phria.*

EUTRESIUM, a town of Arcadia, towards Mantinea.

EUTRETUS portus, a port of Alcyonium mare, near Siphæ. *Bathi.*

EUXINUS pontus, an inland sea, separating Europe from Asia, bet. Bosporus Thracius and Tanais fl. In circuit 2500 m. It is said to have been first named Axenus, "inhospitable," from its tempestuousness, or from the savage character of the population on its shores. Its form the ancients likened to a Scythian bow, of which the coast of Asia Minor was the chord. By the earlier geographers the Euxine was supposed to communicate with the Adriatic, an error arising from the Argonautic migrations up the Danube. *Euxine.*

EVA, a town of Cynuria, Argolis, under Parnon m., N.W. of Thyrea.

EVAGINA, a town of the Trocmi, Galatia, bet. Tavium (16) and Saralium (24). The Phuibagana of Ptolemy.

EVAN m., a summit of Ithome m., E. of Messene.

EVANDRIA, a town of the Turtuli, Bætica, on the Bætis, bet. Dipo and Augusta Emerita.

EVARCHUS (Evechus) fl., a r. of Paphlagonia, running into the Euxine at Cyptasia, the early limit of Paphlagonia and Cappadocia.

EVARIA (Haræ), a town of Palmyrene, bet. Palmyra and Adata.

EVAS m., a summit of Thornax m., Laconia, E. of Sellasia.

EVAZÆ, a people of Sarmatia Asiatica.

EVENUS fl., I. a r. of Æolis Asiatica, rising near Lyrnessus and falling into Adramyttenus sin., near Pitane. Adramyttium was supplied hence with water by an aqueduct. *Tchandeli.* II. *prius* Lycormas, of Ætolia, rising in Callidromus m., near Bomium, and falling into Corinthiacus sin. near Chalcis. Celebrated for the story of Nessus. *Fidari.*

EVII, a town of the Dassaretæ, Illyria.

EVONYMITÆ, a people of Meroe, on the left bank of the Nile, s. of Dodecaschœnus.

EVORAS m., a summit of Taygetus m., Laconiæ.

EVOROLUCUM, a town of the Arverni, Aquitania I., s.e. of Aquæ Neræ.

EX, Bætica, *vide* Saxetanum.

EXAMPÆI regio, a district of Sarmatia e., on Hypanis fl.

EXCISUM, a town of the Nitrobriges, Aquitania II., bet. Trajectus N. and Aginnum s.s.w.

EXOBYGITÆ, a people of Sarmatia, bet. the Roxolani and the Hamaxaboii.

EXOPOLIS, Sarmatia, i. q. Gelonus.

EXTERUM mare, the name given, as being outside Herculis Fretum, to the Atlantic.

F.

FABARIA, i. q. Burchana.

FABARIS fl., i. q. Farfarus.

FABIRANUM, a town of Germania, N.W. of Tecelia.

FABRATERIA, a town of the Volsci, Latium, on Liris fl., bet. Fregellæ (3) and Aquinum (8), on Via Latina. *Falvaterra.*

FACELINUS fl., Siciliæ, i. q. Melas, from *Fax*, the torch of Diana, to whom the river was sacred. The name is sometimes given Fascelinus, as from *fascis*, the bundle of brushwood in which her image was secretly conveyed from the Taurica Chersonesus.

FÆSULÆ (Fæsula), a Tyrrhenian town of Etruria, 3 m. N.E. of Florentia. A colonia of Sylla. The head quarters, in Etruria, of Catiline. *Fiesole.*

FAGITANA, a town of Rhætia.

FALACRINUM (Falacrine), I. a town of Sabinium, on Via Salaria, N. of Interocrea. The birth-place of Vespasian. *Ch. of San Silvestro in Falacrino.* II. of Sabinium, bet. Forum Decii (2) and Vicus Badies (9), on Via Salaria. *Falacrino.*

FALERIA, a town of Picenum, s. of Urbs Salvia. *Falleroni.*

FALERII (Falerium, Falisca), capital of the Falisci, Etruria, on Via Amerina, bet. Nepete (5) and Castell. Amerinum (12). A Siculian town. A colonia of Augustus. Noted for its fertility, for its sausages, and for the story of the treacherous schoolmaster. *Citta Castellana.*

FALERII NOVUM, the later capital of the Falisci, at the foot of the hill on which stood Falerii vetus. *S. Maria Falari.*

FALERNUS ager, a district of Campania, extending from Massici m. to Vulturnus fl. Noted as producing the best wine in the world.

FANESIORUM ins., *vide* Oonæ.

FANUM CARISII, I. a maritime town of the Æsaronenses, Sardinia, bet. Feronia and Viniola. II. FORTUNÆ, a town of Umbria, at the mouth of Metaurus fl., bet. Pisaurum (8) and Ad Pirum. A colonia of Augustus (Julia Fanestris). *Fano.* III. FUGITIVI, of Umbria, on Via Flaminia, bet. Tres Tabernæ (10) and Spoletium (7). *Monte Summo.* IV. MARTIS, of the Nervii, Belgica II., E. of Bagacum. V. of the Osismi, Lugdunensis III., w. of Vorginum. *Sauvagere.* VI. MINERVÆ, of the Remi, Belgica II., bet. Basilia N.W. and Ariola s.E. VII. VACUNÆ, round a T. of Vacuna, near Cures, Sabinium. *On Rocca Giovane.* VIII. VOLTUMNÆ, a temple of Voltumna, Etruria, s.E. of Vulsiniensis lac., where the solemn assemblies of the Tyrrhenian nation were held. *Ch. of Santa Maria in Volturno, at Viterbo.*

FARFARUS (Fabaris) fl., a r. of Sabinium, falling into the Tiber s.E. of Soracte m. *Farfa.*

FASIANA, a town of the Boii, Noricum, on the Danube, bet. Trigesamum and Pirum Tortum.

FAURUS fl., a r. of the Marrucini, falling into the Adriatic at Angulum. *Foro.*

FAUSTIANUS, a village in Falernus Ager of Campania, 6 m. s.E. of Sinuessa. Its district produced the choicest of the Falernian wine.

FAUSTINOPOLIS, a town of Tyanitis, Cappadocia, s.E. of Tyana (12). Built on the site of Halala, by Marcus Aurelius, in honour of his wife Faustina, who died here.

FAVENTIA, a town of Gallia Cispad., bet. Forum Cornelii (10) and Forum Livii (5). *Faenza.*

FAVERIA, a town of Histria, on Arsia fl., opposite Nesaclium. *Peara.*

FAVIANA, a town of Noricum, on the Danube, near Arelate.

FAVONIS portus, a port of Corsica, E. bet. Aleria and Syracusanorum portus. *Porto Favono.*

FELSINA, the name of Bononia, in Gallia Cispad., until its subjugation by the Gauls, 194 B.C.

FELTRIA, capital of the Feltrini, Venetia, near Plavis fl., bet. Ausugum (30) and Ad Cepasias (28). *Feltre.*

FENCHIS, a town of Heptanomis, on the Nile, L., bet. Tacona and Tamontum. *Fechu.*

FERENSE, a town of the Taxaudri, Germania II., bet. Taxaudria and Catualium.

FERENTANA urbs, a town of the Frentani, on Sagrus fl., L. *Foreto.*

FERENTINUM, I. a town of Etruria, bet. Castellum Amerinium and Fanum Voltumnæ. Noted for its stone quarries. A colonia and municipium. The birth-place of the emperor Otho. *Ferenti.* II. of the Hernici, and previously of the Volsci, Latium, on Via Latina, bet. Anagnia (8) and Frusino (7). A municipium. *Frentino.*

FERENTUM, a town of Daunia, Apulia, under Vultur. m., 8 m. s. of Venusium. *Forenza.*

FERETRUS m., a m. of Umbria, s. of Vicus Titiensis. *San Leo.*

FERITOR fl., a r. of Liguria, falling into Ligusticus sin. E. of Genua. *Bisogno.*

FERONIA (Luquidonis portus), a maritime town of the Carenses, Sardinia, bet. Coclearia and Forum Carisii. *Monte Santo.*

FERRARI prom., Tarraconensis, i. q. Artemisium.

FERRARIA, a town of the Siculenses, in Sardinia, bet. Sarabus and Caralis (13). Named from its iron works.

FERRATUS m., m. on the coast of Mauritania Cæsar., bet. Rusucurrum and Audum prom.

FESCENNIUM (Fescennia), a Siculian town of Etruria, towards the Tiber, N.E. of Falerii, taken by the Tyrrheni. Noted for the Carmina Fescennina, or loose nuptial songs, first composed there. *Galese.*

FEVOS fl., a r. of Gallia Cisalpina, falling into the Padus. *Vraita.*

FIBRENUS fl., a r. of Latium, falling into Liris fl., L., below Sora. In it, near its mouth, was the island, the birth-place of Cicero, and the scene of the Dialogues on Legislation. The island (now called San Domenico Abate) subsequently became the property of Silius Italicus. *Fiume della Posta.*

FICANA, a town of the Latini, Latium, near Lanuvium. Destroyed by Ancus Martius, who removed the people to Rome.

FICARIA I. ins., an isl. of Sardinia, at its S.E. extremity. *Serpentera.* II. a town of Corsica S.W., at the mouth of Ficarius fl. *Ficari.*

FICARIUS fl., a r. of Corsica, falling into the sea at Ficaria.

FICOCLÆ, a town of the Lingones, Gallia Cispad., 15 m. s. of Ravenna. *Cervia.*

FICULEA (Ficulnea), a town of Sabinium, on Via Nomentana, E. of Fidenæ, 9 m. from Rome. Taken by the elder Tarquin. *At Monte Gentile.*

FIDENÆ, a town of Sabinium, bet. Rome (5) and Eretum (14), on Via Nomentana. An Etruscan colony from Veii. Destroyed by Æmilius Mamercius 425 B.C. Restored and appointed a municipium. *Near Castel Giubileo.*

FIDENTIA, I. a town of the Anamares, Gall. Cisp., on Via Æmilia, bet. Ad Fonticulos (5) and Ad Tarum (8). A colonia of Augustus. The locality of the defeat of Carbo. *Borgo San Donnino.* II. Hispaniæ, i. q. Ulia.

FIGLINIS, a town of the Allobroges, Viennensis, on the Rhone, bet Vienna and Ursolis.

FILOMUSIACUM, a town of the Sequani, Maxima Sequanorum, bet. Visontio N.N.W. and Ariolica s.

FIRMUM, a town of Picenum, 5 m. N.W. from Castellum Firmanorum, bet. Urbs Salvia (18) and Asculum (24), on Via Flaminia. A colonia of Augustus. *Fermo.*

FISCELLUS m., a portion of the Apennines, separating Sabinium from Picenum. The only district in Italy where wild goats were to be found. *Monte Sibilla.*

FISSENIA (Massice), a town of Babylonia, on the Euphrates, L., bet. Pirisabora (14) and Thelbencane.

FIXTUINUM, a town of the Meldi, Celtica. *Montbout, near Meaux.*

FLACCIANA, a town of Numidia, bet. Signese and Sibus, S.E. of Sicca Venerea.

FLAMONIA, a town of the Veneti, Venetia. *Flagogna.*

FLANATICUS (Polaticus sin.) sin., a gulf of the Adriatic, bet. Histria and Liburnia. *Golfo di Quarnaro.*

FLAVIA BRIGANTIUM (Flaviolambris), a town of the Lucenses, Tarraconensis, at the mouth, R., of Mearus fl. *Ferrol.*

FLAVIA CÆSARIENSIS, a province of Britain, extending bet. Abus fl. and Belisama æstuar. N. and Tamesis fl. s., bounded w. by Britannia II. at Sabrina æstuar. and Seteja æstuar., and E. by Germanicus oc.

FLAVIA MARCI, a town of Numidia, on Bagradas fl., L., bet. Vatari and Vasampus.

FLAVINIUM (Flavina), a town of Etruria, near the Tiber, s. of Capena. *Fiano.*

FLAVIOBRIGA, *prius* Amanus portus, a capital of the Autrigones, Tarraconensis, on the coast, N.E. of Virovesca. A colonia. *Portugalete.*

FLAVIONAVIA, a maritime town of the Pæsici, Tarraconensis, bet. Noega E. and Navilubio fl. w.

FLAVIOPOLIS, a town of Cilicia, near the source of Calycadnus fl.

FLAVIUM AURGITANUM (Giene), a town of the Turtuli, Bætica, E. of Tucci Gemella, N. of Mentesa.

FLAVIUM SOLVENSE, i. q. Virunum.

FLEVA (Phlea) ins., an insulated district of the Frisii, Germ., formed by Flevus fl., near its mouth.

FLEVUM, I. mare, a lake or inland sea of the Frisii, formed by Flevus fl. and other cuts from the Rhine. Zuydersee (S. sea). II. castrum, a citadel built by Drusus at the mouth of Flevus fl., Germaniæ.

FLEVUS fl., the E. issue of the Rhine.

FLORENTIA, I. a town of the Anamares, Gall. Cisp., on Via Æmil., bet. Placentia (15) and Ad Fonticulos (5). Fiorenzuola. II. prius Fluentia, a city of Etruria, on Arnus fl., R., bet. Sena Julia and Solaria (9). A colonia of Jul. Cæsar. Firenze.

FLORIANA, a town of Pannonia Inf., bet. Bregetio and Osones (26).

FLORIUS fl., a r. of Tarraconensis, falling into the Atlantic above Nerium prom.

FLUSOR fl., a r. of Picenum, falling into the sea N. of Tinna fl. Chiento.

FLUVIUS FRIGIDUS, I. a town of the Insubres, in Gall. Transpad., bet. Mediolanum (12) and Argentia (10), on Via Æmilia. Lambro. II. of Pannonia, bet. Aquileia (36) and Longaticum (22).

FOCUNATES, a tribe of Lepontii, in Rhætia. About Vogogna.

FŒNIANA, a town of Germania Magna, on the Danube, above Biriciana.

FOETIBUS, a town of the Isarci, Rhæt., under Alpes Venetæ, N.W. on Athesis fl., L., bet. Pons Drusi and Endidæ.

FONS, I. CAMERATA, baths of Mauritania Cæsar., bet. Berzio and Nobæ Fusciani, N.W. of Cirta. II. POTAMIANUS, of Numidia, on Ubus fl., bet. Gasaupala and Magri. III. SOLIS, vide Ammon. IV. TUNGRORUM, of the Condrusii, Celtica. Spa.

FONTES HERCULIS, baths of the Saldenses, on Tierna fl., near Pons Trajani.

FORATH, a town of Mesene Inf., Babylon., on the Tigris, 14 m. N.W. from Charax. Basra Ferath; Perath Maisun?

FORETANI, a tribe of Carni, Venetia. About Forforcano.

FORMIÆ (Hormiæ), a town of the Ausones, Latium, on Formianus sin., bet. Fundi (12) and Minturnæ (9), on Via Appia. A Laconian settlement. The capital of the Homeric Lestrigones. A colonia and municipium. Noted for its wine. The death-place of Cicero. Mola di Gaeta.

FORMIO fl., a r. of Italy, the boundary, prior to Augustus, of Italy N.E.; the limit of Histria and Venetia, falling into the Adriatic (at Musa Vecchia).

FOROCRINUM, Sabinii, i. q. Forum Decii.

FORTIA MŒNIA prom., a pr. of Sarmatia As., on the Euxine, E. of Thessyrius.

FORTUNATÆ ins., isl. of Africa, S.W. of Gaditanum Fretum. Named from their abounding with the gifts of nature. Canaries.

FORULI, a village of Sabinium, bet. Testrina (3) and Pitinum. Forcella.

FORUM, I. APPII, a town of the Volsci, Latium, on Via Appia, bet. Tres Tabernæ (16) and Ad Medias (9). Mentioned by St. Paul. Borgo Lungo. II. AURELIANUM (Prætorium), of Latium, bet. the mouths of Numicius fl. and Tiber fl. The landing-place of Æneas. Spiaggia d' Ostia. III. AURELII, of Etruria, on Via Aurelia, bet. Marta fl. (14) and Armenta. Torre Aurelia. IV. CASSII, of Etruria, on Via Cassia, bet. Sutrium (11) and Aquæ Passeris. Vetralla. V. CEREALE, a town of the Vagienni, near Pedona. VI. CIGURRORUM, of the Lucenses, Tarraconensis, on Silis fl., R., E. of Nemetobriga. Near La Rua. VII. CLAUDII, of Etruria, on Via Claudii, bet. Sabote and Blera (16). The seat of the prefecture of Novem Pagi. Orivolo. VIII. CLODII, of Gallia Cispadana, bet. Bononia and Florentia. Lojano. IX. CORNELII, of Daunia in Apulia, on Via Frentana, bet. Larinum (26) and Pons Longus (30). X. CORNELII, of Gallia Cispad., on Saternus fl., L., bet. Claterna (13) and Faventia (10), on Via Æmilia Lepida. Founded by Sylla. Imola. XI. DECII, of Sabinium, on Velinus fl., R., bet. Interocrea (12) and Falacria (4), on Via Salaria. Santa Croce. XII. DIANÆ, of the Catavellauni, Britain., N.W. of Verulamium. Dunstable. XIII. DIUGUNTORUM (Tuguntorum), of the Insubres, in Gallia Transpadana, E. of Mediolanum. Crema. XIV. DOMITII, of the Volcæ Arecomici, Narbonensis, bet. Sextatio N.E. and Mesuo S.W. XV. DRUENTINORUM, vel Truentinorum, vel Britonorum, of the Boii, in Gallia Cispadana, s. of Forum Popilii. A municipium. Bertinoro. XVI. FLAMINII, of Umbria, bet. Spoletium (19) and Helvillum (27). S. Giovanni pro fiamma. XVII. FULVII, of the Taurini, in Liguria, on Padus fl., bet. Laumellum and Asta (22).

Villa del Foro. XVIII. GALLORUM, of Gallia Cispad., near Scultenna fl., R., bet. Victuriolæ (5) and Ad Medias (3). The locality of the defeat of Marc Antony by Hirtius and Octavian. *Castel Franco.* XIX. GALLORUM, of the Ilergetes, Tarraconensis, on Gallicus fl., N. of Gallicum. *Garrea.* XX. GIGURRORUM, of the Gigurri, Tarraconensis, w. of Asturica Aug. *Cigarossa.* XXI. HADRIANI, of the Frisii, bet. Lugdunum and Flevium. *Voorburg.* XXII. JULII, of the Oxybii, Narbonensis, at the mouth of Argenteus fl., N.E. of Olbia. A Massilian settlement. A colonia of Julius Cæsar (C. Octavorum, C. Pacensis). *Frejus.* XXIII. JULII, of the Carni, Venetia, on Natiso fl., s.w. of Ad Silanos. Founded by Cæsar. A colonia. *Friuli.* XXIV. LEPIDI, i. q. Regium Lepidum. XXV. LICINII, of the Orobii, Gallia Transpadana, 9 geog. m. N. from Mediolanum. *Lissone.* XXVI. LIGNEUM, of the Osquidates, Novem Populana, in the Pyrenees, s. of Aspaluca. *Lescun.* XXVII. LIMICORUM (Limorum), of the Limici, Tarraconensis, on Limia fl., R., towards its source, s.E. of Bracara. *Santiago.* XXVIII. LIVII, of Gallia Cispadana, on Vitis fl., R., bet. Faventia (5) and Forum Popilii (6). *Forli.* XXIX. NERONIS, of the Memini, Narbonensis II., E.N.E. of Apta Julia. *Mornas.* XXX. NERONIS, of the Volcæ Arecomici, Narbonensis I., bet. Condatomagus N.W. and Araura. XXXI. NOVUM, of the Boii, Gallia Cispadana, on Tarus fl., 10 m. above Bononia. A municipium. *Fornovo.* XXXII. NOVUM, of the Hirpini, Samnium, bet. Beneventum (10) and Equus Tuticus (12), on Via Appia. *Buon Albergo.* XXXIII. NOVUM, of Sabinium, w. of Reate, on the Tiber. *Magliano.* XXXIV. POPILII, of Gallia Cispad., bet. Forum Livii (6) and Cæsena (6), on Via Æmilia Lepida. *Forimpopoli.* XXXV. POPILII, of Lucania, on Tanager fl., L., 9 m. s.w. from Acerronia. *Polla.* XXXVI. POPILII, of the Sidicini, Campania, bet. Teanum and Capua, N. of Appia Via. XXXVII. SEMPRONII, of Umbria, on Metaurus fl., L., bet. Ad Intercisa and Fanum Fortunæ (16), on Via Flaminia. A municipium. The locality of a great battle with Asdrubal. *Fossombrone.* XXXVIII. SEGUSIANORUM, capital of the Segusiani, Lugdunensis I., N.E. of Aquæ Segetæ. *Feurs.* XXXIX. TRAJANI, a town of the Celsitani, Sardinia, on Tyrsus fl., L., bet. Usellis and Ad Medias. A colonia of Trajan. *Fordongianus.* XL. TIBERII, a fortress built by Tiberius, on

an island of Brigantinus lac. *On l'Ile de Reichnau.* XLI. VALENTINUM, a town of Liguria, towards Forum Fulvii. *Valenza.* XLII. VIBII, of the Taurini, in Gallia Transpad., on Cluso fl., s.w. of Augusta Taurinorum. *Envie; or Revello.* XLIII. VOCONII, of the Verrucini, Narbonensis, bet. Forum Julii and Matavonium. *Le Canet.* XLIV. VULCANI, a place in the Campi Phlegræi of Campania, 1 m. E. of Puteoli, which, from its sulphureous exhalations, gave rise to the fables connected with the district. *Solfatara.*

FOSA fl., a r. of the Fosi, Germ., falling into Alara fl.

FOSI, a tribe of Cherusci, Germ., about Fosa fl.

FOSSA, I. a name of Gallicum Fretum. II. AUGUSTA, a canal of Latium, bet. Forum Appii and Tarracina, begun by Augustus, and extended by Nero, for draining the Paludes Pomptinæ. III. CLODIA, a canal from Meduacus Maj. fl., falling into the Adriatic N. of Portus Brundulus. IV. CLUILIA, the camp of Cluilius, 5 m. s.E. of Rome, N.W. of Bovillæ. V. DRUSIANA, *vide* Sala Istæv. VI. MARIANA, TAPHROS, a canal or inlet of Narbonensis, bet. Stomalimne and Astromela. *Marais de Mauguis.* VII. PAPIRIANÆ, a maritime town of Etruria, on Via Aurelia, bet. Pisæ (11) and Luna (12). *Viareggio.* VIII. PHILISTINA. a branch of Padus fl., falling into the Adriatic N. of Carbonaria ost.; hence issued the seven canals constructed by the Tyrrhenians, called Septem Maria, which facilitated the discharge of the waters of the Padus into the sea. *Po Grande.* IX. SCYTHARUM, an artificial cut above Theodosia, insulating the E. extremity of Taurica Chersonesus from the w. portion of the peninsula.

FOSSÆ, a town of Pannonia Inf., on Savus fl., bet. Bassiana and Sirmium.

FOSS WAY, a Roman road in Britain., bet. Totness and Lincoln.

FRANCI, a German people, who invaded Gaul and gave name to France.

FRATRI ins., two islets of Zeugitana, w. of Candidum prom.

FRATUERTIUM, a town of Calabria.

FRAXINUS, a town of the Oretani, Tarraconensis, N.E. of Hactara.

FREGELLÆ, a town of the Volsci, Latium, on Leris fl., R., bet. Frusino (14) and Fabrateria (3), on Via Latina. A colonia 327 B.C. Destroyed for rebellion by L. Opimius. *Ceprano.*

FREGENÆ, a town of Etruria, at the mouth of Larus fl., s.E. of Alsium (9). A colonia. *Torre Maccarese.*

FRENTANI, a tribe of Samnites, settled on the coast of the Adriatic, bet. Frento fl., whence their name, and Aternus fl.

FRENTUS fl., a r. of Daunia, Apul., running into the Adriatic below Teanum. *Fortore.*

FRESCILIA, a town of the Marsi, Ital., near Plestinia. *Civitella.*

FRIGIDÆ, Maurit., i. q. Thymiaterium.

FRIGIDARIUM, a town of the Macrones, Pontus, bet. Pylæ (6) and Patara (8), under Tekes m.

FRIGIDUS fl., a r. of Venetia, running by Fluvius Frigidus. *Urpach.*

FRINIATES, a maritime tribe in Gallia Cispadana, N. of Letus m., on the confines of the Apuani.

FRISIOBONES, a tribe of Frisii, about Flevus lacus.

FRISII (Phreisii, Phrisii, Frisiones, "fresh, new land people"), a tribe of Ingævones, on Germanicus oc., below the Chauci. They were divided into Majores towards the sea, and Minores inland.

FRUSINO, a town of the Hernici, Latium, on Cosa fl., bet. Ferentinum (7) and Fregellæ (14), on Via Latina. *Frusinone.*

FRUSTENIÆ, a town of the Vestini, Picenum, bet. Aveia (2) and Alba Fucentia (18), on Via Valeria. *Ocre.*

FUCINUS lacus, a lake of the Marsi, S.E. of Tibur, in circuit 40 m. Its superfluous waters were diverted to Liris fl., by a canal constructed in the reign of Claudian. *Lago di Celano; L. di Fucino.*

FULGINIUM, a town of Umbria, on Via Flaminia, bet. Trebia (5) and Forum Flaminii (3). *Foligno.*

FULSINIUM, a town of Curicta ins.

FULSULÆ, a town of the Hirpini, Samnium, near Cala fl. *Montepisco.*

FUNDANUS sin., I. i. q. Amyclanus sin. II. lacus, a lake of Latium, at Fundi.

FUNDI, a town of the Volsci, in Latium, near the N.E. extremity of Fundanus lac., bet. Tarracina (13) and Formiæ (12), on Via Appia. A colonia of Augustus. *Fondi.*

FURCONIUM, a town of the Vestini, Picen., on Aternus fl., towards the confines of Sabinium. *Forconio.*

G.

GAASH m., a hill of Ephraim, near Timnath-Sera.

GABA, a town of Galilæa, bet. Ptolemais and Cæsarea (16).

GABACHUS fl., a r. of Meroe.

GABÆ, I. a palace of the kings of Persia, in Persis Prop., on Cyrus fl., S.E. of Pasargada. II. Gabaza, a town of Sogdiana, N. of Maricanda. *Kaibas.*

GABÄLÆ (Giblim), a town of Cassiotis, Syriæ, s. of Laodicea. *Jibili.*

GABALI, I. a town of the Gabali, s. of Anderitum, in Aquitania, and their capital after the destruction of that city. *Javols.* II. a people of Aquitania I., under Cevenna m. w., bet. the Ruteni and the Helvii. *Gevaudan.*

GABALICUS pagus, a district of the Gabali, about Lesara m. Noted for its cheese, and for some silver mines.

GABARA, a town of Galilæa Superior, N. of Dio Cæsarea.

GABAZA, i. q. Gabæ, Sogdiana.

GABELLUS fl., Gall. Cispad. i. q. Secies.

GABIENE, a district of Susiana Elymais, on Coprates fl., above Cissia.

GABII, I. a town of the Latini, Latium, on Via Prænestina, bet. Rome (12) and Præneste (11). A settlement from Alba; sacred to Juno. Nearly destroyed in the civil wars, but restored by Antoninus. The nurture-place of Romulus and Remus. The death-place of Sext. Tarquinius. The locality of the decisive defeat of the Gauls by Camillus. A colonia and municipium. Here was invented the Cinctus Gabinus, a peculiar mode of arranging the toga. *Osteria dello Pantano.* II. a town of Sabinium, N. of Cures, on or near Via Salaria. *Grotte di Torri; Torri.*

GABRA, a town of Persis Prop., near Pasargada, W.N.W.

GABRANTVICI, a tribe of Parisi, Brit., N. of Ocellum prom.

GABRANTVICORUM portus, a haven of the Gabrantvici, Brit. *Bridlington Bay.*

GABRÊTA SILVA, a part of Hercynia Silva, Germaniæ, s. of Sudeti m. *E. Thuringerwald.*

GABRI, a people of Sarmatia Asiat., towards Cissii m.

GABRIS, a town of the Bituriges Cubi, Aquitania I., on the Liger, bet. Tasciaca and Avaricum.

GABROMAGUS, a town of the Taurisci, Noricum, near Anisus fl., R., bet. Ernolatium and Siriate. *Windischgratz.*

GABROSENTUM, a town of the Brigantes, Brit., near the w. termination of Hadriani murus, s. *Drumburgh.*

GABULA, a town of Chalybonitis, Syr., N.E. of Chalcis.

GABULEUS, a town of the Penestæ, Illyria, at the junction of Drilo Niger with Drilo Albus fl.

GAD, a tribe of Israel, bounded N. by the half-tribe of Manasseh, N. of Argob, s. by Reuben, at Bethlehem, w. by the Jordan, E. by Arabia Deserta.

GADANOPYDRES, a people of Carmania, on the confines of Parthia, bet. the Isatichæ and Modomasticæ.

GADARA, capital of Peræa, 8 m. s.E. from Tiberias. The locality of the miracle of the swine. *Om-Keis.*

GADARIS, Palestinæ, i. q. Gath.

GADAUM CASTRA, a town of Mauritania, bet. Mina (25) and Vagal (18). *El Callah.*

GADDA (Gadoras), a town of Palestine, bet. Pella and Philadelphia (13).

GADENI (*Celticè* "robbers,") a people of Britannia Barbara, N. of the Otadeni.

GADES (Cotinussa), I. the isl. on which Gades stood. II. (*Græcè*, Gadeira, *Phœnic.* Gadir, "hedge,") a city of the Turtetani, Bætica, on Gades ins., s. of the Bætis, connected with Erythea ins. by a causeway, and this again, later, with the mainland, by another causeway. Built by the Tyrians 530 B.C. A colonia (Augusta Julia). *Cadiz.*

GADIANA (Gadusena), a town of Chammanene, Cappadociæ.

GADILONITIS, Pont., i. q. Gazelonitis.

GADITANUM FRETUM, Herculis fretum, so named from Gades.

GAEA, a town of the Thaditæ, Arab., N. of Thœmor.

GÆSA, a town of Arabia, towards Persicus sin., s.w. of Mesanites sin. The seat of Jeush, son of Esau.

GÆSATES, a name of the Gauls, bet. the Alps and the Rhone; so designated, either from a Celtic word, meaning "mercenaries," or from their using a particular sort of missile (*Gæsum*).

GÆSON, I. a marsh of Ionia, on Mæander fl., near its mouth, formed by Gæsus fl. II. a village of Ionia, under Mycale m., s.E. of Neapolis, near where the Persians were defeated by the Spartan Leotykides.

GÆSUS (Gessus) fl., a r. of Ionia, rising in Mycale m., above Priene, and falling into Gæson palus.

GÆTARA, a port of Albania, N. of the mouth of Cyrus fl. *Near Baku.*

GÆTULIA, the country of the Gætuli, Libya, occupying the N. portion of Libya Interior, on the borders of Mauritania, Numidia, and Africa Propria. Its population, almost entirely a nomad race, were variously designated Gætuli Nigri, or Melanoi (central), Autololes (w.), Bagi Gætuli (E.). *S. Morocco, Bileldulgerid, and Sahara* w.

GAGÆ, Palæopolis, a maritime village of Lycia, near Menalippe. *Alaja-dagh.*

GAGANÆ, a town of the Potulatenses, Dacia, bet. Mascliana and Ad Pannonias (9). *Flova.*

GAGANDA ins., an isl. of Meroe, in the Nile, below Aboccis.

GAGASMIRA, a town of the Chatriæi, Indiæ, under Apocopa m., s.w. of Clisobra.

GALABATHA, a town of Mesopotamia, on the Euphrates, bet. Nicephorium and Alamatha.

GALABRI, a tribe of Dardani, in Mæsia, on Margus fl., below Naissus.

GALĂCUM, a town of the Brigantes, Brit., on Ituna fl., bet. Brovonacæ and Verteræ. *Near Kendal.*

GALÆGIA, a town of Germania, on the Albis, at the confluence of the Sala.

GALAETOPHAGI, a people of Scythia i. Imaum, under Aspisii m. E.

GALAPHA, a town of Mauritania Ting., on Mulacha fl., towards its mouth.

GALARIA, a town of Sicily, on Gamosurus fl., R., w. of Adranum. *Gagliano.*

GALASA, Palestine, i. q. Gerasa.

GALATA, I. a town of Sicily, w.s.w. of Abacænum. II. ins., an isl. of Zeugitana, N.E. of Tabraca.

GALATIA (Gallo-Græcia), a country of Asia Min., bounded N. by Paphlagonia, s. by Lycaonia and Cappadocia, w. by Bithynia, E. by Pontus. A portion of Phrygia, occupied and named after a body of Gauls, consisting of Tectosages, Tolistoboii, and Trocmi, who, under Leonorius and Latarius, separated from the army of Brennus, in Thrace, and made their way by Byzantium, into Asia Minor, 278 B.C. They were subsequently named Gallo-Græci, from their intermixture with the Greeks of Asia Minor.

GALĂVA (Galana, Alauna), a town of the Brigantes, Brit., bet. Corstopitum and Alone. *Keswick.*

GALEOTIS, a name of Megara Hyblæa, in Sicily, the people of which, reputed seers, were descended from Galeus, son of Apollo.

GALEPSUS, I. a town of the Pieres, Thrace, on Strymonicus sin. A colony of Phasians. II. of Sithonia, Macedonia, on Toronaicus sin., s.E. of Sermyle.

GALESUS (Eurotas) fl., a r. of Italy, falling into the harbour of Tarentum. *Galeso.*

GALIBA prom., a pr. of Taprobane, over against Agara.

GALIBI m., m. of Central Taprobane, N. of Malea m.

GALIL, the Scriptural name of Galilee.

GALILÆA (Galil), "round or encompassed

tract," a district of Palestine, bounded N. by Phœnicia, s. by Samaria, w. by the Mediterranean, E. by Decapolis, at the Jordan. It was divided into two portions, G. Superior, or of the Gentiles, N. of Bersabe, and G. Inferior, or Propria, s.

GALINDÆ, a tribe of Venedæ, E. of the Gothones.

GALLA, a town of the Mardi, Med., on Straton fl. *Amul.*

GALLABA, a town of Osrhoene, bet. Edessa and Minnocerta.

GALLÆCIA. *Vide* Callæcia.

GALLAICE, Thrac., i. q. Creonia.

GALLESUS (Gallesium) m., a s.w. ridge of Corax m., above Colophon. Covered with pines. *M. Aleman.*

GALLI, generally, the Latin form of the Celtic Ghael; specially, the people of Gaul.

GALLIA, I. Cisalpina, Gallia Togata, the northern portion of Italy, including Gallia Transpadana, Gallia Cispadana, and, at one time all, or the greater part of, Liguria. Occupied first by the Etruscans, then circa 600 B.C., by the Cenomanni, and other invaders from Gaul (whence the name), then by the Romans, circa 190 B.C. II. CISPADANA, the portion of Gallia Cisalpina, s. of Padus fl., separated from Liguria by a line, somewhat w. of Trebia fl., from Etruria by the mountains of the Apuani and Magelli, and from Umbria by Rubico fl. III. CITERIOR, Gaul on the nearer (to Rome) side of the Alps, i. q. Gallia Cisalpina. IV. Comata, a name given to Gallia Transalpina, from the long hair worn by its population. V. PARVA, i. q. Galatia; so distinguished by the Greeks from Gallia Europæ. VI. TOGATA, a name given to Gallia Cisalpina, from its citizens having, under a law of Pompeius Strabo, the right of wearing the Toga. VII. TRANSPADANA, the portion of Gallia Cisalpina, N. of Padus fl., separated from Venetia by Atagis fl. VIII. TRANSALPINA, BRACCATA (" wearing trowsers "), Ulterior, Propria, Gaul on the further (from Rome) side of the Alps; bounded s. by the Alps, Mediterranean, and the Pyrenees, N. by Britannicus oceanus, w. by the Atlantic, E. by the Rhine and Alps. *France, the Netherlands, and Switzerland.*

GALLICA, a town of the Ilergetes, Tarraconensis, on Anga fl., at its confluence with Sicoris fl. *Fragua ?*

GALLICANUS fl., a r. of Anthemus, Macedonia, falling into Echedorus fl., below Grestone, 16 m. N. from Thessalonica. *Gallico.*

GALLICUM fretum (Taphros, Fossa), I. the strait separating Corsica from Sardinia. II.

the strait separating Britannia from Gallia.

GALLINARIA ins., an isl. of Liguria, s. of Albingaunium. Named from the abundance there of the Gallina Rustica, the partridge or rail. *Gallinara.*

GALLINARIA sylva, a forest of Campania, on the coast, above Literni Paludes.

GALLITÆ, a tribe of Salyes, Narbonensis, on Varus fl., R., above the Equiturri. *About Gillette.*

GALLUS fl., I. a r. of Bithynia, rising near Modra, and falling into Sangarius fl., below Leucæ. Its water was reported to produce a phrenetic effect, and hence the priests of Cybele were *surnamed* Galli. *Sakaria.* II. of Phrygia Parorea, falling into a lake not named, below Philomelium.

GAMALA, "camel," capital of Gaulonitis Inferior, on Tiberias lacus, S.E., bet. Hippus N.E. and Bethsan s.w.

GAMBOLA, a district of Tenesis, Æthiopia, s. of Pseboa lacus.

GAMBRIUM (Palæ Gambrium), a town of Ionia N., on the confines of Lydia.

GAMBRIVII, a tribe of Marsi, Germaniæ.

GAMMUSIA (Gambria), a town of Phrygia.

GANDARII, a people of Paropamisus, on the confines of Aria.

GANGANI, I. a people of Hibernia, s. of the Autiri. II. of India, on both banks of the Ganges, s. of the Nanichæ.

GANGARIDÆ, a port of India, at the mouth of the Ganges.

GANGARA, a town of Otene, Armenia, S.E. of Sanora. *Gandsak.*

GANGE, capital of the Gangaridæ, Indiæ, on the Ganges.

GANGES fl., I. a r. of India, rising in Imaus m., N. of Catadupa, and after, in a course of 1500 m., separating Hither from Further India, falling into Indicum mare, below Aganagora, by several mouths, according to Virgil 7; according to Ptolemy 5 or 6; but according to Strabo only 1. *Ganges.* II. of Taprobane, falling into the sea at Solis portus. *Mowil-Gonga.*

GANGITICUS sin., a bay of Indicum mare at the mouths of the Ganges, bet. Tyndis fl. w. and Bessynga fl. E. *Bay of Bengal.*

GANGRA, a town of Paphlagonia, s. of Olgasys m., s.E. of Castamon. The royal seat of Morezus. Noted for its apples. *Kangreh.*

GANNARIUM prom., a pr. of Libya, on the Atlantic, bet. Cusarius fl. and Oppiodes fl. *C. Nun.*

GANODURUM, a town of the Helvetii, Maxima Sequanorum, on the Rhine, near its ingress into Brigantinus lacus. *Eschenz.*

GANOS, I. a m. of the Odrysæ, Thrace, on the Propontis. *Tekir-Dagh.* II. a town of Thrace, under the cognominal m. Extinct in Pliny's time.

GAPACHI, a people of Meroe.

GARA fl., a r. of the Garoceli, Alpes Penninæ. *Chiara.*

GARAMA, capital of the Garamantes, Libya Int., s.w. of Saba, towards the source of Cinyps fl. *Gherma.*

GARAMÆI, a people of Chalonitis, Assyriæ, N. of Oricus m.

GARAMANTES, a people of Africa, E. of the Gætuli. *Fezzan, Tuarick, Tibboo, and parts of Soudan and Bornu.*

GARAPHI m., m. of Mauritania Cæsar., E. from Siga fl.

GARBATA m., m. of Æthiopia, about Astapus fl.

GAREA, a town of Arcadia, on Gareates fl., s. of Tegea.

GAREATES fl., a r. of Arcadia, falling into Ænus fl. near Tegea.

GARENDANI, Arabiæ, i. q. Larendani.

GARGANUM prom., a pr. of Daunia, Apul., bet. Urias sin. and Sipontinus sin. *Punta di Viesti.*

GARGANUS (Arion) m., a ridge of the Apennines, in Apulia, terminating in Garganum prom. *Monte Sant' Angelo.*

GARGAPHIA fons, a fountain of Bœotia, on Cithæron m., 1½ m. from Platæa. The scene of Actæon's fate.

GARGARA, I. a summit of Ida m., Troas, 30 m. S.E. from Ilium Novum. *Kasdagh.* II. a headland of Æolis Asiatica, at the N. entrance of Adramyttenus sin. III. a town of Mysia, on Adramyttenus sin., at the cognominal prom. A colonia from Assus, augmented from Miletopolis. Its territory was of peculiar fertility.

GARGAREES, a people of Sarmatia, described as contiguous to the Amazons, and in alliance with them.

GARGARIUS locus, a town of the Salyes, Narbonensis, towards Arelate. *Guarguiez.*

GARGAZA, Taurica Chersonesus, i. q. Cimmerium.

GARGETTUS, a demus of Attica, of the tribe Ægeis, bet. Angele and Cephissus. The birth-place of Epicurus. The burial-place of Eurystheus. *Krabato.*

GARI, a town of Parapomisus, on Sambara fl., N.E. of Bis. *Grisch.*

GARIANONUM, a town of the Iceni, Brit., bet. the Aufona and the Garionus ffl., towards their issue. *Whetacre-burgh.*

GARIANUS fl., a r. of the Iceni, falling into the sea below Garianonum. *Yare.*

GARINDÆI, a people of Arabia Felix, contiguous to the Maranitæ.

GARISCUS, a town of Orbelia, Pæonia, on the Axius fl., about Astipus. *Caratova.*

GARITES, a people of Aquitania, w. of the Rhone. *Diocèse de Montauban.*

GARIUM, a town of Paphlagonia, on the Euxine, E. from Zephyrium prom. 10 m.

GARIZIM (Grisim) m., a m. of Samaria, overlooking Sichem s., whence the voice of Jotham was heard by the Sichemites. On it was a temple erected by Sanballat, in honour of his son-in-law Manasseh, and destroyed by John Hyrcanus.

GARMIAS, a town of Morimene, Cappadocia, bet. Aspana and Parnassus.

GARNA, a port of Apulia, under Garganus m.

GAROCELI, a tribe of Medulli, Alpes Penninæ, bet. the Centrones and the Caturiges, on Gara fl. *Val de Viu.*

GARÆAS fl., Indiæ, i. q. Guræus.

GARSAURA (Garsabora), Cappadociæ, i. q. Orchelais.

GARSAURITIS, a prefecture of Cappadocia, s.E. of Tattæa lac., above Tyanitis.

GARTIA fl., a r. of the Cenomanni, Gallia Cisalpina, running by Brixia. *Garza.*

GARULI, a maritime tribe of Liguria, E. of the Lapicini. *About Gastagnano.*

GARUMNA fl., a r. of Gaul, rising in the Pyrenees towards Aquæ Onesimæ and falling into the Atlantic at Novioregum. *Garonne.*

GARUMNI, a people of Novem Populana, on the Garumna, R., towards its source. *La Rivière.*

GARUS m., m. of Mauritania Cæsar., or N.N.E. continuation of Phrurasus m.

GASANDI, Arabiæ, i. q. Cassanitæ.

GATH (Gittah Hepher), a town of Dan, Judæa, 32 m. w. from Jerusalem. The birth-place of Goliath.

GATH-HEPHER, a town of Zebulun. The birth-place of Jonah.

GATH-RIMMON, I. a town of Dan. II. of Ephraim. III. of Manasseh, s.w. of Tiberias.

GATHEÆ, a town of Arcadia, on Gatheates fl., s.E. of Cromi.

GATHEATES fl., a r. of Arcadia, rising near Gatheæ and falling into Alpheus fl. s. of Megalopolis.

GATHELIN STREET, i. q. Watling Street.

GAUDOS ins., an isl. of Crete, near Hierapytna.

GAUGÆNA (Gauræna), a town of Sargarausene, Cappadocia.

GAUGAMELA, a village of Arbelitis, Assyria, near Arbela. The locality of the battle of Arbela. Allotted (whence the name) by Darius Hystaspes for the maintenance of the camel on which he had effected his escape.

GAULITA, a town of Iberia, s. of Harmozica.

GAULON (Golan), capital of Gaulonitis Superior, bet. Aphek s.s.w. and Neve N.E.

GAULONITIS (Golanitis), a district of Bashan, bet. the Jordan w. and Trachonitis E. It was divided into Superior, N.E., and Inferior, S.W.

GAULOS, I. an isl. of Sicily, in the Mediterranean, 5 m. from Melite. *Gozo.* II. its town; a Carthaginian colony. A municipium.

GAURA m., a m. of the Vocontii, Viennensis, E. of Vologatis.

GAURALEON (Gaurion), a port of Andros ins. *Gauro.*

GAURUS m., I. a ridge of hills in Campania, bordering Avernus lacus. Once noted for its vines, now altogether barren. *Monte Barbaro.* II. of the Troglodytæ, on Arabicus sin.

GAUZACA, a city of Paropamisus, bet. Tazora and Capissa. *Ghazna.*

GAUZANIA, a town of Atropatene, Media, towards Phazaba. *Sofian.*

GAUZONITIS, a district of Mygdónia, Mesopotamia, bet. Osrhoene and Mygdonia. *Gozan.*

GAZA (Aza), I. one of the five cities of the Philistines, Judæa, bet. Ascalon N. and Jenysus s., 12 m. E. from its port Majamas. Destroyed by Alexander, again by Antiochus, and a third time by Alexander Jannæus. *Ghuzzeh.* II. a town of Judæa, E.N.E. of Lydda. III. (Gazaca), capital of Atropatene, Media, midway (90 geog. m.) bet. Ecbatana and Artaxata. *Bet. Tauris and Miana.* IV. a town of Sogdiana, on Jaxartes fl., bet. Cyreschata and Alexandria Ultima.

GAZACA, Mediæ, i. q. Gaza.

GAZACENA, the valley of the Iris, Pontus, towards its source.

GAZARA, Palestine, i. q. Gath.

GAZAUFULA, a town of Numidia, 16 m. w. from Tibilis.

GAZILON (Gadilon), capital of the cognominal district in Pontus.

GAZILONITIS REGIO, a district of the Leuco-Syri, Pontus, on Halys fl., near its mouth, N.W. of Phazemontis, s.w. of Amisus. Noted for the fine wool of its goats and sheep.

GAZIOURA, a royal city of Pontus on Iris fl.,

above its junction with Scylax fl. Deserted in Strabo's time. *Azurni.*

GAZORUM (Zagora), *postea* Calippi, a maritime town of Paphlagonia, 68 m. E. from Gurzubanthon.

GAZŌRUS, a town of the Edones, Thrace, on Augites fl., N.E. of Myrcinus.

GEAPOLIS, a town of Sarmatia Asiatica, on Charienus fl., towards its mouth, s. of Neapolis. *Gonga.*

GEBA, a town of Benjamin, Judæa, bet. Anuath N. and Gophna s.

GEBAL, Phœniciæ, i. q. Byblos.

GEBALENE, a district of Edom. *Djebal.*

GEBANITÆ, Arabiæ, i. q. Cithabanitæ.

GEDRANITÆ, Arabiæ, i. q. Carbæ.

GEDRŌSIA (Cedrosia), a country of Asia, bounded N. by Arachosia, at Bætius m., s. by Indicum mare, w. by Carmania at Persici m., E. by India, at the Indus. *Mekran.*

GEGETA, a town of Numidia, bet. Naraggara and Thagura.

GEIDUNI, a tribe of Morini, Belgica II., on the coast, s.w. of the Grudii.

GELÀ, I. a r. of Sicily, falling into Afric. Pelagus, below Gela, bet. Calvisiana and Camerina. *Fiume de Terra Nova.* II. *prius* Lindus, a city of Sicily, on Gela fl., R., ½ m. from its mouth. Built 690 B.C. by Rhodian and Cretan colonists. Destroyed 210 B.C. by Phintias of Agrigentum, who transferred the inhabitants to Phintiæ. *Near Terra Nova.*

GELÆ, a people of Media, contiguous to the Cadusii. *Guilan.*

GELASIUM PHILOSOPHIANA, a town of Sicily, near the source of Gelas fl., bet. Petiliana and Capitoniana (21). *Piazza.*

GELBES (Gebes) fl., a r. of Bithynia, falling into Propontis, E. of Dascylium.

GELDA, a town of the Gerri, Sarmatia As., at the s. mouth of Gerrus fl. *Near Tarku,* E.

GELDUBA, a town of the Ubii, Germania I., on the Rhine, above Asciburgium. Built by Drusus. *Gelb; Geloub.*

GELOI CAMPI, a plain of Sicily, w. of Gelo, 3 m. from the sea, from which it was separated by a low ridge of hills. Noted for its extreme fertility.

GELONI, a people of Sarmatia, on both sides the Tanais, at its central course. Syracusan settlers, who painted and tattooed their bodies and otherwise adopted the usages of the barbarians.

GELONUS, *postea* Exopolis, capital of the Geloni, Sarmatia, on the Tanais, L. A Milesian colony.

GELOS, a port of Peræa, Caria.

GELUINA, a town of Otene, Armenia, at the s.e. extremity of Lychnitis lac. *Khegha.*

GEMELLÆ, I. a town of Byzacene, bet. Capsa and Thala. II. of Mauritania Cæsar., bet. Sitifis and Nova Petra. III. of Numidia, n.w. of Palladis lac. IV. of Sardinia, 25 m. s. from Tibula. *Claramonte.*

GEMESTARIUM, a town of the Astures, Tarraconensis, w.n.w. of Asturica Augusta.

GEMINÆ, I. a town of the Lucenses, Tarraconensis, near the junction of Chalybis fl., with Minius fl. *Cangas?* II. of the Tricorii, Viennensis, bet. Dea Vocontiorum w. and Gerainæ s.e.

GEMINIACUM, a town of the Aduatuci, Germania II., bet Perviciacum and Bagacum.

GENÄBUM, *postea* Aureliani, a town of the Aureliani, Lugdunensis IV., on the Liger, bet. Salioclita n.n.e. and Avaricum s.s.e. *Orleans.*

GENAUNES (*erroneously* Anaunes, Naunes), a tribe of Euganei, Rhætia, bet. the Brenni and the Vindelici, n. of Tridentum. The Senones of Florus. *Val de Non.*

GENDOS (Chrysorrhoas) fl., a river of Bithynia.

GENESISITIS, Ponti, i. q. Genetes.

GENESIUM, a town of Argolis, on Argolicus sin., near Apobathmi.

GENETÆUM (Boona) prom., a pr. of Pontus, ½ m. e. from Ciliconnesus ins. *C. Vona.*

GENETES (Boona), a port of the Tibareni, Pontus, at the mouth of a cognominal river, 3 m. e. from Genetæum prom. *Vona.*

GENETIUS (Boona), sinus, a bay of the Euxine, at Genetes.

GENEVA, a city of the Allobroges, Viennensis, at the s.w. extremity of Lemanus lac., bet. Noviodunum and Condate. *Geneva.*

GENNESARETH, *i. e.* Cinneroth, lacus (Tiberiädis mare), a lake of Palestine, formed by the Jordan n. of the Dead Sea. In length about 14 m., in breadth about 7. *Lake of Gennesaret ; Sea of Galilee.* II. a town of Galilæa, near the n. extremity w. of the lake, 2 m. w.n.w. from Capernaum.

GENOÆI, a tribe of Molossi.

GENSIS, a town of Mœsia Superior, on Drinus fl., towards its confluence with Savus fl.

GENUA, *prius* Antium, a maritime city of the Euburiates, Liguria, bet. Ad Figlinas (7) and Ricina (7). Destroyed by Mago ; restored by Lucretius the consul. Noted for its timber. *Genova ; Genoa.*

GENUSIUM, a town of Japygia, s. of Mateola. *Ginosa.*

GENUSUS fl., a r. of the Taulantii, Illyria, rising s.e. of Lychnitis and falling into

the Adriatic 14 m. n. of Apsus fl. *Scombi or Tobi.*

GEORGI, a people of Sarmatia Eur., e. of Panticapes fl., n. of Carcinites sin.

GEPHYRA, I. a town of Amphaxitis, on Axius fl., bet. Pella (10) and Ad Decimum (10). II. a village of Attica, on the Via Sacræ, w. of Laciadæ. Noted for the practical tricks upon travellers played there. III. of Paphlagonia, n.w. of Antinoopolis. IV. of Syria, 22 m. from Gindarus. The residence of Cadmus prior to his migration to Greece.

GEPHYRÆI, a tribe of Phœnicians, from Gephyra, in Syria, who followed Cadmus into Bœotia, and settled about Oropus and Tanagra, which they afterwards quitted for Athens.

GEPIDÆ (Gepides), " idle," a tribe of Goths, settled on the Vistula.

GERA, a town of Chaldæa, on the Euphrates, L., bet. Sura and Bethana.

GERÆ (Eræ), I. a maritime town of Ionia, bet. Chytrum and Teos. A Bœotian colony, under Geres. *Erekevi.* II. of the Zygritæ, Marmarica, on the coast, bet. Aratu and Œnesyphira.

GERÆA, a town of the Bracari, Tarraconensis, on Limia fl., L., towards its mouth.

GERÆSTICUS (Gerrhoides, Cherrhoides), the n. port of Teos, Ionia. Named from Geres, its Bœotian colonizer.

GERÆSTUS prom., the s. headland of Eubœa. *C. Mantelo.*

GERAINÆ, a town of the Caturiges, Viennensis, bet. Geminæ n.w. and Caturigæ s.e.

GERANDRUS, a village of Cyprus, near Soli. Noted for its marble.

GERANIA, I. a fortress of Corinthia, on the limits of Megaris, if not actually within Megaris, bet. Tripodiscus and Corinth. II. the highest portion of the Onæi range, in Megaris. *Palæo-vouni.*

GERAR, a city of Judæa, s.w. of Gaza. The seat of the earliest known Philistine kingdom. The locality of the deceit practised upon Abimelech by Abraham and Isaac.

GERARITICA, a toparchy of Judæa, about Gerar.

GERAS (Deras), a fortress of Achaia, bet. Sicyon and Corinthus.

GERASA (Rasa), I. a town of Arabia Petræa, towards Heshbon. II. of Gileaditis, 6 geog. m. n. from Philadelphia. III. of Sarmatia Asiat., on Mæotis palus.

GERASAS (Cœres, Grissia) fl., a r. of Dacia, falling into the Tibiscus.

GERBO, a town of Meroe, on the Nile, R., bet. Berethis and Patæta.

GEREATIS, a town of Marmarica, bet. Ju-
cundia and Tetropyrgia.

GEREN, a town of Lesbos ins. Named from
Geren, son of Neptune.

GERĒNIA (Enope), a town of Messenia, N.E.
of Cardanyle, where Nestor was educated.

GERGIS, a maritime village of Syrtica Regio,
N. of Putea Pallene.

GERGITHA, I. a town of Dardania, under
Marcæus m., E. of Dardanus, near Erythræ. The birth-place of Cephalo, the
historian. Its inhabitants were removed
by Attalus to the more southern cognominal town. II. of Mysia, towards the
source of Caicus fl. Founded by Attalus,
and peopled with the inhabitants of Gergitha Dardaniæ.

GERGITHIUM, a town of Mysia, in the territory of Lampsacus. Noted for its vineyards.

GERGOVIA, I. the early capital of the Arverni,
near Augustonemetum, S.E. Destroyed by
Cæsar. On Mt. Gergoie. II. (Gergobin-
na, Gorgolia, Gortona), of the Boii, Lugdunensis IV., of uncertain position.

GERMA, I. a town of Lydia, bet. Pergamum
(25) and Thyatira (33). Somma. II.
postea Myriangeli, of the Tolistoboii, Galatia, bet. Pessinus and Myricion. A colonia of Vespasian. Yerma.

GERMANI, Tarraconensis, the N. portion of
the Oretani.

GERMANIA, "country of war men" (Germania Magna, Transrhenana, Transda-
nubiana, Barbara), a country of Europe,
bounded N. by Codanus sin., S. by the
Danube, W. by the Rhine, and E. by the
Vistula, though Strabo and Mela appear to
include Noricum and Rhætia in Germany,
while the Bastarnæ, a German people,
were E. of the Vistula.

GERMANIA I., a district of Gaul, bet. Germa-
nia II. N., Maxima Sequanorum s., Belgica
I. W., and the Rhine E. Haut Rhin, Bas
Rhin, &c.

GERMANIA II., a district of Gaul, bet. the
Nervii and the Fretum Gallicum w., the
Rhine N. and E., and Belgica II. and Ger-
mania I. s. Part of Netherlands, &c.

GERMANICIA (Germanicopolis), I. a town of
Cilicia Campestris, towards Adana. II.
(Germanicia Cæsarea), prius Adata, postea
Telesaura, of Commagene, Syria, under
Amanus m.

GERMANICIANA, a town of Zeugitana, bet.
Aqua Regia (24) and Ælia (16).

GERMANICOPOLIS, I. Bithyniæ, i. q. Helgas.
II. a town of Paphlagonia, bet. Gangra
and Halys fl. Named in honour of Germanicus.

GERMANICUM mare (Germanicus Oceanus),
I. the sea washing Germany, w. bet. the
mouths of the Rhine and Albis fl. II. a
town of Vindelicia, on the Danube, near
Celeusum.

GERMANII, apud Herodot., a people of
Persis.

GERME (Hiera Germe), a town of Mysia,
towards Apolloniatis lac. Ghirmasti.

GERMIZERA (Zermizirga), a town of the
Burideenses, Dacia, near Marisus fl., L.,
bet. Blandiana and Petra (9). Kostrinz.

GERODA, Syriæ, i. q. Gerra.

GERONTEUM m., a m. of Arcadia, N. of
Stymphalus.

GERONTHRÆ, a town of the Eleuthero-Lacones, Laconia, on Selinus fl., 27 m. above
Leucæ. Founded by the Achæans. Hier-
aki.

GERONTIA ins., an isl. of Thessaly, in the
Ægean, bet. Halonnesus and Scandile.

GERONTIUS m., a mountain of Arcadia.

GERRA, I. capital of the Gerræi, Arabia
Felix, at the head of Gerraicus sin., S.S.W.
of Katara. Noted for houses built of salt.
Hagar. II. (Gerrum), a maritime town
of Lower Egypt, E. of Pelusium. III. a
town of Meninx ins., Africæ. The birth-
place of the emperor Vibius Gallus, and of
Volusianus. IV. (Geroda), of Syria, towards Damascus.

GERRÆI, a people of Arabia Felix, on Persicus sin., about Gerra. On Bahr el Bahrein.

GERRAICUS sin., a bay of Arabia Felix, in
Persicus sin., s. of Capeus sin. Bahr el
Bahrein.

GERRI, a port of Sarmatia Asiat., on the
Caspian, s. of Gerrus fl.

GERRUS fl., I. a r. of Sarmatia, E., falling
into the Hypacaris fl.; according to Pliny,
into Mæotis palus. II. of Sarmatia A.,
rising from the same source with the
Soana, and falling into the Caspian by
several mouths, N. of Cæsius fl. Koisu.

GERULATA, a town of the Boii, Pannonia,
on the Danube, bet. Carnuntum (14) and
Ad Flexum. Karlburg, or Oroswar.

GERUNDA, a town of the Ausetani, Tarraconens., on Alba fl., R., towards its mouth,
65 m. N.E. from Barcino. Gerona.

GERUNIUM, I. a town of the Pentri, Samnium, bet. Teanum Apulum (18) and Ad
Pirum (9). Taken by Hannibal, and used
as his winter quarters. Girone. II. (Ge-
runs), a town of Phœbotis, Illyria, w. of
Chrysondio.

GERUSA, a maritime town of Dandarica,
Sarmatiæ, s. of Tyrambe.

GESDAS, a town of the Segovii, Gall. Transpad., on Duria Min. fl., bet. Alpis Cottia (5) and Ad Montem (9), on Via Aurelia. *Sezanne.*

GESODANUM, a town of Noricum, near Claudonium. *Poiten.*

GESHUR, a district of Syria, E. of Jordan, towards Hermon m. s.

GESOCRIBATE, a port of the Osismii, Lugdunensis III., s.w. of Vorginum. *Brest.*

GESONIUM, a town of the Tencteri, Germ., on the Rhine, over against Bonna.

GESSORIACUM, *postea* Bononia, a port of the Morini, Belgica II., w. of Taruenna. *Boulogne.*

GETÆ (Gothicè, Gethan, "to get"), I. a people of Dacia, on the Danube, towards its mouth, and extending to Tyras fl. Renowned for their integrity. II. of Mœsia Inf., along the Danube, bet. Jaterus fl. and Atlas fl.

GETARUM DESERTA, a portion of the country of the Getæ, in Dacia, bet. Tyras fl. and Parata fl., towards their mouths.

GETONE ins., an islet on the coast of Troas.

GETTIS (Gath), a maritime town of Syrtica Reg., s. of Meninx ins.

GETULLUM, a maritime town of Tripolis, Africæ, bet. Minna and Aphora.

GEVINI, a people of Sarmatia, N. of the Carpiani.

GEYSA prom., a pr. of India e. Gangem, at the E. extremity of Magnus sinus.

GEZATORIX, a district of Paphlagonia.

GEZER, a town of Ephraim, N.W. of Jerusalem. Rebuilt by Solomon.

GHALADRA, i. q. Chaladra.

GHIMES, a town of the Quadi, on Neta fl., N. of Celmantia.

GHYTANÆ, i. q. Chytona.

GIBBETHON, a town of Dan. The locality of the death of Nadab.

GIBEAH, I. a town of Benjamin, N. of Jerusalem. The birth-place of Saul. *Jebah.* II. of Judah, Judæa, 9 m. s.w. from Jerusalem. *Jebah.*

GIBEON, a Levitical city of Benjamin, 6 m. N. of Jerusalem. Near it was the valley, the locality of the defeat of the two Canaanitish kings. *El Jib.*

GIBRATA, a town of Mesopotamia, on the Tigris, bet. Manchane and Peloriarca.

GIDDA, a town of Tingene, Mesopot., on the Euphrates, bet. Merrhan and Belesi-biblada.

GIGANTIS, an early name of Arcadia.

GIGARTHO fons, a stream of Samos.

GIGARTON, a town of Phœnicia, towards Botrys fl.

GIGIUS m., a m. of Syrtis bet. Cinyps fl. and Triton fl.

GIGŌNUS, a town of Chalcidice, Macedonia, at Heligonium prom.

GIHENINICA, a town of the Macrones, Pontus, bet. Magnana (10) and Pylæ (18). *Ghemishkana.*

GIHON fl., "impetuous," i. q. Oxus; or, according to others, the Araxes.

GILBOA, I. m. of Galilæa and Samaria, extending from Jezreel s.E. nearly to the Jordan. The death-place of Saul and of Jonathan. *Djebel Gilbo.* II. (Gilbus), a town of Galilæa, under Gilboa m. s.E. of Jezreel.

GILDA, a town of Mauritania Ting., on Subur fl., R., bet. Vopisciana and Aquæ Dacicæ (16).

GILEADITIS (Gilead, Galeed, Galeaditis), I. a district extending along the Jordan, L., from Machærus to Gadara. Its name is derived from the mound or monument set up by Laban and Jacob, as a *heap to witness* their covenant. II. a ridge of mountains, 6 m. s. from Jabbok fl. Noted for its balsam-trees. *Djelaad.*

GILGAL, I. a town of Judæa, near Shechem. *Jiljuleh.* II. of Judæa, bet. Jericho N.W. (2) and the Jordan (4). Here the Israelites set up their first encampment after passing the river; and here the tabernacle was for some time kept.

GILIGAMMES, a people of Marmarica, s.E. of the Asbytæ.

GILVA, a maritime town of Mauritania Cæsar., bet. Castra Puerorum and Siga.

GIMZO, a town of Judæa, bet. Lydda w.N.W. and Thumnath E.

GINDANES, a people of Syrtica Regio, w. of the Lotophagi.

GINDARUS, a town of Cyrrhestica, Syriæ, bet. Cephyra (22) and Cyrrhus (36).

GINEA (Engannim, "fountain of gardens"), a town of Issachar, in Galilæa, on the confines of Samaria, bet. Capercopa w. and Gilboa N.E., s. of Jezreel. *Jenin.*

GIR fl., a r. of Africa, s.w. *Om Teiman.*

GIRA, a town of Africa, on Gir fl. *Kaschna.*

GIRBA ins., i. q. Meninx.

GIRATHA, Arabiæ, i. q. Cargatha.

GIRGASITÆ (Girgasæi, Gergasim), one of the seven tribes of Canaan, about Girgasa (Gadara).

GIRGIRIS m., m. of Africa, the s. boundary of Tripolis.

GIRGIS, Africæ, i. q. Hidaphtha.

GISCALA, a town of Palestine, N.W. of Sephet.

GIZAMA, a town of Osrhoene, N.E. of Constantia.

GLANDOMIRUM, i. q. Grandimirum.

GLANOVENDA (Clanoventa, Glannabenta), a

town of the Brigantes, Brit., bet. Vindo-
mora and Vinovium. *Ellenborough.*

GLANUM LIVII, a town of the Desuviates,
Viennensis, bet. Ernagine w. and Pisanæ
S.E. *St. Remi.*

GLAPHYRÆ, I. a town of Cilicia Campestris,
on a cognominal stream, 4 m. from Tarsus.
II. of Pelasgiotis, Thessaly, on the w. shore
of Bæbe lacus, N. of Bæbe.

GLARI, a people of Arabia Felix, towards
Asaborum prom. *About Dsjulfar.*

GLAUCANICÆ (Glausæ), a people of India,
towards Acesines fl.

GLAUCE, Glaucia, a port of Ionia, under
Mycale m., over against Posidium prom.

GLAUCI, a demus of Lycia. Named from the
hero Glaucus.

GLAUCUM prom., a pr. of Marmarica, w. of
Cheimo.

GLAUCUS fl., I. a r. of Achaia, rising in Pana-
chaicus mons, and falling into Corinthia-
cus sin., s.s.w. of Patræ. *Leuka.* II. of
Armenia, rising in Paryadres m., and with
Lycus fl. forming Apsarus fl. *Ichorokson.*
III. of Caria, falling into Glaucus sin.
Meis. IV. (Cludrus), of Phrygia Magna,
rising E. of Eucarpia, and falling into
Mæander fl., w. of Peltæ. V. Sinus, a bay
of the Mediterranean, at Dædala. *Macri.*

GLECON, a town of Phocis, near Panopeus.

GLEMONA, a town of the Carni, Venetia, on
Tilavemptus fl. *Gemona.*

GLESSARIA (Austravia) ins., one of the
Electrides ins., Germ., s.w. of the mouth
of Amisia fl. *Ameland.*

GLESSARIÆ (Glessum, "amber," from *glas*,
Germ. "transparent") ins., the Roman
name of the Electrides ins.

GLEVUM (Clevum, Glebon, Caer Gloew,
Gleau ceaster), a town of the Dobuni,
Brit., on Sabrina fl., L., N.W. of Duro-
cornovium. A colonia (Claudia Castra).
Gloucester.

GLISSAS, a town of Bœotia, under Hypaton
m., N.E. of Thebes. In ruins in Pausanias' time.

GLYKYS portus, "port of sweet water," a
harbour of Epirus, at the mouth of the
Acheron fl. *Glyki.*

GLYMPES (Glyppia), a town of Laconia, near
the source of Marios fl., above Marios.
Cosmopoli.

GLYPHIA, Lacon., i. q. Glympes.

GNOSSUS, *prius* Cæratus and Trilla, the
capital of Crete, established as such by
Minos, on Cæratus fl., 23 m. N.E. from
Gortys. Here was the famous labyrinth. *Longa Candia.*

GOARIS fl., a r. of Arica, India, falling into the
sea 15 geog. m. from the Namadus. *Tapti.*

GOBÆA, a town of Arabia Felix, at Asaborum prom. N. *Cuscan.*

GOB, i. q. Gezer.

GOBANNIUM (Bannio, Abergavenium, Aber-
genium), a town of the Silures, Brit., on
Gobannius fl., w. of Blestium. *Aber-
gavenny.*

GOBANNIUS fl., a r. of the Silures, Brit.,
flowing by Gobannium into the sea. *Gavenny.*

GOBÆUM prom., a pr. of the Osismii, Lugdunensis III., w. of Coriallum. *Cap Go-
bestan.*

GODASA (Gundusa), a town of Armenia Min.,
bet. Eumeis (30) and Zoana (23).

GODIRTHA, a town of Palmyrene, on the
Euphrates, bet. Rahaba and Circesium.

GOGANA, a town of Persis, near the mouth
of Areon fl. *Roncun.*

GOGARENE, a district of Armenia Maj., on
the borders of Colchis and Iberia. Noted
for its abundant harvests. *Gugarkh.*

GOGARI, a people of Sarmatia Asiatica, towards Cissii m.

GOLGI, a Phœnician town of Cyprus, anterior to Cyprus. Colonized by Sicyonians,
under Golgus.

GOMADÆORUM ins., islands of the Troglodytæ, in the Red Sea, N. of Satyrorum
prom. *Daradata and Dolcofallar.*

GOMERA ins., i. q. Capraria.

GOMPHI, a city of Estiæotis, Thessaly, on
Peneus fl., bet. Æginium and Tricca.
Cleisoura.

GONDALI, a people of India i. Gangem,
under Uxentus m.

GONGYLUS fl., a r. of Laconia, falling into
Ænus fl. at Sellasia.

GONNIA, a town of Marmarica, bet. Mecira
and Cardu.

GONNOCONDYLON (Olympias, Condylon), a
fortress of Perrhæbia, Thessaly, near Gonnus, on Peneus fl., L., one of the four
fortresses which guarded the defile of Tempe.

GONNUS (Gonni, Gonussa), a fortress of Perrhæbia, Thessaly, on Peneus fl., L., one of
the four which guarded the defile of Tempe,
20 m. N.E. from Larissa. The birth-place
of Antigonus Gonatas. *Crania.*

GONOESSA, Achæa. *Vide* Donusa.

GONTIANA, a town of Mauritania Tingit.,
N.W. of Babba.

GOPHNA (Gufna), a town of Benjamin, in
Judæa, 15 m. N. of Jerusalem. *Jifna.*

GOPHNITICA, a toparchy of Judæa, about
Gophna.

GORDA, a town of Arabia Felix, under
Zames m. *Aarud.*

GORDĪTĀNUM prom., the N.W. extremity of
Sardinia. *Capo di Monte Falcone.*

GORDIUM, the early name of Juliopolis in Bithynia.

GORDIUTICHOS, a town of Caria, near Aphrodisias. Founded by Gordius, son of Midas.

GORDUS, I. a town of Æolis Asiat., N. of Adramyttium. II. of Lydia, on or near Hyllus fl., 48 m. E. from Thyatira. Surnamed Julia Gorda in compliment to Augustus. *Ghiurdiz.*

GORDYCEI m., i. q. Carduchi.

GORDYENE (Gordene, Corduene), a district of Armenia Major, on the Tigris, L., extending into Assyria, E. of Gordyæi m.

GORDYNESIA, a district of Gordyene, Armen., bet. Nymphæus fl. and Centrites fl., about Tigranocerta.

GORGIPPIA, capital of Sindica, Sarmat., near the Euxine, bet. Sinda and Bate.

GORGUIA, a town of Samos.

GORGODYLENA, a district of Armenia Maj., under Niphates m.

GORGUS, I. (Delas, Diabas, Zillas), a r. of Assyria, falling into the Tigris near Ctesiphon N. *Diala.* II. a fortress of Arcadia, towards Telphusa.

GORNIÆ, a town of Otene, Armenia, N.E. of Artaxata. *Garhni.*

GORTYNIA, a town of Emathia, Macedonia, s. of Idomene.

GORTYNIUS fl., a r. of Arcadia, rising near Thison, and falling into Alpheus fl. at Rheteæ. Remarkable for its excessive coldness. Towards its source it was called Lusius, as the stream in which the infant Jupiter was washed. *Atchicolo.*

GORTYS (Gortyna), I. a town of Arcadia, on Gortynius fl., s. of Megalopolis. Its inhabitants removed to Megalopolis. *Atchicolo Castro.* II. *prius* Larissa, the second city of Crete, on Lethæus fl., 23 m. s.w. from Gnossus, 11¼ N. from Lebena. A Pelasgic city, enlarged by Gortys, son of Rhadamanthus.

GORZUBILA, a town of Taurica Chersonesus, near Chersonesus.

GOSHEN, I. a district of Egypt, bet. the Pelusiac branch of the Nile and the Red Sea. The land given to his father by Joseph. II. a town of Judah.

GOTHINI (Cogni), a tribe of Burii, German., N. of the Visburgii.

GOTHONES (Guttones), a people of Germania Magna, on the Vistula, R., towards its mouth, N. of the Lygii.

GOTTOLENGI, a people of Gallia Cispadana, towards Brixia. *About Godolazzo.*

GOZAN, a r. of Media, falling into the Caspian. *Kizzal Ozan.*

GRACURRIS, *prius* Illurcis, a town of the Vascones, Tarraconensis, near the Iberus,

above Cascantum. A colonia and municipium. Enlarged and new-named by Sempronius Gracchus, in memory of his conquest of the Celtiberi. *Agreda.*

GRADES ins., an isl. of Crete.

GRADUS, the port of Aquilea, at the mouth of Natisus fl. *Porto di Grado.*

GRÆA, I. the country of the Graæi, in Pæonia, N.E. of Orbelia. II. a name given to Pœmandria in Bœotia by its Gephyrean occupants.

GRÆAS-GONY prom., a pr. of Marmarica, w. of Calamæum prom.

GRÆCI, a tribe of Pelasgi in Epirus, bet. Dodona and Achelous fl., whose name the Latins applied to the whole of Greece.

GRÆCIA, I. (Hellas, *biblicè* Javan), a country of Europe, bounded N. by Macedonia, S. by the Mediterranean, W. by the Ionian Sea, E. by the Ægean. It was divided into Græcia extra Peloponnesum, S., and Græcia Propria, N. of the Isthmus of Corinth. II. a name given to the district about Massilia.

GRÆCIA PROPRIA, a region of Europe, bounded N. by the limits of Athamania and Thessaly, S. by Corinthiacus sinus and Corinthia, w. by Arachthus fl. and the Ionium mare, E. by the Ægean. It comprehended Thessaly, Acarnania, Ætolia, Doris, Locris, Phocis, Bœotia, Megaris, Attica, Eubœa, Athamania.

GRAMMOS m., a m. of Macedonia, at Orestia.

GRAMPIUS (Grantzbain) m., m. of Britannia Barbara. Memorable for the defeat of Galgacus by Agricola.

GRANDIMIRUM, a town of the Artabri, Tarraconensis, at the mouth, R., of Ulla fl., 22 m. s. from Ad Duos Pontes.

GRANDESIA, a town of the Leuci, Galliæ. *Grand.*

GRANDIS, a town of Lyncus, Macedonia, bet. Melitonus (14) and Cellæ (14), on the Egnatia Via.

GRANIACUM prom., a pr. of Corsica, S.E. above Rubra. *Punta St. Paolo.*

GRANICUS fl., a r. of Mysia, rising in Cotylus m., and falling into Propontis, 27 m. s. of Priapus. Memorable for the defeat of the Persians by Alexander, B.C. 334, and of Mithridates' army by Lucullus. *Dimotiko.*

GRANIRIANA, a town of the Triballi, Mœsia, on Margus fl., R., bet. Præsidium Pompeii and Naissus.

GRANIS fl., a r. of Persis, falling into Persicus sin. N. of Padargus fl.

GRANNONUM, a port of the Bajocasses, Lugdunensis II., N. of Augustodurum.

GRANUA fl., a r. of the Quadi, Sarmatia

Eur., falling into the Danube at Anabum. *Gran.*

GRAOSGALA, a town of Phrygia, near Charax.

GRASSE, a town of Zeugitana, N.W. of Adrumetum, 10 geog. m. from Carthago. *Paradise.*

GRASTILLUS (Prastillus), a town of Macedonia.

GRATIANOPOLIS, Galliae, i. q. Cularo.

GRAVIACAE, a town of the Taurisci, Noricum, bet. In Muro (17) and Beliandrum. *Pridlet.*

GRAVINUM, a town of the Caleti, Lugdunensis II., N.E. of Juliobona.

GRAVIS m., a m. of the Aequi, bet. Vineae (6) and Carbonarius m. (10.)

GRAVISCAE, "unhealthy," the port of Tarquinii, in Etruria, at the mouth of Minio fl., bet. Rapinium and Marta fl. A colonia 183 B.C. *Torre di Corneto.*

GRAVIONARIUM (Gravisnarium), a town of the Chatti, Germ., S.E. of Nuaesium. *Near Bruckenau.*

GRIDINUS fl., Bactriana, i. q. Tearus.

GRINARIO, a town of German. Mag., bet. Samulocena (22) and Clarenna. *Mengen.*

GRINNES, a town of the Batavi, at the confluence of the Vahalis and Mosa. *Near Drumel.*

GRISELUM (Aquae Griselicae), a town of the Reii, Narbonensis, on the Druentia, s.w. of Reii Apollinares. *Greoul.*

GRIUS m., a ridge of hills in Caria, extending from the s. shore of Latmicus sin. to Euromus. Identified by some writers as the Phthira m. of Homer.

GROARIS ins., one of the Echinades ins.

GRONYCHIA campus, a plain of Bithynia, on the shore of Bosporus Thracius, s. of Amycus.

GROVII, a tribe of Lucenses, Callaecia, bet. Minius fl. and the Artabri.

GRUDII, a tribe of Morini, Belgica II., on the coast, at the mouth, s. of Tabuda ostium. *About Groede.*

GRUMBESTINI, the people of Grumum in Peucetia.

GRUMENTUM, a town of Lucania, on Aciris fl., R., bet. Auxia (18) and Nerulum (27). *Saponara.*

GRUMUM, a town of Peucetia, Apul., near Palio. *Grumo.*

GRUNAEI, a tribe of Sacae.

GRYLIUS fl., a r. of Aeolis Asiat., falling into the Aegean opposite Lesbos.

GRYNAEUM (Grynea), one of the twelve cities of Aeolis Asiat., on Elaeaticus sin., 5 m. s. from Elaea, 5 m. E. from Myrina. Sacred to Apollo Grynaeus. *Calabak-hissar. Glisselik.*

GUGERNI, a people of Germania II., on the Rhine, bet. the Batavi and the Ubii.

GUIZA, a fortress of Mauritania Caesar., 11 m. from Portus Magnus. *Giza, near Oran.*

GULUS fl., a r. of Mauritania, w. of Ampsagas fl.

GUMATHENE, a district of Sophene, Arm., about Amida.

GUNARIA campus, a plain of Paphlagonia, near Castamon.

GUNDUSA, a town of Pontus, s. of Halys fl. bet. Eumaea and Zoana.

GUNTIA, I. a r. of Vindelicia, falling into the Danube at Guntia. *Guntz.* II. a town of Vindelicia, on Guntia fl., at its confluence with the Danube, bet. Pomo and Piniana Castra. *Guntzburg.*

GUNUGIS, a maritime town of Mauritania Caesar., bet. Caesarea (12) and Cartilis. A colonia of Augustus. *Palomas.*

GURAEUS (Goraeus) fl., i. q. Choaspes.

GURBITA, a town of the Pelagones, Macedonia, bet. Stobi (8) and Ad Cephalon (13).

GURGURES m., hills of Sabinium, bet. Reate and Tribula Suffena. Noted as sheep pastures.

GURIANA, a town of Margiana, bet. Susia and Alexandria Margiana.

GURRA, a town of Byzacene, bet. Ulisippira and Hadrumetum (7).

GURTIANA, a town of Valeria, Pannon., on Volcea lac., N.E. bet. Corsio and Vallis Carminiana, 43 m. s. from Bregetio.

GURULIS, I. *surnamed* Nova, a town of Sardinia, bet. Cornus and Macopsisa. *Padria.* II. *surnamed* Vetus, of the Caracenses, in Sardinia, on Ternus fl., N. of Gurulis Nova. *Sassari.*

GURZUBANTHON (Orgibate), a maritime town of Paphlagonia, 18 m. s.e. from Carusa.

GUSAUPALA, a town of Numidia, on Abus fl., bet. Ad Rubras and Tipasa.

GUTTALUS fl., a r. of Sarmatia Europ., falling into Sarmaticus oc. *Pregel.*

GYAROS (Gyrae) ins., an island of the Aegean, one of the Cyclades, bet. Ceos and Tenos, in circuit 12 m. A place of banishment for Roman criminals. *Ghioura.*

GYGAEA palus, *postea* Coloe, an artificial lake of Lydia, bet. Thyatira and Sardes (5). Near it, towards Sardes, was the celebrated tomb of Alyattes. *L. Mermere or Gheul.*

GYMNASIAE, "skilful with the sling," a name of Baleares ins.

GYMNIAS, a city of Armenia, near the s. source of Cyrus fl. *Gole.*

GYNDES (Delas, Dialas) fl., a r. of Assyria, rising in Media, towards Ecbatana? and falling into the Tigris about Ctesiphon. Cyrus, enraged with the river because one of his favourites was drowned in it, or because it retarded his march, divided it into 360 channels. *Kerah.*

GYNÆCOPOLIS, a town of Lower Egypt, on the Canopic branch of the Nile.

GYPSARA (Cæcili portus), a port of Mauritania Cæsar., bet. Artisiga and Siga.

GYPSARIA, a town of Idumæa, towards Hebron.

GYPSITIS ins., an isl. of Æthiopia, s. of Dioscurum portus.

GYRES fl., a r. of Melitene, Cappadocia, running into Euphrates fl. towards Melitene.

GYRINE (Tyrine) ins., an isl. of Carmania, s. of Organa ins.

GYROSENE, a town of the Oretani, Tarraconensis, near Castulo.

GYRTON, *prius* Phlegya, a city of Perrhæbia, near the junction of Titaresius fl. with Peneus fl.

GYRTONA, a town of Stymphalia, in Macedonia, on the confines of Epirus, near Aeas fl. *Konitza.*

GYTARIUM, a town of Tyanitis, in Cappadocia, near Podandus.

GYTHIUM, the port of Sparta, at the head of Laconicus sin., w. bet. Las (5) and Trinasus, 30 m. s. from the capital. Founded by Hercules and Apollo. *Palæopoli.*

H.

HABAR, a town of Media, near Gozan fl., In the district about it the tribes of Israel were located. *Abhar.*

HABITANCUM, a town of the Otadeni, Maxima Cæsar., s. of Bremenium.

HACHILAH, a fortress of Judæa, s. A retreat of David.

HACTARA, a town of the Oretani, Tarraconensis, N.E. of Acci.

HADADRIMMON, "garden of pomegranates," a town of Galilæa, bet. Jezreel (10) and Cæsarea Palæstina (17). The death-place of Josiah.

HADORAM, a district of Aad, Arabia, subsequently occupied by the Adramitæ.

HADORAMUM prom., Arabiæ, i. q. Corodamum.

HADRACH, a district of Syria, near Damascus.

HADRIA (Hatria), I. a Tyrrhenian city of Picenum, bet. Vomanus fl. and Matrinus fl., 7 miles from the sea, s.e. of Interamna. A colony from Hadria, Venetia, strengthen-

ed (*circa* 390 B.C.) by Syracusan immigrants, fugitives from Dionysius, headed by the historian Philistus. A colonia 290 B.C. *Atri.* II. of the Veneti, Venetia, on Hadrianus fl., L., at one time near its mouth, at present 18 m. inland. Founded by the Pelasgi, under Diomed, 1376 B.C. Destroyed 414 B.C., but restored. It gave name to the Adriatic. *Hadria.*

HADRIANI, a town of Mysia, on Rhyndacus fl., R., N.E. of Blaundus. The birth-place of Aristides, the rhetorician. *Edrenos.*

HADRIANI MURUS (Vallum), I. a wall of Britain, constructed by Hadrian, bet. Vedra æstuar. and Ituna æstuar. (80), separating, at that period, Britannia Barbara from Britannia Romana. *The Picts' Wall.* II. of Germania, constructed by Hadrian, from Mœnus fl., below Locoritum, to the Danube at Artobriga.

HADRIANŎPOLIS, I. a town of Bithynia, on Billæus fl., R., above Clitæ. Founded by Hadrian. *Boli.* II. *postea* Justinianopolis, of Chaonia, bet. Amantia (55) and Elæus (24). Built by Hadrian, restored by Justinian. *Drinopoli.* III. (Hadriane), of Pentapolis Cyrenaicæ, bet. Berenice (28) and Teuchira (18). Built or enlarged by Hadrian. IV. of Pisidia. V. *prius* Orestis Uskudama, a town of the Odrysæ, Thrace, at the confluence of Tonskus fl. with Hebrus fl. Rebuilt and renamed by Hadrian. *Edrene; Adrianople.* VI. a name given, under Hadrian, to Neo-Cæsarea, in Pontus.

HADRIANORUM paludes, marshes at the mouth of Padus fl., about Hadria.

HADRIANOTHERÆ, a town of Mysia, bet. Pergamum (8) and Miletopolis. A hunting-retreat of the emperor Hadrian. *Trikala.*

HADRIANUS ager, the district of Hadriæ, Picenum. It was for some time an independent state.

HADRIATICUM (Hadriaticus sinus) mare, a gulf of the Mediterranean, washing the shores of Macedonia and Illyria E. and of Italy w. In St. Paul's time, the appellation was also applied to the sea bet. Crete and Sicily. Named from Hadria, or, according to some antiquaries, from the Greek *adros,* "vehement." *Adriatic.*

HADRUMĒTUM (Adrametum, Adryme, Aldrume), a maritime city of Byzacene, bet. Horrea Cælia and Leptis Min. (18.) A Phœnician settlement. A colonia of Trajan. Named Justiniana by Justinian, and Heraclea by Heraclius. *Hercla.*

HÆMONIÆ, a town of Arcadia, E. of Ladocea. Founded by Hæmon, son of Lycaon.

HÆMOS, Egypti, i. q. Heroopolis.

HÆMUS m., a range of m., the E. continuation of Bertischus m., dividing Thrace from Mœsia, and extending to the w. coast of the Euxine. *Emineh Dagh, or Balkan.*

HAGARENI (Agræi), a people of Arabia, variously situated in Arabia Deserta, and in Arabia Felix, on the shores of Persicus sin. The descendants of Hagar and Ishmael. *Bahrein, &c.*

HAGGÆ VICUS, a port of the Hamirei, Arabiæ, N.E. of Ausara. *Seger.*

HALÆ, "salt," a town of Bœotia, on Opuntius sin., at the m. of Platanius fl. *Alachi.*

HALÆ, I. surnamed Araphenides, a demus of Attica, of the tribe Ægeis, on the Ægean, near Araphen. *Pitchery.* II. *surnamed* Axonides, a demus of Attica, of the tribe Cecropis, on Saronicus sinus, close to Axone; with large salt-works. *Bari.* III. a town of Crete.

HALAH, Assyriæ, i. q. Calah.

HALALA, Cappadociæ, the early name of Faustinopolis.

HALAZIA, the early name of Dascylium, Bithyniæ.

HALCYONE, a town of the Malienses, Thessaly.

HALEJA fl., Paphlagoniæ, i. q. Zalecus.

HALEPORIS (Heloris, Elorus) fl., a r. of Bruttium, falling into Locrensis sin., bet. Altanum (24) and Decastadium (22). Noted for the defeat of the Magna-Grecian allies by Dionysius the Elder, 307 B.C. *Callipari.*

HALES (Halesus) fl., a r. of Ionia, rising in Gallesus m., and falling into Ionium mare s. of Colophon. Its water was extremely cold.

HALESIUM campus, a plain of Troas, on the coast, furnishing salt to the works at Tragasæ. Its springs ceased their supply during the continuance of a tax laid upon salt by Lysimachus. *Near Tusla.*

HALEX fl., a r. of Bruttium, falling into Siculum mare, w. of Caicinus fl. At one time the boundary of the territories of Locria and Rhegium. The cicadæ on its Locrian side were always chirping, on the other bank always mute. *Alece.*

HALIACMON fl., a r. of Macedonia, rising in Canalovii m., and falling into Thermaicus sin. at Alarta. *Inje Carasou.*

HALIARTUS, a town of Bœotia, on the s. shore of Copais lac., at the w. mouth of Termessus fl., 15 m. N.W. from Thebes. Stigmatized for stupidity. The death-place of the Spartan Lysander. Noted for its darts and musical pipes. Destroyed by Lucretius, the prætor.

HALICARNASSUS, *prius* Ziphyria and Isthmus, capital of Caria, at the s. extremity of Ceramicus sin., opposite Arconnesus ins. Founded by a colony from Trœzene, under Anthes. Famous for the tomb of Mausolus, one of the seven wonders of the world. The birth-place of Herodotus, of Dionysius Halicarnassus, and of the poet Heraclitus. Destroyed and restored by Alexander the Great. *Boudroun.*

HALICE, a district of Cilicia Campestris, about Augusta.

HALICUS, a town of Cilicia Campestris.

HALICYRNA (Licyrna), the port of Calydon, Ætolia, under Taphiassus m.

HALISARNA, a fortress of Cos, near Laceter prom.

HALIUSA ins., an isl. of Argolis, in Hermionicus sin., near Bucephala prom.

HALIZONES (Alazones), a tribe of Mysians, the early inhabitants of the coast of Bithynia and Pontus.

HALMUS fl., Armen., i. q. Araxes.

HALMYDESSUS, Thraciæ, i. q. Salmydessus.

HALMYRIS lac., I. an inland bay of the Euxine, at Halmyris, Mœs., near the s. mouth of the Danube. *Rozel See.* II. (Salmorude), a town of Mœsia Inf., on Halmyris lac., w. bet. Salsovia and Vallis Domitiana. *Babadag?*

HALONE ins., an isl. of Ionia, over against Æsepus fl. Noted for an excellent harbour. *Aloni.*

HALONNESUS ins., I. an isl. of Ionia, bet. Argennum prom. and Corycum prom. II. of Thessaly, in the Ægean, N.E. of Scopelos ins. *Chelidromi.* III. the town of the latter isl., on the s. coast. *Chelidromi.*

HALUNS, a town of Arcadia, on Ladon fl., L., above Oryx.

HALUS, Assyria, either Artemita itself, or a small town close to it.

HALYCE, a town of Argolis, on Hermionicus sin., N.E. of Hermione. In ruins in Pausanias' time. *Aleki.*

Halyciæ, a town of Sicily, near the source of Sossius fl.

HALYCIS a district of Argolis, on Hermionicus sin., bet. Hermione and Scyllæum prom.

HALYCUS fl., a r. of Sicily, falling into the sea at Heraclea. *Platani.*

HALYS fl., *quasi* "salt-pits," a r. of Asia Minor, formed by two streams (one rising in Scordiscus m., S.E. of Nicopolis, the other in Taurus m., towards the source of Sarus fl.) which, uniting, intersect Galatia, and, separating Paphlagonia from Pontus, fall into the Euxine N.W. of Amisus. It was the E. limit of the empire of Crœsus. *Kizil-Ermak.*

HAMÆ, a place in Campania, bet. Atella and Cumæ (3), where the Capuans assembled for certain religious celebrations.

HAMATH, Galilæa, i. q. Emmaus.

HAMAXANTEIA, a demus of Attica, of the tribe Hippothoontis.

HAMAXIA, a town of Cilicia, near Jotape.

HAMAXITUS, "highway," I. a town of Caria, on Doridis sin. II. of Troas, on the coast, above Lectum prom.

HAMAXOBII, a name of the Agathyrsi, Sarmatæ, from their custom of living in waggons.

HAMIREI, a people of Arabia, on the s. coast, E. of the Toani Gebanitæ. Descendants of Hamyar, grandson of Joktan. *About Ras Hamier.*

HAMMÆUM littus, a portion of the shore of Arabia Felix, w. of Thamar fl. *About Maham.*

HAMMAMUM, a town of Phazania, S.E. of Garama.

HAMMENUM, a town of the Triballi, Mœsia, bet. Ad Herculem and Ad Fines.

HANES, a city of Egypt, upon an isl. of the Nile, s. of Memphis.

HANNIBALIS ins., an islet of Balearis Maj., s. opposite Palma.

HAPHARAIM, a town of Galilæa.

HARAN, Mesopotamia, i. q. Charan.

HARMA, "chariot," I. a demus of Attica, of the tribe Ægeis, N.W. of Phyle. II. a town of Bœotia, bet. Thebes and Aulis. One of the places claiming to be the scene of Amphiaraus' fate.

HARMÆUM, the port of Harma, Bœotia, on the Euripus, s. of Aulis.

HARMASTIS, i. q. Harmozica.

HARMATELA, a town of the Brachmanes, India.

HARMATOTROPHI, a people of Bactriana, near the Oxus.

HARMATUS prom., a pr. of Æolis Asiatica, the N. entrance of Elæaticus sin., opposite Hydra prom. (10.)

HARMONIA, a town of Macedonia II.

HARMOZA, capital of Harmozia, Carmaniæ, on the coast. *Near Minau.*

HARMOZIA, a district of Carmania, on the coast, about the mouth of Ananis fl.

HARMOZICA (Harmastis, Armatica), capital of Iberia, near the Cyrus, R., towards Leumara. *Armazi-Tsikhe.*

HARMOZON prom., a pr. of Carmania, bet. Saganus fl. and Sabis fl., near Harmoza. *Cape Kuhestek.*

HAROD, a fountain of Jezreel, under Gilboa m.

HAROSHETH, a town of Naphthali, near Hazor. The city of Sisera.

HARPAGIUM (Harphagia), a place in Mysia, E. of Priapus, whence Ganymede was carried off.

HARPASA, a town of Caria, or Harpasus fl., near its junction with Mæander fl. *Harpaz-Calessi.*

HARPASUS fl., I. a r. of Caria, falling into Mæander fl. at or near Harpasa. *Harpaz.* II. (Harpagus), of Siracene, Armen., falling into the Araxes. *Akburean, Arpa.* III. (Harpessus), of Thrace, rising in Rhodope m., N.W. of Nicopolis, and falling into Hebrus fl. at Hadrianopolis. *Arda.*

HARPII, a people of Dacia, bet. the Tyrus and the Parata, N. of the Britolacæ.

HARPINNA, a town of Pisatis, Elis, on Alpheus fl., near its junction with Harpinnates fl., 1 m. s. from Olympia. Founded by Ænomaus.

HARPINNATES fl., a r. of Pisatis, Elis, falling into Alpheus fl. near Harpinna.

HARPIS, a town of Sarmatia, near the N. mouth of the Danube. *Near Adschud.*

HARPLIA, a town of Laconia, at the foot of Taygetus m., 2½ m. s. from Derrhium.

HARPONÆ ins., isl. of Etruria, over against the mouth of Umbro fl. *Formiche.*

HARPYS fl., a later name of Tigres fl., Elid., from the death in it of one of the Harpies.

HASSI (Bassi), I. a people of Belgica. Placed by D'Anville in the district of Haiz, in the diocese of Beauvais. II. of Germania. *In Hesse.*

HASTA, I. a town of Etruria, on Via Aurelia, bet. Telamon (8) and Umbro fl. (2). *Castel Marino.* II. of the Ilvates, Liguria, on the coast, bet. Ad Navalia (7) and Ad Figlinas (3). *Voltri.*

HATERA, a town of Pieria, Macedoniæ, 12 m. N.W. from Dium. *Hateri.*

HATITA, a town of Batanæa, bet. Gadda s.w. and Thantia N.E.

HATRÆ (Bethatræ, Bematra), capital of the Atreni, Mesopotamiæ, towards the Euphrates, S.E. of Singara. Sacred to the sun. *Hatder.*

HATRIANUS (Tartarus) fl., a r. of Venetia, rising s. of Verona, and falling, with Athesis fl., into Fossa Philistina below Hatria. *Tartaro.*

HAURAN, i. q. Auranitis.

HAVILAH, land of, I. Colchis. II. the country about the mouth of the Euphrates. Named from Havilah, son of Cush.

HAVOTH-JAÏR, a district of Gileaditis, with thirty towns, the property of the thirty sons of Jaïr.

HAZARMAVETH, a region of Arabia Felix, towards the s. coast; a portion of Aad.

HAZEZON - THAMARA, "Hazezon of the

Palm Trees" (Thamarus), a town of Simeon, on the s. confines of Judæa.

HAZOR, I. (Haza, Hadata, Hazor Kaine), a town of Judah, Judæa, N.E. of Ascalon. II. (Aza, Azorus), a city of Naphthali, near the sources of the Jordan, s.w. of Laish, "the capital of all the kingdoms N. of Palestine." Destroyed by Joshua. There was a Hazor in Arabia, identified by some with Petra.

HEBA, a town of Commagene, on the Euphrates, bet. Barzula and Cholmadara.

HEBRIDES ins., i. q. Ebudæ.

HEBRON (prius Kirjath Arba, Mamre), a city of Judah, 26 m. s. from Jerusalem. Founded circa 2204 B.C. The locality where Abraham received the angels. El Khalil, Hebroun.

HEBRUS fl., a r. rising in Hæmus m., at the intersection of Rhodope m., in the N.W. angle of Thrace, and falling into the Ægean at Stentoris palus, and also by another mouth, w. of that estuary. Maritza.

HECALE, a demus of Attica, of the tribe Leontis.

HECATOMBÆUM, a town of Achaia, near Dymæ.

HECATOMPEDON, a fortress of Chaonia, on the confines of Illyria, w. of Fauces Antigoneæ.

HECATOMPYLON (Parthyene), capital of Parthia. Named by some geographers Hecatompylan, from the number of roads meeting there. The capital of Arsaces.

HECATONNESI, "hundred islands," a group of islands (Strabo reckons twenty) bet. the N.E. of Lesbos ins. and Pyrrha prom., in Æolis Asiat. Here Hecatus (Apollo) was peculiarly venerated, a circumstance whence Strabo derives the name. Musco-nisi.

HECTODURUM, a town of Vindelicia.

HEDAPHTHA, a town of Syrtis, Africæ, N. of Zuchis.

HEDONACON, a town of Bœotia, on Permessus fl., s.w. of Thespia, where was the fountain of Narcissus. Neochorio.

HEDYLIUM, a town of Bœotia, under Hedylius m.

HEDYLIUS m., a m. of Bœotia, near Chæronea.

HEDYPHAR (Hedypnus) fl., a r. of Susiana, rising in Parachoatras m., and falling into Pasitigris fl.

HEGONIUM prom., a pr. of Chalcidice, Macedonia, N. of Æneum prom. Cara Bourun.

HEGITMATIA, a town of the Diduni, Germ., N.W. of Budorgis. Near Ratibor.

HELCEBUS, a town of the Tribocci, Gaul. Elle.

HELDUA, a maritime town of Phœnicia, bet. Berytus and Platanon.

HELELLUM (Helvetum), a town of the Tribocci, Gallia. Schlestaddt.

HELENA (Macris) ins., an island of Attica, in the Ægean, over against Thoricus. The Cranæ of Homer. Macronisi.

HELENÆ, a town of the Atrebates, Belgica II., bet. Origiacum w.N.w. and Nemetacum S.E.

HELENOPOLIS, a later name of Drepanes, Bithyniæ.

HELES (Hales, Elees, "boggy") fl., a r. of Lucania, falling into Inferum mare, 3 m. N. from Helia (Velia), to which it gave name. Alento.

HELGAS (Booscæte), postea Germanicopolis and Cæsarea, a town of Bithynia, on Gelbes fl., towards Prusa.

HELIA (Hyele), Lucaniæ, the Greek name of Velia.

HELICE (Ilice), I. one of the twelve cities of Achaia, on Corinthiacus sin., bet. Leuctrum and Cerynia. The early capital of Achaia. It was swallowed up by an earthquake 373 B.C. II. palus, an inlet of the Mediterranean, near the mouth of Atax fl. Etang d'Helice; Etang de Bobine d'Aude. III. a town of the Treres, Mœs., near Sardica.

HELISICES (Elysices, Elysii), a tribe of Bebryces, Narbonensis, about Helice palus.

HELICON, I. a r. of Pieria, Macedoniæ, rising in Olympus m., and, after a course of 9½ m., disappearing under ground for the space of 3 miles; on its reappearance, it assumes the name of Baphyrus, and, navigable thence for small vessels, falls into Thermaicus sin. below Dium. Mauro Nero. II. of Sicily, falling into the Tyrrhenian sea at Tyndaris. Olivero. III. a m. of Bœotia, N. of Thisbæ. Sacred to Apollo and the Muses, the worship of whom was brought hither by some Pierian emigrants from Macedonia. Zugora or Palæovouni.

HELICRANIUM, a town of Chaonia, s.e. of Phœnice. Crania.

HELIOSCOPE ins., an isl. of Lycia.

HELIŎPŎLIS, I. (On, Bethsemes), prius Re-ei, a city of Lower Egypt, on the Nile, R., bet. Babylon and Thon, N.E. of Memphis. Famous for the temple of the sun, and as the seat of one of the three sacerdotal colleges of Egypt. Moses was educated here. Near Matareh. II. (Baalbek), a city of Phœnicia, N.W. of Damascus. Sacred to Baal (the sun). Balbec.

HELIOTROPIUM, a village of Phthiotis, Thessaly, near Thebæ.

HELISSUS fl., I. a r. of Arcadia, rising near Helissus, and falling into Alpheus fl. below Megalopolis. II. of Epea, in Elis, falling into Cyllenicus sin. III. a town of Arcadia, near the source of Helisson fl., w. of Mantinea.

HELIUM ost., the s. mouth of the Rhine.

HELLA, a name of the temple of Dodona, from Hellas, a wood-cutter, to whom the sacred dove revealed the oracular oak.

HELLANA, a town of Etruria, bet. Solaria (9) and Pistoria (6), on Via Claudia. *Aglana.*

HELLAS, I. generally, a name of Greece, from Hellas, the wood-cutter, or from Hellen, son of Deucalion; specially, a district of Greece, about Dodona and Achelous fl.; and a district of Thessaly, under Othrys m. II. a town of Phthiotis, capital of Hellas regio, on Enipeus fl., N.E. of Melitæa.

HELLENES (Sellenes), a later name of the Græci, Epirus, and, generally of the Greeks, from Hellas, the wood-cutter, or from Hellen.

HELLENIS prom., a pr. of the Damnonii, Brit., N.E. of Criu Metopon prom. *Berry Head.*

HELLESPONTUS, the strait separating Thrace from Mysia, and communicating between Propontis and the Ægean. In length 60 m., in least breadth 7 furlongs. Named from Helle, daughter of Athamas, drowned here. *Straits of Gallipolis; Dardanelles.*

HELLOMENUM, a port of Leucas ins. *Climeno.*

HELLOPIA regio, i. q. Eleon campus.

HELMODENES, a people of Arabia Petræa, N.E. of Arsinoe.

HELODES ins., islands of Sarmatia As., off Gelda.

HELORIAS campus (Heloria Tempe), the district of Helorum, in Sicily. Noted for its beautiful scenery.

HELŌRUM, a town of Sicily, S.E. at the mouth of Helorus fl. *Muri Ucci.*

HELORUS fl., a r. of Sicily, rising near Acræ and falling into Siculum mare bet. Asinarus fl. and Ichana. Of a very rapid and noisy course. *Abisso.*

HELOS, "marshy," I. a town of Argolis. II. of Elis, near Alpheus fl., towards Arcadia. III. of Laconia, E. of the mouth of Eurotas fl., 10 m. from Trinasus. Founded by Helius, son of Perseus. The Helotes, defeated in an insurrection against the Dorians and Heraclidæ, were reduced to slavery, and their name applied to all Spartan slaves. *Tsyli.* IV. a village 5 furlongs E. from Megalopolis.

HELVILLUM (Suilla), a town of Umbria, on Via Flaminia, bet. Forum Flaminii (27) and Ad Ensem (10). *Near Sigillo.*

HELVECONES (Aelviones), a tribe of Vindeli, on the Vistula, L., near the Burgundiones.

HELVETII, a Celtic people in Maxima Sequanorum. Bounded w. by Jura m., s. by Alpes Penninæ, E. by Alpes Rhætiæ, N. by the Rhine. *Part of Switzerland.*

HELVII (Elui), a Celtic people of Narbonensis I., on the E. slopes of Cevenna m., N. of the Volcæ Arecomici. *Ardèche.*

HELVINUS fl., a r. of Picenum, falling into the sea N. of Balinus fl. *Salinello.*

HELYLICES, i. q. Helisices.

HEMEROSCOPIUM, a name of Dianium, Tarraconensis, from a watch-tower which stood there.

HEMUATÆ, apud Plinium, a corruption of Dumatæ, or people of Domatha, Arabiæ.

HENETI, a maritime people of Paphlagonia, on Parthenius fl., a colony of whom, under the conduct of Antenor, migrated, 1270 B.C., by the Danube to the shores of the Adriatic, called after them Henetia, Venetia.

HENIOCHI, a people of Colchis, on the Euxine, at first towards Mæotis and subsequently removed s. towards the Bechires. Descended from the charioteers of Castor and Pollux.

HEPHA (Sycaminopolis, Sycaminorum Oppid., Sycaminon, Gaba), a maritime town of Galilæa Superior, under Carmelus m., over against Ptolemais. A colonia, enlarged by Herod and appointed by him a settlement of discharged cavalry. *Kopha.*

HEPHÆSTIA, a town of Lemnos ins., on its s. coast, in the neighbourhood of which, according to Pliny, was an extensive and most elaborate labyrinth. *Ponniah.*

HEPHÆSTUS, a town of the Delta Ægypti, towards Tanis. Sacred to Hephæstus (Vulcan).

HEPHESTIADÆ, a demus of Attica, of the tribe Acamantis, near Cephisia.

HEPHER-OPHER, Zabul, i. q. Gath-Hepher.

HEPTACOMETÆ, "seven communities," the general name of the Chalybes, Mosynœci, Tibareni, Drilæ, Macrones, Sanni, and Byzeres, in Pontus.

HEPTANESIÆ ins., isl. of India i. Gangem, over against Mandagora. *Salsette,* &c.

HEPTANOMIS (Heptapolis), Middle Egypt, from the Delta at Cercasura N. to Syène s. Named from its seven nomi and their seven chief cities.

HEPTAPORUS "seven crossings," (Polyporus,

"many crossings,") a r. of Æolis Asiat., falling into Cillæus fl. below Celænæ.

HERACLEA ins., I. an isl. of the Damnonii, Britannia I., off Herculis prom. II. (Heracleotis), of Sicily. *Felicur.* III. a town of Æolis Asiatica, on Adramyttenus sin., w. of Coryphas. IV. of Athamania, Ætolia, on Inachus fl., S.E. of Theodora. V. of Caria, at the head of Latmicus sin., 13 m. S.E. from Miletus. *Oufa Bafi.* VI. (Albace, Salbace), of Caria, under Albacus m. VII. a maritime town of Cassiotis, Syriæ, N. of Laodicea. VIII. of Cyrrhestica, Syriæ, 3 geog. m. N.W. from Hierapolis. IX. of Lucania, at the mouth of Aciris fl. A Tarentine colony, founded 428 B.C. The seat of the general council of the states of Magna Græcia. *Policoro.* X. of Lydia, under Messogis m. XI. of Lydia, near Magnesia. Noted for its magnets, called Heraclei. XII. of Taurica Chersonesus, N. towards the N. entrance of Bosporus Cimmerius. XIII. of the Odrysæ, Thrace, on the Propontis, opposite Ophiusa, bet. Ganos and Tiristasis. *Heraclitza.* XIV. of Pisatis, Elis, on Cytherus fl., 6¼ m. w. from Olympia. XV. (Achais), of Media Ragiana, N. of Ragæ. *Burukkerd.* XVI. of the Salyes, Narbonensis, at the mouth of the Rhone. Its existence, however, is dubious. XVII. (Lyncestis, Lyncus), of Lyncus, Macedonia, at the foot of the Candavii m., on the Psevus fl., bet. Nicia (11) and Cellæ (34), on the Egnatia Via. *Erekli.* XVIII. *surnamed* Minoa, of Sicily, s.w. at the mouth of Halycus fl., L., bet. Thermæ Selinuntiæ and Agrigentum. A colony from Selinus, enlarged by Spartans under Doricus. XIX. *surnamed* Perinthus, *vide* Perinthus. XX. *surnamed* Pontica, of Bithynia, on the Euxine, towards the borders of Paphlagonia, 3 m. E. from Lycus fl. A joint colony from Megara Nisæa and Tanagra, Bœotia. Celebrated for its wine, almonds, and nuts. *Erekli.* XXI. *surnamed* Sintica (ex Sintiis, Strymonis), capital of the Sinti, Macedoniæ, on Strymon fl., 50 m. N.W. from Philippi. Built by Amyntas, brother of Philip. XXII. *surnamed* Trachinia, of Maliensis, Thessaly, bet. Trachis (6 furlongs) and Thermopylæ (7½ m.). Built by a Lacedæmonian colony, 426 B.C.

HERACLEŎPŎLIS MAGNA, I. a town of Heptanomis, S.E. of Arsinoe-Crocodilopolis, on an isl. of the Nile. Sacred to the Ichneumon. II. PARVA, a town of the Delta, s.w. of Pelusium. *Ahnas.*

HERACLEOTICUM OSTIUM NILI, a name of Canopicum Ostium. Named from Heracleum, a village round a temple of Hercules, near Canopus.

HERACLEUM prom., I. a pr. of Pontus, 13 m. E. from Iris fl. *C. Thermeh.* II. a town of Ægina ins., on the E. coast, 2 m. from Tripyrgia. III. a citadel of Caunus, in Caria. IV. of Crete, N., the w. port of Gnossus. *Cartero.* V. of Pieria, Macedoniæ, on Thermaicus sin., bet. Phila (5) and Dium (12), on the Apilas fl. *Platamona.* VI. a port of Pontus, at Heracleium prom. VII. a town of Syria, near Gindarus.

HERACLEUS fl., a r. of Phocis, running into Corinthiacus sin. at Mychos portus.

HERÆA, I. a district of Megaris. II. (Sologorgus), a town of Arcadia, bet. Alpheus fl. and Ladon fl., s.w. of Psophis, towards Epitalium in Elis. Noted for a wine of peculiar potency. *Ajiani.*

HERÆI (Junonis) m., m. intersecting the S.E. portion of Sicily. *Monti Sori.*

HERÆUM, I. a town of the Corsii, Sardinia, N.W. of Olbia. II. of the Odrysæ, Thrace, on the Propontis, E. of Bisanthe. *Karegli.*

HERARASSA, capital of the Malli, India, near the source of Namadus fl. *Dschudpur.*

HERATEMIS fl., a r. of Persia, falling into the sea at or near Ieratis.

HERBANUM (Urbs Vetus), a town of Etruria, N.E. of Vulsinii, at the junction of Clanis and Vallia ffl. *Orvieto.*

HERBESSUS, I. a town of Sicily, N. of Agrigentum. II. of Sicily, near Leontini.

HERBITA, a town of Sicily, bet. Centoripæ and Menænum, according to Ptolemy; or, according to others, E. of Heræi m. *La Citadella;* or, *Nicosia.*

HERCATES, a people of Liguria, towards the Ilvates.

HERCULANEUM, I. an Oscan town of Campania, on Via Domitiana, bet. Neapolis (6) and Oplonti (6). Traditionally founded by Hercules, on his return from Spain. Finally destroyed by an eruption of Vesuvius, after several partial subversions. *Ercolano.* II. (Mars Herculis), a town of the Caudini, Samnium. *Montesarchio.*

HERCULIS FANUM, a town of Etruria, created around a temple of Hercules, towards Luca. *Mazzarosa.*

HERCULIS, I. (Herculareum Columnarum) fretum, the strait separating Africa from Europe, at the entrance of the Mediterranean. So named from the fable of Hercules. *Strait of Gibraltar.* II. ins., an isl. of Bætica, at the mouth of Urius fl.

III. two islets of Sardinia, N. of Gordita-num prom. IV. pagus, a village of Cilicia Camp., near Tarsus. V. portus, a port of Sardinia, s. bet. Nova and Bitia. *Torre del Gigante.* VI. prom., a pr. of Brut-tium, s.w. of Zephyrium prom., E. of Scyla. *C. Spartivento.* VII. a pr. of the Dam-nonii, N., opposite Heraclea ins. *Hart-land Pt.* VIII. a pr. of Mauritania Tin-gitana, bet. Ussadium prom. and Phtut fl. *Cape Mogador.* IX. a pr. of Zeugitana, on Carthag. sin., near Carpis. X. a pr. of the Zichi, Sarmat., on the Euxine, bet. Toreticum prom. and Ampsalis. XI. vicus, a town of Cilicia, near Tarsus. *Erklé.*

HERCUNIATES, a people of Pannonia Inf., on Dravus fl., L.

HERCYNE fl., a r. of Bœotia, rising near Lebadea, and falling into Copais lacus. *Livadia.*

HERCYNIA (Orcynia) silva, a forest covering central and southern Germania Magna, from the Rhine to the sources of the Vistula. The name is the Latin adaptation of the German term for pine-trees. *Schwartz-wald, &c.*

HERDONIA (Ardona, Cerdonia), a town of Daunia, Apulia, on Egnatia Via, bet. Æcæ (18) and Ad Undecim (15). Destroyed by Hannibal; but restored, and appointed a colonia. *Ordona.*

HERIUS fl., a r. of Lugdunensis III., falling into the sea, N.W. of the Liger. *Auray.*

HERMÆA ins., an isl. of Sardinia, E., over against Olbia. *Tavolara.*

HERMÆA ACRA, a pr. of Marmarica, w. of Phœnicus portus.

HERMÆUM prom., I. a pr. of Crete, s., near Pæcilasium. *C. Placo.* II. of Lemnos ins. III. of Mauritania Ting., N. of Asama. *Cape Bon.* IV. of Sardinia, w., above Bosa fl. *Capo della Caccia.* V. of Tri-polis, Afric., at Leptis Magna. VI. of Zeugitana, s. of Carthage. VII. a town of Mysia, on the Hellespont, bet. Lamp-sacus and Parium (8).

HERMAGORA fons, a stream of Bithynia, running into Bosporus Thracius near Chal-cedon.

HERMANTICA, Hispaniæ, i. q. Salmantica.

HERMINIUS m., m. of the Lusitani, the N.E. continuation of Tagus m., N. of the Tagus. *Sierra de Estrella.*

HERMIONE, an autonymous city in Argolis, on the Hermionicus sin., opposite Aperopia ins. Founded by Diopes from Thessaly. The birth-place of the poet Lasus. Near it was a cavern reputed to communicate with Orcus. *Castri.*

HERMIONES, a people of Germania Magna,

bet. the Istævones w. and the Semnones and Hermunduri E.

HERMONIACUS sin., a channel communicating bet. Argolicus sin. and Saronicus sin., and separating Argolis from Hydrea ins.

HERMISIUM, a port of Taurica Chersonesus, s. below Theodosia.

HERMIUS (Smyrnæus) sin., a gulf of the Ægean, bet. the mouth of Hermus fl. and Clazomenæ. *G. of Smyrna.*

HERMOCAPELEIA (Hermopolis), a town of Lydia, in the valley of Hermus fl.

HERMOMACUM, a town of the Nervii, Bel-gica II., bet. Camaracum s.w. and Baga-cum N.E.

HERMON (Aermon, Senior, Shenir, Sion, Scirion, Sarion) m., a s.w. continuation into N.E. Galilæa of Anti-Libanus m. *Jebel es Sheikh.*

HERMONACTIS, a maritime town of Dacia, at the mouth s. of Taras fl. A Milesian colony.

HERMONASSA, I. a town of Sindica, Sar-matiæ, on the Euxine, above Sinda. II. (Liviopolis), of Pontus, 6 m. E. from Cor-dyle. *Platana.*

HERMONTHIS, a town of Thebais, on the Nile, L., bet. Asfinis and Pampanis, above Thebæ. *Erment.*

HERMÖPÖLIS, I. *surnamed* Magna (Mercurii Oppidum), a town of Heptanomis, on the Nile, L., over against Antinoe. Here was a custodia (customs' house), at which goods coming from Thebais paid toll. From this point the schœnus, which lower down con-sisted only of forty stadia, was reckoned at sixty. Named from the worship of Her-mes (Thoth). *Achmunein.* II. *surnamed* Parva, a town of Lower Egypt, on the Canopic branch of the Nile, bet. Archan-dropolis and Andropolis. *Damanhour.*

HERMUNDÜRI (Duri), *postea* Thuringi, a people of Germania Magna, bet. Albis fl. and the Sudeta m. E., the Cherusci N., Visurgis fl. and Sala fl. w., and the Danube s. *Saxony and Anhalt.*

HERMUS, I. a r. of Ionia, rising in Dindy-mene m., or, according to Pliny, near to Dorylæum, and falling into Hermius sin., in Pliny's time, near Leucæ, but after-wards further s. Its sands were said to contain gold. *Sarabat.* II. (Hermoi), a demus of Attica, of the tribe Acamantis, near Athens, on the road to Eleusis.

HERNA, a town of the Contestani, Tarra-conensis, on Illicitanus sin., near Alebus fl.

HERNICI, a tribe of Sabines, settled in La-tium Novum, bet. the Æqui and Marsi N., and Volsci s. Named from the nature of the soil they occupied, *herna*, in the Sabine language signifying a stone.

HERODIUM, I. a fortress of Ammonitis, on the confines of Moabitis. Built by Herod. II. of Judæa, s.e. of Bethlehem. Built by Herod, in memory of the victory over Antigonus.

HEROÖPOLIS, a town of Lower Egypt, on Amari lac. towards Heroopolitis sin., s.w. of Arsinoe.

HEROOPOLITICUM prom., a pr. of Egypt, on Heroopolitis sin. w.

HEROOPOLITICUS sin., the w. termination of the Red Sea, extending from Drepanum prom. to Arsinoe-Cleopatris. The name was sometimes applied to the whole of the Red Sea. *Bahr el Rolsam; Gulf of Suez.*

HEROPHILE, a name of Erythræ, Ioniæ.

HERPA, a town of Sophene, Armenia, on Euphrates fl., L. Assigned to Cappadocia by Lucullus.

HERPEDITANI, I. a people of Hibernia, i. q. Erdini. II. of Mauritania, on both sides of Mulucha fl.

HERPIS, a town of Mauritania Tingit., on Hirpus fl., s.w. of Rusadir.

HERTHÆ ins., an isl. of Scandinavia, in Codanus sin., over against Rugium ins. N.W.

HERTICES, a people of Sarmatia Asiatica, towards the Tanais.

HESBON (Esebon, Esbus), a city, first of Reuben, and then of Gad ; a royal city of the Amorites, s.w. of Rabbath Ammon, 20 m. E. from Bethagla. *Heshban.*

HESIDRUS fl., Indiæ, i. q. Zaradrus.

HESPERIA, the name given by the Greeks to Italy, from its western situation relative to their own country. The name is more commonly met with in the poets, and the epithet *magna* coupled with it, to distinguish it from Spain, which was also denominated Hesperia, with the epithet *ultima.*

HESPERIDUM horti, "the gardens of the Hesperides," a sacred grove at (Hesperis) Berenice, in Cyrenaica.

HESPERIS (Hesperides), the early name of Berenice, in Cyrenaica.

HESPERICORNU prom., a pr. of Libya, s. of Ryssadium prom. *Cape Verd.*

HESPERIUS sin., a bay of the Atlantic, in Africa, at Hespericornu prom.

HESTIAS prom., a pr. of Thrace, near Byzantium.

HETERA, a town of Crete.

HETHITÆ (Hethæi, Hittæi, Chettæi), one of the seven tribes of Canaan, about Hebron. Descendants of Heth, son of Canaan.

HETRICULUM, a town of Bruttium, on Crathis fl., above Uffugum. *Latarico.*

HEVILA, the Scripture name of the country of the Alilæi, Arabia.

HEVILGA, a name of the territories of the Læceni, Astapeni, and Melangitæ, in Arabia Felix.

HEVITÆ (Hevæi, Cadmoneæ), one of the seven tribes of Canaan, in Ephraim, Dan, and Benjamin. Of this people was Cadmus.

HIBE, a village of Libya, at Oasis Magna.

HIBERNIA (Juverna, Iuernia, Ierne, Britannia Minor), an isl. in the Atlantic, w. of Britain. Its principal people, the Hiberni, would appear to have come from Iberia (Spain), and it was their name which Cæsar extended to the whole island. The Scoti, who formed a portion of its later population, were Scandinavian immigrants, and were called by the natives Daoine Gaul or Gaulte, "foreign or barbarous men ;" whence Donegal.

HIBERNICUS OCEANUS, the sea bet. England and Ireland. *Irish Sea.*

HICÆSIA ins., an isl. of Sicily, s. of Strongyle. *Vacheluce.*

HIDDEKEL fl., i. q. Tigris.

HIEMPA, a town of Bætica, near Hispalis, s.e.

HIERA ins., I. an isl. of the Ægean, one of the Sporades, contiguous to Thera. *Neo Caimeni.* II. of Argolis, i. q. Spharia. III. (Hieronesus), *surnamed* Maritima, an isl. of Sicily, one of the Ægates ins., w. of the Buscina ins. *Maritima.* IV. a pr. of Lycia, 4 m. from Calabantia. V. a town of Lesbos, under Olympus m., N.E. *Jero* or *Olivieri.*

HIERA GERME, "True Germe," Mysiæ, i. q. Germe.

HIERA SYCAMINOS, a town of Dodecaschœnus, on the exact border of Egypt and Æthiopia, on the Nile, R., bet. Corte and Premnis, 54 m. from Syene.

HIERABRIGA, a town of the Lusitani, near the Tagus, s.w. of Scalabis.

HIERACHUS, the Greek form of Jericho.

HIERACOME, a town of Caria, on Mæander fl., with an oracle of Apollo, whose responses were given in verse.

HIERACOMETÆ, a people of Æolis Asiat., towards Pergamus N.

HIERACOMPOLIS, a town of Thebais, on the Nile, L., bet. Apollinopolis Magna and Latopolis.

HIERACON, a town of Thebais, on the Nile, R., bet. Pesla (28) and Isium.

HIERACONNESUS, the Greek name of Accipitrum ins.

HIERAPETRA (Girapetra), the port of Arcadia, in Crete.

HIERAPOLIS, I. a town of Chorzene, Armen., N.E. of Dascusa. II. of Crete. III. *prius* Mabog, "city of cotton," *græcè* Bambyce, of Cyrrhestica, bet. Antiochia and Cecilia. Sacred to Atargatis (Astarte, Derceto). Named Hierapolis by Seleucus. *Mambej.* IV. of Phrygia M., on the confines of Lydia, bet. Tripolis and Laodicea (5). Noted for its warm springs, which had a peculiar property in dyeing processes, and for an oracle of Pluto, and for its numerous temples. The locality of the labours of Epaphras, the disciple of St. Paul. *Pambuk-Kalessi.*

HIERAPYTNA, "sacred Pytna," *prius* Cyrba (Camirus, Pytna), a town of the s. coast of Crete, w. of Erythræum prom. Founded by the Corybantes. *Girapietra.*

HIERASUS fl., Daciæ, i. q. Parata.

HIERATIS, a maritime town of Persis, near Mesambria.

HIERAX fl., Cilicia, i. q. Cydnus.

HIERENSES, a tribe of Malienses, in Thessaly, about Irus.

HIEROCÆSAREA, a town of Lydia, w. of Thyatira. Sacred to Diana Persica.

HIEROCEPIS (Hiorecipia), an enclosure near Paphos, sacred to Venus; or, according to Pliny, an island off Paphos.

HIEROLOPHIENSES, a people of Æolis Asiat., towards Pergamum.

HIEROMAX (Jarmoch) fl., a r. of Syria, rising in Alsadamus m. N.E. of Bostra, and falling into Tiberias lacus N. of Bethsan. *Sheriat el Mandour; Yarmouk.*

HIERON, I. a village in Arcadia, s. of Dactylesema. The scene of one of Orestes' phrensies. II. Bithyniæ, i. q. Estia. III. a harbour of the Toreatæ, Sarmat., on the Euxine, bet. Sinda Sorgippia and Pagræ.

HIERON OROS prom., a pr. of Pontus, 12½ m. w. from Trapezus. *C. Toroz.*

HIEROS (Siberis) fl., I. a r. of Asia Minor, falling into Sangarius fl. bet. Juliopolis (13) and Lagania. The limit, in that direction, of Bithynia and Galatia. II. Sardinæ, i. q. Sacer.

HIEROSOLYMA (Salem, "peace;" Jerusalem, "possession of peace," or "dwelling of peace;" Jebus), capital of Judæa, its N. portion in Benjamin, its s. in Judah, 20 m. N. from Hebron. *Jerusalem.*

HIERUS fl., a r. of Æolis, rising in Ida m., and falling into Adramyttenus sin.

HIEZON m., a m. of Crete, a summit of Dicte m.

HILADES ins., isl. in the Caspian, bet. the mouths of Rha and Cyrus ffl.

HILLEVIŌNES, a people of Scandinavia.

HIMELLA fl., a r. of Sabinium, falling into the Tiber above Farfarus fl. *L'Aia.*

HIMĚRA fl., I. a r. of Sicily, falling into the sea w. of Phalerium. The E. boundary of the Syracusan territory. II. *surnamed* Minor, of Sicily, falling into the Tyrrhenian sea at Himera. *San Leonardo; Fiume di Termini.* III. a town of Sicily N., at the extremity of Himera fl., L., bet. Cephaloedium and Soluntum. A Zanclian colony; destroyed by the Carthaginians.

HIMERÆUM, a town of the Edones, Thrace, on Strymon fl., above Amphipolis.

HIMERENSES THERMÆ, a town of Sicily N., at the mouth of Himera fl., R. Built by the inhabitants of Himera, after the destruction of that town by the Carthaginians. A colonia of Augustus. *Termini.*

HIMJAR, the local name of the country of the Homeritæ, in Arabia Felix.

HINNOM, *vide* Ben Hinnom.

HIPPANA, a town of Sicily, bet. Panormus and Mutistratus.

HIPPARENUM, *vide* Borsippa.

HIPPĀRIS fl., a r. of Sicily, falling into Camarina lac. *Carina.*

HIPPI (Equi) ins., I. four isl. of Ionia, over against Erythræ. II. prom., a pr. of Africa P., on Syrtis Maj., w. of Aræ Philenorum, bet. Transmariciolum and Sagazæna. III. of Numidia, N. of Roborrum prom. *Ras el Hamreh.*

HIPPIA, I. a district of Bœotia. II. Thessaliæ, i. q. Phalana.

HIPPICI m., a ridge of m. in Sarmatia As., s.E. of Gelonus.

HIPPICUS lac., a lake of Zeugitana, below Hippo Dyarrhitis.

HIPPO, I. a town of the Carpetani, Tarraconensis, near the Tagus, E. of Toletum. II. *surnamed* Diarrhytis, "watered;" *rectius* Zarytus, of Zeugitana, on Hipponensis sin., near the N. entrance of Hippicus lac., bet. Tinissa and Tabraca. A colonia (Colonia Libera). *Benizert; Bizerta.* III. *surnamed* Nova, of the Turtuli, Bætica, bet. Asimbrum N.W. and Ilipula Magna S.E. IV. *surnamed* Regius, of Numidia, w. of the mouth of Rubricatus fl., 218 m. w. from Carthage. A colonia. *Bona.*

HIPPOCORONA, a town of Æolis Asiat., near Adramyttium.

HIPPOCORONIUM, a town of Crete. *Ampicorna.*

HIPPOCRENE fons, a fountain of Helicon, in Bœotia, springing from the spot where Pegasus struck his hoof. Sacred to the Muses.

HIPPOCURA, capital of Southern Ariaca, Ind., N.E. of Sarimagula. *Hyderabad.*

HIPPOLA, a town of Laconia, at Thyrides prom.

HIPPOLEUM prom., a pr. of Sarmatia Europ., near the inner mouth of the Borysthenes.

HIPPONENSIS sin., a bay of the Mediterranean, at Hippo Dyarrhitis.

HIPPONESUS ins., an isl. of Caria, in Ceramicus sin.

HIPPONIATES sin. (Vibonensis sin.), a bay of Terinæus sin., at Hipponium.

HIPPONIUM, *postea* Vibo Valentia, a city of Bruttium, on Hipponiates sin., s. bet. Amnicia (10) and Tauriana (10) on Via Aquilia. A colony from Locri. Destroyed by Dionysius the Elder; restored by Carthaginian settlers. A colonia (Vibo Valentia, 194 B.C.) and municipium. Here was a grove of Proserpine, where the women assembled once a year to gather flowers in her honour. Here also was the Horn of Amalthea, constructed by Gelo. *Monte Leone.*

HIPPOPHAGI, people of Sarmatia and Parthia, named from their living upon horseflesh.

HIPPOPODUM ins., i. q. Oonæ.

HIPPOS mons, a pr. of Arabia Felix, on the Red Sea, the s. boundary of the Thamuditæ. *Djebel Hassane.*

HIPPOTAMADÆ, a demus of Attica, of the tribe Æneis.

HIPPOTES, a village of Bœotia, on Libethrius m.

HIPPOTHOONTIS, a tribe or ward of Attica, named from Hippothoon, son of Neptune and Alope.

HIPPURI portus, a port of Taprobane.

HIPPURIS ins., an isl. of the Ægean, one of the Sporades, w. of Tragia. *Hermonisi.*

HIPPURIUS fl., a r. of Lydia, falling into Macistus fl. below Blaundus.

HIPPUS, I. a r. of Ecretice, Colchis, falling into Phasis fl. towards Astelephus. *Rion.* II. m. of the Banubari, in Arabia Felix, above Leucecome. III. (Susitha), a town of Gaulonitis Inferior, on Tiberias lac., over against Tiberias (3). *Szammera.*

HIRMINIUS fl., a r. of Sicily, falling into the sea at Cancana. *Fiume di Ragusa.*

HIROTH, a town of Lower Egypt, w. of Arsinoe, bet. Etham and Clysma.

HIRPINI, a tribe of Samnites, settled in the s. portion of Samnium. Named from their predatory character, *hirpus*, in their language signifying a wolf.

HIRPIS fl., a r. of Mauritania Ting., falling into the Mediterranean, w. of Rusadir.

HIRRI, Germaniæ, i. q. Sciri.

HISPA (Ipsa), a town of Armenia Min., bet. Dascusa (18) and Arangæ (18).

HISPALIS, capital of the Turtetani, Bætica, on the Bætis, L., 62 m. from its mouth, bet. Italica and Vergentum. Not improbably the ancient Tartessus. A colonia (Romulea). *Sevilla.*

HISPANIA (Spanjah, *Phœnician,* "rabbits;" Hesperia Ultima, Iberia), a peninsular country of Europe, bounded N. by Cantabricum mare and by Gaul at the Pyrenees, s. and E. by the Mediterranean, w. by the Atlantic. It was divided by the Romans, upon their conquering it from the Carthaginians, into Hispania Citerior (*postea* Tarraconensis) and Hispania Ulterior (*postea* Lusitania and Bætica). Peopled principally by Iberi, from N.E. Asia, and by Celtæ. *España; Spain.*

HISPELLUM, a town of Umbria, s. of Assisium. A colonia (Colonia Julia Hispellum). *Spello.*

HISPIRATIS, a district of Armenia Int., on the confines of the Macrones Ponti. *Sper.*

HISTI, a people of Scythia, on Jastus fl.

HISTIÆA, a demus of Attica, of the tribe Ægeis.

HISTIÆA, a town of Eubœa ins., on the N.W. coast, at the mouth of Callas fl., w. of Dium; an Athenian colony. On the expulsion by the Athenians of its original inhabitants, who withdrew to Macedonia, it was renamed Oreus. *Oreos.*

HISTONIUM, a maritime town of the Frentani, on Via Frentana, bet. Pallanum (12) and Uscosium (15). At first a pirate's haunt, afterwards a colonia. *Vasto d'Ammone.*

HISTRI, a Thracian migration, settled in the country called from them Histria, bet. Venetia (at Formio fl.) and Illyria (at Arsia fl), bounded w. by the Adriatic. By the poets the name is derived from Hister fl. (the Danube), and the primitive Histri are identified with the Argonauts, and, as later immigrants, with the Colchians sent by Ætes in pursuit of the ravishers of Medea. Subjugated by Rome 179 B.C. Included within the limits of Italy by Augustus.

HISTRIA, *vide* Histri.

HITTITÆ, a people of Judæa, about Hebron and Bethel. The descendants of Heth, son of Canaan.

HIULCA lacus, a marsh of Pannonia Inf., s.w. of Mursa. It was drained by Probus.

HOBAH, a village of Cœle-Syria, N.E. of Damascus, whither Abraham pursued Chedorlaomer. *Hobah.*

HODIOPOLIS, a town of Bithynia, towards Heraclea.

HOLMI I. (Hormi, Oani), a maritime town of Cilicia Trachea, 5 m. N.E. of Mylæ. The inhabitants were removed to Seleucia. II. of Phrygia Parorea, E. of Cylla. *Houma.*

HOLMŌNES, a town of Bœotia, ¾ m. E. of Hyettus, on Copais lac. Named after Holmus, son of Sisyphus.

HOLO, a town of the Turtuli, Bæturia, w. of Bæcyla.

HOLOPHYXUS, a town of Crete.

HOMARIUM, a town of Achaia, near Ægium.

HOMERITÆ (Gebanitæ), a people of Arabia Felix, occupying its S.W. angle.

HOMILÆ, a town of the Ænianes, Thessaly, towards the source of Sperchius fl., N.W. of Sperchiæ.

HOMŎLE m., a m. of Magnesia, in Thessaly, the N. termination of Ossa m., on the right of Peneus fl., near the sea. A favourite abode of Pan.

HOMOLĬUM (Homolis), a town of the Lapithæ, in Magnesia, Thessaly, under Homole m. *Ambelakia.*

HOMONADA, a maritime fortress of Cilicia Trachea, on the borders of Pisidia, near the w. source of Calycadnus fl. *Ermenak.*

HONOSCA, a maritime town of Tarraconensis, bet. the Iberus and Carthago Nova.

HOR m., I. a mountain of Idumæa, midway bet. the Red Sea and the Dead Sea. The burial-place of Aaron. *Jebel Haroun.* II. a ridge of Libanus m. N.E.

HOREB m., *vide* Sinai.

HORESTÆ, a tribe of Venicontes, Brit., under Grampius m. *Eskdale.*

HORIM, "dwellers in caves," i. q. Horitæ.

HORISIUS fl., a r. of Bithynia, falling into the Rhyndacus.

HORITÆ (Horim), a people of Idumæa, about Seir m.

HORMA, a town of Almopæia, Pæonia, on Erigonus fl., w. of Ad Herculem.

HORMANUS fl., a r. of Arabia Felix, falling into Erythræum mare S.W. of Abissa. *Harmin.*

HORREA, I. *surnamed* Cælia, Ad Horrea, a maritime town of Byzacene, at the N. limit of that province, bet. Orasse and Hadrumetum (10). II. of Mauritania Cæsar., bet. Choba and Sitifi (18). III. of Mygdonia, Messeniæ, on Arzamo fl., R., below Bebasa. IV. (Margi), a town of the Triballi, Mœsiæ, on Margus fl., R., near Ad Octavum.

HORREUM, a town of Molossis, near the w. bank of Pambotis lacus. *Gardikaki.*

HORTA (Hortanum), a town of Etruria, on

the Tiber, N.E. of Falerii. A military colony of Augustus. *Orta.*

HORTONA (Artona), a town of the Latini, Latium, on the confines of the Æqui, s. of Algidum. *Monte Fortino.*

HOSÆA, a town of Sardinia, on the coast, 10 m. s. from Sacer fl. *Torre di Marchidi.*

HOSSTI, a people of Sarmatia, N. of the Veltæ.

HOSTILIA, a town of the Cenomanni, Gallia Transp., on Padus fl., E.S.E. of Mantua. The birth-place of Cornelius Nepos? *Ostiglia.*

HUCUMBRA, Assyriæ, i. q. Symbra.

HUMATIA fl., a r. of Rhætia, falling into Addua fl. *Serio.*

HUNGUNVERRO, a town of the Volcæ Tectosages, Narbonensis I., bet. Casinomagus w. and Bucco E.

HUNNUM, a town of the Otadeni, Brit., on Hadriani murus N., bet. Procolitia and Vindobula. *Halton-Chesters.*

HYACINTHIA VIA, the road from Sparta to Amyclæ.

HYÆA, a town of the Locri Ozolæ, s. of Tritæa.

HYAMEIA, a town of Messenia.

HYAMPIA m., I. a summit of Parnassus, at Hyampolis. II. a summit of Phædriades m.

HYAMPOLIS, a city of Phocis, bet. Elatæa and Opus, under Hyampia m. Built by the Hyantes. Destroyed by Xerxes, and again by Philip; restored a second time by Hadrian. *Bogdana.*

HYANTES, a tribe of Leleges, in Bœotia, prior to the invasion of Cadmus; named after their king, Hyas.

HYANTIS, an early name of Bœotia, from the Hyantes.

HYBA (Hybadæ), a demus of Attica, of the tribe Leontis.

HYBLA, I. *surnamed* Major, a town of Sicily, on Simæthus fl., L., above Murgantia. Noted for its honey. Extinct in Pausanias' time. *Paterno.* II. *surnamed* Minor, *vel* Heræa, a town of Sicily, under Heræus m., E. of Gela. Noted for its honey. *Calata-Girone.* III. *surnamed* Parva, a name of Megara Hyblæa, in Sicily.

HYCCARA, a maritime town of Sicily, N. bet. Panormus (16) and Parthenicum (8). The birth-place of Lais.

HYDA (Hyla), a town of Caria, on Schœnus sin.

HYDARA, a fortress of Armenia Minor. Built by Mithridates.

HYDASPES fl., a r. of India e. Gangem, rising in Imaus m., and falling into Hyphasis fl. above Alexandria. It was on this river that Alexander built his Indian fleet. *Jylum.*

HYDATA, a town of the Potulatenses, Dac., on Ardiscus fl., towards its source.

HYDE, I. a town of Lycaonia, towards the N. extremity of Tattæa lac. II. of Lydia, near Gygæa palus. Thought by Pliny to be identical with Sardes.

HYDISSUS, a town of Caria, E. of Mylassa.

HYDRA, I. Ætol., i. q. Lysimachia. II. a pr. of Æolis Asiat., the s. extremity of Elæaticus sin., opposite Harmatus prom. (10).

HYDREA ins., an isl. of Argolis, in Myrtoum mare, over against Scyllæum prom. and Buporthmus. *Hydra.*

HYDRÆUM APOLLINIS, a town of Thebais, bet. Phalacrum and Cabalsus, E. of Syene.

HYDRÆUM CÆNON (Hydreum Novum), a town of Thebais, bet. Cabalsus and Berenice.

HYDRANON, Cretæ, i. q. Rhithymna.

HYDRAOTES (Hyarotes, Adris) fl., a r. of India e. Gangem, falling into Hydaspes fl. below Mallorum urbs. *Ravee.*

HYDRAX, a town of Pentapolis, Cyrenaicæ, bet. Limnias and Darnis.

HYDRELA, a surname of Caria, Phrygiæ.

HYDRIACUS (Caudriacus) fl., a r. of Gedrosia, falling into Paragon sin. at Talmena.

HYDRUNTUM (Hydrus), a city of Japygia, on the Adriatic, bet. Lupia (25) and Castrum Minervæ (8). The nearest port to Greece. A Cretan col. *Otranto.*

HYDRUS fl., a r. of Calabria, falling into the sea at Hydruntum. *Idro.*

HYDRUSA ins., an isl. of Attica, in Saronicus sin., N.W. of Zoster prom. *Cambonisi.*

HYELE, Italiæ, i. q. Velia.

HYELIUM, a town of Phrygia Mag., on Mæander fl.

HYETTUS, a town of Bœotia, E. of Tegyra. Named after Hyettus, the Argive.

HYETTUSA ins., an isl. of Ionia, in Icarium mare, over against Panormus. *Gaithnosi.*

HYGASTUS, a town of Caria.

HYGENNA, Lyciæ. *Vide* Ibytenna.

HYGRIS, a town of the Jazyges, Sarmat., on Palus Mæotis, bet. Lycus fl. and Poritas fl.

HYLÆ, a people of Sarmatia Eur., on the Borysthenes, L., towards its mouth.

HYLÆTUS fl., a r. of the Locri Ozolæ, falling into Crissæus sin., s. of Tolophon.

HYLÆUM mare, the strait separating Achillei Cursus, Sarmat., from the mainland.

HYLAS fl., a r. of Bithynia, flowing from Arganthonius m. into Cianus sin. The scene of the story of Hylas.

HYLE, I. a town of Bœotia, N.E. of Thebæ palus. Noted for its shields. II. of Cyprus, near Curium. Sacred to Apollo Hylates.

HYLIAS fl., a r. of Bruttium, falling into the Ionian sea at Paternum ; the limits of the territories of Thurii and Crotona. *Calonato.*

HYLICE palus, a lake of Bœotia, s.E. of Copais palus, formed by a subterraneous stream from that lake. *L. Livadhi; Senzina.*

HYLIUS fl., a r. of Argolis, running into Saronicus sin. below Ilei. *Eileo.*

HYLLAICUS portus, one of the harbours of Corcyra oppidum. Noted for its beautiful scenery.

HYLLARIMA (Hilarema), a town of Caria, N. of Stratonicea. The birth-place of Hierocles.

HYLLINI, a tribe of Dalmatæ, Illyria, about Hyllis prom.

HYLLIS prom., a pr. of the Dalmatæ, in Illyria, N. of Epidaurus. *Sabioncello.*

HYLLUS (Phrygius) fl., a r. of Lydia, rising in Phrygia Epictetus, near the source of Rhyndacus fl., and falling into Hermus fl. above Magnesia ad Sipylum.

HYLLYALA, a village of Caria. The death place of Hyllus.

HYMETTUS m., m. of Attica, the southern range of Pentelicus m., s.E. of Athens. Famous for its honey, and for its marble quarries. *Trelovouni; Monte Matto.*

HYMOS ins., an isl. of Rhodes.

HYNIDOS, a town of Caria, near Alabanda.

HYOESSA f., a stream of Argolis, falling into Taurus fl.

HYPACARIS fl., Sarmat., i. q. Carcinis.

HYPACHÆI, a primitive tribe in Cilicia, afterwards calling themselves Cilices, from Cilix, son of Agenor.

HYPÆA ins, one of the Stæchades ins., Narbonensis, E. of Mese ins. *Isle du Levant; du Titan.*

HYPÆLOCHII, a tribe of Molossi.

HYPÆPA, a town of Lydia, near the source of Caystrus fl., under Tmolus m. Sacred to Venus. Noted for the especial beauty of its women. *Birkhe.*

HYPÆSIA (Æpasium), a district of Triphylia, in Elis, about Lepræum.

HYPANA, a town of Triphylia, Elis, near Pylos. *Upana.*

HYPANIS fl., I. Ind., i. q. Hyphasis. II. of Sarmatia Asiat., i. q. Vardanus. III. *postea* Buges, of Sarmatia E., bet. Axiaces fl. and the Borysthenes. *Bog.*

HYPATA, a town of the Ænianes, Thessaly,

on the right bank of Sperchius fl., opposite Macracomæ, 27 m. s.w. from Pharsalus. Its women were reputed sorceresses. *Castritza.*

HYPANTON m., a m. of Bœotia, N.E. of Thebes. *Klephto Vouni.*

HYPERBOREI m., i. q. Rhiphæi.

HYPERDEXION, a town of Lesbos.

HYPEREA, a name, with Homer, of Liburnia.

HYPEREA fons, a fountain of Pelasgiotis, in Thessaly, near Pheræ.

HYPERESIA, the early name of Ægira, in Achaia.

HYPERIS fl., a r. of Persis, falling into Persicus sin. bet. Aracia ins. and Brisoana fl.

HYPERTALEATON, a village of Laconia, N.E. of Asopus.

HYPHALI, a maritime town of Cyrenaica, w., bet. Liba and Euschœnus.

HYPHĂSIS (Axiaces, Hypanis) fl., a r. of India e. Gangem, falling into the Indus at Alexandria. The boundary of Alexander's eastern conquests, on the banks of which he raised altars. *Beyah.*

HYPHORMUS, a port of Attica, near Sunium. *Enea Pyrga.*

HYPIUS, I. a r. of Bithynia, rising in Hypius m., and, after forming Daphnusis lac., falling into the Euxine 22 m. E. from Sangarius fl. *Mitan.* II. a summit of Olympus m., Bithynia, N.E. of Daphnusis lac.

HYPOCREMNUS prom., Ioniæ, i. q. Apocremnus.

HYPODROMOS prom., a pr. of Libya, on the Atlantic, s. of Masitholus prom. *Cabo Roxo.*

HYPOTHEBÆ, Bœotia, i. q. Potniæ.

HYPPELIUNE, a town of Phrygia, near Carura.

HYPSARNUS fl., a r. of Bœotia.

HYPSAS fl., I. a r. of Sicily, falling into Afric. pelagus, bet. Silinus and Isborus fl. *Belici.* II. of Sicily, falling into the sea near Agrigentum. *Dnago.*

HYPSELE, a town of Thebais, on the Nile, L., bet. Apollinis Minor civitas and Abotis.

HYPSIGORUS m., i. q. Dysorus.

HYPSUS, I. a town of Arcadia, near Thyreum. II. of Laconia, on Smenus fl., N.W. of Las.

HYRCĀNIA, I. a country of Asia, bounded N. by the Caspian and by Sogdiana, at Oxus fl., s. by Parthia, at Labuta m., w. by Media and the Caspian, E. by Margiana. Noted for its tigers, vines, figs, olives, and honey. *Werkana.* II. its capital, on Maxera fl., L. *Werkana.* III. a

town of Lydia, in Hyrcanius campus, on Hyllus fl.

HYRCANIUM, a fortress of Judæa, built by Hyrcanus.

HYRCANIUM mare, i. q. Caspium.

HYRCANIUS campus, a plain of Lydia, watered by Hyllus fl. Colonized by Hyrcanians and Macedonians.

HYRGIS fl., a r. of Sarmatia Asiat., falling into the Tanais above Gelonus. *Donetz.*

HYRIA (Uria), I. a town of Bœotia, in the territory of Tanagra, towards Aulis. II. of Cilicia Trachea, on Calycadnus fl., above Seleucia. III. of Messapia, on Via Appia, bet. Scamnum and Mesochoron, E. of Tarentum. Founded circa 1000 B.C. by some Cretan settlers. *Oria.* IV. according to Pliny, the early name of Zacynthus ins. V. according to Ovid, the name of Conope lac., after Hyrie, mother of Cycnus.

HYRIS prom., a pr. of Bithynia, on Propontis, 14 m. E. from Acritas prom.

HYRMINE, I. a prom. of Epea, Elis, N. of Cyllene, over against Cephallenia. *C. Chiarenza.* II. a town of Epea, Elis, within the cognominal prom. Extinct in Strabo's time.

HYRMINIUS fl., a r. of Sicily, falling into Afric. pelagus w. of Motycanus fl. *Mauli.*

HYRTACINA, a town of Crete.

HYSBE, a town of Lydia.

HYSIÆ, I. a town of Argolis, on the confines of Arcadia, bet. Cenchreæ and Tegea. II. of Attica, near Œnoe.

HYSIÆ, a town of Bœotia, under Cithæron m., 1 m. s.E. from Platæa. Founded by Nycteus, father of Antiope. *Platania.*

HYSPRIATIS, a town of Armenia.

HYSSELINUS m., Argolis, i. q. Arachnæus.

HYSSUS (Susarmia) fl., a r. of Pontus, falling into the Euxine at Hyssus. *Sourmenah.*

HYSSUS portus (Psoron, *postea* Susarmia), a port of Pontus, 22 m. E. from Trapezus, at the mouth of Susarmia fl.

I.

IAPIS, a r. of Græcia extra Peloponnesum, rising in Kerata m., and, after separating Attica from Megaris, falling into Saronicus sin. s.w. of Eleusis.

IAR-IN ("western land," Erin), the early name of Hibernia.

IBĒRA JULIA (Ilercavonia), capital of the Ilercaones, Tarraconensis, on the coast s. of the Iberus. A municipium.

IBERIA, I. a country of Asia, bounded N. by

Sarmatia Asiat., s. by Armenia, w. by Colchis, and at one period by Pontus, E. by Albania. *Georgia.* II. the name given generally to Spain, but more correctly to its southern portion, from the Iberes, whom Scylax designates the earliest people in Europe.

IBERINGÆ, a people of India e. Gangem, on Dorius fl., towards its source.

IBERNI (Iuerni), a people from Iberia (Spain) settled generally in Southern Hibernia.

IBERNIUM, a port of the Durotriges, Brit. *Bere Regis.*

IBERUS fl., a r. of Tarraconensis, rising in Vindius m., above Juliobriga, and falling into the Mediterranean below Dertosa, s. of Tarraco. *Ebro.*

IBETTES fl., a r. of Samos, falling into the sea near Samos.

IBIS, a town of the Contestani, Tarraconensis, N.N.W. of Lucentum.

IBIUM, a town of Heptanomis, on the Nile, L., 24 m. N. from Hermopolis. *Minyeh?*

IBLIGO, a town of Venetia. *Iplis.*

IBLIODURUM, a town of the Mediomatrices, Belgica I., bet. Verodunum w. and Divodurum E.

IBORA, a town of Pontus, bet. Agriane and Pardonesa.

IBYTENNA, a town of Lycia; the Hygenna of Herodotus.

ICARIA, a demus of Attica, of the tribe Ægeis, at the foot of Icarius m., bet. Cecropia and Chastia.

ICARIUM mare, the portion of the Ægean bet. Icarus and Samos ins. N., and Patmos and Lepsia s. Named after Icarus, son of Dædalus, who fell into the sea here.

ICARIUS m., a m. of Attica, w. of Acharnæ, N.W. of Athens. *Tragomano.*

ICARTA, a town of the Bettigi, Ind., under Adisathrus m., N. of Candipatna.

ICARUS (Icaria, Doliche, Macris, Ichthyoessa), I. an isl. of Ionia, in the Ægean, s.w. of Samos. Named from the fate of Icarus, son of Dædalus. Noted for its strong wines. *Nicaria.* II. fl., a r. of Bactriana, falling into the Axus E. *Aederab.*

ICATALÆ, a people of Sarmatia Asiatica, on Mæotis palus.

ICAUNA fl., a r. of Gaul, falling into the Sequana at Condate. *Yonne.*

ICĔNI (Simĕni), a maritime people of Flavia Cæsariensis, bet. the Catavellauni w., the Trinobantes s., Metaris Æstuar. N., and the German ocean E. *Norfolk and Suffolk.*

ICHANA, a maritime town of Sicily, s.E., above Pachynum prom.

ICHARA ins., an isl. of Arabia Felix, in Persicus sin., 130 m. s. from Achana fl.

ICHNÆ (Achnæ), I. a town of Bottiæa, Macedonia, on Thermaicus sin., above the mouth of Ludias fl. II. (Ichnia, Ischnæ), of Osrhoene, on Belias fl., bet. Alagma and Nicephorium. Built by the Macedonians. The death-place of the son of Crassus. III. of Phthiotis, Thessaly, N.W. of Phyllus.

ICHNUSA ins., a name of Sardinia, from its resemblance to a footstep.

ICHTHYOPHAGI, maritime people thus named from their living upon fish, are described by ancient geographers, 1. in Sinica; 2. in Arabia, on Persicus sin.; 3. in Libya, on the Atlantic; 4. in Gedrosia, on Erythræum m.

ICHTHYS prom., a pr. of Epea, Elis, over against Elatus m., Zacynthi. *C. Catacolo.*

ICIANI, a town of the Iceni, Brit., bet. Camboricum and Villa Faustina. *Ickburgh.*

ICIDMAGUS, a town of the Vellavi, Aquitania I., bet. Revessio w. and Aquæ Segetæ N. *Issengeaux.*

ICINIACUM, a town of Germania Mag., on the Danube, bet. Vetoniana and Biriciana.

ICLODURUM, a town of the Caturiges, Viennensis, bet. Vapincum w. and Caturigæ E.N.E.

ICONIUM, capital of Lycaonia, bet. Laodicea and Lystra. Named from the *eikon* or image of Gorgon, brought there by Jason. The scene of the labours of St. Paul and Barnabas. *Konia; Cogni.*

ICORIGIUM, a town of the Ubii, Germania II., bet. Marcomagus and Ausava.

ICOS ins., an ins. of Thessaly, in the Ægean, N.E. of Solimnia. Colonized by Gnossians from Crete. *Iouia.*

ICOSIUM, a maritime town of Mauritania Cæsar., bet. Rusconium and Casæ Calventi. A colonia. Built by twenty of the companions of Hercules. *Shershell.*

ICTIMULA (Castellum Ictimuli), the town of the Ictimuli, a tribe of Salassi, towards Vercellæ.

IGULISMA, a town of the Santones, Aquitania II., E. of Condate. *Angoulême.*

IDA m., I. m. of Asia Minor, extending from about Zeleia N. to Lectum prom. s.w. Named from the Cretan Ida. II. a range of m. running through Crete from w. to E. Its summit, especially called Ida (the modern *Psilorati*), occupies the centre of the island, N.W. of Gortys. Sacred to Jupiter, as his birth-place, and to Cybele.

IDACUS, a town of Chersonesus Thracia, on the Hellespont, s. of Cynossema.

IDÆA, a name of Creta ins., from Ida m.

IDĂLIUM (Idalia), a town of Cyprus, near Pedalium prom., with a grove sacred to Venus.

IDANUSA, a town of Novem Populana, in the Pyrenees. *Indaus.*

IDARA (Arre Vicus), a town of the Malangitæ, Arabiæ, s.w. of Biabanna. *Deraié.*

IDE, a town of Chersonesus Thracia, on Melas sin., N. of Pæon.

IDEESSA, a town of Iberia, on the confines of Colchis. Built by Phrixus, the predecessor of the Argonauts.

IDEX fl., a r. of Gallia Cispadana, falling into Padus fl. w. of Silarus fl. The boundary bet. the Boii and the Lingones. *Idice.*

IDICARA (Diacira), a town of Arabia Felix, on Mesanites sin., at the old mouth of the Euphrates. *El Kader.*

IDICRA, a town of Mauritania, 25 m. s.w. from Mileum.

IDISTAVISUS CAMPUS, a place in the territory of the Cherusci, Germania, on Visurgis fl., L., below Ascalingium. The locality of the defeat of Arminius by Germanicus.

IDOMENE, I. two hills in Amphilochia, Acarnania, on the E. coast of Ambracius sin., N. of Olpæ. II. of Emathia, Macedoniæ, on the confines of Pelagonia. *Idomeni.*

IDOMUS, a town of the Triballi, Mœsia, on Margus fl., R., bet. Jovis pagus and Ad Octavum.

IDORA, a town of Arabia Felix, in the Desert, s.w. of Nascus.

IDRÆ, a people of Sarmatia, s. of the Nasci.

IDREAS, the early name of Euromus, in Caria.

IDUBĒDA m., m. of Tarraconensis, extending from Vindius m., about Juliobriga, S.E., to the Mediterranean at Caprasia prom. *Sierra d' Oca.*

IDUMÆA, the classical name of Edom.

IDUMANIA (Sidumanis) fl., a r. of the Trinobantes, Brit., falling into Germanic. Oc. below Camulodunum. *Blackwater.*

IDYMA, a town of Caria, on Idymus fl.

IDYMUS fl., a r. of Caria.

IDYRUS, a port of Pamphylia, E. of Climax.

IERATIS, a town of Persia, on the coast bet. Sitacus fl. (88) and Padagrus fl.

IERNE, the term given by Strabo to Iar-in (Erin).

IGÆDITA (Egitania), a town of Tarraconensis, near Lancia Oppidana. *Idanha la Vieja.*

IGILGILIS, a town of Mauritania Cæsar., on Numidicus sin., bet. Choba and Pacciana. A colonia of Augustus. *Gigel; Gigeri.*

IGILIUM ins., an isl. of Etruria, w. of Cosanum prom. *Giglio.*

IGILLIONES, a people of Sarmatia, s. of the Sudeni.

IGUVIUM, a town of Umbria, s. of Tifernum Tiberinum, at the foot of the Apennines. The head of an Umbrian confederacy, in alliance with Rome. A municipium. Here, in 1440, were found the famous Eugubbian Tables. In the vicinity was a temple and oracle of Jupiter Apenninus; and Lanzi suggests that the name Iguvium is a corruption of Vicus Jovius. *Eugubbio; Gubbio.*

IJON, a town of Galilæa, on Jordan fl., R., towards its source.

IKENILD STREET (Icenild, Via Vicinalis), a road to London from the territory of the Iceni.

ILA, I. a r. of Britannia Barbara, falling into the German ocean s. of Vervedrum prom.; it separates the Cornavii N. from the Lugi s. *Wick.* II. a maritime town of Carmania-Rudiane, bet. Dara fl. and Tarsias prom.

ILARCURIS, a town of the Carpetani, Tarraconensis, N. of Ilucia.

ILARGUS fl., a r. of Vindelicia, falling into the Danube at Piniana castra? *Iller.*

ILARIS, a town of Lycia.

ILDUM, a town of the Ilercaones, Tarraconensis, N.W. of Etovesa, $7\frac{1}{2}$ m. from the sea. *Salsadella?*

ILEA, a demus of Attica.

ILEI, a town of Argolis, on the Hylius fl., bet. Trœzen and Hermione. *Ileo.*

ILEOSCA, with Strabo, i. q. Osca.

ILERCAONES (Illurgavonenses, Ilergaones), a maritime people of Tarraconensis, E., bet. Tulcis fl. N. and Sepelaci s. *Valencia, and S.E. Arragon.*

ILERCATES, a mountain tribe of Liguria, N. of the Apuani.

ILERDA, capital of the Ilergetes, Tarraconensis, on the Sicoris fl., R., towards its confluence with Cinga fl. A colonia. *Lerida.*

ILERGAVONIA (Hibera Julia), the ancient capital of the Ilercaones, on the Iberus, opposite Dertosa. A municipium.

ILERGĒTES (Ilergetæ, Ilerdetæ), a people of Tarraconensis, on Cinga fl., bet. Sicoris fl. and the Iberus, about Ilerda. *Arragon.*

ILESIUM, a town of Bœotia.

ILESSUS, a town of the Locri Ozoles, s. of Tritæa.

ILICA, a town of Zeugitana, under Cirna m.

ILIENSES, a tribe of Trojans settled in Sardinia, bet. the Sulsitani N. and the Scapitani s. *About Ilena.*

ILIO, Epiri, i. q. Elæus.

ILIOCONE, a town of Mysia, near Parium.

ILION, a town of Phœbotis, in Illyria, on Apsus fl., N.W. of Codrion.

ILIPA, *surnamed* Magna and Ilia, a town of the Turtuli, Bætica, on the Bætis, R., 63 m. above Hispalis, opposite the junction of Singilis fl. *Alcolea; Penaflor?*

ILĬPA (Ilipŭla), a town of the Turtetani, Bætica, on Urius fl., N.E. of Onoba. *Niebla.*

ILIPULA m., m. of Bætica, separating the Turtuli N. from the Bastuli s. *Sierra Nevada, Sierra de Alhamilla, and Sierra de Antequera.*

ILISSUS, a stream of Attica, rising N.E. of Athens, and, at one time, falling into Saronicus sin., but now losing itself, after a short course s., in marshes. Sacred to the Muses, hence called Ilissiades. The lustration of the lesser mysteries was usually performed on its banks. *Ilisse.*

ILISTRA, a town of Lycaonia, bet. Isaurica and Parlais, S.E. of Lystra.

ILIUM NOVUM, a city of Troas, 3¾ m. N.W. from Troja, 21 s. from Abydus. Built *circa* 1180 B.C. Enlarged and walled by Lysimachus. Named after Ilion, son of Troas. *Hissardjick, Eski Kalapfali.*

ILIUS m., a m. of Laconia, w. of Las.

ILLIBERIS fl., I. a r. of Narbonensis, running by Illiberis. *Tech.* II. (Liberini), a town of Bætica, on Singilis fl., S.E. of Ulia. *Granada.* III. (Eliberi), *postea* Helena, a town of the Bebryces, Narbonensis I., on Illiberis fl., bet. Ruscino and Stabula. Enlarged and renamed by Constantine the Great. The death-place of Constans. *Elne.*

ILLICI (Illice, Illicia, Elia), a town of the Contestani, Tarraconensis, 8 m. inland from Illicitanus sin., s.w. of Lucentum. A colonia. The death-place of Hamilcar. *Near Elche.*

ILLICITANUS sin., a bay of the Mediterranean, in Tarraconensis, bet. Saturni prom. s. and Artemisium prom. N. Named from Illici. *G. of Alicant.*

ILLITURGIS, a town of the Turtuli, Bætica, on the Bætis, above Ucia. Destroyed by Scipio. Rebuilt and appointed a colonia (Julium). Appian calls it Ilyrgia. *Baza.*

ILLYRIA, a country of Europe, extending along the E. coast of the Adriatic from Istria to Epirus, and inland to Dravus fl., and the frontiers of Mœsia and Macedonia. Under the Romans it was divided into the provinces of Illyricum and Pannonia.

ILLYRICÆ GENTES, various tribes of Thracian descent occupying Illyria.

ILLYRICUM, a province of Rome, consisting of Illyria Barbara, *postea* Romana, and Illyria Græca, the former comprising Japydia, Liburnia, and Dalmatia; the latter extending from the Drilo to the Aous.

ILLYRIS ins., an isl. of Lycia, in the Lycium mare.

ILORCI (Eliocrora), a town of the Bastitani, Tarraconensis, bet. Carthago Nova (48) and Basti (50). *Lorca.*

ILUCIA, a town of the Carpetani, Tarraconensis, on the Anas, above Metellinum.

ILUNUM, a town of the Bastitani, Tarraconensis, below Turbula.

ILURATUM, a town of Taurica Chersonesus, w. of Panticapæum.

ILŬRO (Eluro, Diluro), I. a town of the Lacetani, Tarraconensis, N.E. of Bætulo. *Mataro.* II. of the Ilergetes, 12 m. from Aspaluca. *Argels.* III. capital of the Osquidates, Novem Populana, bet. Beneharnum N.N.W. and Aspaluca s.

ILUZA, Phrygiæ, i. q. Alydda.

ILVA (Æthalia) ins., I. an isl. of Etruria, 10 m. s.w. of Populonium. Occupied first by the Phœnicians and then by the Tyrrheni. Celebrated for its iron-mines. *Elba.* II. of Sardinia, N.E. above Phintonis ins. *Santa Madalena.*

ILVATES, a people of Liguria, s. of the Statielli.

ILYRGIA, *apud* Appian, i. q. Illiturgis.

IMACHARA, a town of Sicily, N.W. of Eryce.

IMADUCHI, a people of Sarmatia Asiat., in Caucasus m. *Traina.*

IMÆUS, I. a ridge of the Apennines, towards the E. shore of Fucinus lac. II. a village of the Marsi, on the cognominal mountains, bet. Cerfenna (5) and Statulæ (7). *Forca Carrasa.*

IMAUS m., a range of Taurus, dividing Scythia into Scythia i. Imaum and Scythia e. Imaum, and separating Scythia itself from India. *Part of Himalaya.*

IMBARUS m., a portion of Taurus, in Armenia Maj., according to Strabo, or in Cilicia according to Pliny.

IMBRASUS fl., *prius* Parthenius, a r. of Samos ins., falling into the sea at Samos opp. From the temple of Juno on its banks, that goddess was surnamed Imbrasia.

IMBROS, I. an isl. of Thrace, in the Ægean, bet. Samothrace ins. and Mastusium prom., 22 m. N.E. of Lemnos. Settled by the Tyrrheni Pelasgi. A seat of the Cabiric worship, and of the adoration of Mercury Imbranus. Its soldiers excelled in the use of the javelin. *Imbro.* II. its capital, on the S.E. coast, opposite Mastusium prom.

Castro. III. a citadel of Caunus, in Caria.

IMITII, a people of Sarmatia Asiat., on Imitys fl.

IMITYS fl., a r. of Sarmatia Asiat., in Cissii m.

IMMA, a town of Seleucis, Syriæ, E. of Seleucia. The locality of the first victory of Aurelian over Zenobia. *Cuph.*

IMMADRUS ins., an isl. of Narbonensis II., s.w. of Massilia.

IMPHEES, a tribe of Perrhæbi, in Thessaly.

INACHORIUM, a town on the w. coast of Crete, bet. Bienon and Criumetopon prom. *San Niccolo.*

INĂCHUS fl., I. a r. of Argolis, rising in Lyrcæus m., about 10 m. N.W. from Argos, and falling into Argolicus sin. at Temenium. Feigned by the poets to be a continuation of the Amphilochian Inachus. *Xeriadry.* II. of Athamania, rising in Lacmon m., towards the source of Æas fl., and falling into Achelous fl. s.e. of Heraclea. Fabled by some of the ancients to pass under the sea, and to rise again as Inachus fl. of Argolis. *Ariadha.*

IN ALPE, a town of the Ambisontii, in Noricum, near Tamasici. *Tauern.*

IN ALPE JULIA, a town of the Ambidravi, Noricum. *Hotedorchiz.*

INAPÆI, a people of Sarmatia Asiat.

IN APENNINO, a town of Apuani, in Liguria, on Via Aurelia, bet. Monilia (13) and Boron (2). *Matarana.*

INAPHA, a town of Arabia Felix, s.w. of Labris. *Hanifah.*

INARIME, "abounding with apes," the Tuscan name of Ænaria.

INATA, a town of Crete, on Catarrhactes fl., bet. Hierapytna (32) and Lyctus.

INATUS m., a summit of Ida, in Crete, e. of Lyctus.

INCARO, a town of the Segoregii, Narbonensis, on the coast, 12 m. w. from Massilia. *Carry.*

INCOGNITUS sin., a bay of the Red Sea, below Orine.

INDABARA, a town of Surasena, Indiæ, on Diamuna fl., R., above Methora.

INDAPRATHÆ, a people of India e. Gangem, on Doanus fl., R., towards its source.

INDESINA, a town of the Leuci, Belgica I., N.W. of Divodurum.

INDIA, a country of Asia, bounded N. by Scythia at Imaus m. and Serica, s. by Erythræum mare, w. by Erythræum mare and Aria, e. by the Sinæ and Eous oc. It comprehended India extra Gangem e. and India intra Gangem w. Ptolemy assigns for its w. limits Paropamisus, Ara-

chosia, and Gedrosia. *India, Thibet, Birmah, Ava, &c.*

INDICOMORDANA, a town of Sogdiana, towards Bactria, w. of Oxiana.

INDIGĒTES (Indicetæ), a maritime people of Tarraconensis, under the Pyrenees, N.E. of the Ausetani. *Catalonia* N.E., *Ampurdan?*

INDO-SCYTHIA, a district of India e. Gangem, on both sides of the Indus, towards its mouth.

INDUS fl., I. a r. of Asia, rising in Paropamisus m., towards the source of the Ganges, and after separating, in a course of 1300 miles, India from Aria, &c., falling into Indicus oc. by two mouths below Sindomana, w. of Barace ins. *Indus, Sind.* II. of Caria, rising in the m. of the Cybyratæ, and, after receiving 60 rivers and 100 torrents, falling into the Mediterranean at Panormus Caunorum. Named from an Indian who fell into it from his elephant. *Kaignez.*

INDUSTRIA, *Gallicè* Bodincomagus, *prius* Allustria, a town of the Taurini, in Liguria, on Padus fl., bet. Quadratæ and Cestæ. *Monteu di Po, near Verrua.*

INFERUM MARE, a name of Tyrrhenium mare, as being s. of or below the Apennines.

INGÆVONES, a people of Germania Magna, on its N.W. coast, w. of the Vindili and Hermiones.

INGAUNI (Ingaunes), a people of Liguria, bet. the Alpes Maritimæ and the sea, e. of the Intemelii, about Album Ingaunum. Named from the hero Aunus.

INGENA, i. q. Abrincatui.

INGILA, a town of Gumathene-Armenia, N. of Amida.

INGITLINGUM, a town of the Brigantes, Brit., on Abus fl., L., bet. Lavatræ and Cataractonium.

INGRIONES, the s. portion of the Tencteri, Germania.

INICERUM, a town of the Andizetes, Pannoniæ, bet. Menneianæ (28) and Picentinum. *Vucsin.*

INIMURIUM, a town of Noricum, on Murus fl., 14 m. from IN ALPE. *St. Michael.*

INNA fons, I. a fountain of Thrace, on the borders of Pæonia, where Midas caught Silenus. II. a town of Drangiana-Tatacene, on Pharnacotus fl., L., above Phrophtasia.

INOPUS fl., a r. of Delos ins., falling into the sea at Delos oppid.

IN PORTU, a town of Etruria, 17 m. e. from Valvata. *Near La Scala.*

INSĀNI m., m. of Sardinia, N.W. of Forum

Trajani. Named from their rugged impracticability.

INSÜBRES (Isombri, Symbrici, Symbri), I. a colony of the Gaulish Insubres in Gallia Transpadana, on Padus fl., s. of the Orobii, bet. Ticinus fl. w. and Addua fl. E., but extending earlier to Sessites fl. w. and Clusius fl. E. II. a people of Lugdunensis I., on the territory afterwards occupied by the Segusiani.

INSULA SACRA, an isl. at the mouth of the Tiber, formed by its two branches.

INTEMELII, a people of Liguria, bet. the Alpes Maritimæ and the sea, w. of the Ingauni, about Albintemelium.

INTERACRIUM, a town of Sabinium, on Velinus fl., 10 m. from Fisternæ. *Antrodoco.*

INTERAMNESIA, a town of the Vettones, Lusitania, bet. the Durius and Cuda fll.

INTERAMNIA, I. a town of the Frentani, S.E. of Buca. *Termoli.* II. of Latium, on Liris fl., near its confluence with another r., not named, below Arpinum, near Casinum. A colonia 314 B.C. III. of Lucania, at the springs of Laus fl., bet. Nerulum and Muranum. *Firmo.* IV. *surnamed* Prætutiana, of Prætutia, in Picenum, on Batinus fl., L., E. of Vicus Badies. A colonia and municipium. *Teramo.* V. of Umbria, bet. the confluence of Nar fl. and a tributary stream, on Via Flaminia, bet. Narnia (8) and Spoletium (18). Founded 733 B.C. A municipium. Noted for the extreme fertility of its territory. *Terni.*

INTERAMNIUM-FLAVIUM, a town of the Astures, Tarrac., on Silis fl., L., S.E. of Bergidium. *Ponferrada.*

INTERCATIA, a town of the Vaccæi, Tarraconensis, 20 m. S.E. from Brigacium. Memorable in the life of Scipio Æmilianus. *Belver.*

INTERCISA, a town of Valeria, Pannoniæ, on the Danube, bet. Annamatia and Lussonium. *Foldvar ?*

INTERMANANA, a town of Sabinium, 12 m. from Æquum Falsicum. *Magliano.*

INTERUM MARE, i. q. Mediterraneum.

INTEROCREA, a town of Sabinium, on Velinus fl., R., bet. Cutiliæ (6) and Forum Decii (14), on Via Salaria. *Interdoco.*

INTERPROMIUM, a town of the Peligni, on Aternus fl., R., bet. Corfinium (12) and Teate (13) on Via Valeria. *San Valentino.*

INTIBILI, a town of Tarraconensis, 27 m. s.w. from Dertosa.

INTUERGI, a tribe of Alemanni, Germaniæ, bet. the Rhine, Mœnus fl., and Niter fl.

INUCA, a town of Zeugitana, 13 m. from Sicilibba.

IŌLCOS, I. the shore of Pagasæus sin., near the cognominal town. II. a town of Magnesia, Thessaly, 1 m. N. from Demetrias, on Anaurus fl., under Pelion m. The birth-place of Jason. The inhabitants were transferred to Demetrias by Demetrius Poliorcetes. Extinct in the time of Strabo.

IOLASITÆ, a people of Arabia Felix, E. of Zames m., towards the Astapeni. *In El Ahsa.*

ION, I. a r. of Estiæotis, in Thessaly, rising in Cercetius m., and falling into Peneus fl., below Ericinum. *Cachia.* II. a fortress of Sciros, Laconiæ, commanding a pass into Arcadia.

IONES, the Athenians, poetically so called, from Ion, son of Hellen.

IONIA, I. a country of Asia Minor, bounded N. by Æolis, s. by Caria, w. by Ionium mare, E. by Lydia. Peopled first by Leleges and Carians, and then by Iones from Greece, whence the name. II. the name given to Ægialus, in Achaia, by the Iones from Attica, who had blended with its original population, the Ægialees. III. *postea* Cephalus, a town of Cilicia Campestris, on Issicus sin., E. of Pyramus fl.

IONIDÆ, a demus of Attica, of the tribe Ægeis.

IONIUM MARE, the portion of the Mediterranean which washes the shores of Epirus, Acarnania, and Peloponnesus E., and of Magna Græcia w. ; s. of the Adriatic, N. of Libycum mare. Named after Ionia. *Ionian Sea.*

IONIUS sin, i. q. Hadriaticum mare.

IONOPOLIS, a later name of Aboniteichos.

IORI, a tribe of Pæones, Macedoniæ, N. of Almopæia.

IOS ins., I. an island of the Ægean, one of the Sporades, bet. Donysa and Sicinos. The birth-place of Homer's mother, and burial-place of the poet himself. *Nio.* II. a fortress of Laconia.

IPAGRUM (Ægabrum), a town of the Turtuli, Bætica, 43 m. N. of Antiquaria. *Near Santaella.*

IPNI (Hypnus) ins., an island or rocky shoal of Magnesia, Thessaly, off Sepias prom. *Ipnous.*

IPNUS, I. a town of the Locri Ozolæ, s. of Myon. II. of Samos, N. of Samos oppid. *Vathi.*

IPSUS, a town of Phrygia, bet. Synnada and Julia. The locality of the defeat and death of Antigonus.

IRA, a fortress of Messenia, on Neda fl., N.E.

of Dorium. The scene of Aristomenes' last efforts. *Kakoletri.*

IRASA, a town of Cyrenaica, on Triton palus.

IRENE ins., I. an isl. in Argolicus sin. II. of Taprobane, off Nabarba.

IRENOPOLIS, *prius* Neronias, a town of Cilicia II.

IRESLÆ, a town of Pelasgiotis, Thessaly.

IRIA, I. a r. of Liguria, falling into Padus fl. below Iria. *Staffora.* II. VICUS IRIA, a town of the Ananes, Liguria, on Ira fl., L., bet. Dertona (10) and Cameliomagus (16), on Via Posthumia. *Voghera.* III. FLAVIA, a town of the Lucenses, Tarraconensis, at the junction of Sars fl. with Ulla fl. *El Padron.*

IRINON sin., i. q. Canthicus sin.

IRIS fl., a r. of Pontus, rising N.E. of Comana, and enlarged by the Scylax and Lycus, falling into the Euxine 13 m. w. from Heracleum. Remarkable for its circuitous course. *Tokatlu.*

IRUS, I. a m. of Gedrosia, towards the mouth of the Indus. II. the capital of the Malienses Hierenses, in Thessaly, w. of Lamia.

IS fl., I. a r. of Babylon, running into the Euphrates, R., at Is. Hence came the bitumen with which the walls of Babylon were cemented. II. a stream of Lucania, falling into Inferum mare N. of Posidium prom. *Isso.* III. (Sitha, Aiopolis), a town of Babylonia, at the confluence of Is fl. with the Euphrates, bet. Izannesopolis and Pylæ, s.w. of Opis (98½ geog. m.). *Hit.*

ISADICI, a people of Sarmatia, towards the N. coast of the Euxine.

ISÆ portus, the port of Olizon, in Magnesia. *Ise.*

ISALA fl., a r. of Germania, i. q. Salas.

ISAMNIUM prom., a pr. of the Darini, Hibernia, opposite Monarina ins. *Killard Point.*

ISAMUS fl., a r. of India i. Gangem, falling into the sea towards Patala.

ISANUS fl., a r. of Illyria, rising in the m. of the Albani, and falling into the Adriatic below Sesarethus. *Ismo.*

ISĂRA (Isargus) fl., I. a r. of Vindelicia, rising in Alpes Rhæt., towards Parthenum, and falling into the Danube. *Iser.* II. (Æsia, Œsia), a r. of Belgica II., falling into the Sequana at Anderitium. *Oise.* III. a r. of Gaul, rising in Alpes Graiæ, s.e. of Bergintrum, and falling into the Rhone above Valentia. *Isère.*

ISARCI, a tribe on the s. slope of the Alps, towards Mediolanum. *About Arcisate.*

ISARII, a people of Vindelicia, on the Isara.

ILARUS fl., i. q. Athesis.

ISATICHÆ, a people of Carmania, occupying its N.W. angle.

ISATIS, capital of the Isatichæ, Carmaniæ.

ISAURA, the later capital of Isaurica, bet. Caspia and Germanicopolis. Destroyed by Servilius; restored by Amyntas, nearly on the same site, with the surname Euerces, "well-fortified." *Zengi-Bor.*

ISAURIA, a district of Lycaonia, on the borders of Pisidia.

ISAURUS fl., apud Lucan., i. q. Pisaurus.

ISBORUS (Isbures) fl., a r. of Sicily, rising in Coprianus m. and falling into Afric. pelagus w. of Thermæ Selinuntiæ.

ISBUS, a town of Isauria.

ISCA (Isaca, *Celticè* "water,"), I. a r. of the Damnonii, Brit., falling into the sea below Isca Damnoniorum. *Ex.* II. of the Silures, Brit., falling into Sabrinæ æst. below Isca Silurum. III. (Caer-uisk, "city on the Esk," Caer-Rydh, "red city," *postea* Exan-ceaster), *surnamed* Damnoniorum, capital of the Damnonii, Brit., on Isca fl., L., 10 m. from its mouth. A British city. *Exeter.* IV. *surnamed* Silurum (Augusta Silurum), capital of the Silures, Brit., on Isca fl., s.w. of Burrium. The station of the Legio Secunda Augusta, whence its modern name. *Caer-Leon.*

ISCADIA, a town of the Turtuli, Bætica, bet. Tucci-Gemella N. and Ebura Cerealis s.s.e.

ISCARA, the Latin form of Karioth, Galileæ.

ISCHALIS, *postea* Givelceaster, a town of the Belgæ, Brit., s.w. of Sorbiodunum. *Ilchester.*

ISCHIA ins., one of the Œnotrides ins., of Lucania. *Ischia.*

ISCINA, a town of the Psylli, Africa Prop., on Syrtis Maj., bet. Aulahon and Ad Palmam.

ISCOPOLIS, the early name of Tripolis, Pontus.

ISECHI, Insechi, i. q. Zechi.

ISIACORUM portus (Jaco portus), a maritime town of the Tyrangetæ, Sarmatiæ, 11 m. w. from Istrianorum portus.

ISIONDA (Isinda), a town of Milyas, in Pisidia, 12 m. N.W. from Ataleia.

ISIS (Edom), I. an isl. of Arabia Felix, in the Red sea, over against Myos Hormus. II. a r. of Britain, rising w. of Durocornovium, and forming a junction with Tamis fl. at Dorcinia civitas. III. a r. of Colchis, falling into the Euxine N. of Acinacis fl. IV. a r. of Noricum, falling into the Danube below Ad Pontem Isis. *Ips.*

ISIUM, I. a town of Heptanomis, on the Nile, bet. Peme and Coene. II. of Thebais, on the Nile, R., bet. Hieracon and Muthis, below Lycopolis.

Isius m., I. a prom. of the Troglodytæ, Æthiopia, s. of Chersonesus prom. *Ras el Dwaer.* II. a fortress of Lycia, on the coast, 8 m. from Andriace. *Pyrgo.*

Ismarium prom., I. a pr. of the Cicones, Thrace, the termination on the Ægean of Ismarus m. *C. Marogna.* II. a m. of the Cicones, Thrace, terminating in Ismarium prom. Noted for its generous wine. The residence for a time of Orpheus. III. capital of the Cicones, Thrace, under Ismarium m., at Ismarium prom. Taken and plundered by Ulysses.

Ismēne, a village of Oropus, on Ismenus fl.

Ismenus, I. a stream of Bœotia, rising in Ismenus m. and falling into Hylica lac. *Ismeno.* II. a hill of Bœotia, outside Homoloides porta, at Thebes.

Isombroi, the Greek name of the Insubres.

Isoandæ, a people of Sarmatia As., on Soana fl., n. of Gerrus fl.

Isos, a town of Bœotia, on Euripus, n. of Salganeus. By some considered the Nysa of Homer. *Lokisi.*

Isos, a town of Megaris, at the foot of Cithæron m. Extinct in Strabo's time.

Israel, Kingdom of (called also of Ephraim and of Samaria), on both sides of the Jordan, comprising the tribes of Ruben, Simeon, Dan, Issachar, Zebulon, Naphtali, Gad, Asser, Ephraim, Manasseh.

Issa ins., an isl. of the Adriatic, on the coast of the Dalmatæ, one of the Liburnides ins. Colonized by Syracusans. A Roman naval station. Noted for its wines. *Lissa.*

Issa (Hiera), a town of Lesbos ins.

Issachar (Isaschar), a tribe of Israel. Bounded n. by Zebulon, at Dobrath, s. by Ephraim, at Ebal m., w. by the half-tribe of Manasseh, at Thebes, e. by the Jordan.

Issedon, I. capital of the Issedones, Serica, n.e. of the source of Œchardes fl. *Kantscheu.* II. a town of Scythia i. Imaum, s.w. of Ausacia.

Issēdŏnes, a people of Serica, on Æchardes fl.

Issi, a people of Sarmatia Asiatica, towards the Tanais.

Issicus sinus, a gulf of the Mediterranean, at Issus, bet. Megarsus prom. and Rossicus Scopulus. *G. of Iskanderoon.*

Issus, a town of Cilicia Campestris, at the head of Issicus sin. The locality of the great victory of Alexander over Darius.

Istævones, a people of Germania Magna, bet. the Ingævones n. and n.w., Germania II., at the Rhine, w., the Hermiones e., and Germania I., at the Rhine, s.

Ister (Istros) fl., the early Greek name of the Danube, from its mouth to its junction with the Savus.

Isthmia Magnesica, the isthmus at the s. extremity of Magnesia, in Thessaly, at the e. entrance of Pagasæus sin.

Isthmus, an early name of Halicarnassus.

Isti prom., the w. extremity of Icarus ins.

Istone m., a hill of Corcyra, 5 stadia w. from the capital.

Istriana, a town of the Themi, Arabia, near Capeus sinus, s. of Thar. *El Katiff.*

Istriani, a people on Ister fl., towards its mouth.

Istrianorum portus, a port of Sarmatia, 3¾ geog. m. w. from Odessus.

Istrianus fl., a r. of Taurica Chersonesus, falling into the Euxine below Corax prom. *Knup Tepi.*

Istropolis, *postea* Constantia, a town of Mœsia Inferior, below the mouth of the Danube. A Milesian settlement. *Chiustange.*

Istros, I. an isl. of Caria, bet. Cos ins. and Nisyrus ins., over against Triopium prom. *Giali.* II. (Istrona), a town of Crete, s. of Olus. *Istrona.* III. (Istropolis, Istria), a town of Mœsia Inf., s. of the s. or sacred mouth of the Danube, or Ister, whence its name. A Milesian colony.

Isturgi, a town of the Turtuli, Bætica, on the Bætis, above Ripa.

Isumbus, a town of Thospitis, Armenia, n.e. of Artemita.

Isunisca, a town of the Launi, Vindel., bet. Bratananium (12) and Pons Æni. s.w. *of Helfendorff.*

Isura ins., an isl. of Arabia Felix, on the Persicus sin., 50 m. n.e. from Canis fl. *Sheick Sure.*

Isurinum (Isubrigantium), a maritime town of the Brigantes, Brit., s.e. of Cataractonium. *Aldborough.*

Isus, a town of Ætolia. The birth-place of Alexander Isius.

Itabyrius m., Atabyrius, i. q. Thabor.

Italia (Hesperia, Saturnia, Œnotria), a country of Europe, extending bet. Tyrrhenium mare and Hadriaticum mare, and from the Alps to Ionium mare. In length, by the great road through Rome and Capua, 1020 Roman m.; in direct distance 700; in greatest breadth, from Varus fl. to Arsia fl., 410 m.; in least breadth, from Scyllacius sin. to Terinæus sin., 20. n.w. it was bounded at first by Alpes Maritimæ and afterwards by Varus fl.; n.e. at first by Tergeste and afterwards by Arsia fl. By Augustus it was divided into eleven regions: 1. Campania and Latium; 2.

Apulia and part of Samnium; 3. Lucania and Bruttium; 4. Samnium and the countries of the Sabini, Æqui, Marsi, &c.; 5. Picenum; 6. Umbria; 7. Etruria; 8. Flaminia; 9. Liguria; 10. Venetia, Histria, and Carnia; 11. Transpadana. Another distribution is: 1. Liguria; 2. Gallia Cisalpina; 3. Venetia, Carnia, and Histria; 4. Etruria; 5. Umbria and Picenum; 6. the countries of the Sabini, Æqui, Marsi, Peligni, Vestini, Marrucini; 7. Roma; 8. Latium; 9. Campania; 10. Samnium and Frentania; 11. Apulia; 12. Lucania; 13. Bruttium. The peoples of Italy, exhibited in the nearest practicable chronological order, were: Umbri, Opici or Osci, Ænotri, Sicani, Siculi, Ligures, Aurunci, Ausones, Tyrrheni Pelasgi, Etrusci, Latini, Volsci, Campani, Sidicini, Sabini, Picentes, Æqui, Marsi, Hernici, Peligni, Vestini, Marrucini, Liburni, Apuli, Daunii, Peucetii, Pædiculi, Calabri, Japyges, Messapii, Leutarni, Chaones, Itali, Hirpini, Pentri, Caraceni, Frentani, Leucani, Bruttii, Veneti, Galli. The name Italia (*Græc.* "heifer") was at first applied only to the country bet. Lameticus sin. and Scylleticus sin.; its general extension took place under Augustus. *Italy.*

ITALICA, I. a name given for a short time to Corfenium, q. v. II. a town of the Turtetani, Bætica, on the Bætis, above Hispalis (6). Built by Scipio Africanus for the reception of the soldiers wounded in the Spanish war. A municipium and colonia of Hadrian. The birth-place of Trajan, Hadrian, and Silius Italicus. *Sevilla Vieja.*

ITALIUM, a town of the Caudini, Samnium.

ITAMUS portus, a port of the Leanitæ, on Persicus sin., at the mouth of Achana fl., bet. Sacer sin. and Leanitis sin. *Kadema.*

ITANUM prom., a pr. on the E. coast of Crete, N. of Ampelos prom. *C. Yala.*

ITANUS, a town on the E. coast of Crete, s. of Sammonium prom. *Sitano.*

ITHACA, I. an isl. of Acarnania, bet. the continent and Cephallenia ins., 6 m. S.E. from Leucate prom., 30 m. round and 10 long. Named after the hero Ithacus. The country of Ulysses. Here Homer resided for a considerable period with Mentor, one of the island chieftains, and the island itself is one of the seven places which dispute the honour of having been the poet's birth-place. *Theaki.* II. capital of the cognominal island on the E. coast, over against Crithote prom. The residence of Ulysses. *Aito.*

ITHACESIÆ ins., three islets of Bruttium, in Hipponensis sin., off Hipponium. Named from Ulysses. *Brace, Praca, and Torricella.*

ITHAR, a town of Arabia Felix.

ITHOME, I. a m. of Messenia, the citadel of Messene. Named after Ithome, the nurse of Jupiter. *Vourkano.* II. a town of Estiæotis, Thessaly, on the N. bank of Peneus fl., in the territory of Metropolis. *Petchouri.*

ITHORIA, a town of Ætolia, near Achelous fl., bet. Conope and Pæanium. Destroyed by Philip of Macedon. *Ivoria.*

ITIUM prom., a pr. of Belgica, near Itius portus. *C. Grinnez.*

ITIUS portus (Portus Morinorum), a port of the Morini, Belgica, above Gessoriacum. The place whence Cæsar embarked for England. *Witsand; Wissant.* Named by the Flemings *Isten,* and by the local sailors *Essen.*

ITOANA, a town of Caria, S.E. of Antiochia.

ITON, a town of Phthiotis, Thessaly, on Cuarius fl., w. of Alos. *Near Armyro.*

ITONE, I. a town of Bruttium, s.w. of Melæ. II. of Lydia, on Cimpsus fl. III. (Ægonne, Eugone), of Pontus, bet. Choloe and Piala.

ITUCCI, a town of the Turtuli, Bætica, S.E. of Corduba. A colonia (Virtus Julia). Called by Ptolemy Ulia.

ITUNA fl., a r. of Britain, falling into the sea at Itunæ æstuar. *Eden.*

ITUNA æstuar., the mouth of the Ituna fl., separating the Selgovæ, Brit., from the Brigantes. *Solway Firth.*

ITURÆA (Gessur, Jettur), a district of Syria, s. of Trachonitis, including Auranitis and Batanea. Inhabited by the descendants of Jetur, son of Ismael. *Djedour.*

ITURISSA (Turissa), a town of Novem Populana, bet. Pompelo and In Summo Pyrenæo. *Iturin.*

ITYS fl., an æstuary of Brit. Barb., N. of Epidium prom. *Loch Carron.*

IUERNIA, the form given by Ptolemy to Iar-in (Erin).

IUERNIS, a town of the Gangani, Hibern. *Aen* (a former city w. of Cashel).

IULIS, a town of Ceos ins., on Elixus fl. The birth-place of Simonides, Bacchylides, Erasistratus, and Ariston the Peripatetic. It was the law here for every person, on attaining sixty, to poison himself.

IVERNUS fl., a r. of Hibernia. *Kinmore.*

IVES, a town of Spain.

IXIA, a fortress of Rhodes, s. of Lindus.

IXIAS, a town of Bruttium, near Consentia. *Carolei.*

IXUS (Ixia), a port of Rhodus ins., near Lindus. *Uxilico.*

IZALA m., m. of Asia, a ridge of Masius m., bet. Aisumas m. and the Tigris.

IZANNESOPOLIS, a town of Mesopotamia, on the Euphrates, bet. Olabus and Pylæ.

J.

JABADII ins., an isl. of India e. Gangem, S.E. of Bonæ Fortunæ ins. Noted for its barley. *Java.*

JABESH, "dryness" (Jabesh-Gilead, Jabisus, Jabissa), a city of Manasseh, in Gilead, on Tabes fl., 6 m. E. from Pella.

JABBOK fl., a stream of Peræa, rising N.E. of Rabbath Ammon and falling, after a course of 60 miles, into the Jordan, at Succoth. The boundary bet. the Amorites and the Ammonites. *Zerka.*

JABNEEL (Jabneh, Jamnia), a city of the Philistines, 12 m. s. from Joppa. *Yebna.*

JABRIS, a town of the Darechenucæ, Arabia, on Lar fl., E. of Nascus.

JABRUDA, a town of Phœnicia, towards Ocorura. *Hebud.*

JACCA, capital of the Jacetani, Tarraconensis, N.E. of Cascantum. *Jaça.*

JACETANI, Tarraconensis, i. q. Lacetani.

JACO portus, i. q. Isiacorum portus.

JADERA, a town of the Liburni, Illyria, on the Adriatic, N. of Titius fl. A colonia of Augustus. *Zara Vecchia.*

JADUA fl., a r. of the Burgundiones, Germ., falling into Viadrus fl. near its mouth.

JAESAR, a town of Gad, Gileaditis, bet. Rabbath Ammon N.E. and Bethhoron S.W.

JAGATH, a town of Mauritania Ting., near Taluda fl.

JAHZUH (Jahaz, Jahaza), a town of Moabitis, N. of Bezar. The locality of the defeat of Sihon by Moses.

JALA fl., a r. of Gallia Cisalpina, falling into the Padus, towards Latis fl. *Malea.*

JALŸSUS, a Phœnician town of Rhodus ins., N.E. of Mylantia prom. *Jaliso.*

JAMBE ins., an isl. of Thebais, in the Red Sea, under Smaragdus m., S.E. of Nechesia.

JAMBIA, a town of the Arsæ, Arab., on the Red Sea, N. of Zaaram regia. *Yembo.*

JAMNIA, I. a town of Galilæa Sup., N. of Cæsarea. II. *Vide* Jabneel.

JAMNITARUM portus, the port of Jamnia, Judæa, S.W. of Jamnia.

JAMNO (Jamna, *rectius* Jamnorca, "western place"), a town of Balearis Minor, on the N.W. coast. *Ciudadela.*

JAMPHORINA, capital of the Mædi, Thrace, on Angites fl., towards its source, N.E. of Phragandæ.

JANUA, i. q. Genua.

JANUARIUM prom., a pr. of Cilicia Campestris, on Issicus sin., E. of Ionia.

JAPYDES (Japodes), an Illyrian tribe, occupying the coast of the Adriatic from Timavus fl. to Jadera, and extending inland beyond Albius m. towards Pannonia. A colony of these people settled and gave name to Japydia, or Japygia, in Italy.

JAPYGES, descendants of the Japodes of Illyria, settled in Japygia.

JAPYGIA, specially the Greek name of that district of Apulia which occupied the "heel of the boot" of Italy, s. of Peucetia, bet. Tarentinus sin. and Superum mare. Its early colonists, however, Japydes from Illyria, extended their migrations, fusing with the Œnotri, s. as far as Scyllacium, and even beyond it.

JAPYGIUM (Sallentinum) prom., a pr. of Japygia, at the E. entrance of Tarentinus sin. It formed the w. line of separation bet. the Ionian sea and the Adriatic, the E. being Acroceraunum prom. *Capo di Leuca.*

JAPYGUM TRIA PROMONTORIA, three prom. of Bruttium, s. of Lacinium prom. *Capo delle Castella, C. Rizzuto, C. della Nave.*

JAPYX fl., a stream of Calabria, falling into the sea bet. Sybaris and Hydruntum.

JARDANUS fl., Elid., i. q. Acidas.

JARDANUS fl., a r. of Epia, in Elis, running into the sea at Pheia. *Cardamo.*

JARGANON, i. q. Gargara.

JARMUTH (Jeremoth), a town of Juda, Judæa, 4 m. w. from Eleutheropolis. The Ramoth of Joshua.

JASONIUM, I. a prom. of Pontus, 16 m. E. from Side. Named from the Argonauts having anchored here. *C. Jasun.* II. a town of Margiana, on Margus fl., below Alexandria.

JĀSŌNIUS m., m. intersecting Media, N.W. —S.E., parallel w. with Caspius m.

JASSII, I. a people of Dacia, bet. Parata fl. and Ararus fl. N. of the Cotenses. The progenitors of the Wallachians. II. of Pannonia s., bet. Murus fl. and Savus fl., s. of the Coletiani.

JASSIORUM MUNICIPIUM (Petrodava), capital of the Jassii, Dacia, on Parata fl., L., above Palada. *Jassy.*

JASSIUS sin., a gulf of Ionium mare, Caria, bet. Posidium prom. and Zephyrium prom.

Named from Jassus opp. *G. of Hassan-Kalessi.*

JASSUS (Jasus), I. a town of Caria, on a peninsula of Jassicus sin. N. An Argive colony. Noted for its striped red and white marble. *Assem.* II. of Melitene, Cappadocia.

JASTÆ (Histi), a people of Scythia i. Imaum, on Jastus fl.

JASTUS fl., a r. of Scythia i. Imaum, N.W.

JASULONES, a town of Valeria, Pannonia, bet. Acincum and Corsio.

JATHRIPPA, a town of the Darræ, Arabia, N.E. of Jambia. *Yathreb; Medina.*

JATII, a people of Sogdiana, on the Jaxartes.

JATINUM, *postea* Meldi, Fixtuinum, a town of the Meldi, Lugdunensis IV., on Alba fl., R., above Cale. *Meaux.*

JATRUM, a town of the Mœsi, Mœsia Inf., on the Danube, bet. Ad Novas and Trimanium, at the mouth of Jatrus fl.

JATRUS (Iantrus, Athrys) fl., a r. of Mœsia, rising in Hæmus m. near Ad Radices, and falling into the Danube at Jatrum. It separated the Mysi from the Getæ. *Jantra.*

JATTIR (Jethira), a town of Simeon, Judæa, N.W. of Arad.

JAXARTÆ, a people of Scythia, on the Jaxartes.

JAXARTES fl., a r. of Scythia, rising in Imaus m., and, after a course of 1682 m., falling into an inland sea (the sea of Aral) E. of the Caspian. *Sir.*

JAZER, a town of the Ammonites, on Jabbok fl., 15 m. from Heshbon.

JAXAMATÆ (Ixomatæ), a tribe of Asiatic Scythians, on the Tanais.

JAZYGES, a people of Sarmatia Eur., on the coast of Palus Mæotis, bet. Borysthenes fl. and the Roxolani.

JAZYGES METANASTÆ, "wanderers," a tribe of Zazyges, settled in Dacia, bet. Tibiscus fl. and the Danube, s. of the Bastarnæ.

JEBBA, in Pliny, i. q. Hepha.

JEBUSITÆ (Jebusæi), one of the seven tribes of Canaan, about Jebus (Jerusalem). Descendants of Jebus, son of Canaan.

JEHUD, a town of Judæa, bet. Antipatris N. and Lydda w.

JEMERII, a tribe of Caturiges, Galliæ, on Druentia fl. *About St. Jemmes.*

JĒNA æst., an æstuary of the Selgovæ, Brit., E. of Abravannus sin. *Wigton bay.*

JENYSUS, a town of Judæa, near the sea, bet. Gaza N.E. and Rhinocura s.w. (24 geog. m.) *Kan Younes.*

JERABRICA (Hierabrica), a town of the Lusitani, on the Tagus, bet. Scalabis N.E. and Olisippo s.w.

JERACHÆI, Arabiæ, i. q. Minæi.

JERACHÆORUM ins., an isl. of Arabia Felix, on the Red sea, s.s.w. of Mamala. *Serene.*

JERACHÆORUM (Jerachum) vicus, a town of the E. Jerachæi (Minæi), Arabiæ, on Canis fl., L., towards its source. *Djar; Osjan.*

JERICHO (Hierachus, Jericus), a city of Benjamin, bet. Jerusalem (20) and the Jordan (2). Called by Moses "The city of palm-trees." Named from the worship of Jerah (Luna). Destroyed by the Israelites. A new city of the same name (the abode of Elisha) was built in its vicinity. *At or near Riha.*

JERNUS (Juvernus) fl., a r. of Hibernia, w., separating the Velibori from the Coriandi.

JERUSALEM. *Vide* Hierosolyma.

JESPUS, a town of the Lacetani, Tarraconensis, bet. Anatis w. and Egara E.

JETÆ (Jætæ), a town of Sicily, at the source of Bathys fl. *Jato.*

JEZREEL (Esdrael), " God's seed," I. Vallis, i. q. Esdraelon. II. *postea* Stradela (Parvum Gerinum), a royal city of Manasseh, in Esdraelon Vallis, bet. Cæsarea Palestina w. and Bethsan E. Here was a palace of the kings of Israel. *Zerin.* III. of Judah.

JINEUS m., a ridge of Apennines, towards Corfinium.

JOBARES fl., i. q. Jomanes.

JOBARITÆ, *rectiùs* Jobabitæ, a people of Arabia Felix, in the desert, next to the Sachalitæ. Descendants of Job. *Beni-Jubar.*

JOBIA (Zobia), a town of Pisidia, near Termessus.

JOBOB, a district of Arabia Felix, in the desert; occupied by the Jobaritæ.

JOBULA, a town of Albania, on Albanus fl., towards its source.

JOCTAN (Kahtan), the Scriptural name of the region of Arabia Felix, on the borders of the desert, N.E. of Usal and Seba.

JOKLEEL (Petra), a town of the Amalekitæ, s. of Acrabbim m.

JOKNEAM, a town of Zebulun, on Kison fl., s. of Ptolemais, towards its mouth.

JOL, the local name of Cæsarea, in Mauritania Cæsar.

JOLÆI, an early people of Sardinia, N.

JOMANES fl., Indiæ, i. q. Diamuna.

JOMNIUM, a maritime town of Mauritania Cæsar., bet. Rusippisir (38) and Rusucurrum. *Alschier.*

JOMUSA, a town of India, on the Indus, L., below the confluence of the Acesines.

JONTORA, a town of the Commoni, Galliæ. *Jonquières.*

JOPPA (Japho), a maritime city of Ephraim, in Judæa, bet. Cæsarea and Gaza, 36 m. N.W. from Jerusalem, of which it was the port. The locality of the story of Andromeda. *Jaffa; Yaffa.*

JORDANES ("rapid") fl., a r. of Palestine, rising in two springs, one 20 m. N. of Paneas, the other at Laish, and, after flowing through Merom lac. and Tiberias lac., terminating, after the punishment of Sodom and Gomorrah, at the Dead sea; it previously flowed on to the Red sea. *Sheriat el Kebir; Jordan.*

JORUM, the town of the Jori, in Pæonia.

JOSEPHI canalis, a canal parallel with the Nile, extending from Mæridis lacus to Diospolis Parva. Traditionally constructed by Joseph.

JOTABE ins., an isl. of Arabia Pet., in the Red sea, at the entrance of Avalites sin., E. of Phocarum ins.

JOTAPATA, a fortress of Galilæa Inf., 1 m. s. from Gabara. Taken by Vespasian from Josephus the historian and razed.

JOTAPE, a town of Cilicia Trachea, in the territory of Selinus.

JOVALLIUM (Jovalia), a town of the Hercuniatæ, Pannonia, on Dravus fl., R., bet. Berebis and Mursella (8). *Valpo.*

JOVANUS (Ivarus) fl., a r. of Noricum, rising s. of Masciacum, and falling into Ænus fl. below Turum. *Salza?*

JOVAVUM. *Vide* Juvavia.

JOVIA (Bononia), I. a town of the Jassii, Pannonia, on the Danube, R., 18 m. E. from Aqua Viva. *Hersenicza.* II. of the Peligni, Italiæ, 7 m. s. from Sulmo. *Valle Scura.* III. of Pisidia, near Termessus.

JOVIACUM, a town of the Sevaces, Noricum, bet. Itanacum and Ovilaba (27). *Geyersberg.*

JOVIS ins., an isl. of Arabia Petræa, in the Red sea, s. of Modiana.

JOVIS (Jovinus, Janus) mons, I., i. q. Alpes Cottiæ. II. a prom. of Tarraconensis, near Barcino. *Montjui.* III. m. of Zeugitana, N.E. of Usaletus m.

JOVIS pagus, I. a village of the Triballi, Mœsiæ, on Margus fl., R., bet. Municipium and Idomus. II. prom., a pr. of Taprobane, w., below Sindocandæ.

JOVISURA, a town of the Runicates, Vindel., on Isara fl., L., bet. Reginum and Turum. *Braunau.*

JUCARA, a town of Arabia Felix, 20 m. s. from Idicara. *Dsjahhre.*

JUCUNDIU, a town of Marmarica, bet. Cardu and Gereatis.

JUDA m., m. of Judæa, running bet. Jerusalem and Beerseba.

JUDÆA, generally Palestine at large; specially a district of Palestine, bounded N. by Samaria, at Silo, s. by Idumæa, at Arad, w. by the Mediterranean, E. by Peræa, at the Jordan.

JUDA, I. kingdom of, and country of the two tribes Juda and Benjamin, bounded N. by Dan and Ephraim, at Bethsames, and s. by Simeon, at Eskol fl., w. by the Mediterranean, E. by the Dead sea and the Jordan. II. a tribe of Judah, bounded N. by Benjamin (E.) and Dan (w.), s. by Simeon, at Eskol fl., w. by the Mediterranean, E. by the Dead sea.

JUENNA, a town of the Taurisci, Noricum, on Dravus fl., S.E. of Virunum (23). *Jaunstein.*

JUGANTES, a people of Britain, towards the Cangi.

JUHONES, a people named by Tacitus, but of wholly uncertain position.

JULIA, I. a r. of Noricum, falling into Dravus fl. at Santicum. II. CONSTANTIA, Hispaniæ, i. q. Osset. III. *surnamed* Libyca (Livia), a town of the Cerretani, Tarraconensis, on the Pyrenees, N.W. of Egosa, on Sicoris fl., near its source. *Julia? Llivia?* IV. (Jullæ, Juliopolis), of Phrygia, near Philomelium. V. *surnamed* Gordus. *Vide* Gordus. VI. FIDENTIA, a town of Bætica, S.E. of Itucci. *Almodovar.* VII. JOZA, a name of Transducta, Bætica. VIII. MYRTILI, a town of the Cynetes, Lusitania, on the Anas, above Cunistorgis, 40 m. N. from Esuris. A colonia. *Mertola.*

JULIANOPOLIS, a town of Lydia, near Tabula.

JULIAS, Galaaditis, i. q. Bethhoron.

JULIACUM, a town of the Ubii, Germania II., bet. Tiberiacum and Coriovallum. *Julich; Juliers.*

JULIOBONA, I. capital of the Caleti, Lugdunensis II., on the Sequana, bet. Carocolinum w. and Lotum E. *Lillebonne.* II. Pannoniæ, i. q. Vianiomina.

JULIOBRIGA, a town of the Cantabri, Tarraconensis, on Iberus fl., L., near its source. *Retortillo.*

JULIOMAGUS, I. *postea* Andecavi, capital of the Andecavi, Lugdunensis III., bet. Combaristum N.W. and Robrica E.S.E. *Angers.* II. a town of the Lentienses, Vindel., bet. Brigobanna and Tenedo.

JULIOPOLIS, I. *prius* Gordium, a town of Bithynia, on the borders of Paphlagonia, bet. Dadastana (26) and Lagania, on Scopus fl. Built by king Gordius. Here Alexander cut the Gordian knot. Restored and renamed by Cleon of Abrettene. II. a town of Saravene prefect., Cappadocia, on Euphrates fl., s. of Claudiopolis.

JULIOSEBASTE, a town of Cilicia Trachea.

JULIPA, a town of the Turtuli, Bæturia, bet. Contributa s.w. and Corticata N.E.

JULIUM CARNICUM, capital of the Carni, in Venetia, on Tilaventus fl., bet. Loncium (22) and Ad Tricesimum (30). Founded by Julius Cæsar. *Zuglio.*

JULIUS vicus, a town of the Nemetes, Gaul. *Germersheim.*

JUNA, a town of Albania.

JUNCARIA, a town of the Indigetes, Tarraconensis, bet. Ad Summum Pyrenæum and Emporium. *Figueras.*

JUNCARUM campus, a maritime district of Tarraconensis, E., about Juncaria. Named from its fertility in a sort of fine broom.

JUNONIS ins., I. an isl. of Bætica, in Herculeum fretum, s. of Carteia. II. prom., a pr. of Bætica, on the Atlantic, with a temple of Juno, w. of Bælon. *Cabo de Trafalgar.* III. ACREÆ, prom., Corinthiæ, i. q. Olmiæ prom. IV. fontes, *vel* Aquæ, a town, with warm springs, of the Arusnates, Gallia Cisalp. *Caldetio.*

JURA m., m. of Maxima Sequanorum w., N. of Lemanus lac. *Jura.*

JURASSUS m., m. on the N.E. shore of Lemanus lac.

JUROEIPAACH, a fortress of Iberia, near Caucasiæ Portæ.

JUSAGURA ins., an isl. on the w. coast of Crete, over against Cimaros prom. *Pundico.*

JUSTINIANA, a town of the Dassaretæ, Illyria. Built by Justinian. *Achrida.*

JUSTINIANOPOLIS, Epiri. *Vide* Hadrianopolis.

JUSTINOPOLIS, a name given to Ægida, Histriæ, in honour of Justinian.

JUSTIS, a town of Numidia, on Bagradas fl., L., bet. Mercimeris and Altaba.

JUTA (Jota, Jeta, Jettan, Jethan), a sacerdotal town of Juda, 10 m. s.E. from Eleutheropolis.

JUTHUNGI, a tribe of Quadi, Germ., on the Danube.

JUVAVIA (Jovavum, Juvense castellum), capital of the Alauni, in Noricum, on Jovanus fl., L., bet. Artobriga and Cucalle. A colonia of Hadrian. *Salzburg.*

JUVERNA, a Roman name of Hibernia, from the Juverni (incorrectly Uterni), a people in its s.w. angle.

JUVIA fl., a r. of Tarraconensis, N.W., falling into the Atlantic at Ardobrica. *Jubia.*

JYRCÆ, a people of Scythia, near the Thyssagitæ.

K.

KADES BARNEA, a town of Simeon, s.E. of Hazezon Thamar.

KÆDUUM, a town of Germania Magna.

KAHTAN. *Vide* Joctan.

KALANCORUM, a town of Germania Magna, s.E. of Susudata. *Near Schweidnitz.*

KANAH fl., a r. of N. Judæa, falling into the Mediterranean bet. Cæsarea and Assur, s.

KAPHAR ACCO, a town of Galilæa Sup., N.E. of Acco.

KAPHARBARUCHA, a town of Juda, in Judæa, N. of Hebron.

KAFARSOREK, a village of Judæa, on Sorek fl., near Zarea. The birth-place of Samson.

KAPHARSUBA, Judææ, i. q. Antipatris.

KARIOTH, a small town of uncertain position, E. of Jordan. The birth-place of Judas Iscariot.

KEDASA (Kedes, Cedesis, Cedissus), a Levitical city of Naphtali, in Galilæa, s.E. of Tyre (20).

KEDEMOTH, a town of Reuben, in Ammonitis, s.E. of Hesbon.

KEGILA, a town of Palestine, 8 m. E. from Eleutheropolis.

KENASITÆ (Kenisæi), Arabiæ, the descendants of Kenaz, son of Elephaz.

KENITÆ, i. q. Kenasitæ.

KENTUS, a port of the Cinædocolpitæ, Arab., bet. Arga and Zaaram.

KERATA m., a bi-peaked m. of Attica, N.W. of Eleusis. *Kerata.*

KIDRON (Kedron, Cedron) fl., a stream of Benjamin, running from Jerusalem through a cognominal valley into the Dead sea.

KIRMOAB (Charakmoba), a city of Moabitis, s. of Rabbath Moab.

KIRGATHAIM, a town of Reuben, in Ammonitis, 12 m. s.w. of Medba. At one time the capital of the Emim.

KIRGATH ARBA ("the city of Arba"), a famous giant, the early name of Hebron.

KIRGATH JEARIM, " city of the woods" (Kirgath Baal), a town of Judah, in Judæa, bet. Jerusalem s.E. (9) and Emaus. Here the Ark of the Covenant stood for some time after its recovery from the Philistines.

KISON (Chison, Megiddo) fl., a r. of Galilæa, rising in Tabor m., and falling into the Mediterranean near Carmelum prom., E. The locality of the defeat of Sisera.

KISLOTH, *vide* Chesuloth.

KOKABA, a town of Ituræa, s.w. of Damascus.

KOREATHE, a town of Auranitis, N. of Zara.

KOPUR, a town of Arabia, on the Red Sea, towards Arga. *Abu Aijan.*

KRITH fl., a stream of Benjamin, running from near Bethel into the Jordan, below Jericho.

L.

LABANATIS (Labanis) ins., an isl. of the Omanitæ, Arabiæ, at the s. extremity of Duatus sin.

LABARA, a town of Caria.

LABBANA. *Vide* Lebana.

LABEATES, a people of Illyria, extending inland, bet. the Damatæ and the confines of Mœsia.

LABEATIS palus, a lake of the Labeates, Illyria, on the borders of the Dalmatæ, formed by Barbana fl. *Lago di Scutari.*

LABECIA, a town of Arabia Felix, towards the Red sea, s.w. of Nagara. *Al Beish.*

LABERUS, a town of the Chauci, Hiberniæ, s. of Eblana.

LABICUM (Lavici), a town of the Latini, Latium, on Via Labicana, 15 m. s.E. of Rome, bet. Præneste and Algidum. A colonia from Alba, prior in date to Rome. Cæsar had a villa in the neighbourhood. A municipium; a colonia 418 B.C. *Colonna.*

LABISCO, a town of the Allobroges, Viennensis, bet. Lemincum N.E. and Morginnum s.w.

LABONA fl., a r. of Liguria, falling into Ligusticus sin. at Ad Navalia.

LABOTAS fl., a r. of Apamene, Syria, falling into the Orontes, towards Antiochia. *Aswad.*

LABRANDA, a town of Caria, 8 m. from Mylasa. Famous for a temple of Jupiter Labrandenus or Labradeus ("with the hatchet"). Built by Labrandus the Curete.

LABRIS, a town of Arabia Felix, under Marithæ m., s.E., bet. Gerra and Inapha. *El Labrin.*

LABUS m., a m. of Hyrcania, towards Zadracarta.

LABUTA m., a N.E. continuation of Caspius m., separating Hyrcania from Parthia.

LACANITIS, a district of Cilicia, about Tarsus.

LACEDÆMON, a Lacedæmonian town of Cyprus.

LACEDÆMONIA, a name of Laconia, from Lacedæmon its king, son of Semele. The name was afterwards applied to the capital.

LACENE, a town of Byzacene, on Syrtis Minor, bet. Silvani præsidium and Ad Palmam.

LACEREA, a town of Magnesia, Thessaly, at the source of Amyrus fl., N.W. of Melibœa, towards Bæbe lac. The birth-place of Corone, mother of Æsculapius.

LACETANI (Jaccetani), a people of Tarraconensis, s. of the Ceretani. *Part of Catalonia.*

LACHERE, a town of the Homeritæ, Arabiæ, N. of Arabiæ Felicis Emp.

LACHISH, a town of Juda, Judæa, 7 m. s. from Eleutheropolis. The death-place of Amaziah.

LACIACA, a town of the Sevaces, Noricum, bet. Tergolape and Tarnantum (14). *Vockelmarkt.*

LACIACUS lac., a lake of Noricum, at Laciaca. *Traunzee.*

LACIADÆ, a demus of Attica, of the tribe Oeneis, w. of Sciron, on the Via Sacra. Named after the hero Lacius. The birth-place of Miltiades. Here dwelt Phylalus, whom Ceres taught the culture of the fig. *Agia Saba.*

LACIBURGIUM, a town of the Teutones, Germaniæ, on Lagnus sin., E. of Marionis.

LACINA, a town of Phrygia Magna, N.E. of Eriza.

LACINIUM (Naus) prom., a pr. of Bruttium, at the s.w. entrance of Tarentinus sin., s.E. of Crotona (6). Here was a temple of Juno Lacinia, traditionally founded by Hercules, in which was the Helen of Zeuxis, and a famous pillar of gold. *C. Nao, or C. delle Colonne.*

LACIPPO, a town of the Turtetani, Bætica, bet. Oningis N.N.E. and Barbesula s.

LACMON m., a m. of Paroræa, Epirus, E. of Tymphe m. *Politzi.*

LACOBARDI, a tribe of Chatti, Germ., under Rhetico m., E., extending bet. the Rhine, near Confluentes, to the springs of Adrana fl.

LACOBRIGA, I. a town of the Cuneus, Lusitania, E. of Sacrum prom. *Lagos.* II. of the Vaccæi, Tarraconensis, on Pisoraca fl., N. of Pallantia. *Lobera.*

LACONIA (Laconikè, Lacedæmonia), a country of Peloponnesus, bounded N. by Arcadia and Argolis, s. and E. by the Ægean, w.

by Messenia, and Messeniacus sin. Settled first by Leleges, next by Achæi from Thessaly, under Pelops, and then, 1104 B.C., by the Dorians and Heraclidæ. *Maina* (S.W.), *Bardunia* (Central), *Zakounia* (E.).

LACONICUS sin., a gulf of the Ægean, in Laconia, bet. Tænarium prom. and Onegnathus prom., in circuit 106 m., in extreme breadth 39 m. *G. di Colokythia.*

LACONIMURGUM, a town of the Turtuli, Bætica, bet. Calentum N.W. and Ilipa S.S.E. A colonia (Constantia Julia).

LACOTENA, a town of Cappadocia, 28 m. from Messene. *Lacaben.*

LACTARIUS m., a hill of Campania, behind Stabiæ. Named from the fine milk produced from its pastures.

LACTER prom., the S. extremity of Cos ins.

LACTODURUM, a town of the Catavellauni, Brit., on Watling-street, N.W. of Magiovinium. *Towcester.*

LACTORA, a town of the Auscii, Novem Populana, N. of Elimberris. *Lectoure.*

LACURIS (Ilorcum), I. a town of the Oretani, Tarraconensis, near the source of Tader fl. *Huesca.* II. a town of the Bastuli.

LACUS FELICIS, *rectiùs* Lucus Felicis, a town of Pannonia, on the Danube, 18 m. E. from Azaum.

LACUS FUCĪNUS, a lake of the Marsi, Italy, bet. Marrubium E. and Auxantia W., in circuit 40 miles. Its superfluous waters were carried off by a canal constructed under Claudius to Liris fl., 3 m. *Lago di Celano; L. Fucino.*

LACUS REGILLUS, a lake of Latium, N. of Tusculum; the locality of the great defeat of the Latins by Posthumius, 529 B.C. *Laghetto della Colonna.*

LACUS REGIUS, a town of Numidia, on Ampsaga fl., L., bet. Cirta and Visalta.

LACYDON portus, the harbour of Massilia.

LADE, formerly an isl. of Ionia, at the mouth of Mæander fl., but afterwards joined to the mainland by the deposits of that river.

LADEPSI, a people of Bithynia.

LADICUS m., m. of Tarraconensis, on Minius fl., L., towards Bilbilis fl.

LADON fl., I. a r. of Arcadia, rising near Lycuria, and falling into Alpheus fl. near Heræa. Noted for its beautiful scenery, and for the adventures of Daphne and Syrinx. Its fish were reputed vocal. *Laudona.* II. of Epea, Elis, falling into Peneus fl. near Pylos. *Derviche.*

LÆA, a town of Caria.

LÆCENI, a people of Arabia Felix, towards

Persicus sin., w of the Leanitæ. *Beni al Kenaz.*

LÆETANI, a maritime tribe of Lacetani, Tarraconensis, bet. the Ausetani N. and the Cositani S.W.

LÆLIA, a town of the Celtici, Bætica, near the source of Urius fl., N.N.W. of Italica. Founded by Scipio, and named in honour of his friend Lælius. *Aracena?*

LÆMUS (Chabinus) m., m. of Arabia Felix, towards Zaaram Regia. *Zobh.*

LÆPA, a town of the Turtetani, Bætica, bet. the Anas and Onoba fl. *Lepe.*

LAERTES, a fortress of Cilicia Trachea, E. of Syedra, 16¼ m. N.W. from Coracesium. The birth-place of Diogenes Laertius.

LÆRON fl., a r. of Tarraconensis, falling into the Atlantic at Ad Duos Pontes.

LÆSTRIGONES, a very early people of Sicily, occupying the country on Simæthus fl., R., towards its source.

LÆVI, a people of Gallia Cisalpina, bet. Ticinus fl. and Orgus fl., contiguous to the Libicii.

LAGANIA (Regia-Lagania), *postea* Anastasiopolis, a town of the Tectosages, Galatia, on Sangarius fl., R., bet. Gordium (23) and Mnizus.

LAGARIA, a town of Lucania, 12 m. S.W. from Siris. Founded by Phocians, under Epæus, the builder of the wooden horse of Troy. The district was noted for its wine. *Nucara.*

LAGECIUM, Brit., i. q. Legeolium.

LAGINA, a town of Caria, 39 m. from Physcus. *Lakena.*

LAGNARÆ, a town of Mauritania Cæsariensis.

LAGNI, a town of the Arevacæ, Tarraconensis, on Durius fl., above Randa.

LAGNUS sin., a bay of Codanus sin., S.W., on the coast of the Saxones and Teutones.

LAGNUTUM, a town of Mauritania Cæsar., the mouth of Chinalaph, R.

LAGOS, a town of Pisidia, bet. Mandrupolis and Cobulatus fl.

LAGOUS fl., a r. of Sarmatia Asiat.

LAGUSA ins., I. an isl. of the Ægean, one of the Sporades, bet. Pholegandros and Sicinos. *Kardiotissa.* II. of Lycia, near Telmissus. *Isle des Chevaliers.*

LAGUSSA ins., islets on the coast of Troas, s. of Sigæum prom.

LAGYRA (Lampas), a maritime town of Taurica Chersonesus, s.w. of Charax. *Jalta.*

LAI, Liguria, i. q. Levi.

LAIUS (Elæus), a port of Chios ins., N.W. of Notium, 7½ m. w. from Chios oppid. *Mesta.*

LALACÆUM, a town of Melitene, Cappadocia.

LALASSIS regio, a district of Cilicia Trachea, on the borders of Pisidia and Lycaonia, w. of Cetis regio.

LALASTIS (Lalisanda, Dalisanda), a town of Isaurica, bet. Isaura and Germanicopolis.

LALETANI, a people of Tarraconensis, s. of the Ausetani.

LALISANDA, Isaur., i. q. Lalassis.

LALLA, a town of Colthene, Armenia, on the Cyrus, N. of Sanora.

LAMA, a town of the Lusitani, on the Durius, below Roboretum. *Lamego ?*

LAMASBUA, a town of Numidia, w.N.w. of Lambæsa (23). *Nik-Kuse ; Ben-Kuse.*

LAMBÆSA (Lambese), a town of Numidia, bet. Lambiridis and Tamugadis (23). The station of the Legio Augusta Tertia. *Tezzoute.*

LAMBANUS m., Cariæ, i. q. Albacus.

LAMBERITUM, a town of the Vascones, Tarraconensis, bet. Alanton w. and Summum Pyrenæum E.

LAMBIRIDIS, a town of Mauritania Cæsar., bet. Lamasbua and Lamæsa.

LAMBRIACA, a town of the Lucenses, Tarraconensis, at the mouth of Ulla fl. *Caril.*

LAMBRUS (Lamber) fl., a r. of Gallia Transpadana, rising N. of Eupilus lac., and, after passing through that lake, falling into Padus fl. below Ad Rota. *Lambro.*

LAMBULA, a pass in the mountains of N.E. Bruttium, leading from Roscianum into Lucania. *Roseto.*

LAMELLI præsidium, a fortress of Mauritania Cæsar., in the mountains s.w. of Equizetum.

LAMETES fl., a r. of Bruttium, falling into Lameticus sin., s. of Tempsa. *Lamato.*

LAMETIA (Lametum), a town of Bruttium, on Lametes fl., 3 m. above its mouth. A Crotonian colony. *Sant' Eufemia.*

LAMETINUM prom., a pr. of Bruttium, at the N. entrance of Lameticus sin. *Capo Suvero.*

LAMETICUS sin., a bay of Terinæus sin., at the mouth of Lametes fl. *G. di St. Eufemia.*

LAMIA ins., I. an islet on the coast of Troas. II. a city of the Malienses-Hierenses, in Thessaly, 4 m. N. from Anticyra. Its territory was the principal seat of the Lamiac war between Antipater and the confederate Greeks. *Zeitoun.*

LAMIACUS sin., i. q. Maliacus sin.

LAMINIÆ, a town of Gætulia, bet. Ad Templum and Veri, w. of Sabrata.

LAMINIUM, a town of the Oretani, Tarra-

conensis, bet. Murus N.w. and Arcilacis s.E., 7 m. from the source of the Anas, 95 m. s.E. from Toletum. *Alhambra.*

LAMNÆ, a town of the Æqui, Latium, on Anio fl., R., bet. Mandela (3) and Carseoli (10), on Via Valeria. *Ferrata.*

LAMNÆUS fl., a r. of India e. Gangem, falling into Barygazenus sin.

LAMOTIS, a district of Cilicia Trachea, on Lamus fl., towards its mouth.

LAMPAS, I. an isl. bet. Melita ins. and Gaulos ins. *Comino.* II. Tauricæ Cherson., i. q. Lagyra.

LAMPE m., I. a summit of Erymanthus range; the particular m. on which Hercules killed the boar. II. a town of Acarnania. III. (Lapha), of Crete, under Ida m., s.w. IV. of Phrygia Magna, near Celænæ.

LAMPES fl., Mysiæ, i. q. Rhyndacus.

LAMPETES prom., a pr. of Bruttium, s. of Clampetia. *Capo di Lamantia.*

LAMPETIA, the Greek name of Clampetia in Bruttium.

LAMPONIUM, a town of Æolis Asiat., bet. Gargara and Antandros.

LAMPRA INFERIOR, a demus of Attica, of the tribe Erectheis, on Saronicus sin., near Æxone.

LAMPRA SUPERIOR, a demus of Attica, of the tribe Erectheis, on Hymettus m., N.E. of Lampra Inf. The burial-place of Cranaus. *Lamprica.*

LAMPSACUS, *priùs* Pityusa, a city of Mysia, on the Hellespont, over against Callipolis in Thrace (5). Enlarged by colonies from Phocæa and Miletus. Noted for its wines, and therefore given by Artaxerxes to Themistocles for his cellar. The birth-place of Charon the historian, Anaximenes the orator (whose address saved it from the destruction menaced by Alexander), and Metrodorus the epicurean. Here was the recumbent lion of Lysippus, removed by Agrippa to Rome. *Lamsaki.*

LAMPSEMANDUS (Lepsemandus) ins., an isl. of Caria, in Ceramicus sin.

LAMPSUS, I. a town of Estiæotis, Thessaly, E. of Lisinæ. II. of Ionia, in the territory of Clazomenæ.

LAMUS fl., a r. separating Cilicia Campestris from Cilicia Trachea, and falling into the sea at Antiochia Lamotis. *Lamas.*

LANCE (Lancia), a town of the Astures, Tarraconensis, 2 m. s.E. from Legio.

LANCIA, I. *surnamed* Oppidana, a town of the Vettones, Lusitania, s.E. of Augustobriga, near the source of Munda fl. *Guarda.* II. *surnamed* Transcudana, a town of the Lusitani, E. of Lancia Oppidana and of Cuda fl. *Ciudad Rodrigo.*

LANDI, a tribe of Chatti, Germ., E. of the Lacobardi.

LANDŌBRIS (Lanucris) ins., isl. of Lusitania, N.W. of Olisopense prom. *Berlinguas.*

LANDOSIA, a town of the Tectosages, Galatiæ.

LANGIA (Adrastia) fons, a fountain of Argolis, near Nemea.

LANGOBARDI, a tribe of Vindili, German., on Albis fl., L., bet. the Viruni and the Hermiones, W. of the Semnones. Named from their long beards; and noted for their valour and their love of independence. D'Anville does not consider them the progenitors of the Italian Langobards or Lombards.

LANGOBRIGA, I. a town of the Celtici, Hispaniæ, on Tagus fl., L., near its mouth. *Near Benevente.* II. of Lusitania, near the mouth of Durius fl. *Near Villa Feira.*

LANGONES, a maritime tribe of Astures, on Salia fl.

LANGOSA, a town of Laviniasene, in Cappadocia.

LANISE ins., an isl. of the Ægean, one of the Sporades.

LANOS fl., a r. of Asia, rising in Emodi m., and falling into the Eous oceanus at Rabana. Towards its source it is called Ambastus. It is the boundary of India and Serica.

LANTOLAETES, i. q. Laletani, Tarraconensis.

LANUVIUM, a city of Latium, near Appia Via, R., N.W. of Ardea, S.E. of Corioli. Founded by Diomed. A municipium; a colonia of Sylla and of Cæsar, with a famous temple of Juno Sospita, in whose grove was a dragon, which detected unchastity in women. The birth-place of Annius Milo, of Roscius, Q. Catulus, the Elder; of the Cyrenius of St. Luke (P. Sulpicius Quirinius), and of the three Antonines. *Citta Lavinia* or *Della Vigna.*

LAODAMANTIUS portus, a port of Marmarica, bet. Leuce Acte (3) and Calamæum prom. (5.) *Lagusi.*

LAODICEA, I. a town of Arcadia, bet. Megalopolis and Orestium. II. of Lycaonia, bet. Tyrcæum and Iconium. III. of Persia. IV. *surnamed* Catacecaumene vel Combusta, of Phrygia Parorea, and later in Lycaonia, bet. Antiochia (28) and Iconium. Surnamed from the volcanic nature of the district. *Ladik.* V. *surnamed* ad Lycum, *prius* Diospolis and Rhoas, of Phrygia, on Lycus fl., 40 m. E. from Ephesus. Enlarged by Antiochus, and renamed after his wife, Laodice. Noted for its fine wool. One of the Seven Churches. *Eski Hissar.* VI. *surnamed* Ad Libanum, and also Sca-

brosa or Cabrosa, of Cœle-Syria, N.E. of Heliopolis. Built by Seleucus Nicator. VII. *surnamed* Ad Mare, of Syria, on the coast, N. of Gabala. Built by Seleucus Nicator; and beautified by the emperor Severus. *Latikia.*

LAPADON fl., a sacred stream of Bruttium, one of the seven streams falling into Metaurus fl. E. of Portus Orestis.

LAPERSA m., a m. of Laconia.

LAPETHUS (Lapathus), a town of Cyprus, on the N. coast, E. of Crommyon prom. Founded by Belus, and named from Lapethus, an attendant of Bacchus. Enlarged by a Lacedæmonian colony.

LAPHYSTIUS m., a summit of Helicon near Coronca.

LAPICINI, a mountain tribe of Liguria, N.E. of the Garuli. *About Picciana.*

LAPIDARIA, a town of the Venonetes, Rhætia, bet. Curia (32) and Cuneus Aureus (17).

LAPITHA m., a m. of Arcadia.

LAPITHÆ, a tribe of Pelasgi, about Pelion m., who usurped Pelasgiotis from the Perrhæbi. Noted as horse-tamers.

LAPITHÆUM, a village of Laconia, on Taygetus m., towards Derrhium.

LAPURDUM, a town of the Tarbelli, Novem Populana, at the mouth, L., of Aturis fl. *Bayonne.*

LAR, I. a r. of Arabia Felix, i. q. Canis. II. *postea* Germanorum Castrum, a maritime town of Mauritania Cæsar., bet. Cartilis and Apollinis prom.

LARANDA (Læandis), I. a town of Cataonia, Cappadocia, bet. Cocussus (18) and Daban. II. of Lycaonia, S.W. of Derbe. The birth-place of the poet Nestor and of his son Pisander. *Karaman.*

LARENDANI (Garendani), a people of Arabia Felix, contiguous to the Gebonitæ. *In Karje.*

LARES, a town of Numidia, on Bagradas fl., 16 m. N.E. from Altiburus. *Lorbus.*

LARGA, a town of the Rauraci, Maxima Sequanorum, bet. Cambete E. and Epamanduorum W.

LARIAGARA, a town of the Nangalogæ, Indiæ, on Dorius fl., L.

LARICE, a district of India e. Gangem, on the coast of Barygazenus sin., and extending inland N.E.

LARINA, a village of Cestrine, especially noted for its oxen.

LARINUM, I. a town of Corsica, on Tavola fl., R., above Mariana. II. *prius* Arenium, of Italy, bet. Uscosium (14) and Teanum (18). A municipium. The birth-place of A. Cluentius. *Larino Vecchio.*

LARISSA, I. a town of Adiabene, Assyriæ, on

the Tigris, bet. Ninus and Cænæ. The Resen of Scripture. II. one of the twelve cities of Æolis Asiat., bet. Cyme and Neontichos. Surnamed Phriconis, from Phricius m. in Locris, the previous seat of its Æolian colonizers. Originally a Pelasgic town. A colony of Egyptian soldiers was settled here by Cyrus. III. of Attica, at the foot of Hymettus. A settlement of Pelasgi. *Syriani.* IV. of Campania, near Forum Popilii. In ruins in Pliny's time. V. of Epea in Elis, on Larissus fl. VI. of Lydia, on Caystrus fl., L., 20 m. above Ephesus. VII. *surnamed* Cremaste, *vel* Pensilis (Pelagia), perhaps the Argos Pelasgicum of Homer, a city of Phthiotis, Thessaly, bet. Pteleum and Echinus (14), at the extremity of Aphetæ portus. The capital of Achilles. *Makalla.* VIII. (Argos Pelasgicum), a city of Pelasgiotis, in Thessaly, on the R. bank of Peneus fl., bet. Elatia and Atrax. Long the seat of a republic. The city of Achilles and of the Aleuadæ of Herodotus. *Larissa.* IX. Maced., i. q. Arnissa. X. a city of Apamene, Syria, on the Orontes, bet. Epiphania (16) and Apamea (16). Built by Seleucus Nicator. *Sjaizar.* XI. of Troas, near Alexandria, whither its inhabitants were transferred.

LARISSUS fl., a r. of Peloponnesus, rising in Scollis m., and, after separating Achaia from Elis, falling into Ionium mare below Araxus prom. *Risso* or *Mana.*

LARIUS lacus, a lake of the Orobii, Gallia Transpadana, partly formed by Addua fl. In length, from Summus lacus to Comum, 60 m. On its shores Pliny had two villas. Much frequented by coots, whence its name. *Lago di Como.*

LARIX, a town of Noricum, 27 m. s. from Santicum. *Plez.*

LARNA, a town of the Arevacæ, Tarraconensis, E. of Porta Augusta.

LARNUS fl., a r. of Tarraconensis, falling into the Mediterranean at Blanda, N.E. of Iluro. *Tordera.*

LARUNESIÆ ins., two islets of Byzacena, N. of Thapsus.

LARYMNA, I. *surnamed* Inferior, a town of Bœotia, on Opuntius sin., s. of Larymna Sup. *Martini.* II. *surnamed* Superior, a town of Bœotia, on Opuntius sin., N. of Larymna Inferior. *Proschyna.* III. of Peræa, Caria.

LARYSIUM m., a m. of Laconia, behind Gythium. Sacred to Bacchus.

LAS (Laas), a town of Laconia, on Laconicus sin. w., on Ilius m., bet. Arainus and Trinasus. Founded by the hero Las.

LASIA ins., an isl. of Argolis E., one of Pelopidis ins.

LASONII, a tribe of Mæones in Lydia.

LASOS, a town of Crete, on Oaxes fl., below Pergamus. *Laso.*

LASSIRA, a town of Tarraconensis, N. of Belsinum.

LASSUNNI, a people of Aquitania. *Vallée de Baigorry.*

LASTIGI, a town of the Turtetani, Bætica, N.W. of Acinipo.

LATEÆ (Latania), a town of Bithynia, bet. Nicomedia (24) and Demetrium, on Sangarius fl., L.

LATERA, a port of the Volcæ Arecomici, Narbonensis, N.E. of Agatha, at the mouth of Ledus fl. *Lattes.*

LATHRIPPA, Arabiæ, i. q. Jathrippa.

LATINA, a town of the Triballi, Mœs., bet. Remessiana and Turres.

LATINI, descendants of the Umbri, settled in Latium. Named from their king Latinus (of date anterior to Hesiod).

LATIS fl., a r. of Gallia Cisalpina, falling into the Padus, R. *Maira.*

LATIUM ANTIQUUM, the early distribution of Latium, as bounded s. by Circeum prom.

LATIUM, *Celticè* "fen-country," a region of Italy, bounded N. by Etruria and Sabinium, s. and w. by Tyrrhen. mare, E. by Samnium. Occupied, 1. by the Sicani; 2. by the Siculi; 3. by the Umbri or Osci, with whom became associated a colony of Tyrrhenian Pelasgi from Ænos, in Thrace, under a chief called Æneas. The name is poetically derived, according to Virgil, *à latendo,* Saturn having hidden himself here from Jupiter.

LATIUM NOVUM, the later distribution of Latium, when its s. boundary was extended to Liris fl., and still later to Vulturnus fl.

LATMICUS lacus, formerly a bay of Ionium mare, at the mouth of Mæander fl., extending from Miletus to Heraclea (12½); subsequently an inland lake, s. of Miletus. *Lago d'Oufa Bafi.*

LATMOS, I. a m. of Caria, overlooking Heraclea; the scene of the story of Endymion. Identified by some as the Phthira m. of Homer. *Betchek Parmak.* II. a town of Ionia, on Latmicus lacus, S.E. of Miletus.

LATO, the early name of Camara, Crete.

LATOBRIGI, a people of Vindelicia, towards the Danube, contiguous to the Rauraci. *About Donauschingen.*

LATOPOLIS, a town of Thebais on the Nile, L., bet. Hieracompolis and Asfinis. Named from the worship of the fish *latos. Esne.*

LATOVICI, a people of Pannonia s., on Savus fl., R.

LATRIS ins., an isl. of Germania Magna, in Cylipenus sin.

LATRONES, a people of Aurea Chersonesus, at its s. extremity.

LATURUS sin., Mauritaniæ, i. q. Portus Magnus.

LATUSATES, a people of Aquitania. *About Latus.*

LATYMNIUS m., a summit of the Apennines, towards Crotona. *Monte di Crotona.*

LAUMELLUM (Gaumellum), a town of the Lævi, in Gallia Transpad., on Novaria fl., near its junction with Padus fl., bet. Durii and Forum Fulvii. *Lomello.*

LAUNI, a people of Vindelicia, on Isara fl., towards its source.

LAURENTUM, a town of the Latini, in Latium, on Via Severiana, bet. Ostia (6) and Lavinium (6). The capital of Latinus, Picus, and Faunus. Named from its laurel groves. Noted for its wild boars. In Lucan's time, the population had removed to Lavinium. *Paterno.*

LAURIACUM, a town of the Boii, Noricum, on the Danube, at the confluence of Anisus fl., bet. Lentia and Lacus Felicis. A colonia. Founded by Marcus Aurelius. Noted for its shields. *Lorch.*

LAURITANUS portus, a haven of Etruria, bet. Populonium and Cosa.

LAURIUM m., hills of Attica, extending from about Azenia to Prasiæ. Rich in silver mines.

LAURON, a town of the Contestani, Tarraconensis, on the coast, N.W. of Dianium. *Laury.*

LAUS, I. a r. of Italy, separating Lucania from Bruttium, and falling into Laus sin. at Laus. *Lao.* II. a bay of Inferum mare, at Laus. *Golfo di Policastro.* III. a town of Lucania, at the mouth of Laus fl., 5 geog. m. from Pyxus. Founded by Sybarites escaped from the destruction of their own city. Extinct in Pliny's time. *Scalea.* IV. *surnamed* Pompeia, a town of the Insubres, Gall. Transpad., bet. Ad Nonum (7) and Tres Tabernæ (9), on Via Æmilia. A colonia of Pomp. Strabo. *Lodi Vecchio.*

LAUSANNA, a town of the Helvetii, near the s. shore of Lemanus lacus, bet. Noviodunum and Viviscus. *Lausanne.*

LAUTULÆ, a defile in Latium, bet. Tarracina and Fundi.

LAUZUDA, a town of Cilicia Trachea.

LAVARA, Lusitaniæ, i. q. Talabriga.

LAVATRÆ, a town of the Brigantes, Brit.,

bet. Verteræ and Ingetlingum. *Burgh under Stanmore.*

LAVINIASENE PREFECTURA, a prefecture of Cappadocia, E. of Sargarausene prefec., extending to the Euphrates. *Arabkir.*

LAVINIUM, a town of the Latini, Latium, on Via Severiana, bet. Laurentum (6) and Antium (17). Founded by Æneas, and named after his wife. The seat of the Dii Penates. The death-place of Tatius. Surnamed Lauro-Lavinium upon the removal hither of the people of Laurentum. *Pratica.*

LAVINIUS fl., a r. of Gallia Cispadana, falling into Vatrenus fl. towards Bononia. In it was the isl. on which the Triumvirs met. *Lavino.*

LAZI, a later people of maritime Colchis.

LEA ins., an isl. of the Ægean, one of the Sporades.

LEANA, a town of Arabia, on Leanites sin., bet. Itamus port. and Mallaba.

LEANDIS, a town of Cappadocia, S.E. of Cocusus.

LEANITÆ (Chaulanitæ, Havilitæ), a people of Arabia Felix, on Persicus sin., bet. Itamus portus and Chersonesus Acra. *Havilah.*

LEANITES sin., a gulf of Persicus sin. at Leana, Arab.

LEBADEA, *prius* Midea, a town of Bœotia, under Laphystius m., w. of Coronea. Enlarged by Lebadus the Athenian. Famous for the oracle of Trophonius. *Libadha.*

LEBENA, a town on the s. coast of Crete, E. of Leon prom., the E. port of Gortys. *Mitropoli.*

LEBEDOS, one of the twelve cities of Ionia, bet. Teos and Colophon, E. of Myonnesus prom. Almost destroyed by Lysimachus. It became the abode or rendezvous of the Ionian comedians, who here celebrated annual games in honour of Bacchus. Noted for its mineral baths. *Xingi; Ecclesia.*

LEBINTHUS ins., an isl. of the Ægean, one of the Sporades, N.E. of Cinarus. *Levita.*

LEBORINI campi, a district of the Phlegræi campi, bet. Cumæ and Puteoli. Hence was derived the modern name of Campania. *Terra di Lavoro.*

LECCUM, a demus of Attica, of the tribe Antiochis.

LECHIENI, a people of Arabia Felix, near the Dachareni. *Beni Lahyan.*

LECTUM prom., the s. extremity of Troas, at the N. entrance of Adramyttenus sin.; the termination, in this direction, of Ida m. Here Juno and the god of sleep landed. *C. Baba.*

LECYTHUS, a fortress of Torone, in Sithonia, Macedonia.

LECHÆUM, the w. port of Corinth, on Corinthiacus sin., 2 m. N. from the city.

LEDERATA (Leterita turris), a town of the Albocenses, Dacia, on the Danube, bet. Viminacium and Punicum.

LEDON, a town of Phocis, s. of Tryia. The birth-place of Philomelus. In ruins in Pausanias' time.

LEDUS, a r. of Narbonensis, falling into the Mediterranean at Latera. *Lez.*

LEGÆ, a people of Albania As., bet. its N.W. portion and Cœsius fl. *Lekh.*

LEGEDIA, a town of the Osismii, Lugdunensis III., bet. Cosedia w.s.w. and Condate E.S.E. *Lezeau.*

LEGEOLIUM, a town of the Brigantes, Brit., bet. Calcaria and Danum (16). *Castleford.*

LEGIO, Galilææ, i. q. Megiddo.

LEGIO SEPTIMA GEMINA (Brigæcium), a town of the Astures, Tarraconensis, N.E. of Asturica Augusta. A colonia. *Leon.*

LEGUM, a town of Sicily, on Halycus fl., R., below Ancyra.

LEIA ins., an isl. of Cyrenaica, off Apollonia.

LEINIACUM, a town of Rhætia, 8 m. from Mediana, at the confluence of the Licus and Danubius. *Monastery of Nieder-Schonfeld.*

LEINUM, a town of the Bastarnæ, Sarmat., near the source of Hypanis fl. *Near Bracklow.*

LELANNONIUS sin., a bay of the Atlantic, on the coast of the Epidii, Brit. *Loch Fin.*

LELANTUS campus, I. a plain of Eubœa, above Chalcis. In it were springs of hot mud. II. fl., a r. of Eubœa, rising in Lelantus campus and falling into Euripus s. of Chalcis.

LELEGES, an original people of Greece, prior to the Pelasgi, occupying Acarnania, Locris, Eubœa, Bœotia, Laconia, several islands in the Ægean, and portions of Mysia and Ionia.

LELEGIA, the early name of Laconia, from its Lelegian settlers.

LEMANUS lacus, a lake of Maxima Sequanorum, formed by the Rhone bet. Geneva w. and Viviscus E. *L. of Geneva.*

LEMBUS prom., a pr. of Bithynia, on Bosporus Thracius, N. of Potamonium.

LEMINCUM, a town of the Allobroges, in Gaul, bet. Aquæ Gratianæ and Labisco.

LEMNIS, a port of Mauritania Cæsar., bet. Mulucha fl. and Ad Fratres.

LEMNUS fl., Bœotia, i. q. Olmius.

LEMNOS ins., surnamed Dipolis, prius Æthalia, an isl. of Thrace, in the Ægean, bet. Athos m., from which it is distant 37 m.,

and Imbros ins. In circuit 100 m. From its volcanic nature, sacred to Vulcan. Occupied first by Sintii, then, prior to the Trojan war, by Tyrrheni Pelasgi, and afterwards colonized by Athenians. Noted for a peculiar astringent earth. *Stalimene.*

LEMOVICES, a people of Aquitania I., bet. the Pictones and Santones w. and the Arverni E. *Haute Vienne.*

LEMOVII, postea Heruli, a tribe of Rugii, Germania, on Venedicus sin. w.

LENTIA, a town of the Boii, Noricum, on the Danube, N.E. of Ovilia. Built by Gratian. *Lintz.*

LENTIANA, a town of Mysia, under Pelecas m.

LENTIANI colles, m. of Mysia, an E. range of Temnus m., bet. Cyzicus and Lopadium.

LENTIENSES, a tribe of Vindelici, N. and s. of Brigantinus lac.

LENTULA, a town of the Jassii, Pannonia, bet. Piretæ and Jovia (32). *Berzentz.*

LENUS, a town of Pisatis, Elis.

LEON, I. a pr. on the s. coast of Crete, w. of Lebena. *Lionda.* II. a headland of Eubœa, on the w. coast, s. of Styra, over against Cynosura prom. *C. Daron.* III. a maritime village of Sicily, 2 m. N. from Syracuse.

LEONICA, a town of the Edetani, Tarraconensis, w. of Dertosa. A colonia. *Villar Luengo.*

LEONTARNE, a town of Bœotia, near Coronea.

LEONTECEPHALE (Leontos-come), a town of Phrygia, near Alexandri Diversorium. Noted for its warm springs.

LEONTES fl., a r. of Phœnicia, falling into the sea above Tyrus. *Lanto.*

LEONTINI, I. a later name of the Læstrigones, Sicily, from the lion impressed on their coins. II. (Leontium), their capital, on Terias fl., R., towards its source. *Lentini.* III. campi (Læstrigonii campi), the country of the Leontini in Sicily.

LEONTIS, a tribe or ward of Attica. Named after the three daughters of Leos.

LEONTIUM, one of the Twelve Cities of Achaia, on the confines of Elis, s.w. of Pharæ. *Gifto Castro.*

LEONTOPOLIS, I. vide Nicephorium. II. a town of Lower Egypt, on the Busiritic branch of the Nile, 3 geog. m. s. from Thmuis. Here lions were worshipped.

LEONTOSCOME, Phrygiæ, i. q. Leontecephale.

LEONTION, a town of Phœnicia, on Leontes fl., R., towards its source.

LEOPODON, a portion of the coast of Ionia, about Erythræ.

LEPAVISTUM, a town of the Amantini, Pannoniæ, bet. Bregetium (5) and Sardellaca (13).

LEPENUS m., a chain of m. in Latium, bet. Præneste and Tarracina. Noted for its wines.

LEPETYMNUS m., a range of m. on the N. coast of Lesbos ins. *Leptimo.*

LEPIDOTONPOLIS, a town of Thebais, on the Nile, R., 4 geog. m. s. from Chenoboscia.

LEPONTII (Leipontii), a tribe of Taurisci, Rhætia, on the s. slope of the Alpes Lepontiæ, N.W. of the Orobii. Fabled to have been so named from having been left behind by Hercules, because frostbitten. *Bet. Gt. St. Bernard and St. Gothard.*

LEPRÆA ins., an isl. of Ionia, off the mouth of Caystrus fl.

LEPRÆUM, a town of Triphylia, Elis, s. of Pylos. Built by the Caucones. *Strobitzi.*

LEPSIA ins., an isl. of Ionia, in the Icarium mare, bet. Pharmacusa and Palmos ins. *Lepso.*

LEPTE (Syrias) prom., a pr. of Paphlagonia, the most N. point of Asia Minor, w. of Sinope, 15 m. E. from Potami. *C. Inje.*

LEPTIS, I. *surnamed* Magna, *postea* Neapolis, a city of Tripolis, Africa, on the Mediterranean, w. of the mouth of Cinyps fl., bet. Sugolin and Ad Palmam, at Hermæum prom. A Sidonian settlement. A colonia (Victrix Julia). The birth-place of Septimius Severus. *Libada.* II. *surnamed* Minor, vel Parva, a maritime city of Byzacene, bet. Ruspina and Thapsus. A municipium. *Lemta.* III. Bæticæ, i. q. Ilipa.

LERAMUSA, a town of Pontus, on the borders of Cappadocia, towards Mazaca (16).

LERETISCA, a town of the Treres, Mœsia, bet. Media and Sardica.

LERINUS ins., an isl. of the Ligauni, Narbonensis, s. of Lero ins.

LERNE, I. a stream of Argolis, discharging its waters through Lerne palus into Argolicus sinus. *Maloi.* II. a lake of Argolis, towards the mouth of Erasinus fl., wherein Minerva purified the daughters of Danaus, and in which the Argives performed religious ablutions. The scene of the contest between Hercules and the hydra. III. a town of Argolis, at Lerne palus.

LERON ins., an isl. of the Ligauni, Narbo-

nensis, s.E. of Ad Horrea. *St. Marguerite.*

LEROS (Leria) ins., an isl. of Caria, in the Icarium mare, one of the Sporades, bet. Lepsia and Colymna. Colonized by Milesians ; with a temple of Diana, where the birds called Melæagrides were kept. *Lero.*

LESA, a town of the Ruacenses, Sardinia, on Tyrsus fl., L., above Forum Trajani. *Ales.*

LESBOS (Pelasgia) ins., an isl. of Æolis Asiat., bet. Adramyttenus sin. and Cumæus sin., in circuit 195 m. Colonized by Pelasgi, and next by Æolians, under Lesbus, grandson of Æolus. *Metelin.*

LESORA m., a summit of Cevenna m., N. of Andusia. *Mt. Lozere.*

LESSA, a town of Argolis, bet. Argos and Epidaurus. *Likurio.*

LESTIADÆ, a town of Naxos ins., towards the s. coast.

LETANDROS ins., an isl. of the Ægean, one of the Sporades, N.W. of Amorgos. *Stenosa.*

LETE, a town of Amphaxitis, Macedonia, s.E. of Carabia.

LETES (Læti), a tribe of Sarmatians, settled in the territory of the Nervii.

LETHÆUS fl., I. a r. of Crete, rising in Ida m. and falling into Libycum m. at Metallum. *Messara.* II. (Lethe), of Cyrenaica, rising in the Desert and falling into the sea towards Tritonis palus. It was the name of this river which the poets adopted as that of the river of forgetfulness. *Lathon.* III. of Estiæotis, falling into Peneus fl. below Tricca. IV. of Ionia, rising in Pactyas m. and falling into Mæander fl. below Magnesia. V. of Callæcia, i. q. Limia.

LETHE fons, a sacred spring of Bœotia, rising in Liphystius m., near Libadia, and forming, with Mnemosyne fons, the river Hercine.

LITHRUS m., a m. of Pontus, s. of Amasia.

LETOIA (Lotoia) ins., an islet of Cephallenia, on the s. coast, over against Bæa m.

LETOPLIS (Latonæ urbs), a town of Lower Egypt, on the Saitic channel of the Nile, w.N.w. of Heliopolis.

LETRINA (Letrini), a town of Pisatis, Elis, on Alpheus fl., rising near its mouth, with a temple of Diana Alpheia a Alpheiusa. Named from Letrinus, son of Pelops.

LETUS m., a summit of the Apennines, in the territory of the Apuani, Etruria, N.E. of Luna. *M. Pellegrino.*

LEUCA, I. a town of Ionia, on a peninsula (at one period an island) in Hermæus sin., s. of Phocæa. II. of Bithynia, on Sangarius fl., bet. Nicæa and Agrillium. *Lefkè.* III. of Laconia, N.E. of Acriæ. IV. of the Salentini, Halice, towards Japygium prom. *Santa Maria di Leuca.*

LEUCADIA. *Vide* Leucas.

LEUCÆ ins., three isl. bet. the N.E. extremity of Lesbos ins. and Hecatonnesi ins.

LEUCAPIS, a haven of Marmarica, 2 geog. m. w. from Glaucum prom.

LEUCARISTUS, a town of the Diduni, Germania, N.E. of Budorgis.

LEUCARUM, a maritime town of Britain, 15 m. N.E. from Isca Damnoniorum. *Cinnington.*

LEUCAS, I. *prius* Neritis, Epileucadii, a peninsula of Acarnania, s. of Anactorium. Partly colonized by Corinthians from Ambracia, who afterwards separated it from the mainland by a cut, called Dioryctus, through the connecting isthmus. In the time of Strabo a bridge had been thrown across this channel. *Santa Maura.* II. its capital, at the N.E. extremity. A Corinthian colony from Ambracia and Anactorium. At one time the capital of Acarnania. *Santa Maura.*

LEUCASIA fl., a r. of Messenia, falling into Pamisus fl. N.w. of Stenyclerus. *Melegala.*

LEUCASIUM, a town of Arcadia, on Ladon fl., L., above Mesoboa.

LEUCATAS prom., Bithyniæ, i. q. Acritas.

LEUCATE, "white," I. prom., the s.E. headland of Leucas ins., with a temple of Apollo on its summit, in honour of whom a condemned criminal was once a year thrown from the cliff. The Lover's Leap, fatal, among others, to Sappho and to Artemisia, queen of Caria. *C. Ducato.* II. a port of the Volcæ Tectosages, Narbonensis I., N. of Ruscino.

LEUCE, I. the coast of Caria, bet. Halicarnassus and Myndus. II. an isl. on the N. coast of Crete, over against Minoa. III. an isl. of Sarmatia Europ., near Achillei Cursus. IV. an isl. of India i. Gangem, off Cottiara.

LEUCE ACTE, I. the s.w. coast of Eubœa, towards Petalia prom. II. a pr. of Marmarica, 2 geog. m. from Hermæum prom. III. a headland of Thrace, on the Propontis, bet. Tiristasis and Pactya. *C. Kerkiriacou.*

LEUCECOME, a town of Arabia Felix, on the Red sea, bet. Hippus and Raunathus, opposite Nechesia, in Egypt. *Haura.*

LEUCERA, a town of the Orobii, Gallia Cisalpina, at the s.E. extremity of Larius

lac., bet. Bergomum (20) and Brixia (35). *Lovere.*

LEUCI, "white," I. a s.w. continuation of Ida m., in Crete, terminating in Criumetopon prom. *Aspro Vouni.* II. a people of Belgica I., bet. the Mediomatrices and the Verodunenses N. and the Sequani s. *N.E. Haute Marne; N.W. Vosges; S. Meuse and Meurthe.*

LEUCIMNA prom., a headland of Corcyra ins., the s.E. extremity of the island, over against Sybotæ ins. *C. Bianco.*

LEUCOCIDIA, a town of the Novantæ, Brit., at the mouth of Jena fl., R.

LEUCOGAI colles, hills of Campania, about Neapolis.

LEUCOLLA, I. a pr. of Pamphylia, E. of Capria lac. II. a port of Cyprus, N. of Pedalium prom. *Armida.*

LEUCONIUS fons, a stream of Arcadia, near Tegea.

LEUCONOIUM, I. a demus of Attica, of the tribe Leontis. The birth-place of Meton, the mathematician. II. a town of Chios ins.

LEUCONUM, a town of Pannonia Inf., bet. Cirtisa (12) and Picentinum (26). *Rasboistje.*

LEUCOPETRA, "chalk" (Bruttianum), I. a pr. of Bruttium, at the extreme toe of Italy, over against Tauromenium, Sicily. The termination of the Apennines. · *C. dell' Armi.* II. a town of Bruttium, at Leucopetra prom.

LEUCOPHRYS, "white-cliffed," I. a name of Tenedos ins. II. a town of Lydia, 15 m. s. from Ephesus, towards Priene, with a famous temple of Diana Leucophrys. Hither the people of Magnesia removed and built a new city. *Inek-bazar.*

LEUCOPIBIA (Casæ Candidæ), a town of the Novantæ, Britan. *Wigton.*

LEUCOPOLIS, a town of Caria, on Doridis sin.

LEUCOPYRA, a demus of Attica, of the tribe Antiochis.

LEUCOS portus, a port of Thebais, on the Red sea, s. of Aias prom.

LEUCOSIA (Leucasia), I. an isl. of Lucania, off Posidium prom. Named from one of the sirens buried there. *Licosa; Isola piana.* II. a town of Cyprus.

LEUCO-SYRI, "white Syrians," the colonists from Upper Asia of Asia Minor, E. of Halys fl.

LEUCOTHEA fons, a stream of Samos.

LEUCOTHEUM prom., a pr. of Pamphylia, 6 m. s.E. from Cibyra parva. *C. Karabournou.*

LEUCTRA, a town of Bœotia, bet. Thespiæ

and Platæa, where the Lacedæmonians, under Cleombrotus, were defeated by the Thebans under Epaminondas, B.C. 371. *Lefka.*

LEUCTRUM, I. a town of Achaia, on the Meganitas fl., S.E. of Rhypæ. II. of Arcadia, on the confines of Laconia, the inhabitants of which removed to Megalopolis. *Leontari.* III. (Leuctra), a town of Messenia, on Messeniacus sin., E., 8 m. below Cardamyle. Founded by Pelops. *Leutro.*

LEUCUS fl., a r. of Pieria, Macedoniæ, falling into the Thermaicus sin. below Pydna.

LEUCYANIAS fl., a r. of Elis, rising in Pholoe m. and falling into Alpheus fl. E. of Olympia.

LEUGÆSA (Leutæsa), a town of Melitene, Cappadocia.

LEUNI, a people of Vindelicia, contiguous to the Runicatæ. *About Leutkirch.*

LEUPAS portus, a port of Arabia Felix, N. of Thamar fl. *Lua.*

LEUPHĀNA, a town of the Langobardi, Germania, towards the mouth of Albis fl. *Near Buxtehude.*

LEUTARNIA, a city of the Lucania, towards Lagaria. *Albidona.*

LEUTERNI, a tribe of Japyges, occupying the coast of Japygia, about Leuca, and that of Lucania, about Leutarnia. Strabo describes them as giants who had escaped the destruction of their brethren in the Campi Phlegræi.

LEUTOANUM, Pannoniæ, i. q. Ad Labores.

LEVACI, a tribe of Morini, Belgica II., on the Scaldis, towards its mouth.

LEVI, a people of Gallia Transpadana, on Padus fl., bet. Ticinus fl. and Novaria fl.

LEVONI, a people of Scandinavia.

LEXOVII (Lexobii), a people of Lugdunensis II., on the Sequana, L., at its æstuary. *Calvados.*

LIANUM, a town of the Jazyges, Sarmatiæ, near Coretus sin. w. of Byces fl.

LIBA, I. a town of Cyrenaica, w. above Crocodilum prom. II. of Mygdonia, Mesopotamia, S.E. of Nisibis.

LIBANA (Labbana), a town of Arabene, Mes., on the Tigris, bet. Betuma and Mespyla. *Mosul?*

LIBANESIA, a name of Cœle-Syria, from Libanus m.

LIBANOTOPHOROS regio, a district of Arabia Felix, on the S.E. coast, below the Omanitæ. Named from its incense. *Mountains of Sciorm.*

LIBANUS (Lebanon) m., a range of m. in Syria, parallel w. with Antilibanus, be-

ginning near Tripolis and blending with the m. of Trachonitis. *Lebanon.*

LIBARNA (Libarnum), a town of the Statielli, Liguria, bet. Caristum and Genua. *Lavezzara.*

LIBERO, a town of the Libicii, Gallia Transpad., N.W. of Vercellæ, on a cognominal lake. *Viverone.*

LIBETHRA, I. a stream sacred to the Muses, on Himolium m., Thessaliæ. II. (Libethrum), a town of Pieria, Macedoniæ, in Olympus m., near the source of the Enipeus, s.w. of Dium. The burial-place of Orpheus. *Palæo Castro.*

LIBETHRUS m., a summit of Helicon, Bœotia, towards Coronea, on which was a grove and temple of the Muses, and of the nymphs Libethrides.

LIBETHRUS m., a summit of Olympus m., overlooking Libethra, Pieria. Sacred to the Muses.

LIBIA, a town of the Autrigones, Tarraconensis, bet. Cigurri N.N.E. and Termantia S.S.W.

LIBICI, a tribe of Salyes, Gallia Transpadana, on Padus fl., w. of the Levi, bet. Novaria fl. and Duria Maj. fl. *About Vercellæ.*

LIBINIUS fl., a r. of Hibernia, falling into the sea at Eblana. *Liffey.*

LIBISOSA (Forum Augusti), a town of the Oretani, Tarraconensis, E. of Laminium. A colonia. *Lesuza.*

LIBNAH (Shilo Libnath), I. a town of Asher, w. of Shilo. II. of Arabia, near Sinai m. III. (Lobna), of Judah, Judææ, bet. Eleutheropolis N.N.E. and Eglon w.s.w. A Levitical city.

LIBNEUS æst., an æst. of Hibernia, 5 geog. m. s.w. from Magnata. *Sligo Bay.*

LIBORA (Talabriga), a town of the Carpetani, Tarraconensis, on the Tagus, R. *Talavera.*

LIBUI, i. q. Libici.

LIBUM, a town of Bithynia, bet. Nicomedia (21) and Nicæa.

LIBUNCA, a maritime town of the Callæci, Tarraconensis, bet. Navilubio fl. E. and Nabius fl: w.

LIBURNI, a people of Illyria, along the Adriatic, s. of the Japydes, from Jadera to Titius fl.

LIBURNIDES ins., forty islands of the Adriatic, along the coast of Illyria, s. of Absyrtides ins.

LIBURNUS m., a ridge of Apennines, Daunia Apul., bordering the valley of Tifernus fl., N. *Monte della Serra.*

LIBYA, with the Greeks and with the Latin poets, the continent of Africa; with the Roman prose writers, the N. coast of

Africa, from Syrtis Major to Egypt, and extending inland to the Desert. The country of the Lubim or Lehabim of Scripture, whence probably the name was derived.

LIBYA ÆGYPTI, I. a maritime region of Africa, bet. Marmarica, at Parætonium, and Egypt, at Plinthine. II. palus, a lake of Gætulia, s.w. of Palladis pal. Formed by Triton fl.

LIBYCA ora, a name of the coast of the Delta of the Rhone.

LIBYCUM mare, the portion of the Mediterranean, bet. the coast of Peloponnesus and Africa, extending E. as far as Crete.

LIBYSSA, a village of Bithynia, on Astacenus sin. N., at the mouth of Libyssus fl., bet. Calchedon (37) and Nicomedia (23). The burial-place of Hannibal. Extinct in Pliny's time. *Malsum.*

LIBYSSUS fl., a r. of Bithynia, falling into Astacenus sin. at Libyssa.

LICATES, a people of Vindelicia, on Licus fl., s. of the Catenates.

LICHADES ins., three islets of the Locri Epicnemidii, in Maliacus sin., bet. Cnemius and Cenæum prom. Named from the fate of Lichas.

LICUS (Licius) fl., a r. of Rhætia, rising S.E. of Brigantium and falling into the Danube below Drusomagus. *Lech.*

LIDE m., a m. of Caria, near Pedasa.

LIGAUNI, a maritime tribe of Salyes, Narbonensis, bet. the Deciates and the Oxybii. *About St. Vallier.*

LIGEA ins., an isl. of Bruttium, in Hipponiates sin. Named from a siren buried there. *Pietra della Nave.*

LIGER fl., a r. of Gaul, rising in Lesora m., S.E. of Anderitum, and falling into the Atlantic at Portus Namnetum. *Loire.*

LIGUES, the Greek name of the Ligures.

LIGURES, "mountaineers," a Celtic people, settled in Liguria and portions of Etruria, long prior to the Tyrrhenian invasion, ranking, in order of Italian colonization, next to the Siculi. They were distributed into Capillati, those dwelling on the coast, and Montani, those occupying the mountains.

LIGURIA, a region of Italy, bounded N. by Gallia Transpadana, at Padus fl., s. by Ligusticus sin., w. by Alpes Maritimæ, E. by Gallia Cispadana, w. of Trebia fl. At one period the Ligurian territory extended to the confines of Spain.

LIGURRUS pagus, the district about Ad Navalia, in Liguria.

LIGUSTICUS sinus, the upper portion of Tyrrhenium mare, on the coast of Liguria. *Golfo di Genoa.*

LILÆA, a town of Phocis, at the N. foot of Parnassus, 22 m. N. from Delphi, near the source of Cephissus fl. *Palæocastro.*

LILÆUM, a port of Bithynia, on the Euxine, 5 m. E. from Dia, at the mouth of Lilæus fl.

LILÆUS fl., a r. of Bithynia, rising in Hypius m. and falling into the Euxine at Lilæum.

LILYBÆUM, I. a pr. of Sicily, w. over against Carthage (125 m.). *C. Boeo.* II. a city of Sicily, at Lilybæum prom. A colonia of Augustus. *Marsala.*

LIMANUS fl., a r. of Britannia, s., falling into the sea at Novus portus. *Rother.*

LIMAGUS fl., a r. of the Helvetii, running by Turicum. *Limmat.*

LIMAX fl., a r. of Arcadia, falling into the Neda, near Phigalea.

LIMENÆ, a town of Pisidia.

LIMENIA, a town of Cyprus, 4 m. S.E. from Soli.

LIMENEIUM, a town of Caria, in the territory of Miletus.

LIMIA (Belion, Lethe), I. a r. of Callæcia, rising in Medullus m. E. of Forum Limiorum and falling into the Atlantic below Geræa. Noted for the exploit of Decimus Brutus. *Lima.* II. a town of the Bracari, Tarraconensis, on Limia fl., L., below Aquæ Querquennæ, 19 m. from Bracara. *Puente de Lima.*

LIMICI, a tribe of Bracari, Tarraconensis.

LIMIOSALIUM, a town of the Diduni, Germania Magna, N. of Budorgis. *Oppeln.*

LIMMOCHORUS, a town of Phrygia Magna, on Mæander fl.

LIMNÆ, a village of Messenia, on the border of Laconia, N. of Alagonia, where the festival of Diana Limnadis was celebrated.

LIMNÆA (Limne), I. a town of Acarnania, on the S. shore of Ambracius sin., w. of Argos Amphilochum. *Lutraki.* II. of the Bechires, Pontus, at the mouth of Prytanis fl. III. of Chersonesus Thracia, on Melas sin., N. of Alopeconnesus. A Milesian colony. IV. of Estiæotis, in Thessaly, towards Metropolis.

LIMNIAS, a town of Pentapolis, Cyrenaicæ, bet. Cyrene and Hydrax.

LIMNUS ins., an isl. of Hibernia, s. of Oboca fl. *St. Patrick's Island.*

LIMOBRAMA, a town of Pamphylia.

LIMON, I. an islet of Campania, near Nesis ins. II. a cavern of Lydia, near Charonium specus, with which it was said to be connected. Sacred to Pluto and Proserpine.

LIMŌNUM (Lemuno), *postea* Pictavi, capital of the Pictones, Aquitania II., bet. Cæsarodunum N.N.E. and Raurannum s.s.w. *Poitiers.*

LIMUSA, a town of Pannonia.

LIMYRA, a town of Lycia, on Limyrus fl., 3 m. above its mouth. The death-place of Caius Cæsar.

LIMYRICA, a maritime district of India i. Gangem w., bet. N. of Calliane and Coreura.

LIMYRUS fl., a r. of Lycia, falling into the Mediterranean below Limyra.

LINDUM (Lindocolina civitas, Clidum), I. capital of the Coritani, Brit., bet. Agelocum and Ad Pontem. A colonia. *Lincoln.* II. a town of the Damnii, Brit., on Bodotria æstuar., bet. Alauna and Alaterva. *Kirkantulloch.*

LINDUS, a city of Rhodus ins., on its E. coast, s. of Rhodus opp. One of the three Dorian cities, with a temple of Minerva, founded by Danaus, the image being a shapeless stone. The birth-place of the sage Cleobulus. *Lindo.*

LINDUS, the early name of Gela, in Sicily, from its Lindian colonists.

LINGON m., Epiri, i. q. Polyanus m.

LINGŌNES, I. a colony of Lingones from Gaul, who, dispossessing the Umbri, occupied the extreme E. part of Gallia Cispadana, bet. Padus fl. and Rubico fl. II. a people of Lugdunensis I., on the Arar, R., towards its source, N. of the Ædui. *N. Côte d'Or, S. Aube and Haute Vienne, N. Haute Saone.* III. Their capital. *Langres.*

LINTOMAGUS, a town of the Menapii, Belgica II., bet. Castrum Morinorum N. and Ad Lullia.

LINUM, I. a pr. of Bruttium, N. of Clampetia. *Capo Verre.* II. a town of Mysia, on the Hellespont, bet. Parium and Priapus. Noted for its shell fish.

LIPĂRA, "fertile," *postea* Lycandus, a district of Cappadocia. II. chief of the Æoliæ ins. *Lipari.*

LIPĂRĒÆ ins., i. q. Æoliæ.

LIPAXUS, a town of Chalcidice, Macedonia, on Thermaicus sin., bet. Combria and Potidæa.

LIPORIS fl., a r. of Cilicia Campestris, falling into the sea at Soli. It rose near some pitch-springs, and its water was accordingly very unctuous, as the name imports.

LIPSYDRIUM, a fortress of Attica, N. of Pæonia, near Aphidna.

LIQUENTIA (Liquetia) fl., I. a r. of Venetia, rising in the Alps and falling into the Adriatic by several mouths, bet. Plavis fl.

and Romatinus fl. *Livenza.* II. portus, a town of the Veneti, Venetia, at the mouth of Liquentia fl. *Porto di Margarita.*

LIRIA, Tarraconensis, i. q. Edeta.

LIRIMIRIS, a maritime town of the Saxones, Germ., over against Saxonum ins. *Two m. N. of Hamburgh.*

LIRINATES, the people of Interamna ad Lirin.

LIRIS fl., *prius* Clanis, a r. of Latium, rising in the territory of the Marsi, w..of Lacus Fucinus, and falling into Tyrrhenium m. below Minturnæ. Noted for its sluggish course. *Garigliano.*

LIRUSA, a town of the Hercuniatæ, Pannon., bet. Sopianæ and Silacenæ.

LISÆ, a town of Chalcidice, Macedonia, on Thermaicus sinus, s. of Smila.

LISIA ins., an isl. of Britain.

LISINÆ, a town of Estiæotis, Thessaly, s. of Thimarum.

LISSA ins., an isl. of the Adriatic, one of the Liburnides ins., over against Jadera. *Isola Grossa.*

LISSA, a northern town of the Ilergetes, Tarraconensis.

LISSA (Exilissa), a town of Mauritania Ting., on Herculis Fretum, bet. Tingis and Abyla.

LISSÆ, a town of the Odrysæ, Thrace, on Hebrus fl., above Bessapara.

LISSE ins., a rock on the s. coast of Crete, towards Metallum.

LISSUS fl., I. a r. of the Cicones, Thrace, falling into the Ægean bet. Stryme and Mesembria. One of the rivers exhausted by the army of Xerxes. II. a r. of Sicily, flowing by Leontini into the Terias. *Lentini.* III. (Lissa), a town on the s.w. coast of Crete, bet. Bienon and Calamydes. *Castel Selino.* IV. of the Taulantii, Illyria, on Drilon fl. near its mouth. Founded by a colony of Syracusans under Dionysius. A colonia.

LISTA, capital of the Pelasgi, in Sabinium, 3 m. s.E. of Tiora.

LITANA silva, a forest of Gallia Cispadana, extending along the base of the Apennines from Scultenna fl. to Secies fl. The locality of the destruction of the Roman army, under L. Posthumius Albinus, by the Gauls. *Litana.*

LITANOBRIGA, a town of the Silvanectes, Belgica II., bet. Cæsaromagus N.W. and Augustomagus s.E.

LITERNA palus, a marsh of Campania, formed by Liternus fl. just above its mouth. *Lago di Patria.*

LITERNUM, a maritime town of Campania,

on Via Domitiana, bet. Sinuessa (14) and Cumæ (6). A colonia 196 B.C. The death-place of Scipio Africanus. *Patria.*

LITERNUS fl., a r. of Campania, rising near Abella and falling into the sea at Liternum. *Lagno.*

LITHRUS m., a ridge of Paryadres m., in Pontus, N.W. of Amasia.

LITTAMUM, a town of the Isarci, Rhætiæ, bet. Setalum (23) and Aguntum (23). *Prunecken.*

LITUBIUM, Liguriæ, i. q. Ritubium.

LIVIANI, a town of the Volcæ Tectosages, Narbonensis I., bet. Tricesimum w. and Usuerva E.

LIVIAS, Galaaditis, i. q. Bethhoran.

LIVINIANA, a town of Numidia, bet. Popletum and Vicus Aureli.

LIVIOPOLIS, i. q. Hermonassa of Pontus.

LIXUS, I. a r. of Mauritania Ting., rising in Atlas Minor, and falling into the Atlantic at Lixus. *Luccos.* II. of Libya w. *St. Cyprian.* III. (Linx), a port of Mauritaniæ Ting., at the mouth of Lixus fl., L., bet. Thymiaterium and Zilia (32). The abode of Antæus. *L'arais* or *L'arache.*

LIZIZIS, a town of the Biephi, Dacia, N.W. of Berzovia.

LOBETANI, a tribe of Celtiberi, Tarraconensis, N. of the Suessetani, about Lobetum.

LOBETUM, capital of the Lobetani, Tarraconens., on Turia fl., L., near its source. Built by the Lybian Hercules. *Albarazin? Riquena?*

LOBUNI, Brit., i. q. Dobuni.

LOCANUS fl., a r. of Bruttium, falling into Locrensis sin. N. of Locri. *Locano.*

LOCHA, a town of Zeugitana, inland of Utica.

LOCHIAS prom., a pr. of Egypt, at Alexandria.

LOCORITUM, a town of the Tursones, Germ., on Mœnus fl., R., below the junction of Sala fl. *Gemund.*

LOCOGUS, a town of Phrygia, on Mæander fl. Destroyed by an inundation.

LOCRAS fl., a r. of Corsica, falling into the sea at Paula. *Talavo.*

LOCRI, surnamed Epicnemidii, I. a tribe of Leleges, settled on the N. shore of Maliacus sin., w. of the Locri Opuntii and N.E. of their colonists, the Locri Ozolæ. II. *surnamed* Epizephyrii, a body of slaves, who, escaping from Locris Epicnemid. with their masters' wives, settled circa 710 B.C., under the conduct of Evanthes, in Bruttium, about Zephyrium prom., whence their surname. III. *surnamed* Opuntii, a tribe of Leleges,

settled about Opus, in Phocis, whence their name. Their territory extended along Opuntius sin. from Cnemis to Halæ. IV. *surnamed* Ozolæ, "stinking Locrians," a colony from Eastern Locris, occupying Locris Prop., nicknamed from the fable that some of the streams in their territory, rising in Taphius m., under which Nessus, the centaur, was buried, were fetid with his blood; or, from the stench diffused by the burning in the district of the arrows of Hercules, dipped in the blood of Hydra. They were also, from their position with regard to the parent tribe, called Locri Zephyrii. *About Malandrino.* V. capital of the Locri Epizephyrii, Bruttium, on Locrensis sin., bet. Subsicivum and Altanum. Founded by Evanthes, the Locri-Ozolian or Epicnemidian, circa 710 B.C. Celebrated for its ruler, Zaleucus, the first who compiled a code of laws. *Pagliapoli.*

LOCRIS, a country of Græciæ. Peloponnesum, bounded N. by Doris, s. by Corinthiacus sin., w. by Ætolia, E. by Phocis. The country of the Locri Ozolæ.

LOD, i. q. Lydda Diospolis.

LODEBAR, a town of Gad, near Mahanaim. The dwelling-place of Mephibosheth.

LOGANA (Lohana) fl., a r. of Germania Magna, falling into the Rhine. *Lahn.*

LOGI, a people of Britannia Barbara, bet. the Cantæ and the Cornavii. *S.E. Sutherland and S. Caithness.*

LOGIA (Lugia) fl., a r. of the Darini, Hibern., falling into the sea N.W. of Novantum prom. *Lagan.*

LONCIUM, a town of the Ambidravi, Noricum, on Dravus fl., L., bet. Aguntum (18) and Julium Carnicum (22). *Luccau.*

LONDINIUM, capital of the Trinobantes, on Tamesis fl. A colonia (Augusta Trinobantum). *London.*

LONGANUS fl., a r. of Sicily, falling into the Tyrrhenian sea bet. Tyndaris and Mylæ. *Fiume di Castro Reale.*

LONGATICUM, a town of the Latovici, Pannonia, bet. Nauportus (6) and Ad Castra, at the source of Nauportus fl. *Logatez.*

LONGINIA, a village of Cilicia Camp., near Tarsus.

LONGONES, a maritime town of the Corsii, Sardinia, on Gallicum fretum, at Erebantium prom.

LONGOVICUM, a town of the Brigantes, s. of Moricambe æstuar.

LONGULA, a town of the Volsci, E. of Ardea.

LONGUM prom., a pr. of Sicily, s.E. of Syracuse. *Capo Lungo.*

LONGUM æstuarium, an æstuary of the Caledonii, Brit. w., falling into the sea at Malea ins. *Loch Linnhe.*

LOPADIUM, a Lower Age Greek town of Mysia, on Rhyndacus fl., below Apolloniatis lacus. *Lubad.*

LOPHIS fl., a stream of Bœotia, falling into Copais lac., w. of Haliartus.

LOPOSAGUM, a town of the Sequani, Maxima Sequanorum, on Dubis fl., R., bet. Velatodurum and Visontio. *Luxiol.*

LORACINA fl., a stream of Latium, near Astura, which the prætor, C. Lucretius, diverted into the grounds of his villa.

LORIUM, a town of Etruria, bet. Rome (12) and Alsium (10), on Via Aurelia. The death-place of Antoninus Pius. *Castel Guido.*

LORYMA, a port of Caria, in Ædimus sin., within Cynossema prom. E. *Porto Cavaliere* or *Aplotheka.*

LORNE, a town of Mygdonia, Mes., bet. Antoninopolis and Maride.

LOSA, a town of the Bercarates, Novem Populana, s. of Boii.

LOSODICA, a town of Rhætia, bet. Septemiaca (7) and Mediana (11). *Lustnau.*

LOSSONUS, Thess., i. q. Oloossoon.

LOTADOS, a town of the Ambilici, Noricum, 12 m. E. of Ragindum.

LOTEVA, Narbonensis, i. q. Forum Neronis.

LOTOPHAGI, "lotus-eaters," a people of Syrtis Reg., bet. Cynyphs fl. and Triton fl. Named from living upon the lotus.

LOTOPHAGORUM (Lotophagitis) ins., a name of Meninx ins., Byzac., from the inhabitants being lotus-eaters.

LOTUM, a town of the Caleti, Lugdunensis II., on the Sequana, bet. Juliobona w. and Rotomagus E.

LOXA fl., a r. of the Caledonii, falling into the Germ. oc. above Abona æstuarium. *Loth; Lossie.*

LUCA, a Teutanian city of Etruria, on Ausar fl., L. A colonia and municipium, 179 B.C. *Lucca.*

LUCANI, a tribe of Samnites, settled in Lucania.

LUCANIA, a region of Italy, separated from Apulia by Bradanus fl., from Campania by Silarus fl., from Bruttium s.w. by Laos fl., and s.E. by Crathis fl. Bounded w. by Inferum mare and E. by Tarentinus sin.

LUCERIA, a town of Daunia Apulia, 12 m. w. of Arpi. Built by Diomed, with a temple consecrated by him to Minerva. A colonia 314 B.C. Noted for its wool. *Lucera.*

LUCENSES, a tribe of Callæci, Tarraconensis, L. of Minius fl.

LUCENTUM (Lucentia), a town of the Contestani, Tarraconensis, on Illicitanus sin., bet. Tader fl. s. and Castrum Album. A colonia. *Lucante ; Alicant.*

LUCINA (Elethia), a town of Thebais, on the Nile, R., bet. Contra-Latopolis and Toum. Sacred to Elethia (Lucina).

LUCIPEA, a town of the Vettones, Lusitania, 20 m. N.E. of Augusta Emerita.

LUCRETILIS m., a hill of Sabinium, on Farfarus fl. *Monte Libretti.*

LUCRĪNUS lacus, a lake of Campania, at Baiæ, originally an inlet of the sea, but inclosed by a dyke a mile long, the work of Hercules. Noted for its oysters. The creation of an earthquake in 1538 now occupies its site. *Monte Nuovo.*

LUCRIS, a town of the Arevacæ, Tarraconensis. *Soria.*

LUCULLIANA, a town of Numidia, bet. Visalta and Salviana.

LUCUS, I. a r. of Liguria, falling into Ligusticus sin. at Lucus Bormanni. II. a town of the Marsi, on Lacus Fucinus s.w. Named from a sacred grove of Augitia, sister of Circe. *Luco.* III. (Ovetum), *surnamed* Asturum, of the Astures, Tarraconensis, s.w. of Noega. *Oviedo.* IV. *surnamed* Augusti, capital of the Lucenses, Tarraconensis, on Minius fl., L., above Salientes. A municipium. *Lugo.* V. of Narbonensis, bet. Vapincum and Ad Deam Vocontiorum. VI. *surnamed* Augusti, of the Vocontii, Viennensis, bet. Dea Vocontiorum N.N.W. and Vologatis S.E. *Luc.* VII. *surnamed* Bormanni, of the Ingauni, Liguria, at the mouth of Lucus fl., L., bet. Costa Balæna (16) and Albingaunum (16). VIII. *surnamed* Feroniæ, a grove of Feronia, Latium, 3 m. w. from Tarracina. In it was a fountain sacred to the goddess and a temple dedicated to her by some Lacedæmonian exiles, in which was a stone seat, on which deserving slaves received their freedom. IX. *surnamed* Feroniæ, a town of Etruria, erected around a temple of Feronia, s. of Vesidia fl. A colonia. *Pietra Santa.* X. *surnamed* Semnonum, a sacred forest of the Semnones, Germania. The locality of the general assemblies of the Suevic tribes. *Sonnewald and Finsterwald.*

LUDIA (Audia), a town of Arabia Petræa, under Hor m. w. The Eldaah of Genesis. *Eldij.*

LUENNA, a town of Noricum, 23 m. from Virunum. *Volkermarkt.*

LUENTIUM (Loventinum, Luentinum), a

town of the Demetæ, on Tuerobis fl.,
near its mouth. Supposed to have been
swallowed up by an earthquake and to
have occupied the site of lake Llyn Sava-
tan. By some, however, identified with
Llan-dewy-brevis.

LUGDUNENSIS (Gallia Celtica), a division of
Gaul, comprising Lugdunensis I. *Lyon-
nais, Bourgogne, Nivernois, and part of
Champagne.* II. *Normandie, Seine Infé-
rieure, &c.* III. *Touraine, Maine, &c.*
IV. *Isle de France, &c.*

LUGDUNUM, I. a town of the Convenæ,
Novem Populana, on the Garumna, L., towards its source. *St. Bertrand.* II. of
Germania, near the mouth of the N. issue
of the Rhine. *Leyden.* III. capital of
the Segusiani, Gaul, at the confluence of
Rhodanus and Arar ffl. A Gaulish town,
enlarged by Munatius Plancus, 42 B.C.
Burned A.D. 64; rebuilt by Nero. The
birth-place of Claudius. *Lyon.* IV. *surnamed* Clavatum, a town of the Veromandui, bet. Augusta Veromanduorum and
Durocortorum. *Laon.*

LUGEUS lacus, a lake of Pannonia Sup., on
the confines of Liburnia, s.w. of Emona,
near the source of Arsia fl. It becomes
empty in the summer months, and the
people then grow corn on it. *L. Zirich-
nitz.*

LUGI (Lygii), a people of Britannia Barbara,
on the E. coast, bet. the Cornavi N. and
the Meretæ s.

LUGIDUNUM, a town of the Lygii, Germ.,
N. of Stragona.

LUGIO (Lugionum), a town of Valeria-
Pannon., bet. Antiana (12) and Alta Ripa
(22). *Batta.*

LUGUBALLUM (Caer-Luel), a town of the
Brigantes, Brit., on Ituna fl., L., towards
its mouth. *Carlisle.*

LUMA, I. a town of Arabia Deserta, near
Sabe. A seat of the Leummim of Scripture. II. of Arabia Felix. III. a fortress
of Phrygia Magna, on Mæander fl.

LUMBERITA, a town of the Berones, Tarraconens., bet. Barbariana N. and Numantia s.

LUMO, a maritime town of the Intemelii,
Liguria, bet. Alpis Summa (6) and Albintemelium (10), on Via Aurelia.

LUNA, I. a town of the Apuani, Etruria, on
Macra fl., near its mouth. A municipium.
Noted for its marble (the Carrara), its
wine, and its large cheeses. *Luni.* II. of
the Segusiani, Lugdunensis I., on the
Arar, bet. Matisco and Assa Paulina.

LUNÆ m., I. m. of Libya Int., of uncertain
position. II. portus, the harbour of Luna,

Etruria. *Golfo di Spezzia.* III. prom.,
a pr. of Etruria, at Luna (N.W.). *C. Corvo.*
IV. of Lusitania, N. of Magnum Promontorium. *Cabo Corbociro.* V. silva, m.
of Germania Magna, on each side of
Marus fl. *Manhartsberg.*

LUNARIUM prom., a pr. of Tarraconensis, s.
bet. Iluro N.E. and Bætulo s.w. *Punta
de Maladayre.*

LUPATIA, I. a ridge of Apennines, separating
Messapia from the Peuceti. II. a town of
Messapia, under Lupatia m., s.w. of Blera.
Altamura.

LUPHARDUM, a town of the Bonochæmæ,
Germ., on Albis fl., s.E. of Calæpa.

LUPIA (Luppia), I. a r. of Germania Mag.,
rising in Teutoburgus Saltus, w. of the
springs of the Amisus, and after separating
the Bructeri Maj. from the Bructeri Min.,
falling into the Rhine above Castra Vetera.
Lippe. II. *prius* Sybaris, *postea* Lycium,
a town of Calabria, on Teuthras fl., bet.
Baletium (15) and Hydruntum (25). A
Rhodian colony. *Lecce.*

LUPODUNUM, a town of the Vangiones,
Germ., on Niter fl., R., near its junction
with the Rhine. Built by Valentinian.

LUPTA, a town of the Cherusci, Germ., w. of
Melibocus m.

LUQUIDO, a town of the Balari, Sardinia,
bet. Macopsisa and Olbia, with a port
called Portus Luquidonis. *Lugodor.*

LURA, a town of the Veromandui, Belgica
II., on the Isara, R., below Noviomagus.

LURIA fl., a r. of Bætica, falling into the
Atlantic bet. the Anas and Urius fl.

LURINUM, a town of Corsica, s.w. of Mariana.

LUSI, a town of Arcadia, N.W. of Clitor, at
the source of Aroanius fl. Almost extinct
in Pausanias' time.

LUSIA, a demus of Attica, of the tribe
Æncis.

LUSIAS fl., a r. of Bruttium, falling into
Tarentinus sin. s. of Crathis fl. Much
used by the Sybarites for their baths, on
account of the softness and purity of its
water. *Lucido.*

LUSITANI, the N.W. population of Lusitania,
bet. Durius and Tagus ffl.

LUSITANIA, a division, under Augustus, of
Hispania Ulterior, bet. the Anas and the
Durius, separated from Tarraconensis by a
line drawn from Sarabris N. to Ilucia s.
*Portugal (except Entre Douro y Minho,)
and Tras os Montes.*

LUSIUS fl., the name of Gortymus fl., towards
its source.

LUSONES, an early people of Tarraconensis,
on the Tagus, towards its source.

LUSONIANA, a town of Valeria, Pannoniæ, bet. Sardellaca (13) and Acincum (12).

LUSSONIUM, a town of Valeria, Pannon., on the Danube, bet. Intercisa and Annamatium. *Near Paks.*

LUTETIA, *postea* Parisii, capital of the Parisii, Lugdunensis IV., on an island in the Seine, above Anderitium. *La Cité at Paris.*

LUTEVA, a town of the Volcæ Arecomici, bet. Agatha and Segedunum. *Lodève.*

LUTIA, a town of the Lusones, Tarraconens., on Tagonius fl., R., 38 m. S.E. from Numantia.

LUTOSA fl., a r. of Gaul, flowing by Alesia. *Lose.*

LUTUDĀRUM, a town of the Brigantes, Britannia. *Leeds.*

LUXIA fl., a r. of Spain, bet. the Anas and the Bætis. *Odiel.*

LUXOVIUM, a town of the Sequani, w. of Magetobria. *Luxeuil.*

LUZ, the early name of Bethel.

LYCABETTUS m., a m. of Athens, s.w. of the Acropolis.

LYCADIUM (Cycladium) sin., a rivulet of Bosporus Thracius, Bithynia, N. of Nausimachium.

LYCÆA, a town of Arcadia, on Helisson fl., B. of Megalopolis, whither the inhabitants removed.

LYCÆUS, I. campus, a plain of Bithynia, on Lycus fl. II. m., a m. of Arcadia, overlooking Lycosura. The birth-place of Jupiter, according to Arcadian tradition, with a grove sacred to him, in which animals were said to cast no shadow. There was also a grove sacred to Pan, where the rites, called at Rome Lupercalia, were first celebrated. *Tetragi.*

LYCAON, a town of Phrygia, near Themisonium.

LYCAONIA, I. an early name of Arcadia, from Lycaon. II. a country of Asia Minor, bounded N. by Galatia, s. by Cilicia, w. by Phrygia and Pisidia, E. by Cappadocia. Originally settled by Solymi.

LYCAPSUS, a town of Lydia.

LYCASTUS, I. a town of Crete, bet. Miletus and Olus. Extinct in Strabo's time. *Lakida.* II. of Pontus, at the mouth of a cognominal river, 3 m. E. from Amisus.

LYCHNIDUS, capital of the Dassaretæ, Illyria, on the E. shore of Lychnitis palus, bet. Patræ (14) and Brygias (13), on the Egnatia Via. Founded by Cadmus. Nearly destroyed by an earthquake in the time of Justinian. *Near the Monastery of St. Naum.*

LYCHNITIS palus, I. *prius* Dassaretis, a lake of the Dassaretæ, Illyria, formed by the Drilon Niger, abounding in fish. *Lago d'Ochrida.* II. of Otene, Armen., N.E. of Artaxata. *Gaghamai.*

LYCIA, a country of Asia Minor, bounded N. by Phrygia, at Cadmus m., s. by the Mediterranean, w. by Caria, E. by Pisidia and Pamphylia. Settled by Termilæ or Tremilæ from Crete, under Sarpedon, brother of Minos, and then by Greeks, under Lycus, son of Pandion. The Lycians excelled as archers.

LYCIUM, Calabriæ, i. q. Lupia.

LYCOA, a village of Arcadia, at the foot of Mænalus m., near the junction of Alpheus and Sapheates ffl.

LYCONE m., a m. of Argolis, s.w. of Argos.

LYCŌPŌLIS, a town of Thebais, on the Nile, L., bet. Cusæ and Apollinis Minor Civitas. Named from the worship there of wolves. *Syouth.*

LYCOREA, "wolves' height," a town of Phocis, on Parnassus, N. of Cyparissus, whither the people of Delphi retreated in Deucalion's flood, guided by the howling of wolves, whence the name. *Lyakoura.*

LYCORMAS fl., the earlier name of Evenus fl., Ætoliæ.

LYCOSTHENE, a town of Lydia.

LYCOSURA, a town of Arcadia, under Lycæus m., w. of Megalopolis. Founded by Lycaon, and the royal residence of his successors. Deemed by Pausanias the oldest city in the world. *Agios Giorgios.*

LYCTUS (Lyttus), a town of Crete, under Dicte m., bet. Prasus and Chersonesus, 10 m. from Libycum mare. Upon its being destroyed by the Gnossians, the inhabitants removed first to Lampe and then to Diatonium.

LYCUNTES, a town of Arcadia, bet. Argiathæ and Scotane.

LYCURIA, a town of Arcadia, s.w. of Pheneus, at the source of Ladon fl. *Likori.*

LȲCUS, *prius* Zabatus, Zaba, I. a r. of Assyria, rising in Chiliocomum and falling into the Tigris below Larissa. Named by the Macedonians from the Lycus of Phrygia. *Zab Ala,* or *Greater Zab.* II. of Bithynia, falling into the Euxine 3 m. w. from Heraclea. III. of Cyprus, falling into the sea at Curium. IV. (Chersus), of Cilicia Campestris, falling into Issicus sin. N. of Issus. V. of Colchis, forming, with Glaucus fl., Apsarus fl. *Gorgoro.* VI. of Lydia, falling into Hyllus fl. VII. of Phœnicia, running into the Mediterranean near Berytus. *Nahel-Kelb.* VIII. of Phrygia Magna, rising in Cadmus m.,

Lycia, and falling into Mæander fl. towards Tripolis. In its course, it disappears for some time under ground. *Djok-Bounai.* IX. of Pontus, rising in Armenia Minor, w. of Aza, and falling into the Euxine s.w. of Amisus. *Yeshil-Ermak.* X. of Sarmatia As., falling into the Tanais above Tanais. XI. of Sarmatia E., falling into Palus Mæotis E. of Agaris fl. *Kalmius.*

LYDDA (Lud), *postea* Diospolis, a town of Judæa, bet. Joppa N.W. and Emmaus S.E. The scene of the cure of Æneas by St. Paul. *Lud.*

LYDIA, I. *prius* Mæonia, a country of Asia Minor, bounded N. by Mysia, at Hermus fl., s. by Caria, at Mæander fl., w. by Ionia, E. by Phrygia Magna. Peopled successively from Syria (from towards Babylon), and from Phœnicia, by Leleges, Caucones, and Pelasgi, and by Mœsi from Thrace and Thessaly. Under Crœsus, the kingdom extended from Halys fl. to the Ægean. Named from Lydus, son of Atys, or from Lud, son of Shem. II. a town of Cassiotis, Syriæ, E., on the Orontes, E. of Bacataili. *Schoghor.*

LYDIAS fl., a r. of Bottiæa, Macedonia, rising in Pellæus lacus and falling into Thermaicus sin. below Ichnæ. *Carismaik.*

LYGDAMUM, a town of Mysia.

LYGIES, i. q. Ligures.

LYGII (Lugii, Lugiones), a people of Germania Mag., bet. Vistula and Viadrus fll., s. of the Vindili, E. of Asciburgius m. Named from the close league subsisting among their various tribes.

LYGON, a town of Pisidia, w. of Caralitis pal. near the source of Lysis fl.

LYLE, a town of Arcadia.

LYMNÆUS lacus, a lake of Acarnania, below Lymnæa N.W. and Argos Amphilochum, 6 m. long. *Nizero.*

LYNCESTIS aqua, an acidulous spring bet. Heraclea Lyncestis and Beva, the waters of which were said to have an inebriating effect. *Eceisso Verbeni.*

LYNCEUS, I. a r. of Etruria, rising N.E. of Vetulonii and falling into the sea E. of Populonium. *Corina.* II. a lake of Etruria, formed by Lynceus fl. just above its mouth. *L. Caldano.*

LYNCUS (Lyncestis), the country of the Lyncestæ, Macedonia, on the borders of Illyria. Bounded N. by Deuriopus, s. by Orestis and Eordæa, w. by Dassaretia, E. by Bottiæa and Emathia.

LYNCUS, i. q. Heraclea Lyncestis.

LYPERUS m., a summit of Olympus in Bithynia.

LYNXAMA, a town of Meroe.

LYRBE (Lyrope), a town of Pamphylia, towards Etenna.

LYRCÆA (Lyrcæum), a town of Argolis, under Lyrcæus m., bet. Argos (7½) and Orneæ (7½).

LYRCÆUS m., a m. of Argolis, 10 m. N.W. of Argos.

LYRNATIA, a fortress of Lycia, on a cognominal peninsula.

LYRNAS, Pamphyliæ, i. q. Lyrnessus.

LYRNESSUS, I. a Syro-Phœnician town of Æolis Asiat., on Evenus fl., 10 m. s. from Adramyttium. The town of Bryseis, destroyed by Achilles. II. (Lyrneas), a maritime town of Pamphylia, s. of Attaleia. Founded by Cilicians of Troas. *Ernatia.* III. a name of Tenedos ins.

LYSIAS (Lysinia), a town of Phrygia Mag., on Lysis fl., E. of Themisonium. Founded by Alexander.

LYSIMACHIA, I. a town of Ætolia, s.w. of Trichonius lac., bet. Chalcis and Arsinoe. Built by Arsinoe, and named by her in honour of her first husband Lysimachus. II. a city of Chersonesus Thracia, on Melas sin. Founded by Lysimachus, and partly peopled from Cardia. It was restored by Antiochus, and again by Justinian, who named it Hexamilion, the isthmus at that point being six miles across.

LYSIMELIA, a lake or marsh formed by Anapus fl., Siciliæ, near its mouth.

LYSINOE (Lysinia), a town of Pisidia, N.E. of Cormasa, near Pisidicus lacus.

LYSIS fl., a r. of Pisidia, falling into Catarrhactes fl.

LYSTRA, a town of Lycaonia, 30 m. s. of Iconium, N.W. of Derbe. Noted in the history of St. Paul. *Khatoun Serai.*

LYTÆ, a town of Thessaly, near Tempe.

LYTARNIS prom., a pr. of Sarmatia, on Borealis Oceanus.

M.

MAAGRAMMUM, a city of Taprobane, under Galibi m., E. towards Procuri.

MAARSARES fl., i. q. Naarsares.

MACÆ, I. a tribe of Omanitæ, Arab., on Persicus sin. The Naumachæi of Pliny. II. a people of Africa Prop., on the s.w. coast of Syrtis Major, towards Cinyps fl.

MACALA, a town of Bruttium, 3 m. inland from the Ionian Sea, 15 m. N. from

Crotona. Founded by Philoctetes, who was worshipped there.

MACANITÆ, a people of Mauritania Ting., s. of Atlas Minor, bet. the Bacuates and the Herpeditani.

MACAREÆ, a town of Arcadia, on the left bank of Alpheus fl., 2½ m. s.w. from Megalopolis.

MACARIA, I. ins., an isl. of Egypt, in the Red Sea, N. of Pani ins. II. regio, a district of Messenia, on Pamisus fl., w. of Calamæ. III. (Nagidos), a town of Cyprus, 2½ m. E. of Ceronia.

MACARIÆ fons, the fountain of Macaria, daughter of Hercules, at Marathon, in Attica.

MACHARTA, a town of Mygdonia, Mesop., on Arzamo fl., bet. Ressaina and Nisibis.

MACCALA, a maritime town of the Adramitæ, Arab., bet. Cane and Sochor. *Maculla.*

MACCARÆ, a town of Phthiotis, in Thessaly, N. of Pharsalus.

MACCOLALINGÆ, a tribe of Calingæ, India, E. of the Ganges.

MACEDNI, the early name of the Macedones and of the Dores, in their original seat in Estiæotis, in Thessaly, under Pindus m.

MACEDNON, a district of Macedonia, near Pindus m. The original seat, especially, of the Macedones.

MACEDONES ASCHYLICÆ, i. q. Myso-Macedones.

MACEDONIA (Macetia), *prius* Emathia, a country of Europe, bounded N. by Mœsia, s. by Thessaly and the Ægean, w. by Illyria, and E. by Thrace. An original seat, with Thrace, of the Pelasgi or Tyrrheni. Established as a kingdom, according to some authors, by Caranus or Gavanus, descendant of Temenus, son of Hercules; but, according to Herodotus and Thucydides, by Perdiccas, another of the Temenidæ of Argos. The name, traditionally derived from Macedo, son of Jupiter or Osiris, at first designated only the district of Macednon, near Pindus m.

MACEDONIA ADJECTA, the portion of Macedonia and Thrace bet. Strymon fl. and Nestus fl. So called because added to the Macedonian territory by Philip, son of Amyntas.

MACELA prom., a pr. of Arabia Felix, at the entrance of Persicus sin.

MACELLA, a town of Sicily, s.E. of Segesta.

MACEPRACTA, a town of Babylonia, on the Euphrates, L., above Pirisabora.

MACEPRACTA (Maifarekin), a paved canal, communicating bet. the Euphrates and the Tigris, s. of Medius Murus.

MACESTUS (Magestus) fl., a r. of Mysia, rising in Abbaitis regio, and, after passing through Miletopolis palus, falling into Rhyndacus fl. below Lopadium. *Mikalick.*

MACETA prom., a pr. of Arabia, N. of Asaborum prom.

MACHELONES, a people of Colchis, on the Euxine, at first towards Mæotis, and, subsequently, removed s. towards the Macrones.

MACHORBÆ, a town of Arabia Felix, on Persicus sin., w. of Cuscan. *Regama,* or *Ramah Rums.*

MACHLYES, a people of Africa, contiguous to the Lotophagi.

MACI, a people of Bactria, bet. Caucasus Indicus and Oxus fl. *Maka.*

MACISTUS m., a summit of Lepetymnus m.

MACISTUS (Platanistus), a town of Triphylia in Elis, N.E. of Lepidæum. Built by the Caucones; with a temple of Hercules Macistius. *Mofkitza.*

MACNA, a town of the Nabathæi, in Arabia Petræa, s.E. of Ælana.

MACOLIUM, a town of the Iverni, Hibern., N.E. of Iuernis. *Near Kilbeggan.*

MACOMADES, I. a town of Byzacene, on Syrtis Min., bet. Thunæ (27) and Cella Picentina (26). A municipium. II. *surnamed* Psyllorum, a town of the Psylli, in Africa Propria, on Syrtis Maj., bet. Euphranta and Sur.

MACOPSISA, a town of the Æchilenenses, Sardinia, bet. Gurulis Nova and Luquido.

MACORABA, capital of the Macoritæ, Arab., N.E. of Zaaram Regia. *Mecca.*

MACORITÆ, a people of Arabia Felix, s. of the Salapeni.

MACPHA, a town of the Chatramotitæ, Arab., on Prion fl., N. of Abisama.

MACRA fl., I. a r. of Italy, rising in Balista m., and falling into Tyrrhenium mare at Luna. The boundary of Liguria and Etruria. *Magra.* II. ins., an isl. of Sarmatia Europ., on Carcinites sin.

MACRA COME, a town of the Ænianes, in Thessaly, N. of Sperchius fl., E. of Sperchiæ. *Macresi.*

MACRA STOA, the emporium of Athens, at Piræus.

MACRÆ PETRÆ, rocks N.W. of the Acropolis of Athens, where was a grotto sacred to Apollo and Pan.

MACRI, I. a town of Mauritania Cæsar., bet. Cellæ and Zabi. II. the people occupying Macri Campi, in Italy. III. campi, the plain bet. Regium Lepidi and Sicimina and Papinius montes. A great cattle fair was held here every year. IV. ins., an isl. of Lycia, on Glaucus sin. *Makri.*

MACRIS, "long," I. the early name of Eubœa ins., of Helena ins., of Icarus ins., of Aspis ins., of Chios. II. an isl. of Ionia, off Myonnesus prom.; with warm springs.

MACROBII, "long livers," a people of Æthiopia, on the s. coast of Mare Erythræum, E. of the Avalitæ.

MACROCEPHALI, Colch., i. q. Macrones.

MACROCREMMI m., m. towards the N.W. coast of the Euxine.

MACRONES (Macrocephali, Colchi), a people of Pontus, on the coast, bet. the Mosynœci and the Bechires, and in the m. above Trapezus. They afterwards became identified with the Sauni. They were Colchian immigrants, and practised circumcision.

MACRONTEICHOS, "long wall," I. a wall extending from Selymbria, in Thrace, to the Euxine; built by Miltiades. II. the wall built across the isthmus of Chersonesus Thracia, by Dercyllidas, the Lacedæmonian.

MACROPAGONES, a people of Sarmatia, towards the N.E. coast of the Euxine.

MACRUM prom., Siciliæ, i. q. Plemmyrium.

MACTIADUM, i. q. Mattium.

MACTORIUM, a town of Sicily, N. of Gela. *Mazzarino.*

MACYNIA (Macynium), a town of Ætolia, on the E. slope of Taphiassus m.

MADAI, the scriptural name of s. Media.

MADAIN SABATH, a town of Babylonia, bet. Besuchis and Seleucia.

MADASARA, *rectiùs* Vadasara, a district of Arabia Felix, s. of Thumna. *Wady Dowaser.*

MADASSUMA, a town of Byzacene, bet. Septimunicia and Nora.

MADAURA, the birth-place of Apuleius, in Numidia, i. q. Ad Medera.

MADETHUBADUS m., a N.E. continuation of Atlas Maj. m., separating central Mauritania from Gætulia.

MADIUS fl., a r. of Pontus, towards Petra.

MADOCE, Arabiæ, i. q. Arabiæ Felicis Emporium.

MADUS, a town of the Cantii, Brit., above Durobrivæ. *Maidstone.*

MADYTUS, a town of Chersonesus Thracia, on the Hellespont, N. of Cynossema. *Maito.*

MÆANDER fl., a r. of Asia Min., rising in Aulocrene m., near Celænæ, and, after separating Ionia and Lydia from Caria, falling into Ionium mare below Miletus. Remarkable for the sinuosity of its course, and for its excessive deposits of mud. *Mendere.*

MÆANDRIA, a fortress of Chaonia.

MÆANDRIUS campus, *postea* Mænomenus campus, the plain of the Mæander, on the R. bank of that river, towards its source. By Herodotus and Pliny stated to have been at first a bay of Ionium mare, reaching to Magnesia ad Mæandrum.

MÆANDRUS m., m. of India e. Gangem, on the E. coast of Gangeticus sin., and extending N.E. to Bepurrus m.

MÆATÆ, a general name of the tribes bet. Hadriani Vallum and Severi Vallum. The predecessors of the Picts.

MÆCHÆRUS, a city of Ammonitis, towards the Dead sea. Destroyed by Gabinius; restored by Herod. The death-place of John the Baptist.

MÆDI (Mædobithyni), a people of Thrace, bounded N. by the Dentheletæ, s. by the Odomanti, w. by Strymon lacus, E. by the Bessi.

MÆDICA, the country of the Mædi, in Thrace.

MÆNALIA regio, a plain of Arcadia, under Mænalus m.

MÆNALUS, I. a town of Arcadia, near Mænalus m.; with a temple of Minerva. The inhabitants removed to Megalopolis. II. m., a m. overlooking a cognominal plain, in Arcadia, N.E. of Megalopolis, 2 m. from Peræthia. Sacred to Pan, who much frequented it. *Roino.*

MÆNARIA ins., I. an isl. of Balearis Maj., off Palma. II. of Etruria, near Urgo ins. *Meloria.*

MÆNIA MILESIORUM, a wall bet. Buticus lacus and the sea, E. of Canopus.

MÆNŎBA fl., I. a r. of Bætica, falling into the Mediterranean at Mænoba. *Velez.* II. (Mænaca), a town of the Turtuli, Bætica, at the mouth of Mænoba fl., bet. Malaca w. (12) and Caviclum E. *Velez Malaga.*

MÆNOSGADA, a town of the Hermunduri, Germ., near Mænus fl., R.

MÆONES, probably a Phœnician people, the primitive colonizers of Mæonia or Lydia.

MÆONIA, I. the early name of Lydia, from Manes, one of its kings. II. a town of Lydia, in Catacecaumene regio.

MÆOTÆ (Mæotici), a people of Sarmatia, on the E. coast of Mæotis palus, to which they gave name.

MÆOTIS palus, a bay of the Euxine, at its N.E. angle, approached by Cimmerius Bosporus. *Sea of Azof; Assow More.*

MÆPHA, capital of the Mæpharitæ, Arabiæ. *Meqna.*

MÆPHARITÆ, a people of Arabia Felix, N. of the Adramitæ. *In Wady Mayfah.*

MÆRA, a village of Arcadia, N. of Mantinea.

MÆRAS, a portion of Argus campus, in Arcadia.

MÆSOLIA, I. a maritime district of India i. Gangem, about the mouth of Tyndis fl. Noted for its diamond-mines. II. a town of India i. Gangem, near the mouth of Mæsolus fl., L.

MÆSOLUS fl., a r. of India, rising in Bettigus m., and falling into Indicum mare bet. Tynna fl. and Tyndis fl. *Krishnah.*

MAETHATH, a maritime town of Arabia Felix, w. of the mouth of Prion fl.

MÆTONIUM, a town of Sarmatia, on or near the Euxine, towards Dacia. *Near Halitsch.*

MAGABA m., *postea* Modiacus, a m. of Galatia, bet. Ancyra and Halys fl.

MAGALASSUS (Mogarissus), a town of Cappadocia, on Halys fl., above Marandara.

MAGDALA (Migdol), a town of Galilæa, on Tiberias lac. w., bet. Capernaum N. and Tiberias s. The birth-place of Mary Magdalene.

MAGDOLUM (Magdalum, Migdol), a town of Lower Egypt, s. of Pelusium (12). *Ras el Moyeh.*

MAGELLI, I. a people under Alpes Cottiæ, E. towards the Vibelli. *Val de St. Martin.* II. *postea* Macellum, Magedellum, their town. *Magers, near Prali.*

MAGETOBRIGA, a town of the Sequani, Maxima Sequanorum, on Arar fl., N.W. of Visontio. *Morgte de Broie.*

MAGIA, a town of Rhætia, 16 m. N. from Curia. *Near Mayenfeld.*

MAGI, a town of the Brigantes, Brit., on Dunum fl., bet. Vinovium and Cataractorium.

MAGIOVINTUM, a town of the Catavellauni, Brit., bet. Lactodurum and Verolamium. *Fenny Stratford.*

MAGITÆ, a people of Arabia Felix, N. of the Salapeni.

MAGLONA, a town of the Ordovices, Brit., on Stucia fl., L.

MAGNA, I. a town of the Brigantes, Brit., on Hadriani murus, s. bet. Æsica and Amboglanna. *Carvoran.* II. of the Silures, Brit., N.W. of Uriconium. *Kentchester.*

MAGNA GRÆCIA, the name given to the maritime portion of S. Italy, from the number of Greek colonies established there.

MAGNANA, a town of the Macrones, in Pontus, bet. Trapezus (20) and Giheninica (10). *Machka.*

MAGNATA, capital of the Magnatæ, Hibern., N. of Regia. *Castlebar.*

MAGNATÆ, a people of Hibernia w., bet. the Erdini N. and the Autiri s. *Mayo.*

MAGNESIA, I. the territory of Philoctetes and Eurypylus, in Thessaly, along the Ægean, from Peneus fl. to Magnesiæ prom., and bounded inland by Ossa and Pelion m. II. a city of Lydia, near Mæander fl., s.E. of Ephesus. Founded by a Magnesian colony from near Dotium, in Thessaly, that afterwards removed to the neighbouring village of Leucophrys. The territory, noted for its wine, figs, and cucumbers, was assigned to Themistocles, who died here, to furnish his table with bread. Here was a temple of Dindymene (Cybele). *Inek-Bazar.* III. a town of Magnesia, in Thessaly, towards Methone. IV. a city of Lydia, on Hermus fl., L., near Sipylus m. A colony of Magnesians, from Thessaly. Memorable for the defeat of Antiochus by the Scipios. *Manissa.*

MAGNESIUM prom., a headland of Thessaly, the s.E. extremity of Magnesia, s. of Sepias prom. *Hagios Giorgios.*

MANETES, the people of Magnesia, in Thessaly; a primitive race.

MAGNOPOLIS (Megalopolis), i. q. Eupatoria in Pontus.

MAGNUM OSTIUM, a mouth of the Ganges, bet. Cambys ost. and Chambericum ost.

MAGNUM LITTUS, the coast of Arabia Felix, on Erythræum mare, bet. Abisama and Parvum littus.

MAGNUM PROM., I. the s.E. extremity of Aurea Chersones. *Point Romania.* II. of Mauritania Cæsar., N.W., near Ad Fratres. *Ras Houneine; Cabo Hone.* III. (Olisipense), of Lusitania, at the mouth, R., of the Tagus, N.W. of Olisipo. The westernmost point of the peninsula. *Cabo da Roca.*

MAGNUS portus, I. a haven of the Mediterranean, in Bætica, bet. Abdera and Charidemi prom. *Golfo de Almeria.* II. a haven of the Atlantic, in Callæcia, bet. Artabrum prom. and Caranicum. III. a harbour of the Regni, N.E. of Vectis ins. *Portsmouth Harbour.* IV. (Cirnaba) sin., a bay of Eous oceanus, at Aspithra. *Gulf of Siam.*

MAGO, I. a town of Balearis Minor, on the s.E. coast. Built by Mago. *Port Mahon.* II. fl., a r. of Prasiaca regio, Indiæ, falling into the Ganges, L., above its junction with Diamuna fl. *Ramgonga.*

MAGON ins., an isl. of the Colobi, in the Red sea, N. of Sabæ.

MAGORUM, I. portus, a city of the Themi, Arabiæ, on Magorum sin. *Magas.* II.

sin., a bay of Persicus sin., N. of Capeus sin. *Bahr al Magas.*

MAGRADA fl., a r. of Tarraconensis, falling into Cantabricum mare, E. of Aturia fl. *Vidasoa.*

MAGRI, a town of Numidia, bet. Fons Potamianus and Rustici.

MAGULABA, Arabiæ, i. q. Magusa.

MAGUR, a town of the Arvarni, Ind., W. of Sabura.

MAGUSA (Magulaba), a town of the Cassanitæ, Arabiæ, under Cassanites m., N.E. of Tabala. *Korn el Maghsal.*

MAGUZA (Thillada, Mirrhada?), a town of Mesopotamia, on the Euphrates, bet. Galabatha and Basilia. *Makesin.*

MAGYDUS (Masythus, Mygdala), a maritime town of Pamphylia, E. of Attalia. *Laara.*

MAHANAIM ("hosts"), a town of Gad, on Jabbok fl., L., bet. Pniel and Succoth, where the two hosts of angels appeared in a vision to Jacob. It was the capital of Ishbosheth, and the retreat of David during the rebellion of Absalom.

MAHATANZUR, a town of Gætulia, on Tritonis palus, bet. Thimesegiri turres and Puteus.

MAIS (Mophis) fl., a r. of India i. Gangem, falling into Barygazenus sin. *Mahi.*

MAJA ins., one of the Scopelites ins. of Cyrenaicæ.

MAJORCA, the larger of the Baleares ins., Tarraconensis. *Majorca.*

MAJAMAS (Portus Gazæus), the port of Gaza, Judæa, 6 m. from its metropolis. Enlarged by Constantius, and named by him Constantia.

MAJAS, a town of the Venosti, Rhæt., on Athesis fl., L., bet. Teriolis and Præsidium Tiberii. *Merano.*

MAJIA, a town of the Rugusci, Rhæt., on the Rhine, bet. Curia and Clunia. *Meyenfeld?*

MAKKEDAH, a royal city of the Canaanites, in Judah, 8 m. E. of Eleutheropolis. In the vicinity is a singular cavern, where the five kings hid from Joshua.

MALA, a town of Colchis, on Phasis fl., R., above Æa.

MALĂCA fl., I. a r. of Bætica, falling into the Mediterranean at Malaca. *Guadalmedina.* II. a town of the Turtetani, Bætica, bet. Suel s. and Mænoba E., at the mouth, L., of Malaca fl. *Malaga.* III. Lucaniæ, i. q. Macala.

MALÆA, a village of Arcadia, on the confines of Laconia, the inhabitants of which removed to Megalopolis.

MALACI COLON. prom., a pr. of Aurea Chersonesus, W., at the N. extremity of Perimulicus sin.

MALÆTAS fl., a r. of Arcadia, near Methydrium, falling into Gortynius fl.

MALAMANTUS fl., a r. of India, falling into the Cophen.

MALANA prom., I. a pr. of Gedrosia, on Indicum mare, bet. Bagisara and Cocala. II. a port of the Oritæ, Gedrosia, at Malana prom. *Malan.*

MALANGA, a maritime town of India i. Gangem, E., bet. Maliarpha and Tynna fl. *Madras.*

MALANGITÆ, a people of Arabia Felix, bet. Zames m. and the Uadeni. *Beni Lam.*

MALAO, a town of the Macrobii, Æthiop., on Erythræum mare, W. of Mundu. *Barbara.*

MALATHA, a town of Judæa, S. of Hebron.

MALCECA, a maritime town of the Celtici, Lusitania, E. of Cetobriga.

MALE, I. a district of India i. Gangem, W., towards Calliana. II. a town of Colchis, i. q. Æa.

MALEA m., I. m. of Taprobane, s. II. prom., the S.E. extremity of Laconia. Noted for its dangerous navigation. *C. Malio, or C. Sant' Angelo.* III. the S.E. extremity of Lesbos ins. IV. a town of the Celtiberi, Tarraconensis, near the Iberus, above Ælia castra.

MALEAS ins., an isl. of Britain, off Longum æstuarium. *Mull.*

MALEANA, a town of Mauritania Cæsariensis, bet. Tigava castra and Suffasar (15).

MALENE, a village of Æolis Asiat., near Atarneus.

MALETUM, a fortress of the Euganei, in Gall. Transp. *Maleto.*

MALEUM prom., a pr. of India, at Barygazenus sin.

MALEUS m., I. m. of the Suari, Indiæ. II. ins., one of the Ebudæ ins., Britanniæ.

MALEVENTUM, the early name of Beneventum.

MALI (Malichæ), a people of Arabia Felix, s. of Jathrippa. *About Malai.*

MALIA, I. a maritime town of Lesbos, on the E. coast, near Mitylene. II. the early capital of Maliensis, in Thessaly, of uncertain position. III. a town of Tarraconensis, near Numantia. IV. prom., the s. extremity of Lesbos ins.

MALIACUS (Meliacus, Melis, Lamiacus, Ænianum) sin., a gulf of the Ægean, washing the coasts of Thessaly, Phocis, and Eubœa. *G. d Zeitoun.*

MALIANA, a town of Mauritania Cæsar., on Chinalaph fl., R., above Tigava.

MALIARPHA, a maritime town of India i. Gangem, E., bet. Sabura and Malanga. *Maliapur.*

MALICHUS ins., islands of Arabia Felix, on the Red sea, bet. Sacatia and Musa. *Sokar.*

MALIENSIS (Meliensis), a district of Thessaly, on the borders of Locris, s. of Phthiotis and Dolopia, E. of Æniania; the country of the Malienses; the territory of Protesilaus.

MALISSA, a town of Corsica, N.W. of Rubra.

MALLABA, a town of the Themi, Arabia, on Persicus sin., s. of Chersonesus prom.

MALLÆA, a town of Perrhæbia, in Thessaly, bet. Mylæ and Azorus, w. of Titaresius fl., whither Chiron the centaur withdrew when he was driven from Pelion m.

MALLI (Mali), a people of India, on Hydaspes fl., towards its confluence with Hydraotes fl.

MALLORUM metropolis, capital of the Malli, Indiæ, on Hydraotes fl., above its junction with Hydaspes fl. It was at the siege of this place that Alexander so endangered his life. *Moultan.*

MALLUS fl., I. a r. of Arcadia, falling into Alpheus fl. towards Phædria. II. a town of Cilicia Campestris, on Pyramus fl., near its mouth. Founded by the soothsayers Amphilochus and Mopsus. *Malo.* III. of Troas, bet. Palæscepsis and Troja.

MALOTHA, a town of Arabia Felix, bet. Serrain and Nagara. *Tabala.*

MALUA (Mulva, Malvana) fl., a r. of Mauritania Cæsar., falling into the sea E. of Mulucath fl. *Mulul?*

MALUM, a town of Cyprus, near Citium. Destroyed by Ptolemy.

MAMALA, a town of the Alilæi, on the Red sea, bet. Ambe (23 geog. m.) and Thebæ. *Haly.*

MAMERTINA, the early name of Messana, in Sicily.

MAMERTINI, an early people of Sicily, about Messana. Named from the god Mamers.

MAMERTIUM, an Oscan town of Bruttium, in Sila Silva, N.E. of Rhegium. Sacred to Mamers (Mars). *Oppido.*

MAMMA, Byzacene, i. q. Byzacium.

MAMMIDA, a town of Persis Prop., N.W. of Pasargada.

MAMORTHA, the early name of Sichem.

MAMPSARUS m., m. of Numidia and Byzacene, E. of Aurasius m.

MAMRE (Mambre, Ogyta? Terebinthus?) vallis, the plain of Hebron, wherein was the sacred grove called the oak of Mamre. The seat of superstitions which Constantine the Great abolished. Hebron itself appears to have been called Mamre.

MAMUGA (Mammisca), a town of Phœnicia, 1 m. w. from Laodicea.

MANA (Mandas) fl., a r. of India i. Gangem, falling into Gangeticus sin. S.E. of Callingum prom. *Mahanuddy.*

MANACA, a town of Bætica, bet. Carteja and Malaca. Extinct in Strabo's time.

MANADA fl., a r. of India, falling into the sea, 6 geog. m. N. from Canagara.

MANAMBIS regia, a town of Arabia Felix, s. of Labecia. *Ibu Main.*

MANANGE, a town of Byzacene, bet. Uzappa and Aggar.

MANARMANIS portus, a port of the Frisii, Germ., at the mouth, R., of Unsingis fl. *Groningen?*

MANASSEH, a tribe of Israel, occupying districts on both sides the Jordan. The w. half-tribe was bounded N. by Asser at Jokniam, s. by Ephraim at Kana fl., w. by the Mediterranean, E. by Issachar at Thibez. The E. half-tribe was bounded N. by Cœle-Syria, s. by Gad, s. of Argob, E. by Arabia Deserta, w. by the Jordan.

MANCHANE, a town of Mesopotamia, on the Tigris, bet. Cænæ and Gibrata.

MANCUNIUM, a town of the Sentantii, Brit., bet. Coccium and Condate. *Manchester.*

MANDAETH, a town of the Adulitæ, on the Red sea, s. of Antiochi Solen.

MANDAGARSI, a port of the Mardi, Med., on the Caspian, w. of Charinda fl.

MANDAGORA, a town of Limyrica, Ind., S.E. of Aramagara. *Bassain.*

MANDALÆ, a people of India i. Gangem, on the Ganges, towards its mouth.

MANDANE, Cilicia, i. q. Myanda.

MANDARÆ, a tribe of Emathians, in Macedonia, about Cyrius.

MANDAS fl., Indiæ, i. q. Mana.

MANDELA, a village of Sabinium, on Digentia fl. The locality of Horace's Sabine farm. *Bardela.*

MANDOBRIGA, a town of the Celtici, Lusitania, bet. Norba Cæsarea, N.E., and Medobriga.

MANDRAHIPPI ("stall"), a town of Abrettene, in Mysia, on Lycus fl. Here Paris was nursed. *Mandrakora.*

MANDRUENI, a people of Bactriana, near the Oxus.

MANDRUM, capital of the Mandrueni Bactriana.

MANDRUFNUM (Mandropolis), a town of Pisidia, near Caralitis lac.

MANDRUS m., a southern ridge of Atlas m. in Western Libya.

MANDUBII, a people of Lugdunensis I., s. of the Vadicasses, w. of the Lingones. *In Auxois.*

MANDUESSEDUM, a town of the Cornavii, Brit. Rom., s.e. of Etocetum. *Mancetter.*

MANDURIA, a town of the Salentini, in Japygia, bet. Neretum (29) and Tarentum (24). The death-place of Archidamus of Sparta. Near it was a singular well, the water of which always retained the same level, whatever quantity was added to or taken from it. *Mandura.*

MANEGORDIUM, a town of the Tectosages, in Galatia, bet. Minizus (28) and Ancyra (24).

MANESIUM, a town of Phrygia.

MANGARUD. *Vide* Melinda.

MANIÆ ("mad"), a place in Arcadia, s. of Megalopolis, where Orestes' madness first displayed itself.

MANICELUM, a town of the Langenses, Liguria. *Manicelo.*

MANII, a tribe of Dalmatæ, in Illyria.

MANIMI, a tribe of Lygii, Germania.

MANIOLÆ ins., isl. of India e. Gangem, w. of Agatho Dæmon ins. *The Philippines.*

MANITÆ, a people of Arabia Felix, s. of the Salapeni, e. of Jathrippa. *Beni Mezeyne.*

MANLIANA (Manilia), a maritime town of Etruria, on Via Aurelia, bet. Salebro (9) and Aquæ Populoniæ (9). *Pienza.*

MANLIANUS saltus, a forest of the Lobetani, Tarraconensis, under Idubeda m., s.w.

MANNARITIUM, a town of Germania I., 15 m. from Trajectum. *Maurik.*

MANORIS, a town of Bithynia, 20 m. e. from Claudiopolis.

MANSA, a town of Narbonensis, near the mouth of the Rhone. *Massillargues.*

MANTALA, a town of the Centrones, Alpes Penninæ, on Isara fl., R., bet. Lemincum and Ad Publicanos.

MANTELUS, a town of Phrygia.

MANTHUREA, a village of Arcadia, near Tegea.

MANTHURICUS campus, the district about Manthurea, in Arcadia.

MANTIANA palus, i. q. Arsissa.

MANTINEA, capital of Arcadia, on Ophis fl., at the foot of Artemisius m., w. of Argos. Founded by Mantineus, son of Lycaon. Celebrated for the death-battle of Epaminondas, 363 B.C. The name of Mantinea was changed to that of Antigonea by Antigonus Doson, but restored by Hadrian.

At Mantinea were the statues of Juno, Minerva, and Hebe, by Praxiteles; the tomb of Arcas, and the temple of Antinous, favourite of Hadrian, in whose honour annual games were celebrated. *Goritza.*

MANTINIUM, a town of Paphlagonia.

MANTINORUM oppid., a maritime town of Corsica, e., bet. Clunium and Mariana. *Bastia.*

MANTITUR, a town of Pandionis reg., Ind., N.E. of Bambala.

MANTREI, a people of Sarmatia Asiatica.

MANTUA, I. a city of the Carpetani, Tarraconensis, near the Tagus, s.w. of Complutum. *Mondejar.* II. of Gallia Transpad., on an isl. of Mincius fl., bet. Bedriacum and Verona, on Via Posthumia. In the time of the Etruscans, the capital of Etruria Transpadana. Named from Manto, daughter of Tiresias, or from Mantus, the Etruscan Pluto. Its territory was distributed by Augustus among his veterans. *Mantova; Mantua.*

MANURRHOA, a town of Cyrrhestica, on the Euphrates, bet. Serrhæ and Ceciliana.

MAOCOSMOS (Meliopolis, Maoscopus, Nascus, Jaîo), a town of Arabia Felix, s. of Mariaba. *Jemama.*

MAOGAMALCHA (Besuchis), a town of Messene, Babyl., w. of Ctesiphon (12).

MAON, a town of Judah, bet. Carmel, N.N.W. and Arad s.

MAPHARITÆ, I. a people of Arabia Felix, towards Arabicus sin., w. of Musa. II. a tribe of Homeritæ, Arabiæ, towards Cane emporium. *About Wady Mayfah.*

MAPPURA, a town of Mæsolia, Indiæ, N. of Calliga.

MAPSA (Mibsa), a town of Arabia Petræa, on the borders of Palestine. The seat of the descendants of Mibsam.

MARABINA, a town of Cyrenaica, s.e. of Drepanum prom.

MARABIUS fl., a r. falling into Mæotis palus, s.e. of Paniardis.

MARACANDA, capital of Sogdiana, on Polytimetus fl., L., N. of Alexandria Oxiana. *Samarcand.*

MARACODRA, a town of the Orsipi, Bactriana, s.w. of Alexandria.

MARACCA, a town of Phœnicia, 16 m. N. from Antaradus. *Merakieh.*

MARALIANI, a people of Sogdiana.

MARANDARA, a town of Morimene, Cappadocia, on Halys fl., bet. Armaxa (28) and Scanatus (38).

MARANITÆ, a people of Arabia, on Ælanites sin., w. The progenitors of a tribe of the same name, called also Anaritæ,

Epimaranitæ, and Ramanitæ, on Persicus sin., bet. Canis fl. and Asaborum prom.

MARANTHIS, a town of Cyrenaica, S.E. of Cocynthion.

MARARMANUS æstuar., the mouth of Viadrus fl.

MARASIA, a town of Cilicia. *Marash.*

MARATA (Marah), a town of the Themi, Arabiæ, under Zames m., N.W. *Ramah.*

MARATHA, a village of Arcadia, bet. Buphagium and Gortys.

MARATHE ins., an isl. on the S.E. coast of Zacynthus ins. *Marathonisi.*

MARATHESIUM, a town of Ionia, bet. Ephesus and Magnesia.

MARATHON, a demus of Attica, of the tribe Leontis, on the Ægean, 20 m. N.E. of Athens. Famous for the victory of the Athenians over the Persians 490 B.C., and for the Marathonian bull slain by Perseus. *Marathona.*

MARATHUS, I. Phœniciæ, i. q. Arvad. II. a town of Phocis, on the coast bet. Medeon and Bulis. *Metochi.*

MARATHUSA, a town of Crete.

MARATHUSSA ins., an isl. of Ionia, in Hermius sin., opposite Clazomenæ.

MARAZANÆ, a town of Byzacene, bet. Aqua Regia (15) and Sufes (28).

MARCADA (Carmada), a town of Melitene, in Cappadocia.

MARCÆUM m., a N. ridge of Ida m., E. of Abydos.

MARCI, a port of the Morini, N.E. of Portus Superior.

MARCIA, a town of the Turtetani, Bætica, bet. Hiempa N.W. and Urso S.E. A colonia.

MARCIANA (Eremus Helvetiæ) silva, a portion of Hercynia silva, Germ., bet. the Rhine and the sources of the Danube. *Schwartzwald.*

MARCIANŎPŎLIS, I. a town of Caria. II. of the Crobyzi, Mœs., bet. Palmata and Pannisus, w. of Odessus. Named from Trajan's sister. *Eski Stamboul; Prithlara; Marcenopoli.*

MARCILIANA, a town of Lucania, on Silanus fl., bet. Calor fl. and Cæsariana (14), on Via Aquilia. *Sala.*

MARCINA, a Tyrrhenian town of the Picentini, Campania, on Pæstanus sin., w. of Salernum. *Vietri.*

MARCODAVA, a town of the Burideenses, Dac., on Marisus fl., L., bet. Salinum (12) and Brucla (12). *Mirizlo.*

MARCODURUM, a town of the Ubii, Germania II., N.W. of Tolbiacum. *Duren.*

MARCOMAGUS, a town of the Ubii, Germania II., bet. Tolbiacum and Icorigium. *Markmagen.*

MARCOMANNI, "men of the marches or confines," a people of Germania Mag., who flying, under their king Marobodunus, from the Romans, from about the springs of the Danube, expelled the Boii from Bojohemum, and occupied that country.

MARDI, I. a people of Armenia Maj., on the E. shore of Arsissa lac., N. of Caspius m. *Mardistan.* II. of Persis Prop., s. of the Messabatæ.

MARDULA fl., a r. of Pontus, towards Athenæ.

MARDUS fl., i. q. Amardus.

MARDYENI, a people of Sogdiana, E. of Sogdii m., on the confines of Bactria.

MAREIA, I. palus, i. q. Mareotis. II. (Palæmareia), a town of Lower Egypt, on Mareotis (Mareia) lac., s. bet. Taposiris and Apis.

MARE MORTUUM, Palestinæ, i. q. Asphaltites lacus.

MAREONIS, a town of the Suardones, Germ., on Codanus sin., at the mouth, L., of Treva fl., w. of Laciburgium.

MAREOTIS (Mareia, Arapotes) lac., a lake of Lower Egypt, at Alexandria s., in breadth 150 stad., in length 300. It communicated by numerous cuts with the Nile. The Alexandrians had a port on it richer than their port on the Mediterranean. The adjacent district was noted for its wine.

MARES, a tribe of Mosynœci, in Pontus.

MARESNAH, a town of Judah, Judæa, 2 m. s. from Eleutheropolis. Fortified by Rehoboam; restored by Gabinius. The residence of the prophet Micah.

MAREURA, a town of Argentea regio, Indiæ, on Dorius fl., R., S.E. of Berabonna.

MARGÆA, ELID, i. q. Margana.

MARGALA (Margalæ, Elid), i. q. Margana.

MARGANA, (Margæa, Margalæ, Margala), I. a town of Pisatis, in Elis, on Alpheus fl., R., E. of Olympia. II. a port of Taprobane, w. bet. Anarismundi prom. and Modulla.

MARGASI, a people of Atropatene, Med., N.W., on the s. shore of Spauta lac.

MARGASTANA ins., an isl. of Persis, over against the mouth of Cataderbis fl.

MARGIANA, a country of Asia, bounded N. by Sogdiana at Oxus fl., s. by Aria and Parthia at Sariphi m. and Mosdoranus m., w. by Hyrcania at Labuta m., E. by Bactriana w. of Zariaspes fl. Noted for its grapes. *A portion of Khorasan; Marghush.*

MARGIANE, a district of Media-Atropatene, on its w. border.

MARGIDUNUM, a town of the Coritani, Brit.,

bet. Ad Pontem and Verometum (13). *Near Bridgeford.*

MARGIUM, the early name of Apollonia in Phrygia Magna.

MARGASUS (Magarsa, Malchos), a town of Cilicia, near the mouth of Pyramus fl.

MARGUS fl., I. a r. of Margiana, rising in Paropamisus m., w. of Maracodra, and falling into Oxus fl. N.W. of Alexandria Marg. *Murghab; Meru-rud.* II. of Mœsia Sup., rising in Scordus m. s.w. of Ulpiana, and falling into the Danube at Margus. *Morawa.* III. a town of the Triballi, Mœs., on the Danube, at the mouth, L., of Margus fl., bet. Aureus mons and Viminacium. The locality of the defeat of Carinus by Diocletian. *Pobritzar.*

MARIABA, "metropolis," a town of the Colingæi, Arabiæ, bet. Zames m. and Muranimal. *Mareb.*

MARIABA (Baramalcum, Maruba, Baraba, Taraba), a town of the Sabæi, Arabiæ, E. of Tamacus. *Taraba.*

MARIAMA, Arabiæ, i. q. Mariaba.

MARIAMNE, I. a town of Phœnicia, w. of Emesa. *Chesn al Akrad.* II. of Syria, near Damascus.

MARIANA, a city of Corsica E., at the mouth of Tavola fl., bet. Mantinorum oppid. and Ara Tutelæ. A colonia of Marius. *At Stagno di Biguglia.*

MARIANUM, I. a town of the Oretani, Tarraconensis, N.E. of Oretum. II. prom., a pr. of Corsica, s.w. below Pitanus fl. *Capo di Casa Barbarica.*

MARIANUS (Montes Ariani) m., m. of Spain, separating Bæturia N. from Bætica s. *Sierra Morena.* II. (Ariorum), of Bætica and Tarraconensis, parallel with the Bætis N. *Sierra Morena.* III. a town of Corsica, s.w. at Marianum prom.

MARICI, a people of Liguria, contiguous to the Lævi. *About Marengo.*

MARIDE, a town of Mesopotamia, 5 geog. m. N.W. from Nisibis. *Mardin.*

MARIDUNIUM (Dunium), a town of the Durotriges, Brit., bet. Isca Damnoniorum and Durnovaria.

MARIDUNUM, a town of the Demetæ, on Tobius fl., R., towards its mouth. *Caermarthen.*

MARIMATHA (Marmetha), a port of Smyrnophoros regio, Arabiæ, E. of Ausara. *Merbat, or Morebat.*

MARINIANA, a town of Pannonia Inf., on Dravus fl., R., bet. Serota (20) and Vereæ (20). *Near Szara.*

MARINIANÆ, Norici, i. q. Stanacum.

MARIŌNIS, a maritime town of the Saxones,

Germ., on Albis fl., R., near its mouth. *Hamburg.*

MARIOS, I. fl., a r. of Laconia, rising near Glympes, and falling into Laconicus sin. at Acriæ. II. a town of the Eleuthero-Lacones, in Laconia, on the cognominal r., 12 m. above Geronthræ. With a temple of Diana and of all the gods. *Marios.*

MARIS (Marisus) fl., a r. of Dacia, rising in Carpathus m. N. of the source of Aluta fl., and falling into Tibiscus fl. by two mouths s. of Ziridava. *Marosch.*

MARITHI m., m. of Arabia Felix, towards Persicus sin., w. of Gerrha. *Mountains of Yemama.*

MARITIMA ins., Siciliæ, i. q. Hiera.

MARIUM, the early name of Arsinoe, Cyprus.

MARMARENSIUM rupis, a fortress of Lycia, near Climax.

MARMARICA (Marmarida), a region of Africa, bounded N. by the Mediterranean, s. by Libya, E. by Egypt, w. by Cyrenaica at Chersonesus Magna.

MARMARIUM, the marble quarries of Carystus, in Eubœa, on the w. coast, under Oche m., nearly opposite Halæ Araphenides. Here was a temple of Apollo Marmarius.

MARMATHA, Arabiæ, i. q. Marimatha.

MARO m., m. of Sicily, a w. continuation of Heræi m.

MAROBUDUM, a town of the Marcomanni, Germ., E. of Monosgada. Named from king Marobodus. *Budweis.*

MAROHÆ, a people of India i. Gangem, about the source of Nagaruris fl.

MARONEA, *prius* Ortaguera, a maritime town of the Cicones, Thrace, w. of Ismarium prom. A Greek city, founded by Chians, or, according to fable, by Maro, a follower of Bacchus. So noted as a depot of the fine wines grown in its vicinity, that it was humorously called the tavern. *Marogna.*

MARONEIA, a village of Attica, on Laurium m.

MARONIA, I. a town of the Pentri, Samnium, on Trinius fl., R., below Treventum. *Campo Marano.* II. of Syria, towards Palmyra.

MAROSCUS m., a summit of Olympus, Bithynia, s.E. of Nicomedia.

MAROZA (Masora), a town of Sargarausene, Cappadocia.

MARPESSA m., a m. of Paros, in which were the famous marble quarries.

MARRUBIUM, capital of the Marsi, Italy, on Fucinus lac. E., bet. Alba Fœcentia (13) and Cerfennia (7), on Via Valeria. *San Benedetto.*

MARRUVIUM, a Pelasgic town of Sabinium, N. of Reate. *Morro Vecchio.*

MARRHASIUM, a town of Persis Prop., near Persepolis N.E.

MARRICHE, a town of Parthia-Nisæa, S. of Parbara.

MARRUCINI, a tribe of Marsi, on Aternus fl., R., bet. the Peligni w., the Adriatic E., the Vestini N., and the Frentani S.

MARSACII, a tribe of Frisii, on the Rhine.

MARSARA, a town of Armenia Minor.

MARSI, I. a tribe of Istævones, Germ. bet. the Chasuarii N., the Bructeri Maj., at Amisia fl. w. and s., and the Cherusci E. II. a tribe of Sabines, bet. Sabinium Proper and the Peligni. Bounded N. by Picenum and s. by Latium. Solinus calls them descendants of Marsyas, a Phrygian; Pliny says they derived from Marsus, son of Circe, and were enchanters, having power over serpents. They are historically famous as the leaders in the Marsic war against Rome.

MARSIGNI, a tribe of Lygii, Germ., under Asciburgius m., bet. the Silingi and the Visburgii.

MARSILLA, Paphlagonia, i. q. Callistratia.

MARSINGI, a tribe of Chatti, Germ., on Visurgis fl., L., towards its source.

MARSONIUM, a town of Pannonia Inferior, on Savus fl., 30 m. from Siscia. *Jessenoviz.*

MARSYABA (Sabia), capital of the Rhamanitæ-Sabæi, Arabiæ, s. of Manambis regia. *Sabe.*

MARSYAS fl., I. a r. of Caria, rising towards Stratonicea and falling into Mæander fl. *China.* II. of Phrygia, i. q. Catarrhactes. III. of Syria, falling into the Orontes towards Apamea. IV. of Syria, falling into the Euphrates. V. a name of the portion of Phœnicia from the coast about Tripolis inland towards Palmyra and Libanus.

MARTA fl., a r. of Etruria, falling into Tyrrhenium mare bet. Centumcellæ (10) and Forum Aurelii (14). *Marta.*

MARTÆ, a town of Syrtica Reg., bet. Tacape and Asas Lupeici.

MARTANUM, a town of Etruria, at the mouth of Marta fl., bet. Graviscæ (3) and Quintiana (3), on Via Aurelia. *Bocca di Marta.*

MARTENI, a people of Arabia Felix, S.E.

MARTHYLA, a town of the Bizeres, Pontus, at the mouth of Pyxites fl., 11 m. N.E. from Limne.

MARTIALIS, a town of the Arverni, Aquitania I., near Augusta Nemetum, N.W.

MARTIANI m., an E.S.E. ridge of Caspius m., in Media, N.

MARTIANUS palus, a salt lake of Media, under Martianus m. *Urmi.*

MARTILUS sinus, a bay of the Ægean, in Crete, bet. Psacum prom. and Corycum prom. *G. di Kisamo.*

MARTIUS collis, a m. of the Latini, Latium, 5 m. from Lanuvium. The locality of the defeat of the Volsci by Camillus. *Colle Marzo.*

MARTYROPOLIS, I. a town of Cilicia, in Cappadocia, towards Cæsarea Mazaca. II. of Sophanene, Mesopotamia, on Nymphius fl., 30 m. N.E. from Amida. Fortified by Justinian. *Meia Farekin.*

MARUBIUS fl., a r. of Sarmatia As., falling into Palus Mæotis below Tanais.

MARUCA, a town of Sogdiana, s.w. of Oxiana.

MARUNDÆ, I. a people of Atropatene, Media, occupying its w. angle, under Caspius m. II. of India e. Gangem, bet. the Ganges and Œdanes fl.

MARUS (Morus) fl., a r. of the Quadi, Germ., rising in Asciburgius m. and falling into the Danube at Anduætium. *Marowa.*

MARUSIUS, a town of the Taulantii, Illyria, on the Egnatia Via, bet. Apsus fl. (14) and Clodiana (13).

MARYANDINI, a tribe of Bithynians, on the coast, E. of the Thyni, from whom they were separated by Sangarius fl. Reduced to slavery by the colonizers of Heraclea.

MARYNÆI, a people of Bactriana, s. of the Tambyzi.

MASADA, a fortress of Judæa, on the Dead sea, s. of Engaddi. Built by Jonathan Maccabæus ; strengthened by Herod. *Sebbeh.*

MASÆI (Masani), a people of Mesopotamia, towards the borders of Arabia. The descendants of Massa.

MASÆMANES, a people of Arabia Felix, immediately N. of Zames m. The descendants of Masma, fifth son of Ishmael. *Beni Shaman.*

MASANI, Arabiæ, *vide* Masæi.

MASATICA, a town of the Heniochi, Sarmat., on the Euxine, bet. Achæus fl. and Nesis.

MASCA fl., a r. of Mesopotamia s., falling into the Euphrates, R., opposite Merrhan.

MASCIACUM, a town of the Genauni, Rhæt., on Ænus fl., R., bet. Veldidena (38) and Pons Æni (26). *Gemund.*

MASCLIANÆ, a town of the Potulatenses, Daciæ, bet. Gaganæ (11) and Tiviscum (14). *Near Kirpa.*

MASCULA, a town of Numidia, bet. Vegesela and Claudis.

MASDORANI, a people of Margiana, on the borders of Aria.

MASETHOLUS fl., a r. of Libya, falling into the Atlantic s.s.e. of Hesperium prom. *Gambia.*

MASICYTES m., m. of Asia Minor, separating Lycia from Pamphylia and Pisidia.

MASIUS m., m. of Asia, separating Armenia Maj. N. from Mesopotamia s. *Karadjidagh.*

MASORA (Basora), a port of Arabia Felix, near Corodamum prom. s.w. *Mizi.*

MASREH, a town of Nabatene, s.s.e. of Joktheel.

MASSA (Masasat), fl., I. a r. of Libya, falling into the Atlantic s. of Soloentium prom. II. VETERNENSIS, a town of Etruria, N.E. of Vetulonia, raised on the ruins of Veterna. The birth-place of Constantine's nephew, Gallus. *Massa.*

MASSABATICE, a district of Elymais, Susianæ.

MASSÆI, a people of Scythia i. Imaum.

MASSAGA (Massaca), a town of India, near Guræus fl.

MASSAGETÆ, a Scythian tribe in Sogdiana, on Oxus fl., E. of the Chorasmii.

MASSALIA, I. (Messapus) fl., a r. of Crete, rising near Lampe and falling into the Libycum mare w. of Psychium. *Meglia.* II. a town of the Ananes, Liguria, on Trebia fl. towards Placentia. *Marsaglia.*

MASSAVA, a town of the Senones, Lugdunensis IV., on the Liger, bet. Condate and Noviodunum.

MASSIA (Maxilua), a town of the Celtici, Lusitania, s.w. of Pax Julia.

MASSICE, Mesopotamiæ, i. q. Fissenia.

MASSICUS m., a ridge of hills separating Campania from Latium, extending, in length 10 m., in breadth 3, bet. Sinuessa and Suessa Auruncorum. Celebrated for its wines.

MASSICYTES m., m. of Lycia, on the coast above Gagæ.

MASSICYTUS, a town of Lycia, on Massicytes m.

MASSIENA, the earlier name of Carthago Nova, Tarraconensis.

MASSIENUS sin., a bay of the Mediterranean, in Tarraconensis, bet. Charidemi prom. s.w. and Massiena (Carthago Nova) N.E. *Bay of Carthagena.*

MASSILIA, capital of the Salyes, Narbonensis, on the coast bet. Solarium and Portus Zao. Built upon a peninsula by the Phocæans, 600 B.C. The death-place of Maximinian. Noted for its literature. *Marseilles.*

MASSONITÆ, a people of Arabia Felix, towards the Maphoritæ.

MASTAURA, a town of Lydia, on Chrysorrhoas fl., E. of Nysa. *Mastauro.*

MASTHALA, a town of Arabia Felix, E. of Sata. *Mascalat.*

MASTIANI, a people of Tarraconensis, contiguous to the Olcades.

MASTROMELA, i. q. Astromela.

MASTUSIA m., a m. of Lydia, E. of Smyrna, bet. Temnus m. and Draco m. *Tartali.*

MASTUSIUM prom., the s. extremity of Chersonesus Thracia, below Elæus. *C. Greco.*

MASTYA, a town of Paphlagonia. A Milesian colony.

MASUMA (Masma), capital of the Masæmanes, Arabiæ. *Sumama.*

MASURA, a maritime town of Pamphylia, 9 m. E. from Magydus.

MATASARUM, a town of the Celtici, Lusitania, bet. Septem Aræ w.n.w. and Augusta Emerita s.e.

MATASTANA, a town of Araxene, Armen., s. of Artaxata. *Maku.*

MATAVONIUM, a town of the Sueltri, Narbonensis, on Argenteus fl., L., bet. Forum Voconii and Ad Turres.

MATETA, a maritime town of the Conapseni, Sarmat., s. of Gerusa.

MATENI, a people of Scythia, on the Rha, above Nesiotis regio.

MATEOLA, a town of Japygia, s. of Silvium. *Matera.*

MATERNUM, I. a town of Etruria, on Via Claudia, bet. Tuscana (17) and Saturnia (18). *Farnese.* II. of the Euganei, Gallia Transpad., on Benacus lac. *Materno.*

MATHIS fl., a r. of Illyria, rising in the m. w. of Drilon fl. and falling into the Adriatic below Bassania. *Matt.*

MATILICA, a town of Umbria, at the source of Æsis fl. *Matilica.*

MATINUS m., a pr. of Daunia Apul., N.E. of Sipontum. Noted for its honey. *Monte Matinata.*

MATINUM, a town of Daunia Apul., at Matinum prom. The burial-place of Archytas of Tarentum. *Matinata.*

MATISCO, a town of the Ædui, Lugdunensis I., on the Arar, bet. Tinurtio and Luna. *Macon.*

MATIUM, I. a town of Colchis, s. II. of Crete, on the N. coast, E. of Apollonia.

MATREIUM, a town of the Breuni, Rhætia, bet. Veldidena (18) and Vipitenum (20). *Matray.*

MATRINUM, the port of Hadria Picen., at the mouth of Matrinus fl. *Porto d'Atri.*

MATRINUS fl., a r. of Picenum, falling into the sea s.e. of Hadria. *Piomba.*

MATRONA m., I. i. q. Alpes Cottiæ. II. fl., a r. of Gaul, rising towards Andematunum and falling into the Sequana above Lutetia. *Marne.*

MATTECORÆ, a people of India e. Gangem, about the head of Barygazinus sin.

MATTHANA, a town of Palmyrene, bet. Palmyra N.E. and Circesium.

MATTIACI, a tribe of Chatti, Germ., on Mænus fl., E. of the Vispii. They were the allies of Rome, and their territory was fortified with citadels and a vallum, erected by Drusus.

MATTIUM (Mattiacum, Mactiadum), capital of the Mattiaci, Germ. *Baden.*

MATUCAGUM, a town of the Taurisci, Noricum, bet. Noriga and Virunum (14). *Hohenfeld.*

MATYLUS, i. q. Magydus.

MAURI (Mauresii), the people of Mauritania.

MAURITANIA, I. a country of Africa, extending from the Atlantic to Numidia, at Ampsaga fl. Bounded N. by the Mediterranean and S. by Libya, at Atlas Major. *Morocco and Fez.* II. CÆSARIENSIS, the E. division of Mauritania, as settled by Claudius, separated from Mauritania Tingitana by Mulucha fl. So named from its capital, Cæsarea. *Vide* Numidia. III. SITIFENSIS, a division, in the Lower Age, of Mauritania Cæsariensis. The country about Sitifis. IV. TINGITANA, the w. division of Mauritania, as settled by Claudius, separated from Mauritania Cæsariensis by Mulucha fl. So named from its capital, Tingis.

MAURUSIA, the Greek form of Mauritania.

MAUSOCA, a town of Hyrcania, E. of Zadracarta.

MAUSUS, a town of Corinthia, s.w. of Chersonesus prom., towards Tenea. *Mertese.*

MAXERA fl., a r. of Hyrcania, rising in Coronus m. and falling into the Caspian below Zadracarta. *Eskar; Korkan.*

MAXIMA CÆSARIENSIS, I. a province of Britain, extending across the island, bet. Alanus fl. and Ituna æstuar. N. and Abus fl. and Belisama æstuar s. II. SEQUANORUM, a district of Gaul, bet. the Rhine E., the Arar w., Germania I. N., and Gallia Cisalpina s. *Franche Comté; W. Switzerland; S. Alsace.*

MAXIMIANOPOLIS (Porsulæ), I. a maritime town of the Cicones, Thrace, on the Egnatia Via, bet. Dicæa (12) and Brendice (10). *Mycena Kalis.* II. of Egypt, near Coptos. III. Galilæeæ, i. q. Hadadrimmon. IV. a town of Pamphylia.

MAXITANI, a people of Numidia, towards Carthage.

MAXULA, a town of Zeugitana, 1½ m. from Tunes. *Rhodes.*

MAXYES, a people on the coast of Syrtis Minor.

MAZACA, I. a town of Elegosine, Armen., s.w. of Arsamosata. II. (Cæsarea, Eusebia, Metropolis), of Cappadocia, under Argæus m., 28 m. s.w. from Armaxa, near the source of Melas fl. Founded by Mesech, son of Japhet, or by Mosoch, a Cappadocian chief. *Kaisirieh.*

MAZACÆ, a people of Sarmatia Asiatica.

MAZÆUM, a village of Bithynia.

MAZES, a town of Argolis, on Argolicus sin., s. of Didymus. The haven of Hermione. *Bisati.*

MAZICES, a people of Mauritania Cæsariensis, under Waneseris m.

MAZINIAMAN, a town of Media Magna, N.E. of Ecbatana.

MAZZĂRA, a port of Sicily, s.w. at the mouth of Mazzarus fl. *Mazzara.*

MAZZARUS fl., a r. of Sicily, falling into the sea bet. Lilybæum and Selinus. *Fiume di Mazzara.*

MEADIA, a town of Dacia, 10 m. N. from Tierna.

MEARAH, a cavern bet. Sarepta and Sidon.

MEARUS fl., a r. of Tarraconensis, falling into Magnus portus at Flavia Brigantium. *Mero.*

MECHLESSUS, a town of Colchis, on the confines of Sarmatia, towards the source of Surius fl.

MECIRA, a maritime town of Marmarica, bet. Paliurus and Gonia.

MECISSA fl., a sacred stream of Bruttium, falling into Metaurus fl. E. of Portus Orestis, q. v.

MEDABA (Medba), a town of Reuben, in Ammonitis, s.E. of Hesbon. *Madaba.*

MEDEON, I. a town of Acarnania, N.w. of Phytia, near the coast. *Medenico.* II. surnamed Phœnicis, of Bœotia, at the foot of Phœnicius m., E. of Haliartus. *Megalo Mulchi.* III. of the Labeates, Illyria, on Barbana fl., bet. Berziminum and Alata. *Medani.* IV. of Phocis, on the coast bet. Anticyra and Marathus. Destroyed in the sacred war. *Palæo Castro.*

MEDERIACUM, a town of the Ubii, Germania II., bet. Mediolanum and Teudurum.

MEDIA, I. a country of Asia, bounded N. by Armenia, at Cyrus fl., s. by Susiana, at Carbanus m., E. by Hyrcania and Parthia, at Coronus m., and w. by Assyria, at Zagrus m. It was distributed into Media Atropatëne, the N.w. portion, Media Magna, its s. portion, and Northern Media.

Named from Madai. *Azerbijan; Shirvan; Ghilan; W. Mazandaran and N. Irak.*

MEDIANA, a town of Rhætia, bet. Losodica (11) and Leiniacum (8). *Donauwarth.*

MEDIANUM, a town of the Triballi, Mœs., on Margus fl., R., bet. Naissus and Ulmus.

MEDIOCERA (Mediccara), a town of Zeugitana, bet. Bibæ and Aggersel, N.W. of Hadrumetum.

MEDIOLANUM, I. a town of the Bructeri Maj., Germ., in Cæsia silva, E. of Asciburgium. *Meteln.* II. *postea* Eburovices, of the Aulerci Eburovices, Lugdunensis II., bet. Uggade N. and Condate S.S.W. *Evreux.* III. of the Bituriges Cubi, Aquitania I., bet. Argantomagus W. and Aquæ Neræ S.E. IV. capital of the Insubres, Gallia Transpadana, bet. Forum Licinii and Laus Pompeia. Built by the Insubres on their arrival in Italy, and named from Mediolanum, Galliæ. A municipium. In the time of Ausonius, it was considered the sixth city of the empire. Procopius characterizes it as second only to Rome. Noted for its encouragement of learning, whence it was called Novæ Athenæ. *Milano; Milan.* V. of the Ordovices, Brit., bet. Bovium and Rutunium. VI. of the Cornavii, Brit., N.W. of Uriconium (23). *Chesterton.* VII. of the Gugerni, Germania II., bet. Vetera Castra and Sablones. *Mayland.* VIII. *postea* Santones, capital of the Santones, Aquitania II., on Carantonus fl., L., bet. Portus Santonum and Condate. *Saintes.* IX. of the Segusiani, Lugdunensis I., bet. Assa Paulina and Forum Segusianorum. *Roanne.*

MEDIOMATRICES, a people of Belgica I., bet. the Treveri and the Leuci. *Department of Moselle.*

MEDIUS murus, a wall separating Mesopotamia from Babylonia, extending bet. the Euphrates, at Pirisabora, and the Tigris N. of Opis. Erected by Semiramis.

MEDMA (Mesma) fl., I. a r. of Bruttium, falling into the Tyrrhenian sea N. of Metaurus fl. *Medama; Mesama.* II. (Mesma), a town of Bruttium, bet. Nicotera and Medma fl. A Locrian colony. Named from a great fountain near it. *Rossano?*

MEDMASA, a town of Caria, near Halicarnassus.

MEDOBRIGA (Medubrica, Meribriga), a town of the Celtici, Lusitania, N.E. of Ebora. Here were lead-mines, whence the people were surnamed Plumbarii. *Marvao.*

MEDOSLANIUM, a town of the Juthungi, Germaniæ, 1 m. N. from Vindobona.

MEDUACI, a tribe of Euganei or Veneti, in Venetia, towards the sources of Meduacus Maj. and Minor. *About Bassano.*

MEDUACUS MAJOR fl., I. a r. of Venetia, rising near Tridentum and falling into the Adriatic at a cognominal port. *Brenta.* II. MINOR, of Venetia, rising N.E. of Sarni and falling into the Adriatic at a cognominal town. *Bachiglione.*

MEDUANA fl., a r. of Gaul, falling into the Liger, near Andecavi. *Mayenne.*

MEDUANTUM, a town of the Treveri, Belgica I., bet. Epoissum S.S.W. and Orolaunum S.S.E.

MEDULLI, I. a people of Alpes Maritimæ, N. of the Caturiges. *Val. de la Maurienne.* II. a tribe of Bituriges Vivisci, Aquitania, on the Garumna, L., at its mouth.

MEDULLIA, a town of Latium, towards Alba Longa.

MEDULLIUS m., a continuation of Vindius m., Tarraconensis, on Minius fl. s. *Sierra las Medulas.*

MEDULLUM, a town of the Genauni, Rhæt., on Ænus fl., N.E. of Veldidena. *Farwar; Schamior.*

MEDUS fl., a r. of Persis, falling into the Araxes at Persepolis.

MEFULA, a Pelasgic town of Sabinium.

MEGABARI, a people of Meroe, on the Nile, R., about Napata.

MEGALASSUS, a town of Pontus, on Halys fl., R., above Zara.

MEGALE ins., an isl. of Bithynia, one of the Demonisi group.

MEGALIA ins., an islet of Campania, at Neapolis. *Castel del Ovo.*

MEGALOPOLIS, "great city," I. a town of Zeugitana, bet. Carthago and Tunes. II. the capital of Arcadia, on Helisson fl., near the confines of Laconia. Founded by Epaminondas circa 370 B.C. *Sinano.* III. an early name of Aphrodisias, in Caria. IV. Pont., i. q. Eupatoria.

MEGANITAS fl., a r. of Achaia, falling into the Corinthiacus sin. below Leuctrum. *Gaidouriari.*

MEGARA, I. capital of Megaris, on Saronicus sin., over against Salamis, 26½ m. N.W. from Athens. Under the Romans a colonia. Destroyed by Alaric. The birthplace of Euclid the Socratic and Theognis the Gnomist. The seat of a school of philosophy. *Megara.* II. (Parva Hybla), *surnamed* Hyblæa Galaōtis, a maritime town of Sicily, E., at the mouth of Alabon fl. A colony from Megara Nisæa. Extinct in Strabo's time. Noted for its honey. III. of Molossis. IV. an ancient district of Megaris. V. a town of Thessaly.

MEGARICE, Taurica Cherson., i. q. Chersonesus.

MEGARICUS sinus, the strait bet. Megaris and Salamis ins.

MEGARICUS, a town of Bithynia, on the Propontis, E. of Posidium prom. A colony from Megara Nisæa.

MEGARIS, I. a country of Græcia e. Peloponnes. Bounded N. by Bœotia, s. by Saronicus sin., w. by Corinthiacus sin., Achaia, and Argolis, E. by Attica. Established as a kingdom by Megarus, son of Apollo. II. an isl. of Italy, bet. Neapolis and Pausilippum.

MEGARSUS prom., a pr. of Cilicia Campestris, at the w. mouth of Pyramus fl., with a temple of Minerva Megarsus, where were the tombs of the soothsayers, Mopsus and Amphilochus. C. Karadash.

MEGATICHOS (Myrson), a town of Egypt, on the confines of Æthiopia.

MEGIDDO, I. Galilææ, i. q. Kison. II. postea Legio, a town of Manasseh, Galilæa, on Kison fl., L., 15 m. s.w. from Nazareth. The death-place of Ahaziah and Josiah. Fortified by Solomon. Lejjun.

MEGERTHIS, a maritime town of Tripolis, Afric., bet. Aphora and Œa.

MEGISTANI, a people of Armenia, in the mountains E. of Melitene.

MEGISTE ins., I. an isl. of Lycia, near Rhope ins. Castelorizo. II. (Cisthene), a town of Megiste ins., Lyciæ. Extinct in Pliny's time.

MEGISTUS fl., i. q. Macestus.

MEJACORIRE, salt baths of Mesopotamia, under Masius m., bet. Samachis and Maride, at the springs of Arzamo fl.

MELA (Melanoros), m., a chain of m., extending 20 m. along the coast of Arabia Felix, E. of Agmanisphe. Gibul Fouthelee; Gibul Harrasse.

MELADULA (Megaluda), a town of Pontus, towards Comana.

MELÆ, I. a town of Bruttium, near Mamertium. A Locrian colony. Mella. II. of the Caudini, Samnium, s. of Telesia, near Vulturnus fl., L. Melissano.

MELÆNA prom., I. a pr. of Bithynia, on the Euxine, 19 m. E. from Rhebas fl. II. the N.W. extremity of Chios ins., over against Psyra ins. (6¼.) C. San Niccolo. III. the N. extremity of Melas m., m. of Ionia. C. Karabouroun. IV. a town of Bithynia, on the Euxine, within the cognominal prom.

MELÆNÆ, a town of Lycia.

MELÆNÆ, a town of Arcadia, on Alpheus fl., bet. Heræa and Megalopolis. Founded by Melæneus, son of Lycaon. Anaziri.

MELÆNEIS (Melænæ), a demus of Attica of the tribe Antiochis.

MELAMBIUM, a town of Pelasgiotis, Thessaly, s.E. of Scotussa.

MELAMPEA, a town of Lydia.

MELAMPHYLLUS, a name of Samos, Ionia.

MELANCHLÆNI, "wearing black," a people of Sarmatia As., on the Rha, bet. Mithridatis regio and the Sapothrenæ.

MELANE ins., an isl. of Ionia, towards the mouth of Caystrus fl.

MELANEA, a maritime village of Cilicia Trachea, near Myanda.

MELANGÆ, capital of the Arvarni, Indiæ.

MELANGÆA fons, a spring of Arcadia, E. of Mantinea, whence water was supplied to the city.

MELANGEA, a town of Bithynia.

MELANIPPE, a town of Lycia, 4 m. w. from Sacrum prom.

MELANITES m., Arabiæ, the m. terminating in Asaborum prom.

MELANO ins., I. an isl. of Caria. II. GÆTULI, a people of Libya Int., s. of the Daræ.

MELANOS prom., a pr. of Mysia, on Propontis, at Cyzicus.

MELANTHIUS fl., a r. of Pontus, falling into the Euxine, 8 m. E. from Cotyora, and dividing Tibarenia from Mosynœcia.

MELANTII SCOPULI, I. rocks on the N. coast of Patmos ins., s. of Corassiæ ins. II. rocks on the coast of Thera, where Apollo appeared to the Argonauts.

MELAPONTIS, an early name of Syme ins.

MELAS fl., I. a r. of the Apsynthii, Thrace, falling into Melas sin. at its N.E. extremity. Cavatcha. II. of Bœotia, rising N.W. of Orchomenus and losing itself in Pelecania regio. Its water dyed fleece black. III. of Cappadocia, rising in Argæus m. and falling into Euphrates fl. at Melitene. Karasou. IV. of Cilicia Trachea, falling into the sea 5 m. N.E. from Cruni prom. V. of Maliensis, in Thessaly, 2¾ m. s. of Dyras fl., falling into Maliacus sin. below Trachis. VI. of Pamphylia, falling into the sea 6 m. E. from Side. Remarkable for the coldness of its water. Menoughat. VII. (Facelinus), of Sicily, falling into the Tyrrhen. sea, s.w. of Naulochus. The oxen of the sun were pastured on its banks. VIII. sin., a bay of the Ægean, along the N. coast of the Chersonnesus Thracia. G. di Saros.

MELDI, I. a people of Lugdunensis IV., on Matrona fl., N. of the Senones. II. of Celtica, contiguous to the Tricasses. E. Seine et Marne. III. their town. Meldfelt, near Bruges.

MELDIA, a town of the Treres, Mœs., bet. Ballanstra and Seretisca.

MELENICUM, a town of the Mædi, in Thrace, N.E. of Desudaba. *Melenik.*

MELES fl., I. a r. of Ionia, rising in Mastusia m., and falling into Hermius sin. below Smyrna. On its banks is the cave in which Homer arranged his poem. II. a town of Sicily. III. a t. of the Pentri, near Maronea.

MELETES sin., a bay of Hermius sin., at the mouth of Meles fl.

MELFEL fl., a r. of Latium, falling into the Liris, 4 m. E. from Fabrateria. *Melfa.*

MELGUNIS ins., i. q. Æoliæ.

MELIA, a town of Caria.

MELIBŎCUS m., m. of the Cherusei, Germ., E. of Lupta. *The Hartz.*

MELIBŒA, I. ins., an isl. of Syria, at the mouth of the Orontes. II. a town of Estiæotis, in Thessaly, N.E. of Gomphi. III. of Magnesia, in Thessaly, bet. Rhizus and Casthanæa. Assigned by Homer to Philoctetes. *Castri.*

MELINDA (Mangarud), a maritime town of India i. Gangem, w., bet. Bacari and Corcura.

MELIODUNUM, a town of the Corcontii, Germ., on Mariscus fl. *Near Olmutz.*

MELIOSEDUM (Mecledum), *postea* Melodunum, a town of the Senones, Lugdunensis IV., on the Seine, above Lutetia. *Melun.*

MELISSE (Melitæa, Melitara), a town of Phrygia M., bet. Synnada and Metropolis. The burial-place of Alcibiades.

MELISURGIS, a town of Chalcidice, in Macedonia, bet. Thessalonica (20) and Apollonia (17), on the Egnatia Via.

MELITA, I. ins., an isl. of the Adriatic, one of the Liburnides ins., s. of Corcyra. Noted for the Catuli Melitæi. *Meleda.* II. of the Mediterranean, 60 m. s.E. from Sicilia. Peopled by Phœnicians 1500 B.C., and therefore at first regarded as belonging to Africa. Noted for its linen manufactures. The scene of the shipwreck of St. Paul. *Malta.*

MELITÆA, *prius* Pyrrha, a town of Achaia, in Thessaly, 1½ m. w. from Hellas, on the opposite side of Enipeus fl. Here was the tomb of Hellen, son of Deucalion. *Goura.*

MELITARA, Phrygia, i. q. Melisse.

MELITE, I. a suburban demus of Athens, of the tribe Cecropeis. The residence of Phocion. The place of rehearsal for the tragic actors. II. palus, a salt lake of Acarnania, on its s. coast, E. of the E. mouth of Achelous fl., 4 m. long by 1 m. broad.

MELITENE, I. a district of Susiana Elymais, bet. Tigris and Choaspes ffl., above Characene. II. prefectura, a prefect. of Cappadocia, or, according to Ptolemy, of Armenia Minor, on Euphrates fl., R., N. of Commagene. Noted for a fine wine called Monarites. III. capital of Melitene pref., in Cappadocia. Built by Trajan, enlarged by Justinian. The station of the Legio XII., or Fulminifera; subsequently the metrop. of Armenia Minor. *Malatia.*

MELITONUS, a town of Lyncus, in Macedonia, bet. Heraclea (13) and Grandis (14), on the Egnatia Via.

MELIZIGARA ins., an isl. of India i. Gangem, over against Balepatna.

MELLA fl., Gallia Cisalpina. *Vide Melo.*

MELLARIA, I. a maritime town of the Turtetani, Bætica, bet. Transducta s.w. and Carteja N.E. *Torre de la Penna.* II. a town of the Turtuli, Bætica, w.N.w. of Corduba. Named from its fine honey. A colonia from Mellaria ad Mare.

MELFIS fl., a r. of Latium, falling into Liris fl. near Aquinum. *Melfa.*

MELINA, a town of Argolis, with a temple of Venus. *Melinea.*

MELLOSECIUM, a town of the Tricorii, Viennensis, bet. Catorissium w. and Durotincum E. *Mella.*

MELO fl., a r. of Gallia Cisalp., passing through Brixia into the Ollius. *Garza; Melone.*

MELOBOTEIRA, i. q. Ægæ.

MELOCABUS (Melomabus), a town of the Marsingi-Chatt., Germ., s.E. of Gravionarium. *Near Fulda.*

MELODUNUM. *Vide* Meliosedum.

MELOROME (Mesorome), a town of Pontus, on the confines of Galatia, towards Tavia.

MELOS (Mimallis), ins., an island of the Ægean, one of the Cyclades, s. w. of Cimolus. For some time a dependency of Lacedæmon. *Mili.* II. capital of the cognominal isl., on the N.w. coast. The birth-place of the Atheist Diagoras. *Milo.* III. a maritime village of Acarnania. *Mela.*

MELPEA, a village of Arcadia, on Nomii m., where Pan invented his pipe.

MELPHES fl., I. a r. of Lucania, falling into Inferum m. s.E. of Palinurus prom. *Molpa.*

MELPUM, a town of the Cenomanni, in Gallia Transpad., on Addua fl., bet. Mediolanum and Bergomum.

MELSUS (Nœlus) fl. a r. of Tarraconensis, falling into Navilubio fl., L., towards its mouth. *Abono.*

MELTA, a town of the Mœsi, Mœs., bet. Doriones and Sostra.

MELTENE, a town of Zeugitana, towards Mescela.

MILTOS, a town on Sogdiana ins., Carm.

MEMBRISSA (Membresa), a town of Zeugitana, on Bagradas fl., L., bet. Musti (35) and Thureis (12).

MEMBRO, a maritime village of Zeugitana, N.W. of Utica (6).

MEMINI, a tribe of Vocontii, Viennensis, bet. the Vulgientes w. and Druentia fl. E.

MEMNON, a town of Mysia, E. of Æsepus fl., where was the tomb of Memnon.

MEMNONIA, the fortress of Susa, Susianæ; from Memnon, son of Tithonus.

MEMNONES, a people of Æthiopia, bet. the Tangaitæ and Meroe ins.

MEMNONIUM (Memnon, Phaturis, Patros), a suburb of Thebes, in Egypt, on the left bank of the Nile, where once stood two colossal figures of Memnon, destroyed by Cambyses, or by an earthquake; the remaining portion of one of these emitted a sound when struck by the rays of the rising sun.

MEMPHIS (Momf, Memf, Mefi; Moph, Noph), capital of Heptanomis, on the Nile, L., bet. Cercasura (15) and Tasdrum. Built by Menes, on the ancient bed of the Nile, the course of the river having been changed by him for that purpose. The seat of the sacred Apis. *Near Fostat.*

MENÆNUM (Menæ), a town of Sicily, on Eryces fl., R., above Eryce. *Mineo.*

MENALIPPE, a naval station of Lycia, on Limyrus fl. Sacred to Minerva.

MENAMBIS, a district of Arabia Felix, bet. the Sabæi and the Sappharitæ.

MENANATHA (Minois), a town of Idumæa, E.S.E. of Raphia.

MENAPIA (Menevia), I. a town of the Demetæ, Brit., w. of Ad Vigesimum. *St. David's.* II. capital of the Menapii, Hiberniæ. *Wexford.* III. a town of the Zariaspæ Bactr., on Zariaspes fl., above Zariaspe. Probably the original seat of the Menapii. *Andechud.*

MENAPII, a colonia of the continental Menapii, settled in Hibernia, E., bet. the Chauci and the Brigantes. They were called by the natives Fir-bolgs (Viri-Belgici). II. a people of Germania II., bet. the Rhine, the Mosa, and the Scaldis; afterwards settled in Belgica II., s. of the Marini.

MENAPIORUM castrum, a fortress of the Menapii, Germania II., on the Mosa, bet. Blariacum and Catuatium. *Cassel.*

MENAVII, a town of the Aduatuci, Germania II., N.W. of Genuacum.

MEN-CARUS, a village of Caria, E. of Carura, towards Laodicea. Founded around a celebrated temple of Men-Carus by the disciples of Herophilus the physician.

MENDE, a town of Pallene, in Macedonia, at Posidium prom. A colony from Eretria in Eubœa. Famous for its wines.

MENDES, a town of Lower Egypt, on the Mendesic branch of the Nile, near its mouth. Here Pan and a goat were worshipped. *Achmoun.*

MENDESIUM OSTIUM NILI, the fifth greater mouth of the Nile, E. from Alexandria. Named from Mendes. It separates from Phatmeticum ostium at Diospolis. *Menzaleh Canal.*

MENDICALEJA, a town of the Ilergetes, Tarraconensis.

MENDRION, a town of Cyrenaica, on Syrtis Maj., bet. Ad Puteum and Boreum prom.

MENEBRIA, the early name of Mesambria, in Thrace.

MENECINA, a town of Bruttium, near Consentia.

MRNEDEMIUM, I. a town of Lycia. II. of Melyas, in Pisidia.

MENEGERE, a town of Byzacene, on the borders of Numidia, bet. Scillium and Theveste.

MENEGESIS, a town of Numidia, N.E. of Thebeste.

MENELAI portus, a port of Marmarica, at Ardanis prom. Named from the landing here of Menelaus. The death-place of Agesilaus. *Toubrouk.*

MENELAIS, I. fons, a fountain of Arcadia. Noted for a very splendid plane-tree. II. a town of Athamania, in Ætolia, on Achelous fl.

MENELAIUM m., m. of Laconia, on Eurotas fl., terminating in Malea prom. A continuation of Thornax m., from about Sparta. *Malevo.*

MENELAUS, a name of Canopus Ægypti, from Menelaus, brother of Ptolemy Lagus.

MENEPHESE, a town of Zeugitana.

MENEPIA. *Vide* Menapia.

MENESTHEI portus, a maritime town of the Turtetani, Bætica, N.E. of Gades. Here was the oracle of Menestheus. *Near Puerto Real.*

MENINX (Girba, Lothophagorum) ins., I. an isl. of Byzacene, in Syrtis Minor, opposite Tacape. *Gerbi; Zarbi.* II. capital of Meninx ins., on the N. coast. The birth-place of Vibius Gallus and of Volusianus.

MENLASCUS fl., I. a r. of Europe, falling into Cantabricum m. at Menosca. The boundary, in that direction, of Spain and Gaul. *Orio.*

MENNEIANÆ, a town of the Andizetes, Pannonia, bet. Inicerum (28) and Varianæ (26). *Patraez.*

MENNIS, a town of the Garamæi, Assyriæ, s. of Arbela. *Near Dus-Churmula.*

MENOSCA, a town of the Varduli, Tarraconensis, at Olarsum prom. *Sumaya.*

MENOTHARUS fl., a r. of Sarmatia Asiatica.

MENRALII, a people of Colchis. The progenitors of the Mingrelians.

MENTESA, a town of the Oretani, Tarraconensis, s.e. of Tucci-Gemella.

MENTESA-BASTIA (Mentosa), a town of the Bastitani, Tarraconensis, on the Bætis, L., towards its source, e. of Castulo.

MENTOVENES, a people of Liguria, N. of Genua.

MENUTHIAS ins., an isl. of Africa, s.e. *Peruba.*

MEPHAATH, a Levitical city of Reuben, in Silbonitis, bet. Lydia N.W. and Anitha s. The Romans erected a fortress here.

MERCIMERIS, a town of Numidia, bet. Macomades and Justis.

MERCURIALES, Byzac., i. q. Thenæ.

MERCURII (Hermæum) prom., I. the N.E. extremity of Africa. II. of Byzacene, over against Cercina ins. *Cape Bon.* III. of Sicily, s. of Nymphæum prom. IV. oppidum, *vide* Hermopolis Magna.

MERETÆ, a people of Britannia Barbara, on the E. coast, bet. the Lugi N. and the Decantæ s.

MERGABLUM, a maritime town of the Turtetani, Bætica, bet. Gades N. and Junonis prom.

MERGANA, a town of Sicily, on Himera Min. fl., L., under Cratas m. N. *Margana.*

MERIABA, Arabiæ, i. q. Mariaba.

MERINUM, a maritime town of Daunia, Apul., at Garganum prom. N. *Ch. of Santa Maria di Merino, near Viesti.*

MERMODAS (Mermadalis) fl., a r. of Sarmatia, rising in Caucasus m., and falling into Mæotis palus.

MEROBRIGA, a town of Lusitania, N. of Sacrum prom. *Sines.*

MĔRŎE, I. a kingdom of Æthiopia, on the Nile, bet. Dodecaschœnus at Hiera Sycaminos N. and Astapus and Astaborus ffl. The name is an extension of that of Meroe ins., q. v. II. capital of Meroe, on the Nile, R., above Primis Magna. Josephus says that its ancient name was Saba, and that it was renamed by Cambyses in honour of his son, who died there. At this point, according to Pliny, the shadow decreases twice a year; when the sun is in the 18th degree of Taurus and in the 14th of Leo. III. ins., an insular district of Meroe,

formed by the Nile, the Astapus, and the Astaboras ffl., from Primis Magna N. to about Sirbitium.

MEROM lacus, *vide* Samachonitis.

MEROPIA ins., an early name of Acis ins.

MEROTH, a town of Dan, w.s.w. of Hazor.

MEROZ, I. a place near Kison fl. II. a town of Galilee, of uncertain position.

MERRHAN (Corsote), a town of Tingene, Mesop., on the Euphrates, bet. Zarta and Giddara.

MERULA fl., a r. of Liguria, falling into Ligusticus sin., at Albintemelium. *Arosoia.*

MERUS, "thigh," m., I. a m. of India i. Gangem, at Nyssa. Here Bacchus and his army were preserved from a pestilence which raged in the plain below, and hence the fable of Bacchus having been inserted in Jupiter's thigh. II. a town of Phrygia.

MERUSIUM, a town of Sicily, towards Syracuse.

MESANITES sin., the mouth of the Euphrates next to Arabia. Named from Mizzah, son of Reuel. *Phrat Misan.*

MESARFILIA, a town of Numidia, bet. Aquæ Herculis and Piscina.

MESATE, I. ins., an isl. of Ionia, off the cognominal prom. II. prom., a pr. of Ionia, at the s. entrance of Erythræus sin.

MESAMBRIA, a maritime district of Persis Prop., s. of Taocene.

MESCELE, a port of Zeugitana, towards Hippo Regius.

MESE (Pomponiana) ins., one of the Stoechades ins., Narbonensis, E. of Prote ins. *Portcros.*

MESECH (Meshech), the Scriptural name of the N.E. angle of Asia Minor, as colonized by Mesech, son of Japheth, supposed to be the progenitor of the Muscovites.

MESEMBRIA, I. a maritime town of the Cicones, in Thrace, at the mouth, E. of Lissus fl. A Samothracian colony. II. a town of the Crobyzi, in Thrace, on the Euxine, N. of Anchialus. A colony from Megara Nisæa. *Misioria.*

MESENE, I. a peninsular district of Chaldæa and Susiana, formed by Tigris fl. and Naarmalcha canalis. II. a peninsular district at the mouth of the Tigris.

MESHA m., Arabiæ, i. q. Zames. Named from Mishma or Masma.

MESIATES, a tribe of Lepontii, N. of Verbanus lac. *Val de Misox; Val di Misocco.*

MESINIUM, a town of the Cherusci, on Albis fl.

MESMA, Italiæ, i. q. Medma.

MESOBOA, a town of Arcadia, on Ladon fl., L., above Oryx.

MESOCHORION, a town of the Salentini, in Japygia, on Via Appia, bet. Tarentum (10) and Uria (10). *Grottoglie.*

MESOLA, a town of Messenia.

MESONACTE, a town of Phrygia Parorea, near Philomelium.

MESOPOTAMIA (*biblicè* Aram Naharaim, Padan Aram), a country of Asia, bet. the rivers Euphrates and Tigris, bounded N. by Armenia Maj. at Masius m. and the Tigris, S. by Babylonia at Medius murus, w. by Syria at the Euphrates, E. by Assyria at the Tigris. Its southern portion was included by the earlier Greeks in the name of Arabia, and its northern in that of Syria.

MESOPOTAMIUM, a town of Sicily, bet. Gela and Hybla Heræa.

MESOTIMOLITÆ (Mesotmolitæ), a tribe occupying the centre of the ridge Tmolus, in Lydia.

MESPHE, a town of Tripolis, Africa, bet. Leptis Mag. and Thenadassa.

MESPYLA, a town of Assyria, near Nineveh.

MESSA, a town of Laconia, on Messeniacus sin., 19 m. s. from Œtylus. *Maino? Mezapo?*

MESSABA, a town of Caria.

MESSABATICE (Mesabatenes), a district of Susiana Elymais, on Choaspes fl., L., w. of Corbiene.

MESSANA (*prius* Zancle, Mamertina), a city of Sicily, on Siculum fretum, over against (N.W.) Rhegium, in Italy. Founded by a colony from Messene, or, according to Thucydides, by Anaxilas the Messenian, tyrant of Rhegium. Enlarged by Mamertine exiles. The birth-place of Euemerus the historian. *Messina.*

MESSAPIA, I. the Greek name for the portion of Apulia on the coast of Tarentinus sin. II. a district of Japygia, extending over its central and N. portions. III. a town of Messapia, on Via Appia, bet. Hyria and Brundusium. *Messagna.* IV. a town of the Locri Ozolæ, w. of Chaleon. V. an early name of Bœotia, from Messapius m.

MESSAPII, I. descendants of the Osci, settled in Messapia. Named from their leader Messapus. II. a tribe of Japyges, occupying the interior of Japygia.

MESSAPIUS m., a m. of Bœotia, w. of Anthedon, giving name to Messapus, the colonizer of Messapia, in Italy, and also to Bœotia. *Ktypia.*

MESSATIS, a town of Achaia, near Patræ, whither its inhabitants were removed by Patreus.

MESSENE, I. a district of Babylonia, about Seleucia. *Kutha.* II. the later capital of

Messenia, at Ithome m., 7 m. E. from Cyparissia. Founded by Epaminondas; and named from Messene, daughter of Triopas. The burial-place of Aristomenes. *Mauromati.*

MESSEIS fons, a fountain of Pelasgiotis, in Thessaly, near Pheræ.

MESSENIA, a country of Peloponnesus, bounded N. by Elis and Arcadia, S. and w. by the Ionium mare, E. by Laconia. Under Menelaus a portion of Laconia. Named after Messene, wife of Polycaon.

MESSENIACUS sin., a bay of the Ægean, on the S. coast of Messenia. *Golfo di Coron.*

MESSOGIS m., a range of m. in Lydia, running parallel with Tmolus m. w.—E. Noted for its wine. *Kestenous Dayh.*

MESSUA collis, a peninsular prom. of Gaul, on the Mediterranean, E. of Setium prom. *Near Mèse.*

MESTLETA, a town of Iberia, on the Aragus, at its junction with the Cyrus, bet. Caspia and Scumara, N.E. of Harmozica. *Mtskhetla.*

MESTRIANA, a town of the Amantini, Pannonia, bet. Sabaria and Mogentiana (30). *Mindsent.*

MESUO, a town of the Volcæ Arecomici, Narbonensis, bet. Forum Domitii N.E. and Araura S.w.

MESYLA, a town of Pontus, bet. Gaziura and Comana.

METABOLE, a fortress of Bithynia, on Sophon m.

METABUM, the name of Metapontum, Lucan., from the hero Metabus.

METACHÆUM, a fortress of Bœotia, bet. Coronea and Orchomenus.

METACOMPSO (Tacompso), *postea* Contra Pselchis, a town of Dodecaschœnus, on the Nile, R., opposite Pselchis.

METAGONITÆ, a people of Mauritania Tingitana, on the coast, bet. Tænia Longa and Metagonium prom.

METAGONITIS (Metheg, *heb.* "bridle"), I. a name of Numidia as a subjugated country. II. prom., a pr. of Mauritania Ting., E. of Rusadir prom.

METAGONIUM prom., a pr. of Numidia, near the mouth of Ampsaga fl. *Cape Honneine?*

METALLA, a town of the Celsitani, in Sardinia, bet. Populum and Neapolis. Named from its (silver) mines. *Antas.*

METALLIFERI m., a chain of Carpatæ m., in Germania Magna. *Erzgebirge.*

METALLINUM (Metellina Castra), a town of the Turtuli, Bætica, on the Bætis, above Augusta Emerita (24). It once stood on the Lusitanian side of the Bætis. *Medelin.*

METALLUM prom., I. a pr. on the s. coast of Crete, at the cognominal town. *C. Matala.* II. a town of the Colapini, Pannonia, s.e. of Emona. III. of Crete, within the cognominal prom., at the mouth of Lethæus fl. The dockyard of Gortys. *Castel Priotissa.*

METAPA, a town of Ætolia, at the s. shore of Trichonius lacus, n.e. of Phyteum. *Metarga.*

METAPONTUM, *prius* Metabum, Aliso, a city of Lucania, on Tarentinus sin., s. of Bradanus fl. Colonized, *circa* 1000 b.c., by Pylians, and afterwards by Achæans, who named it Metapontum. There was a temple of Minerva, where were shown the tools with which Epæus made the wooden horse. The district was the abode for many years of Pythagoras, and the scene of the reappearance of Aristias of Proconnesus. Celebrated for its agriculture. In ruins in the time of Pausanias. *Torre di Mare.*

METARIS æstuar., an estuary of Germanicus oc., at the mouths of Trivona and Aufona ffl., s. of Abus fl. *The Wash.*

METARUS fl., I. an arm of the Cantabricum mare, within Trileucum prom. II. a r. of Tarraconensis, falling into Cantabricum mare, bet. Burum e. and Trileucum prom. w. *Rio de Vivero.*

METAUM, a town of Lesbos ins. Founded by Metas, a Tyrrheno-Pelasgic chief.

METAURUS fl., I. a r. of Bruttium, falling into the Tyrrhenian sea at Metaurum, s. of Medma fl. Noted for the thunny-fishing at its mouth. *Marro* or *Petrace.* II. of Umbria, rising w. of Tifernum Metaur., and falling into the Adriatic 2 m. s. of Fanum Fortunæ. Memorable for the defeat of Asdrubal by Livius Salinator and Claudius Nero, b.c. 207. *Metauro.*

METAURUM, a town of Bruttium, on Metaurus fl., near its mouth. A Locrian, or, according to Solinus, a Zanclæan colony. The birth-place of Stesichorus. *Gioja.*

METELIS, *postea* Bechis, a town of Lower Egypt, on the Bolbitic branch of the Nile, L., below Bolbitene. *Abu Mandur.*

METHATH, a port of Arabia Felix, e. of Cane Emporium. *Muglidah.*

METHEG-AMMAH, i. q. Gath.

METHONE (Methana) I. a peninsula of Argolis, bet. Pogon portus and Epidaurus. Enlarged by a volcanic eruption in the reign of Antigonus Gonatas. With hot springs. The volcanic exhalations from this place were intolerable from their stench by day, but not by night. II.

prom., a pr. of Messenia, s. of Pylos. III. (Methana), a town of Argolis, on the cognominal peninsula, bet. Epidaurus and Trœzen. With a temple of Isis. *Methana.* IV. of Eubœa. V. of Magnesia, in Thessaly, on Pagasæus sin., bet. Spalathra and Ormenium. A town of Philoctetes. VI. (Mothone), of Messenia, at the cognominal prom. Named from Mothone, daughter of Æneas. The Pedasus of Homer. A colonia of Trajan. Here was a well sacred to Diana, the water of which, mixed with pitch, formed a fine ointment. *Modonpalaio.* VII. of Pieria, in Macedonia, on the Thermaicus sin., bet. Pydna (5 m.) and Alorus. A Greek colony. It was razed by Philip of Macedon, who at its siege lost one of his eyes. *Leuterochori.*

METHORA, a town of Surasena, Ind., on Diamuna fl., R., bet. Indabura and Clisobra.

METHYMNA, a town of Lesbos, on its n. coast, over against Polymedium (7½). The birth-place of Arion and of Myrsilus. Noted for its wine. *Molivo.*

METHYRIADES ins., islets of Megaris, bet. Nisæa and Salamis ins. *Revitousa.*

METHYDRIUM, I. a town of Arcadia, 16 m. n. from Megalopolis, w. of Mantinea, built by Orchomenus, bet. Malætas and Mylaon ffl. The inhabitants were transferred to Megalopolis. *Palatia.* II. of Thessaly.

METIBI, a people of Sarmatia, towards the n.e. coast of the Euxine.

METINA ins., an isl. of Narbonensis, off the Metapinian mouth of the Rhone. *Jamatan.*

METINE, a district of Tenesis, in Æthiopia, s.e. of Agame.

METIOSEDUM, a town of the Senones, in Gaul, at the confluence of the Matrona with the Sequana.

METITA, a town of Laviniasene, in Cappadocia, on Euphrates fl.

METOPES fl., a r. of Arcadia.

METORES, a people of Persis Prop., s.w. of Persepolis.

METROPOLIS, I. a town of Acarnania, on the R. bank of Achelous fl., s. of Stratus. Burned by Philip III. of Macedon. *Ligustorika.* II. of Dolopia, Thessaliæ, n.w. of Sosthenis. III. a city of Estiæotis, Thessaly, on the n. bank of Peneus fl., n.e. of Tricca. IV. a fortress of Histiæa, in Eubœa. V. a town of Lydia, under Gallesus m. e. *Cabadja.* VI. of Phrygia, n. of Synnada. Sacred to Cybele. *Tchoulabad.* VII. Scythiæ, i. q. Olbia. VIII. i. q. Argos Amphilochum.

METROUM, a port of Bithynia, on the Euxine, 10 m. n.e. from Heraclea.

METUBARRIS ins., an isl. of Pannonia, on Savus fl. *Colubara ?*

METULUM, capital of the Japydes, in Illyria, at the siege of which Augustus Cæsar was wounded. *Metling.*

MEVANIA, a town of Umbria, on Tinia fl., bet. Spoletium (12) and Forum Flaminii (16). Noted for its rich pastures and its white sacrificial bulls. The birth-place of Propertius. *Bevagna.*

MEVANIOLA, a town of Umbria, w. of Sarsina. *Galeata.*

MIACŌRUS (Milcōrus), a town of Chalcidice, in Macedonia.

MIACUM, a town of the Vaccæi, Tarraconensis, bet. Segobia N.W. and Complutum s.s.w.

MIBA, a town of the Sammei, Arabia Felix, bet. Labecia and Arabicus sin. *Niab.*

MICHMASH, a town of Judæa, 9 m. from Jerusalem. The abode of Jonathan Maccabæus. *Mukhmas.*

MICODES fl., a sacred stream of Bruttium, one of the seven streams falling into Metaurus fl. E. of Portus Orestis.

MIDEA, I. the Medea or Epimedea of Xenophon, *olim* Persepolis, a town of Argolis, bet. Argos and Lessa. Named after the wife of Electryon. *Agios Adrianos.* II. the early name of Lebadia, in Bœotia.

MICYBERNA, the port of Olynthus, in Sithonia, Macedonia, on the Toronaicus sin., which, after it, was sometimes called Micybernicus sin. *Medjid Barna.*

MIDÆUM (Mygdone), a royal city of Phrygia Epict., E. of Doryleum (28). Named from Midas, one of the kings of Phrygia. *Caragamous.*

MIDIAN, I. a country of Arabia Petræa, on both sides of Ælanites sin. The seat of the descendants of Midian, fourth son of Abraham. *Madian.* II. (Modiana), capital of Midian, on the E. shore of Ælanites sin.

MIDUS, a town of Bithynia, on Sangarius fl., bet. Nicæa (16) and Totaium.

MIEZA, *olim* Strymonium, *postea* Mediana, a town of Emathia, Macedonia, on the Olganus fl., s.e. of Ægæ. Named after Mieza, grand-daughter of king Macedon. The birth-place of Peucestas. Here was a school established for the exiled Stagirites by Alexander. *Near Cailari.*

MIGDOL, a fortress of Arabia Petræa, near Arsinoe, N. *Bir Suez.*

MIGO, a town of Cyrenaica, N.E. of Augila.

MIGRON, a place near Michmash, Judæa.

MIJOS (Mophis) fl., a r. of India i. Gangem, falling into Barygazenus sin.

MILĂTA (Milatæ, *postea* Bononia), a town of Pannonia Inf., on the Danube, s. of Acincum. *Illok; Ujlak.*

MILCORUS, Maced., i. q. Miacorus.

MILETOPOLIS, a town of Mysia, s. of Cyzicus, 20 m. s.w. from Apollonia ad Rhyndacum. A colony of Mitylenians from Cyzicus. *Melté.*

MILETUM, a town of Attica, of the tribe Cecropeis.

MILETUS (Lelegeis), I. capital of Ionia, on the coast, 40 m. s. of Ephesus, towards the mouth of Mæander fl., but removed some distance from it by its deposits. Founded by Sarpedon, brother of Minos. Colonized by Ionians under Neleus. The birth-place of Thales, Anaximander, Anaximenes, of Timotheus, the musician, and the historians Cadmus and Hecatæus. Noted for its carpets and tapestry. *Palat.* II. a town on the N. coast of Crete, E. of Amnisus. The parent of Miletus, in Ionia. *Milato.* III. of Paphlagonia, 15 m. from Cereæ.

MILEUM, a town of Numidia, on the borders of Mauritania Cæsariensis, bet. Numiturianum and Nobæ Fasciani, w. of Cirta (30). *Milah.*

MILICHUS fl., a r. of Achaia, rising in Panachaicus m. and falling into the Corinthiacus sin. E. of Patræ. On its banks was a temple of Diana Triclaria.

MILIZEGERIS ins., an isl. of India i. Gangem, w. of Comaria prom.

MILOLITUM, a town of the Cicones, Thrace, on the Egnatia Via, bet. Brendice (15) and Tempyra (15).

MILONIA, a town of the Marsi, Italy, w. of Alba Fucentia.

MILTŌDES m., a m. of Thebais, on the Red sea, N. of Myos Hormus.

MILTOPÆ, a naval station of Calabria, bet. Valetium and Portus Tarentinus. Constructed by Hadrian. *Torre di San Cataldo.*

MILYAS regio, *postea* Cabalis and Cibyra, I. a district of Lycia, settled by the Solymi of Phœnicia. II. of Pisidia, about Termessus and Isionda. III. capital of the cognominal district in Pisidia, s.e. of Pisidicus lacus.

MIMAS m., a m. of Ionia, on the w. side of Hermius sin., N. of Erythræ, and extending through Asia Minor for 250 m. Full of wild beasts. Hence the Bacchantes were called Mimallones. *Caravouno.*

MIMATE, the later capital of the Gabali, after the destruction of Gabali. *Mende.*

MIMIZA, a town of Syria, bet. Cyrrhus (20) and Beræa (22). *Aazaz ?*

MIN, a town of Drangiana, on Etymandrus fl., above Ariape.

MINA fl., I. a r. of Mauritania Cæsar., falling into Chinalaph fl., L., towards its mouth. II. a town of Mauritania Cæsar., on Mina fl., R., near its source.

MINARIACUM, a town of the Menapii, Belgica II., bet. Castrum Morinorum N.W. and Turnacum E.

MINÆI, a people of Arabia Felix, E. of the Cinædocolpitæ, Alitæi, and Cassanitæ, extending from the Red sea towards Zames m. *Beni Ateybe.*

MINCIUS fl., a r. of Gallia Transpadana, rising in Alpes Rhætiæ, s.w. of Anonium, and, after passing through Benacus lac., falling into Padus fl. below Mantua. *Mincio.*

MINERVÆ prom., Campaniæ, i. q. Surrentinum.

MINERVIUM, I. Bruttii, i. q. Castrum Minervæ. II. a town of the Cenomanni, Gallia Transp., on Mela fl., R. *Manerbio.*

MINIO (Mindo) fl., a r. of Etruria, falling into Tyrrhenum mare at Graviscæ. *Mignone.*

MINIUS (Bainis) fl., a r. of Callæcia, rising N. of Lucus Augusti and falling into the Atlantic s. of Abobrica. Named from its minium, "red-colouring earth." *Minho.*

MINIZUS (Regemnezus, Mizagus), a town of the Tectosages, Galatia, bet. Lagania (21) and Manegordium (28). Here Arcadius published his code of laws.

MINNA, a maritime town of Tripolis Africæ, bet. Quintiliana and Getullum.

MINNAGARA, a town of Larica, Indiæ, 28 geog. m. from Barygaza, on Namadus fl. *Mahmudabad.*

MINNETH, a town of Peræa, bet. Heshbon (4) and Philadelphia. Noted for its wheat.

MINNI, a people of Armenia, in Taurus m.

MINNOCERTA, a town of Osrhoene, bet. Gallaba and Nisibis.

MINOA, I. a pr. of Megaris, in the Saronicus sin., over against Nisæa. It was at one period an island. II. a town of Amorgos ins., s. of Ægiale. The birthplace of Simonides. *Porto Bathy.* III. of Crete, in Didymi sin., E. of Camara, 7½ m. N.W. from Hierapytna. *Porto Triani.* IV. (Minoum), of Crete, at the N. of Minous sin. Built by Minos. *Sirda.* V. of Laconia, at a cognominal prom. on the Ægean, N. of Epidaurus. *Monembasia* or *Nauplia di Malvasia.*

MINODUNUM, a town of the Ambrones, Maxima Sequanorum, bet. Aventicum N.E. and Bromagus s. *Mouton.*

MINORCA ins., the "smaller" of the Baleares ins., Tarraconensis. *Minorca.*

MINOUS sin., a bay of the Ægean, in Crete, E. of Drepanum prom. *G. di Suda.*

MINTHE m., a m. of Triphylia, Elis, s.E. of Scillus, whither some of the centaurs retired on the death of Chiron. *M. Smyrne.*

MINTURNÆ, a town of the Ausones, Latium, on Liris fl., 3 m. from its mouth, bet. Formiæ (9) and Sinuessa (9), on Via Appia. A colonia 298 B.C. Surrounded by marshes, the refuge of Marius. *Minturni.*

MINYA, *prius* Almon, Almonia, a town of Thessaly.

MINYÆ, I. a tribe of Thessalians who emigrated to Bœotia, under Minyas, and settled in Orchomenus, surnamed after them Minyan. II. descendants of the Argonauts, first settled in Lemnos and then in Laconia and Triphylia, on the confines of Arcadia, whence they expelled the Paroreatæ.

MINYAS (Minni), a district of Armenia Maj., on the Euphrates, L., towards its source, N. of Arsissa. *Manavazean.*

MINYEUS fl., Elid., i. q. Anigrus. Named after the Minyæ.

MIROBRIGA, I. a town of the Cynetes, Lusitania, N. of Lacobriga. II. of the Turtuli, Bætica, N., bet. Contosolia N.W. and Sisapo E.S.E. *Capilla.*

MIRYANDRUS, a Phœnician town of Cilicia Campestris, s.w. of Alexandria ad Issum.

MISĒNUM, I. a pr. of Campania, s. of Cumæ, over against Prochyta ins. The burial-place of Misenus, the trumpeter of Æneas ; or, according to Strabo, a companion of Ulysses. *Capo Miseno.* II. the port of Cumæ, Campan., within Misenum prom. Under the empire the naval station of the fleet of the Mare inferum. Near it was Cicero's Cumæan villa, and a magnificent villa of C. Marius, afterwards the property of Tiberius, and the scene of that emperor's death. It was at Misenum that the elder Pliny was stationed, as commander of the fleet, when he perished.

MISĒTUS, a town of Macedonia.

MISEUS (Mises, Misis) fl., a r. of Picenum, falling into the sea N. of Potentia. *Muscone.*

MISGOMENÆ, a town of Thessaly.

MISNA, a town of Zeugitana, on Carthaginensis sin., over against Clypia, 8½ geog. m. from Carthage. *Sidy Doude.*

MISPAH, "place of observation," I. the highest summit of Gilead m. II. (Maspha, Mizbeh), a town of Judah, Judæa, 20 m. s. of Jerusalem. The dwelling-place of Samuel. III. of Gad. The residence of

Jephtha. IV. of Moab. The retreat of David's parents.

MISTHEA, a town of Lycaonia, bet. Lystra and Vasata.

MISUS fl., a r. of Umbria, falling into the sea at Seno Gallia.

MITHRIDATIS regio, a district of Sarmatia As., on the Rha, above the Melanchlæni.

MITHRIDATIUM, a town of the Trocmi, Galatia, on the borders of Pontus, and within the limits of that kingdom, until dismembered from it by Pompey.

MITIBI, a people of Sarmatia As., on Vardanes fl., R.

MITYLENE (Mytilene), capital of Lesbos ins., on the E. coast, over against Attalia. Named from Mitylene, daughter of Macareus. The birth-place of Sappho, of Alcæus, of Myrsilus, of Hellanicus, and of Theophanes. Under Rome a free city. A colonia of Trajan. Noted for its wine, the beauty of its women, and for its shell fish. *Metelin.*

MITYS fl., a r. of Pieria, Macedonia, falling into the Haliacmon below Æane.

MIZAGUS, Galat., i. q. Minizus.

MIZI, the people of Masora, Arabiæ.

MIZREPHOTH-MAIM, i. q. Sarepta.

MNASYRIUM prom., the s. extremity of Rhodus ins. *C. Tranquillo.*

MNEMIUM prom., the termination of Isius m., on the Red sea, opposite Zaaram, in Arabia. *Cape Calmes.*

MNEMOSYNE fons, a sacred spring of Bœotia, rising close to Lethe fons, and forming with it the river Hercyne.

MOCATA, a town of Bithynia, towards Heraclea.

MOAB m., a ridge of Abarim m., separating Moabitis from Idumæa.

MOABITIS (Moab), a district of Arabia Petræa, bounded w. by Ammonitis at Arnon fl., s. by Sared fl., E. by Abarim m., w. by the Dead sea. Named from Moab, son of Lot, whose descendants wrested it from the Emim, a race of giants.

MOCCALESII, the people of Moccle, Phrygia.

MOCCLE (Molpe, Molte), a town of Phrygia Epict., on the borders of Bithynia.

MOCISSUS, a town of Morimene, Galatia, on Halys fl. above Nyssa. *Mochiour.*

MODIA, a town of Colchis, s. of Cytæa.

MODIANA, i. q. Midian.

MODICIA, a town of the Insubres, in Gallia Transpadana, 12 m. N.E. from Mediolanum. *Monza.*

MODIN (Modim), a village of Judæa, bet. Lydda N.W. and Emaus S.E. Here was the sepulchre of the Maccabees.

MODIUS fl., a r. of Pontus, towards Petra.

MODOCÆ, a people of Sarmatia Asiat., E. of the Scythæ Regii.

MODOGALINGÆ, i. q. Maccocalingæ.

MODOGALLA, a town of Ariarica, Ind., s.w. of Sarimagula. *Modgull.*

MODOLANA, a town of Mauritania Cæsar., bet. Berzeo and Caput Budelli, w. of Cirta.

MODOMASTICE, a district of Carmania, occupying its N.E. angle.

MODŎNUS (Modnunnus) fl., a r. of Hibernia, N. of Sacrum prom., separating the Menapii from the Brigantes. *Slaney.*

MODRA, a town of Phrygia Epictetus.

MODUBÆ, a people of India i. Gangem.

MODUTTU, a port of Taprobane, w., bet. Galiba prom. and Margana. *Moladiva.*

MODURA, capital of Pandionis reg., Ind., E. of Cottiara. *Madura.*

MŒNUS fl., a r. of Germania Mag., rising N.W. of Rhiusiana by a double spring, and falling into the Rhine at Mogunciacum. *Maine.*

MŒRITÆ, a people of Arabia Felix, s. of Macoraba. *About Mehkra.*

MŒRIDIS (Mœrios, Myris) lacus, an artificial lake of Heptanomis, near the Nile, s. of Arsinoe-Crocodilopolis. Said, but it would seem erroneously, to have been constructed by king Mœris. *Birket el Korn.*

MŒSI, a people of Mœsia, who colonized Mysia.

MŒSIA (Mysia in Europa), a country of Europe, bounded N. by Dacia, at the Danube, s. by Macedonia and Thrace, at Scordus m. and Hæmus m., w. by Illyria, at Drinus fl., E. by the Euxine. It was divided into Mœsia Superior (w.), and Mœsia Inferior (E.) by Ciabrus fl. *Servia and Bulgaria.*

MŒSIA SILVA, a forest of Etruria, conquered from the territory of Veii by Ancus Marcius. It was infested with dormice. *Bosco di Baccano ?*

MOGARON, a town of the Trocmi, in Galatia, bet. Tavium (36) and Daranon.

MOGITIANA (Mogentiana), a town of the Amantini, Pannon., bet. Mestriana (30) and Vulcum. *Szalaber.*

MOGONTIACUM (Magontiacum), capital of the Vangiones, Germania I., on the Rhine, above Bingium. Founded by Drusus B.C. 13. *Maintz; Mayence.*

MOGRUS (Nigrus) fl., I. a r. of Colchis, falling into the Euxine s. of Phasis. II. (Nigrus), a town of Colchis, at the mouth of Mogrus fl.

MOLADA (Malatha), a town of Simeon, Judæa, s.w. of Arad.

MOLARIA, a town of Sardinia, bet. Hafa (24) and Ad Medias (12). *Mulargia.*

MOLOCIS fl., a r. of Bœotia, rising in Cithæron m.

MOLOE, a town of Cilicia Trachea.

MOLOGENI, a people of Scythia i. Imaum, s. of the Sætiani.

MOLORCHI nemus, a grove at Nemea, in Argolis, where the Nemean games were celebrated. Named after Molorchus, the host of Hercules.

MOLOSSI, a tribe of Pelasgi, in Epirus, named after Molossus.

MOLOSSIS, I. a district of Epirus, extending along the coast bet. Cassiopeia and Amphilochia, and inland along the Arachthus fl., towards the source of the Æas fl. Noted for its breed of large dogs. *Jannina.* II. (Molossia), a name of Epirus, from Molossus, son of Pyrrhus I. by Andromache.

MOLURIS, a rock of Megaris, on the s. coast, w. of Megara, whence Ino leaped into the sea.

MOLYBODES, the Greek name of Plumbia ins., Sardiniæ.

MOLYCRIA (Molycrium), a town of Ætolia, on the coast, w. of Antirrhium. Colonized by Corinthians. *Cavrolimne.*

MOLYNDÆA, a town of Lycia.

MOMEMPHIS (Therenuthis), a town of Lower Egypt, on Agathos Dæmon fl., R., bet. Nicium and Letoplis. Here Venus was worshipped under the form of a heifer. *Teraneh.*

MONA ins., an isl. of the Ordovices, in Britannia II., s. of Monarina ins. The chief seat of the British Druids. *Anglesey.*

MONABÆ, a town of Isauria.

MONACHA ins., an isl. of India i. Gangem, s. of Comaria prom.

MONADES, an Illyrian tribe, whom, with the Dardi, Diomed found in occupation of a portion of Daunia Apul., about Apina, and whom he destroyed.

MONALUS fl., a r. of Sicily, falling into the Tyrrhenian sea, bet. Cephaloedium and Alæsa. *Pollina.*

MONAPIA ins., i. q. Monarina.

MONARINA (Monagria, Monadia) ins., an isl. of Maxima Cæsariensis, s.E. of Novantorum prom. The Mona of Cæsar. *Man.*

MONASTRA, a village of Bithynia, near Heracleum.

MONATE, a town of the Taurisci, Noricum, on Murus fl., 30 m. from Candalica. *Oberwohls.*

MONDELA, a town of the Aii, Ind., bet. Cottiara and Modurla.

MONESI, a people of Novem Populana. *About Moneins.*

MONETIUM, a town of the Japydes, in Illyria.

MONILIA, a maritime town of the Apuani, in Liguria, on Via Aurelia, bet. Ad Solaria (6) and In Apennino (13). *Moneglia.*

MONOCALINI, a people of Histria. *About Montona.*

MONOCANUNON, a port of Egypt, 10 m. s. from Alexandria.

MONODACHYLUS m., a prom. of the Troglodytæ, on the Red sea, above Deorum Salutaris portus, E.N.E. of Meroe. *Cap. Assiz.*

MONOGISSA, a town of Caria, with a temple of Diana Monogissene. Built by Dædalus.

MONOGLOSSA, a town of Larica, near Mophis fl. *Cambay?*

MONOLEUS lacus, a lake of the Colobi, near Ptolemais-Theron.

MONOSGADA, a town of Germania Magna, towards Bergium.

MONS BALABUS, I. a town of Lucania, bet. Polentia and Forum Popilii (5). *Pietra Fesa.* II. BRISIACUS, a town of the Tribocci, Germania I., on the Rhine, above Argentoratum. *Breisach.* III. MARIANUS, a town of the Turtuli, Bætica, under Marianus m., N. of Lælia. IV. SACER, hills of Sabinium, on Anis fl., near its junction with the Tiber, and extending along the latter river to Crustumerium. Celebrated as the spot whither the Roman commons were accustomed to retire from the oppression of the nobles. V. SANCTUS, i. q. Teches m. VI. SELEUCUS, a town of the Vocontii, Narbonensis, bet. Vapincum N.E. and Theopolis S.S.W. VII. SILICIS (Ilicis), a town of the Veneti, in Venetia, under a cognominal m., s. of Patavium. *Monselice.*

MONTEFEREBRUM, a town of Umbria, 2 m. E. from Sarsina. *Montefeltro; San Leo.*

MOPH, the Scriptural name of Memphis.

MOPHIS fl., a r. of India i. Gangem, falling into Barygazenus sin. *Mhye; Mahi.*

MOPSIUM, a town of Pelasgiotis, in Thessaly, S.E. of Larissa. *Eremo.*

MOPSOPIA, I. an early name of Attica, from the hero Mopsopus or Mopsops. II. a name of Pamphylia, from the soothsayer Mopsus.

MOPSUCRENE, a district of Cilicia, N.

MOPSUESTIA, *postea* Mamista, a town of Cilicia Campestris, on Pyramus fl., above Mallus. Founded by Mopsus the soothsayer. Under Rome a free city. *Messis.*

MORA, I. a town of Corsica, under Aurius

m., E. of Urcinium. II. of Numidia, bet. Vasampus and Thebeste.

MORBIUM, a maritime town of the Brigantes, Brit., at the s. entrance of Ituna æstuar., below Virosidum.

MORDULA, a port of Taprobane, N., bet. Procuri and Aburatha.

MORDULI, a people of Taprobane, on the E. coast, bet. the Tarachi and the Bocani.

MOREH ("high oak"), a grove of oaks near Shechem.

MORENE, a district of Mysia, towards Abrettene.

MORGES, an early name of a portion of Œnotria.

MORGINNUM, a town of the Allobroges, Viennensis, bet. Tarecionum, N.W., and Cularo.

MORIAH m., a hill at Jerusalem, on which the Temple was built.

MORICAMBE æstuar., an æstuary of Britain, s. of Setantiorum portus, bet. Longoricum and Morbium. *Morcambe Bay.*

MORIDUNUM, a town of the Damnonii, Brit., on the coast, N.E. of Ad Durium. *Seaton.*

MORIMARUSA mare ("Dead sea"), the portion of Borealis oceanus w. of Rubeas prom.

MORIMENE (Muriana), a prefecture of Cappadocia, on the confines of Galatia. *Kircher.*

MORÏNI, a people of Belgica II., on the seacoast, bet. the Ambiani and Nervii, N.W. of the Atrebates. *Part of Pas de Calais.*

MORIUS fl., a r. of Bœotia, rising in Thurium m., and falling into Cephissus fl.

MORON, a town of the Vettones, on the Tagus, s.w. of Norba Cæsarea. *Montalvao.*

MORONTOBARA. *Vide* Portus Mulierum.

MOROSGI, a town of the Varduli, Tarraconensis, on the coast.

MORU, a town of Meroe, on the Nile, L., bet. Satachta and Nakis. *Near Koraigh.*

MORTUUM mare, Palestinæ, i. q. Asphaltitis lacus.

MORUNDA, a town of Atropatene, Mesopot., s. of Rubena. *Marand.*

MORUM lac., a salt lake of Lycia, on the coast bet. Sacrum prom. and Crambusa.

MORYLLUS, a town of Anthemus, in Macedonia, s.e. of Thessalonica.

MOSA, I. a r. of Germania II., rising s. of Andematunum, and falling into the Rhine below Grinnes. *Meuse.* II. a town of the Lingones, Lugdunensis I., N.E. of Andematunum. III. of the Remi, Belgica II., on the Mosa, R., bet. Vungo vicus s.w. and Epoissum.

MOSÆUS fl., a r. of Susiana, falling into Per-

sicus sin. bet. the Eulæus and the Tigris.

MOSCHA portus, a port of Arabia Felix, on Sachalites sin., bet. Tretus portus and Syagrium prom. *Kesem.*

MOSCHI, a people of Colchis and Iberia, about Moschici m. *Moskethi.*

MOSCHICI (Mesech) m., a N.E. extension of Paryadres m., on the N.W. border of Armenia Inf., in Iberia. *Mesidji-Dagh.*

MOSCHIUS fl., a r. of Mœsia, falling into the Danube at Tricornium.

MOSCONNUM, a town of the Tarbelli, Novem Populana, bet. Aquæ Tarbellicæ, s.e. and Segosa N.

MOSDORANUS m., mountains of Asia, separating Aria from Parthia.

MOSEGA, a town of Albania, on Albanus fl., towards its source.

MOSEROTH (Mosera), a village of Idumæa, s.e. of Kades Barnea. Here the Israelites encamped.

MOSON, a town of Paphlagonia, w. of Andrapa.

MOSILEA fl., a r. of Gaul, rising s.w. of Argentovaria, and falling into the Rhine at Confluentes.

MOSSINE, i. q. Mostene.

MOSTENE, a town of Hyrcanius campus, in Lydia. Noted for its nuts.

MOSTEVIA, a town of the Damnonii, Brit., near Herculis prom.

MOSYCHLUS m., a volcanic m. of Lemnos ins.

MOSYLICUM prom., a pr. of Æthiopia, on Erythræum mare, E. of Munda.

MOSYLUM, a port of Æthiopia, at Mosylicum prom. A cinnamon emporium.

MOSYNA, a town of Phrygìa, N. of Laodicea.

MOSYNŒCIA ("dwellers in *mosuni*, wooden towers"), the country of the Mosynœci, in Pontus, on the coast, bet. the Tibareni and the Drilæ. Singular for a custom of starving their king into good order. *Heldir.*

MOTENE, Armen. Maj., i. q. Otene.

MUNICHIATIS, a town of the Nabathæi, Arabia, E. of Petra. *Maan.*

MOTHO ("place of death"), a village of Arabia. The death-place of Antigonus the Macedonian.

MOTYA (Motye), a maritime town of Sicily, w., on an island, joined to the mainland by a causeway 6 furlongs in length, bet. Drepanum and Ægithallus. The oldest Phœnician settlement in the island. Remarkable for the beauty of its architecture. The inhabitants were removed by Himilco to Lilybæum.

MOTYCANUS fl., a r. of Sicily, falling into

Africum pelagus w. of Odysseum prom. *Sicali.*

MOTYCE (Motuca), a town of Sicily, near the source of Motycanus fl. *Modica.*

MOTYUM, a fortress of Sicily, near Agrigentum.

MOURGISCE, a town of the Cicones, in Thrace, near Hebrus fl.

MOXIANI, a tribe of Phrygians towards Peltæ.

MOXŒNE, a district of Assyria, on the confines of Chiliocome.

MUCAPORIS sinus, an inlet of Bosporus Thracius, in Bithynia, N. of Amycus.

MUCHIRESIS, a district of Colchis, on Phasis and Rheion ffl.

MUCRÆ, a town of the Pentri, in Samnium, s. of Sepinum. *Morcone.*

MUGILONES, a tribe of Semnones, about Semnon lacus.

MUHARUR, a maritime town of Numidia, bet. Tacatria and Zaca.

MULIADUS fl., Tarraconensis, i. q. Monda.

MULIERUM portus, Morontobara, a port of India i. Gangem, bet. Salaca and Arabis fl. *Sonmany.*

MULUCHA (Molochath), I. a r. of Mauritania Ting., rising in Atlas Maj., and falling into the Mediterranean E. of Metagonitis prom. It separates Mauritania Tingitana from Mauritania Cæsariensis. *Mulivia; Mohalon.* II. a town of Mauritania Tingit., on Mulucha fl. Of uncertain position.

MUMASTUS, a town of Caria.

MUNDA (Monda, Muliadus) fl., a r. of Lusitania, rising near Lancia Oppidana, and falling into the Atlantic midway bet. the Tagus and the Durius. *Mondego.*

MUNDA, I. a town of the Carpetani, Tarraconensis, bet. Alce w.s.w. and Paterniana N.E. II. of the Turtetani, Bætica, bet. Certima N.E. and Salduba s.w. Memorable for the battle bet. Cæsar and the sons of Pompey. *Monda.*

MUNDU ins., I. an isl. of Æthiopia, in Erythræum mare, w. of Mosylicum prom., opposite Arabiæ Felicis Emp. II. (Mundi Emporium), a port of Æthiopia, on Mundu ins. *Mete.*

MUNICIPIUM, a town of the Triballi, Mœs., on Margus fl., R., bet. Ad Novas and Jovis pagus, 16 m. s. from Viminacium.

MUNIMENTUM SUETONII, a fortress of Mauritania Ting., on Mulucha fl., L., towards its source.

MUNITIUM, a town of the Bructeri Maj., Germ., N. of Aliso. *Near Bielefeld.*

MUNYCHIA portus, a fortified harbour of Attica, constituting, with Piræus and Phalerum, the port of Athens. With a temple of Diana Munychia, built by Munichus of Orchomene. *Stratioki.*

MURANIMAL, a town of the Calingii, Arabiæ, towards Capeus sin. *Al Borani.*

MURANUM, a town of Lucania, bet. Interamnia and Aprustum. *Castro Villari.*

MURATIUM, a town of the Ambrones, Maxima Sequanorum, bet. Petenisca N.E. and Aventicum s.w.

MURBOGII, i. q. Turmodigi, Curgonii.

MUREOLA, a town of Pannonia Sup., on Murus fl., R., above Ad Vicesimum, N.W. of Poetovium

MURGANTIA (Murtantia), I. a town of Samnium. *Baselice.* II. (Murgantium, Morgantia, Morgantium), a town of Sicily, on Simæthus fl., R., towards its mouth.

MURGILLUM. *Vide Mursa.*

MURGIS (Murgi, *postea* Almerja), a maritime town of the Bastuli, Bætica, bet. Abdera w. and Turaniana N. *Almeria.*

MUROCENATA, a town of Pannonia Inf., 100 m. from Brigetium. The residence of the empress Justina and Valentinianus her son.

MUROELA, a town of Pannonia Sup., on Murus fl. *Mureck?*

MURRA, a town of the Chætuari, Germ., on Niter fl., R., below Clarenna.

MURSIA (Mursa), a town of Pannonia Inf., on Dravus fl., bet. Mursella (10) and Teutoburgium. A colonia of Hadrian. *Eszeg.*

MURSELLA, a town of Pannonia Inf., bet. Mursa (10) and Jovallium. *Petrovicz.*

MURUS, I. a town of the Oretani, Tarraconensis, 27 m. N.W. of Laminium. Near it the Anas, having run some way under ground, reappears. *Mortales.* II. of the Venonetes, in Gallia Transp., bet. Tinetio (15) and Summus lac. (20). III. fl., a r. of Pannonia Sup., rising in Noricum, and falling into Dravus fl. at Carrhodunum.

MURZUPALE, a town of Ariaca Ind., N.E. of Aramagara.

MUSA, *prius* Mesa, a port of the Homeritæ, Arabia Felix. on the Red sea, towards its mouth. *Moosa.*

MUSÆ, a town of Heptanomis, on the Nile, R., bet. Alyi and Cynopolis.

MUSAGORÆ ins., three islets of Crete, off Criumetopon prom.

MUSARNA, capital of the Musiranæi, Gedros., under Bætius m., N.W. of Cottobara.

MUSARNA, a port of Gedrosia, bet. Badara and Cissa. *Sucedur.*

MUSEUM, a place in Macedonia, near Olympus m.

MUSIRANÆI, a people of Gedrosia, on the confines of Arachosia, above Pardene.

MUSIS fl., a r. of Armenia Inf., rising in Scordisces m., and falling into the Araxes w. of Artagera. *Arpasu.*

MUSLUBIUM, a maritime town of Mauritania Cæsar., bet. Salde and Choba.

MUSONES, a people of Mauritania Cæsar., under Buzara m., s.w.

MUSTI, a town of Zeugitana, on Bagradas fl., R., bet. Thacia (7) and Tisnica (13). The place where Regulus killed the great serpent.

MUSTILIA, a town of Cilicia prefect., in Cappadocia.

MUSULA, a town of the Macæ, in Africa Prop., s. of Auzui.

MUTENUM, a town of the Boii, Pannon., bet. Scarabantia (12) and Vindobona (22). *Eisenstadt.*

MUTHA, a town of Mauritania Tingit., at the mouth of Mulucha fl.

MUTHIS, a town of Thebais, on the Nile, R., bet. Isium and Antæopolis (8).

MUTHUL, a town of Numidia, on Bagradas fl., R., bet. Ad Medera and Orba.

MUTILA, a town of Histria, on Flanaticus sin., N.E. of Polaticum prom. *Medolino.*

MUTÍNA, a town of Gallia Cispad., bet. Pons Secies (5) and Victuriolæ (3), on Via Æmilia Lepida. A colonia (151 B.C.) and municipium. Noted for its wool; and memorable for its siege by Mark Antony 45 B.C. *Modena.*

MUZIRITIS, a maritime town of Limyrica, Ind., bet. Callicorias prom. (5 geog. m.) and Pseudostoma fl. *Mirdschno.*

MYA ins., an isl. of Caria, in Ceramicus sin.

MYANDA (Myas, Mandane), a maritime town of Cilicia Trachea, 7 stadia w. from Posidium prom.

MYCALI m., a w. ridge of Tmolus m., in Ionia, parallel with Mæander fl., terminating in Trogilium prom. *Samsoun.*

MYCALESSUS, a town of Bœotia, bet. Harma and Aulis.

MYCENÆ, I. a city of Argolis, and formerly, in the time of Agammemon, its cap., bet. Argos (6¼) and Cleonæ. Named after Mycene, daughter of Inachus. Established as a kingdom by Perseus, 1313 B.C.; destroyed by Argives 468 B.C. Nearly extinct in Strabo's time. It was famed for its breed of horses. *Krabata.* II. a town of Crete, founded by Agamemnon.

MYCHOS portus, the port of Bulis, in Phocis, E. of Pharygium prom. *Hagios Lukas.*

MYCONIUS m., a N.E. continuation of Taurus m., in Sicily, above Tauromenium.

MYCONUS ins., an isl. in the Ægean, one of the Cyclades, bet. Tenos and Naxos. Beneath it the last of the centaurs, slain by Hercules, was buried. The people were noted for baldness. *Myconi.*

MYGDONES, a tribe of Thracians, contiguous to the Bryges or Briges, in Thrace, towards Bermius m.

MYGDONIA, I. a district of Macedonia, bounded on the N. by Pæonia, on the s. by Chalcidice, on the w. by Emathia and Bottiæa, on the E. by Thrace. II. a region of Mesopotamia, N.E., on Mygdonius fl., E. of Osrhoene. *Dyar-rabiah.*

MYGDONIUS fl., a r. of Mesopotamia, rising in Masius m., N.E. of Nisibis, and falling into Chaboras fl. at Thubida. *Nahr al Hauali.*

MYGDUNE, i. q. Midæum.

MYLA fl., a r. of Sicily, falling into Siculum mare bet. Alabon fl. and Thapsus. *Marcellino ? San Guliano ?*

MYLÆ, I. an isl. on the w. coast of Crete, over against Phalasarna. *Sordi or Pelatidi.* II. a maritime village of Cilicia Trachea, on a peninsula N.E. of Nesulium. *Aghaliman.* III. a town of Perrhæbia, in Thessaly. IV. a maritime city of Sicily N., on a cognominal peninsula, bet. Artemisium and Tyndaris. A Zanclean colony. *Melazzo.*

MYLANTIA prom., a pr. of Rhodus ins., s. of Camirus. *C. Candura.*

MYLAON fl., I. a r. of Arcadia, rising in Thesoa reg., and falling into Alpheus fl. II. of Arcadia, near Methydrium, falling into Gortynius fl.

MYLAS fl., a r. of Sicily, falling into the sea at Mylæ. *Mela.*

MYLASA, a city of Caria, and at one time its capital. Here was a celebrated temple of Jupiter Carius. The birth-place of the orators Euthydemus and Hybreas. *Melasso.*

MYNDUS (Neapolis), a port of Caria, on Jassicus sin., w. of Caryanda, 56 m. s. from Miletus. A colony from Palæmyndus. Ridiculed for its enormous gates. *Menlesha.*

MYON, a town of the Locri Ozolæ, on the confines of Phocis, bet. Chaleon and Amphissa (4 m.).

MYONNESUS, I. one of the Pisistratidæ ins. of Ionia. II. an island of Thessaly, at the w. entrance of Pagasæus sin. *Argyro.* III. a town of Ionia, on a cognominal prom., s. of Teos, of which it was a dependency. For a time the abode of the comedians expelled from Teos. *Hysili-Bounos.*

MYOS-HORMOS (Aphrodite, Portus Veneris),

"port of the mouse," a port of Thebais, on the Red sea, bet. Arsinoe and Philotera. Named from the intricacy of its entrance. *Suffange al Bahri.*

MYRA, one of the six cities of Lycia, on Andriacus fl., 2½ m. from its mouth.

MYRÆ, a town of Magnesia, in Thessaly, on the coast, bet. Peneus fl. and Eurymnæ.

MYRCINUS, a town of the Edones, in Thrace, on Strymon fl. Rich in timber and in mines. It was granted by Darius to Histiæus of Miletus. Cleon the Athenian was killed at the siege of this place. *Orphano.*

MYRHINA, a town of Lemnos ins., opposite Athos m., the shadow of which, according to Pliny, was visible in the forum of this town, a distance of 37 m., in the summer solstice. *Castro.*

MYRIANDRUS, a town of Cilicia, near Alexandria ad Issum, w. A Phoenician settlement.

MYRIANGELI, a later name of Germa, in Galatia.

MYRCION, a village of the Tolistoboii, in Galatia, bet. Germa and Vindia.

MYRINA, *postea* Sebastopolis, the most ancient of the twelve cities of Æolis Asiat., on Elæaticus sin., 5 m. w. from Gryneum. Built by Myrinus. *Nemourt.*

MYRINA, a town of Crete, N. of Lyctus. *Mirina.*

MYRINUS campus, the district about Myrina, in Æolis Asiat.

MYRIOCEPHALUS, Phrygiæ, i. q. Holmi.

MYRLIA, the early name of Apamea, in Bithynia, from Myrleus, the Colophonian general, or from the Amazon Myrlea. Destroyed by Philip, son of Demetrius. The birth-place of Asclepiades the grammarian.

MYRLIANUS sin., Bithyniæ, i. q. Cianus sin.

MYRMECES ins., islets of Ionia, in Hermius sin., s. of Leucæ, opposite the former mouth of Hermus fl.

MYRMECIUM, a town of Taurica Chersonesus, on Bosporus Cimmerius, E. of Panticapæum.

MYRMEX ins., an isl. of Cyrenaica, off Phycus prom. w.

MYRMIDONES, *vide* Ægina ins.

MYRMISSUS (Mermessus), a town of Mysia, near Gergithium.

MYRONIS ins., an isl. of the Troglodytæ, in the Red sea, N. of Deorum Salutaris portus. *Marata.*

MYRRHIFERA REGIO EXTERIOR, a region of Arabia Felix, on the s. coast, bet. Macpha and Saphar.

MYRRHIFERA REGIO INTERIOR, a mountain-

ous district of Arabia Felix, towards the Red sea, w. of Saba. *Mountains* E. *of Tayf.*

MYRRHINUS, "full of myrtles," a demus of Attica, of the tribe Pandionis, on the Ægean, s. of Halæ Araphenides.

MYRSINUS, *postea* Myrtuntium, a town of Epea, in Elis, towards the coast, 9 m. N.W. from Elis. *Kaloteichos.*

MYRTIUM, a town of the Cicones, in Thrace.

MYRTOS ins., an isl. of Euboea, lying w. of its s. extremity. Named after Myrto, and itself giving name to Myrtoum mare.

MYRTOUM mare, the portion of the Ægean bet. Argolis and Attica w., and the Cyclades E., extending s. to the extremity of Laconia.

MYRTUNTIUM, I. a salt lake of Acarnania, s. of Actium. *Lago di Valkharia.* II. a town of Acarnania, on Myrtuntium lacus. *Murtari.*

MYSARIS prom., the s. extremity of Achillei cursus, Sarmatia.

MYSECROS (Masora) fl., a r. of the Omanitæ, Arabia Felix, falling into the sea bet. Acilla and Damnia. *Moiesar.*

MYSI (Moesi), the people of Moesia, along the Danube to Jaterus fl.

MYSIA, "beech," I. a country of Asia Minor, bounded N. by the Propontis and Hellespont, s. by Lydia, w. by the Ægean, E. by Bithynia and Phrygia. Settled by Moesi from Thrace, some time before the siege of Troy. II. a town of Aria, on the confines of the Masdora m.

MYSIA MAJOR, the s. portion of Mysia in Asia Minor.

MYSIA MINOR, or Olympena, the N. portion of Mysia in Asia Minor.

MYSIUS fl., a r. of Mysia, rising in Temnus m., and falling into Caicus fl.

MYSOCORAS portus, a port of Maurit. Tingit., w. bet. Phthuth fl. and Solis m. *Safi.*

MYSO-MACEDONES (Aschilacæ), a people of Central Mysia.

MYSTIA, a town of Bruttium, N. of Cocynthum prom. *Monasteraci.*

MYSTUS ins., one of the Echinades ins.

MYTHELOPIS (i. q. Basilinopolis), a town of Bithynia, on Ascania palus, N.W. *Dscheranite.*

MYTISTRATUM (Amistrata), a town of Sicily, E. of Paropus. *Mistretta.*

MYUS, Cilic., i. q. Myanda.

MYUS, one of the twelve cities of Ionia, bet. Priene and Miletus. Founded by Cydrelus, son of Codrus. It was bestowed by Artaxerxes upon Themistocles, to supply the cost of his table. It became so infested with gnats, owing to the accumulation of mud, that the inhabitants removed.

N.

NAANA, a town of Sarmatia Asiat., near the source of Corax fl.

NAARATHA, a town of Ephraim, in Samaria, 5 m. N.N.W. from Jericho.

NAARDA, Mesopotamiæ, i. q. Naharra.

NAARMALCHA, "royal river," a canal bet. the Euphrates at Fissenia, and the Tigris at Seleucia.

NAARSARES (Maarsares, Baarsares), a canal of the Euphrates, bet. Pirisabora, through Babylon, and above Sura. *Narsi.*

NABÆUS (Nabarus) fl., a r. of Britannia Barbara. *Navern.*

NABALIA fl., Germaniæ, i. q. Sala.

NABARTA, a port of Taprobane E., bet. Jovis prom. and Azanus fl.

NABATENE (Nabatæorum regio, Nebajoth), generally, the country of the Nabathæi, bet. the head of the Red sea and Babylonia, comprising all Arabia Deserta and part of Arabia Petræa; specially, the district on the Red sea, s. of the Midianitæ. Named from Nebajoth, the first-born of Ismael.

NABATHÆI, *vide* Nabatene.

NABIA, a town of the Lucenses, Tarrac., at the mouth, R., of Nabius fl., bet. Liburnia and Burum. *Navia.*

NABIANI, a people of Sarmatia, towards the N.E. coast of the Euxine.

NABIUS fl., a r. of Tarraconensis, falling into Cantabricum mare at Navia. *Navia.*

NABLIS (Bacus) fl., a r. of Germania Magna, falling into the Danube. *Naabe.*

NACARRORUM palus, a marsh on the E. coast of Tarraconensis, near the mouth of the Iberus s.

NACOLÉA, a town of Phrygia Epict., s. of Dorylcum (20). The locality of the defeat of Procopius by Valens.

NACROSA, a town of Lydia, N.E. of Germa. *Bakhir.*

NADRA fl., a r. of Gallia Cisalpina, falling into the Padus near Placentia.

NÆANDRIA, an Æolic town of Troas, bet. Hamaxitus and Ilium Novum (16¼). Its inhabitants were transported to Alexandria Troas. *Enai.*

NÆBIS fl., a r. of Callæcia, falling into the Atlantic bet. Limia fl. and Celadus fl. *Neya.*

NÆBUS fl., Tarraconensis, i. q. Melsus.

NÆVA, a town of the Turtuli, Bætica, on the Bætis, above Axati.

NAGADIBA, a port of Taprobane N., bet. Anubingara and Oxia prom.

NAGARA, a town of the Minæi, Arabiæ, N.E. of Labecia. *Nedjram.*

NAGARURIS, a town of the Badiamæi, Ind., N.E. of Hippocura. *Nagaram.*

NAGIA, a town of the Gebanitæ, Arabiæ, S.E. of Nagara. *Nagiah.*

NAGIDUS, a Samnian town of Cilicia Trachea, on Arymagdus fl., just above its mouth.

NAGIDUSA ins., I. an islet of Cilicia Trachea, off the mouth of Arymagdus fl. II. Cypri, i. q. Macaria.

NAHARRA (Naarda, Narraga, Neardia), a town of Ancobaritis, Mes., on an isl. of the Euphrates, bet. Besechana and Macepracta. In the Lower Age the Jews had a famous school here. *Haditha.*

NAHARVALES, a tribe of the Lygii, Germ., bet. the Omani and the Arii.

NAHARVALORUM lacus, a sacred grove of the Naharvali, Germ., near the Vistula, L.

NAIN, I. a town of Judah, in Judæa, N.E. of Hebron. II. of Manasseh, in Galilæa, near Capernaum. The scene of the restoration to life of the widow's son.

NAISSOPOLIS, a town of the Jazyges Metanastæ, on the Tibiscus, above its junction with the Danube.

NAISSUS (Nessum), a town of the Triballi, Mœs., on Margus fl., R., bet. Graniriana and Medianum. *Nezza; Nissath.*

NAKIS, a town of Meroe, on the Nile, L., bet. Moru and Tadu, s.w. of Napata. *Sannab.*

NAMADUS fl., a r. of India i. Gangem, rising in Vindius m. s., and falling into Barygazenus sin. at Barygaza. *Nerbuddha.*

NAMARE, a town of the Boii, in Noricum, on the Danube, bet. Arelate (7) and Trigesimum (16). *Molch.*

NAMASTÆ, a people of Scythia i. Imaum, bet. the Jaxartes and the Oxus.

NAMNÉTES, a people of Lugdunensis III., on the Liger fl., R., from its mouth to the Andecavi. *Part of Loire Inférieure.*

NANAGUNA fl., a r. of India i. Gangem, falling into Barygazenus sin. *Tiptee.*

NANASA fl., a r. of Tarraconensis, falling into Cantabricum mare bet. Saunium fl. E. and Deva fl. w. *Nausa.*

NANDE, a town of the Matiani, Media. *Selmas.*

NANICHÆ, a people of India e. Gangem, on the Ganges, L., towards its source.

NANIGIRI, a people of Taprobane, on the S.E. coast.

NANIGERIS ins., Taprob., i. q. Epinos.

NANTUÁTES, a people of Alpes Penninæ, on the s. shore of Lemanus lacus, E. of the Allobroges. The Chalbici of Avienus. *About Faucigny.*

NAPATA, a city of the Megabari, in Meroe, on the Nile, R., bet. Arabis and Sacole, 300 English m. S.E. of Syene. The capital of queen Candace; destroyed by Petronius. *Dongola; Gibel el Birkel?*

NAPATÆI, i. q. Nabathæi.

NAPARUS fl., a r. of Dacia, falling into the Danube above Troesmis. *Ardschisch.*

NAPE, a town of Lesbos ins., near Methymna.

NAPEGUS, a town of the Sabæi, in Arabia Felix, on the Red sea, bet. Aelu (6 geog. m.) and Sacatia.

NAPETINUS sin., i. q. Terinæus.

NAPHILUS fl., a r. of Arcadia, rising in Thesoa regio, and falling into Alpheus fl.

NAPHTHALI, a tribe of Israel, bounded N. by Antilibanus m., s. by Zebulon below Migdol, w. by Asser w. of Kedes, E. by the Jordan.

NAPITIA, a town of Bruttium, on Napetinus sin., E. of Hipponium. *Pizzo.*

NAPITÆ, a people of Sarmatia Asiatica.

NAPOCA (Napuca), a town of the Ratacenses, Dac., on Marisus fl., L., bet. Patavissa (24) and Salina (36). A colonia. *Maros Masarbhely.*

NAR fl. (*Sabin.* "sulphur"), a r. of Italy, rising in Fiscellus m., and, after separating Sabinium from Umbria, falling into the Tiber above Ocriculum. Noted for its sulphureous quality, and for its headlong current. *Nera.*

NARA, a town of Byzacene, bet. Madassuma and Suffetula (15).

NARACON OSTIUM, the s. mouth of the Danube.

NARAGGARA (Navaggara), a town of Numidia, bet. Sicca Venerea and Gegeta, 20 m. E. from Thagura. Here Scipio and Hannibal had an interview.

NARBA (Narhavan) fl., a canal connecting the Tigris, at Opis, with the Euphrates above Aserga.

NARBATA, a town of Judæa, S.E. of Cæsarea Palestina.

NARBO, I. i. q. Atax fl. II. *surnamed* Martius, capital of the Bebryces, Narbonensis I., near the coast, bet. Beterræ N.E. and Ad Vicesimum s., on Atax fl. The first colonia of Rome in Gaul (Colonia Atacinorum). It was also surnamed Colonia Decumanorum, as the settlement of the Legio Decumana. *Narbonne.*

NARBONENSIS I., a Roman division of Gaul, bet. the Rhone and the Pyrenees. *Languedoc and Rousillon.*

NARBONENSIS II., a Roman division of Gaul, E. and S.E. of Narbonensis I. *Provence.*

NARCASUS, a town of Caria.

NARDINIUM, a town of the Vaccæi, Tarraconensis, N.E. of Ocellodurum.

NARES, a town of Lucania, 9 m. E. from the mouth of Silarus fl. *Soccorso.*

NARIBUS, a town of Meninx ins., Byzac., E. below Uchium.

NARISCI (Nariscæ, Varisti), a people of Germania Mag., on the Danube, below the Hermunduri. *Under the Fichtelgebirge.*

NARMALIS, a town of Pisidia.

NARNIA, *prius* Nequinum, a town of Umbria, on Nar fl., L., bet. Ocriculum (12) and Interamnia (8), on Via Flaminia. A colonia 300 B.C. Famous for a bridge constructed by Augustus. *Narni.*

NARO fl., a r. of the Dalmatæ, falling into the Adriatic opposite Pharos ins. *Narenta.*

NARONA, a town of the Dalmatæ, in Illyria, on the Naro fl., 10 m. above its mouth. A colonia, and the seat of a conventus juridicus. *Castel Norin.*

NARRABO, i. q. Arrabo.

NARRAGA canalis, i. q. Macepracta.

NARTHAKION m., a hill of Phthiotis, in Thessaly, S.E. of Pharsalus. The scene of a defeat of the Thessalians by Agesilaus. *Nartakion.*

NARTHECUSA ins., an isl. of Rhodes.

NARTHECIS ins., an isl. of Samos, N.E. of Posidium prom.

NARTIA fl., a r. of Tarraconensis, falling into Minius fl. below Lacus Augusti.

NARYCIA (Naryx), a town of the Locri, in Bruttium, near Locri. Noted for its pitch.

NARYX (Narycium), a town of the Locri Opuntii, s.w. of Opus. The birth-place of Ajax, son of Oileas. Destroyed by the Phocians.

NASAMONES, the predominant people of Marmarica and Cyrenaica. A nation of robbers and wreckers, almost extirpated by Domitian. Their only object of worship was the manes of the dead.

NASCUS, *vide* Maocosmus.

NASCI, a people of Sarmatia Asiatica, s. of the Borusci.

NASI, a town of Arcadia, on Ladon fl., above Mesoboa.

NASICA, a town of the Marohæ, Ind., N. of Omenagora. *Nassuk.*

NASIUM, a town of the Leuci, Belgica I., S.E. of Caturigæ. *Nas, near Grand-Nancy.*

NASONACUM, a town of the Pæmani, Belgica I., s.s.w. of Tullum. *Nassogne.*

NASOS (Nesos, Naxos), a town of Acarnania, the port of Æniadæ, at the w. mouth of Achelous fl.

NASOTIANI, a people of Sogdiana.

NASSUNIA, a town of Sarmatia, S.E. of Corusia.

NATHABUR fl., a r. of Libya Interior, towards Girgiris m.

NATIOLUM, a maritime town of Peucetia, on Via Frentana, bet. Turenum (6) and Barium (19). *Bisceglie.*

NATISO fl., a r. of Venetia, rising in Alpes Carnicæ, S.W. of Larix, and falling into the Adriatic E. of Aquileia. *Natisone.*

NAUBARUM, a town of Sarmatia, on the Euxine, near Carcine.

NAUBOLUS, the early name of Drymæa, in Phocis.

NAUCRATICUM OSTIUM NILI, i. q. Canopicum.

NAUCRĂTIS, a town of the Delta Egypti, on the Canopic branch of the Nile, R. Enlarged by Milesian settlers, and long the sole trading mart of the Greeks in Egypt. Noted for its silver-plated cups. The birth-place of Athenæus and Julius Pollux. *Salhadschar.*

NAUGALOGÆ, a people of India e. Gangem, on Dorius fl., s. of the Damasæ.

NAULIBIS, a town of the Rhammæ, Gedrosia, s. of Sosxetra.

NAULŎCHUS, I. portus, Phocid., i. q. Mychos. II. a maritime town of the Selletæ, Thrace, on the confines of Mœsia. III. (Naulocha), a town and naval station of Sicily, N. bet. Porthmus and Melas fl.

NAUMACHÆI (Macæ), a people of Arabia, about Naumachæorum prom. *Beni Jowaser.*

NAUMACHÆORUM (Asabæorum) prom., a pr. of Arabia Felix, at the inner entrance of Persicus sin. *C. Mussendom; Ras Musandam.*

NAUNI, a people of Rhætia I., on Athesis fl., R., below the Venosti. *Val di Non.*

NAUPACTUS, "ship-building place," a town of the Locri Ozolæ, on Corinthiacus sin., E. of Antirrhium, bet. Molycria and Erythræ; where the Heraclidian fleet of invasion was built. Here were temples of Neptune and of Diana. Nearly destroyed by an earthquake, *temp.* Justinian. *Lepanto;* loc. *Enebacthi and Nepacto.*

NAUPLEIA m., one of the summits of Phædriates m.

NAUPLIA, "full of ships," a town of Argolis, at the head of the Argolicus sin., bet. Prosymna and Temenium (6). Founded by Nauplius, son of Neptune and Amymone. The inhabitants were removed by the Spartans to Methone Messen. *Napli di Romania.*

NAUPORTUS, I. a r. of Pannonia Sup., rising 6 m. s.w. of Nauportus, and falling into Savus fl. below Emona. *Laybach.* II. a Tauriscan town of Pannonia Sup., bet. Emona and Longaticum, on Nauportus fl. Named from the circumstance that the ship Argo having sailed so far down the Danube, Savus, and Nauportus ffl. towards Italy, was carried hence on men's shoulders to the Adriatic. *Ober Laybach.*

NAURA m., a ridge of Oxii m., on the N. frontier of Sogdiana.

NAUS prom., i. q. Lacinium.

NAUSIMACHIUM, "sea-fight," a pr. of Bithynia, on Bosporus Thracius, N. of Ciconium.

NAUSTALO, a port of Narbonensis, E. of Mansa vicus. *Mauguis.*

NAUSTATHMUS, I. a pr. of Cyrenaica, bet. Erythron and Apollonia. II. a port of Pentapolis, Cyrenaicæ, at Naustathmus prom. III. of Sicily, at the mouth of Cacyparis fl., s. of Syracuse. IV. of Pontus, 11½ m. S.E. from Halys fl., on the border of a cognominal marsh or lake.

NAUTACA, a town of Oxiana, Sogdian., S.E. of Maracanda.

NAVA fl., a r. of Germania I., falling into the Rhine at Bingium. *Nahe.*

NAVÆ, a town of the Estiones, Vindel., bet. Rostra Nemaviæ and Viaca.

NAVALE (Nandea), the port of Cythera, in Cythera ins. *Port' Antemona.*

NAVALIA, a haven at the mouth of the Rhine.

NAVARI, a people of Sarmatia Europ., bet. the Amadoci and the Jazyges.

NAVARUM (Naubarum), capital of the Navari, Sarmat., on Panticapes fl. Ptolemy places it on the Palus Mæotis.

NAVIA, a town of the Lucenses, in Callæcia, at the mouth of Nabius fl.

NAVIAN fl., i. q. Aroanius.

NAVILUBIO fl., a r. of Tarraconensis, falling into Cantabricum mare bet. Flavionavia E. and Libunea w. *Nalon.*

NAVOE, a town of Rhætia, 18 m. from Campodunum. *Raufbeuren.*

NAXIA, a town of Caria.

NAXOS (Strongyle, Dia, Callipolis, Dionysias), I. an island of the Ægean, one of the Cyclades, bet. Paros and Lelandros, in circuit 75 m. Settled by Carians. The birth-place of Bacchus. *Naxia.* II. capital of the cognominal island, on the N.W. coast. With a temple of Bacchus. III. a maritime town of Sicily, s. of Tauromenium. A Chalcedian colony. Destroyed by Dionysius.

NAXUANA, a town of Araxene, Armen., on the Araxes, L., below Artaxata. *Nakhdschavan.*

NAXUS, a town of Crete. Noted for its whetstones.

NAZADA, a town of Media-Atropatene, near the source of Gorgus fl., w. of Alinza, bet. Marziniaman and Seva Vicina. *Derbend*.

NAZARETH, a town of Galilæa, bet. Dio Cæsarea and Chesuloth, w. of Tabor m. The birth-place of our Saviour. *Nazaret*.

NAZARINI, a people of Syria, on Marsyas fl.

NAZARIS, *vide* Azilis.

NAZIANDUS, a town of Caria, towards Myndus.

NAZIANZUS, a town of Garsauritis, in Cappadocia, bet. Archelais (24) and Sesama (25).

NEA COME, *vide* Ænea.

NEÆ ins., an isl. of the Ægean, s.w. of Lemnos ins. *Stratia*.

NEÆ PATRÆ, a town of the Ænianes, in Thessaly, near Hypata. *Patragick*.

NEÆTHUS fl., a r. of Bruttium, falling into the Ionian sea bet. Crimisa (12) and Targines fl. (24.) Named from the captive Trojan women having here set fire to the Greek fleet. *Nieto*.

NEANDRIA, a town of Æolis Asiatica, on Adramyttean sin.

NEAPOLIS, I. a town of Babylonia, on the Euphrates, L., over against Fissenia. II. (Parthenopeia), a city of Campania, at the s.w. extremity of Cumanus sin. A colony from Cumæ, under Eumelus, but otherwise ascribed to the Phocæans and Rhodians, and, poetically, to the syren Parthenope (whose tomb was shown here in Strabo's time), and to Hercules. Noted for its luxury and its learning, and as the burial-place of Virgil. The sun was worshipped here in the form of a man-faced bull named Hebon. *Napoli; Naples.* III. Cariæ, i. q. Myndus. IV. a maritime town of the Celsitani, Sardinia, w. bet. Metalla and Othoca. *Sardara.* V. a maritime town of the Edones, in Thrace, E. of Scapte-hyle, the port of Philippi, where St. Paul landed on his way from Samothrace. VI. a town of Colchis, on the Euxine, at the mouth of Cyaneus fl. *Nabbakki.* VII. a town of Ionia, on the coast, 12 m. s.w. from Ephesus. *Scala Nova.* VIII. a town of Pallene, in Macedonia, on the Toronaicus sin., s.e. of Ægæ. IX. Cyrenaicæ, i. q. Cænopolis. X. a maritime town of Peucetia, Apul., 1 m. from Apanestæ, 50 m. s.e. from Canusium. *Polignano.* XI. a town of Pisidia, near Antiochia. XII. Syrtic. reg., i. q. Leptis. XIII. Samariæ, i. q. Sichem. XIV. a town of Taurica Chersonesus, N.E. of Argoda. XV. Egypti, i. q. Cænopolis. XVI. a

town of Zeugitana, on Neapolitanus sin., bet. Curubis and Putput (12). A Phœnician settlement. A colonia. It was for the most part swallowed up by the sea. *Nabal.*

NEAPOLITANUS sin., a bay of the Mediterranean, bet. Neapolis, Zeugitan., and Horrea Byzacen. *Gulf of Hamamet.*

NEARCHI, a people of Gaul, at the mouth of the Rhone.

NEATUM, a district of Sicily. *Val di Noto.*

NEAULE, a town of Lydia.

NEBAJOTH, the Scriptural name of Nabatene.

NEBALLAT, a town of Judæa, N.E. of Lydda.

NEBIUS (Nebis) fl., Tarraconensis, a r. of Tarraconensis, N. of Durius fl. *Cavado.*

NEBO m., I. a summit of Abarim m., in Peræa, whence Moses surveyed the Promised Land. II. a town under Nebo m.

NEBRISSA, a town of the Turtetani, near the Bætis, L., bet. Ugia N.E. and Carissa s.w. A colonia (Augusta Venerea). *Librija.*

NEBRŌDES, "doe-frequented?" m., m. intersecting the N.E. portion of Sicily, s.w. of Ætna.

NECHESIA, a haven of Thebais, on the Red sea, E. of Apollinopolis Magna. *Gualibo.*

NECICA (Sice, Sycea), a town of Lalassis, in Cilicia Trachea.

NECTA, Arabiæ, i. q. Nagara.

NĔDA fl., a r. of Peloponnesus, rising in Lycæus m., and, after separating Elis from Messenia, falling into the Ionian sea below Pyrgi. *Buzi? Paulizza?*

NEDAD (Nedao) fl., a r. of Pannonia.

NEDE, a town of Arcadia.

NEDIBUS, a town of Numidia, bet. Rusicada and Hippo Regius.

NEDON, I. a r. of Messenia, rising in Laconia E. of Denthela, and falling into Messeniacus sin. near Pheræ. On its banks was a temple of Minerva Nedusia. II. prom., a headland of Eubœa, on the E. coast, above Chersonnesus prom.

NEETUM, a town of Sicily, near the source of Erincus fl., N.W. of Helorum. The Anagrana of Strabo. *Noto.*

NEGA, a town of Albania, on Alazonius fl., near its mouth.

NEGRA, Arabiæ, i. q. Nagara.

NEION m., a m. in the N. of Ithaca ins. *Stefano-vouni? Oxoi?*

NELCYNDA, a town of India i. Gangem, N. of Elancum.

NELIA, a town of Magnesia, in Thessaly, on Pagasæus sin.; the inhabitants of which were removed by Demetrius Poliorcetes to Demetrias.

NELUS fl., a r. of Callæcia, falling into the Adriatic s.e. of Vir fl.

NEMALONI, a tribe of Albiæci, Alpes Maritimæ, under Cema m. N. *About Miolan.*

NEMASUM, a town of the Carni, in Venetia, on Tilavemptus fl. *Mazo.*

NEMAUSUS, capital of the Volcæ Arecomici, Narbonensis, N.W. of Arelate, bet. the Rhodanus (12½) and Narbo (90). The birth-place of Antoninus Pius. Noted for its amphitheatre. *Nismes.*

NEMEA, I. a r. of Peloponnesus, which, rising in the m. of Argolis, near Nemea, separates Achaia from Corinthia, and falls into the Corinthiacus sin. at Coronea. *Kutchmadi.* II. a town of Argolis, bet. Cleonæ and Mycenæ. The scene of the story of the Nemæan lion was a wood bet. Nemea and Cleonæ. Here were celebrated the Nemæan games. There was a temple of Jupiter Nemæus here. *Kutchumadi.* III. a town of Elis.

NEMENTURI, a tribe of Salyes, Narbonensis, N.W. of the Brigiani. *About Demandols.*

NEMETACUM, *postea* Atrebates, capital of the Atrebates, W.N.W. of Camaracum. *Arras.*

NEMETES, a people of Germania I., on the Rhine, bet. the Vangiones and the Tribocci.

NEMETOBRĪGA, a town of the Astures, Tarraconensis, 47 m. S.W. from Bersidum, on Silis fl., near its confluence with Minius fl. *Mendaya.*

NEMICOME, a town of Bithynia.

NEMORENSIS (Triviæ lacus, Dianæ Stagnum) lacus, a lake of Latium, at Nemus, N.E. of Aricia. Sacred to Diana. *Lago di Nemi.*

NEMOSSUS, the Greek name of Augustonemetum, in Aquitania.

NEMUS, a town of the Latini, in Latium, on Nemorensis lacus, N.E. of Aricia, where were a sacred grove and temple of Diana, whose priest held his office only by the tenure of superior force.

NEO CÆSAREA, I. the name given to Ameria, in Pontus, when renovated by Tiberius. On Lycus fl., L., below Colonia. *Niksar.* II. a town of Chalybonitis, Syria, on the Euphrates. Fortified by Justinian.

NEOCLAUDIOPOLIS, Paphlagoniæ, i. q. Andrapa.

NEOGEIALLA NAVALE, a port of the Sachalitæ, Arabiæ, N.E. of Marmatha. *Ainad.*

NEOMAGUS. *Vide* Noviomagus.

NEON, a city of Phocis, on the N. declivity of Parnassus, under Tithorea m., on Cachales fl., N.E. of Delphi. With a temple of Minerva. The burial-place of Phocus. Burned by Xerxes. *Velitza.*

NEONIUM, i. q. Niconium.

NEONTICHOS ("new walls"), I. a city of

Æolis Asiat., bet. Larissa (3¾) and Cyme, on Hermus fl., R. Founded eight years later than Cyme. *Near Guzzel-Hissar.* II. of the Odrysæ, in Thrace, on the Propontis, bet. Bisanthe and Ganos.

NEOPTOLEMI turris, a fortress of Dacia, on the Euxine, bet. Æpolium and Hermonactis.

NEPETE (Nepe), a town of Etruria, on Via Amerina, bet. Baccanæ (9) and Falerii (5). A colonia 383 B.C., and municipium. *Nepi.*

NEPHILIS (Nephillum) prom., a pr. of Cilicia Trachea, with a cognom. town.

NĒPHĒRIS, a fortress of Zeugitana, on Carthaginensis sin., over against Carthage (7½ m.). Taken by Scipio, previous to the taking of Carthage, after a siege of twenty-two days.

NEPISTA, a town of Carmania Paræpaphytis, bet. Carmana and Portospana.

NEPTUNI ara, I. an altar of Neptune, on the N. coast of Zeugitana, w. of Candidum prom. II. ins., an isl. of Carmania, s. of Agidana ins.

NEPTUNIUS m., m. of Sicily, in the N.E. angle of the island, terminating in Pelorum prom.

NERACOME, Arabiæ, i. q. Jambia.

NEREIDUM CHORI, a place in Thrace, on Strymon fl., near Amphipolis.

NERETUM, a town of the Salentini, on Tarentinus sin., bet. Aletium (10) and Manduria (29). *Nardo.*

NĒRĪEUM, the early capital of Leucas ins., on its s. coast, within Leucate prom. Besieged and taken by Laertes, father of Ulysses.

NERIGOS, a supposed island of Scandinavia. *Norway.*

NERII, a people of Tarraconensis, towards Nerium prom.

NERIPI, a people of Sarmatia Asiatica.

NERIS, I. a town of Argolis, on Tanus fl., w. of Thyrea. II. a town of Messenia.

NERITIS, the early name of Leucas ins.

NERITUS m., a m. in the s. of Ithaca ins. *Anoi.*

NERIUM (Artabrum, Celticum) prom., a pr. of Callæcia, on the Atlantic, s.w. of Magnus portus. *Cabo di Finisterra.*

NEROASSUS, Cappad., i. q. Nara.

NERONIA, a town of Gallia Cispad., bet. Sagis ad Padum (4) and Cornicularia (6). *Codigoro.*

NERTEREANI, a tribe of Cherusci, on Adrana fl., L., towards its source.

NERTOBRIGA (Nergobriga, Centobriga), a town of the Celtiberi, Tarraconensis, on Salo fl., R., 22 m. s.w. from Cæsar Augusta. *Almuria.* II. of the Celtici, Bæturia, bet. Aruci N.N.W. and Contributa N.E. A colonia (Concordia Julia). *Valera la Vieja.*

NERULUM, a town of Lucania, N.W. of Muranum. *Rotonda.*

NERVA fl., a r. of Tarraconensis, falling into Cantabricum mare at Flaviobriga. *Tina; Nansa.*

NERVESIA (Nursæ), a town of the Æqui, in Latium.

NERVII, a people of Belgica II., bet. the Morini N., the Veromandui S., the Atrebates W., and the Aduatici E. *Hennegan, &c.*

NERUSCI, a maritime tribe of Salyes, Narbonensis II., bet. Varus fl. and Aprus fl. *About Vence.*

NESACTUM, a town of Histria, on Arsia fl., L., near its mouth. *Castel Vecchio.*

NESCA, a town of Arabia Felix, N.N.W. of Miba. *Sancan.*

NESCANIA, a town of the Turtetani, Bætica, bet. Ilipula Magna N.E. and Antiquaria S.W.

NĒSIS ins., an isl. of Campania, in Cumanus sin., S.E. of Puteoli. The favourite retreat of Brutus. *Nisida.*

NESIS, a town of the Heniochi, Sarmat., at the mouth of Burcas fl.

NESIOPE ins., an islet of Lesbos ins., W., opposite Antissa.

NESIOTIS regio, a district of Scythia, on the Rha, above the Orgasi.

NESSA, Arabiæ, i. q. Maoscopus.

NESSON, a town of Pelasgiotis, in Thessaly, near Nessonis palus. *Nezero.*

NESSONIS palus, a marsh of Pelasgiotis, in Thessaly, on the right bank of Peneus fl., N.E. of Larissa. *L. Nezero.*

NESTÆI, a tribe of Dalmatæ, in Illyria.

NESTANE (Nostia), a village of Arcadia, at the entrance of Prinus saltus.

NESTUS (Nessus, *postea* Mestus) fl., a r. of Thrace, rising in Scomius m., and falling into the Ægean, over against Thasos opp., W. of Abdera. Under Philip and Alexander, and under the Romans, the boundary bet. Thrace and Macedonia. *Mesto; Carasou.*

NESULIUM, a port of Cilicia Trachea, N.E. of Philæa.

NEOCLAUDIOPOLIS, a later name of Andrapa, in Paphlagonia.

NEVE, a town of Gaulonitis Sup., bet. Gaulon S.W. and Œere N.E.

NETAD fl., a r. of the Quadi, Germ., falling into the Danube at Celmantia.

NETINDAVA, a town of the Cotenses, Dac., on Parata fl., above its junction with the Danube.

NETIUM, a town of Peucetia, on Via Egna tia bet. Celia (9) and Norba (10). *Rotigliano.*

NETUM, a town of Sicily, S.W. of Syracuse. *Noto Antico.*

NEUDRUS fl., a r. of India, falling into the Hydraotes.

NEURI, a people of Sarmatia, towards the Euxine, bet. the mouths of Tyras fl. and Borysthenes fl.

NEZIAZUSA prom., a pr. of Cilicia Trachea, 1 m. N.E. from Selinus.

NIA fl., a r. of Libya, falling into the Atlantic N. of Hesperium prom. *Senegal.*

NIARA, a town of Cyrrhestica, Syriæ.

NIBARUS (Imbarus) fl., a r. of Armenia, falling into Arsissa palus.

NICÆA, I. capital of Bithynia, at the E. extremity of Ascanius lacus, 25 m. N.E. from Prusa. A colony of Bottiæi from Thrace, and named by them Anchore. Enlarged by Antigonus, son of Philip, and called by him Antigonia; named Nicæa by Lysimachus, in honour of his wife. The birthplace of Hipparchus the astronomer, and of Dio Cassius. The death-place of Philistion the comedian. *Isnik.* II. a town of the Vediantii, Alpes Maritimæ, on the coast, 1 geog. m. E. from the mouth of Varus fl. A Massilian settlement. *Nizza; Nice.* III. of Bœotia, near Leuctra. IV. a town of the Locri Epicnemidii, on Maliacus sin., bet. Thermopylæ and Scarphæa. *Apano Molo.* V. of India i. Gangem, on Hydaspes fl., over against Bucephala. Founded by Alexander as a memorial of his victory over Porus. *Udinagur.*

NICASIA ins., an isl. of the Ægean, one of the Sporades, bet. Naxos and Amorgos. *Karo.*

NICATORUS m., m. of Armenia, running S.E. of Arbela, towards the Tigris. *Karadsjog.*

NICE (Nicæ), a town of the Cælatæ, in Thrace, on Harpessus fl., bet. Darphaba and Tarpodizus.

NICĒPHŌRIUM (Callinicum, *prius* Philiscum), a town of Osrhoene, S. of Carrhæ, at the junction of Belias fl. with the Euphrates. Begun by Alexander, and completed and named by Seleucus Nicator. Named by the emperor Leo, Leontopolis. *Near Racca.*

NICEPHORUS fl., a r. of Armenia Mag., falling into Nymphæus fl. below Tigranocerta.

NICER (Niger) fl., a r. of Germania Magna, rising near the source of the Danube, and falling into the Rhine. *Neckar.*

NICIA (Nigella) fl., a r. of the Boii, in Gallia Cispad., falling into Padus fl. at Brixellum. *La Lenza.*

NICIUM, a town of Lower Egypt, on Agathos Dæmon fl., bet. Andropolis and Momemphis.

NICII VICUS, a town of Marmarica, E. of Plenthine.

NICONIS DROMOS (Niconis), a port of Azania, s. of Serapis.

NICOMEDIA, capital of Bithynia, at the head of Astacenus sin. Founded by Nicomedes, *circa* 260 B.C. Destroyed by an earthquake before A.D. 314; restored by Justinian. The birth-place of Arrian. The death-place of Constantine the Great. *Ismid ; Isnikmid.*

NICONIUM (Niconia, Neonium), a town of the Tyrangetæ, Sarmat., on Tyras fl., a few miles from its mouth, over against Tyras. A Milesian colony.

NICOPOLIS, I. a town of Bithynia, on Bosporus Thracius, at the mouth of Azaritia fons. The bridge of Darius was constructed between this town and Potamonium, at a point where the breadth of the strait was 5 stadia. II. of Cilicia Campestris, near Issus, and by Stephanus identified with that town, as so named after the victory of Alexander. III. of Lydia. IV. (Ad Istrum), of the Mœsi, Mœsia Inf., at the junction of Jatrus fl. with the Danube. Built by Trajan, in commemoration of his victory over Decebalus. *Nicopoli.* V. of the Sapæi, in Thrace, on Nestus fl., N.E. of Philippi. *Nicopoli.* VI. *surnamed* Achaia and Actia, a city of Molossis, on an isthmus at the N. mouth of the Ambracius sin., bet. Elæa and Anactorium. Built by Augustus, in memory of the victory of Actium; restored by Julian. Here the Actian games were celebrated. *Prevesa Vecchia.* VII. *postea* Tephrice, of Armenia Minor, on the frontier of Pontus, s.E. of Colonia. Built by Pompey; restored by Justinian. *Deoliki.* VIII. of Palestine, i. q. Emmaus.

NICOTERA, a town of Bruttium, on Via Aquilea, bet. Ad Angitulam (25) and Rhegium.

NIDUM, a town of the Silures, Brit., on Nidus fl., towards Bovium. *Neath.*

NIDUS fl., a r. of the Silures, falling into the sea below Nidum. *Neath; Nedd.*

NIGAMA, a town of India i. Gangem, at one of the s. mouths of Chaberis fl. *Near Cottapatam.*

NIGELLA fl., Gall. Cispad., i. q. Nicia.

NIGER m., a prom. of Arabia Felix, at Abisama.

NIGER PULLUS, a town of Gallia Belg., on the Rhine, bet. Albiniana and Lauri.

NIGER fl., a r. of Libya Interior, supposed to rise in the territory of the Garamantes, and to fall into a lake E. of Mandrus m. *Niger; Quorra.*

NIGIRA, capital of the Nigritæ, Libyæ, on Niger fl., E. of Thamonda Kana. *Gana.*

NIGRI m., I. m. of Arabia Felix, on the coast, E. ; a s. continuation of Asabo m. II. of Arabia Petræa, bet. Heroopolites sin. and Ælanites sin.

NIGRITÆ, a people of Libya Interior, s. of the Gætuli, on Niger fl. *Part of Soudan.*

NIGRINIANA, a town of the Getæ, Mœsia, on the Danube, bet. Tegulicium and Candidiana.

NILEUS fl., a r. of Eubœa, which rendered the fleece of the sheep that drank of it black.

NILOPOLIS, a town of Heptanomis, 5 geog. m. N.E. from Heracleopolis.

NILOPTOLOMÆUM, a port of Æthiopia, on Erythræum mare, bet. Cobe and Daphnon.

NILUS fl., a r. of Africa, rising in the mountains of Æthiopia, and falling into the Mediterranean, by numerous mouths, E. of Alexandria. *Nile.*

NIMRAH (Beth Nimrah), a town of Moabitis, N., on a cognominal stream. *Nimrein.*

NINÆA, a town of Bruttium, near Balbia. *San Donato.*

NINEVEH ("dwelling of Ninus"), Ninus. capital of Assyria, on the Tigris, L., above the confluence of Lycus fl., N.E. of Babylon. Founded by Ninus (Nimrod), or, according to some writers, by Asshur. Destroyed by Cyaraxes; restored, nearly on the same site, but it is uncertain on what exact spot. There are ruins identified with Nineveh at Konyunjik, over against Mobul, at Nimroud, lower down the Tigris, and at Khorsabad.

NINGUM, a town of Histria, bet. Tergeste (28) and Parentium (18). *Montona.*

NINITACUM, a town of the Remi, Belgica II., bet. Catusiacum N. and Axuenna s.

NINUS fl., a r. of Asia Minor, falling into Glaucus sin. near Dædala. The ancient boundary of Caria and Lycia.

NIOBE fons, a fountain of Argolis.

NIOSSUM, a town of the Chuni, Sarmat., N.E. of Azagarium.

NIPHATES ("snow-clad") m., a ridge of Taurus, in Armen. Maj., on the border, w. and s. of Arsissa lacus, s. of Abus m. *Npat.*

NISACUS, a town of Persis Prop., bet. Siacus and Portipa.

NISÆA, I. a district of Parthia, on the confines of Margiana and Aria. Famous for its horses. *Nisaya.* II. (Asaac), its capital, under Masdoranus m., N. of Parbara. *Near Herat.* III. the port of Megara, on the Saronicus sinus, opposite Minoa ins., 2¼ m. s. from the city. Built by Nisus, son of Pandion. *Dodeca Ecclesiai.*

NISÆI, the people of Megara, so called from their port Nisæa, to distinguish them from the Megarians of Sicily.

NISBARA, a town of Apolloniatis, Assyr., on the Tigris, bet. Opis and Symbra.

NISERGE, a town of Persis Prop., s.w. of Persepolis.

NISĪBIS, *Semiticè*, "fortress," capital of Mygdonia, Mes., on Mygdonius fl. Founded by Nimrod ; the Achad of Scripture. Named by the Macedonians Antiochia. A colonia, and the bulwark of Rome against the Parthians and Persians until delivered up by Jovian. *Nezib.*

NISUS, a town of Commagene, w. of Samosata.

NISŸRUS ins., an isl. in Icarium mare, 8 m. s.w. from Triopium prom., in Caria. One of the Sporades. Said to have been torn from Cos by Neptune as a weapon against the giant Polybotes. *Nisari.* II. its capital, on the w. coast. *Nisari.* III. a town of Calymna ins.

NITAZUS, I. a town of Morimene, in Cappadocia, s. of Ozzalas (18).

NITHÏNE, a town of Lower Egypt, bet. Andropolis and Hermupolis (25).

NITICE, a town of the Heniochi, Sarmat., on the Euxine, N. of Pityas.

NITIOBRIGES, a people of Aquitania II., on the Garumna, bet. the Vasates w. and the Cadurci E.

NITRA (Naura, Mitrias), a maritime town of Limyrica, Ind., bet. Calliane and Tyndis. *Niuti.*

NITRARIÆ FODINÆ, nitron lakes of Egypt, s.E. of Alexandria.

NIVARIA, I. an isl. of Africa, one of the Fortunatæ ins. *Teneriffe.* II. a town of the Vaccæi, Tarraconensis, bet. Septimanca N.N.W. and Cauca.

NIVIRNIS fl., a r. of Lugdunensis I., falling into the Liger at Nevirnum. *Nièvre.*

NIVIRNUM (Noviodunum), a town of the Ædui, Lugdunensis I., on the Liger, R., at the confluence of the Nivirnis, bet. Condate and Decetia. *Nevers.*

NIVIRTIGAB, a maritime town of Tripolis, Afric., bet. Sugolin and Simnana.

NOÆ, a town of Sicily, near the source of Melas fl., L., bet. Abacænum and Tauromenium. *Noara.*

NOARUS (Odra) fl., a r. of Pannonia, falling into the Danube.

NO-AMMON, the Scriptural name of Thebes, in Egypt.

NOB, a Levitical city of Benjamin, 15 m. N. from Jerusalem. Here the Ark of the Covenant stayed for some time.

NOBÆ FUSCIANI, a town of Mauritania Cæsar., bet. Fons Camerata and Mileum.

NOBOCUS fl., a r. of the Careni, Brit., s. of Orcas prom.

NOCHETI, a tribe of shepherds in Arabia, of uncertain position.

NOEGAS, a town of the Astures, on the coast, N.E. of Lucus Asturum.

NOELA, Tarraconensis, i. q. Novium.

NOELUS fl., Tarraconensis, i. q. Melsus.

NOES fl., a r. of Mœsia Inf., rising in Hæmus m., and falling into the Danube. *Kara Lom.*

NOETU, a town of Cyrenaica, E. of Drepanum prom.

NOIDENOLEX, a town of the Ambrones, Maxima Sequanorum, s.E. of Filomusiacum.

NOLA, a town of Campania, on Via Aquilia, bet. Suessula (9) and Teglanum (5), N.E. of Herculaneum. A col. from Cumæ, or, perhaps, immediately from Cyme. Noted for its resistance to Hannibal. Destroyed in the social war, but restored. A colonia of Vespasian. The death-place of Augustus, and of his father Octavius. Here, later, bells ("nolæ") were invented. *Nola.*

NOLADA, a town of the Macæ, in Africa Proper, on Syrtis Maj., w., bet. Cisternæ and Aspis.

NOLASENE, a town of Laviniasene, in Cappadocia.

NOLIBA, a town of the Oretani, Tarraconensis, bet. Oretum s.w. and Murus N.N.E.

NOMÆ, a town of Sicily, s. of Alesa.

NOMASO, a town of Venetia.

NOMENTUM, a town of Sabinium, E. of Crustumerium. A colony from Alba ; a municipium 337 B.C. The district was noted for its wines. *Lamentana Vecchia.*

NOMII m., a N. continuation of Lycæus m., in Arcadia. Sacred to Pan.

NOMISTERIUM, a town of the Batini, Germ., w. of Strevinta.

NONACRIS, a village of Arcadia, on the confines of Achaia, N.W. of Pheneus, under Aroanius m., with a temple of Mercury. *Vounari.*

NOORDA, a town of Adiabene, Mesopotamia, towards Diala fl.

Noph, the Scriptural name of Memphis, in Egypt.

Nora, I. a maritime town of the Coracenses, in Sardinia, w., bet. Nymphæus portus and Turris Libyssonis. Named from (Sardus) Norax. *Torre Forcadizo.* II. a maritime town of Sardinia, s., bet. Caralis and Herculis portus. Founded by Norax. *Pula.* III. (Neroastus), a fortress of Tyanitis, in Cappadocia, near Castabala. *Nor, or Yengibar.*

Norba, a town of the Vettones, Lusitania, on the Tagus, above Fraxinus. Memorable for a bridge constructed here by a number of the adjacent towns in honour of Trajan. A colonia (Cæsariana). *Alcantara.* II. of Calabria, on Via Egnatia, bet. Netium (10) and Ad Veneris (8). *Conversano.* III. of the Volsci, s. of Cora. A colonia. Destroyed by Sylla. *Norma.*

Noreia, capital of Noricum, N. of Celeia. Noted for its gold-mines. *Noring, near Gmund.*

Norĭcum, the country of the Norici (Taurisci, Taurini, Carni), bounded N. by Germania Mag., at the Danube, s. by Italy and Illyria, at the Alpes Venetæ and Carnicæ, w. by Rhætia, at Œnus fl., E. by Pannonia, at Cetius m. It was, probably by Diocletian, divided into two provinces, Ripense, N. (*Carinthia*), and Mediterraneum, s. (*Stiria*). It was noted for its iron.

Norossi m., I. m. of Scythia i. Imaum, s.E. of Rymmici m. *Part of Ural m.* II. a people of Scythia i. Imaum, under Norossi m.

Noscopium, a town of Lycia.

Nosala ins., an isl. of Gedrosia, on the coast of the Ichthyophagi. The reputed abode of a Nereid, whose wont it was to transform all men who approached the island into fish.

Nostana, a town of Drangiana.

Nostrum mare, a name of the Mediterranean.

Noticornu, *vide* Aromata.

Notium prom., I. the s.w. extremity of Hibernia. *Mizen Head ; Cape Clear.* II. a pr. of the Sinæ, E. of the mouth of Lanos fl. III. a town of Calymna ins., on the E. coast. IV. portus, a roadstead of Chios ins., N.W. of Phanæ prom. *Mastico.* V. the port of Colophon, in Ionia, 2 m. s.w. from its metropolis.

Nova Augusta, Tarraconensis, i. q. Augustobriga.

Nova Mœnia, a town of the Jazyges, Sarmatia, at the mouth of Pasiaces fl.

Nova Petra, a village of Mauritania Cæsar., bet. Gemellæ and Diana Veteranorum, s.E. of Sitifis.

Novana, a town of Picenum, on Suinus fl. *Monte di Nove.*

Novantæ, a tribe of Selgovæ, Brit., on the w. coast, opposite the Darini, Hibern. *Galloway.*

Novantum portus, I. a port of the Novantæ, Brit. *Port Patrick.* II. prom., a pr. of the Novantæ, Britt., opposite Monarina ins. *Mull of Galloway.*

Novanus fl., a r. of the Vestini, Picen., falling into Aternus fl. near Pitinum. Remarkable for being dry in winter, but overflowing in summer. *Laghetto di Vetojo.*

Novara fl., a r. of Gallia Transpadana, falling into Padus fl. below Laumellum. *Gogna.*

Novaria, capital of the Vertacomicori, in Gallia Transpadana, on Novara fl., L., bet. Vercellæ (16) and Mediolanum (33). A municipium. *Novara.*

Novem Craræ, a town of the Tricastini, Viennensis, on the Rhone, above Senomagus.

Novem Pagi, a prefecture of Etruria, at the head of which was Forum Clodii.

Novem Populana, a division of Gaul, bet. Aquitania s., Narbonensis I. E., the Pyrenees s., and the Atlantic w.

Novem Viæ (Ennea Odoi), a place on the Strymon, Thrace, close to Amphipolis, where nine roads met. The point at which Xerxes crossed the river after sacrificing to its divinity nine young men and women, and nine white horses.

Novesium, a town of the Eburones, Germania I., on the Rhine, 24 m. from Colonia Agrippina. Built by Drusus. *Nuitz.*

Noviciana, a town of Pannonia Inf., on Savus fl., bet. Altina (11) and Bassianum (12).

Novida (Norba), a town of Sittacene, on Gyndes fl., R., towards its junction with the Tigris.

Noviodunum, I. a town of the Aulerci Diablintes, Lugdunensis III., N.W. of Suindinum. II. of the Helvetii, Maxima Sequanorum, on Lemanus lacus, N.E. of Geneva. A colonia (C. Equestris). *Nyon.* III. of the Latovici, Pannonia, on Savus fl., R., bet. Ad Prætorium (30) and Romula (10). *Novigrad.* IV. of Mœsia Inf., on the Danube, bet. Dinogetia and Ægyssus. *Nivorz?* V. of the Bituriges Cubi, Aquitania I., bet. Genabum N.N.W. and Avaricum s.E. *Neuvy-sur-Baranjon.*

Noviodunum Suessionum, i. q. Augusta Suessionum.

NOVIOMAGUS, I. a town of the Cantii, Brit., w. of Durobrivæ. *Holwood Hill, near Farnborough.* II. of the Cavares, Viennensis, N. of Vasio. *Nion.* III. of the Gugerni, Germ. II., on the Rhine, bet. Grinnes and Quadriburgium. IV. of the Leuci, Belgica I., on the Mosa, R., towards its source, bet. Solimariaca and Mosa. V. of the Remi, Belgica II., bet. Durocortorum w.s.w., and Vungo vicus. VI. of the Treveri, Belgica I., on the Mosella, R., bet. Taberna and Ad Decimum. *Nimeguen.* VII. of the Vadicassi, Lugdunensis I., w.n.w. of Andematunum. VIII. of the Suessiones, near Augusta Suessionum, s. *Neyon.* IX. of the Veromandui, Belgica II., on the Isara, R., below Contra Acincum. X. of the Bituriges Vivisci, Aquitania II., N.w. of Burdigala. XI. capital of the Batavi, on the Vahalis. *Nimegen.* XII. *postea* Lexovii, of the Lexovii, Lugdunensis II., N.w. of Condate. *Lisieux.* XIII. *postea* Augusta Nemetum and Spira, of the Nemetes, Germania I., on the Rhine, above Alta Ripa. *Spire; Speyer.*

NOVIOREGUM, a town of the Santones, Aquitania II., at the mouth, R., of the Garumna. *Royan.*

NOVIUM, a town of the Artabri, in Callæcia, at the mouth of Tamaris fl. *Noya.*

NOVIUS fl., a r. of the Selgovæ, Brit., falling into Ituna æst. opposite Olenaum. *Nith.*

NOVUM COMUM, a name given to Comum, when recolonized by Julius Cæsar.

NUÆSIUM, a town of the Danduti, Germ., s.w. of Mattium.

NUBA lacus, a lake of Æthiopia, formed by Gir fl., w. of Aboccis.

NUBÆ (Nubi), a people of Libya, on the Nile, L., below the Evonymitæ, and about Nuba lac.

NUCERIA, I. a town of the Boii, in Gallia Cispadan., 10 m. N.E. of Brixellum. *Luzzara.* II. *surnamed* Alfaterna, a Pelasgic town of Campania, on Sarnus fl., 12 m. s.E. from Nola. Burned by Hannibal; restored and colonized by Nero. *Nocera de Pagani.* III. of Umbria, s.E. of Iguvium. Noted for its wooden ware. *Nocera.*

NUCERIOLA, a town of the Caudini, in Samnium, on Calor fl., bet. Beneventum (4) and Calor (6), on Via Appia. *Ricerola.*

NUCHUL fl., a r. of Libya Int., of uncertain position; supposed by the ancients one of sources of the Nile.

NUCRIA, a Tyrrhenian town of Bruttium, on Sabbatus fl., 5 m. from the sea. *Nocera.*

NUDIUM, a town of Triphylia, in Elis. Destroyed by the Eleans.

NUITHONES, a tribe of Vindili, Germ., on Albis fl., N. of the Calucones.

NUIUS fl., a r. of Libya, falling into the Atlantic N. of Soloentium prom.

NUMANA, a Siculian town of Picenum, at the mouth of Miseus fl., bet. Cumerium prom. and Potentia (10). *Humana.*

NUMANTIA, capital of the Arevaci, Tarraconensis, on Durius fl., L., towards its source, bet. Clunia w. and Augustobriga E. Distinguished for its fourteen years' resistance to Rome. Destroyed by its inhabitants, to prevent its falling into the hands of Scipio Æmilianus; but restored. *Puente Don Garay, near Soria.*

NUMICIUS (Numicus) fl., a r. of Latium, running into the sea s. of Lavinium. Sacred to the nymph Anna Perenna, sister of Dido. At its source was a temple of Æneas, under the title of Jupiter Indiges. *Rio Torto.*

NUMIDIA (Nomadia), a region of Africa, bounded N. by the Mediterranean, s. by Libya Int., w. by Mauritania, E. by Africa Propria. It was by some writers divided into Numidia Propria, *vel* Massylorum and Numidia Massæsylorum; but the latter region is more generally described as Mauritania Cæsariensis. *Algiers.*

NUMIDIA MASSÆSYLORUM, the w. division of Numidia, bet. Ampsaga fl. and Mulucha fl. The kingdom of Scyphax, and afterwards of Bogud.

NUMIDIA PROPRIA (Nova), the E. division of Numidia, bet. Tusca fl. and Ampsaga fl. The kingdom of Masinissa, and afterwards of Bocchus.

NUMIDĬCUS sin., a bay of the Mediterranean, at the mouth of Tapsus fl. *Golfo di Stora.*

NUMISTRO, a town of Lucania, N. of Volceium, on the confines of Apulia. *Muro.*

NUMITURIANUM, a town of Numidia, bet. Mileu and Aquartille.

NURSÆ, Æquor., i. q. Nervesia.

NURSIA, a town of Sabinium, near the source of Nar fl., N.E. of Spoletium. Noted for its extreme coldness. The birth-place of Polla Vespasia, Vespasian's mother. *Norcia.*

NUS fl., a r. of Arcadia, rising in Thisoa regio, and falling into Alpheus fl.

NYMBÆUM palus, a pool of Laconia, near Malia prom. Sacred to Neptune. *Nymbiko.*

NYMPHÆA, I. a town of Taurica Chersonesus, on the s. coast, s. of Panticapæum. *Kazeka.* II. ins., an isl. of Samos, towards Ampelus prom. III. of Sardinia, s. of

Nymphæus portus. IV. of Sardinia, in Gallicum fretum, N. of Herculis ins.

NYMPHÆUM, I. the S.W. headland of Acte penins., in Macedonia. *C. San Giorgio.* II. a village of Bithynia, on the Euxine, 2 m. N.E. from Tyndaridæ. III. a maritime town of Cilicia Campestris, towards Celenderis. IV. a place in Illyria, on Æas fl., above Apollonia. Remarkable for bituminous exhalations, which were reputed to do no injury to vegetation; and for an oracle, which consumed or rejected frankincense according as it favoured or rejected the sacrificer. *Selenitza.* V. a town of the Taulantii, in Illyria, S.W. of Sissus. VI. a hunting-seat of the Byzantine emperors, in Lydia, under Sipylus m. *Nif or Nymfi.* VII. a cavern on the N.W. slope of Casius m., in Casiotis, Syriæ.

NYMPHÆUS, I. a r. of Armenia Maj., rising in Taurus m., S.E. of Arsamosata, and falling into the Tigris near Amida. II. of Latium, rising near Norba, and falling into the sea w. of Tarracina. *Nimfio.* III. portus, a port of the Coracenses, Sardinia w., bet. Carbia and Nura. *Porticuolo? Porto di Conte?*

NYMPHAS, a town of Arcadia, 2½ m. s.w. from Cromi.

NYMPHASIA fons, a fountain of Arcadia, 4½ m. N.E. from Methydrium.

NYSA, I. a town of Bœotia, on Helicon, s. of Coronea. II. of Eubœa, where the vine was reputed to send forth leaves and fruit on the same day. III. Indiæ, i. q. Nagara. IV. (Pythopolis), a city of Caria, E. of Tralles, under Messogis m., on both sides of a torrent descending from the m. Founded by Athymbrus the Spartan. Noted for its school of philosophy. *Sultan or Eski-hissar.* V. a town of Naxos ins., on the N. coast.

NYSSA, a town of Morimene, in Cappadocia, on Halys fl., bet. Parnassus (24) and Osiana (32).

O.

OADITÆ (Aditæ), a tribe of Saraceni, Arabiæ. The descendants of Adah, mother of Eliphaz. *Beni Ad.*

OANUS fl., a r. of Sicily, falling into Africum pelagus, below Camerina. *Fresculari.*

OARACTA ins., *vide* Agidana.

OARUS fl., a r. of Sarmatia Asiat., falling into Mæotis palus.

OASIS (Auasis). There are three oases described by ancient geographers in the Li-

byan desert. 1. Oasis Ammonii, at Ammon. 2. Oasis Major, s. of Abydus Thebais, near which the army of Cambyses was overwhelmed with sand. *Wah el Kharbeh.* 3. Oasis Minor, in Heptanomis, N. of Oasis Major. Here was a fountain resembling in character the Fons Solis of Ammon. *Wah el Behnessa.*

OAXES fl., a r. of Crete, rising in Ida m., and falling into the Ægean below Oaxus. *Mylopotamo.*

OAXUS (Axus), a town of Crete, on Oaxes fl., towards Eleutherna.

OBASA (Olbasa), a town of Pisidia, towards Seleucia Sidera; under Rome, a colonia.

OBBANE, a town of Chalybonitis, Syriæ, on the Euphrates, 5 m. from Barbalissus. *Balis.*

OBIDIACENI, a people of Sarmatia Asiat., towards the Tyrambæ.

OBILA, a town of the Vettones, Lusitania, on the Tagus, R., above Turmuli.

OBLIMUM, a town of the Centrones, Alpes Graiæ, on Isara fl., bet. Ad Publicanos and Darantasia.

OBŎCA fl., a r. of the Cauci, Hibern. E., falling into the sea opposite Canganorum prom. *Avoca.*

OBOTH, a village of Arabia Deserta, s. of Arindela. One of the stations of the Israelites on their return from Egypt.

OBRIMA fl., a r. of Pisidia, towards Apamea.

OBRINGA fl., a r. of Gaul, at or near Moguntiacum. *Ahr.*

OBRIS fl., a r. of Narbonensis, flowing by Beterræ. *Orbe.*

OBUCULA, a town of the Turtetani, Bætica, E. of Carmona. *Fuentes.*

OBULCUM, surnamed Pontificense, a town of the Turtuli, Bætica, 36 m. E. from Corduba. A statue of a sow with thirty pigs was found here, whence the modern name. *Porcuna.*

OCALEA fl., I. a r. of Bœotia, falling into Copais lac. at the cognominal town. II. a town of Bœotia, on the s. shore of Copais lac., w. of Haliartus. *Brastamiotis.*

OCCARABA (Coara), a town of Apamene, Syriæ, bet. Apamea and Palmyra.

OCCULTUS PORTUS, a port of Arabia, on Omanni sin.

OCE, i. q. Taoce.

OCELIS (Acila), a harbour of Arabia Felix, near the E. entrance of the Red sea, bet. Ammonii prom. and Palindromos prom. *Ol Cella.*

OCELA (Ocella), capital of the Garoceli, Narbonensis. *Near Lans le Bourg.*

OCELLODURUM, a town of the Astures, Tarraconensis, on Durius fl., below Sarabris.

OCELLUM prom., a pr. of the Parisi, Brit., at the mouth of Abus fl., N. *Spurn Head.*

OCELUM, I. a town of the Belaci, in Gallia Transpad., under Alpes Cottiæ, on Duria Min. fl., L., above Segusio. *Uxeau.* II. of the Vettones, Lusitania, on the Durius, above Acontia, N.W. of Salmantica.

OCETIS (Scutis) ins., one of the Orcades ins. *South Ronalsha.*

OCHARUS (Opharus) fl., a r. of Sarmatia Asiatica.

OCHE m., I. a hill of Eubœa, on the s. coast, at Carystus. On its summit was a temple of Neptune. *Monte Sant Elias.* II. a name of Eubœa ins.

OCHOSBANES (Ocheraenos) fl., a r. of Paphlagonia, falling into the sea near Armene.

OCHUS fl., I. a r. of Bactriana, rising near Arius fl., L., and falling into the Oxus. II. m., a m. of Persis, on the coast, w. of Apostana.

OCHYROMA, *prius* Achaia, a Phœnician town of Rhodus ins., 10 m. from Jalysus.

OCILIS, a town of the Carpetani, Tarraconensis, E. of Hippo.

OCINARUS fl., Bruttii, i. q. Sabbatus.

OCOLUM, a village of Eubœa, near Eretria.

OCORURA, a town of Phœnicia, bet. Damascus and Emesa. *Karaw.*

OCRA m., a ridge of Alps in Pannonia, on the confines of Noricum. *Birnbaumer.*

OCRICULUM, a town of Umbria, on the Tiber, L., bet. Rostrata Villa (25) and Narnia (12), on Via Flaminia. *Ocricoli.*

OCRINUM prom., Damnonium, a pr. of the Damnonii, E. of Bolerium prom. *Lizard Point.*

OCTAPITARUM prom., the s.w. extremity of Britannia II. *St. David's Head.*

OCTAPOLIS, a town of Lycia.

OCTODURUM, a town of the Veragri, Alpes Penninæ, on the Rhone, L., above Tarnacæ. *Sion.*

OCTOGESA, a town of the Ilercaones, Tarraconensis, on Iberus fl., at the confluence of Sicorus fl. *Mequinenza.*

OCTOLOPHUS, I. a place in Perrhæbia, in Thessaly, under Olympus m., near Lapathus. II. a town of Lyncus, in Macedonia, near Athacus.

OCULMA, a town of Mauritania Cæsar., bet. Sitifis and Vaccæ.

ODEA ins., an isl. of the Ægean, one of the Sporades, near Amorgos.

ODESSUS, *vide* Ordessus.

ODIANA, Numid., i. q. Onellana.

ODIATES, a people of Liguria. *About Obieta.*

ODINTUS, Pont., i. q. Adienus.

ODOCA, a port of Taprobane, s. bet. Orneum prom. and Azanus fl.

ODOGRA (Odoga), a town of Chammenene pref., in Cappadocia.

ODOMANTI, a Pæonian tribe in Thrace, N. of the Edones.

ODRA fl., i. q. Noarus.

ODRYSÆ, the people of Odrysia, in Thrace.

ODRYSIA, the country of the Odrysæ, in Thrace, occupying, in the time of its king Sitalces, son of Teres, the whole s. and E. coast of that country, from Abdera to the mouth of the Danube, and inland from Strymon fl. to the Euxine.

ODRYSSES (Horisius) fl., a r. of Bithynia, rising in Olympus m. near Prusa, and, after forming Dascylitis palus, falling into Rhyndacus fl. near its mouth. *Oufersou or Niloufer.*

ODUBRIA fl., Liguriæ, i. q. Urbs.

ODUGIA, a town of Bætica, N.W. of Ilipa.

ODYSSEA (Ulyssea), a maritime town of Sicily s., at Odysseum prom. Named after Ulysses.

ODYSSEUM (Ulysseum) prom., a pr. of Sicily, w. of Pachynum prom. *Capo di Marzo; C. di Castelluccio.*

OE (Oie), I. a demus of Attica, of the tribe Pandion, near Ægaleus m. II. (Œa), a village of Ægina ins., on Panhellenius m., where the Æginates destroyed the statues of Damia and Auxesia, and gave rise to the war bet. the Athenians and the Epidaurians.

OEA (Acrocon), a fortress of Mysia, commanding a cognominal defile, s. of Apollonia ad Rhyndacum.

ŒA, I. a town of Thessaly. II. (Œenses civitas), a maritime city of Tripolis, Africa, bet. Megerthis and Pisindon. A Sicilian settlement. A colonia (Ælia Augusta Felix). *Tripoli.*

ŒANEUM nem., a sacred grove near Opus Locrid.

ŒANIS fons, a sacred fountain near Opus Locrid.

ŒANTHE (Euanthia), a town of the Locri Ozolæ, on Corinthiacus sin., over against Ægeum in Achaia. With temples of Diana, Venus, and Æsculapius. *Veternitza.*

ŒBALIA, I. *vide* Arena. II. (Œbaliæ turres), a name of Tarentum, from Œbalus, king of Lacedæmon, son of Helen.

ŒCÆ, a town of Daunia, in Apulia, on Via Egnatina, bet. Aquilo and Herdonia (8). *Troja.*

ŒCHALIA, I. a town of Arcadia. II. of Estiæotis, in Thessaly, near Tricca. III. Mess., i. q. Andania.

ŒCHARDÆ, a people of Serica, on Œchardes fl.

ŒCHARDES fl., a r. of Serica, rising in Asmiræi m., and falling into the sea N.E. of Bautisus fl. *Selinga.*

ŒCHOLIA, a town of Eubœa, s.e. of Chalcis. Destroyed by Hercules.

ŒCUS, a town of Caria.

ŒDANES (Dyardanes) fl., a r. of India e. Gangem, rising in Emodi m., and falling into Gangeticus sin. close to Antibole ostium e.

ŒNÆ, a demus of Attica, of the tribe Attalis or Ptolemais.

ŒNANTHIA, a town of the Heniochi, in Sarmatia Asiat., on the Euxine, bet. Pityus and Dioscurias.

ŒNARIA, Etruria, i. q. Volaterræ.

ŒNEUM nemus, I. a forest of Lycia. II. a fortress of the Penestæ, in Illyria, on Ardaxanus fl., bet. Draudacum and Caravantis. *Near Orocho.*

ŒNIADÆ, a town of Acarnania, above the e. mouth of Achelous fl., on its left bank, near Melite lacus. Uncertain whether *Kuria Irene* or *Gardako.*

ŒNIANDUS, the early name of Epiphania, in Cilicia.

ŒNION, a town of the Locri Ozolæ, on Corinthiacus sin., e. of Naupactus. Near it was a temple of Jupiter Nemæus, wherein Hesiod died. *San Nicolo.*

ŒNOANDA, Lyciæ, i. q. Balbura.

ŒNOBARAS fl., a r. of Syria, falling into the Orontes.

ŒNOE, "wine-growing," I. a name of Sicinus ins. II. a town of Argolis, on the Charadrus fl., bet. Argos and Mantinea, under Artemesius m. Named after Œneus, son of Diomed, its founder. *Enoa.* III. a demus of Attica, of the tribe Œantis, n.w. of Probalinthus. With a temple of Apollo. *Œnoe.* IV. a demus of Attica, of the tribe Hippothoontis, towards the borders of Bœotia, on the Cephissus-Eleusinius, bet. Thria and Eleutheræ. Extinct in Pliny's time. *Blachi.* V. a fortress of Corinthia, on Corinthiacus sin., on the confines of Megaris. VI. a town of Icarus ins., n.e. of Isti prom. Near it was a temple of Diana Tauropolos. VII. of Pontus, 5 m. w. from Phigamus fl. *Unisch.* IX. i. q. Ephyre. X. Lacon., i. q. Œnus.

ŒNOPHYTÆ, a town of Bœotia, in the territory of Tanagra.

ŒNOTRIDES ins., two isl. of Lucania, in Eleates sin.

ŒNOTRI, the name given by the Arcadian colonists to the Umbrian or Oscan inhabitants of Magna Græcia.

ŒNOTRIA, "wine-land," a name given by its Arcadian colonists to Magna Græcia, from its rich vineyards. Dion Halicarnassus derives the name from Œnotrus, son of Lycaon, the Arcadian leader; and Herodotus says that Œnotria was the previous name of the region.

ŒNUS, I. a r. of Germania, rising in Alpes Rhætiæ, e. of Cuneus Aureus, and, after separating Rhætia from Noricum, falling into the Danube at Bojodurum. *Inn.* II. of Laconia, rising n. of Sellasia, and falling into Eurotas fl. above Sparta. *Tchlesina.* III. a town of Laconia, on the cognominal river, n. of Sparta. Noted for its wine. IV. (Œnoe, Cœna), a maritime town of Pontus, 4 m. e. from Thoaris fl. *Unieh.*

ŒNUSSÆ ins., I. isl. of Chios, over against Pteleum, n.w. of Hippi ins. *Spalmadores.* II. two isl. of Messenia, in the Asinæus sin., s.e. of Methone. *Sapienza* (w.) *and Cabrera* (e.).

ŒNUTRIUM, a town of the Breuni, Rhæt., on Œnus fl., R., above Veldidena.

ŒNYRA, a town of Thasos ins., on the e. coast, opposite Samothrace.

ŒON, a demus of Attica, of the tribe Hippothoontis, near Deceleia.

ŒEROE (Peroe) fl., a r. of Bœotia, rising in Cithæron m., near Platææ, and falling into Alcyonium mare at Creusis.

ŒSCUS (Escius, Cius), I. a r. of Mœsia Inf., rising in Scomius m. s.e. of Sardica, and falling into the Danube at Castra Nova. *Isca.* II. a town of the Mœsi, Mœsia Inf., on Œscus fl., R., bet. Ad Putea and Storgosia.

ŒSO, I. a pr. of Tarraconensis, at the n. extremity of the Pyrenees at the mouth of Magrada fl. *Cabo de Machicaco.* II. a town near the cognominal prom. on Bagradas fl. *Ilea.*

ŒSPORIS (Anbureum), a village of the Psylli, Africa P., on Syrtis Maj., bet. Charax and Aulahon.

ŒSTRYMNES, the people occupying Cassiterides ins., hence called Œstrymnides.

ŒSYME, *vide* Æsyme.

ŒTA m., a continuation of Pindus, on the n. frontiers of Ætolia, Doris, and Phocis, extending s. to the m. of Bœotia. *Katavothra.*

ŒTEUS sinus, i. q. Maliacus sin.

ŒTYLUS (Tylus, Bityla), a town of Laconia, on Messeniacus sin., 10 m. s. from Thalamæ, with a temple of Serapis. Named from the hero Œtylus. *Vitulo.*

ŒUS, a village of Arcadia, under Parthenius m. e. of Tegea.

OGDAMUS m., m. of Marmarica.

OGÏA ins., an isl. of Aquitania, n.w. of Radis, 10 m. from the land. *D'Yeu; Dieu.*

OGLASA ins., an islet of Etruria, s. of Ilva ins., w. of Igilium ins. *Monte Cristo.*

OGYGIA, "ancient," I. an early name of Bœotia, from Ogyges. II. a name of Thasos ins. III. an islet of Bruttium, near Japygum Tria prom. The fabled abode of Calypso, and prison-place of Ulysses. Now submerged. Mela places the Ogygia of Calypso in the Siculum Fretum.

OGYRES ins., Arabiæ, i. q. Sarapis.

OIBONION, the Greek name of Vibinum, Apulia.

OION, " egg shape," a fort of Opus, Locris, above Cynus.

OLABUS, I. a town of Auranitis, Babyl., on the Euphrates, bet. Colorina and Paraxmalcha. II. of Ancobaritis, Mes., on an island of the Euphrates, bet. Aboron and Tzannesopolis. A treasure fortress of the Parthians. *Eluce ?*

OLACHUS fl., Bithyniæ, i. q. Bryazon.

OLANA fl., *postea* Volana, a branch of Padus fl., falling into the Adriatic N. of Ostium Sagis. *Po di Volano.*

OLARSO prom., a pr. of Tarraconensis, w. of Œaso prom. *Oiarço ; Olearçon.*

OLBE (Olbasa), a town of Lycaonia, 6 m. E. from Laranda (placed by Strabo in Cilicia). Famous for a temple of Jupiter, founded by Ajax, son of Teucer. A colonia of Severus.

OLBELUS, a town of Macedonia.

OLBIA, I. the early name of Astacus, Bithynia. II. a town of the Commoni, Narbonensis II., on the coast bet. Telo Martius and Alconis. *Euoubo ; Oubies.* III. of Pamphylia, at the mouth of Catarrhactes fl., R., opposite Attaleia. IV. (Borysthenis, Olbiopolis, *prius* Savia, Miletopolis), a city of Sarmatia Europea, on Hypanis fl., L., near its junction with the Borysthenes. A Milesian colony. *Kudac.* V. of the Corsii, Sardinia, at the head of Olbianus sin. A Greek colony.

OLBIANUS sinus, I. Bithyniæ, i. q. Astacenus. II. a gulf of the Tyrrhenian sea, at Olbia, Sardiniæ.

OLBIUS fl., Arcad., i. q. Aroarius.

OLCADES, an early people of Tarraconensis, on Anas fl., towards its source, about Althæa.

OLCHACHITES sin., a bay of the Mediterranean, at Rusicada. *Gulf of Stora.*

OLCIMUS fl., Emathiæ, i. q. Olganus.

OLCINIUM (Ulcinium), a town of the Dalmatæ, Illyria, N.W. of Scodra. *Dulcigno Vecchio.*

OLCIUM, an old town of the Olci (Volsci), on the site of Cosa.

OLEASTRUM, I. a pr. of Byzacene, on Syrtis Min., bet. Macomades and Cellæ Picentinæ. II. (Barbari), a pr. of Mauritania Ting., on the Mediterranean, bet. Aquila Maj. and Tænia Longa. III. a maritime town of the Cosetani, Tarraconensis, bet. Tarraco N.E. and Tria Capita prom. s. IV. of the Turtetani, Bæticæ, near Gades.

OLENAUM, a town of the Brigantes, Brit., bet. Virosidum and Luguballum.

OLENUS, I. one of the Twelve Cities of Achaia, at the mouth of Olenus fl., bet. Dymæ and Patræ. Deserted in Pausanias' time. *Palaio-Achaia.* II. a town of Ætolia, N.E. of Uria lacus. Destroyed by the Æolians. III. of the Tectosages, Galatia.

OLERUS, a town of Crete, near Hierapytna, where a festival was held in honour of Minerva Oleria.

OLESIA, a town of the Boii, Gallia Cispad. A municipium. *Mirandola ?*

OLGANUS (Olcimus), fl., a r. of Emathia, rising in the m. of Deuriopæa and falling into the Astræus below Ægæ. *Polora.*

OLGASSYS m., a chain of m. extending through the centre of Paphlagonia, from Parthenius fl. to Halys fl. *Ulgaz.*

OLIA, a town of Cyprus.

OLIAROS ins., an isl. of the Ægean, one of the Cyclades, bet. Paros (1½) and Siphnos. *Antiparo.*

OLICANA, a town of the Brigantes, Brit., w. of Eboracum.

OLIGYRTUS (Ologontum) m., a m. of Arcadia, s.w. of Stymphalus lacus.

OLINTIGI, a town of the Turtetani, Bætica, at the mouth of Urium fl. *Moguer.*

OLINUM, a town of the Rauraci, Maxima Sequanorum, s.w. of Augusta Rauracorum.

OLISIPO (Ulippona), capital of the Celtici, Lusitania, on the Tagus, R., 10 m. from its mouth. Traditionally founded by Ulysses, and, to favour this origin, written by Mela Ulysippo. A municipium (Felicitas Julia). *Lisbon.*

OLISIPONENSE prom., i. q. Magnum.

OLIVA, a town of Mauritania Cæsar., bet. Salda and Sava.

OLIVULA, a port of the Vediantii, Alpes Maritimæ, bet. Nicæa and Anaum E.

OLIZON, "small," a town of Magnesia, Thessaly, on Pagasæus sin., under Tisæus m. A town of Philoctetes. *Argalasti.*

OLKION, the Greek name of Volci, Etruria.

OLLIUS fl., I. a r. of Æolis Asiat., falling into the Ægean s. of Grylius fl. II. of Gallia Transpadana, rising in the territory of the Camuni, and, after forming Serbinus lacus, falling into Padus fl. below Bedriacum. *Oglio.*

OLMIÆ prom., a headland of Corinthia, on

Corinthiacus sin., 7 m. N.E. from Corinth, on which stood a temple of Juno Acræa. *C. Malangara.*

OLMIUS (Lemnus) fl., a stream of Bœotia, rising from Helicon m. and falling into Permessus fl. Sacred to the Muses. *Talatzi.*

OLOBAGRA, a town of Macedonia.

OLOCRUS m., a summit of Olympus, near Pydna.

OLONDÆ, *vide* Alontæ.

OLOOSSOON (Lossonus), "white," a town of Perrhæbia, Thessaly, on Titaresius fl., above Cyretiæ, 30 m. N. of Peneus fl. *Alassona.*

OLOPHYXUS, a town of Acte penins., Macedonia, on the Strymonicus sin., N.W. of Apollonia.

OLPÆ, I. a fortress of the Amphilochi, Acarnania, on the S.E. shore of Ambracius sin., 3 m. N. from Argos Amphilochum. Noted for the victory gained here by the Acarnanians and Amphilochians, under Demosthenes, over the Ambraciots and Peloponnesians. *Arapi.* II. (Alope), a town of the Locri Ozolæ, N. of Œanthe.

OLTIS fl., a r. of the Cadurci, Aquitania I., running to Cadurcorum opp. *L' Olt.*

OLURIS, Messeniæ, i. q. Dorium.

OLURUS, a town of Achaia, S.W. of Pellene.

OLUS, a town of Crete, on the w. shore of Didymi sin., 7½ m. s. from Chersonesus. *Mirabel.*

OLYMPENI, a people of Mysia, under Olympus m., N.E.

OLYMPIA (Litrinea) regio, a place in Pisatis, Elis, on Alpheus fl., S.E. from Elis, where was the great temple and oracle of Jupiter Olympius, and the seat of the Olympic games. Here was the Jupiter of Phidias.

OLYMPIAS fons, a fountain of Arcadia, near Basilis. The scene of a battle between the gods and the giants. Here the mysteries of Ceres and Proserpine were celebrated, on a spot called Bathos. *Bathureuma.*

OLYMPUS m., I. a summit of Thornax m., Laconia, w. of Sellasia. II. a circular m. of Cyprus, s. above Palæa. *M. Santa Croce.* III. a summit of Lepetymnus m., in Lesbos, S.E. of Hiera. IV. (Phænicus, Solymæi), m. of Lycia, on the coast. Hence Neptune watched Ulysses. *Adratchan.* V. of Macedonia, along the coast of the Thermaicus sin., from the Haliacmon fl. to the Peneus fl. From their extreme altitude adopted by the poets as the abode of the gods. VI. a range of m. in Mysia and Bithynia, the

chief summit of which overlooks Prusa ad Olympum. Its forests were infested with robbers and wild beasts. *Anadoli Dagh.* VII. prom., Cypri, i. q. Dinaretum. VIII. a port, and latterly pirate fortress, of Lycia, E. of Crambusa, under Olympus m. One of the six chief communities of Lycia. Destroyed by Servilius Isauricus. *Deliktash.*

OLYNTA ins., an isl. of the Adriatic, one of the Liburnides ins. *Sotta.*

OLYNTHIACUS fl., a r. of Chalcidice, Macedonia, falling into Bolbe palus w. of Ammites fl. On its banks was the monument of Olynthus, son of Hercules. Noted for a periodical influx of fish from the lake.

OLYNTHUS, capital of Sithonia, Macedonia, at the head of the Toronaicus sin., 8 miles N.E. from Potidæa. Founded by the Eretrians of Eubœa, on their return from the siege of Troy. Long the seat of a powerful republic. Destroyed in Strabo's time. *Agios Mamas.*

OLYSIA (Olyca), a fortress of Olynthus, in Sithonia, Macedonia, N. of the city.

OMANI (Manimi), a tribe of Lycii, German., bet. Viadrus fl. and Vistula fl., s. of the Burgundiones.

OMANITÆ, a people of Arabia Felix, under Didymi m., w. and N.

OMANUM (Omana) emporium, capital of the Omanitæ, Arabiæ, w.s.w. of Abissa.

OMANUS sin., a gulf of Erythræum mare, leading into Persicus sin.

OMARIUM, a town of Thessaly, with temples of Jupiter and Minerva.

OMBI (Ambi), a town of Thebais, on the Nile, bet. Silsilis and Syene (30). Here crocodiles were worshipped, the inhabitants warring in their defence with the people of Apollinopolis Magna and Tentyra, who were hostile to these animals. *Rum-Ombu.*

OMBRÆA, a town of Mesopotamia, E. of Edessa.

OMBRIKOI, the Greek name of the Umbri.

OMBRION ins., i. q. Pluvialia.

OMBRONES, a people of Sarmatia. Probably a migration of Ambrones.

OMENAGORA, a town of the Marohæ, Ind., on Renda fl., 10 m. s. of Nasica. *Amednagur.*

OMIRAS fl., a name of the Euphrates, towards its source. *Jephrat.*

OMŒNIUS ins., an isl. of Arabia Felix, in Persicus sin., towards Isura ins. *Bumose.*

OMPHALE, Siciliæ, i. q. Dædalium.

OMPHALIUM, a town of Chaonia, on the borders of the Paravæi, N.E. of Hadrianopolis. *Ruins near Spilio.*

OMPHALIUS campus, "plain of the navel," a plain of Crete, bet. Ida m. and Gnossus, where Jupiter's navel dropped off.

ON, a Scriptural name of Heliopolis, in Egypt.

ONABRISATES, a people of Aquitania. *About Nebousan.*

ONÆI m., a chain of hills traversing Megaris from Cithæron m. to Scironides Petræ. *Macriplayi.*

ONAGRINUM, a town of the Jazyges Metanastæ, near the confluence of the Tibiscus with the Danube. *Neusatz.*

ONCHESMUS, a harbour of Chaonia, opposite Cassiope, Corcyra. Dionysius of Halicarnassus calls the place Anchisæ portus, as having been built in honour of the father of Æneas. *Agioi-Saranta.*

ONCHESTUS fl., I. a r. of Pelasgiotis, Thessaly, rising N.W. of Scotussa and falling into Bæbe lacus. *Patrassi.* II. a town of Bœotia, in Tenericus campus, s.w. of Copais lac. With a grove and temple of Neptune.

ONCHOBRICA ins., an isl. of Arabia, in Persicus sin., N.W. of Asaborum prom. *Tuumbs.*

ONEIUM, a fortress of Corinthia, on Oreius m. N. of Mausus. *Hexamili Apano.*

ONEIUS m., a range of hills in Corinthia, on the coast towards Mausus.

ONELLANA (Odiana), I. a town of Numidia, bet. Simithu and Hippo Regius. II. a town of Zeugitana, bet. Athicna and Bibæ.

ONESII, a tribe of Convenæ, in Gaul. *About Ozon.*

ORINGIS (Aurinx), a town of the Turtetani, Bætica, bet. Sæpona N. and Lacippo s.

ONISIA ins., an isl. on the E. coast of Crete, over against Itanum prom. *Cophonisi.*

ONNE (Esiongeber), a town of the Nabathæi, Arabia Petræa, on Ælanites sin., E., below Ælana. *Aszioun.*

ONO, a town of Judæa, 5 m. from Lydda.

ONOBA, *surnamed* Æstuaria, Onabalisturia, a town of the Turtetani, Bætica, opposite Herculis ins. *Huelva.*

ONŎBALUS fl., i. q. Taurominius.

ONOCHONUS fl., a r. of Pelasgiotis, Thessaly, rising near Scotussa and passing through Nesonis palus into Peneus fl. towards Tempe. One of the rivers drained by Xerxes' army. *Rejani.*

ONOGLI, a village of Laconia, near Sparta. Noted for its wine.

ONOPNICTES fl., a r. of Cappadocia, N. of Sarus fl.

ONTHIS palus, a lake or marshes near Calydon, Ætolia, abounding with fish.

ONTHYRIUM, a town of Thessaly, near Arne.

ONUGNATHOS, "ass's jawbone," I. a peninsula of Laconia, at the E. entrance of Laconicus sin., over against Platanistus prom., with a temple of Minerva, built by Agamemnon, and the tomb of Cinadus, the pilot of Menelaus. *Isola dei Servi.* II. prom., Cariæ, i. q. Cynossema.

ONUPHIS, a town of Lower Egypt, on the Mendesic branch of the Nile, N.E. of Busiris.

ONYCHIUM, a town of Crete.

OONÆ (Hippopodum, Fanesiorum) ins., isl. placed somewhere in the Borealis oceanus.

OPHARUS fl., i. q. Ocharius.

OPHARITÆ, i. q. Ocharitæ.

OPHELTES prom., a headland of Eubœa, on the E. coast, N. of Caphareus prom.

OPHIOGENEIS, a race of snake-charmers, in Mysia, near Parium.

OPHIONENSES, a people of Ætolia, occupying the country between the Apodoti and Maliacus sin.

OPHIOTES ins., an isl. of Egypt, in the Red sea, S.E. of Berenice.

OPHIR (Appa), capital of a cognominal district of Arabia Felix, inland of Hammæum littus. The seat of the children of Ophir, son of Joktan, and the locality of the gold quest of Solomon. *Ofor; Afi.*

OPEIS fl., I. a r. of Arcadia, flowing by Mantinea. II. of Colchis, 7 geog. m. E. from Trapezus.

OPHITES fl., a stream of Bœotia, falling into Copais lacus w. of Haliartus.

OPHITIA, the name given by a decree of the Amphictyonic council to Amphicæa in Phocis.

OPHIUS (Orphis) fl., I. a r. of Pontus, falling into the Euxine at Ophius portus. The limit of the Macrones and Bechires. *Caouchi.* II. a town of the Bizeres, Pontus, at the mouth of the cognominal river.

OPHIUSA, I. an early name of the N.W. coast of Spain. II. (*Latinè* Colubraria, also Ebusus) ins., the smaller of the Pityusæ ins., Tarraconensis, s. of Ebusus. So named from its abounding in snakes, or from its large production of snake-wort, or from the figure of the island. *Formentera.* III. a town of Dacia, on Tyras fl., above Tyra. The original settlement of the Milesians, who founded the latter city, with which, indeed, some geographers identify it.

OPHIUSSA ins., an isl. in the Propontis, S.E. of Proconnesus. *Afzia.*

OPHLIMUS m., a m. of Pontus, N. of Amasia.

OPHLONES, a people of Sarmatia E., bet. Tanais fl. and the Gerrus ?

OPHNI, i. q. Gophna.

OPHRADUS fl., a r. of Drangiana, falling into Aria lacus bet. Pharnacotus fl. and Etymandrus fl.

OPHRAH, I. a town of Benjamin. II. of Manasseh. The birth-place of Gideon.

OPHRYNIUM, a town of Dardania, Mysia, near Dardanus, with a grove sacred to Hector.

OPICI, the Greek name of the Osci.

OPIE, a town of Rhætia, on the Danube, w. of Mediana. *Dillingen.*

OPINUM, I. a town of Corsica, E.N.E. of Cenestum. *Opini.* II. of Lucania, bet. Venusia (15) and Bradanus fl. (9). *Oppido.*

OPIS, a town of Assyria, of uncertain position.

OPISTHO-LEPRE, a suburb of Ephesus, under Prion m.

OPITERGIUM, a town of the Veneti, Venetia, on Plavis fl., R., bet. Ad Cepasias (28) and Concordia (15). *Oderzo.*

OPIZAS, a town of the Odrysæ, Thrace, s. of Hebrus fl., bet. Cellæ and Assus.

OPLONTÆ (Salinæ Herculeæ), a town of Campania, on Via Domitiana, bet. Herculaneum (6) and Pompeii (3). *Torre della Nunziata.*

OPŌNE, a port of Æthiopia, on Indicus oceanus, N. of Zingis prom.

OPPIDUM CAMELORUM, Arabiæ, i. q. Fons Emischabalis.

OPPIDUM DECIATUM, capital of the Deciates, Gaul. *St. Paul de Vence.*

OPPIDUM NOVUM, a town of Mauritania Cæsar., on Chinalaph fl., L., bet. Tigauda (32) and Tigava (12). A colonia. *El Cadara.*

OPPIDUM NOVUM, a town of Mauritania Ting., bet. Ad Novas (32) and Tremula (2), on Lixus fl. *Narandscha.*

OPPIDUM NOVUM, a town of the Bigerrones, Novem Populana, bet. Beneharnum N.W. and Aquæ Convenarum S.E.

OPSIKELLA, a town of the Cantabri, Tarraconensis. Founded by Opsikellas, follower of Antenor.

OPTATIANA, a town of the Ratacenses, Dac., on Marisus fl., R., bet. Napoca (10) and Cargiana (15). *Gernyezseg.*

OPUNTIUS sinus, a bay of the Ægean, bet. Locris Opunt. and Eubœa. *Golfo di Talanta.*

OPUS, I. a town of Acrorea, Elis. II. (Opoes), capital of the Locri Opuntii, on the confines of Bœotia, 2 m. from the sea, 7½ S.E. from Cynus. The city of Deucalion and Pyrrha. The birth-place of Patroclus. *Kardenitza.*

ORA, I. a town of Gedrosia, towards the coast. *Fohredj.* II. (Rhambacia), capital of the Oritæ, Gedrosia, 7 days' journey inland.

ORACANA, a fortified town of Media, N.E. of Galla. *Balfrusch.*

ORANI, a people of Sarmatia, on Mæotis palus.

ORASSE, a town of Zeugitana, on Neapolitanus sin., bet. Horrea and Putput.

ORBA, a town of Numidia, on Bagradas fl., R., bet. Mutia and Lares.

ORBADURA, a town of Meroe, on the Nile, R., bet. Sandace and Primis Magna.

ORBALISSENE regio, a district of Armenia Minor, N.

ORBANASSA, a town of Pisidia, s. of Dyrcela.

ORBELIA, a district of Pæonia, Macedonia, under Orbelus m. *Caratova.*

ORBELUS m., a s.w. continuation of Scomius m., separating Mœsia from Orbelia. The name was sometimes extended to Hæmus and Rhodope. *Egrisou Dagh.*

ORBESINE, a district of Asia Minor, s.

ORBITANIUM, a town of the Caudini, Samnium, near Melea. *Ducenta.*

ORCADES ins., isl. of Britannia Barbara, N.E. of Orcas prom. They were known to the ancients prior to the circumnavigation of Britain by Agricola. *Orkneys.*

ORCAORICI, a tribe of Tectosages, Galatia, towards Tattæa lac.

ORCAS prom., i. q. Tarvidium.

ORCELIS, a town of the Contestani, Tarraconensis, on Tader fl., L., towards its mouth. *Murcia?*

ORCHENI, a people of Arabia, towards the Euphrates.

ORCHOE (Urchoa), a town of Chaldæa, S.E. of Vologesia. The seat of an astronomical college. By some supposed the Ur of Abraham.

ORCHOMENUS, I. a town of Arcadia, bet. Mantinea and Pheneus. Built by Orchomenus, son of Lycaon, on a hill, and gradually removed to its foot. Extinct in Strabo's time. Noted for its sheep. Here were temples of Neptune and Venus. *Kalpaki.* II. *prius* Andreis, *surnamed* Minyæus, the second city of Bœotia, and at one time its capital, on Cephissus fl., near its mouth, N. of Coronea. Primarily occupied by the Phlegyæ, and then by the Minyæ. Named after Orchomenus, son of Minyas. The burial-place of Hesiod. The first city in which a temple to the Graces was consecrated. The territory was almost undermined by moles. *Skripou.* III. a port of Eubœa, within Geræstus prom.

ORCIA, a town of the Bastetani, Tarraconensis, bet. Fraxinus s.w. and Ad Morum N.E.

ORCISTUS, a town of Phrygia Epict., w. of Pessinus.

ORCUS fl., Thess., i. q. Titaresius fl.

ORDESSUS fl., I. a r. of Dacia, rising E. of Castrum Trajani and falling into the Danube. *Sereth*. II. a port of the Callipidæ, on Sagaricus sin., w. of Olbia. Ptolemy assigns it to the mouth of the Axiaces. III. of the Crobyzi, Mœsia, on the Euxine, s. of Tomi. *Varna*.

ORDOVICES (*Celticè*, Ord-tuavich, "northern mountaineers"), a people of Britannia II., occupying the upper portion of the province, N. of Stucia fl. *N. Wales*.

ORDYMNUS (Ordynus) m., a summit of Lepetymnus m., in Lesbos, w., overlooking Antissa.

OREIA m., a m. of Ætolia, one of Corax m.

OREOPHANTA, a town of the Mandalæ, Ind., on the Ganges, bet. Celydna and Aganagora.

OREI, Mesopotamiæ, i. q. Orrhoeni.

ORESTE, a town of Eubœa.

ORESTHEIUM (Oresthasium), a town of Arcadia, s.E. of Ladocea.

ORESTIA (Argos Oresticum), capital of Orestis, Macedonia, on the s.E. shore of Celetrius lacus. Founded by Orestes. The birth-place of Ptolemy Lagus. *Sdreotza*.

ORESTIS, the country of the Orestæ, a Molossian tribe, in Macedonia. Bounded on the w. by Atintania, on the N.E. by Lyncus, on the E. by Eordæa and Elymæa, on the s. by Stymphalia.

ORETANI, a people of Tarraconensis, on the borders of Bætica, bet. Anas fl. and Bætis fl.

ORETHUS fl., a r. of Sicily, falling into the sea at Panormus. *Orfeto*.

ORETUM GERMANORUM (Oria), capital of the Oretani, Tarraconensis, N. of Mirabriga. *Chapel of Nuestra Señora de Oreto, near Calatrava*.

OREUS, a village of Ellopia, Eubœa, on Callas fl., above Histiæa, to which city the Athenians extended its name, on the expulsion of its former inhabitants. It was extinct in Pliny's time.

OREXIS m., a m. of Arcadia, on the confines of Achaia, N. of Pheneus.

ORGANA ins., an isl. of Carmania, off Harmuza. *Ormus*.

ORGASI, a people of Scythia, on the Rha, above the Erymmi.

ORGESSUS (Orgysus), a town of the Pissantini, Illyria, on Genusus fl., N.w. of Pelion.

ORGIA, a town of the Lacetani, Tarraconens., N.E. of Æsona.

ORGIBATE, Paphlagoniæ, i. q. Garzibanthon.

ORGOCYNI, a people of Taurica Chersonesus.

ORGUS fl., a r. of Phrygia M., falling into Mæander fl., L., below Euphorbium.

ORIA, Hispaniæ, i. q. Oretum.

ORICUM, a town of Illyria, at the s.E. extremity of Aulonicus sin., at the mouth of Celydnus fl. Founded by the Abantes of Eubœa, on their return from Troy, extended by a Colchian colony, and restored by Herodes Atticus. A Roman naval and commercial station. Noted for its turpentine. *Ericho*.

ORĪCUS m., m. of Chalonitis, Assyriæ, bet. the Tigris and the Gyades.

ORIEUS MEDIUS, Midus, a town of Bithynia, 16 m. from Nicæa.

ORIGIACUM, capital of the Ambiliati, Belgica II., towards Turnacum. *Orchies*.

ORINÆI, a people of Sarmatia A., on the Rha, above the Vali.

ORINE CHERSONESUS, a rugged pr. of the Adulitæ, on the Red sea, at the s. entrance of Adulitanus sin.

ORINGIS, a town of Bætica, near Hispalis. Noted for its silver-mines.

ORIPPO, a town of the Turtetani, Bætica, bet. Hispalis N. (9) and Salpesa s. *Dos Hermanos*.

ORISETI, a people of Bactriana, s. of the Scordæ.

ORISSI, a people of Tarraconensis, in Orospeda m.

ORITÆ (Ori), a people of Gedrosia, occupying the coast for 250 m. w. of Arbis fl. The Asiatic Æthiopes of Herodotus.

ORIUM prom., a pr. of Tarraconensis, on the Atlantic, bet. Evora and Cambetum.

ORIUNS fl., a r. of Illyria, formed by the junction below Scodra of Barbana and Clausula ffl., and, after separating the Dalmatæ from the Taulantii, falling into the Adriatic s.E. of Olcinium. *Bojana*.

ORMENIUM, a town of Magnesia, Thessaly, at the N.E. extremity of Pagasæus sin., 3½ m. s.E. from Demetrias, whither its inhabitants were transferred by Demetrius Poliorcetes. A town of Eurypylus. The birth-place of Phœnix, the tutor of Achilles. *Goritza*.

ORMINIUS m., a ridge of Olympus, separating Salon regio, of Bithynia, from the Tectosages of Galatia.

ORMIZA, a town of Trachonitis, near Canatha, E.

ORNÆUM prom., the s. extremity of Taprobane.

ORNEÆ fl., a r. of Argolis.

ORNEON ins., Arabiæ, i. q. Avium ins.

ORNITHIAS, *vide* Chelidonias.

ORNITHŌNPOLIS (Avium Oppidum), a maritime town of Phœnicia, bet. Sidon (12) and Tyrus (12).

OROANDA, a town of Pisidia, N.E. of Pisidicus lacus, towards Galatia. *Hawiran.*

OROATIS fl., i. q. Arosis.

OROBATIS, a town of Arachosia, s.w. of Peucela.

OROBIÆ, a town of Eubœa, on the w. coast, s. of Ægæ, with an oracle of Apollo Selinuntius. *Rovies.*

OROBII, "mountain-dwellers," generally the name given by the Greeks to the Alpine tribes of Italy ; specially, the people about Larius lacus, among whom Greek colonies were settled by Pompeius Strabo, Cornel. Scipio, and Julius Cæsar.

OROBIS fl., a r. of Gaul, falling into the Mediterranean E. of the Rhone. *Orb.*

OROBIUM forum, i. q. Forum Licinii.

OROLAUNUM, a town of the Treveri, Belgica I., bet. Meduantum w.N.w. and Augusta Trevirorum N.E.

OROMA fl., a name of the Euphrates, near its source.

OROMANDRUS, a town of Armenia Minor.

OROMARSACI, a tribe of Morini, Gaul, about Gessoriacum.

OROMEDON m., a m. of Cos.

ORONTES (Axius), I. a r. of Syria, rising in Libanus m. and falling into the Mediterranean 14 m. s. of Antiochia. *Aasi.* II. a m. of Media, towards Ecbatana. *Alwend.*

OROPUS, a city of Bœotia, on Asopus fl., R., 4¼ m. E. from Tanagra. The port of Thebes, 1 m. from the sea. Stigmatized for avarice. Near it was a temple of Amphiareus, the spot where he and his chariot were swallowed up. *Ropo.*

OROSANA, a town of Serica, near the source of Bautissus fl.

OROSPEDA m., i. q. Ortospeda.

OROVA, a town of the Silices, Assyr., on Lycus fl., N.E. of Arbela.

ORPHEI tumulus, a large conical tumulus, 20 stadia from Dium, raised over the remains of Orpheus after their removal to Libethra. *Near Khatera.*

ORRA, Italiæ, i. q. Aria.

ORREA, a maritime town of the Venicontes, Brit., within the N. entrance of Bodotria æstuar. *Orrock ?*

ORRHOE, the early name of Edessa, Mesopotamia.

ORRHOENE, i. q. Osroene.

ORROTHA, a district of India i. Gangem, contiguous to Sinthu. *In Guzerat.*

ORSA (Orsara), I. a town of Armenia Minor. II. of Bisaltia, in Macedonia, on Bisaltes fl., N.w. of Bolbe. *Soho.* III. m., a m. of Arabia Felix E., towards the head, N., of Duatus sin.

ORSENA, I. a district of Armenia Minor (central).

ORSINUS fl., a r. of Caria, falling into Mæander fl. below Antiochia. *Gongere.*

ORSIPI, a town of Bactriana, under Parapomisus m., s.w. of the Amarispi.

ORSON, Bætica, i. q. Ursao.

ORTACEA fl., a r. of Susiana, falling into the sea on the eastern coast.

ORTHE (Corseæ), the citadel of Phalanna, in Perrhæbia, on the right bank of Titaresius fl.

ORTHRONIENSES, a people of Caria.

ORTHOSIA, I. a town of Caria. *Ortaki.* II. of Phœnicia, s. of Eleutherus fl.

ORTHURA, capital of the Soringæ, Ind., N.E. of Carura. *Utatur.*

ORTONIA, the naval arsenal of the Frentani, bet. Augulus and Anxanum. *Ortona.*

ORTOSPANA (Cabura), capital of the Cabolitæ, Arachos, on Cophes fl., near its source. *Candahar.*

ORTOSPEDA (Orospeda, Tugiensis saltus) m., a continuation of Idubeda m., running s.E. to Spartarius campus, and w. (as Marianus m.), and s.w. as (Ilipula m.) through Bætica.

ORTYGIA, I. a town of Ætolia, whence Delos obtained its surname of Ortygian. II. ins., an isl. of Sicily, at Syracuse. Here was the fountain Arethusa, fabled to communicate with the river Alpheus of Greece.

ORTYGIA, I. a grove of Ionia, on the coast, below Ephesus. One of the spots claiming to be the birth-place of Apollo and Diana. II. an early name of Ephesus.

ORUDII m., m. of India e. Gangem, N. of Callinga.

ORXANTES fl., i. q. Jaxartes.

ORYCHIUM, a village of Attica.

ORYX, a town of Arcadia, on Ladon fl., L., above Nasi.

OSA fl., a r. of Etruria, falling into the sea s. of Telamon port. *Osa.*

OSÆA, a maritime town of the Celsitani, in Sardinia, w. of Neapolis. *Oseo ?*

OSCA, I. a town of Bætica, s.w. of Tucci. II. capital of the Ilerjetes, Tarraconensis, N.N.E. of Cæsar-Augusta. A colonia (Victrix). The death-place of Sertorius, who here established a school of Greek and Roman literature. *Huesca.*

OSCELLA, capital of the Lepontii, in Rhætia, N.w. of Umana. *Domo d' Ossola.*

OSCI (Obsci, Opici), a people of Italy descendants of the Umbri. So named, according to Festus, from their loose manners and language.

OSCINÆUM, a town of the Sotiates, Novem Populana, N.N.E. of Elusa.

OSERIATÆ, a people of Pannonia, s., on Savus fl., E. of the Jassi.

OSI, a people of Germania Magna, towards the Quadi.

OSIANA, a town of Morimene, in Cappadocia, bet. Nyssa (32) and Saccasena (28).

OSICERTA (Ossigerda), a town of the Ilergetes, Tarraconensis, on the Iberus, w. of Leonica. A colonia of veterans, and a municipium.

OSII (Ossii), a people of Sarmatia, N. of the Vettæ.

OSINCUM, a town of Corsica, near the source of Circidius fl.

OSISMII (Sismii), a people occupying the w. extremity of Lugdunensis IV., w. of the Curiosilites and Veneti. *Finisterre, N.*

OSONES, a town of the Amantini, Pannon., bet. Floriana (26) and Cæsariana (29). *Bank.*

OSOPUM, a town of the Carni, in Venetia, on Tilavemptus fl. *Osopo.*

OSPHAGUS fl., a r. of Lyncus, in Macedonia, rising s.w. of Heraclea, and falling into the Erigonus at Alcomenæ.

OSQUIDATES, I. *surnamed* Campestri, a people of Aquitania, contiguous to the Tarusates. *Vallée d'Ossan.* II. *surnamed* Montani, a tribe of the same people, in Aquitania, contiguous to the Elusates.

OSRHOENE (Orrhoene), a district of Mesopotamia, about Epessa. Named from Osroes, who established it as a principality 120 B.C.

OSSA m., a ridge of mountains in Thessaly, the s. continuation of Olympus (from which they are said to have been severed by the earthquake which gave a mouth to Peneus fl.), forming, with Pelion m., the w. boundary of Magnesia. The chief abode of the Centauri. *Kissovo.*

OSSADII, a people of India i. Gangem, on Acesines fl.

OSSARENE, a district of Armenia, on Cyrus fl.

OSSET, *apud* Plin., i. q. Hispalis.

OSSIGI, *surnamed* Laconicun (Civitas Ossigitana), a town of the Turtuli, Bætica, on the Bætis, above Illiturgis. *Near Ubeda.*

OSSONOBA, a maritime town of the Cynetes, Lusitania, bet. Hannibalis portus and Balsa (16). *Faro.*

OSTEODES ins., an isl. of Sicily, 75 m. N.E. from Soli. *Alicur.*

OSTIA, a town of Latium, at the fork of the double mouth of the Tiber. The port of Rome; founded by the tribune Ancus Martius; the harbour, called Portus Augusti, begun by Julius Cæsar, was completed by Claudius. A colonia. *Ostia.*

OSTIÆ lacus, a salt lake of Latium, near Ostia. *Stagno di Levante.*

OSTIÆI, a people of Northern Germany.

OSTIDAMNII, i. q. Timnii.

OSTIMII (Ostionestimii, Ostsimii), i. q. Timii.

OSTIONES (Ostiæi), i. q. Timnii.

OSTIPPO, a town of the Turtetani, Bætica, bet. Hispalis s.w. and Astigi E.N.E.

OSTIUM SACRUM, the southernmost issue of the Danube.

OSTIUM HISPANICUM, the w. mouth of the Rhone.

OSTIUM MASSILIENSE, a mouth of the Rhone, bet. Ostium Metapinum w. and Stomalimne E.

OSTIUM METAPINUM, a mouth of the Rhone, bet. Ostium Hispanicum and Ostium Massiliense.

OSTRA, a town of Umbria, s. of Suasa. *Corinaldo.*

OSTRACINA m., a m. of Arcadia, 4 m. w. from Mantinea.

OSTRACINE, a maritime town of Casiotis, in Egypt, at the extremity of Sirbonis palus, on the confines of Palestine, E. of Pelusium (65).

OSTRUS (Otrus), a town of Phrygia Salutaris.

OSTUDIZUM, a town of the Odryzæ, in Thrace, bet. Tarpodizus and Burtudizum.

OSTUR, a town of the Ilercaones, Tarraconens., w. of Ildum.

OSYLI, a people of Sarmatia Europ., bet. the Ophlones and the Roxolani.

OTADENI (Ottadini), a maritime people of Britain, in Valentia and Maxima Cæsar., E. bet. Bodotria æstuar. and Hadriani murus.

OTENE (Motene), a district of Armenia Maj., on Cyrus fl. *Uti.*

OTESINI, a people of Gallia Cisalpina, towards the Padus.

OTHACA, a town of the Celsitani in Sardinia, above the mouth of Tyrsus fl., L., bet. Neapolis (18) and Cornus. *Oristano.*

OTHONA portus, a port of the Regni, bet. Portus Novus and Anderida. The station of the Milites Fortenses. *Hastings.*

OTHRYS m., a ridge of Pindus, extending E. from Tymphrestus m., on the south border of Thessaly, separating Dolopia from Æniania and Phthiotis from Maliensis. The ancient seat of the Centaurs. Noted for a peculiar serpent called *seps.* Variously *Hellovo, Varbovo, Goura.*

OTHRONUS ins., an isl. of Corcyra, over against Phacrum prom. *Fano.*

OTHRYTÆ, a Thessalian tribe inhabiting the gorges of Othrys m.

OTREA, a town of Bithynia, near Agrilium. Built by Otreus the Phrygian. *Ortakevi.*

OTRYNE, a demus of Attica, of the tribe Ægeis. Famous for its gudgeons.

OTTAVIOLCA, a town of the Autrigones, Tarraconensis, on Nerva fl., below Flaviobriga.

OTTOROCORRÆ, a people of Serica, s. of the Batæ.

OVETUM, a later name of Lucus Asturum.

OVILABIS (Ovilia), capital of the Sevaces, in Noricum, bet. Joviacum (27) and Tergolape (14). A colonia (Aurelia Colon. Antonia). *Wels.*

OXEÆ (Thoæ) ins., isl. on the w. coast of Acarnania, bet. Echinades ins. and Ithaca ins. *Curzolari.*

OXIA prom., a pr. of Taprobane, N. above Rizala.

OXIANA, I. a town of Sogdiana, on Oxus fl. *Termed.* II. palus, a lake of Sogdiana, formed by Polytimetus fl., on the borders of Margiana, with an issue into Oxus fl.

OXIANI, a people of Sogdiana, on the Oxus.

OXII m., m. of Sogdiana N.

OXIMAGIS fl., a r. of India e. Gangem, falling into the Ganges below Corygaza.

OXIMUM, a town of the Sesuvii, in Gaul, towards Noviomagus. *Eximes.*

OXINAS (Zoonautes) fl., a r. of Bithynia, falling into the Euxine 2 m. N.E. from Nymphæum.

OXIONES, a people of Northern Germany.

OXTHRACA, a town of the Celtici, Lusitania, S.E. of Arandis.

OXUS fl., a r. of Asia, rising N.W. of the source of the Indus, and, after separating Sogdiana N. from Bactriana and Margiana s., falling into a lake E. of the Caspian (the Sea of Aral). Remarkable for the quantity of soil it carried down with it. *Amoo; Jihon.*

OXYBII, a maritime tribe of Salyes, Narbonensis, N.E. of the Suelteri.

OXYDRACÆ, a people of India i. Gangem, on Hydraotes fl., towards the Malli.

OXYNEIA, a town of Estiæotis, in Thessaly, on Ion fl., 15 m. w. from Azorus. *Euskineh.*

OXYOPUM, a town of Mysia.

OXYRRHOUM prom., a headland of Bithynia, on Bosporus Thracius, N. of Phrixus portus.

OXYRYNCHUS, a town of Heptanomis, near the Nile, L., bet. Heracleopolis Magna and Co. Here the fish oxyrynchus was worshipped with peculiar veneration. *Beneseh.*

OZĒNE, a town of India i. Gangem, under Vindius m. N. *Uzen.*

OZERA fl., a r. of Gaul, flowing by Alesia. *Ozerain.*

OZOGARDANA (Zaragardia, Pacoria, Aniobaritis), a town of Mesop., on the Euphrates, bet. Pylæ and Besechanna. Here was shown a judgment-seat of Trajan in stone.

OZZALA (Togola), a town of Morimene, in Cappadocia, bet. Archelais (17) and Nitazus (18).

P.

PAALA fl., a r. of Gallia Cisalpina, flowing by Bononia. *Savena.*

PABLIA fl., a r. of Etruria, falling into the Clanis at Urbs Vetus. *Paglia.*

PACCIANA, a town of Numidia, at the mouth of Ampsaga fl., bet. Chullu and Igilgilis.

PACHIUM (Crassum) prom., a pr. of Sardinia, N.E. of Accipitrum ins.

PACHNAMUNIS, a town of Lower Egypt, on the Athribitic branch of the Nile, R., towards its mouth. *Handahur.*

PACONIA ins., an isl. of Sicily N.W.

PACHYNUM (Pachynus) prom., the S.E. extremity of Sicily; a flat tongue of rocky land. *C. Passaro.*

PACTIUS fl., a r. of Apulia, falling into the Adriatic s. of Brundusium. *Canale del Cefalo.*

PACTOLUS (Chrysorrhoas) fl., a r. of Lydia, rising in Tmolus m., and falling into Hermus fl. near Sardes. Its sands were mixed with gold. On its banks was a temple of Cybele. *Bagouly.*

PACTYA, a town of Chersonesus Thracia, at the entrance to the Propontis. Founded by Miltiades. The retreat of Alcibiades on his second banishment.

PACTYES m., a m. of Ionia, bet. Magnesia and Ephesus.

PACYRIS fl., i. q. Hypacaris.

PADARGUS fl., a r. of Persis Prop., falling into Persicus sin. N. of Hieratis.

PADASIA, a town of Cilicia Campestris, s.w. of Callipolis.

PADINUM, a town of the Boii, in Gallia Cispadana, on Scultenna fl., above its junction with Padus fl. *Bondeno.*

PADAN fl., i. q. Padusa.

PADUS (Eridanus) fl., a r. of Italy, rising in Vesulus m., and after a course of 288 m. falling into the Adriatic by two principal and five smaller mouths, together called Septem Maria, s. of Athesis fl. *Po.*

PADUSA (Padoa) fl., i. q. Spineticum Ostium Padi.

PADYANDUS, i. q. Podandus.

PÆANIA, Superior and Inferior, two villages forming a demus of Attica, of the tribe Pandionis, near Aphidna. The birth-place of Demosthenes, and of Phya, the personifier of Minerva.

PÆANIUM, a town of Ætolia, on Achelous fl., bet. Ithoria and Œniadæ. Destroyed by Philip of Macedon. *Stamna.*

PÆCILE petra, a headland of Cilicia Trachea, 5 m. E. of Sarpedon prom., with a cognominal town. *Pershendy.*

PÆESSA, a town of Ceos ins., on the s.w. coast. With a temple of Minerva built by Nestor. *Kabia.*

PÆMÆNIUM, a town of Macedonia.

PÆMANDRIA, the early name of Tanagra, Bœotia, from its founder Pæmander.

PÆON, a town of Chersonesus Thracia, on Melas sin., s. of Ide.

PÆONES, a nation of Macedonia, at one time occupying also a large portion of Thrace and Emathia. A colony of Dardani and Teucri.

PÆONIA, the northern portion of Macedonia, from the Erigonus to the Strymon, bounded N. by Mœsia, s. by Lyncus, Deuriopæa, and Emathia, w. by Illyria, E. by Thrace. An early name also of Emathia.

PÆOPLÆ, a people of Thrace, on Strymon fl., E. of the Doberes.

PÆSICI, a tribe of Astures, Tarraconensis, N., occupying a peninsula E. of Navilubio fl.

PÆSTANUS sin., a gulf of the Tyrrhenian sea, at Pæstum, bet. Minervæ prom. and Posidium prom. *Golfo di Salerno.*

PÆSTUM (Posidonia), a city of Lucania, 4 m. s. from the mouth of Silarus fl. A Tyrrhenian city, enlarged by a Sybarite colony circa 500 B.C. A colonia 274 B.C. Celebrated for its temple of Neptune, and for its roses, which bloomed twice a year. *Pæstum.*

PÆSULA, a town of the Turtetani, Bætica, w.n.w. of Italica.

PÆSUS, Mysiæ, i. q. Apæsus.

PÆTANION ins., an isl. of Cuneus, Lusitaniæ, off the mouth of the Anas. *Caes.*

PÆTI, a people of Thrace, on Hebrus fl.

PAGÆ (Pegæ), a town of Megaris, on the Alcyonium mare, bet. Ægosthenæ and Creusis (20). The burial-place of Ægialeus. *Psato.*

PAGASÆ ("full of springs"), the port of Iolcos, and, later, of Pheræ, at the s. extremity of Pagasæus sin., to which it gave name, 11 m. s. from Pheræ. Sacred to Apollo. The port where the ship Argo

was built, and whence she sailed on her famous voyage. *Volo.*

PAGASÆA regio, the district about Pagasæ, in Thessaly. The territory of Eumelus.

PAGASÆUS (Pagaseticus, Pagasites, Pagasicus, Iolciacus, Demetriacus) sin., a gulf of the Ægean, on the s.E. coast of Thessaly, bet. Magnesia and Phthiotis. *Golfo di Volo.*

PAGRÆ, a town of the Toreatæ, Sarmatiæ, bet. Bate and Toricus portus.

PAGRASA, a port of the Sindi, Indiæ, above Sinda.

PAGULA, a maritime town of the Oritæ, Gedrosia, bet. Cabana and Arbis fl.

PAGUS m., a m. of Lydia, overlooking Smyrna.

PAGUS ILIENSIUM, a town of Troas, bet. Troja and the sea. Built by Ilus, son of Troas, 1314 B.C.

PAGUS INSUBER, a district of the Ædui, in Gaul.

PAGUS TROJANUS, the district about Hadria, Venetiæ.

PAGYRITÆ, a people of Sarmatia, contiguous to the Aorsi.

PAIPERTA, a fortress of Phrygia, near Philomelium.

PALA, a town of the Odrysæ, in Thrace, on Harpessus fl., bet. Beræa and Castra Zarba.

PALACENTI, a town of Drangiana, on Etymandrus fl., R., above Tazarene.

PALACIUM, a maritime town of Taurica Chersonesus, s.E., above Criumetopon prom.

PALÆ TYRUS, "old Tyre," the earlier city of that name, on the Mediterranean, 3¾ m. s. from Tyre. Its materials were applied by Alexander to the formation of the mole by which he connected the island on which Tyre stood with the mainland.

PALÆA, I. a village of Æolis Asiat., 16 m. from Andeira, with which town it was said to be connected by a subterranean passage. Here was a temple of Cybele. II. a maritime town of Cyprus, at the foot of Olympus m., N.E. of Curias prom. III. (Pleia), a town of Laconia, on Selenus fl., N. of Leucæ.

PALÆBYBLOS, a town of Phœnicia, near Byblus, of which it was the predecessor.

PALÆMARIA, Ægypti, i. q. Maria.

PALÆMYNDUS, a maritime town of Caria, near Astypalæa prom. A colony from Trœzene.

PALÆOPOLIS, I. (Panemotichos), a town of Pamphylia. II. a city of Campania, bet. Neapolis and Vesuvius m. A mixed colony (anterior to Neapolis), of Chalcidians, Pithecusans, and Athenians, under Diotimus. Apparently destroyed by the Romans 325 B.C. III. a town of Lydia.

PALÆOTRIUM (Palæorium), a town of Acte penins., in Macedonia.

PALÆPAPHOS, the parent city of Paphos, in Cyprus, 7¼ m. E. from the later city, 1¼ m. from the sea, E. of Drepanum prom., on Bocarus fl. The landing-place of Venus, and pre-eminently sacred to her. *Conclia.*

PALÆPHATUS, a town of Pelasgiotis, in Thessaly.

PALÆRUS (Palirus), a town of Acarnania, on the w. coast, bet. Thyreum and Solium. *Zaverda.*

PALÆSCEPSIS, "old Scepsis," the capital of Æneas, 7½ m. above Scepsis. The inhabitants were removed by Ascanius to Scepsis. Extinct in Pliny's time.

PALÆSIMUNDI ins., i. q. Taprobane.

PALÆSTE (Pharsalia), a harbour of Chaonia, under Acroceraunii m., bet. Oricum (20) and Chimæra, 25 m. S.E. from Acroceraunium prom. *Paleassa.*

PALÆSTINA, "land of the Philistines," a country of Asia, bounded N. by Syria, s. by Arabia Petræa, w. by the Mediterranean, E. by Arabia Deserta. *Palestine.*

PALAMNUS fl., a r. of the Taulantii, in Illyria, falling into the Adriatic N.E. of Epidamnus. *Stefano.*

PALANDA, I. a r. of Aurea Chersonesus, falling into Perimulicus sin. at Palanda. II. a port of Aurea Chersonesus, w., at the mouth of Palanda fl., within Malaci prom.

PALANTA, a town of Corsica, N.w. of Cersunum. *Balagna.*

PALANTHRUS, a town of Magnesia, in Thessaly.

PALAS, a district of Germany, on Mænus fl.

PALATINUS m., one of the seven hills of Rome. The locality of the city of Romulus, and of his palace, whence its name.

PALATIUM, I. a town of Rhætia, bet. Tridentum (24) and Verona (36). II. (Palantium), an aboriginal town of Sabinium, w. of Reate. It gave name to Mons Palatinus at Rome. *Palazzo.*

PALATIOLUM, a town of the Treviri, Belgica I., near Augusta Trevirorum N.

PALFURIANA, a town of the Cosetani, Tarraconensis, E.N.E. of Tarraco.

PALI, the eastern Pelasgi, progenitors of the Philistæi.

PALIANA, a town of Serica, towards the source of Bautisus fl.

PALICORUM lacus, a lake of Sicily, the crater of an extinct volcano, near Palice. Sacred to the Palaci. Remarkable for always retaining the same level. The oath by its waters was deemed very sacred.

PALĬCE, a town of Sicily, s.w. of Leontini, on Palicanus lac. Built by Dacetius of Menæ, round the temple of the Palici.

PATALIPUTRA, capital of the Prasii, Indiæ, on the Ganges, near the confluence of Sonus fl. The residence of Sandracottus. *Near Patna.*

PALINDROMOS prom., the s.w. extremity of Arabia, at the E. entrance of the Red sea, over against Dire prom. *Bab el Mandeb.*

PALINURUM prom., a pr. of Lucania, s. of Velia. Named from the pilot of Æneas, who perished there. *Capo di Palinuro.*

PALINURUS AD MELPHEM (Palinurus Molpis), a town of Lucania, at the mouth of Melphes fl.

PALINURUS, a town of Samos, near Panormus.

PALIO, a town of Peucetia, Apul., 4 m. s. of Butuntum. *Palo.*

PALISCIUS, a town of Arcadia, 4½ m. E. from Megalopolis.

PALIURI palus, a lake of Marmarica, N.w. of Paliurus.

PALIURUS, I. a town of Marmarica, w. of Batrachos. II. fl., a r. of Marmarica, rising in Paliuri palus, and falling into the Mediterranean at Paliurus, bet. Chersonesus Magna and Batrachos portus.

PALLA (Palæ), a maritime town of Corsica, bet. Rubra and Albiana. *San Bonifacio.*

PALLACOPAS canalis, an artificial issue of the Euphrates, cut by Alexander, above Besechana, 100 m. N. of Babylon, to Persicus sin., w. of Diridotis.

PALLADIA, a surname of Tolosa, from Pallas there worshipped, and generally from its cultivation of learning.

PALLANTIA, I. a city of the Astures, Tarraconensis, on Astura fl., s.E. of Asturica Augusta. *Villa Moros.* II. capital of the Vaccæi, on Pisoracus fl. *Palencia.* III. fl., Tarraconensis, i. q. Turis.

PALLANTIUM (Palatium), a town of Arcadia, N.w. of Tegea. Named from Pallas, greatgrandfather of Evander. Made a free town by Antoninus, as having been the place whence Evander led his colonists to Italy. Here were temples of Evander, Pallas, and the great goddesses. *Thana.*

PALLADIS (Pallantias) lac., a lake of Africa, s.w. of Tritonis palus, formed by Triton fl. Named from Pallas (Minerva).

PALLANUM, a town of the Frentani, on Via Frentana, bet. Annum (12) and Histonum (12). *Pallano.*

PALLE (Pale), a town of Cephallenia ins., on a gulf on the s. coast, N.W. of Zacynthus ins., under Bœa m. *Lixuri.*

PALLENE, *prius* Phlegra, I. the w. peninsula of Chalcidice, in Macedonia, bet. Thermaicus sin. and Toronaicus sin. Colonized and named by Pallenians of Achaia, after the siege of Troy. The scene of the battle bet. the gods and the Titans. II. (Pallenis, Pallenium), a demus of Attica, of the tribe Antiochis, bet. Angele and Braurion. Here Minerva Pallene was especially worshipped. *Pala.* III. Maced., i. q. Scione.

PALLIA fl., a r. of Etruria, falling into Clanis fl. at Herbanum. *Paglia.*

PALLON (Bilbana), a town of the Gerræi, Arabiæ, on Persicus sin., s. of Thar. *Hims.*

PALMA, I. a town of Balearis Mag., on the s.w. coast. Founded by Metellus. A colonia. *Palma.* II. Siciliæ, i. q. Tamaricium.

PALMARIA ins., an island of Latium, 5 m. w. from Sinonia ins. *Palmaruola.*

PALMARUM CIVITAS, i. q. Jericho.

PALMATA, a town of the Getæ, Mœsia, N. of Marcianopolis.

PALMYRA (Tadmor), capital of Palmyrene, s. of Thapsacus, s.w. of Circesium ; 140 m. E.N.E. from Damascus. Founded or fortified by Solomon ; restored by Hadrian, and called Hadrianopolis. The royal city of Zenobia.

PALMYRENE, a district of Syria, about Palmyra, bounded N. and E. by the Euphrates, s. by Arabia Deserta, w. by Syria propria.

PALODA, a town of the Jassii, Dacia, on Parata fl., R., below Jassiorum Municipium.

PALSATIUM, i. q. Palatium, Rhætiæ.

PALTOS, a town of Phœnicia, bet. Balanea (8) and Gabala (8). *Boldo.*

PALUMBINUM, a town of the Caudini, in Samnium.

PALURA, I. a port of the Gangaridæ, Ind., on Magnum ostium, Ganget. II. a town of the Calingæ, Ind., N. of Pitynda.

PAMBOTIS lacus, a lake of Molossis, on the confines of Athamania, E. of Dodona, on whose shores Neoptolemus settled after the taking of Troy. *Lago di Jannina.*

PAMISUS fl., I. a r. of Dolopia, in Thessaly, rising in Othrys m., s. of Acharræ, and falling into Peneus fl. E. of Tricca. *Fanari.* II. of Messenia, rising towards Thuria, and falling, after a course of 12½ m., into Messeniacus sin., w. of Pheræ. The water at its source was good in children's disorders. *Pirnatza.*

PAMPELO. *Vide* Pompelon.

PAMPHIA, a town of the Eurytanes, in Ætolia, on or near the s.E. shore of Trichonius lacus, 3½ m. N.W. from Thermus.

PAMPHYLIA, "all nations" (Mopsopia), a country of Asia Minor, bounded N. by Pisidia, s. by the Mediterranean, w. by Lycia, at Climax, E. by Cilicia, at Coracesium. Settled by Solymi from Phœnicia, and after the siege of Troy by Greeks under Calchus, Amphilochus, and other leaders. *Téké-ili.*

PAMPHYLIUM mare, a bay of the Mediterranean, on the coast of Pamphylia, from Sacrum prom. to Anemurium prom. *G. of Attalia.*

PAMPONIS (Papa, Repampane), a village of Thebais, w. of the Nile, 3 geog. m. N.W. from Memnonium. A station of the Ala Prima Jovia Cataphracta Legio.

PAMPORTUS, Pannoniæ, i. q. Nauportus.

PAMPOTADÆ, a demus of Attica, of the tribe Erectheis.

PACTYAS m., a N.E. ridge of Mycale m., bet. Panionium and Ephesus.

PANACHAICUS m., a m. of Achaia, above Patræ. *Voidia.*

PANACRA, I. a summit of Ida m., in Crete. Peculiarly sacred to Jupiter. II. a district of Cyprus, about Olympus m.

PANACTUM, a fortress of Attica, on the frontier of Bœotia, bet. Phylæ and Thebæ. Razed by the Bœotians. *Kako Sialesi.*

PANÆI, a tribe of Edones in Thrace, near Amphipolis.

PANAGRA, a town of Libya Interior.

PANAPIO, a town of Etruria, 7 m. E. from Castrum Novum.

PANCALIA campus, a plain of Cappadocia, on Halys fl.

PANCHÆA ins., an isl. of Arabia Felix, s.

PANDA, I. a town of the Aorsi, Sarmatia Asiat., towards Uspe. II. Sogdianæ, i. q. Maracanda.

PANDASA, a town of the Nangalogæ, Ind., N.E. of Lariagara.

PANDĀTĀRIA ins., an isl. on the coast of Campania. The exile-place of Julia, daughter of Augustus ; of the Elder Agrippina, and of Octavia, wife of Nero. *Vandotina.*

PANDION prom., Cariæ, i. q. Paridion.

PANDIONIS regnum, the kingdom of Pandion, occupying the s. extremity of India i. Gangem, below Chaberis fl.

PANDIONIS, a tribe or ward of Attica, named after Pandion, son of Erectheus.

PANDOSIA, I. an Œnotrian city of Bruttium, on Acheron fl., bet. Consentia and the Tyrrhenian sea. The death-place of Alexander of Epirus. *Near Mendocino.* II. a town of Cassopæa, in Epirus, on the right bank of Acheron fl., s.e. of Buchetium. *Paramythia.* III. of Lucania, on Aciris fl., 5 m. above Heraclea. Near it the footsteps of Hercules were shown in the soil. *Anglona.*

PANGÆUM m., a s.e. ridge of Rhodope m., extending along the coast of Thrace, and terminating in Acontisma. Noted for its gold and silver mines. *Pundhar Dagh; Castagnats.*

PANEAS, I. a district of Galilæa Sup., about Paneas fl. II. fl., a stream of Galilæa, n. of Samachonitis lac., one of the sources of the Jordan. *Banias.* III. m., a m. of Galilæa Sup., at the source of Paneas fl. On it was a temple, erected by Herod in honour of his benefactor Augustus.

PANEPHYSIS, a town of Lower Egypt, 3 geog. m. n. from Tanis.

PANHELLENIUS m., a m. of Ægina ins., 2½ m. from the capital, on which was a temple of Jupiter Panhellenius, erected by Æacus, where were kept the statues of Damia and Auxesia, which occasioned the war of Ægina with Epidaurus.

PANIA, a port of Cilicia Campestris, towards Aleius campus.

PANIARDII, a people of Scythia i. Imaum, n. of Conadipsas regio.

PANIARDIS, a town of Sarmatia A., on the Palus Mæotis, s. of Tanais.

PANIONIUM templum, a temple of Neptune Heliconius, in Ionia, on the sea-shore, under Mycale m., bet. Trogilium prom. and Neapolis. Here were held the general assemblies of the Ionian states. *Tchangeli.*

PANIS antrum, a stalactite cavern near Marathon. Sacred to Pan.

PANNISUS, I. a r. of the Crobyzi, Mœs., falling into the Euxine at Crite. II. (Panyssus), a town of the Crobyzi, Mœs., on Pannisus fl., R., bet. Marcianopolis and Soatræ.

PANNONA, a town of Crete, s. of Gnossus. *Panon.*

PANNONIA, a country of Europe, bounded n. and e. by the Danube, s. by Illyricum and Mœsia, at the Savus, w. by Noricum. *Sclavonia, Lower Austria, Illyria, Croatia, &c.*

PANNŎNII, a Celtic or Germanic people, occupying a portion of Illyria, and Pannonia, to which they gave name.

PANŌN (Taba), a port of Æthiopia, on Indicus oceanus, s. of Aromatum prom.

PANOPEUS (Phanoteus), a town of Phocis, on the right bank of Cephissus fl., 2½ m.

w. from Chæronea. Destroyed by Xerxes. *Agios Blasios.*

PANOPHYSIS, a town of Lower Egypt, on the Mendesic branch of the Nile, below Mendes.

PANOPIS fons, a fountain of Athens, near the Lyceum. Named after the hero Panops.

PANOPOLIS (Chemmis), a town of Thebais, on the Nile, R., bet. Selanus and Thomu, below Ptolemais Hermii. The inhabitants, chiefly linen-weavers and stone-cutters, were especial worshippers of Pan. *Athenyn.*

PANORMUS, I. a port of Achaia, on the Corinthiacus sin., 11 stadia w. of Erineus portus, bet. Argyra and Patræ. II. the harbour of Acanthus, in Acte of Macedonia. III. a port of Attica, n.e. of Sunium. IV. of Caria, n. of Posidium prom. *Kobella.* V. CAUNIORUM, the port of Caunus, in Caria, 6 m. from Cymaria. VI. a harbour of Chaonia, under Acroceraunii m., bet. Chimæra and Photice. *Panormo or Palermo.* VII. a port of Cephallenia ins., on its n.e. coast, opposite Ithaca. VIII. a haven of Chersonnesus Thracia, on the Hellespont, near Cælus. IX. a town of Crete, towards Zephyrium prom. X. a harbour of Cyzicus, in Mysia. *Panormo.* XI. a harbour of Marmarica, 4 m. w. of Syce. XII. the port of Ephesus, at the mouth of Caystrus fl. XIII. a port of Samos, n. of Posidium prom. XIV. a town of Scopelus ins., on the s.w. coast, opposite Eubœa. *Panormo.* XV. a maritime city of Sicily, n., bet. Eleutherus fl. and Hyccara. A Phœnician settlement. A colonia. *Palermo.*

PANOS ins., an isl. of Egypt, in the Red sea, towards Ælaniticus sin.

PANOTÆ, a people on the n. coast of Sarmatia, having monstrous eyes.

PANTAENSES, a people of Æolis Asiat., towards Pergamum.

PANTAGIAS fl., a r. of Sicily, falling into Siculum mare, s. of Megara. *Porcari.*

PANTALIA, a town of the Dentheletæ, Mœsia, on Margus fl., s. of Naissus.

PANTANUS lacus, a lake of Daunia Apul., e. of the mouth of Frentus fl., below Teanum. *Lago di Lesina.*

PANTI sin., a bay of Indicum mare, in Taprobane, bet. Axia prom. and Nagadiba.

PANTICAPÆUM (Bosporus), a city of Taurica Chersonesus, on Bosporus Cimmerius, opposite (n.w.) Phanagoria. Capital of the European Bosporani. A Milesian colony. *Kerché; Wospor.*

PANTICAPES (Samara) fl., a r. of the Navari, Sarmatiæ, falling, according to Herodotus, into the Borysthenes, but more
probably into the Danapris. *Ingalez.*

PANTICHIUM, I. a town of Bithynia, in
Propontis, bet. Calchedon (15) and Li-
byssa (22). *Pantiki.* II. a village of
Bithynia, on Bosporus Thracius, E. of
Estia prom.

PANTOMATRIUM (Amphimatrium), a town
on the N. coast of Crete, w. of Dium
prom.

PANTYENE, a town of Carmania Deserta,
N. of Carmana.

PANYASIS fl., a r. of the Taulantii, in Illyria, falling into the Adriatic s. of Epidamnus. *Spirnitza.*

PANXANI, a people on Mæotis palus, towards the Siraci.

PAOS, a town of Arcadia, S.E. of Psophis,
where Euphorian received the Dioscuri.
Ayio Anastasio.

PAPA, i. q. Pampanis.

PAPHARA, a town of Cyrrhestica, in Syria.

PAPHLAGONIA, a country of Asia Minor,
bounded N. by the Euxine, s. by Galatia
(at Olympus w. and Halys fl. E.), w. by
Bithynia, at Parthenius fl., or, according
to some geographers, at Halys fl. Occupied first by Cappadocians (Leuco-Syri),
and then, contemporaneously with their
settlement in Mysia, Bithynia, and Phrygia, by Thracians. Named from Phaleg.

PAPHOS, capital of Cyprus, 8 m. w. from
Palæpaphos, on the shore, within Zephyrium prom. Founded by Agenor the Arcadian, on his return from the siege of
Troy. Restored by Augustus, after an
earthquake, and named Augusta. Sacred
to Venus. The locality of the punishment of Elymas, and of the conversion of
Sergius Paulinus. *Baffa.*

PAPIA, i. q. Ticinum.

PAPICA prom., a pr. of Syrastrene, Ind., on
Barygazenus sin.

PAPINUS m., a summit of the Apennines, in
Gallia Cispadana, on Secies fl., R., below
Pons Secies.

PAPIRA, a town of the Tolistoboii, Galatia,
bet. Vindia (32) and Ancyra (27).

PAPPA, a town of Isauria, bet. Carallia and
Isaura.

PAPPUA m., Africæ, i. q. Thambes.

PAPREMIS, Ægypti, i. q. Xois.

PAPYRII castrum, a fortress of Cilicia Campestris, near Tarsus.

PAPYRON pylæ, a pass in the m. of Galeaditis,
bet. Ramoth Gilead and Rabbath Ammon.

PARABÆSIUM, the monument of the Arca-

dians, who fell in battle against Cleomenes,
bet. Gortys and Megalopolis.

PARACANDA, i. q. Maracanda.

PARACHELOITIS regio, the district of Acarnania, watered, as the name imports, by
Achelous fl.

PARACHOANA, a town of Media Magna, E.
of Ecbatana.

PARACHOATRAS m., m. of Susiana, separating it s. from Persis Prop.

PARADA (Phara), a town of Zeugitana, bet.
Thapsus and Utica.

PARADISUS (Triparadisus), a town of Syria,
near the source of Orontes fl. Noted for
its fine gardens.

PARADISUS fl., a r. of Cilicia Campestris.

PARÆPAPHYTIS, a district of Carmania, E.
of the Soxotæ.

PARÆTACENE, I. the N. portion of Persis
Prop. Its population was agricultural.
II. a district of Sogdiana, E. of Sogdii
m.

PARÆTONIUM, a city of Libya Ægypti, on
the Mediterranean, within Pythis prom.,
bet. Laodamantias portus and Apis, w. of
Catabathmus Minor (36). *Baretoun.*

PARAGON sin., a bay of Indicum mare, at
the entrance of Persicus sin.

PARALAI ins., islands on the E. coast of
Africa, s. of Azania.

PARALAIS, a maritime town of Lycaonia,
near Iconium.

PARALIA, a district of India e. Gangem, w.
of Malanga.

PARALII (Enalii), "along the sea," a tribe
of Malienses, in Thessaly, along the coast
bet. Larissa Cremaste and Sperchius fl.

PARALISSUM, i. q. Porolissum.

PARALUS, a town of Lower Egypt, w. of
Sebennyticum ost.

PARAN, *vide* Pharan.

PARANTANI, i. q. Carantani.

PARAPIOTÆ (Parapiani), a people of India
e. Gangem, bet. Sambus fl. and Sittocacis fl.

PARAPOMISUS (Paraponisus) m., m. of Asia,
a ridge of Taurus, dividing Bactria from
Arachosia. Out of compliment to Alexander, the Macedonians called them Caucasus.

PARAPOTAMIA, a district of Assyria, occupying its s. extremity.

PARAPOTAMII, "on the river," a town of
Phocis, on Cephissus fl., 5 m. N.W. from
Chæronea. Destroyed by Xerxes. *Pelesi.*

PARAS, "horsemen," the Scriptural name
of Persia.

PARATA (Pyretus, *prius* Hierasus) fl., a r. of
Dacia, rising above Arcodabara, and falling
into the Danube below Netindava. *Pruth.*

PARATIANÆ, a town of Numidia, on Numidicus sin., s. bet. Callucitanæ and Rusicada.

PARATII, a town of Ariaca, Ind., s. of Modogulla.

PARAVÆI, "near the Aous," a part of Epirus, on the borders of the Atintani and Orestæ (N.), of Thresprotia (s.), of Chaonia (w.), of the Tymphæi (E.).

PARAXIA, a district of Mygdonia, on the Axius.

PARBARA, a town of Parthia Nisæa, bet. Saphri and Armiana.

PARCA, a town of the Jazyges Metanastæ, s.E. of Acincum.

PARDENE, a district of Gedrosia, N. of the Rhammæ.

PARDOSERIA, a town of the Trocmi, in Galatia, bet. Corniaspa and Ibora.

PAREMBOLE, I. Illyr., i. q. Castra. II. a fortress of Dodecaschœnus, on the Nile, bet. Syene (16) and Tzitzi (2). *Debot.* III. a town of the Odryssæ, in Thrace, bet. Cyrnota and Cillium.

PARENTIUM, a maritime town of Istria, bet. Ningum (18) and Silvium (9). *Parenzo.*

PARICANI, a port of Arachosia, under Paryeti m. w. *Voekareta.*

PARISII, a people of Lugdunensis IV., on the Sequana, N. of the Carnutes and Senones. *About Paris.*

PARIDION (Posidium, Paurdon, Paudron) prom., a pr. of Peræa, in Caria, 6 m. E. of Phalarus. *C. Marmorice.*

PARIENNA, a town of Northern Germany, on Granua fl.

PARIETINA, a maritime town of Mauritania Ting., N., bet. Cobucta and Cannarum prom. *Velez.*

PARIETINUM, a town of the Celtiberi, Tarraconensis, 22 m. N.W. from Libisosa.

PARISI, a tribe of Brigantes, Brit., on the N. shore of Abus fl.

PARIUM, I. a m. of Cilicia Campestris, N. of Serrepolis. II. a town of Mysia, on Hellespont, w. of Priapus; a colony of Milesians, Erythræans, and Parians. Under Rome, a colonia, as Colonia Julia, and Colonia Antonia. The birth-place of Neoptolemus the grammarian. *Kamares.*

PARMA (Paala), I. a r. of the Boii, in Gallia Cispadana, falling into Padus fl., below Parma. *Parma.* II. a town of the Boii, in Gallia Cispadana, on Parma fl., R., bet. Ad Tarum (7) and Tannetum (8), on Via Æmilia. A colonia 185 B.C., and again of Augustus (as Col. Jul. Augusta). Noted for its wool. The birth-place of Cassius Severus. *Parma.*

PARMÆCAMPI, a people of Germania Mag., N. of the Varduli, under Gabreta silva.

PARNASSUS (Par Nahas, "hill of augury"), I. an E. continuation of Corax mons, extending from above Amphissa through Phocis, N.E. to Œta m., s.E. to Helicon. Surnamed Dicophura, Biceps, Bicornis, Bivertex, from its "two-headed" summit Phædriades. Its earlier name was Larnassus, as having borne the Larnax, or ark of Deucalion, during his flood. Sacred to Bacchus. II. a town of Morimene, Cappadocia, on Halys fl., R., s. of Nysa, N. of Archelais.

PARNES m., a m. of Attica, on the frontiers of Bœotia, a central range bet. Pentelicus and Cithæron m., with the temple of Jupiter Parnethius, and another of Jupiter Semaleus. The highest m. of Attica. Famous for boar and bear-hunting. *Nozea.*

PARNI (Aparni), a tribe of Dahæ, in Margiana, E. of the Deibiccæ.

PARNON m., a m. of Peloponnesus, dividing Argolis from Laconia s.E. and Arcadia. *Bourboura,* or *Berbena.*

PAROLISSUM, a town of the Teurisci, Dac., N. of Ulpianum.

PAROPUS, a town of Sicily, near the coast, s.E. of Himera. *Colisano.*

PARORÆA, "near the mountains," I. a district of Epirus, on the confines of Athamania, N.E. of Pambotis lac. II. of Paroræa, in Epirus. III. a town of Arcadia, 1¼ m. N. from Zætia.

PAROREATÆ, "mountain-bordering," an Arcadian tribe, occupying a portion of Triphylia, on the borders of Arcadia, until expelled by the Minyæ.

PAROS (Pactyæ, Minoa, Demetrias, Zacynthus, Hyria, Hyliessa, Cabarnis) ins., an isl. of the Ægean, one of the Cyclades, bet. Olearus and Naxos. Named after Paros, leader of its first Arcadian colony. Famous for its marble. The birth-place of Archilochus the poet. Thence came the Arundelian marbles. *Paro.*

PARÔSTA, a town of Taurica Chersonesus, N.W. of Theodosia. The earth here was said to cure all wounds.

PARRADUM, a town of the Catenates, Vindel., s.W. of Drusomagus.

PARRHASIA, an early name of Arcadia, from Parrhasius, son of Lycaon.

PARRHASII, a people of Arcadia, w. and N.W. of Megalopolis. Named from Parrhasius, s. of Lycaon.

PARRHASINI, a people of Sogdiana.

PARSIA, capital of the Parsii, Ariæ, s.E. of Alexandria Arion.

PARRODUNUM, Rhætiæ, i. q. Parthanum.

PARSII, a people of Aria, E. of Alexandria Arion.

PARTA, a town of Persis Prop., N.E. of Chersonesus prom.

PARTHANUM (Parrodunum), a town of the Genauni, Rhæt., bet. Coveliace and Scarbia. *Parten Kirchen.*

PARTHENIA, "virgin," a name of Samos.

PARTHENICUM, a maritime town of Sicily N.W., near the mouth of Bathys fl. (E.) *Near Palamita.*

PARTHENIUM prom., I. a pr. of Taurica Chersonesus s.w., above Palacium. II. a town of Eubœa. III. a town of Mysia, near Pergamum. IV. a town of Taurica Chersonesus, on Bosporus Cimmerius, bet. Panticapæum and Heraclea.

PARTHENIUS ("of the maiden," Diana), I. a r. of Asia Minor, rising in Pœmen m., and, after dividing Bithynia from Paphlagonia, falling into the Euxine, w. of Amastris. *Bartan.* II. of Pisatis, in Elis, falling into Alpheus fl., E. of Harpinna. III. the early name of Imbrasus fl., in Samos. IV. mons, a m. of Peloponnesus, w. of Cynuria, separating in that direction Argolis from Arcadia. On the Arcadian side were the sacred grove of Telephus, and a temple of Pan. *Partheni.*

PARTHENOPE, the Greek name of Neapolis Campaniæ.

PARTHENOPOLIS, I. a town of the Crobyzi, Mœs., w. of Calatis. II. of Bithynia, on Parthenius fl., extinct in Pliny's time.

PARTHIA (Parthiene), "land of exiles," a county of Asia, bounded N. by Hyrcania at Labuta m. and Mosdonius m., s. by Persis Prop. and Carmania at Parachoatras m., w. by Media and Susiana at Parachoatras m., E. by Aria and Drangiana. At one time reckoned a part of Hyrcania, but rendered a great kingdom by Arsaces. The people were noted for their archery, and for a peculiar skill in shooting as they retreated. *Parthiva.*

PARTHENI, a people of Illyria, bet. the Taulantii and the Albani.

PARTHISCUS fl., i. q. Tibiscus.

PARTHISCUM, a town of the Jazyges Metanastæ.

PARTHÖN, a town of Numidia, s.w. of Sicca Venerea.

PARTHUS, capital of the Parthini, in Illyria, w. of Isanus fl. *Presa.*

PARVUM littus, I. the coast of Arabia Felix, bet. Magnum littus and Cane emporium. II. prom., a pr. of Thebais, on the Red sea, E. of Syene.

PARYADRES m., m. of Asia, in Pontus and Armenia Maj., parallel with Scordisci m. N.

PARYETÆ, a people of Arachosia E., about Paryeti m. *Parutah.*

PARYETI m., m. of Arachosia, a N.E. extension of Baetius m., towards the Indus.

PASACARDA, a town of Parthia Choroana.

PASADA, a port of Caria, 4 m. from Caunus.

PASAGE, a town of the Bettigi, Ind., w. of Candipatna.

PASALÆ, a people of India e. Gangem, N. of the Tiladæ.

PASARGADA, a royal city of Persis Prop., and its ancient capital, on Cyrus fl. Built by Cyrus, in commemoration of the defeat of Astyages, s.E. of Persepolis. The burial-place of Cyrus. *Farsa.*

PASARNE, a town of Laviniasene, in Cappadocia.

PAS-DAMMIM (Ephes-Dammim), a valley of Judah, N.W.

PASIACES fl., a r. of Sarmatia Eur., falling into the Coretus sin., w. of Lianum.

PASIANI, a people of Sogdiani, towards the Caspian.

PASICÆ, a tribe of Massagetæ, Sogdiana, on Oxus fl., w. of Maracanda.

PASIDA, a port of Gedrosia, on Paragon sin., bet. Dagosira and Salarus fl.

PASIRA, a maritime town of Gedrosia, bet. Calyba and Bagisira.

PASIRIS, a town on the Euxine.

PASITIGRIS, the name of the Tigris, after its junction with the Euphrates. *Shat al Arab.*

PASGUSA lac., i. q. Caralitis.

PASSALA, the port of Mylasa, in Caria, 10 m. from the city.

PASSALON, a town of Thebais, on the Nile, R., bet. Antæopolis (2 geog. m.) and Panopolis (2 geog. m.).

PASSARON, capital of Molossus, in Epirus, on the Thyamis fl., about 15 m. s.w. from Euræa. *Dramitzi.*

PASTONA, i. q. Ciaca.

PASYRIS, a town of the Jazyges, Sarmat., bet. Carcines fl., towards its source, and Pasiaces fl.

PATÆTA, a town of Meroe, on the Nile, R., bet. Gerbo and Ponteris.

PATĀLA (Pattala), a town of Patalene Ind., at the separation of the two mouths of the Indus. *Tatta.*

PATALENE (Indo-Scythia), the Delta of the Indus, an isl. formed by the two mouths of that river; in size larger, according to Arrian, than the Delta of the Nile.

PATARA, *prius* Sataros, a town of Lycia, on Xanthus fl., L., near its mouth. With a celebrated temple of Apollo Lycius or

Pataræus, where the god gave answers for the six winter months. Named after Pataræus, son of Apollo. Enlarged by Ptolemy Philadelphus, and called by him Arsinoe. *Patera.*

PATAREUM littus, the coast of Lycia, towards Patara.

PATARVE, a town of Sarmatia As., on the Palus Mæotis, N. of Rhombites Maj. fl.

PATAVISSA, i. q. Patruissa.

PATAVIUM, capital of Venetia, on Meduacus Min. fl., L., bet. Ad Finem (10) and Ad Duodecim (12), on Via Æmilia. Founded by Antenor. Noted for its woollen-manufactures. The birth-place of Thrasea Pætus. *Padova, Padua.*

PATERNIANA, a town of the Celtiberi, Tarraconens., bet. Certima s.w. and Valeria N.E.

PATHISCUS fl., i. q. Tibiscus.

PATMOS ins., an isl. in Icarium mare, s.w. of Samos, w. of Lepsia ins. One of the Sporades. The place of St. John's banishment. *Patimo; Patmosa.*

PATRÆ, I. one of the twelve cities of Achaia, 60 m. w. of Corinth, on the Corinthiacus sin., bet. Olenus and Panormus. It was formerly called Aroe, but, enlarged by Patreus, took the name of Patræ. A colonia of Augustus. *Patras.* II. a town of the Dassaretæ, in Illyria, on the N.E. shore of Lychnitis palus, bet. Pons Servilii (9) and Lychnidas (14), on the Egnatia Via.

PATRASYS, a town of Pontus.

PATRIDAVA, a town of the Cistoboci, Dac., on Tyras fl., above Carsidava.

PATROCLI ins., an isl. of Attica, in the Ægean, off Sunium. Named after Patroclus, the admiral of Ptolemy Philadelphus. *Gaidoro-Nesi.*

PATROS, i. q. Memnonium, Thebaid.

PATRUISSA (Patavissa), a town of the Burideenses, Dac., on Mariscus fl., 12 m. from Salinæ. *Mar-Ujvar.*

PATREUS, a town of Taurica Chersonesus, s. of Achilleum.

PATUMOS (Pithom), a town of Lower Egypt, on the Athribitic branch of the Nile, 2 geog. m. s. from Bubastus. *Belbeys.*

PATUS, Sericæ, i. q. Batæ.

PATYCUS, a town of the Œnotri, in Bruttium, 24 m. s. from Cerillæ. *Paolo.*

PAUCA, a maritime town of Corsica w., at the mouth of Locra fl. *Casa di Valinco.*

PAULON fl., a r. of Liguria, falling into the sea near Nicæa (E.). *Poglion.*

PAUSULÆ, a town of Picenum, 10 m. N.E. of Urbs Salvia. *Monte dell'Olmo.*

PAUSILYPUS m., a ridge of hills in Campania, separating Cumanus sin. from Puteolinus sin., through which a tunnel, called Crypta Neapolitana, was cut by the Neapolitans (attributed by Strabo to L. Cocceius), between Neapolis and Puteoli, large enough to admit carriages. At its entrance is the tomb of Virgil. Upon the m. stood the villa of Vedrus Pollio. *Posylipo.*

PAX AUGUSTA, a town of the Celtici, Bæturia, on the Anas, w. of Augusta Emerita. *Badajoz.*

PAX JULIA, a town of the Celtici, Lusitania. A colonia (Pacensis) N.W. of Myrtilis. *Beja.*

PAXUS ins., an isl. of Corcyra, 5 m. s. from Leucimna prom. *Paxo.*

PE-BISETH, the Scriptural name of Bubastus, in Egypt.

PEDALIA, a maritime town of Cilicia, towards Adana.

PEDALIUM prom., I. a pr. of Caria, 10 m. from Artemisium prom. *C. Contouri.* II. (Ammochostos) of Cyprus, N.E. of Thronium prom. *C. Grego.*

PEDASA, a Lelegian town of Caria, N.E. of Halicarnassus, near Stratonicæa. With a temple of Minerva, the priestess of which had a beard sprout from her chin whenever danger threatened the town. *Peitchin.*

PEDASUS, Æolid. Asiat., i. q. Adramyttium.

PEDLÆA, a town of Phocis, N.W. of Tritæa.

PEDIÆUS fl., a r. of Cyprus.

PEDIEIS, a town of Caria.

PEDNELISSUS, a town of Pisidia, on Eurymedon fl., above Aspendus.

PEDONA, a town of the Vagienni, near Caburro. *Borgo San Dalmazzo.*

PEDONIA (Pezone) ins., an isl. of Marmarica, N.W. of Antiphra.

PEDUM, a town of the Latini, Latium, N.W. of Præneste. Destroyed by Camillus. *Zagarolo.*

PEDYLI, a people of Narbonensis, towards the Magelli. *About Piegu, near Tallard.*

PEGASEUM stagnum, a marsh of Ionia, above Ephesus, formed by Phyrites fl. at its junction with Caystrus fl.

PEGILLA, a town of Lycaonia, bet. Egdevama (20) and Congustus (20).

PEIRÆ, a village of Achaia, near Olenus.

PEISO (Pelso, Pelsodis) lac., a lake of Valeria, Pannonia; its waters communicated with the Danube. *S. Balaton; Plattensee.*

PEIUM, the treasure-fortress of Deiotarus, in Galatia, near Bloucium.

PELAGONES, a tribe of Pæonians, formerly occupying the country bet. the Strymon and the Peneus, and afterwards settled more particularly in the cognominal district of Pæonia. Named after Pelagon, father of Asteropæus.

PELAGONIA, I. the country of the Pelagones, in Pæonia, bounded w. by Illyria, E. by Mygdonia, N. by Dardania, s. by Deuriopæa, Lyncus, and Emathia. II. capital of the cognominal district in Pæonia, on the confines of Dassaretia, near the source of the Bevus fl. *Monastir.*

PELAGONIA TRIPOLIS (Ager Tripolitanus), "three-towned Pelagonia," a district of Perrhæbia, in Sicily, under Cambunii m. Settled by Pelagonians from Macedonia.

PELAGUS nemus, a wood of Arcadia, bet. Mantinea (4) and Pallantium. The site of the battle of Mantinea. Here was the tomb of Epaminondas.

PELASGI, a Scythian or eastern people, deriving their name, according to the Greeks, from Pelasgus, son of Jupiter and Niobe, who rapidly spread themselves over Thessaly, Epirus, parts of Macedonia and Thrace, Mysia, Troas, the Cyclades, Crete, Attica, Bœotia, Achaia, Argolis, Arcadia, and Italy. Named from their migratory habits (Pelargi, " storks"). Extinct as a people in the time of Herodotus.

PELASGIA, I. an early name of Arcadia, from its Pelasgic settlers. II. the early name of Epirus, Macedonia, Acarnania, Thessaly, Ætolia, and the adjacent countries of N. Greece. The ancient name also of Lesbos, and, according to some writers, of Peloponnesus.

PELASGIOTÆ, the people of Pelasgiotis, in Thessaly, a combination of Lapithæ and Perrhæbi.

PELASGIOTIS, a district of Thessaly, bet. Estiæotis and Magnesia.

PELASGIS, a name of Chaonia.

PELE ins., an isl. of Ionia, in Hermius sin., opposite Clazomenæ.

PELECANIA lacus, a marshy lake on the borders of Copais lacus, formed by the r. Melas, Cephissus, and Probatia. Peculiarly productive of the large reeds used in the manufacture of darts, flutes, Pan's pipes, &c.

PELECAS m., an E. summit of Temnus m., towards Macestus fl.

PELECES, a demus of Attica, of the tribe Leontis, bet. Athens and Cropia. *Pelica.*

PELENDONA, a town of the Saldenses, Dac., bet. Amutrium (35) and Castra Nova (20).

PELENDONES, a tribe of Celtiberi, Tarraconensis, on Durius fl., towards its source.

PELETHRONIUM, *quasi* "flower under Pelion," a town of Magnesia, in Thessaly, under Pelion m. A town of the Lapithæ.

PELIGNI, a Liburnian people settled in the country bet. the Vestini (N.), the Caraceni (S.), the Marrucini (E.), and the Marsi (W.). They were reputed to have great skill in magic.

PELINÆUS m., a m. on the N. coast of Chios ins., N.E. of Melæna prom. Noted for its marble. On its summit was a temple of Jupiter. *M. Sant' Elias.*

PELINNA (Pelinnæum), a city with a celebrated temple of Jupiter Pelinnæus, in Estiæotis, Thessaly, bet. Tricca (10) and Phareadon. *Plocovo.*

PELION m., I. a range of m. of Magnesia, in Thessaly, the s. continuation of Ossa m., from Bæbe lacus to Magnesiæ prom. The abode, first of the Centauri, and then of the Lapithæ ; the summits clothed with pine forests, the sides with oak and ash. Hence the favourite haunt of Chiron. *Zagora.* II. the highest summit of the cognominal range, in Thessaly, behind Iolchos and Ormenium. At its top was a temple of Jupiter Actæus, where the young nobles of Demetrias celebrated an annual sacrifice. III. (Pelium), a fortress of the Pissantini, in Illyria, commanding a pass into Macedonia, near the source of Eordaicus fl. *Plia.*

PELIUM nemus, a wood on the w. slope of Pelion m., towards Iolchos.

PELLA, I. a town of Achaia. II. *prius* Bunomus, Bunomeia, a city of Bottiæa, in Macedonia, a royal city, and afterwards metropolis of Macedonia III., on a cognominal lake, 15 m. N.W. from Ichnæ, on the Egnatia Via, bet. Ægæ (28) and Thessalonica (27). The birth-place of Philip of Macedon and of Alexander the Great. Founded by Pellas. A colonia of Julius Cæsar. Under Diocletian called Diocletianopolis. *Palatisa* or *Alaklisa.* II. *prius* Butis, the southernmost city of Decapolis Peræa. Built by Seleucus. The retreat of the Christians of Jerusalem, who were divinely admonished to flee before the siege of that city by Titus. *El Budsche.*

PELLACONTA fl., a r. of Mesopotamia, falling into the Euphrates.

PELLALA, a town of Mesopotamia, on Saocoras fl., s. of Nisibis.

PELLANE, a town of Laconia, on Eurotas fl., bet. Characoma and Belemina (12½). The residence of the exiled Tyndareus. Here was a temple of Æsculapius.

PELLENE, a town of Achaia, on Sythas fl., 7½ m. from Corinthiacus sin., N.E. of Olurus. Named from Pellen, son of Phorbas. Games were celebrated here in honour of

Mercury and Apollo Theoxenius. Noted for its woollen cloaks. *Tricala.*

PELODES ("muddy haven") portus, a bay of Cestrine, in Epirus, at Buthrotum.

PELONTIUM, a town of Tarraconensis, bet. Ovetum w. and Concana s.e.

PELOPIA, an early name of Thyatira in Lydia.

PELOPIDIS scopuli, rocks off Methone penin., in Argolis.

PELOPONNESUS, "the island of Pelops," *prius* Apia, a peninsula of Europe, the portion of Greece s. of the Isthmus Corinthiacus, bounded n. by Corinthiacus sin., s. by Libycum mare, w. by Ionium mare, e. by the Ægean. Named after Pelops, who migrated hither from Phrygia. In area 7800 m.; in circumference, the sinuosities of the coast included, 700 m. In shape resembling a mulberry-leaf, whence its modern appellation. *Morea.*

PELORIARCA, a town of Mesopotamia, on the Tigris, bet. Gibrata and Dura.

PELORIAS (Peloritana regio), a district of Sicily, adjacent to Pelorum prom.

PELORUM (Pelorias, Peloris, Pelorus) prom., the extreme e.n.e. prom. of Sicily, over against Scylla prom. *Capo Faro.*

PELŌRUS fl., a r. of Armenia Maj., falling into the Cyrus, n. of the w. extremity of Lychnitis lacus. *Arazi.*

PELTÆ, a town of Phrygia Mag., bet. Mæander fl., near its source (n.), and Glaucus fl., n.w. of Apamea Cibotus (26).

PELTENUS campus, the country about Peltæ, in Phrygia Mag.

PELTUINUM, a town of the Vestini, Picen., on Aternus fl., L. *Church of San Paolo or Peltuino, at Prata.*

PELUSIACUM OSTIUM NILI, the e. mouth of the Nile. Named from Pelusium.

PELUSIUM (Sin, Pheromi), "marshy," a city of Lower Egypt, on Pelusiacum ostium, R., 2 m. from its mouth, s.e. of Damiathis. The key of Egypt in that direction.

PEME, a town of Heptanomis, Egypt, on the Nile, bet. Tasdrum and Iseum (20). *Bembe.*

PENELOCUS, a town of the Nantuates, Alpes Penninæ, on Lemanus lacus, e. below Viviscus.

PENESTÆ, I. a tribe of aborigines in Thessaly, who became slaves to the triumphant invaders, as the Helotes in Lacedæmon. II. a people of Illyria, bounded n. by the Cavii, s. by the Dassaretæ and Eordeti, w. by the Albani, e. by Macedonia.

PENEUS fl., I. a r. of Epea, in Elis, rising in Erymanthus m., and falling into the Ionian sea below Coryne. *Igliaco.* II. a r. of Thessaly, rising in Pindus m., and falling into the Thermaicus sin. n. of Myræ, by what is called the Lycastomo "wolf's mouth." *Salembria.*

PENIEL (Penuel), a town at the ford of Jabbok fl., where Jacob wrestled with the angel. Rebuilt by Jeroboam.

PENNINI m., i. q. Alpes Penninæ.

PENOCRUCIUM, a town of the Cornavii, Brit. Rom., bet. Uxacoma and Etocetum.

PENOXULLUM prom., a pr. of Britannia Barb. n.e. *Ord Head.*

PENPEDUNNI, a maritime people of Novem Populana, towards the Pyrenees. *About Pinede.*

PENTACHIRA, a fortress of Phrygia Mag., on Mæander fl.

PENTACHOMIA, a town of Chalybonitis, on the Euphrates.

PENTADEMITÆ, a people of Mysia s.

PENTAPOLIS, the maritime frontier of Cyrenaica, bet. Eccius fl. and Poliurus fl. Named from its five chief towns, Berenice, Arsinoe, Ptolemais, Cyrene, and Apollonia.

PENTAPŌTĂMIA, the district of India watered by the five rivers, Hydaspes, Acesines, Hydraotes, Hyphasis, and Xeradrus. *Punjaub.*

PENTASCHŒNON, a town of Casiotis, in Egypt, on Sirbonis palus, s. bet. Pelusium (20) and Casium.

PENTEDACTYLUS m., a m. of Dodecaschœnus, on the Red sea, s. of Berenice.

PENTELE, a demus of Attica, of the tribe Antiochis, at the s. foot of Pentelicus m. *Monastery of Penteli.*

PENTELICUS m., a m. of Attica, the centre of the Brilessus, Hymettus, &c., range. Famous for its marble-quarries. *Pentelikon.*

PENTELOPHOI, a village of Laconia, 7 furlongs from Sparta.

PENTHILE, a town of Lesbos ins.

PENTRI, a tribe of Samnites, occupying the central or more hilly (whence their name) portion of Samnium.

PEOR (Phogor) m., a summit of Abarim m., in Amoritis, w. of Hesbon. On it was a temple of Baal.

PEOS-ARTEMIDOS, *vide* Speos.

PEPARETHUS, I. *prius* Evænus, an isl. of Thessaly, in the Ægean, e. of Halonnesus ins. Settled by Cretans, under Staphylus. Noted for its wine and oil. *Piperi.* II. its town on the n. coast. Destroyed by the Romans.

PEPERENE ins., an isl. of India i. Gangem, in Colchicus sin.

PEPHNUS ins., I. an isl. of Laconia, close to the cognominal town. The birth-place of the Dioscuri. *Pekno.* II. a town of Laconia, on Messeniacus sin., 2½ m. from Leuctra. *Pekno.*

PEPUZA, a town of Phrygia Pacatiana. Destroyed in the second century. The seat of the heretics called Cataphryges or Pepuziani.

PERA, a town of Pisidia.

PERÆA, I. *surnamed* Rhodiorum, the coast of Caria, E. of Cynossema prom., opposite Rhodes. II. generally, the portion of Israel E. of Jordan; specially, the district bet. Arnon fl. and Hieromax fl.

PERÆTHIA, a village of Arcadia, E. of Paliscius. With a temple of Pan.

PERANTHE collis, a hill of Epirus overlooking Ambracia.

PERCE, the early name of Thrace.

PERCEJANA, a town of the Turtuli, Bæturia, s. of Augusta Emerita.

PERCOTE, a town of Mysia, on Practius fl. near its mouth. Given to Themistocles by Artaxerxes for his wardrobe. *Bergan.*

PERCRI, a town of the Mardi, Armenia, at the E. extremity of Arsissa lacus.

PERDICES, I. a town of Mauritania Cæsar., 25 m. w. from Sitifis. *Near Sidy Embarack.* II. of Mauritania Cæsar., s.E. of Sitifis.

PERDICIÆ, a port of Lycia, 6½ m. from Cissides.

PERGA, a town of Pamphylia or of Pisidia, on Cestrus fl., L., 7½ m. above its mouth. Sacred to Diana Pergæa. Noted in the history of St. Paul. Later the metropolis of Pamphylia. *Eski Kalesi.*

PERGAMUM, a city of Mysia, on Caicus fl., at its junction with Ceteius fl. Established as a principality by Philetærus, uncle of Attalus. The seat of the ninth conventus juridicus of Asia Romana; with a temple of Æsculapius. Memorable for the library of 200,000 volumes, formed by Eumenes, and given by Antony to Cleopatra. One of the Seven Churches of Asia. Here parchment was invented. The birth-place of the physicians Galen and Oribasius; the death-place of P. Scipio. *Bergamah.*

PERGAMUS, I. a town of Crete, on Oaxus fl., below Oaxus. Founded by Æneas or by Agamemnon. The burial-place, according to some writers, of Lycurgus. *Peramo.* II. a fortress of the Pieres, in Thrace, s.E. of Amphipolis.

PERGANTIUM, a town of the Commoni, Narbonensis, on an island E. of Olbia. *Breganson.*

PERGUSA (Pergus) lacus, a lake of Sicily, 5 m. s. from Enna, in circuit 4 m. The locality of the rape of Proserpine. *Lago di Goridano.*

PERGUSE, a demus of Attica, of the tribe Erectheis.

PERIERBIDI, a people of Sarmatia Asiat., on the Tanais, above the Jaxamatæ.

PERIMULA, a town of Aurea Chersonesus, s. bet. Coli and Samarada, on Perimulicus sin.

PERIMULICUS sin., the strait bet. Aurea Chersonesus and Bonæ Fortunæ ins.

PERINCARI, a town of India i. Gangem, s.w. of Carura.

PERINTHUS, *postea* Heraclea, a town of the Odrysæ, in Thrace, on the Propontis, bet. Silymbria and Ærea.

PERIONOTUS m., a prom. of the Troglodytæ, on the Red sea, E. of Hiera Sycaminos. *Schaab al Jadayn.*

PERIPOLIUM, a town of Bruttium, on Halex fl., L. The birth-place of Praxiteles?

PERIRRHENSA ins., an isl. of Ionia, on Hermius sin., opposite Clazomenæ.

PERIRRHOUS prom., a pr. of Bithynia, on Bosporus Thracius, N. of Lycadium sin.

PERISADII, a tribe of the Parthini, in Illyria.

PERITHOIDÆ, a demus of Attica, of the tribe Œneis. The birth-place of Hyperbolus.

PERMESSUS fl., a r. of Bœotia, rising in Helicon, and falling into Copais lacus near Haliartus. Sacred to the Muses. *Xero Mais.*

PERIZZITÆ, "lowlanders," a tribe of Canaanites, of unascertained locality.

PERORSI, a people of Æthiopia Interior.

PERPERENA regio, a district of Æolis Asiat., about Perperon. Noted for its copper and its wines.

PERPERON (Parparon, Perperene), *postea* Theodosiopolis, a town of Æolis Asiat. The death-place of Thucydides.

PERRE, a town of Commagene, 24 m. N. from Samosata. *Pharin.*

PERRHÆBI, a tribe of Pelasgi settled in Perrhæbia of Thessaly, and at one time occupying Pelasgiotis also.

PERRHÆBIA, a district of Thessaly, bet. Pelasgiotis and Timarus m. At one period comprising Pelasgiotis also.

PERRHÆBUS, a town of Perrhæbia, in Thessaly, N. of Pharsalus.

PERRHIDÆ, a demus of Attica, of the tribe Antiochis, near Aphidna.

PERSARUM EMPORIUM, a port of Arabia Felix, at the entrance of Persicus sin.

PERSEPOLIS (Persæpolis), capital of Persis Prop., near the junction of Medus fl. with Araxes fl. Built out of the spoils of Thebes, in Egypt; its palace was burned by Alexander.

PERSEUS, a port of Attica.

PERSICI m., m. of Asia, separating Carmania from Gedrosia, and terminating in Carpella prom.

PERSICUM, a citadel of Caunus, in Caria.

PERSĬCUS sin., a gulf of Erythræum mare, washing the shores of Arabia w., and of Susiana, Persis, and Carmania E. Theophrastes calls it Arabicus sin. *Persian Gulf.*

PERSII SPECULA prom., a pr. of Lower Egypt, near Agni Cornu prom.

PERSIS (Persia Propria, Paras), a country of Asia, bounded N. by Parthia and Media at Parachoatras m., s. and s.w. by Persicus sin., w. by Susiana, and E. by Carmania. The Persians were noted for excellent horsemanship and archery. *Fars.*

PERTA, a town of Lycaonia, bet. Congestus (15) and Ubinnaca (20).

PERTUSA, I. a town of the Ilergetes, Tarraconensis, E. of Æsona. II. of Zeugitana, 13 m. from Carthage.

PERUSIA, one of the twelve cities of Etruria, near Tiberis fl., R., N.w. of Vettona (10). A colonia 45 B.C. Nearly destroyed by fire, *circa* 40 B.C., on the occasion of its being taken by Octavius from Antony. *Perugia.*

PERVICIACUM, a town of the Segni, Germania II., bet. Aduatuca and Geminiæ.

PESLA (Pescla), a town of Thebais, on the Nile, R., bet. Antinoopolis (24) and Hieracon (28).

PESSIDE, a town of the Nigritæ, Libya Int., on the Niger, L. *Tombuctoo ?*

PESSINUS, capital of the Tolistoboii, Galatia, on the Sangarius fl., on the borders of Phrygia Epict., s.w. of Ancyra (99), bet. Germa and Amorium, under Agdistus m. Sacred to Angistis (Cybele), whose statue, a great stone said to have dropped from heaven, was removed hence to Rome 547 A.U.C. Subsequently the metropolis of Galatia Salutaris. *Balahissar.*

PESSIUM, a town of the Jazyges Metanastæ, Daciæ, over against Acincum. *Pesth.*

PETALIA prom., the s.w. extremity of Eubœa, opposite Ceos ins. *C. Carysto.*

PETALIÆ ins., isl. of Eubœa, off Leon prom. *Petaliora.*

PETAVONIUM, I. a town of the Astures, Tarraconensis, 29 m. s.w. from Asturica Augusta. II. (Patæonium), a town of Pannonia, on Dravus fl., w. of Ramista. *Pettau.*

PETELIA, a town of Bruttium, on Tarentinus sin., bet. Malaca and Crotona (13). Founded by Philoctetes. Memorable for its resistance to Hannibal. A municipium. *Strongoli.*

PETENISCA, a town of the Ambrones, Maxima Sequanorum, on Arula fl., R., bet. Solodurum and Muratium.

PETEON, a town of Bœotia, bet. Hyle and Thebes.

PETHOR, a town of Mesopotamia. The birthplace of Balaam the diviner.

PETILIA (Phistelia), an Oscan town of Lucania, s.E. of Pæstum. *On Monte della Stella.*

PETILIANA, a town of Sicily, on or near Himera Maj. fl., R., bet. Agrigentum (28) and Gelasium (27). *San Cataldo.*

PETILINUS m., a m. of Lucania, s.E. of Pæstum. *Monte della Stella.*

PETIRGALA, a town of Ariaca, Ind., s.E. of Murzupale.

PETITARUS fl., a r. of Acarnania, rising in the territory of the Agræi and falling into Achelous fl., 5 m. N. of Stratus. *Vounicovo.*

PETOBIS (Petovio, Petano), i. q. Patavonium.

PETRA (Sela), "rock," I. capital of the Nabathæi, Arabiæ, N.E. of the head of Ælanites sin., w. of Munichiatis. *Wady Musa.* II. a village of Corinthia. The birth-place of Eetion, father of Cypse. III. a fortress of the Mædi, Thrace, near Strymon fl., on the confines of the Denthetetæ. IV. of Pieria, Macedonia, commanding the Pass in Olympus m., leading to Pythium. V. a town of the Potulatenses, Dacia, on Marisus fl., L., bet. Ad Aquas (13) and Germihera (9). *Pad.* VI. a suburb of Elis. The burial-place of Pyrrho. VII. a town of Pontus, bet. Bathys fl. and Acinacis fl. VIII. of Sicily, bet. Pirina and Enna. IX. of the Taulantii, Illyria, on a cognominal prom. s. of Epidamnus. *C. di Lachi.* X. (Pertusa, Intercisa), a defile of Umbria, s. of Urbinum Hortense. Cut through the rocks which at that point came down to the edge of the river (Cantiano). *Furlo* or *Sasso Ferato.*

PETRASANGUINIS, a pass in the mountains of N.E. Bruttium, leading from Roscianum into Lucania. *Morano.*

PETRACHUS, the Acropolis of Chæronea, Bœotia, where Rhea deceived Saturn.

PETRÆ MAGNÆ portus, a port of Marmarica, bet. Euria and Ardanis prom.

PETRÆ PARVÆ portus, a port of Marmarica, bet. Antipyrgos and Batrachos.

PETRÆA, a town of Bithynia, bet. Sophon lac. and Nicæa (2).

PETRIANA, a town of the Brigantes, Brit., on Hadriani murus, s., bet. Amboglanna and Aballaba. *Cambeck.*

PETRINA, a town of Sicily, bet. Piciniana and Pirina (24).

PETROCORII, a people of Aquitania II., on Duronius fl., R., bet. the Santones, N., and the Nitiobriges s. *Perigord.*

PETRODAVA, Dac., i. q. Jassiorum municipium.

PETROMANTALUM, a town of the Velio-casses, Lugdunensis II., bet. Ritumagus w.n.w. and Briva Isara e.s.e.

PETRONII VICUS, a town of the Memini, Narbonensis, near the Druentia, s.e. of Apta Julia.

PETROSACA, a town of Arcadia, under Ostra-cena m., s.

PETROSSA ins., an isl. of Cilicia.

PETUARIA, a town of the Parisi, Brit., on Abus fl., L., bet. Delgovitia and Ad Abum. *Beverley?*

PEUCE, I. an isl. formed by the mouths of the Danube. II. m., i. q. Teuce.

PEUCELA (Peucelaotis, Peucolaetis), a town of Arachosia, on Cophen fl., L., towards its junction with the Indus.

PEUCELLA fl., a rivulet of Phrygia Epictetus, rising in Dindymene m. and falling into Hermus fl. below Cadi.

PEUCETI, a tribe of Illyrians, occupying the coast of Apulia, bet. Aufidus fl. and Brun-dusium, and extending inland to Lapatia m. *Terra di Bari.*

PEUCETIA, the country occupied by the Peuceti, in Italy.

PEUCINI, a tribe of Bastarnæ, occupying Peuce ins., Daciæ.

PHACIUM (Phacus), a town of Perrhæbia, Thessaly, on the left bank of Peneus fl., w. of Larissa. *Coutzochero.*

PHACUSA, a town of Lower Egypt, on the Tanitic branch of the Nile, s. of Tanis, at the point of junction of Bubasticus fl. *Tell Phacus.*

PHADISANA (Phadissa, Phauda), a maritime town of Pontus, 19 m. e. from Amele-tum. *Fatsah.*

PHÆACES, a people of Liburnia, on the coast opposite Corcyra Nigra, a colony of whom settled in Corcyra Epiri.

PHÆDRIA, a village of Arcadia, w. of Cromi.

PHÆDRIADES m., a bi-forked summit of Parnassus, N. of Delphi, whence crimi-nals were hurled. The death-place of Æsop.

PHÆNIANÆ, a town of Rhætia, on the Danube.

PHÆNO, a town of Arabia Petræa, bet. Zoar and Petra.

PHÆSANA, a town of Arcadia, on Alpheus fl., near Olympias.

PHÆSTUS, I. a town of Crete, bet. Metallum (5) and Gortys. The birth-place of Epi-menides the poet. Founded by Minos. Extinct in Strabo's time. *Hodyitria.* II. of the Locri Ozolæ, at the w. entrance of Crissæus sin. With a temple of Apollo Phæstii. III. of Perrhæbia, Thessaly, w. of Larissa.

PHAGRES, a fortress of the Pieres, Thrace, s.e. of Amphipolis, w. of Pergamus.

PHAGRORIOPOLIS, i. q. Phalacum.

PHALACRI, "bald-heads," *apud* Herodotum, i. q. Argippæi.

PHALACRIUM, I. a prom. of Sicily, N., bet. Pelorus prom. and Porthmus. *C. di Rasi-culmo.* II. a m. of Pontus, N. of Co-mana. III. a headland of Corcyra ins., the N.w. extremity of the island s.e. of Oth-ronus ins. *C. Drasti* or *Apocripiti.* IV. a fortress of Cilicia Prefect., Cappadocia. V. a town of Thebais, bet. Ariston and Hydræum Apollinis, e. of Ombi.

PHALACTHIA, a town of Dolopia, Thessaly, N.w. of Xynias pal., w. of Thaumaci. *Falaclia.*

PHALANNA, I. a town of Crete. The birth-place of Phæniades. II. (Hippia), a city of Perrhæbia, Thessaly, bet. Titaresius fl. and Peneus fl., N. of Larissa. *Tor-novo.*

PHALANTHUS m., I. a m. of Arcadia, at the cognominal town. II. a town of Arcadia, beyond Tricoloni.

PHALARA, a port of the Malienses Paralii, on Maliacus sin., 2½ m. N. of the mouth of Sperchius fl. *Stilidi.*

PHALARIUM, a maritime fortress of Sicily, s. bet. Phintiæ and Chalis. Built by Phalaris, and the receptacle of his brazen bull. *Chiesa di Santa Caterina.*

PHALARUS, I. a r. of Bœotia, rising from Laphystius m. and falling into Copais lacus. II. a town of Peræa, Caria, 6½ m. e. of Elæusa ins.

PHALASARNA, a town on the w. coast of Crete, bet. Cimaros prom. and Chersone-sus. *Hagios Kirghiani.*

PHALASIA prom., a headland of Eubœa, on the e. coast, N. of Chersonesus prom. *C. Kandili.*

PHALCARA, a town of Mesopotamia, bet. Sabbis and Gibrata.

PHALERUM, a demus of Attica, of the tribe Antiochis, constituting, with Piræus and Munychium, the port of Athens. The s. and earliest used of the three harbours. The birth-place of Demetrius Phalereus. The burial-place of Aristides. Here was a large aphyæ-fishery. *Porto Fanari.*

PHALESIÆ, a town of Arcadia, on Thius fl., s. of Megalopolis, 2½ m. from the confines of Laconia.

PHALORIA (Phalerias), a town of the Æthi-ces, Thessaly, under Cercetius m. Burned by Flaminius. *Malacassi.*

PHALORIAS, a town of the Locri Opuntii.

PHALYCON (Alycon), a town of Megaris.

PHAMIZON, *vide* Phazemon.

PHANA, a town of Ætolia, on the coast, N.E. of Cynia lacus. *Kuria Irene.*

PHANÆ ins., I. an isl. of Chios, over against the cognominal promontory. *Venetico.* II. prom., the S. extremity of Chios ins. *C. Mastico.* III. portus, a port of Chios, within the cognominal promontory. The district was peculiarly noted for its wine.

PHANAGŎRIA, a town of Sarmatia Asiatica, on Bosporus Cimmerius, over against Panticapæum. A Milesian colony. The capital of the Asiatic Bosporani. *Taman.*

PHANO, a town of Trachonitis, bet. Damascus N.N.W. and Canatha S.E.

PHANORÆA regio, a district of Pontus, on Iris and Lycus ffl. Bounded E. by Paryadres m. and w. by Lithrus and Ophlimus mm. *Niksar.*

PHANOTE, I. a fortress of Chaonia, on the Dodon fl. w. of Antigonea. *Gardiki.* II. (Phanoteus), i. q. Panopeus.

PHARÆ (Pheræ), I. one of the twelve cities of Achaia, on Pirus fl., 9 m. from Olenus. With an oracle of Mercury. II. a town of Bœotia, in the territory of Tanagra, near Hyria. III. of Crete. A colony from Pheræ, in Messenia.

PHARAN, I. a pr. of Arabia, at the entrance w. of Ælanites sin. *Ras Mohammed.* II. capital of the Pharanitæ, Arabiæ, above Pharan prom. *Tor.*

PHARANITÆ, a people of Arabia Petræa, on and N. of Ælanites sin., extending from Sinai m. to Seir m. The descendants of Epher. The wilderness of Paran was in their territory.

PHARAZANA (Phra), capital of Drangiana Anabon, on Pharnacotus fl., L.

PHARBÆTHUS, a town of Lower Egypt, on the Tanitic branch of the Nile, above Phacusa.

PHARBELUS, a village of Eubœa, near Eretria.

PHARIS (Pharæ), a town of Laconia, on Phillias fl., s. of Amyclæ.

PHARMACIAS fl., a r. of Bithynia, falling into Ascanius lac. near Nicæa.

PHARMACUSA ins., an isl. of Caria, off Posidium prom. The scene of Julius Cæsar's capture by the pirates. The death-place of Attalus. *Farmaco.*

PHARMACUSÆ ins., two islets of Attica, off Amphiale prom. One of them was the burial-place of Circe. *Kyra.*

PHARMATENUS fl., a r. of Pontus, falling into the Euxine, 19 m. E. from Melanthius fl.

PHARNACIA, *prius* Chærades, a maritime town of the Mosynœci, in Pontus, 15 m. E. from Pharmatenus fl. Enlarged by Pharnaces, grandfather of Mithridates Eu-

pator, who transferred hither the population of Cotyora. *Keresoun.* II. a town of Phrygia.

PHARNACOTUS fl., a r. of Drangiana, rising E. of Astasana and falling into Aria palus below Prophtasia.

PHAROS (Pharia) ins., I. an isl. of the Adriatic, one of the Liburnides, E. of Lissa. Colonized from Pharos. The birth-place of Demetrius Pharius. *Lessina.* II. capital of the cognominal island. III. an isl. of Egypt, at Alexandria, on which stood the great lighthouse.

PHARODINI, i. q. Varini.

PHARSALIA, Epiri, *vide* Palæste.

PHARSALUS (Phanalius), I. a town of Pamphylia. II. (Pharsalia), a city of Phthiotis, Thessaly, in the district Thessaliotis, on Enipeus fl., near its junction with Apidanus fl., s. of the elder city of the same name, 27 m. N.E. from Hypata. On the plain, between and about the two, was fought the battle in which (May 12, B.C. 48) Julius Cæsar defeated Pompey. It was for some time the seat of a republic. *Phersale.* III. vetus (Palæo-Pharsalus), a city of Phthiotis, Thessaly, a short distance N. from its younger sister of the same name.

PHARUSII, a people of Æthiopia, bet. the Æthiopes N. and the Gætuli s.

PHARYCADON (Pharcadon), a town of Estiæotis, Thessaly, at the junction of Cuarius fl. with Peneus fl. *Zarco.*

PHARYGÆ, I. a town of Phocis, at Pharygium prom. II. the latter name of Tarphe, in Locris Epicnemid.

PHARYGIUM prom., a headland of Phocis, w. of Bulis, over against Ægira. *C. Agia.*

PHARYTRA, a town of India i. Gangem, N. of Pitynda.

PHASELIS, I. a town of Judæa, in a cognominal valley of Judæa, N.E. of Jericho. Built by Herod in honour of his brother Phasælus. Noted for its plantation of palm-trees, given by Salome to Livia. II. *prius* Pityussa, an autochthonous city of Lycia, on a peninsula. With a temple of Minerva, in which was shown the spear of Achilles. A Dorian colony, enlarged by Argives. Noted for its attar of roses. The birth-place of Theodectes the poet. Immediately contiguous was a cognominal lake, the exhalations from which rendered the place very unhealthy. *Tekrova.*

PHASIA (Phausia), a town of Armenia Maj., on Phasis Min. fl. *Pasean.*

PHASIANE, *prius* Bæsean, a district of Colchis, on Phasis fl. The people were famous for their hospitality. Hence came the pheasant.

PHASIANUM mare, the s. portion of the Euxine, on the coast of Phasiane.

PHASIS, a r. of Colchis, rising in Iberia, towards Sura, and falling into the Euxine at Phasis. Remarkable for its gentle course. By Herodotus and some others considered the boundary of Asia and Europe. It was up this river the Argonauts sailed to plunder the golden fleece. *Don.* II. capital of Phasiana, Colch., on a lake formed by Phasis fl., near its mouth, N. of Mogrus. A Milesian colony. Here was the temple of Phryxus, and the grove celebrated for the golden fleece. III. a town of Taprobane, N.E., bet. Talucory and Anubingara. IV. MINOR, *prius* Phison, a r. of Armenia Maj., falling into the Araxes below Phasia. *Pasin.*

PHATAREI, a people of Sarmatia Asiat., towards the Tanais.

PHATISANA (Phauda), a fortress of Pontus, 1½ m. w. from Polemonium.

PHATMETICUM OSTIUM NILI (Phatnicum, Pathmeticum, Phatmicum), the fourth larger mouth of the Nile, E. from Alexandria.

PHATRUA, a town of Bactriana, near the source of the Oxus. *Fyzabad.*

PHATURIS, Patros, i. q. Memnonium Thebaid.

PHATUSA, a town of Tingene, Mes., on the Euphrates, bet. Belesi and Rhescipha. *Hena?*

PHAURA ins., an isl. of Attica, in Saronicus sin., s.w. of Zoster prom. *Flega.*

PHAUSIA, a remarkable stalactite cavern in Peræa Rhodiorum.

PHAVONÆ, a people of Scandia ins., E.

PHAZANIA, the country of the Phazanii, in Libya Int. *Fezzan.*

PHAZEMON (Phamizon), a city of Pontus, N.W. of Amasia. *Mazifun.*

PHEBOL ins., an isl. of Arabia Felix, s.

PHECA, a fortress of Estiæotis, in Thessaly, under Pindus m., w. of Gomphi. *Clinovo.*

PHEGAIA, I. a demus of Attica, of the tribe Pandionis. II. of Attica, of the tribe Æantis, on the Saronicus sin., towards Sunium. *Kataphekai.*

PHEGEA, an early name of Psophis, in Arcadia.

PHEGUS, a demus of Attica, of the Erectheis tribe, on the Ægean, bet. Marathon and Halæ Araphenides.

PHEIA prom., I. a pr. of Epea, in Elis, s. of Ichthys prom. *C. Scaphidia.* II. a town of Epea, in Elis, at the cognominal prom. *Pundico Castro.*

PHELLIAS fl., a r. of Laconia, falling into Eurotas fl., R., s. of Amyclæ.

PHELLINE, a town of Zeugitana, bet. Tochæ and Mescela.

PHELLOE, a fortress town of Achaia, 5 m. s. of Ægira, with temples of Bacchus and Diana. *Zakoula.*

PHELLUS, a port of Lycia, nearly opposite Megiste. *Sevedo.*

PHENEA palus, a lake at Pheneus, in Arcadia, formed by Aroarius fl. *Kokinobouno.*

PHENEUS, a town of Arcadia, N.W. of Stymphalus. An abode of Hercules. The residence of Evander and his ancestors. With temples of Minerva Tritonia, Mercury, and Ceres Eleusinia, and the tomb of Iphiclus. *Phonia.*

PHERÆ, I. a town of Ætolia. II. of Messenia, at the head of Messeniacus sin., E. of Pamisus fl. The abode of Diocles, the host of Telemachus. III. a city of Pelasgiotis, at the s. extremity of Bæbe lac. Built by Pheres, father of Admetus and Eumetus. For some time the seat of a republic. The capital of Alexander Pheræus. *Velestina.*

PHERESITÆ (Pheresæi), one of the seven tribes of Canaan, w. of Manasseh and Issachar.

PHERINUM, a town of Estiæotis, in Thessaly, s.E. of Argenta.

PHEUGARUM, a town of the Cherusci, Germania. *Halberstadt.*

PHIALA lac., a pool of Gaulonitis, Palestine, formed by Jordan fl., 10 m. from its source. Now a marsh. *Birket el Ram.*

PHIALEA, Arcadia, i. q. Phigalia.

PHIARA, I. a town of Pontus, bet. Sebastia and Berissa. II. of Sargarausene prefecture, in Cappadocia.

PHIBESETH, i. q. Bubastus.

PHICIUS m., Bœotia, i. q. Sphingius.

PHIGALEA (Phialea), a town of Arcadia, under Elæus m., on Lymax fl. Founded by Phigaleus, son of Lycaon, or by Phialus, son of Bucolion. With a temple of Bacchus Acratophorus and Diana Sospita. The inhabitants were noted for their gluttony and drunkenness. *Paulizza.*

PHIGAMUS fl. a r. of Pontus, falling into the Euxine, 5 m. E. from Œnœ.

PHILA, a town of Pieria, in Macedonia, on the Thermaicus sin., bet. Heraclium and Tempe. Built by Antigonus Gonatas, and named after his mother Phila. *Platamona?*

PHILACUM, a town of Thebais, bet. Xeron (24) and Apollinis Hydreum (24).

PHILADELPHIA, I. a town of Cilicia Trachea, on Calycadnus fl., above Diocæsarea. *Mout.* II. of Lydia, on Cogamus fl., un-

der Tmolus m., on the borders of Catacecaumene regio. Built by Attalus Philadelphus. One of the seven churches of
Asia. *Allah-Sher.*

PHILADELPHIA, Palestinæ, i. q. Rabbath
Ammon.

PHILÆ (Philak, "end"), a town of Thebais, on the Nile, on a cognominal isl.;
the southernmost town of Egypt. *Djesiret
el Birbe.*

PHILÆA, a maritime village of Cilicia Trachea, 16 m. N.E. from Zephyrium prom.

PHILÆUM, a name given to Thria Attic. in
honour of Phila, mother of Demetrius.

PHILAIDÆ, a demus of Attica, of the tribe
Ægeis, under Anchesmus m., N.W. of Alo-
pece. Named after Philæus, son of Ajax.
The birth-place of Pisistratus. *Philiati.*

PHILANORIUM, a town of Argolis, on the
Argolicus sin., bet. Boli and Asine.

PHILARIUS fl., a stream of Bœotia, falling
into Copais lac., w. of Haliartus.

PHILÆ prom., a headland of Astica, in
Thrace, on the Euxine, S.E. of Halmydessus.

PHILEA (Phrygia), a town of Astica, in
Thrace, on the Euxine, at the cognominal
prom., E. *Philine.*

PHILEATINA palus, a lake near Philea, in
Thrace.

PHILECIA, a town of the Corcontii, Germ.,
N. of Eburodunum. *Filek?*

PHILENORIUM, a town of Bœotia, near
Chæronea. Named from Philenor the
Ætolian.

PHILIPPI, a city of the Edones, in Thrace,
on the Egnatia Via, bet. Ad Duodecim
(12) and Neapolis (10). Founded by
Thasians; rebuilt and renamed by Philip
of Macedon. Memorable as the first
place in Europe where the Gospel was
preached (A.D. 51) by St. Paul; and for the
great victory here of Mark Antony and
Octavian over Brutus and Cassius. Noted
for its rich mines, its fertility, and its
beautiful roses. A Roman colonia. The
birth-place of Adrastus the peripatetic.
Filibah.

PHILIPPOPŎLIS, I. a town of Batanæa, near
Bostra. *Ghereyah.* II. of Estiæotis, in
Thessaly, bet. Tricca and Phalaria. III.
Poneropolis (*prius* Eumolpias), a town of
the Odrysæ, in Thrace, on Hebrus fl.,
below Bessapara. Enlarged and renamed
by Philip of Macedon.

PHILISCUM. *Vide* Nicephorium.

PHILISTÆI (Philistini, Palæstini), descendants of the Pali, who from Egypt took
possession of the E. coast of the Mediterranean, named from them Palestine.

Their special locality was between Joppa
and Egypt.

PHILLITÆ, a people of India i. Gangem, on
Namadus fl., L., towards its source.

PHILLON, a town of Triphylia, in Elis, near
Scillus.

PHILOCALEA, a port of the Mosynœci, in
Pontus, 12 m. N.E. from Tripolis. *Hele-
hou.*

PHILOMELIUM, a town of Phrygia Parorea,
bet. Antiochia and Tyriæum, on Gallus fl.
Ilgan.

PHILONOS, a town of Cyrenaica, bet. Arimanthos and Augila.

PHILOTERA, a port of Egypt, on Heroopolitis sin., 3 geog. m. s. from Myos Herma.
Named from the son of Ptolemy Philadelphus.

PHILYRCIS ins., an isl. of Pontus, off Tripolis. Settled by the Philyres, the off-
spring of Philyra and Saturn.

PHINEA (Phinopolis), a town of Thrace,
near the mouth of the Bosporus. *Der-
cus.*

PHINNI, a people of N.W. Sarmatia. *The
Fins.*

PHINTIÆ, a maritime town of Sicily, s., bet.
Dædalium and Phalarium. Built 210 B.C.
by Phintias of Agrigentum, who populated
it with the inhabitants of Gela.

PHINTONIS ins., an isl. of Sardinia, N.E.,
above Arcti prom. *Isola di Figo.*

PHIRÆSI, a town of Scandia Ins., E.

PHISTELIA, the Oscan name of Petitia Luca-
norum.

PHAZEMONITIS (Phanuzonitis) regio, a district of Pontus, on the border of Galatia,
S.E. of Gazelonitis.

PHLA ins., an isl. of Africa, in Tritonis
palus.

PHLEGRÆI CAMPI, "burning plains," a district of Campania, extending from above
Puteoli to Vesuvius. Full of volcanic fis-
sures, whence issued fiery and sulphureous
exhalations, which gave rise to the fables
connected with the district.

PHLEGYÆ, a predatory tribe of Bœotia, the
early inhabitants of Orchomenus. Named
after Phlegyas, son of Mars. Destroyed
by the gods for their impiety.

PHLEUM, i. q. Flevum.

PHLIUS, *olim* Aræthyria, I. a district of Peloponnesus, on the confines of Arcadia and
Achaia. Once independent, but afterwards subject to Argolis. II. mons, a
branch of Arachnæus m., in Argolis, on
the Asopus fl., above the cognominal
town. III. an autonymous city of Argolis,
capital of the cognominal district, on Asopus fl., w. of Bembina. Named from

Phlius, son of Asopus. With a temple of Dia or Hebe. *Agios Giorgios.* IV. a town of Argolis, on the Argolicus sin., bet. Asine and Prosymna. *Drepano.*

PHLYÆ, a demus of Attica, of the tribe Cecropis, bet. Castra and Panactum. With temples of Apollo, Dionysodotus, &c. The birth-place of Euripides. *Phillea.*

PHLYGONIUM (Phlygone), a town of Phocis.

PHOCÆA, one of the twelve cities of Ionia, at the head of a bay of Ionium mare, s.w. of Cyme, near the E. entrance of Hermius sin. Founded by a col. from Phocis. *Palæo-Phoggia.*

PHOCAICA ORA, the coast of Gaul, about Massilia.

PHOCARUM ins., an isl. of the Red sea, towards Myos Hormus. *Tiran.*

PHOCE ins., an isl. of Crete, off Sammonium prom.

PHOCEÆ, a name of Leontini, in Sicily.

PHOCENSES, a tribe of Pelasgi, who from Thessaly superseded the Leleges in Phocis.

PHOCICUM, a place bet. Delphi and Cyparissus, in Phocis, where the Phocian states assembled.

PHOCIS, a country of Græcia e. Peloponnesum, bounded N. by the Locri Epicnemidii and Locri Opuntii, s. by Corinthiacus sin., w. by Doris and the Locri Ozolæ, E. by Bœotia. Named after Phocus, son of Æacus. First settled by the Leleges, then by the Phocenses.

PHOCRA m., a range of m. in Mauritania Ting., running parallel with Mulucha fl., L., towards its source.

PHOCUSSA ins., an isl. of the Ægean, one of the Sporades, bet. Naxos and Nicasia. *Gaiphonisi.*

PHODA, a town of Arabia Felix, E.N.E. of Thumata. *Soda.*

PHŒBATIS regio, a district of Illyria, on the confines of Macedonia, bet. the Pissantini and the Atintanes.

PHŒBI prom., a pr. of Mauritania Ting., on the Mediterranean, bet. Aquila Min. and Aquila Maj., s. of Abyla.

PHŒBIA, a town of Achaia, towards Sicyon.

PHŒCIA ins., i. q. Corcyra ins.

PHŒNICE, I. a city of Chaonia, on the Dodon fl., s. of Phanote, bet. Acroceraunium m. (41) and Buthrotum (26). Restored by Justinian. *Phenikè.* II. (Pinaca), a town of Gordyene, Armen., on the Tigris, L., above Bezabde. III. a name of Tenedos ins.

PHŒNICIA (Phœnicè, "land of the sons of Anak"), a province of Syria, on the Mediterranean, extending from Seleucis, N. of Berytus, to Album prom., in length 80 m., in breadth 12 m. The Phœnicians, descendants of the Canaanites, were the fathers of commerce and navigation, and probably the inventors of letters.

PHŒNICIUS m., a summit of Helicon, towards Haliartus. A name contemporary with Cadmus.

PHŒNICON, I. a town of Thebais, bet. Coptos (25) and Aphrodites (24). II. of Thebais, bet. Apollinopolis parva and Didymis.

PHŒNICUS m., I. Lyciæ, i. q. Olympus. II. a port of Cythera, on the E. coast. III. of Ionia, under Mimas m., s. of Erythræ. *Egri-limen.* IV. of Libya Ægypti, 17 m. w. from Pnix. V. of Messenia, in Asinæus sin., N. of Acrias prom. *Marathy.* VI. a haven of Sicily, s.E., bet. Helorum and Ichana. VII. of Lycia, E. of Patara (1½ m.). *Kalamaki.*

PHŒNICUSA ins., an isl. of Sicily, N. of Didyme. *Lisca Bianca.*

PHŒNIX, I. a r. of Achaia, falling into the Corinthiacus sin. at Erincus portus. *Salmenico.* II. a stream of Bœotia, rising in Delos m. Sacred to Apollo. III. a fortress of Caria, on Phœnix m., over against Elæussa ins. IV. a r. of Dolopia, in Thessaly, rising near Sosthenis, and falling into Apidanus fl. s.w. of Cranon. *Emicassos.* V. of Maliensis, in Thessaly, 2 m. w. of Thermopylæ, falling into Asopus fl. VI. m., m. of Caria, running along the s. coast, from Cynossema prom. to Caunus. VII. portus, a harbour on the s. coast of Crete, w. of Sulia prom., the port of Lampe. Mentioned by St. Luke. *Castel Franco.*

PHOEZON, a village of Arcadia, near Mantinea, in which was the tomb of Areithous.

PHOGOR m., a summit of Abarim m., 6 m. from Livias.

PHOLEGANDROS (Sideria) ins., an isl. of the Ægean, one of the Sporades, bet. Melos and Sicinos. *Policandro.*

PHOLOE m., a m. of Epea, in Elis, overlooking Pylos. Named from Pholus the Centaur. *Maurovouni.*

PHORBÆ, a town of Thessaly.

PHORBANTIA ins., Siciliæ, i. q. Bucina.

PHORCYS portus, a town of Ithaca ins., the port of Ithaca oppid. *Porto Molo.*

PHORIAMI, a town of Elis, near Parthenius fl.

PHORICA, a town of Arcadia.

PHORMISIUM (Phormisii), a demus of Attica.

PHORON portus, a port of Attica, N.W. of Piræus.

PHOTICE, a town of Chaonia, towards the coast, bet. Panormus and Phœnice. Restored by Justinian. *Sopoto.*

PHOTINÆUM, a town of Thessaly.

PHRAGANDÆ, a town of the Mædi, in Thrace, s.w. of Jamphorina.

PHRATERIA, a town of the Ciagisi, Dac., s.e. of Arcinna.

PHREARRII, a demus of Attica, of the tribe Leontis. The birth-place of Themistocles.

PHREATA, "wells," a village of Garsauritis, towards Sesama.

PHRICIUM, a town of Perrhæbia, in Thessaly, bet. Mylæ and Orthe, N.W. of Larissa.

PHRICONIS, a surname of Cyme and of Larissa, in Æolis Asiat.

PHRIXA (Phæstus), a town of Triphylia, in Elis, on Alpheus fl., E. of Olympia; with a temple of Minerva Cydonia. *Palaio Phamari.*

PHRITTII, a demus of Attica.

PHRIXUS, I. a r. of Argolis, rising in Chaon m., and falling into the Argolicus sin. below Trochos. II. a port of Bithynia, in Bosporus Thrac., N. of Lembus prom.

PHRUDIS fl., a r. of Gaul, falling into Gallicum Fretum, w. of Samarobriva; the maritime boundary bet. Belgica II. and Lugdunensis. *Somme.*

PHRUGUNDIONES, an eastern division of the Burgundiones, in Germany.

PHRURÆSON m., m. of Mauritania Cæsar., towards Sitifis.

PHRURI, a people of Serica.

PHURION, a town of the Arvarni, Ind., s. of Poleur.

PHRURIUM prom., a pr. of Cyprus, bet. Drepanum prom. and Curium.

PHRYGIA, a country of Asia Minor, bounded N. by Bithynia, s. by Pisidia and Lycia, w. by Mysia, Lydia, and Caria, E. by Galatia and Lycaonia. Settled first by Leuco-Syri, and afterwards, circa 1280 B.C., by Bryges, or Briges, under Midas, from about Bermius m., in Thrace. It was distributed into Ph. Epictetus, Ph. Magna, and Ph. Parorea, and later, into Ph. Pacatiana and Ph. Salutaris.

PHRYGIA EPICTETUS, "acquired," the N. portion of Phrygia, on the confines of Galatia, N.W., Bithynia and Mysia s.e., and Lydia N.E. Named as having been *acquired* by Attalus of Pergamus from Rome. It at one time extended into Bithynia and Mysia, N., and into P. Magna s.

PHRYGIA HELLESPONTIACA, i. q. P. Minor.

PHRYGIA MAGNA, the division of Phrygia extending from its s. frontier to Hermus fl. w., and Alander fl. E., having P. Paroria s.e.

PHRYGIA MINOR (Hellespontiaca), the districts of Bithynia and Mysia towards Hellespont, which more anciently belonged to the Phrygiæ Brygi.

PHRYGIA PAROREA, the district of Phrygia, in its s.e. angle, under Taurus m.

PHRYGIA (Phrygii), a village of Attica, towards Bœotia.

PHRYGIUS fl., Phryx, i. q. Hyllus.

PHTHIA (Phæa), a maritime district of Marmarica, bet. Paliurus fl. and Chersonesus Magna.

PHTHIOTIS, a district of Thessaly, bounded N. by Pelasgiotis, s. by Dolopia and Maliensis, w. by Estiæotis, E. by Magnesia. Comprising the Homeric districts of Pthia and Hellas, and representing the dominions of Achilles, Protesilaus, and Eurypylus.

PHTHIROPHAGI, "louse-eaters," a people of Sarmatia, on the N.E. coast of the Euxine.

PHTHONTIS, a town of Thebais, N.W. of Contra-Toum.

PHTHURIS, a town of the Evonymitæ, on the Nile, bet. Autoba and Pitara. *Faras.*

PHTHUTH (Fut) fl., a r. of Mauritania Tingit., rising in Atlas Maj., and falling into the Atlantic, s. of Mysocoras portus. *Tensift.*

PHUIBAGANA, *vide* Evagina.

PHUNDUSI, a people of Cimbrica Chersonesus, w.

PHUPHUENA (Euspæna), a town of Armenia Min., bet. Blaundus (28) and Aranis (24).

PHURGISATIS, a town of the Juthungi, Germania, N.W. of Medoslanium. *Znaim.*

PHUSIPARA, I. a town of Melitene, in Cappadocia. II. (Physcus), a town of Pentapolis, Cyrenaicæ, at Phycus prom.

PHYCUS prom., a pr. of Cyrenaica, w. of Apollonia (25), over against Tænarum prom. (350). *Cape Sem.*

PHYLACÆUM, a town of Phrygia.

PHYLACE, I. *surnamed* Hermopolitana, a village of Heptanomis, on the Nile, w. bet. Hermopolis and Phylace Thebaica. II. a town of Molossis, bet. Dodona and Horreum. *Ruins near Velchizta.* III. of Phthiotis, in Thessaly, on Pagasæus sin. With a temple of Protesilaus, in whose honour games were celebrated here. IV. of Pieria, in Macedonia, on the Haliacmon fl., N.W. of Bala. *Phili.*

PHYLACE THEBAICA, a town of Thebais, on Josephi canalis, bet. Phylace Heptanomica and Cusæ.

PHYLACTRIS, a town of Arcadia, the citadel of Tegea.

PHYLE, a demus and citadel of Attica, of the tribe Æneis, 15 m., N.W. of Athens. Hither Thrasybulus retired. *Bigla Castro.*

PHYLLEIUS m., a hill of Phthiotis, in Thessaly, bet. Demetrias and Phyllus.

PHYLLIS regio, a district of Thrace, in the territory of the Edones, bet. Pangæus m. and Angites fl.

PHYLLUS, a town of Phthiotis, in Thessaly, under Phylleius m., N.W. of Demetrias. With a famous temple of Apollo Phylleius.

PHYRCON, a fortress of Elis.

PHYRITES fl., a r. of Ionia, rising in Tmolus m. S.W., and falling into Caystrus fl. at Pegaseum Stagnum.

PHYROCASTRUM, a fortress of Cilicia prefectura, in Cappadocia.

PHYSCA, I. a town of Grestonia, in Macedonia, N.W. of Terpillus. II. a maritime town of the Tyrangetæ, Sarmatia, bet. Hermonactis and Isiacus portus.

PHYSCELLA, a town of Sithonia, near Toron.

PHYSCON (Tornadotus) fl., a r. of Assyria, falling into the Tigris at Opis.

PHYSCUS m., I. the termination, towards the Ionian sea, of Clibanus m., in Bruttium. II. prom., i. q. Phycus. III. a town of Eordæa, in Macedonia. Named after Physcus, the first chief of the Eordi or Leleges. IV. (Physca), a port of Peræa, in Caria. The Rhodian emporium of Ephesus. With a grove of Latona. *Castra Marmora.*

PHYTEUM, a town of the Eurytanes, Ætolia, near the S.W. shore of Trichonius lacus, S.W. of Metapa. Named after Phœtius, son of Alcmæon. II. a town of Elis.

PHYTIA (Phœtiæ), a town of Acarnania, on or near Anapus fl., N.W. of Metropolis. Founded by Phœtius, son of Alcmæon. *Aeto.*

PIALA (Piada), a town of Serica, on Œchardes fl., bet. Amasia (15) and Coloe (12).

PIALIA, a town of the Æthices, in Thessaly, under Cercetius m., N. of Phaloria. *Pali.*

PICENI (Picentes), a tribe of Sabines settled in the country bet. Sabinium Proper and the Adriatic, N. of the Vestini. Named, according to Festus, from the bird picus, under the guidance of which they fixed upon this settlement; according to Silius Italicus, from a leader so named.

PICENSES, an early people of Dacia.

PICENTIA, an Etruscan city, capital of the Picentini, in Campania, on Via Aquilia, bet. Salernum (7) and Ad Tanarum, on Pæstanus sin. *Vicenza.*

PICENTINI, the descendants of those inhabitants of Picenum, whom the Romans, after the conquest of that city, settled in Campania, on and above Pæstanus sin.

PICENTINUM, a town of the Andizetes, Pannonia, bet. Leuconum (26) and Iniccrum (25). *Orhovicz.*

PICENUM, the country of the Piceni, in Italy, bounded N.E. and E. by the Adriatic, N.W. by Umbria, S.W. by the Sabini and Marsi, s. by the Peligni and Marrucini at Aternus fl. Subjugated by Rome 270 B.C. By Augustus it was nominated the fifth region of Italy. It was noted for its agricultural produce, and peculiarly for its apples.

PICINIANA, a town of Sicily, 9 m. from Agrigentum. *Aragona.*

PICI, a people of Sarmatia Asiatica, on Mæotis palus.

PICIS lacus, a lake of Zacynthus, near Arcadia.

PICTI (Pecht-dich, *Gaelic*, "thieves"), a tribe of Scandinavians, who settled on the E. shores of Britannia Barbara, and were ultimately exterminated by, or fused with, the Picts. Some of the Roman writers imagined that the term, as they rendered it, meant that the people painted themselves.

PICTONES (Pictavi), a people of Aquitania II., on the Liger, L., towards its mouth. *La Vendée and Loire Inférieure*, s. and s.w., &c.

PICTONUM prom., a pr. of Aquitania II., s. of the mouth of the Liger. *Pointe de l'Aiguillon; Pointe de Boisnivet?*

PICUENTUM, a town of Istria.

PICUS, a town of Zeugitana, under Cirna m., s. bet. Aquilianis and Teglata.

PIDOSUS ins., an isl. of Caria, off Halicarnassus.

PIENGITÆ, a people of Sarmatia, under Carpathus m.

PIEPHIGI, a tribe of Getæ, on the Danube, E. of the Ciagisi, on Ordessus fl. and Naparis fl.

PIERA fons, a stream of Pisatis, in Elis, N.W. of Olympia.

PIERES, a Pelasgic people settled in Pieria, Macedonia, who, expelled by the Temenidæ, formed a new settlement beyond Strymon fl.

PIERIA, I. the country of the Pieres, Macedonia, bounded N. by Bottiæa, s. by Thessaly, w. by Elymæa, Eordæa, and Olympus m., E. by Thermaicus sin. II. a district of Syria, towards Issicus sin. Named from its mountain range Pierius. III. a town of Estiæotis, in Thessaly, N.W. of Metropolis. IV. silva, a wood near Pydna, in Macedonia. Noted for its pitch.

PIERICUS sin., i. q. Strymonicus sin.

PIERIS m., a summit of Helicon, in Bœotia. Sacred to the Muses.

PIERIUM, a town of Thessaly.

PIETAS JULIA, Histriæ, i. q. Pola.

PIGELASSUS, a town of Caria.

PIGINDA, a town of Caria.

PIGRUM mare, i. q. Coretus sin.

PIMOLOSENE regio, a district of Paphlagonia, on Halys fl., N.W. of Amasia.

PIMOLOSA, a fortress of Paphlagonia, on Halys fl., N.E. of Andrada. In ruins in Strabo's time.

PIMPLEA m., I. a summit of Helicon, in Bœotia, near Astra. Sacred to the Muses. II. a village of Pieria, in Macedonia, S.E. of Dium, bet. Libethra and Hatera. The birth-place of Orpheus.

PIMPLEUS m., a summit of Olympus, overlooking Pimplea in Pieria. Sacred to the Muses, hence surnamed Pimpleæ.

PINACA, Armen., i. q. Phœnice.

PINARA, "round hill," I. one of the Echinades ins. II. a town of Pieria, Syriæ, N. of Pagræ. III. a maritime town of Cilicia, towards Adana. IV. prius Artymnesus, a Xanthian city of Lycia, under Cragus m. N. With a temple of Pandarus, the Homeric archer. Named from Pinarus, son of Tremilus.

PINARUS fl., a r. of Cilicia Campestris, falling into Issicus sin. below Issus. Delisou.

PINDASUS m., a summit of Temnus m., in Mysia, N.E. of Pergamum.

PINDENISSUS, a town of the Eleuthero Cilices, in Amanus m.

PINDUS, I. a r. of Doris, falling into Cephissus fl. w. of Lilæa. Mauro Potamos. II. m., a s. continuation of Scardus m., separating Thessaly from Athamania and Aperantia, and extending E. to Œta m. III. (Acyphas), a town of Doris, one of the Dorica Tetrapolis, on Pindus fl., w. of Lilæa.

PINEPTIMI OSTIUM NILI, one of the two lesser mouths of the Nile, E. of Diolcos ostium.

PINETA, a town of the Lusitani, N. of Lancia Transcudana.

PINIANA CASTRA, a town of Vindelicia, on the Danube, at its confluence with Ilargus fl.

PINNA, capital of the Vestini, Picenum, N.W. of Teate Marruc. A colonia. Citta di Penna.

PINTIA (Vallis Oletana), a town of the Vaccæi, Tarraconensis, 4 m. S.E. from Intercatia. Valladolid.

PINUM, a town of Dacia, on Aluta fl., near its mouth.

PION m., a m. of Ionia, near Ephesus.

PIPLAS ins., islets of Gaul, in Rubresus lacus. Isles d'Ouillous.

PIONIA, a town of Æolis Asiat., N. of Antandrus.

PIORUM campus, the district about Catana, in Sicily. Named in honour of the brothers Amphinomus and Anapius.

PIQUENTUM, a town of Histria, E. of Ningum. Piquento.

PIRÆA, an ancient district of Megaris.

PIRÆUM, a fortress of Corinthia, on Corinthiacus sin., towards Megaris.

PIRÆUS, I. a demus of Attica, and constituting (from the time of Themistocles) with Phalerum and Munychium, the port of Athens. The burial-place of Themistocles. With temples of Jupiter Soter, Venus, &c. II. (Anthedon portus, Atheniensium portus) a harbour of Corinthia, on Saronicus sin., s: of Bucephalus. Francolimni.

PIRAÏCE regio, Bœotia, probably Graïce.

PIRATARUM (Lestorum) regio, a district of India e. Gangem. Pegu?

PIRATORTUM, a town of Noricum, 8 m. E. from Trigisamum.

PIRESLÆ (Asterium), a town of Phthiotis, in Thessaly, N. of Titanus m., s.w. of Pheræ.

PIRETÆ (Pirræ), a town of the Jassii, Pannonia, bet. Sunesta and Lentula.

PIRI m., a m. of Germany, towards Lupodunum.

PIRIAS, Eubœa, i. q. Pyrrha.

PIRINA, a town of Sicily, bet. Panormus (13) and Petra (23). Near Cattamo.

PIRINE fons, a stream, sacred to the Muses, bet. Corinth and Lechæum. Named after Pirene, mother of Cenchria. Used in tempering the celebrated Corinthian brass. Here Pegasus was seized by Bellerophon.

PERIPHOSIUS portus, a port of Libya, on the Atlantic, s. of Hesperium prom.

PIRISABORA (Birsabora), a town of Messene Sup., Babyl., on the Euphrates, L., bet. Macepracta and Fissenia.

PIROBORIDAVA, a town of the Britolagæ, Dacia, on Parata fl., above Netindava. Near Gerschany.

PIROSSUS m., a m. of Mysia, above Zelica. The Terea of Homer.

PIRUM, a town of the Cotenses, Dacia, s.w. of Augustia. Piteschty.

PIRUM TORTUM, a town of the Boii, Noric., on the Danube, bet. Fasiana and Comagene. Pixendorf.

PIRUS, I. a r. of Achaia, rising in Erymanthus m., and falling into Corinthiacus sin. at Olenus. Camenitza. II. m., a m.

of Germania Mag., on the R. bank of Niter fl., s.e. of Borbetomagus.

PIRUSTÆ, a tribe of the Dassaretæ, in Illyria.

PISA, capital of Pisatis, in Elis, of uncertain position; no traces, indeed, of any such distinct place existing in the time of Strabo. It was probably an early name of Olympia, from Pisos, son of Æolus.

PISÆ (Pisa, Pithsa), *prius* Teuta, a city of Etruria, on Arnus fl., R., at its junction (formerly) with Auser fl., bet. Portus Herculis Lab. (12) and Fossæ Papirianæ (11). Traditionally founded by the followers of Nestor. A Teutanian settlement, colonized by Etruscans. A colonia 182 B.C. Noted for its timber and marble. *Pisa.*

PISANÆ, a town of the Anatili, Viennensis, bet. Terisiæ w. and Aquæ Sextiæ E.S.E.

PISATIS, a district of Elis, bet. Epea, or Elis Propria, and Triphylia. Named from its capital, Pisa.

PISAURUM, a town of Umbria, at the mouth of Pisaurus fl., bet. Fanum Fortunæ (8) and Ariminum (24) on Via Flaminia. A colonia 184 B.C. Denounced for its bad climate. *Pesaro.*

PISAURUS (Isaurus) fl., a r. of Umbria, falling into the sea at Pisaurum. *Foglia.*

PISCENÆ, a town of the Volcæ Arecomici, Narbonensis I., N.w. of Araura.

PISCINA, I. a town of Numidia, bet. Mesarfilia and Gemellæ. II. *postea* Pesenatium, a port of Narbonensis. *Pesenas.*

PISCINÆ, a maritime village of Etruria, bet. Ad Fines (6) and Triturrita (8).

PISCURI, a tribe of Dahæ.

PESENDARÆ, a people of Ethiopia, s. of the equator.

PISGAH (Phasga) m., m. N.w. of Machærus, in Amoritis.

PISIDIA, I. a country of Asia Minor, bounded N. and N.w. by Phrygia, s. by Pamphylia, at Taurus m., s.w. by Lycia, e. by Lycaonia. Settled first by Solymi, and next by a tribe of Leleges. *Hamed.* II. (Fisinda, Pisinda), a town of the Psylli, in Africa Prop., on Syrtis Maj., bet. Sagazæna and Taberna, w. of Aræ Philænorum.

PISIDICUS lacus, i. q. Acrioteri palus.

PISILIS (Pilisis), a port of Peræa, in Caria, at the mouth of Calbis fl. *Couindji.*

PISINDA (Isinda, Isionda), a town of Pisidia, 5 m. w. from Termessus.

PISINDON, a port of Tripolis, Afric., bet. Æa and Assaria.

PISINGARA, a town of Armenia Min.

PISISTRATI ins., three islets of Ionia, off the mouth of Caystrus fl., Anthine, Myonnesus, and Diarrheusa.

PISON fl., a r. of Arabia, an arm of the Euphrates, which, running parallel with Persicus sin., emptied itself into that gulf towards Gerra.

PISORACA fl., a r. of Tarraconensis, falling into Durius fl. below Septimanca. *Pisuerga.*

PISSANTINI, a tribe of Dassaretæ, in Illyria, bet. the s.e. extremity of Lychnitis palus and Macedonia.

PISSAUM, a town of Pelagonia Deuriopis, in Pæonia.

PISSURI, a people of Sogdiana, towards the Caspian.

PISTORIA, a town of Etruria, bet. Hellana (6) and Ad Martis (8), on Via Claudia. Memorable for the defeat in its vicinity of Catiline. *Pistoia.*

PISTRA (Pitara), a town of Meroe, on Gagauda ins., 106 m. N. of Tergidum.

PISTYRUS lacus, I. a salt lake of the Bistones, in Thrace, at the cognominal town. Drained by the beasts of burden of Xerxes' army. II. (Bistyrus, Bisterta, Pardi), a town of the Bistones, in Thrace, on Cadetus fl., 5 m. N.E. from Abdera.

PISURGIA, a maritime town of Cilicia Trachea, 6¼ m. N.E. from Berenice. Named from its pitch-manufacture.

PISYE, a town of Caria.

PITAIUM, a town of Caria, towards Halicarnassus.

PITANE, I. a maritime town of Mysia, bet. Evenus fl. and Canaius fl. The birthplace of the philosopher Arcesilas. Noted for its porous bricks. *Tchandeli.* II. a demus of Laconia, on Eurotas fl., N.w. of Sparta.

PITANUS fl., I. a r. of Corsica, falling into the sea s. of Pitanus portus. *Talabo.* II. portus, a port of Corsica w., at or near the mouth of Pitanus fl.

PITHECUSA, a town of Zeugitana, w. of Meltine.

PITHECUSÆ, "ape-abounding," the Greek name of Ænaria and Prochyta ins. Here apes lived in society with the human population.

PITHOLAI prom., a pr. of Aromatopheros regio, Æthiopia.

PITHOM, the Scriptural name of Patumos, in Lower Egypt.

PITHSA, "crescent," the Etruscan name of Pisæ, in Etruria.

PITHUS, a demus of Attica, of the tribe Cecropis. The birth-place of Melitus, the accuser of Socrates.

PITHYCUS fl., a r. of Æolis Asiat., falling into Cumæus sin. at Myrina. *Condoura.*

PITINUM, I. a town of the Vestini, in Picenum, bet. Foruli (7) and Prifernum (12). *Torre di Pitino.* II. *surnamed* Pisaurense, a town of Umbria, on Pisaurus fl. L. *Piagnino.*

PITNISSUS, a town of the Tectosages, in Galatia, on the borders of Lycaonia.

PITONIUS fl., a stream of the Marsi, rising S.E. of Lacus Fucinus, and after passing through that lake, its water (peculiarly cold and pure in its character) remaining unmixed with it, said to rise again near Tibur, as Aqua Marcia; a statement disputed, but not disproved. *Giovenco.*

PITULUM, a town of Umbria, s.w. of Matilica. *Piolo.*

PITYEA, a town of Mysia, s.w. of Parium, under Pityus m.

PITYNDA, a town of the Calingæ, Ind., on Tyndis fl., at the separation of its E. mouth.

PITYODES (Pityusa) ins., one of the Demonisi ins. of Bithynia, in Propontis, s. of Calchedon. *Prinkipo.*

PITYONESUS ins., an isl. of Argolis, in the Saronicus sin., bet. Epidaurus and Ægina ins. *Angistri.*

PITYUS "fir-growing," I. a m. of Mysia, overlooking Pityea. II. *surnamed* Magna, a town of Sarmatia Asiat., on the Euxine N.E., 44 m. N.W. from Dioscurias. A Milesian colony. At one time the boundary in this direction of the Roman empire. *Drandar.*

PITYUSA I. a district of Mysia, about Pityea. II. in., isl. of Argolis, in the Argolicus sin., over against Phlius. III. of Cilicia Trachea, off Zephyrum prom., s.E. from Aphrodisia. IV. an early name of Chios ins. V. an early name of Salamis.

PITYUSÆ ins., "pine islands," two islands of Tarraconensis, E. of the mouth of Sacro fl.; Ebusus N., and Ophiusa s.

PLACENTIA, a city of the Anamares, in Gall. Cisp., near Padus fl., R., bet. Ad Rotas (11) and Florentia (15), on Via Æmilia. A colonia 219 B.C. A municipium. Burned by Hamilcar; restored by Valerius 197 B.C. *Piacenza.*

PLACIA, a Pelasgic town of Mysia, on Propontis, E. of Scylace.

PLACUS (Plax) mons., a mountain of Mysia, near Thebæ.

PLAGA CALVISIANA, a district of Sicily, near Gela.

PLAGA MESOPOTAMIA, a district of Sicily, 12 m. from Plaga Calvisiana.

PLAGA HEREA (Cymbæ), a district of Sicily, 24 m. from Plaga Mesopotamia.

PLAGRARIA, a town of the Vettones, Lusitania, N.W. of Emerita.

PLANÆ ins., three islands of Tarraconensis, in Illicitanus sin., near Plumbaria ins. *St. Pola, and two others.*

PLANASIA (Planarea) ins., an isl. of Etruria bet. Ilva and Corsica. The exile-place of Augustus' nephew, Agrippa. *Pianosa.*

PLANARIA ins., Africæ, i. q. Canaria.

PLANESIA ins., an isl. of Tarraconensis E., near Plumbaria ins.

PLANIUS, a town of Caria.

PLARASSA, a town of Caria, in the territory of Eunomus.

PLATÆA ins., I. an isl. of the Ægean, one of the Sporades. *Bomba.* II. of Marmarica, off Paliurus.

PLATÆÆ, a city of Bœotia, bet. Leuctra and Eleutheræ, at the foot of Cithæron m., near the springs of Asopus fl., 6 m. s.w. from Thebes. Stigmatized for arrogance. Famous for the defeat of Mardonius by Pausanias and Aristides, 479 B.C., in memory of which a temple was raised here to Jupiter Eleutherius. *Palæo Castro, near Kockla.*

PLATAMODES prom., a pr. of Messenia, s. of Erana.

PLATANEA, a town of Bithynia, on Plataneus fl., bet. Calchedon and Nicomedia.

PLATANEUS fl., a r. of Bithynia, flowing by Platanea into Astacenus sin.

PLATANISTUS, "plane-tree-bordered," I. a r. of Arcadia, falling into Neda fl., near Phigalia. II. (Platanus), the coast of Cilicia Trachea, bet. Cragus prom. and Anemurium. Peculiarly rugged and dangerous. III. prom., the N. pr. of Cythera ins., opposite Onugnathus prom. IV. Elid, i. q. Macistus.

PLATANIUS fons., a r. of Bœotia, falling into Opuntius sin. at Halæ, separating Bœotia from the Locri Opuntii.

PLATANOS, a town of Cassiotis, Syriæ, bet. Cathela (24) and Antiochia (25).

PLATEÆ ins., I. three islets on the coast of Troas. II. two islands on the E. coast of Crete, above Sammonium prom. *Lassa.*

PLAVIS fl., a r. of Venetia, rising in Alpes Rhæticæ, near the source of Tilavemptus fl., and falling into the Adriatic s.E. of Altinum. *Piave.*

PLEGRA, a village of Paphlagonia, N. of Andrapa.

PLEISTUS fl., a r. of Phocis, rising near Cyparissus, and falling into Crissæus sin. at Cirrha. *Sizaliska.*

PLEMMYRIUM prom., I. (Macrum), a pr. of Sicily E., below Syracusæ. *Massa d' Olivero.* II. a town of Sicily E., in an isl. off Plemmyrium prom., s. of Syracuse.

PLERÆI, a tribe of Dalmatæ, in Illyria, contiguous to the Ardiæi, on Naro fl.

PLESTINIA, a town of the Marsi, Ital., near the source of Sagrus fl. *Pesco-Asserolo.*

PLEUMAUS, a town of Pontus.

PLEURON nova, I. a town of Ætolia, under Aracynthus m., N.E. of Olenus. Founded by the fugitive population of Pleuron vetus. II. vetus, a town of Ætolia, on Evenus fl., w. of Calydon, at the foot of Curium m. With a celebrated temple of Minerva; deserted by its inhabitants in consequence of the ravages of Demetrius II., of Macedon. Thestius, the grandfather of Helen, was king of this place. *Missolonghi.*

PLINTHINE, a maritime town of Marmarica, bet. Antiphra and Alexandria.

PLINTHINĒTIS sin., a bay of Marmarica, at Plinthine. *Bahr al Araba.*

PLISTARCLEA, a surname of one of the Heracleas, in Caria.

PLISTIA, a town of the Caudini, in Samnium, 4 m. from Saticula. *Presta.*

PLITANIÆ ins., two islets on the coast of Troas.

PLITENDUS, a town of Phrygia Epictetus, on Alander fl., bet. Midæum and Tricomia.

PLOTHEIA, a demus of Attica, of the tribe Ægeis.

PLOTINOPOLIS, a town of the Cælatæ, in Thrace, bet. Zerinca and Hadrianopolis. Built by Hadrian, and named in honour of his wife, Plotina. *Dijisr-Erkene.*

PLUBIUM, a port of Sardinia, s. of Phintonis ins. *Cala Angionela.*

PLUINA, a town of Lyncus, in Macedonia, near Octolaphus.

PLUMBARIA, I. penins. of Sardinia, i. q. Plumbea. II. an isl. of Tarraconensis, E. of Dianium prom. III. a town of Numidia, w.s.w. of Hippo Regius.

PLUMBEA (Molybodes) ins., "lead-producing," a penins. of Sardinia s.w., below Accipitrum ins. *Isola Sant'Antioco.*

PLUVIALIA ins., Aprositos, one of the Fortunatæ ins., Africæ. *Palma.*

PLYNOS, Marmaricæ, i. q. Panormus.

PNIEL (Pnuel, Peniel, "face of God"), a town of Gileaditis, on Jabbok fl., L., near Succoth. Here Jacob wrestled with the angel.

PNIX (Pnigeus), a pr. of Marmarica, s. of Portus Phœniceus. There was a town of the same name somewhat inland.

PNUPS, a town of Meroe, on the Nile, R., bet. Premnis and Boon. *Aarnara.*

POCRINIUM, a town of the Ædui, Lugdunensis I., bet. Telonnum N.E. and Sitilia.

PODALIA, a town of Lycia, towards Masycetes m.

PODANDUS, a town of Tyanitis, Cappadocia, bet. Cœna (12) and the Pylæ Ciliciæ (14), on a cognom. stream. *Podend.*

PODIUM (Anicium), a town of the Villavi, Galliæ. *Puy en Velay.*

PODOCA, a maritime town of India i. Gangem E., bet. Chaberis and Sabura.

PODOPERURA, a maritime town of India i. Gangem w., bet. Pseudostomus fl. and Bacari.

PŒCILASIUM, a town on the s. coast of Crete, bet. Tarrha and Hermæum prom.

PŒCILE mons., I. a m. of Attica, on the Via Sacra, near Gephyre. II. of Cilicia, near Coracesium.

PŒDICULI, descendants of the Osci, settled with the Peucetii, in Peucetia.

PŒDOPIDES fl., a r. of Bithynia, falling into the Euxine, w. of Sandaraca.

PŒESSA ins., an early name of Rhodes.

PŒMANENUS (Pœmanentus, Pomenion), a town of Mysia, s.E. of Cyzicus, under Lentiani collis. With a temple of Æsculapius. *Doulokcui.*

PŒMANI, a tribe of Tungri, Germania II., bet. the Mosa and the Sura fll.

PŒONIDÆ, a demus of Attica, of the tribe Leontis.

POGLA (Socla), a demus of Milyas, in Pisidia, s.w. of Cormasa.

POGON portus, the outer port of Trœzene, in Argolis, on a headland resembling a beard.

POLA, "exile," the capital of Histria, on the Adriatic, N. of Polaticum prom. Founded circa 1350 B.C. by the Pelasgi. Traditionally founded by the Argonauts. A colonia (Pietas Julia). *Pola.*

POLATICUM prom., the s.w. extremity of Histria, s. of Pola. *Punta di Promontore.*

POLATICUS sin., i. q. Flanaticus.

POLEMARTIUM, a town of Etruria, towards the Tiber, s.E. of Ferentinum. *Bomarzo.*

POLEMONIACUS reg., a district of Pontus, extending along the w. border of the kingdom of Polemo, the client of Augustus.

POLEMONIUM, i. q. Side, in Pontus.

POLENTIA, a town of Balearis Mag. ins., on the N. coast. *Pollenza.*

POLEURA, a town of the Arvarni, Ind., N.W. of Malanga.

POLI campus, a plain of Arcadia, N. of Tricoloni.

POLICHNA, I. a town of Crete, bet. Cydonia and Gortys. *Ipoli.* II. a town of Laconia, on the borders of Argolis.

POLICHNE, a town of Megaris.

POLICHUA, a town of Troas, s. of Ida m., w. of Scepsis.

POLIS, a town of Locris Ozol., in the territory of Hyæa.

POLISMA, Troad., i. q. Polium.

POLITIA, a town of Achaia.

POLITORIUM, a town of the Latini, Latium, near Lanuvium. Destroyed by Ancus Martius, who removed the inhabitants to Rome, assigning them Mons Aventinus for their residence.

POLIUM, I. a town of Lesbos ins., under Tantalus m. Sacred to Tantalus. II. (Polisma), a town of Troas, on Simois fl. An Astypalæan colony.

POLLENTIA, I. a town of Picenum, bet. Urbs Salvia and Treja. *Monte Melone.* II. of the Taurini, in Liguria, on Tanarus fl., at its confluence with Stura fl., bet. Augusta Taurinorum (35) and Alba Pompeia. A municipium. The locality of the defeat of Stilicho, by Alaric. Noted for its black wool. *Pollenzá.*

POLLITIUM, a town of the Marrucini, Ital., w. of Teate. *Sant'Agatopo.*

POLLUSCA (Pollustia), a town of the Volsci, s.w. of Lanuvium.

POLME fl., a sacred stream of Bruttium, falling into the Taurus fl., E. of Portus Orestis, q. v.

POLOSON, a village of Bœotia, near Delium. The birth-place of Atlas.

POLTYOBRIA, an early name of Ænos, in Thrace.

POLYANTHES fl., a r. of Illyria, rising in Acroceraunii m., and falling into Æas fl. at Nymphæum. *Sutchitza.*

POLYANUS m., Lingon, a branch of Pindus, N.W. of Tymphe. *Palæo-Vouni.*

POLYARA, a town of Caria.

POLYÆGOS ins., "many-goated," an isl. of the Ægean, one of the Sporades, bet. Cimolos and Pholegandros. *Polino.*

POLYBOTUS, a town of Phrygia Parorea, N. of Julia. *Bulwudun.*

POLYGIUM, Galliæ, i. q. Maritima Colonia.

POLYMEDIUM, a maritime fortress of Æolis Asiat., bet. Lectum prom. (5) and Assus (5).

POLYPHAGI, a people of Sarmatia, on the N.E. coast of the Euxine.

POLYTIMETUS fl., a r. of Sogdiana, rising in Sogdii m., and falling into Oxiana palus. *Soghda.*

POLYRRHENIA, a town of Crete, bet. Phalasarna (7½) and Rhamnus. *Priniaco.*

POMANUS fl., a r. of Gedrosia, falling into Indicum mare, bet. Cophas and Badara.

POMETIA, *vide* Suessa Pometia.

POMODIANA, a town of the Mœsi, Mœs., on the Danube, bet. Almus and Ciabrus.

POMONA, a town of Rhætia, bet. Ad Lunam (40) and Augusta Vindelicorum (12).

POMPEII, an Oscan town, on Cumanus sin., Campania, on Via Domitiana, bet. Oplonti (3) and Stabiæ (3). Traditionally founded by Hercules, on his return from Spain. A colonia and municipium. Finally destroyed by an eruption of Vesuvius, after several partial subversions. *Pompeii.*

POMPEIOPOLIS, I. a name of Solis, in Cilicia. II. a town of Paphlagonia, on Amnias fl., below Dadybra, 27 m. s.w. from Sinope. Founded by Pompey the Great. *Tash-Kupri.*

POMPELON (Pampelon), a town of the Vascones, Tarraconens., s.s.e. of Turissa. The name, which it might seem should rather be Pompeion, indicates in the Basque language "place or monument of Pompey." *Pampeluna.*

POMPONIANA, i. q. Mese, in Gaul.

POMPONIUS portus, a port of Narbonensis, near Alconis. *In Isle de Gien.*

POMPTINÆ PALUDES, marshes on the coast of the Volsci, at first confined to the vicinity of Suessa Pometia, or Pomtia, whence they derived their name, but gradually covering a large extent of country. They were successively drained, with more or less effect, by Cethegus, Augustus, Trajan, Nerva, and Cæcilius Decius. They were infamous as the haunt of banditti.

PONS ÆLII, a town of the Brigantes, Brit., on Vedra fl., w. of Segidunum. *Newcastle.*

PONS ÆRARIUS, a town of the Volcæ Arecomici, Narbonensis, bet. Nemausus N.W. and Arelate S.E.

PONS ALUTÆ (Alitti), a town of the Potulatenses, Dac., on Aluta fl., R., bet. Buridava (13) and Rusidava (12).

PONS ARGENTEUS, a town of the Oxybii, Narbonensis, on Argenteus fl., L., below Forum Voconii.

PONS AUFIDI, a town of the Hirpini, in Samnium, on Aufidus fl., L., bet. Sub Romula (17) and Venusia (19), on Via Appia. *Ponte Santa Venere.*

PONS AUGUSTI, Zeugma, a town of Dacia, bet. Agnava (8) and Zarmizegethusa (15). *Bonizar.*

PONS AUREOLI, a town of the Cenomanni, in Gallia Transp., on Addua fl., bet. Argentia (10) and Tollegata (12). Named from the defeat of Aureolus. *Pontiruolo.*

PONS CAMPANUS, a bridge over Savo fl., in Campania, on Via Appia, bet. Sinuessa (3) and Urbana (3). *S. Giovanni.*

PONS DRUSI, a town of the Isarci, in Rhæ-

tia, on Isarus fl., L., bet. Sublavium (13)
and Endidæ (11). *Botzen.*

PONS DUBIS, a town of the Sequani, Maxima
Sequanorum, on Dubis fl., R., bet. Crusinia and Cabillonum.

PONS LONGUS, a village of Daunia, in Apulia, below Arpi. *Ponte del Candelaro.*

PONS MANSUETUS, a town of Pannonia, 30 m.
from Tricciana. *Dombovar.*

PONS MOSÆ, a town of the Eburones, on
the Mosa, L., bet. Coriovallum and Aduatuca.

PONS NARTIÆ, a town of the Lucenses,
Tarraconensis, on Nartia fl., s.w. of Lucus
Augusti.

PONS NOVIA, a town of the Lucenses, Tarraconensis, on Nabia fl., 34 m. E. from
Lucus Augusti. *Navia de Suarna.*

PONS ŒNI, I. a town of the Launi, Vindelicia, on Œnus fl., above Carrhodunum.
Muhldorff. II. a town of Vindelicia, on
the Œnus, 20 m. from Isunisca. *Innspruck.*

PONS SARAVI, a town of the Mediomatrices,
Belgica I., on Saravus fl., bet. Decem
Pagi and Tres Tabernæ.

PONS SCALDIS, a town of the Nervii, Belgica II., on the Scaldis, L., above Turnacum.

PONS SECIES, a town of Gallia Cispad., on
Secies fl., L., bet. Regium Lepidum (13)
and Mutina (5), on Via Æmilia Lepida.
La Secchia.

PONS SERVILII (Claudanum), a town of the
Dassaretæ, in Illyria, on Drilon Niger fl.,
at the N.W. extremity of Lychnitis palus,
on the Egnatia Via, bet. Tres. Tabernæ
and Patræ.

PONS SOCIORUM, a town of Valeria, Pannon., bet. Jovia and Sopianæ.

PONS TRAJANI, a bridge erected by Apollo-
dorus Damascenus, under the auspices of
Trajan, over the Danube, bet. Tierna and
Ad Aquas, below Viminiacum, s. of Zarmizegethusa. It consisted of twenty piers
of hewn stone, 170 feet distant from each
other, the arches being 150 feet above the
foundation. The arches were removed by
Hadrian.

PONS USCAR, Pannoniæ, i. q. Ad Labores.

PONS VETUS, a village of the Burideenses,
Dac., on a river not named, bet. Stenarum
(44) and Prætorium (9).

PONTERIS, a town of Meroe, on the Nile,
R., 10 geog. m. N.E. from Abuncis.

PONTES, *prius* Zita, Pontezita, i. q. Tarichia.

PONTES RENSES, *rectius* Isareneses, a town
of Rhætia, on Isarus fl., E. of Serviodurum.

PONTIA ins., I. one of the Ænotrides ins. of
Lucania. *Ponza.* II. one of the Scopelites
ins., Cyrenaicæ. III. an isl. of Latium,
s.w. of Sinonia ins. Colonized by Rome
313 B.C. The death-place of Nero, son of
Germanicus. The exile-place of Caligula's
sisters. *Ponza.*

PONTICUM mare, i. q. Euxinus.

PONTINUS fl., I. a stream of Argolis, rising
in the cognominal m. II. m., a m. of
Argolis, towards Lerne. With a temple
of Minerva Saitis, and by it the tomb of
Hippomedon.

PONTIUM, Africæ, i. q. Thymiaterium.

PONTUS fl., a r. of the Sinti, in Macedonia,
rising in the mouth of the Agrianes, towards
Æstræum, and falling into Strymon fl.
near Heraclea Sintica. Remarkable for a
red pebble, which ignited when thrown
into other water, and sent forth a fetid
odour. *Stroumnitza.*

PONTUS (regio Pontica), at first a designation
of the coast of Asia, from Colchis to
Halys fl. Established as a kingdom by
Mithridates Ctistes (founder) 338 B.C.
Bounded N. by the Euxine, s. by Cappadocia and Armenia, at Moschici m., w. by
Paphlagonia (at Halys fl.) and Galatia, E.
by Colchis (at Acampsis fl., or, according
to Pliny, at Apsarus fl., or, according to
Strabo, at Trapezus) and Armenia (at
Paryadres, &c. m.). Principally settled
by Syrians (called from the lighter com-
plexion they acquired in their new seat,
Leuco-Syrians, "white Syrians") and Ar-
menians. Named from the Pontus Euxinus.

PONTUS EUXINUS (Cimmerium mare, Bo-
reale mare, Ponticum mare, Colchicum
mare, Caucasium mare, Sarmaticum mare).
Vide Euxinus.

PONTUS, Mæsiæ, *vide* Scythia Minor.

POPLETUM, a town of Numidia, bet. Thamugadis and Liviniana.

POPULI, a town of the Jassii, Pannon., bet.
Aqua Viva and Jovia-Bononia.

POPULONIUM (Pupluna), I. a pr. of Etruria,
at Populonium. *Capo di Campana.* II.
a town of Etruria, at the cognom. prom.
on Via Aurelia, bet. Aquæ Populoniæ (3)
and Aquæ Vetuloniæ. The naval arsenal
of the Etrusci. Noted for its metallic
works. *Porto Baratto.*

PORAS fl., i. q. Pyretos.

PORCIFERA (Procobera) fl., a r. of Liguria,
falling into Ligusticus sin., below Ad
Figlinas. *Polcevera.*

PORCIUS m., a hill of Latium, near Tusculum. Named from, or giving name to, the
Porcius family. *Monte Porzio.*

PORDOLOSENE (Porolesene) ins., chief of Hecatonnesi ins., Æolid. With a cognominal town. *Mosco.*

PORINAS, a village of Arcadia, on the frontier of Achaia, towards Pellene.

PORITUS fl., a r. of Sarmatia E., falling into Palus Mæotis, w. of Tanais. *Mius.*

POROLISSUM (Paralissum), a town of Dacia, on Mariscus fl., 4 m. E. from Cersie. *Micaz.*

POROS, a demus of Attica, of the tribe Acamantis.

PORPHYRION, a maritime town of Phœnicia, bet. Platana N. and Sidon.

PORPHYRIS, a name of Cythera ins., and of Nysirus ins., from the purple dye produced there.

PORPHYRITES m., m. of Thebais, on the coast of the Red sea, bet. Philotera and Nechesia. Noted for their porphyry. *Dgebel el Dokkan.*

PORSICA, a town of Osrhoene, Mesop., N.W. of Edessa.

PORSULÆ, Thraciæ, i. q. Maximianopolis.

PORTACRA, a town of Taurica Chersonesus, N. of Tazus, E. of Eupatoria. *Akmetschet.*

PORTHMION, a town of Taurica Chersonesus, N.W. of Parthenium.

PORTHMUS, "ferry," I. a port of Eubœa, on the w. coast opposite Rhamnus, s. of Dystus. *Bufalo.* II. a port of Sicily N., bet. Phalacrium prom. and Naulochus.

PORTICENSES, a maritime town of the Ilienses, in Sardinia, above Saralapis.

PORTIPA, a town of Persis Prop., bet. Nisacus and Persepolis.

PORTOSPANA, a town of the Camelobosci, Carmania, E. of Gabæ.

PORTUARI, a people of India i. Gangem, under Uxentus m. N.

PORTUS (In portu), a town of Etruria, on Arnus fl., below Arnus. *Empoli.*

PORTUS ACHIVORUM, a haven of Æolis Asiat., on Elæaticus sin., bet. Gryneum and Myrina. Here was an altar of the twelve gods.

PORTUS AGASUS, a port of Daunia, Apul., at Garganum prom. s. *Porto Greco.*

PORTUS ALBURNUS, a haven of Lucania, at the mouth of Silarus fl.

PORTUS ALBUS, I. the harbour of Carteja, Bætica. II. a port of Thebais, on the Red sea, bet. Philotera and Nechesia.

PORTUS ALTUS, a town of the Lazi, in Colchis, on the Euxine, N. of Apsarus.

PORTUS APOLLINIS PHÆSTII, the harbour of Phæstus, in Locris. *Porto Monasteraki.*

PORTUS AUGUSTI, the corn emporium of Rome, at the right mouth of Tiberis fl. Here was a celebrated light-house, constructed by Claudius, and repaired by Trajan. *Porto.*

PORTUS AUGUSTI, a town of the Vaccæi, Tarraconens., on Pisoraca fl. N.N.E. of Pallantia. *Torre Quemada? Los Valrases?*

PORTUS BRIVATES, a port of the Namnetes, Lugdunensis III., N. of Portus Namnetum.

PORTUS BRUNDULUS, a haven of Venetia, at the mouths of Athesis and Togisonus ffl. *Porto Brondolo.*

PORTUS CLASSIS, the s. port of Ravenna, in Gallia Cispad., at the mouth of Candianus fl., communicating with Padus fl. by a canal called Fossa Augusti, and with Ravenna by a causeway called Via Cæsaris. It was filled up by continuous deposits of soil from the river. The monastery now on its site is distant more than two miles from the sea. *Classe.*

PORTUS DELPHINI, a town of the Garuli, in Liguria, on Via Aurelia, bet. Genua (12) and Tegulia (21). *Porto Fino.*

PORTUS DEORUM, a port of Mauritania Cæsar., bet. Portus Magnus and Castrum Puerorum. *Sigalo.*

PORTUS DEON SOTERON, a port of Thebais, on the Red sea, bet. Thrissilides ins. and Portus Evangelion.

PORTUS EDRO, a port of Venetia, bet. Fossa and Meduacus Min.

PORTUS ERIDANUS (Vatrenus), a port constructed in the 4th century, as a substitute for Portus Classis, which was becoming filled up with sand and other deposit from Padus fl. It was hence the Emperor Claudian sailed on his mock triumph.

PORTUS EVANGELION, a port of Thebais, on the Red sea, bet. Portus Soteron and Ptolemais Theron.

PORTUS FALESIA, the harbour of Populonium, in Etruria. *Porto Falese.*

PORTUS HADRIANUS, Hadrianum, the port of Hadria, in Venetia, on Carbonaria Ost. *Ariano.*

PORTUS HANNIBALIS, a maritime town of the Cuneus, Lusitan., bet. Lacobriga w. and Ossonoba E.

PORTUS HERACLEA (Caccabaria, Porbaria), capital of the Camatullicini, Narbonensis, E. of Alconis.

PORTUS HERCULIS (Heraclea), the port of Alyzia, in Acarnania, opposite Leucas ins. Here was a grove sacred to Hercules, in which stood a group by Lysippus, " the

Labours of Hercules," transferred to Rome. *Porto Candili.*

PORTUS HERCULIS, a town of Bruttium, N. of Medma. *Le Formicole.*

PORTUS HERCULIS COSANUS, the harbour of Cosa, in Etruria. *Porto Ercole.*

PORTUS HERCULIS LIBURNI, *vel* Labronis (Liburnum), a port of Etruria, bet. Vada Volaterrana (18) and Pisæ (12), on Via Aurelia. *Livorno, Leghorn.*

PORTUS, *vel* ARX HERCULIS MONŒCI, a Greek town of the Vediantii, in Liguria, bet. Albintemelium and Avisio portus. Traditionally built by Hercules, who was especially worshipped here. *Monaco.*

PORTUS GARNÆ, a port of Daunia, Apul., E. of Uria.

PORTUS INFERIOR, a port of the Morini, Belgica II., s.w. of Itius portus.

PORTUS LACYDON, a haven of Narbonensis II., s. of Massilia.

PORTUS LEMANUS (Lemanianus), a port of the Cantii s., bet. Dubræ and Portus Novus. *Lymne.*

PORTUS LUNÆ, the port of Luna, in Liguria, 5 m. s. of Portus Veneris. *Spezzia.*

PORTUS MAGNUS, a bay of the Mediterranean, in Bætica and Tarraconensis, bet. Murgis w. and Charidemi prom. E. *Golfo d'Almeria.*

PORTUS MAGNUS, a port of Mauritania Cæsar., on Laturus sin. w. of Quiza (11). A colonia. *Marsel Kibir.*

PORTUS MAURITII, a maritime town of the Intemelii, in Liguria, at the mouth of Lucus fl., R., bet. Lucus Bormanni and Costa Balæna. *Porto Maurisio?*

PORTUS NAMNETUM, a port of the Namnetes, Lugdunensis III., at the mouth of the Liger.

PORTUS NOVUS, a port of the Regni, bet. Lemanis portus L. and Othona portus.

PORTUS ORESTIS, a haven of Bruttium, s. of Metaurus fl. Named from Orestes, who, having landed here, was purified from his mother's blood, in seven streams falling E. of N. into Metaurus fl., 8 m. from its mouth. *Porto Ravagloso?*

PORTUS OXYBIORUM, the town of the Oxybii, Narbonensis, bet. Ad Horrea and Forum Julii.

PORTUS PARTHENIUS, a town of Bruttium, in Terinæus sin., s. of Laus fl. *Cirella.*

PORTUS PISANUS, the port of Pisæ, in Etruria, at the mouth of Arnus fl.

PORTUS POMPONIANIS, a port of the Commoni, Narbonensis II., E. of Telo Martius.

PORTUS ROMATINUS, a port of the Veneti,

in Venetia, at the mouth of Romatinus fl. *Porto Lemetino.*

PORTUS ROSCIA, a port of Bruttium, belonging to Thurii, s. of Lasias fl.

PORTUS SCABRIS, a port of Etruria, bet. Alma fl. and Salebra. *Scarlino.*

PORTUS SUPERIOR, a port of the Morini, Belgica II., N.E. of Itius portus.

PORTUS SYMBOLORUM, a port of Taurica Chersonesus s.

PORTUS TESSENII, a town of the Licates, Vindel., on a lake not named, formed by Ambra fl., E.N.E. of Abodiacum.

PORTUS TITIANUS, a port of Corsica, s. of Rhium prom. *Porto Tiziano.*

PORTUS TRAJANUS, a port built by Trajan, on a prom. of Etruria, over against Portus Longus, in Æthalia, s.w. of Alma fl. *Torre di Troja.*

PORTUS VATRENUS, a name of Portus Eridanus, in Gallia Cisalp., from Vatrenus fl.

PORTUS VELINUS, the port of Velia, Lucaniæ, at the mouth of Heles fl.

PORTUS VENERIS, a maritime town of the Apuani, in Liguria, bet. Segesta Tiguliorum (30) and Luna (5). *Porto Venere.*

PORTUS VENERIS, *vide* Myos-Hormus.

PORTUS VICTRIX (Victoriæ), the port of Juliobriga, Tarraconensis, on Cantabricum mare. *Santonna.*

PORTUS ZAO, a port of the Commoni, Narbonensis, s. of Massilia.

POSA, a town of the Japydes, in Illyria.

POSIDARION prom., a pr. of Lycia, 4 m. from Crambusa.

POSIDEA, a town of Æolis Asiatica.

POSIDIUM (Neptunium) prom., I. a pr. of Arabia Felix, bet. Palindromos prom. and Cabubathra prom. II. of Bithynia, on the Euxine, 12½ m. N.E. from Heraclea. *Tschantsche-Aggisi.* III. of Caria, s.w. of Miletus, over against Leros ins. *C. Arbora.* IV. of Cestrine, in Epirus, opposite the N.E. extremity of Corcyra ins. *Coperta.* V. of Chios ins., over against Argennum prom. in Ionia. *C. Catomeria, or Masticio.* VI. of Cilicia Trachea, E. of Arsinoe. *C. Kizilman.* VII. (Enipeum), of Lucania, at the s. entrance of Pæstanus sin. *Punta di Licosa.* VIII. *vel* Therambium, a headland of Pallene, in Macedonia, on the Thermaicus sin., s. of Cassandræa. *C. Cassandra.* IX. a headland of Phthiotis, in Thessaly, over against Æantium prom., at the w. entrance of Pagasæus sin. *Cape Stauro.* X. a pr. of Samos, N.E. of Samos oppid. Here was a temple of Neptune. XI. a town of Carpathus ins., at Ephialtium prom. XII. a town of Syria, near Heraclea N. *Poseda.*

POSIDONIA, Lucaniæ, *vide* Pæstum.

POSIDONIATES (Pæstanus) sin., a gulf of Inferum mare, at Pæstum, extending from Minervæ prom. to Posidium prom. *G. di Salerno.*

POSIDONIUM, I. a pr. of Bithynia, the N. entrance of Cianus sin., the termination of Arganthonius m. *Bozburun.* II. a temple of Neptune, in Bruttium, near Columna Rhegina. A town by degrees grew around it.

POSIRION, a town of Marmarica, on the coast, bet. Plinthine (1) and Cheimo.

POSTIGIA, a town of Taurica Chersonesus.

POTACHIDÆ (Botachidæ), a town of Arcadia, near Tegea.

POTAMI, a maritime town of Paphlagonia, 8 m. E. from Stephane.

POTAMIA regio, a district of Paphlagonia, at its S.W. angle.

POTAMONION, a village of Bithynia, on Bosporus Thracius, N. of Nicopolis.

POTAMOS, a demus of Attica, of the tribe Leontis, on the Ægean, N. of Thoricus. *Potamoi.*

POTAMOSACON fl., a r. of Æolis Asiat., with a cognominal island.

POTENTIA (Flosis) fl., I. a r. of Picenum, falling into the sea at Potentia. *Potenza.* II. a city of Lucania, towards the source of Casuentus fl., E. of Volceja. *Potenza.* III. a town of Picenum, at the mouth of Potentia fl., bet. Numana (10) and Castellum Firmanorum (12), on Via Flaminia. A colonia 186 B.C. *Abb. of S. Maria Potenza.*

POTHEREUS (Theron) fl., a r. of Crete, bet. Gortys and Gnossus.

POTIDANIA, a town of the Apodoti, in Ætolia, on the confines of Locris Ozol., N.W. of Œneon. *Clima.*

POTIDÆA, *postea* Cassandria, a city of Chalcidice, on the isthmus connecting Pallene with the mainland. Founded by the Corinthians; and afterwards recolonized from Athens.

POTNÆUM, a fortress of Athamania, in Ætolia, on the frontier of Thessaly, N. of Athenæum.

POTNIÆ (Hypothebæ), a town of Bœotia, 1¼ m. S.W. from Thebes. With a grove consecrated to Ceres and Proserpine. The scene of Glaucus' fate. In ruins in the time of Pausanias. *Taki.*

POTNIUS fons, a stream of Bœotia, at Potniæ.

POTOMIA CEPORA, a town of Bithynia, 32 m. from Manoris. *Bayandir.*

POTULATENSES, a people of Dacia, about Aluta fl., N. of the Saldenses.

PRACA, a town of Cilicia Campestris, near Seleucia.

PRACTIUS fl., a r. of Mysia, rising in Ida m., and falling into the Hellespont below Lampsacus, 37 m. w. from Parium. The ancient boundary (N.) of Troas. *Bergan.*

PRÆDAVENSES, a people of Dacia, on the Tibiscus, S. of the Anarti.

PRÆNESTE (Polustephane), a town of the Latini, in Latium, on Via Latina, bet. Gabii (11) and Anagnia (24). A settlement from Alba, traditionally founded by Prænestus, grandson of Ulysses, B.C. 1500; or, according to others, by Cæculus, son Vulcan. A colonia and municipium. The death-place of the younger Marius; the birth-place of Ælian, the naturalist. Noted for its walnuts. Here was a temple of Fortune, whence was taken the celebrated Barberini pavement. *Palestrina.*

PRÆNETUS (Pronetios, Pronectus), a town of Bithynia, on Propontis, 28 m. N.E. from Nicæa. A Phœnician colony. *Debrende.*

PRÆPELISSUS, a town of Phrygia Epictetus, near Alydda.

PRÆPENISSUS (Propniasa), a town of Galatia.

PRÆSIDIUM, I. a fortress of Syrtica regio, on Zuchis lacus E. II. of the Turtetani, Bætica, on the Anas, towards its mouth.

PRÆSIDIUM POMPEII, a fortress of the Triballi, Mœsia, on Margus fl., bet. Cametas and Graniriana.

PRÆSIDIUM TIBERII, a fortress of the Isarci, Rhæt., on Athesis fl., above its confluence with Isarus fl.

PRÆTORIUM, I. a town of the Albocenses, Dac., bet. Fontes Herculis and Ad Pannonias (9). *Cornia.* II. of the Burideenses, Dac., bet. Pons Vetus (9) and Arutela (13). III. (Præsidium), of the Coritani, Brit., bet. Ad Abum and Lindum. IV. of the Psylli, in Africa Prop., on Syrtis Maj., s. bet. Ad Ficum and Astiagi. V. of the Varciani, Pannon., bet. Siscia and Servitium (33). *Neustadel.* VI. of the Lemovices, Aquitania I., bet. Augustoritum s.w. and Acitodunum N.E.

PRÆTORIUM LAVERIANUM, a town of Daunia, in Apulia, bet. Arpi and Lucerea (8). *Laconicello.*

PRÆTORIUM LATOVICORUM, a fortress of the Latovici, Pannon., on Savus fl., bet. Emona (34) and Noviodunum (31).

PRÆTUTIA, the country of the Prætutii, in Picenum. Noted for its fertility, and peculiarly for its wines. The name, corrupted in later ages to Aprutia, Aprutium, and this again to Abruzzium, indicates the modern district of which it forms a part.

PRÆTUTII, a people of uncertain origin, occupying the portion of Picenum, bet. Batinus fl. and Matrinus fl., N. of the Vestini.

PRAMNUS m., a hill of Icarus ins. Noted for its wine.

PRAS, I. a hill of Phthiotis, in Thessaly, S.E. of Pharsalus, on which Agesilaus erected a trophy of his victory at Narthakion. II. a town of Phthiotis, in Thessaly, on the cognominal m. near Narthakion.

PRASIACA regio, a district of Central India, on both sides the Ganges.

PRASIÆ, I. a demus of Attica, of the tribe Pandionis, on the Ægean, N. of Potamos. Here was the monument of Eresychthon. *Prassa.* II. (Brasiæ), a town of the Eleuthero Lacones, in Laconia, on Argolicus sin., 25 m. N. from Cyphanta. With temples of Æsculapius and Achilles, and with annual games in honour of the latter. *S. Rheontas.*

PRÆSIMARII, a people on the coast of Tarraconensis, about Tamaris fl.

PRASIAS palus, a lake of Doberæa, in Pæonia, near Doberus, the inhabitants of which lived in huts raised on lofty piles in the centre of the lake, and fed their horses and cattle on fish, with which the place abounded. Near it was a rich silver-mine. *Lake Doiran.*

PRASMON, a village of the Tectosages, in Galatia, bet. Cenaxe palus (13) and Minizus (10).

PRASODIS sin., a bay of Indicum mare, at Jovis prom., Taprob.

PRASSÆBI, a people of Epirus.

PRASUM prom., a pr. of Africa, on Indicus oceanus, s. of Rhaptum prom. *Cabo del Gardo.*

PRASUS (Præsus, Prosis), a town of Crete, on Catarrhactes fl., 17½ m. E. from Gortys, 7½ from the sea. Founded by Eteocrates. Destroyed by the Hierapytnians. Here swine were sacrificed at weddings.

PRECIANI (Pitani, Pitiani, Prociani, Laciani), a people of Aquitania.

PREMNIS, i. q. Premis.

PREMUTHIS, a town of the Nubæ, on the Nile, bet. Pistra and Aboccis. *Kait.*

PRENDAVESTI, a people of Dacia.

PREPESINTHUS ins., an isl. of the Ægean, one of the Cyclades, bet. Cimolus ins. and Olearus ins. *Spotiko.*

PRIAMON (Promona), a town of the Dalmatæ, in Illyria, near Issa ins.

PRIANSUS, a town of Crete, near Hierapytna.

PRIAPIDIS portus, a harbour of Taprobane w., at Sindocanda.

PRIAPONESUS ins., an isl. of Caria, in Ceramicus sin.

PRIAPUS, I. an islet of Ionia, towards the mouth of Caystrus fl. II. a port of Mysia, within the s. entrance of Propontis, opposite Ophiusa ins. A colony from Miletus. Named after the god Priapus, especially venerated here. Noted for its fine wines. *Karaboa.*

PRIATICUS campus, Thrac., i. q. Ciconia.

PRIENE (Cadme), one of the twelve cities of Ionia, under Mycale m. on Gæson palus, bet. Magnesia and Miletus. A Carian city. Founded by Æpytus, son of Neleus; enlarged by the Theban Philotas. The birth-place of the sage Bias. It at one time stood on the sea-shore, but in Strabo's time had been removed 5 m. from it, by the deposits of the Mæander. Here was a famous temple of Minerva. *Samsoun.*

PRILE (Prelius) lac., a lake of Etruria, on the coast, s.w. of Rusellæ, formed by Prile fl., bet. Cosa (22) and Salebro (12). *Lago Castiglione.*

PRIMIS MAGNA (Premnis), a town of Meroe, on the Nile, R., bet. Arbadura and Meroe, at the point where the peninsula of Meroe begins. Sacred to Papremis (Mars).

PHIMIS PARVA, a town of Meroe, on the Nile, R., bet. Ponteris and Arabis. *Ibreem.*

PRIMOPOLIS, Pamphyliæ, i. q. Aspendus.

PRINASSUS, a town of Caria.

PRINCASTELLA, a town of Gallia Belgica, on Mosella fl., bet. Cardena and Noviomagus.

PRINOESSA ins., an isl. of Acarnania, towards Achaia. *Nodieri.*

PRINUS saltus, a defile in Artemisium m., bet. Mantinea and Argos.

PRION, "saw," I. a r. of Arabia Felix, falling into Erythræum mare E. of Methath. II. a m. of Ionia, overlooking Ephesus s.

PRIONOTUS, "serrated," a pr. of Arabia Felix, E. of the mouth of Prion fl. *Ras Brum.*

PRISCA TABERNA, a maritime village of Cyrenaica, N. of Boreum prom.

PRIVERNUM, I. a town of the Vestini, in Picenum, bet. Pitinum (12) and Aveia (7). *Asserge.* II. a city of the Volsci, or rather of a separate tribe of Latins (Privernates), on Ufens fl., s.E. of Setia. Memorable for its resolute assertion of independence. The birth-place of Virgil's Camilla. A præfectura and military colonia. *Piperno Vecchio.*

PROANA, a town of the Malienses Paralii, in Thessaly, E. of Echinus, near Pteleum.

PROBALINTHUS, a demus of Attica, of the tribe Pandionis, under Brilessus m., bet. Tricorythus and Œnoe. In ruins in Pliny's time.

PROBATIA fl., a r. of Bœotia, losing itself in Pelecania regio.

PROCERASTES, the early name of Calchedon, in Bithynia.

PROCHYTA ins., an isl. of Campania, bet. Misenum prom. and Ænaria ins., from which latter it is supposed to have been rent; whence the name. *Procida.*

PROCLE, a town of Lydia.

PROCOLITIA, a town of the Otadeni, Brit., on Hadriani murus N., bet. Cilurnum and Borcovicus. *Carraw-burgh.*

PROCONNESUS ins., I. an isl. of Mysia, in Propontis, opposite the mouth of Æsepus fl. Noted for its white and black marble. *Mamara.* II. capital of the cognominal isl. The birth-place of the poet Aristias. Burned by Darius.

PROCURI, a port of Taprobane, N. bet. Rizala and Mordula.

PROENE ins., an isl. of Rhodes.

PROERNA, a town of Phthiotis, in Thessaly, bet. Thaumaci and Pharsalus.

PROFUNDUS portus, a haven of the Troglodytæ, Æthiop., N. of Bathys portus.

PROGASIA, a town of Lydia. Named from Progasus, son of Melampus.

PROLAQUEUM, a town of Umbria, on a small lake, not named, bet. Dubii (8) and Septempeda (15), on Via Flaminia. *Piovaco.*

PROMONTORIUM MAGNUM, a pr. of Mauritania Cæsar., N.W. of Siga.

PROMONTORIUM SACRUM, the w. extremity of Achillei Cursus.

PRON m., a m. of Argolis. With a temple of Juno (Hermione), and one of Ceres, built by Clymenes, son of Phoroneus, an inviolable sanctuary.

PRONASTÆ, a people of Bœotia.

PRONESUS (Pröni), a town of Cephallenia ins., on the S.E. coast, over against Chelonites prom., in Elis. Named after Promnesus, son of Cephalus.

PROPHTASIA, capital of the Zarangi, Drangiana, on Etymandrus fl. *Zarend.*

PROFONTIS, "before the sea," the inland sea leading from the Ægean to the Euxine, by two straits, the Hellespont w. and the Bosporus E. In length 120 m., in extreme breadth 40. *Sea of Marmara.*

PROPUS m., a m. of Arcadia, near Olygyrtus m.

PROSCHIUM, a town of Ætolia, on Corinthiacus sin., w. of Chalcis. Founded by the people of Pylene. *Kurtaga.*

PROSÆA, a town of Arcadia.

PROSILEMMENITÆ, a name given by Ptolemy to the southern population of Galatia.

PROSOPITIS ins., an isl. of Lower Egypt, off the Canopic mouth of the Nile, s.

PROSPALTA, a demus of Attica, of the tribe Acamantis, near Zoster prom. With temples of Ceres and Proserpine. *Palæo Spata.*

PROSTAMA, a town of Pisidia, E. of Baris.

PROSTROPÆA, AD TROPÆA, a town of Bruttium, on Hipponiates sin., w. of Hipponium. *Tropea.*

PROSYMNA, a town of Argolis, bet. Phlius and Nauplia. With a temple of Juno.

PROTE ins., I. an isl. of Bithynia, in Bosphorus Thracius, over against Calchedon. *Prote.* II. of Messenia, in Ionium mare, over against Erana. *Prodano.* III. one of the Stœchades ins., Narbonensis, s. of Olbia.

PROTONACRA, a town of Bithynia, bet. Nicæa and Dadastana.

PROTOPACHIUM, a fortress of Paphlagonia, under Scorobas m.

PRUSA AD OLYMPUM, a city of Bithynia, at the foot of Olympus m., on Odrysses fl., bet. Apollonia and Modra. Built by Prusias, on the recommendation of Hannibal. Noted for its warm baths. *Broussa.*

PRUSIANUM, *postea* Bresium, a town of the Volcæ Arecomici, on Vardo fl. *Bresis.*

PRUSIAS AD HYPIUM, a town of Bithynia, on Hypius fl., between its source and Daphnusis pal. Founded by Prusias. *Uskub.*

PRUSIAS AD MARE, *vide* Cius, Bithyniæ.

PRYMNESIA (Prymnessus), a town of Phrygia Mag., on Bathys fl., bet. Doryleum and Docimia. *Afiom Carahissar.*

PRYTANIS (Pordanis) fl., a r. of Pontus, falling into the Euxine at Limne.

PSACUM prom., a pr. of Crete, at the E. entrance of Myrtilus sin. On its summit was a temple of Britomartis Dictynna. *C. Spada.*

PSAMATHE fons, a fountain of Argolis.

PSAMATHUS, Laconiæ, i. q. Amathus.

PSAPHIS, a demus of Attica, of the tribe Æantis, S.E. of Oropos.

PSAPOS (Psadius) fl., a r. of Dandarica, Sarmat., falling into Atticitus fl. above Tyrambe.

PSELCIS (Pselchis, Pselcha), a town of Dodechaschœnus, on the Nile, L., bet. Tutzis and Premnis. *Dakkeh.*

PSESSII, a people of Sarmatia A., on Vardanes fl., L., below the Agoritæ.

PSEUDOCELIS, a port of Arabia Felix, bet. Musa (8) and Ocelis (6). *Near Mocha.*

PSEUDO CORASIUM, Cilic., i. q. Pulchrum Coracesium.

PSEUDO ostium, a mouth of the Danube, bet. Pulchrum ost. and Boreum ost.

PSEUDOPENIAS prom., a pr. of Cyrenaica, at Berenice.

PSEUDOSTOMUS fl., a r. of India i. Gangem, falling into Indicum mare bet. Muziris and Podoperura.

PSILE ins., an isl. of Ionia, in Hermius sin., opposite Clazomenæ.

PSILIS (Psillus, Phyllis), I. a r. of Bithynia, falling into the Euxine at Psillis. II. a port of Bithynia, on the Euxine, at the mouth of Psilis fl., 18 m. E. from Artanes.

PSILON, I. the N. mouth of the Danube, forming an island at its issue. II. an islet of Ionia, off Trogilium prom.

PSIMADÆ, a town of Isauria.

PSITARAS fl., a r. of Serica, falling into Eous oceanus.

PSOPHIS, *prius* Erymanthus and Phegea, I. a town of Arcadia, on Erymanthus fl., E. of Eupagium, Elis. With temples of Erymanthus and Venus Eracina, and the tomb of Alcmæon. *Tripotamia.* II. the citadel of Zacynthus opp. Named after Psophis, in Arcadia.

PSYCHIUM, a town on the s. coast of Crete, w. of Metallum.

PSYCHRUS fl., a r. of the Toreatæ, Sarmat., falling into the Euxine bet. Toricus portus and Achæa.

PSYLLA, a port of Bithynia, on the Euxine, 4 m. E. from Crenides.

PSYLLI (Seli), a people of Africa Prop., on the s. coast of Syrtis Major, bet. the Macæ and the Nasamones, by the latter of whom they were extirpated. According to Herodotus, however, they were overwhelmed by sand from the desert. They had the faculty of charming serpents.

PSYRA ins., an isl. of Chios, over against Melæna prom. (6¼ m.). In circuit 5 m. *Psara.*

PSYTTALEIA ins., an isl. of Attica, off Piræus. Sacred to Pan. *Lipsocontalia.*

PTANDARIS, i. q. Tanadaris.

PTANIAS, a town of Umbria, 7 m. from Helvillum. *Near Gualdo.*

PTELEA, I. a demus of Attica, of the tribe Æneis. II. an early name of Ephesus.

PTELEUM, I. a town of Dardania, Mysia, on a cognominal lake, near Ophrynium. II. a fortress of Ionia, N. of Erythræ. III. a town of Messenia. A colony from Pteleum, Thess. Extinct in Strabo's time. IV. of Phthiotis, Thessaly, near the w. entrance of Pagasæus sin., 14 m. s. of Alos. Destroyed by the consul Licinius. *Pteleo.*

PTERIA, a town of the Trocmi, Galatia, s.E. of Tavium.

PTERON prom., a pr. of Mœsia Inf., s. of Biecrum ost.

PTEROS ins., an isl. of Arabia Felix, off Hammæum littus, N.E.

PTEROTONE, a town of the Vacomagi, Brit., on Tuæsis fl., R.

PTOLEDERMA, a town of Arcadia, near Eutresium.

PTOLEMAIS, I. a port of the Colobi, on the Red sea, above Sabæ, E. of Meroe. Surnamed Iberon, Epitheras Ferarum, from the wild beasts chased in its vicinity. Famous in connexion with the astronomical calculations of Eratosthenes, Marinus, and Ptolemy. *Near Mirza Bombarrik.* II. (Augæ), a maritime town of Pamphylia, 6¼ m. s.E. of Leucotheum prom. III. one of the chief towns of Pentapolis Cyrenaica, bet. Arsinoe and Ausigda, N.W. of Barce, of which city it was the port. According to Strabo, its own early name would seem to have been Barce. *Tolemata.* IV. Phœniciæ, i. q. Acco. V. *surnamed* Hermii, a city of Thebais, on the Nile, L., bet. Crocodilopolis and Thinitis, above Panopolis. *Mensieh.* VI. the port of Arsinoe Crocodilopolis, on the Nile, bet. Iseum and Cœne.

PTOLIS, a village of Arcadia, N. of Mantinea. One of the hamlets which contributed to the aggrandisement of that city. *Palæopoli.*

PTOSON, a town of Melitene, Cappadocia.

PTOUS m., a m. of Bœotia, s. of Anchoe. With an oracle of Apollo, which ceased to operate after the taking of Thebes. *Ptoo.*

PTYCHIA ins., an isl. of Corcyra, bet. Corcyra opp. and Buthrotum. *San Vito.*

PUCINUM, a maritime town of Istria, bet. Timavus fl. and Tergeste. Noted for its wines, to the use of which Julia Augusta attributed her long life. *Pucino Vecchio.*

PUDAPATANA, a maritime town of India i. Gangem, w., above Comaria prom.

PUDNU, a town of the Cassanitæ, Arabia, on the Red sea, bet. Adedu and Aelu.

PULCHER portus, Tauricæ Cherson., i. q. Calos limen.

PULCHERIANOPOLIS, a town of Phrygia. Named after the empress Pulcheria.

PULCHRUM, I. prom., Zeugitan., i. q. Apollonium. II. ostium, a mouth of the Danube, N. of Naracon ost.

PULCHRUM CORACESIUM portus, a port of Cilicia Trachea, w. of Corycus, 9 m. E. from Pœcile.

PULERUS, a town of Amphaxitis, in Macedonia.

PULINDA, a district of India i. Gangem, N. of Barygazenus m.

PULLARIÆ ins., three islets of Histria, off Pola (N.W.). *Brioni, Conversana, and San Nicolo.*

PULLOPIX, a maritime town of the Ingauni, in Liguria, on Via Aurelia, bet. Albingaunum (15) and Vada Sabata (12). *Finale.*

PUMENTUM, a town of Bruttium, on Neæthus fl., R., towards Chone. Founded by Philoctetes. *Cerenza.*

PUNICUM, I. i. q. Panapis. II. a town of the Triballi, Mœs., on the Danube, bet. Lederata and Cuppa.

PUPLUNA, the Etruscan name of Populonium.

PUPULUM, a maritime town of Sardinia, w., over against Sulcis. *Massacara.*

PURA (Parsis, Persis), the capital of Gedrosia, of uncertain position, but assigned by Arrian to the R. bank of Arbis fl. More probably inland, s.e. of Rhagæa.

PURATA, a town of the Soræ, Ind., on Chaberis fl., R., below Tennagora.

PURGUM, a town of Noricum, 5 m. from Faviana. *Burgk.*

PURPURARIÆ ins., isl. of Africa, in the Atlantic, N. of Fortunatæ ins. Named from the purple-manufactories established there by Juba. *Madeira, &c.*

PUTEA, a town of Syrtica regio, bet. Tumalleni turres and Ad Templum, s.e. of Zuchis.

PUTEA NIGRA, a town of the Psylli, in Africa Prop., on Syrtis Maj., bet. Astiagi and Euphranta.

PUTEA PALLENE, a maritime town of Syrtica reg., bet. Zuchis and Zitha.

PUTEOLANUS sin., an inlet of Cumanus sin., bet. Puteoli and Mysenum prom.

PUTEOLI, " wells" (Dicæarchia), the E. port of Cumæ, in Campania, on Cumanus sin., 3 m. s.e. from Cumæ. A settlement of Samians. A col. of Nero. It was named Puteoli about the period of Hannibal, from the sulphureous exhalations about it. *Pozzuoli.*

PUTEUS, a village of Gætulia, on Tritonis palus, bet. Mahatanzar and Aggersel.

PUTPUT (Pupput), a town of Zeugitana, on Neapolitanus sin., bet. Neapolis and Orasse. *Hamamet ?*

PYCNUS fl., a r. of Crete.

PYDES, a town of Pisidia.

PYDNA, I. Lyciæ, i. q. Cydna. II. a town of Pieria, in Macedonia, on the Leucus fl., at its junction with the Æson fl., bet. Dium (20) and Methone (5). Noted for the definitive victory of Paulus Æmilius over the Macedonians under Perseus. *Kitros.*

PYGELA, "piles" (Phygela, "flight"), a town of Ionia, on the coast, bet. Ephesus and Neapolis. Built by some deserters from Agamemnon, 1186 B.C. Noted for its wine. Here was a temple of Diana Munychia.

PYLÆ, I. a town of Arcadia. II. of Ancobaritis, Mes., on the Euphrates, bet. Tzamiesopolis and Ozogarda.

PYLÆ SARMATICÆ, a defile of Caucasus, bet. the Sanari and the Diduni.

PYLÆ SYRIÆ, a defile of Cilicia Campestris, in Amanus m., bet. Alexandria ad Issum and Antiochia.

PYLÆMENIA, a name of Paphlagonia.

PYLENE, a town of Ætolia, on the Corinthiacus sin., s.w. of Chalcis, the inhabitants of which removed to Proschium.

PYLLEUM, a town of Thessaly.

PYLON, a fortress of the Dassaretæ, in Illyria, on the borders of Macedonia, bet. Scirtiana (4) and Nicia (11).

PYLORA ins., an isl. of Carmania, in Persicus sin., w. of Asaborum prom.

PYLORUS, a town of Crete.

PYLOS, I. a town of Epea, in Elis, 10 m. E. from the capital, 12 m. from Olympia, at the foot of Pholoe m., towards the source of Peneus fl. Founded by Pylus of Megara. *Portes.* II. of Triphylia, in Elis, on Amathus fl., 3⅜ m. from its mouth, s.w. of Macistus. The royal city of Nestor. *Piskini.* III. of Messenia, at the foot of Ægialeus m., s.w. The earlier portion founded by Pylus, son of Æeson ; the later portion, built by Demosthenes the Athenian, stood on Coryphasium prom. *Pyla, and Old Navarino.*

PYRA, the spot in Maliensis in Thessaly, on Œta m., on Dyras fl., where Hercules lay down on the funeral pyre.

PYRÆ, a Greek town of the Ausones, in Latium, on the coast bet. Formiæ and Minturnæ.

PYRÆA lacus, a sacred grove of Achaia, on Asopus fl., near Titane, in which were a grove and temple of the Furies.

PYRAMA, Ciciliæ, i. q. Pirina.

PYRAMUS, I. fl., a r. of Cilicia Campestris, rising in Catαonia, near Cucusus, and, after forcing a passage through Taurus m., falling into Issicus sin., formerly near Mallus, but now 23 m. further E. ; a change effected by the enormous quantities of mud carried down by its strong and rapid current. *Gihoon.* II. a village of Cilicia Campestris, above Serrepolis.

PYRANTHUS, a village of Crete, near Gortys.

PYRASUS, the harbour of Thebæ Phthiotica, 2½ m. from the city, on Pagasæus sin. In ruins in Strabo's time.

PYREA, a district of Thessaly.

PYRENÆA, a town of Locris.

PYRENÆI m., m. of Europe, separating Gallia from Hispania, and in various ridges intersecting the northern portion of the latter country; in total extent 294 m. *The Pyrenees.*

PYRENÆUS (Aphrodisium) portus, a port of the Indigetes, Tarraconensis, within Aphrodisium prom.

PYRETUS fl., Poras, i. q. Parata.

PYRGENSES, a people of Achaia.

PYRGI, I. a maritime town of Etruria, on Via Aurelia, bet. Ad Turres (12) and Castrum Novum (8). A Pelasgic settlement. Noted for its luxury. The port of Cære. A colonia. Here was a temple of Lucina, plundered by Dionysius of Syracuse 386 B.C. *Santa Severa.* II. (Pyrgos), a town of Triphylia in Elis, at the mouth of Neda fl. *Bouzi.*

PYRGITÆ, a name of the Cretans.

PYRGUM prom., a pr. of Celtica, Lusitania, N. of Sacrum prom.

PYRGUS EUPHRANTA, a maritime town of Syrtis Reg., bet. Macodama w. and Aræ Philænorum E.

PYRINTHUS, a town of Caria.

PYRNUS, a maritime town of Peræa, in Caria, E. of Pisilis.

PYRONÆA, a town of the Locri Opuntii.

PYRRHA, I. an isl. of Caria. II. a pr. of Æolis Asiat., at the S. entrance of Adramyttenus sin., over against Gargara prom. (15). With a temple of Venus. *Karatape-bouroun; C. San Nicolo.* III. a headland of Phthiotis, in Thessaly, E. of Pyrasus. *Ankistri.* IV. a town of Caria, on Laconicus sin., S.E. of Miletus. *Sarikomer.* V. (Pirias), of Eubœa. Named after Pyrrha, wife of Deucalion. VI. of Lesbos, at the head of Euripus, 10 m. N.W. from Mitylene. *Caloni.* VII. an early name of Thessaly, after Pyrrha, wife of Deucalion.

PYRRHI CASTRA, Lacon., i. q. Xarax.

PYRRHICUS, a town of Laconia, N.W. of Teuthrone. With a temple of Diana Astrateia, and Apollo Amazonius; whence Achilles sailed to marry Hermione. Here Silenus was educated. *Pirrhichina.*

PYRRON, a district of Mauritania Ting., bet. Diur m. and Phocra m.

PYSTUS, a town of Caria.

PYTHANGELON portus, a port of Æthiopia, towards Avalites sin. Noted for its elephant-hunts.

PYTHECA, a fortress of Bithynia, at one of the passes of Olympus m.

PYTHIS prom., a pr. of Libya Ægypti, at Paraetonium.

PYTHIUM, I. a town of Pelagonia Tripolis,

in Thessaly, N.E. of Dodona. Named after a celebrated temple here of Apollo. II. i. q. Pythopolis, of Bithynia.

PYTHO, the early name of Delphi.

PYTHOPOLIS, I. the early name of Antiochia ad Mæandrum. II. (Pythium), a town of Bithynia, on Ascanius lac., N., 15 m. E. from Cius. Remarkable for springs which failed in winter and overflowed in summer. Built by Theseus.

PYTNA m., I. a summit of Ida Asiat., towards Scepsis. Named from the Cretan Pytna. II. an early name of Hierapytna, in Crete.

PYXAS, a village of Cos, sacred to Apollo.

PYXIRATES fl., a r. of Armenia Int., rising in Scordisci m., E. of Theodosiopolis, and falling into the Euphrates above Dascusa. According to Pliny, a name of the Euphrates; while Strabo says the Euphrates rises in Caranitis towards its source.

PYXITES fl., a r. of Pontus, falling into the Euxine at Marthyla.

PYXUS prom., I. a pr. of Lucania, s. of Melphes fl. *Capo degli Infreschi.* II. (Puxoes), the Greek name of Buxentum opp., and of Buxentus fl., in Lucania.

Q.

QUADI, a people of Germania Magna, bounded E. by Sarmatia, at Granua fl., N. by the Lygii, at Asciburgius m., s. by the Danube, and w. by the Marcomanni.

QUADIATII, a people of Alpes Maritimæ. *In Vallée de Queyras.*

QUADRATA (Quadratum), I. a town of the Boii, Pannon., bet. Ad Flexum and Stailucum. II. of the Colapini, Pannon., on Colapis fl., L., bet. Noviodunum and Romula castrum (4). *Voinich.* III. of Gallia Cisalpina, on the Padus, at the confluence of the Ticinus.

QUADRIATES, a tribe of Caturiges, Alpes Maritimæ, N.W. of Vesulus m. *About Forcalquier.*

QUADRIBURGIUM, a town of the Gugerni, Germ. II., on the Rhine, bet. Noviomagus and Burginatium.

QUARTEUSLOCUS, a town of the Nervii, Belgica II., bet. Bagacum N.N.W. and Duronum s.

QUATUORSIGNANI, an appellation of the Tarbelli, from the four cohorts stationed among them.

QUERCUS (Ad Quercum), a town of Rhætia, on Plavis fl., below Belunum. *Quer.*

QUERQUANI, the people of Quercus, in Rhætia.

QUERQUETULANI, an early people of Latium.

QUINDA, a town of Cilicia, N. of Anchiale.

QUINTANA (Quintiana) castra, a town of Rhætia, on the Danube. *Osterhoven.*

QUINTANÆ, Latium, i. q. Ad Quintanas.

QUINTIANA, a maritime town of Etruria, on Via Aurelia, bet. Martanum (3) and Villa Regis (3).

QUINTILIANA, a maritime town of Tripolis, Afr., bet. Ad Palmam and Minna.

QUINTODEMUS, a town of the Ciagisi, Dac., on the Danube, E. of Aluta fl.

QUIZA, *surnamed* Xenitana, a town of Mauritania on Laturus sin., S., bet. Arsinaria and Portus Magnus. *Oran.*

R.

RAABENI, a people of Arabia Deserta, on the confines of Arabia Felix.

RAAMAH, Arabia Felix, i. q. Machorbæ. A seat of Raamah, son of Cush.

RABANA, a town of the Ambastæ, at the mouth of Lanos fl.

RABANÆI, a people of Serica, E. of Annibi m.

RABBATH AMMON, Philadelphia, capital of Ammonitis, near the source of Arnon fl. Restored and renamed by Ptolemy Philadelphus. *Amman; Rabba.*

RABBATH MOAB (Ar, Areopolis), capital of Moabitis, near Arnon fl., N. of Kir-Moab. Nearly destroyed by an earthquake in the time of St. Jerome. *Rabba.*

RABDIUM, a town of Mesopotamia, towards the Tigris. *Tur-rabden.*

RACHÆ, a town of Sittacene, Assyr., near Ctesiphon.

RADIS (Ratis) ins., an isl. of Aquitania, N. of Uliarus. *Ré.*

RAEBLÆ, a town of Hibernia, 12 geog. m. w. of Eblana. *Enniskillen.*

RAEMSES (Rameses), a fortress and granary of Egypt, 40 m. w. of Arsinoe-Heroopolitana. *Aben-Keyshed.*

RAGÆ (Ragan, Europus), capital of Media-Ragiana, bet. Bithia and Charax, 6 m. N.W. of Caspiæ Pylæ.

RAGÆA, a town of Parthia-Arcticene, N. of Nios. *Raghan?*

RAGIA, a town of Arabia, E. of Chiriphe.

RAGIANE (Raga), a district of Media Magna, bet. Jasonius m. and Caspius m., N.W. of Choarene.

RAGONDO, a town of the Ambilici, Pannonia, bet. Celeja (18) and Petavio (18). *Windischferstritz.*

RĂHĂBA (Rabbath, Rehoboth, "great"), a town of Arabia, on the Euphrates, bet. Zaita and Auzara, 10 m. below the confluence of the Chaboras. There appears to have been a city of the same name higher up. *Mesjia.*

RAMA, "eminence," a town of Benjamin, in Judæa, 6 m. N. from Jerusalem. The locality of the story of the Levite and his concubine. The birth-place of Saul. *Er-râm.*

RAMATHAIM-ZOPHIM, a town in the land of Zuph. The birth and burial-place of Samuel.

RAMBACIA, Gedrosiæ, i. q. Ora.

RAME, a town of Alpes Cottiæ, bet. Brigantium (19) and Ebrodunum (17). *Casse-Rom.*

RAMI, a people of Sarmatia, on the Mæotis palus.

RAMIDAVA, a town of the Cotenses, Dac., on Ararus fl., S.W. of Jassiorum municipium.

RAMISBA, a town of the Jassii, Pannon., on Dravus fl., 18 m. E. from Petovium. *Sauritsch.*

RAMOTH-GILEAD (Ramoth Mispeh, "watchtower"), capital of Gileaditis, on Jabbok fl., N.W. of Rabbath Ammon (15). A city of refuge.

RANARIA ins., one of the Fortunatæ ins., Africæ.

RANDAMORCOTTA, a district of Serica, on Lanos fl., L., N. of Chalcitis regio.

RAPÆ, a town of Rhætia, bet. Navoæ (23) and Aug. Vindelicorum (18). *Schwab-munchen.*

RAPHANEA, a town of Syria, w. of Epiphaniā, 33 m. from Apamea. *Rafaniat.*

RAPHIA, a maritime town of Judæa, bet. Jenysus, N.E., and Rhinocura. The locality of the battle between Antiochus the Great and Ptolemy IV.

RAPIDI, a village of Mauritania Cæsar., bet. Trinadi and Auzia.

RAPINIUM (Rapio), a maritime town of Etruria, on Via Aurelia, bet. Algæ (3) and Graviscæ (3). *Torre Ortando.*

RAPTA (Rhapta), capital of Azania, Libyæ, on the coast, at Raptum prom.

RAPTUM prom., a pr. of Azania, on Barbarum sin., S. of Paralai ins. *Cape Formoso.*

RARAPIA, a town of the Celtici, Lusitania, w. of Pax Julia. *Ferreira.*

RARASSA, a town of the Chatriæi, Ind., s. of Gagasmira.

RARIUS campus, a portion of the Thriasius campus, in Attica, near Eleusis, where corn was first sown by Triptolemus, and where were his threshing-floor, his altar, and temple.

RASENA, the name given by Dionysius Halicarn. to the Pelasgi Tyrrheni, a corruption of Tyrseni (Tyraseni).

RATACENSES, a tribe of Agathyrsi, in Dacia, on Carpathus m., n.w. of the Cotenses.

RATÆ, a town of the Coritani, Brit., bet. Veromelum and Venonæ (12). *Leicester.*

RATES, a maritime town of the Cantii, Brit., n., bet. Durobrivæ and Regulbium.

RATIARIA (Rætiaria), a town of the Mœsi, Mœs. Sup., on the Danube, bet. Ad Malum and Remetodia. *Arzea-Palanca.*

RATIATUM, a town of the Pictones, Aquitania II., on the Liger. *St. Pierre et St. Opportune de Retz.*

RATOMAGUS, i. q. Augustomagus.

RATTA, a town of Mesene Inf., Babyl., w. of Diridotis.

RAUDA, a town of the Vaccæi, Tarraconensis, on Durius fl., 26 m. w. from Clunia. *Roa.*

RAUDII campi, plains of Gallia Transpadana, 10 m. n.w. of Milan. The locality of the defeat of the Cimbri by Marius, 100 B.C. *About Rho.*

RAUGONIA, a town of Siracene, Armen., on the Araxes, at the junction of the Harpasus. *Erevandaschat.*

RAUMATHI VICUS, a town of the Banizomenes, Arab., on the Red sea, bet. Leucecome and Charamuthas. *Mher.*

RAUNONIA ins., i. q. Abalus.

RAURACI, a people of Maxima Sequanorum, on the Rhine, bet. the Tribocci and the Helvetii. *About Bâle.*

RAURANUM, a town of the Pictones, Aquitania II., bet. Limonum n.n.e. and Brigiosum s.w. *Raum.*

RAURARIS fl., i. q. Arauris.

RAVENNA, a city of the Lingones, in Gallia Cispadana, on Utis fl., near its mouth, bet. Padunum and Ariminum, on Via Flaminia. Founded by the Thessalian Tyrrheni Pelasgi, and subsequently occupied by the Umbri, and again by the Tyrrheni Etrusci. It was built at first upon piles, among a number of small marshy islets, close to the shore ; but afterwards, by the encroachment of the land upon the sea, brought gradually three miles inland (the communication between the houses being by boats and bridges). It was so healthy, that the gladiators were trained there. A col. of Pompeius Strabo, and the chief naval station of Rome on the Adriatic. Under the eastern empire it was the seat of an exarchate. *Ravenna.*

RAVIUS, I. a r. of Hibernia, the issue of Ravius lacus, N. of Libneus fl., separating the Erdini from the Venicnii, 5 geog. m. from Magnata. II. lacus, a lake of the Erdini, Hibernia. *Loch Ern.*

RAX ins., an isl. of Lycia.

REATE, a town of Sabinium, on Velinus fl., bet. Vicus Novus (16) and Cutiliæ (8), on Via Salaria. The first settlement of the Arcades Pelasgi. Named from Rhea. A municipium. Noted for its fine mules and asses, some of which were sold for between 400*l.* and 500*l.* *Rieti.*

RECHEM, a name of Petra, in Arabia.

RĔDONES (Rhĕdones), a people of Lugdunensis, N.E. of the Veneti. *Departments of Ille and Villaine.*

REDUNA ins., an isl. of Lugdunensis II., N.E. of Sarnia ins.

REFUGIUM CHALE, a haven of Sicily, 18 m. E. from Plintæ.

REFUGIUM APOLLINE, a haven of Sicily, 20 m. E. from Plaga Herea. *Spaccafurno.*

REGAMA, Arabiæ, i. q. Machorbæ.

REGEMNEZUS, Galat., i. q. Minizus.

REGESALAMARA, a town of Pamphylia.

REGETA, a later name of Forum Appii.

REGIA, I. a town of Hibernia, on Argita fl. *Armagh.* II. *surnamed* Altera, a town of Hibernia, N.E. of Juvernis, on Bubinda fl., R. *Limerick.*

REGIÆ, a town of Mauritania Cæsar., on Cartenna fl., bet. Thaisacora and Ad Dracones.

REGIANA, a town of the Turtuli, Bætica, bet. Curgia s.w. and Arsa N.E.

REGIANUM (Forum Augusti, Augusta), a town of the Mœsi, Mœs. Inf., on the Danube, bet. Camistrum and Variana, 18 m. E. from Ciabrus.

REGIAS, a town of Syria.

REGIATES, the early name of the Velejates.

REGILLUM (Regilli), a town of Sabinium, near Eretum. The birth-place of Appius Claudius (Atta Clausus), the founder of the Claudian family.

REGILLUS lacus, a lake of Latium, bet. Labicum and Gabii. *Laghetto della Colonna.*

REGINEA, a town of the Osismii, Lugdunensis III., s.w. of Cosedia.

REGINUM (Regina Castra, *prius* Artobriga, *postea* Radaspona), a town of Germania

Mag., on the Danube, below Artobriga, opposite the confluence of Reginus fl. The station of the Ala Secunda Valeria. *Ratisbon; Regensburg.*

REGINUS (Campus) fl., a r. of German. Mag., falling into the Danube at Reginum. *Regen.*

REGIO STRATA, a district of Syria, s. of Palmyra.

REGIO ATTENE, a peninsula of Arabia, on Persicus sin., N.E. of Gerra. *Khalt.*

REGIUM, surnamed Lepidum, prius Forum Lepidi, a town of Gallia Cispad., bet. Ta- netium (10) and Pons Secies (13), on Via Æmil. Lepida. Founded by M. Æmilius Lepidus. The death-place of the Elder Brutus. *Reggio.*

REGIUM, a town of the Odrysæ, in Thrace, on the Propontis, s.w. of Byzantium.

REGNI, a people of Britannia I., bet. the Thames, the Atrebatii, and the Belgæ N., the Durotriges w., the Cantii E., and the sea s. *Surrey, Sussex, and part of Hants.*

REGNUM, capital of the Regni, towards the coast. *Chichester.*

REGULBIUM, a maritime town of the Cantii, Brit., N., bet. Rates and Cantium prom. *Reculver.*

REHOB (Beth-rehob), a town of Asher, N. of Cæsarea Philippi.

REII APOLLINARES, the later capital of the Albiœci, Narbonensis, N.E. of Griselum. A colonia. *Riez.*

REMESSIANA (Remisiana, Romausiana), a town of the Triballi, Mœs., bet. Ulmus and Latina, S.E. of Naissus. *Piri?*

REMETODIA, a town of the Mœsi, Mœs. Sup., on the Danube, bet. Ratiaria (20) and Almus.

REMI (Rhemi), a people of Belgica II., bet. the Veromandui and Tungri, N., the Sues- siones and Tricasses w., the Lingones s., and the Treveri and Leuci E. *In Bel- gium.*

REPANDUNUM, a town of the Cornavii, Brit. Rom., bet. Margidunum and Etocetum.

REPHAIM, "valley of the giants," a valley of Judæa, bet. Bethlehem and Jerusalem. Famous in the history of David.

REPHIDIM (Meribah), a station of the Israel- ites, on the Red sea, near Mount Sinai. The locality of the miraculous supply of water, and of the defeat of Amalek by Joshua.

RERIGONIUM (Retegonium), a maritime town of the Novantæ, Brit., N., on Reri- gonius sin. *Strathnaver.*

RERIGONIUS sin., a bay of Clota Æstuar., at Rerigonium. *Loch Rain.*

RESAPHA (Reseph), postea Sergiopolis, a town of Chalybonitis, Syriæ, S.E. of Bar- balissus, 20 m. w. from the Euphrates. *El Ressafa.*

RESPA, a town of Peucetia, bet. Aufidus fl. (23) and Barium (13), on Via Frentana. *Molfeta.*

RESPUBLICA RURADENSIS, a town of the Oretani, Tarraconensis, E.N.E. of Castulo.

RESSAINA (Ressania), "head of the spring," Callirrhoe, a town of Gauzonitis, Mes., at the principal source of Chaboras fl., 27 m. s. of Masius m., bet. Nisibis, 50½ geogr. m., and Carrhæ, 48 geogr. m. The lo- cality of the defeat of Sapor by Gordian. It was named by Theodosius, Theodosio- polis. *Ras al Ain.*

RETINA, a villa at Misenum, in Campania, where Pliny the Elder received the first intelligence of the great eruption of Vesu- vius.

RETOVINUM, a town of Gallia Cisalpina, in Albana regio. The mart of the Lana Re- tovina. *Retovino; Rebbio.*

REUNIA, a town of the Carni, in Venetia, on Tilavemptus fl. *Rean.*

REVESSIO (Ruesium), a town of the Vellavi, Aquitania I., bet. Condate w. and Icid- magus E. *St. Paulien.*

RHA fl., a r. of Asia, which, after separating Sarmatia A. from Scythia, falls into the Caspian by numerous mouths. On its banks grew the plant rhabarbarum, cog- nate with the rhubarb, which derives its name from it. *Wolga; Rama.*

RHABA fl., I. i. q. Arrabo. II. (Sargelia, Gilfil), a r. of Dacia, falling into the Danube. *Syl.*

RHABANA REGIA, a town of Arabia Felix, W.N.W. of Ophir. *Gabrin.*

RHABANITÆ, i. q. Rhamanitæ.

RHACATÆ, a tribe of Quadi, S.E., on the Danube, and on Granua fl.

RHACOTIS, the early name of Alexandria, in Egypt.

RHADAMÆI, a people of Arabia Felix, E. of Labris. *Beni Maddar.*

RHACELUS m., m. intersecting Chalcidice, in Macedonia, from w. to E.

RHÆTEUM prom., a pr. of Mysia, separating Dardania from Troas.

RHÆTI, a tribe of Tyrrhenians, driven by the Gaulish invasion of Italy to the Alps, called, from their leader Rhætius, Alpes Rhætiæ, and extending some distance N. of those mountains bet. the Helvetii and Vindelicii. They were subdued by Drusus and Tiberius Nero.

RHÆTIA, a country of Europe, bounded N. by Germania Mag., at the Danube, s. by

Gallia Cisalpina, at the Alps, w. by Gallia, at the Rhine, E. by Noricum, at Œnus fl. It was formed by Dioclesian into two provinces, Rhætia Propria, and Vindelicia. *Tyrol and E. Switzerland.*

RHÆTIUS m., m. on the w. coast of Corsica, about Urcinium. *Monte Rosso.*

RHÆXUS, a port of Cilicia Campestris, at the mouth of Sarus fl.

RHAGA, a town of Pentapolis Cyrenaicæ, N.E. of Ptolemais.

RHAGIANA, a town of Arachosia, N. of Chodda.

RHAMÆ, a town of the Odrysæ, in Thrace, on Harpessus fl., bet. Castra Zarba and Burdextium.

RHAMANITÆ (Manaritæ, Anariti), I. a people of Arabia Felix, on Persicus sin., w.N.W. of Naumachæorum prom. II. of Arabia Felix, towards Arabicus sin., s. of the Elisari.

RHAMMÆ, a people of Gedrosia, w. of Arbitius m., above the Oritæ and Arbitæ.

RHAMNÆ, a people of India i. Gangem, about Namadus fl., towards its source.

RHAMNUS, I. a demus of Attica, of the tribe Æantis, on the Ægean, 8 m. N. of Marathon. Here was a temple of Nemesis, in which was the statue of the goddess by Phidias. Named from the plant rhamnus. The birth-place of the orator Antipho. *Vræo Castro.* II. a town on the w. coast of Crete, bet. Chersonesus and Inachorium. *Stomio.*

RHANIUS, a town of Crete, N.E. of Hierapytna. *Roucaca.*

RHAPSES, a people of Persis Prop., E. of the Messabatæ.

RHATHINI, a people of Arabia Felix, N.W. of the Homeritæ. *Beni Jerha.*

RHATOSTATHIBIUS fl., a r. of the Silures, falling into Sabrina Æstuar., w. of Isca Silurum. *Tav.*

RHAUNATI, a port of Arabia Felix, on Arabicus sin., s. *Hank-Krue.*

RHAUSÆ, a people of Tenesis, in Æthiopia, s.w. of Avalites.

RHEBAS (Rhesus) fl., a r. of Bithynia, falling into the Euxine, 12½ m. from Estia prom. *Ruva.*

RHEDA, a town of Arabia Felix. *Rodda.*

RHEDINTUINUM, a town of the Batini, Germ., on Albis fl., L., N.E. of Marobudum.

RHEGINUM prom., a pr. of Bruttium, at Rhegium. According to Thucydides, the nearest point to Sicily. *Capo Pittaro.*

RHEGIUM, *prius* Recion, a city of Bruttium, on Siculum Fretum, at Rhegium prom., bet. Scyllæum (13) and Leucopetra, on

Via Aquilia. An Auruncian town, enlarged by Zanclean, Chalcidian, and Messenian col. 700 B.C. Traditionally named from the earthquake that separated Sicily from the continent. Destroyed by Dionysius; restored by Dionysius the Younger, and called by him Phætra. A col. of Augustus, as Colonia Julia. The birth-place of the historians Theagines, Hyppis, Butera, Glaucus; of the poet Ibycus; of Pythagoras the statuary, &c. *Reggio.*

RHEGMA lac., I. a salt lake or bay of the Mediterranean, formerly at the mouth of Cydnus fl., in Cilicia. Now a marsh, 7 m. from the sea. II. a town of Arabia Felix, on Persicus sin., s. of Solis prom., E. of Gerrha.

RHEIMIA, a town of Trachonitis, N.W. of Canatha.

RHEITHRON portus, a haven of Ithaca ins., N. of Phorcys portus. *Bathy.*

RHEITI, salt springs or ponds of Attica, on the w. coast of Attica, near Thria. Sacred to Ceres and Proserpine.

RHEITUM prom., a headland of Corinthia, on Saronicus sin., w. of Bucephalus.

RHENUS fl., I. a r. of Europe, rising in Adula m., on the confines of Gaul, towards the source of the Rhone, and, after separating Gaul from Rhætia and Germania Magna, falling into Germanicus oc. by three mouths (Helium ostium s., Flevus fl. N., and Rhenus Prop.), below Manaritium. *Rhine.* II. (Rigonus, *surnamed* Bononiensis), of Gallia Cispadan., falling into Vatrenus fl. below its junction with Lavinius fl. Noted for its reeds, which were much used for arrows. In an island of this river, 2 m. w. of Bononia (hence called Triumvirorum insula), occurred the meeting of the Second Triumvirate, 45 B.C. *Reno.*

RHESCIPHA, a town of Tingene, Mes., on the Euphrates, bet. Phatusa and Thilutha. *Elersi.*

RHESUS fl., a r. of Troas, falling into Granicus fl.

RHETICO m., a range of mountains in Germania Magna, extending E.S.E. from the Rhine, over against Bonna. *Rothhaargebirge.*

RHEUCA (Celadussa, Artemis) ins., an isl. of the Ægean, ½ m. w. from Delos, to which Polycrates is said to have fastened it with a chain. The burial-place of the Delians. *Sdili.*

RHEUCALANI (Rheucacalci), a people of Sarmatia E., above the Chuni.

RHEUDIGNI, a maritime tribe of Vindili, Germ., bet. the Viruni w. and the Sideni E.

RHEUPUS, a village of Arcadia, N.W. of Orchomenus.

RHIBII, a people of Scythia i. Imaum, bet. the Oxus and the Jaxartes.

RHIDAGUS fl., a r. of Parthia, falling into Zioberis fl.

RHINNEA ins., an isl. of Arabia Felix, in Persicus sin., 5 m. E.N.E. from Isara ins. Remarkable for several stone columns, with inscriptions in some unknown characters.

RHINOCORURA (Rhinocularia), "mutilated-noses," a town of Palestine, on the confines of Egypt, 26 m. E. from Ostracine. A place of exile for criminals, their noses having been previously slit. *El Areesh.*

RHIPE, a town of Arcadia, near the junction of Ladon fl. with Alpheus fl. Extinct in Strabo's time.

RHIPHÆI (Hyperborei) m., m. of Europe and Asia, of uncertain identification.

RHIS fl., i. q. Phasis.

RHITEÆ, a town of Arcadia, at the junction of Alpheus and Gortynius ffl.

RHITTIUM (Ricti), a town of Pannonia, on the Danube, bet. Cusum and Burgena. *Ratza ?*

RHIUM, I. a pr. of Achaia, *surnamed* Achaicum, over against Anti-Rhium, in Ætolia. *Castle of the Morea.* II. of Corsica, w., above Paula. *C. di Feno.* III. a town of Messenia, on Thuriates sin.

RHIUSIAVA, a town of Germania Mag., on Hadriani vallum, N. of Losodica.

RHIZIUS, a r. of Pontus, falling into the Euxine bet. Athenæ and Archabis fl. II. (Bechireus) portus, a town of the Bechires, in Pontus, at the mouth of Rhizius fl. Enlarged by Justinian. *Rizieh.*

RHIZON, I. a r. of the Dalmatæ, in Illyria, falling into Rhizonicus sin. II. (Rhizinium), a town of the Dalmatæ in Illyria, S.E. of Epidaurus, on the N. shore of Rhizonicus sin. *Risano.*

RHIZONICUS sin., a bay of the Adriatic, at Rhizon, Dalmat. *Bocca di Cattaro.*

RHIZUS, a town of Magnesia, in Thessaly, on the E. coast, bet. Eurymenæ and Meliboea. *Pesi.*

RHOBOSCI, a people of Scythia i. Imaum, N. of Conadipsas regio.

RHODA (Rhodanusia), I. an early name, according to some writers, of Arelate. Walcknaer identifies it, however, with Aigues-Mortes. II. (Rhodope), a maritime town of the Indigetes, Tarraconensis, bet. Aphrodisium prom. N. and Clodianus fl. s.w. A Massilian and Rhodian colony. *Rosas.*

RHODĂNUS fl., a r. of Gaul, rising in Adula m., and falling into the Mediterranean, by several mouths, below Arelate. *Rhone.*

RHODANUSIA, a town of the Salyes, Narbonensis, on Massiliense Ostium Rhodani, L., near its issue.

RHODE fl., i. q. Sagaris.

RHODIA (Rhodiopolis), a town of Lycia, towards Massicytes m.

RHODIUS fl., I. a r. of Troas, rising in Ida m. II. of Mysia, falling into the Hellespont below Abydos, over against Cynossema, in Thrace. *Scultanie; river of the Dardanelles.*

RHODOMERUS, a village of Bithynia, near Heracleum.

RHODOPE m., a s.E. continuation of Scomius m., commencing in the N.W. angle of Thrace, and traversing the centre of Thrace far beyond the Hebrus fl. Sacred to Mars, said to have been born amidst them. *Despoto Dagh.*

RHODOPOLIS, a town of Colchis, towards Archæopolis.

RHODUNTIA, a fortress of Maliensis, in Thessaly, on Œta m.

RHODUS, I. *prius* Ophiussa, Telchinis, an isl. of Caria, in the Mediterranean, off Cynossenia prom. (9). In circuit 125 m. Settled by Telchines, Phœnicians, and afterwards by Æolian Pelasgi, under Tlepolemus, son of Hercules. Sacred to the sun, and fabulously peopled by the Heliadæ, children of Apollo by the nymph Rhoda. The Rhodians excelled in war as darters and stringers. II. its capital, at the N. extremity. Built by Hippodamus of Miletus. Celebrated for its Colossus, one of the seven wonders of the world, cast in bronze by Chares of Lindus. The birth-place of Panætius, Stratocles, Andronicus, Eudemus, Hieronymus, &c.

RHODUSSA, I. an islet of Bithynia, one of the Demonisi group. II. (Rhopusa), an isl. of Caria, bet. Caunus (13) and Samos (12). *Limosa; Karagash.* III. a town of Argolis.

RHOE, a port of Bithynia, on the Euxine, 3 m. E. from Calpe.

RHŒTACES fl., a r. of Albania, falling into the Cyrus.

RHŒTĒUM, I. a prom. of Troas, N. of Rhœteum. *Cape St. Ghelmes.* II. a town of Troas, 7½ m. from Sigæum. *Et-Ghelme.*

RHOGMI (Rhegmi), a port of Cilicia.

RHOGONIS (Rogomannis) fl., a r. of Persis falling into Persicus sin. N. of Granis fl.

RHOMBITES MAJOR fl., a r. of Sarmatia A., falling into the Palus Mæotis, s. of Tanais (100). *Jea; Jei.*

RHOMBITES MINOR fl., a r. of Sarmatia A.,

falling into the Palus Mæotis, s. of Rhombites Maj. (100). *Iselbasch.*

RHOPE (Rhoge) ins., an isl. of Lycia, 6 m. w. from Megistus. *Is. San Giorgio.*

RHOPEI, a people of Pamphylia.

RHOSPHODUSA ins., an isl. of Sarmatia, in Carcinites sin. *Terlagon.*

RHŌSUS, a town of Seleucia, Syriæ, on Issicus sin., 15 m. s. from Seleucia. Noted for its earthenware. *Arsus.*

RHOTANUS fl., a r. of Corsica, falling into the sea N. of Alista. *Tavignano.*

RHOZICUS SCOPULUS, a prom. of Cilicia Campestris, on the confine of Syria; the s. termination of Issicus sin., and of Amanus m. *C. Hynzir.*

RHUANA, a town of Arabia Felix, in the desert, s. of Gerrha.

RHUBON fl., a r. of Sarmatia Europæa, falling into Sarmaticus oc. *Duna.*

RHUCANTII, a tribe of Rhæti, noted for their predatory habits.

RHUDIÆ (Ad Quindecim), a Greek town of Peucetia, in Apulia, on Via Egnatina, bet. Canusium (15) and Rubi (10). *Andria.*

RHUGII, a people of Germania Magna, on Borealis oceanus.

RHUGIUM, capital of the Rhugii, Germania, near the E. mouth of Viadrus fl. *Stettin.*

RHUS, "rushing water," a village of Megaris, near Megara. *Palaio-Kondoura.*

RHUTICLII, a tribe of Rugii, Germania.

RHYMMI, a people of Scythia, on Rhymmus fl., under Rhymmici m.

RHYMMICI montes, m. of Scythia, towards the coast of the Caspian.

RHYMMUS fl., a r. of Scythia, falling into the Caspian, E. of the Rha. *Cjasuri.*

RHYMOZOLI, a people of Sarmatia Asiatica, on Mæotis palus.

RHYNCUS, a town of Acarnania, near Stratus.

RHYNDACUS, I. a r. of Asia Minor, rising in Azanitis reg., and, after passing through Apolloniatis palus, falling into Propontis, on the confines of Mysia and Bithynia, opposite Besbicus ins. *Lubad.* II. a town of Mysia, on the confines of Bithynia, at the mouth of the cognominal river, where was the tomb of Briareus.

RHYPÆ, one of the twelve cities of Achaia, on Meganitas fl., 4 m. s.w. from Ægium. The birth-place of Myscellus of Crotona. In ruins in Pausanias' time. *Patræ.*

RHYPARA ins., an isl. of Samos, towards Ampelus prom.

RHYTIUM, a town of Crete, near Gortys, whence the inhabitants were driven by noxious insects.

RIBLAH, a town of Syria, on the Orontes, 30 m. s. from Hamath (Epiphania). The abode of Nebuchadnezzar during the siege of Jerusalem.

RICCIACUM, a town of the Treveri, Belgica I., bet. Augusta Treverorum N.E. and Corenusca s.w.

RICINA, I. an isl. of Britannia Barbara, w., below Ebudæ ins. II. a maritime town of the Garuli, in Liguria, on Via Aurelia, bet. Genua (7) and Ad Solaria (15). *Recco.* III. (Helvia Ricina), a town of Picenum, on Flosis fl., L., bet. Urbs Salvia (12) and Auximum (14). A col. of Severus. *Near Macerata.*

RICINUM, a town of the Carni, in Venetia, on Tergestinus sin., bet. Fons Timavi and Tergeste. Noted for its fine, wholesome wine. *Castel Duino.*

RICONIUM, a town of Lycaonia.

RIDUNA ins., an isl. of Gaul, N.E. of Sarnia. *Alderney; Aurigny.*

RIGÆ, a town of the Celtiberi, Tarraconensis, on Salo fl., L., s.E. of Numantia.

RIGODULUM, *postea* Regiodola, a town of the Treveri, Belgica I., on the Mosella, R., bet. Ad Decimum and Augusta Treverorum. *Reol.*

RIGODUNUM (Coccium), a town of the Setantii, Brit., on Belisama fl., R., towards its mouth. *Ribchester.*

RIGOMAGUM, a town of Germania, on the Rhine, s. of Bonna. *Rimagen.*

RIGOMAGUS, a town of the Taurini, in Liguria, bet. Cestiæ (8) and Ad Medias (10). *Rinco.*

RIMMON (En-remmon), I. a town, first of Juda, and then of Simeon, Judæa, N.N.E. of Beerseba. II. of Zebulun. A Levitical city.

RIOBE, a town of the Senones, Lugdunensis IV., bet. Calagum N.N.E. and Agenticum s.E.

RIPA, a town of the Turtuli, Bætica, on the Bætis, L., above Ebora.

RIPEPORA, a town of the Oretani, Tarraconensis, s. of Arcilacis.

RISARDIR portus, Libyæ, i. q. Mysocoras.

RISINA, a town of Osrhoene, on the Euphrates, w. of Edessa.

RITHYMNA, a town on the N. coast of Crete, N.E. of Eleuthernæ. *Retimo.*

RITTIUM (Rictium), a town of Rhætia, 8 m. s. of Acimincum. *Banonze.*

RITUBIUM (Litubium), a town of the Ananes, in Liguria, s. of Tria. Noted for its wool. *Retorbio.*

RITUMAGUS, a town of the Veliocasses, Lugdunensis II., bet. Ritomagus w. and Petromantalum E.

Rivus, a town of Venetia, near Ateste.

Rizala, a port of Taprobane, N., bet. Oxia prom. and Procuri.

Rizenia, a town of Crete, w. of Prasus.

Roana (Ragan), a town of the Parni Marg., s. of Nisæa.

Robogdii, a people occupying the N.E. angle of Hibernia.

Robogdium prom., a pr. of Hibernia, 8 geogr. m. from Argita fl. *Fair Head.*

Robororia, a town of the Hernici, in Latium, on Via Latina, bet. Ad X. (6) and Ad Pictas (7). *Molara.*

Roborētum, a town of the Bracari, Tarraconensis, on Durius fl., below Acontia. *On Mt. Rovoredo.*

Roborrum prom., a pr. of Numidia, N. of Hippo Regius.

Robrica, a town of the Andecavi, Lugdunensis III., bet. Juliomagus w.n.w. and Cæsarodunum e.

Robur, a town of Germania Mag., on the Rhine, below Augusta Rauracorum. Built by Valentinian. *Eichen.*

Rodium, a town of the Ambiani, Belgica II., bet. Setucis N.W. and Noviomagus S.E.

Rodumna, à town of the Segusiani, in Gaul. *Roanne.*

Rogandini, a people of Taprobane, on the s. coast.

Roidonna, a town of the Aulerci Brannovices, Lugdunensis I., bet. Ariolica N. and Mediolanum S.E.

Roma, the capital of Italy. A Siculian city, enlarged by the Arcadian (Tyrrhenian) Evander, 1240 B.C. Further enlarged by Romus or Romulus, a Latin chief, who expelled the Tyrrhenians circa 790 B.C. Taken by the Gauls 387 B.C.; by the Visigoths, A.D. 411 ; by the Vandals, 455 ; by the Heruli, 476 ; by the Goths, 547. It was *surnamed* Septicollis from its seven hills : Aventinus, Capitolinus, Cœlius, Esquilinus, Palatinus, Quirinalis, Viminalis. In circuit, in the time of Honorius, 21 m. ; with 644 towers on the walls (31 gates, Agonensis, Aurelia, Capena, Carmentalis, Catularia, Cœlimontana, Esquilina, Fenestrella, Ferentina, *vel* Piacularis, Flaminia, Flumentana, Frumentaria, Janualis, Lavernalis, Metia, Minutia, Mugonia, Nævia, Ostiensis, Pinciana, Portuensis, Querquetulana, Ratumena, Randusculana, Romunula, Salutaris, Sanqualis, Septemiana, Trigemina *vel* Navalis, Trigonia, Viminalis), and seven bridges (Ælius, Cestius, Fabricius, Janiculensis, Palatinus, Sublicius, Triumphalis, Viminalis). The city of Romulus occupied M. Palatinus ; M. Capitolinus, Cœlius, and Quirinalis, were taken in by Tatius ; the other three by Servius Tullius. *Roma ; Rome.*

Romatinus fl., a r. of Venetia, rising in Alpes Carnicæ, and falling into the Adriatic by two mouths, Major and Minor, bet. Liquentia fl. and Tilavemptus fl. *Lumino.*

Romatinus portus, a port of Venetia, at the mouth of Romatinus fl. *Porto di Falconera.*

Romechium, a town of Bruttium, on Locrensis sin., s. of Caulonia. *Romechi.*

Romula castra, a town of Pannonia, bet. Noviodunum (10) and Quadrata (14). *Carlstadt.*

Romulia (Sub Romula), a town of the Hirpini, in Samnium, on Via Appia, bet. Eclanum (21) and Aquilonia (10). *Bisaccia.*

Ropicum, a town of Corsica, s.w. of Palanta. *Near Calvi.*

Roschinus fl., i. q. Ruscino.

Roscianum, a town of Bruttium, on Tarentinus sin., bet. Thurii (16) and Crimisa (27), on Via Trajana. *Rossano.*

Rosei campi, the meadows on Velinus fl., in Sabinum, about Reate. *Le Rose.*

Rosologia, a town of the Tectosages, in Galatia, bet. Corbeus (12) and Aspona.

Rostrum Nemaviæ, a town of Rhætia, bet. Augusta Vindelicorum (25) and Cambodunum (35). *Dillishausen.*

Rostrata villa, a town of Etruria, near Capena, bet. Rome (24) and Ocriculum (25), on Via Flaminia. *Rignano.*

Rotomagus, capital of the Vellocasses, Lugdunensis II., on the Sequana, R., bet. Lotum w. and Ritumagus e. *Rouen.*

Roxolani (Rhoxolani), a people occupying with the Jazyges the w. and N. shores of Mæotis palus.

Ruacenses, a people of Sardinia, on Tyrsus fl., s. of the Canusitani.

Ruanni, a tribe of Quadi, s.w., on the Danube.

Rubeas prom., a pr. of Sarmatia Europæa, on Sarmaticus oceanus.

Ruben, a tribe of Israel, e. of the Jordan, bet. Gad N., at Bethharan, Moabitis s., at Arnon fl., and Arabia e.

Rubi, a town of Peucetia, on Via Egnatia, bet. Rudiæ (15) and Butuntum (11). *Ruvo.*

Rubico fl., a r. of Italy, rising s.w. of Solina, and, after being joined by a number of other small streams, falling into the Adriatic bet. Ad Confluentes and Ariminum. The boundary of Gallia Cispadana and Umbria. Memorable from its association with the history of Cæsar. *Rigone,* or *Urgone,* called towards its mouth *Pisciatello,* a tributary of the *Fiumecino;* according to some antiquaries, the Fiumecino itself.

RUBRA, a maritime town of Corsica, bet. Syracusanorum portus and Graniacum prom.   *Torre Pinarello.*

RUBRESUS lacus, an inlet of Narbonensis, at the mouth of Atax fl.   *Etang de Sigean; Etang le Gruissan.*

RUBRICATA, a town of the Læetani, Tarraconensis, near Rubricatus fl., L., above Fines.   *Near Monresa.*

RUBRICATUS fl., I. Numidiæ, i. q. Ubus fl. II. a r. of Tarraconensis, falling into the Mediterranean bet. Barcino N. and Tarraco S.W.   *Llobregat.*

RUBRUM mare, generally the same with Erythræum mare; specially, the gulf of the Erythræum mare, bet. Egypt and Arabia. The boundary of Asia and Africa. The name arose from a misconception on the part of the Romans of the meaning of Erythræum, which they supposed to indicate a colour.

RUCCONIUM, a town of Dacia, towards Doricava.

RUCENATES (Rucantii, Runicatæ), a people of Vindelicia, on Lycus fl., contiguous to the Leuni.   *About Reusach.*

RUDA, I. a town of the Ariaspæ, Draugianæ, on Etymandrus fl., L., above Palacenti. II. a town of Parthia Choroana, s. of Apamea.

RUDIANE, a maritime district of Carmania, bet. the Camelobosci and Agdanitis.

RUESIUM, Galliæ, i. q. Revessio.

RUFFRIUM, a town of the Pentri, in Samnium, near Allifæ.   *Sant' Angelo Raviscanino.*

RUFIANA, a town of the Rauraci, Maxima Sequanorum, W.S.W. of Argentovaria.

RUFRÆ, a town of the Hirpini, Samnium, near Comsa.   *Ruvo.*

RUGUSCI, a people of Rhætia, s. of the Calucones.   *Vallée de Bellinzone.*

RUMA (Rimmon), a town of Galilæa, N.E. of Dio Cæsarea.

RUMBODONA, a town of the Cicones, in Thrace, on the Egnatia Via, bet. Epyrus (10) and Bistonia (10).

RUMON, an early town of the Tiber.

RUNICATES, a people of Vindelicia, on Isara fl., towards its junction with the Danube.

RUSADIR (Sestiaria), I. a pr. of Mauritania Ting., N. above Rusadir.   *Capo di Tres Forcas.* II. a town of Mauritania Tingit., within Rusadir prom.   *Melilla.*

RUSAZU, a town of Mauritania Cæsar., bet. Salda (35) and Rusippisir (23). A municipium.

RUSCINO (Roschinus), I. a r. of Narbonensis,

falling into the sea at Ruscino.   *Tet.* II. a port of the Sardones, Narbonensis I., on Ruscino fl., bet. Combusta N. and Illiberis s.   *Roussillon.*

RUSCINONA, a town of Zeugitana, on Carthaginensis sin., bet. Carthago and Ad Gallum.

RUSCOPODA fl., a r. of Pamphylia, falling into the sea E. of Attaleia.

RUSELLÆ, a town of Etruria, on Via Claudia, bet. Saturnia and Ad Mensula, 2½ m. N.E. of Prile lacus. A colonia.   *Roselle.*

RUSGONIUM (Rustonium), a maritime town of Mauritania Cæsar., bet. Rusubricari (14) and Icosium (15). A colonia of Augustus.

RUSIBIS (Rutubis), a port of Maurit. Ting., s. of Asama fl.   *Azamur.*

RUSICADA (Rusicade, Rusiccadæ), a town of Numidia, on Numidicus sin., bet. Paratianæ and Cullu. A colonia.   *Sgegada.*

RUSIDAVA, a town of the Potulatenses, Dac., on Aluta fl., L., bet. Pons Alutæ and Acidava.

RUSIPPISIR (Rusubesa), a maritime town of Mauritania Cæsar., bet. Rusazu (23) and Jomnium (42). A municipium.

RUSPÆ, a maritime town of Byzacene, bet. Brachodes prom. and Usilla.

RUSPÏNA, a town of Byzacene, bet. Hadrumetum and Leptis Min.

RUSTICANA, a town of the Vettones, Lusitania, E. of Tgædila.   *Corchucha.*

RUSTICI, a town of Numidia, bet. Magri and Ad Pisinas.

RUSUBICARI (Rusucibar, Rusubricari, *surnamed* Matidia), a maritime town of Mauritania Cæsar., bet. Cissi (12) and Rusconium.   *Tefessad.*

RUSUCURRUM (Rusuccoræ), a maritime town of Mauritania Cæsar., bet. Jomnium (18) and Cissi (12), near the mouth of Serbes fl., R. A municipium.   *Algiers?*

RUSUGUNUM, i. q. Rusconium.

RUTENI, a people of Aquitania, contiguous to the Cadurci. They were previously in Narbonensis, towards the Allobroges.

RUTTARATA, a town of Susiana Messabatice, on Tigris fl., above Sabata.

RUTUBA fl., a r. of Liguria, falling into Ligusticus sin. at Albintemelium.   *Rotta.*

RUTUBIS portus, a port of Libya, on the Atlantic., bet. Sala fl. and Soloentum prom.

RUTULI, descendants of the Umbri and Pelasgi, settled on the coast of Latium, about Ardea.

RUTUPIÆ (Rutupæ), a maritime town of the Cantii, Brit., E. bet. Cantium prom. and Dola. Celebrated by Juvenal for its oysters.

The birth-place of the usurper Maximus. *Richborough.*

RUTUNIUM, a town of the Ordovices, Brit., bet. Mediolanum (12) and Uriconium (11). *Rowton.*

RYGMANA, Cilic., i. q. Arymagdus.

RYNCHÆ, a town of Eubœa.

RYSSADIUM prom., a pr. of Libya, s. of Magnus portus. *Cape Blanco.*

S.

SAANA, a town of Syria, near Damascus, N. *Seneiah.*

SABA (Sabatha, Sabas), I. capital of the Sabæi, in Arabia Felix, on Prion fl., towards its source, N. of Cane Emporium. *Mareb.* II. a town of Phazania, N.E. of Garama.

SABADICÆ (Sabadibæ) ins., three isl. of India e. Gangem, bet. Aurea Chersonesus and Jabadii ins. Inhabited by anthropophagi. *Langan, &c.*

SABADII, a people of Bactria, on the confines of Margiana, bet. the Scordi and Parapomisus m.

SABÆ, a city of the Colobi, on the Red sea, N. of Adulis.

SABÆÆ ARÆ, temples of the fire-worshippers, in Media, on the Caspian, bet. the Cambyses and the Cyrus. *Howe-Lemur.*

SABÆI (Siba), I. a people of Arabia Felix, on the Red sea, bet. the Cassanitæ and the Homeritæ. II. (Gabæi), a people of Persis Prop., on the borders of Carmania, N.E. of the Sazæi.

SABÆON, a town of Pamphylia.

SABAGENA, a town of Laviniasene Cappadociæ.

SABAIÆ, a people of India i. Gangem, on Mana fl., L.

SABALASSUS, a town of Sargarausene Cappadociæ.

SABALINGII, a people of Northern Germania, on Germanicus oc., s. of the Sigulones.

SABANA, a pr. of Aurea Chersonesus, w. above Malaci prom. *Near Tantan Velha.*

SABARIA, I. i. q. Savus. II. a town of the Boii, Pannon., bet. Mogetiana (36) and Scarabantia (34), on Guntia fl., L. A colonia of Claudius. *Stein.*

SABARUS fl., a r. of India, falling into the Ganges bet. Diamuna fl. and Soanus fl. *Gagra.*

SABÄTA (Savo), I. a maritime town of the Ingauni, Liguria, bet. Vicus Virginis and Alba Docilia. *Savona.* II. Æthiopiæ, i. q. Saba. III. Arabiæ, i. q. Mariaba.

SABÄTE, a town of Etruria, on Sabatinus lacus, s.w. bet. Ad Nonum and Forum Claudii. Submerged by the lake.

SABATICA regio, the district of Sabe, Arabiæ.

SABATINCA, a town of the Taurisci, Noricum, on Murus fl., 18 m. N. from Monate. *Irdning.*

SABATINUS lacus, a lake of Etruria, at Sabate. *Lago di Bracciano.*

SABATIUM, a town of the Caudini, in Samnium, on Sabatus fl. *Near Prato.*

SABATRA (Soatra), a town of Lycaonia, bet. Laodicea and Coropissus, N.E. of Iconium (25). Noted for its great deficiency of water.

SABATTHA MINAS (Sabattra), a town of Babylonia, s. of Seleucia.

SABATUS fl., I. a r. of Samnium, falling into Calor fl. near Beneventum. *Sabbato.* II. (Ocinarus), a r. of Bruttium, falling into Terinæus sin. s. of Tyllesium prom. III. of Phœnicia, bet. Arca and Raphanæa.

SABBIS, a town of Mesopotamia, bet. Atra and Phalcara.

SABE (Sabbia, Maryaba), I. capital of the Rhamanitæ Sabæi, Arabiæ, s. of Manambis Regia. The seat of Sheba, grandson of Cush. II. a town of Arabia, towards the Euphrates. The seat of Sheba, son of Jokshan. III. *surnamed* Regia, a town of Arabia Felix, w. of Sabatha.

SABELLI, i. q. Sabini.

SABINÆ, a town of Pisidia.

SABINI, a branch of the Umbri, settled originally about Testrina, and thence spreading over Picenum, Samnium, and the contiguous districts. Named from their god Sabus, the Medius Fidus of the Latins. They were finally subjugated by Rome, 292 B.C. Sabinium Proper, as fixed by Augustus, was bounded N. by Umbria at Fiscellus m., s. by Latium, w. by Etruria at the Tiber, E. by Picenum and the country of the Peligni.

SABINIUM, *vide* Sabini.

SABIRI, a people of Colchis, N. of the Sagidæ.

SABÏRA, i. q. Savatra, Lycaoniæ.

SABIS, I. (Sethis, Sandis) a r. of Carmania, i. q. Corius. II. a r. of Gaul, falling into the Mosa at Namurcum. *Sambre.* III. (Sabo), a town of Carmania, on Corius fl.

SABIUM, a town of the Triumpilini, Gallia Transp., on Cleusis fl. A municipium. *Sabio.*

SABLONES, a town of the Gugerni, Germania II., s.w. of Mediolanum.

SABORA, a town of the Turtetani, bet. Teba N.E. and Sitia S.W.

SABOCÆ, a people of Sarmatia.

SABOTHA, Arabiæ, i. q. Saba.

SABRATA, *prius* Abrotonum, a maritime city of Tripolis, Afric., bet. Pontes and Ad Ammonem. A colonia. *Sabart.*

SABRINA (Sabriana) fl., a r. of Britain, rising near Dorum urbs, and, after separating Britannia II. from Flavia Cæsariensis, falling into the sea below Glevum. *Severn.*

SABRINA ÆSTUARIUM, the mouth of Sabrina fl., bet. Herculis prom., s., and Octopitarum prom., N. *Bristol Channel.*

SABTAH, Arabiæ, i. q. Zabida.

SABURA, a maritime town of India i. Gangem, E. bet. Podoca and Maliarpha.

SABUS, a town of Cappadocia, bet. Teucila (28) and Dascusa (18). The station of the Equites Sagittarii.

SACÆ, a Scythian people, bounded N. and E. by Scythia, w. by Sogdiana, s. by Imaus m. Ptolemy describes them as having no towns, but living in woods and caves. Their name was applied by some of the ancients to all the Asiatic Scythians, and by the Persians to the Scythians generally.

SACANI, a people of Sarmatia Asiat., under Hippici m., S.E.

SACALA, a port of Gedrosia, towards Arabis fl.

SACAPENE (Sacasene), a district of Armenia Maj., towards the source of Araxes fl. Hence came the gum sacapenum.

SACASTENE, a district of Drangiana, on Etymandrus fl.

SACATIA, a town of the Homeritæ, in Arabia Felix, on the Red sea, bet. Aelu (16 geog. m.) and Musa (7). *Hodeida.*

SACCASENA, a town of Morimene, in Cappadocia, bet. Osiana (28) and Cæsarea-Mazaca (30).

SACCEA, a district of Arabia Des., on the borders of Auranitis.

SACCOPODES, a people of Assyria, N. of the Absidri.

SACE (Sale), a town of Hyrcania, S.W.

SACER, I. a r. of Corsica, falling into the sea at Aleria. *Orbo.* II. of Sardinia, falling into the sea at Neapolis. *Uras.* III. a m. of Tarraconensis, w. of Asturica Augusta. IV. of the Cicones, in Thrace, towards Tempyra. V. a bay of Persicus sin., towards its N.W. extremity, at Coromanis.

SACHALITES sin., a gulf of Erythræum mare, in Arabia Felix, towards Syagrus prom. *Bahr Seger.*

SACHLE, a maritime village of Arabia Felix, w. of Saphar.

SACIS AD PADUM, a town of Gallia Cispad., on one of the branches of Padus fl., s. of

Olane ostium, bet. Augusta (12) and Neronia (4). *Fisiaglia.*

SACOLE, a town of Meroe, on the Nile, R., bet. Napata and Sandace.

SACORSA, a town of Paphlagonia, w. of Andrapa.

SACRA ins., the island formed by the two mouths of the Tiber.

SACRANI, i. q. Aborigines Ital.

SACRARIA, a town of Umbria, on Via Flaminia, bet. Spoletium (7) and Trebia (4). *Vene.*

SACRIPORTUS, a place in Latium, towards Signia, where occurred the great battle between Sylla and Marius the Younger.

SACRUM OSTIUM (Peuce, Teuce), the s. mouth of the Danube.

SACRUM prom., I. the w. extremity of Achillei cursus penins., Sarmatiæ. II. the N.N.W. extremity of Corsica. *Capo Corso.* III. the S.E. extremity of Hibernia, over against Octopitarum prom. *Grenore Point.* IV. the S.W. extremity of Lusitania, s. of Barbarium prom. Named from the belief that the sun plunged into the sea over against this point. *Cape St. Vincent; Cabo San Vicente.* V. (Chelidonium, Tauri), a pr. of Lycia, at one time popularly regarded as the termination, in this direction, of Taurus m. *C. Kelidonia.*

SACUS, a village of Laconia.

SADA, a maritime town of Argentea regio, Indiæ, 25 m. s. from Baracurra.

SADAGENA (Salagena), a town of Sargarausene prefectura, Cappadociæ.

SADAGOTHINA, a village of Morimene, near Parnassus.

SADAME, a town of Astica, in Thrace, bet. Deultus and Tarpodizus.

SADANÆ (Sadanes), a maritime district of Ariaca, Indiæ, towards Goaris fl.

SADARUS fl., a r. of Gedrosia, falling into the Cophen.

SADUS fl., a r. of India e. Gangem, falling into Gangeticus sin. at Sada.

SÆFES, an early people of Hispania, contiguous to the Cempsi.

SÆPINUM, a town of the Pentri, Samnium, on Via Numicia, bet. Allifæ (16) and Sirpium (6). A colonia of Nero; a municipium. *Attilia, near Sepino.*

SÆPONA, a town of the Turtetani, Bætica, on Barbesula fl., N. of Oningis.

SÆPRUS fl., a r. of Sardinia, falling into the sea below Sarabus. *Flamendoso.*

SÆTABICULA, a town of the Edetani, Tarraconensis, on Sucro fl., above Sucro.

SÆTABIS, I. a r. of Tarraconensis, falling into the Mediterranean. *Montesa.* II. a town of the Contestani, Tarraconensis, near Sucro fl., s.s.e. of Valentia (29). A colonia. Noted for its fine linen. *Xativa; San Filipe.*

SAETTÆ (Saittæ, Sitæ), a town of Lydia, on Hermus fl., near its junction with Hyllus fl.

SAGA, Scythiæ, i. q. Chaurana.

SAGADAVA, a town of Mœsia Inf., on the Danube, bet. Succidava and Dorostolium, at the mouth of Atlas fl.

SAGALA (Sangala, Euthymedia), a town of India, towards the junction of Hydaspes fl. and Acesines fl.

SAGALASSUS (Silgessus), a city of Pisidia, on the borders of Phrygia, n.e. of Cormasa. *Aglasoun.*

SAGAPOLA m., m. of Western Libya, n. of Mandrus m.

SAGARAUCÆ, a people of Scythia, towards the mouth of Oxus fl.

SAGARICUS sin., a bay of the Euxine, at the mouth of Sagaris fl.

SAGARIS (Rhode) fl., I. a r. of Sarmatia E., falling into Sagaricus sin. at Istrianorum portus. II. of Asia, i. q. Sangarius.

SAGARTII (Asagartya), a people of Media Magna, on its w. border, above Cambadene.

SAGASAMA, a town of Syrtica regio, e. of Iscina.

SAGDIANA ins., an isl. of Carmania, in Persicus sin., off the mouth of Dara fl.

SAGEDUNUM, the easternmost town on Hadriani vallum. *Cousin's house ?*

SAGIDA, a town of India, near the source of Soanus fl. *Sohagepur.*

SAGIDÆ, a people of Colchis, about Dioscurias.

SAGII, Gallia, i. q. Essui.

SAGIS OSTIUM, a mouth of Padus fl., bet. Caprasiæ Ostium and Olane Ostium. *Fossage.*

SAGRAS fl., a r. of Bruttium, falling into Locrensis sin. below Caulonia. Memorable for a great defeat of the Crotonians, by a comparatively small force of Locrians and Rhegians. *Alaro.*

SAGRUM, capital of the Sagii, Lugdunensis II., s.e. of Argenus.

SAGRUS fl., a r. of Samnium, running into the sea. *Sangro.*

SAGUNTUM, *postea* Muri Veteres, a city of the Edetani, Tarraconensis, 1 m. from the mouth of Turis fl., R., 16 m. n. from Valentia. A colony from Zacynthus, enlarged by immigrants from Ardea. Noted for its fine clay ; and memorable for its resistance to Hannibal, whose conduct towards it occasioned the second Punic war. A municipium. *Morviedro.*

SAGYLIUM, a fortress of Pontus, n.w. of Phazemon.

SAHAL, a town of Osrhoene, bet. Carrhæ and Ressaina.

SAIACE, a town of the Saraceni Zamareni, Arabiæ. *Saiak.*

SAIS, the early capital of Lower Egypt, on Buticus lacus, s., bet. Butos (2 geog. m.) and Cabasa, at the Saitic mouth of the Nile, R. Neith (Minerva) was worshipped here. *Sa.*

SAITICUM OSTIUM NILI, the branch of the Nile, falling into Buticus lacus at Sais.

SALA, I. a r. of the Hermunduri, Germaniæ, falling into Albis fl. below Calægia. II. (Isala), of the Istævones, Germaniæ, falling into Flevo lacus. It was connected with the Rhine, below the separation of Vahalis fl., by a canal 8 m. long, the construction of Drusis, called after him Fossa Drusiana, or Nabalia, the Latin form of the local Na-waal, "hitherwahal." *Yssel.* III. of Libya, falling into the Atlantic, bet. Agna fl. and Subur fl. IV. of Mauritania Ting., rising in Diur m., and falling into the Atlantic 50 m. s. of Subur fl. V. of the Tursones, Germ., flowing through the territories of the Hermunduri and Chatti into the Mœnus. *Saale.* VI. a town of Mauritania Ting., at the mouth of Sala fl., L. *Sallee.* VII. of Pannonia Sup., s.e. of Sabaria. *Szala Egerssek.* VIII. of Phrygia Magna.

SALACIA, a town of the Celtici, Lusitania, on Calipus fl., bet. Olisipo (60) and Ebora (44). A municipium, *surnamed* Urbs Imperatoria.

SALACENI, a people of India i. Gangem, s. of the Drillophillitæ.

SALÆ, a name given by Ptolemy to the people of Taprobane.

SALAMBINA, a maritime town of the Bastuli, Bætica, bet. Caviclum w. and Saxetanum e.

SALAMBRIA (Salaberina), a town of Garsauritis, Cappadocia, bet. Coropissus (20) and Ubinnaca, 20 m. s.e. of Archelais.

SALAMII, the people of Sylæum, Arabiæ. *Beni Salem.*

SALAMINIAS, a town of Syriæ, 18 m. n.e. from Emesa. *Salemjat.*

SALAMIS (Sciras, Cychrea), I. an isl. of Attica, in Saronicus sinus, between Megaris and Athens. Named from Salamis, mother of Asopus. Settled prior to the siege of Troy by the Æacidæ ; in length 9 m. Celebrated for the defeat, in its bay, of the fleet of Xerxes by Themistocles, 480 b.c. *Colouri.* II. *surnamed* Nova, the later capital of Salamis ins., on a neck of land towards Attica. *Ampelachi.* III. *surnamed* Vetus, the early capital of Salamis ins., at the mouth of the Boccarus fl. With a temple of Ajax, son of Telamon, who was born here. The birth-place also of Solon. IV. a city of Cyprus, at the mouth of Pediæus fl., N. of Leucolla. Founded by a colony from Salamis ins., under Teucer, son of Telamon, upon the site of a village called Coronis. Restored after an earthquake by Constantine, and named Constantia. Here were temples of Jupiter and of Venus, where human victims were sacrificed. Noted for its embroidery, and for its salt-works. *Constanza.*

SALANIANA, a town of the Grovii, Tarraconensis, on Minius fl., L., below Aquæ Origenis.

SALAPENI, a people of Arabia Fel., N. of the Manitæ. Descendants of Saleph. *Beni Meteyer.*

SALAPIA (Salpia), I. a port of Daunia, Apulia, on Salapinus lacus, S.E. of Arpi, of which it was the S. emporium. Noted for the debaucheries of Hannibal. Founded by Rhodians, under Elpias. The inhabitants, in consequence of the insalubrity of the place, removed to Salapia Nova. *Salpi.* II. *surnamed* Nova, a port of Daunia, Apul., E. of Salapia Vetus, by the population of which it was, under the auspices of M. Hostilius, built and settled. *Salpia.*

SALAPINUS palus, a lake of Daunia, Apulia, bet. Salapia Vet. and Salapia Nova. *Lago di Salpi.*

SALARIA, a town of the Bastitani, Tarraconensis, bet. Apiarium E. and Turbula W. A colonia.

SALARUS fl., a r. of Gedrosia, falling into Paragon sin., bet. Carpella prom. and Pasida.

SALASSI, a people of Gallia Transpadana, bet. the Libicii and Lepontii, bet. Duria Min. fl. S., Padus fl. E., Alpes Penninæ N., and Alpes Graiæ w.

SALATE, a district of Æthiopia, S.E. of Avalites.

SALATERRÆ, a people of Margiana, on Oxus fl., w. of the Trybactæ.

SALAURIS (Sellus) m., a m. on the coast of Tarraconensis, near Tarraco S.

SALCHA, a town in the S.E. territory of Manasseh, E. of the Jordan. *Salchat.*

SALDE (Saldis), a maritime town of Mauritania Cæsar., bet. Vabar and Muslubium. A colonia of Augustus. *Bugia.*

SALDENSES, a people of Dacia, on the Danube, bet. the Albocenses and the Ciagisi.

SALDIS, a town of Pannonia, on Savus fl., R., bet. Tarsium and Basante.

SALDUBA, I. a r. of Bætica, falling into the Mediterranean at Salduba. *Gordo.* II. a town of the Turtetani, Bætica, at the mouth of Salduba fl., L., bet. Cilniana w. and Suel. N.E. III. the early name of Cæsar Augusta, Tarraconensis.

SALE (Saloe), I. a lake or marsh of Lydia, on the site of Sipylus. Near it was the tomb of Tantalus. II. a town of the Cicones, in Thrace, N.W. of the mouth of Hebrus fl. A Thasian colony.

SALEBRA, a maritime town of Etruria, on Via Aurelia, bet. Prile lacus (12) and Manliana (9). *Burriano.*

SALEM, I. i. q. Jerusalem. II. (Shalem), a town of Judæa, S. of Bethshan, w. of Œnon. The city of Melchizedek.

SALEMIA, a town of Arabia Felix, under Zames m., S.E. of Idara.

SALERA, a town of Zeugitana, near Carthage.

SALERNUM, a maritime town of the Picentini, Campania, on Via Aquilia, bet. Nuceria (8) and Picentia (7). A colonia. Noted, later, for its school of medicine.

SALETIO, a town of Germania, bet. Brocomagus (27) and Tabernæ (16½). *Seltz.*

SALGANEUS, a town of Bœotia, on Euripus, N. of Aulis. Named in honour of the pilot Salganeus, unjustly put to death here. *Karababa.*

SALIA fl., a r. of Tarraconensis, falling into Cantabricum mare, bet. Nanasa fl. E. and Noeja w. *Sella.*

SALICE ins., i. q. Taprobane.

SALIENTES, a town of the Lucenses, Tarraconensis, on Minius fl., R., above Lucus Augusti.

SALII, i. q. Batavi.

SALINÆ, I. isl. of India e. Gangem, off the mouth of Sabaricus sin. II. a salt lake of Africa, on Syrtis Maj., at Macomades. III. a town of the Catavellauni, Brit. IV. salt-works of Daunia, in Apulia, on the coast, bet. Anxanum and Aufidena (11). *Saline.* V. salt marshes of Etruria, on the Tiber, bet. Rome and Veii. *Campo di Saline.* VI. *surnamed* Ostienses, salt-pits at Ostia, formed by Ancus Martius. *Near Casone del Sale.* VII. (Salinum), a village of the Prædavenses, Dac., bet. Marcodava (12) and Patavissa (12). Named, as now, from its salt-works. *Saltzwerk.* VIII. capital of the Sueltri, Narbonensis, S.E. of Sanitium. *Castellane.* IX. a village, with salt springs, of the Tursones, Germaniæ, on Sala fl., L., near its source. X. *surnamed* Thubunenses, salt-works, near Thubuna Maurit., on a large lake not named.

SALINARUM VALLIS, a valley of Idumæa, at the s. extremity of the Dead sea.

SALINUM (Vetusallum), a town of Valeria Pannoniæ, on the Danube, bet. Campona (25) and Cinium (14). *Hansabek.*

SALIOCLITA, a town of the Carnutes, Lugdunensis IV., bet. Lutetia N.E. and Genabum s.s.w.

SALISSA, i. q. Zoar.

SALISSO, a town of the Treveri, Germania I., on the Rhine, above Bontobrica.

SALITIA, a town of the Tribocci, Germania I., on the Rhine, above Tabernæ.

SALIXA, i. q. Taxila.

SALLENTIA (Soletum), capital of the Sallentini, Japygia, 12 m. s. of Sybaris. *Soleto.*

SALLENTINI (Salentini), a migration of Cretans, settled, circa 1000 B.C., under their chief, Idomeneus, on the coast of Japygia, from below Tarentum to below Hydruntum.

SALLENTINUM prom., i. q. Japygium.

SALMA, a town of the Melangitæ, Arab., on Zametus m.

SALMACIS, the citadel of Halicarnassus, on Salmacis fl., a stream, the fine water of which determined the selection of the site of the city. Rendered memorable by the story in Ovid.

SALMALASSUS, a town of Armenia Interior, bet. Satala and Theodosiopolis.

SALMANTICA (Elmantica, Hermantica), a town of the Vettones, Tarraconensis, on Tormes fl., bet. Sibaria N.N.E. and Sentica s. *Salamanca.*

SALMON (Zalmon) m., a m. of Judæa, at Shechem.

SALMONE, a town of Pisatis, in Elis, near Letrini N.E. Founded by Salmoneus.

SALMONIUM prom., i. q. Sammonium.

SALMYDESSUS (Halmydessus), a town of Astica, in Thrace, on the Euxine, s. of Thynias. *Midjeh.*

SALO (Bilbilis) fl., a r. of Tarraconensis, falling into the Iberus, R., at Augustobriga. It was noted for its excellence in tempering steel. *Xalon.*

SALODURUM, a town of the Helvetii, Maxima Sequanorum, s.w. of Turicum, on Arola fl. *Solothurn, Soleurne.*

SALOIA, a town of the Ambilici, Noricum, on Dravus fl., R., bet. Tarvisetum and Virunum (11). *Selch.*

SALOMACO, a town of the Belendi, Novem Populana, bet. Burdigala N. and Tellonum s.

SALONA, a town of the Dalmatæ, in Illyria, on the Adriatic, s. of Tragurium. A co-

lonia. The retreat of Diocletian, the ruins of whose palace are at Spalatro, 3 m. from the ancient town. *Salona.*

SALONE, a district of Bithynia, on the confines of Paphlagonia, s. of Hypius m. Noted for its cheese.

SALONIUM, a town of the Allobroges, Viennensis, on Isara fl., below Ventia.

SALOPIA (Pengwern, Scrobbesberig), a town of the Cornavii, Brit., near Uriconium. *Shrewsbury.*

SALPINUM, a town of Etruria, N.E. of Fanum Voltumnæ. *Ch. of San. Giov. in Selina.*

SALSOVIA, a town of Mœsia Int., at the N.W. extremity of Halmyris lacus.

SALSULÆ, a town with salt-pits, in Narbonensis I., bet. Leucate N. and Ruscino s., 30 m. from Narbo. *Salces.*

SALSUM fl., I. a r. of Arabia, falling into the Persicus sin., near the Euphrates. II. of Bætica, falling into Singulis fl., above Astigi. *Guadiato.* III. (Cathraps), of Carmania, falling into Persicus sin., bet. Tarsiana and Oaracta fl. It separates Rudiane from Agdanitis. IV. of Mauritania, flowing into the Mediterranean, E. of Siga fl.

SALTICUM (Saltiga), a town of the Bastitani, Tarraconensis, w. of Bigerra. *Suorniglia?*

SALTUARES (floating, "dancing") ins., isl. of Latium, on the small lake whence the river Nymphæus rises.

SALTUS GALLIANUS, a town of the Boii, in Gallia Cispad., near Mutilum. *Saltino.*

SALUCE, a town of Libya, on Nigir fl.

SALTUS SAPÆORUM, i. q. Acontisma.

SALURNUM, a town of the Tridentini, Rhætia, on Athesis fl., below Balzanum. *Salorno.*

SALUTARIS portus, a port of the Troglodytæ, on Arabicus sin.

SALVA, a town of Valeria Pannon., on the Danube, 9 m. N.W. from Ad Herculem.

SALVIA, a town of Liburnia, near Sirmium.

SALVIANA, a town of Numidia, bet. Luculliana, L., and Thabutis.

SALYES (Saluvii, Salyci), a people of Narbonensis II., bet. the Vocontii, near Dea Vocontiorum N., the Vocontii w., the Mediterranean s., and the Avantici and Bodiontici E. *Departments of Rhone and Var.*

SAMACHIS, a town of Agstanitis, Armeniæ, under Aisumas m., bet. Arcairis and Mejacarire.

SAMAMYCII, a town of Syrtica, bet. Syrtis Magna and Cinyphs fl.

SAMANOCHITIS lacus, i. q. Merom.

SAMARA (Sumina, Somma), a r. of Belgica

II., falling into Gallicum fretum, N. of Phrudis fl. *Somme.*

SAMARADA, a town of Aurea Chersonesus s.w., below Perimula.

SAMARIA (Samaritis), I. a district of Palestine, bounded N. by Galilæa at Ginea, s. by Judæa at Silo, w. by Judæa at Bethar, E. by Peræa at the Jordan. *Areta and Nabloos.* II. *prius* Sehemron, "hill of Semer," capital of Samaria, 40 m. N. from Jerusalem. The royal residence of the kings of Israel. Built by Omri; destroyed by the Assyrians, and again by John Hyrcanus; restored by Herod, and called by him Sebaste, "august, royal." A colonia of Severus.

SAMARIANE (Saramanne), a town of Hyrcania, on the Caspian, bet. Maxera fl. and the confines of Media. *Fehrabad.*

SAMARITIS, i. q. Samaria.

SAMAROBRIVA, *postea* Ambiani, capital of the Ambiani, Belgica II., on Samara fl., R., bet. Teucera and Curmiliaca. *Amiens.*

SAMBĂNE (Sabata), a town of Adiabene, Assyriæ, E. of Artemita.

SAMBATÆ, a people of Apolloniatis, Assyriæ, on Gyndes fl., L.

SAMBATUS m., m. of Chalonitis, Assyr., s. of Chala.

SAMBRA, a town of India, near Sadus fl.

SAMBRACATE, I. an isl. of Arabia, off Sambracate. *Burka.* II. a town of Arabia, at the s. extremity of Hammæum littus. *Burka.*

SAMBRACITANUS sin., a bay of the Mediterranean, s.s.w. of Forum Julii, Narbonensis.

SAMBROCA fl., Tarraconensis, i. q. Betullo.

SAMBUS fl., a r. of India i. Gangem, rising in Vindius m., and falling into Diamuna fl. below Clisobra. *Sambul.*

SAME (Samos), I. the early name of Cephallenia ins. II. a town of Cephallenia ins., on the E. coast, over against Neritus m. The only town on the island mentioned by Homer. *Samo.*

SAMENI, a people of Arabia Felix, N. of the Masæmanes. *Beni Shaman.*

SAMIA, Elidis, i. q. Samos.

SAMICUM m., a m. of Triphylia in Elis, s. of Samos.

SAMINTHUS, a town of Argolis, N.w. of Œnoe.

SAMMEI, a maritime people of Arabia Felix, towards Miba.

SAMMITÆ, a people of Scythia i. Imaum, s. of the Mologeni.

SAMMESUMIM, a race of giants, the early occupants of Ammonitis.

SAMMONIUM (Salmonium) prom., the E. extremity of Crete, s. of Platiæ ins., 15 m. from Dionysiades ins. *C. Salmone.*

SAMNAGES (Samnagenses), a people of Narbonensis, bet. Glanum and Cabellio. *About Senas.*

SAMNITES (Saunites, Sabelli), a tribe of Sabines, settled, in fulfilment of a vow, and under the guidance of a bull, in that portion of the Oscan territory to which they communicated their name. They consisted of three tribes; the Caraceni, Pentri, and Hirpini. They were destroyed as a nation, and nearly extinguished as a race, by Sylla.

SAMNIUM, I. the country of the Samnites, in Italy, bounded N. by the Peligni and Marruceni, s. by Campania and Lucania, w. by Latium and Campania, E. by the Frentani and Apulia. II. (Samnia, Samne) the ancient capital of Samnium, on Vulturnus fl., near its source. Taken by Scipio Barbatus. *Corro.*

SAMONIUS CAMPUS, a plain of Troas, in the territory of Næandria. *Bairamisch.*

SAMONOCHITIS lacus, i. q. Merom.

SAMORNA, an early name of Ephesus.

SAMOS, "eminence" (Parthenia, Dryusa, Anthemisa, Melamphyllus, Cyparissia), I. an isl. of Ionia, bet. Panionium and Icarus ins., in circuit 87 m. Sacred to Juno. Originally occupied by Leleges. Colonized by Samians (Cephallenians), Epidaurians, and Ephesians. Traditionally named after Samia, daughter of Mæander. *Samo.* II. its capital, on the s.E. coast, over against Mycale prom. (5). The birth-place of Pythagoras. *Megalochora.* III. (Samia), *prius* Arene, a town of Triphylia, in Elis, near Anigrus fl., towards its mouth. IV. a port of Peræa, in Caria, 8 m. E. from Posidium prom. V. (Same), the early name of Cephallenia ins. VI. i. q. Samothrace.

SAMOSĂTA, capital of Commagene, on the Euphrates, bet. Cholmandara and Singa. The birth-place of Lucian. *Schemisath.*

SAMOTHRACE (Samos, Dardania, Electris, Melite, Leucosia), I. an isl. of Thrace, towards the mouth of Melas sin., 62 m. s.E. from Thasos ins. Hence Dardanus introduced the Cybelean mysteries upon the continent. Originally settled by the Daii, and afterwards by Tyrrheni Pelasgi, but named after a colony from Samos. *Samandraki.* II. its capital, on the N.w. coast, opposite Ismarium prom. Here was a great temple of Cybele.

SAMULIS, Palestinæ, i. q. Seleucia.

SAMULOCENIS, i. q. Alcimunnis.

SAMUNIS, a town of Albania, on Albanus fl., towards its source.

SAMYDACE, a port of Gedrosia, on Paragon sin., at the mouth of Samydacus fl.

SAMYDACUS fl., a r. of Gedrosia, falling into Paragon sin. at Samydace.

SAMYTIA, a town of Caria. Founded by Motylus.

SANA fl., a r. of the Ambilici, Noricum, falling into Savus fl., below Celeja.

SANAA, *prius* Uzal, Arabiæ, i. q. Sabe regia.

SANARA (Perischabur), a town of Zabdicene, Armeniæ, on the Tigris, L., below Bezabde.

SANARI, a people of Sarmatia, in the mountains towards Albania.

SANAUS (Sanis, Sanaos), i. q. Anava, in Phrygia.

SANCTIO, a town of the Rauraci, Germania I., on the Rhine, above Augusta Rauracorum. *Seckingen.*

SANDA fl., a r. of Tarraconensis, falling into Saunium fl., L., near its mouth. *Saja.*

SANDACE, a town of Meroe, on the Nile, R., bet. Sacole and Orbadura.

SANDALEON ins., an isl. bet. Æolis Asiat., and Lesbos.

SANDALIOTIS (Ichnusa), a name given by the Greeks to Sardinia, from its fancied resemblance to a footstep or sandle.

SANDALIUM, a fortress of Pisidia, bet. Cremna and Sagalassus.

SANDARACA (Sandara), a port of Bithynia, on the Euxine, 11 m. E. from Oxinas fl.

SANDARACURGIUM, the celebrated mine of Sandarach, in Olgasys m., near Pompeiopolis, Paphlagoniæ.

SANDAVA, a town of the Caucoenses, Dac., N.W. of Utidava.

SANDIUS COLLIS, a m. of Lydia, bet. Magnesia Ad Mæandrum and Priene.

SANDOBANES fl., a r. of Armenia, falling into the Cyrus.

SANDRABITIS, a district of India, E. of the Caspiræi. The territory of Sandrocottus.

SANE, I. a town of Acte, in Macedonia, at the N.E. extremity of the Singiticus sin., the point at which the canal cut by Xerxes, to avoid the dangerous promontories of Athos, commenced. A colony of Andrians. *Problakas.* II. of Pallene, on the Thermaicus sin., s. of Cassandria.

SANGADA, a district of the Arbitæ Gedros., on Terabdon sin. E.

SANGALA, i. q. Sagala.

SANGARIUS fl., a r. of Asia Minor, rising in Adoreus m. at Sangra, in Phrygia Magna, and after traversing a portion of Galatia, and separating the Thyni from the Maryandini, in Bithynia, falling into the Euxine, 22 m. E. from Chelæ. Noted for its immense supply of fish. *Sakaria.*

SANGRA, a town of Phrygia Min., 19 m. s. from Pessinus, near the source of Sangarius fl.

SANINA, a town of Armenia Mag., on the Cyrus, below Taga.

SANISENE, a district of Paphlagonia.

SANISĔRA, a tribe of Balearis Minor. *Alajor.*

SANITIUM, a town of the Albiœci, Alpes Maritimæ, N.E. of Reii Apollinares. *Senez.*

SANNI, a people of Pontus, under Moschici m., E. of the Macrones, who ultimately became fused with them, and adopted their name.

SANNIGÆ, a people of Sarmatia, towards the Pontus Euxinus.

SANORA, a town of Otene, Armeniæ, bet. Lalla and Geliuna.

SANTABARIS, a town of Phrygia, near Doryleum. *Seid Ghazi.*

SANTICUM (Sianticum), a town of Pannonia, on the Dravus, bet. Larix (27) and Virunum (30). *Federaun.*

SANTŎNES, a people of Aquitania II., bet. the Garumna, towards its mouth, and the Liger. *Depts. of Charente Inférieure and Charente Supérieure.*

SANTONUM portus, I. a port of the Santones, Aquitania II., near the mouth of Carantonus fl. *Rochelle.* II. prom. a pr. of the Santones, Aquitania II., s. of Uliarus ins. *Pointe d'Arvert.*

SANUA, a town of Albania, 7 m. N. from Deglane.

SAOCE m., a m. of Samothrace, whence Neptune contemplated the Greeks and Trojans on the plain of Troy.

SAOCORAS fl., Masca, a r. of Mesopotamia, rising E. of Nisibis, and falling into the Chaboras, below Thubida. Now a dry bed. *Wady al Sebaa,* "ravine of fallow game."

SAPÆI (Saï), a maritime people of Thrace, s. of the Odomanti, E. of the Edones.

SAPARNUS fl., a r. of India, N. of Cophen fl.

SAPATMA, a maritime town of the Calingæ, Indiæ, bet. Caltigardama and Canagara.

SAPHAR (Sephar, Taphar), I. a mountain of Arabia, on Sachalites sin., E. of Prionotus prom. The boundary of the sons of Joktan. II. a m. of Arabia Felix, N.N.E. of Ocelis. *Sabber.*

SAPHER, a town of Judah, in Sephela Campus, E.N.E. of Ascalon.

SAPINIA tribus, a tribe of Umbri, occupying the country on the borders of Gallia Cispadana, about Sapis fl., towards its source. *About Sapigno.*

SAPIS fl., a r. of Gallia Cispadana, rising in the Apennines N. of Tifernum, and falling into the Adriatic s. of Utis fl. *Savio.*

SAPORDA saltus, a defile of Taurus m., in Pisidia, towards Phrygia.

SAPOTHRENÆ, a people of Sarmatia Asiat., on the Rha, above the Orinæi.

SAPPHA, Armen., i. q. Bezabde.

SAPPHARITÆ, a people of Arabia Felix, about Saphar m.

SAPPIRENE (Saspirene) ins., an isl. of Thebais, in the Red sea, N.E. of Myos-hormus. Named from the sapphire which it produced. *Sheduan.*

SAPRA lacus, a salt lake of Æolis Asiat., near Astyra.

SAPYSELATON m., the early name of Arachnæus m.

SARACA, a town of the Homeritæ, Arabiæ, N. of Sava.

SARABICUS sin., a bay of Indicum mare.

SARABRIS, a town of the Vaccæi, Tarraconensis, on Durius fl., below Septimanca.

SARABUS (Agoranis), I. a r. of India e. Gangem, falling into the Ganges at Boracta. II. a maritime town of Sardinia, bet. Saralapis and Ferraria, on Sæprus fl., a few miles from its mouth.

SARACA, I. a town of Colchis. II. of Media-Choromitrene, N.W. of Sincar. III. of Arabia Felix, N.W. of Sabe regia. Named from Sara, wife of Abraham. *Ayal Sara.* IV. capital of the Saraceni, Arabiæ, S.E. of Bacas Chamiry. *Karacar.*

SARACENI (Zamareni), a tribe of Nabathæi, Arabiæ, N. of the Thebani. Named from Sarah, wife of Abraham ; or, according to some authorities, from the Arabic word indicating ' robber.'

SARAGINA, a town of Cyrenaica, E. of Augila.

SARALAPIS, an inland town of the Ilienses, in Sardinia. *Burgus.*

SARALIUM, a town of the Trocmi, Galatiæ, s. of Evagina (24).

SARAMENE, a district of Pontus, bet. Gazelonitis and Amisus.

SARANGÆ, a town of Sogdiana.

SARANGES fl., a r. of Colchis, falling into the Phasis.

SARANTIUM, a town of Noricum, bet. Tartursana (10) and Siriate (15).

SARAPANA, a town of Colchis, S.E. of Dioscurias. *Scharapani.*

SARAPARÆ, i. q. Zariaspæ.

SARAPIS (Serapis, Ogyris) ins., an isl. of Arabia Felix, s.w. of Abissa. *Mazeir or Midjar.*

SARAVENE (Ravene, Avarene) præfect., a prefecture of Cappadocia, in its S.E. angle, on the confines of Commagene. *Malatia.*

SARAVUS fl., *postea* Sarra, a r. of Belgica I., falling into the Mosella, s. of Augusta Treverorum. *Saar.*

SARBACUM (Barsacum), a town of Sarmat., w. of Niossum. *Near Konietzpol.*

SARBANISSA, a town of Pontus, towards Sinope.

SARDÆUM, a town of Bœotia.

SARDELLACA, a town of the Amantini, Pannoniæ, bet. Lepavist (13) and Lusomana (13).

SARDEMISUS m., a m. of Pamphylia, bet. Perga and Aspendus, with a cognominal town.

SARDENE m., a m. of Æolis Asiat., S.E. of Cyme.

SARDES, capital of Lydia, on Pactolus fl., under Tmolus m. Fortified by Meles. Enlarged by Crœsus ; destroyed by the great earthquake under Tiberius, but repaired by that emperor. One of the Seven Churches of Asia. The seat of the Fifth Asiatic Conventus Juridicus. The birthplace of the poet Alcman, of Diodorus the orator, of Polyænus, and of Eunapius the historian. *Sart.*

SARDESSUS, Pamphyliæ, i. q. Sardemisus.

SARDEVA, a town of Agstanitis, Armeniæ, on the Tigris, above its junction with Nymphæus fl.

SARDICA (Ulpia Sardica), capital of the Treres, in Mœsia, under Scomius m. E., bet. Ælia and Helice, near the source of Œscus fl. Enlarged by the inhabitants of Ulpia, in Dacia, transferred hither. *Triaditza.*

SARDINIA (Sardon, Sandaliotis, Ichnusa), an isl. in the Tyrhenian sea, s. of Corsica, in length 170, in breadth 90, in circuit 560 m. Named from Sardus, son of the Lybian Hercules, leader of the Libyan colonists who first occupied it. It received also at various periods Iberian, Trojan, Greek, and Carthaginian settlers, the latter of whom chiefly possessed it at the period of its subjugation by Rome, 231 B.C. Its fertility caused it to be considered one of the granaries of Rome. It was exempt from wolves, and from all venomous creatures except a sort of spider, the *ranunculus sceleratus*, which it produced in large quantities, and which, from its effect in causing a convulsive contraction of the facial nerves, gave rise to the expression *risus Sardonicus. Sardinia.*

SARDONES, *vide* Sordi.

SARDONIX m., a m. of India i. Gangem, bet. Namadus fl. and Nanaguna fl.

SARDOPATORIS FANUM, a town of the Celsitani, in Sardinia, w., around a temple of Sardus Pater, bet. Metalla and Neapolis.

SARED fl., a r. of Moabitis, falling into the Dead sea below Zoar.

SAREPTA (Sarephtha), a maritime town of Phœnicia, bet. Sidon and Ornithonpolis. Noted in the history of Elijah, and for its wines. *Zerpha; Surafend.*

SARGARAUSENE (Sargasena), a prefecture of Cappadocia, S.E. of Chamanene prefectura, towards Armenia, on Melas fl.

SARGATII, a people of Sarmatia.

SARGAVENE, Cappadociæ. i. q. Garsauritis.

SARGENTIUM, i. q. Ergetium.

SARGETIA fl., i. q. Rhabo.

SARIMAGULA, a town of Ariaca, Indiæ, on Mæsolus fl., s.w. of Hippocura.

SARIPHÆA, a town of Judæa, bet. Joppa N.W. and Lydda S.E.

SARIPHI m., m. of Asia, separating Aria from Margiana. *Sahar.*

SARITÆ, Arabiæ, the people of Southern Saraca.

SARMADILLUM, an inland town of the Sallentini, in Japygia. *Muro.*

SARMALIA, a town of the Trocmi, in Galatia, bet. Ancyra and Lascoria.

SARMATA, a town of the Triballi, Mœsia, on Margus fl. R., bet. Horrea and Præsidium Dasmum.

SARMATÆ, I. (Saar-Madai, "sons of the Medes," Sauromatæ, Samatæ), the people of Sarmatia; descended from the Medes. II. portæ, i. q. Caucasiæ.

SARMATIA ASIATICA, a country of Asia, extending from Tanais fl. w. and the Euxine to Rha fl. E., bounded N. by Terra Incognita, s. by Armenia, Iberia, and Colchis at Caucasus m.

SARMATIA EUROPÆA, a country of Europe, extending from Tyras fl. w. to Tanais fl. E., bounded N. by Terra Incognita, and s. by Palus Mæotis.

SARMATICA ins., an isl. at the mouth of the Danube.

SARMATICUS OCEANUS, the s. portion of Suevicum mare.

SARNACA, a town of Mysia.

SARNÆ, a town of Rhætia, 20 m. from Tridentum. *Ala.*

SARNIA ins., an isl. of Lugdunensis II., bet. Reduna ins. N. and Cæsarea ins. s. *Guernsey.*

SARNII, a people of Gallia Cisalpina, towards Rhætia. *About Sarniga.*

SARNIUS fl., a r. of Hyrcania.

SARNUCA, a town of Osrhoene, on the Euphrates, below Eragiza.

SARNUM, a town of Dacia, E. of Pinum.

SARNUS (Draco) fl., a r. of Campania, falling into the sea 1 m. s. of Pompeii. *Sarno.*

SARON campus, the plains on the coast of Judæa, bet. Cæsarea Palestina N. and Lydda s.

SARONICUS sin., a gulf of the Ægean, washing the coasts of Argolis (E.), Megaris (s.), and Attica (w.). *G. d'Engia.*

SARONIS palus, *prius* Phœbea, a salt lake of Argolis, on the E. coast, N. of Trœzen. Named, with Saronicus sinus, after Saron, an early king of Argolis.

SARPEDON (Calycadnus), I. a sandy prom. of Cilicia Trachea, at the mouth of Calycadnus fl. *C. Lissan el Capheh.* II. a port of the Apsynthii, in Thrace. III. a headland of the Apsynthii, in Thrace, at the N. entrance of Melas sin. *C. Dragoatina.*

SARRA, the Roman form of the Phœnician Tsar (Tyrus).

SARRACA (Caracca), a town of the Euganei, on Mincius fl., above Benacus lacus. A municipium. *Sarca.*

SARRÆ, a town of the Treveri, on Saravus fl., near its confluence with the Mosella.

SARRASTES, the people on Sarnus fl., in Campania.

SARRUM, a town of the Santones, Aquitania II., bet. Condate N.W. and Vesunna S.E.

SARS fl., a r. of Tarraconensis, falling into Ulla fl. at Turres Augusti.

SARSINA, capital of the Sarsinates, a people of Gallia Cisalpina, towards Ariminum, on Sapis fl., L., towards its source. The birth-place of Plautus. A municipium. *Sarsino.*

SARTALI, a town of the Volcæ Tectosages, Narbonensis, bet. Lactora N.W. and Tolosa S.E.

SARTE, a town of Acte, in Macedonia, on Singiticus sin., near Pilorus.

SARTUM, capital of the Serdi, Mœsiæ, bet. Sardica and Lissæ.

SARUENA (Sacoela), Cappadociæ, i. q. Aquæ Aravenæ.

SARUM, a town of the Amadoci, Sarmatiæ, on the Borysthenes, L., below Amadoca. *Near Novomoskowsk.*

SARUNETES, a people of Maxima Sequanorum, bet. the Tugeni and the Lepontii.

SARUS fl., a r. of Cilicia Campestris, rising in Cataonia, and falling into the Mediterranean, 26 m. w. of Pyramus fl. *Sihoon.*

SARXA, a town of the Odomanti, in Thrace, bet. Drabescus (20) and Scotussa (18).

Sasa (Sesea), a district of Æthiopia, s.e. of Pseboa lacus.

Sasala, a town of Latium, towards Tibur.

Sasīma, a town of Cappadocia, 24 m. from Dio Cæsarea. *Ingesu.*

Sasina portus, a haven of the Sallentini, in Japygia, on Tarentinus sin., n.w. of Neretum. *Porto Cesareo.*

Saso ins., an isl. of the Adriatic, on the coast of Illyria, n. of Acroceraunium prom. *Saseno.*

Sasones, a people of Scythia, under Alani m.

Saspires, a people of Pontus, towards Colchis.

Sata, a town of Arabia Felix, near Persicus sin., s. of Catara. *Sata.*

Satachta, a town of the Nubæ, on the Nile, bet. Erchoas and Moru. *Ambucote.*

Satala, I. a town of Armenia Minor, bet. Domana (18) and Suissa. The station of the Legio Apollinaris. *Sukme.* II. of Lydia, 5 m. from Mæonia. *Kula.*

Satarche, capital of the Satarchei, in Taurica Chersonesus, near Eupatoria. *Near Mangut.*

Satarchei, a tribe of Tauro-Scythæ, occupying the n. portion of Taurica Chersonesus. Mela describes them as living in caves during winter, with their bodies covered up to their eyes.

Sataros, the early name of Patara, in Lycia.

Satiani, a people of Scythia e. Imaum, s. of Alani m.

Saticula, a town of the Caudini, in Samnium, on the borders of Campania, towards Calatia. *Sant' Agata dei Goti.*

Satifis, a town of Mauritania Cæsar., bet. Horrea and Sitifis (16).

Sation, a town of the Dassaretæ, in Illyria, on Lychnitis palus, bet. Euchelanæ and Boium.

Satnioeis (Saphnioeis) fl., a r. of Æolis Asiat., rising in Ida m., n. of Antandrus, and falling into the Ægean below Tragasæ. *Tuzla.*

Satrachus, a town of Cyprus, on a cognominal river.

Satræ, a people of Thrace, extending e. from the Odomanti, Mœdi, and Danthaletæ, and n. from the Sapæi to Rhodope m. A fierce predatory nation, who remained unconquered and independent until subjugated by the Romans in the reign of Augustus.

Satrapēne, a division of Assyria, s.

Satricum, a town of the Volsci, in Italy, bet. Velitræ and Antium. Destroyed by the Romans.

Sattagydæ, a people of Paropamisus, on the borders of Bactria n. and of Aria w. *Thataghush.*

Saturium, a maritime town of Messapia, 7 m. e. from Tarentum. *Saturio.*

Saturni (Scombraria, Traete), a pr. of Tarraconensis, near Strongyle ins. *Cabo de Palos.*

Saturnia, I. a name poetically given to Italy, from Saturn, who took refuge there from Jupiter. II. *prius* Aurinia, a city of Etruria, on Albinia fl., near its source, bet. Maternum (18) and Rusellæ, on Via Claudia. A Pelasgic city. A colonia 185 b.c. *Saturnia.*

Satutanda, i. q. Siatutanda.

Satyrorum ins., I. three isl. of Aurea Chersonesus, n.e. of Magnum prom. Named, according to Ptolemy, from the resemblance of the inhabitants to satyrs. *Borneo, Palawan, Celebes.* II. prom., a pr. of the Sinæ, n.e. of Theriodes sin. III. of the Troglodytæ, on the Red sea, above Monodactylus m. *Point Condor.*

Saucona fl., a later name of the Arar.

Saudaratæ, a people of Sarmatia Europ., on the Borysthenes, L., above the Thissamatæ.

Sauloe, the local name of Nisæa, Parthiæ.

Saunites (Sannites), the Greek name of the Samnites.

Saunium fl., a r. of Tarraconensis, falling into Cantabricum mare at Vereasueca. *Besaya.*

Saura, a town of Persis, n.e. of Taoce. *Shapur ?*

Sauromatæ, the Greek name of the Sarmatæ.

Saurus fl., a r. of Crete.

Saus fl., a r. of Mauritania Cæsar., falling into the Mediterranean bet. Icosium w. and Ruscosium e.

Sava (Cholabus), I. a town of the Homeritæ, in Arabia Felix, bet. Taphar and Musa. II. of Mauritania Cæsar., bet. Oliva and Tamununa.

Savara, a town of Mesopotamia, on the Tigris, bet Mardis and Nineveh.

Savari, a people of Sarmatia, s. of the Pagyritæ.

Savia, a town of the Pelendones, Tarraconensis, w. of the source of Durius fl., bet. Larna n.w. and Visontium s.e. *Near Salas.*

Savincatui, a people of Alpes Cottiæ. *About Sapet.*

Saviona, a town of the Isarci, Rhæt., on Isaurus fl., R., bet. Sebatum and Pons Drusi.

Savo, I. (*surnamed Piger,* from its sluggish course), a stream of Campania, falling into

the sea s. of Sinuessa (3). *Savone.* II. a
town of Liguria, near Vada Sabata.

SAVUS (Saus) fl., a r. of Pannonia, rising in
Tullus m., and falling into the Danube at
Taurunum.

SAXA RUBRA, the early name of Ad Rubras,
in Etruria.

SAXETANUM (Ex, Sexi), a maritime town of
the Exetani Bastuli, Bætica), bet. Salam-
brua w. and Abdera E. A colonia (Sexti
Firmum Julium). *Castro de Ferro.*

SAXŎNES, a people of Northern Germany,
definitively settled bet. Germanicus oc. and
the rivers Albis, Luppia, and Rhine.
Named from *Sass*, settled, domestic; or
from *Seax*, short sword; or from *Sache*,
legal process; or from the Sacæ, their pre-
sumed progenitors. Ancestors and progenitors of the English.

SAXONUM ins., three isl. of Germania Mag.,
at the mouth of Albis fl. *Eiderstedt,*
Norstrand, &c.

SAXULA, a town of the Latini, Latium, in
the territory of Tibur. *Near Castel Ma-*
dama.

SCABALA, a village of Eubœa, near Eretria.

SCABINE, a town of Media, towards Armenia.

SCAIDAVA, a town of the Getæ, Mœsiæ, on
the Danube, bet. Tegræ and Trimanium.

SCALA TYRIORUM, a pr. of Galilæa Sup., 12
m. N. from Acco.

SCALABIS (Scalabiscus), a town of the Lusi-
tani, on the Tagus, R., 62 m. above
Olisippo. A colonia (Præsidium Julium).
Sant' Irene; Santarem.

SCALDIS fl., a r. of Belgica I., rising towards
Bagacum, and falling into the sea at Tabuda æstuarium. *Scheldt; Escaut.*

SCAMANDER (Xanthus) fl., I. a stream of
Troas, rising E. of Troja, at a place now
called *Kirk Guezler*, and, in the Homeric
ages, joining Simois fl. above Ilium Novum.
It now enters the sea by a separate course
near Sigæum prom. Named from Sca-
mander, father of Teucer. *Bournabachi.*
II. a r. of Sicily, falling into Simois fl. at
Segesta. Named by Æneas from the
Trojan river.

SCAMANDRIA, a town of Troas, on Scamander
fl.

SCAMBONIDÆ, a demus of Attica, of the tribe
Leontis, on Cephissus Eleusinius fl., near
Eleusis. The birth-place of Alcibiades.

SCAMNUM, a town of Messapia, on Via
Appia, bet. Uria (8) and Brundusium (15).
Latiano.

SCAMPIS, a town of the Eordeti, Illyria, on
Genusus fl., bet. Clodiana (20) and Tres
Tabernæ (28), on Egnatia Via.

SCANATUS, a town of Ætulane, Armenia
Minor, between Marandara (38) and Sebastia.

SCANDA, a town of Colchis, towards Iberia.
Scander.

SCANDARIUM prom., a pr. of Cos, over
against Termerium prom., in Caria.

SCANDEA, a town of Cythera ins., on the
w. coast. *Kapsali.*

SCANDIA ins., four isl. and supposed isl. in
Codanus sin., E. of Cimbrica Chersonesus.
Zeeland, Part of Sweden, &c.

SCANDILE ins., an isl. of Thessaly, in the
Ægean, S.E. of Halonnesus. *Scangero.*

SCANDINAVIA, a district of Northern Ger-
many, on Borealis oceanus, comprising
Scandia ins. and a part of the mainland.
Sweden. Norway, &c.

SCANTATE, a town of the Saraceni, Arabiæ,
s.w. of Saraca. *Kin.*

SCAPITANI, a people of Sardinia, bet. the
Iienses N. and the Siculenses s.

SCAPTE-HYLE, a town of the Edones, in
Thrace, on Strymonicus sin., over against
Thasos ins., w. of Neapolis. Noted for
its gold-mines, the dowry which Thucydides received with his wife, and as the
place where he prepared his history.

SCAPTIA, a town of the Latini, Latium,
near Pedum. *Passerano.*

SCARABANTIA, a town of the Boii, Pannoniæ, bet. Mutenum (12) and Sabaria (23).
A colonia (Julia). *Oldenburg; Sopron.*

SCARBIA, a town of the Genauni, Rhætiæ,
bet. Parthanum (11) and Veldidena (19).
N. of Scharnitz.

SCARCĂPOS, a town of Sardinia, at the
mouth of Sæprus fl. *Scarabo.*

SCARDONA, I. an isl. of the Adriatic, one of
the Liburnides ins. *Arba.* II. the capital
of the Liburni, Illyriæ, on Titius fl., a few
miles above its mouth. *Scardona.*

SCARDUS (Scordus, Scobius) mons, a s. continuation of Bertischus m. dividing central
Illyria from Mœsia and Almopeia. *Tchar-*
dagh.

SCARI, a village of Lycia, on a cognominal
stream.

SCARPHE, I. Bœotiæ, a later name of Eteonus. II. a town of the Locri Epicnemidii, at the mouth of Boagrius fl., E. of
Nicæa. Nearly destroyed by an earthquake. *Andera.*

SCARPONA, a town of the Leuci, Belgica I.,
on the Mosella, L., bet. Divodurum and
Tullum. *Scarpone; Charpeigne.*

SCATEBRA fl., Latii, i. q. Vinius.

SCENÆ, capital of the Scenitæ, Arabiæ, s.
of Babylon.

SCENÆ MANDRÆ, a town of Heptanomis,

on the Nile, R., bet. Aphroditopolis (20) and Babylon (12).

SCENÆ VETERANORUM, a town of Lower Egypt, bet. Heliopolis (18) and Vicus Judæorum (12).

SCENITÆ, a Nomadic people, wandering over the country bet. Arabia Deserta and the Euphrates.

SCEPSIS, a city of Dardania, in Mysia, on Æsepus fl., 7½ m. below Palæscepsis; the capital of Ascanius, son of Æneas. Memorable as the place where the works of Aristotle and Theophrastus were recovered by Sylla. The birth-place of Demetrius the grammarian, of Erastus and Coriscus the Socratics, of Nelius, disciple of Aristotle and Pythagoras, and of Metrodorus Scepsius. *Eskiupschi.*

SCHÆDIA, a village of Lower Egypt, on the Canopic branch of the Nile, at the junction of a canal leading to Alexandria (6). The king's river-barges were stationed here.

SCHERA, a town of Sicily, near Hypsa Maj. fl.

SCHERIA, the early name of Corcyra ins., Epiri.

SCHIDIAS, a village of Rhodus ins., near Jalysus.

SCHINUSSA ins., an isl. of the Ægean, one of the Sporades, bet. Donysa and Nicasia. *Skinosa.*

SCHISTE ODOS, "divided way" (Triodos, "three ways"), a defile of Parnassus m., in Phocis, where the roads from Delphi, Daulis, and Ambryssus unite. The scene of Laius' murder. *Derbeni.*

SCHŒNUS, I. a r. of Bœotia, falling into Hylice palus. II. of the Cicones, in Thrace, rising in Rhodope m., and falling into the Ægean at Maronea. III. a bay of Doridis sin., N., separated from Thymnias sinus by Aphrodisias prom. IV. a town of Arcadia, s. of Methydrium. Built by Schœnus, father of Atalanta. V. of Bœotia, E. of Hylice palus, on Schœnus fl., bet. Anthedon and Thebes (6¼). *Morikios.* VI. a port of Corinth, on Saronicus sinus, at the narrowest point of the isthmus, 8½ m. s.E. from the city. *Kokosi.*

SCIA, a town of Eubœa.

SCIAS, a town of Arcadia, 1½ m. N. from Megalopolis.

SCIATHIS, I. a m. of Arcadia, on the confines of Achaia, N. of Pheneus. II. a town of Lower Egypt, s. of Alexandria.

SCIATHOS, I. an isl. of Thessaly, in the Ægean, 4 m. E. from Magnesiæ prom., in circuit 15 m. Settled by Pelasgi from Thrace, and afterwards by Chalcidians

from Eubœa. Noted for its wine. *Skiathos.* II. its capital, on the N.E. coast. Destroyed by Philip, son of Demetrius.

SCIDRUS, a maritime town of Lucania, s.E. of Buxentum. Founded by some Sybarites, escaped from the destruction of their own city. *Sapri.*

SCILLIUM, a town of Byzacene, bet. Thala and Suffetula. A colonia.

SCILLUS, a town of Triphylia, in Elis, towards the coast, bet. Olympia (2½) and Samia. The retreat and burial-place of Xenophon, with a temple of Diana Ephesia erected by him. *Brina.*

SCILLUSTIS ins., Psilloustis, Indiæ, i. q. Cilluta.

SCINCOMAGUS, a town of Alpes Cottiæ. *Servières.*

SCIONE (Pellene), a town of Pallene, in Macedonia, on Toronaicus sin., s.E. of Neapolis. Founded by Pellenian colonists from Achaia. Its inhabitants were destroyed by the Athenians, and the town given to Platæan fugitives.

SCIRAS, a name of Salamis ins., after the hero Scirus.

SCIRI, a tribe of Vindili, Germaniæ, on Vistula fl., L., towards its mouth.

SCIRITIS, a town of Caria.

SCIRON, a village of Attica, s.w. of Athens, on a cognominal stream. Named after Sciron the soothsayer.

SCIRONIDES PETRÆ (Scironia Saxa), a defile of Megaris, on the s. coast, bet. Megara and Crommyon. The haunt of the robber Sciron, killed by Theseus. *Kaki Scala.*

SCIROS (Sciritis), a district of Laconia, on the borders of Arcadia.

SCIRPHÆ, a town of Phocis.

SCIRTHÆA, a town of Sicily, near Triocala.

SCIRTIANA, a town of Illyria, on the Egnatia Via, bet. Brygias (4) and Pylon (4).

SCIRTONIUM, a village of Arcadia, in the territory of Ægys of Laconia. Its inhabitants removed to Megalopolis.

SCIRTUS fl., a r. of Osrhoene, Mesopotamiæ, rising N. of Edessa, and falling into Carrha fl. below Carrhæ. *Daisan.*

SCITTIUM (Sotium), capital of the Sotiates, Novem Populana, near Elusa, N.W. *Sos.*

SCODRA, capital of the Labeates, in Illyria, on Barbana fl., at the s. extremity of Labeatis lacus. A colonia. *Fortress of Scutari.*

SCOLLIS, I. a mountain of Elis, on the borders of Achaia, s.w. of Pharæ. *Santa Meri.* II. a town of Achaia, under the cognominal mountain.

SCOLOPÆIS, a village of Ionia, in Mycale m., towards Gæson.

SCOLOTÆ, a name of the Scythæ, from one of their kings, Scolotes.

SCOLUS, I. a town of Bœotia, bet. Platæa (5) and Thebæ. Its territory was proverbially barren. In ruins in Pausanias' time. II. of Sithonia, Macedonia, N.E. of Olynthus.

SCOMBRARIA (Herculis ins.), I. an isl. of Tarraconensis, 3 m. s.w. from Carthago Nova. Named from the great quantities of scombri (mackerel) taken there. Islota. II. a prom., i. q. Saturni prom.

SCONII (Siconii), a people of Narbonensis, bet. the Tricorii and the Medulli, N. of the Vocontii and Caturiges. Val Oysans.

SCOMIUS (Scombrus) m., a N.W. continuation of Rhodope m., separating Mœsia from the Graæi. Cadja Balcan.

SCOPELITES ins., islets of Cyrenaica, above Boreum prom.

SCOPELOS, I. an isl. of Ionia, in Hermius sin., opposite Clazomenæ. II. a town of Sarmatia, near the mouth of Vardanus fl. Temrook. III. an isl. of Paphlagonia, off Sinope. IV. of Thessaly, bet. Sciathos ins. and Halonnesus ins. Scopelo. V. of Troas.

SCOPIA prom., Cariæ, i. q. Zephyrium.

SCOPIA CERERIS prom., a pr. of the Troglodytæ, on the Red sea, N. of Aspis prom.

SCOPIUM, a village of Phthiotis, in Thessaly, near Thebæ.

SCOPOLURA, a town of the Bettigi, Indiæ, N.W. of Candipatna.

SCOPOS fl., a r. of Bithynia, falling into Sangarius fl. below Juliopolis.

SCORDI, a people of Bactria, on the confines of Margiana, bet. the Zariaspæ and the Sabadii.

SCORDISCI (Scoedisces) m., m. of Asia, intersecting the N. districts of Armenia Major. II. a people occupying the S.E. angle of Pannonia I., and the w. portion of Mœsia to Scordus m., and later, all the country bet. Thrace and the Adriatic.

SCOROBAS m., a summit of Olympus, in Paphlagonia, on the confines of Bithynia. Beinder dagh.

SCORUS (Scoras) fl., the early name of the Isara.

SCOTANE, a town of Arcadia, s.w. of Clitor.

SCOTI (Gaelic, "contemptible, little"), a tribe of Daione Ghael from Hibernia, who invaded the w. coast of Britannia Barbara, after the withdrawal of the Romans from Britain, and gradually fusing with the Picts, whom they had permitted to survive, obtained possession of the country named after them Scotland.

SCOTITAS, a town of Laconia, on the confines of Arcadia, N. of Caryæ.

SCOTUSSA, I. a town of Pelasgiotis, Thessaly, bet. Larissa and Pheræ. The birthplace of the athlete Polydamus. Sarliki. II. of the Siropæones, in Thrace, near Strymon fl., bet. Sarxa (13) and Heraclea Sintica (18).

SCULTENNA (Scutana) fl., a r. of Gallia Cispadana, falling into Padus fl. below Padunum. Panaro.

SCULTERII (Selterii, Celtorii), a tribe of Salyes, in Gaul. About Sterel.

SCURGUM, a town of the Burgundiones, Germaniæ, near Jadua fl., E.

SCUTIS ins., i. q. Ocetis.

SCYBRUS, a town of Macedonia.

SCYDISCES (Scotius) m., m. of Asia, a range of Scordisci m., S.E. of the Macrones, in Pontus.

SCYDRA (Chydræ, Scurio), a town of the Byrsi, in Emathia, on the Egnatia Via, bet. Ægæ (15) and Pella (15).

SCYLACE, a Pelasgic town of Mysia, on Propontis, bet. Cyzicus and Placia.

SCYLACIUM (Scylletium), a city of Bruttium, on Scylleticus sin., bet. Targines fl. (22) and Corinthum (22), on Via Trajana. Founded by Athenians under Mnestheus. A colonia. The birth-place of Cassiodorus. Squillace.

SCYLAX fl., a r. of Galatia, falling into Iris fl., 10 m. above Amasia. Gulkiras.

SCYLLA prom., a peninsulated rock of Bruttium, at the N. entrance of Siculum fretum, peculiarly subject to storms, whence the fable. The abode of the Homeric Scylla.

SCYLLÆUM, I. the S.E. prom. of Argolis, over against Bucephala prom. Named from Scylla, daughter of Nisus. Capo Skyllo. II. a town of Bruttium, within Scylla prom., bet. Arceades fl. (7) and Rhegium (13), on Via Aquilia. Built by Anaxitas of Rhegium. Here Spartacus was hemmed in by Crassus. Scilla.

SCYLLETICUS sin., a bay of the Ionian sea, at Scylletium, bet. Japygia promontoria and Cocynthum prom. G. di Squillaci.

SCYMNITÆ, a people of Sarmatia Asiatica, N. of the Sacani.

SCYPPIUM (Scypha), a village of Ionia, towards Colophon. The temporary settlement of the founders of Clazomenæ.

SCYRAS fl., a r. of Laconia, falling into Laconicus sin. 5 m. N. from Pyrrhicus.

SCYRMUS, a town of the Doliones, in Mysia, towards Cyzicus.

SCYROS ins., "rocky," a town of Thessaly, in the Ægean, E. of Eubœa. Settled by Dolopians, and afterwards by Athenians; the country of king Lycomedes. The birth-place of Neoptolemus. The scene of Achilles' adventure with Deidamia, and of Theseus' death. Noted for its goats and its veined marble. *Skyro.*

SCYRTHÆA, a town of Sicily, on Allava fl., towards Tricala. Noted in the Servile war. *Acristia.*

SCYTHÆ AGRICOLÆ, a tribe of Scythians, settled as husbandmen in Sarmatia Europæa on both sides the Borysthenes, s. of the Amadoci.

SCYTHÆ REGII, Basilii, a tribe of Scythians in Sarmatia, E., on the Tanais and Mæotis palus, towards Taurica Chersonesus.

SCYTHÆ SCOLOTÆ, a tribe of Scythians in the country N. and N.E. of Mæotis palus. Traditionally named from Scythes, son of Hercules.

SCYTHIA, at first a country of Europe, bet. Carpathus m. and the Tanais; afterwards, as Scythia Propria, understood by Ptolemy to be a country of Asia, extending bet. the Tanais and Serica, bounded s. by Sogdiana, Hyrcania, Margiana, &c. It was intersected by Imaus m., and distributed accordingly into Scythia intra Imaum w. and Scythia extra Imaum E.

SCYTHIA MINOR, a province of Mœsia Inferior, on the Euxine, bet. the Danube and Hæmus m., occupying the country previously called Pontus, and named from its original Scythian population.

SCYTHINI (Scythæ, Cercetæ, Cæti), a people of Asia, separated from the Macrones of Pontus by Glaucus fl., N.W. of Harpasus fl.

SCYTHOPOLIS, i. q. Bethsan.

SCYTHRANIUS (Cyrthanius) portus, a port of Marmarica, bet. Catæonium prom. and Antipyrgos.

SEBA, the Scriptural name of the Sabæi, in Arabia.

SEBAGENA, a town of the Trocmi, in Galatia, bet. Soanda and Ochria.

SEBARDÆ, a people of Æthiopia, w. of the Nile, N. of the Radapi. *In Sennaar.*

SEBASTE, I. a maritime town of Cilicia Trachea, 3 m. E. from Corycus, opposite Elæussa ins. Built by Archelaus of Cappadocia. *Ayash.* II. a town of Phrygia Mag., bet. Acmonia and Blaundus. III. Samariæ, i. q. Samaria. IV. of the Tectosages, in Galatia, E. of Ancyra.

SEBASTIA (Carana), capital of Caranitis, in Pontus, E. of the source of Halys fl., S.E. of Cabira. *Siwas.*

SEBASTOPOLIS, I. a town of the Bessi, in Thrace, w. of Cillium. II. of Colchis, i. q. Dioscurias. III. a later name of Myrina, in Æolis Asiat. IV. of Pontus, i. q. Cabira.

SEBATUM, a town of the Breuni, in Rhætia, bet. Sublavium and Littamum (23). *Sabs.*

SEBENNYTICUM OSTIUM NILI, Thermuchicum, the third mouth of the Nile, E. from Alexandria. Named from Sebennytus.

SEBENNỸTUS, a town of Lower Egypt, on the Sebennytic branch of the Nile, E. of Sais. *Semmenud.*

SEBETHUS fl., a r. of Campania, falling into Cumanus sin. near Neapolis. Named from the nymph Sebethis. *Fornello, Fiume della Maddalena.*

SEBĪNUS lacus, a lake of Gallia Transpad., bet. Larius lac. and Benacus lac. *Lago d'Iseo.*

SEBOUNTA, Arabiæ, i. q. Esbuta.

SEBRITÆ, a people of Tenesis, in Æthiopia, s. of the Memnones.

SEBUDINUM, Galliæ, i. q. Vindinum.

SEBUM, a town of the Euganei, in Gallia Transpad., at the s. extremity of Sebinus lac. A municipium. *Iseo.*

SECERRÆ, a town of the Ausetani, Tarraconensis, near Ausa.

SECIES (Secia, Gabellus) fl., a r. of Gallia Cispadana, rising in Letus m., and falling into Padus fl. above Hostilia. *Secchia.*

SECOR, a port of the Pictones, Aquitania II., S.E. of Pictonum prom.

SECURISCA, a town of the Mœsi, Mœsia Inferior, on the Danube, bet. Nicopolis and Dunum.

SECUSSES, a people of Histria, bet. Pola and Tergeste. *About Saguria.*

SEDATUM, a town of Germania Mag., on Alcius fl., N. of Vetoniana.

SEDIBONIATES, a people of Novem Populana, towards the Pyrenees. *About Sebi.*

SEDISSA (Scydissa), a town of Pontus, bet. Thea (17) and Domana (24).

SEDULA, a town of Liguria, on Padus fl.

SEDUNI, a people of Alpes Penninæ, contiguous to the Veragri. *Val d'Aoste.*

SEDUNUM, capital of the Seduni, on the Rhone, R., above Octodurum. *Sion.*

SEGALAUNI, a tribe of Cavares, Viennensis, on the Rhone and Druna ffl.

SEGEDA, I. a town of the Arevacæ, Tarraconensis, N.W. of Lobetum. A colonia (Julia Restituta). II. *surnamed* Augurina, a town of Bætica, bet. Urgao N. and Tucci s.

SEGEDUNUM, a town of the Otadeni, Brit., on Hadriani murus, towards its E. termination.

SEGELOCUM, Brit., i. q. Agelocum.

SEGESTA (Egesta, Acesta), a city of Sicily, on Scamander fl., R., at its confluence with Simois fl. II. *surnamed* Tiguliorum, the port of Tigulia, in Liguria. *Sestri.*

SEGESTANUM EMPORIUM, the port of Segesta, in Sicily, at or near the mouth of Simois fl., L.

SEGESTICA, I. Tarraconensis, i. q. Segida. II. Pannoniæ, i. q. Siscia.

SEGGO, a town of Byzacene, bet. Zama (20) and Avula (10). *Kissor.*

SEGISA, a town of the Contestani, Tarraconensis, on Tader fl., R., above Vergilia. A colonia (Julia).

SEGISAMA, a town of the Vaccæi, s.w. of Segisamum.

SEGISAMUM (Egisamum), a town of the Turmogidi, Tarraconensis, 92 m. E. from Legio. *Sasamon.*

SEGISAMUNCLUM, a town of the Autrigones, Tarraconensis, 2 geog. m. E. from Virovesca.

SEGISSERO, a town of the Lingones, Lugdunensis I., bet. Corobilium N.W. and Andematunum S.S.E.

SEGNI, a people of Germania II., bet. the Eburones and the Treveri.

SEGOBIA, I. a town of the Carpetani, Tarraconensis. II. of the Vaccæi, Tarraconensis, N. of Augustobriga. A settlement of Gaulish Segobrigians. *Cigudosa.*

SEGOBODIUM, a town of the Sequani, Maxima Sequanorum, on the Arar, bet. Varcia N.W. and Visontio S.E. *Seveux.*

SEGOBRIGA, I. a town of the Edetani, on Pallantius fl., N.W. of Saguntum. *Segorbe.* II. capital of the Celtiberi, Tarraconensis, near the Tagus, L., towards its source, bet. Mantua N.W. and Valeponga E. Founded by Segobrigian colonists from Massilia. Noted for its excellent *lapis specularis. Priego.*

SEGOBRIGII, a Ligurian people, occupying the country about Massilia, in Gaul, at the time of the Phocæan immigration.

SEGODUNUM, I. a town of the Curiones, Germaniæ, on Mœnus fl., R., above Locoritum. *Wurtzburg.* II. *postea* Ruteni, capital of the Ruteni, Aquitania I., bet. Carantomagus w. and Ad Silanum N.E. *Rhodez.*

SEGONTIA (Saguntia), I. a town of the Arevacæ, Tarraconensis, S.E. of Clunia. *Siguenza.* II. of the Celtiberi, Tarraconensis, w. of Cæsar Augusta. III. of the Turtetani, Bætica, bet. Ceret N.W. and Asindum S.E.

SEGONTIUM, a port of the Ordovices, Brit., opposite Mona ins.

SEGORA, a town of the Cambolectri, Aquitania II., bet. Condivicnum N.W. and Limonum S.E.

SEGOREGII, a tribe of Salyes, Narbonensis, on the S.E. shore of Astromela stagnum.

SEGOVINI, a people of Alpes Cottiæ, contiguous to the Segusini. *Vallée de Sezane.*

SEGOVINUM, capital of the Segovini. *Seguin.*

SEGUSIANI (Sebusiani, Segusini), a people of Lugdunensis I., on the Arar and Rhone ffl., R., bet. Assa Paulini and Vienna.

SEGUSIUM, capital of the Segusini, in Gallia Transpadana, on Duria Min. fl., bet. Ad Martem (16) and Ad Duodecim (12), on Via Aurelia. The death-place of Cottius. *Suza.*

SEGUSTERO, a town of the Vulgientes, Narbonensis, on Druentia fl., bet. Epotium and Alaunium. *Sisteron.*

SEGUSTO, a town of Narbonensis, towards Nemausus. *Sagriers.*

SEÏRÆ, a village of Arcadia, E. of Psophis.

SEIR mons, I. a range of m. extending bet. Asphaltites lacus and Ælanites sinus. II. a m. near Kirjath-jearim.

SELACHUSA ins., an isl. of Argolis, in Saronicus sin., over against Spiræum prom.

SELAIM, "rock," the Punic name of Soluntum, in Sicily.

SELAMPURA, a town of India e. Gangem, on Œdanes fl., L.

SELANUS, a town of Thebais, on the Nile, R., bet. Passalon and Panopolis.

SELÄSIA, a town of Laconia, at the confluence of Œnus and Gorgylus ffl., in a defile bet. Evas and Olympus. Noted for the defeat of Cleomenes. In ruins in Pausanias's time.

SELBONITIS, a district of Ammonitis, on Arnon fl.

SELE (Sile), a town of Lower Egypt, 28 m. E. from Thaubasium. The station of the Ala Prima Ægyptiorum. *Salehieh.*

SELEDIBA ins., Selandiba, the local name of Taprobane.

SELENESPOLIS, the Greek name of Luna, in Etruria.

SELENSIS, a town of the Lacetani, Tarraconensis, N.W. of Cortona. *Solsona.*

SELEMNUS fl., a r. of Achaia, falling into Corinthiacus sin. w. of Boline.

SELEOBOREIA, a town of Armenia Minor, bet. Nicopolis (21) and Caltiorissa (15).

SELEUCIA, I. *prius* Zochasia, a city of Babylonia, on the Tigris, 45 m. N. from Babylon, over against Ctesiphon. Enlarged by Seleucus Nicator. *El Madain.* II. Trachea, *surnamed* Tracheotis, a city of Cilicia Trachea, on Calycadnus fl., R., towards its mouth. Founded by Seleucus Nicator. The seat of a distinguished school of philosophy and literature. The birth-place of the peripatetics, Athenæus and Xenarchus. *Selefkieh.* III. (Samulias), town of Palestine, on Merom lacus. IV. a port of Pamphylia, at the mouth of a river not named, 12 m. E. of Eurymedon fl. V. capital of Seleucis, Syriæ, near the Orontes, w̄. of Imma. Built by Seleucus Nicator, and his burial-place. *Kepsé.* VI. *surnamed* Sidera, a town of Pisidia, on the borders of Phrygia. VII. (Sele, Soloce), a city of Susiana Elymais, on Hedyphon fl. *Sultanabad.* VIII. a name of Tralles, in Lydia. IX. *surnamed* ad Belum, *postea* Seleucopolis, a town of Apamene, Syriæ, on the Orontes, near Belus mons, N.W. of Apamea. *Sehjun.*

SELEUCIS, a district of Syria, about Seleucia.

SELGE, a city of Pisidia, on Eurymedon fl., above Pidnelissus. Founded by Calchas, and enlarged by a Lacedæmonian colony.

SELGOVÆ (Selgovich, *Celticè*, "hunters, freebooters," Elgovæ), a people of Valentia, Brit., bet. the Damnii and Otadeni, N. and Ituna æst. s. *On the Solway (hence named), in Kircudbright and Dumfriesshire.*

SELIA, a town of the Turtuli, Bætica, N.E. of Mænoba.

SELINITIS (Selentis), the district about Selinus, in Cilicia.

SELINUS, I. a r. of Achaia, rising S. of Trilæa, and falling into Corinthiacus sin. S.E. of Ægium. *Vostizza.* II. of Cilicia Trachea, falling into the sea at Selenus. *Selenty.* III. of Mysia, rising in Pindasus m., and falling into Caicus fl. towards Pergamum. *Tabaklar-Tchay.* IV. of Sicily, falling into the sea at Selinus. Named from the parsley that covered its banks. V. (Sellenus), of Triphylia in Elis, falling into the sea S.W. of Scillus. VI. a town of Cilicia Trachea, N.E. of Syedra, at the mouth of Selinus fl. The death-place of Trajan, and hence, for a time, named Trajanopolis. *Selenty.* VII. of Laconia, on Marios fl., 2¼ m. N.W. from Geronthræ. VIII. a port of Marmarica, bet. Zagylis and Trisarchi villa. IX. a city of Sicily, S.W., at the mouth of Selinus fl., bet. Pintia and Thermæ Selinantiæ. Surnamed Palmosa, from its palm-trees. *Pulci.*

SELINUSIA palus, a marsh of Ionia, formed by Caystrus fl. at its mouth.

SELLEIS fl., I. a r. of Achaia, falling into Corinthiacus sin., E. of Elisson fl. II. of Epea in Elis, rising in Pholoe m., and falling into Ionium mare below Ephyre. *Alepochori.* III. of Mysia, falling into the Hellespont at Arisbe.

SELLETÆ, a people of Thrace, on the Euxine, bet. the Crobyzi and the Thyni.

SELLI, a Pelasgic tribe in Epirus, about Dodona, descendants of the Tyrrheni, who worshipped Jupiter in a peculiar way.

SELLIUM, a town of the Lusitani, E. of Collippo.

SELUR, a town of Pandionis regnum, Ind., s. of Modurla.

SELYMBRIA (Selybria, "town of Selys"), a town of the Odrysæ, in Thrace, on the Propontis, bet. Regium and Perinthus Heraclea. A colony from Megara Nisæa. *Selibria.*

SEMACHIDÆ, a demus of Attica, of the tribe Antiochis, in Epacria regio.

SEMANA SILVA, a portion of Hercynia Silva, in the territory of the Hermiones, on the confines of the Hermunduri.

SEMANTHINI mons, m. of Asia, extending N.W. from Sinarum sin., and separating the Seres from the Sinæ.

SEMBOBITIS, a town of Tenesis, in Æthiopia, on Pseboa lac., S.W.

SEMENE, a district of Tenesis, in Æthiopia, N.E. of Pseboa lac.

SEMINETHUS (Simmethus), a town of Caria, near Antiochia, whither its inhabitants were transferred by Antiochus.

SEMIRAMIDIS mons, m. of Carmania, N. of Harmozia.

SEMIRUS fl., a r. of Bruttium, falling into Scylleticus sin., 12 m. N.E. from Scylletium. *Simmari.*

SEMISUS, a town of Metelene, in Cappadocia.

SEMNA, a town of Limyrica, Ind., 4 geog. m. from Podoperura. *Mangalor.*

SEMNI, a people of Taprobane, about Panti sin.

SEMNON lacus, a sacred grove of the Semnones, Germaniæ, on Viadrus fl., w. of Viritium.

SEMNŌNES, a tribe of Suevi, in Germania Magna, bet. Albis fl. and Viadrus fl., s. of the Vindili. *Mecklenburg, Brandenburg, Lusace, Part of Poland, &c.*

SEMNUS fl. Lucaniæ, i. q. Siris.

SENA, I. a r. of Umbria, falling into the sea at Ad Pirum. *Cesano.* II. ins., an isl. of the Osismii, Lugdunensis III., s. of Gobæum prom. *Sène.*

SENAGALLICA (Senogallia, Sena), a town of Umbria, at the mouth of Misus fl., bet. Ad Pirum (8) and Ancona. The first Roman colony beyond the Apennines (283 B.C.). Sacked by Pompey. *Sinigaglia.*

SENA JULIA, a town of Etruria, on Via Claudia, bet. Ad VI. and Florentia. A col. of Julius Cæsar. *Sienna.*

SENÆ, a town of Sicily, bet. Porthmus and Messana.

SENNABRIS, a town of Galilæa, on Tiberias lac., s.w., bet. Hamath and Tarichæa.

SENNATES, a people of Novem Populana. *About Sennac.*

SENOMAGUS, a town of the Volcæ Arecomici, Narbonensis, bet. Arausio (15) and Acunum (18). *St. Pierre de Senos.*

SENŌNES, a people of Lugdunensis IV., in Gaul, N.E. of the Lingones. A colony of them settled in Umbria, on the Adriatic, after pillaging Rome under Brennus. *Seine et Oise: Seine et Marne.*

SENONIA, a later name of Lugdunensis IV.

SENSES, a tribe of Getæ, Dac., bet. the Cotenses and the Piephigi.

SENTIANUM, a town of Samnium, 33 m. s.e. from Equus Tuticus. *Bisaccio.*

SENTICA, a town of the Vettones, Lusitania, s. of Salmantica. *Zamora.*

SENTII, a people of Alpes Cottiæ, about Sanitium.

SENTINATES, a tribe of Senones, in Umbria, about Sentinum.

SENTINUM, capital of the Sentinates, in Umbria, s. of Ad Ensem, towards the Apennines. Memorable for the devotion of the consul Decius. *Sasso Ferrato.*

SENUS (Scena) fl., a r. of Hibernia, w., separating the Hiberni from the Autiri. *Shannon.*

SEPELACI, a town of the Edetani, Tarraconensis, on Sucronensis sin., bet. Etovesa N. and Saguntum s.

SEPHAR. *Vide* Saphar.

SEPHARAD, a district of Asia Minor, towards the Bosporus.

SEPHARAIM, i. q. Sepphara.

SEPHET, a town of Galilæa Sup., w.n.w. of Bethsaida.

SEPHITA campus, the plains on the coast of Judæa, bet. Lydda N. and Gaza s.

SEPIA, I. a m. of Arcadia, bet. Stymphalus and Pheneus, where Æpylus, son of Elatus, was killed by the serpent. II. a village of Argolis, near Tirynthus. The scene of a great defeat of the Argives by Cleomenes.

SEPIAS prom., a headland of Magnesia, in Thessaly, bet. Casthanæa and Magnesiæ prom., whence Peleus carried off Thetis. The scene of the wreck of a considerable portion of Xerxes' fleet. *C. Hagios Demetrios.*

SEPĪNUM, a town of Samnium, s.e. of Bovianum. A colonia of Nero. *Attilia.*

SEPIUSSA ins., an isl. of Caria.

SEPORAS fl., a r. of Paphlagonia, rising in Pæmen m., and falling into Parthenius fl. *Beinder Sou.*

SEPONTIO (Paramica), a town of the Vaccæi, Tarraconensis, s.e. of Pallantia.

SEPPHORIS, i. q. Dio Cæsarea, Galileæ.

SEPTÆ (Setæ, Salala), a town of Phrygia, towards Attalia.

SEPTEM AQUÆ, springs of Sabinium, near Velinus fl., formerly the lake now called Lago di Santa Susanna.

SEPTEM ARÆ, a town of the Celtici, Lusitania, bet. Medobriga N. and Arunci s.e.

SEPTEM FRATRES m., seven hills of Mauritania Ting., on the coast bet. Lissa and Abyla; so named from their resemblance to one another.

SEPTEM MARIA, a town of the Veneti, in Venetia, bet. Hadrianum (6) and Fossa (6). *Marozzo.*

SEPTEM PAGI, a district of Etruria, bet. Cremera fl. and the Tiber.

SEPTEMIACI, a fortress of Vindelicia, on Hadriani vallum, 7 m. N. of Opie. *Near Hochstadt.*

SEPTIMUNICIA, a town of Byzacene, bet. Tabalta (20) and Madassuma (25).

SEPTEMPEDA, a town of Picenum, on Flosis fl., R., bet. Prolaquem (15) and Treia (9). *S. Severino.*

SEPTENTRIONALIS oceanus, i. q. Borealis.

SEPTIMANCA, a town of the Vaccæi, Tarraconensis, on Durius fl. below Rauda. *Simancas.*

SEPTONIA, a town of the Belgæ, Brit., w. of Sorbiodunum.

SEPYRA, a fortress of the Eleuthero Cilices, in Amanus m.

SEQUĂNA fl., a r. of Gaul, rising towards Andematunum and falling into the Atlantic at Carocotinum. *Seine.*

SEQUĂNI, a Celtic people of Maxima Sequanorum, bounded N. by Vogesus m., s. by the Rhodanus, w. by the Arar, and E. by Jura m. *Departments of Ain, N. Saone, E., Jura and Doubs, and Haute-Saone, s.*

SERA, capital of the Issedones, Sericæ. *Pekin. Singan?*

SERACA, a town of Sarmatia, near the source of Vardanus fl. *Procznoi.*

SERANUSSA, a town of Pontus, bet. Comana and Cabira.

SERAPIDIS ins., an isl. of Arabia Felix, in Erythræum mare, bet. Didymi prom. and Corodamum prom.

SERAPIS, a mart of Azania, on the coast, under the line.

SERAPIUM, I. a maritime village of Cyrenaica, s. of Drepanum prom. II. (Suchoth), a town of Lower Egypt, on the w. bank of Amarus lacus, bet. Heroopolis (18) and Etham.

SERBES fl., a r. of Mauritania Cæsar., falling

into the Mediterranean, bet. Rusucurrum and Rusubicar.

SERBI, a people of Sarmatia As., on the Caspian, bet. the Vali and the Udæ.

SERDI, a people of Mœsia, on Scomius m., bet. the Thunatæ and the Tilatæi, s. of the Treres.

SERES, the people of Serica.

SERGETIA fl., a r. of Dacia, rising N.E. of Zarmizegethusa, and falling into the Danube above Taurunum.

SERGIOPOLIS, a town of Chalybonitis, Syriæ, 3 geog. m. s. from Sura.

SERIA, a town of the Celtici, Bæturia, near the Anas, w.n.w. of Nertobriga. A colonia (Fama Julia). *Seria*.

SERIANE (Chalybon), capital of Chalybonitis, Syria, bet. Chalcis (45) and Androna, 32 m. s.e. from Salaminias.

SERICA, a country of Asia, bounded N. by Terra Incognita, s. by India e. Gangem, w. by Scythia e. Imaum, and E. by the Sinæ. Named, like its people the Seres, from the silkworm (Sēr), whose product formed a staple of the country. *Bucharia, Kotschotei, and part of China*.

SERĪMUM, a town of the Bastarnæ, Sarmat., near the Borysthenes, L., below Sarum. *Ekaterinoslav*.

SERINDA, a district of Serica, with a cognominal capital. *Sirhind*.

SERIO, I. a r. of Novem Populana, falling into the Garumna at Alingo. II. a town of the Bituriges Vivisci, Aquitania II., on the Garumna, L., bet. Stomata and Ilingo. *Rions*.

SERIPHUS, I. an isl. of the Ægean, one of the Cyclades, bet. Cythnus and Siphnus. In circuit 12 m. Under the Romans a place of banishment. The scene of the punishment by Perseus of Polydectes. The frogs here were dumb. *Serpho*. II. its capital, on the s.e. coast. *Serpho*.

SERMANICOMAGUS, a town of the Santones, Aquitania II., bet. Aunedonacum w. and Cassinomagus E.

SERMITIUM, a town of Corsica, near Circidius fl., L., under Aureus m., N.

SERMO, a town of the Edetani, Tarraconensis, s.w. of Cæsar Augusta.

SERMYLE, a town of Sithonia, Macedonia, at the N.E. extremity of the Toronaicus sin.

SERNA (Senna), a town of Pamphylia.

SEROTA, a town of Pannonia Inferior, on Dravus fl., R., bet. Berebis and Mariniana (20). *Draus*.

SERPA, a town of the Celtici, Bæturia, on the Anas, above Præsidium. *Serpa*.

SERRAPILLI, a people of Pannonia, on Dravus fl.

SERRE (Gerre), a town of Cyrrhestica, Syr., 13 m. s. from Bethammaria.

SERREPOLIS (Seretile), a town of Cilicia Campestris, on Issicus sin., E. of Januaria prom.

SERRETES, a people of Pannonia, on Dravus fl.

SERRHEUM prom., I. a headland of the Cicones, Thrace, E. of Ismarium prom. *C. Makri*. II. a fortress of the Cicones, Thrace, at Serrheum prom., under Ismarus m. *Makri*.

SERRI, a people of Sarmatia, on the N.E. coast of the Euxine.

SERUS fl., a r. of India e. Gangem, falling into Sinus Magnus. *Menam*.

SERVIODURUM, a town of Rhætia, bet. Reginum (28) and Pontes Renses (27). *Straubing*.

SERVITIUM (Serbinum), a town of the Varciani, Pannon., on Savus fl., R., at the confluence of Verbas fl., bet. Prætorium (23) and Urbate (25).

SESAMA, a town of Cappadocia, bet. Nazianzus (25) and Andabilis (16).

SESAMUS, "sesame-growing," the early name of Amastris, in Paphlagonia.

SESARETHUS, a town of the Taulantii, 10 m, s.e. from Acrolissus, on Isanus fl. *Sersdit*.

SESECRIENÆ ins., Indiæ, i. q. Heptanesiæ.

SESIPPI (Sibi) portus, a port of Arabia Felix, on the Red sea, near Zabida.

SESSĪTES fl., a r. of Gallia Transpad., rising N.E. of Vitricium and falling into Padus fl. below Ad Medias. *Sessia*.

SESTIARIUM prom., Mauritaniæ, i. q. Cannarum.

SESTINATES, a people of Umbria, about Sestinum.

SESTINUM, capital of the Sestinates, Umbria, on Pisaurus fl. above Pitinum. *Sestino*.

SESTIUM, an inland town of the Œnotri, in Bruttium.

SESTOMAGUS, a town of the Volcæ Tectosages, Narbonensis I., bet. Ad Fines w. and Ebromagus.

SESTOS, I. a city of Chersonesus Thracia, on the Hellespont, over against (N.E.) Abydos, in Troas, from which it is distant 3 m. 6 furlongs. Celebrated for the loves of Hero and Leander, and for Xerxes' bridge, which, however, commenced on the European side, lower down the coast, towards Madytus, where the breadth of the Hellespont is only 7 furlongs. II. a town of Cyprus, towards Tamasus.

SESUVII, *postea* Saii, Sagii, a tribe of Aulerci, in Lugdunensis. *About Seez.*

SETANTII, a tribe of Brigantes, Brit., w.,
bet. Moricambe æstuar. and Belisama æstuarium.

SETANTIORUM portus, an æstuary of the
German ocean, in Britain, bet. Belisama
æstuarium and Moricambe æstuarium.
Lancaster Bay.

SETATUM, Rhætiæ, i. q. Sullavio.

SETE, a town of Bithynia.

SETEJA fl., a r. of Britain, falling into the
sea below Deva, the N. boundary of Britannia II. and Flavia Cæsariensis. *Dee.*

SETHRUM (Tochpanhes), a town of Lower
Egypt, on Bubasticus fl. below Daphne.

SETHIS fl., Carmaniæ, i. q. Sabis.

SETIA, a town of the Volsci, 3 m. S.E. of
Sulmo. A colonia. Noted for its wine.
Sezza.

SETIDAVA, a town of Northern Germany, N.
of Calisia. *Posen.*

SETINUS sinus, a bay of the Tyrrhenian sea
at Sinuessa.

SETIUS m., a pr. of Narbonensis, N.E. of
Agatha. *Cape Sette.*

SETOVIA, a town of Germania, under Carpathus m.

SETUACATUM, a town of the Marcomanni,
in Germany, over against the mouth of the
Œnus fl.

SETUCIS, a town of the Ambiani, Belgica II.,
bet. Samarobriva N.W. and Rodium E.S.E.

SETUIA, a town of the Sidones, Sarmatiæ,
on Aucha fl. above Parienna. *Sittau?*

SEUMARA (Seusamora), a town of Iberia, on
Aragus fl. *Samthauro.*

SEUTLEUSA (Teutleusa) ins., an isl. of
Rhodes, N. of Chalcea. *Limonia.*

SEVA THABAS, a town of Media Magna, S.
of Seva Vicina.

SEVA VICINA, a town of Media Sigriane,
bet. Nazada and Bithia.

SEVACES, a tribe of Boii, Noricum, N.W.,
bet. the Danube N. and the Alauni s.

SEVERI murus, an earth-wall, constructed
by Severus 121 A.D., from Bodotria Æstuar. to Clota Æstuar. (32), separating
Britannia Barbara from Valentia.

SEVERUS m., a summit of Fiscellus m., in
Italy, adjoining Tetricus m. *Monte Sibilla.*

SEVO m., m. of Western Scandinavia. *M.
Kjolen.*

SEX INSULÆ, six isl. of Mauritania Ting.,
in the Mediterranean, off Cannarum prom.

SEXI, Bætica, *vide* Saxetanum.

SEXTANTIO (Sostentio), a town of the Volcæ
Arecomici, Narbonensis, bet. Ambrussum
N.E. and Forum Domitii S.W. *Castelnau.*

SHAARAIM, a port of Juda and then of
Simeon.

SHARON vallis, a valley extending along the
coast of Palestine, bet. Cæsarea and Joppa.
Noted for its beauty and fertility.

SHECHEM (Sichem, Sychem, Sychar, *postea*
Neapolis), a city of Samaria, 35 m. N.
from Jerusalem, under Garizim m. N.
Destroyed by Abimelech; restored by Jeroboam, and appointed by him the capital
of Israel. A colonia (Flavia). *Naploos.*

SHILOH, a city of Ephraim, bet. Lebanon
and Bethel, 25 m. N. from Jerusalem.
Here Samuel began to prophesy, and here
Joshua set up the tabernacle.

SHINAAR, a plain on the Euphrates, bet.
Mesopotamia and Persia.

SHOCHOCH, *vide* Socho.

SHUNEM, a town of Issachar. The locality
of Elisha's miracle. *Solam.*

SHUSHAN, i. q. Susa.

SIAGUL (Siagu), a town of Zeugitana, bet.
Vina and Putput (3). *Kassir-Asseite.*

SIACUS, a town of Persis Parætacene, bet.
Aspadana and Nisacus.

SIALA, a town of Tyanitis, in Cappadocia.

SIANTICUM, i. q. Santicum.

SIARUM, a town of the Turtetani, Bætica,
near Salpesa, S.E.

SIASURA (Ziazur), a town of Chalonitis,
Assyr., under Zagrus m., S.E. of Arbela.

SIATA ins., I. an isl. of Britain. II. of the
Veneti, Lugdunensis III., N. of Vindilis
ins.

SIATUTANDA (Satutanda), a town of the
Frisii, Germ., on Amisia fl., R., towards
its mouth. *Asenhaus.*

SIATA ins., an isl. of the Veneti, Lugdunensis III., N. of Vindilis ins.

SIAZUROS, a town of Adiabene, Assyria.
Sehrzur.

SIBACENE, Armeniæ, i. q. Siracene.

SIBARIA, a town of the Vettones, Lusitania,
bet. Sarabris N.N.E. and Salmantica.

SIBERĒNA, a city of the Œnotri, in Brut-
tium, on the s. declivity of Clibanus m.
Noted for its wine (Vinum Severianum).
Santa Severina.

SIBERIS fl., Bithyniæ, i. q. Hieros.

SIBDE, a town of Caria, near Halicarnassus.

SIBI, a people of Gedrosia, under Bætius m.,
E. of the Musarinæi.

SIBIDUNDA (Sibindus), a town of Phrygia
Salutaris.

SIBMAH, a town of Reuben, near Heshbon.
Noted for the vines of its district.

SIBRUS (Subes), the early name of Xanthus
fl., Lyciæ.

SIBUS, a town of Numidia, bet. Flacciana
and Ad Arvalla.

SIBUTZATES, a people of Aquitania, N.E. of Lapurdum. *About Sobusse.*

SIBYLLATES, a tribe of Tarbelli, w. of the Osquidates. *Vallée de Soule.*

SIBYRTUS (Sybrita), a town of Crete, 8 m. s.w. from Eleuthernæ. *Hagios Basilios.*

SICAMBRI (Sugambri, Sygambri, Salii), a tribe of Istævones, Germ., bet. the Chattuarii w., the Cherusci E., the Bructeri N., and the Chatti s. Under Augustus they were removed into Belgica II., and later, under the name of Gugerni, and the epithet excisi, "separated," occupied a district of Germania II., N. of the Ubii.

SICANI, a Celto-Ligurian people, who settled in w. Italy, and, after the Umbri and Osci, or Opici, were probably its earliest inhabitants. From Italy, colonies of them passed into Sicily, circa 1300 B.C., occupying its w. parts.

SICANIA, a name of Sicily, from its Sicanian colonists.

SICANUS (Silana), I. a r. of Tarraconensis, falling into the Mediterranean N. of Sicoris fl. Named from the Sicani. II. of Sicily, falling into Afric. pelagus, E. of Agrigentum. Named from the Spanish Sicanus.

SICCA VENEREA, a town of Numidia, on Bagradas fl., s. of Vacca. A Phœnician settlement, and named from a temple of Venus. *Keft.*

SICDELIS ins., an isl. of Britain.

SICELIOTÆ, i. q. Siculi.

SICELLA, Jud., i. q. Ziklag.

SICILIA (Sicania, Trinacria) ins., an isl. of Italy, in the Mediterranean, bet. Italy and Africa. Named Sicilia from the Siculi, Sicania from the Sicani, and Trinacria from the three great promontories marking its triangular outline. By some writers it is considered to be the Thrinakria of Homer. *Sicily.*

SICILIPPA (Sicilibra), a town of Zeugitana, 11 m. N.E. from Vallis. *Bazilbah.*

SICILIUM, a town of the Hirpini, in Samnium.

SICIMINA m., a summit of the Apennines, in Gallia Cispad., on Secies fl., s. of Papinus m.

SICINA, Hyrcaniæ, i. q. Zadracarta.

SICINOS, *prius* Œnoe, I. an isl. of the Ægean, one of the Sporades, bet. Photegandros and Ios. Noted for its wine. *Sikyno.* II. its capital, on the s.E. coast. *Sikyno.*

SICORIS fl., a r. of Tarraconensis, rising near Julia Libyca, and falling into Iberus fl. above Octogesa. *Segre.*

SICULENSES, a tribe of Siculi, settled in the s.E. angle of Sardinia.

SICULI, a Celto-Ligurian people, who settled in w. Italy, coming next in order of colonization to the Sicani. From Italy colonies of them passed into Sicily, circa 1260 B.C., and gave name to it. They occupied, more especially, its E. parts.

SICULIUM, an early name of Tibur, from its Siculian founders.

SICULUM FRETUM, the straits separating the extremity of Italy from Sicily. Called also Porta, i. e. the door admitting the Tuscan sea into the Ionian.

SICYON, *olim* Ægialea, Demetrias, *postea* Mecone, a maritime city of Achaia, bet. Aristonautæ and Goras; formerly the capital of a distinct kingdom, founded by Ægialus. The birth-place of Aratus. Noted for its water, marble, and conger eels. *Basilica.*

SICANABIS (Siganeum, Neapolis), a town of the Manrali, Colchid., at the mouth of Singames fl.

SIDACE, a town of Lycia.

SIDAS, a district of Bœotia, on the confines of Attica, 8 m. E. of Platæa.

SIDDIM VALLIS, the site of Sodom and Gomorrah, covered by the s. extremity of Asphaltites lacus.

SIDE, I. a town of Laconia, on the Ægean, N. of Malea prom. Named from Sida, daughter of Danaus. II. a maritime town of Pamphylia, 10 m. E. from Seleucia. A colony of Cumæans from Æolis. Sacred to Minerva. The chief harbour and emporium of the Pamphylian and Cilician pirates. Later, the metropolis of Pamphylia II. *Eski Adalia.* III. (*postea* Polemonium), a town of Pontus, in Sidene regio, at the mouth of Sidenus fl., 1¼ m. E. from Phadisana. Renamed from King Polemo, the client of Augustus.

SIDELE, a town of Ionia.

SIDENE, I. a district of Pontus, E. of Themiscyra regio. II. a town of Lycia. III. of Mysia, on Rhesus fl. Destroyed by Crœsus.

SIDENI, I. a people of Arabia Petræa, on the Red sea, s. of the Thamuditæ. *Beni Djeheyne.* II. a maritime tribe of Vindili, Germ., on Viadrus fl. w., bet. the Rugii and the Semnones.

SIDENUS fl., a r. of Pontus, falling into the Euxine at Side. *Sidin.*

SIDERIS fl., a r. of Hyrcania, falling into the Caspian, w. of Socanas fl.

SIDERUS, the haven of Olympus, in Lycia. *Porto Genovese.*

SIDICES, a people of Media Magna, N.w. of Choarene.

SIDICENI, descendants of the Umbri, or

Osci and Pelasgi, settled in Campania, N. of Vulturnus fl.

SIDOLOCUM (Sedelaucum), a town of the Ædui, Lugdunensis I., bet. Aballo N.W. and Augustodunum S.E. *Saulieu.*

SIDON (Zidon), a maritime city of Asher, in Phœnicia, at the mouth of Bostrenus fl., bet. Porphyrias N. and Sarepta s., 25 m. N. of Tyrus. Built by Sidon, s. of Canaan. The Sidonians, the Poludaidaloi of Homer, were famous for their commercial enterprise and their manufacturing ingenuity. Sidon was the birth-place of Moschus, the atomic philosopher. *Sidon; Saide.*

SIDONES, a tribe of the Bastarnæ, Sarmat., N. of the Carpi.

SIDŌDŌNA, a town of Carmania w., on the coast. Its population, human and animal, still subsist, as of old, on fish. *Lundje.*

SIDUMANIS fl., Brit., i. q. Idumania.

SIDUS, a fortress of Corinthia, on Saronicus sin., bet. Crommyon and Schoenus. Noted for its apples.

SIDUSSA ins., an islet of Ionia, towards the mouth of Caystrus fl., with a cognominal town.

SIDYMA, a maritime village of Lycia, near Patara.

SIELEDIVA, i. q. Taprobane.

SIGA (Sardabale), I. a r. of Mauritania Cæsar., falling into the Mediterranean bet. Gypsara and Ad Salsum (25). *Tafua; Tremesen.* II. a city of Mauritania Cæsar., on Siga fl., L., near its mouth. The capital of Syphax. Destroyed in Strabo's time, but afterwards restored, and made a colonia and municipium. *Tremesen.* III. a town of the Segovini, in Gaul. *Sause.*

SIGÆUM, I. a prom. of Troas, 7½ m. s. from Rhæteum prom. The burial-place of Achilles. *Yeni-cher.* II. a town of Troas, at the cognominal prom. An Æolian colony. Built with the stones of Troja. The retreat of Hippias. Destroyed by the people of Ilion Novum.

SIGALA, a town of the Mandalæ, Indiæ, on the Ganges, bet. Boracta and Palimbothra.

SIGARRA, a town of the Ilercaones, Tarraconensis, N.W. of Dertosa.

SIGIA, the original name of Alexandria Troas.

SIGIUNÆ, a tribe of Scordisci, on the Danube.

SIGMANUS ÆST., an æstuary of Gaul, at Curianum prom. *Bassin d'Arcachon.*

SIGNIA, I. a m. of Phrygia Magna, overlooking Celenæ. II. (Signa, "standards"), a Tyrrhenian town of the Volsci, s. of Præneste. A military col. of Tarquinius

Superbus. It was noted for a peculiar sort of astringent wine, for its pears, and for its brick flooring (opus Signinum). *Segni.*

SIGRÆUM prom., the N.W. extremity of Lesbos ins. *C. Sigri.*

SIGRIANE, a district of Media Magna, about Jasonius m., N.W. of Choarene.

SIGULONES, a tribe of Saxones, Germ., on Germanicus oc., s. of the Angli.

SIGUM fl., a r. of Germania Magna, falling into the Danube. *Sieg.*

SIGUS (Sega, Segoha), a town of Numidia, bet. Cirba (25) and Thigisis. *Temluk.*

SIGYNNES, an early people of Germania, according to Herodotus, N. of the Veneti. Described by Herodotus as colonists from Media.

SIHER, a town of Aturia, Assyriæ, N.W. of Ninus.

SIHINNUS, a town of Mygdonia, Mesopotamiæ, under Singara m. N., bet. Thigubis and Singara.

SILA fl., a r. of Messenia, falling into Asinæus sin. s. of Methone. *Siloso.*

SILA SILVA, a fir forest of Bruttium, 87 m. in extent, bet. Consentia and Rhegium. From it chiefly came the pix Brutia.

SILACENÆ, a town of the Aravisci, Pannoniæ, bet. Limusa (16) and Valcum (28). *Near Koposvar.*

SILANDUS, a town of Lydia, on Hermus fl., above Bagæ. *Selendi.*

SILARUS, I. a r. of Gallia Cispadana, falling into Vatrenus fl. below Silarus. II. of Italy, dividing Lucania from Campania, rising in the Apennines, s. of Sub Romula, and falling into Tyrrhen. mare N. of Pæstum. Its water was of a petrifying quality. *Sele.* II. a town of the Boii, in Gallia Cispadana, on Silarus fl., R.

SILAS (Silias) fl., a r. of India.

SILBIUM (Sybleum, Syblas), a town of Phrygia Magna, N.E. of Apamea Cibotus, at the source of Mæander fl.

SILDA, Maurit. Ting., i. q. Gilda.

SILE, Ægypti, *vide* Sele.

SILEUM, a town of Lycia.

SILICES, a people of Assyria, on Lycus fl., above the Orontes.

SILINGÆ, a tribe of Vindili, Germania, on Viadrus fl., L., above the Diduni.

SILIS fl., I. a r. of Tarraconensis, rising in Vindius m., and falling into Minius fl. below Gemestarium. II. a name of the Jaxartes. III. a r. of Venetia, rising near Tarvisium, and falling into the Adriatic at Altinum. *Sile.*

SILLAS fl., a canal of the Tigris, running by Artemita.

SILLIGUS, a town of Ionia, near Smyrna.

SILOAM (Siloah, Shiloah), a pool or stream of Benjamin, near En-rogel, under Sion m.

SILSILIS, a town of Thebais, on the Nile, R., bet. Toum and Ombi.

SILURES (*Celtice*, siol-uri, "race of the river"), a people of Britannia II., on Sabrina æstuar. and Sabrina fl., E. of the Demetæ.

SILURUM ins., i. q. Cassiterides.

SILVA GALLINARIA, a pine forest of Campania, above Literna palus, whence came the timber for the fleet of Sextus Pompeius. Infamous as the haunt of banditti. *Pineta di Castel Volturno.*

SILVANECTES (Subanecti, Ubanecti), a tribe of Bellovaci, Belgica II., on the Isara, above Briva Isara. *About Senlis.*

SILVANI PRÆSIDIUM, a fortress of Byzacene, on Syrtis Min., bet. Cellæ Picentinæ and Lacene.

SILVIUM, I. a town of Istria, bet. Parentium (9) and Pola (21). *Telcovich.* II. of Messapia, on Via Appia, bet. Venusia (20) and Blera (16). *Garagnone.*

SIMARA (Ismara), a town of Armenia Min., on the Euphrates, bet. Analiba (15) and Zenocopi (18).

SIMBRIVIUS (Simbruinus) lacus, a lake of the Æqui, in Latium, formed by Anio fl. at Sublaqueum. Noted for its cooling property. *Lago di Subiaco.*

SIMENA, a town of Lycia, 8 m. from Aperlæ.

SIMĒNI, Britanniæ, i. q. Iceni.

SIMEON, a tribe of Israel, bet. Juda N. at Sorek fl., Idumæa, s., the Mediterranean w., and the Jordan E.

SIMITU (Simisthu), a town of Numidia, bet. Bulla Regia (7) and Ad Aquas (5). A colonia.

SIMNANA, a town of Africa, on Syrtis Maj., w. bet. Nivirgitab and Thubactis.

SIMOIS fl., "shelving-banked," I. (Simus), a r. of Sicily, falling into the Tyrrhenian sea at or near Segestanum Emporium. Named by Æneas from the Trojan river. II. of Troas, rising in Gargara m., 30 m. S.E. from Troja, and, in the Homeric ages, joining Scamander fl. above Ilium Novum, whence they together flowed to the sea under the name of Stomalimne. Since called Scamander, and losing itself in a marsh on the coast. *Mendere.*

SIMOISIUS campus, a plain of Troas, bet. Scamander and Simois ffl.

SIMONIAS, a town of Galilæa, near Kison fl., s.w. of Nazareth.

SIMOS, a town of Pontus, bet. Agriane and Sebastia.

SIMPSIMIDA, a town of Parthia, w. of Tabas.

SIMMUNDU ins., i. q. Taprobane.

SIMYLLA prom., I. a pr. of India i. Gangem, w. bet. Nanaguna fl. and Calliane. *C. St. John.* II. a port of India i. Gangem, at Simylla prom.

SIMYRA, a town of Phœnicia, towards the mouth of Eleutherus fl.

SIN, "mire," the Scriptural name of Pelusium, and of the wilderness towards Sinai m.

SINA ins., I. an isl. of Britain. II. a town of Margiana, on Thus fl.

SINACA, a town of Hyrcania, E. of Maxera fl.

SINÆ, a people of Asia, bounded N. by Serica, w. by India, E. by Terra Incognita. *Cambodia, Cochin-China, &c.; and also in the province of Thensi-si.*

SINAI m., a m. of Arabia Petræa; the particular summit of Mount Horeb whence God published his law. *Ras-Sufsafeh.*

SINARA (Sinera, Sinorega, Sinebra, Sinerva), a fortress of Armenia Min., bet. Carsagis (28) and Analiba (28). Built by Mithridates. *Senarvir.*

SINARUM sin., a bay of Eous oceanus, w. of Colliarius fl.

SINARUS fl., a r. of India, falling into the Hydaspes.

SINCAR, a town of Media Ragiana, N.E. of Ecbatana.

SINDA, I. a town of Lycia, towards Cibyra. Strabo assigns it to Pisidia. II. of Phrygia Mag., near the source of Lysis fl., w. of Themisonium. III. capital of Sindica, Sarmatiæ, on Bosporus Cimmerius. IV. capital of the Sindi, Indiæ, on Magnus sin., over against Bramma.

SINDÆ ins., isl. of India e. Gangem, towards Malaci prom. Inhabited by anthropophagi.

SINDESSUS, a town of Caria.

SINDI, a people of Aurea Chersonesus, on Magnus sin., w.

SINDICA, a district of Sarmatia Asiat., on the Euxine, towards the s. mouth of the Vardanes.

SINDICUS portus, a port of the Sindi, Sarmatiæ, 4½ geog. m. from Corocondama.

SINDOMANA, a town of the Arbitæ, Gedrosia, on the Indus, below Susicana.

SINDUS (Sinthus, ad Decimum), a town of Mygdonia, in Macedonia, on the Egnatia Via, bet. Gephira (10) and Thessalonica (10), at the mouth of Echedorus fl.

SINDOCANDA, a port of Taprobane, w. below Soanus fl.

SINGA (Sugga), a town of Cyrrhestica, on Singas fl., L., at its junction with the Euphrates, 48 m. N. from Doliche.

SINGAMĒS fl., Colch., i. q. Cyaneus.

SINGANEUM, Colchid., i. q. Cyaneus.

SINGARA, a town of Mygdonia, Mesopotamia, N.W. of Cænæ. The locality of the defeat of Constantius II. by Sapor. *Sinjar.*

SINGARAS m., m. of Mygdonia, Mesopotamia, towards Singara. *Sindjar.*

SINGAS fl., a r. of Cyrrhestica, falling into the Euphrates at Singa. Named Marsyas by the Macedonians. *Sengia.*

SINGIDAVA, a town of the Prædavenses, Dac., on Marisas fl., R., s.w. of Apulum. *Deva.*

SINGIDUNUM (Sigindunum, Sengidon), a town of Mœsia Sup., on the Danube, at its confluence with the Savus. *Belgrade.*

SINGITICUS sin., a bay of the Ægean, bet. Acte penins. and Sithonia penins., in Macedonia. *G. di Monte Santo.*

SINGONE, a town of the Rheatæ, in Germania, between Celmantia and Arsicua. *Schemnitz.*

SINGOS, a town of Sithonia, in Macedonia, near the s. extremity of the Singiticus sin., to which it gave name, N.E. of Torone. *Sigga.*

SINGULIS, I. a r. of Bætica, rising in Ilipula m., s.e. of Illiberis, and falling into the Bætis near Carbula. The boundary bet. the Turtuli E. and the Turtetani w. *Xenil.* II. a town of the Turtetani, Bætica, on Singulis fl., above Astigi. *Puente di Don Gonzalo?*

SINGYA, a town of Pamphylia.

SINIM, the Scriptural name of China.

SINIS, a town of Melitene prefect., in Cappadocia. Made a colonia by the interest of Pompey.

SINITHANDUS (Siniandus), a town of Pisidia.

SINNA, a town of Acabene, Mesopotamia, on the Tigris, under Masius m.

SINNIUS fl., a r. of Gallia Cispadana, falling into Vatrenus fl. N.W. of Ravenna. *Senno.*

SINONIA ins., an isl. of Latium, 20 m. s.e. of Circæum prom. *Senone.*

SINOPE, I. a city of Paphlagonia, on a peninsula at the E. entrance of a small bay of the Euxine, over against Lepte prom., 88 m. E. from Carambis prom. Founded by Autolycus, the Argonaut; enlarged by a Milesian colony. Latterly the capital of the king of Pontus. A Roman colonia. The birth-place of Mithridates Eupator, Diogenes the Cynic, Baton the historian, and Diphilus the dramatist. *Sinub.* II. the Greek name of Sinuessa, in Latium.

SINORIA, Armeniæ, i. q. Sinara.

SINTHU, a district of India, on the western arm of the Indus (Sinthus).

SINTHUS fl., the w. mouth of the Indus. *Darraway.*

SINTI (Sinties), a people of Thrace, extending into Macedonia, on both banks of Strymon fl., N.W. of the Siropæones.

SINTICA, the country of the Sinti, in Pæonia, formerly a part of Thrace.

SINUESSA (Sinope), a town of the Ausones, in Latium, on Sinus Vesanus, bet. Minturnæ (9) and Pons Campanus, on Via Appia. A colonia 298 B.C. Noted for its wines. *Mondragone.*

SINZITA (Sindita), a town of Morimene, in Cappadocia.

SION m., a name of Hermon m.

SIONIA, a town of Pontus.

SIODA, a town of Albania, on Cyrus fl.

SIPH, a town bet. Hebron N.W. and Karmel s.

SIPHÆ (Typhæ), a port of Bœotia, on Alcyonium mare, w. of Creusis. The birthplace of Tiphys, the Argonaut pilot. *Agiani.*

SIPOR, a district of India, towards Calliane. *About Goa.*

SIPHNUS (Meropia) ins., an isl. of the Ægean, one of the Cyclades, bet. Olearus and Cimolus. In circuit 28 m. Noted for its gold and silver mines, and for a peculiarly soft stone, yielding to the turning-lathe. *Siphanto.*

SIPIA, a town of the Redones, Lugdunensis III., bet. Condate N.W. and Combaristum s.e.

SIPONTUM (Sipus), a maritime city of Daunia, in Apulia, on Via Frentana, bet. Ergitium and Anxanum. Founded by Diomed, an Etruscan chief, and named from the sepia (cuttle-fish) found on the coast in great abundance. A colonia 196 B.C.

SIPPHARA (Siphavaim), a district of Mesopotamia.

SIPUS, the Greek name of Sipontum.

SIPYLUS, I. a m. of Lydia, N. of Mastusia m., s. of Magnesia. The optical effect of a portion of this eminence, fancied to resemble a woman weeping, gave rise to the story of Niobe. Here was a rock called the Throne of Pelops. *Savounidje Dagh.* II. *prius* Tantalis, a city of Lydia, under Sipylus m. Submerged beneath Sale palus by an earthquake. The residence of Tantalus, and birth-place of Pelops.

SIRACENE, I. a district of Armenia Maj., about Harpasus fl. *Schirak.* II. of Parthia, bet. Astabene and Nisæa.

SIRACES (Siraceni), a people of Sarmatia Asiat., bet. the Tanais and Caucasus.

SIRBITUM, a town of Æthiopia, on Astaboras fl., s. of Meroe.

SIRBONIS (Barathra) palus, a lake of Casiotis,

Ægypti, on the sea-coast, bet. Gerrha and Ostracene. At one time 25 m. in length, and of extreme depth. Connected with the story of Typhon, whence the Egyptians named it "the exhalations of Typhon." *Sebaket Bardoil.*

SIRENUSÆ (Sirenes, Sirenum Petræ) ins., islets of Campania, off Surrentinum prom. The abode of the sirens. *Galli.*

SIRENUSARUM prom., a name of Surrentinum prom., in Campania, from the Sirens who frequented that coast.

SIRIATE, a town of Noricum, 15 m. from Sarantium. *Liezen.*

SIRIS (Semnus), I. a r. of Lucania, falling into Tarentinus sin. s. of Aciris fl. *Sinno.* II. a town of Lucania, at the mouth of Siris fl., L., 3 m. from Heraclea. Founded by a Trojan colony, and taken from them by Colophonians from Ionia, who changed its name to Poliæum, from Minerva Polias, whose palladium had been brought hither. Its inhabitants, who rivalled the Sybarites in luxury, were removed by the Tarentines to Heraclea, of which city Siris became the port. III. the town of the Siropæones, in Thrace, near Strymon fl. *Serres.*

SIRMIUM, I. a village, on a peninsula at the s. extremity of Benacus lac., bet. Beneventum and Ardelica. A favourite retreat of Catullus. *Sirmione.* II. a city of Pannonia Inf., on Savus fl., at its confluence with Bacuntius fl. *Mitrovitz; Schabacz.*

SIRNIDES ins., an isl. of Crete, off Sammonium prom.

SIROCE, a town of the Tapuri, Margiana, s.w. of Guriana.

SIROPÆONES, a Pæonian tribe, in Thrace, bet. the Odomanti and Strymon fl. Perhaps a tribe of the Odomanti themselves.

SIROTA, a town of Pannonia Inf., bet. Bolentum and Jovia.

SIRPIUM, a town of the Pentri, in Samnium, on Via Numicia, bet. Sæpinum (6) and Beneventum (18).

SISÁPO, I. *surnamed* Novus, a town of Tarraconensis, N.E. of Mirobriga. *Guadalanar.* II. *surnamed* Vetus, a town of Tarraconensis, S.E. of Mirobriga. Both noted for their silver and cinnabar mines. *Almaden.*

SISAR fl., Mauritaniæ, i. q. Audus.

SISARA lacus, a lake of Zeugitana, below Hippicus lacus.

SISAURA, a town of Mesopotamia, near Dara.

SISCIA (Segestica), a town of the Varciani, Pannoniæ, on Savus fl., R., at its confluence with Colapis fl. *Szissek.*

SISIUM, a fortress of Cilicia.

SISMII, *vide* Timii.

SISSA, i. q. Cissa.

SITACE, a town of Babylonia, 6 m. N. from Medius murus, 15 furlongs from the Tigris. *Eski-Bagdad.*

SITACUS fl., a r. of Susiana, falling into the sea bet. Gogana (100) and Teratis.

SITHONIA, a district of Chalcidice, in Macedonia, comprising the country at the head of the Toronaicus sin., and the peninsula bet. that gulf and the Singiticus sinus. Peopled by a gigantic tribe from Thrace. The Egyptian bean grew here naturally.

SITIA, I. a town of the Ilergetes, Tarraconensis, S.E. of Osca. II. of the Turtetani, Bætica, N.W. of Alostigi.

SITIBERIS, a town of the Cudupæ, Indiæ, on Serus fl.

SITIFIS (Sitifi), a city of Mauritania Cæsar., s. of Igilgilis (80). A colonia. *Setéf.*

SITILIA, a town of the Ædui, Lugdunensis I., on the Liger, bet. Aquæ Bormonis w. and Ariolica s.

SITIOGAGUS (Sitacus) fl., a r. of Persis, falling into Persicus sin. N. of Chersonesus prom.

SITOMAGUS, a town of the Iceni, Brit., on the coast, near Ad Taum. *Dunwich.*

SITONES, a people of Northern Germany. *In Norway.*

SITTACE (Sitta), a town of Adiabene, Assyriæ, 8 geog. m. S.E. from Artemita.

SITTACENE, a district of Assyria, about Sittace.

SITTIANI, a name of the people of Cirta, Numidiæ, from its colonizer, Sittius.

SITTIM, "acacias," a town of Moabitis, in the valley of Abel Sittim, over against Jericho.

SITTOCACIS fl., a r. of India i. Gangem, rising in Vindius m., and falling into Diumana fl. below its junction with Sambus fl. *Sind.*

SITUPOLIS, a town of Phrygia.

SIUPH, a town of Lower Egypt, near Sais. The birth-place of King Amasis.

SIUR portus, a port of Numidia, N.W. of Hippo Regius.

SIVA, a town of Cilicia prefectura, in Cappadocia, bet. Campe (22) and Sermusa (16).

SMARAGDUS m., m. of Thebais, on the Red sea, N. of Berenice. The kings of Egypt derived a large revenue from the emeralds found here. *Djebel Zabarah.*

SMENUS fl., a r. of Laconia, rising in Taygetus m., and falling into Laconicus sin. ½ m. from Las. Its water was peculiarly sweet.

SMILA, a town of Chalcidice, in Macedonia, on the Thermaicus sin., bet. Æneia and Combrea.

SMYRNA, "myrrh-producing," I. the capital

of Ionia. on Hermius sin. There were two successive cities of the name; the elder, named after the Amazon Smyrna, was built by the Ephesians, at the mouth of Meles fl.: the second, commanded by Alexander the Great in consequence of a dream, commenced by Antigonus, and completed by Lysimachus, stood 2½ m. higher up the river, under Pagus m. The birth-place of Homer and of Quintus Calaber. *Smyrna.* II. the early name of Ephesus, from the Amazon Smyrna.

SMYRNÆUS sin., i. q. Hermius.

SMYRNOPHOROS regio, a maritime district of Arabia Felix, N. and w. of Marmatha.

SOANAREI, a people of Sarmatia Asiatica, about Soanus fl.

SOANDA, a town of the Trocmi, in Galatia, bet. Therma (18) and Sacoena (32).

SOANUS fl., I. a branch of Gerrus fl., Albania, falling into the sea s. of Gerrus fl. *Sudak.* II. a r. of Taprobane, falling into Indicum mare bet. Sindocanda and Anarismundi prom.

SOARA, a town of the Phillitæ, India, near the source of Sonus fl.

SOATRÆ, I. a town of the Crobyzi, Mœsia, bet. Pamisus and Cahalet. II. of Lycaonia, i. q. Sabatra.

SOATRIX, a town of the Odrysæ, in Thrace, N.W. of Mesymbria.

SOBALA, a town of Caria.

SOBANUS fl., a r. of Aurea Chersonesus, running through the country of the Latrones. *Tenasserim?*

SOBIDÆ, a people of Parthia, on its s. border, E. of Choroana.

SOBURA, a port of India i. Gangem, E. *Near Elimpora.*

SOCANAA fl., Sarnius, I. a r. of Hyrcania, falling into the Caspian E. of Ochus fl. *Abiscoun.* II. a town of Hyrcania, at the mouth of Socanaa fl. *Meshed.*

SOCHI, a town of Commagene.

SOCHO (Shochoh), a town of Juda, Judæa, bet. Eleutheropolis (9) and Jerusalem. The death-place of Goliath.

SOCHCHOR, a town of Arabia Felix, near Sabe regia. *Shehra.*

SOCRATIS ins., an isl. of Arabia Felix, in the Red sea, opposite Ptolemais-Theron, in Egypt. *Firan.*

SODOBRIA, a town of the Carnutes, in Gaul. *Suèvre.*

SODOM, *vide* Asphaltites lacus.

SOGANA, a town of Gaulonitis, near the Jordan, N.E. of Bethsaida.

SOGANUS fl., a r. of Carmania, falling into Paragon sin. s. of Anamis fl.

SOGDIANA (Sogdias), a country of Asia, bet.

Jaxartes fl. and Oxus fl., having Scythia and Oxii m. w. and Comedarum m. E. The people were remarkable for their contempt of life. *Turkestan and Bokhara.*

SOGDII m., m. intersecting Sogdiana N.E.—s.w.

SOGIONTII, a tribe of Albiœci, Alpes Maritimæ, w. of the Vellauni. *About Sigonce.*

SOLANA, a town of Serica. *Lingtao.*

SOLANIDÆ ins., isl. of Arabia Felix, off Hammæum littus. *Isles of Sohar.*

SOLARIA, a town of Etruria, on Via Claudia, bet. Florentia (9) and Hellana (9).

SOLARIUM, a town of the Segoregii, Narbonensis, bet. Calcaria N.W. and Massilia S.E.

SOLEN fl., a r. of India, falling into the sea 12 m. E. from Colchis. *Vaygaru.*

SOLENTUM, Siciliæ, *vide* Solus.

SOLETUM, Apulia, i. q. Sallentia.

SOLI (Soloeis, *postea* Pompeiopolis), I. a maritime town of Cilicia Campestris, N.E. of Antiochia Lamotis, at the mouth of Liparis fl. A colony of Achæans and Rhodians from Lindus; enlarged by Pompey with a colony of Cilician pirates. The birth-place of Chrysippus, Philemon, and Aratus. *Mezetlu.* II. a city of Cyprus, on the N. coast, w. of Crommyon prom. With a temple of Venus and Isis. Founded by Demophoon, son of Theseus; or by an Athenian colony, under Phalerus and Acamas. The death-place of Solon. *Solea.*

SOLIA (Sollurco), a town of the Turtetani, Bætica, w. of Hispalis.

SOLICINUM, a town of Germania Mag., towards the Rauraci.

SOLIMNIA ins., an isl. of Thessaly, in the Ægean, bet. Halonnesus and Teos ins. *Pelagnisi.*

SOLIMARIACA, a town of the Leuci, Belgica I., on the Mosa, R., bet. Tullum and Noviomagus. *Soulosse.*

SOLIS, I. an island of India i. Gangem, E. above Cory ins. II. prom., a pr. of Arabia Felix, on Persicus sin., N. of Rhegma. III. (Soloeis, Soluntis), a pr. of Mauritania Tingit., w. bet. Vala and Mysocoras portus. *Cape Cantin.* IV. portus, a port of Taprobane, N. bet. Procuri and Mordala. V. fons, Africæ, *vide* Ammonum.

SOLIUM, a town of Acarnania, on the w. coast, bet. Palærus and Medeon. A Corinthian colony. *Selavena.*

SOLMISSUS m., a hill of Ionia, near Ephesus, s.w. above Ortygia nemus, where, according to the local tradition, the Curetes, by clashing their weapons, concealed from Juno the cries of Latona, during her confinement in the adjacent grove.

Soloce (Sodome), Susianæ, i. q. Seleucia.

Solodurum (Salodurum), a town of the Rauraci, Maxima Sequanorum, on Arula fl., bet. Ultinum and Petinesca. *Solothurn, Soleure.*

Soloe, *vide* Soli.

Soloeis prom., I. a pr. of Maurit. Ting., i. q. Solis m. II. the Greek name of Soluntum in Sicily and of Soli.

Soloentum prom., a pr. of Libya, on the Atlantic, s. of Nujus fl. *C. Bogador.*

Solona, a town of the Boii, in Gallia Cispadana, on Utis fl., below Forum Livii. *Solaria.*

Solonium, I. a town of the Allobroges, in Gaul, w. of the Rhone. The locality of the defeat of the Allobroges by Pomptinus. *Scillonaz.* II. a Tyrrhenian town of Latium, near Ardea.

Solonius campus, the district about Solonium, in Latium.

Soloon fl., a rivulet of Bithynia, running by Pythopolis into Ascanius lacus. Named after one of the companions of Theseus.

Solorius m., a s.w. continuation of Ortospeda m., in Bætica, n. of the Bastuli, the w. boundary of Tarraconensis. *Sierra di Solaria.*

Solus (Solentum, *prius* Selaim, Soloeis), a maritime town of Sicily, n. bet. Himera and Panormus. A Phœnician colony. *Solanto.*

Solygia, a village of Corinthia, on Saronicus sin., bet. Chersonesus and Rheitum, under Solygius m. *Mertese.*

Solygius m., a hill of Corinthia, one of Oneius m., on the s.e. coast, above Solygia.

Solyma, I. a summit of Taurus, in Lycia, at Phaselis. II. a town of Auranitis, e. of Seleucia.

Solymi, *postea* Milyæ, a tribe of Phœnicians, first settlers of Lycia, especially in Milyas, and of Pisidia, about Pisidicus lacus.

Solymos m., Pisidiæ, i. q. Sardemisus.

Sonisera, a town of Balearis Min., on the s.e. coast.

Sontia, a town of Lucania, s. of Tegianum. A Sybarite colony. *Sanzo.*

Sontius fl., a r. of Venetia, rising in Tullus m., and falling into the Adriatic e. of Aquileia. *Isonzo.*

Sonus (Eronobaos) fl., a r. of India i. Gangem, rising in Vindius m., and falling into the Ganges near Gange. *Sone.*

Soonautes fl., Bithyniæ, i. q. Oxinas.

Sopei, a people of Sarmatia Asiat., on Ocharius fl.

Sophanitæ, a people of Arabia Felix, partially on the desert, e. of the Minæi. *Beni Sephian.*

Sophene, a district of Armenia Maj., occupying its s.w. extremity, w. of Gordiene, s. of Armenia Minor. *Dzophkh.*

Sophon (Siphones, Sunonensis, Sumonensis, Boane), I. a lake of Bithynia, s.e. of Nicomedia. *Shabanja.* II. m. of Bithynia, w. and s. of Nicomedia.

Sophtha ins., an isl. of Persis, s. of Tabiena ins.

Sopianæ, a town of the Hercuniatæ, Pannon., 30 m. n.w. from Antiana. *Funfkirchen.*

Sōra, I. a town of Paphlagonia. II. capital of the Soræ, Indiæ, on Chaberis fl., towards its source. *Arcot?* III. a town of the Volsci, in Latium, on Liris fl., R., on the confines of the Marsi. A colonia 302 b.c., and again of Augustus. *Sora.*

Sorabile, a town of the Barbaricini, in Sardinia, n.e. of Forum Trajani.

Soracte m., a m. of Etruria, s.e. of Falerium, on which was a grove and temple of Apollo. Near it was a sulphureous lake, the exhalations from which were fatal to birds. *M. San Silvestro,* or *Preste.*

Soræ, a people of India i. Gangem, s. of the Ambastæ.

Sorba, a town of Hyrcania, on Maxera fl.

Sorbiodunum, "dry hill," a town of the Belgæ, on Alaunus fl., w. of Brigæ. *Old Sarum.*

Sordi (Sordiceni, Sordones, Sardones), a people of Narbonensis, on the Mediterranean, contiguous to the Pyrenees, about Illiberis.

Sordicen Stagnum, an inlet of the Mediterranean, in the territory of the Sordi. *Etang de Leucate.*

Sordus fl., a r. of Narbonensis, falling into Sordicen Stagnum.

Sorek (Sorech, "fine shapes") fl., a r. of Judæa, running through a cognominal valley, and falling into the Mediterranean, n. of Ascalon. Dalilah dwelt on its banks.

Soricaria (Soriba), a town of Bætica, near Corduba, n. of the Bætis.

Soringæ, a maritime people of India i. Gangem, e., bet. the Arvarni and the Bati.

Soriphæa, a town of Palestine, bet. Joppa and Rama. *Serpheat.*

Sornum, a town of the Senses, Dac., e. of Acidava.

Soroba (Sobara), a town of Cilicia prefect., in Cappadocia, bet. Cæsarea (13) and Foroba (14).

Soron fl., a r. of Galilæa, rising in Thabor m., and falling into the Jordan n.e. of Bethsan.

Soronius nemus, a woody district of Arcadia, on the right bank of Ladon fl., towards Clitor. Abounding in bears, boars, and tortoises.

Sosicuri, a maritime town of India i. Gangem, s.e., opposite Anarismundi prom.

Sosimathris Arx, a fortress of the Massagitæ, Sogdianæ, n.w. of Maracanda.

Sosippi portus, a port of Arabia, on the Red sea, bet. Ocelis and Musa.

Sossius fl., a r. of Sicily, falling into the sea below Lilybæum. *Fiume di Marsala.*

Sosthenis, a town of Dolopia, in Thessaly, w. of Phalacthia, towards the source of Phœnix fl. *Sostene.*

Sostra, a town of the Tilatæi, Mœsiæ, on Jatrus fl., R., towards its source, bet. Melta and Ad Radices.

Sosxetia, a town of Gedrosia-Pardene, s.w. of Badara.

Sota, a town of Scythia e. Imaum.

Soter limen, Ægypt., i. q. Salutaris portus.

Sotera, a town of Parthia.

Soteriopolis, i. q. Dioscurias.

Sotiates, a people of Novem Populana, n. of the Elusates. *Diocèse d'Eause.*

Sotium, *vide* Scittium.

Soxotæ, Carmaniæ, i. q. Camelobosci.

Sozopolis, I. a town of Phrygia Parorea, n.w. of Antiochia, near the n. extremity of a large lake not named. II. Thraciæ, i. q. Apollonia.

Sozusa, Cyrenaicæ, i. q. Apollonia.

Spælæum, a town of Bottiæa, in Macedonia, near Pella.

Spalathra, a town of Magnesia, in Thessaly, on Pagasæus sin., bet. Olizon and Methone.

Spalei, a people of Sarmatia Asiat., on the Tanais.

Spaneta, a village of Pannonia, 8 m. w. from Vidulia.

Sparta, "scattered," Lacedæmon, the capital of Laconia. Founded by Lacedæmon, its fourth Lelegian king, 1490 b.c., and named after his wife Sparta. Subjected to Rome 147 b.c. For 800 years it remained without walls. *Near Misitra.*

Spartarius campus, a district along the coast of the Contestani, Tarraconensis, s.e. of Tader fl. Named from its fertility in Spartum or Spanish broom. *La Mancha.*

Spartolus, a fortress of Olynthus, in Sithonia, Macedonia.

Spasinu, Babyloniæ, i. q. Charax.

Spatana, a port of Taprobane e. *Trincomalee.*

Spauta lacus, a salt lake of Media. *Lake of Urmi.*

Specia, a town of Eubœa.

Speculum, a town of Byzacene, bet. Tiges (16) and Turres (18). *Sbekka.*

Spelunca, a villa of Tiberius, in Latium, constructed in a cavern on the coast, e. of Tarracina. The fall of a portion of the roof was nearly fatal to the Emperor, and killed some of his guests. *Sperlonga.*

Speluncæ (Sturni), a port of Calabria, on Via Egnatia, bet. Ad X. (11) and Brundusium (14). *Grotta Rossa.*

Speos-Artemidos, an artificial grotto, sacred to Pasht (Diana), s. of Cynopolis, Heptanomis.

Sperchiæ, a town of the Ænianes, in Thessaly, n. of Sperchius fl., w. of Macracome.

Sperchius fl., a r. of Thessaly, rising in Tymphrestus m., w. of Homilæ, and falling into Maliacus sin. at Antícyra. *Hellada.*

Sphacteria (Sphagia) ins., an isl. of Messenia, in the Ionium mare, over against Pylus. *Sphagia.*

Sphæria (*postea* Hiera) ins., an isl. of Argolis, close to Calauria ins.

Sphagia ins., i. q. Sphacteria.

Sphendale (Sphendalus), a demus of Attica, of the tribe Hippothoontis, n. of Deceleia.

Sphettus, a demus of Attica, of the tribe Acamantis, e. of Athens. A Trœzenian colony. Named after Spettus, son of Trœzen. The birth-place of Æschines. Noted for its vinegar.

Sphingius m., a hill of Bœotia, bet. Hylaka lacus and Copais lacus. The haunt of the Sphynx. *Phaga.*

Spina, a city of Gallia Cispadana, on the s. branch of Padus fl. (Spineticum Ostium), Founded circa 1376 b.c. by Thessalian Pelasgi, who were driven thence by the Tyrrheni, at an uncertain period, the latter being, in their turn, expelled by the Gauls, 393 b.c. It stood, at first, on the sea-shore, but, in the time of Strabo, was removed by continuous deposits of Padus fl., and by the formation of the Roman road bet. Ravenna and Hatria Venet., 11 miles inland. Become a mere village, it was finally submerged by an inundation. *Vestiges in the Lagune of Commachio, near Corezzo.*

Spinæ, a town of the Atrebatii, Brit., n.w. of Calleva. *Speen.*

Spineticum Ostium (Eridanum), the southernmost branch of Padus fl., so named from Spina. *Po di Primaro.*

Spiræum prom., a promontory of Argolis, on Saronicus sin., n. of Epidaurus. *Cape Franco.*

Spireo-Stoma, Danubii, i. q. Psilon Stoma.

Spoletinum, a town of the Turtuli, Bæturia, N.E. of Mirobriga.

Spoletium, a town of Umbria, on Via Flaminia, bet. Interamnia (18) and Forum Flaminii (19). A colonia 242 B.C., and a municipium. Besieged by Hannibal 217 B.C. *Spoleto.*

Spondolici, a people of Sarmatia Asiat., on the Tanais.

Sponsæ, a town of the Volsci, in Latium, on Astura fl., bet. Tres Tabernæ (9) and Aricia (7), on Via Appia. *Tor Vergata.*

Sporades ins., isl. in the Ægean, around and interspersed with the Cyclades, and on the coasts of Crete and Asia Minor. The islands comprehended within this designation were Amorgos, Anaphe, Ascania, Astypalæa, Automate, Azibintha, Calymna, Camina, Carpathus, Casus, Chalcia, Cinarus, Donysa, Hiera, Hippuris, Ios, Lagusa, Lanise, Lea, Letandros, Libinthus, Nisyrus, Nicasia, Odia, Phacussa, Pholegandrus, Platæa, Polyægos, Schinussa, Sicinus, Techedia, Telos, Thera, Therasia, Thia, Tragia.

Sporgilus, a demus of Attica.

Stabatio, a town of the Medulli, Viennensis, N.W. of Brigantio.

Stabiæ, a town of Campania, on Cumanus sin., bet. Pompeii (3) and Surrentum. Celebrated for its fountains and its medicinal milk. The death-place of Pliny the Elder. Destroyed by Sylla. *Castelamare.*

Stabula, I. a town of the Morini, Belgica II., s. of Gessoriacum. *Etaples.* II. of Pontus, between Comana (37) and Neo Cæsarea (38). *Near Tunkal.* III. of the Sordones, Narbonensis I., under the Pyrenees, s.w. of Illiberis. IV. of the Rauraci, Germania I., on the Rhine, below Cambete.

Stachis fl., a stream of Libya, falling into the Atlantic near Ryssadium prom. *Rio San Juan.*

Stadia, Cariæ, i. q. Cnidus.

Stadisis, Ægypti, i. q. Tasitia.

Stagira (Stagirus), a town of Chalcidice, in Macedonia, in the Strymonicus sin., s.e. of Posidium. A colony of Andros. The birth-place of Aristotle. *Stauros.*

Stagnum Lucanum, salt marshes of Lucania, near Pæstum, the scene of the defeat of Spartacus by Crassus.

Stailucum, a town of the Boii, in Pannonia, bet. Ad Flexum (13) and Arrabona (14). *Hochstrass.*

Staliocanus, a port of the Osismii, Lugdunensis III., N.E. of Coriallum. *Liocan; Tour Blanche.*

Stanacum, a town of the Boii, in Noricum, on the Danube, bet. Bojodurum (20) and Joviacum (18). *Reigersberg.*

Staseros fl., a sacred stream of Bruttium, falling into Metaurus fl., E. of Portus Orestis.

Statanus ager, a district of Campania, on Vulturnus fl., contiguous to Falernus ager. Also noted for its wine.

Stathmi, a village of Laconia, near Sparta.

Statielli, a people of Central Liguria, bet. the Vagienni w., the Cerdiciates and Euburiates E., the Taurini N., and the Ilvates s.

Statonia, a town of Etruria, on Armenta fl., L., above Volci. A prefectura. *Castro.*

Statoniensis lacus, a lake of Etruria, at Statonia. *Lago di Mezzano.*

Statulæ, a town of the Marsi, in Italy, bet. Mons Imæus (7) and Corfinium (7). *Goriano.*

Statumæ, a town of Narbonensis, bet. Briginna and Virinna. *Sumènes.*

Stauri, a people of Northern India.

Stectorium, a town of Phrygia, on Mæander fl.

Steganos ins., an isl. of Rhodes.

Stelæ, a town of Crete, near Rithymna.

Stelis (Stylis), i. q. Columna Rhegina.

Stellatinus ager, a district of Etruria, in the territory of Capena.

Stellatis Campus, a district of Campania, bet. Appia Via and the sea, and Vulturnus and Savo ffl. *Mazzella, Mazzone?*

Stempeum (Astalephus), a town of Ecretice, Colchid., at the mouth of Astelephus fl.

Stenarum, a town of the Burideenses, Daciæ, bet. Cedonie (12) and Pons Vetus (44).

Steno-Stoma, Danubii, i. q. Psilon-Stoma.

Stentoris palus, an estuary of Thrace, at the E. mouth of Hebrus fl. *G. d'Enos.*

Stenyclerus, the capital of Messenia, under Cresphontis, s.w. of Amphæa. Named from the hero Stenyclerus. *Nisi?*

Stenyclerius campus, the district about Stenyclerus, in Messenia. The scene of Aristomenes' achievements.

Stephanaphana, a town of the Taulantii, on Egnatia Via, bet. Apollonia (18) and Apsus fl. (12).

Stephane lacus, I. a lake of Pontus, N.E. of Amasia. Now dried up. II. a town of Paphlagonia, on the Euxine, 19 m. E. from Anticinolis. III. of Phocis.

Stereontium, a town of the Bructeri Majores, Germ., on Amisia fl., w. of Munitium. *Steynfurt.*

Steunos Antrum, a cavern of Dindymene

m., in Phrygia. Sacred to Cybele. Hence flows Peucella fl.

STIBOETES fl., i. q. Zioberis.

STILIDA prom., i. q. Cocinthum.

STIMO, a town of Estiæotis, in Thessaly, N.E. of Lisinæ.

STIRA, I. a demus of Attica, of the tribe Pandionis, on the road bet. Brauron and Prasiæ. The birth-place of Theramenes and Thrasybulus. Near it was the tomb of Hipparchus. II. a town of Eubœa, on the w. coast, s. of Porthmus, opposite Marathon. A colony from Stira of Attica. Destroyed by the Persians. *Stoura.*

STIRIA fl., a r. of Noricum, falling into Anisus fl., above Laureacum.

STIRIATE, a town of Noricum, on Stiria fl., towards its source. *Steyrmark?*

STIRIS, a town of Phocis, E. of Anticyra. With a temple of Ceres. A colony from Stira in Attica. Destroyed in the sacred war. *Palæo Stiri.*

STOBI, a town of Pelagonia, in Pæonia, on the Erigonus fl., towards its junction with the Axius fl., bet. Gurbita and Antigonea. The salt-mart for Dardania. A colonia and municipium, and afterwards the metropolis of Macedonia Secunda or Salutaris. The birth-place of Stobæus.

STOBORRUM prom., a pr. of Numidia, at the w. entrance of Numidicus sin.

STOECHÄDES "in a row" ins., five islets of Narbonensis II., off Olbia. *Isles d'Hieres.*

STOENI, a people of Gallia Cisalpina, towards Benacus lacus.

STOMA-LIMNE, I. the issue of Astromela palus, in Gallia Narbonensis. II. the name of Simois and Scamander fll., after their junction at Troas. III. the E. mouth of the Rhone, towards Fossæ Marinæ. IV. a port of Cos, on the s. coast, w. of Drecanum prom. *Stafodino.*

STOMATA, a town of the Bituriges Vivisci, Aquitania II., on the Garumna, L., bet. Burdigala and Serio.

STONI, I. a tribe of Euganei, Gallia Transpad., bet. Sebinus lac. and Benacus lac., N. of the Triumpilini. *Val di Steneco.* II. their town, on Cleusis fl., above Sebinus lac. A municipium.

STORGASIA, a town of the Mœsi, Mœsia Inferior, bet. Œscus and Doriones.

STRAGONA, a town of the Diduni, Germaniæ, N.E. of Strevinta.

STRAPELLUM, a town of Daunia, Apulia, N. of Venusium. *Rapolla.*

STRATIA (Stratus), a town of Arcadia, on Ladon fl.; towards Telphusa. Named after a daughter of Phaneus. Extinct in Strabo's time.

STRATOCLEA, a town of Sarmatia, near Phanagoria, on Thracius Bosporus.

STRATON fl., a r. of Media, falling into the Caspian. It separates the Drybices from the Anariacæ.

STRATONICE, I. a town of Acte penins., Macedonia, on the Singiticus sin., N.W. of Cleonæ. II. of Caria, s.E. of Mylasa. Founded by Antiochus Soter, in honour of his queen Stratonice. Named by Hadrian, Hadrianopolis. The birth-place of the orator Menippus Calochas. *Eski-hissar.*

STRATONIS ins., an isl. in the Red sea, N. of Saba.

STRATUS, the capital of Acarnania, on the right bank of Achelous fl., N. of Metropolis. The river was navigable up to this point. *Porta.*

STRAVIANÆ, a town of the Andizetes, Pannon., bet. Mursa (30) and Inicerum (24).

STREPSA, a town of Mygdonia, in Macedonia, near Thessalonica.

STREVINTA, a town of the Corcontii, Germ., under Asciburgius m., s., bet. Stragona and Meliodunum. *Jagerndorf.*

STROBILUS m., a summit of Caucasus, E. of Pityas.

STROGOLA, a town of Lydia.

STRONGYLE "round island" ins., I. an isl. of Sicily, one of the Lipari ins. The fabled residence of Æolus, from the circumstance that the population knew beforehand which way the wind was about to blow, from the direction of the smoke from the volcano. *Stromboli.* II. of Tarraconensis, in Illicus sin., N. of Saturni prom. *Grosa.*

STRONGYLUS m., Carman., i. q. Semiramidis.

STROPHADES (Cyparissiæ) ins., two islands in the Ionium mare, s.E. of Zacynthus ins., over against Cyparissium prom. Named from the return hence of Zetes and Calais from the pursuit of the harpies. *Strivali.*

STROPHI, a town of Babylonia, on the Tigris, over against Melitene, Susianæ.

STRUTHIA, a town of Phrygia, on the borders of Lycaonia.

STRUTHNUS prom., a pr. of Argolis, N. of Mases. *C. Koraka.*

STRYME, a maritime town of the Cicones, Thrace, at the mouth, w., of Lissus fl., opposite Mesembria. A Thasian colony.

STRYMON fl., a r. of Europe, rising in Scomius m., towards Ælea, and after separating Thrace from Macedonia, in a course of 200 miles, falling into the Strymonicus sin. below Amphipolis. Fabled to have had its navigation impeded by rocks thrown into it by Hercules. Noted for its eels. *Carasou* or *Orphano.*

STRYMONICUS sinus, *prius* Conozus, a gulf of the Ægean, on the coast of Thrace. Named after Strymon fl., which falls into it. *Golfo di Contessa.*

STUBERA (Stymberra), a town of Pelagonia, Pæonia, on the Erigonus fl., above Athacus.

STUCIA fl., a r. of the Ordovices, Brit., falling into the sea s.e. of Canganorum prom. *Duffi.*

STUINUS, capital of the Stoeni, Galliæ. *Storo.*

STURA, I. a r. of Liguria, rising in Alpes Maritimæ and falling into Tanarus fl. above Pollentia. *Stura.* II. a district of Gedrosia, towards Patala.

STURGON, a town of Northern Germany. *Near Stargard.*

STURII, a maritime tribe of Frisii, e. of Flevus lacus.

STURIUS fl., a r. of Flavia Cæsariensis, falling into the German ocean n. of Idumania. *Stour.*

STURNI, a people of Sarmatia.

STURNIUM, a town of Messapia, s. of Sybaris. *Sternaccio.*

STYMPHÆA, i. q. Tymphæa.

STYMPHALIA, a district of Macedonia, bounded on the n. and w. by Orestis, on the s. by Thessaly, Athamania, and Epirus, on the e. by Elymæa. *Konitza.*

STYMPHALIA fons, a stream of Arcadia, falling into Stymphalius lacus. The fabled source of Erasinus fl. of Argolis. *Kephalobrusi.*

STYMPHALIS palus, a lake of Arcadia, at its extreme n.e. angle, infested with robbers, extirpated by Hercules; these were the fabled Stymphalides. *L. di Zaraka.*

STYMPHĀLUS, a town of Arcadia, and afterwards of Argolis, on Stymphalus lacus, n. Founded by Stymphalus, a descendant of Arcas.

STYMPHE m., i. q. Tymphe.

STYRACIUM m., a m. of Crete.

STYX, I. a stream of Arabia Felix, falling into Prion fl. at Saba. II. of Arcadia, falling into the Crathis, near Nonacris. Its waters were deemed poisonous and corrosive. *Mauronero.*

STYLLANGIUM, a town of Triphylia, in Elis.

SUANA, a town of Etruria, on Armenta fl. n.w. of Vulsinii. *Soana.*

SUANETÆ (Suanitæ, Sarunetes), a tribe of Rhæti, on the Rhine, towards its source. *Val de Seriana.*

SUANI (Suano-colchi), a people of Colchis, in Caucasus m., e. of the Coraxi.

SUARATARATÆ, a people of India i. Gangem, s. of Nanaguna fl.

SUARDENI, a people of Sarmatia Asiatica, contiguous to the Zacatæ.

SUARDONES, "long-sworded people," "dark people," a maritime tribe of Vindili, Germ., e. of Chalusus fl.

SUARDURENSE PRÆSIDIUM, a town of Mauritania Cæsar., s. of Sitifis.

SUARÆ, Indiæ, i. q. Sabaræ.

SUARNI, i. q. Suanes.

SUASA, a town of Umbria, on Sena fl. *Castel Leone.*

SUASTENE, a district of India, about Suastus fl.

SUASTUS fl., Indiæ, i. q. Choaspes.

SUBANECTI, i. q. Sylvanectes.

SUBCISIVUM, a town of Bruttium, on Locrensis sin., bet. Caulonia and Noricia, on Via Trajana.

SUB COSA, a village near Cosa, in Etruria, on the sea.

SUBDINNUM, i. q. Siundinum.

SUBIS, a town of the Læetani, Tarraconensis, near Rubricatus fl., L., above Egara.

SUB LANUVIO, a town of the Latini, in Latium, near Lavinium, bet. Aricia and Sponsæ, on Via Appia.

SUBLAQUEUM, a town of the Æqui, in Latium, on Simbruinus lacus, created around a villa of Nero, on Via Sublacensis, bet. Lamnæ (7) and Vineæ (5). *Subiaco.*

SUBLAVIUM, a town of the Isarci, in Rhætia, on Isarus fl., R., bet. Vipitenum (32) and Pons Drusi (13). *Monastery of Seben, near Clausen.*

SUBLUPATIA, a village of Messapia, near Lupatia, bet. Blera (14) and Ad Canales (13). *Anticaglie.*

SUBOCRINI, a people of Venetia, n.e. of Aquileia.

SUB ROMULA, *prius* Romules, a town of the Hirpini, on Via Appia, bet. Eclanum (21) and Pons Aufidi (17). *Formicoso.*

SUBSOLANUS. *Vide* Solanus.

SUBUR, I. a r. of Mauritania Ting., rising in Atlas Min., and falling into the Atlantic at Banasa. *Seboo.* II. a town of the Cosetani, 2 geog. m. w. from Rubricatus fl., towards its mouth. A colonia (Julia Valerna). *Sitiges.*

SUBURBICANUM, in Italy, i. q. Ad Centesimum, as marking the limit of the Provincia Suburbicana.

SUBZUPARA, a town of the Odrysæ, in Thrace, on Hebrus fl., bet. Assus and Burdipta.

SUCALCI villa, a maritime village of the

Siculenses, in Sardinia, s.e., below Sarabus.

SUCCASES, a people of Novem Populana. *About Succos.*

SUCCASINI (i. e. Sub Casinum), the people of Interamna ad Lirim.

SUCCEIANUM, a town of Bruttium, on Locrensis sin., bet. Cocinthum (20) and Subcisivum (24).

SUCCIDAVA, a town of Mœs. Inf., on the Danube, bet. Axiopolis and Sagadava.

SUCCINIUM, a town of Etruria, submerged by Ciminus lac.

SUCCOTH, I. a town of Galeaditis, on the Jordan, at the confluence of Jabbok fl., E. of Zarthan. Named from Jacob's fixing his tent there. II. the Scriptural name of Serapium, Egypt.

SUCCUBAR (Zuchabbari), Mauritaniæ, i. q. Tubusuptus.

SUCHE, a town of the Adulitæ, on Adulitanus sin., bet. Sabæ and Adulis.

SUCRO, I. a r. of Tarraconensis, rising towards Segobriga, and after a course of 200 m. falling into Sucronensius sin. below Sucro. *Xucar.* II. a town of the Sedetani, Tarraconensis, on Sucro fl., near its mouth, below Saguntum. Extinct in Pliny's time. *Cultera.*

SUCRONENSIS sinus, a bay of the Mediterranean, in Tarraconensis, at Sucro, bet. Caprasia prom. N. and Artemisium prom. s. *G. of Valencia.*

SUDAVA, a town of Mauritania Cæsar., towards Nasabath.

SUDERTUM (Sudernum), a town of Etruria, near Volci. *Sorano.*

SUDĒTI m., m. of Germania Mag., separating the Hermunduri N.W. from the Boii S.E. *Fichtelberg.*

SUDENI, a people of Germania Magna, s. of the Marcomanni.

SUEL, *Phœnicè,* "fox," a port of the Turtetani, Bætica, 21 m. s.w. from Malaca. A Phœnician colony. A municipium. *Castro de Fumgirola.*

SUELLENI, a people of Arabia, N. of the Salapeni.

SUELTRI, a tribe of Salyes, Narbonensis, N. of the Commoni. *About Esterel.*

SUERNI, a tribe of Ubii, about Tolbiacum.

SUESSA AURUNCORUM, a town of the Aurunci, bet. Minturnæ and Teanum. A municipium. A colonia 313 B.C. (Julia Felix.)

SUESSA POMETIA (Pomtia), a town of the Volsci, s. of Appia Via, towards Forum Appii. An Alban col., the spoils of which were applied by Tarquin to the foundation of the Capitol.

SUESSETANI, a tribe of Edetani, Tarraconensis, on Turia fl.

SUESSIONES, a people of Belgica II., s.w. of the Remi, s. of the Veromandui. *Departments of Oise and Aisne (Central), and Marne, N.*

SUESSULA, a town of Campania, on Via Aquilia, bet. Calatia (3) and Nola (9). A colonia. *Sessola.*

SUETRI, a people of Alpes Maritimæ, E. of the Var.

SUEVI, in general the people of Germania Magna; specially, with Cæsar, the Chatti; with Tacitus, the people occupying the country bet. the Danube and Codanus sin., the Albis, and the Vistula.

SUEVICUM mare, i. q. Codanus sin.

SUEVUS fl., the central issue of Viadrus fl.

SUFFASAR, a town of Mauritania Cæsar., on Chinalaph fl., R., above Maliana.

SUFFETULA, a city of Byzacene, 25 m. s. from Sufes. *Sfaitla.*

SUFES, a town of Byzacene, 25 m. s. from Tucca. *Sbiba.*

SUGA, the early name of Drepane, in Bithynia.

SUGOLIN, a town of Tripolis, Africa, at the mouth of Cynyphs fl., bet. Leptis Magna and Nivirtigab.

SUIA, a town on the s. coast of Crete, w. of Hierapytna; the port of Elyrus.

SUILLUM, Umbriæ, i. q. Helvillum.

SUINDINUM (Subdinnum, *postea* Cenomanni), capital of the Aulerci Cenomanni, w.N.w. of Genabum.

SUINUS (Tessuinus) fl., a r. of Picenum, falling into the sea s. of Truentus fl. *Sino.*

SUIONES, a people of Northern Germany. *In Sweden.*

SUISMONTIUM, a ridge of Apennines, in Liguria, N. of Genua.

SULANES (Bulanes), a people of Sarmatia Asiatica.

SULATHA, a town of the Basanaræ, Ind., on Lanos fl.

SULCI (Solci, Sylci, Sulchi), a city of Sardinia, on the isthmus connecting Plumbea ins. with the mainland. Next to Colaris, the most ancient town of Sardinia. A Carthaginian or Tyrrhenian settlement. *Sant' Antioco.*

SULCITANUM (Sulcense) prom., a pr. of Sardinia, E., at Sulci. *Punta dell' Ulga.*

SULGAS fl., a r. of Viennensis, falling into the Rhone above Avenio. *Sorgue.*

SULIA (Sulena) prom., a pr. on the s. coast of Crete, w. of Psychium. *C. San Paolo.*

SULIOTES, a town of Thesprotia. *About Suli ?*

SULIUM, a town of the Veneti, Lugdunensis III., s.w. of Condate.

SULLECTIS, a maritime town of Byzacene, bet. Thapsus and Acholla (12). Here was the Turris Hannibalis, or castle, whence Hannibal took his departure on his flight from Africa.

SULLONIACÆ, a town of the Catavellauni, Brit., bet. Verolamium and Londinium. *Brockley Hill, near Edgeware.*

SULLUCU (Sublucu), a maritime town of Numidia, w. of Siur portus (30). *Sullect.*

SULMO, I. a town of the Peligni, in Italy, on Via Valeria, bet. Corfinium (7) and Temp. Jovis Palenæi (7). Founded by Solymus, a companion of Æneas. A colonia. The birth-place of Ovid. *Sulmone.* II. (Sermona), a town of the Volsci, on Nymphæus fl., L., s. of Norba. Extinct in Pliny's time. *Sermonetta Vecchia.*

SULSIS, a maritime town of the Sulsitani, Sardinia, E., bet. Viniola and Saralapis.

SULPICIUS portus, a port of Sardinia, on Sæprus fl., 2 geog. m. from its mouth.

SUMA (Sumera, Samara), a town of Apolloniatis, Assyriæ, on the Tigris, bet. Carcha and Opis.

SUMATIA, a town of Arcadia, under Mænalus m. Founded by Sumatæus, son of Lycaon. The inhabitants removed to Megalopolis.

SUMMONTORIUM (Submontorium), a town of Rhætia, bet. Abusina (18) and Vallatum (16). *Reichershofen.*

SUMMURANUM, a town of Lucania, 14 m. from Nerulum. *Murano.*

SUMMUS LACUS, a town of the Orobii, in Gall. Transp., at the N. extremity of Larius lac., bet. Clavenna (10) and Comium (60). It was nearly destroyed by a landslip. *Samolico.*

SUNA, a Tyrrhenian town of Sabinium, N. of Mons Lucretilis. *Nerola.*

SUNEM (Sonna), a town of Issachar, 6 m. N.W. from Gilboa. The birth-place of Abisag, and the abode of the hostess of Elisha.

SUNICI, a people on Mosa fl.

SUNISTA, a town of the Jassii, Pannoniæ, bet. Jovia and Piretæ.

SUNIUM, I. the s. extremity of Attica, on the Ægean. Sacred to Minerva and Neptune. *C. Colonna.* II. a demus of Attica, of the tribe Leontis, at Sunium prom.

SUOBENI, a people of Scythia i. Imaum, towards the Agathyrsi.

SUPER EQUUM, a town of the Peligni, Ital., w. of Corfinium. A colonia. *Castel Vecchio Subequo.*

SUPERNATES, a name of the Italians N. of, or *above*, the Apennines.

SUPERUM MARE, a name of the Adriatic, as being N. of, or *above*, the Apennines.

SUPHTA, the local name of Susia, Parthiæ.

SURA (Surra), I. a town of Iberia, on Cyrus fl., N. of Mestleta. *Zeheta.* II. a village of Lycia, bet. Myra and Phellus, where auguries were given by means of a fish. III. (Ura), a town of Mesopotamia, w. of Philiscum. V. of Palmyrene, on the Euphrates, near Thapsacus. IV. fl., a r. of Germania II., falling into the Mosella, L., above Augusta Treverorum.

SURAGANA, a town of Bactriana, on Oxus fl.

SURANI, a people of Sarmatia Asiatica, under Hippici m., s.w.

SURAPURU, Indiæ, i. q. Clisobra.

SURASÈNE, a district of India i. Gangem, bet. Diamuna fl. and Sambus fl.

SURDAONES, a tribe of Ilercaones, Tarraconensis, on Sicoris fl., N.W. of the Cosetani.

SURIUM, a town of the Manrali, in Colchis, on Surius fl., at its junction with Phasis fl., above Mala. *Asmuleti.*

SURIUS fl., a r. of Colchis, falling into the Phasis 37 m. from the sea.

SURRENTINUM (Minervæ, Sirenusarum) prom., a pr. of Campania, at the s. entrance of Cumanus sin., below Surrentum. On it was a temple of Minerva. *Punta della Campanella.*

SURRENTUM, a town of Campania, on Cumanus sin., s.w., below Æqua. Noted for its medicinal wines (which, however, Tiberius denounced as a better sort of vinegar, and Caligulus as a noble vapidity), and for its beautiful scenery. *Sorrento.*

SURUBA, a town of the Metibi, Sarmatiæ, on Vardanes fl., above Corusia. *Ekatirmodar.*

SUS fl., a r. of Pieria, in Macedonia, an inundation of which, in fulfilment of the oracle, overwhelmed the adjacent town of Libethra. Leake identifies it with the Enipeus.

SUSA (Susan, "lilies"), capital of Susiana, on Choaspes fl., 30 m. w. from Seleucia. The winter residence of the kings of Persia. Founded by Tithonius, father of Memnon; completed by Memnon; restored by Darius Hystaspes. In circuit 15 m. The burial-place of Daniel. *Sus.*

SUSALEUS vicus, a town of Sardinia, near Caralis.

SUSARMIA, i. q. Hyssus, in Pontus.

SUSIA (Suphtha), a town of Parthia, N.E. of Nisæa-Sauloe, on the confines of Aria.

SUSIADES PYLÆ, Persides, i. q. Susianæ portæ.

SUSIANA (Susis), a country of Asia, bounded N. by Media, at Charbanus m., s. by Persicus sin., w. by Assyria, E. by Persis. Sometimes described as a part of Persis, and its extent N. limited to Cissia. The people were famous for their skill in archery. *Khusistan.*

SUSIANÆ portæ, defiles bet. the s. extremity of Susiana Cabandene and Persis Prop.

SUSICANA, a town of Gedrosia, on the Indus, L., bet. Sindomana and Alexandria Sogdiorum.

SUSUDATA, a town of the Silingi, Germ., under Vindilici m. N.

SUTHUL, a treasure fortress of Numidia.

SUTRIUM, a town of Etruria, on Via Cassia, bet. Baccanæ (12) and Forum Cassii (11). A colonia. Considered the key of Etruria. Memorable for its rapid capture by Camillus. *Sutri.*

SUZÆI, a people of Persis, occupying its s.w. angle.

SUZAN, "lilies," the Scriptural name of Susa, from the abundance of those flowers in its vicinity.

SYAGELA, "royal tomb," a Lelegian town of Caria, near Pedasa. The burial-place of Car.

SYAGRA, a village of Cilicia Trachea, near Laertes.

SYAGRIUS prom., a pr. of Arabia Felix, N. of Dioscorides ins., midway bet. Persicus sin. and Rubrum mare. Described by Arrian to be the largest prom. in the world. *Ras Fartask.*

SYBARIS, I. a r. of Lucania, falling into Crathis fl. above Sybaris, at present 14 m. from the sea, but its ancient junction must have been 8 or 10 m. lower down. Its water made sheep and oxen black, caused horses to sneeze and shy, and gilded the human hair. *Cochile.* II. Calabriæ, i. q. Lupia. III. a city of Lucania, on Crathis fl., below its junction with Sybaris fl. Founded circa 1160 B.C. by Trœzenians; enlarged circa 720 B.C. by Áchæans under Isiliceus. Infamous for its luxury. Destroyed by the people of Crotona, who submerged it beneath the waters of the Sybaris circa 510 B.C.

SYBOTA, a harbour of Thesprotia, opposite Leucimna prom., in Corcyra. *Sivota.*

SYBOTÆ "swine-feeding" ins., three small islands of Thesprotia, opposite the cognominal town. It was on one of them that the Corcyræans erected a trophy after their victory, aided by the Athenians, over the Corinthians.

SYBRIDÆ, a demus of Attica, of the tribe Erectheis.

SYCAMINOPH (Chepha), a town of Phœnicia, N. of Ecbatana. Named from its wild figtrees. *Kaffa.*

SYCÆ, *postea* Justiniana, a bay of the Bosporus, at Byzantium.

SYCE, a town of the Zygritæ, in Marmarica, on the coast, bet. Anæsyphira and Tetrapyrgia.

SYCEON, a town of Galatia, near the confluence of Hieros fl. with the Sangarius.

SYCURIUM, an encampment of Perseus, in Pelasgiotis, in Thessaly, N.E. of Scotussa, on the s. slope of Ossa m. *Sariniki.*

SYCUSSA ins., an isl. of Ionia, in Hermius sin., opposite Clazomenæ.

SYDROS, a town of India i. Gangem, near the E. mouth of the Indus. *Nusserpur.*

SYEBI (Sycbi), a people of Scythia i. Imaum, towards the Suobeni.

SYEDRA, a maritime town of Cilicia Trachea, S.E. of Coracesium.

SYENE, a city of Thebais, on a peninsula of the Nile, R., bet. Ombi and Phylæ. Near it (s.) was a well which indicated the summer solstice, being under the tropic of Cancer. The Romans maintained a garrison at Syene, deeming it one of the keys of the empire. *Assuan.*

SYESSA, a village of Lycia, named from the hostess of Latona.

SYGELA (Suagela), a town of Caria, towards Myndus.

SYLEUS campus, a district of Bisaltia, in Macedonia, on the Strymonicus sinus, bet. Bromiscus and Argilus.

SYLINÆ ins., i. q. Cassiterides.

SYLLÆUM (Sulacum), Arabiæ, i. q. Labecia.

SYLLEUM (Syllium), a town of Pamphylia, on Cestrus fl., R., 3 m. below Perga.

SYMÆTHA, a town of Thessaly.

SYMÆTHUS, I. a r. of Sicily, falling into Siculum mare N. of Amenanus r. Noted for its mullets. *Jaretta.* II. a town of Sicily, on Symæthus fl., towards its source.

SYMBOLAS, a village of Arcadia, near Tegea.

SYMBOLI portus, a harbour of Taurica Chersonesus, at Palacium.

SYMBRA, a town of Apolloniatis, Assyriæ, on the Tigris, bet. Nysbara and Sittace.

SYMBRI, the name given by Strabo to a remnant of the Cimbrian invasion, settled in the hills above Verona.

SYME (*prius* Metapontis, Ægle), I. an isl. of Caria, at the entrance of Doridis sin. *Symi.* II. its capital, the abode of Homer's Nereus.

SYMMACHI, a town of Numidia, bet. Basilica Diadumene and Ad Duo Flumina.

SYMPLEGADES ins., i. q. Cyaneæ.

SYNDROMADES ins., i. q. Cyaneæ.

SYNHIETÆ, a people of Sarmatia Asiatica, on the Tanais.

SYNNADA, a city of Phrygia Magna, bet. Eucarpia and Ipsus, N.E. of Apamea Cibotus. Noted for its fine purple-veined marble.

SYNNAUS, a town of the Abbaites, Phrygia Epictetus, S.E. of Ancyra.

SYNOBRA, a town of Lycia.

SYNORIA, a fortress of Armenia Minor, built by Mithridates. *Senarvir.*

SYPALETTUS, a demus of Attica, of the tribe Cecropis.

SYPHÆUM, a town of Bruttium, 25 m. N. from Consentia. *Montalto.*

SYPICIUS portus, Sardiniæ, i. q. Saralapis.

SYRACELLA, a town of the Apsynthii, Thrace, on the Egnatia Via, bet. Drippa (14) and Zesutera (10). *Malgara.*

SYRACUSÆ (Syracusa, Syracossæ, Syracosa), a city of Sicily, on the E. coast, at the mouth of Anapus fl., L. Founded by a joint colony of Corinthians, under Archias, and Dorians. It was a five-fold city, its divisions being respectively named Nasos or Ortygia (S.E.), Achradina (E.), Tyche (central), Neapolis (S.W.) and Epipoplæ (W.). The latter, being but thinly inhabited, was not taken notice of by many topographers. The circuit of the city was 15 m. Restored by Augustus. The birth-place of Archimedes, Theocritus, Philemon, Vopiscus, &c. *Syracusa.*

SYRACUSANORUM portus, a port of Corsica, E., bet. Favonius portus and Palla.

SYRAPUS fl., a r. of Lucania, falling into Siris fl. *Serrapotamo.*

SYRASTRENE, a district of India e. Gangem, bet. Canthy sin. and Barygazenus sin.

SYRGIS fl., a r. of Sarmatia, falling into Mæotis palus E. of the Tanais.

SYRIA, I. an isl. of Ionia, at the mouth of Caystrus fl. In Pliny's time joined to the mainland by deposits of the river. II. a country of Asia, bounded N. by Amanus m., S. by Arabia and Egypt, w. by the Mediterranean, E. by the Euphrates and Arabia. The Aram of Scripture, as peopled by the children of Aram. *Syria; Belad el Scham.*

SYRIAS prom., Paphlagoniæ, i. q. Lepte.

SYRIENI, a people of India, near the mouth of the Indus.

SYRINTHUS, a town of Crete.

SYRINX, Hyrcaniæ, i. q. Zadracarta.

SYRNA, a town of Caria, founded by Podalirius.

SYRNOTA, a town of the Odrysæ, Thrace, bet. Philippopolis and Parembole. *Stanimak.*

SYRO-MEDIA, a district of Media Magna, on the borders of Susiana and Parthia.

SYRTĬCA regio, a maritime district of Africa, bet. Syrtis Minor, at Triton fl., and Syrtis Major, at Cynyps fl. *Serb; Tripoli.*

SYRTIS MAJOR, a gulf of the Mediterranean, in Africa, bet. Boreum prom. and Cephalæ prom. In extent 230 geog. m. *G. of Sidra.*

SYRTIS MINOR, a gulf of the Mediterranean, in Africa, bet. Meninx ins. and Brachodes prom., w. of Syrtis Major. In length 60 geog. m. *G. of Khabs.*

SYRUS, I. a r. of Arcadia, falling into Alpheus fl. towards Phædria. II. an isl. of the Ægean, one of the Cyclades, bet. Cythnus and Rhenea. In circuit 20 m. *Syra.* III. its capital, on the E. coast. The birth-place of Pherecydes. *Syra.*

SYTHAS fl., a r. of Achaia, rising in Geronteum m. and falling into Corinthiacus sin. at Aristonautæ. *Xylo Castro.*

T.

TAANACH, a town of Manasseh, near Megiddo.

TABÆ, "a rock," I. a port of Æthiopia, on Indicus oceanus, E., bet. Panon and Opone. II. a town of Persia, towards Ecbatana. III. (Tiaba), a town of Phrygia, on the borders of Pisidia. Founded by the hero Tabus. *Thaous* or *Davas.*

TABALA (Gabala), a town of Lydia, on Hermus fl.

TABALTA (Thasbalte), a town of Byzacene, bet. Macomades (15) and Septimunicia (15).

TABANA, a town of Taurica Chersonesus.

TABASSÆ, a people of India i. Gangem, bet. Nanaguna fl. and Tyndis fl., w. of the Adisathri. *In Popal and Berar.*

TABELLARIA, a town of Etruria, bet. Graviscæ (5) and Forum Aurelii (3).

TABERNA, a valley of the Psylli, Africa, bet. Pisidium and Tagulis.

TABERNA FRIGIDA, a maritime town of Etruria, on Via Aurelia, bet. Fossæ Papirianæ (12) and Luna (10). *Frigido.*

TABIDIUM (Thabudis), a town of Libya, near the springs of Bagradas fl.

TABIENA ins., an isl. of Persis, N.W. of Mesambria.

TABIENI, a people of Scythia i. Imaum.

TABIS (Tamos) prom., a pr. of India e. Gangem, towards Serica.

TABLÆ, a town of the Batavi, on the Rhine, R., bet. Caspingium and Flevum. *Ablas.*

TABLATÆ, a town of Africa, 156 m. s.e. from Turris Tamellini.

TABOR, *vide* Thabor.

TABRACA, a town of Numidia, towards the mouth of Tusca fl. A colonia. *Tabarca.*

TABUDA æstuarium, the mouth of the Scaldis fl., s.w. of Helium ostium. *Aas.*

TABULA, a town of Lydia, on Hermus fl., L., bet. Attalea and Sattala. *Toubaili.*

TABURNUS m., a m. of Samnium, e. of Saticula. Covered with olive-trees. *M. Taburno.*

TACAPE, a town of Byzacene, on Syrtis Minor, s. of the mouth of Triton fl. A colonia. *Tegé; Gabe?*

TACAPITANÆ aquæ, baths of Byzacene, w. of Tacapa.

TACARSATA (Tacaseri), a town of Lower Egypt, on Bubasticus fl., R., bet. Thon (24) and Daphnon (18).

TACATUA, a maritime town of Numidia, bet. Sullucu and Muharur. *Mabra.*

TACHORI, i. q. Tochari.

TACOLA, a port of Aurea Chersonesus, w. above Aurea Cherson. prom. *Tavai.*

TACOLOSIDA, a town of Mauritania Ting., s. of Volubilis. *Maghila.*

TACOMPSO, "island of crocodiles" (Tachemso, Tacompsos, contra Pselchis), ins., i. q. Metacompso.

TACONA, a town of Heptanomis, on the Nile, L., 24 m. n. from Oxyrinchus.

TACORÆI, a people of India e. Gangem, on Œdanes fl., R.

TACOSANNA, a town of India e. Gangem. *Arracan.*

TADMOR, "palm-tree," *vide* Palmyra.

TADER (Tereps) fl., a r. of Tarraconensis, rising in Ortospeda m. and falling into Illicitanus sin. s. of Illici. *Segura.*

TADINA (Ptanias), a town of Umbria, on Via Flaminia, bet. Nuceria (8) and Helvillum (7). The death-place of Totila. *S. Maria Tadina.*

TADNOS, a mineral spring at Myoshormus.

TADU ins., an isl. of Meroe, on the Nile, L., near Meroe.

TÆNARUM, I. a pr. of Laconia, at the w. entrance of Laconicus sin. With a temple of Neptune: an inviolable sanctuary. Noted for its marble. The place at which Hercules dragged forth Cerberus, and where Arion was landed by the Dolphin. *C. Matapan.* II. *postea* Cænopolis, a town of Laconia, bet. Thyrides prom. (2) and Tænarum prom. (5). *Near Cyparisso.*

TÆNIA LONGA, I. prom., a pr. of Mauritania Tingit., on the Mediterranean, w. of Cobucta. Named from its form, a long tongue of land running out into the sea. II. a town of Mauritania Ting., at Tænia longa prom. *Torga.*

TÆPA, a town of Susiana, on Arosis fl., R., towards its mouth.

TÆZALI, a maritime people of Britannia Barbara, e., bet. the Caledonii and the Venicontes, towards Tæzalum prom.

TÆZALUM prom., a pr. of the Tæzali, Brit., e., at the s. entrance of Tuæsis æstuar. *Kinnaird's Head.*

TAGA, a town of Armenia Maj., on the Cyrus, at the junction of the Araxes.

TAGABA, a town of Judah, Judæa, on Eskol fl., R., below Eglon.

TAGÆ (Tapæ), a town of Parthia, on Labuta m., bet. Hecatompylon and Hyrcania. *Dameghan.*

TAGAMA, a town of Libya Interior.

TAGARA, a town of Ariaca, Indiæ, 15 m. n.e. from Bætana. *Deoghir.*

TAGASTE (Thagaste), a town of Numidia, on Rubricatus fl., R., bet. Hippo Regius and Naraggara. A municipium.

TAGODA, a town of Albania, near the source of Alazonius fl. (8).

TAGONIUS fl., a r. of Tarraconensis, falling into the Tagus above Toletum.

TAGORI, I. a people of Sarmatia Asiatica, towards Tanais. II. of Sarmatia Europæa, on Tyras fl., towards the Tyrangetæ.

TAGULIS (Tugulus, Thagulis), a town of the Psylli, Africa, on Syrtis Maj., 25 m. w. from Aræ Philænorum.

TAGURA, a town of the Tabassæ, Indiæ, e. of Nasica.

TAGUS, *Phœnic.* "fish," I. a r. of Spain, rising in Idubeda m., towards Urbiaca, and falling into the Atlantic at Olisipo. It once abounded with gold and precious stones. *Tejo; Tajo; Tagus.* II. m., m. of the Lusitani, on the coast, n. of the Tagus.

TAHAPANES (Tehaphnehes, Tahpanhes, Hanes), the Hebrew name of Daphne in Lower Egypt.

TAIFALGI, a tribe of Pictones, in Gaul. *In Tifauge.*

TAIPHALI, a people of Dacia.

TALABRIGA (Ercobrica), a maritime town of the Lusitani, on Vacua fl., near its mouth. *Eveiro.*

TALABROCA, a town of Hyrcania.

TALACORY, a port of Taprobane, n.e., under Boreum prom. *Near Pospyl.*

TALARES, a colony from Tomarus m., of Molossis, settled in Estiæotis, of Thessaly, on the slopes of Pindus, contiguous to the Æthices. Extinct in Strabo's time.

TALARGA, a town of the Marundæ, Indiæ, bet. the Ganges, near its mouth, and Œdanes fl.

TALARIA, a town of Sicily, 9 m. from Syracusæ.

TALBENDA, a town of Pisidia.

TALCA ins., an isl. of Hyrcania, in the Caspian, off the mouth of Maxera fl.

TALCINUM, a town of Corsica, on Tavola fl., L., towards its source. *Talsini.*

TALETUM m., the loftiest summit of Taygetus m., behind Bryseæ. Sacred to the sun, in whose honour horses were annually sacrificed. *M. Agio Elio.*

TALIATA (Talia), a town of Dacia, 4 geog. m. from Tierna.

TALLARA, a town of the Bati, Indiæ, on Chaberis fl.

TALLATA (Tanatis), a town of the Mœsi, Mœsia Sup., on the Danube, bet. Ad Scrofulas and Pons Trajani, 25 m. E. from Ad Novas.

TALMENA, a port of Gedrosia, on Paragon sin., at the mouth of Hydriacus fl., bet. Cyiza (125) and Canasis (50).

TALMIS, a city of Dodecaschœnus, on the Nile, L., bet. Taphis and Tutzis (20). The residence of the priests and chieftains of the surrounding districts. *Kalabsche.*

TALUBATH, a town of Libya Inf.

TAMALA, a port of India e. Gangem, near Tabis prom. *Baroban.*

TAMALLENI turris, a fortress of Syrtica reg., bet. Agariaba (30) and Putea.

TAMALLUMA, a town of Mauritania Cæsar., w. of Sitifis. *Callah.*

TAMARA, a town of the Damnonii, at the mouth of Tamarus fl., w. of Ad Durium. *Tamerton.*

TAMARI OSTIUM, an estuary of Britain, at the mouth of the Tamarus. *Plymouth Sound.*

TAMARICI, a people of Tarraconensis, on Tamarus fl.

TAMARICIUM PALMAS, a maritime town of Sicily, bet. Messana (25) and Taurominium (15). *Torre di Palma.*

TAMARUS fl., I. a r. of the Damnonii, falling into the sea below Tamara. *Tamar.* II. of Samnium, rising above Ad Tamarum and falling into Calor fl. above Beneventum. *Tamaro.* III. of Tarraconensis, falling into the Atlantic at Novium, bet. Grandimurum N. and Ebora s. *Tambre.*

TAMASCANUM, a town of Mauritania Cæsar., on Audus fl., 10 m. from Tamunana.

TAMASICI, a town of the Taurisci, Noricum, on Murus fl., near its source.

TAMASIDA, a maritime town of Mauritania Ting., w., bet. Sala and Banasa.

TAMASIDAVA, a town of the Harpii, Daciæ, on the Parata, s.w. of Ophiusa. *Near Faltschy.*

TAMASIS (Thanusar), a town of the Nanichæ, Ind., w. of Catadupa.

TĂMĂSUS, an inland city of Cyprus, bet. Limenia and Leucosia. Noted for its copper and its calcanthum. Here grew the golden apples of Hippomenes.

TAMBRAX, Hyrcaniæ, i. q. Talabroca.

TAMBYZI, a people of Bactriana.

TAMERÆ, a people of India e. Gangem, s. of the Tiladæ.

TAMĔSIS (Tamĕsa) fl., the combined waters of the Tamis and Tamis fll., Britanniæ, falling into the sea at Toliatis ins. According to some writers, it was throughout entitled Tamĕsis, and no such name as Isis was known in connexion with this river.

TAMIA, a town of the Caledonii, Brit., N.W. of Victoria. *Dunkeld.*

TAMIATHIS, a maritime town of Lower Egypt, on the Phatmetic branch of the Nile, near its mouth. *Damietta.*

TAMIS (Tamh, *Celticè*, "great water"), fl., a r. of the Dobuni, Brit., falling into Isis fl. at Dorciniæ Civitas.

TAMISA, a town of Elegosine, Armen., on the Euphrates, bet. Corne and Claudias.

TAMMACUM (Agdami), a town of Arabia Felix, near Carman regia, N.E. *Al Tayf.*

TAMNA (Thamna, Thomna), capital of the Gebanitæ, Arabia Fel., s.s.w. of Nagia. *Shibam?*

TAMNUM, a town of the Santones, Aquitania II., on the Garumna, bet. Novioregum and Blavium. *Mortagne.*

TAMONTUM, a town of Heptanomis, on the Nile, L., bet. Oxyrynchus and Co.

TAMOS prom., Indiæ, i. q. Tabis.

TAMUDA (Taluda) fl., a r. of Mauritania Ting., falling into the Mediterranean at Aquila Major.

TAMUGADIS, a town of Numidia, bet. Popletum and Lambæse.

TAMUNUNA, a town of Mauritania Cæsar., bet. Sava and Sitifis.

TAMYNÆ, a town of Eubœa, on the w. coast, s.E. of Eretria. With a temple of Apollo, erected by Admetus.

TAMYRACE, a town of the Hylæ, Sarmat., on Hylæum mare, s.w. of Carcina.

TAMYRAS fl., a r. of Phœnicia, falling into the Mediterranean at Platanon, bet. Heldua and Porphyrion. *Damer.*

TANADARIS (Ptanadari), a town of Cataonia, Cappadocia, bet. Comana (24) and Cucusus (38).

TANAGER (Tanagrus) fl., a r. of Lucania, rising s. of Casilinum and falling into Silarus fl. above Ad Silarum. Two miles of its course are subterraneous. *Negro.*

TANAGRA, *prius* Græa or Gephyræa, and

Pæmandria, a town of Bœotia, on Asopus fl., bet. Thebæ and Oropus. With temples of Bacchus, Apollo, Venus, &c. Under Rome a free city. The birth-place of Corinna. Stigmatized for envy. Noted for its fighting-cocks and its wine. *Grimathi.*

Tanais, "water," fl., I. a r. of Sarmatia, dividing Sarmatia Europæa from Sarmatia Asiatica. The boundary, in this direction, of Europe and Asia, falling into the N.E. extremity of the Palus Mæotis by two mouths. *Don.* II. a town of Sarmatia Europæa, at the mouth of the Tanais. A Milesian colony. *Azof; Assow.*

Tanarus fl., a r. of Liguria, rising in the territory of the Casmonates and falling into Padus fl. w. of Ira fl. *Tanaro.*

Tanatis (Tanetos) ins., an insulated district of the Cantii, in Brit. I., on the N.E. coast. *I. of Thanet.*

Tanetum (Canetum), a town of Gallia Cispadana, on Nicia fl., R., bet. Parma (8) and Regium (10), on Via Æmilia Lepida. Noted in connexion with the defeat of the prætor Manlius by the Boii. *St. Ilario.*

Tangala, a town of India e. Gangem, s. of Carura.

Tangaitæ, a town of Æthiopia, bet. the Colobi and the Memnones.

Tanis, *prius* Zoan, a city of Lower Egypt, on the Tanitic branch of the Nile, E. of Thmuis. The locality of the miracles of Moses. *Sau.*

Taniticum ostium, the sixth larger mouth of the Nile, E. from Alexandria. Named from Tanis.

Tanos fl., I. a r. of Argolis, rising in Parnon m. and falling into Thyreates sin. at Thyrea. *Hagios Petros.* II. a town of Crete.

Tantabra fl., Indiæ, i. q. Hydraotes.

Tantalus, I. the early name of Sipylus, in Lydia. II. a m. of Lesbos ins. Named from the hero Tantalus.

Tanupolis, i. q. Trajanopolis.

Tanusiga, a town of Mauritania Tingitana, at the mouth of Una fl., R., within Herculis prom., s.

Tanuitæ (Tanuchitæ), a people of Arabia Felix, s.w. of Inapha.

Taoce (Oca), I. a port of Persis, ᶰ. of Brizana fl. II. Oce (capital), of Taocene, in Persia, E. of Taoce prom., on Rhogomanis fl.

Taocene, a maritime district of Persis Prop., about Taoce.

Taochi, a tribe of Scythæ, in Armenia Int., about Boas fl., towards its source. *Taikh.*

Tapæ, I. a town of the Potulatenses, Daciæ, s.e. of Tiriscum. II. of Hyrcaniæ, i. q. Tagæ.

Taphar, Arabiæ, i. q. Saphar.

Taphiassus m., a m. on the coast of Ætolia, bet. Calydon and the sea. The scene of Nessus' death, whose blood communicated a fetid odour to the many springs that issue from its sides. *Kakiscala.*

Taphii, a tribe of Leleges, named after Taphius, son of Neptune.

Taphiorum ins., i. q. Teleboarum.

Taphis (Tahis), a town of Dodecaschœnus, on the Nile, L., bet. Tzibzi and Talmis (8). *Tafa.*

Taphitis prom., Zeugitana, i. q. Clypea prom.

Taphnis, the name, with Ezekiel, of Zoan.

Taphos (Taphius, Taphiusa), I. chief of the Teleboarum ins. of Acarnania, w. of Carnus ins. *Meganisi.* II. a town of Cephallenia, on the w. coast, under Beræa m. *Taphios.*

Taphros, "close," I. a name of Gallicum Fretum and Fossa Mariana. II. a town of Taurica Chersonesus, at its isthmus.

Taphrura, a maritime town of Byzacene, bet. Thenæ and Usilla. *Sfax.*

Tapis fl., a stream of Attica, rising in Kerata m., and, after separating Attica from Megaris, falling into Saronicus sin. w. of Megara.

Taposiris Magna, a town of Lower Egypt, at the s.e. extremity of Mareotis lac. Its name indicates it to be the burial-place of Osiris. *Abusir.*

Taposiris Parva, a town of Lower Egypt, at the N.E. extremity of Mareotis lac.

Tappuah, i. q. Thappuah.

Taprobane (Palæsimundi, Salice, Sielediva) ins., an isl. of India i. Gangem, at its s.e. extremity. Supposed by Mela and other geographers to be the first part of another continent. *Ceylon.*

Tapsus fl., a r. of Numidia, falling into Numidicus sin. E. of Rusicada.

Tapura, a town of Armenia Minor, bet. Salala and Nicopolis.

Tapuri (Tapari, Tapurei), a people of Hyrcania, on the borders of Margiana. *Taberistan.*

Tarabenorum vicus, a town of Corsica, on Circidius fl., R., s. of Palanta. *Vico.*

Tarachi, a people of Taprobane, on the E. coast, bet. the Semni and the Morduli.

Tarantus (Darantus), a town of Bithynia.

Taras fl., L. a r. of Messapia, falling into the sea w. of Tarentum. *Tara.* II. the

Greek name of Tarentum, from Taras, son of Neptune.

TARASCO, a town of the Desuviates, Viennensis, on the Rhone, above Arelate. *Tarascon.*

TARBELLI, a people occupying the s. coast of Novem Populana, from about Segosa to the Pyrenees.

TARCUNA, the Etruscan name of Tarquinii.

TARENTINUS portus, I. a harbour of Calabria, N. of Hydruntum. Now a lake, somewhat inland. *L. Limene.* II. sinus, a gulf of the Mediterranean, at Tarentum. *Golfo di Tarento.*

TARENTUM (Taras, Œbalia), a city of Messapia, at the N.E. head of Tarentinus sin., at the mouth of Galesus fl., on Via Appia, bet. Ad Canales (20) and Mesochoria (10). Colonized by the Spartan Parthenii, under Phalanthus, circa 700 B.C. Subjugated by Rome circa 71 B.C. The birth-place of Archytas the geometrician; of Aristoxenas the musician, &c. *Taranto.*

TARGINES (Tacina) fl., a r. of Bruttium, falling into Scylleticus sin., bet. Neæthus fl. (24) and Scylacium (22), on Via Trajana. *Tacina.*

TARETICA prom., Sarmatiæ, i. q. Herculis.

TARICHIA (Zuchis, Pons Zitha, Pontezita, Zeucharin), a salt lake of Byzacene, on the coast of Syrtis Major, at Zitha prom., where a large trade in salted fish was carried on. Named from the pickled fish which formed the chief trade of the town. It was nearly depopulated by Vespasian. II. ins., an islet of Byzacene, over against Leptis. *Tschuries.*

TARNADÆ (Tarnacæ), a town of the Nantuates, Alpes Penninæ, on the Rhone, L., bet. Penelocus N. and Octodurum S.S.E. *St. Maurice.*

TARNANTO, a town of the Alauni, Noricum, bet. Laciaca (14) and Juvavia (14). *Nieumarkt.*

TARNASIS, a town of Noricum, bet. Graviasi (14) and Biliandrum (14). *Murau.*

TARNE, I. the source of Pactolus fl. II. a town of Achaia.

TARNIS fl., a r. of Gaul, rising in Cebenna m., and falling into the Garumna, 22 m. above Aginnum. *Tarn.*

TARODUNUM, a town of Germania Mag. *Freyburg.*

TARONA, a town of Taurica Chersonnetus.

TARPETES, a people of Sarmatia Asiat., towards the Tyrambæ.

TARPHE, an inland town of the Locri Epicnemidii; resettled by a colony from Argos, and called Pharygæ.

TARPODIZUS, a town of the Odrysæ, in Thrace, on Artiscus fl., bet. Sadame and Ostudizum. There appears to have been another town of the same name in the neighbourhood (s.w.).

TARQUINII (Tarcuna), a town of Etruria, on Marta fl., L., w. of Blera. One of the twelve cities. Founded by Tarchon (Tages). The birth-place of Tarquinius Priscus. A colonia and municipium. Noted for its timber and flax. *Turchina.*

TARRACINA (Anxur, Trachas, Trachina), a maritime town of the Volsci, in Latium, on Via Appia, bet. Ad Medias (10) and Fundi (13). A colonia and municip. Galba was born near it. *Terracina.*

TARRACO, a city of the Cosetani, and capital of Tarraconensis, on the Mediterranean, at the mouth, L., of Tulcis fl., bet. Tolobis and Oleastrum, 45 m. s.w. from Barcino. Enlarged by Cneius and Publius Scipio. A colonia of Cæsar (Julia Victrix). *Tarragona.*

TARRACONENSIS, the name given by Augustus to Hispania Citerior, from Tarraco, its capital; separated from Bætica by a line from Portus Magnus to Ilucia, on the Anas, and from Lusitania by the Durius, and a line from Sarabris on that r., N., to Ilucia, s.

TARRAGA, a town of the Vascones, Tarraconensis, bet. Ulavola and Cascantum. *Tauste.*

TARRAS, a town of Sicily, towards Coracodes portus.

TARRHA, a town on the s. coast of Crete, bet. Calamydes and Pæcilasium (7½). The birth-place of the grammarian Lucius Tarrhæus. *Temegna.*

TARRHA, a town of Lydia.

TARSATICUM, a town of Liburnia, at the head of Tarsaticus sin., s. of Ad Titulos (17).

TARSHISH, i. q. Tartessis.

TARSIANA, a port of Carmania, on Persicus sin., at Tarsias prom., w. of Agedana ins.

TARSIAS (Themistias) prom., a pr. of Carmania, on Persicus sin., opposite Pylora ins.

TARSIUM, a town of the Scordisci, Pannon., on Drinus fl., at its junction with Savus fl. The death-place of Maximianus.

TARSIUS fl., a r. of Mysia, rising in Ida m., and falling into Propontis. Extremely sinuous in its course. *Tarza.*

TARSURAS (Tassirus), I. a r. of Colchis, falling into the Euxine, 18½ m. s. from Hippus fl. II. a town of Ecretice, Colchid., at the mouth of Tarsuras fl.

TARSUS, I. a town of Bithynia. II. capital

of Cilicia, on Cydnus fl., at one time near
its mouth, but now 13 m. inland. Built
" in one and the same day with Anchiale,"
by Sardanapalus. A celebrated seat of
learning. The birth-place of St. Paul; of
the stoics Antipater, Archedamus, and
Nestor; of Athenodorus and Cordylion;
of Nestor, the tutor of Marcellus; of Plu-
tiades and Diogenes; of the grammarians
Artemidorus and Diodorus; and of the
dramatist Dionysiades. *Tersoos.*

TARTARUS fl., the later name of Hatrianus
fl., in Venetia.

TARTESSIS fl., Hispaniæ, i. q. Bætis.

TARTESSIS, the coast of Bætica, on both
sides of Tartessis fl. (Bætis).

TARTESSIS, a maritime city of Hispania,
variously identified with Hispalis, Carteia,
and Gades; but the circumstance, that the
bay on which Cadiz stands was called
Tartessius sinus, would argue in favour of
the title of Gades to be at once the Tartessis of the classics, and the Tarshish of
Scripture.

TARTURSANÆ, a town of the Taurisci, in
Noricum, on Murus fl., below Inimurium,
9 m. N. from Viscella. *Heilbad.*

TARUANA, a town of Carmania, on Saganus
fl., L.

TARUENNA, a town of the Morini, Belgica II., E. of Gessoriacum. *Terou-
anne.*

TARUS fl., a r. of Gallia Cispadana, rising
in the Apennines, N.w. of Boron, and falling into Padus fl. below Parma. It separated the territory of the Anamani from
that of the Boii. *Taro.*

TARUSATES, a people of Novem Populana,
w. of the Elusates. *In Tursan.*

TARVIDIUM prom., i. q. Orcas.

TARVISEDUM, I. a town of the Venonetes,
Rhæt., bet. Cuneus Aureus (10) and Clavenna (15). *Madese.* II. (Tasinemetum),
a town of the Japodes, in Pannonia, bet.
Ad Silanos and Saloca. *Tarvis.*

TARVISIUM, a town of the Veneti, in Venetia, on Silis fl., L., N.w. of Altinum.
A municipium. *Treviso.*

TASA, Lycaon, i. q. Caspia.

TASCIACA, a town of the Carnutes, Lugdunensis IV., bet. Cæsarodunum w.N.w.
and Gabris.

TASCONI, a tribe of Tectosages, in Aquitania I., on Tarnis fl. *On the Tescon.*

TASDRUM, a town of Heptanomis, on the
Nile, L., bet. Memphis and Peme.

TASINEMETUM, Pannoniæ, i. q. Tarvesedum.

TASITIA, a town of the Evonymitæ, on the
Nile, bet. Pselcis and Autoba. *Samne.*

TATACENE, a district of Drangiana, on Pharnacotus fl., towards Aria palus.

TATHILBA, a town of the Badiamæi Ind.,
s.w. of Nagaruris.

TATITTI, a town of Mauritania Cæsar., bet.
Auzia and Aræ.

TATTA palus, a lake of Lycaonia, on the
borders of Cappadocia, N.E. of Iconium;
in length 18 m., in circuit 45. Noted for
its intense impregnation with brine. *L.
Tuzla,* or *Duslag.*

TAUCHIRA (Teuchira), the early name of
Arsinoe, in Cyrenaica.

TAULANTII, a people of Illyria, occupying
the sea-coast bet. Lissus and Chaonia.

TAUM ÆSTUARIUM, *vide* Tava.

TAUNUS m., a ridge of Abnoba m., on the
confines N. of the Mattiaci, Germaniæ.
Hohe; Heyrich.

TAURANIA (Thora), a town of Campania,
near Stabiæ. Destroyed by Spartacus.

TAURANITIUM, a district of Armenia Mag.,
towards the eastern source of the Tigris.
Taron.

TAURASIA, the early name of Augusta Taurinorum.

TAURASIUM, a town of the Hirpini, in
Samnium, on Calor fl., s. of Eclanum.
The locality of the defeat of Pyrrhus, by
Curius Dentatus, 277 B.C. In this dis-
trict the senate settled a colony of Ligu-
rians. *Taurasi.*

TAURESIUM, a town of Mœsia Sup., s.E. of
Sardica. The birth-place of Justinian.
Giustendil.

TAURI m., I. m. of the Colobi, on the w.
coast of the Red sea, N. of Ptolemais
Theron. *Ras Akik.* II. prom., a pr. of
Lycia, i. q. Sacrum. III. of Sicily E.,
above Xiphonia.

TAURIANA, a town of Bruttium, on Metaurus fl., R., bet. Hipponium (12) and
Arciades fl. (12), on Via Aquilia. *Tra-
viano.*

TAURIANUM (Tauroentum), I. a pr. of Bruttium, on the Tyrrhenian sea, N. of Metaurum. II. a town of Bruttium, at the
cognominal prom.

TAURIANUS ager, a district of Bruttium,
between Thurii and Besidiæ. *About Ti-
riolo.*

TAURICA CHERSONESUS (Scythica, Magna),
a peninsula of Sarmatia E., forming the
w. and partly the s. shore of Palus
Mæotis. Named from its inhabitants the
Tauro-Scythæ, or, fabulously, from the
yoke of bulls with which Osiris is said to
have ploughed there.

TAURINI (Taurisci, "mountaineers;" Taur,
Tor, *Celticè,* "high mountain"), a people

of Italy, who from the high country about Augusta Taurinorum, gradually extended themselves, with the decline of Etruscan power, over the plains below as far as Tanarus fl. The name was applied also to the people of Noricum ; and generally to the inhabitants of mountainous districts.

TAURIS ins., an isl. of Illyria, the locality of the defeat of Cn. Octavius, by Vatinius. *Torkola.*

TAURISCI, i. q. Taurini.

TAUROEIS (Taurentum), a port of the Commoni, Narbonensis, bet. Citharista w. and Portus Æmines. Built by a Phocæan colony, circa 600 B.C., and named after the bull, which constituted the ensign of their ship. *Taurenti.*

TAUROMENIUM (Tauromenia), a maritime city of Sicily, E., under Taurus m., bet. Argenum prom. and Tauromenius fl. Built 336 B.C., by Andromachus, father of Timæus the historian, and partly constructed with the ruins of Naxos, an adjacent town destroyed by Dionysius. *Taormina.*

TAUROMENIUS (Onobala) fl., a r. of Sicily, falling into Siculum mare at Tauromenium. *Cantara.*

TAUROPOLIS, a town of Caria, in the territory of Eunomus.

TAURO-SCYTHÆ, a tribe of Scythians, inhabiting Taurica Chersonesus, and the adjacent portion N.W. of the mainland of Sarmatia, E. to the Borysthenes.

TAURUBULÆ SCOPULI, cliffs of Capreæ ins., Campaniæ. *Toro grande ; Toro piccolo.*

TAURUNUM, a city of Pannonia Inf., on the Danube, at its confluence with Savus fl., L. *Semlin.*

TAURUS, *postea* Hyleius, I. a r. of Argolis, falling into the Ægean, near Trœzen. II. of Pisidia, falling into Cestrus fl. or Eurymedon fl. III. m. intersecting Asia, in various ridges and under various names, Imaus, Caucasus, Caspius, Niphates, &c., from the Mediterranean, at Chelidonium prom., and thence up to the Ægean to the Caspian, s. of the mouth of Araxes fl. Strabo assigns its w. commencement to Caria. Named either as being generally bull-like, or from the fancied shape of Chelidonium prom. *Enamas; Ramadan; Gourin, &c.* IV. a ridge of Nebrodes m., in Sicily, N.W. of Tauromenium.

TAUS fl., a r. of the Iceni, Brit., falling into Garianus fl. below Garianonum.

TAUSES fl., i. q. Aluta.

TAVA (Taus) ÆSTUAR., the mouth of Tava fl., bet. Deva fl. and Tina fl. *Frith of Tay.*

TAVA (Taus), I. a r. of the Venicontes, Brit., falling into Germanic. oc. at Tava Æstuar. *Tay.* II. a town of Lower Egypt. bet. Andropolis and Sebennistus.

TAVANA, a town of Taurica Chersonesus, E.N.E. of Cercinetis.

TAVIA fl., a r. of Liguria, falling into Ligusticus sin., E. of Costa Balæna.

TAVIUM (Tavia), capital of the Trocmi, in Galatia, bet. Ancyra (124) and Amasia (73). Noted as an emporium, and for a grove of Jupiter, a sanctuary, with a colossal bronze statue of the god. *Jeuzgatt.*

TAVOLA fl., a r. of Corsica, falling into the sea at Mariana. *Golo.*

TAXARIS, a later name of Colonia, in Cappadocia.

TAXGÆTIUM, a town of Rhætia, on the Rhine, N.W. of Brigantia. *Lindau.*

TAXILA (Taxiana), a town of Caspiria Ind., on the Indus, N.W. of Agalassa. The death-place of Calanus.

TAXIMYRA, Phœniciæ, i. q. Simyra.

TAYGETUS m., a chain of m. in Laconia, a continuation of Lycæus m., separating that country from Messenia, and terminating in Tænarum prom. A celebrated hunting-ground, with a peculiarly fine breed of hounds. Noted also for its green marble. *Pentedactylos.*

TAZARENE, a town of Drangiana, on Etymandrus fl., R., above Alexandria.

TAZORA, a town of the Gandarii, Arachosiæ, s.w. of Gazaca.

TAZUS, I. a town of the Achæi, Sarmat., bet. Achæa and Toreticum prom. II. of Taurica Chersonesus, in the centre of the peninsula.

TEANUM, I. capital of Daunia, Apulia, on Frento fl., R., 10 m. above its mouth, bet. Larinum (18) and Ergitium, on Via Frentana. A colonia and municipium. *Civitate.* III. of the Sidicini, in Campania, on Via Latina, bet. Venafrum (18) and Cales (4). A colonia of Augustus. A favourite retreat of the Roman aristocracy. *Teano.*

TEARI JULIENSES (Tiara Julia), a town of the Ilercaones, Tarraconensis, s. of Dertosa.

TEARUS fl., a r. of Thrace, rising with thirty-eight springs in Hæmus m., and falling into Contadesdus fl. below Burtudizum. At its source was a pillar, erected by Darius, commending its waters as the purest and best in the world. *Tekedere.*

TEATE, I. a town of Daunia, Apulia, 12 m. E.S.E. from Larinum, 6 m. from the sea. *Chieti Vecchio.* II. capital of the Marrucini, in Italy, on Aternus fl., R., bet.

Interpromium (13) and Hadria (24), on Via Valeria. *Chieti.*

TEBA, a town of the Turtetani, Bætica, bet. Attegua N.N.E. and Sabora S.W.

TEBAVII, a tribe of Caturiges, Alpes Maritimæ, w. of the Medulli. *Vallée d'Allevard.*

TEBENDA (Tebenna, Tomba), a town of Pontus, towards Comana.

TECELIA, I. one of the Electrides ins., Germ., off the mouth of Flevus fl. II. a town of the Marsi, in Germany, S. of the mouth of the Visurgis.

TECMON, a town of Molossis, near Passaro. *Gastrizza.*

TECOA, Palestinæ, i. q. Thecoa.

TECTOSĀGES, a colony of the Tectosages, of Gaul, established in Central Galatia, bet. the Tolistoboii and the Trocmi.

TECTOSAGES, Galliæ, *vide* Volcæ Tectosages.

TEDANIUS fl., a r. of Illyria, the boundary of Japydia. *Zermagna.*

TEDIUM, a town of Arabia Deserta, on the confines of Chaldæa. *El Tediun.*

TEGEA, I. a town of Crete. Founded by Agamemnon. II. a city of Arcadia, bet. Argos and Megalopolis. Founded by Tegeus, son of Lycaon; consolidated as a state by Aleus. Here was a temple of Minerva Alea, built by Scopas; in it was preserved the hide of the Calydonian boar. Near it was the tomb of Orestes, whence the Spartans removed his bones. *Piali.*

TEGESSUS, a town of Cyprus, at a cognominal prom.

TEGEUM, a town of Mysia.

TEGLANUM, a town of Campania, on Via Aquilia, bet. Nola (5) and Nuceria (9). *Palma.*

TEGLATA, a town of Zeugitana, under Cirna m. S., bet. Picus and Vaga.

TEGNA, a town of the Allobroges, Viennensis, on the Rhone, bet. Ursolis and Valentia.

TEGRÆ, a town of the Getæ, in Mœsia, on the Danube, bet. Appiaria and Scaidava.

TEGRANUM, a town of Lucania, on Tanager fl., L., N. of Sontia. *Diano.*

TEGULA, a maritime town of Sardinia S., within Chersonesus prom. *Teulada.*

TEGULICIUM, a town of the Getæ, Mœsiæ, on the Danube, bet. Dorostolum and Nigriniana.

TEGYRA, a town of Bœotia, in Pelicania regio. The birth-place, according to some traditions, of Apollo; with a temple and oracle of that god.

TEKES m., "the sacred mountain," a summit of Scydisces m., overlooking Frigidarium at a distance of about 50 m., whence the Ten Thousand first saw the sea (the Euxine) on their return. *Cop Dagh.*

TEKOAH, a city of Judah, S.E. of Jerusalem, near Bethlehem. Founded by Ashur; fortified by Rehoboam.

TELA, I. a town of the Vaccæi, Tarraconensis, above Amallobriga. *Santoio?* II. of Mesopotamiæ, i. q. Antoninopolis.

TELABIB, a town on Chaboras fl., of uncertain identification.

TELAEBA, a town of the Olondæ, Sarmatiæ, on the Caspian, N. of Gelda.

TELAMO, I. a pr. of Etruria, at Telamo portus. II. (Portus Telamonis), a port of Etruria, on Via Aurelia, bet. Albinia (4) and Hasta (8). An Argonautic and Pelasgic settlement under Telamon. *Talamone.*

TELANDRUM prom., a pr. of Caria.

TELANDRUS, a town of Caria, at Telandrum prom.

TELCHINES, the primitive inhabitants of the N. coast of Crete. An ingenious and inventive people, they passed as enchanters, having control of the elements. They were among the first who practised the Cabiric worship.

TELCHINIA, a name of Creta ins., from its Telchinian settlers.

TELEBOÆ (Taphii), a tribe of Leleges, settled in the islands on the S. coast of Acarnania; conquered by Amphytrion.

TELEBOARUM, *vel* TAPHIORUM ins., a group of islands of Acarnania, within Leucate prom. w. and Crithote prom. E. Settled by the Teleboæ. Remarkable for their fertility, and notorious for the pirates who frequented them.

TELEBA, a town of Albania, bet. Gerrus fl. and Soana fl.

TELEMÆA, a village of Bithynia, near Sophon lacus.

TELENDOS ins., an isl. of Lycia, in Lycium mare.

TELEPHI fons, a stream of Lycia, near Patara.

TELEPTE (Thala), a town of Numidia, 20 m. N.W. from Vicus Gemellæ. A treasure fortress of Jugurtha, taken by Metellus. *Ferreanah.*

TELESAURA, Syriæ, a later name of Germanicia.

TELESIA, a town of the Caudini, in Samnium, bet. Allifæ (25) and Beneventum (16). A colonia. The birth-place of Caius Pontius, the Samnite general, and of C. Pontius, the opponent of Sylla. *Telese.*

TELETHRIUS m., a m. of Ellopia, in Eubœa, S.E. of Histiæa. *Plokovouni.*

TELLENÆ, a town of the Latini, Latium, near Lanuvium. Destroyed by Ancus Martius, who removed the inhabitants to Rome.

TELLUR, a maritime town of the Bati, Indiæ, on Agaricus sin. N.

TELMESSICUS sin., i. q. Glaucus sin.

TELMESSUS, I. a pr. of Lycia. II. a town of Caria, towards Halicarnassus, whose inhabitants had the gift of divination. III. a city of Lycia, on Telmessicus sin. S.E. Celebrated for its augurs. *Myes ; Meis.*

TELOBIS, a town of the Jacetani, Tarraconensis.

TELO MARTIUS, capital of the Commoni, Narbonensis, on the coast, bet. Tauroeis w. and Olbia E. *Toulon.*

TELONIUS fl., Italiæ, i. q. Tolenus.

TELONNUM, I. a town of the Ædui, Lugdunensis I., bet. Augustodunum N.E. and Pocrinium S.S.E. II. a town of the Tarbelli, Novem Populana, bet. Salomaco N. and Coequosa S.

TELOS, I. an isl. of Icarium mare, S.E. of Nisyrus ins., s. of Cnidus, in circuit 17 m. Noted for its unguents. *Tilo, or Piscopi.* II. its capital, on the N. coast. *Tilo.*

TELPUSA (Thelpusa), a town of Arcadia, on Ladon fl., L., 5 m. s. from Caus. Named from Telphusa, daughter of Ladon. *Katzioula.*

TEMALA fl., one of the mouths of Dorius fl., Indiæ, falling into Sarabicus sin. at Temala.

TEMAN, *vide* Thaman.

TEMATHIA m., a m. of Messenia, an E. continuation of Tomæus.

TEMBROGIUS fl., Phryg., i. q. Thymbres.

TEMBRUS, a town of Cyprus.

TEMENEIA, Phryg., i. q., Eumenia.

TEMENICUM agrum, a district of Gaul, on the Rhone, contiguous to Lemanus lacus. *Vallée de Simmenthal.* .

TEMENIUM, a town of Argolis, on the Argolicus sin., at the mouth of Inachus fl., bet. Nauplia and Argos. The burial-place of its founder, Temenus.

TEMENUTHYRÆ, a town of Lydia, or, according to Ptolemy, of Mysia. Its early occupants were giants.

TEMERINDA, a local name of Mæotis palus.

TEMESA, *vide* Tempsa.

TEMISDIA, a district of Persis, about Persepolis.

TEMMICES, a tribe of Leleges, in Bœotia, about Chæronea.

TEMNUS, I. m. intersecting Mysia. *Tchumus Dagh ; Kudj Dagh.* II. one of the twelve cities of Æolis Asiat., on Hermus fl., towards its mouth. The birth-place

of Hermagoras, the rhetorician. Extinct in Pliny's time. *Menimen.*

TEMPE (Temenos, Tempos), *postea* Lycostomo, a valley of Thessaly, on both sides of the Peneus, towards its mouth ; for the extent of two miles, a narrow and rugged defile bet. Ossa and Olympus ; then for 3 m. a beautiful vale, in breadth about 2½ m. The narrower portion of the valley, now called Bogaz, " defile," is considered to have been the effect of an earthquake. In the valley was a sacred grove, Temenos, Æolicè Tempos, giving name to the place.

TEMPOS, Æolicè " sacred grove," the Æolian designation of Tempe in Thessaly ; whence the Latin tempus, tempulum, templum.

TEMPSA, *prius* Temesa, I. a maritime town of Bruttium, bet. Clampetia (10) and Terina, on Via Aquilia. An Ausonian town, enlarged by Ætolian settlers, under Thoas. A colonia 192 B.C. Near it was the heroon of Polites, to whose manes a virgin was annually sacrificed. *Torre del piano del Casale.* II. *surnamed* Montana, a town of Bruttium, near Crimisa.

TEMPYRA (Tympora), a town of the Cicones, in Thrace, on the Egnatia Via, bet. Milolitum (12) and Trajanopolis (8).

TEMUS fl., a r. of Sardinia, falling into the sea at Bosa.

TENCTĚRI, a tribe of Istævones, Germ., on the Rhine, bet. the Chattuarii N. and the Sicambri and Chatti S.

TENDEBA, a fortress of Caria, in the territory of Stratonice.

TENEA, a town of Corinthia, on the Contoporia Via, bet. Corinth (7½ m.) and Mycenæ (9). With a temple of Apollo. A colony from Tenedos, and for some time the seat of a republic. Here Œdipus was brought up by Polybus.

TENEBRESTE, a town of Numidia, bet. Thigisis and Ad Centenarias.

TENEBRIUM, I. a prom. of Tarraconensis E., at the mouth of the Iberus s. II. a town of the Ilercaones, Tarraconens., at Tenebrium prom., s. of Iberus fl. *Alfaques.*

TENEDOS, *prius* Leucophrys, an isl. of Troas, s. of Sigæum, 5 m. from the coast, in circuit 10 m. Settled by Phœnicians, and afterwards by Æolians. Named from Tennes, son of Cycnus. The scene of one of the strategics of the Greeks against Troy. Noted for the beauty of its women, and for its red pottery. *Tenedo.* II. its capital. III. a maritime town of Pamphylia, bet. Climax and Lyrnessus.

TENERICUS campus, a plain of Bœotia, on Copais lacus, N.W. of Thebes. Named from the soothsayer Tenerus.

TENESIS (Axomitarum regnum), a country of Æthiopia, S. of Meroe, bet. Astaboras fl. and the Red sea. Settled by the Egyptian military caste, emigrants from their native country, in the time of Psammitichus.

TENIUM, a town of Achaia.

TENNAGORA, a town of the Soræ, Indiæ, on Chaberis fl., L., above Parata.

TENNYS ins., an isl. in Tanis lacus, Ægypti.

TENOS (Hydrussa, Ophiusa), I. an isl. of the Ægean, one of the Cyclades, bet. Andros and Myconus. *Tino.* II. its capital, on the S. coast. Here was the tomb of the sons of Boreas. *Tino.* III. a village of Laconia. Reputed by some the birthplace of the poetess Erinna.

TENTȲRA (Tei-n Athor, "abode of Athor"), a town of Thebais, on the Nile, L., bet. Contra Coptos and Diospolis Parva. Sacred to Athor (Venus). The inhabitants, who were great enemies to the crocodile, had the power of charming them, so that, when these animals were introduced into the public shows at Rome, they were always attended by Tentyrite keepers. From the temple of Isis here came the celebrated zodiac, of date circa A.D. 40. *Denderah.*

TENUPSIS, a town of Meroe, S. of Semberrita.

TEOS, a maritime city of Ionia, on a peninsula, bet. Chytrium and Myonnesus. Colonized by Orchomenian Minyæ, Ionians, and Bœotians. Sacred to Bacchus. The birthplace of Anacreon, of Hecatæus the historian, of Protagoras the sophist, of Scythinus the poet, of Andron the geographer, of Apellicon, the preserver of the works of Aristotle. Noted for its wine. *Boudroun.*

TERABDON sin., a bay of Indicum mare, at the mouth of Arabis fl., Gedros., bet. Malana prom. and Bibacte ins.

TERACATRIÆ, a tribe of Quadi, Germania, about Medoslanium.

TEREA m., a m. of Mysia, 5 m. S. from Lampsacus.

TEREDON (Diridōtis), a town of the Orrheni, in Chaldæa, at the E. mouth of the Tigris. Noted as a mart for Arabian produce. *Dorah.*

TERENTUM, a town of Byzacene, bet. Aquæ Regiæ and Ælia.

TEREPS fl., i. q. Tader.

TERGIDUM, a district of Meroe, on the Nile, 80 m. above Napata.

TERGESTE, a city of the Carni, in Venetia, on Tergestinus sin., E. bet. Timavus fl.

(12) and Ningum (28). Founded by Colchians, 1350 B.C. At one period it marked the limit in this direction of Italy. A colonia. *Trieste.*

TERGESTINUS sin., a bay of the Adriatic, at Tergeste. *Golfo di Trieste.*

TERGOLAPE, a town of the Sevaces, in Noricum, bet. Ovilia (14) and Laciaca (18). *Buchheim.*

TERIAS fl., a r. of Sicily, falling into Siculum mare N. of Megara. *San Lionardo.*

TERINA, a town of Bruttium, on Sabbatus fl., L., towards its mouth. A colony from Crotona, giving name to Terinæus sin. Destroyed by Hannibal, but restored. *Near Nocera.*

TERINÆUS (Napitinus, Lametinus, Hipponiates) sin., a bay of the Tyrrhenian sea, bet. Terina and Hipponium. *Golfo di Sant' Eufemia.*

TERIOLI, a town of the Vennonetes, in Rhætia, near Athesis fl., L., S.W. of Vipitenum; hence the name of the Tyrol.

TERISLÆ, a town in the Campi Lapidei, Viennensis, w. of Pisanæ.

TERMANTIA (Termes, Termessus), a town of the Arevacæ, Tarraconensis, N.W. of Numantia. The ally of Numantia against Scipio Æmilianus. According to Ptolemy more E. (near Palacios). *Lerma.*

TERMERA, I. a prison fortress of Caria, at Termerium prom. *Carbaglar.* II. of Lydia, i. q. Permere.

TERMERIUM prom., a pr. of Caria, over against Scandarium prom., in Cos (5). *C. Carabaglar.*

TERMES, Tarraconensis, i. q. Termantia.

TERMESSUS, I. a grove of Bœotia, near Thebes. II. a city of Pisidia, N.W. of Attaleia, commanding one of the leading defiles of Taurus m., bet. Pisidia, Pamphylia, and Lycia.

TERMOLUS, a town of the Damnonii, N.W. of Isca. *Molland.*

TERPO, a town of the Latovices, Pannonia, on Lugeus lac., S.E.

TERPONUS, a town of the Japydes, in Illyria.

TERVIUM, a port of Picenum, N. of Truentum. *Grotto a Mare.*

TESANA, a town of Rhætia, on the confines of Venetia. *Tezza.*

TESTONA, a town of Liguria, near Augusta Taurinorum. *Moncalieri.*

TESTRINA, a town of Sabinium, bet. Interocrea (10) and Foruli (3). The first seat of the Sabine nation. *Citta Tommassa.*

TETARION (Tetradrum, Tyriæum), a town of Lycaonia, 15 geog. m. w. from Iconium. *Akshehr.*

TETELLUS, a town of the Cenomanni, in

Gallia Transpadana, bet. Tollegata (10) and Brixia (10), on Via Æmilia. *Baitella.*

TETHRINUS fl., a r. of Crete.

TETIOPOLIS, a town of Cilicia Trachea.

TETIUS fl., a r. of Cyprus, falling into the sea w. of Citium. *Simeone.*

TETRACIS, a maritime town of Paphlagonia, bet. Stephane and Potami.

TETRAPHYLLIA, the treasure city, and, probably, the capital of Athamania, in Ætolia, on Campylus fl.

TETRAPOLIS, *prius* Hyllenia, a district of Attica, containing the four demi of Œnoe, Marathon, Probalinthus, and Tricorythus, all built by Xuthus.

TETRAPYRGIA, I. a town of Garsauritis, in Cappadocia, on the confines of Cilicia. II. of Marmarica, bet. Gereatis and Catabathmus Major.

TETRICUS, "rugged," m., a summit of Fiscellus m., adjoining Severus m., in Italy. *Monte Sibilla.*

TETRISIA (Tiriza Acra), a port of the Crobyzi, Mœsia, bet. Callatis and Cruni.

TETUS fl., I. a r. of Narbonensis, falling into the sea below Ruscino. *Tet.* II. ins., an isl. of the Curiosolites, Lugdunensis III., N.E. of Alauna.

TEUCERA, a town of the Ambiani, Belgica II., bet. Dolucens N.W. and Samarobriva.

TEUCRI, a tribe of Pelasgi from Mœsia, who colonized the N.W. portion of Mysia. Named from their chief Teucer, son of Scamander.

TEUDERIUM, a town of the Eburones, Germania II., bet. Mederiacum and Coriovallum. *Detcern.*

TEUMESSUS, I. a m. of Bœotia, bet. Thebes and Chalcis, where Hercules slew the lion, whose skin he afterwards wore. II. a town of Bœotia, under the cognominal m., bet. Thebes and Harma, where Jupiter concealed Europa.

TEURIOCHÆMÆ, a tribe of Hermunduri, in Germany, on Visurgis fl., R., towards its source.

TEURISCI (Taurisci), a tribe of Bastarnæ, in Dacia, in Carpathus m., N. of the Ratacenses.

TEURNIA, Norici, i. q. Tiburnia.

TEUTANI, a people from Peloponnesus, who occupied the country about Pisæ (Teuta), in Italy, prior to the Tyrrhenian immigration.

TEUTERIUM, a town of the Ansibarii, in Germany, N. of Siatutanda.

TEUTHEA, a town of Achaia, on Teutheas fl.

TUTHEAS fl., a r. of Achaia, rising in Scollis

m., and, after a junction with the Caucon, falling into the Pirus fl. above Olenus.

TEUTHIS, a town of Arcadia, on Gortynius fl., below Thisoa. *Dimitzana.*

TEUTHRANIA, I. a district of Mysia, on Caicus fl., about Teuthrania. II. its capital, on Ceteius fl., 9 m. E. from Elæa. Named from Teuthras, foster-father of Telephus.

TEUTHRONE, a town of Laconia, on Laconicus sin., w., 19 m. above Tænarum prom. Founded by Teuthras.

TEUTOBODIACI, a tribe of Tectosages, in Galatia.

TEUTOBURGIENSIS saltus, woody m. of the Cherusci, Germania, bet. Amisia fl. and Visurgis fl.

TEUTOBURGIUM (Tutisurgion), I. a town of the Cherusci, Germania, under Teutoburgiensis saltus E., S.W. of Ascalingium. *Dithmold—Dietmellen ?* II. (Tittoburgium), of Pannonia, on Dravus fl., above its junction with the Danube, 16 m. from Mursia.

TEUTŌNES "men of Teuto," or merely Teut, Tut, Dit, Thod, "people:" generally, the people of Germany; specially, a tribe E. of Albis fl., bet. the Saxones and the Semnones. There was a people called Teutani in Peloponnesus.

TEUTONOARI, i. q. Teutones.

TEUTRIA ins., one of the Diomedeæ ins., Apuliæ. *San Nicolo.*

TEXALI, a people of Britannia Barbara, s. of the Vacomagi. *Aberdeenshire and part of Kincardineshire.*

THABALATI, a town of the Bagi Gætuli, in Libya, bet. Thebellami and Augemmi.

THABENI, a people of Arabia Felix, towards Chaldæa. *Beni Thaaba.*

THABILACA, a town of Albania, on Cæsius fl., S.W. of Gelda.

THABUNAGDI, a town of the Garamantes, in Libya, near Adaugmadum.

THABOR (Tabor, Itabyrius, Atabyrius) m., a m. of Galilæa, 50 m. N. from Jerusalem, 6 from Nazareth. Here Barak assembled his army; and here, according to some, took place the Transfiguration. *Djebel Tur.*

THABUSION, a fortress of Caria, on Indus fl., towards Cibyra. *Tabu ?*

THABUTHIS, I. a town of Æthiopia. II. of Numidia, N.W. of Tipasa. III. of Numidia, 18 m. N.W. of Lambæsa. *Tattubt.*

THACIA, a town of Zeugitana, on Bagradas fl., R., bet. Drusillana and Musti.

THADITÆ, Arab., *vide* Thaij.

THÆMI, a people of Arabia Felix, towards Magorum sin.

THÆMICOTÆ, a people of Sarmatia Asiatica, s. of the Psessii.

THAGORA, a port of Aurea Chersonesus, at Magnum prom.

THAGULIS, Africæ, *vide* Tagulis.

THAGURA (Tagora), a town of Numidia, bet. Gegeta and Vasidica.

THAGURON m., m. of Serica, running from N. to S.

THAHUITÆ, a people of Arabia Felix, s. of the Salapeni, on the edge of the desert, under Zametus m.

THAIJ, a district of Arabia Deserta, s. of Nabatene; subsequently occupied by the Thaditæ.

THALA, *vide* Telepte.

THALALATI, a town of the Bagi Gætuli, in Libya, bet. Thenadassa and Vinaza.

THALAMÆ, I. a fortress of Epea, in Elis, s.w. of Pylos. II. a town of Laconia, on Messeniacus sin., 2½ m. s. from Pephnos. A colony of Bœotians. Here was an oracle of Pasiphæ. *Calamo.*

THALASSA (Lisea), a town on the s. coast of Crete, w. of Calolimen.

THALIADÆ, a town of Arcadia, on Ladon fl.

THALLABA, a town of Gauzonitis, Mesopotamiæ, on Chaboras fl., s. of Ressaina. *Thalaban.*

THALLUSA (Daphnusa) ins., an isl. of Ionia, one of the Œnussæ ins.

THAMADA (Duma, Themma), Arabia Deserta, i. q. Thaman.

THAMAN, I. a district of Edom, E. of Petra, about Thaman; subsequently occupied by the Thamidemi. II. its capital, 15 m. E. from Petra. Named from Thaman, son of Esau. The birth-place of Eliphaz. The Romans had a garrison here.

THAMAR fl., a r. of Arabia Felix, falling into the sea N. of Acilla. *Sib.*

THAMARA, a town of Chaldæa, bet. Curraphus and Cybate.

THAMARICETUM, a town of Mauritania Cæsar., bet. Tigisis and Thanaramusa.

THAMBES m., a ridge of m. in N. Numidia, running E.N.E. from about Cirta.

THAMIA (Thamicia), a town of Thessaly.

THAMONDACANA, a town of Libya Int., s. of Thuppa, on Niger fl., R. *Haussa?*

THAMUDITÆ, a people of Arabia Felix, on Arabicus sin., s. of the Banizomenes. *Beni Thamud.*

THAMUSCALDI, a town of the Garamantes, in Libya, bet. Thentei and Thamusdusis.

THAMUSDUSIS, a town of the Garamantes, in Libya, bet. Tabunagdi and Thamuscaldi.

THANARAMUSA, a town of Mauritania Cæsar., bet. Thamaricetum and Suffasar.

THANTIA, a town of Batanæa, 24 m. s. from Bostra. *El Dschemal.*

THAPPUAH (Thephua, Thaffu, Taphua), a town of Judah, Judæa, w.N.W. of Hebron.

THAPSĂCUS (Thapsach, "passage"), I. a r. of Cilicia, i. q. Diaphanes. II. a city of Palmyrene, on the Euphrates, s.E. of Resapha. Greatly enlarged by Seleucus. Named Amphipolis by the Macedonians, who crossed the Euphrates here. It was the boundary in this direction of Solomon's kingdom. *Opposite Racca.*

THAPSA, Numidiæ, i. q. Rusicada.

THAPSIS fl., a r. of Taurica Chersonesus, falling into the Euxine near Cimmerium. *Salgir.*

THAPSUS, I. a maritime town of Byzacene, bet. Leptis Min. (8) and Turris Hannibalis. The locality of the defeat of Scipio and Juba by Cæsar. II. a town of Sicily, E., on a cognominal peninsula, bet. Myla fl. and Syracusæ. *Mauchisi.*

THÆMEOTÆ, a people of Sarmatia Asiat., on Theophanius fl., R.

THAR, a port of the Themi, Arabia, on Persicus sin., s. of Capeus sin. *Tarut.*

THARO ins., Arabiæ, i. q. Asgilia.

THARRANA, Osrhoene, i. q. Carrhæ.

THARROS, a maritime town of the Æchilenenses, in Sardinia, w., opposite the mouth of Tyrsus fl. *Torre di San Giov. di Sinis.*

THASARTE, a town of Byzacene, bet. Viresve and Silesua.

THASIA, a district of Armenia Major, on Pelorus fl., N.W. of Lychnitis lacus. *Taschir.*

THASOS (Chryse, Ogygia, *prius* Æria), I. an isl. of Thrace, on the Ægean, 22 m. s.w. from Abdera. Rich in gold and silver mines, marble, and wine. Colonized originally by Phœnicians, under Thasus; recolonized by Parians. Here was a temple of Hercules, built by the Phœnicians who were in search of Europa, five generations before the assigned period of the Theban Hercules. *Tasso.* II. its capital, on the N. coast, s.E. of Neapolis. *Castro.*

THASSACORA, a town of Mauritania Cæsar., bet. Castra Nova and Regiæ, s. of Cartenna.

THAUBASTUM, a town of Lower Egypt, at the N. extremity of Amarus lacus, 8 m. N. from Serapium. The station of the Ala Ulpia Afrorum.

THAUMACIA, *quasi* "wondrous view," I. a town of Dolopia, in Thessaly, N.E. of Melitæa, bet. Xynias lacus and Pharsalus, situated on an isolated rock commanding a most extensive and varied prospect, whence the name. Fabled to have been named from Thaumacus, father of Pæan. *Thamako.* II. of Magnesia, in Thessaly, N.E. of Olizon. Built by Philoctetes.

THAUMACIUS m., a m. of Arcadia, on Malætus fl., near Methydrium, in which was the cave of Rhea, where Saturn swallowed the stone.

THEA, a town of Laconia.

THEANGELA, a town of Caria, in the territory of Halicarnassus. The birth-place of Philip the historian.

THEBÆ, I. a town of the Alilæi, Arabiæ, i. q. Debæ. II. of Attica. III. *prius* Calydnus and Cadmeia, *surnamed* Heptapylos from its seven gates, a city of Bœotia, bet. Thespiæ and Aulis, N.E. of Platæa. The birth-place of Bacchus and of Hercules; of Pelopidas and of Pindar. Founded, or rather enlarged by Cadmus, B.C. 1493; walled by Amphion and Zethus, 1386; destroyed by Alexander, 335 B.C.; restored by Cassander, 315 B.C. In Strabo's time a village. Stigmatized for insolence. *Thiva.* IV. a town of Lucania, near the source of Laus fl. Extinct in Pliny's time. *Casteluccio.* V. a city of Phthiotis, in Thessaly, near Pagasæus sin., s.w. of Demetrias. Taken by Philip, son of Demetrius, and named by him Philippopolis. *Near Armiro.* VI. (Tape, "head," Diospolis Magna, No-Ammon), capital of Thebais, and later of all Egypt, on both banks of the Nile, bet. Apollinopolis Parva and Tuphium, below Hermonthis. Built by Busiris. Surnamed Hecatompylos traditionally from its 100 gates, each of which, it was said, could send forth 200 men, with horses and chariots; but in reality Thebes was a city without walls. The gates in question were probably those of its many temples. In the quarter called Tathyris, "sacred to Athor," on the left bank of the Nile, was the famous Memnonium. The city was almost entirely destroyed by Cambyses. *Luxor, Carnac, Gournou, and Medeenet-Haboo.*

THEBAIS, I. (Ægyptus Superior), Upper Egypt, from Phylace N. to Philæ s., N. from its capital, Thebæ. II. a rivulet of Lydia, falling into Eudon fl. below Tralles.

THEBASA, a town of Lycaonia, on the confines of Cilicia.

THEBE, I. *surnamed* Hypoplacia (under Placos), a Syro-Phœnician town of Æolis Asiat., under Placos m., 7½ m. N. from Adramyttium, 6½ m. N.E. from Chrysa. The city of Eetion, father of Andromache; destroyed by Achilles. II. a town of Cap-

padocia. III. of Ionia, near Miletus. IV. a maritime town of Pamphylia, E. of Climax. Founded by Cilicians of Troas.

THEBELLAMI, a town of the Bagi Gætuli, in Libya, bet. Thillabari and Thabalati.

THEBES campus, the district around Thebe, in Æolis Asiat.

THEBETA, a town of Mygdonia, Mesopotamia, near Nisibis.

THEBEZ, a town of Ephraim, N.E. of Shechem. The death-place of Abimelech.

THECOA (Thecua, Thecos), a town of Judæa, 6 m. s. from Bethlehem. The birth-place of the prophet Amos.

THEGANUSA ins., an isl. of Messenia, off Acritas prom. *Venetico.*

THEGIBA, a town of Numidia, near Tibilis.

THEGŌNIUM, a town of Thessaly.

THEIUM, a fortress of Athamania, Ætolia, on Achelous fl., N.W. of Cranon.

THELBENCANE, a town of Babylonia, on the Euphrates, R., bet. Fissenia and Bithna.

THELDA, Mesopotamiæ, i. q. Zaitha.

THELINE, a name of Arelate, in Gaul.

THELME, a town of Amordocia, Babyloniæ, s. of Aserga.

THELSAPHATA, a town of Acabene, Mesopotamiæ, bet. Singara and Ninus.

THELSEÆ, a town of Damascene, Syr., bet. Damascus (24) and Geroda.

THEMA, a town of the Asilæ, Arabia.

THEMACI, a demus of Attica, of the tribe Erectheis.

THEMANI, Arabiæ Desertæ, i. q. Thamideni.

THEMENOTHYRÆ (Timeni Venationes), a town of Phrygia, on the confines of Lydia.

THEMI, I. a people of Arabia Felix, on Persicus sin., bet. the Leanites sin. and Gerrha. II. under Zames m., w. III. in Arabia Deserta, amongst the Saraceni. Descendants of Temer, son of Ishmael.

THEMISCYRA, I. the district about Themiscyra, in Pontus, bet. Thermodon fl. and Iris fl. Noted for its abundant vegetable and animal life. It belonged to Amisus. II. a town of Pontus, near the mouth of Thermodon fl. The capital of the Amazons.

THEMISONIUM, a town of Phrygia Magna, on the borders of Pisidia, and latterly within its limits, bet. Laodicea (34) and Olbasa. Near it was a large cavern, sacred to Hercules, Apollo, and Mercury.

THEMISSUS, a town of Caria.

THEMUD, a district of Arabia Felix, on the

borders of Arabia Deserta, E. of the Darræ. Subsequently occupied by the Thameditæ.

THENADASSA, a town of the Bagi Gætuli, Libya, bet. Mesphe and Thalalati.

THENÆ, I. a town of Byzacene, on Syrtis Min., at Mercurii prom., bet. Macomades and Taphrura. A colonia of Hadrian (Ælia Augusta Mercurialis). *Tainah.* II. a village of Crete, N.E. of Gnossus. *Castel Temeno.*

THENATH (Thaanath-Silo), a village of Ephraim, in Samaria, 10 m. E.N.E. from Sichem.

THEODORIA, a town of Athamania, Ætolia, bet. Ambracia and Argithea. *Theodora.*

THEODOSIA, I. a town of the Epidii, Brit., at the w. termination of Severi murus. II. (Ardauda, " Ardauda, "city of the seven gods ") of Taurica Chersonesus, S., under Cimmerius m., N.E. A Milesian colony. *Eski-Caffa.* III. a town of Phrygia.

THEODOSIOPOLIS, I. capital of Armenia, near Arzes. Built by Theodosius II., enlarged by Anastasius and Justinian. *Achlalh.* II. a town of Cappadocia I. III. of Heptanomis, bet. Ibium and Hermopolis. IV. a later name of Perperene, in Æolis. V. i. q. Ressaina.

THEON OCHEMA prom., a pr. of Æthiopia, on the Atlantic, N. of Noti Cornu prom.

THEOPHANIUS fl., a r. of Sarmatia As., falling into Mæotis palus, N. of Rhombites Min. fl.

THEOPOLIS, I. a later name of Antiochia. II. a town of Narbonensis II., w. of Alabon.

THEOPOMPUS, a town of Phlius, in Argolis.

THERA, *prius* Calliste, I. an isl. of the Ægean, one of the Sporades, bet. Anaphe and Sicinus. In circuit 22 m. Named from Theras, chief of the colony of Minyæ sent hither by the Lacedæmonians. Of volcanic origin. Traditionally described as having been created by a lump of earth thrown from the ship Argo. *Santoria.* II. a town of Caria, on Chaus fl. III. i. q. Aulæi-tichos.

THERAMBUS, a town of Pallene, Chalcidice, on Thermaicus sin., at Posidium prom., s.

THERANDA, a town of the Dardani, Illyria, on the Drilo Albus fl., bet. Gabuleus and Vicianum.

THERAPNE, "hollow," I. a valley of Bœotia, on Asopus fl., L., towards Thebes. II. a town of Crete. III. of Laconia, on Eurotas fl., L., S.E. of Sparta ; with the tombs of Menelaus and Helen, and a temple of the Dioscuri, in which the Ephori

sacrificed to Mars. Named after the daughter of Lelex. *Chrysapha.*

THERAS m., a summit of Taygetus m.

THERASIA ins., an isl. of the Ægean, one of the Sporades, separated from Thera by an earthquake. *Therasi.*

THERENUTHIS, *vide* Momemphis.

THEREX, a town of Palestine, near Jericho.

THERIODES regio, I. the s. portion of Numidia. II. sin., a bay of Eous ocean., bet. Satyrorum prom. and Notium.

THERIONARCE ins., an isl. of Rhodes, towards Cnidus.

THERMÆ, I. baths of Byzacene, on the Mediterranean, near Ruspina. II. *surnamed* Himerenses, *vide* Himerenses. III. (Chytri), of Maliensis, Thessaly, issuing from Œta m., near and giving name to Thermopylæ. *Thermæ.* IV. *surnamed* Perticianenses, i. q. Thermæ Segestanæ. V. *surnamed* Phazemonitarum, of Pontus, bet. Phazemon and Amisus. *Gouzu.* VI. *surnamed* Segestanæ, Perticianenses, of Sicily, on the N.W. coast, near Segestanum emporium. VII. *surnamed* Selenuntiæ, of Sicily, bet. Selinus and Allava. A Carthaginian settlement. A colonia. VIII. of Tauranitium, under Capotes m. IX. of the Trocmi, Galatia, bet. Tavia (19) and Soanda (18).

THERMAÏCUS sinus, a bay of Macedonia, at the mouth of the Haliacmon. *Golfo di Saloniki.*

THERMODON fl., I. Hæmon, a r. of Bœotia, falling into Asopus fl. towards Tanagra. II. of Pontus, rising in Paryadres m., s.w. of Thia, and enlarged in its course by 96 streams, falling into the Euxine below Themiscyra, 12 m. E. from Heracleum prom. The chief seat of the Amazons. Its banks produced jasper and crystal. *Thermeh.*

THERMOPYLÆ, "gates of the warm springs," a defile of Maliensis, Thessaly, bet. Œta m. and Maliacus sin. The scene of the death-fight of Leonidas. The place of assembly of the Amphictyonic council.

THERMUS, I. a r. of Sardinia, falling into the sea N.E. of Plubium. II. a city of the Eurytanes, Ætolia, 4 m. N.W. from Trichonius palus. With an oracle of Ulysses. The general assemblies of the Ætolians were held here. Peculiarly rich in temples and statues. It was nearly destroyed by Philip of Macedon. *Vlokho ?*

THERMUTHIACUM OSTIUM NILI, i. q. Sebennyticum. Named from Thermuthis.

THERMUTHIS, a town of Lower Egypt, on the Thermuthic (Sebennytic) branch of the Nile.

THERON fl., Cretæ, i. q. Pothereus.

THERSITÆ, a people of Tarraconensis, contiguous to the Olcades.

THERVINGI, a people of Dacia, contiguous to the Taiphali.

THESEIS, a place bet. Hermione and Trœzen, in Argolis, where was the altar of Jupiter Sthenius, under a rock near which Theseus found his father's sword.

THESPIÆ, a town of Bœotia, under Helicon m., bet. Ascra (5) and Eutresis. Sacred to the Muses. Stigmatized for contention. The birth-place of Phryne the courtesan. *Eremo Castro.*

THESPIS, a town of Carmania, bet. Carmana and Portospana.

THESPROTI, a Pelasgic tribe in Epirus. Named after their king Thesprotus.

THESPROTIA, a district of Epirus, extending along the coast from Thyamus fl. to Acheron fl., and inland towards the confines of Illyria. *Calama and Souli.*

THESSALIA (Æmonia, Æolis), *prius* Pyrrha, a country of Græcia e. Peloponnesum, bounded N. by Macedonia, s. by Ætolia, Locris, and Phocis, w. by Athamania and Aperantia, E. by the Ægean. Settled by Æolian Pelasgi from Thesprotia. Named after Thessalus. The people were noted as the first tamers of horses, for their gluttony, and their skill in the preparation of poisonous drugs.

THESSALIOTIS, an early division of Thessaly.

THESSALIS, the early name of Bithynia.

THESSALONICA, *prius* Thermæ, a city of Amphaxitis, Macedonia, at the N.E. extremity of the Thermaicus sin., on the Egnatia Via, bet. Pella (27) and Mellisurgis (20). Enlarged by Cassander and named Thessalonica by him in honour of his wife. Under the Romans it became the capital of Macedonia II., and later the residence of the prefect of Illyricum. The seat of some of St. Paul's most successful exertions. *Saloniki.*

THESTIÆ, Ætoliæ, i. q. Thermus. Named from Thestius, a chief of the Curetes.

THESTIUS, an early name of Achelous fl., from Thestius.

THETIDIUM, a village of Phthiotis, Thessaly, N. of Pharsalus. Sacred to Thetis.

THEUDOLIS (Theudole), a town of Zeugitana, on Sisara lacus E.

THEUMA, a town of Dolopia, Thessaly, on Pamisus fl., above Acharræ, N.W. of Calathana. *Thauma.*

THEUPROSOPON (Dei facies) prom., a pr. of Phœnicia, s. of Tripolis.

THEVESTE, a town of Numidia, bet. Tim-

phadis and Menegere, near the source of Ardali fl. A colonia.

THIA, I. an isl. of the Ægean, one of the Sporades, contiguous to Thera. It emerged in Pliny's time. *Palaio Caimeni.* II. a town of Pontus, s. of Zigana.

THIAGOLE lac., a lake of Dacia, formed by the Danube towards its mouth.

THIAUNA, a town of Albania, N. of Alamus.

THIBA, a town of Pontus, on Thermodon fl., the people of which were sorcerers, whom it was impossible to drown. Named from the amazon Thiba.

THICATH (Œcath), a town of Mauritania Ting., on Cusa fl.

THIGES, a town of Libya Int., bet. Thasuri and Speculum.

THIGESIS, a town of Numidia, bet. Sigus and Tenebreste.

THIGUBIS, a town of Mesopotamia, N.E. of Nicephorium.

THILATICOMUM (Tillacama), a town of Osrhoene, near the Euphrates, 22 m. w. from Balnæ. *Scharmely.*

THILBIS, a town of the Isondæ, Sarmatiæ, on Gerrus fl., below the junction of Soanus fl.

THILLABARI, a town of the Bagi Gætuli, Libya, bet. Adaugmadum and Thebellami.

THILSAPHATA, a town of Mesopotamia, towards Nisibis. *Tellaafar.*

THILUTHA, Mesopot., i. q. Olabus.

THIMARUM, a town of Estiæotis, Thessaly, s. of Pherinum.

THIMESEGERI turres, a fortress of Gætulia, on Tritonis pal., bet. Aves and Mahatanzur.

THIMNATH (Thamna, Thamathsare, Thamnasarach, Thamuasachar), I. a town of Ephraim, Judæa, N.E. of Lydda. The property and burial-place of Joshua. II. a town of Judah, afterwards assigned to Dan, in Judæa, on Sorek fl., L., above Jamnia. The birth-place of Samson's wife. The place where Judah sheared his sheep.

THIMONEPSI, a town of Lower Egypt, on the Nile, R., bet. Aphroditopolis (16) and Alyi (16). The station of the Ala Tingitana.

THINÆ, capital of the Sinæ. Of altogether uncertain position.

THINGRUS, a Dorian town of Perrhæbia, on Lacmon m.

THINNESUS, a town of Lower Egypt, on Tennys ins. (nesos).

THINTIS, a town of Pentapolis, Cyrenaicæ, s.E. of Cyrene.

THIPSACH, i. q. Thapsacus.

THIRMIDA, a town of Numidia. The death-place of Hiempsal.

THIRZA (Tirzah, Thersa, Tharse), a city of Samaria, E.N.E. of Samaria. The capital of the kings of Israel, before Omri built Samaria.

THIS (Thonis), a town of Thebais, on the Nile, L., bet. Ptolemais Hermii and Aby-dus.

THISBÆ, a town of Bœotia, bet. Bulis and Siphæ. Noted for its wild pigeons. The birth-place of Ismenias the minstrel. *Ka-kosia.*

THISBE (Haroseth), a town of Dan, E. of Giscala, near Jordan fl., R. The birth-place of Elias.

THISOA, a town of Arcadia, near the source of Gortynius fl. Its inhabitants removed to Megalopolis.

THISSAMATÆ, a tribe of Neuri, Sarmat., bet. Axiaces fl. and the Borysthenes fl.

THIUS fl., a r. of Arcadia, falling into Al-pheus fl. 5 m. s. from Megalopolis.

THMUIS, "goat," *postea* Augustamnica, a town of Lower Egypt. Here the goat was worshipped with peculiar veneration. *Tel-el-Mai.*

THOANA (Thormia), a town of Arabia Pe-træa.

THOANTIUM prom., I. the s. prom. of Car-pathus ins. II. the coast of Rhodes ins., bet. Camirus and Jalysus.

THOARIS fl., a r. of Pontus, falling into the Euxine 7½ m. from Bires fl.

THOCNIA, a town of Arcadia, on Alpheus fl., bet. Brenthea and Megalopolis.

THOEMA, a town of the Thaditæ, Arabiæ, s. of Gaea.

THOGARA, a town of Serica.

THOLUS, a town of Zeugitana, w. of Car-thage.

THOMU, a town of Thebais, on the Nile, R., bet. Panopolis and Lepidotonpolis.

THONIS, a town of Lower Egypt, E. of Ni-copolis.

THONITES pal., Armen., i. q. Thospites.

THORA, I. a town of Parthia Comisene, s.w. of Hecatompylos. II. Campaniæ, i. q. Taurania.

THORÆ, a demus of Attica, of the tribe An-tiochis, s. of Zoster prom. The birth-place of Andocides.

THORAX, I. a m. of Lydia, above Magne-sia ad Mæandrum, on which Daphidas was crucified for lampooning the successor of Antiochus. II. of Sicily, a N.E. continua-tion of Myconius m., towards Messana. III. a town of Ætolia. IV. a town of Magnesia, Thessaly.

THORICUS, a demus of Attica, of the tribe Acamantis, on a cognominal prom. on the Ægean, bet. Potamos and Pantomatria. Famous for its emerald and silver mines. *Therico.*

THORNAX m., I. i. q. Coccygius. II. a m. of Laconia, extending N. from Menelaium, E. of Sparta, to Parnon m. *Thornika.*

THOSPIS, a town of Carmania Agdanitis, on Dara fl., L., towards its source.

THOSPITIS, I. a district of Armenia Maj., on the S.S.E. shore of Arsissa Thospitis lac. *Tosp.* II. lacus, a lake of Sophene, Arm., N.W. of Amida, near the source of the Tigris, or, according to Pliny, traversed by that river. Arsissa palus seems also to have been called Thospitis.

THON, a town of Lower Egypt, 12 m. E. of Vicus Judæorum.

THRACI, the descendants of Tiraz, son of Japhet, whence their designation; or, ac-cording to Greek tradition, named after Thrax, son of Mars. Settled in Thrace, whence, at various periods, bands of them migrated to Phocis, Bœotia, Eleusis in Attica, Bithynia, Samothrace, Mœsia, and Phrygia; the country receiving, on the other hand, prior to the Trojan war, immi-grants, and, according to Herodotus, con-querors from Troas and Mysia.

THRACIA, a country of Europe, extending generally between Strymon fl. and Danu-bius fl. from w. to E. and bet. Hæmus m. and the Ægean, the Euxine and the Pro-pontis from N. to s. Specially, bounded N. by Mœsia, s. by the Ægean and the Propontis, w. by Macedonia, E. by the Euxine. Annexed to Macedonia 335 B.C., to Rome 168 B.C. *Roumelia.*

THRACIA mare, the portion of the Ægean washing the coast of Thrace, s.

THRÆSTUS (Thraustus), a town of Acroria, Elis.

THRASYLLUM, a mining village of Attica, on Laurium m.

THRIA (Philæum), a demus of Attica, on Cephissus Eleusiacus fl., near its mouth, bet. Cecropia and Oenoe. The birth-place of Crates the philosopher.

THRISSILIDES ins., an isl. of the Colobi, in the Red sea, s.E. of Ptolemais Theron.

THRIUS, a town of Achaia, near Patræ.

THROANA, a port of Serica, on Œchardes fl.

THROASCA, a town of Carmania, w. of Ora *Djirost.*

THRONI, I. a pr. of Cyprus, E., near Ammo-chostum. II. a town of Cyprus, at Throni prom.

THRONIUM, I. a town of the Atintanes,

Illyria, in Abantis regio. Built by the Abantes of Euboea, on their return from Troy. Destroyed by the Apolloniatae. II. of the Locri Epicnemidii, on Boagrius fl., s.e. of Scarphe. *Longachi.*

THROSMOS collis, a hill of Troas, near Troja, on Scamander fl., L.

THRYANDA, a town of Lycia.

THUARIA, a town of Zeugitana, on Bagradas fl., L., bet. Tuburbis Min. and Cicisa.

THUBACTIS, a town of Africa, on Syrtis Magna, w., bet. Cephalae prom. and Trieron prom.

THUBANA (Tubonae), a town of Mauritania Caesar., s. of Vaccae. *Tubna.*

THUBIDA, a town of Gauzonitis, Mes., at the junction of Mygdonius fl. with Chaborras fl. *Al Nahraim.*

THUBURNICA (Thubursica, Tuburnicense opp.), a town of Numidia, s. of Hippo regius. A colonia.

THUBURSICA, Numidiae, i. q. Thuburnica.

THUBUSCUM, Mauritaniae, i. q. Tubusuptus.

THUCCABORI, *vide* Tucca Terebinta.

THULE (Thyle, "darkness,") ins., an isl. situate towards the n. extremity of Germanicum mare. Supposed by some to be Shetland; from the description of Pytheas of Marseilles, others suppose it to be Iceland; and others again take it to be the district of Telemark in Scandinavia.

THULCIS, *vide* Tulcis.

THUMATA, a town of the Macoretae, Arab., e. of Macoraba.

THUNATÆ, a people of Moesia Superior, under Scordus m., about Ulpiana.

THUNELILLIA, a town of Libya Int., s. of Girgiris m. *Kanem.*

THUNODROMUM, a town of Numidia, s. of Rusicada. A colonia.

THUNUIDA (Thunisidense oppid.), a town of Numidia, w.s.w. of Tabraca.

THUPPA, a town of Libya Int., on Niger fl.

THURCIS, a town of Zeugitana, bet. Membrossa (12) and Sicilibba. *Tuccubar.*

THURIA, I. a town of Messenia, w. of Lymnae, towards the sea. The Æpeia of Homer. *Pedrina.* II. chief town of Cynuria, Argolis, on the Thuriates sin., at the mouth of the Tanus fl., 1 m. from the sea. The scene of the celebrated combat of 300 Lacedaemonians and 300 Argives. *Astro.*

THURIATES sin., I. a bay of Messeniacus sin., below Thuria. *Golfo d'Astro.* II. ins., islets of Messenia, s. of Theganusa. *Formignes.* III. prom., the s.w. extremity of Laconia, on Messeniacus sin., 20 m. s. of Œtylus. The early boundary of Messenia. *C. Grosso.*

THURII, *postea* Copia, a city of Lucania, bet. Crathis and Sybaris ffl., n.w. of Sybaris. Founded, circa 460 b.c., by a colony of Athenians and other Greeks (among whom were Herodotus and the orator Lysias), under Lampon and Xenocritus. It was celebrated for its laws, based on those of Zaleucus and Charondas. A colonia (Copia) and municipium.

THURIUM, I. a m. of Boeotia, near Chaeronea. II. a town of Laconia, midway bet. Sparta and the sea. III. of Acarnania, on the w. coast, bet. Echinus and Palaerus. One of the towns the inhabitants of which were transferred by Augustus to Nicopolis.

THUSURI, a town of Libya Int., bet. Aggarsel Nepte and Thiges.

THYA, a town of Phocis, on Cephissus fl., near its junction with Cachales fl., w. of Elataea. Named from the death of Cephissus. The district was noted for its oil. *Thiva.*

THYAMIA, a town of Phlius, Argolis, bet. Phlius and Titane.

THYAMUS, I. a r. of Epirus, dividing Cestrine from Thesprotia, rising w. of Pambotis lac. and falling into the Adriatic s.e. of Thyamus prom. *Calama.* II. a pr. of Cestrine, in Epirus, n. of Thyamus fl. *C. Nissi.* III. a m. of Acarnania, on the confines of the territory of the Agraei.

THYARIS fl., Phrygiae, i. q. Thymbris.

THYATIRA, I. one of the Echinades ins. II. *prius* Pelopia, Euhippa, a town of Lydia, on Lycus fl., n. of Magnesia ad Sipylum. A Macedonian colony. *Akhissar.*

THYDA fl., a r. of Sicily, falling into the sea bet. Calacte and Aluntium. *Furiano.*

THYDONOS, a town of Caria, bet. Miletus and Halicarnassus.

THYESSUS, a town of Lydia.

THYIA, a village near Elis, where the festival of Bacchus was celebrated.

THYMBRA, I. a town of Mysia. II. of Troas, n. of Troja. With a temple of Apollo Thymbraeus, in which Achilles received his death-wound.

THYMBRARA (Thymbra), a town of Lydia, n. of Pactolus fl. The scene of the decisive defeat of Croesus.

THYMBRES (Thymbrius, Thyaris, Tembrogius) fl., a r. of Phrygia Epict., rising w. of Cotiaeum and falling into Sangarius fl. below Doryleum. *Pursek.*

THYMBRIA, a town of Caria, near Myus.

THYMBRIUS, I. a plain of Troas, about Thymbra. II. a r. of Troas, falling, in the Homeric ages, into Scamander fl., R., but, later, joining the sea near Æanteum. *Tumbek.*

THYMENA (Teuthrania), a port of Paphlagonia, 5 m. N.E. from Climax.

THYMIATERIUM, *postea* Frigidæ, a port of Mauritania Ting., on Emporicus sin., w. of Babba Julia, 26 m. from Lixus.

THYMNIA, a town of Caria, near Ceramicus sin.

THYMNIAS sin., a bay of Doridis sin., E., separated from Schœnus sin. by Aphrodisias prom.

THYMŒLADÆ, a demus of Attica, of the tribe Hippothoontis, on Saronicus sin., near Alimus. Stigmatized as litigious.

THYNI, a people of Thrace, on the Euxine, about Thynia, a migration of whom settled in and gave name to Bithynia.

THYNIAS, I. the early name of Apollonia ins., Bithyniæ. II. a headland of Astica, Thrace, at Thynias. III. a town of Astica, Thrace, on the Euxine, s. of Aulæi Tichos. *Tiniada.*

THYNUS (Tyrus), a maritime town of Cilicia Campestris, w. of Pyramus fl.

THYRÆUM, a town of Arcadia, 2 m. N. from Parorea.

THYRGONIDÆ, a demus of Attica, of the tribe Antiochis, near Aphidna.

THYRSUS fl., a r. of Sardinia, falling into the sea towards Usellis. *Tirsis.*

THYSDRUS, *vide* Tisdra.

THYSSAGETÆ, a people of Sarmatia Asiatica, of uncertain position.

THYSSUS, a town of Acte penins., on Singiticus sin., under Athos m.

TIABA, Phrygiæ, i. q. Tabæ.

TIAMA, a district of Tenesis, Æthiopia, w. of Pseboa lac.

TIANA ins., an isl. of Susiana, in Persicus sin., E. of Cataderbis.

TIARANTUS fl., a r. of Dacia.

TIARE, a town of Mysia.

TIASAS (Tiasus) fl., a r. of Laconia, falling into Eurotas fl. N. of Amyclæ. *Tzoka.*

TIASUM, a town of the Senses, Daciæ, w. of Netindava.

TIATURA, a town of Larice, Ind., E. of the mouth of Mophis fl. *Tchampanir.*

TIBARENI, I. a tribe of Eleuthero Cilices, in Amanus m. II. (Tibari), a people of Pontus, on the coast, bet. Sidene and Mosynœcia. Noted for their light-heartedness. *Djanik.*

TIBERIACUM, a town of the Ubii, Germania II., bet. Colonia Agrippina and Juliacum.

TIBERIADIS lacus, *vide* Gennasareth.

TIBERIAS, a town of Lower Galilee, on Tiberiadis lac., s.w., bet. Migdala N. and Emmaus s., 15 m. N. from Bethsan. Built by Herod Antipas, and named after Tiberius.

TIBERIOPOLIS, a town of Phrygia, on Tilius fl., s. of Eumenia. Founded by Tiberius.

TIBERIS fl., *prius* Albula, a r. of Italy, rising in the Apennines above Arretium and, after a course of 147 m., falling into Tyrrhenium mare at Ostia, by two mouths, the right now called Fiumecino, the left Fiumara. The boundary of Etruria from Umbria, Sabinium, and Latium. Named from Thybris, a Tyrrhenian chief, drowned in it. Servius observes that on solemn occasions it is called Tyberinus; on ordinary occasions Tiberis; and poetically Tibris. *Tevere; Tiber.*

TIBILIS, a town of Numidia, bet. Capraria and Aquæ Tibilitanæ (25). *Hamise.*

TIBISCUM, a town of Dacia, bet. Mascliana (14) and Agnavæ (14). *Cavaran.*

TIBISCUS (Pathissus, Parthiscus, Tibissus, Tisianus) fl., a r. of Dacia, rising in Carpathus m. and falling into the Danube N. of the confluence of Savus fl. *Theiss.*

TIBIUM, I. a m. of Phrygia, whence the appellation Tibius, given to a slave, a slavish person. II. a town of Otene, Armeniæ, E. of Artaxata. *Dovin.*

TIBOURA, the Greek name of Tibur, in Latium.

TIBŪLA, a maritime town of the Corsii, Sardinia, s. of Erebantium prom. *Castro Aragonese.*

TIBUR, *prius* Siceleon, a city of the Latini, Latium, on Anio fl., L., bet. Ad Aquas Albulas (6) and Varia (10). A Sicilian settlement, enlarged by Catellus, a Pelasgic chief, said to be a son of Amphiaraus, and named after his brother Tiburtus. Sacred to Hercules, with a temple of the Tiburtine sibyl, assigned by some antiquaries to Vesta. A municipium. An asylum for Roman criminals. Noted for its orchards. *Tivoli.*

TIBURNEA (Teurnia), capital of the Ambidravi, Noricum, on Dravus fl., L., below Loncium.

TICARĪUS fl., a r. of Corsica, falling into the sea on the w. coast. *Tigari.*

TICHILLA (Ticelia), a town of Zeugitana, on Bagradas fl., L., bet. Membrissa and Tionica.

TICHIS fl., a r. of Narbonensis, falling into the Mediterranean below Illiberis. *Muga.*

TICHIUS, a fortress of Maliensis, Thessaly, on Œta m.

TICHIUSSA, a town of Caria, on Jassicus sin., N. Noted for its sprats.

Tichos, a fortress of Achaia, in the territory of Dymæ, near Araxus prom. Built by Hercules. *Palaio-Castro.*

Ticinum, *postea* Papia, a town of the Insubres, in Gall. Transp., on Ticinus fl., L., near its junction with Padus fl., bet. Laumellum (22) and Mediolanum (22). A municipium. Pliny erroneously ascribes it to the Levi. *Pavia.*

Ticinus fl., a r. of Gallia Transpadana, rising in Alpes Lepontiæ, and, after passing through Verbanus lacus, falling into Padus fl. below Ticinum. Celebrated for the purity of its water. On its right bank, s.e. of Novara, occurred the defeat of Scipio by Hannibal. *Tesino.*

Tierna, I. a r. of Dacia, falling into the Danube at Transtierna. II. (Zerna), a town of the Mœsi, Mœsia Sup., on the Danube, bet. Ad Scropilas and Pons Trajani, over against Transtierna. A colonia. *Czernez.*

Tifata m., a ridge of the Apennines, in Campania, 1 m. e. of Capua, on which was a temple of Diana consecrated by Sylla, and a temple of Jupiter Tifatinus. *Monte di Caserta; Monte Maddaloni.*

Tifernum, I. a town of the Pentri, in Samnium, on Tifernus fl., R., n.e. of Bovianum. *Near Ponte di Limosano.* II. *surnamed* Metaurense, a town of Umbria, on Metaurus fl., L., towards its source, above Urbinum Met. *Sant' Angelo in Vado.* III. *surnamed* Tiberinum, a town of Umbria, on Tiber fl., L., towards its source. Near it, on the opposite, or Etrurian side of the river, was Pliny's Tuscan villa. *Citta di Castello.*

Tifernus fl., I. a r. of Samnium, rising in Tifernus m., and falling into the Adriatic, s.e. of Buca. *Biferno.* II. m., a summit of the Apennines, in Samnium, above Bovianum. *Monte Matese.*

Tiganda, a town of Mauritania Cæsar., on Chinalaph fl., L., bet. Castrum Tingitii and Oppidum Novum. *Sinaab.*

Tigava, a town of Mauritania Cæsar., on Chinalaph fl., R., bet. Oppidum Novum (12) and Maliana (19). *El Herba.*

Tiges (Tigisis), I. a town of Mauritania Cæsar., bet. Bida (27) and Rusucurrum (12). II. of Numidia, 16 m. e. from Speculum. *Tegeiose.*

Tigrana, a town of Atropatene, in Media.

Tigranocerta, "city of Tigranes," a town of Armenia, on Nicephorius fl., 37 m. n.e. from Nisibis. Built by Tigranes. *Sered.*

Tigris "arrow" fl., a r. of Asia, rising in Arsissa-Elegosine, Armenia Maj., on the s.w. shore of Thospites lac., e. of Metelene, Cappadocia, and, after separating Mesopotamia and Babylonia w. from Assyria and Susiana e., falling, joined by the Euphrates, into Persicus sin., below Charax. For some portion of its earlier course it was said to run under ground. At Seleucia it divided into two channels, which re-united at Apamea, after forming the island called Mesene Sup. *Tigris.* II. Elid, i. q. Harpys. III. Susianæ, i. q. Pasitigris.

Tigulia (Tegolata), a town of the Garuli, in Liguria, on Entella fl., 3 m. from its mouth, bet. Portus Delphini (21) and Bodetia (12), on Via Aurelia. *Tregosa.*

Tigurini, a tribe of Helvetii, s. of the Verbigeni. *About Lac Morat.*

Tigurinus pagus, the country of the Tigurini, in Helvetia.

Tiladæ, a people of India e. Gangem, on Œdanes fl., bet. the Corancali and the Cirrhadi.

Tilatæi, a people of Mœsia Inf., under Hermus m., e. of the Treres.

Tilaventus fl., a r. of Venetia, rising n. of Julium Carnicum, and, after separating the Veneti from the Carni, falling into the Adriatic, by two mouths, Major and Minor, below Apicilia. *Tagliamento.*

Tilena, a town of the Lingones, Lugdunensis I., bet. Andematunum n. and Dibia s.w.

Tili castrum, a fortress of Cilicia Campestris, near Tarsus.

Tilium, a maritime town of the Coracenses, in Sardinia, n.w. of Nura. *Argentera.*

Tilius fl., a r. of Phrygia, falling into Mæander fl. s.e. of Eumenia.

Tilogramum, a town of the Gangaridæ, Indiæ, on Chamberichum ostium, Ganget.

Tilox prom., a pr. of Corsica, w. of the mouth of Volerius fl. *Punta Martella.*

Tilphossa fons, a stream issuing from Tilphossus m., and falling into Copais lac. 1½ m. e. from Alalcomenæ. The excessive coldness of its water occasioned the death of the soothsayer Tiresias.

Tilphossus m., a summit of Helicon, in Bœotia, overlooking Alalcomenæ.

Timacus, I. a r. of Mœsia Sup., rising in Scomius mons, s.e. of Naissus, and falling into the Danube below Dorticum, bet. Ad Aquas and Bononia. *Timak.* II. *surnamed* Major, a town of the Triballi, Mœsia, on Timacus fl., above Timacus Min., n.n.e. of Naissus. III. *surnamed* Minor, a town of the Triballi, Mœsia, on Timacus fl., R., below Timacus Major.

TIMÆA, a village of Bithynia, E. of Dadastana.

TIMAGENIS ins., an isl. of Arabia Felix, in the Red sea, S.W. of Leucecome.

TIMALINUM (Talamina), a town of the Lucenses, in Callæcia, N.E. of Lucus Augusti.

TIMAVI fons (Timavi lacus), a small lake of Venetia, 1 m. from Tergestinus sin., near Pucinum, where Timavus fl. rises, for the second time, in seven springs. *Lago della Pietra Rossa, near Castel Duino.*

TIMAVUS fl., I. a stream of Venetia, rising in the hills N.E. of Aquileia, and then, after a subterraneous course of 14 m., rising again, in seven springs, at Fons Timavi, and, after a further course of about a mile, falling into Tergestinus sin., N.W. On its banks was a grove and temple of Diomed. *Timao.*

TIMELES fl., a r. of Caria.

TIMETHUS fl., a r. of Sicily, falling into the Tyrrhenian sea, w. of Tyndaris. *Fiume di Naso.*

TIMICI, a town of Zeugitana, bet. Tabraca and Bagradas fl., s. of Carthage.

TIMII, an early people of Cimbrica Chersonesus.

TIMII (Sismii, Ostidamnii, Osismii), a people of Lugdunensis, w. of the Veneti, about Calbium prom. *About Ouessant.*

TIMISCUM, a town of the Potulatenses, Dac., w. of Zarmizegethusa.

TIMNATH. *Vide* Thumath.

TIMOLÆUM, a town of Paphlagonia, on the Euxine, 7½ m. E. from Climax.

TIMONITIS, a district of Paphlagonia, on the borders of Bithynia, N. of Potamia reg.

TIMONIUM, Paphlagoniæ, i. q. Hadrianopolis.

TIMPHADES, a town of Numidia, bet. Thebeste and Vegesela.

TIMYRA, a town of Isauria, near Isaura.

TINA fl., a r. of the Venicontes, Brit., falling into the sea bet. Tava æstuar. and Bodotria æstuar. *Tyne.*

TINCI (Corniclanum), a town of the Ausari, in Cyrenaica, bet. Liba and Prisca Taberna.

TINCONIUM, a town of the Bituriges Cubi, Aquitania I., bet. Avaricum N.W. and Aquæ Bormonis S.E.

TINDION, a maritime town of Lower Egypt.

TINGENE, a district of Mesopotamia, on the Euphrates, bet. Chaborras fl. and Saocorus fl.

TINGENTERA (Tingitera, Tingi Cetaria), a maritime town of the Turtetani, Bætica, bet. Mellaria and Transducta. The birthplace of Pomponius Mela.

TINGIS (Tinge, Tingi), a city of Mauritania Tingitana (to which it gave name), at the s. entrance of Herculis Fretum, within Ampelusia prom. Built by Antæus, whose vast elephant's hide buckler was long preserved there. A colonia of Claudius (Traducta Julia). *Tangier.*

TINIA fl., a r. of Umbria, falling into the Tiber, below Perusia. *Timia.*

TINIODIRUM, a town of Cyrenaica, on Syrtis Mag., bet. Anabucis and Cocynthion.

TINISSA (Tuniza, Tumsa), a maritime town of Zeugitana, bet. Utica (10) and Hippo Diarrhytus (20).

TINNA fl., a r. of Picenum, falling into the sea below Cluana. *Tinna.*

TINNETIO, a town of the Venonetes, Rhætiæ, bet. Curia (20) and Murus (15). *Tintzen.*

TINOA fl., a r. of the Damnonii, Brit., falling into the sea, w. of Isaca fl. *Teign.*

TINTAGIUM, a maritime town of the Damnonii, N.W., below Herculis prom. *Tintagell.*

TINURTIUM, a town of the Ædui, Lugdunensis I., on the Arar, bet. Cabillonum and Matisco. The locality of the battle between Albinus and Septimius Severus. *Tournus.*

TIONICA, a town of Zeugitana, R., bet. Agbia and Tichilla.

TIORA MATIENA, *postea* Thora, Tyra, a Pelasgic town of Sabinium, 37 m. S.E. from Reate. *Torano.*

TIPARENUS ins., an isl. of Argolis, in Argolicus sin., w. of Tricrana ins. *Spezzia.*

TIPASA (Tipasus), I. a maritime town of Mauritania Cæsar., bet. Casæ Calventi (19) and Cæsarea. A colonia. *Damus.* II. a town of Meninx ins., Byzacene, S.W., opposite Veneris Templ. III. of Numidia, bet. Ad Malas and Capraria (43), s. of Hippo Regius.

TIPHÆ (Syphæ), a port of Bœotia, on Mare Alcyonium. The birth-place of Tiphis, the pilot of the Argonauts. *Agiani.*

TIQUADRA ins., an isl. of Balearis Mag., off Palma.

TIRACIA (Trinacia), a town of Sicily, of uncertain position, destroyed and afterwards restored by the Syracusans.

TIRESIAS, an inland town of Crete.

TIRIDA (Turris Diomedis), a town of Chalcidice, Thrace, near Abdera, N.W. The residence of the tyrant Diomedes, killed by Hercules.

TIRISCUM, a town of the Biephi, Daciæ, w.N.w. of Zarmizegethusa.

TIRISTASIS, a town of the Odrysæ, in Thrace,

on the Propontis, bet. Heraclea and Leuce Acte. *Peristi.*

TIRIZA, a town of Paphlagonia.

TIRYNS (Tirynthus), *prius* Halieis, a city of Argolis, 1½ m. from Nauplia. Built for king Prætus, by the Cyclopes, and famous for its massive walls. Destroyed by the Argives, and most of the inhabitants removed to Argos. The people were stigmatized for extreme buffoonery. Hercules was surnamed Tirynthius from this city.

TIRZA, i. q. Shechem.

TISÆUS m., a ridge of m. at the extremity of Magnesia, in Thessaly, extending from Magnesiæ prom. to Æantium prom. Sacred to Diana. *Trikkeri.*

TISANUSA, a port of Peræa, in Caria.

TISAPATINGA, a town of the Caspiræi, Indiæ.

TISDRA (Tisdrus, Thysdrus, Tusdrus), a town of Byzacene, N. of Usala (32). A colonia. *El Jemni.*

TISEBARICA, a district of Ethiopia, w. of the Ichthyophagi.

TISIA, a town of Bruttium, of uncertain position.

TISSA (Tissæ, Tisse), a town of Sicily, on Acesines fl., R., towards its source. *Randazzo.*

TISTILA fl., Liguriæ, i. q. Feritor.

TITACIDÆ, a demus of Attica, of the tribe Antiochis, near Aphidna. Named after Titacus, the revealer of Helen.

TITANE (Teutanion), a town of Achaia, on Asopus fl., 7½ m. s.w. from Sicyon. *Alopeki.*

TITANUS, "chalk," I. a r. of Mysia, near Pitane. II. m., a hill of Phthiotis, in Thessaly, N.W. of Demetrias.

TITARESIUS (Eurotas, Orcus), a r. of Perrhæbia, in Thessaly, rising in Titarus m. Of a thick oily substance, so that, when it joined Peneus fl., near Gyrton, it did not mix with the water of that river, but floated on its surface. Mopsus, the Argonaut augur, was born on its banks. *Saranta Poros.*

TITARISSUS, a town of Meletene pref., in Cappadocia.

TITARUS m., a ridge of Olympus m., separating Pelagonia Tripolis from Macedonia. *Saranta.*

TITHOREA m., a summit of Parnassus, overlooking Neon.

TITHRAS, a demus of Attica, of the tribe Ægeis. Famous for its figs.

TITHRONIUM, a town of Phocis, 1¾ m. from Amphicæa. Destroyed by Xerxes. *Moulki.*

TITIANI, a maritime people of Corsica, s.w. of Ticarius fl.

TITIUS fl., I. a r. of Cyprus, falling into the sea s.w. of Citium. II. (Catarbates), of Illyria, separating the Liburni from the Dalmatæ, and falling into the Adriatic below Scardona. *Kerka.*

TITONIUS fl., a r. of Latium, near Circæum. Swallowed up by the earth.

TITTHIUM mons, a hill of Argolis, near Epidaurus.

TITUA, a town of the Carei, Indiæ, w. of Colchi.

TITULEIA, a town of the Vaccæi, Tarraconensis, on the Tagus, at the junction of Tagonius fl., bet. Toletum and Complutum. *Torrejon.*

TITYASSUS (Pityassus), a town of Pisidia.

TITYRUS m., m. of Crete, terminating in Psacum prom.

TIUM, a town of Bithynia, on a penins., at the mouth of Billæus fl. A Milesian col. The birth-place of Philetærus. *Tilios; Tios.*

TLŌS, I. a city of Caria, N.E. of Xanthus, near Xanthus fl. *Doover.* II. a town of Pisidia.

TMOLUS, I. a m. of Lydia, bet. Draco m. and Cadmus m. Named from Tmolus, a king of Lydia. Noted for its wines, its saffron, and its minerals. *Bouz - Dagh.* II. a town of the Mesotimolitæ, on Tmolus m. Destroyed by the great earthquake under Tiberius.

TMUNDUS sin., a gulf of the Red sea, at Berenice.

TNYSSUS, a town of Caria.

TOANI, a people of Arabia, N.E. of Macpha.

TOB (Tobi, Tubin, Ish-tob, Tabæ), a town of Syria, s.E., bet. Gadara N.W. and Jabes Gilead, s.E. Hither Jephtha fled from his kindred.

TOBATA, a town of central Paphlagonia, under Olgasys m.

TOBIUS fl., a r. of the Demetæ, in Britain, falling into the sea below Maridunum, w. of Leucarum. *Tovy.*

TOCÆ, a town of Zeugitana, bet. Musti and Utica.

TOCHARI, *Heb.* Togarmah, a people of Bactria, s.w. of the Maci.

TOCOLOSIDA, a town of Mauritania Ting., s. of Volubilis.

TOCOSANNA fl., a r. of India e. Gangem, falling into Gangeticus sin., 36 geog. m. s. from Catabeda fl. *Aracan?*

TŒMPHŒMBIUS fl., a r. of Mauritania Cæsar., falling into Savus fl. below Labdia.

TŒSOBIS (Tisobis) fl., a r. of the Ordovices,

Brit., falling into the sea at Conovium, E. of Mona ins. *Conway.*

TOGARMAH, the Scriptural name of the To-chari, in Bactria.

TOGISONUS fl., a branch of Eridanus fl., falling into the Adriatic at Portus Brundulus. *Canal Bianco.*

TOGRINSES, a tribe of Carni, in Venetia, *About Torsa.*

TOLBIACUM (Colbiacum), Calbiacum, a town of the Superni, Germania II., W. of Bonna. *Suernich, near Zulpich,* N.

TOLE, a town of Meroe, bet. Meroe and Esar.

TOLENUS (Telonius) fl., a r. of Sabinium, falling into the Nar. *Turano.*

TOLERIA, a town of the Latini, in Latium, near Labicum.

TOLETUM, capital of the Carpetani, Tarraconensis, on the Tagus, R., above Libora. A municipium. *Toledo.*

TOLIATIS ins., an isl. of the Cantii, Brit., at the mouth of the Thames, R., off Rates. *Sheppey.*

TOLINA, a town of Daranissa, Armeniæ, on Lycus fl., R.

TOLISTOBOII, a tribe of the Boii of Gaul, established in south-western Galatia.

TOLLEGATA, a town of the Cenomanni, in Gallia Transpadana, on Ollius fl., R., bet. Bergamum (12) and Tetellus (10), on Via Æmilia. *Talgato.*

TOLLENTINUM, a town of Picenum, on Flusor fl., L., N.W. of Urbs Salvia. A municipium. *Tolentino.*

TOLMIDESSA (Teleda), a town of Syria, towards Palmyra.

TOLOPHON, a town of the Locri Ozolæ, at the w. entrance of Crissæus sin., N.E. of Æanthe. *Galadixi.*

TOLOSA, capital of the Volcæ Tectosages, on the Garumna, R., below Vernasole. *Toulouse.*

TOLOUS, a town of the Ilergetes, Tarraconensis, on Cinga fl., L., N.E. of Segestica.

TOMABEI, a people of Arabia Felix, on the coast, W. of the Soritæ. *Beni Tehama.*

TOMÆUS m., a m. of Messenia, E. of Pylos. *Pilau.*

TOMARA, a town of the Bari, Indiæ, on Serus fl.

TOMARENE, a town of Lydia.

TOMÄRUS (Tamarus, Tmarus) m., a m. of Thesprotia, in Epirus, s. of Dodona. Remarkable for the many streams issuing from it. *Chamouri.*

TOMERUS (Tuberus) fl., a r. of Gedrosia, falling into Indicum mare bet. Bagisara and Malana prom. *Busul.*

TOMI (Tomis, Miletis, Metropolis), a town of Mœsia Inferior, on the Euxine, bet. Constantiana and Callatis. A Milesian colony. The place of Ovid's banishment. Named from the mangled remains of Apsyrtus. Near it is a lake called Ouvidouve Jesero, "lake of Ovid." *Babba.*

TOMISAS, i. q. Melitene.

TONOSA, a town of Pontus, s. of Halys fl., bet. Zoana (25) and Comana Aurea.

TONSKUS (Tonzus) fl., a r. of Thrace, rising in Hæmus m., and falling into Hebrus fl. at Hadrianopolis. *Tonja.*

TOORNÆ, a people of Scythia, bet. the Jaxartes and Imaus m.

TOPHET, a place in the valley of Ben-Shinnom, where children were sacrificed to Baal. The name, meaning "drum-beating," has reference to the noise made to drown the cries of the victims.

TOPIRUS (Ulpia Topiris), a maritime town of the Bistones, in Thrace, on Egnatia Via, bet. Acontisma (18) and Bistonia (22).

TOPIS, a district of Laconia.

TOPIUM, a town of the Veneti, in Venetia, N. of Opitergium. *Topo.*

TOREATÆ, a maritime people of Sarmatia Asiatica, on the Euxine, N.W. of the Achæi.

TORÆATICUM prom., a pr. of the Toreatæ, Sarmatia, on the Euxine, N.W. of Herculis prom.

TORÆATICUS portus, a port of the Toreatæ, Sarmatia, bet. Pagræ and Psychrus fl.

TORECADÆ, a people of Sarmatia, towards Byce lacus.

TORHARI, a people of Bactriana.

TORNADATUS fl., Assyr., i. q. Physcon.

TORNATES, a tribe of Auscii, Novem Populana, N.W. of the Convenæ. *About Tournay, near Bagneres.*

TOROCCA, a town of the Hylæ, Sarmatiæ, on Carcines fl., below Ercabum.

TORONAÏCUS (Mecybernæus sin.), a bay of the Ægean, in Chalcidice, Macedonia, separating Pallene penins. from Sithonia penins. *G. di Cassandria.*

TORÖNE, I. a town of Sithonia, in Macedonia, on the Toronaicus sin., towards the s. extremity of the peninsula. Noted for its fish. II. (Toryne), a port of Thesprotia, within Chimerium prom., S.E. *Palæo-Parga.*

TORRHÆBI, a tribe of Mæones, in Lydia, named from Torrhæbus, son of Atys. Extinct in the time of Herodotus.

TORRHÆBIUS lacus, a lake at Torrhæbus, in Lydia.

TORRHÆBUS, a town of Lydia, on Torrhæbius lacus, under Carius m. With a temple the hero Carius. Named from Torrhebus, son of Atys.

TOSALE, a town of the Pasalæ, India, near Athenagura. *Near Tipra.*

TOTAIUM, a town of Bithynia, on Sangarius fl., bet. Nicæa (40) and Dablæ (28).

TOUM (Thmui), a town of Thebais, N. of Ombi. Sacred to the goat.

TOXANDRI, a people of Germania II., s. of the Batavi, bet. the Rhine, the Mosa, and the Scaldis.

TRABALA, a town of Lycia.

TRACANA, a town of the Jazyges, Sarmatiæ, N.E. of Ercabum.

TRACHAS (Trachina), the Greek name of Tarracina, in Latium.

TRACHEA, an early name of Ephesus.

TRACHINII, a tribe of Malienses, in Thessaly, about Heraclea Trachinia.

TRACHIS (Trechis, "rugged"), I. a town of Maliensis, on Melas fl., 6 furlongs w. from Heraclea Trachinia, 7½ m. from Thermopylæ. A town of Achilles. The adopted scene of one of Sophocles' tragedies. II. (Thracis), of Phocis, on the confines of Bœotia, near Chæronea. Destroyed in the sacred war.

TRACHONITIS, "rugged," a district of Decapolis, on the borders of Arabia Deserta, N. of Batanæa.

TRACHYS m., a m. of Arcadia, N. of Orchomenus.

TRACTARI, a people of Taurica Chersonesus.

TRÆLIUM, a town of the Edones, in Thrace, s.w. of Philippi.

TRAETE prom., the early name of Saturni prom., Tarraconensis.

TRAGASÆ, "voracious," a salt-manufacturing town of Troas, near the mouth of Satnioeis fl. *Tuzla.*

TRAGEÆ, a town of Naxos ins.

TRAGIA ins., an isl. of the Ægean, one of the Sporades, bet. Astypalæa and Hippuris. The birth-place of Theogiton. *Tragonisi.*

TRAGURIUM, a town of the Dalmatæ, in Illyria, on the Adriatic, s. of Scardona, on a piece of land separated from the continent by an artificial canal. Noted for its marble quarries. *Trau.*

TRAGUS fl., a r. of Arcadia, rising at Nasi, and falling into Ladon fl. near Mesoboa.

TRAIS fl., a r. of Bruttium, falling into the Ionian sea N. of Hylias fl. The scene of two great defeats of the Sybarites. *Trionto.*

TRAJANI MUNIMENTUM, a fortress built by Drusus and repaired by Julian, on Mænus fl., Germania, towards its junction with the Rhine. *Aschaffenberg.*

TRAJANOPOLIS, I. a town of the Cicones, in Thrace, on the Egnatia Via, bet. Tempyra

(8) and Dyme (13). II. of the Tremenothyritæ, in Phrygia Magna, on the borders of Lydia, bet. Acmonia and Salala. The Tanupolis of Hierocles. III. of Cilicia, *vide* Selinus.

TRAJECTUM (Trajectus Rheni, Vetus Trajectus), a town of the Batavi, towards the N. issue of the Rhine, bet. Albiniana and Manaritium. *Utrecht, Oud-trecht,* "old passage."

TRAJECTUS, I. a village of the Belgæ, on Avona fl., below Abone (8). *Keynsham.* II. a town of the Petrocorii, Aquitania II., on the Duronius, below Diolindum.

TRAJECTUS GENUSI, a town of the Eordeti, in Illyria, on the Genusus fl., bet. Scampis (9) and Ad Dianam (7).

TRALLES, *prius* Anthea, Euanthia, *aliter* Erynina, Seleucia, Antiochia, a city of Lydia, s.w. of Magnesia, on Eudon fl. A colony of Argives and Thracians. One of the wealthiest emporia of the ancient world. The birth-place of Queen Pithodoris and of Alexander Trallianus. *Ghiuzel Hissar.*

TRALLICON, a town of Caria, on Harpasus fl. Extinct in Pliny's time.

TRAMPE, a town of Ionia.

TRAMPYA, a town of the Tymphæi, in Epirus, E. of Bunima, where Hercules, son of Alexander, was murdered by Polysperchon. *Mezzovo.*

TRANIPSI, a tribe of Bithynians, in Bithynia.

TRANSCELLENSIS m., m. on the coast of Mauritania Cæsariensis, below Cæsarea.

TRANSDUCTA (*Arabicè*, Joza), a town of the Turtetani, Bætica, on Herculeum fretum, bet. Tingintera w. and Mellaria E. Named from the circumstance that it was populated by the inhabitants of Zilis, in Mauritania, brought over hither by the Romans. A colonia (Julia). *Tarifa.*

TRANSLITÆ, a town of the Triballi, Mœsia, bet. Turres and Ballanstra.

TRANSMARICIOLUM, a town of the Psylli, in Africa, on Syrtis Maj., bet. Ad Palmam and Hippi prom.

TRANSMARISCA, a town of the Getæ, Mœsiæ, on the Danube, bet. Candidiana and Appiaria.

TRANS TIERNA, a town of the Albocenses, Dacia, on the Danube, at the mouth of Tierna fl., opposite Tierna.

TRANUPARA, I. a town of the Galabri, Mœsiæ, under Scordus m., bet. Astibus and Scopi. II. of the Pelagones, at the junction of Axius fl. with Erigonus fl., 30 m. N.E. from Stobi.

TRAPERA, a port of India i. Gangem, near Barygaza.

TRAPEZOPOLIS, a town of Caria, bet. Alabanda and Mæander fl. *Carpuseli.*

TRAPEZU prom., Dardaniæ, i. q. Dardanium.

TRAPEZUS, "table shape," I. a m. of Taurica Chersonesus, s., above Charax. II. a town of Arcadia, on the left bank of Alpheus fl., N.W. of Megalopolis, the inhabitants of which withdrew to Trapezus, on the Euxine. III. a maritime city of the Macrones, in Pontus, 7½ m. from Hermonassa. A Sinopian colony. In the Lower Age, the seat of a petty empire. About it the people made a sort of honey from the rhododendron, of a peculiarly intoxicating quality. *Trebizond.*

TRAPHIA, a town of Bœotia.

TRARIUM, I. a town of Æolis Asiat., s. of Cisthene. II. (Trallium), a town of Bithynia, on Astacenus sin., bet. Pantichium and Libyssa.

TRASIMENUS lacus, a lake of Etruria, s. of Cortona, W. of Perusia. The locality of the defeat of Flaminius by Hannibal, 217 B.C. Named from the youth Thrasimenus. *L. di Perugia.*

TRAUSI, a tribe of the Cælelatæ in Thrace.

TRAVUS fl., a r. of the Bistones, in Thrace, rising in Rhodope m., and falling into the Ægean at Bistonis lacus, E. of Bistonia.

TREBA, a town of the Æqui, in Latium, near the source of Anio fl. A colonia of Augustus. *Trevi.*

TREBELLICUM, a village of Campania, near Neapolis. Noted for its wine.

TREBIA, I. a r. of Gallia Cispadana, rising in the m. of the Euburiates, of Liguria, and, after a course of 50 m., falling into Padus fl. W. of Placentia. Memorable for the defeat on its left bank, about 8 m. from Placentia, of Scipio and Sempronius Gracchus by Hannibal. *Trebia.* II. a town of Umbria, on Via Flaminia, bet. Sacraria (4) and Fulginium (5). *Trevi.*

TREBULA (Trebia), *surnamed* Balinea, I. a town of the Sidicini, in Campania, 5 m. N.E. of Forum Popilii, under Callicula m. *Treglia.* II. *surnamed* Suffena, of Sabinium, N. of Reate. *Monte Leone della Leonessa.* III. *surnamed* Mutusca, of Sabinium, near Eretum. With a temple of Feronia, plundered by Hannibal. *Monte Leone della Sabina.*

TREIA, a town of Picenum, on Flosis fl., L., bet. Septempeda (9) and Auximum (18). A municipium. *Montecchio.*

TREMILÆ (Termilæ), a body of Cretans who, under the command of Sarpedon, brother of Minos, colonized Lycia long prior to the Trojan war. Named from one of their early chiefs.

TREMITHUS (Trimethus), an inland town of Cyprus, bet. Leucosia and Salamis. *Tremiti.*

TREMITUM ins., Apuliæ, i. q. Diomedeia.

TREMULA, a town of Mauritania Tingit., bet. Oppidum Novum (12) and Vopisciana (19), s.w. of Babba Julia. *Ezadschen.*

TRERES, a people of Mœsia Inferior, under Scomius m., E. about Sardica.

TRERUS fl., a r. of Latium, rising near Præneste, and falling into Liris fl. below Fabrateria.

TRES ARBORES, a town of the Vasates, Novem Populana, on Serio fl., bet. Cossio N.W. and Oscineium S.E.

TRES INSULÆ, three isl. of Mauritania Ting., in the Mediterranean, at the mouth of Mulucha fl.

TRES TABERNÆ, I. a town of the Dassaretæ, on the Egnatia Via, bet. Candavia (9) and Pons Servilii (9). II. of the Insubres, in Gallia Transpad., bet. Laus Pompeia (9) and Ad Rotas (5), on Via Æmilia. III. of Umbria, on Via Flaminia, bet. Interamnia (3) and Ad Tine Recina. IV. of the Volsci, in Latium, on Astura fl., bet. Aricia (7) and Forum Appii (16), on Via Appia. Mentioned by St. Paul. *Castella.* V. of the Tribocci, Germania I., bet. Pons Saravi and Argentoratum (21). *Rhein Zabern.*

TRESENA, a town of Pamphylia.

TRETA (Phrurion) prom., a pr. of Cyprus, W. of Curium, whence persons who had desecrated the altar of Apollo were thrown into the sea. *C. Bianco.*

TRETUM prom., I. a pr. of Numidia, at the w. entrance of Olchachites sin. *Ras Sebba Rus.* II. of Crete, at the w. entrance to Martilus sin. *C. Buso.* III. (Sambracate) prom., a pr. of Arabia Felix, on Sachalites sin., E. of Saphar.

TRETUS saltus, a mountain defile of Argolis, bet. Nemea and Corinth. Near it was the den of the Nemæan lion.

TREVA, a town of the Suardones, Germania, on Treva (Chalusus) fl. *Near Gluckstadt.*

TREVENTINUM, a town of the Pentri, in Samnium, on Trinius fl., s. of Maronea. A colonia of Cæsar and municipium. *Trivento.*

TREVERI, a people of Belgica I., extending into Germania I., on both banks of the Mosella, bet. the Mosa and the Rhine, s. of the Tungri. *About Treves.*

TREVIDON, a town of the Gaballi, Aquitania I., N.W. of Vindomagus. *St. Laurent de Treves.*

TRIA CAPITA, a maritime town of the Cosetani, Tarraconensis, 18 m. N.E. from Dertosa.

TRIARE, a district of Armenia Magna, on the confines of Iberia, N. of Thasia. *Thregkh.*

TRIBACTRA, capital of the Tribactræ, Sogdiana, on Polytimetus fl., above Oxiana palus. *Near Bokhara.*

TRIBALA, a town of the Lusitani.

TRIBALLI, a people of Mœsia Superior, N.W. and central. Their eyes, when excited by passion, were reputed to have the power of killing people.

TRIBANTA, a town of Phrygia Epict., near Nacolea.

TRIBOCCI (Tribŏci), a people of Germany, on the Rhine, bet. the Mediomatrices and the Lirici. *Alsace.*

TRICA, a town of Daunia, Apulia, towards Arpi. Destroyed by Diomed.

TRICAMEROS, a town of Zeugitana, 20 m. from Carthage.

TRICARANA ins., an isl. of Argolis, w. of Hydrea ins. *Trikkera.*

TRICARANUM, a fortress of Phlius, in Argolis, on the borders of Achaia, bet. Phlius and Orneæ.

TRICASSES, a people of Lugdunensis IV., bet. the Remi N. and the Vadicasses s., the Senones w. and the Remi and Lingones E. *About Troyes.*

TRICASTINI, a tribe of Cavares, Viennensis, on the Rhone, E. of the Segelauni.

TRICCA, I. a city of Estiæotis, on the confines of Pelasgiotis, on Lethæus fl., 12 m. S.E. from Gomphi. The birth-place of Æsculapius, and of his sons Podilarius and Machaon. *Tricala.* II. a village of Messenia. The birth-place, according to the Messenians, of Æsculapius.

TRICCIANA, a town of Pannonia, bet. Mansuetinapons (30) and Cimbriana (25). *Mezo-Romarom.*

TRICESIMA, a town of the Gugerni, Germania I., near Castra Vetera. *Drich.*

TRICESIMUM, a town of the Volcæ Tectosages, Narbonensis I., bet. Carcasso w. and Liviana E.

TRICHONIUM, a town of Ætolia, on or near the s. shore of Trichonius lacus, to which it gave name.

TRICHONIUS lacus, a lake of Ætolia, E. of Trichonium. *L. Vrachori.*

TRICOLONI, a town of Arcadia, 1¼ m. N. from Charisia. With a temple of Neptune.

TRICOMIA, I. a township of Attica, formed of the three demi Cropia, Pelices, and Euripydæ. II. a town of Phrygia Epictetus, bet. Midæum (28) and Pessinus (21).

TRICORNIUM, a town of the Triballi, Mœsia, on the Danube, bet. Singidunum (14) and Aureus mons. *Galumbatz ?*

TRICORII, a tribe of Medulli, N. of Vapin-

cum, a colony of whom settled among the Salyes, Narbonensis, s.E. of the Anatili.

TRICORYPHUS (Triphyllus) prom., a pr. of Arabia Felix, E., at the N. extremity of Duatus sin. *Chorfakan.*

TRICORYTHUS (Tricorynthus), a demus of Attica, of the tribe Œantis, bet. Phegus and Probalinthus, near Marathon. The residence of the Heraclidæ in Attica. *Souli.*

TRICRENA "three fountains" fons, a fountain of Arcadia, rising from three springs bet. Stymphalus and Pheneus, in which Mercury was washed after his birth.

TRICRORUM prom., a pr. of Africa, on Syrtis Major, w. bet. Simnana and Thubactis.

TRIDENTINI, a tribe of Rhæti, on both sides of Atagis fl., about Tridentum.

TRIDENTUM (Tridentinum), capital of the Tridentini, in Venetia, on Atagis fl., L., bet. Endidæ (16) and Ad Palatium (24). *Trent.*

TRIERON prom., a pr. of Syrtica regio, N.W. of Cephalæ prom. *Cape Mesurata.*

TRIERIS, a town of Phœnicia, near Tripolis.

TRIFANUM, a town of Latium, bet. Minturnæ and Sinuessa.

TRIGABOLI, a town of Gallia Cispadana, on Padus fl., below Padinum, where the river separates into Spineticum ostium and Olana ostium.

TRIGÆCINI, a people of Tarraconensis.

TRIGISAMUM (Augustiniana Castra), a town of the Boii, in Noricum, on the Danube, bet. Namare (16) and Piratortum (8). *Trasmauer.*

TRIGLA, a suburban demus of Athens.

TRIGLYPHUM (Trilengon), a town of the Tiladæ, India, s.E. of Talarga.

TRIGUNDUM, a town of the Artabri, Tarraconensis, on Nelus fl., L., near its source.

TRILEUCI scopuli, three rocks of Tarraconensis, off Trileucum prom.

TRILEUCUM (Cornu) prom., the N.W. extremity of Hispania, N.E. of Artabrum prom. *C. Ortiguera,* or *Ortegal.*

TRIMANIUM, a town of the Getæ, Mœsia, on the Danube, bet. Scaidava and Jatrum. *Drimago ?*

TRIMETARIA, a surname of Laodicea, in Phrygia.

TRIMONTIUM, a town of the Selgovæ, N. of Blatum-Belgium. *Near Loughholm.*

TRIMULOPOLIS, i. q. Aspendus, Pamphyliæ.

TRINACRIA, a name of Sicily, from its three promontories ; and also of Rhodes.

TRINADI, a town of Mauritania Cæsar., bet. Caput Cellane and Auzia.

TRINASUS, "three islands," a town of Laconia, at the head of Laconicus sin., bet.

Gythium (4) and Helos (10), over against which were the three islets which gave name to it. *Trinisi.*

TRINE ins., an isl. of Argolis.

TRINEMEIS, a demus of Attica, of the tribe Cecropeis, at the source of the Cephisius Atticus fl. *Agios Soleros.*

TRINESIA ins., three isl. of India i. Gangem, 5 geog. m. N. from Musiris prom. *Andschidive Islands.*

TRINESSA, a town of Phrygia.

TRINIUS fl., a r. of Samnium, rising N. of Æsernia, and falling into the Adriatic S.E. of Histonium. *Trigno.*

TRINOBANTES (*Celticè,* trion-oban, "marshy district"), a people of Flavia Cæsariensis, bet. the Cenimagni N., the Tamesis S., the Dobuni and Catevallauni w., and the Germ. Oc. E. *Essex and Middlesex.*

TRINION, i. q. Canthy, India.

TRINYTHIS, a town of Libya, in Oasis Min.

TRIOBRIS fl., a r. of Gaul, falling into the Oltis. *Truyère.*

TRIOCALA (Tricala), a town of Sicily, on Isborus fl., L. Named from its three good things; its plentiful and fine water, the fertility of its district, and its strength. The seat of the slave-king, Tryphon. *Near Calata Bellota.*

TRIOPIUM prom., a pr. of Caria, over against Istros ins. Here was a temple of Apollo, where the assemblies of the Dorian states were held. *C. Krio.*

TRIPARADISUS, i. q. Paradisus.

TRIPHYLIA, I. a district of Elis, from Alpheus fl. to Messenia. The kingdom of Nestor. Named, traditionally, from Triphylus, the Arcadian; but rather, as being settled by colonists from three tribes, the Elei, Epei, and Minyæ. II. a town of Orestis, in Macedonia, on Æas fl., w. of Gyrtone.

TRIPHULUM, a town of the Cistoboci, Dac., on the Tyras, above Patridava.

TRIPODISCUS, I. an ancient district of Megaris. II. *prius* Tripodi, a town of Megaris, at the E. foot of Geranea mons. Founded by the Argive Corœbus. The birth-place of Susarion, the comic writer.

TRIPOLIS (Tripolitana), I. a district of Africa, on the Mediterranean, bet. Sabrata and Cynyps fl. Named from its three chief towns, Æa, Sabrata, and Leptis Magna. *Tripoli.* II. of Arcadia, comprising Calliæ, Dipœna, and Nonacris. III. of Laconia, S.E. of Megalopolis, comprehending the towns of Belmina, Ægys, and Pellane. IV. a maritime district of Phœnicia, comprehending the territories of the three towns, Tyre, Sidon, and Aradus. V.

(Antoninopolis), a town of Lydia, on Mæander fl., bet. Sardes and Laodicea, s. of Callibetus. *Ostraven?* VI. *prius* Ischopolis, a port of the Mosynœci, in Pontus, 11 m. E. from Zephyrium. *Tireboli.* VII. a town of Pelasgiotis, in Thessaly, on Peneus fl., 3 m. above Larissa.

TRIPOLISSI, a people of Epirus, on the confines of Thessaly.

TRIPOLUS, a town of Crete. The birth-place of Plutus.

TRIPONTIUM, I. a town of the Coritani, Brit., on Aufona Maj. fl., bet. Venonæ and Beneventum. *Dovebridge.* II. of the Volsci, near Appii Forum. *Treponti.*

TRIPYRGIA, a village of Ægina ins., on its E. shore, 2 m. from Heracleium.

TRISANTON fl., a r. of the Regni, Brit., falling into the sea at Anderis. *Tees.*

TRISARCHIS vicus, a maritime village of Marmarica, bet. Selinus portus and Apis.

TRISCA, a village of Bithynia, under Maroscus m.

TRISSUM, a town of the Jazyges Metanastæ.

TRISTOLUS, a town of the Sinti, in Thrace, S.E. of Parthicopolis.

TRITÆA, I. one of the Twelve Cities of Achaia, near Pirus fl., 15 m. above Pharæ Tritæ. Built by Menalippus, son of Mars. *Agios Andria.* II. a town of the Locri Ozolæ, s.w. of Chalion. III. of Phocis, s.w. of Elatæa.

TRITIUM, *surnamed* Metallum, I. a town of the Berones, Tarraconensis, 18 m. w. of Varia. *Treton, near Najera.* II. *surnamed* Tuboricum, Tobolicum, of Tarraconensis, on Deva fl., 2 geog. m. w. from Virovesca. *Near Mondragon.* III. a town of the Autrigones.

TRITON fl., I. a r. of Africa, rising in Usargala m., and, after forming Libya palus, Palladis lacus, and Tritonis palus, falling into the Mediterranean s. of Tacape. The name is erroneously connected by some with the Greek Minerva, said to have been born on its banks. *Kabes.* II. of Bœotia, falling into Copais lacus, w. of Alalcomenæ. III. of Crete.

TRITONIS palus, I. a lake of Africa, receiving Triton fl. w. of Tacape. *Shibkah-Ellowdiah.* II. lacus, a lake of Cyrenaica, at Berenice, formed by the mouth of Eccius fl.

TRITONUS, a town of Macedonia.

TRITTA, an early name of Gnossus, in Crete.

TRITTIA, a town of the Salyes, Narbonensis II., near Aquæ Sextiæ. Sacred to the goddess Trittia. *Tretz.*

TRITURRITA, a town of Etruria, bet. Piscinæ (8) and Pisæ (12), on Via Aurelia, E. of Portus Herculis Labronis.

TRIULATTI, a people of Alpes Maritimæ, on Var fl.

TRIUMPILI, a tribe of Euganei, bet. Larius lacus and Benacus lacus. *Val Troppia.*

TRIUMVIRORUM ins., an isl. in Rhenus fl., Galliæ Cispad., 2 m. w. of Bononia, in which occurred the meeting of the Second Triumvirate. *Crocetta del Trebbo.*

TRIVONA fl., a r. of Britain, falling into Metaris Æstuarium. *Ouse.*

TRIVĬCUM, a town of the Hirpini, Samn., S.E. of Beneventum. *Trivico.*

TRIVIÆ lacus, the grove of Diana, on Nemorensis lacus, in Latium.

TROAS, a region of Mysia, extending along the coast from Rhæteum prom. to Adramyttenus sin., and inland to the range of Ida. Peopled by Pelasgi, Treres, Æoles, &c.

TROCHOS, a town of Argolis, under Chaon mons, on the Phryxus fl., bet. Argos and Hysiæ.

TROCMI, a tribe of Gallo-Græci, occupying the E. portion of Galatia.

TROEA, a port of Gedrosia, on Paragon sin., bet. Canasis and Talmena.

TROESMIS (Trismis), a town of Mœsia Inf., on the Danube, bet. Arrubium and Bereum.

TRŒZENE, I. *prius* Orea, Hyperia, Posidonia, a city of Argolis, N.E. of Hermione, 2 m. from the sea. Renamed after Trœzen, son of Pelops. The birth-place of Theseus. *Damala.* II. (Troizen, Trezen, Trœzenide), a town of Gallia Cisalpina, N. of Alpes Maritimæ, near Massalia. *Tracaro.*

TROGILIA ins., an islet of Ionia, off Trogilium prom.

TROGILIUM prom., a pr. of Ionia, opposite Samos oppidum, the w. termination of Mycale m. *C. Santa Maria.* II. a maritime village of Sicily, N. of Syracusæ.

TROGILUS, a town of Macedonia. The birth-place of Asclepiades, the critic.

TROGITIS palus, a lake of Isauria, s.w. of Iconium. Noted for concreting salt naturally.

TROGLODYTÆ, generally dwellers in caverns; specially, a people of Æthiopia, on the coast of the Red sea, from the Tropic of Cancer N. to Avalites sin. s.

TROGLODYTICUS sin., a gulf of the Red sea, bet. Mnemium prom. and Satyrorum prom.

TROILIUM, Etrur., *apud* Livium, i. q. Trossulum.

TROJA, I. a town of Lower Egypt, on the Nile, R., bet. Scenæ Mandræ and Babylon, opposite Memphis. II. (Ilium vetus), a city of Troas, near the source of Scamander fl. Built by Tros 1374 B.C. Taken by the Greeks, after a ten years' siege, June 11, 1184 B.C. *Bournarbachi.* III. the early name of Xypete, in Attica.

TROJANUS PAGUS, the primitive settlement of the Veneti, in Italy, about Hadria Venet.

TROMILIA, a town of Achaia. Noted for its goats' milk cheese.

TRONIS, a district within the territory of Aulis Phocis.

TROPÆA DRUSI, a town of Germany, on the Vistula, towards its source.

TROPHONII ORACULUM, the oracle of Trophonius, in a cavern near Lebadea, of Bœotia; those who consulted it never smiled again ; or, at least, not for a long period.

TROPINA, a port of India w., 750 m. N. from Perimula prom.

TROSSULUM, a town of Etruria, w. of Ferentinum; it was taken by a squadron of Roman horse, unaided by infantry, whence the surname of Trossuli was given to the former force. *Trosso.*

TROTILUM, a town of Sicily, at the mouth of Pantagias fl. Built 700 B.C.

TRUENTUS fl., a r. of Picenum, falling into the sea at Castrum Truentinum. *Tronto.*

TRULLA, "spoon," I. an isl. of Arabia Felix, off Cane. *Barruhggur.* II. a port of the Adramitæ, Arab., E. of Cane emporium.

TRUTULENSIS portus, a haven of Britannia Barbara. *Firth of Tay ?*

TRYCHAS, a town of Eubœa, towards Chersonesus prom.

TUÆSIS ÆSTUARIUM, I. the mouth of Tuæsis fl., bet. Vara Æstuar. and Tæzalum prom. *Murray Frith.* II. a town of the Decantæ, Brit., near the mouth of Tuæsis fl. *Nairn.*

TUBANTES, a tribe of Istævones, in Germany, bet. the Rhine and the Sala ffl., afterwards on Luppia fl., L., and finally in the territory of the Marsi.

TUBERUS fl., Gedrosiæ, i. q. Tomerus.

TUBLINATIUM, a town of the Genaunes, Rhætiæ. *Toblino.*

TUBONÆ, i. q. Thubonæ.

TUBURBIS (Tubarbo) majus, I. a town of Zeugitana, 28 m. s.E. from Carthage. *Tubersole.* II. minor, of Zeugitana, on Ampsagas fl., L., bet. Cluacaria (15) and Cigisa (15). *Tuburbo.*

TUBUSUPTUS (Thubuscum, Succubar), a

town of Mauritania Cæsar., 25 m. s.e. from Salda. A colonia of Augustus.

TUCABATH, a town of Libya Interior.

TUCCA TEREBINTHINA (Thugga, Tuccabora, Thuccabori), I. a town of Byzacene, bet. Sufes (25) and Assuræ (12), s.w. of Zama. II. of Mauritania Cæsar., on Ampsaga fl., near its mouth, 46 m. s.e. from Teibeilis. *Dugga.* III. of Zeugitana, N. of Zama.

TUCCI (Tacubis), I. a town of the Lusitani, on the Tagus, R., above Scalabis. II. a city of the Turtuli, Bætica, s.e. of Corduba, bet. Segeda N. and Iscadia s. A colonia (Augusta Gemella). III. a town of the Turtetani, Bætica, w. of Italica (18). *Tejada.*

TUDÆ (Tyde), a town of the Grovii, Tarraconensis, on Minius fl., R., towards its mouth, 22 m. N. from Limia. Built by Diomedes, and hence surnamed Ætola. *Tuy.*

TUDER, a town of Umbria, on the Tiber, L., bet. Ameria (16) and Vettona (14), on Via Amerina. Sacred to Mars. A colonia (Fida). *Todi.*

TUDERIUM, a town of Northern Germany, on the Amisus fl. *Meppen.*

TUEROBIS fl., a r. of the Demetæ, Brit., falling into the sea s. of Luentium. *Teify.*

TUFICUM, a town of Umbria, on Sena fl. *Near Pergola.*

TUGENI, the people of Tugenus pagus, Maxima Sequanorum, bet. the Tigurini and the Sarunetes. *About Tugen.*

TUGIA, a town of the Oretani, Tarraconensis, 35 m. s.e. from Castulo. *Toia.*

TUGMA, a town of the Tiladæ, Indiæ, N. of Triglyphum. *Koduascan.*

TULCIS fl., a r. of Tarraconensis, falling into the Mediterranean at Tarraco. *Francoli.*

TULINGI, a tribe of Vindelici, in Rhætia, w. of Brigantinus lacus, under Abnoba m.

TULIPHURDUM, a town of the Dulgibini, Germ., on Visurgis fl., on the confines of the Angrivarii. *Verden.*

TULISURGIUM, a town of Northern Germany. *Bodenworder.*

TULLINA fl., a r. of Noricum, flowing near Comageni. *Tuln.*

TULLONIUM, a town of the Varduli, Tarraconensis, bet. Velia s.w. and Alba N.E.

TULLUM, a town of the Leuci, Belgica I., on the Mosella, L., bet. Scarpona and Solimariaca. *Toul.*

TULLUS m., a ridge of the Alpes Carnicæ, on the confines of Pannonia, w. of Carvancas m.

TUMERA, a town of Assyria, near Sumera.

TUNES (Thunis), a town of Zeugitana, on Carthag. sin., bet. Carthage (15) and Maxula (7½). The locality of the defeat of the Romans, under Regulus, by the Carthaginians, under Xantippus. *Tunis.*

TUNGRI, a German people who crossed the Rhine, and took possession of the country of the Eburones and Aduatici.

TUNIZA, Numidiæ, i. q. Tinissa.

TUNNOCELUM, a town of the Selgovæ, Brit., at the w. termination of Hadriani murus N. *Boulness.*

TUPHIUM, a town of Thebais, on the Nile, over against Hermonthis. *Tod.*

TURANIANA, a town of Bætica, on Portus Magnus, bet. Murgis and Urci.

TURBA (Tarba, Tarvia), a town of the Bigerrones, Novem Populana, bet. Bigerra N. and Aquæ Convenarum s. *Tarbes.*

TURBULA, a town of the Bastitani, Tarraconensis. *Tabarra.*

TURCÆ, Sarmatiæ, *vide* Tusci.

TURCILINGI, a tribe of Rugii, Germaniæ.

TURECIONUM, a town of the Allobroges, Viennensis, bet. Vienna N.W. and Morginum s.e.

TURENUM, a maritime town of Peucetia, on Via Frentana, bet. Aveldius fl. (9) and Natiolum (6). *Trani.*

TURIA (Tucia), I. a r. of Sabinium, passing by the town of Feronia, near Eretum, and falling into the Tiber, L., 6 m. N.E. from Rome. II. (Tyria), a town of the Edetani, Tarraconensis, on Turis fl., w. of Valentia.

TURIASO, a town of the Celtiberi, Tarraconensis, s. of Ergavica. A municipium and colonia. Noted for its steel-manufactures. *Tarazona.*

TURICUM, a town of the Helvetii, on Limagus fl. *Zurich.*

TURIS (Turulis, Tyrius, Duria) fl., a r. of Tarraconensis, rising towards Lobetum, and falling into Sucronensis sin. below Valentia. Its banks were the locality of the defeat of Sempronius by Pompey. *Guadalaviar.*

TURISSA (Iturissa), a town of the Varduli, Tarraconensis, on Magrada fl., 22 m. N.N.W. from Pompelo. *Ituren.*

TURMEDA, i. q. Thapsacus.

TURMODIGES, a tribe of Cantabri, s. of the Iberus, w. of the Berones.

TURMULI, a town of the Vettones, Lusitania, on the Tagus, R., above Norba Cæsarea.

TURNACUM, a town of the Nervii, Belgica II., on the Scaldis, L., bet. Viroviacum N.W. and Origiacum s.w. *Tournai.*

TUROBOLIS, a maritime town of the Corsii, in Sardinia E., bet. Olbia and Elephantaria.

TURONES, a people of Lugdunensis III., bet. the Liger and the Sequana, having the Carnutes N.E. and the Pictones S.W.

TUROQUA, a town of the Grovii, Tarraconensis, on Læron fl., L., above Ad Duos Pontes. *Vedra.*

TURRES, a town of the Triballi, in Mœsia, bet. Latina and Translitæ.

TURRIS, I. a town of Zeugitana, bet. Sicilibba and Vallis. II. *surnamed* Ad Algam, a fortress of Tripolis, Afric., E. of Oea. III. *surnamed* Augusti, a town of the Artabri, Tarraconensis, on Sars fl., w. of Iriaflavia. IV. *surnamed* Cæsaris, Turris Aureliana, a maritime town of Calabria, on Via Frentana, bet. Barium (15) and Dertum (9). *Ripagnola.* V. *surnamed* Cæsaris, a fortress of Numidia, 15 m. S.E. from Sigus. VI. *surnamed* Ferrata, a fortress of Pannonia, near Sirmium. VII. *surnamed* Hannibalis, *vide* Sullectis. VIII. *surnamed* Juliana, a fortress of Peucetia, on the Adriatic, bet. Barium (11) and Turris Aureliana (9), on Via Egnatia. *Torre Pelosa.* IX. *surnamed* Libyssonis, Ad Turrim, a maritime town of the Coracenses, in Sardinia, S.E. of Gorditanum prom. *Porto Torre.* X. *surnamed* Stratonis, Judææ, i. q. Cæsarea. XI. *surnamed* Veledæ, a citadel of the Bructeri Min., Germ., on Lupia fl., below Bogadium.

TURRUS fl., a r. of Venetia, falling into Natiso fl. above Ad XII. *Torre.*

TURSONI, a tribe of Hermunduri in Germany, on Mœnus fl., R., bet. the Chatti N. and the Curiones s.

TURTETANI, a maritime people of Bætica, S.W., bet. Luria fl. and the Mediterranean, w. of the Turtuli and Bastuli.

TURTULI, a people of Bætica, on Bætis fl., R. and L., and extending S.E. to Ilipual. *Algarves.*

TURULIS fl., a r. of Tarraconensis, falling into Sucro fl., L., above Sucro.

TURULLUS, a town of the Odrysæ, in Thrace, near Drusipara. *Tehorlu.*

TURUM, I. a town of Peucetia, in Apulia, near Norba. *Turo.* II. of the Sevaces, in Noricum, on Œnus fl., bet. Jovisara (63) and Pons Œni.

TURUNTES fl., a r. of Sarmatia, N.E. of Rhabon fl. *Windau.*

TUSCA, I. a r. of Africa, falling into the Mediterranean at Tabraca. The boundary of Numidia and Africa Propria. *Zain; Wad-el-Barbar?* II. a town of Numidia, on Tusca fl.

TUSCANA, a town of Etruria, on Marta fl.,

R., bet. Blera (9) and Maternum (17), on Via Claudia. Built by Ascanius. *Toscanella.*

TUSCI (Turci, Turcæ), "devastators," a people of Sarmatia As., bet. Caucasus and Ceraunii m. The progenitors of the modern Turks.

TUSCULANUM, a town of the Stoni, in Gallia Transpad. near the w. shore of Benacus lac. A municipium. *Toscolano.*

TUSCULUM (Tysclum), a city of the Latini, in Latium, 12½ m. S.E. of Rome, E. of Bovillæ. Founded by Telegonus, son of Ulysses and Circe. A favourite summer retreat of the Roman aristocracy. Near it (above the convent of Grotta Ferrata), among other villas there of Lucullus, Mæcenas, &c., was the villa Tusculana, previously belonging to Sylla, in which Cicero wrote his Tusculan Disputations. Tusculum was the birth-place of M. Porcius Cato, of T. Coruncanius, Cn. Plancius, &c. *Tuscolo, above Frascati.*

TUTATIO, a town of the Alauni, in Noricum, on Stiria fl., bet. Gabromagus (20) and Ernolata (12). *Near Schlierbach.*

TUTHOA fl., a r. of Arcadia, falling into Ladon fl., L., bet. Telphusa and Herææ.

TUTIA, a town of the Edetani, Tarraconensis, near Sucro fl., L., above Sætabicula. *Tous.*

TUTINI, the people of Turum, in Apulia.

TUTZIS (Thosch, Pthah-ei, "abode of Pthah"), a town of Dodecaschœnus, on the Nile, L., bet. Talmis (20) and Pselcis (12). *Kish; Gyrsche.*

TYANA (Dana, *postea* Eusebia), capital of Tyanitis, in Cappadocia, on the causeway of Semiramis, bet. Archelaus (75) and Podandus (34), 12 m. from Cadyna. Built by Thoas, king of the Tauro Scythi, in his pursuit of Orestes and Pylades. Named Eusebia from the worship of Jupiter Asmabæus. The birth-place of Apollonius Tyanæus; subsequently the metropolis of Cappadocia II. *Ketchhissar.*

TYANITIS præfectura, a prefecture of Cappadocia, about Tyana.

TYBA, a town of Palmyrene, bet. Cholle and Adatha, w. of Circesium.

TYBRACÆ, a people of Bactriana.

TYCÆ, a town of Paphlagonia, 15 m. from Cereæ.

TYDII, a people of Sarmatia Asiatica.

TYLANGII (Tulangii), a people of Gaul, on the Rhone, towards Lemanus lacus. *Vallée de Turnange in Le Valais.*

TYLISSUS, a town of Crete.

TYLLESIUM prom., a pr. of Bruttium, S. of Clampetia. *Capo Corica.*

Tylos ins., Major et Minor, two islands of Arabia Felix, on Persicus sin., over against Gerra. *Bahrein isl.*

Tymandrus, a town of Pisidia.

Tymbrium (Tymbrias, Tembrium, Tembricum), a town of Pisidia, on the borders of Phrygia, near Philomelium. In its vicinity was the fountain in which Midas caught Silenus.

Tymenæum m., a m. of Phrygia.

Tymenna, a town of Lycia.

Tymnessus, Tymnus, Cariæ, i. q. Thymnia.

Tymphæa (Stymphæa), the district of the Tymphæi, in Epirus. *About Mezzovo.*

Tymphæi, a people of Epirus, N. of the Molossi, about Tymphe m.

Tymphe (Stymphe) m., a branch of Pindus, occupying the N.E. angle of Epirus. Noted for a peculiar species of gypsum used to cleanse cloth. *Zagora.*

Tymphrestus m., a S.E. continuation of Pindus, separating Æniania from Athamania and Aperantia. *Klytzos* or *Smocovo.*

Tyndaridæ, a town of Bithynia, on the Euxine, 6 m. N. from Posidium prom.

Tyndaris, I. a prom. of Sicily, N., at Tyndaris. II. a city of Sicily, N., at the mouth of Helicon fl. ; founded by Dionysius the Elder. Named from Tyndarus, father of Leda. More than half the city was submerged by the sea. *Tindaro.*

Tyndarii Scopuli, four islets of Marmarica, off Chetæa.

Tyndis (Tundis), I. a r. of India i. Gangem, falling into Gangeticus sin. by two mouths, N.E. of Mæsolus fl. II. a maritime town of Limyrica, Indiæ, bet. Nitra and Aramagara (5). *Goa.*

Tynna, a town of Cataonia.

Typæum m., an eminence N.E. of Scillus, the place of execution assigned for women who had infringed the Olympic regulations.

Typana, a town of Triphylia in Elis, under Typæum m.

Tyra, a town of Dacia, on Tyras fl., towards its mouth (17½ m.). A Milesian colony. By some identified with Ophiusa, but discriminated by Ptolemy. *Acraman?*

Tyrambe, a town of Dandarica, Sarmat., on Palus Mæotis, at the mouth of Atticitus fl., S.E. of Phanagoria. A Milesian colony.

Tyrangetæ, a people of Sarmatia, on Tyras fl., towards its mouth.

Tyras (Trisses, Danastrus) fl., a r. of Europe, which separates Dacia from Sarma-

tia, and falls into the Euxine below Tyras, at one time, it would appear, by two mouths. *Dniester.*

Tyria, Lydiæ, i. q. Metropolis.

Tyriæum, i. q. Titarion.

Tyricteca Dia, a town of Taurica Chersonesus, on Bosporus Cimmerius, bet. Panticapæum and Nymphæa.

Tyrissa (Tauriana), a town of Emathia, on Axius fl., bet. Bærus and Alindea. *Aurethissar.*

Tyritæ, a people of Dacia and Sarmatia, E., about the mouth of Tyras fl.

Tyrmidæ, a demus of Attica, of the tribe Œneis.

Tyrrhena ins., i. q. Ogyris.

Tyrrheni, I. a tribe of Pelasgi in Epirus, about Dodona, the progenitors of the Selli. II. (Tyrseni), a colony of the Greek Tyrrheni, who, circa 1280 B.C., established themselves, by the aid of the Umbri, in (Tyrrhenia) Etruria, where they formed a confederacy of twelve principal cities. Thence, crossing the Apennines, they extended their conquests to the Alps, occupying the whole country between the two seas, with the exception of Venetia. In this New Etruria (afterwards Gallia Cisalpina) they formed a second confederacy of twelve principal cities, representing, and respectively colonized by, the twelve Tyrrhenian cities, s. of the Apennines. Their conquests s., which probably reached Lucania, are extended by some antiquaries to the very extremity of the Peninsula; it is tolerably clear that, at all events, Rome was a Tyrrhenian foundation. The decided decline of the Tyrrhenian power began 453 B.C., when the Syracusans took Æthalia ins., and was consummated by the conquests of the Gauls 403—388 B.C.

Tyrrhenia, the Greek form of Etruria.

Tyrrhenium mare, the upper portion of Inferum mare, on the coast of Etruria.

Tyrsus, I. ins., i. q. Tylos. II. fl., a r. of Sardinia, falling into the sea below Othoca. *Tirso; Oristagni?*

Tyrus, I. a city of Phœnicia, on the coast, 25 m. s. from Sidon, 90 m. N.W. from Jerusalem. Built 1300 B.C. Destroyed by Nebuchadnezzar. The later cognominal city, destroyed by Alexander, was afterwards restored. *Soor.* II. a town of Laconia.

Tyscon, a town of Phrygia Epict., on Alanda fl., towards Plitendus.

Tziamo, a district of Æthiopia, on Astaboras fl., L., towards its source.

Tzitzi, a town of Dodecaschœnus, on the Nile, L., bet. Parembole and Taphis (14).

TZINISTA, a name of the country of the Sinæ (China).

U.

UADENI, a people of Arabia Felix, under Zames m. s. *Wady Sarr.*

UBARTUS fl., a r. of Rhætia. *Brembo.*

UBAZA castrum, a fortress of Byzacene, bet. Ad Media and Thala.

UBII, a people of Germania II., on the Rhine, bet. the Gugerni and the Treveri.

UBINUM, a town of the Arverni, Aquitania I., bet. Augusta Nemetum s.e. and Ad Fines n.w.

UBUS (Rubricatus) fl., a r. of Numidia, falling into the Mediterranean 12 m. w. of Armoniacus fl. *Zenati; Seibus.*

UCENI, a tribe of Medulli, Alpes Maritimæ, n.w. of Brigantio. *Vallée d' Oz.*

UCERA (Noega, Gigia), a town of the Astures, on Cantabricum mare, bet. Salia fl. e. and Flavionavia. *Gigon.*

UCETIA (Castrum Uticense, Eutica), a town of the Volcæ Arecomici, Narbonensis, near Luteva. *Uzes.*

UCHIMERIUM, a fortress of Colchis, near Cytæa.

UCHIUM, a town of Meninx ins., Byzacene e., above Naribus.

UCIA, a town of the Turtuli, Bætica, on the Bætis, above Isturgi.

UCULTUNIACUM, a town of Bætica.

UDACESPES m., m. of Asia, separating Assyria from Armenia Maj.

UDÆ (Udini), a people of Sarmatia Asiat., on Udon fl., towards its mouth.

UDON fl., a r. of Sarmatia Asiat., rising w. of Strobilus m., and falling into the Caspian n. of Alontas fl.

UDUBA fl., a r. of Tarraconensis, falling into the sea s. of the Iberus. *Mijares.*

UFENS (Oufens) fl., a r. of Latium, rising n. of Prifernum, and falling into the sea w. of Tarracina. Noted for its sluggish course. *Aufente.*

UFFUGUM, an inland town of Bruttium, on Crathis fl., below Hetriculum. *Fagnano.*

UGERNUM, a town of the Volcæ Arecomici, Narbonensis, on the Rhine, over against Tarasco. *Beaucaire.*

UGGADE, a town of the Veliocasses, Lugdunensis II., on the Sequana, R., bet. Rotomagus and Mediolanum.

UGIA, a town of the Turtetani, Bætica, bet. Asta s.w. and Hispalis n.e. A colonia (Cæsaris Salutarensis). *Las Cabezas de San Juan.*

ULAI fl., *vide* Eulæus.

ULAMA, a town of Galilæa, s. of Tarichæa.

ULCÆA lacus, a lake of Pannonia, formed by the Savus, near Cibalis.

ULEA, a town of the Turtuli, Bætica, 10 m. n. from Ipagrus. *Rambla.*

ULIAMBUS, a town of Pamphylia.

ULIARUS ins. *postea* Olero, an isl. of the Santones, Aquitania II., at the mouth of Carantonus fl., n. of Antros ins. *Oleron.*

ULISIPPIRA (Ulizibirra), a town of Zeugitana, bet. Aggersel (8) and Gurra.

ULLA fl., a r. of Tarraconensis, falling into the Adriatic below Iria Flavia.

ULMANETES, a tribe of Treveri, on the Rhine. *About Ulmersbach.*

ULMERUGI, a maritime tribe of Northern Germany, towards the Rhugii.

ULMUM, I. a town of the Boii, Pannon., bet. Carnuntum (14) and Scarabantia (25). *Jois*, or *Niyulas.* II. of Pannonia Inf., on Bacuntius fl., bet. Spaneta (10) and Celena (11). *Sid.* III. of the Triballi, Mœs., bet. Naissus (19) and Remessiana.

ULPIA PANTALIA, a town of Graæa, in Pæonia, bet. Ælia (20) and Gariscus (40). *Ghiustendil.*

ULPIANA, capital of the Thunatæ, in Mœsia, on Drinus fl., L., towards its source, s.w. of Sardica. *Prisren.*

ULPIANUM, a town of the Prædavenses, in Dacia, n. of Apulum. *Peterwaradin?*

ULTINUM, a town of the Rauraci, Maxima Sequanorum, on Arula fl., bet. Vindonissa and Soladurum.

ULŬBRÆ, a village of the Volsci, in Latium, s. of Velitræ, on the edge of the Paludes Pomptinæ; wherefore Cicero calls its people *little frogs. Near Velitri.*

ULYSSIUM prom., Siciliæ, i. q. Odysseum.

UMBENNUM, a town of the Segelauni, Viennensis, on the Rhone, bet. Valentia and Batiana.

UMBRANICI, a tribe of Ruteni, Aquitania, e. of Tolosa. *Diocèse d' Albi.*

UMBRANUM, a town of the Boii, in Gallia Cispadana. *Marano.*

UMBRI (Ombrikoi), the most ancient people of Italy, of uncertain origin (by some antiquaries considered cognate with the Gauls), who, from about Reate, in Sabinium, extended themselves over the central and mountainous portions of the peninsula. By the Tyrrheni they were restricted (n.w.) within the left bank of the Tiber; by the Senones they were driven from the sea-coast into the mountains. Their subjugation by Rome took place 308—295 B.C. Umbria, as arranged by Augustus, was separated from Gallia Cispadana by Rubico fl., from Etruria by the Tiber, from Sabinium by Nera fl., and from Picenum by Æsis fl. Its E. boundary was the Adriatic. Pliny says their name was given to them by the Greeks, upon their having escaped from some great inundation.

UMBRIA, *vide* Umbri.

UMBRO fl., a r. of Etruria, falling into the sea, bet. Hasta (2) and Aprile lacus. The locality of a defeat of the Gauls, by Paulus Æmilius, 225 B.C. *Ombrone.*

UNA fl., a r. of Mauritania Tingit., falling into the Atlantic s. of Usadium prom. *Iguzul.*

UNELLI, a people occupying the N.W. angle of Lugdunensis II., N. of the Lexovii. *Cotentin.*

UNSINGIS fl., a r. of the Frisii, Germ., falling into Germanicus ocean. s.w. of Amisia fl., below Manarmanis portus. *Hunsing ?*

UNUCA, a town of Zeugitana, on Bagradas fl., R., bet. Ad Mercurium and Sicilibba.

UPELLI, a town of the Ambilici, in Noricum, on Sana fl., bet. Collatio and Celeja.

UR (Orche, Orchoe, *postea* Edessa), a town of Mesopotamia, towards Nisibis, 25 m. from Haran. The residence of Abraham.

URA, I. Syriæ, i. q. Sura. II. prom., Cypri, i. q. Dinaretum.

URANOPOLIS, I. a town of Acte penin., in Macedonia, on the Strymonicus sin., opposite Calarna. Built by Alexander, brother of Cassander. *Callitza.* II. a town of Pisidia, w. of Termessus.

URANIA, a town of Cyprus, near Carpasia.

URBA, capital of the Verbigeni, Maxima Sequanorum, bet. Ariolica and Lacus Lausonius. *Orbe.*

URBANA, a town of the Sidicini, in Campania, on Via Appia, bet. Pons Campanus (3) and Ad Nonum (6). A colonia of Sylla ; the inhabitants were transferred to Capua.

URBANATES, a people of Gallia Cisalpina, towards the Veliates. *About Marano.*

URBATE, a town of Pannonia Inf., on Savus fl., R., bet. Servitium (25) and Marsonia. *Brod.*

URBIACA, a town of the Celtiberi, Tarraconensis, s.E. of Arcobriga.

URBIGENI, *vide* Verbigeni.

URBINUM, *surnamed* Hortense, a town of Umbria, bet. Metaurus fl. and Pisaurus fl., 8 m. N.E. of Urbinum Met. The deathplace of Valens, the general of Vitellius. *Urbino.* II. *surnamed* Metaurense, a town of Umbria, on Metaurus fl., R., towards its source. *Urbania.*

URBICUS, a r. of Tarraconensis, falling into Durius fl. below Ocellodurum. *Orbigo.*

URBS (Odubria) fl., a r. of Liguria, rising N.W. of Hasta, and falling into Tanarus fl. w. of Dortona. *Orba.*

URBS SALVIA, a town of Picenum, on Via Flaminia, bet. Septempeda (12) and Firmum (18). *Urbisaglia.*

URCE (Urgi, Virgi), a town of the Bastitani, Tarraconensis, on Portus Magnus, bet. Turaniana and Charidemi prom. *Near Vera.*

URCESA, i. q. Althæa.

URCHOA, Chaldeæ, i. q. Ur.

URCINIUM, a maritime town of Corsica w., below Circidius fl. *Ajaccio.*

UREMA, a town of Cyrrhestica, Syriæ, near the mouth of Singas fl.

URGAON (Alba), a town of Bætica, N.W. of Bastia. A municipium. *Arjona, near Andujar.*

URGI, a people of Sarmatia Europæa, towards Mæotis palus.

URGO ins. *postea* Gorgona, an isl. of Etruria, 25 m. w. from Portus Herculis Liburni. *Gorgona.*

URIA, I. a salt lake of Acarnania, on the s. coast, E. of Cynia palus, forming with this lake and Melite lacus the marshes of Missolonghi. II. (Ureium, Hyrium), a town of Daunia, Apul., on Urias sin., N. of Garganus m. *Rodi.* III. (Orra), a maritime town of the Locri, in Bruttium, s. of Locri. Founded by Idomeneus, circa 1100 B.C. *Palazzi.* IV. a town of Messapia, on Via Appia, bet. Mesochorion (10) and Scamnum (8). *Rodi.*

URIAS sin., a bay of the Adriatic, at Uria.

URICONIUM (Viroconium), a town of the Cornavii, Brit., on Sabrina fl., L., bet. Rutunium and Magna. *Wroxeter.*

URIMA (Urma Giganti), a town of Cyrrhestica, on the Euphrates, bet. Zeugma and Arulis.

URINCÆ, a town of the Rauraci, Maxima Sequanorum, N.W. of Cambete.

URIUM, a town of the Turtetani, Bætica, on Urius fl., near its mouth. *Veos.*

URIUS fl., a r. of Bætica, falling into the Atlantic at Onoba. *Rio Tinto ; Rio Azige.*

URPANUS fl., a r. of Pannonia, falling into the Savus. *Verbas.*

URSA prom., Sardiniæ, i. q. Arcti.

URSENTUM, a town of Lucania, near the source of Laus fl. *Orso Marso.*

URSO (Ursaon, Orso, *surnamed* Genua Urbanorum), a town of the Turtetani, Bætica, bet. Callensis respublica, N.W., and Astapa E. *Ossuna.*

URSOLIS, a town of the Allobroges, Viennensis, on the Rhone, bet. Figlinis and Tegna.

URUS fl., a r. of the Brigantes, Brit., falling into Abus fl. at Isurnum. *Ouse.*

URUSA, a town of Rhætia, bet. Abodiacum (13) and Bratananium (12).

USAL, I. a district of Arabia Felix, N. of the Sabæi. II. its capital, E. of Napegus.

USALETUS (Vasaletum) mons, m. of Zeugitana, extending s.w. into Byzacene.

USALITANUM oppidum, *vide* Uzan.

USARGALA m., m. of Gætulia, a s.E. continuation of Madethubadus m.

USBIUM, a town of the Boii, in Noricum, on the Danube, bet. Arelate and Isis fl. *Ips.*

USCANA, capital of the Penestæ, on the Drilo niger, bet. Diborus Superior and Draudacum. *Near Isturga.*

USCARDEI, a people of Sarmatia Asiatica.

USCENUM, a town of the Jazyges Metanastæ, towards Granua fl.

USCETA, *vide* Uzita.

USCOSIUM, a town of the Frentani, on Tifernus fl., L., bet. Histonum (15) and Larinum (14), on Via Frentana. *Vicoso.*

USDIÆ, a people of Hibernia, w. of the Menapii. *Part of Cork co.*

USELLIS, a city of the Celsitani, in Sardinia, w., bet. Neapolis and Forum Trajani. A colonia of Augustus, as Col. Jul. Aug. *Torre Fontanamar.*

USILLA, a maritime town of Byzacene, bet. Ruspæ and Taphrura.

USIPII (Usipĕtes), a tribe of Germania, on the Rhine; of varying locality; at one time occupying the territories of the Menapii, Eburones, and Condrusi. They finally became fused with the Alemanni.

USITA (Usceta), a town of Zeugitana, near Ruspina.

USLUNTII, a people of Hibernia E., bet. the Darini N. and the Eblani s.

USPE, capital of the Siraci, Sarmatiæ.

USSADIUM prom., a pr. of Mauritania Tingitana, s. of Herculis prom., 15 m. N. of Onellana.

USSUBIUM, a town of the Vasates, Novem Populana, on the Garumna, R., bet. Alingo and Ad Fines.

USTICA ins., one of the westernmost of the Æoliæ ins.

USUERVA, a town of the Volcæ Tectosages, Narbonensis I., bet. Liviana w. and Narbo E. *Aubère.*

UTELLABRI, i. q. Velibori.

UTHISNA, a town of Zeugitana.

UTICA, "old" (Ityca), a maritime city of Zeugitana, within Apollonium prom., on Bagradas fl., close to its mouth. A Tyrian settlement, older than Carthage, and, after the destruction of that city, the capital of Africa Prop. The death-place of Cato. *Biserta.*

UTIDAVA, a town of the Cistoboci, in Dacia, on Parata fl., L., below Arcobadara.

UTIDORSI, i. q. Aorsi.

UTIS (Utens, Vibis) fl., a r. of Gallia Cispadana, falling into the Adriatic at Classis. *Montone.*

UTOCETUM, a town of the Cornavii, Brit. Romana, bet. Condate and Ripandunum.

UTUS (Artenes), I. a r. of Mœsia Inferior, rising in Hæmus m., and falling into the Danube at Utus. II. a town of the Mœsi, in Mœsia Inf., on the Rhine, bet. Castra Nova and Anasamus, at the mouth, L., of Utus fl.

UXACONA, a town of Britain, bet. Uriconium (11) and Pennocrucium (12).

UXAMA, *surnamed* Argella, Vasama, Auxima, Auxierium, Uxamabarca, a town of the Arevacæ, Tarraconensis, on Areva fl., L., at its junction with Durius fl., 24 m. E. of Clunia. Noted for its horses. *Osma.*

UXANTIS ins., i. q. Uxisama.

UXELA, a town of the Damnonii, Brit., w. of Isca Damnoniorum.

UXELLODUNUM, a town of the Cadurci, Aquitania I., N.E. of Divona. *Capdenac.*

UXELUM, a town of the Selgovæ, Brit., at the mouth of Novius fl., R. *Near Drumlanrig.*

UXENTUM, a town of the Salentini, in Japygia, on Tarentinus sin., bet. Veretum (10) and Aletium (12), N.W. of Japygium prom. *Ugento.*

UXENTUS m., m. of India i. Gangem, bet. the Ganges and Mana fl.

UXIA (Uxiana), the country of the Uxii, in Susiana.

UXII (Oxii, Uskangli), a tribe of Elymæi, on Aroatis fl., in the N.E. division of Susiana.

UXIORUM ARX (Climax), a fortress of the Uxii Susian., at Susianæ portæ.

UXISAMA ins., an isl. of Lugdunensis, near Calbium prom. *Ouessant.*

UZ (Huz, Ausitis), a district of Arabia Deserta, on the confines of Edom. Named after Uz, grandson of Shem, by whose posterity it was colonized. The country of Job.

UZAL, Arabiæ, i. q. Sabe Regia.

UZAN (Usalis, Usalitanum oppidum), a town of Zeugitana, w. of Utica. A colonia.

UZAPPA, a town of Byzacene, bet. Autipsida and Manange.

UZELA, I. a town of the Damnonii, Brit., E. of Voliba. *Launceston.*

UZICATH (Thusicath), a town of Numidia, bet. Culucitani (18) and Rusicada (25).

V.

VABAR fl., a r. of Mauritania Cæsar., falling into the sea w. of Salda. *Giffer.*

VACCA (Vacua, Vacus), a r. of Lusitania, falling into the Atlantic bet. the Durius N. and the Munda S. *Vouga.*

VACCÆ (Vaga, Baga), a town of Mauritania Cæsar., s. of Sitifi. The principal mart of Numidia.

VACCÆI, a people of Tarraconensis, on the Durius, R. and L., bet. the Astures w. and the Arevacæ E.

VACOMAGI, a people of Britannia Barbara, s.E. of the Caledonii. *Nairn, Elgin, and Banff.*

VACUA fl., i. q. Vacca.

VADA SABATA, a maritime town of the Ingauni, in Liguria, on Via Aurelia, bet. Albingaunum (29) and Vicus Virginis (9). *Vadi.*

VADA VOLATERRANA, the port of Volaterræ, in Etruria, at the mouth of Cæcina fl., on Aurelia Via, bet. Populonium (25) and Ad Fines. *Vada.*

VADASI, a people of Media Magna, on the borders of Parthia, bet. Syro Media and Choarene.

VADATA, a town of Chammenene prefectura, in Cappadocia.

VADEI, Arabiæ, the people of Badia.

VADENI, Arabiæ, i. q. Uadeni.

VADICASSES, a people of Lugdunensis I., bet. the Senones w. and the Lingones E.

VADIMONIS lacus, a lake of Etruria, at Castellum Amerinum, on which were some floating islands. The locality of the decisive defeat of the Etruscans by the Romans; and of the Senones by Dolabella, 310 B.C. It is now a marsh. *Lago di Bassano.*

VADRIUS fl., Indiæ, i. q. Hydraotes.

VADUM ARUNDINIS, a town of the Belgæ, Brit. *Near Redbridge.*

VÆSAPA (Varsapa), a town of Armenia Minor.

VAGA, I. Mauritaniæ Cæsar., i. q. Vaccæ. II. (Baga), a town of Zeugitana, under Cirna m. s., bet. Teglata and Elephantaria.

VAGÆ, a town of Mauritania Cæsariensis, 18 m. N. of Gadaum Cast.

VAGIENNI, a people of Liguria, occupying its N.W. angle, bet. the Statielli E., Alpes Maritimæ w. and s., and the Taurini N.

VAGNIACÆ, a town of the Cantii, Brit., bet. Noviomagus and Durobrivæ.

VAGORITUM, a town of the Arvii, Lugdunensis III., w. of Suindinum.

VAGUM prom., a pr. of Corsica E., above Mariana.

VAHĀLIS fl., the left or s. issue of the Rhine. *Waal.*

VALA fl., a r. of Mauritania Ting., bet. Hermæum prom. and Solis prom.

VALCUM, a town of Pannonia, bet. Mogetiana (30) and Silacenæ (28). *Bottyan.*

VALDASUS fl., a r. of Pannonia, falling into the Savus fl. *Bosna.*

VALENTIA, I. a province of Britain, extending across the island bet. Bodotria Æst. N., Ituna Æst. N.W., and Alaunus fl. N. II. a town of Phrygia. III. a surname of Rome. IV. Calabriæ, i. q. Baletium. V. a town of Sardinia, s. of Aquæ Neapolitanæ. *Iglesias.* VI. of the Edetani, Tarraconensis, on Turia fl., R., towards its mouth. Assigned by Junius Brutus to the soldiers of Viriathus. Destroyed by Pompey; restored by Cæsar, and appointed a colonia (Julia Valentia). *Valencia.* VII. of Mauritania, i. q. Banasa. VIII. capital of the Segelauni, Viennensis, on the Rhone, bet. Tegna and Umbennum. *Valence.*

VALEPONGA, a town of the Celtiberi, Tarraconensis, s.w. of Lobetum.

VALERIA, I. a pr. of Pannonia Inf., along the Danube. So named by Galerius, in honour of his wife. II. a town of the Celtiberi, Tarraconensis, on Sucro fl., L., towards its source, s.E. of Ergavica. A colonia. *Cuenca?* III. with Strabo, i. q. Varia, in Latium, and Valentia, in Sardinia.

VALI, a people of Sarmatia Asiat., on the Rha, about its mouth.

VALLA, Pieriæ, i. q. Bala.

VALLATA, a town of the Astures, Tarraconensis, bet. Legio Septima Gemina N.E. and Asturica Augusta s.w.

VALLATUM, a town of the Catenates, in Vindelicia.

VALLI, a town of Zeugitana, 11 m. s.w. from Sicilibba.

VALLIS CARINIANA, a town of the Aravisci, in Pannonia, bet. Gurtiana and Joviana.

VALLIS DOMITIANA, a town of Mœsia Inferior, bet. Halmyris and Ad Salices, w. of Halmyris lacus.

VALLIS JULIÆ, a valley of the Ambidravi, in Noricum, bet. Dravus fl. and Julia fl.

VALLIS JUNONIS, a valley of the Ambilici, in Noricum, bet. Dravus fl. and the Alps.

VALOBRIA, a town of the Astures, in Tarraconensis, s.w. of Asturica Augusta.

VALVA m., a N. ridge of Phrurasus m., in Mauritania Cæsar., leading to Garus m.

VALVATA, a town of Etruria, on Arnus fl., R., above Pisæ (9). *Fornacette.*

VANDABANDA, a district of Bactria, s. of Babacene, under Caucasus Indicus N.

VANDALI, i. q. Vindili.

VANDALII m., m. of Northern Germany, at the source of the Albis. *Riesengebirge.*

VANDOGARA (Vanduaria), a town of the Damnii, Brit., near Clota fl., R., towards its mouth. *Paisley.*

VANESIA, a town of the Auscii, Novem Populana, bet. Elusa N.W. and Elimberris S.E.

VANGANIA ins., an isl. of India i. Gangem, s. of Milizegeris.

VANGIONES, a people of Germania I., on the Rhine, E. of the Treveri, N. of the Nemetæ, about Borbetomagus.

VANIENSES, a people in the mountains of Northern Histria. *About Venzone.*

VANNIA (Vennum), a town of the Bechuni, in Gallia Transpad. A municipium. *Lavezine.* II. capital of the Vanienses, in Histria. *Venzone.*

VAPANES, a town of Corsica, on or near Tavola fl., L., above Larinum.

VAPINCUM, a town of the Caturiges, Narbonensis, bet. Eburodunum N.E. and Mons Seleucus. *Gap.*

VARA ÆSTUARIUM, the mouth of Vara fl., bet. Alta-Ripa and Tuæris æstuar. *Frith of Cromarty.*

VARA fl., a r. of Britannia Barbara, falling into the German ocean at Vara æstuar.

VARADETUM, a town of the Cadurci, Aquitania I., bet. Divona w. and Carantomagus E. *Varaye.*

VARÆ, a town of the Ordovices, Brit., bet. Conovium (19) and Deva. *Bodfari.*

VARAMUS fl., a r. of Venetia, falling into the Adriatic E. of Tilavemptus fl. *Stella.*

VARBARI (Varvani), a people of Venetia. *About Valvasone.*

VARCIA, a town of the Sequani, Maxima Sequanorum, bet. Andematunum N.W. and Segobodium.

VARCIANI, a people of Pannonia Sup., bet. Savus fl. and Illyria, E. of the Colapini.

VARDACATENSIUM, *postea* Gavardatensium, a town of the Cenomanni, in Gallia Cisalpina, N. of Brixia. *Gavardo.*

VARDANUS (Varadanus) fl., a r. of Sarmatia As., rising in Caucasus, s. of Corusia, and falling by several mouths, one of which is

Atticitus fl., into the Mæotis palus and the Euxine, towards Phanagoria. *Kuban.*

VARDO fl., a r. of Narbonensis I., falling into the Rhone E. of Nemausus. *Gardon.*

VARDULI, a people of Tarraconensis, bet. the sea N., the Iberus s., the Caristi w., and the Vascones E.

VARIA, I. a town of the Æqui, in Latium, on Anio fl., R., bet. Tibur (10) and Mandela. *Vicovaro.* II. (Vcrela), of the Berones, Tarraconensis, on the Iberus, R., above Calagurris, over against Contrebia. *Varea.* III. of Messapia.

VARIANA, a town of the Mœsi, in Mœsia Inferior, on the Danube, bet. Regianum (12) and Castra Nova.

VARIANÆ, a town of the Oseriatæ, Pannon., bet. Siscia (23) and Menneianæ (26).

VARIANUM. *Vide* Vicus Varianus.

VARICA, a town of Iberia.

VARII, a people of Germany, s. of the Chauci.

VARINI, Germaniæ, i. q. Pharodini.

VARISTI, i. q. Naristi.

VARNI, a people of Bactria, E. of the Zariaspæ.

VARSA, the district of India about Taxila.

VARUS fl., a r. of the Ananes, in Líguria, falling into Padus fl. at Ad Padum. *Stura.* II. of Alpes Maritimæ, falling into the Mediterranean w. of Nicæa.

VARUTHA, a town of the Taochi, Arm., s.w. of Chorsa.

VASALA, Lycaoniæ, i. q. Caballicome.

VASAMA, i. q. Uxama, Tarraconensis.

VASAMPUS, a town of Numidia, bet. Flavia Marci and Mora.

VASANDA, a town of Iberia.

VASĀTES (Vasarii), a people of Novem Populana, N.E., about Cossio.

VASCŌNES, a people of Tarraconensis, bet. the Pyrenees N., the Iberus s., the Varduli w., and the Ilergetes E. Large numbers of them were driven over the Pyrenees into Gaul. *Biscay.*

VASIDICA, a town of Numidia, bet. Thagura and Ad Malas.

VASIO, capital of the Vocontii, Viennensis, E. of Ad Lectoce. *Vaison.*

VASODA, a town of Lycaonia, near Misthea.

VASSEI, a people of Novem Populana. *About Basas.*

VATARI, a town of Numidia, bet. Velefis and Flavia Marci.

VATEDO, a town of the Bituriges Vivisci, on Duronius fl., bet. Condate and Burdigala. *About Mont Vassia.*

VATICANUM prom., a pr. of Bruttium, at Portus Herculis. *Capo Vaticano.*

VATRENUS (Vaternus) fl., a r. of Gallia Cis-

padan., falling into Padus-Eridanus, w. of
Sinnius fl. *Santerno.*

VATRUTE, a town of Narbonensis, bet. Tedusia and Ugerni. *Valleraugue.*

VEAMINI, a tribe of Albiœci, Alpes Maritimæ, s. of the Bodiontici. *In Toramenos.*

VECTIS (Ouectis, Vecta, *Grœcè*; *Celticè,*
Gwydh) ins., an isl. of the Regni, bet.
Magnus portus and Alaunus fl. Taken
by Vespasian under Claudius. According
to Diod. Siculus, here was a Carthaginian
depôt for the tin of the Cassiterides ins.,
on its way to Gades. *Isle of Wight.*

VEDIANTII, a tribe of Albiœci, Narbonensis II., on the Varus, L., towards its
mouth.

VEDĪNUM, a town of the Carni, in Venetia.
Udine.

VEDRA fl., a r. of the Brigantes, Brit., falling into the Germanicus oceanus bet.
Alaunus fl. and Dunum sin. *Weare.*

VEGESULA, I. a town of Byzacene, bet. Me-
negesem (20) and Sufetula (30). *Fusana.*
II. of Numidia, bet. Timphadis (20) and
Mascula (18).

VEII, one of the twelve cities of Etruria, on
Via Cassia, bet. Roma (11) and Baccanæ
(9). Noted for the slaughter of the 300
Fabii, and for its ten years' siege by Camillus. A colonia of Julius Cæsar, and a
municipium. *Isola Farnese, near La
Storta.*

VEITURII, a town of Liguria, E. of Genua.
Voltaggio.

VELATHRI, the Tyrrhenian name of Volaterræ.

VELATODURUM, a town of the Sequani,
Maxima Sequanorum, on Dubis fl., R.,
bet. Epamanduodurum and Loposagum.

VELDIDENA, capital of the Breuni, in
Rhætia, on Œnus fl., bet. Scarbia (19)
and Matreium (18). *The monastery of
Wilden, near Innspruck.*

VELEFIS, a town of Numidia, bet. Ad Pisinas and Vatari.

VELEIA, a town of the Anamanes, in Gallia
Cispadana, on Nura fl., R., 18 m. s. of
Placentia. Overwhelmed by a land-slip.
Above Mancinesso and Liveia.

VELIA (Veleja), I. a town of the Caristi,
Tarraconensis, on the Iberus, R., above
Contrebia. *Viana.* II. (Helia, Hyele), a
city of Lucania, on the coast, 3 m. s. from
Heles fl. Founded by Phocæans from
Ionia, under Creontiades, circa 540 B.C.;
enlarged by a col. from Thurii B.C. 440.
The birth-place of Zeno and Parmenides,
and seat of the Eleatic sect. A col. circa
270 B.C. It was noted for its salubrity.
Castel a mare della Bruca.

VELIATES, *surnamed* Vecteri, Veleiaci, a
people of Gallia Cispadana, on the confines of Liguria.

VELĪBARI (Utelabri), a people of Hibernia.
In Kerry.

VELINÆ, i. q. Vada Volaterna.

VELINUS fl., I. a r. of Sabinium, falling into
Nar fl. below Cutiliæ. *Velino.* II. lacus,
a lake of Sabinium, formed by Velinus fl.
A channel to drain its waters into Nar fl.
was constructed by Curius Dentatus, and
produces the Fall of Terni (Caduta delle
Marmore). *Lago di pie di Lugo.*

VELITRÆ, a city of the Volsci, in Latium, on
the left of Appia Via, bet. Aricia and Ulubræ, 20 m. s.e. from Rome. A colonia
494 B.C. The birth-place of Augustus.
Velletri.

VELLAUNI, a tribe of Salyes, Narbonensis,
on Varus fl., R., bet. the Egdini and the
Bericini. *About Vevelause.*

VELLAUNODUNUM, a town of the Senones,
Lugdunensis IV., s.e. of Agedincum.
Beaune.

VELLAVI, a people of Aquitania I., on the N.
slopes of Cebenna m., N.E. of the Gabali.
About Velay.

VELLICA (Belgica), a town of the Turmodigi, Tarraconensis, on Iberus fl., R., 1 m.
from its source. *Near Valdearroyo.*

VELLOCASSES, a people of Lugdunensis II.,
on the Sequana, bet. the Bellovaces N.E.
and the Lexovii and Aulerci Eburovices
S.W.

VELPA m., m. of Cyrenaica, 25 geog. m.
from the sea.

VELTÆ, a people of Sarmatia, N. of the Venedæ.

VEMANIÆ castrum, a town of Rhætia, bet.
Cambodunum (15) and Brigantium. *Wan-
gen.*

VENAFRUM, a town of the Pentri, in Samnium, on Via Lat., bet. Ad Flexum (8)
and Cluturnum. A colonia. Noted for
its olive-oil.

VENAMAXODURUM, a town of Vindelicia, w.
of Augusta Vindelicorum.

VENASA, a town of Cappadocia, s.e. of Parnassus. Noted for its temple of Jupiter.

VENDELIA, a town of the Autrigones, N.E.
of Virovesca, s. of the Iberus.

VENDENÆ, a town of the Galabri, in Mœsia,
bet. Ad Fines and Vicinianum.

VENDUM, a town of the Japydes, in Illyria.
Vendo.

VENĒDÆ (Venedi, Winidi), a people of Sarmatia E., on Venedicus sinus, extending
for some distance s. along the Vistula.
The progenitors of the Wends.

VENEDICUS sin.; I. the E. extremity of Sarmaticus oceanus. *G. of Riga.* II. mons, m. of Sarmatia, towards Venedicus sinus.

VENENI, a people of Narbonensis, N. of the Ectini. *About Vinadio.*

VENERIS ins., I. an isl. of Thebais, in the Red sea, above Parvum prom. II. prom., Ciliciæ, i. q. Zephyrium.

VENETI (Venetes, Henetes), a colony of Paphlagonian Heneti, who, circa 1270 B.C., crossing the Bosphorus under the command of Antenor, made their way by Danubius fl. and Savus fl., and thence by land to the mouths of Eridanus and Padus ffl., where, having expelled the Euganei, they formed a settlement, at first called Trojanus Pagus, and in its extension bounded N. by Alpes Venetæ and Carnicæ, s. by the Adriatic and Padus fl., w. by Athesis fl., and E. by Formio fl. and Alpes Juliæ. Strabo calls them Gauls, Herodotus speaks of them as Illyrians. It is to be observed, that the various peoples in Paphlagonia, Italy, Gaul, and Germany, who were anciently called Veneti or Heneti, all occupied the same description of country—marshy districts on the coast. This district was especially celebrated for its breed of fleet horses, and for its cattle. After the second Punic war, Venetia was included within Gallia Cisalpina. By Augustus it was created the tenth region of the empire. II. a people of Lugdunensis IV., on the coast, s., bet. the Osismii w. and the Namnetes E.

VENETIA, Italiæ. *Vide* Veneti.

VENETICÆ ins., islands on the coast of the Veneti, Lugdunensis. *Belleisle, Houat, Hedic, Groa, &c.*

VENETUS lacus, the w. portion of Brigantinus lacus. *Bodenzee.*

VENIATIA, a town of the Bracari, Tarraconensis, s.w. of Petavonium. *Torre di Vezzavona.*

VENICAMORI, a people of Narbonensis. *About Col Maurin.*

VENICIUM, a town of Corsica, S.E. of Talcinum.

VENICNII, a people occupying the N.W. angle of Hibernia. *Donegal.*

VENICNIUM prom., the N. extremity of Hibernia, bet. Vidua fl. and Boreum prom. *Bloody Foreland.*

VENICONTES, a tribe of Caledonii, about Tava æstuar. and Bodotria æstuar. N.

VENIDATES, a people of Venetia. *About Udino.*

VENNENSES, a people of Tarraconensis, near the Caristi.

VENNONES, a tribe of Rhæti, on the Alps, above Larius lacus. *Valteline.*

VENNONETES, a tribe of Rhæti, N. of the Naunes. *Val di Venosia.*

VENONÆ, a town of the Cornavii, Brit. Rom., bet. Etocetum and Tripontum. *Near Highcross.*

VENNUM. *Vide* Vannia.

VENOSTÆ, a people of Rhætia, near the Camuni. *Val di Venosta; Winthgau Thal.*

VENTA BELGARUM (Caer-Gwent), capital of the Belgæ, Brit., bet. Brigæ and Vindomis. *Winchester.*

VENTA ICENORUM, capital of the Iceni, Brit., near Garianus fl., w. of Garianonum. *Caistor.*

VENTA SILURUM, capital of the Silures, Brit., E. of Isca Silurum. *Caerwent.*

VENTIA. *Vide* Vintium.

VENTISPONTE, a town of the Turtetani, Bætica, bet. Astigi and Hispalis.

VENUSIA, a town of Daunia, in Apulia, on Via Appia, bet. Pons Aufidi (19) and Silvium. A colonia. The refuge of Varro after the defeat of Cannæ. The birthplace of Horace. *Venosa.*

VER fl., a r. of Britain, running by Verulamium.

VERA, Mediæ, i. q. Phraspa.

VERĀGRI, a people of Alpes Penninæ, bet. the Nantuates and the Salassi.

VERBANUS lacus, a lake of the Lepontii, in Rhætia, chiefly formed by Ticinus fl., in length 50 Roman miles. *Lago Maggiore.*

VERBIGENUS (Urbigenus) pagus, a district of Maxima Sequanorum, about Urba.

VERBINUM, a town of the Veromandui, Belgica II., bet. Duronum N. and Catusiacum s. *Vervins.*

VERCELLÆ (Vercellum), capital of the Libicii, in Gallia Transpad., on Sessites fl., L., s.w. of Novaria. A municipium. *Borgo Vercelli, 2 m. from Vercelli.*

VERCELLIUM, a town of the Hirpini, in Samnium.

VEREÆ, a town of Pannonia, bet. Marianæ (20) and Mursa (26). *St. Gyorgy.*

VEREASUECA, a maritime town of the Cantabri, Tarraconensis, at the mouth of Saunium fl., bet. Portus Juliobrigensium E. and Nanasa fl. w. *Suances.*

VEREDRUM prom., a pr. of the Cornavii, Brit. Barb., midway bet. Verubium prom. and Orcas prom.

VERENTUM, a town of Etruria, on Vulsiniensis lac. w., below Visentium. *Varentano.*

VERESIS fl., a r. of Latium, falling into the Tiber.

VERESVI, a town of Byzacene, bet. Capsa and Thasarte.

VERĒTUM, *prius* Baris, a town of Japygia, somewhat inland, bet. Castrum Minervæ (15) and Uxentum (10). *Santa Maria di Vereto.*

VERGÆ, a town of Bruttium, on Crathis fl., L. *Roggiano.*

VERGENTUM (Julii Genius), a town of the Turtetani, Bætica, on the Bætis, above Caura. *Gelves?*

VERGILIA, I. a town of the Bastuli, Bætica, N.E. of Abdera. II. of the Contestani, Tarraconensis, on Tader fl., L., above Thiar.

VERGILLUS fl., a r. of Daunia, in Apulia, falling into Aufidus fl. near Cannæ. Memorable for its Hannibal bridge of Roman corpses.

VERGIUM, Tarraconensis, i. q. Bergidum.

VERGUNNI, a tribe of Salyes, Narbonensis, N. of the Nementuri. *About Vergon.*

VERI, a town of Gætulia, bet. Laminiæ and Berezei.

VERLUCIO, a town of the Belgæ, Brit., bet. Aquæ Solis and Cunetio. *Sandy Lane; Leckham?*

VERNASOLE, a town of the Volcæ Tectosages, on the Garumna, R., bet. Calagorris and Tolosa.

VERODUNENSES, a people of Belgica I., bet. the Treveri and the Leuci.

VERODUNUM, capital of the Verodunenses, Belgica, bet. Ibliodurum E. and Axuenna w. *Verdun.*

VEROMANDUI, a people of Belgica II., bet. the Nervii N., the Suessiones and Remi s., the Ambiani w., and the Remi E. *Vermandois.*

VEROMETUM (Vernemetum), a town of the Coritani, Brit., bet. Margidunum and Ratæ. *Near Willoughby.*

VERONA, a city of the Cenomanni, in Gallia Transp., on Atagis fl., R., bet. Ariolica and Cadiana. A Euganean city. A colony of Pompeius Strabo, enlarged under Gallienus. The birth-place of Catullus Macer, Corn. Nepos, Pomp. Secundus, Vitruvius, and Pliny the Elder. Noted for its wine. Here was a magnificent amphitheatre, capable of containing 22,000 spectators. *Verona.*

VERRUCINI, a maritime tribe of Salyes, Narbonensis, bet. the Oxybii and the Camatullicini.

VERRUGO, a town of the Volsci, of uncertain position. The locality of the defeat of the consul Sempronius.

VERTACOMICORI, a tribe of Vocontii, Viennensis, N. of Dea Vocontiorum.

VERTĒRÆ, a town of the Brigantes, Brit., near the source of Ituna fl., bet. Galacum and Lavatræ. *Brough.*

VERTINÆ, a town of Bruttium, on Neæthus fl., L. *Verzine.*

VERUBIUM prom., the extreme N.E. prom. of Britannia Barbara, s. of Orcades ins. *Noss Head.*

VERUCA, a fortress of Rhætia, on the Athesis.

VERULÆ, a town of the Hernici, in Latium, towards Arpinum. A col. Assigned to the soldiers of Gracchus, but restored to the colonists by Nerva. *Veroli.*

VERULAMIUM, capital of the Catavellauni, Brit., bet. Magiovinum and Sulloniacæ. A British town., A municipium. *Close to St. Alban's.*

VERURIUM, a town of the Lusitani, bet. Conimbrica w.N.w. and Egetania.

VERVASSIUM, a town of the Genaunes, Rhætia. *Vervo.*

VESASPE, a town of Media Choromitrene, E. of Phraaspa. *Rasbin.*

VESCELIA, a town of the Oretani, Tarraconensis, bet. Silpia N. and Elingas s.w.

VESCELLIUM, a town of the Hirpini, in Samnium.

VESCIA, a town of the Ausones, in Latium, on Liris fl., L., s.E. of Minturnæ. Near it was Vescinum, Cicero's villa.

VESCINUS ager, the territory of Vescia, in Latium. *Demanio di Sessa.*

VESCITANIA (Œscitania), a district of Tarraconensis, about Osca.

VESERIS fl., a r. of Campania, running from Vesuvius m. into the sea at Herculaneum. It was overwhelmed in the great eruption of A.D. 79. The locality of the self-devotion of the elder Decius.

VESIDIA fl., a r. of Etruria, falling into the sea N. of Fossæ Papirianæ. *Versiglia.*

VESIONICA, a town of Umbria, towards the Tiber, s.w. of Nuceria. *Benezzone.*

VESPASIÆ, a village of Sabinium, bet. Nursia and Spoletium; belonging to the Vespasian family. *Monte Vespio.*

VESPASIANA, a province of Britannia Barbara, bet. Bodotria æst. and the Caledonii.

VESPERIES, a maritime town of the Caristi, Tarraconensis, E. of Blendium.

VESTINI, a tribe of Sabines, settled in the extreme s. portion of Picenum, bet. the Prætutii and the Marrucini.

VESTULA, a Pelasgic town of Sabinium.

VESUBIANI, a tribe of Salyes, Narbonensis II., N. of the Vediantii. *Vallée de Vesubia.*

VESULUS m., a summit of the Alpes Cottiæ, in the extreme N.w. angle of the territory of the Vagienni, in Liguria. Two small lakes on its slopes form the source of Padus fl. Its base was covered with firs. *Monte Viso.*

VESUNNA, *postea* Petrocorii, capital of the Petrocorii, Aquitania II., bet. Sarrum N.W. and Diolindum. *Perigueux.*

VESUVIUS m., *prius* Vesevus, Vesvius, Vesbius, a m. of Campania, above Herculaneum and Pompeii. The great eruption, after many centuries' quiescence, which overwhelmed these cities, destroying 250,000 persons, among whom was the elder Pliny, occurred under Titus, A.D. 79.

VETERA castra, a town of the Gugerni, Germ. II., on the Rhine, bet. Col. Trajana and Asciburgium.

VETERNA (Vetar), a Tyrrhenian town of Etruria, the predecessor of Massa Veternensis.

VETESTUM, a town of Lycaonia, bet. Bagrum (20) and Egdavama (20). *Egdana ; Ecdaumana.*

VETLUNA, the Tyrrhenian name of Vetulonii.

VETOMANÆ, a town of Noricum, bet. Tutatio (11) and Ovilabis (11). *Kremsmunster.*

VETONIANA, a town of Rhætia, on the Danube, bet. Biriciana E. and Germaniacum (12). *Irsnig.*

VETTONA, a town of Umbria, on Tiberis fl., L., bet Tuder (14) and Perusia (10). *Bettona.*

VETTONES, the E. population of Lusitania, on the confines of Tarraconensis.

VETULONII (Vetluna), one of the twelve Tyrrhenian cities of Etruria, on Lynceus fl., R., towards its source, N.E. of Aquæ Vetuloniæ. Here first were used the Etruscan insignia of magistracy afterwards adopted by Rome. *Ruins in the Selva di Vetleta.*

VETURI, a Gaulish people, of uncertain position, who migrated to Galatia.

VETUSALIUM, Pannoniæ, i. q. Salinum.

VEXALA æstuar., the mouth of Vexala fl., in Sabrina æstuar. *Bridgewater Bay.*

VIA ÆMILIA, a continuation of Via Aurelia, from Pisa to Dertona, constructed circa B.C. 115, by the consul Æmilius Scaurus, and afterwards extended to Arelate. The whole road was, however, generally termed Aurelia.

VIA ÆMILIA LEPIDA, a double road from Mediolanum in Gallia Transpad., the one to Aquileia, the other to Ariminum. Constructed by M. Æmilius Lepidus 187 B.C.

VIA AMERINA, a branch road from Via Cassia, at Baccanæ, through Ameria, to Perusia.

VIA APPIA, a road constructed from Rome to Capua by Appius Cæcus, censor 312 B.C.; extended to Beneventum by Appius Claudius Pulcher, 250 B.C. ; and to Brundusium (by two roads, the one through Venusium, the other through Tarentum) by another member of the same family, 214 B.C.

VIA AQUILIA, a road from Capua, through Campania, Lucania, and Bruttium, to Rhegium. Constructed by M. Aquilius Gallus, proconsul, and prætor in Sicily.

VIA ARDEATINA, the road from Rome to Ardea.

VIA AURELIA, a road from Rome to Pisa, constructed by the consul Aurelius, circa B.C. 149.

VIA CAMPANA, i. q. Via Consularis.

VIA CASSIA, a road from Rome to Florence, through Vulsinii and Clusium.

VIA CLAUDIA (Clodia), a road from the sixth mile-stone from Rome, on Via Æmilia, to Luna, through Florentia and Luca.

VIA CONSULARIS (Via Campana), the road bet. Capua and Cumæ, with a branch to Puteoli.

VIA DOMITIANA, the coast road from Sinuessa to Surrentum, constructed by Domitian.

VIA EGNATIA, a branch of Via Appia, from Beneventum, through Canusium and Egnatia, to Brundusium.

VIA FICULENSIS, the early name of Via Nomentana.

VIA FLAMINIA NEPOTIS, a branch road bet. Arretium and Bononia, constructed by C. Flaminius Nepos, 187 B.C.

VIA FLAMINIA, a road from Rome to Ariminum, constructed by the censor Caius Flaminius, 221 B.C. There were branches from Narnia to Mevania and Spoletium, uniting at Fulginia ; from Fulgeria to Nuceria ; and from Nuceria, two to Ariminum, one through Picenum, the other through Forum Sempronii.

VIA FRENTANA, *vel* Flaminia Apula, a continuation of Via Salaria, from Aternum, along the coast, to Brundusium.

VIA GRÆCA (Herculea), a road in Campania, near Lucrinus lacus.

VIA HADRIANA, a road from Minturnæ to Teanum Sidicin. Constructed by Hadrian.

VIA LAURENTINA, a road from the Via Ostiensis, 2 m. from Rome to Laurentum.

VIA LAVICANA (Latina), a road from Rome, through Lavicum to Ad Bivium, on Via Latina.

VIA NOMENTANA, a road from Rome, through Fidenæ and Nomentum, to Eretum.

VIA NUMICIA, a road from Corfinium, through N. Samnium, to Venusia.

VIA OSTIENSIS, the road from Rome to Ostia.

VIA POSTHUMIA, a road from Genoa to Verona. Constructed by A. Posthumius Albinus, B.C. 182.

VIA PRÆNESTINA, a road from the Porta Esquilina at Rome, through Præneste, to Anagnia.

VIA PYTHIA, the road leading through Thessaly from Thermopylæ to Pythium.

VIA SACRA, a road of Attica, from Athens to Eleusis.

VIA SALARIA, a road from Hadria in Picenum to the Porta Collina at Rome.

VIA SEVERIANA, a coast road from Ostia to Tarracina. Constructed or repaired by Severus.

VIA SPHETTIA, the road bet. Athens and Sphettus.

VIA SUBLACENSIS, a branch-road from Via Valeria at Lamnæ to Sablaqueum, and thence to Narrubium.

VIA TIBURTINA, the road from Rome to Tibur.

VIA TRAJANA, a branch of Via Appia, bet. Tarentum and Rhegium, on the coast. Repaired by Trajan.

VIA BELOIO, a town of Noricum, bet. Aquileia (30) and Larix (24).

VIACA, a town of Vindelicia, bet. Cælius m. and Augusta Vindelicorum (20).

VIADRUS fl., a r. of Germania Magna, rising in Asciburgius m., above Eburum, and falling by three mouths into Codanus sin. w. of Rugium. Oder.

VIANA, a town of Vindelicia, on Ilargus fl., L., towards its confluence with the Danube.

VIANIOMINA, i. q. Vindobona.

VIBAGINA, i. q. Evagina.

VIBANDOVARIUM, a town of Daunia.

VIBELLI, a people of Italy, contiguous to the Vagienni.

VIBERI (Juberi), a people near the source of the Rhone. About Wisbach.

VIBINUM, a town of Sarmatia, on the confines of Dacia.

VIBIONES, a people of Sarmatia Europæa, s. of the Nasci.

VIBONENSIS sin., Bruttium, i. q. Hipponiates sin.

VICENTIA, prius Vicetia, a town of the Veneti, in Venetia, bet. Ad Aureos (11) and Ad Finem (11), on Via Æmilia. A municipium. Vicenza.

VICINIANUM, a town of the Galabri, in Mœsia, under Scordus m., bet. Vendenæ and Theranda.

VICTOPHALÆ, a people of Germany, of uncertain position.

VICTORIA, a town of the Damnii, Brit., N.W. of Lindum. Kinross.

VICTUMVIÆ, a town of the Insubres, in Gallia Cisalpina. Vicevano.

VICTURIOLÆ, a village of Gallia Cispadana, bet. Mutina (3) and Forum Gallorum (5), on Via Æmilia Lepida.

VICUMNIÆ, a town of the Anamares, in Gallia Cispadana, near Placentia. Taken and plundered by Hannibal. Vicomune.

VICUS AMBIATICUS, a town of the Treveri, Germania I., on the Rhine, above Confluentes.

VICUS AQUARIUS, a town of the Astures, s.w. of Albucella. Viseo?

VICUS AUGUSTI (Cæsaris), a town of Byzacene, bet. Hadrumetum (25) and Aquæ Regiæ. Kairwan.

VICUS AURELI, a town of Numidia, bet. Liviniana and Zyrna Maseli.

VICUS BADIES, a town of Picenum, on Truentus fl., R., bet. Falacrinum (9) and Ad Centesimum (10), on Via Salaria. Accumulo.

VICUS CUMINARIUS, a town of the Carpetani, Tarraconensis, near the Tagus, E. of Titulcia. Named from its fertility in cummin. Zarza?

VICUS ICTYMULORUM (Vicus Longæ Viæ), a gold-mining town of the Libicii, in Gallia Transpadana, on Sessites fl., above Vercellæ. The miners were limited by law to 5000 in number. Santia, Sant' Agata.

VICUS JUDÆORUM, a town of Lower Egypt, bet. Scenæ Veteranorum and Thou.

VICUS JULIANI, a town of Numidia, bet. Capraria and Hippo Regius.

VICUS JULII, a town of the Atures, Novem Populana, on the Aturis, s.w. of Elusa.

VICUS JULIUS, a town of the Nemetes, Germania I., on the Rhine, above Noviomagus.

VICUS LONGÆ VIÆ, Gallia Transpad., i. q. Vicus Ictymulorum.

VICUS MATRINI, a town of Etruria, on Via Cassia, bet. Sutrium and Forum Cassii. Capanaccia.

VICUS METIDICOLCUS, a town of Lucania, bet. Cæsariana and Nerulum. At Lago Negro.

VICUS NOVUS (Forum Novum), a town of Sabinium, on Farfa fl., bet. Eretum (14) and Reate (16), on Via Salaria. S. Maria in Vico Nuovo.

VICUS SERNINUS, a town of Gallia Cispadana, on Padus fl., bet. Mutina (23) and Vicus Varianus (20), on Via Æmilia.

VICUS SPACORUM, a maritime town of the

Grovii, Tarraconensis, N. of the mouth of Minius fl. *Vigo.*

VICUS TITIENSIS, a town of Umbria, on Ariminus fl., L. *Castel Sicchiano.*

VICUS VALERIANI, a town of Numidia, on or near Bagradas fl., L., bet. Ad Arvalla and Vatari.

VICUS VARIANUS, a town of the Cenomanni, in Gallia Transpadana, on Atagis fl., R., bet. Vicus Serninus (20) and Anneianum (18) on Via Æmilia. *Bariano.*

VICUS VATOLANUS, a maritime village of Lucania, s. of Pæstum. *Vatolla.*

VICUS VIRGINIS, a maritime town of the Ingauni, in Liguria, on Via Aurelia, bet. Vada Sabata (9) and Alba Docilia (13). *Veragine.*

VIDOGARA sin., a bay of Clota æstuar., N. of Rerigonius sin.

VIDRUS fl., the northern branch of the Rhine, falling into Flevus lacus. *Vecht.*

VIDŪA fl., a r. of Hibernia, N., separating the Robogdii from the Venicnii. *Foyle.*

VIDUBIA, a town of the Ædui, Lugdunensis I., near Augustodunum N.E.

VIDUCASSES, I. a people of Lugdunensis II., bet. the Lexovii E. and the Bajocasses w. II. their capital. *Vieux, near Caen.*

VIDULIA, a town of Pannonia, bet. Sirmium (8) and Spaneta (8).

VIENNA, capital of the Allobroges, Viennensis, on the Rhone, L., below Lugdunum. *Vienne.*

VIGNÆ, a town of Latium, 7 m. N.W. from Sublaqueum. *Agosta.*

VIGENNA fl., a r. of Gaul, rising among the Lemovices, and falling into the Liger near the junction of the Caris. *Vienne.*

VILLA FAUSTINA, a town of the Trinobantes, Brit., 18 m. from Iciani. *Thetford.*

VILLA REGIS, a town of Etruria, erected around a maritime palace of the Tyrrhenian king Malæotis, on Via Aurelia, bet. Quintiana (3) and Armenta (3).

VILLA SELE, a town of Numidia, on Tapsus fl., L., bet. Rusicada and Ad Palmam.

VILLA SERVILIANA, a village of Numidia, bet. Hippo Regius and Aquæ Tibilitanæ.

VILLAGAI, a town of the Boii, in Pannonia, on the Danube, bet. Vindobona (18) and Æquinoctium (4). *Near Schwochat, E.*

VILLARIUM, a town of the Jemerii, in Gaul. *Valluvoire.*

VIMINACIUM, a town of the Triballi, Mœsia, on the Danube, bet. Margus (10) and Lederata. *Widin.*

VINA, a town of Zeugitana, bet. Ad Mercurium and Siagul.

VINAZA, a town of the Bagi Gætuli, in Libya, bet. Thalalati and Auru.

VINCELA, a town of the Tectosages, in Galatia.

VINDALUM, a town of the Cavares, Viennensis, near the Rhone, above Avenio. The locality of the defeat of the Allobroges by Domitius Ænobarbus. *Videne.*

VINDAMA, a port of the Osismii, Lugdunensis III., S.E. of Coriallum.

VINDELIA prom., a pr. of Britain, E. of Hellenis prom. *Portland Bill.*

VINDELICIA, the N. portion of Rhætia, named from its inhabitants, the Vindelici, who themselves were so called from their rivers the Vindo and Licus.

VINDERIUS fl., a r. of the Darini, in Hibernia, falling into the sea opposite Monarina ins.

VINDIA, a town of the Tolistoboii, in Galatia, bet. Germa and Papira (32).

VINDILI (Vandali), a people of Northern Germany, on the coast of Codanus oc., bet. Albis fl. and Vistula fl. There was a tribe of them on the Danube.

VINDILICI m., m. of Germania Magna, on the confines of the Vindili, bet. Sudeta m. and Asciburgius m. *Riesengebirge.*

VINDILIS ins., an isl. of the Namnetes, Lugdunensis III., off the mouth of the Liger, N.W.

VINDINUM, i. q. Sebudinum Aulercorum.

VINDIUS m., I. m. of India i. Gangem, parallel with Namadus fl. II. of Tarraconensis, a w. continuation of the Pyrenees, parallel with Cantabricum mare.

VINDO fl., a r. of Rhætia, falling into the Licus near Augusta Vindelicorum. *Wertach.*

VINDOBALA, a town of Britain, at Hadriani murus. *Ronchester.*

VINDOBONA (Vianomina, Vindomina, *postea* Juliobona), a town of the Boii, Pannonia, on the Danube, bet. Citium and Villagai (10). The station of the Legio Decima Germaniana. *Wien; Vienna.*

VINDOCLADIA (Vindelia), a town of the Durotriges, Brit., bet. Durnovaria and Venta Belgarum. *Gussage.*

VINDOLANA, a town of the Brigantes, Brit., at Hadriani murus. *Little Chesters.*

VINDOMAGUS, a town of the Volcæ Arecomicæ, towards Nemausus. *Vendemiaise.*

VINDOMĀRA, a town of the Brigantes, Brit., bet. Corstopitum and Glanoventa. *Near Ebchester.*

VINDOMIS (Caer-Segont), a town of the Regni, Brit., bet. Venta Belgarum and Acela. *Finkley Farm.*

VINDONISSA, a town of the Tigurini, Maxima Sequanorum, on Arula fl., L., bet. Augusta Rauracorum and Vitodurum. *Windisch.*

VINEÆ, a town of the Æqui, in Latium, bet. Sublaqueum (5) and Gravis m. (6), on Via Sublacensis. *Jenna.*

VINIOLA, a maritime town of Sardinia, E., bet. Fanum Carisii and Sulsis.

VINIOLA, a maritime town of the Corsii, in Sardinia, w., bet. Erucium and Tibula.

VINIOLÆ, a town of the Turtuli, Bætica, N. of Mentesa.

VINIUS (Scatebra) fl., a r. of Latium, running through the estate of Terentius Varro, near Casinum. *Rapido.*

VINOVIUM, a town of the Brigantes, Brit., bet. Glanoventa and Magi. *Binchester.*

VINTIMILIUM, a later name of Albium Intemelium.

VINTIUM (Ventia, Ventium), a town of the Nerusci, Alpes Maritimæ, near Varus fl., bet. Cemenelium and Deceates. *Vence.*

VINZELA (Unzela), a town of Pamphylia, near Lyrbe.

VIPITENUM, a town of the Breuni, in Rhætia, bet. Veldidena (36) and Sublavium (32). *Sterzing.*

VIR fl., a r. of Tarraconensis, falling into the Atlantic s.w. of Caranicum.

VIRACELUM, a fortress of Etruria, near the source of Ausar fl. *Verrucola.*

VIRGA, a village of Africa, bet. Nivirgitab and Macomades.

VIRGANTIA, i. q. Brigantia.

VIRIBALLUM prom., a pr. of Corsica, w., below Ropicum. *C. di Calvo ; C. Rosso.*

VIRINNA, a town of Narbonensis, bet. Statumæ and Ucetia. *Luc, or Vissec.*

VIRITIUM, a town of the Burgundiones, Germania, on Viadrus fl. *Gripswald ? Piritz ?*

VIROCONIUM, Brit., i. q. Uriconium.

VIROSIDUM (Volantium), a maritime town of the Brigantes, Brit., bet. Morbium and Olenaum. *Preston.*

VIROVESCA (Viruesca, *postea* Verveca), a town of the Autrigones, Tarraconensis, bet. Segisamo w. and Cigurri E. *Bribiesca.*

VIROVIACUM, a town of the Menapii, Belgica II., bet. Castrum Morinorum w. and Turnacum s.E.

VIRTA, Mesopotamiæ, i. q. Bithiga.

VIRUNI (Pharodeni), a people of Northern Germany, on the Albis, bet. the Saxones and the Semnones.

VIRUNUM, I. capital of the Viruni, Germania, N.E. of Astuia. II. a town of the Taurisci, in Noricum, bet. Santicum (30) and Candalicas (20). A colonia of Claudius. *Solfeld, near Klagenfurt.*

VIRUTIUM, a town of Northern Germany, on Viadrus fl. *Near Crossen.*

VISALTA, a town of Numidia, on Ampsaga fl., L., bet. Baduxi and Luculliana.

VISBURGII, a tribe of Lygii, Germania, under Asciburgius m., N. of the Quadi.

VISCELLÆ, a town of the Taurisci, in Noricum, on Murus fl.,bet. Ad Pontem (14) and Tartursanæ (9). *Oberwolz.*

VISENTIUM, a town of Etruria, on Vulsiniensis lacus, w. above Verentum. *Bisentino.*

VISONTIO, capital of the Sequani, Maxima Sequanorum, on Dubis fl., L., bet. Loposagum and Crusinia. *Besançon.*

VISONTIUM, a town of the Pelendones, Tarraconensis, bet. Savia N.w. and Numantia s.E. *Burgos.*

VISPII, a tribe of Chatti, Germania, on the Rhine, N. of Moguntiacum, w. of the Mattiaci.

VISTULA (Bisla) fl., a r. of Europe, rising in Carpathus m., and, after separating Germany from Sarmatia, falling into Venedicus sin. *Weichsel ; Ursla ; Vistula.*

VISULA, i. q. Vistula.

VISURGIS (Bisurgis, Visutros) fl., a r. of Germania Magna, rising in Sudeta m., towards the source of Moenus fl., and falling into Germanicus oc. s. of Albis fl. *Weser.*

VITIANUM, a town of Rhætia, w. of Tridentum. *Vezzano.*

VITELLIA, a town of the Latini, in Latium, E. of Labicum. A colonia.

VITII, Mediæ, i. q. Drybices.

VITIS fl., i. q. Utis.

VITODURUM, a town of the Tugeni, Maxima Sequanorum, bet. Vindonissa w. and Ad Fines E. *Ober-Winterthur.*

VITRICIUM, a town of the Salassi, in Gallia Transpadana, on Duria Maj. fl., L., bet. Augusta Prætoria (25) and Eporedium (21). *Verrez.*

VIVARIUM, a town of the Helvii, Narbonensis I., on the Rhone, bet. Umbennum and Senomagus.

VIVISCUS, a town of the Ambrones, Maxima Sequanorum, at the E. extremity of Lemanus lacus. *Vevay.*

VOBARNA, a town of the Triumpili, in Gallia Transpadana, on Cleusis fl. A municipium. *Vobarno.*

VOCARIUM, a town of the Ambisontii, in Noricum, on Jovanus fl., bet. Cuculli (17) and in Ani (17). *Werfen.*

VOCATES, a tribe of Tarbelli, Novem Populana, on the confines of the Vasates.

VOCETIUS m., m. of Maxima Sequanorum, parallel with Arula fl., s. of Augusta Rauracorum.

VOCONTII, a people of Viennensis, bet. the Cavares w., the Avantici and Salyes E., and the Mediterranean s.

VODONA, a town of Arabia Felix, bet. Thumna and Nazara. *Kond.*

Vogĕsus (Vosegus) m., m. of Gaul, commencing in the territory of the Lingones, and forming the boundary bet. the Leuci and the Sequani, and bet. the Mediomatrici and the Rauraci. *Vosges; Vogesen.*

Volana, a town of the Caudini, in Samnium.

Volana Ostium, one of the mouths of the Padus. *Po di Ferrara.*

Volandum, Armeniæ, i. q. Olane.

Volaterræ (Velathri), one of the twelve Tyrrhenian cities of Etruria, on Cæcina fl., R., 15 m. above its mouth. Memorable for its two years' siege by Sylla. A colonia and municipium. The birth-place of Persius. *Volterra.*

Volcæ Arecomici, a people of Narbonensis I., on the Mediterranean, bet. the Atax and the Rhone. The term Volcæ is simply the German Volk "folk."

Volcæ Tectosages, a people of Narbonensis I., bet. the Volcæ Arecomici and the Mediterranean E. and Novem Populana w. A colony of them migrated to Asia Minor, and settled in Galatia.

Volcarum stagnum, an inlet of the Mediterranean, in Narbonensis I., E. of Agatha.

Volcea (Peiso) lacus, a lake of Pannonia Inferior, extending s.w.—n.e. from above Valcum towards Acincum. *Plaaten-see.*

Volci (Olkion), a Tyrrhenian town of Etruria, bet. Tuscania and Tarquinii. *Piano di Volci.* II. (Vulceium, Volcentum, Ulci), a town of Lucania, N. of Tanager fl. *Buccino.*

Volenes, a fortress of Rhætia, on the Athesis. *Volano.*

Volerius fl., a r. of Corsica, falling into the sea s. of Tilox prom. *Cigno.*

Voliba, a town of the Damnonii, Brit., at the mouth of Cenion fl. *Falmouth.*

Vologatis, a town of the Vocontii, Viennensis, bet. Lucus Augusti n.n.w. and Cambonum E.

Vologesia (Vologesocerta, Bolagasus), a town of Babylonia, on Naarsares canal, s.w. of Babylon (18). Built by Vologesus, king of Parthia. *Rufa.*

Volsas sin., a bay of the Atlantic, on the coast of the Carnonacæ, Brit., s. of Nobocus fl. *Calvay Bay.*

Volsci, a tribe of Umbri, or of Osci, in Latium, extending along the coast from Antium to Tarracina, and about thirty miles inland.

Volubiani m., m. of Mauritania, s. of Volubilis.

Volubilis, a town of Mauritania Ting., on a branch of Subur fl., 35 m. s.e. from Banasa. *Gualili.*

Voluntii (Usbintii), a maritime people of Hibernia, s. of the Darini. *On Dundalk Bay.*

Volustana, i. q. Cambunius saltus.

Vomanus fl., a r. of Picenum, falling into the° sea s. of Castrum Novum. *Vomano.*

Vopisciana, a town of Mauritania Ting., on Subur fl., R., bet. Tremula (19) and Gilda (24).

Vordenses, a tribe of Vocontii, Viennensis, on Sulgas fl. *About Gordes.*

Vorĕda, a town of the Brigantes, Brit., bet. Luguvallum and Brovonacæ. *Near Plumpton Wall.*

Vorgium (Vorganium), capital of the Osismii, Lugdunensis III., bet. Gesocribatæ s.w., and Ad Fines E. *Variously placed at Concarneau, Treguier, &c.*

Vorincus, *postea* Brocincus, a town of the Volcæ Arecomici, on Vardo fl. *Brocen.*

Vorogium, a town of the Aulerci Brannovices, Lugdunensis I., w. of Ariolica.

Vosavia, a town of the Treveri, Germania I., on the Rhine, above Salipo. *Ober-Wesel.*

Voturi, a people of Galatia; predecessors of the Tectosages.

Vulcaniæ ins., i. q. Æoliæ.

Vulchalo, a town of Narbonensis, bet. Tolosa and Narbo.

Vulgientes, a tribe of Vocontii, Viennensis, w. of the Memini.

Vungo Vicus, a town of the Remi, Belgica II., L., bet. Noviomagus w.s.w. and Mosa N.E.

Vulsiniensis lacus, Tarquiniensis, a lake of Etruria, at Vulsinii. On it were two floating islands.

Vulsinii, one of the twelve cities of Etruria, on Vulsiniensis lacus, N.E., bet. Aquæ Passeris and Clusium (30), on Via Cassia. Sacred to Nartia. The birth-place of Sejanus. *Bolsena.*

Vultur m., a volcanic m. of Daunia, Apulia, s. of Venusium. Celebrated by Horace as a scene of his boyish sports. *Monte Vulture.*

Vulturia (Vulturnia), a town of the Cenomanni, in Gallia Transpad., on Padus fl., below Cremona. *Valdoria.*

Vulturnum, I. a town of Campania, at the mouth of Vulturnus fl., n.w. of Liternum. II. the Etruscan name of Capua.

Vulturnus fl., a r. of Campania, rising in Samnium, towards Aufidena, and falling into the Tyrrhenian sea at Vulturnum. Noted for its rapid course, and for the magnificent bridge thrown over it on Via Domitiana by Domitian. *Volturno.*

X.

XALOTH, a town of Samaria, w. of Cæsarea Palestina.

XANTHUS, I. a r. of Cestrine, in Epirus, falling into the Pelodes palus s. of Buthrotum. *Saronia.* II. *prius* Sibrus, Sirbes, a r. of Lycia, falling into the Mediterranean 8 m. from Cydna. III. a stream of Æolis Asiat., falling into Elæaticus sin., near Cyme. IV. a town of Lesbos ins. V. capital of Lycia, on Xanthus fl., 7½ m. from its mouth. Twice destroyed by its inhabitants to save it from hostile occupation. Hence came the Xanthian marbles. *Aksenide.*

XAURUS, a town of Macedonia.

XENAGORÆ (Enagoræ) ins., isl. of Lycia, off Phœnicus portus. *Patara; Volo and Okendra.*

XENITANA, *vide* Quiza.

XENIPPA, a district of Sogdiana, on the borders of Scythia, about Alexandria Ultima.

XERA, a town of the Turtetani, Bætica, bet. Asta Regia N.W. and Ceret S.S.E. *Xera de la Frontera.*

XERADRUS fl., a r. of India, falling into Indicus oceanus, towards the Indus. *Sutlej.*

XERXENE (Derxene), a district of Armenia Int., on Pyxirates fl., w. of Carenitis. Named from Xerxes. *Terdschan.*

XIMENE, a district of Galatia, on Halys fl., R. Here were the salt-mines which gave name to that river.

XIPHONIA, a town of Sicily, at Xiphonium prom. *Augusta.*

XIPHONIUM prom., a pr. of Sicily E., above Thapsus.

XOANA, a town of Paphlagonia, N.E. of Pompeiopolis.

XOIS, I. an isl. of Lower Egypt, on the Sebennytic branch of the Nile, w. of Sebennytus. II. a town of Lower Egypt, on Xois ins.

XUTHIA, a name from King Xuthus, of the Leontini Campi in Sicily.

XYLENOPOLIS, a port of Gedrosia, near the mouth of the Indus.

XYLINE, Pont., i. q. Archabis.

XYLOCASTRUM, a fortress of Cilicia prefect., in Cappadocia.

XYLOPOLIS, a town of Grestonia, in Macedonia, near the source of the Echedorus fl.

XYLUS, a town of Caria.

XYMETHUS, a town of Cyrenaica, E. of Artamis.

XYNIAS lacus, a lake of Dolopia, in Thessaly, s.w. of Pharsalus. *L. Daoukli.*

XYNIAS (Xyniæ), a town of Dolopia, in Thessaly, on the s. shore of Xynias lacus, on the confines of Aniania. *Daoukli.*

XYPETE, *olim* Troja, a demus of Attica, of the tribe Cecropis, on Saronic. sin., s. of Alimus. Founded by Teucer.

XYSTIS, a town of Caria.

Z.

ZAA, a district of Tenesis, in Æthiopia, w. of Adulis.

ZAANANNIM, a city of Naphthali, N.E. of Kedesh.

ZAANAN (Zenan), "place of the flock," a city of Judah, towards the sea.

ZAARAM, a port of the Darræ, Arab., on the Red sea, 20 m. s. of Jambia. *Djar.*

ZABA, I. a district of Mauritania, about Sitifis. II. a town of India e. Gangem, near Magnum prom. *Senasar.*

ZABALUS fl., Assyriæ, i. q. Caprus.

ZABAZ, a town of Aurea Chersonesus, at its s. extremity.

ZABBOK fl., a r. of Peræa, rising near Rabbath Ammon, and falling into the Jordan s.w. of Amathus. The boundary of Decapolis N., and Ammonitis s. *Zerka.*

ZABDA, Mesopotamiæ, i. q. Bezabda.

ZABDICENE, a district of Armenia Maj., on Masius m., extending into Mygdonia, Mesopotamiæ.

ZABES, "wolf," Assyriæ, i. q. Lycus.

ZABIDA (Sabala), a town of Arabia Felix, near Sesippi portus. *Zebid.*

ZACA, a maritime town of Numidia, bet. Muharur and Callucitanæ.

ZACATÆ, a people of Sarmatia Asiatica.

ZACYNTHUS, I. an island of Peloponnesus, off Elis, 40 m. in circuit. Named after Zacynthus, son of Dardanus, the Arcadian. Within the territory of Ulysses. Noted for its great fertility, its fine woods, and its pitch. *Zante.* II. its capital, on the E. coast opposite Ephyre, in Elis. *Zante.*

ZADRACARTA (Carta), capital of Hyrcania, on the confines of Media. Supposed to be the Tape of Strabo, and the Syrinx of Polybius. *Zaryah.*

ZADRIS (Surapona), a town of Colchis, on Phasis fl., L., towards its source. *Scharapani.*

ZÆA, a town of Bœotia.

ZÆTIA, a town of Arcadia, 2 m. N.W. from Tricoloni.

ZAGAZAMA, *vide* Sagasama.

ZAGORA, Paphlagoniæ, i. q. Gazorum.

ZAGRI portæ, defiles of Zagrus m., bet. Media and Assyria, w. of Ecbatana.

ZAGRUS (Zarcæus) m., m. of Asia, separating central Assyria from Media.

ZAGURA, I. a r. of Mesopotamia, falling into the Saocoras below Zagura. II. a town of Gauzonitis, Mesopotamia, on Zagura fl., bet. Singara and Ad Pontem.

ZAGYLIS, a maritime village of Marmarica, bet. Selinus and Chetæa.

ZAITHA (Zaita, Zitha, Zautha, "oil-producing," Asaca), a town of Tingene, Mesopot., on the Euphrates, below Chabura. Between it and Dura, at a place now called Zoxo-Sultaun, "the prince's tomb," still subsists the tumulus of Gordian, raised by the devotion of a single soldier.

ZALACE, a town of Media, on Amardus fl. *Langarud.*

ZALACUS m., m. of Mauritania Cæsar., E. of Ancorarius m.

ZALECUS (Zaliscus, Halega), a r. of Paphlagonia, falling into the Euxine, 12½ m. E. from Gazorum. II. a town of Paphlagonia, at the mouth of the cognominal river.

ZALISSA, a town of Iberia, on Cyrus fl., towards Albania.

ZALMON "shady" (Salmon) m., a m. of Palestine, w. of Shechem.

ZAMA, *surnamed* Regia, I. a city of Numidia, s.w. of Sitifis. The capital of Jugurtha. The locality of the decisive defeat of Hannibal by Scipio. A colonia of Hadrian (Ælia Hadriana). *Zainah.* II. a town of Chammenene prefect., in Cappadocia, bet. Tavium and Cæsarea Mazaca.

ZAMARENI, Arabiæ, i. q. Saraceni.

ZAMES (Zamelas, Mesha) m., m. of Arabia Felix, intersecting the desert from s.w. to E., from about Marata to about Giratha. *Ajam.*

ZAMUCHANA, a town of Aria, on Arios fl., s.w. of Alexandria Arion.

ZAMZUMMINS (Zuzims, "turbulent"), a gigantic race, N. of the Emims, s. of the Rephaim, E. of Jordan. Conquered by Chedorlaomer, and ultimately expelled by the Ammonites.

ZANCLE, "sickle," the early name of Messana, in Sicily, from King Zanclus, or from the sickle of Saturn, or from the curved character of the coast.

ZANOAH, "marsh," a city in the m. of Judah.

ZAO prom., a pr. of Narbonensis, E. of Massilia. *Bec de Sormion; Cap de la Croisette.*

ZAPARA, a town of Macedonia II.

ZAPETIA, a town of Commagene, towards the Euphrates. *Zabatra.*

ZAR fl., I. Arabiæ, i. q. Canis. II. ins., an isl. of Arabiæ, at the mouth of Zar (Canis) fl. *Sharedsje.*

ZARA, I. a town of Pontus, on Halys fl., above Sebastia. II. (Zorava), capital of Trachonitis, N.E. of Astaroth-Karnaim. ZARADRUS fl., i. q. Hydaspes.

ZARAGARDIA, Mes., *vide* Ozogarda.

ZARAI, a town of Numidia, bet. Predices (12) and Lamasbua (25).

ZARANGIA, an oriental form of Drangiana, produced by the Eastern substitution of the *zain* for the *daled.*

ZARATH, a town of Mauritania Cæsar., E. of Sitifis.

ZARATÆ (Zeretæ), a people of Scythia, under Alani m.

ZARAX prom., I. a headland of Eubœa, on the E. coast, N. of Opheltes prom. II. (Pyrrhi-Castra), a fortress of the Eleuthero Lacones, in Laconia, on the Ægean, under Barbosthenes m., 10 m. s.E. from Sparta. In the first instance a fortified camp of Pyrrhus, son of Achilles. *Kari.*

ZARCÆUS, *vide* Zagrus.

ZARCOA, a town of Arabia, on Zar (Canis) fl. *Seer.*

ZAREA, a town of Judah, in Judæa, N.N.E. of Bethsemes.

ZARED "embowered" (Zered) fl., a r. of Moab, rising in Abarim m., and falling into the Dead sea s. of Arnon fl. On its banks the Hebrews encamped on their way from Egypt.

ZARGIDAVA, a town of the Harpii, Dacia, N. of Tamasidava.

ZARIASPA, i. q. Bactra.

ZARIASPÆ, a people of Drangiana, about Bactrus.

ZARIASPIS, the early name of Bactrus fl.

ZARMIZEGETHUSA (Sarmisogethusa, Zarmigethusa, Sarmategte), capital of Dacia, 15 m. from Pons Augusti. A colonia of Trajan (Ulpia Trajana, Augusta Dacica). *Varhely.*

ZARPATH, *vide* Sarepta.

ZARTAN (Zaretan, Zartanah, Zarereth, Zereda, Zeredathah, Sarthan), a town on Jordan fl., near Bethshean; the place where the river retrograded to give passage to the Israelites. The birth-place of Jeroboam.

ZARUANA, a town of Minyas, Armeniæ, s.w. of Ararat. *Zarchavan.*

ZARUG, Mesopot., *vide* Batnæ.

ZARZELA, *vide* Zorzila.

ZAU TABERNA, a maritime village of Cyrenaica, w., above Drepanum prom.

ZEBOIM, a town of Benjamin, in a cognominal valley.

ZEBOIM, "harts," one of the cities of the plain, destroyed with Sodom and Gomorrha.

ZEBULON (Zibulon), I. a tribe of Israel, bounded N. by Asser (w. above Rana) and Napthali (E. above Migdol), s. by Issachar, at Dobrath, w. by Asser, w. of Kana, E. by the Jordan and Tiberias lacus. II. its chief town, on the Mediterranean, near Ptolemais.

ZEDAH (Zedad), "broad," a town on the N.E. frontier of Israel.

ZEDE, a town of Cilicia Trachea.

ZEERITÆ, a people of Arabia Felix, under Zarares m., E. *Beni Zerah.*

ZELA, capital of Zelitis regio, in Pontus, on the left bank of Iris fl., bet. Gazioura and Daranon. With temples of Anaitis and of Omanus and Anandates, the former erected on the mound of Semiramis. Enlarged by Pompey, after the defeat of Mithridates. The locality of the "Veni, vidi, vici," of Cæsar. *Zeleh.*

ZELASIUM prom., a headland of Magnesia, in Thessaly, on Pagasæus sin., opposite Cicynethus ins.

ZELEIA,• a town of Mysia, on Æsepus fl., 10 m. from its mouth, near Aphnitis lacus ; the city of Pandarus. *Biga.*

ZEMARAIM, I. a town of Benjamin, near Bethel. II. of Ephraim, on Ephraim m.

ZEMYTHUS, a town of Pentapolis, Cyrenaicæ, s.w. of Cyrene.

ZENOBIA, i. q. Thapsacus.

ZENOBII ins., seven islets of Arabia Felix, on Sachalites sin.

ZENODORI domus, i. q. Gaulonitis.

ZENODOTIUM (Zenodotia), a town of Osrhoene, Mesopotamiæ, near Nicephorium. Noted for its treachery to Crassus.

ZENONIS CHERSONESUS, an elongated peninsula of Taurica Chersonesus, on Palus Mæotis, w.

ZEPHATH, a city of Simeon.

ZEPHATH PYLÆ, a pass in Akrabbim m., Idumææ, s.e. of Arad.

ZEPHATHAH vallis, a valley of Judah, near Mareshah, in which occurred the battle between the Jews and the Ethiopians.

ZEPHYRE ins., an isl. of Crete, off Sammonium prom.

ZEPHYRIA, an early name of Halicarnassus.

ZEPHYRIUM prom., I. a pr. of Bruttium, N. of Heracleum prom. It gave name to the

Locri Epizephyrii. *Capo di Bruzzano.* II. of Caria, at the s. entrance of Jassicus sin. III. of Ciliciæ, i. q. Anemurium prom. IV. (Veneris prom.), of Cilicia Trachea, E. of Cruni prom. *C. Cavaliere.* V. of Crete, at the w. entrance of Didymi sin. *C. San Giovanni.* VI. of Cyprus, w. of Paphos. VII. of Cyrenaica, N.W. of Darnis. *Cabo Derne.* VIII. of Marmarica, near Derris prom. IX. of Paphlagonia, 5 m. E. from Callistratia. X. of Pontus, 15 m. E. from Aretias ins., with a cognominal town. *Zefré.*

ZEPRYRICUM, a town of Taurica Chersonesus.

ZERBIS " goat " fl., i. q. Caprus, Assyr.

ZEREDA, i. q. Zartan.

ZEREDATHAH, i. q. Zartan.

ZERERATH, i. q. Zartan.

ZERINIA, a town of the Cicones, in Thrace, on Hebrus fl., bet. Dyme and Plotinopolis.

ZERMIZIRGA, a town of Dacia, s.E. of Ziridava.

ZERNESIUM (Zernis), i. q. Tierna.

ZERYNTHUS, a town of the Apsynthii, in Thrace, where Apollo was peculiarly worshipped, and where was also, according to Lycophron, a cave sacred to Hecate, hence surnamed Zirynthia. Ovid, however, assigns this cave to Samothrace.

ZESUTERA, a town of the Apsynthii, in Thrace, on the Via Egnatia, bet. Syracella (10) and Apri (12).

ZETHIS, Carmaniæ, i. q. Salmunti.

ZEUDRACARTA, i. q. Zadracarta.

ZEUGISA prom., a pr. of Azania, on Barbaricus sin.

ZEUGITANA (Zeugis), the N. division of Africa Propria, separated from Byzacene by a line drawn from Horrea, and from Numidia by Tusca fl.

ZEUGMA, I. a town of Cyrrhestica, on the Euphrates, bet. Europus and Urima, opposite Apamea, with which it communicates by a bridge, whence its name. *Zegme.* II. of Dacia, i. q. Pons Augusti.

ZICHI (Zigæ), a people of Sarmatia Asiat., on the Caspian, N. of the Abasgi. The progenitors of the Circassians.

ZIGANA, a town of Pontus, s. of Cerasus.

ZIKLAG "pressed" (Siclag, Sicella), a town of Simeon, but locally in Judah, where David took refuge from Saul, by permission of Achish, king of the Philistines, in whose possession it was at that period.

ZILIA (Zilis) fl., I. a r. of Mauritania Tingit., falling into the Atlantic near Ampelusia prom., s. II. a port of Mauritania Tingit., at the mouth of Zilia fl., R. A colonia of Augustus (Colonia Julia Constantia). *Arzilla.*

ZIMARA, a town of Armenia Minor, towards the w. source of the Euphrates.

ZIN, "shield," a wilderness of about 5 m. in breadth, extending from the Dead sea to the Red sea. *El Ghor.*

ZINCHI (Zingi), i. q. Zichi.

ZINGIS, I. a district of Ethiopia, s. of Azania. *Zendge, Zanguebar.* II. prom., a prom. of Azánia, Africæ, under Phalangis m., N. of Noti Cornu prom. *Cape Delgada.*

ZIOBERIS fl., a r. of Parthia Comisene, on the confines of Hyrcania, which, in its course towards Rhidagus fl., alternately flowed on and under ground. *Adschizu.*

ZION "sunny" (Sion) m., one of the hills of Jerusalem, having Kedron vallis E., Hinnom vallis s. and w., Acra N., and Moriah N.E. Upon it stood a fortress of the Jebusites which, taken by Joab, became the city of David on his removal from Hebron. Here subsequently arose the temple of Solomon and Herod's palace. It was only pregnable on the N. side.

ZIPH, I. a wilderness of Judah, E. of Hebron, where David concealed himself from Saul. II. a town of Judah, E. of Hebron, on the border of the wilderness of Ziph, fortified by Rehoboam.

ZIPHRON, a town of Israel, near Zedad.

ZIRAS fl., a r. of the Crobyzi, Mœs., falling into the Euxine, at Cruni.

ZIRCA fl., a r. of Phœnicia, falling into the sea towards Darum.

ZIRIDAVA, a town of the Prædavenses, in Dacia, on Tibiscus fl., L., above the junction of Marisus fl. *Near Muhlenbach.*

ZITHA, a maritime town of Syrtica regio, bet. Gittis and Putea Pallene.

ZITTA (Zetta), a town of Byzacene, near Thapsus.

ZOAN "low," (Tanis,) the metropolis of the Nomos Tanaitis, on the Tanaitic branch of the Nile. The residence of the Pharaohs, and the scene of Moses' miracles. Founded circa 1997 B.C. *Zan.*

ZOANA, a town of Pontus, s. of Halys fl., bet. Gundusa (23) and Tonosa (25).

ZOAR, "small" (Bela, Salissa), a town of Moabitis, at the s.E. extremity of the Dead sea; the refuge of Lot, at whose prayer it had been exempted from the fate of Sodom.

ZOBAH (Aram Zobe), a city of Syria, the capital of a cognominal district on the Euphrates, N. of Damascus, the king of which, Hadarezer, was smitten by David.

ZOGORRA, a town of Gauzonitis, Mesopotamiæ, on Saocoras fl., bet. Sergora and Dicate.

ZOLLANA, a town of the Apsynthii, in Thrace, bet. Colla and Syracella.

ZONE, a town of the Cicones, in Thrace, w. of the mouth of Hebrus fl., where Orpheus by his strains drew after him the woods, alike with their living tenants.

ZOPORASTUS, a town of Melitene pref., in Cappadocia, N.w. of Melitene.

ZORAH, "hornets' nest" (Zoreah, Zoran), a city of Judah, afterwards transferred to Dan, on the borders of either tribe, 10 m. from Emmaus. Fortified by Rehoboam. The birth-place of Samson. *Surah.*

ZORALUS fl., a r. of the Odrysæ, in Thrace, falling into the Propontis at Perinthus.

ZORAMBUS fl., a r. of Gedrosia, falling into Indicum m. at Cophas.

ZOROPASSUS, i. q. Arabissus.

ZOSTER prom., a headland of Attica, on Saronicus sinus, in form like the Needles, bet. Œxone and Anagyrus; so called from Latona's here loosening her girdle. *Halikes.*

ZUCHIS, Africæ, i. q. Tarichea.

ZUCHUBARI m., m. of Tripolis, Africæ, an E. continuation of Girgiris m.

ZUMI, a tribe of Hermunduri, Germ., s. of the Bonochæmæ.

ZUPH, a district of Palestine, named after Zuph, the ancestor of Samuel.

ZUPHON, a town of Zeugitana, 10 geog. m. s. from Carthage. *Zowan.*

ZUR, a town of the Psylli, in Africa Prop., on Syrtis Maj., bet. Macomades and Charax.

ZUROBARA, a town of the Biephi, in Dacia, on the s. mouth of Marisus fl., above its junction with Tibiscus fl.

ZUSIDAVA, a town of the Cotenses, Dacia, N.E. of Netindava. *Near Buseo.*

ZUTHI, a people of Carmania Deserta, s. of the Gadanopydres.

ZUZIMS, i. q. Zuzummims.

ZYDRETÆ, a people of Sarmatia, near the Lazi.

ZYGANA ins., an isl. of Thebais, in the Red sea, off Parvum prom. *Jambo.*

ZYGANTES (Gyzantes), a people on the w. coast of Syrtis Minor, Africæ.

ZYGATIS (Zagatis) fl., a r. of Pontus, falling into the Euxine, 7 furlongs E. from Athenæ.

ZYGIANI, a people of Bithynia.

ZYGOPOLIS, i. q. Cissa in Pontus.

ZYGRÆ, capital of the Zygritæ, Marmarica, on the coast bet. Chetæa and Aratu.

ZYGRITÆ (Zygres, Zyritæ), a people of Marmarica, on the coast bet. Chetæa and Catabathmus Major.

ZYPÆTIUM, a town of Bithynia, under Lyperus m. Founded by king Zipætes.

ZYRNA MASELI, a town of Numidia, bet. Vicus Aureli and Ad Cahalis.

THE END.